HALSBURY'S
Laws of England

FOURTH EDITION
REISSUE

Volume 11(1)

HALSBURY'S
Laws of England

FOURTH EDITION
REISSUE

LORD HAILSHAM OF ST. MARYLEBONE

Lord High Chancellor of Great Britain
1970–74 and 1979–87

Volume 11(1)

BUTTERWORTHS

LONDON   1990

UNITED KINGDOM   Butterworth & Co (Publishers) Ltd
88 Kingsway, **London** WC2B 6AB and
4 Hill Street, **Edinburgh** EH2 3JZ

AUSTRALIA   Butterworths Pty Ltd, **Sydney, Melbourne, Brisbane, Adelaide, Perth, Canberra** and **Hobart**

CANADA   Butterworths Canada Ltd, **Toronto** and **Vancouver**

IRELAND   Butterworth (Ireland) Ltd, **Dublin**

MALAYSIA   Malayan Law Journal Sdn Bhd, **Kuala Lumpur**

NEW ZEALAND   Butterworths of New Zealand Ltd, **Wellington** and **Auckland**

PUERTO RICO   Equity de Puerto Rico, Inc, **Hato Rey**

SINGAPORE   Malayan Law Journal Pte Ltd, **Singapore**

USA   Butterworth Legal Publishers, **Austin**, Texas; **Boston**, Massachusetts; **Clearwater**, Florida (D & S Publishers); **Orford**, New Hampshire (Equity Publishing); **St Paul**, Minnesota; and **Seattle**, Washington

---

FIRST EDITION

Published in 31 volumes between 1907 and 1917 under the Editorship of the Rt. Hon. the Earl of Halsbury, Lord High Chancellor of Great Britain, 1885–86, 1886–92 and 1895–1905

SECOND EDITION

Published in 37 volumes between 1931 and 1942 under the Editorship of the Rt. Hon. the Viscount Hailsham, Lord High Chancellor of Great Britain, 1928–29 and 1935–38

THIRD EDITION

Published in 43 volumes between 1952 and 1964 under the Editorship of the Rt. Hon. the Viscount Simonds, Lord High Chancellor of Great Britain, 1951–54

FOURTH EDITION

Published in 56 volumes between 1973 and 1987 under the Editorship of the Rt. Hon. Lord Hailsham of St. Marylebone, Lord High Chancellor of Great Britain, 1970–74 and 1979–87

ISBN   (complete set, standard binding) 0 406 03400 1
(this volume, standard binding) 0 406 03464 8

Printed in Great Britain by
Thomson Litho Ltd, East Kilbride, Scotland

Editor in Chief

THE RIGHT HONOURABLE

LORD HAILSHAM OF ST. MARYLEBONE

LORD HIGH CHANCELLOR OF GREAT BRITAIN

1970–74 and 1979–87

The Title Criminal Law, Evidence and Procedure has been contributed by:

The Right Hon. Sir FREDERICK LAWTON,

a former Lord Justice of Appeal;
a Master of the Bench of the
Inner Temple

DIANE BIRCH, LL.B.,

Reader in the Law of Evidence, University of Nottingham

MICHAEL GUNN, LL.B.,

Lecturer in Law, University of Nottingham

LYNNE KNAPMAN, LL.B.,

of the Middle Temple, Barrister;
Deputy Registrar of Criminal Appeals,
Criminal Appeal Office

MAGGY PIGOTT, M.A.,

of the Middle Temple, Barrister;
Senior Principal Legal Officer,
Criminal Appeal Office

The law stated in this volume is in general that in force on 1 November 1989.

TABLE OF CONTENTS

CRIMINAL LAW, EVIDENCE AND PROCEDURE

VOLUME 11(1)

REFERENCES AND ABBREVIATIONS

ACT	Australian Capital Territory
A-G	Attorney-General
Adv-Gen	Advocate General
affd	affirmed
Alta	Alberta
App	Appendix
art	article
Aust	Australia
B	Baron
BC	British Columbia
BCC	British Company Cases
BCLC	Butterworths Company Law Cases
BFSP	British and Foreign State Papers
BS	British Standard
Bk	Book
C	Command Paper (of a series published before 1900)
c	chapter number of an Act
CA	Court of Appeal
CA in Ch	Court of Appeal in Chancery
CCA	Court of Criminal Appeal
CC Fees Order 1982	County Court Fees Order 1982 (SI 1982/1706) as subsequently amended (see the current County Court Practice)
CC Funds Rules 1965	County Court Funds Rules 1965 (SI 1965/1500) as subsequently amended (see the current County Court Practice)
CCR 1981	County Court Rules 1981 (SI 1981/1687) as subsequently amended (see the current County Court Practice)
CCR	Court of Crown Cases Reserved
CCT	Common Customs Tariff
C-MAC	Courts-Martial Appeal Court
Can	Canada
Cd	Command Paper (of the series published 1900–18)
Cf	compare
ch	chapter
cl	clause
Cmd	Command Paper (of the series published 1919–56)
Cmnd	Command Paper (of the series published 1956 to date)
Commons Journals	Journals of the House of Commons

Court Forms (2nd Edn)........	Atkin's Encyclopaedia of Court Forms in Civil Proceedings, 2nd Edn. See note 2, p *16* post
Cr App Rep.................	Criminal Appeal Reports, 1908—(current)
Cr App Rep (S)..............	Criminal Appeal Reports (Sentencing), 1979—(current)
Crim LR (preceded by date).....	Criminal Law Review, 1954—(current)
DC........................	Divisional Court
Digest (Reissue)	The Digest Reissue Volumes (Green Band). Continuation Volume D includes cases reported 1971–75; Continuation Volume E includes cases reported 1976–79; Continuation Volume F includes cases reported 1980–83; Continuation Volume G includes cases reported 1984–85
EAT.......................	Employment Appeal Tribunal
EC	European Communities
ECJ.......................	Court of Justice of the European Communities
ECSC.....................	European Coal and Steel Community
EEC......................	European Economic Community
ECt HR	European Court of Human Rights
Edn.......................	Edition
EFTA.....................	European Free Trade Association
Euratom...................	European Atomic Energy Community
Ex Ch.....................	Court of Exchequer Chamber
FC........................	Full Court
Fed	Federal
Forms & Precedents (5th Edn) ...	Encyclopaedia of Forms and Precedents other than Court Forms, 5th Edn. See note 2, p *16* post
HC.......................	High Court
HL	House of Lords
H of C	House of Commons
Halsbury's Statutes (4th Edn)....	Halsbury's Statutes of England, 4th Edn. See note 2, p *16* post
ILO......................	International Labour Organisation
IMF	International Monetary Fund
Ir........................	Ireland
J.........................	Justice
JA.......................	Judge of Appeal
LA	Lord Advocate
LC	Lord Chancellor
LCJ......................	Lord Chief Justice
LJ	Lord Justice of Appeal
LoN	League of Nations
MR......................	Master of the Rolls
Man	Manitoba
n	note
NB......................	New Brunswick
NI.......................	Northern Ireland
NIRC....................	National Industrial Relations Court
NS	Nova Scotia

NSW	New South Wales
NZ	New Zealand
Nfld	Newfoundland
OJ	The Official Journal of the European Communities published by the Office for Official Publications of the European Communities
Ont.	Ontario
Ord.	Order
P	President
PC	Judicial Committee of the Privy Council
PCC	Palmer's Company Cases
PEI	Prince Edward Island
Qld.	Queensland
Que	Quebec
r	rule
RPC	Restrictive Practices Court
RSC	Rules of the Supreme Court 1965 (SI 1965/1776) as subsequently amended (see the current Supreme Court Practice)
reg	regulation
Res	Resolution
revsd.	reversed
s	section
SA.	South Africa
S Aust.	Southern Australia
SC.	Supreme Court
SC Fees Order 1980	Supreme Court Fees Order 1980 (SI 1980/821) as subsequently amended (see the current Supreme Court Practice)
SC Funds Rules 1975	Supreme Court Funds Rules 1975 (SI 1975/1803) as subsequently amended (see the current Supreme Court Practice)
SI	Statutory Instruments published by authority
SR & O	Statutory Rules and Orders published by authority
SR & O Rev 1904.	Revised Edition comprising all Public and General Statutory Rules and Orders in force on 31 December 1903
SR & O Rev 1948.	Revised Edition comprising all Public and General Statutory Rules and Orders and Statutory Instruments in force on 31 December 1948
SRNI	Statutory Rules of Northern Ireland
Sask	Saskatchewan
Sch	Schedule
Sess.	Session
TS.	Treaty Series
Tas	Tasmania
ULFIS	Uniform Law on the International Sale of Goods
UN.	United Nations
Vict.	Victoria
W Aust.	Western Australia

NOTE 1. The abbreviations of law reports and other sources used in this work are listed in vol 1(1) (Reissue) at p 15 et seq.

NOTE 2. Where references are made to other publications, the volume number precedes and the page number follows the name of the publication; eg the reference '12 Forms & Precedents (5th Edn) 44' refers to volume 12 of the Encyclopaedia of Forms and Precedents, page 44.

NOTE 3. An English statute is cited by short title or, where there is no short title, by regnal year and chapter number together with the name by which it is commonly known or a description of its subject matter and date. In the case of a foreign statute, the mode of citation generally follows the style of citation in use in the country concerned with the addition, where necessary, of the name of the country in parentheses.

NOTE 4. A statutory instrument is cited by short title, if any, followed by the year and number, or, if unnumbered, the date.

TABLE OF STATUTES

This Table consolidates statutes cited in Volume 11(1) (paragraphs 1–800)
and Volume 11(2) (paragraphs 801–1592).

TABLE OF STATUTORY INSTRUMENTS

This Table consolidates statutory instruments cited in Volume 11(1) (paragraphs 1–800) and Volume 11(2) (paragraphs 801–1592).

TABLE OF NON–STATUTORY PROCEDURAL RULES AND
DIRECTIONS

TABLE OF CODES OF PRACTICE

This Table consolidates Codes of Practice cited in Volume 11(1) (paragraphs 1–800) and Volume 11(2) (paragraphs 801–1592).

TABLE OF
EC LEGISLATION

This Table consolidates EC legislation cited in Volume 11(1) (paragraphs 1–800) and Volume 11(2) (paragraphs 801–1592).

TABLE OF
CONVENTIONS

This Table consolidates conventions cited in Volume 11(1) (paragraphs 1–800)
and Volume 11(2) (paragraphs 801–1592).

TABLE OF CASES

This Table consolidates cases cited in Volume 11(1) (paragraphs 1–800) and
Volume 11(2) (paragraphs 801–1592)

A

PARA

M

PARA

Pais v Pais [1971] P 119, [1970] 3 All ER 491, [1970] 3 WLR 830, 114 Sol Jo 720   1163
Palace-Clark v Standen [1964] 1 QB 294, [1963] 3 All ER 627, [1963] 3 WLR 917, 128 JP 28, 107 Sol Jo 811, 48 Cr
    App Rep 20, DC   380
Palmer v R [1971] AC 814, [1971] 1 All ER 1077, [1971] 2 WLR 831, 115 Sol Jo 264, 55 Cr App Rep 223, 243n, 16
    WIR 499, 511, PC 455, 456, 1063, 1065
Pamplin v Fraser [1981] RTR 494, 127 Sol Jo 786, 80 LS Gaz R 3243   320
Paprika Ltd v Board of Trade [1944] KB 327, [1944] 1 All ER 372, 113 LJKB 209, 170 LT 269, 108 JP 104, 60 TLR
    203, 42 LGR 131, DC   1469
Parker v Green (1862) 2 B & S 299, 31 LJMC 133, 6 LT 46, 26 JP 247, 8 Jur NS 409, 10 WR 316, 9 Cox CC 169 . . . 2, 1096
Parker v R [1964] AC 1369, [1964] 2 All ER 641, [1964] 3 WLR 70, 108 Sol Jo 459, PC   438
Parker v Smith [1974] Crim LR 426, DC   1065
Parkes v Prescott (1869) LR 4 Exch 169, 38 LJ Ex 105, 20 LT 537, 17 WR 773, Ex Ch   47
Parkes v R [1976] 3 All ER 380, [1976] 1 WLR 1251, 140 JP 634, 120 Sol Jo 720, 64 Cr App Rep 25, PC 1121, 1123
Parkin v Norman [1983] QB 92, [1982] 2 All ER 583, [1982] 3 WLR 523, 126 Sol Jo 359, [1982] Crim LR 528, DC . .   152
Parlement Belge, The (1880) 5 PD 197, [1874–80] All ER Rep 104, 42 LT 273, 28 WR 642, 4 Asp MLC 234, CA . . . 38, 626
Pate's Case (1850) 8 State Tr NS 1   31
Patel v Comptroller of Customs [1966] AC 356, [1965] 3 All ER 593, [1965] 3 WLR 1222, 109 Sol Jo 832 1099
Patel and Patel v Blakey (1987) 151 JP 532, [1988] RTR 65, [1987] Crim LR 683   1527
Paton v British Pregnancy Advisory Service Trustees [1979] QB 276, [1978] 2 All ER 987, [1978] 3 WLR 687, 142 JP
    497, 122 Sol Jo 744   465
Patterson v Block (1984) Times, 21 June   167
Paul v Luton Justices, ex p Crown Prosecution Service (1989) 153 JP 512, [1989] Crim LR 660, DC   396
Pearks, Gunston and Tee Ltd v Ward [1902] 2 KB 1, [1900–3] All ER Rep 228, 71 LJKB 656, 87 LT 51, 66 JP 774, 20
    Cox CC 279   35
Pearson v Lemaitre (1843) 5 Man & G 700, 6 Scott NR 607, 12 LJCP 253, 1 LTOS 170, 7 JP 336, 7 Jur 748   91
Pearson's Case (1835) 2 Lew CC 144   29
Pedro v Diss [1981] 2 All ER 59, 145 JP 445, 72 Cr App Rep 193   320
Pellew v Wonford Inhabitants (1829) 9 B & C 134, 7 LJOSMC 84, sub nom Pellew v East Wonford Hundred 4 Man
    & Ry KB 130, 2 Man & Ry MC 127   786
Penny v Nicholas. See Nicholas v Penny
People, The (A-G) v Carney and Mulcahy [1955] IR 324   997
People, The (A-G) v Casey (No 2) [1963] IR 33   1140
People, The (A-G) v Dunleavy [1948] IR 95, 82 ILTR 70, CCA   445
People, The (A-G) v Keating [1953] IR 200, CCA   1166
People, The (DPP) v Mulvey [1987] IR 502, CCA   1141
People, The (A-G) v Thomas [1954] IR 319   625
Perkins v Jeffery [1915] 2 KB 702, [1914–15] All ER Rep 172, 84 LJKB 1554, 113 LT 456, 79 JP 425, 31 TLR 444, 25
    Cox CC 59, DC 418, 1091, 1092, 1094, 1095, 1096
Peters, Re [1988] QB 871, [1988] 3 All ER 46, [1988] 3 WLR 182, 132 Sol Jo 966, CA   1316
Pharmaceutical Society v London and Provincial Supply Association (1880) 5 App Cas 857, [1874–80] All ER Rep Ext
    1363, 49 LJQB 736, 43 LT 389, 45 JP 20, 28 WR 957, HL   35
Pharmaceutical Society of Great Britain v Storkwain Ltd [1985] 3 All ER 4, 149 JP 625; affd [1986] 2 All ER 635,
    [1986] 1 WLR 903, 150 JP 385, 130 Sol Jo 481, [1986] BTLC 135, 83 Cr App Rep 359, [1986] LS Gaz R 2238,
    [1986] Crim LR 813, HL   18
Phelon and Moore Ltd v Keel [1914] 3 KB 165, 83 LJKB 1516, 111 LT 214, 78 JP 247, 24 Cox CC 234, 12 LGR
    950, DC   56
Phillips v Eyre (1869) LR 4 QB 225; affd (1870) LR 6 QB 1, 10 B & S 1004, 40 LJQB 28, 22 LT 869, Ex Ch   1449
Phillips v R [1969] 2 AC 130, [1969] 2 WLR 581, 113 Sol Jo 14, 53 Cr App Rep 132, 13 WIR 356, PC   439
Piddington v Bates [1960] 3 All ER 660, [1961] 1 WLR 162, 105 Sol Jo 110, DC   320
Pine's Case (1628) Cro Car 117, 3 State Tr 359   81
Pippet v Hearn (1822) 5 B & Ald 634, 1 Dow & Ry KB 266   315
Pittard v Mahoney [1977] Crim LR 169, DC   167
Plancq v Marks (1906) 94 LT 577, 70 JP 216, 22 TLR 432, 50 Sol Jo 377, 4 LGR 503, 21 Cox CC 157, DC   1140
Plunkett v Cobbett (1804) 5 Esp 136   91
Pointing v Wilson [1927] 1 KB 382, [1926] All ER Rep 523, 96 LJKB 309, 136 LT 307, 91 JP 5, 43 TLR 44, 70 Sol Jo
    1091, 28 Cox CC 291, DC   320
Pointon v Hill (1884) 12 QBD 306, 53 LJMC 62, 50 LT 268, 48 JP 341, 32 WR 478, 15 Cox CC 461, DC   417
Police v Emirali [1976] 1 NZLR 286   398
Police v Reid [1987] Crim LR 702   145
Police Comr v Cartman [1896] 1 QB 655, 65 LJMC 113, 74 LT 726, 60 JP 357, 44 WR 637, 12 TLR 334, 40 Sol Jo
    439, 18 Cox CC 341 . . . . 55, 56
Pomeroy v Baddeley (1826) Ry & M 430   1002
Poole v R [1961] AC 223, [1960] 3 All ER 398, [1960] 3 WLR 770, 104 Sol Jo 868, PC   941
Poole v Stokes (1914) 110 LT 1020, [1914–15] All ER Rep 1083, 78 JP 231, 30 TLR 371, 24 Cox CC 169, 12 LGR
    629, DC   537
Popkin v Popkin (1794) 1 Hag Ecc 765n   515
Portsea Island Mutual Co-operative Society Ltd v Leyland [1978] ICR 1195, [1978] IRLR 556, 122 Sol Jo 486, 77 LGR
    164, [1978] Crim LR 554   55

Table of Cases

PARA

PARA

CRIMINAL LAW, EVIDENCE AND PROCEDURE

Volume 11(1)

3. OFFENCES AGAINST THE PERSON

Volume 11(2)

9. HEARING OR PRELIMINARY INQUIRY BEFORE JUSTICES

10. BAIL

14. SENTENCE

Appendix

NOTE – For particulars of crimes and offences, not included in the above table (which does not purport to be complete), see the appropriate titles.

1. PRINCIPLES OF CRIMINAL LIABILITY

(1) THE NATURE OF CRIME

1. Definition of 'crime'. 'Criminal' and 'crime' are words of ordinary English usage. There is no satisfactory definition of crime which will embrace the many acts and omissions which are criminal, and which will at the same time exclude all those acts and omissions which are not[1]. Ordinarily a crime is a wrong which affects the security or well-being of the public generally so that the public has an interest in its suppression[2]. A crime is frequently a moral wrong in that it amounts to conduct which is inimical to the general moral sense of the community. There are, however, many crimes which exhibit neither of the above characteristics[3]. An act may be made criminal by Parliament simply because it is criminal, rather than civil, process which offers the more effective means of controlling the conduct in question.

1 Whether conduct amounts to a crime may be determined by whether it is followed by criminal or civil proceedings: see para 2 post.
2 See *Mogul SS Co v McGregor, Gow & Co* (1889) 23 QBD 598 at 606, CA per Lord Esher MR ('an illegal act which is a wrong against the public welfare seems to have the necessary ingredients of a crime').
3 See *Sherras v De Rutzen* [1895] 1 QB 918 at 922 per Wright J ('acts which . . . are not criminal in any real sense, but are acts which in the public interest are prohibited under a penalty').

2. Criminal and civil proceedings distinguished. Civil proceedings have for their object the recovery of money or other property, or the enforcement of a right or advantage on behalf of the plaintiff, whereas criminal proceedings have for their object the punishment of a person who has committed a crime[1]. Criminal proceedings are not to be used as a means of enforcing a civil right[2]. Whether conduct amounts to a crime may be determined by ascertaining whether the conduct in question is followed by criminal or civil proceedings. If the proceedings will result in the punishment of a party, the conduct in question will be a crime notwithstanding that it may be a matter of small consequence[3]. Where an act is commanded or prohibited by statute, disobedience is prima facie criminal unless criminal proceedings manifestly appear to be excluded by the statute[4]. An act may be prohibited or commanded by statute in such a manner that the person contravening the provision is liable to a pecuniary penalty which is recoverable as a civil debt; and in such an instance contravention is not a crime[5].

1 *A-G v Radloff* (1854) 10 Exch 84 at 101 per Platt B. See also *Re Douglas* (1842) 3 QB 825; *A-G v Bradlaugh* (1885) 14 QBD 667, CA; *R v Hausmann* (1909) 73 JP 516, 3 Cr App Rep 3, CCA.
2 *R v Peel* [1943] 2 All ER 99, 29 Cr App Rep 73, CCA. As to the powers of criminal courts to award compensation see para 1238 et seq post.
3 *Parker v Green* (1862) 2 B & S 299 at 311; *Mellor v Denham* (1880) 5 QBD 467, CA; *R v Sullivan* (1874) IR 8 CL 404.
4 *R v Hall* [1891] 1 QB 747; *Willingale v Norris* [1909] 1 KB 57, DC; *Rathbone v Bundock* [1962] 2 QB 260, [1962] 2 All ER 257, DC; *R v Lennox-Wright* [1973] Crim LR 529.
5 See *Brown v Allweather Mechanical Grouting Co Ltd* [1954] 2 QB 443, [1953] 1 All ER 474, DC. See also *Atcheson v Everitt* (1776) 1 Cowp 382; *Ex p Beeching* (1825) 4 B & C 136 at 137; *A-G v Siddon* (1830) 1 Cr & J 220; *A-G v Radloff* (1854) 10 Exch 84 at 96; *Parker v Green* (1862) 2 B & S 299; *R v Hawkhurst Inhabitants* (1862) 1 New Rep 88; *A-G v Bradlaugh* (1885) 14 QBD 667, CA; *Newman v Jones* (1886) 17 QBD 132 at 136; *R v Tyler and International Commercial Co* [1891] 2 QB 588 at 594, CA per Bowen LJ; *St Helen's District Tramways Co v Wood* (1891) 60 LJMC 141, DC.

Whether a statute creates a criminal offence is a question of interpretation; eg if the word 'penalty' as distinct from the word 'fine' is used, the general rule is that the penalty must be recovered as a debt in a civil court: see *Brown v Allweather Mechanical Grouting Co Ltd* supra at 446 and at 475 per Lord Goddard CJ; but cf *R v Paget* (1881) 8 QBD 151. The Common Informers Act 1951 s 1 (3) substituted fines for the penalties previously recoverable in many common informer actions and made the acts for which the penalties had been recoverable into crimes.

The word 'offence' is sometimes used to describe a criminal act (see *R v Paget* supra) and sometimes to describe an act which is not criminal (see *A-G v Radloff* supra; *Brown v Allweather Mechanical Grouting Co Ltd* supra). There is a rule of statutory interpretation that 'a man is not to be put in peril upon an ambiguity': *London and North Eastern Rly Co v Berriman* [1946] AC 278 at 313, 314, [1946] 1 All ER 255 at 270, HL per Lord Simonds.

3. Legal punishment. Legal punishment is punishment awarded in a process instituted at the suit of the Crown standing forward as prosecutor on behalf of the subject on public grounds[1]. Such process, once instituted, may be stayed only at the instance of the Attorney General acting on behalf of the Crown[2], or during the preliminary stages of the proceedings, and, subject to statutory conditions, by the Director of Public Prosecutions[3]; and the punishment, when imposed, may be remitted only by the Crown[4] or by Parliament.

1 *Burdett v Abbot* (1811) 14 East 1 at 162 per Bayley J. In the absence of statutory provision to the contrary any person may of his own initiative, and without any preliminary consent, institute criminal proceedings with a view to an indictment: see para 639 post. The prosecution is, however, always at the suit of the Crown. Hence criminal proceedings were known as Pleas of the Crown. As to the circumstances in which consent is required to proceedings being brought see para 639 post; as to the right of any person to prefer an indictment see para 916 post; as to the penalties which may be imposed in criminal proceedings see para 1192 et seq post; and as to sentencing principles see paras 1187–1189 post.
2 As to the entry of a nolle prosequi by the Attorney General see para 939 et seq post.
3 See the Prosecution of Offences Act 1985 s 23 and para 871 post.
4 See para 1449 post and CONSTITUTIONAL LAW vol 8 para 949 et seq.

(2) THE ELEMENTS OF CRIME

(i) In general

4. The constituents of crime in general. A person is not to be convicted of a crime unless he has, by voluntary conduct, brought about those elements which by common law or statute constitute that crime. In general a person does not incur criminal liability unless he intended to bring about, or recklessly brought about, those elements which constitute the crime. The above concepts are traditionally expressed in the maxim 'actus non facit reum nisi mens sit rea'[1].

In some instances a person may be convicted of a crime if he has negligently brought about its constituent elements[2].

In certain crimes, nearly all of which are created by statute, a person may incur criminal liability even though he has acted without intention, recklessness or negligence in relation to one or more of the elements of that crime[3]. Such crimes are known as crimes of strict liability. Notwithstanding that the statute creating an offence contains no expression indicating that a mental element is a necessary constituent, there is a presumption in favour of the requirement of mens rea[4]; and, before criminal liability without fault can be imposed, this presumption must be displaced.

1 The maxim originated with Coke: see 3 Co Inst 6. Stephen (2 History of the Criminal Law 95) thought that 'the maxim not only looks more instructive than it really is, but suggests fallacies which it does not precisely state'. See also *Haughton v Smith* [1975] AC 476 at 491, 492, 58 Cr App Rep 198 at 206, 207, HL per Lord Hailsham of St Marylebone LC ('the phrase means "an act does not make a man guilty of a crime unless his mind be also guilty". It is thus not the actus which is reus but the man and his mind respectively . . . it is well to record this as it has frequently led to confusion'); *Sweet v Parsley* [1970] AC 132 at 162, 53 Cr App Rep 221 at 245, HL per Lord Diplock. As to voluntary conduct see para 6 note 2 post.
2 See para 17 post.
3 See para 18 post.
4 *Sherras v De Rutzen* [1895] 1 QB 918 at 921, 922; this presumption was categorically affirmed by the House of Lords in *Sweet v Parsley* [1970] AC 132, 53 Cr App Rep 221, HL.

(ii) The Criminal Act

5. The actus reus. Every crime has specified elements, prescribed by the common law or by the statutory definition of the offence, which together make up its actus reus. Mere intention will not suffice for criminal liability[1]; but the actus reus may be so defined as to include acts of omission as well as acts of commission, and a person may incur criminal liability for failing to do that which the law enjoins[2] as much as by doing that which the law proscribes.

In a criminal trial the prosecution must prove the existence of all those elements constituting the offence; failure to prove the existence of any particular element necessarily involves a failure to establish the commission of the crime[3]. Where, on the other hand, it is proved that the accused brought about all the constituent elements of the particular crime, he is not entitled to be acquitted merely because certain facts exist which, had he been aware of them, would have provided justification or excuse[4].

1 Under the Treason Act 1351 (as amended) it is an offence to 'compass or imagine' the death of the Sovereign; but the courts have required that the intention be manifested by some overt act: *R v Thistlewood* (1820) 33 State Tr 681. See further para 81 post.
2 See para 9 post.
3 *R v Deller* (1952) 36 Cr App Rep 184, CCA (conviction for obtaining by false pretences quashed where prosecution could not prove statement to be untrue though accused believed it to be untrue); *R v Dyson* [1908] 2 KB 454, 1 Cr App Rep 13, CCA (conviction for manslaughter quashed where judge directed jury that accused could be found guilty though death resulted from injuries inflicted more than a year before the death). Cf *Haughton v Smith* [1985] AC 476, 58 Cr App Rep 198, HL.
4 *R v Dadson* (1850) 2 Den 35, 4 Cox CC 358, CCR (constable, unaware of circumstances which would have justified his use of force, convicted of wounding with intent to cause grievous bodily harm). As to justification and excuse see para 19 et seq post.

6. Involuntary conduct; automatism. In general[1], no crime is committed unless a person brings about its constituent elements by a voluntary act or omission[2]. A person does not incur criminal liability for acts done in a state of automatism, as when in his sleep he kills someone[3] or sets fire to a house[4], or where he causes harm to someone during a mental blackout induced by an external factor[5] such as violence or drugs, including anaesthetics, alcohol and hypnotic influences[6], or by disease (not being a disease of the mind) or injury[7] or by forces outside his control[8]. If, however, the accused's state of automatism results from self-induced intoxication due to alcohol or drugs, it is not a defence to crimes of 'basic intent'[9], although it may negative mens rea in crimes requiring a 'specific intent'[10]. Automatism which is self-induced by other means may be a defence even to a crime of 'basic intent'[11].

An act is not, however, involuntary merely because it is done in circumstances of constraint which affect the freedom of action of the person doing it, as where an act is done under threats[12] or on the command of a superior[13]. For an act to be regarded as involuntary, the person doing it must not only be deprived of a free choice as to what to do, he must also be divested of the ability to control what he does. Automatism has been said to postulate complete absence of voluntary control[14] and the category of such involuntary acts is very limited[15].

There is no burden upon the defence to establish automatism where insanity is not involved; the burden is upon the prosecution to exclude it[16]. Before the prosecution is required to negative the assertion that conduct on the part of the accused was involuntary, the defence must, in the course of the evidence, lay a proper foundation for that assertion[17]. The accused's own evidence will rarely be enough and should be supported by medical evidence[17]. The prosecution may call medical evidence to rebut a plea of automatism[18].

1 An offence may be so defined as apparently to require no proof of any voluntary act or omission on the part of the accused: see the much criticised case of *R v Larsonneur* (1933) 24 Cr App Rep 74, CCA, although that case is probably unique. However, on a charge of driving while unfit through drink or drugs under the Road Traffic Act 1988 s 4, or of driving with an excessive blood-alcohol concentration under s 5, it seems that the accused may be convicted notwithstanding that he was unaware of the consumption of alcohol, though the unwitting consumption may constitute a special reason for not disqualifying him from driving: *Brewer v Metropolitan Police Comr* [1969] 1 All ER 513, 53 Cr App Rep 157, DC; *R v Shippam* [1971] Crim LR 434, CA; *Williams v Neale* [1971] Crim LR 598, DC.
   Even though some conduct on the part of the accused may have been involuntary, he may incur criminal liability in respect of voluntary conduct which took place before the involuntary conduct: see eg *Kay v Butterworth* (1945) 173 LT 191, DC (driver continuing to drive when overcome with drowsiness). See also *Henderson v Jones* [1955] Crim LR 318, DC; *R v Sibbles* [1959] Crim LR 660; *R v Jarmain* [1946] KB 74, 31 Cr App Rep 39, CCA. As to vicarious liability see para 52 et seq post.
2 See 2 Stephen's History of the Criminal Law 100; 4 Bl Com (14th Edn) 20. 'The requirement that it should be a voluntary act is essential, not only in a murder case, but also in every criminal case': *Bratty v A-G for Northern Ireland* [1963] AC 386 at 409, 46 Cr App Rep 1 at 16, HL per Lord Denning.
3 *R v Boshears* (1961) (unreported but noted in The Times, 18 February).
4 See 2 Stephen's History of the Criminal Law 100; 1 Hale PC 434.
5 Stress, anxiety and depression are not in themselves, separately or together, external factors of the kind capable of causing or contributing to a state of automatism: *R v Hennessy* [1989] 2 All ER 9, 89 Cr App Rep 10, CA.
6 *R v Quick, R v Paddison* [1973] QB 910 at 922, [1973] 3 All ER 347 at 356, CA. Cf *R v Kemp* [1964] 2 QB 341, 48 Cr App Rep 131, CCA.
7 *Hill v Baxter* [1958] 1 QB 277 at 286, 42 Cr App Rep 51 at 61, DC.
8 1 Hale PC 434; *Hill v Baxter* [1958] 1 QB 277, 42 Cr App Rep 51, DC.
9 *DPP v Majewski* [1977] AC 443, 62 Cr App Rep 262, HL. '"Crimes of basic intent" . . . mean those crimes whose definition expresses (or, more often, implies) a mens rea which does not go beyond the actus reus': *DPP v Morgan* [1975] 2 All ER 347 at 363, 61 Cr App Rep 136 at 152, HL per Lord Simon of Glaisdale; approved in *DPP v Majewski* supra at 471 and at 267 per Lord Elwyn-Jones LC.
   As to self-administration of a soporific or sedative drug see *R v Hardie* [1984] 3 All ER 848, 80 Cr App Rep 157, CA (accused charged with an offence under the Criminal Damage Act 1971 s 1 (2); self-administration of valium did not raise a conclusive presumption that proof of intoxication was not to be admitted for the purpose of showing that mens rea was lacking).
10 'A crime of specific intent requires something more than contemplation of the prohibited act and foresight of its probable consequences. The mens rea in a crime of specific intent requires proof of a purposive element': *DPP v Majewski* [1977] AC 443 at 479, 480, 62 Cr App Rep 262 at 274, HL per Lord Simon of Glaisdale. As to the consequences of self-induced intoxication see para 28 post.
11 *R v Bailey* [1983] 2 All ER 503, 77 Cr App Rep 76, CA (diabetic accused was in a state of automatism due to hypoglycaemia); but quaere whether this case is consistent with *R v Sullivan* [1984] AC 156, 77 Cr App Rep 176, HL or *R v Hennessy* [1989] 2 All ER 9, 89 Cr App Rep 10, CA.
12 As to the defence of duress, however, see para 24 post.
13 See para 27 post.
14 *Watmore v Jenkins* [1962] 2 QB 572 at 587, [1962] 2 All ER 868 at 874, DC.

15 *Bratty v A-G for Northern Ireland* [1963] AC 386 at 410, 46 Cr App Rep 1 at 18, HL per Lord Denning. Cf *R v Pantelic* [1973] 1 ACTR 1 at 3.
16 *Bratty v A-G for Northern Ireland* [1963] AC 386, 46 Cr App Rep 1, HL. See also para 7 note 4 post. As to the burden of proof generally see para 1062 et seq post.
17 *Bratty v A-G for Northern Ireland* [1963] AC 386, 46 Cr App Rep 1, HL.
18 *R v Smith* [1979] 3 All ER 605, 69 Cr App Rep 378, CA.

7. Automatism and insanity contrasted. A person's conduct may be involuntary[1] where he brings about the elements of a crime but, owing to a defect of reason arising from a disease of the mind within the M'Naghten Rules[2], does so without any awareness of the act, or without any rational control over his actions. In such a situation the accused is entitled to an acquittal in relation to what would otherwise be a guilty act, and the proper verdict is one of not guilty by reason of insanity[3]. Where the sole cause assigned for involuntary conduct is insanity, it follows that the defence of automatism is inapt and inapplicable[4]. Where, however, on the evidence issues of both insanity and automatism arise, it is necessary for the trial judge to distinguish clearly between them as a matter of law[5], and to explain that, while the accused carries the burden of proving insanity, it is for the prosecution to negative the defence of automatism[6].

1 See para 6 ante.
2 See para 31 post; *R v Sullivan* [1984] AC 156, 77 Cr App Rep 176, HL (assault committed during an epileptic fit); *R v Hennessy* [1989] 2 All ER 9, 89 Cr App Rep 10, CA (accused was insulin-dependent diabetic suffering from hyperglycaemia). See also *R v Kemp* [1964] 2 QB 341, 48 Cr App Rep 131, CCA (mental blackout due to cerebral tumour). *R v Charlson* [1955] 1 All ER 859, 39 Cr App Rep 37, CCA (another cerebral tumour case) is inconsistent with *R v Sullivan* supra and should no longer be followed.
3 See para 1040 post.
4 *Bratty v A-G for Northern Ireland* [1963] AC 386, 46 Cr App Rep 1, HL. Where the defence of insanity is raised, the evidence may be such that, while it fails to support a finding that the accused was suffering from a disease of the mind, a jury may nevertheless be left in doubt whether the crime was the result of a conscious and deliberate act or omission on the part of the accused. Insanity is an answer in the nature of confession and avoidance, and must in general be raised and proved by the defence: see para 33 post. Where the evidence tendered by the defence is such as to show that the accused was suffering from a defect of reason arising from a disease of the mind, the accused cannot avoid a verdict of not guilty by reason of insanity by seeking to rely exclusively upon a defence of automatism: see *Bratty v A-G for Northern Ireland* supra at 411 and at 19 per Lord Denning. See also *R v Sullivan* [1984] AC 156, 77 Cr App Rep 176, HL (accused who inflicted grievous bodily harm during an epileptic fit sought to rely on a defence of automatism; held that the proper verdict was one of not guilty by reason of insanity); *R v Hennessy* [1989] 2 All ER 9, 89 Cr App Rep 10, CA.
5 *R v Sullivan* [1984] AC 156, 77 Cr App Rep 176, HL.
6 *R v Burns* (1973) 58 Cr App Rep 364, CA, applying *R v Quick, R v Paddison* [1973] QB 910, [1973] 3 All ER 347, CA. See also para 6 text to notes 15–17 ante.

8. Causation. To give rise to criminal liability it is not enough that the accused had a culpable state of mind; it must be proved that the crime was caused by some conduct on his part[1]. That conduct need not be a direct cause of the crime, for a person may cause an event through the agency of others[2]; nor need the conduct of the accused be the sole or the effective cause of the crime. It is sufficient if it is a cause, that is a cause which cannot be dismissed as trivial, or as merely part of the history of the events leading up to the commission of the crime[3].

1 *R v Dalloway* (1847) 3 Cox CC 273.
2 *R v Tyler* (1838) 8 C & P 616. As to the use of an innocent agent see para 44 post; and as to vicarious liability see para 52 et seq post.

3 *R v Hennigan* [1971] 3 All ER 133, 55 Cr App Rep 262, CA; *R v Pagett* (1983) 76 Cr App Rep 279, CA; and see generally para 430 post.

9. Omissions. Save in exceptional circumstances the criminal law imposes no obligation on persons to act so as to prevent the occurrence of harm or wrongdoing. There is no general duty to prevent the commission of crime[1]; nor does a person commit a crime or become a party to it solely because he might reasonably have prevented its commission[2]. Omission to act in a particular way will give rise to criminal liability only where a duty so to act arises at common law or is imposed by statute[3]. Such a duty is exceptional and the criminal law does not ordinarily require a person to be his brother's keeper[4]. Nevertheless, if a person assumes that role, he may incur criminal liability not only for any subsequent acts but also for omissions[5]. In such circumstances there is no need to prove that the accused had been obliged by law to undertake the particular duty, or that he was bound by contract to care for the other; it is sufficient that he voluntarily undertook the care of another in circumstances in which that other was unable to fend for himself[6].

Where a person, with the requisite mens rea, by his conduct brings about the actus reus of a crime, he commits that crime, and conduct in this sense includes acts of omission as well as commission[7]. It is unnecessary to characterise the act immediately causing harm as one of commission or omission if that act forms part of a course of conduct undertaken by a person. If the course of conduct is such that other persons, or possibly the property of other persons, are harmed by its performance, the accused will be criminally liable in respect of his acts, whether they are of commission or omission[8]. A crime may be so defined that it is impossible or difficult to conceive of circumstances in which the actus reus could be constituted by an omission[9]; but it would seem that, in conjunction with the appropriate mens rea, most offences against the person and most offences against property, including theft[10] and dishonest handling[11], may be so constituted.

1 A constable has a duty to prevent crime (*Crouther's Case* (1599) Cro Eliz 654); and it is an offence for a person to refuse without reasonable excuse to assist in quelling a breach of the peace when called upon by a constable (*R v Brown* (1841) Car & M 314); and see para 322 post.
2 Cf *Rice v Connolly* [1966] 2 QB 414, [1966] 2 All ER 649, DC (person refusing to answer questions is not 'wilfully obstructing' a police officer even though this may hamper inquiries). See also *Swallow v LCC* [1916] 1 KB 224, DC.
3 Where pursuant to an Act of Parliament an order is made requiring a corporation to effect certain works, an indictment lies for failure to comply: *R v Birmingham and Gloucester Rly Co* (1842) 3 QB 223.
4 At common law a parent has a duty to act for the welfare of his child and, if harm is caused to the child by his failure to act, he may be criminally liable for the resulting harm: *R v Bubb, R v Hook* (1850) 4 Cox CC 455; *R v Gibbins and Proctor* (1918) 13 Cr App Rep 134, CCA. Cf *R v Knights* (1860) 2 F & F 46.
5 *R v Smith* (1826) 2 C & P 449. See also *R v Stone, R v Dobinson* [1977] QB 354, 64 Cr App Rep 186, CA (the occupier of a house and the woman with whom he was living were both convicted of manslaughter for failing to provide nursing care for the occupier's sister who lodged with them).
6 'In this case, as in most cases, the legal duty can be nothing else than the taking upon oneself the performance of a moral obligation': *R v Instan* (1893) as reported in 17 Cox CC 602 at 603, CCR per Lord Coleridge. Thus a woman who assumes responsibility for the care of another's child may be liable in respect of a failure to provide food (*R v Gibbins and Proctor* (1918) 13 Cr App Rep 134, CCA); or to provide medical aid (*R v Lee and Parkes* (1917) 13 Cr App Rep 39, CCA). See also *R v Instan* [1893] 1 QB 450, CCR; the Children and Young Persons Act 1933 s 1 (as amended); and para 537 post.
7 See eg *R v Pittwood* (1902) 19 TLR 37 (a railway level-crossing keeper who forgot to close the gates was convicted of manslaughter). See also *R v Miller* [1983] 2 AC 161, 77 Cr App Rep 17, HL

(accidentally setting fire to mattress and, with knowledge of the fire, taking no steps to put it out; guilty of arson).

8 No mere omission, however, can constitute a battery: see para 488 text and note 11 post.

9 Eg offences under the Forgery and Counterfeiting Act 1981 Pt I (ss 1–13): see para 605 et seq post.

10 An appropriation includes 'keeping . . . [the property] as owner': see the Theft Act 1968 s 3 (1) and para 543 post.

11 *R v Pitchley* (1973) 57 Cr App Rep 30, CA.

(iii) The Mental Element

10. Mens rea in general. As a general rule every crime requires a mental element[1], the nature of which will depend upon the definition of the particular crime in question. Expressions connoting the requirement of a mental element include: 'with intent'[2]; 'recklessly'[3]; 'unlawfully'[4]; 'maliciously'[5]; 'unlawfully and maliciously'; 'wilfully'[6]; 'knowingly'[7]; 'knowing or believing'; 'fraudulently'[8]; 'dishonestly'[9]; 'corruptly'; 'allowing'; and 'permitting'. Each of these expressions is capable of bearing a meaning which differs from that ascribed to any other. The meaning of each must be determined in the context in which it appears, and the same expression may bear a different meaning in different contexts[10].

Although the view has been expressed that it is impossible to ascribe any particular meaning to the term mens rea[11], concepts such as those of intention, recklessness and knowledge are commonly used as the basis for criminal liability and in some respects may be said to be fundamental to it. Generally, subject to both qualification and exception, a person is not criminally liable for serious crime[12] unless he intends to cause, foresees that he will probably cause, or at the lowest, foresees that he may cause, the elements which constitute the crime in question[13].

1 See, however, *R v Larsonneur* (1933) 24 Cr App Rep 74, CCA and para 6 note 1 ante. Even in crimes of strict liability some mental element is required: see para 18 post.

2 See paras 11, 16 post.

3 See para 14 post.

4 For the meaning of 'unlawfully' see *R v Kimber* [1983] 3 All ER 316, 77 Cr App Rep 225, CA; *R v Williams* [1987] 3 All ER 411 at 413, 414, 78 Cr App Rep 276 at 279, CA. 'We cannot accept that the word "unlawful" when used in a definition of an offence is to be regarded as "tautologous". In our judgment the word "unlawful" does import an essential element of the offence': *R v Kimber* supra at 320 and at 230 per Lawton LJ; disapproving dictum of Hodgson J in *Albert v Lavin* [1982] AC 546 at 561, 562, [1981] 1 All ER 628 at 639, DC.

5 For the meaning of 'maliciously' in the context of the Offences against the Person Act 1861 s 23 see *R v Cunningham* [1957] 2 QB 396, 41 Cr App Rep 155, CCA (held to import intention or recklessness: see further para 475 post). *R v Caldwell* [1982] 2 AC 341, 73 Cr App Rep 13, HL (see para 14 post) does not affect the decision in *R v Cunningham* supra: *R v Caldwell* supra at 351 and at 17, 18 per Lord Diplock; *W (a minor) v Dolbey* (1983) 88 Cr App Rep 1, DC. Cf, however, *DPP v K (a minor)* [1990] 1 All ER 331, DC (cited in para 488 note 10 post). In the context of the Offences against the Person Act 1861 s 20 'maliciously' was held to postulate intent or recklessness as to the causing of physical harm but not as to wounding or the causing of grievous bodily harm: *R v Mowatt* [1968] 1 QB 421, 51 Cr App Rep 402, CA (now to be considered in the light of the Criminal Justice Act 1967 s 8: see para 16 post).

6 For the meaning of 'wilfully' in the context of the Children and Young Persons Act 1933 s 1 (as amended) (wilfully neglecting a child: see para 537 post) see *R v Sheppard* [1981] AC 394, 72 Cr App Rep 82, HL.

7 For the meaning of 'knowingly' in the context of the Explosive Substances Act 1883 s 4 (1) (see para 482 post) see *R v Hallam* [1957] 1 QB 569, 41 Cr App Rep 111, CCA; overruling *R v Dacey* [1939] 2 All ER 641, 27 Cr App Rep 86, CCA.

Knowledge includes the state of mind of a person who shuts his eyes to the obvious: see *James & Son Ltd v Smee* [1955] 1 QB 78 at 91, [1954] 3 All ER 273 at 278 per Parker J; *Warner v Metropolitan Police Comr* [1969] 2 AC 256 at 279, 52 Cr App Rep 373 at 389, HL per Lord Reid; *Atwal v Massey*

[1971] 3 All ER 881, 56 Cr App Rep 6, DC. See also *R v Hall* (1985) 81 Cr App Rep 260, CA; and for the meaning of 'knowledge' in the context of handling stolen goods see para 561 post.

8 For the meaning of 'fraudulently' see *R v Sinclair* [1968] 3 All ER 241 at 246, 52 Cr App Rep 618 at 622, CA; and see para 605 et seq post.

9 See para 542 post.

10 See notes 4–8 supra.

11 See 2 Stephen's History of the Criminal Law 95 and para 4 note 1 ante.

12 There is no precise definition of what amounts to 'serious' crime, but cf the classification favoured by older authorities (eg 1 Bl Com (14th Edn) 54, 57, 58) into offences mala in se and offences mala prohibita. Offences falling within the first class were those described as offending against divine law or natural law, or as contrary to the moral sense of the community. Offences falling within the second class were those described as not in themselves immoral but offending against laws which enjoin positive duties and to which was annexed a penalty for non-compliance without making the transgression a moral offence.

For the meaning of 'serious crime' in the Interception of Communications Act 1985 see s 10 (3) and para 271 note 6 post; and for the meaning of 'serious arrestable offence' see para 704 post.

13 See *DPP v Beard* [1920] AC 479 at 504, HL per Lord Birkenhead; *Sweet v Parsley* [1970] AC 132, 53 Cr App Rep 221, HL; *Warner v Metropolitan Police Comr* [1969] 2 AC 256 at 271, 52 Cr App Rep 373 at 376, 377, HL per Lord Reid; *R v Taaffe* [1984] AC 539, 78 Cr App Rep 301, HL (accused who mistakenly believed he was committing one offence did not necessarily have the mens rea for another offence with which he was charged).

11. Intention. The mental element required to constitute many serious crimes is intention to bring about the elements of the crime in question; such crimes can be committed only by intention[1]. Attempted murder is confined to an intention to kill[2]; and attempts generally require intention[3]. Many statutory offences require intention as to all[4] or some[5] of their elements. A person intends the commission of a crime only where it is his aim or purpose to bring about its constituent elements[6]. Where he has this aim or purpose, he acts intentionally, though, to his knowledge, the chances of his causing the result are small. If he does not have this aim or purpose, he does not act intentionally[7] though to his knowledge the chances of causing the result are high. A person cannot be said to intend the unlawful conduct of others merely because it is a foreseen consequence of his own conduct[8].

Intention is not the same thing as motive[9]. The mental element of a crime ordinarily involves no reference to motive[10].

1 Cf those serious crimes where the requisite mental element is intention to bring about the elements of the crime or recklessness as to whether they are brought about. For a discussion as to what constitutes intention see *R v Hancock, R v Shankland* [1986] AC 455, 82 Cr App Rep 264, HL. See also *R v Moloney* [1985] AC 905, 81 Cr App Rep 93, HL; *R v Nedrick* [1986] 3 All ER 1, 83 Cr App Rep 267, CA; *R v Donnelly* [1989] Crim LR 739, CA.

2 *R v Whybrow* (1951) 35 Cr App Rep 141, CCA.

3 See para 73 post.

4 Eg the Infant Life (Preservation) Act 1929 s 1 (see para 452 post) requires an 'intent to destroy the life of the child'; under the Offences against the Person Act 1861 s 59 (see para 464 post), the poison or thing must be supplied 'knowing that the same is intended to be unlawfully used'. The offences created by the Aviation Security Act 1982 ss 2, 3 (see AVIATION) require that the specified acts should be done 'unlawfully and intentionally'.

5 Under the Offences against the Person Act 1861 s 18 (as amended) (where it deals with wounding or causing grievous bodily harm with intent to resist arrest: see para 469 post), the first part of the actus reus (wounding or causing grievous bodily harm) must be done unlawfully and maliciously; but the second part (doing some grievous bodily harm, resisting or preventing arrest) must be done intentionally. Where a crime requires the proof of an ulterior mental element, eg as in the Theft Act 1968 s 9 (1) (a) (entering a building with intent to steal etc: see para 552 post), this is ordinarily expressed to require intention.

6 Such aim or purpose is not to be equated with desire: see *R v Moloney* [1985] AC 905 at 926, 81 Cr App Rep 93 at 106, 107, HL per Lord Bridge; *R v Nedrick* [1986] 3 All ER 1 at 3, 83 Cr App Rep 267 at

270, CA. In so far as desire predicates something that is wanted because it causes pleasure or involves gain, desire in this sense is not essential to criminal intention; a killing is no less intentional where it is done by a parent to spare a child pain and suffering: *R v Simpson* (1915) 11 Cr App Rep 218, CCA; *R v Gray* (6 October 1965, unreported); cf *R v Steane* [1947] KB 997, 32 Cr App Rep 61, CCA.

7 See paras 15, 16 post. A result is not intended merely because it is foreseen as certain: see eg *R v Adams* (unreported but see [1957] Crim LR 365).

8 See *Beatty v Gillbanks* (1882) 9 QBD 308, DC; cf *Duncan v Jones* [1936] 1 KB 218, DC; *Dwyer v Mansfield* [1946] KB 437, [1946] 2 All ER 247, DC; *Fabbri v Morris* [1947] 1 All ER 315, DC; *Arrowsmith v Jenkins* [1963] 2 QB 561, [1963] 2 All ER 210, DC.

9 For the meaning of 'motive' see *Crofter Hand Woven Harris Tweed Co Ltd v Veitch* [1942] AC 435 at 452, [1942] 1 All ER 142 at 152, 153, HL per Viscount Maugham; *Hyam v DPP* [1975] AC 55 at 73, 59 Cr App Rep 91 at 100, 101, HL per Lord Hailsham of St Marylebone LC. As to foresight of consequences generally see para 16 post.

10 A bad motive is no more reason for convicting a person of crime than a good motive is an excuse for acquitting him: see eg *R v Simpson* (1915) 11 Cr App Rep 218, CCA; *R v Gray* (6 October 1965, unreported); and see *R v Sharpe* (1857) Dears & B 160, CCR; *R v Hicklin* (1868) LR 3 QB 360; *R v Booth* (1872) 12 Cox CC 231; *Steele v Brannan* (1872) LR 7 CP 261; *R v Jarrett* (1885) Times, 9, 11 November; *Chandler v DPP* [1964] AC 763, 46 Cr App Rep 347, HL; *Hyam v DPP* [1975] AC 55 at 73, 59 Cr App Rep 91 at 100, 101, HL per Lord Hailsham of St Marylebone LC.

12. Conditional intention. Where a person intends to bring about the elements of a crime conditionally upon the occurrence of some event, the fact that his intention is conditional in this sense does not prevent his action from being intentional for the purpose of criminal liability[1].

1 *R v Bentham* [1973] QB 357, 56 Cr App Rep 618, CA (possession of firearms with intent to endanger life when occasion arose); *R v Collins* [1973] QB 100, 56 Cr App Rep 554, CA (entering building to have intercourse against will of girl if she did not consent). However, in *R v Easom* [1971] 2 QB 315, 55 Cr App Rep 410, CA, it was said, of the intent permanently to deprive required to constitute theft, that a conditional intent would not do.

R v Easom supra was distinguished in *A-G's References (Nos 1 and 2 of 1979)* [1980] QB 180, 69 Cr App Rep 266, CA, in which it was held that, if an offence requires an intention to steal, it is irrelevant that the intention is conditional upon finding anything worth stealing. Hence it is no defence for the accused to show that he did not intend to steal any specific objects. See also *R v Walkington* [1979] 2 All ER 716, 68 Cr App Rep 427, CA (burglary); *Scudder v Barrett* [1980] QB 195n, 69 Cr App Rep 277, DC (attempted theft). As to attempts see now the Criminal Attempts Act 1981 s 1 and para 71 et seq post.

13. Transferred intention. Where a person intends to commit a particular crime and brings about the elements which constitute that crime, he may be convicted notwithstanding that the crime takes effect in a manner which was unintended or unforeseen[1]. The intent and the act must coincide[2].

1 See *R v Latimer* (1886) 17 QBD 359, CCR; cf *R v Pembliton* (1874) LR 2 CCR 119. See also *R v Mitchell* [1983] QB 741, 76 Cr App Rep 293, CA (accused's unlawful act directed at one person led to the death of another; conviction for manslaughter upheld). Presumably the rule applies where the accused acts recklessly but not intentionally, so that he might incur criminal liability where, foreseeing but not intending harm to A, he causes harm to B. It has been held that, where the accused intends to assault A, a private person, and by accident strikes B, a constable acting in the execution of his duty, the accused may be convicted of the aggravated assault which does not require knowledge that the person assaulted is a constable acting in the execution of his duty: *McBride v Turnock* [1964] Crim LR 456, DC.

2 *R v Gross* (1913) 23 Cox CC 455; cf *R v Monger* [1973] Crim LR 301.

14. Recklessness and foresight. Recklessness on the part of the accused is sufficient mens rea for certain statutory offences[1] and the common law crime of manslaughter[2]; and for these purposes a person is reckless if he has done an act which in fact involves an obvious[3] and serious risk of causing injury or damage and either (1) he fails to give any thought to the possibility of there being any such risk; or (2) having recognised that there is some risk involved, he nonetheless goes on to take it[4]. In relation to rape and indecent assault, however, being reckless as to whether the woman consents to sexual intercourse or to the indecent act means being indifferent to the feelings and wishes of the victim and giving no thought to the possibility that she might not be consenting[5].

Where a statute prohibits the doing of an act 'maliciously', this imports intention or such recklessness as is mentioned in head (2) above[6].

1 Eg criminal damage contrary to the Criminal Damage Act 1971 s 1 (see para 594 post); reckless driving contrary to the Road Traffic Act 1988 s 2 (see ROAD TRAFFIC).
2 See para 436 et seq post.
3 'Obvious' means obvious to an ordinary prudent individual rather than obvious to the particular accused having regard to his age, mental capacity and experience: *Elliott v C (a minor)* [1983] 2 All ER 1005, 77 Cr App Rep 103, DC; *R v Stephen Malcolm R* (1984) 79 Cr App Rep 334, CA. See also *R v Lawrence* [1982] AC 510, 73 Cr App Rep 1, HL; *R v Caldwell* [1982] AC 341, 73 Cr App Rep 13, HL; *R v Miller* [1983] 2 AC 161, 77 Cr App Rep 17, HL; *Chief Constable of Avon and Somerset Constabulary v Shimmen* (1986) 84 Cr App Rep 7, DC; *R v Sangha* [1988] 2 All ER 385, 87 Cr App Rep 88, CA. For a discussion as to whether the test of recklessness is 'subjective' or 'objective' see *R v Caldwell* supra at 352–354 and at 19, 20 per Lord Diplock.
4 *R v Lawrence* [1982] AC 510 at 527, 73 Cr App Rep 1 at 12, HL; *R v Caldwell* [1982] AC 341 at 354, 73 Cr App Rep 13 at 20, HL per Lord Diplock.
5 *R v Kimber* [1983] 3 All ER 316, 77 Cr App Rep 225, CA; *R v Satnam S, R v Kewal S* (1983) 78 Cr App Rep 149, CA; and see para 517 post.
6 See *R v Cunningham* [1957] 2 QB 396, 41 Cr App Rep 155, CCA and para 10 note 5 ante. Cf *DPP v K (a minor)* [1990] 1 All ER 331, DC (cited in para 488 note 10 post).

15. Extent to which intention or recklessness is required. In order to establish guilt of a common law or statutory offence which is defined as requiring intention or recklessness, there must be proof of intention or recklessness in relation to all the elements which constitute the offence; it is not enough that a person intended to do an act, the natural and probable consequences of which would be to bring about those elements[1]. An offence may, however, be defined in such a manner as to require intention or recklessness to be shown as to one or more elements, but not to be shown in relation to every one[2]. Even in the case of offences of strict liability, some mental element must be proved[3].

1 *R v Pembliton* (1874) LR 2 CCR 119; *R v Smith (David)* [1974] QB 354, 58 Cr App Rep 320, CA.
2 On a charge of assault occasioning actual bodily harm contrary to the Offences against the Person Act 1861 s 47 (as amended) (see para 490 post), it must be shown that the accused intended to commit the assault, but not that he intended or foresaw that the assault would occasion actual bodily harm: *R v Roberts* (1971) 56 Cr App Rep 95, CA; cf *Bolton v Crawley* [1972] Crim LR 222, DC. See also the Offences against the Person Act 1861 s 23 (administering a noxious thing so as thereby to endanger life: see para 475 post); s 27 (exposing a child whereby life is endangered: see para 537 note 7 post); the Explosive Substances Act 1883 s 2 (substituted by the Criminal Jurisdiction Act 1975 s 7(1), (3) (causing explosion likely to endanger life or property: see para 478 post); the Police Act 1964 s 52 (2) (amended by the Criminal Justice Act 1982 ss 38, 46) (wearing articles calculated to deceive others into thinking the wearer is in police uniform: see para 99 post); the Administration of Justice Act 1970 s 40 (as amended) (harassment of debtors in a manner calculated to cause distress: see para 423 post); the Aviation Security Act 1982 s 2 (1) (so damaging an aircraft as to be likely to endanger its safety in flight: see AVIATION). In *Turner v Shearer* [1973] 1 All ER 397, [1972] 1 WLR 1387, DC, it was held that 'calculated to deceive' under the Police Act 1964 s 52 (2) (as so amended) meant 'likely to deceive' and that accordingly it was not a defence that the accused did not intend to deceive. See also *R v Davison* [1972] 3 All ER 1121, 57 Cr App Rep 113, CA.

In such cases as those above it may be said that the particular statute lends itself to the interpretation that intention or foresight is not required as to the ulterior element in the offence. A statutory provision may, however, be interpreted so as to require intention or recklessness as to some of the elements of the offence but not as to others, although the statute does not naturally lend itself to such an interpretation. On a charge of malicious wounding contrary to the Offences against the Person Act 1861 s 20 (see para 471 post), it is necessary to show only that the accused intended or foresaw some physical harm to another, and not that he intended or foresaw the wounding: *R v Mowatt* [1968] 1 QB 421, 51 Cr App Rep 402, CA; but see para 10 note 5 ante. On a charge of assaulting a constable in the execution of his duty contrary to the Police Act 1964 s 51 (1) (amended by the Criminal Law Act 1977 ss 15, 30, 31, Schs 1, 6; the Criminal Justice Act 1982 s 46) (see para 320 post), it is necessary to show that the accused intended to assault another but not that he knew or foresaw that the other was a constable acting in the execution of his duty: *McBride v Turnock* [1964] Crim LR 456, DC; see para 320 note 1 post.

3 See para 18 note 3 post.

16. Proof of intention and foresight. Whenever an offence is defined so as to require proof that a person intended or foresaw a particular result, the court or jury is not bound in law to infer that such person intended or foresaw that result by reason only of its being a natural and probable consequence of his actions, but must decide whether he did intend or foresee that result by reference to all the evidence, drawing such inferences from the evidence as may be proper in the circumstances[1]. Foresight of the consequences of an act does not necessarily imply the existence of intention but it may be a factor from which, when considered together with all the other evidence, the jury may infer that the accused had the alleged intention[2]. The probability of the result is another factor, and an important one, for the jury to consider when deciding whether the result was intended[2]. When directing juries about the mental element in any crime of specific intent, judges should avoid any elaboration or paraphrase as to what is meant by intent[3]. Some further direction may, however, be necessary if the prosecution invites the jury to infer intent from the foresight of a consequence[4]. As a matter of evidence, the greater the probability of a consequence, the more likely it is that the consequence was foreseen and, if that consequence was foreseen, the more likely it is that that consequence was also intended[4].

1 See the Criminal Justice Act 1967 s 8 which in effect reversed the decision in *DPP v Smith* [1961] AC 290, 44 Cr App Rep 261, HL, to the effect that there was an irrebuttable presumption that a man is presumed to intend the natural and probable consequences of his acts; and see *Frankland v R, Moore v R* [1987] AC 576, 86 Cr App Rep 116, PC. The Criminal Justice Act 1967 s 8 deals not with substantive law but with the law of evidence: see *DPP v Majewski* [1977] AC 443, 62 Cr App Rep 262, HL. See also *R v Moloney* [1985] AC 905, 81 Cr App Rep 93, HL; *R v Hancock, R v Shankland* [1986] AC 455, 82 Cr App Rep 264, HL; *R v Nedrick* [1986] 3 All ER 1, 83 Cr App Rep 267, CA.
2 *R v Hancock, R v Shankland* [1986] AC 455, 82 Cr App Rep 264, HL.
3 *R v Moloney* [1985] AC 905, 81 Cr App Rep 93, HL.
4 *R v Hancock, R v Shankland* [1986] AC 455, 82 Cr App Rep 264, HL.

17. Negligence. Criminal liability for negligence is exceptional at common law; manslaughter appears to be the only common law crime which may result from negligence[1]. Crimes of negligence may be created by statute[2], and a statute may provide that it is a defence to charges brought under its provisions for the accused to prove that he was not negligent[3]. Conversely, negligence with regard to some subsidiary element in the actus reus of a crime may deprive the accused of a statutory defence which would otherwise have been available to him[4].

Whether negligence involves a mental element, or whether it is conduct assessed by reference to an impersonal standard, is arguable[5]. What is or is not negligent involves a consideration of that which a reasonable person would or would not have done in the circumstances; this does not invariably rule out of consideration subjective factors such as a person's knowledge, physical condition or age[6]. A statutory provision may be so phrased as to require consideration of the accused's intelligence or maturity in order to determine whether it was negligent for him to have acted as he did[7].

Degrees of negligence are recognised; thus negligence which was sufficient to sustain a charge of driving without due care and attention[8] is not sufficient to found a charge of reckless driving[9].

1 See para 436 post.
2 See eg the Road Traffic Act 1988 s 3 (driving without due care and attention: see ROAD TRAFFIC).
3 See eg the Trade Descriptions Act 1968 s 24; the Misuse of Drugs Act 1971 s 28; the Food and Environment Protection Act 1985 s 22.
4 See eg *R v King* [1964] 1 QB 285, 48 Cr App Rep 140, CCA (accused's unreasonable belief that prior marriage void no defence to a charge of bigamy).
5 Differing views have been expressed. Cf *Tesco Supermarkets Ltd v Nattrass* [1972] AC 153 at 199, [1971] 2 All ER 127 at 155, HL per Lord Diplock ('Due diligence is in law the converse of negligence and negligence connotes a reprehensible state of mind—a lack of care for the consequences of his physical acts on the part of the person doing them') and *McCrone v Riding* [1938] 1 All ER 157 at 158, DC per Lord Hewart CJ ('The question is not a question dependent upon inexperience or lack of skill. It is a question dependent upon lack of care and attention . . . "Due care and attention" is something not related to the proficiency of the driver but governed by the essential needs of the public on the highway').
6 On a charge of driving a vehicle without due care and attention the accused's physical infirmity or lack of experience may be irrelevant since by driving a motor vehicle he has undertaken to conform to an objective and impersonal standard: *Simpson v Peat* [1952] 2 QB 24, [1952] 1 All ER 447, DC. On a charge of manslaughter based upon gross negligence in the use of firearms it may be relevant to consider the accused's knowledge of firearms: see eg *R v Lamb* [1967] 2 QB 981, 51 Cr App Rep 417, CA.
7 See *R v Hudson* [1966] 1 QB 448, 49 Cr App Rep 69, CA (on a charge of unlawful sexual intercourse with a defective, the proper question for the jury is whether it was reasonable for the accused, having regard to his mental or physical limitations, to have been unaware that the woman was a defective).
8 See notes 2, 6 supra.
9 *R v Lawrence* [1982] AC 510 at 526, 73 Cr App Rep 1 at 10, 11, HL per Lord Diplock.

18. Strict liability. Despite the general rule that criminal liability is not imposed unless a person intends to, or foresees that he may, bring about the constituents of a crime[1], there are instances in which strict liability is imposed. Such instances mainly arise under statute[2]. Where strict liability is imposed, the accused incurs criminal liability though he was ignorant of one or more of the factors which rendered his conduct criminal[3], and even though his ignorance is not attributable to any default or negligence on his part.

In determining whether a statutory provision does or does not impose strict liability the following considerations are relevant:
(1) the language of the provision creating the offence, and in particular any expression indicating that some mental element is required[4], although the absence of any such expression does not give rise to a compelling inference that mens rea is excluded[5];
(2) whether the act is criminal in the generally accepted sense or is an act which, in the public interest, is prohibited under a penalty[6];
(3) the nature of the mischief at which the provision is aimed and whether the imposition of strict liability will tend to suppress that mischief[7], although strict liability will not be inferred simply because the offence may be described as a grave social evil[8].

Where the offence is one which is truly criminal in character[9], strict liability as to any element or elements of the offence will be imposed only where the language of the provision creating the offence is incompatible with any other interpretation; but, where the age of the victim is an element in such an offence, strict liability is ordinarily imposed as to that element[10].

It is not unusual to find strict liability imposed in relation to offences which are not criminal in any real sense by legislation concerned with matters such as the sale of food[11], the supply of intoxicating liquor[12], the safety of those employed in factories[13], the control of weights and measures[14], and the less serious road traffic offences[15].

1 See para 10 ante.

2 There are some instances of strict liability imposed at common law: eg public nuisance (see NUISANCE), which may be justified on the ground that the proceedings are substantially civil in character, and the aim is to put an end to the nuisance; and contempt of court (see CONTEMPT vol 9 para 25). It has also been suggested that, as a result of the majority decision in *Whitehouse v Gay News Ltd, Whitehouse v Lemon* [1979] AC 617, 68 Cr App Rep 381, HL, blasphemy is a common law offence of strict liability: cf the minority judgments of Lords Diplock and Edmund–Davies and the majority judgments of Viscount Dilhorne and Lords Russell and Scarman. Quaere whether the minority opinion is to be preferred. As to blasphemy and blasphemous libel see para 348 post.

The imposition of vicarious criminal liability (see para 52 et seq post) may be regarded as a common law development of strict liability. In *Churchill v Walton* [1967] 2 AC 224, [1967] 1 All ER 497, HL, a suggestion that a conspiracy to commit an offence of strict liability was itself an offence of strict liability was firmly rejected by the House of Lords.

3 An offence may be so defined as to require intention or knowledge as to certain of its elements but not as to others (cf para 15 ante). On a charge of abduction of an unmarried girl under 16 (see para 532 post), it need not be proved that the accused knew the girl to be under that age; but it must be proved that he knew the girl to be in the possession of her parents or guardian: *R v Prince* (1875) LR 2 CCR 154. A licensee commits an offence in selling liquor to a drunken person even though he did not know that person to be drunk; but it must be proved that he intended to sell the liquor to the particular customer who was drunk: *Cundy v Le Cocq* (1884) 13 QBD 207, DC.

4 *R v Prince* (1875) LR 2 CCR 154 (see note 3 supra), where Blackburn J laid stress on the absence of any word such as 'knowingly', indicating that knowledge of the girl's age was required. See also *A-G v Lockwood* (1842) 9 M & W 378; affd sub nom *Lockwood v A-G* 10 M & W 464; *R v Bishop* (1880) 5 QBD 259, CCR.

5 *Roper v Taylor's Central Garages (Exeter) Ltd* [1951] 2 TLR 284 at 288, 289, DC per Devlin J. See also *Sherras v De Rutzen* [1895] 1 QB 918, DC; *Brend v Wood* (1946) 175 LT 306, DC; *Lim Chin Aik v R* [1963] AC 160, [1963] 1 All ER 223, PC.

6 *Sherras v De Rutzen* [1895] 1 QB 918 at 924, DC per Wright J; *Sweet v Parsley* [1970] AC 132, 53 Cr App Rep 221, HL; *Alphacell Ltd v Woodward* [1972] AC 824, [1972] 2 All ER 475, HL. See also *Gammon (Hong Kong) Ltd v A-G of Hong Kong* [1985] AC 1, 80 Cr App Rep 194, PC; *Wings Ltd v Ellis* [1985] AC 272, [1984] 3 All ER 577, HL; *R v Wells Street Metropolitan Stipendiary Magistrate, ex p Westminster City Council* [1986] 3 All ER 4, [1986] 1 WLR 1046, DC; *Pharmaceutical Society of Great Britain v Storkwain Ltd* [1986] 2 All ER 635, 83 Cr App Rep 359, HL.

7 *Hobbs v Winchester Corpn* [1910] 2 KB 471, CA; *Reynolds v G H Austin & Sons Ltd* [1951] 2 KB 135, [1951] 1 All ER 606, DC; *R v St Margaret's Trust Ltd* [1958] 2 All ER 289, 42 Cr App Rep 183, CCA; *Yeandel v Fisher* [1966] 1 QB 440, [1965] 3 All ER 158, DC; *Lockyer v Gibb* [1967] 2 QB 243, [1966] 2 All ER 653, DC; *Warner v Metropolitan Police Comr* [1969] 2 AC 256, 52 Cr App Rep 373, HL.

8 *Lim Chin Aik v R* [1963] AC 160, [1963] 1 All ER 223, PC. No rule, or set of rules, relating to offences of strict liability can be formulated which would not be subject to qualification or exception. A factor of growing importance, however, is the overall policy of the courts towards the recognition of offences of strict liability, and it may be that, following the decision in *Sweet v Parsley* [1970] AC 132, 53 Cr App Rep 221, HL, new offences of strict liability will be recognised only within the classes of offences where the acts are not truly criminal, but are prohibited in the public interest, under a penalty; see *R v Gosney* [1971] 2 QB 674, 55 Cr App Rep 502, CA. Causing the pollution of a stream was regarded as an act falling into this class in *Alphacell Ltd v Woodward* [1972] AC 824, [1972] 2 All ER 475, HL. See also *Gammon (Hong Kong) Ltd v A-G of Hong Kong* [1985] AC 1, 80 Cr App Rep 194, PC; *R v Wells Street Metropolitan Stipendiary Magistrate, ex p Westminster City Council* [1986] 3 All ER 4, [1986] 1 WLR 1046, DC.

9 See para 10 note 12 ante.
10 *R v Prince* (1875) LR 2 CCR 154.
11 Eg the Food Act 1984 ss 1, 2: see FOOD. See also *Smedleys Ltd v Breed* [1974] AC 839, [1974] 2 All ER 21, HL.
12 Eg the Licensing Act 1964 ss 59, 160 (as amended): see INTOXICATING LIQUOR vol 26 paras 375, 341 respectively.
13 See eg the Factories Act 1961 ss 12–28 (as amended) and HEALTH AND SAFETY AT WORK vol 20 para 549 et seq.
14 See the Weights and Measures Act 1985 (as amended) and WEIGHTS AND MEASURES.
15 See eg the Road Traffic Act 1988 ss 24, 37, 170 and ROAD TRAFFIC.

(3) GENERAL DEFENCES TO CRIME

19. In general. The general principle of the common law is that the prosecution must prove the guilt of an accused beyond all reasonable doubt[1]; it is not incumbent upon an accused to establish his innocence[2]. Where one of those matters affording justification at common law, such as accident[3], consent[4], duress[5], drunkenness[6], self-defence[7], or non-insane automatism[8] is set up as a defence, the burden of proving the absence of such justification lies upon the prosecution[9]; this is also the rule in the case of provocation such as to reduce a killing from murder to manslaughter[10]. The burden of proving insanity[11] or the statutory defences of diminished responsibility[12] or marital coercion[13] lies upon the defence; but the standard of proof is not as high as that required of the prosecution to prove guilt[14].

1 *Woolmington v DPP* [1935] AC 462, 25 Cr App Rep 72, HL; and see paras 1063, 1066 post.
2 See para 1062 et seq post.
3 See para 22 post.
4 See para 23 post.
5 See para 24 post.
6 See para 28 post. The same principles apply in relation to intoxication through drugs: see para 28 post.
7 See paras 456, 498 post.
8 See para 6 ante.
9 See para 1062 et seq post.
10 See paras 438, 439 post.
11 See para 33 post. As to insanity alleged by the prosecution where the defence set up diminished responsibility see para 440 post.
12 See paras 440, 441 post.
13 See para 25 post.
14 As to the standard of proof see para 1066 post.

20. Mistake or ignorance of law. Ignorance of the law is no defence to a criminal charge; a criminal intent does not involve knowledge on the part of an accused that his acts or omissions were against the law and constituted a crime[1].

Where a person acts under a mistake of law which precludes him from having the requisite mental element for a particular offence, he cannot be guilty of that offence[2]. This is the case so long as such a mistake was honestly entertained, whether or not it was reasonable to make it[3].

1 *R v Bailey* (1800) Russ & Ry 1, CCR: *R v Esop* (1836) 7 C & P 456; *Re Barronet and Allain* (1852) 1 E & B 1. Ignorance of the law may be a ground for mitigation of sentence: *R v Crawshaw* (1860) Bell CC 303, CCR. See also *R v Derriviere* (1969) 53 Cr App Rep 637, CA. A mistaken belief that a prosecution will not be instituted in respect of the offence is not a defence: *R v Arrowsmith* [1975] 1 All ER 463, 60 Cr App Rep 211, CA. Where a person is charged with contravening a statutory

instrument, it is a defence if he proves that the instrument had not been issued by Her Majesty's Stationery Office at the date of the alleged contravention, unless it is proved by the prosecution that at that date reasonable steps had been taken for the purpose of bringing the purport of the instrument to the notice of the public, or of the persons likely to be affected by it, or of the person charged: Statutory Instruments Act 1946 s 3 (2); *Defiant Cycle Co Ltd v Newell* [1953] 2 All ER 38, [1953] 1 WLR 826, DC; *R v Sheer Metalcraft Ltd* [1954] 1 QB 586, [1954] 1 All ER 542.

A continuing act or proceeding, not originally unlawful, commenced before the passing of a statute which prohibits it, cannot be treated as unlawful by reason of the passing of the statute until a reasonable time has been allowed for its discontinuance: *Burns v Nowell* (1880) 5 QBD 444 at 454, CA per Baggallay LJ.

2 See *R v Hall* (1828) 3 C & P 409; *R v Knight and Roffey* (1781) 2 East PC 510, CCR: *R v Twose* (1879) 14 Cox CC 327; *R v Rutter* (1908) 25 TLR 73, CCA: *R v Langford* (1842) Car & M 602, CCR; *R v Day* (1844) 8 JP 186; *R v Smith (David)* [1974] QB 354, 58 Cr App Rep 320, CA.

3 *R v Day* (1844) 8 JP 186; *Wilson v Inyang* [1951] 2 KB 799, [1951] 2 All ER 237, DC; *R v Waterfall* [1970] 1 QB 148, 53 Cr App Rep 596, CA; *R v Smith (David)* [1974] QB 354, 58 Cr App Rep 320, CA. Honest mistake about legal rights does not extend to refusal to accept an order of the court in the belief that it has been fraudulently obtained: *R v Barrett and Barrett* (1981) 72 Cr App Rep 212, CA.

21. Mistake of fact. Where an offence is so defined that proof of intention or foresight is necessary[1], mistake of fact is a defence[2] provided that, on the facts as the accused believed them to be, he did not have the mens rea required to constitute the offence charged[3]. The defence is made out provided that the accused's belief was honestly, even if unreasonably, held[4]. Where, however, an offence is so defined that negligence[5] constitutes sufficient mens rea, mistake of fact affords a defence only if the mistaken belief was honestly held and there were reasonable grounds for holding it[6].

Mistake of fact does not afford a defence to crimes of strict liability[7].

1 See paras 5, 6 ante.
2 1 Hale PC 42; 4 Bl Com (14th Edn) 27; *Levett's Case* (1639) cited in Cro Car 538; *Nichols v Hall* (1873) LR 8 CP 322; *R v Rose* (1844) 15 Cox CC 540; *R v Gould* [1968] 2 QB 65, 52 Cr App Rep 152, CA; *DPP v Morgan* [1976] AC 182, 61 Cr App Rep 136, HL.
3 *Cook's Case* (1638) cited in Cro Car 537.
4 The reasonableness of the accused's belief is material to the question of whether the belief was held by him at all; but, if it was in fact held, its unreasonableness is irrelevant: *DPP v Morgan* [1976] AC 182, 61 Cr App Rep 136, HL; *R v Kimber* [1983] 3 All ER 316, 77 Cr App Rep 225; *R v Williams* [1987] 3 All ER 411, 78 Cr App Rep 276, CA; *Beckford v R* [1987] 3 All ER 425, 85 Cr App Rep 378, PC.
5 Ie negligence as to all, or some only, of the elements of the actus reus: see para 17 ante. See eg *R v Tolson* (1889) 23 QBD 168, CCR; *R v King* [1964] 1 QB 285, 48 Cr App Rep 140, CCA.
6 'There is nothing unreasonable in requiring a citizen to take reasonable care to ascertain the facts relevant to his avoiding doing a prohibited act': *Sweet v Parsley* [1970] AC 132 at 165, 53 Cr App Rep 221 at 249, HL per Lord Diplock. See eg the Sexual Offences Act 1956 s 19 (abduction of unmarried girl under 18 from parent or guardian: see para 531 post).
7 As to crimes of strict liability see para 18 ante.

22. Accident. In offences for which a particular mental element is required, it is a defence that, although the accused did the acts which would be criminal if done with intent, they were done by accident or inadvertence so that the mental element was absent[1]. Inadvertence which is reckless[2] or negligent[3] may, however, give rise to criminal liability.

1 1 Hale PC 38; 4 Bl Com (14th Edn) 26; *Batting v Bristol and Exeter Rly Co* (1860) 3 LT 665, CCR.
2 See para 14 ante.
3 See para 17 ante.

23. Consent. In relation to offences against the person or against property it is the general rule[1] that acts are criminal only when they are done without the consent of the person affected or the owner of the property concerned. If a person agrees to physical contact or consents to an appropriation of property or is willing that his property be destroyed or damaged, there is no offence of assault, theft or criminal damage[2]. Consent is a defence only to the extent that the act constituting the alleged offence falls within that which is freely permitted by the other[3]. Consent obtained by threats is no consent[4]. Whether consent is nullified by fraud depends upon whether the fraud goes to some matter fundamental to the consent or to something which is merely collateral to it. Consent is not negatived merely because the victim would not have agreed to the act had he known all the facts[5]; nor is consent negatived where the victim is deceived in some collateral matter[6]. Consent is negatived where the victim is deceived as to the nature of the act; and as to the identity of the doer[7].

A victim's ability to consent to what would otherwise be the unlawful infliction of bodily harm is limited by considerations of public policy[8].

Consent is no defence to murder, or to a charge arising from an illegal prizefight[9], or to certain statutory offences involving children or young persons[10].

1 As to exceptions in the case of offences against the person see text to notes 8–10 infra.

2 In relation to offences against property, it appears that the consent of the owner to the act causing harm will always be a defence where the gravamen of the offence consists in the appropriation or destruction of, or damage to, the property. Where the gravamen of the offence consists in putting life at risk, the consent of the owner of the property is immaterial: see eg the Criminal Damage Act 1971 s 1(2) and para 594 post.

3 Cf *Donnelly v Jackman* [1970] 1 All ER 987, [1970] 1 WLR 562, DC. A person who consents to play football does not thereby consent to deliberate and dangerous kicking (see *R v Bradshaw* (1878) 14 Cox CC 83; *R v Moore* (1898) 14 TLR 229); nor does a person who consents to property being taken thereby consent to its being appropriated. In the absence of specific statutory provision, however, (eg the Theft Act 1968 s 12 (taking motor vehicle or other conveyance without authority: see para 556 post)) the use, as opposed to the appropriation, of property without the consent of the owner is not a criminal offence.

4 It is immaterial what form the threats take if the will of the victim is overborne; and submission is not consent: *R v Day* (1841) 9 C & P 722; *R v Lock* (1872) LR 2 CCR 10; *R v Olugboja* [1982] QB 320, 73 Cr App Rep 344, CA. As to consent as a defence to rape see para 517 post.

5 At least where that ignorance is due to a failure on the part of the accused to disclose all the facts: *R v Clarence* (1888) 22 QBD 23, CCR.

6 As where a man gives a prostitute bad money: *R v Clarence* (1888) 22 QBD 23 at 28, CCR per Wills J.

7 *R v Rosinski* (1824) 1 Mood CC 19; *R v Case* (1850) 1 Den 580, CCR; *R v Lock* (1872) LR 2 CCR 10; *R v Barratt* (1873) LR 2 CCR 81; *R v Flattery* (1877) 2 QBD 410, CCR; *R v Williams* [1923] 1 KB 340, 17 Cr App Rep 56, CCA; *Burrell v Harmer* [1967] Crim LR 169, DC. As to impersonation of a married woman's husband in the context of rape see the Sexual Offences Act 1956 s 1 (2) and para 514 post.

8 See *R v Donovan* [1934] 2 KB 498, 25 Cr App Rep 1, CCA (infliction of bodily harm for the purpose of sexual gratification unlawful even if the victim consents); *R v Cato* [1976] 1 All ER 260, 62 Cr App Rep 41, CA (accused who injected consenting victim with heroin convicted of manslaughter); *A-G's Reference (No 6 of 1980)* [1981] QB 715, 73 Cr App Rep 63, CA (two youths agreed to fight in the street; conviction of one participant for assault upheld because it is not in the public interest that people should try to cause, or should cause, each other actual bodily harm for no good reason).

The infliction of bodily harm in the course of medical or surgical procedures, even with consent, may be unlawful if these are not performed for bona fide medical reasons: see eg the Prohibition of Female Circumcision Act 1985 ss 1, 2 and para 503 post; *Bravery v Bravery* [1954] 3 All ER 59 at 67, [1954] 1 WLR 1169 at 1180, CA obiter per Lord Denning. It seems, however, that this does not extend to cosmetic surgery or, at the present day, to sterilisation procedures, both of which have now become routine. The court's jurisdiction should be invoked whenever it is proposed to perform a sterilisation operation on an adult woman disabled by mental incapacity, since, while a doctor may lawfully operate on such a patient if it is in her best interests, a declaration will establish by judicial process whether the proposed operation is in her best interests and therefore lawful: *F v West Berkshire Health Authority (Mental Health Act Commission intervening)* [1989] 2 All ER 545; sub nom *Re F (Mental Patient; Sterilisation)* [1989] 2 WLR 1025, HL. As to consent to medical treatment generally see MEDICINE vol 30 para 38.

9 *R v Coney* (1882) 8 QBD 534, CCR.
10 See eg the Sexual Offences Act 1956 ss 14, 15 and paras 522, 521 respectively post; the Tattooing of Minors Act 1969 s 1 and para 539 post.

24. Duress; compulsion. Duress provides a defence to a charge of any offence[1] other than murder[2] and some forms of treason[3]. Duress postulates the existence of threats of immediate[4] death or serious personal violence so great as to overbear the ordinary power of human resistance to the doing of acts which would otherwise be criminal[5]. A threat of such harm to another may suffice[6], but a threat to property is not sufficient to constitute duress[7]. The defence is available only where the threat was operative and effective at the time of the act or omission alleged to constitute the offence[8].

The test of duress is not purely subjective but includes the objective test of whether a sober person of reasonable firmness, sharing the accused's character-istics, would have responded to whatever he reasonably believed was said or done by the other person taking part in the crime[9]. The erosion of the will of the accused by the voluntary consumption of alcohol or drugs is irrelevant to this objective test[9]. Whether a plea of duress is open to the accused may involve consideration of the extent to which the accused voluntarily placed himself under the dominance of the person making the threat, and whether it was open to him to withdraw himself from the situation creating the threat[10]. Where a person has voluntarily joined an illegal paramilitary organisation or a gang of armed criminals, the defence of duress will not normally be available to him[11]; but, where the violent nature of the organisation was unknown to him at the time of joining and he subsequently attempts to withdraw from the association but is compelled by threats of violence to continue, then he may plead duress with regard to any offences committed after the threats were made[12].

Where it is sought to rely on duress as a defence, the accused must show a proper foundation for the defence so that the issue is fit and proper to be considered by the jury; once this is done, it is for the prosecution to establish beyond reasonable doubt that the defence is not made out[13].

1 See *R v Crutchley* (1831) C & P 133; *A-G v Whelan* [1934] IR 518 (offences against property); *R v Bourne* (1952) 36 Cr App Rep 125, CCA (offences against the person); *R v Hudson, R v Taylor* [1971] 2 QB 202, 56 Cr App Rep 1, CA (offences against the administration of justice); *R v Steane* [1947] KB 997, [1947] 1 All ER 813, CCA (offences against the state).
2 *R v Howe* [1987] AC 417, 85 Cr App Rep 32, HL; overruling *Lynch v DPP for Northern Ireland* [1975] AC 653, [1975] 1 All ER 913, HL. See also *Abbott v R* [1977] AC 755, 63 Cr App Rep 241, CA.
3 There appears to be no decision which unequivocally denies the defence to the principal in treason (see *R v M'Growther* (1746) 18 State Tr 391; *R v Oldcastle* (1419) 1 Hale PC 50) and, while there are dicta to this effect (see eg *R v Hudson, R v Taylor* [1971] 2 QB 202 at 206, 56 Cr App Rep 1 at 4, CA), the point may now be regarded as open; cf the observations of Lord Morris of Borth-y-Gest and Lord Edmund-Davies in *Lynch v DPP for Northern Ireland* [1975] AC 653 at 672 and at 707, 708, [1975] 1 All ER 913 at 919 and at 949, HL. It is submitted that duress is not a defence to treason involving the death of the Sovereign, but may be a defence to less serious forms of treason: see para 76 et seq post.
4 See, however, note 8 infra.
5 *Lynch v DPP for Northern Ireland* [1975] AC 653 at 711, [1975] 1 All ER 913 at 952, HL; *A-G v Whelan* [1934] IR 518, CCA.
6 *R v Hurley and Murray* [1967] VR 526, Vict FC (threat to woman living with accused as his wife).
7 *R v M'Growther* (1746) 18 State Tr 391.
8 *Lynch v DPP for Northern Ireland* [1975] AC 653, [1975] 1 All ER 913, HL; *R v Hudson, R v Taylor* [1971] 2 QB 202, 56 Cr App Rep 1, CA. Provided that the threat is operative at the time of the alleged offence, the defence is available although the threat is of injury which may not necessarily follow instantly but after an interval: see *Subramaniam v Public Prosecutor* [1956] 1 WLR 965, PC.

9 *R v Graham* [1982] 1 All ER 801, 74 Cr App Rep 235, CA.
10 *Lynch v DPP for Northern Ireland* [1975] AC 653 at 670, [1975] 1 All ER 913 at 918, HL per Lord
Morris of Borth-y-Gest, at 679 and at 925 per Lord Wilberforce, and at 705 and at 947 per Lord
Edmund-Davies.
11 *R v Sharp* [1987] QB 853, 85 Cr App Rep 207, CA; *R v Shepherd* (1988) 86 Cr App Rep 47, CA; see
also *R v Fitzpatrick* [1977] NI 20, CCA.
12 *R v Shepherd* (1988) 86 Cr App Rep 47, CA.
13 *R v Gill* [1963] 2 All ER 688, 47 Cr App Rep 166, CCA; *R v Bone* [1968] 2 All ER 644, 52 Cr App Rep
546, CA; *Subramaniam v Public Prosecutor* [1956] 1 WLR 965, PC. As to burden of proof generally,
and standard of proof required, see para 1062 et seq post.

25. Marital coercion. Where a married woman[1] is charged with any offence
other than treason or murder, it is a defence to prove that the offence was
committed in the presence of[2], and under the coercion of, her husband[3].
The burden of proving coercion lies upon the accused[4].

1 'Married woman' is construed strictly and a belief, even on reasonable grounds, that the accused was
married when she was not, is not sufficient: *R v Ditta, Hussain and Kara* [1988] Crim LR 43, CA.
2 See *R v Hughes* (1813) 2 Lew CC 229; *R v Connolly* (1829) 2 Lew CC 229.
3 Criminal Justice Act 1925 s 47. This provision replaced the presumption at common law, in relation
to certain crimes, that, where such a crime was committed by a wife in the presence of her husband,
the wife acted under the coercion of her husband: see s 47. The provision does not affect the common
law rule as to duress (see para 24 ante) which is capable of application between husband and wife: see
R v Bourne (1952) 36 Cr App Rep 125, CCA.
4 Although the defence of coercion is in this respect less favourable to the accused than that of duress
(see para 24 ante), coercion includes threats or intimidation less than threats of death or personal
injury. Thus it may be sufficient for the accused to show that she was in no position to defy her
husband or ignore his orders: see *Lynch v DPP for Northern Ireland* [1975] AC 653 at 713, [1975] 1 All
ER 913 at 954, HL obiter per Lord Edmund-Davies.
As to the burden of proof see para 1062 et seq post.

26. Necessity. There are some circumstances in which it is not criminal for a
person to cause harm to the person or property of another[1]; and apart from these
the defence of necessity in extreme circumstances is recognised where it arises from
objective dangers threatening the accused or others amounting to duress of circumstances[2]. The defence is available only if, from an objective standpoint, the accused
can be said to have acted reasonably and proportionately in order to avoid a threat
of death or serious injury[3]. Where such a defence is open to the accused on his
account of the facts, it should be left to the jury with a direction to determine (1)
whether the accused was, or might have been, impelled to act as he did because, as a
result of what he reasonably believed to be the situation, he had good cause to fear
that otherwise death or serious physical injury would result: and (2) if so, whether a
sober person of reasonable firmness, sharing the characteristics of the accused,
would have responded to the situation by acting as the accused did[3]. If both
questions are answered affirmatively, the defence of necessity is established[3].

1 These cases include self-defence (see paras 456, 498 post), defence of property (see para 499 post),
force used in the prevention of crime (see para 455 post) duress (see para 24 ante) and marital coercion
(see para 25 ante). Traditionally it has been held lawful to pull down a house in order to prevent the
spread of fire; it is apparently permissible to jettison cargo to lighten a ship in a storm (*Mouse's Case*
(1608) 12 Co Rep 63); or to carry an infected child through the streets to seek medical aid (*R v
Vantandillo* (1815) 4 M & S 73). See also *Burns v Nowell* (1880) 5 QBD 444, CA.
2 *R v Martin* [1989] 1 All ER 652, 88 Cr App Rep 159, CA, applying *R v Conway* [1989] QB 290, 88 Cr
App Rep 343, CA; not following *R v Dudley and Stephens* (1884) 14 QBD 273, CCR; *R v Kitson*
(1955) 39 Cr App Rep 66, CCA; *Buckoke v Greater London Council* [1971] 1 Ch 655 at 668, [1971] 2 All

ER 254 at 258, CA. See also *Southwark London Borough v Williams* [1971] Ch 734 at 743, 744, [1971] 2 All ER 175 at 179, CA; *Johnson v Phillips* [1975] 3 All ER 682, [1976] 1 WLR 65, DC (constable has the right to direct a driver to disobey traffic regulations where it is necessary to protect life and property).

3 *R v Martin* [1989] 1 All ER 652, 88 Cr App Rep 343, CA.

27. Superior orders. The mere fact that a person does a criminal act in obedience to the order of a duly constituted superior does not of itself excuse the person who does it from criminal liability[1]. A person acting under superior orders which he carries out in good faith may, however, lack the mental element required for criminal liability[2]. The orders may have led the accused to make a mistake of fact or to believe that he had a claim of right to do as he did[2]; and obedience to orders may be a factor in disproving criminal negligence[3].

Those subject to military law are amenable to the criminal law to the same extent as other subjects; obedience to superior orders is not in itself a defence to a criminal charge[4].

1 See *R v Thomas* (1816) Ms of Bayley J, CCR, Turner and Armitage, Cases on Criminal Law 67 (sentry killing intruder under mistaken impression that it was his duty so to do; convicted of murder); *Lewis v Dickson* [1976] RTR 431, DC (security officer causing obstruction of highway by checking all the vehicles entering his employer's premises; no defence that he was obeying his employer's instructions).

2 A person who, under orders, appropriates, destroys or damages property may have a defence of claim of right so to act: *R v Knight and Roffey* (1781) 2 East PC 510, CCR; *R v James* (1837) 8 C & P 131.

3 *R v Trainer* (1864) 4 F & F 105; *R v Hutchinson* (1864) 9 Cox CC 555.

4 See the Manual of Military Law (12th Edn) Pt I 156, 157; and cf the Charter of the International Military Tribunal art 8. For a discussion of the defence of superior orders see [1989] Crim LR 396–411. The orders of a superior officer afford no excuse for consorting with rebels: *R v Axtell* (1660) 5 State Tr 1146 at 1175 (cited in para 79 post).

28. Effect of voluntary intoxication. The voluntary taking of alcohol or drugs cannot of itself excuse the commission of a crime; and it is not a defence to prove that a person's mind was so affected by alcohol that he acted in a way he would not have done had he been sober[1]. Whether the alleged intoxication is induced through alcohol or through drugs, the principles to be applied are the same[2]. Intoxication is, however, relevant to the proof of mens rea[3] and voluntary intoxication may therefore negative mens rea in crimes requiring proof of specific intent[4] or where a statute provides that a specific belief is a defence to a charge[5].

Voluntary intoxication is not a defence where recklessness[6] on the part of the accused constitutes sufficient mens rea for the crime with which he is charged[7], unless such intoxication arises from the taking of a soporific or sedative drug[8], or a drug which has been lawfully prescribed or administered by a doctor[9]. In such cases an issue may arise as to whether the accused was reckless in taking the drug in the circumstances or quantities in which he took it[10].

Where the essence of the crime consists in negligence, it seems that drunkenness can never excuse. Nor will drunkenness be a defence in cases of strict liability, since, if an honest and reasonable mistake by a sober person cannot afford a defence, a mistake while drunk cannot do so.

Self-induced drunkenness at the time of committing an offence causing death can at most operate to reduce the crime from murder to manslaughter[11].

Drunkenness which is self-induced with a view to committing crime, as where a person drinks to give himself courage to carry out an intention to kill, does not excuse even though at the time of committing the act the accused could not, because of the drink taken, form the mens rea required for that crime[12].

1 *DPP v Majewski* [1977] AC 443, 62 Cr App Rep 262, HL; and see *R v Sheehan, R v Moore* [1975] 2 All ER 960, 60 Cr App Rep 308, CA. See also *DPP v Beard* [1920] AC 479, 14 Cr App Rep 159, HL.
2 *R v Lipman* [1970] 1 QB 152, 53 Cr App Rep 600, CA; but see text to notes 8–10 infra.
3 *DPP v Majewski* [1977] AC 443, 62 Cr App Rep 262, HL.
4 As to crimes of specific intent see para 6 note 10 ante.
5 *Jaggard v Dickinson* [1981] QB 527, 72 Cr App Rep 33, DC. An honest belief which results from a drunken mistake may not, however, be relied upon for the purposes of self-defence: see para 456 note 3 post.
6 See para 14 ante.
7 *DPP v Majewski* [1977] AC 443, 62 Cr App Rep 262, HL; *R v Caldwell* [1982] AC 341, 73 Cr App Rep 13, HL. As to voluntary intoxication in the context of sexual offences see *R v Woods (W)* (1982) 74 Cr App Rep 312, CA.
8 See *R v Hardie* [1984] 3 All ER 848, 80 Cr App Rep 157, CA cited in para 6 note 9 ante.
9 *R v Quick, R v Paddison* [1973] QB 910, [1973] 3 All ER 347, CA; *R v Bailey* [1983] 2 All ER 503, 77 Cr App Rep 76, CA.
10 *R v Bailey* [1983] 2 All ER 503 at 507, 77 Cr App Rep 76 at 80, 81, CA; *R v Hardie* [1984] 3 All ER 848, 80 Cr App Rep 157, CA.
11 *DPP v Beard* [1920] AC 479 at 499, 14 Cr App Rep 159 at 192, 193, HL per Lord Birkenhead LC, approving the view of Stephen J in *R v Doherty* (1887) 16 Cox CC 306 at 307; *R v Lipman* [1970] 1 QB 152, 53 Cr App Rep 600, CA; *R v Howell* [1974] 2 All ER 806. However, cf *R v Sheehan, R v Moore* [1975] 2 All ER 960, 60 Cr App Rep 308, CA.
12 *A-G for Northern Ireland v Gallagher* [1963] AC 349 at 382, 45 Cr App Rep 316 at 344, HL per Lord Denning.

29. Involuntary intoxication. Intoxication produced by others, as where an accused's drink was 'laced' with alcohol without his knowledge, is a defence provided that it negatives mens rea[1]; if it does not, it cannot be a defence, but may well be a substantial mitigating factor[2]. It would seem that involuntary intoxication may be available as a defence even in crimes of basic intent[3].

Once the issue of involuntary intoxication has been raised, the burden of proof is generally on the prosecution to show that the intoxication was voluntary[4].

1 1 Hale PC 32; *R v Pearson* [1835] 2 Lew CC 144.
2 See *R v Davies* [1983] Crim LR 741 and the commentary thereon.
3 See *DPP v Majewski* [1977] AC 443, 62 Cr App Rep 262, HL. As to the position where intoxication arises from a drug prescribed or administered by a doctor see para 28 text to notes 8–10 ante. For the meaning of 'crime of basic intent' see para 6 note 9 ante.
4 *R v Stripp* (1978) 69 Cr App Rep 318 at 323; *R v Bailey* [1983] 2 All ER 503 at 507, 77 Cr App Rep 76 at 81, CA. See, however, the Public Order Act 1986 s 6 (5) and para 149 note 5 post.

30. Drunkenness and insanity contrasted. The criminal law is concerned with the effect, not the origin, of disease of the mind[1]. If insanity supervenes as a result of alcoholic excess, it is as much a defence to a criminal charge as insanity from any other cause[2].

The defences of insanity and drunkenness are otherwise in no way analogous. Where the defence raises drunkenness as negativing mens rea, it is immaterial whether or not the accused knew that what he was doing was wrong[3].

1 See *R v Kemp* [1957] 1 QB 399, 40 Cr App Rep 121 and para 31 note 4 post.
2 *DPP v Beard* [1920] AC 479 at 500, 14 Cr App Rep 159 at 193, HL; *R v Davis* (1881) 14 Cox CC 563; *R v Baines* (1886) Times, 25 January.
3 *DPP v Beard* [1920] AC 479, 14 Cr App Rep 159, HL.

31. Insanity. Where, on a criminal charge, it appears[1] that, at the time of the act or omission giving rise to the offence alleged[2], the accused was labouring under a defect of reason[3] owing to a disease of the mind[4] so as not to know the nature and quality of his act[5], or, if he knew this, so as not to know that what he was doing was wrong[6], he is not regarded in law as responsible for his act[7].

The question whether, owing to a defect of reason due to disease of the mind, the accused was not responsible for his act is a question of fact to be determined by the jury[8]. Where the jury finds insanity is made out, the verdict takes the special form of not guilty by reason of insanity[9].

The above principles have in many ways lost the importance they once had, but they are still relevant in so far as they may affect the defence of automatism[10].

1 As to the burden and mode of proof of insanity see para 33 post.
2 The accused's state of mind before or after that time is irrelevant except in so far as it tends to establish or negative insanity at the time of the act. Where a defect of reason is self-induced, as where a psychopath takes drink to give himself the courage to kill, he cannot rely on insanity at the time of the act if he was responsible when he formed the intent to kill: *A-G for Northern Ireland v Gallagher* [1963] AC 349 at 382, 45 Cr App Rep 316 at 344, HL per Lord Denning.
3 The defence of insanity is not available to a person who retains the power of reasoning, but who in a moment of confusion or absentmindedness fails to use that power to the full: *R v Clarke* [1972] 1 All ER 219, 56 Cr App Rep 225, CA. As to uncontrollable impulse see also para 32 post.
4 The criminal law is not concerned with the origin of the disease but with its effect; it matters not whether the defect of reason is due to a degeneration of the brain cells, or to some other form of mental derangement, or to a physical disorder, such as arteriosclerosis, which, by cutting off the supply of blood to the brain, impairs the reasoning process. Nor does it matter whether the disease is curable or incurable, temporary or permanent: *R v Kemp* [1957] 1 QB 399, 40 Cr App Rep 121; *R v Sullivan* [1984] AC 156, 77 Cr App Rep 176, HL (epileptic seizure held to be a disease of the mind); *R v Hennessy* [1989] 2 All ER 9, 89 Cr App Rep 10, CA (hyperglycaemia caused by inherent defect and not corrected by insulin is a disease capable of falling within the M'Naghten Rules); and see the observations of Lord Denning in *Bratty v A-G for Northern Ireland* [1963] AC 386 at 412, 46 Cr App Rep 1 at 20, HL and para 30 ante.
   There must be a malfunctioning of the mind caused by disease; a malfunctioning caused by an external factor such as alcohol, drugs or injury does not constitute a disease of the mind: *R v Quick, R v Paddison* [1973] QB 910, [1973] 3 All ER 347, CA.
5 The expression 'nature and quality' has always been held to refer to the physical nature and consequences of the act, and does not refer to its moral aspects: *R v Codere* (1916) 12 Cr App Rep 21, CCA.
6 For this purpose a person knows that an act is wrong if he knows that it is contrary to law: see the dicta in *R v Windle* [1952] 2 QB 826, 36 Cr App Rep 85, CCA; *R v Holmes* [1953] 2 All ER 324, 37 Cr App Rep 61, CCA. Cf the answers of the judges to questions 2 and 3 in *M'Naghten's Case* (1843) 10 Cl & Fin 200 at 210 and the view of Lord Reading CJ in *R v Codere* (1916) 12 Cr App Rep 21, CCA, that the test is whether the act is right or wrong according to the standard accepted by reasonable men.
7 *M'Naghten's Case* (1843) 10 Cl & Fin 200, HL; *R v Layton* (1849) 4 Cox CC 149; *Pate's Case* (1850) 8 State Tr NS 1; *R v Richards* (1858) 1 F & F 87; *R v Davies* (1858) 1 F & F 69; *R v Law* (1862) 2 F & F 836; *R v Vyse* (1862) 3 F & F 247; *R v Townley* (1863) 3 F & F 839; *R v Southey* (1865) 4 F & F 864; *R v Leigh* (1866) 4 F & F 915; *R v Atherley* (1909) 3 Cr App Rep 165, CCA; *R v Smith* (1910) 5 Cr App Rep 123, 26 TLR 614, CCA; *R v True* (1922) 16 Cr App Rep 164, 127 LT 561, CCA; *R v Kopsch* (1925) 19 Cr App Rep 50, CCA; *R v Flavell* (1926) 19 Cr App Rep 141, CCA; *R v Rivett* (1950) 34 Cr App Rep 87, CCA.
   The defence of insanity also applies where a person acts under an insane delusion as to existing facts. If he labours under a partial delusion only and is not in other respects insane, his responsibility must be determined as if the facts with regard to which the delusion exists were real: *M'Naghten's Case* (1843) 10 Cl & Fin 200, HL. Cf *R v Townley* (1863) 3 F & F 839: *Pate's Case* (1850) 8 State Tr NS 1 at 47 per Alderson B.
   The above principles apply only to insanity as a substantive defence; as to the raising of the issue of unfitness to plead see paras 962, 963 post.
8 *R v Rivett* (1950) 34 Cr App Rep 87, CCA; *R v Kemp* [1957] 1 QB 399 at 406, 40 Cr App Rep 121 at 126 per Devlin J; approved by Lord Denning in *Bratty v A-G for Northern Ireland* [1963] AC 386, 46

Cr App Rep 1, HL. See also *R v Sullivan* [1984] AC 156, 77 Cr App Rep 176, HL and para 441 note 4 post.
9 Trial of Lunatics Act 1883 s 2 (1) (amended by the Criminal Procedure (Insanity) Act 1964 s 1). The amendment by the latter Act replaces the verdict of guilty but insane introduced by the former. As to the court's order for the accused's admission to hospital where such a special verdict has been returned see para 1256 post; and as to appeal against a verdict of not guilty by reason of insanity see para 1397 post.
10 *R v Hennessy* [1989] 2 All ER 9 at 12, 89 Cr App Rep 10 at 13, CA per Lord Lane CJ. As to the defence of automatism see paras 6, 7 ante.

32. Uncontrollable impulse. The defence of insanity[1] is not established by showing merely that the accused suffers from a disease of the mind and because of that he more readily gives way to passion or is less able to control his reactions. It is no defence that a person is mentally defective[2] or may be regarded as morally defective or displays lack of moral judgment[3], or that he cannot control his impulses owing to a disease of the mind[4].

1 See para 31 ante.
2 *R v Alexander* (1913) 9 Cr App Rep 139, 109 LT 745, CCA.
3 *R v Burton* (1863) 3 F & F 772.
4 *R v Barton* (1848) 3 Cox CC 275; *R v Holt* (1920) 15 Cr App Rep 10, CCA; *R v Quarmby* (1921) 15 Cr App Rep 163, CCA; *R v Kopsch* (1925) 19 Cr App Rep 50, CCA; *R v Flavell* (1926) 19 Cr App Rep 141, CCA. Cf *R v Hay* (1911) 75 JP 480; *R v Fryer* (1915) 24 Cox CC 403, in which the defence was allowed, but which cannot stand in the light of the later authorities.
   The defence of insanity as defined by the M'Naghten Rules does not apply to the case of an accused who knew what he was doing and that it was wrong, but was unable, owing to disease of the mind, to prevent himself from doing what he did. In this class of case, in charges of murder, the defence of diminished responsibility is available: see the Homicide Act 1957 s 2 and paras 440, 441 post.

33. Burden and mode of proof of insanity. It is for the defence to raise the question of insanity[1]; and, if the prosecution has evidence of insanity, it must make that evidence available to the defence[2]. Where, however, the defence raises a plea of diminished responsibility[3], the prosecution may adduce or elicit evidence of insanity by way of rebuttal[4], and the burden of proving insanity in these circumstances rests on the prosecution[5]. Otherwise it is for the defence to prove insanity on the balance of probabilities[6].

Medical evidence in support of the issue of insanity, though usual, is not a requirement[7]. The fact that the act of the accused was without apparent motive is not enough to prove insanity[8]; the issue may be raised and the defence established by cross-examination of the prosecution witnesses and any other relevant evidence.

Where the medical evidence is all to the effect that the accused was insane so as not to be criminally responsible, and that evidence is uncontroverted, a verdict of guilty may be set aside on the ground that no reasonable jury could have reached such a verdict[9]; but a conviction will not be quashed merely because the jury has chosen to disagree with expert medical opinion[10] or because the medical evidence tends to support the defence, if there is other evidence to the contrary[11].

1 See, however, para 7 note 4 ante. In certain exceptional circumstances, and provided that there is evidence of the factors to be taken into account under the M'Naghten Rules (see para 31 ante), the judge may raise the issue of insanity of his own volition and leave the issue to the jury: see *R v Dickie* [1984] 3 All ER 173, 79 Cr App Rep 213, CA.
2 *R v Dickie* [1984] 3 All ER 173, 79 Cr App Rep 213, CA.
3 See paras 440, 441 post.

4 See the Criminal Procedure (Insanity) Act 1964 s 6 and para 440 note 3 post.
5 See *R v Bastian* [1958] 1 All ER 568n, [1958] 1 WLR 413; *R v Grant* [1960] Crim LR 424.
6 *M'Naghten's Case* (1843) 10 Cl & Fin 200, HL; *R v Stokes* (1848) 3 Car & Kir 185; *R v Layton* (1849) 4 Cox CC 149; *R v Smith* (1910) 6 Cr App Rep 19, CCA; *R v Casey* (1947) 32 Cr App Rep 91, 63 TLR 487, CCA; *Bratty v A–G for Northern Ireland* [1963] AC 386, 46 Cr App Rep 1, HL. As to the standard of proof see paras 1065, 1066 post.
7 *R v Dart* (1878) 14 Cox CC 143.
8 *R v Barton* (1848) 3 Cox CC 275; *R v Haynes* (1859) 1 F & F 666. Cf *R v Vyse* (1862) 3 F & F 247.
9 *R v Matheson* [1958] 2 All ER 87, 42 Cr App Rep 145, CCA. Cf *R v Latham* [1965] Crim LR 434, CCA. Both cases were decided on diminished responsibility but similar principles are applicable in the case of insanity. See also para 440 post.
10 *R v Rivett* (1950) 34 Cr App Rep 87, CCA; *R v True* (1922) 16 Cr App Rep 164, 127 LT 561, CCA.
11 *R v Latham* [1965] Crim LR 434, CCA.

(4) CRIMINAL CAPACITY

34. Children under fourteen. There is a conclusive presumption that no child under the age of ten years can be guilty of a criminal offence[1]. A child between the ages of ten and 14 cannot be convicted unless it is proved not only that the child did the act in circumstances which would involve an adult in criminal liability but also that he knew that he was doing wrong. That knowledge is not to be presumed from the mere fact of the commission of the act, but must be proved by the circumstances attending the act, the manner in which it was done and evidence as to the nature and disposition of the child concerned[2]. There is an irrebuttable presumption that a boy under the age of 14 years is incapable of having sexual intercourse; he cannot therefore be convicted as a principal of rape[3], buggery[4] or of any offence involving sexual intercourse[5].

The Children and Young Persons Act 1969 makes provision for the prohibition of criminal proceedings for all offences other than homicide in respect of anything done by a child under the age of 14[6]. The provision may, however, be brought into effect[7] with reference to such age between ten and 14 as may be specified[8].

1 Children and Young Persons Act 1933 s 50 (amended by the Children and Young Persons Act 1963 s 16 (1)). As to the rule at common law see 1 Hale PC 27; 4 Bl Com (14th Edn) 23. See also *Marsh v Loader* (1863) 14 CBNS 535. A person attains a particular age at the commencement of the relevant anniversary of the date of his birth: Family Law Reform Act 1969 s 9(1).
2 Eg by evidence of design, concealment, exceptional ferocity: 1 Hale PC 25, 26; Fitzherbert, Grand Abridgement, Corone, pl 57; *R v York* (1748) Fost 70, CCR; *R v Owen* (1830) 4 C & P 236; *R v Wild* (1835) 1 Mood CC 452, CCR; *R v Smith* (1845) 1 Cox CC 260; *R v Vamplew* (1862) 3 F & F 520; *R v Kershaw* (1902) 18 TLR 357; *R v Gorrie* (1919) 83 JP 136. This includes home background: *F v Padwick* [1959] Crim LR 439, DC. See also *R v B, R v A* [1979] 3 All ER 460, 69 Cr App Rep 362, CA (evidence of child's previous convictions admissible); and see the cases cited in para 1069 note 6 post.
3 *R v Groombridge* (1836) 7 C & P 582. He may be convicted as a secondary party: *R v Eldershaw* (1828) 3 C & P 396. As to rape see para 514 et seq post. Quaere whether he may now be convicted of attempted rape: see the Criminal Attempts Act 1981 s 1(2), (3) and paras 71, 73 post.
4 *R v Tatam* (1921) 15 Cr App Rep 132, CCA.
5 *R v Waite* [1892] 2 QB 600, CCR; *R v Williams* [1893] 1 QB 320, CCR. If he is charged with an offence involving sexual intercourse, he may be found guilty of indecent assault or of common assault: *R v Brimilow* (1840) 9 C & P 366; *R v Williams* supra.
6 See the Children and Young Persons Act 1969 ss 4, 70 (1).
7 Ie by order made by the Secretary of State.
8 See the Children and Young Persons Act 1969 s 34 (1), (4). An order must be laid before Parliament in draft and, if the effect of the order is to prohibit criminal proceedings against a child who has attained an age of more than 12, it may not be made unless the draft is approved by resolution of each

House of Parliament: s 34 (7). At the date at which this volume states the law no order had been made bringing s 4 into force. With respect to an offence other than homicide a child may be brought before the court in care proceedings: see s 1(1), (2) (f) and INFANTS.

35. Corporations. In general, a corporation is in the same position in relation to criminal liability as a natural person and may be convicted of common law[1] and statutory[2] offences including those requiring mens rea[3]. There are, however, crimes which a corporation is incapable of committing[4] or of which a corporation cannot be found guilty as a principal[5]; nor can a corporation be convicted of a crime for which death or imprisonment are the only punishments[6].

Criminal liability of a corporation arises where an offence is committed in the course of the corporation's business by a person in control of its affairs to such a degree that it may fairly be said to think and act through him so that his actions and intent are the actions and intent of the corporation[7]. It is not enough that the person whose conduct it is sought to impute to the corporation is a manager or responsible agent or high executive[8]; whether persons are the 'directing mind and will' of a corporation, so that their conduct in its affairs becomes the conduct of the corporation, must depend on all the circumstances[9]. An important circumstance is the constitution of the corporation to the extent to which it identifies the natural persons who, by the memorandum and articles of association or as a result of action taken by the directors or by the corporation in general meeting pursuant to the articles, are entrusted with the exercise of the powers of the corporation[10].

A corporation is vicariously liable for a crime committed by its servant or agent in the course of his employment or agency in the same circumstances as an employer or principal who is a natural person[11].

1 *R v J G Hammond & Co Ltd* [1914] 2 KB 866 (contempt of court); *R v ICR Haulage Ltd* [1944] KB 551, 30 Cr App Rep 31, CCA (conspiracy to defraud); *Triplex Safety Glass Co Ltd v Lancegaye Safety Glass (1939) Ltd* [1939] 2 KB 395, [1939] 2 All ER 613, CA.
2 Unless the contrary intention appears, 'person' includes a body of persons corporate or unincorporate: Interpretation Act 1978 s 5, Sch 1. This definition, so far as it includes bodies corporate, applies to any provision of an Act passed relating to an offence punishable on indictment or on summary conviction: s 22 (1), Sch 2 para 4 (5). See also *R v Birmingham and Gloucester Rly Co* (1842) 3 QB 223 (non-repair of highway); *R v Great North of England Rly Co* (1846) 9 QB 315 (obstruction of highway); *R v Tyler and International Commercial Co* [1891] 2 QB 588 at 592–594, CA (default in forwarding list of members to registrar); *A-G v London and North Western Rly Co* [1900] 1 QB 78, CA (excessive speed of trains); *Pearks, Gunston and Tee Ltd v Ward* [1902] 2 KB 1, DC; *R v Ascanio Puck & Co and Paice* (1912) 76 JP 487 (sale of food); *Provincial Motor Cab Co Ltd v Dunning* [1909] 2 KB 599 (breach of road traffic regulations); *R v Gainsford Justices* (1913) 29 TLR 359 (breach of Factory and Workshop Acts); *Evans & Co Ltd v LCC* [1914] 3 KB 315 (breach of the Shops Act 1912 s 4 (repealed)); *Mousell Bros v London and North Western Rly Co* [1917] 2 KB 836 (giving false account of goods to toll collector); *Brentnall and Cleland Ltd v LCC* [1945] 1 KB 115, [1944] 2 All ER 552, DC (offence against the Weights and Measures Act 1889 s 29 (repealed)); *Orpen v Haymarket Capitol Ltd* (1931) 145 LT 614; *Houghton-Le Touzel v Mecca Ltd* [1950] 2 KB 612, [1950] 1 All ER 638 (offence against the Sunday Observance Act 1780). Cf *Hawke v E Hulton & Co Ltd* [1909] 2 KB 93, DC; *A-G v Walkergate Press Ltd* (1930) 142 LT 408 (corporation not liable to be convicted under the Lotteries Act 1823 s 42 (repealed)); but see *Green v Kursaal (Southend-on-Sea) Estates Ltd* [1937] 1 All ER 732 at 734 per Goddard J; and *Houghton-Le Touzel v Mecca Ltd* [1950] 2 KB 612 at 614, 615, [1950] 1 All ER 638 at 640, 641 per Birkett J.
3 *DPP v Kent and Sussex Contractors Ltd* [1944] KB 146, [1944] 1 All ER 119, DC; *R v ICR Haulage Ltd* [1944] KB 551, 30 Cr App Rep 31, CCA. As to corporate personality generally see CORPORATIONS.
4 *R v ICR Haulage Ltd* [1944] KB 551 at 554, 30 Cr App Rep 31 at 34, CCA (perjury, bigamy); *DPP v Kent and Sussex Contractors Ltd* [1944] KB 146, [1944] 1 All ER 119, DC (treason); *Wych v Meal* (1734) 3 P Wms 310 (perjury). A corporation cannot be convicted of conspiracy where the only other party thereto is the sole director of the corporation: *R v McDonnell* [1966] 1 QB 233, 50 Cr App Rep 5. A limited company could not be convicted of driving a lorry without a Greater London Council

permit since the act of driving a lorry was a physical act: *Richmond upon Thames London Borough Council v Pinn & Wheeler Ltd* (1989) Times, 14 February, DC. The decision in *R v Cory Bros & Co Ltd* [1927] 1 KB 810, that a corporation cannot be indicted for manslaughter or for an offence involving personal violence, was questioned in *R v ICR Haulage Ltd* supra; and in *R v HM Coroner for E Kent, ex p Spooner* (1987) 88 Cr App Rep 10, DC the court was of the opinion that a corporate body is capable of being found guilty of manslaughter.

5 A corporation cannot be guilty as a principal of reckless driving or of driving without due care and attention. In *R v Robert Millar (Contractors) Ltd, R v Millar* [1970] 2 QB 54, 54 Cr App Rep 158, CA, the corporation was convicted as a secondary party to the offence of causing death through dangerous driving (now replaced by 'reckless' driving: see the Road Traffic Act 1988 s 1 and para 449 post).

6 *R v ICR Haulage Ltd* [1944] KB 551 at 554, 30 Cr App Rep 31 at 34, CCA; *Pharmaceutical Society v London and Provincial Supply Association* (1880) 5 App Cas 857 at 869, HL per Lord Blackburn; *R v Cory Bros & Co Ltd* [1927] 1 KB 810; *Law Society v United Service Bureau Ltd* [1934] 1 KB 343 at 350, DC per Avory J.

   Except for crimes such as murder and treason where the punishment is fixed by law, the courts generally have power to fine: see para 1232 post. Accordingly limitation on a corporation's criminal liability by reference to punitive sanctions is of little practical importance.

7 *Tesco Supermarkets Ltd v Nattrass* [1972] AC 153, [1971] 2 All ER 127, HL. See also *DPP v Kent and Sussex Contractors Ltd* [1944] KB 146, [1944] 1 All ER 119, DC; *R v ICR Haulage Ltd* [1944] KB 551, 30 Cr App Rep 31, CCA; *Moore v I Bressler Ltd* [1944] 2 All ER 515, DC; *Magna Plant Ltd v Mitchell* (1966) 110 Sol Jo 349, DC; *John Henshall (Quarries) Ltd v Harvey* [1965] 2 QB 233, [1965] 1 All ER 725, DC; *H L Bolton (Engineering) Co Ltd v T J Graham & Sons Ltd* [1957] 1 QB 159, [1956] 3 All ER 624, CA. Where in accordance with this principle a corporation is guilty of a crime, the person whose actions and intent are those of the corporation must himself also be criminally liable. See also the specific provisions of eg the Official Secrets Act 1920 s 8 (5) (see para 268 post), the Theft Act 1968 s 18 (see para 567 note 1 post); and as to the criminal liability of a company and its officers see further COMPANIES vol 7 (1) (Reissue) para 1001 et seq.

8 *R v Andrews Weatherfoil Ltd* [1972] 1 All ER 65, [1972] 1 WLR 118, CA.

9 *Tesco Supermarkets Ltd v Nattrass* [1972] AC 153, [1971] 2 All ER 127, HL; *R v Andrews Weatherfoil Ltd* [1972] 1 All ER 65, [1972] 1 WLR 118, CA. As to the directing mind of a company see COMPANIES vol 7 (1) (Reissue) para 1000.

10 *Tesco Supermarkets Ltd v Nattrass* [1972] AC 153 at 199, 200, [1971] 2 All ER 127 at 155, HL per Lord Diplock.

11 See para 52 et seq post. Where it is a defence for an employer or principal to prove that the offence was due to the act or default of another, and that he took all reasonable precautions, this defence is available to a corporation; in such circumstances 'another person' is a person other than the directors or other superior officers who control the corporation's affairs: *Tesco Supermarkets Ltd v Nattrass* [1972] AC 153, [1971] 2 All ER 127, HL.

36. Unincorporated associations. Criminal liability may be imposed by statute on unincorporated associations[1].

1 See eg the Trade Union and Labour Relations Act 1974 s 12, which makes both trade unions and employers' associations liable for refusing or wilfully neglecting to perform certain statutory duties.

   Unless a contrary intention appears, 'person' in any Act passed after 1 January 1979 includes a body of persons unincorporate: see the Interpretation Act 1978 ss 5, 22 (1), 26, Sch 1, Sch 2 para 4 (5). A statute may make special provision for criminal proceedings against unincorporated associations: see eg the Insurance Companies Act 1982 s 92; the Banking Act 1987 s 98 (1).

   It is uncertain whether criminal proceedings may be instituted against an unincorporated body at common law; but see *A-G v Able* [1984] QB 795 at 810, 78 Cr App Rep 197 at 206 per Woolf J ('the society is an unincorporated body and there can be no question of the society committing an offence').

37. Members of Parliament. Except in relation to anything said in debate[1], a member of the House of Lords or of the House of Commons is subject to the ordinary course of criminal justice[2]; the privileges of Parliament[3] do not apply to criminal matters[4].

1 Although members are probably subject to the jurisdiction of the courts in respect of other conduct in Parliament, they cannot be made criminally responsible in the courts for what is said by them in Parliament while it is sitting; see the Privilege of Parliament Act 1512 (as amended). 'The freedom of speech and debates or proceedings in Parliament ought not to be impeached or questioned in any Court or place out of Parliament': Bill of Rights (1688) s 1. Members of Parliament are not subject to the jurisdiction of the courts for a conspiracy to deceive Parliament by making false speeches in the House: *Ex p Wason* (1869) LR 4 QB 573.
2 See *Bradlaugh v Gossett* (1884) 12 QBD 271 at 283 per Stephen J; *R v Elliott, Hollis and Valentine* (1630) Cro Car 181, 605 (revsd on other grounds (1668) 3 State Tr 294, HL); *Jay and Topham's Case* (1689) 12 State Tr 822.
3 As to these privileges see PARLIAMENT.
4 The privilege of members of Parliament from arrest does not apply to criminal process: *Wellesley v Duke of Beaufort* (1831) 2 Russ & M 639 at 665; and see Erskine May, Parliamentary Practice (21st Edn) 95–97.

38. The Queen and foreign sovereigns. The Queen is exempt from all criminal process, and no court has any coercive power over Her[1].

By the comity of nations the reigning sovereign of another state is treated as being exempt from the criminal and civil jurisdiction of all other states[2]; and this is accepted as being a rule of English law[3].

1 *Cooke's Case* (1660) 5 State Tr 1077 at 1113; *Tobin v R* (1864) 33 LJPC 199 at 205 per Erle CJ. See further CONSTITUTIONAL LAW vol 8 para 966. As to the liability of Crown servants for criminal acts done by them see CONSTITUTIONAL LAW vol 8 para 971.
2 Wheaton's International Law (6th Edn) 220; Dicey and Morris, Conflicts of Laws (11th Edn) 236 et seq; 1 Oppenheim's International Law (8th Edn) 757 et seq; *The Parlement Belge* (1880) 5 PD 197, CA; *Mighell v Sultan of Johore* [1894] 1 QB 149, CA.
  A sovereign or other head of state, members of his family forming part of his household, and his private servants are entitled to diplomatic immunity: see the State Immunity Act 1978 s 20 and FOREIGN RELATIONS.
  A deposed, exiled or fugitive sovereign who takes refuge in England may, it seems, be liable to the criminal jurisdiction of the country: see *R v Mary, Queen of Scots* (1586) 1 State Tr 1161.
3 *R v Madan* [1961] 2 QB 1, 45 Cr App Rep 80, CCA.

39. Ambassadors and diplomatic staff. Ambassadors and persons entitled to claim diplomatic immunity[1] are immune from the criminal process of the English courts[2].

This immunity is a privilege of the sending state or other international organisation[3]; as such it may be waived by that state or organisation, though not by the representative himself[4].

1 As to those persons who are entitled to diplomatic immunity see FOREIGN RELATIONS. Diplomatic immunity is extended to observers, inspectors and auxiliary personnel exercising functions under international agreements or arrangements for furthering arms control or disarmament: see the Arms Control and Disarmament (Privileges and Immunities) Act 1988. See also para 38 note 2 ante.
2 Proceedings instituted against such persons where the immunity is not waived are therefore null and void as being without jurisdiction: *R v Madan* [1961] 2 QB 1, 45 Cr App Rep 80, CCA. See also *R v Guildhall Magistrates' Court, ex p Jarrett-Thorpe* (1977) Times, 5 October, DC.
  Since the immunity is from the process of English courts, a person would not act unlawfully eg in using reasonable force to prevent the commission of a crime by a person protected from prosecution by diplomatic immunity.
3 See, however, *R v Governor of Pentonville Prison, ex p Teja* [1971] 2 QB 274 at 282, [1971] 2 All ER 11 at 17, DC (acceptance of the representative by the host country is a condition precedent to his immunity).
4 *R v AB* [1941] 1 KB 454, CCA; sub nom *R v Kent* (1941) 28 Cr App Rep 23, CCA; *R v Madan* [1961] 2 QB 1, 45 Cr App Rep 80, CCA. See further FOREIGN RELATIONS.

40. Visiting forces. Members of the armed forces of certain countries, visiting the United Kingdom, and members of some international headquarters and defence organisations are, in certain respects, exempt from the criminal jurisdiction of the English courts[1].

1 See the Visiting Forces Act 1952 ss 3, 4 (amended by the Aviation Security Act 1982 s 40, Sch 2 para 3); the International Headquarters and Defence Organisations Act 1964 s 1, Schedule: the International Headquarters and Defence Organisations (Designation and Privileges) Order 1965, SI 1965/1535 (amended by SI 1987/927); and see FOREIGN RELATIONS; ROYAL FORCES. These provisions do not affect any power of arrest, search etc with respect to offences believed to have been committed against English law: Visiting Forces Act 1952 s 5; and see ROYAL FORCES.

41. Aliens. In general, aliens are subject to the jurisdiction of the English courts only for crimes committed within England, or within territorial waters of Her Majesty's dominions, or on British ships or British controlled aircraft[1].

1 See para 620 et seq post.

(5) PARTICIPATION IN CRIME

(i) Classification of Offences

42. Classification of offences. At common law crimes were classified as treasons, felonies and misdemeanours.

Treason is the name still given to certain offences against the security of the Crown and the State[1].

All distinctions between felony and misdemeanour were abolished by the Criminal Law Act 1967[2]; and on all matters in which a distinction was formerly drawn the law and practice is assimilated to that formerly applicable to misdemeanours[3]. Offences are now classified:

(1) for the purposes of the power to arrest without warrant[4], as arrestable[5] or non-arrestable offences; and

(2) for procedural purposes, as (a) indictable offences[6]; (b) summary offences[7]; and (c) offences triable either way[8].

1 See para 76 et seq post.
2 Criminal Law Act 1967 s 1 (1).
3 Ibid s 1 (2). Subject to any express amendment or repeal made by the Criminal Law Act 1967, an enactment passed before that Act creating an offence by directing it to be a felony is to be read as directing it to be an offence, and an enactment referring to felonious stealing is to be read as referring merely to stealing; the punishment provided for an offence by the enactments specially relating to that offence is not affected: s 12 (5). At common law a distinction was drawn in relation to felonies between the principal in the first degree, the principal in the second degree (the aider or abettor) and the accessory before the fact (the counsellor or procurer). In the case of felonies, the accessory after the fact was also guilty of an offence. As to aiding, abetting, counselling or procuring an offence see now the Accessories and Abettors Act 1861 s 8 (amended by the Criminal Law Act 1977 s 65 (4), Sch 12; the Magistrates' Courts Act 1980 s 44) and para 43 et seq post. In treason all persons who participate are regarded as principals, as is any person who receives or assists the traitor, knowing him to be such: see para 82 post.
4 As to arrest without warrant see para 703 et seq post.
5 For the meaning of 'arrestable offence' see para 703 post. Where a person has committed an arrestable offence, another person who knowingly does any act with intent to impede his apprehension or prosecution, or who conceals information about the offence for gain, is himself guilty of an offence: see the Criminal Law Act 1967 ss 4, 5 and paras 51, 319 respectively post.

6 'Indictable offence' means an offence which, if committed by an adult, is triable on indictment, whether it is exclusively so triable or triable either way: Interpretation Act 1978 s 5, Sch 1. As to trial of indictments see para 942 et seq post.

7 'Summary offence' means an offence which, if committed by an adult, is triable only summarily: ibid Sch 1. As to summary trial see para 805 et seq post.

8 'Offence triable either way' means an offence, other than an offence triable on indictment only by virtue of the Criminal Justice Act 1988 Pt V (ss 37–70), which, if committed by an adult, is triable either on indictment or summarily: Interpretation Act 1978 Sch 1 (amended by the Criminal Justice Act 1988 s 170 (1), Sch 15 para 59). As to offences triable either way see paras 804, 809 et seq post.

(ii) Complicity in Crime

43. Complicity in crime generally. A person who participates in a crime with the mens rea of that crime[1] may be convicted as a party to it if he is the perpetrator[2] of it, or if he assists the perpetrator at the time of its commission, or if he assists or encourages the perpetrator before its commission[3].

Any person who aids, abets, counsels or procures the commission of any indictable offence[4], whether an offence at common law or by statute, is liable to be tried and punished as a principal offender[5]. A person who aids, abets, counsels or procures the commission by another person of a summary offence[6] is guilty of the like offence and may be tried, whether or not he is charged as a principal, either by a court having jurisdiction to try that other person or by a court having by virtue of his own offence jurisdiction to try him[7]; and any offence consisting in aiding, abetting, counselling or procuring the commission of an offence triable either way[8] is triable either way[9].

The words 'aids, abets, counsels or procures' should be construed in their ordinary meaning and not in a technical sense[10]. To 'procure' the commission of an offence there must be a causal connection between the act constituting the procurement and the commission of the offence, but there need be no agreement or discussion as to the form which the offence should take[10]. In the case of 'counselling', it is not necessary to show that the counselling was a substantial cause of the commission of the offence, but it must be proved that there was counselling, that the principal offence was committed by the person counselled and that the person counselled was acting within the scope of his authority and not accidentally[11].

Except in treason[12], a person who gives assistance after the commission of a crime does not become thereby a party to the crime[13].

1 As to mens rea see para 10 et seq ante.

2 See para 44 post.

3 See Fost 341, 347; hence, if the crime is committed in England, a secondary party commits that crime though the acts of abetting or counselling took place outside the jurisdiction: *R v Robert Millar (Contractors) Ltd, R v Millar* [1970] 2 QB 54, 54 Cr App Rep 158, CA; *R v Wall* [1974] 2 All ER 245 at 249, [1974] 1 WLR 930 at 935, CA.

4 For the meaning of 'indictable offence' see para 42 note 6 ante.

5 Accessories and Abettors Act 1861 s 8 (amended by the Criminal Law Act 1977 s 65 (4), Sch 12); and see paras 45–49 post. As the Accessories and Abettors Act 1861 s 8 (as so amended) is essentially procedural, it does not affect the common law rule that a person can be convicted of abetting or counselling a crime only if the crime is thereafter committed (*R v Gregory* (1867) LR 1 CCR 77), although he may incur liability for incitement or conspiracy (see para 58 et seq post). See also *R v De Marny* [1907] 1 KB 388, CCR; *R v Burton* (1875) 13 Cox CC 71, CCR; *R v Waudby* [1895] 2 QB 482, CCR; *Benford v Sims* [1898] 2 QB 641, DC.

6 For the meaning of 'summary offence' see para 42 note 7 ante.

7 Magistrates' Courts Act 1980 s 44 (1).

8 Ie other than an offence listed in ibid s 17 (1), Sch 1: see para 804 post. Aiding, abetting, counselling or procuring the commission of an offence so listed, except an offence under the Criminal Law Act 1967 ss 4 (1), 5 (1), is triable either way by virtue of the Magistrates' Courts Act 1980 Sch 1 para 33: see para 804 post.

9 Ibid s 44 (2).

10 *A-G's Reference (No 1 of 1975)* [1975] QB 733, [1975] 2 All ER 684, CA.

11 *R v Calhaem* [1985] QB 808, 81 Cr App Rep 131, CA; see also *A-G v Able* [1984] QB 795 at 812, 78 Cr App Rep 197 at 208 per Woolf J (the fact that the person counselled would have tried to commit suicide anyway made no difference to a charge under the Suicide Act 1961 s 2 (1): see para 443 post).

12 Any person who assists a traitor knowing him to be such is guilty of treason: see para 82 post.

13 *R v M'Makin and Smith* (1808) Russ & Ry 333n; *R v King* (1817) Russ & Ry 332, CCR; *R v Dyer and Disting* (1801) 2 East PC 767; *R v McPhane* (1841) Car & M 212; and see para 42 note 3 ante. He may, however, be guilty of assisting an arrestable offender: see the Criminal Law Act 1967 s 4 and para 51 post.

44. Principal or perpetrator. A principal is a person who by his own act or omission directly brings about the actus reus[1], or any part of the actus reus, of a crime[2]. A person may be a principal, notwithstanding the fact that he is not present when the crime is committed, if he causes the actus reus by some contrivance[3], or by the use of an innocent agent[4].

If several persons act together in a common unlawful enterprise and the actus reus of the crime is caused by one of them, but it is not known by whom, all are principals in its commission[5].

1 As to the actus reus see para 5 ante.

2 *R v Sheppard* (1839) 9 C & P 121; *R v Kelly and M'Carthy* (1847) 2 Car & Kir 379; and see *R v Dyer and Disting* (1801) 2 East PC 767. If several persons combine to forge an instrument, each of them who executes any part is a principal though he may not know by whom the other parts are executed: *R v Bingley* (1821) Russ & Ry 446, CCR; *R v Kirkwood* (1831) 1 Mood CC 304; *R v Dade* (1831) 1 Mood CC 307, CCR.

There is no statutory definition of a principal. The Accessories and Abettors Act 1861 s 8 (amended by the Criminal Law Act 1977 s 65 (4), Sch 12) (see para 43 text to note 5 ante) recognises the principal but does not define him. Notwithstanding the abolition of the distinctions between felonies and misdemeanours and the assimilation of the law to that applicable to the latter (see the Criminal Law Act 1967 s 1 and para 42 text and note 3 ante) it would seem that one who would formerly have been a principal in the first degree to felony will now be a principal or perpetrator whatever the offence. Cases decided under the former law accordingly remain authoritative in defining a principal.

3 See eg Fost 349; Kel 52. See also Russell on Crime (12th Edn) 128, 129 cited in *R v Robert Millar (Contractors) Ltd, R v Millar* [1970] 2 QB 54 at 72, 54 Cr App Rep 158 at 165, CA.

4 Fost 349; Kel 53; *R v Tyler* (1838) 8 C & P 616; *R v Michael* (1840) 2 Mood CC 120, CCR; *R v Manley* (1844) 1 Cox CC 104; *R v Bannen* (1844) 2 Mood CC 309; *R v Bull and Schmidt* (1845) 1 Cox CC 281; *R v Clifford* (1845) 2 Car & Kir 202; *R v Blaesdale* (1848) 2 Car & Kir 765; *R v Butcher* (1858) Bell CC 6. See also *R v Bourne* (1952) 36 Cr App Rep 125, CCA (procuring act of bestiality by a woman acting under duress); *R v Cogan, R v Leak* [1976] 2 QB 217, 61 Cr App Rep 217, CA (procuring sexual intercourse without the woman's consent by a man who has reason to believe she was consenting). Both cases have been criticised as being contrary to principle but until overruled by the House of Lords they state the law as it is.

5 *R v Salmon* (1880) 6 QBD 79, CCR; *R v Pridmore* (1913) 77 JP 339, CCA; but there is no criminal liability for acts going beyond the scope of the common unlawful enterprise: *R v Borthwick* (1779) 1 Doug KB 207; and see para 47 post.

45. Secondary parties; the actus reus. A person who aids, abets, counsels or procures the commission of a crime and is liable to be tried and punished as a principal offender[1] may be termed a secondary party[2].

A person who is present abetting the principal when the crime is committed is liable as a secondary party even though he takes no part in the actual perpetration of the crime[3]. Mere presence at the commission of the crime is not enough to create criminal liability[4], nor is it enough that a person is present with a secret intention to assist the principal should assistance be required[5]. Some encouragement or assistance must have been given to the principal either before or at the time of the commission of the crime with the intention of furthering its commission[6].

Presence without more may, however, afford some evidence of aid and encouragement[7].

Knowledge that a crime is to be committed does not of itself make a person a secondary party. He must by his conduct have aided, abetted, counselled or procured the crime[8]. Thus it is enough if a person supplies materials in order that a crime of the particular kind may be committed but without knowing the details of the crime[9], or supplies information to enable the crime to be carried out[10]. Rendering assistance knowing that one of several crimes is going to be committed, without knowing which crime, is enough[11]; but not if the only knowledge is of an intention to do something illegal[12]. Any assistance which enables the crime to be committed, given with knowledge of the relevant circumstances, will suffice[13], unless the person was not in law entitled to withhold that assistance[14], or the assistance did not contribute to the commission of the crime[15].

A person who conspires to commit, or who incites the commission of, a crime, is without more a secondary party to that crime if and when it is committed, unless before its commission he has effectively withdrawn from the conspiracy or has effectively countermanded or nullified the incitement[16]. Where assistance or encouragement is given, however, a person may be a secondary party, although it cannot be shown that he conspired with the principal, or that he had been in direct communication with him[17].

A person who renders assistance after the commission of the crime does not thereby become a party to it[18].

1 See the Accessories and Abettors Act 1861 s 8 (amended by the Criminal Law Act 1977 s 65 (4), Sch 12); the Magistrates' Courts Act 1980 s 44. See also paras 48, 50 post. Since the Accessories and Abettors Act 1861 s 8 (as so amended) is essentially procedural and neither enlarges nor restricts the common law rules relating to participation in crime, any person who would formerly have been a principal in the second degree or an accessory before the fact to felony (see para 42 note 3 ante) continues to be a party to crime, but not otherwise.

2 It is unimportant, so far as criminal liability is concerned, to determine in what character a person participates in crime and the words 'aid, abet, counsel or procure' may all be used in an indictment against a secondary party: *Ferguson v Weaving* [1951] 1 KB 814, [1951] 1 All ER 412, DC.

  All persons who incite or abet an act of treason are, however, themselves guilty of treason as principals and may be indicted accordingly: see para 82 post.

3 *Coal-Heavers' Case* (1768) 1 Leach 64, CCR; *R v Towle* (1816) Russ & Ry 314.

4 1 Hale PC 439; *R v Coney* (1882) 8 QBD 534, CCR.

5 1 Hale PC 439; *R v Allan* [1965] 1 QB 130, 47 Cr App Rep 243, CCA.

6 There must be an intent to aid and also an act or omission that amounts to an aiding or encouraging. Mere presence in pursuance of an agreement to commit the crime will suffice, but, where there is no prior counselling or procuring, mere presence will not suffice without some evidence of active assistance or encouragement given. An apparent exception to this rule is where a person has a right to control the actions of another, when his failure to do so may afford evidence of encouragement by means of tacit approval of the other's actions: *Du Cros v Lambourne* [1907] 1 KB 40 DC; *Rubie v Faulkner* [1940] 1 KB 571, [1940] 1 All ER 285, DC; *Tuck v Robson* [1970] 1 All ER 1171, [1970] 1 WLR 741, DC.

7 *Wilcox v Jeffrey* [1951] 1 All ER 464, DC. See also *R v Young* (1838) 8 C & P 644. An intent to aid or encourage may be inferred from the fact that the parties were engaged in a joint unlawful enterprise (*R v Baldessare* (1930) 22 Cr App Rep 70, 144 LT 185, CCA); but a party is nevertheless criminally liable only if he has mens rea; cf *R v Borthwick* (1779) 1 Doug KB 207.

8 *R v Taylor* (1875) LR 2 CCR 147 (stakeholder for prize fight not a party to the offence).

9 *R v Bainbridge* [1960] 1 QB 129, 43 Cr App Rep 194, CCA (supplying cutting equipment for use in a breaking offence without knowing the details).

10 *R v Bullock* [1955] 1 All ER 15, 38 Cr App Rep 151, CCA; *Cook v Stockwell* (1915) 84 LJKB 2187, DC; *Cafferata v Wilson* [1936] 3 All ER 149, DC. Where the selling of particular goods is a criminal offence, the buyer may be guilty of abetting the seller: *Sayce v Coupe* [1953] 1 QB 1 at 8, [1952] 2 All ER 715 at 718, DC per Lord Goddard CJ. It is necessary for requisite mens rea to be proved in each case of the offence of aiding, abetting, counselling or procuring suicide: *A-G v Able* [1984] QB 795, 78 Cr App Rep 197 (supply of booklets describing methods of suicide). As to the ingredients of the offence of counselling a person to commit an offence see *R v Calhaem* [1985] QB 808, 81 Cr App Rep 131, CA. As to whether a doctor who gives contraceptive advice to a girl under 16 without parental consent is party to an offence against the Sexual Offences Act 1956 s 6 see *Gillick v West Norfolk and Wisbech Area Health Authority* [1986] AC 112, [1985] 3 All ER 402, HL.

11 *DPP for Northern Ireland v Maxwell* [1978] 3 All ER 1140, 68 Cr App Rep 128, HL (the accused drove another to an inn knowing that his passenger intended either to plant a bomb or to shoot someone).

12 *R v Bainbridge* [1960] 1 QB 129, 43 Cr App Rep 194, CCA; *R v Patel* [1970] Crim LR 274, CA.

13 *National Coal Board v Gamble* [1959] 1 QB 11, 42 Cr App Rep 240, DC; *Garrett v Arthur Churchill (Glass) Ltd* [1970] 1 QB 92, [1969] 2 All ER 1141, DC.

14 *R v Lomas* (1913) 110 LT 239, 9 Cr App Rep 220, CCA. See also *R v Bullock* [1955] 1 All ER 15 at 17, 38 Cr App Rep 151 at 155 per Devlin J, explaining *R v Lomas* supra. However, cf *Garrett v Arthur Churchill (Glass) Ltd* [1970] 1 QB 92, [1969] 2 All ER 1141, DC.

15 See *Lloyd v Johnson* (1798) 1 Bos & P 340.

16 *R v Croft* [1944] 1 KB 295, 29 Cr App Rep 169, CCA; mere repentance or withdrawal is insufficient: *R v Fletcher* [1962] Crim LR 551, CCA. See also *R v Grundy* [1977] Crim LR 543, CA; *R v Whitefield* (1983) 79 Cr App Rep 36; *R v Becerra, R v Cooper* (1976) 62 Cr App Rep 212, CA.

17 *R v Cooper* (1833) 5 C & P 535. The procurement may be personal or through the intervention of a third person: see *M'Daniel's Case* (1755) 19 State Tr 745 at 804 per Foster J; *R v Earl of Somerset* (1616) 2 State Tr 965, HL. See also *Mohan v R* [1967] 2 AC 187, [1967] 2 All ER 58, PC.

18 See para 43 ante.

46. Secondary parties; the mental element. A person cannot be convicted as a secondary party[1] unless he was aware of all the essential matters which make the act done a crime; but he need not have known that the act amounted in law to a crime[2]. Whether an accused was aware of essential matters is to be decided on all the relevant evidence. He can be adjudged to have known if he deliberately closed his eyes to the circumstances[3]. Criminal liability as a secondary party arises by virtue of the common law; hence mens rea is required of that party, even though the offence is one of strict liability as regards the principal[4]. It is not enough that the secondary party does acts which in fact aid or encourage the commission of the crime; it must be proved that he intended that the crime should be committed[5] or was indifferent whether it would be committed or not[6]. It is not necessary, however, to prove that there was a shared intention between the secondary party and the principal[7]. A person does not become a secondary party to a particular crime by rendering assistance to others knowing merely that the others have some criminal objective in view; it must be shown that he knew[8] that the crime contemplated was of the same kind or one of several kinds as that in fact committed[9].

1 See para 45 ante.

2 *Johnson v Youden* [1950] 1 KB 544, [1950] 1 All ER 300, DC; *Ackroyds Air Travel Ltd v DPP* [1950] 1 All ER 933, DC; *Thomas v Lindop* [1950] 1 All ER 966, DC; *Davies, Turner & Co Ltd v Brodie* [1954] 3 All ER 283, [1954] 1 WLR 1364, DC. See also *Ferguson v Weaving* [1951] 1 KB 814 at 821, [1951] 1 All ER 412 at 415, DC per Lord Goddard CJ; *Carter v Richardson* [1974] Crim LR 190, DC.

3 *R v Griffiths* [1974] 60 Cr App Rep 14 at 18; *Ross v Moss* [1965] 2 QB 396, [1965] 3 All ER 145.

4 *Ferguson v Weaving* [1951] 1 KB 814, [1951] 1 All ER 412, DC; *Callow v Tillstone* (1900) 83 LT 411, DC. See also *Gillick v West Norfolk and Wisbech Area Health Authority* [1986] AC 112, [1985] 3 All ER 402, HL and para 45 ante.

5 *R v Bainbridge* [1960] 1 QB 129, 43 Cr App Rep 194, CCA. See also *A-G v Able* [1984] QB 795, 78 Cr App Rep 197. As to the distinction between intention and motive see para 11 text and notes 9, 10 ante.

6   *National Coal Board v Gamble* [1959] 1 QB 11, 42 Cr App Rep 240, DC. Cf *R v Fretwell* (1862) Le & Ca 161, CCR.

7 *A-G's Reference (No 1 of 1975)* [1975] QB 773, [1975] 2 All ER 684, CA.

8 See para 10 note 7 ante.

9 *R v Bainbridge* [1960] 1 QB 129, 43 Cr App Rep 194, CCA; *R v Patel* [1970] Crim LR 274, CA; *DPP for Northern Ireland v Maxwell* [1978] 3 All ER 1140, 68 Cr App Rep 128, HL. See further para 47 post.

47. Collateral acts. If several persons pursue a common unlawful object, and one of them does a criminal act within the scope of the common purpose, all are responsible for that act whether it was originally contemplated or not[1]. Where, however, one of them does an act which was not contemplated by the others and which is outside the common purpose, the others are not criminally liable in respect of that act, even though they may all have been engaged in an unlawful enterprise[2]; but in such circumstances secondary parties remain liable for any crime which is in fact committed and for which they have the necessary mens rea[3].

A person is not liable as a secondary party if he procures another to commit an offence and that other knowingly commits a different offence[4]; but, if that other, although varying the manner, place or time of performance, does in substance that which he is procured to do, the instigator is liable as a secondary party[5].

1   If two persons intend to assault all who pass along a road, both are guilty of manslaughter if one kills in the course of an assault (*R v Harrington* (1851) 5 Cox CC 231); if two persons race one another on the highway both are guilty of manslaughter if one runs over a pedestrian and kills him (*R v Swindall and Osborne* (1846) 2 Car & Kir 230; cf *R v Baldessare* (1930) 22 Cr App Rep 70, 144 LT 185, CCA). If two persons go out to rob and one kills in the course of it, both are guilty of robbery, even though the one uses more force than, or violence of a character different from that which, the other contemplated; but both will be guilty of murder only if the common design was to kill or to cause grievous bodily harm (*R v Jackson* (1857) 7 Cox CC 357; *Sissinghurst House Case* (1673) 1 Hale PC 462; *R v Betts and Ridley* (1930) 22 Cr App Rep 148, 144 LT 526, CCA; *Mohan v R* [1967] 2 AC 187, [1967] 2 All ER 58, PC). See also *R v Becerra, R v Cooper* (1976) 62 Cr App Rep 212, CA; *R v Whitefield* (1983) 79 Cr App Rep 36, CA (a person may dissociate himself from a common design only by a timely communication of his intention to abandon the common purpose).

2   Where a number of men assaulted a gamekeeper and left him senseless and one of them went back to steal the gamekeeper's pocket-book, those who did not steal were held to be not guilty of the theft committed by their companion: *R v Hawkins* (1828) 3 C & P 392; *Anon* (1723) 8 Mod Rep 164. In *R v Hodgson* (1730) 1 Leach 6, a number of persons who assembled with weapons to frustrate a distress were held not guilty of the killing of an onlooker by one of their party; and see *R v Plummer* (1701) 12 Mod Rep 627. See also *R v Skeet* (1866) 4 F & F 931 (persons trespassing in pursuit of game not liable where gamekeeper killed by one of their number); and cf *R v Edmeads* (1828) 3 C & P 390 (all of a number of poachers were held parties to wounding a gamekeeper with intent to murder, since all were armed and intended to shoot any keeper who resisted them). See also *R v Smith (Wesley)* [1963] 3 All ER 597, [1963] 1 WLR 1200, CCA; cf *R v Anderson, R v Morris* [1966] 2 QB 110, 50 Cr App Rep 216, CCA; *R v Lovesey, R v Peterson* [1970] 1 QB 352, 53 Cr App Rep 461, CA.

3   If in the course of a concerted attack without intent to kill or cause grievous bodily harm one participant develops an intention to kill, he may be convicted of murder while the other participants may be convicted of manslaughter (*R v Smith (Wesley)* [1963] 3 All ER 597, [1963] 1 WLR 1200, CCA) but the other participants are not liable to be convicted of manslaughter if the perpetrator uses a weapon or acts in a way not contemplated by the other participants (*R v Anderson, R v Morris* [1966] 2 QB 110, 50 Cr App Rep 216, CCA). See also *R v Lovesey, R v Peterson* [1970] 1 QB 352, 53 Cr App Rep 461, CA; *Chan Wing-siu v R* [1985] AC 168, 80 Cr App Rep 117, PC; *R v Ward* (1986) 85 Cr App Rep 71, CA; *R v Slack* [1989] 3 All ER 90, 89 Cr App Rep 252, CA; and see para 435 post. As to whether a secondary party may be convicted of a higher degree of crime than the perpetrator see para 50 post.

4 Fost 469. Thus if A procures B to burn C's house, and B in so doing steals, A will be liable as a secondary party in respect of the burning, but not in respect of the theft: see 1 Hale PC 617, 4 Bl Com 37; and see *R v Saunders and Archer* (1573) 2 Plowd 473.

5 Fost 369, 370; 2 Hawk PC c 29 s 20; Bacon's Maxims, Regula 16. Foster suggests that, if the offence committed by the perpetrator is a natural and probable consequence of following the instigator's instructions, the instigator is liable (Fost 370; see also *Parkes v Prescott* (1869) LR 4 Ex 169 at 182, Ex Ch per Byles J; and *R v Cooper* (1846) 8 QB 533), but this rule appears to have been superseded by the provisions of the Criminal Justice Act 1967 s 8 (see para 16 ante).

48. Official collaboration in crime. There is no defence of entrapment in English law[1]. A person charged with crime is accordingly not entitled to an acquittal by reason only of the fact that the crime has been instigated by another[2], whether he be a person holding an official position or not[3]; or by reason of the fact that the conduct of the police or their agents contributed to the commission of the crime[4]. It may, however, be lawful to take part in an offence which has already been planned and is going to be committed if the participation is for the purpose of trapping the offender[5]; and it makes no difference that police participation in these circumstances may have affected the time for the commission of the offence[6].

It is doubtful whether a police officer, or a person acting under the directions of the police, who aids, abets, counsels or procures the commission of a crime for the purpose of detecting offenders and bringing them to justice thereby becomes a secondary party to the crime[7].

1 *R v Sang* [1980] AC 402, 69 Cr App Rep 282, HL.

2 Such conduct may, however, amount to a defence where eg consent is in issue: see *R v Macro* [1969] Crim LR 205, CA (conviction for robbery quashed where owner of property, acting under police directions, was not put in fear).

3 It is, however, improper for the police (and, presumably, other persons holding official positions) to instigate crime: *Brannan v Peek* [1948] 1 QB 68, [1947] 2 All ER 572, DC; *R v Birtles* [1969] 2 All ER 1131n, 53 Cr App Rep 469, CA; *R v McCann* (1971) 56 Cr App Rep 359, CA. See also Report to the Home Secretary from the Commissioner of Police of the Metropolis on the Actions of Police Officers concerned with the case of Kenneth Joseph Lennon (H of C Paper (1974) No 351) Appendix C, Extract from Home Office Consolidated Circular to the Police on Crime and Kindred Matters.

4 *R v Sang* [1980] AC 402, 69 Cr App Rep 282, HL. At common law there is no judicial discretion to rule that the prosecution may not lead evidence of offences so instigated, except possibly in the exceptional circumstances where the prosecution amounts to an abuse of the court; a trial judge has always a discretion to refuse to admit evidence if in his opinion its prejudicial effect outweighs its probative value, but, save with regard to admissions and confessions and generally with regard to evidence obtained from the accused after commission of the offence, he has no discretion to refuse to admit relevant admissible evidence on the ground that it was obtained by improper or unfair means: *R v Sang* supra at 437 and at 291 per Lord Diplock, explaining dicta in *Kuruma Son of Kaniu v R* [1955] AC 197, [1955] 1 All ER 236, PC. As to admissibility of evidence generally see para 1059 et seq post; and as to the statutory discretion to exclude relevant prosecution evidence see the Police and Criminal Evidence Act 1984 s 78 and para 1060 post.

In determining sentence, however, the court may have regard to the fact that the crime would not, or might not, have been committed but for official participation: *R v Sang* supra; and see also *Browning v J H Watson (Rochester) Ltd* [1953] 2 All ER 775 at 779, [1953] 1 WLR 1172 at 1177, DC per Lord Goddard CJ; *R v Birtles* [1969] 2 All ER 1131n, 53 Cr App Rep 469, CA; *R v McCann* (1971) 56 Cr App Rep 359. See further para 1189 text and note 16 post.

Infiltration of suspect societies by the police is lawful and proper in appropriate cases: *R v Mealey, R v Sheridan* (1974) 60 Cr App Rep 59, CA. See also *R v Bickley* (1909) 73 JP 239, CCA.

5 *R v McCann* (1971) 56 Cr App Rep 359, CA.

6 *R v McEorlly* (1973) 60 Cr App Rep 150, CA.

7 A dishonest policeman who induces a third person to commit a crime in order to improve his detection record will himself incur criminal liability: see *R v Sang* [1980] AC 402 at 443, 69 Cr App Rep 282 at 296, HL obiter per Lord Salmon. Otherwise it seems that such persons do not become secondary parties; and this rule probably applies to any person engaged in the enforcement of the law

in an official capacity, and to persons employed by them as agents (*R v Mullins* (1848) 3 Cox CC 526; *R v Bickley* (1909) 73 JP 239, CCA; *Sneddon v Stevenson* [1967] 2 All ER 1277, [1967] 1 WLR 1051, DC; *R v Birtles* [1969] 2 All ER 1131n, 53 Cr App Rep 469, CA; *R v McCann* (1971) 56 Cr App Rep 359, CA) but does not seem to apply to persons acting in a purely private capacity (*R v Smith* [1960] 2 QB 423, 44 Cr App Rep 55, CCA).

Extracts from the Home Office guidelines on this subject are published in (1969) 119 NLJ 513.

49. Victims as parties to crime. Where conduct has been made criminal with a view to the protection of a particular class of persons, it would appear that, in general[1], any member of that class of persons, such as children and young persons under 16, who is the victim of such a crime is not to be regarded as a party to it, although he was willing that it be committed or has in fact instigated its commission[2].

Though in such a case a willing victim is not to be regarded as a party to an offence committed upon himself, he may, if of the age of criminal responsibility[3], be criminally liable for abetting or counselling the commission of the offence upon another[4].

1 It has not been settled whether the rule applies outside the field of sexual offences where conduct is made criminal for the protection of young persons; but the reference to 'women' by the court in *R v Tyrrell* [1894] 1 QB 710, CCR may mean that a woman who has abetted a person to procure her for the purposes of prostitution contrary to the Sexual Offences Act 1956 s 22 cannot be convicted of abetting. See also *Grace Rymer Investments Ltd v Waite* [1958] Ch 831, [1958] 2 All ER 777, CA, where the court rejected the proposition that a tenant who paid a premium illegally required by the landlord was debarred by participation in that criminal act from exercising any right she might have under the tenancy.

2 *R v Tyrrell* [1894] 1 QB 710, CCR (girl under 16 years of age could not be convicted of aiding and abetting a male person to have carnal knowledge of her contrary to the Criminal Law Amendment Act 1885 s 5 (repealed: see now the Sexual Offences Act 1956 ss 5, 6)). See also *R v Whitehouse* [1977] QB 868, 65 Cr App Rep 33, CA (daughter under 16 could not be convicted of aiding and abetting father to commit incest with her, therefore father could not be convicted of inciting her to commit offence; the latter proposition is abrogated by the Criminal Law Act 1977 s 54 (1): see para 511 post).

3 See para 34 ante.

4 *R v Eldershaw* (1828) 3 C & P 396; *R v Cratchley* (1913) 9 Cr App Rep 232, CCA; *R v Tatam* (1921) 15 Cr App Rep 132, CCA.

50. Indictment etc of secondary parties. In general, a secondary party may be tried and convicted whether or not the principal has been tried and whether or not the court has jurisdiction to try the principal[1]. The fact that the alleged principal has been acquitted, whether on a procedural point[2] or on the merits, is no bar to the conviction of a secondary party[3]; there may be cases where the conviction of a secondary party must be quashed as inconsistent[4] or unsafe[5] where the principal is acquitted; but, where the offence can be proved against the secondary party, he is not entitled to be acquitted because the offence is not proved against the alleged principal[6]. A secondary party cannot, moreover, be convicted unless the crime to which he is alleged to have been a party is proved to have been committed[7]; and, unless he is the real perpetrator and has used the apparent principal as an innocent agent[8], he cannot be convicted where the principal is in law guilty of no offence[9]. It seems, however, that a secondary party may be convicted of an offence of a more serious degree than that for which the principal has been convicted[10].

1 See para 45 ante.

2 See *R v Daily Mirror Newspapers Ltd, R v Glover* [1922] 2 KB 530, 16 Cr App Rep 131, CCA; considered in *Minister of Food v O'Rourke* [1951] NI 97.

3 'It does not in the least follow because a principal is acquitted that another person may not be convicted of aiding and abetting': *Morris v Tolman* [1923] 1 KB 166 at 169, DC per Lord Hewart CJ; and see *R v Hughes* (1860) Bell CC 242, CCR; *R v Burton* (1875) 13 Cox CC 71, CCR; *R v Anthony* [1965] 2 QB 189, 49 Cr App Rep 104, CCA; *R v Humphreys and Turner* [1965] 3 All ER 689.

4 *Surujpaul (called Dick) v R* [1958] 3 All ER 300, 42 Cr App Rep 266, PC (evidence same against both).

5 *R v Quick, R v Paddison* [1973] QB 910, [1973] 3 All ER 347, CA (possibility that secondary party unaware that principal acted without conscious volition).

6 *R v Humphreys and Turner* [1965] 3 All ER 689. Cf *DPP v Shannon* [1975] AC 717 at 770, 771, 59 Cr App Rep 250 at 275, HL, which deals with the analogous case of the conviction of one conspirator after the acquittal of another on an earlier or later occasion. With regard to conspiracy, the acquittal of one accused is now no bar to the conviction of the other at the same time (see the Criminal Law Act 1977 s 5 (8), (9) and para 66 post); but there is no direct authority on this point with regard to secondary participation, and it was left open in *DPP v Shannon* supra.

7 *R v Gregory* (1867) LR 1 CCR 77; and see para 43 note 5 ante.

8 *R v Cogan, R v Leak* [1976] 2 QB 217, 61 Cr App Rep 217, CA. Cf *R v Quick, R v Paddison* [1973] QB 910, [1973] 3 All ER 347, CA.

9 *Morris v Tolman* [1923] 1 KB 166, DC; *Thornton v Mitchell* [1940] 1 All ER 339, DC. Cf *R v Bourne* (1952) 36 Cr App Rep 125, CCA.

10 The decision to the contrary in *R v Richards* [1974] QB 776, 58 Cr App Rep 60, CA was heavily criticised, although not expressly overruled, in *R v Howe* [1987] AC 417 at 457, 458, 85 Cr App Rep 32 at 65, HL obiter per Lord Mackay, and it is submitted that *R v Richards* supra no longer represents the law on this point.

(iii) Impeding the Apprehension or Prosecution of Arrestable Offenders

51. Impeding the apprehension or prosecution of arrestable offenders. Where a person has committed an arrestable offence[1], any other person commits an offence who, knowing or believing him to be guilty of the offence[2] or of some other arrestable offence[3], does, without lawful authority or reasonable excuse[4], any act[5] with intent to impede his apprehension or prosecution[6].

This offence is punishable on indictment according to the gravity of the arrestable offence, as follows:

(1) if that offence is one for which the sentence is fixed by law, the offender is liable to imprisonment for not more than ten years;

(2) if it is one for which a person, not previously convicted, may be sentenced to imprisonment for a term of 14 years, the offender is liable to imprisonment for not more than seven years;

(3) if it is an offence, not included in heads (1) and (2) above, but for which a person, not previously convicted, may be sentenced to imprisonment for a term of ten years, the offender is liable to imprisonment for not more than five years; and

(4) in any other case, the offender is liable to imprisonment for not more than three years[7].

No proceedings may be instituted for such an offence except by or with the consent of the Director of Public Prosecutions[8].

1 For these purposes, 'arrestable offence' has the meaning assigned to it by the Police and Criminal Evidence Act 1984 s 24 (as amended) (see para 703 post): Criminal Law Act 1967 s 4 (1A) (added by the Police and Criminal Evidence Act 1984 s 119 (1), Sch 6 para 17).

2 The offence must be specified in the charge: *R v Morgan* [1972] 1 QB 436, 56 Cr App Rep 181, CA. A prior conviction of the principal offender is not a prerequisite to a conviction under the Criminal Law Act 1967 s 4 (1): *R v Donald (J) and Donald (L)* (1986) 83 Cr App Rep 49, CA.

3 It is only necessary that the person charged should have known all the facts which constitute the arrestable offence; it is not necessary that he should have known that the facts constituted an arrestable offence in law: see para 46 note 2 ante.

4 Whether given facts are capable of constituting lawful authority or reasonable excuse is a matter of law for the judge (*R v Johnson* (1873) LR 2 CCR 15; *Dickins v Gill* [1896] 2 QB 310, DC); whether they do is for the jury.

5 Some positive act is required but it is presumably enough that the act is done through an agent: see *R v Jarvis* (1837) 2 Mood & R 40.

6 See the Criminal Law Act 1967 s 4 (1). A person commits this offence only where his intent is to impede the arrest etc of another. It is presumably not enough that his intention is to impede his own arrest even though he realises that this incidentally impedes the arrest of another (cf *R v Jones* [1949] 1 KB 194, 33 Cr App Rep 33, CCA, decided on the former law relating to accessories after the fact: see para 42 note 3 ante); or that his intention is to make a profit for himself (*R v Andrews, R v Craig* [1962] 3 All ER 961, 47 Cr App Rep 32, CCA). See also *R v Woods* [1969] 1 QB 447, 53 Cr App Rep 30, CA. It is not necessary to prove that the person charged knew the identity of the offender provided that he intended to impede the apprehension etc of that person: *R v Brindley, R v Long* [1971] 2 QB 300, 55 Cr App Rep 258, CA.

7 Criminal Law Act 1967 s 4 (3). As to the power to fine see para 1232 post. The offence is triable either way where the offence to which it relates is triable either way: Magistrates' Courts Act 1980 s 17 (1), Sch 1 para 26 (a). As to offences triable either way see paras 804, 809 et seq post; and as to the circumstances in which a verdict of an offence under the Criminal Law Act 1967 s 4 (1) (see text to notes 1–6 supra) may be returned on an indictment for an arrestable offence see s 4 (2) and para 1031 post.

8 Criminal Law Act 1967 s 4 (4) (amended by the Criminal Jurisdiction Act 1975 s 14 (5), Sch 6 Pt I). As to the effect of this limitation see para 639 post.

(iv) Criminal Liability for the Acts of Others

52. Vicarious liability; the general rule. In general a master or principal is not criminally liable for an offence committed by his servant or agent[1] even though it is committed in the course of the employment or agency[2]. There is no presumption that a crime committed by a servant or agent in the course of his duties has been authorised by the master or principal[3].

To this general rule, however, there are exceptions both at common law[4] and under statute[5].

1 Unless expressly imposed by statute it seems that vicarious liability cannot be implied unless there is a master and servant or principal and agent relationship: see *Crawford v Haughton* [1973] QB 1, [1972] 1 All ER 535, DC (where, in a case which turned on the construction of the Road Traffic Act 1960 s 64 (2) (substituted by the Road Traffic (Amendment) Act 1967 s 6 (1) (see now the Road Traffic Act 1988 s 42 (1)), it was held that, although an owner may be 'using' a vehicle when it is driven by his employee, he is not 'using' it where it is being driven by another who is not his servant, although it is being driven with the owner's consent). In *Brandish v Poole* [1968] 2 All ER 31, [1968] 1 WLR 544, DC, it was held that a licensee was not liable, under a provision which prohibited a sale by 'the holder of the licence or his servant', in respect of a sale made by his wife who was helping out in his absence; but, where a provision prohibits a sale 'by the licensee', the licensee may be vicariously liable for a sale by one whom he has authorised to sell even though that person is not a servant; cf *Linnet v Metropolitan Police Comr* [1946] KB 290, [1946] 1 All ER 380, DC. As to liability for the acts of an independent contractor, see *Quality Dairies (York) Ltd v Pedley* [1952] 1 KB 275, [1952] 1 All ER 380, DC; cf *United Dairies (London) Ltd v Beckenham Corpn* [1963] 1 QB 434, [1961] 1 All ER 579, DC. For an example of the express imposition of vicarious liability for the conduct of one who is neither servant nor agent see the Road Traffic Offenders Act 1988 s 64 (5) and ROAD TRAFFIC.

2 *R v Stephens* (1866) LR 1 QB 702 at 710 per Blackburn J; *Hardcastle v Bielby* [1892] 1 QB 709 at 712 per Collins J.

3 *R v Huggins* (1730) 2 Ld Raym 1574; *R v Holbrook* (1877) 3 QBD 60 at 63 per Lord Cockburn CJ; *R v Pearson (No 2)* (1908) 1 Cr App Rep 77, 72 JP 451, CCA; *R v Key* (1908) 1 Cr App Rep 135, 52 Sol Jo 784, CCA.

4 See para 53 post.
5 See paras 54–56 post.

53. Vicarious liability at common law. Public nuisance constitutes an exception at common law to the general rule as to vicarious liability[1]. A master is criminally liable where a nuisance is created in the ordinary course of his servant's employment[2] and he cannot escape liability on the ground that he was ignorant of the nuisance or that it was created contrary to his orders[3].

1 See para 52 ante. As to common law nuisances see NUISANCE. The offences of criminal libel and blasphemous libel formerly constituted other exceptions (see *R v Walter* (1799) 3 Esp 21; *R v Gutch, Fisher and Alexander* (1829) Mood & M 433), but the strictness of the rule has been modified by statute, and a master is not liable if he proves that the publication was without his authority and that he took reasonable care to prevent it (Libel Act 1843 s 7). See also *Whitehouse v Gay News Ltd, Whitehouse v Lemon* [1979] AC 617, 68 Cr App Rep 381, HL.
2 *R v Medley* (1834) 6 C & P 292.
3 *R v Stephens* (1866) LR 1 QB 702. As to strict liability in relation to the offence of public nuisance see para 18 note 2 ante.

54. Vicarious liability in relation to statutory offences. Criminal liability may be imposed by statute on a master or principal for the acts or omissions of his servant or agent either expressly or by implication[1]. The implication may arise either because a person has delegated to another the performance of his own statutory duties[2] or because the acts of another may be in law his own acts[3]. Such liability may arise where the offence is one requiring mens rea[4] or one imposing strict liability[5].

1 To determine whether a statute impliedly imposes vicarious liability, regard must be had to 'the object of the statute, the words used, the nature of the duty laid down, the person upon whom it is imposed, the person by whom it would in ordinary circumstances be performed, and the person upon whom the penalty is imposed': *Mousell Bros v London and North Eastern Rly Co* [1917] 2 KB 836 at 845 per Atkin J. It is not to be lightly presumed that the legislature intended that one person is to be punished for the fault of another (see *Chisholm v Doulton* (1889) 22 QBD 736 at 741 per Cave J; see also *Reynolds v G H Austin & Sons Ltd* [1951] 2 KB 135 at 149, [1951] 1 All ER 606 at 611 per Devlin J); and vicarious liability can be imposed only where from consideration of the terms of the statute and other relevant circumstances it appears clearly that that must have been the intention of Parliament (*Vane v Yiannopoullos* [1965] AC 486, [1964] 3 All ER 820, HL).
2 See *Allen v Whitehead* [1930] 1 KB 211; *Vane v Yiannopoullos* [1965] AC 486, [1964] 3 All ER 820, HL. In the latter case doubt was cast on the validity of the delegation principle; but the principle was reaffirmed in *R v Winson* [1969] 1 QB 371, [1968] 1 All ER 197, CA; *Howker v Robinson* [1973] QB 178, [1972] 2 All ER 786, DC.
3 Many examples are provided by cases arising under statutes dealing with the sale, use, keeping and possession of goods under statutes such as the Trade Descriptions Act 1968 and the Food Act 1984. See *Coppen v Moore (No 2)* [1898] 2 QB 306 (selling goods with a false trade description contrary to the Merchandise Marks Act 1887 s 2 (2) (repealed: see now the Trade Descriptions Act 1968 s 1)); *James & Son Ltd v Smee, Green v Burnett* [1955] 1 QB 78, [1954] 3 All ER 273 (using a motor vehicle in contravention of the Motor Vehicles (Construction and Use) Regulations 1951, SI 1951/2101 (revoked: see now the Road Vehicles (Construction and Use) Regulations 1986, SI 1986/1078 (amended by SI 1986/1597; SI 1987/676; SI 1987/1133; SI 1988/271; SI 1988/1102; SI 1988/1177; SI 1988/1178; SI 1988/1287; and by the Road Traffic (Consequential Provisions) Act 1988 s 3, Sch 1 Pt II)). See also para 56 note 2 ante.
4 See para 55 post. In *Chisholm v Doulton* (1889) 22 QB 736 at 742, Cave J thought that vicarious liability could not be imposed where the crime was one of negligence (as to which see para 17 ante) but this view was doubted by Lord Parker CJ in *G Newton Ltd v Smith* [1962] 2 QB 278, [1962] 2 All ER 19 at 22. See also *Niven v Greaves* (1890) 54 JP 548, DC; *Armitage Ltd v Nicholson* (1913) 108 LT 993.
5 See para 56 post. The express imposition of strict liability is exceptional; but, for examples, see the Licensing Act 1964 s 59 and INTOXICATING LIQUOR; the Road Traffic Offenders Act 1988 s 64 (5) and ROAD TRAFFIC.

55. Statutory offences involving mens rea. Where a statutory offence is one involving mens rea, vicarious liability can arise only where there has been delegation[1]. Where the legislature places a duty upon one person and he delegates the performance of that duty to another, whether a servant or agent[2], the principal is criminally liable for the failure of his delegate to perform that duty, at least where the performance of the duty cannot be properly secured without the imposition of vicarious liability[3]. For vicarious liability to arise there must be a real and effective delegation[4]; to constitute such a delegation the activity delegated must be under the exclusive control of the delegate, free from the principal's supervision[5]. If the principal remains in control of the activity he is liable for his own acts and omissions but not for those acts of his servant or agent which he does not actually counsel or abet[6].

1 See *Vane v Yiannopoullos* [1965] AC 486 at 503, [1964] 3 All ER 820 at 827, HL per Lord Evershed ('In my judgment, it can and should now fairly be taken as established by the authorities that, where by the terms of the relevant statutory provision "knowledge" is required as a condition of liability, none of the decided cases has accepted or imposed liability in the absence of the knowledge on the licensee's part or in the absence on the licensee's part of real "delegation" of his powers and duties'). See also *R v Winson* [1969] 1 QB 371 at 382, [1968] 1 All ER 197 at 202, CA per Lord Parker CJ ('The principle of delegation comes into play, and only comes into play, in cases where, though the statute uses words which import knowledge or intent . . . nevertheless it has been held that a man cannot get out of the responsibilities which have been put on him by delegating those responsibilities to another'). As to the expressions of doubt concerning the validity of the principle of delegation see, however, para 54 note 2 ante and *Vane v Yiannopoullos* supra. See also *Portsea Island Mutual Co-operative Society Ltd v Leyland* (1978) 122 Sol Jo 486, [1978] Crim LR 554, DC (employer not liable for illegal employment of minor by unauthorised employee).
2 *Linnett v Metropolitan Police Comr* [1946] KB 290, [1946] 1 All ER 380, DC.
3 *Allen v Whitehead* [1930] 1 KB 211, DC (where, if the owner of the premises had not been liable for the conduct of his manager in knowingly allowing prostitutes to remain on the premises, the statute would have been rendered ineffective). See also *Police Comrs v Cartman* [1896] 1 QB 655 at 658, DC per Lord Russell CJ; *R v Winson* [1969] 1 QB 371, [1968] 1 All ER 197, CA.
4 *Vane v Yiannopoullos* [1965] AC 486, [1964] 3 All ER 820, HL (no delegation where licensee retained overall control of the premises though he was in the basement at the time when his servant did the prohibited act on the ground floor). A master may, however, delegate control though he remains on the premises: see *Howker v Robinson* [1973] QB 178, [1972] 2 All ER 786, DC.
5 *Somerset v Hart* (1884) 12 QBD 360, DC.
6 *Vane v Yiannopoullos* [1965] AC 486, [1964] 3 All ER 820, HL; *Somerset v Hart* (1884) 12 QBD 360, DC; *Ross v Moss* [1965] 2 QB 396, [1965] 3 All ER 145, DC.

56. Statutory offences of strict liability. Even where an offence is one of strict liability[1], vicarious liability can arise only where this appears clearly to have been the intention of the legislature. Where the offence is so defined as to impose a strict duty upon a person, that person may be liable in respect of the performance of that duty by his servant or agent, whether there has been a delegation or not[2], if to hold otherwise would be to render the statutory provision ineffective[3]. Where a master or principal is thus made vicariously liable, he cannot escape his liability by showing that he took all reasonable care that the law should not be contravened, and he is liable notwithstanding that his servant or agent may have disobeyed his instructions, so long as the conduct of the servant or agent remains in the course of his employment or agency[4].

1 As to offences of strict liability see para 18 ante.
2 'When an absolute offence has been created by Parliament, then the person on whom a duty is thrown is responsible, whether he has delegated or whether he has acted through a servant; he is absolutely liable regardless of any intent or knowledge or mens rea': *R v Winson* [1969] 1 QB 371 at

382, [1968] 1 All ER 197 at 202, CA per Lord Parker CJ. In determining whether such a duty is created, a factor of importance appears to be whether the expression used is capable in its context of describing both the activity of the master or principal, and that of the servant or agent. Such expressions include 'sells' (*Coppen v Moore (No 2)* [1898] 2 QB 306, DC); 'keeps' (*Strutt v Clift* [1911] 1 KB 1, DC); 'possesses' (*Melias Ltd v Preston* [1957] 2 QB 380, [1957] 2 All ER 449, DC); 'uses' (*James & Son Ltd v Smee, Green v Burnett* [1955] 1 QB 78, [1954] 3 All ER 273, DC).

3 *Coppen v Moore (No 2)* [1898] 2 QB 306, DC. Where a provision makes it an offence for a licensee to sell or supply liquor to a drunken person, the licensee will be liable for such a sale through his servant or agent without his knowledge, for otherwise the provision would be rendered largely nugatory: *Police Comrs v Cartman* [1896] 1 QB 655, DC.

4 *Coppen v Moore (No 2)* [1898] 2 QB 306, DC; *Police Comrs v Cartman* [1896] 1 QB 655, DC. The master is not liable where the servant acts outside the course of his employment; while the master may be liable where the servant does what he is employed to do albeit in an unauthorised manner (*Police Comrs v Cartman* supra), he is not liable where the servant does something which he is not employed to do at all (*Boyle v Smith* [1906] 1 KB 432, DC; *Phelon and Moore Ltd v Keel* [1914] 3 KB 165, DC).

57. No vicarious liability in relation to abetment or attempt. A master is not, it seems, vicariously liable for an attempt by his servant to commit a crime, even in cases where the master would incur criminal liability for that crime if it were completed[1]; nor is a master vicariously liable for the aiding, abetting, counselling or procuring of a crime by his servant and this is so even where the master would be liable had the crime been perpetrated by the servant as a principal[2]. This rule applies in the case both of crimes at common law[3] and statutory offences. As criminal liability both for an attempt and for aiding and abetting, although statutory, derives from the common law, both require mens rea[4] and these principles are equally applicable where the substantive offence is one of strict liability[5].

1 Cf *Gardner v Akeroyd* [1952] 2 QB 743 at 751, [1952] 2 All ER 306 at 311, DC per Lord Goddard CJ.
2 *Ferguson v Weaving* [1951] 1 KB 814, [1951] 1 All ER 412, DC.
3 Except in the case of public nuisance, there is no vicarious liability at common law for a substantive offence: see para 53 ante.
4 As to the mental element in aiding and abetting and in attempt see para 46 ante and para 73 post.
5 In the case of attempt, a further ground of exclusion of vicarious liability is that the master might otherwise be liable for his servant's attempt even though he intervened to prevent the completion of the servant's offence: *Gardner v Akeroyd* [1952] 2 QB 743 at 751, [1952] 2 All ER 306 at 311, DC per Lord Goddard CJ.

(6) INCHOATE CRIMES

(i) Incitement

58. Incitement. It is an indictable offence at common law for a person to incite or solicit another to commit an offence[1], even though no such offence is either committed or attempted[2]. The penalty for incitement is imprisonment or a fine or both at the discretion of the court[3].

For an incitement to be complete there must be some form of actual communication with a person whom it is intended to incite; where, however, a communication is sent with a view to incite, but does not reach the intended recipient, the sender may be guilty of an attempt to incite[4]. Incitement is complete though the mind of the person incited is unaffected and notwithstanding that the person incited intends to inform on the inciter[5]; but there can be no incitement unless one person seeks to persuade or encourage another[6].

In order to prove incitement it is necessary to show that the accused sought to persuade or encourage another to commit an act that would constitute a crime if done by that other[7]; but it is no defence that, at the time of the incitement, the offence incited could not have been committed[8] or that it could not thereafter be committed owing to physical impossibility or police action[9].

If the person who incites believes that the crime can be accomplished by the means suggested, he commits an offence although the crime incited cannot be accomplished by those means; but there is no offence of incitement where he does not believe that the crime can be thus accomplished even if the person incited believes that it can[10].

1   *R v Higgins* (1801) 2 East 5; *R v Gregory* (1867) LR 1 CCR 77. For statutory forms of incitement see the Incitement to Mutiny Act 1797 s 1 (see para 92 post); the Offences against the Person Act 1861 s 4 (as amended) (incitement to murder: see para 433 post); the Perjury Act 1911 s 7 (2) (see para 308 post); the Official Secrets Act 1920 s 7 (see para 257 post), the Post Office Act 1953 s 68 (see POST OFFICE vol 36 para 786). Such statutory forms of incitement appear to add nothing to the substantive law of incitement at common law. For a consideration of the meaning of the word 'incite' see *Invicta Plastics Ltd v Clare* [1976] RTR 251, DC (company which advertised a device which could detect police radar traps properly convicted of the common law offence of inciting people who read the advertisement to use unlicensed apparatus for wireless telegraphy contrary to the Wireless Telegraphy Act 1949 s 1 (1) (amended by the Post Office Act 1969 s 4; the Ministry of Posts and Telecommunications (Dissolution) Order 1974, SI 1974/691)).
     Incitement to commit the offence of conspiracy, whether the conspiracy incited would be an offence at common law or under the Criminal Law Act 1977 s 1 (amended by the Criminal Attempts Act 1981 s 5 (1)) (see para 59 post) or any other enactment is no longer an offence: see the Criminal Law Act 1977 s 5 (7) (amended by the Criminal Attempts Act 1981 s 10, Schedule Pt I). However, it is submitted that an incitement to incite is an offence except perhaps where it amounts to an incitement to conspire: see *R v Sirat* (1986) 83 Cr App Rep 41 at 44 ('Lest there be any doubt, we do not intend to indicate that the common law offence of inciting to incite no longer exists').
2   *R v Higgins* (1801) 2 East 5; *R v Johnson* (1678) 2 Show 1; *R v Vaughan* (1769) 4 Burr 2494. However, at common law incitement to commit an offence cannot be committed where it was impossible to commit the offence alleged to have been incited. It is therefore necessary to analyse the evidence in order to decide the precise offence which the accused is alleged to have incited and whether it was possible to commit that offence: *R v Fitzmaurice* [1983] QB 1083, 76 Cr App Rep 17, CA; applying *DPP v Nock, DPP v Alsford* [1978] 2 All ER 654, 67 Cr App Rep 116, HL.
3   As to penalties see paras 1200, 1232 post.
     Without prejudice to any other enactment by virtue of which any offence is triable only summarily, any offence consisting in the incitement to commit a summary offence is triable only summarily: Magistrates' Courts Act 1980 s 45 (1), (2). On conviction of an offence consisting in the incitement to commit a summary offence, a person is liable to the same penalties as he would be liable to on conviction of such offence: s 45 (3). See also *R v Curr* [1968] 2 QB 944, 51 Cr App Rep 113, CA (decided under the Magistrates' Courts Act 1952 s 19 (1), Sch 1 para 20 (repealed)).
     Any offence consisting in the incitement to commit an offence triable either way, except an offence mentioned in the Magistrates' Courts Act 1980 s 17 (1), Sch 1 para 33 (see para 804 head (28) post) is triable either way: s 17 (1), Sch 1 para 35 (amended by the Criminal Attempts Act 1981 s 10, Schedule Pt I). On summary conviction of an offence consisting in the incitement to commit an offence triable either way, a person is not liable to any greater penalty than he would be liable to on summary conviction of such offence: Magistrates' Courts Act 1980 s 32 (1) (b). See further MAGISTRATES.
4   *R v Banks* (1873) 12 Cox CC 393; *R v Ransford* (1874) 13 Cox CC 9, CCR; *R v Cope* (1921) 16 Cr App Rep 77, 38 TLR 243, CCA.
5   *R v De Kromme* (1892) 66 LT 301, CCR; *R v Krause* (1902) 66 JP 121.
6   The persuasion need not be directed to a particular person: see *R v Most* (1881) 7 QBD 244, CCR (newspaper article); *Invicta Plastics Ltd v Clare* [1976] RTR 251, DC (advertisement in motoring journal).
7   *R v Curr* [1968] 2 QB 944, 51 Cr App Rep 113, CA. See also *R v Whitehouse* [1977] QB 868, [1977] 3 All ER 737, CA (daughter under 16 could not commit crime of aiding and abetting father to commit incest with her; accordingly father could not be convicted of inciting her to commit offence). It is now an offence, however, for a man to incite to have sexual intercourse with him a girl under the age

of 16 whom he knows to be his granddaughter, daughter or sister: Criminal Law Act 1977 s 54 (1). See further para 511 post.

8 In *R v Shephard* [1919] 2 KB 125, 14 Cr App Rep 26, CCA, it was held that, to support a charge of inciting to murder contrary to the Offences against the Person Act 1861 s 4, it was not essential that the intended victim should be in existence at the time of the incitement. See also *R v McDonough* (1962) 47 Cr App Rep 37, CCA (on a charge of inciting to receive stolen goods, it was held not to be necessary that goods of that description should be in existence at the time of the incitement); *R v Fitzmaurice* [1983] QB 1083, [1983] 76 Cr App Rep 17, CA (on a charge of inciting a person to commit a robbery, it was held sufficient that the accused believed a robbery would take place, albeit that the robbery was a fiction).

9 Cf the position in relation to attempt: see para 72 post.

10 *R v Brown* (1899) 63 JP 790.

(ii) Conspiracy

A. STATUTORY CONSPIRACY

59. Statutory conspiracy. If a person agrees with any other person or persons that a course of conduct is to be pursued which, if the agreement is carried out in accordance with their intentions, either (1) will necessarily amount to, or involve the commission of, any offence[1] or offences by one or more of the parties[2] to the agreement; or (2) would do so but for the existence of facts which render the commission of the offence or any of the offences impossible, he is guilty of conspiracy to commit the offence or offences in question[3]. A person is not, however, so guilty of conspiracy to commit any offence if he is an intended victim of that offence[4].

Where, in pursuance of any agreement, the acts in question in relation to any offence are to be done in contemplation or furtherance of a trade dispute[5], that offence is to be disregarded[6] provided that it is a summary offence which is not punishable with imprisonment[7].

Incitement to commit the offence of statutory conspiracy is not an offence[8].

1 For the purposes of the Criminal Law Act 1977 Pt I (ss 1–5 (as amended: see infra and paras 64–70 post)), 'offence' means an offence triable in England and Wales, except that it includes murder notwithstanding that the murder in question would not be so triable if committed in accordance with the intentions of the parties to the agreement: s 1 (4).

2 As to parties to the agreement see para 66 post.

3 Criminal Law Act 1977 s 1 (1) (substituted by the Criminal Attempts Act 1981 s 5 (1)). See also *R v Anderson* [1986] AC 27, 81 Cr App Rep 253, HL (a person is guilty of conspiracy if, and only if, it is shown that, when he entered into the agreement, he intended to play some part in the agreed course of conduct in furtherance of the criminal purpose which the agreed course of conduct was intended to achieve); *R v Levitz, R v Mbele, R v Vowell* (1989) Times, 1 June, CA ('. . . a criminal conspiracy was an agreement between two or more persons to effect a common unlawful purpose. The kernel of the offence was the agreement. The crime was complete once the agreement was made, even though it was usually necessary to prove acts done pursuant to the agreement to show that it was made'); *R v Di Carlo* (1989) Times, 12 June, CA ('the essence of the crime of conspiracy was the agreement and an agreement to import heroin could not be proved by an agreement to import cannabis . . . If the facts suggested that the agreement was to import drugs of more than one class, that could be appropriately laid because the Criminal Law Act 1977 s 1 (1) expressly provided for the agreed course of conduct to involve the commission of more than one offence'). The Criminal Attempts Act 1981 s 5 (1) does not apply where an agreement was entered into before 27 August 1981, unless the conspiracy continued to exist after that date: ss 5 (2), 11 (1). As to the mental element in conspiracy see para 65 post.

4 Criminal Law Act 1977 s 2 (1).

5 Ie within the meaning of the Trade Union and Labour Relations Act 1974 s 29 (amended by the Trade Union and Labour Relations (Amendment) Act 1976 s 1; the Criminal Law Act 1977 s 65 (5), Sch 13; the Employment Act 1982 s 18): see TRADE AND LABOUR vol 47 para 572.
6 Ie for the purposes of the Criminal Law Act 1977 s 1 (1) (as substituted: see note 3 supra).
7 Ibid s 1 (3). As to the penalty for statutory conspiracy see para 70 post.
8 Ibid s 5 (7) (amended by the Criminal Attempts Act 1981 s 10, Schedule Pt I). As to incitement see para 58 ante. The rules laid down by the Criminal Law Act 1977 ss 1, 2 (as amended: see note 3 supra) (see supra and paras 65, 66 post) apply for determining whether a person is guilty of an offence of conspiracy under any enactment other than s 1 (as so amended); but conduct which is an offence under any such other enactment is not also an offence under s 1 (as so amended): s 5 (6).

B. COMMON LAW CONSPIRACY

60. In general. A person who enters into an agreement with any other person or persons (1) to defraud[1]; (2) to corrupt public morals[2]; or (3) to outrage public decency[3], is guilty of an offence at common law; but an agreement to engage in such conduct as is mentioned in heads (2) and (3) above is a common law conspiracy only where it does not amount to or involve the commission of an offence if carried out by a single person otherwise than in pursuance of such an agreement[4]. Subject to the above exceptions, the offence of conspiracy at common law has been abolished[5]; and incitement to commit the offence of common law conspiracy is not an offence[6].

1 See para 61 post.
2 See para 62 post.
3 See para 63 post.
4 See the Criminal Law Act 1977 s 5 (3) (b) and paras 62, 63 post.
5 Ibid s 5 (1).
6 Ibid s 5 (7) (amended by the Criminal Attempts Act 1981 s 10, Schedule Pt I).

61. Conspiracy to defraud. A person who agrees with one or more other persons by dishonesty[1] (1) to deprive a person of something which is his or to which he would be or might be entitled; or (2) to injure some proprietary right of a person[2], is guilty of conspiracy to defraud[3] at common law[4].

If a person agrees with any other person or persons that a course of conduct shall be pursued, and that course will necessarily amount to or involve the commission of any offence or offences by one or more of the parties[5] to the agreement if the agreement is carried out in accordance with their intentions, the fact that it will do so does not preclude a charge of conspiracy to defraud being brought against any of them in respect of the agreement[6].

1 For the meaning of 'dishonesty' in the context of the Theft Act 1968 see para 542 post. Many conspiracies to defraud are conspiracies to commit offences under the Theft Act 1968 (see note 6 infra); if the offence is charged as a common law rather than a statutory conspiracy, it is submitted that the same meaning of 'dishonesty' applies: see *R v Ghosh* [1982] QB 1053 at 1059, 75 Cr App Rep 154 at 158, CA.
2 'Where the intended victim of a conspiracy to defraud is a person performing public duties as distinct from a private individual, it is sufficient if the purpose is to cause him to act contrary to his public duty and the intended means of achieving this purpose are dishonest. The purpose need not involve causing economic loss to anyone': *Scott v Metropolitan Police Comr* [1975] AC 819 at 841, 60 Cr App Rep 124 at 131, HL per Lord Diplock. See also *Welham v DPP* [1961] AC 103, 44 Cr App Rep 124, HL.
  As to whether the victim may be a stranger outside the contemplation of the parties to the conspiracy see *R v Hollinshead* [1985] AC 975, 81 Cr App Rep 365, HL.

3 For the meaning of 'defraud' see *Welham v DPP* [1961] AC 103 at 123, 124, 44 Cr App Rep 124 at 141, 142, HL per Lord Radcliffe and at 133 and at 155 per Lord Denning. See also *Scott v Metropolitan Police Comr* [1975] AC 819, 60 Cr App Rep 124, HL; *R v Terry* [1984] AC 374, 78 Cr App Rep 101, HL.

4 *Scott v Metropolitan Police Comr* [1975] AC 819 at 840, 60 Cr App Rep 124 at 131, HL per Viscount Dilhorne. The Criminal Law Act 1977 s 5 (1) (abolition of offence of conspiracy at common law: see para 60 ante) does not affect the offence of conspiracy to defraud: s 5 (2) (amended by the Criminal Justice Act 1987 s 12 (2).

   See also *R v Carlisle* (1854) Dears CC 337, CCR; *R v Brown* (1858) 7 Cox cc 442; *R v Lewis* (1869) 11 Cox CC 404; *R v Gurney* (1869) 11 Cox CC 414; *R v Warburton* (1870) LR 1 CCR 274; *R v Aspinall* (1876) 2 QBD 48, CA; *R v Taylor and Boynes* (1883) 15 Cox CC 268; *R v Whiteley* (1907) 148 CC Ct Cas 267; *R v Whitaker* [1914] 3 KB 1283, 10 Cr App Rep 245, CCA; *R v Clucas* [1949] 2 KB 226, 33 Cr App Rep 136, CCA; *R v Fountain* [1965] 2 All ER 671n, 49 Cr App Rep 315; *R v Sinclair* [1968] 3 All ER 241, 52 Cr App Rep 618, CA. As to conspiracies to defraud by officers of companies see COMPANIES vol 7 (1) (Reissue) para 1002.

5 As to parties to the agreement see para 66 post.

6 Criminal Justice Act 1987 s 12 (1). Section 12 (1) gives statutory confirmation to *R v Cooke* [1986] AC 909, 83 Cr App Rep 339, HL (conspiracy to defraud at common law may be charged where the evidence discloses a conspiracy to defraud although there is also evidence of a distinct statutory conspiracy to commit a substantive offence, whether under the Theft Act 1968 or any other enactment or at common law) and resolves the ambiguities arising from the Criminal Law Act 1977 ss 1 (1), 5 (2) as originally enacted and interpreted in *R v Ayres* [1984] AC 447, 78 Cr App Rep 232, HL. For an illustration of previous difficulties see *R v Tonner, R v Evans* [1985] 1 All ER 807, 80 Cr App Rep 170, CA. See also *R v Levitz, R v Mbele, R v Vowell* (1989) Times, 1 June, CA.

   As to the mental element in conspiracy to defraud see para 65 post; and as to the penalty for conspiracy to defraud see para 70 post.

62. Conspiracy to corrupt public morals. A person who enters into an agreement with any other person or persons to engage in conduct[1] which tends to corrupt public morals[2], but which would not amount to or involve the commission of an offence[3] if carried out by a single person otherwise than in pursuance of an agreement, is guilty of conspiracy at common law[4].

No person may, however, be proceeded against for an offence at common law of conspiring to corrupt public morals in respect of an agreement to present or give a performance of a play, or to cause anything to be said or done in the course of such a performance[5].

1 See eg *Shaw v DPP* [1962] AC 220, 45 Cr App Rep 113, HL (publication of magazine containing advertisements by prostitutes). Other examples of such conduct might be (1) publicly advocating and encouraging, by pamphlet and advertisement, homosexual practices not in themselves illegal; (2) encouraging and promoting lesbianism; (3) encouraging 'fornication and adultery': *Shaw v DPP* supra at 268 and at 149 per Viscount Simonds, at 285 and at 169 per Lord Tucker and at 294 and at 179, 180 per Lord Hodson. See also *Knuller (Publishing, Printing and Promotions) Ltd v DPP* [1973] AC 435, 56 Cr App Rep 633, HL (publication of advertisements inducing readers to meet advertisers for the purpose of homosexual practices and encouraging readers to indulge in such practices).

2 Whether or not conduct 'tends to corrupt public morals' is a question of fact for the jury: *Shaw v DPP* [1962] AC 220 at 269, 45 Cr App Rep 113 at 150, HL per Viscount Simonds, at 289 and at 173, 174 per Lord Tucker, at 292 and at 177, 178 per Lord Morris of Borth-y-Gest and at 294 and at 180 per Lord Hodson.

3 Ie an agreement which would not constitute a statutory conspiracy: see para 59 ante.

4 Criminal Law Act 1977 s 5 (3). Section 5 (1) (abolition of offence of conspiracy at common law: see para 60 ante) does not affect the offence of conspiracy to corrupt public morals: s 5 (3). See also *Shaw v DPP* [1962] AC 220, 45 Cr App Rep 113, HL; *Knuller (Publishing, Printing and Promotions) Ltd v DPP* [1973] AC 435, 56 Cr App Rep 633, HL. As to the mental element in conspiracy to corrupt public morals see para 65 post; as to parties to the agreement see para 66 post; and as to the penalty see para 70 post.

5 Theatres Act 1968 s 2 (4). See THEATRES vol 45 para 954. A similar restriction applies in the case of an agreement to give a film exhibition (see para 355 note 8 post) or to cause a programme to be included in a cable programme service (see para 371 text to note 9 post).

63. Conspiracy to outrage public decency. A person who enters into an agreement with any other person or persons to engage in conduct[1] which tends to outrage public decency[2], but which would not amount to or involve the commission of an offence[3] if carried out by a single person otherwise than in pursuance of an agreement, is guilty of conspiracy at common law[4]. No person may, however, be proceeded against for an offence at common law of conspiring to do any act contrary to public morals or decency in respect of an agreement to present or give a performance of a play, or to cause anything to be said or done in the course of such a performance[5].

1 The insertion of outrageously indecent matter on the inside pages of a book or magazine which is sold in public or is capable of being seen by more than one person may constitute such conduct: *Knuller (Publishing, Printing and Promotions) Ltd v DPP* [1973] AC 435, 56 Cr App Rep 633, HL per Lords Kilbrandon, Morris of Borth-y-Gest and Simon of Glaisdale, Lords Diplock and Reid dissenting.
2 '"Outrage" is a very strong word: and "outraging public decency" goes considerably beyond offending the susceptibilities of, or even shocking, reasonable people... Recognised minimum standards of decency... are likely to vary from time to time... Public decency must be viewed as a whole... the jury should be invited, where appropriate, to remember that they live in a plural society, with a tradition of tolerance towards minorities, and this atmosphere of toleration is itself part of public decency': *Knuller (Publishing, Printing and Promotions) Ltd v DPP* [1973] AC 435 at 495, 56 Cr App Rep 633 at 698, HL per Lord Simon of Glaisdale.
3 Ie an agreement which would not constitute a statutory conspiracy: see para 59 ante. As to the offence of outraging public decency see para 372 post.
4 Criminal Law Act 1977 s 5 (3). Section 5 (1) (abolition of offence of conspiracy at common law: see para 60 ante) does not affect the offence of conspiracy to outrage public decency: s 5 (3). As to the mental element in conspiracy to outrage public decency see para 65 post; as to parties to the agreement see para 66 post; and as to the penalty see para 70 post.
5 Theatres Act 1968 s 2 (4). See THEATRES vol 45 para 954. A similar restriction applies in the case of an agreement to give a film exhibition (see para 355 note 8 post) or to cause a programme to be included in a cable programme service (see para 371 text to note 9 post).

C. THE CRIMINAL ACT; THE MENTAL ELEMENT

64. The actus reus in conspiracy. The essence of the offences of both statutory[1] and common law[2] conspiracy is the fact of combination by agreement. The agreement may be express or implied, or in part express and in part implied. The conspiracy arises and the offence is committed as soon as the agreement is made; and the offence continues to be committed so long as the combination persists, that is until the conspiratorial agreement is terminated by completion of its performance or by abandonment or frustration or however it may be[3]. The actus reus[4] in a conspiracy is therefore the agreement to execute the unlawful conduct, not the execution of it[5]. It is not enough that two or more persons pursued the same unlawful object at the same time or in the same place; it is necessary to show a meeting of minds, a consensus to effect an unlawful purpose[6]. It is not, however, necessary that each conspirator should have been in communication with every other[7].

1 See para 59 ante.
2 See paras 60–63 ante.
3 See *DPP v Doot* [1973] AC 807, 57 Cr App Rep 600, HL; *R v Reilly* [1982] QB 1208, 75 Cr App Rep 266, CA (the offence of conspiracy continues to exist while the planned acts are carried out even though the offence of conspiracy was committed and completed when the conspirators made their agreement).
4 As to the actus reus of a crime see para 5 ante.

5 See *Poulterers' Case* (1610) 9 Co Rep 55b; and see *Kamara v DPP* [1974] AC 104, 57 Cr App Rep 880, HL. The offence is completely constituted when the agreement is made; it matters not that it is never carried out: *R v Doot* [1973] QB 73 at 81, 57 Cr App Rep 13 at 20, CA; revsd on other grounds sub nom *DPP v Doot* [1973] AC 807, 57 Cr App Rep 600, HL. Where the conduct agreed upon could not possibly result in the commission of an offence, there may nevertheless be a statutory conspiracy: see the Criminal Law Act 1977 s 1 (1) (b) (substituted by the Criminal Attempts Act 1981 s 5 (1)) and para 59 ante.
6 See *R v Walker* [1962] Crim LR 458, CA: *R v Mills* [1963] 1 QB 522, 47 Cr App Rep 49, CCA.
7 *R v Parnell* (1881) 14 Cox CC 508 at 515: *R v Meyrick, R v Ribuffi* (1930) 21 Cr App Rep 94, CCA. As to 'wheel conspiracies' see *R v Griffiths* [1966] 1 QB 589, 49 Cr App Rep 279, CCA (a conspiracy between B and C is not to be inferred from the fact that A has conspired with B in the same terms as A has conspired with C; nor do B and C conspire with one another because each knows of the other's agreement with A; to constitute a conspiracy between B and C each must know that, through the medium of A, there is a common plan which goes beyond the unlawful act he has agreed to do with A).

65. The mental element in conspiracy. The Criminal Law Act 1977 defines the mens rea[1] in all statutory conspiracies[2]. Mens rea is present where there is an intention that the requisite course of conduct shall be pursued[3]. It follows that it is no defence for the accused to plead that the intended course of conduct could not in fact have been pursued[4]. Where liability for any offence may be incurred without knowledge on the part of the person committing it of any particular fact or circumstance necessary for the commission of the offence, a person is nevertheless not guilty of conspiracy to commit that offence unless he and at least one other party to the agreement intend or know that that fact or circumstance will exist at the time when the conduct constituting the offence is to take place[5].

The mens rea which is an essential ingredient of the remaining common law offences of conspiracy[6] consists in the intention of executing the unlawful elements in the conduct contemplated by the agreeement, in the knowledge of those facts which render the conduct unlawful[7].

A person may not be convicted of conspiracy, however, unless it is shown that he intended to carry the agreement into effect; but, if he did so intend, it is immaterial that nothing was done in pursuance of it[8].

While it seems that a mistake of law will not afford a defence to conspiracy, belief in a state of facts, which, if true, would render the unlawful conduct lawful, would be an answer to the indictment[9].

1 As to the mens rea of a crime see para 10 et seq ante.
2 See the Criminal Law Act 1977 s 1 (1) (substituted by the Criminal Attempts Act 1981 s 5 (1)) and para 59 ante.
3 See the Criminal Law Act 1977 s 1 (1) (as substituted: see note 2 supra); *R v Anderson* [1986] AC 27, 81 Cr App Rep 253, HL; *R v Di Carlo* (1989) Times, 12 June, CA ('the mens rea sufficient to support the commission of a substantive offence would not necessarily be sufficient to support a charge of conspiracy to commit that offence. An intent to cause grievous bodily harm was sufficient to support a charge of murder but was not sufficient to support a charge of conspiracy to murder, or of attempt to murder. If the prosecution charged a conspiracy to contravene [the Customs and Excise Management Act 1979] s 170 (2) by the importation of heroin, then the prosecution had to prove that the agreed course of conduct was the importation of heroin. That was because the essence of the crime of conspiracy was the agreement and, in simple terms, one did not prove an agreement to import heroin by proving an agreement to import cannabis').
4 At common law, if the conduct agreed upon could not possibly have resulted in the commission of an offence, the parties were not guilty of conspiracy though they believed otherwise: see *DPP v Nock, DPP v Alsford* [1978] AC 979, 67 Cr App Rep 116, HL ('possible' meant physically or legally possible); *R v Bennett* (1979) 68 Cr App Rep 168, CA. However, the Criminal Law Act 1977 s 1(1) (b) (as substituted: see note 2 supra) reversed the common law position.

5 Ibid s 1 (2) enacting the common law rule in *Churchill v Walton* [1967] 2 AC 224, 51 Cr App Rep 212, HL. See also *R v Clayton* (1943) 33 Cr App Rep 113, CCA; *R v Jacobs* [1944] KB 417, 30 Cr App Rep 1, CCA.
6 See paras 60–63 ante.
7 See *Kamara v DPP* [1974] AC 104 at 119, 57 Cr App Rep 880 at 895, HL per Lord Hailsham of St Marylebone LC; *R v Allsop* (1976) 64 Cr App Rep 29, CA (intention in the context of conspiracy to defraud). However, a person cannot be party to an agreement by virtue of an uncommunicated intention to enter into that agreement: *R v Scott* (1978) 68 Cr App Rep 164, CA. As to parties to the agreement see para 66 post.
8 *R v Thomson* (1966) 50 Cr App Rep 1.
9 See *Kamara v DPP* [1974] AC 104 at 119, 57 Cr App Rep 880 at 895, HL per Lord Hailsham of St Marylebone LC; *DPP v Nock, DPP v Alsford* [1978] AC 979, 67 Cr App Rep 116, HL.

D. PARTIES TO THE AGREEMENT

66. Parties to the agreement. A person is not guilty[1] of conspiracy to commit any offence or offences if the only other person or persons with whom he agrees are, both initially and at all times during the currency of the agreement, persons of any one or more of the following descriptions, that is to say (1) his spouse[2]; (2) a person under the age of criminal responsibility[3]; and (3) an intended victim of that offence or of each of those offences[4].

A person is not guilty of conspiracy at common law[5] where the only parties to the agreement are husband and wife[6]; but husband and wife may be guilty as co-conspirators where others are involved[7].

A director of a company who is solely responsible for the conduct of the company's business cannot be convicted of conspiring with the company, since only one mind is involved despite the fact that the company has a separate legal personality[8]. Where, however, a director conspires in the course of the company's activities with other persons, the company may be indicted as a party to the conspiracy[9].

Where a statute exempts a particular person or a particular class of persons from liability for an offence, whether as principal or as a secondary party, it does not necessarily follow that that person, or a person belonging to that class, cannot be convicted of conspiring with another to commit that offence. In such a case, the question must be determined by considering the purpose of the statute, whether it would be defeated by holding that such a person may be party to such a conspiracy or whether the immunity was not intended to extend to the case where he agrees with others to commit the offence[10].

Where a person is immune from liability whether in respect of the crime itself or in respect of conspiracy to commit the crime, another who agrees with him to commit that crime may be convicted of conspiracy notwithstanding the immunity of the former[11]. The fact that the person or persons who, so far as appears from the indictment on which any person has been convicted of conspiracy, was or were the only other party or parties to the agreement on which his conviction was based have been acquitted of conspiracy by reference to that agreement, whether after being tried with the person convicted or separately, is not a ground for quashing his conviction unless under all the circumstances of the case his conviction is inconsistent with the acquittal of the other person or persons in question[12].

Where two persons are arraigned together for conspiracy and one pleads guilty and one pleads not guilty, their trials from that moment are separate[13].

1 Ie for the purposes of the Criminal Law Act 1977 s 1 (amended by the Criminal Attempts Act 1981 s 5): see para 59 ante.

2 Criminal Law Act 1977 s 2 (2) (a). A husband and wife may, however, be guilty as co-conspirators where others are involved: see 1 Hawk PC c 27 s 8; *R v Whitehouse* (1852) 6 Cox CC 38 (conspiracy of husband, wife and daughter). They may also be guilty of a conspiracy entered into before their marriage: *R v Robinson* (1746) 1 Leach 37. The rule has been applied to a polygamous marriage: see *Mawji v R* [1957] AC 126, 41 Cr App Rep 69, PC.

3 Criminal Law Act 1977 s 2 (2) (b). A person is under the age of criminal responsibility for these purposes so long as it is conclusively presumed, by virtue of the Children and Young Persons Act 1933 s 50 (amended by the Children and Young Persons Act 1963 s 16 (1)) (see para 34 ante) that he cannot be guilty of any offence: Criminal Law Act 1977 s 2 (3).

4 Ibid s 2 (2) (c). See also s 2 (1) and para 59 ante.

5 See paras 60–63 ante.

6 Ie because of the fiction that husband and wife are one person: see *Kowbel v R* [1954] 4 DLR 337, Can SC. See also *Mawji v R* [1957] AC 126, 41 Cr App Rep 69, PC.

7 See the cases cited in note 2 supra.

8 *R v McDonnell* [1966] 1 QB 233, 50 Cr App Rep 5.

9 *R v ICR Haulage Ltd* [1944] KB 551, 30 Cr App Rep 31, CCA.

10 *R v Whitchurch* (1890) 24 QBD 420, CCR (woman convicted of conspiring to procure her own abortion though she was not pregnant and could not commit the substantive offence); *R v Wakefield* (1827) 2 Lew CC 1; *R v Crossman, ex p Chetwynd* (1908) 98 LT 760; *R v Mackenzie and Higginson* (1910) 75 JP 159, 6 Cr App Rep 64, CCA.

11 *R v Duguid* (1906) 70 JP 294, CCR (accused was convicted of conspiring with a mother to remove her child from her guardian's possession contrary to the Offences against the Person Act 1861 s 56 (repealed), though the mother, had she been charged, might have been immune from liability).

12 Criminal Law Act 1977 s 5 (8). Any rule of law or practice inconsistent with the provisions of s 5 (8) has been abolished: see s 5 (9). See also *R v Holmes* [1980] 2 All ER 458; sub nom *R v Holmes, Merrick, Thornton and Wood* (1980) 71 Cr App Rep 130, CA. This provision abolished the former common law rule of law whereby, if two persons were tried together for conspiring with each other, and there was no allegation of conspiring with any other person, they had both either to be convicted or acquitted: see *R v Grimes* (1688) 3 Mod Rep 220; *R v Nichols* (1742) 13 East 412n; *R v Cooke* (1826) 5 B & C 538, CCR; and see also *DPP v Shannon* [1975] AC 717 at 754, 59 Cr App Rep 250 at 262, HL per Lord Morris of Borth-y-Gest.

13 See *DPP v Shannon* [1975] AC 717 at 762, 59 Cr App Rep 250 at 267, HL per Viscount Dilhorne.

E. PROCEDURE; PENALTY

67. Indictment in conspiracy. Where an indictment contains substantive counts and a related conspiracy count, the judge should require the prosecution to justify the joinder, or, failing justification, to elect whether to proceed on the substantive or on the conspiracy counts[1]. Joinder is justified if the judge considers that the interests of justice demand it[1].

There are no rigid rules governing the inclusion of a conspiracy count in an indictment with other charges[2]. The guiding principles are (1) a conspiracy charge should not be included where it adds nothing to an effective charge of a substantive offence[3]; (2) all offences charged should not only be supported by the evidence but should also represent the criminality disclosed by the evidence[4]; (3) only those charges should be included which make for simplification of the issues and avoid complexity[5]; and (4) a count for conspiracy should not be included if it will lead to unfairness to the defence[6]. A single count which charges what are distinct though overlapping conspiracies is bad for duplicity[7].

In an indictment for conspiracy to defraud it is unnecessary to specify the particular overt acts of the conspiracy so long as the accused understands the allegations against them[8]; but the particulars should be such as to enable the accused and the judge to know precisely the prosecution's case. The archaic words 'and by divers other false and fraudulent devices' should not be used[9].

1 *Practice Note* [1977] 2 All ER 540; sub nom *Practice Direction* [1977] 1 WLR 537, DC.

2 *R v Jones* (1974) 59 Cr App Rep 120, CA.
3 *Verrier v DPP* [1967] 2 AC 195, 50 Cr App Rep 315, HL; *R v Cooper and Compton* [1947] 2 All ER 701, 32 Cr App Rep 102, CCA; *R v Boulton* (1871) 12 Cox CC 87; *R v Luberg* (1926) 135 LT 414, 19 Cr App Rep 133, CCA.
4 *R v Jones* (1974) 59 Cr App Rep 120, CA. Hence the inclusion of a charge of conspiracy is proper where the conspiracy is a distinct and more serious crime: see *Verrier v DPP* [1967] 2 AC 195, 50 Cr App Rep 315, HL.
5 *R v Jones* (1974) 59 Cr App Rep 120, CA; *Verrier v DPP* [1967] 2 AC 195, 50 Cr App Rep 315, HL; *R v Cooper and Compton* [1947] 2 All ER 701, 32 Cr App Rep 102, CCA.
6 *R v Jones* (1974) 59 Cr App Rep 120, CA. Adding what may be called a 'rolled up' conspiracy charge is a wrong practice: *R v Griffiths* [1966] 1 QB 589, 49 Cr App Rep 279, CCA; cf *R v Hammersley* (1958) 42 Cr App Rep 207, CCA (one conspiracy consisting of more than one overt act); *R v Greenfield* [1973] 3 All ER 1050, 57 Cr App Rep 849, CA.
7 *R v West* [1948] 1 KB 709, 32 Cr App Rep 152, CCA; *R v Davey* [1960] 3 All ER 533, 45 Cr App Rep 11, CCA; cf *R v Hammersley* (1958) 42 Cr App Rep 207, CCA (one conspiracy consisting of more than one overt act); *R v Greenfield* [1973] 3 All ER 1050, 57 Cr App Rep 849, CA.
8 *R v Addis* [1965] 2 All ER 794n, 49 Cr App Rep 95, CCA; *R v Churchill* [1965] 2 All ER 793, 49 Cr App Rep 317; affd in *R v Churchill (No 2)* [1967] 1 QB 190 at 195, 196, [1966] 2 All ER 215 at 217, 218, CCA; revsd on other grounds sub nom *Churchill v Walton* [1967] 2 AC 224, 51 Cr App Rep 22, HL.
9 See *R v Landy* [1981] 1 All ER 1172, 72 Cr App Rep 237, CA; but quaere whether the Court of Appeal was right to suggest that the words 'falsely representing' and 'to the prejudice' should not be used in indictments for conspiracy to defraud.

68. Restrictions on the institution of proceedings. Proceedings for conspiracy[1] to commit any offence or offences may not be instituted against any person except by or with the consent of the Director of Public Prosecutions if the offence or, as the case may be, each of the offences in question is a summary offence[2].

Any prohibition by or under any enactment on the institution of proceedings for any offence which is not a summary offence otherwise than by, or on behalf or with the consent of, the Director of Public Prosecutions or any other person applies also in relation to proceedings for conspiracy to commit that offence[3].

Where an offence has been committed in pursuance of any agreement and proceedings may not be instituted for that offence because any time limit applicable to the institution of any such proceedings has expired, proceedings for conspiracy to commit that offence may not be instituted against any person on the basis of that agreement[4].

1 Ie under the Criminal Law Act 1977 s 1 (amended by the Criminal Attempts Act 1981 s 5 (1)): see paras 59, 65 ante.
2 Criminal Law Act 1977 s 4 (1). As to the effect of this limitation see para 639 post. In relation to the institution of proceedings under s 1 (as amended: see note 1 supra) for conspiracy to commit (1) an offence which is subject to a prohibition by or under any enactment on the institution of proceedings otherwise than by, or on behalf or with the consent of, the Attorney General; or (2) two or more offences of which at least one is subject to such a prohibition, s 4 (1) has effect with the substitution of a reference to the Attorney General for the reference to the Director of Public Prosecutions: s 4 (2). Consent must be proved before the summons is issued, and the point that consent is lacking cannot be taken for the first time after the case for the prosecution has closed: *Price v Humphries* [1958] 2 QB 353, [1958] 2 All ER 725. As to proof of consents to prosecutions see para 1155 post.
3 Criminal Law Act 1977 s 4 (3).
4 Ibid s 4 (4).

69. International conspiracies. A conspiracy to commit a crime abroad is not indictable in England and Wales unless the contemplated crime is one for which an indictment would lie in England and Wales[1]. Where a conspiracy in England is intended wholly to be carried out abroad, an indictment may lie in England on proof that the main purpose of the act is to produce a public mischief in England or injure a person in England by causing him damage abroad[2]. However, where such consequences are merely incidental to, rather than the object of, the conspiracy, no indictment lies in England[3].

A conspiracy between a person in England and a person abroad to commit a crime in England is a conspiracy which is indictable in England[4]; and, where conspirators in England agree to do an unlawful act in England with the intent to defraud a person or persons abroad, the conspiracy is indictable in England[5].

Where a conspiracy is formed out of English jurisdiction to commit a crime in England, it is indictable in England if acts in furtherance of that agreement are committed in England[6].

1 See *Board of Trade v Owen* [1957] AC 602, 41 Cr App Rep 11, HL (no indictment for such a conspiracy would lie in England since the unlawful means and the ultimate object were both outside the jurisdiction; such a conspiracy would be indictable, however, if the acts were designed to be done and the object were to be achieved in England as a government department would act to its detriment and be defrauded if it issued a licence which enabled something to be done which it was charged with the duty to prevent).

2 See *Board of Trade v Owen* [1957] AC 602 at 634, 41 Cr App Rep 11 at 55, HL per Lord Tucker. See also *R v Cox* [1968] 1 All ER 410, 52 Cr App Rep 106, CA; *R v Governor of Brixton Prison, ex p Rush* [1969] 1 All ER 316, [1969] 1 WLR 165, DC; *R v McPherson and Watts* [1985] Crim LR 508, CA.

3 See *A-G's Reference (No 1 of 1982)* [1983] QB 751; sub nom *A-G's Reference (No 1 of 1983)* 77 Cr App Rep 9, CA (applying the test in *Board of Trade v Owen* [1957] AC 602, 41 Cr App Rep 11, HL and a dictum of Lord Wilberforce in *DPP v Doot* [1973] AC 807 at 818, 57 Cr App Rep 600 at 606, HL).

4 See *R v Parnell* (1881) 14 Cox CC 508 at 515; *R v Meyrick, R v Ribuffi* (1930) 21 Cr App Rep 94 at 99; *R v Hammersley* (1958) 42 Cr App Rep 207 at 217, CCA.

5 See *R v Hornett* [1975] RTR 256, CA.

6 See *DPP v Doot* [1973] AC 807, 57 Cr App Rep 600, HL, where various judicial views were expressed as to the basis of the jurisdiction. See also *R v Raud* [1989] Crim LR 809, CA. As to the ambit of criminal jurisdiction generally see para 620 et seq post.

70. Penalties for conspiracy. A person guilty[1] of conspiracy to commit any offence or offences is liable on conviction on indictment:

(1) where the relevant offence[2] or any of the relevant offences[2] is (a) murder or any other offence for which the sentence is fixed by law; (b) an offence for which a sentence extending to imprisonment for life is provided; or (c) an indictable offence punishable with imprisonment for which no maximum term of imprisonment is provided[3], to imprisonment for life or for any shorter term;

(2) where in a case other than one to which head (1) above applies the relevant offence or any of the relevant offences is punishable with imprisonment, to imprisonment for a term not exceeding[4] the maximum term[5] provided for that offence or, where more than one such offence is in question, for any of those offences[6];

(3) in any other case, to a fine[7].

A person guilty of conspiracy to defraud[8] is liable on conviction on indictment to imprisonment for a term not exceeding ten years or a fine, or to both[9]. A person guilty of conspiracy to corrupt public morals[10] or to outrage public decency[11] is liable on conviction on indictment to imprisonment or a fine, or to both at the discretion of the court[12].

1 Ie by virtue of the Criminal Law Act 1977 s 1 (amended by the Criminal Attempts Act 1981 s 5 (1)): see para 59 ante.

2 Ie the offence or offences in question.

3 An indictable offence at common law not subject to any specific penalty is punishable by fine and imprisonment and the term of imprisonment is not fixed; but in the case of statutory offences, where the sentence is not limited to a specified term or expressed to extend to imprisonment for life, it is fixed at two years by virtue of the Powers of Criminal Courts Act 1973 s 18 (1) (see para 1200 post). Such offences do not therefore fall within head (1)(c) supra.

4 Ie taking the longer or the longest term as the limit for these purposes where the terms provided differ.

5 In the case of an offence triable either way the references in head (2) supra to the maximum term provided for that offence are references to the maximum term so provided on indictment: Criminal Law Act 1977 s 3 (3).

6 Ibid s 3 (1) (a), (2), (3). In a case falling within s 3 (2), (3) (see heads (1), (2) supra) a person is liable to imprisonment for a term related in accordance with those provisions to the gravity of the offence or offences in question: s 3 (1) (a). See also *R v Ashbee* [1989] 1 WLR 509, 88 Cr App Rep 357, CA. Where the agreement in question was entered into before 1 December 1977, the Criminal Law Act 1977 s 3 (2) is to be read without the reference to murder in s 3 (2) (a) and any murder intended under the agreement is to be treated as an offence for which a maximum term of imprisonment of ten years is provided: ss 5 (5), 65 (7); Criminal Law Act 1977 (Commencement No 3) Order 1977, SI 1977/1682, art 2, Sch 1.

7 Criminal Law Act 1977 s 3 (1) (b). Section 3 (1) (b) is not to be taken as prejudicing the application of the Powers of Criminal Courts Act 1973 s 30 (1) (amended by the Criminal Law Act 1977 s 65 (5), Sch 13) (general power of the court to fine offenders convicted on indictment: see para 1232 post) in a case falling within the Criminal Law Act 1977 s 3 (2) or (3): s 3 (1).

8 Ie at common law: see para 61 ante.

9 Criminal Justice Act 1987 s 12 (3).

10 Ie at common law: see para 62 ante.

11 Ie at common law: see para 63 ante.

12 See paras 1200, 1232 post.

(iii) Attempt

71. Attempting to commit an offence. A person is guilty of attempting to commit an offence[1] if, with intent[2] to commit any offence which, if it were completed, would be triable as an indictable offence, he does an act which is more than merely preparatory to the commission of the offence[3].

A person may be guilty of attempting to commit such an offence even though the facts are such that the commission of the offence is impossible[4].

A person is guilty of an attempt under a special statutory provision[5] if, with intent[6] to commit the relevant full offence, he does an act which is more than merely preparatory to the commission of that offence[7]; and a person may be guilty of an attempt under a special statutory provision even though the facts are such that the commission of the relevant full offence is impossible[8].

1 Ie an offence other than (1) conspiracy at common law (see paras 60–63 ante) or under the Criminal Law Act 1977 s 1 (as amended) (see para 59 ante) or any other enactment; (2) aiding, abetting, counselling, procuring or suborning the commission of an offence; or (3) offences under the Criminal Law Act 1967 s 4 (1) (assisting offenders: see para 51 ante) or s 5 (1) (accepting or agreeing to accept consideration for not disclosing information about an arrestable offence: see para 319 post): Criminal Attempts Act 1981 s 1 (4). Thus the 1981 Act prevented the creation of the separate offence of attempting to aid and abet the commission of a crime; but it did not remove from criminal responsibility the offence of aiding and abetting an attempt to commit a crime: *R v Dunnington* [1984] QB 472, 78 Cr App Rep 171, CA.

    A charge of attempting to procure an act of gross indecency is not precluded by the Criminal Attempts Act 1981 s 1 (4) because the offence is itself a substantive offence under the Sexual Offences Act 1956 s 13 (see para 506 post): *Chief Constable of Hampshire v Mace* (1986) 84 Cr App Rep 40, DC.

2 In any case where (1) apart from the Criminal Attempts Act 1981 s 1 (3) a person's intention would not be regarded as having amounted to an intent to commit an offence; but (2) if the facts of the case had been as he believed them to be, his intention would be so regarded, then for the purposes of

s 1 (1), he is to be regarded as having had an intent to commit the offence: s 1 (3). As to the mental element in attempt see para 73 post.

3 Ibid s 1 (1), (4). Where, in proceedings against a person for an offence under s 1, there is evidence sufficient in law to support a finding that he did an act falling within s 1 (1), the question whether or not his act so fell is a question of fact: s 4 (3). In any case in which a court may proceed to summary trial of an information charging a person with an offence and an information charging him with an offence under s 1 of attempting to commit it or an attempt under a special statutory provision (see note 5 infra), the court may, without his consent, try the informations together: s 4 (2). The offence of attempt at common law and any offence at common law of procuring materials for crime are abolished for all purposes not relating to acts done before 27 August 1981; ss 6 (1), 11 (1). Except as regards offences committed before 27 August 1981, references in any enactment passed before the Criminal Attempts Act 1981 which fall to be construed as references to the offence of attempt at common law are to be construed as references to the offence under s 1: s 6 (2).

The physical presence of an offender in England is not an essential element of an offence committed in England: see *R v Baxter* [1972] 1 QB 1 at 8, 55 Cr App Rep 214, CA; *DPP v Stonehouse* [1978] AC 55, 65 Cr App Rep 192, HL.

Provisions of any of the following descriptions made by or under any enactment, whenever passed, have effect with respect to an offence under the Criminal Attempts Act 1981 s 1 of attempting to commit an offence as they have effect with respect to the offence attempted:

(1) provisions whereby proceedings may not be instituted or carried on otherwise than by, or on behalf or with the consent of, any person, including any provisions which also make other exceptions to the prohibition;

(2) provisions conferring power to institute proceedings;

(3) provisions as to the venue of proceedings;

(4) provisions whereby proceedings may not be instituted after the expiration of a time limit;

(5) provisions conferring a power of arrest or search;

(6) provisions conferring a power of seizure and detention of property;

(7) provisions whereby a person may not be convicted or committed for trial on the uncorroborated evidence of one witness, including any provision requiring the evidence of not less than two credible witnesses;

(8) provisions conferring a power of forfeiture, including any power to deal with anything liable to be forfeited;

(9) provisions whereby, if an offence committed by a body corporate is proved to have been committed with the consent or connivance of another person, that person is also guilty of an offence:

s 2 (1), (2).

4 Ibid s 1 (2). See *R v Shivpuri* [1987] AC 1, 83 Cr App Rep 178, HL (a person is guilty of an attempt if he did an act which was more than merely preparatory to the commission of the offence which he intended to commit, even if the facts were such that the actual offence was impossible); overruling *Anderton v Ryan* [1985] AC 560, 81 Cr App Rep 166, HL.

5 For these purposes, an attempt under a special statutory provision is an offence which (1) is created by an enactment other than the Criminal Attempts Act 1981 s 1 (see supra), including an enactment passed after the 1981 Act; and (2) is expressed as an offence of attempting to commit another offence ('the relevant full offence'): s 3 (1), (2). See also note 3 supra.

Section 3 (2)–(5) (see infra) does not have effect in relation to an act done before 27 August 1981: ss 3 (6), 11 (1).

6 In any case where (1) apart from ibid s 3 (1) a person's intention would not be regarded as having amounted to an intent to commit the relevant full offence; but (2) if the facts of the case had been as he believed them to be, his intention would be so regarded, then for the purposes of s 3 (3), he is to be regarded as having had an intent to commit that offence: s 3 (1), (5).

7 Ibid s 3 (1), (3). Where, in proceedings against a person for an attempt under a special statutory provision, there is evidence sufficient in law to support a finding that he did an act falling within s 3 (3), the question whether or not his act so fell is a question of fact: s 4 (4).

8 Ibid s 3 (1), (4).

72. The actus reus of attempt. A person is guilty of an attempt if he does an act which is more than merely preparatory[1] to the commission of the offence which he intended to commit, even if the facts were such that commission of the actual offence was impossible[2]. The act must be immediately, and not merely remotely, connected with the commission of the offence[3]. Whether an act is more than merely preparatory so as to be capable of amounting to an attempt is a question of law; and whether the act amounts in the circumstances to an attempt is a matter of fact for the jury[4].

1 For the meaning of 'more than merely preparatory' see note 3 infra; and for an example of an act which was 'merely preparatory' see *R v Widdowson* (1985) 82 Cr App Rep 314, CA.
2 See the Criminal Attempts Act 1981 s 1 (1), (2) and para 71 ante. As to the actus reus of an offence see para 5 ante.
3 Interpretation of the Criminal Attempts Act 1981 ss 1 (1), 4 (3) involves a blend of decisions some of which are not easily reconcilable. At common law there seem to have been two lines of authority (see *R v Ilyas* (1984) 78 Cr App Rep 17, CA): (1) where the accused has reached a point from which it is impossible for him to retreat (see *R v Eagleton* (1855) Dears CC 515, CCR; *DPP v Stonehouse* [1978] AC 55, 65 Cr App Rep 192, HL); (2) where an attempt to commit an offence is an act done with intent to commit that offence and forming part of a series of acts which would constitute its actual commission if it were not interrupted (see *Davey v Lee* [1968] 1 QB 366, 51 Cr App Rep 303, DC; *Jones v Brooks* (1968) 52 Cr App Rep 614, DC; *R v Easom* [1971] 2 QB 315, 55 Cr App Rep 410, CA). 'In deciding whether an act is more than merely preparatory to the commission of an offence the court is entitled to look back to the law as it existed before 1981 and to see the tests that were then applied. This court expresses some doubt whether the first of the tests . . . set out in *R v Eagleton* supra is now the test that should be applied. It seems to be inconsistent with the Act, which requires only an act "more than merely preparatory to the commission of the offence", to apply the test of looking to see whether the defendant has done all the physical acts towards the commission of the offence that lay within his power so that there was nothing more left for him to do': *R v Boyle and Boyle* (1987) 84 Cr App Rep 270 at 273, CA. 'The words of the 1981 Act sought to steer a midway course. They did not provide that the test in *R v Eagleton* supra was to be followed or, as Lord Diplock had suggested (in *DPP v Stonehouse* supra at 68 and at 208) that the defendant must have reached a point from which it was impossible for him to retreat before the actus reus of an attempt was proved': *R v Gullefer* [1987] Crim LR 195 at 196, CA. The question now appears to be one of fact, viz whether the accused has gone beyond mere preparation so as to be in the course of committing the offence. See also *R v Widdowson* (1985) 82 Cr App Rep 314, CA.
4 See the Criminal Attempts Act 1981 s 4 (3), (4) and para 71 notes 3, 7 respectively ante; *R v Miskell* [1954] 1 All ER 137, 37 Cr App Rep 214, C-MAC.

73. The mental element in attempt. In order to support a charge of attempting to commit a crime, it must be shown that the accused intended to commit the completed crime to which the charge relates[1]. Notwithstanding that the completed crime might be established by proof of recklessness, an attempt to commit it requires a specific intention[2]. In any case where a person's intention would not be regarded[3] as having amounted to an intent to commit an offence but, if the facts of the case had been as he believed them to be, his intention would be so regarded, he is to be regarded[4] as having had an intent to commit that offence[5].

1 See the Criminal Attempts Act 1981 s 1 and para 71 ante. See also *R v Mohan* [1976] QB 1, 60 Cr App Rep 272, CA; *R v Pearman* (1984) 80 Cr App Rep 259, CA; *R v Nedrick* [1986] 3 All ER 1, 83 Cr App Rep 267, CA. Therefore, on a charge of attempted murder it must be proved that the accused intended to kill; it is a misdirection to direct the jury that the charge may be supported by evidence of an intent to cause grievous bodily harm: *R v Whybrow* (1951) 35 Cr App Rep 141, CCA. See also *R v Millard and Vernon* [1987] Crim LR 393, CA; *R v Walker and Hayles* (1989) Times, 11 August, CA (cited in para 431 note 5 post). As to the mens rea of an offence see para 10 et seq ante.
2 *R v Mohan* [1976] QB 1, 60 Cr App Rep 272, CA. As to the mental element in attempted rape see *R v Khan, R v Dhokia, R v Banga, R v Faiz* (1990) Times, 3 February, CA (cited in para 514 note 4 post).
3 Ie apart from the Criminal Attempts Act 1981 s 1 (3) or s 3 (5): see para 71 notes 2, 6 respectively ante.

4 Ie for the purposes of ibid s 1 (1) or s 3 (3): see para 71 ante.
5 Ibid ss 1 (3), 3 (5). See also para 71 ante; *R v Shivpuri* [1987] AC 1, 83 Cr App Rep 178, HL.

74. Conviction for attempt on charge of full offence. Where, on a person's trial on indictment for any offence except treason or murder, the jury finds him not guilty of the offence specifically charged in the indictment, but the allegations in the indictment amount to or include, expressly or by implication, an allegation of another offence falling within the jurisdiction of the court of trial, the jury may find him guilty of that other offence or of an offence of which he could be found guilty on an indictment specifically charging that other offence; and for these purposes any allegation of an offence is to be taken as including an allegation of attempting to commit that offence[1]. On an indictment for murder a person found not guilty of murder may be found guilty of, inter alia, an attempt to commit murder[2]. Where a person is charged on indictment with attempting to commit an offence, or with any assault or other act preliminary to an offence, but not with the completed offence, then, subject to the court's discretion to discharge the jury with a view to preferring an indictment for the completed offence, he may be convicted of the offence charged notwithstanding that he is shown to be guilty of the completed offence[3].

Where on summary trial for an attempted offence the commission of the completed offence is proved, the attempted offence does not merge with the completed offence and the magistrates' court may convict of the attempt[4].

1 Criminal Law Act 1967 s 6 (3), (4); and see para 1029 post.
2 See ibid s 6 (2) (c) and para 1030 post.
3 Ibid s 6 (4).
4 *Webley v Buxton* [1977] QB 481, 65 Cr App Rep 136, DC; explaining *Rogers v Arnott* [1960] 2 All ER 417, 44 Cr App Rep 195, DC.

75. Penalty for statutory attempt. A person guilty[1] of attempting to commit an offence:
(1) if the offence attempted is murder or any other offence the sentence for which is fixed by law, is liable on conviction on indictment to imprisonment for life or for any shorter term;
(2) if the offence attempted is indictable but does not fall within head (1) above, is liable on conviction on indictment to any penalty to which he would have been liable on conviction on indictment of that offence; and
(3) if the offence is triable either way[2], is liable on summary conviction to any penalty to which he would have been liable on summary conviction for that offence[3].

1 Ie by virtue of the Criminal Attempts Act 1981 s 1: see para 71 ante.
2 As to offences triable either way see paras 804, 809 et seq post.
3 Criminal Attempts Act 1981 s 4 (1). Section 4 (1) has effect: (1) subject to the Sexual Offences Act 1956 s 37, Sch 2 (mode of trial and penalties for attempts to commit certain offences under that Act); and (2) notwithstanding anything (a) in the Criminal Law Act 1977 s 32 (1) (no limit to fine on conviction on indictment: see para 1232 note 5 post); or (b) the Magistrates' Courts Act 1980 s 31 (1), (2) (maximum of six months' imprisonment on summary conviction unless express provision made to the contrary: see MAGISTRATES): Criminal Attempts Act 1981 s 4 (5).

2. OFFENCES AGAINST THE GOVERNMENT AND THE PUBLIC

(1) OFFENCES AGAINST THE SOVEREIGN

(i) Treason

76. Acts constituting treason. By statute a person[1] is guilty of treason who:

(1) levies war against the Sovereign[2] in Her realm, or is adherent to the Sovereign's enemies in Her realm giving them aid and comfort in the realm, or elsewhere[3];

(2) compasses or imagines the death of the Sovereign[4];

(3) within the realm or without, compasses, imagines, invents, devises, or intends the death or destruction, or any bodily harm tending to the death or destruction, maiming or wounding, imprisonment or restraint of the Sovereign, Her heirs and successors, and who expresses, utters, or declares any such compassings, imaginations, inventions, devices, or intentions by publishing any printing or writing or by any overt act or deed[5];

(4) compasses or imagines the death of the King's wife or of the Sovereign's eldest son and heir[6];

(5) violates the King's wife or the Sovereign's eldest daughter unmarried or the wife of the Sovereign's eldest son and heir[7];

(6) endeavours to deprive or hinder any person who is next in succession to the Crown for the time being[8] from succeeding after the demise of the Sovereign to the Crown and the dominions and territories belonging to the Crown and attempts the same maliciously, advisedly and directly by overt act or deed; or, knowing such offence to be done, is an abettor, procurer and comforter of the offender[9];

(7) slays the chancellor, treasurer, or the king's justices[10], being in their places, doing their offices[11].

Marital coercion is not a defence to a charge of treason[12].

1 Ie a person under a duty of allegiance to the Sovereign: see para 77 post.
2 In any Act a reference to the Sovereign reigning at the time of the passing of the Act is to be construed, unless the contrary intention appears, as a reference to the Sovereign for the time being: Interpretation Act 1978 s 10. The Sovereign de facto for the time being is within the provision of the Acts relating to treason and protected thereby: see 3 Co Inst 7; Bac Abr, Prerogative (A). The Sovereign de jure is not within the provision of the Acts: see 1 East PC 54. See, however, 1 Hale PC 103 where it is stated that an act of hostility against the de facto Sovereign in assistance of the rightful heir to the Crown who afterwards obtains the Crown is not treason. Cf *Sir Harry Vane's Case* (1662) 5 State Tr 120 (treason to prevent Sovereign's restoration to rightful throne). As to service in war under the de facto Sovereign see para 79 post.
3 Treason Act 1351; and see paras 79, 80 post.
4 Treason Act 1351; and see para 81 post.
5 Treason Act 1795 s 1 (amended by the Treason Felony Act 1848 s 1); Treason Act 1817 s 1; and see para 81 post.
6 Treason Act 1351. As to the extent to which the Act applies to the Sovereign's spouse and to the Sovereign's heir who is not Her first-born son see 3 Co Inst 8, 9; 1 East PC 64.
7 Treason Act 1351 (as amended). As to this provision of the Treason Act 1351 see Vin Abr, Prerogative (Be); 3 Co Inst 8, 9; 1 East PC 65.
8 Ie according to the Bill of Rights (1688) and the Act of Settlement (1700): see CONSTITUTIONAL LAW vol 8 paras 849, 850.
9 Treason Act 1702 s 3.

10 'Chancellor' means the Lord Chancellor. 'Treasurer' means the Lord High Treasurer; the office has been in commission since 1714: see CONSTITUTIONAL LAW vol 8 para 1165. The Treason Act 1351 (as amended) refers to 'the King's justices of the one bench or the other, justices in eyre, or justices of assise, and all other justices assigned to hear and determine'. These descriptions of the Queen's justices are no longer applicable and it is not clear how the statute might now be held to apply.

11 Treason Act 1351 (as amended).

12 See para 25 ante. As to whether duress may be a defence to a charge of treason see para 24 note 3 ante and para 79 note 8 post.

77. Duty of allegiance. The essence of the offence of treason lies in the violation of the allegiance owed to the Sovereign[1]. Natural allegiance is due from all British subjects[2] at all times wherever they may be[3]; local allegiance is owed by an alien under the protection of the Crown so long as he is resident within the realm and by a resident alien who goes abroad leaving his family or effects within the realm or goes abroad in possession of a British passport[4]. An alien enemy may also be convicted of treason if he accepts British protection during a war[5]. An ambassador who is not a subject of the state to which he is accredited does not owe any temporary allegiance to that state[6].

1 See *Joyce v DPP* [1946] AC 347 at 365, 31 Cr App Rep 57 at 85, HL per Lord Jowitt LC.

2 For the meaning of 'British subject' see the British Nationality Act 1981 s 51 (1) and BRITISH NATIONALITY AND ALIENAGE. A British subject is not, however, exempt from the penalties of treason because he holds a commission in the enemy forces: see *Napper Tandy's Case* (1800) 27 State Tr 1191; *Macdonald's Case* (1747) Fost 59, 183, 18 State Tr 857; *R v Townley* (1746) Fost 7, 18 State Tr 329; *R v Lynch* [1903] 1 KB 444. As to the limitation of liability of British subjects who are not also citizens of the United Kingdom and colonies for offences against the law of the United Kingdom committed elswhere see BRITISH NATIONALITY AND ALIENAGE vol 4 para 904.

3 See *R v Casement* [1917] 1 KB 98 at 137, 12 Cr App Rep 99 at 119, CCA.

4 *Joyce v DPP* [1946] AC 347 at 367, 31 Cr App Rep 57 at 87, 88, HL per Lord Jowitt LC. An alien who goes abroad may withdraw from his allegiance, possibly even though he holds a passport; but an act of treason cannot itself constitute such a withdrawal: see *Joyce v DPP* supra at 371 and at 89, 90 per Lord Jowitt LC. The duty of allegiance is not dependent upon a person's having taken the oath of allegiance: see *R v Arrowsmith* [1975] 1 All ER 463 at 469, 60 Cr App Rep 211 at 216, 217, CA. As to allegiance generally see CONSTITUTIONAL LAW vol 8 paras 862–864.

5 *Joyce v DPP* [1946] AC 347 at 374, 375, 31 Cr App Rep 57 at 96–99, HL per Lord Porter.

6 As to ambassadors and diplomatic agents generally see FOREIGN RELATIONS. Ambassadors and persons attached to embassies are, it seems, amenable to the English laws of treason only if they are British subjects: see Fost 187; 1 Hale PC 96; 1 Hawk PC c 2 s 5; *Story's Case* (1571) 3 Dyer 300b; *R v Owen (alias Collins)* (1615) 1 Roll Rep 185.

78. Penalty for treason. The penalty for treason is death by hanging[1].

1 See the Treason Act 1790 s 1 (amended by the Offences against the Person Act 1828 s 1; the Forfeiture Act 1870 s 31); the Treason Act 1814 s 1 (amended by the Forfeiture Act 1870 s 31). A male traitor may no longer be beheaded: see the Treason Act 1814 s 2 (repealed). As to disqualifications consequent upon a conviction for treason see para 1340 post; and as to the death penalty see para 1199 post.

79. Levying war against the Sovereign. The treason of levying war against the Sovereign in Her realm[1] may be of two kinds: (1) express and direct, as where war is raised against the Sovereign or Her forces with a view to injure Her person or to imprison Her or to force Her to remove any of Her ministers or counsellors; or (2) constructive, as where there is a rising for some general public purpose[2]. A rising for a limited or local purpose[3], or directed against private persons, does not amount to a levying of war[4].

A bare conspiracy or consultation with a view to a levying of war is not a levying of war[5]. To constitute a levying of war it is not, however, necessary that there should be an engagement; it is sufficient if there is arming, enlisting and marching, or if large numbers assemble with warlike intent[6], or if a small number use sufficiently violent means in carrying out their treasonable intent[7].

In an actual insurrection it is a levying of war to join with rebels in any act of rebellion[8]. In the case of war levied directly against the Sovereign, all persons assembled and marching with the rebels are guilty of treason, whether they are aware of the purpose of the assembly, or aid and assist in committing acts of violence, or not[9]. Service in war under the Sovereign de facto is not an act of treason against the Sovereign de jure[10].

1 See para 76 ante. 'The realm' formerly included only the realm of England and Wales: see 1 Hale PC 154, 155; 1 East PC 76, 77; *Lord MacGuire's Case* (1645) 4 State Tr 653. The Treason Act 1351 (as amended) was extended to Ireland (see Poynings' Law 1495) and to Scotland (see the Treason Act 1708 s 1) but not to the Channel Islands or the colonies (see 1 Hale PC 156). The Treason Act 1795 was extended to Ireland by the Treason Felony Act 1848 s 2. The Republic or Ireland is not, however, part of Her Majesty's dominions: see COMMONWEALTH vol 6 para 883. A person committing acts of war in any part of Her Majesty's dominions or abroad in conjunction with a foreign enemy would be guilty of the treason of adhering to the Queen's enemies (see para 80 post): *R v Vaughan* (1696) 13 State Tr 485; *R v Lynch* (1903) as reported in 67 JP 41 at 44.
2 Fost 210, 213; 1 Hale PC 131, 132. Among general public purposes instanced are: to effect an alteration of the law; to alter religion established by law; to open all prisons; to pull down all meetinghouses: see Fost 210, 213; 1 Hale PC 131, 132. Constructive levying of war is in truth more directed against the government than the person of the Sovereign: 1 East PC 72. See also *R v Dammaree* (1710) 15 State Tr 521; *R v Purchase* (1710) 15 State Tr 651 at 699; *R v Lord George Gordon* (1781) 21 State Tr 485 at 644; *R v Thistlewood* (1820) 33 State Tr 681 at 684, 955.
3 Eg to maintain a private claim or right, to release particular persons (unless persons imprisoned for treason), to destroy the machinery of a particular trade: see Fost 210; 1 Hale PC 133, 143, 149. Release of a person imprisoned for treason may constitute treason: see para 82 note 2 post.
4 Fost 208, 210; 1 Hale PC 131, 133, 143, 149. See also *R v Hardie* (1820) 1 State Tr NS 609 at 765; *R v Frost* (1839) 4 State Tr NS 85 at 444. It is the treasonable purpose which distinguishes treason from riot: see *R v Hardie* supra.
5 1 Hale PC 131; 3 Co Inst 9. It may, however, amount to an overt act of compassing the Sovereign's death: see para 81 post.
6 Fost 208; 1 Hale PC 131, 144; *R v Vaughan* (1696) 13 State Tr 485 at 532; *R v Dammaree* (1710) 15 State Tr 521 at 606. Open violence may amount to levying war though there are no regular operations: 3 Co Inst 9.
7 *R v Gallagher* (1883) 15 Cox CC 291 at 315, 317. 'If three men with . . . explosive materials did the same acts with the same objects as it required 3,000 men to do in an earlier period when it was a levying of war, it seemed . . . that the acts of the three men were equally a levying of war': *R v Gallagher* supra at 315 per Lord Coleridge CJ.
8 3 Co Inst 10; Fost 216; 1 East PC 70. It appears uncertain whether duress affords a defence (see para 24 note 3 ante); but, if the joining with rebels is from fear of present death and while the party is under actual force, such force and compulsion will excuse him: see 1 Hale PC 70. However, mere apprehension of loss of property or injury not endangering the person is not an excuse: see *M'Growthers Case* (1746) 18 State Tr 391; 1 East PC 71; *R v Gordon* (1746) 1 East PC 71. The orders of a superior officer afford no excuse for consorting with rebels: see *R v Axtell* (1660) 5 State Tr 1146 at 1175; 1 East PC 71.
9 See *R v Earls of Essex and Southampton* (1600) 1 State Tr 1334; *R v Purchase* (1710) 15 State Tr 651. However, in the case of a constructive levying of war, only those who actually aid and assist in doing those acts of violence which form the constructive treason are traitors; the rest are merely rioters: *R v Messenger* (1668) 6 State Tr 879 at 913; see also *R v Willis* (1710) 15 State Tr 613 at 650.
10 11 Hen 7 c 1 (Treason) (1495) s 1; and see para 76 note 2 ante.

80. Adherence to the Sovereign's enemies. A person commits the treason of adherence to the Sovereign's enemies[1] if he is adherent to the Sovereign's enemies by giving them aid or comfort in Her realm or if he is adherent to the Sovereign's enemies elsewhere by giving them aid or comfort elsewhere[2]. Adherence must be evidenced by an overt act done with intent to aid and assist the Sovereign's enemies[3].

A person is adherent to the Sovereign's enemies who does an act which strengthens or tends to strengthen the Sovereign's enemies in the conduct of a war against the Sovereign or which weakens or tends to weaken the power of the Sovereign and of the country to resist or attack the enemies of the Sovereign and the country[4]; or who sends the Sovereign's enemies money or provisions or renders them any kind of aid or comfort which, when given to a rebel within the realm, would make the subject guilty of levying war[5]; or who, in conjunction with the Sovereign's enemies, commits hostile acts upon an ally of the Sovereign who is also at war with the Sovereign's enemies[6].

Communications with the Sovereign's enemies[7] from which they may derive information to shape their attack or defence constitutes an adherence to the enemy[8]. A British subject adheres to the Sovereign's enemies if he takes an oath of fidelity to them, or makes a declaration of willingness to take up arms on their behalf, or becomes naturalised in the hostile state while it is at war with the Sovereign, unless he acts under compulsion and returns to his allegiance as soon as possible[9]. Acts of piracy committed in wartime, if there is an intention to take the Sovereign's ships as well as those of subjects, may be charged as treason[10].

A person does not adhere to the Sovereign's enemies by giving assistance to rebels within the realm[11]; or, unless war results from the incitement, by inciting a foreign state not at war with the Sovereign to invade the realm[12]; or by mere acts of submission to force majeure in case of an invasion[13]; or by refusing to give personal assistance to the Sovereign or Her forces against an invading enemy[14].

1 See para 76 ante. 'Enemies' means foreign states in actual hostility against the Sovereign (see 1 East PC 77; but see also 1 East PC 78 ('if the subject of a foreign state in amity with us acts in a hostile manner against us without commission from his Sovereign or under commission from a state at enmity with us, he is so far an enemy that a subject . . . adhering to him is a traitor')). There need not have been any formal declaration of war: 1 Hale PC 162. Whether a particular state is in actual hostility or not is a question of fact for the jury, which may judge of the matter from public notoriety: Fost 219; 1 East PC 77. A certificate of the Secretary of State given on behalf of the Crown as to the existence of a state of war involving the Sovereign is, however, conclusive evidence: see *R v Bottrill, ex p Kuechenmeister* [1947] KB 41, [1946] 2 All ER 434, CA.

2 Treason Act 1351; *R v Casement* [1917] 1 KB 98, 12 Cr App Rep 99, CCA. See also *Joyce v DPP* [1946] AC 347, 31 Cr App Rep 57, HL; *R v Lynch* [1903] 1 KB 444; *R v Vaughan* (1696) 13 State Tr 485. As to trading with the enemy see the Trading with the Enemy Act 1939 and WAR para 148 et seq.

3 See *R v Ahlers* [1915] 1 KB 616, 11 Cr App Rep 63, CCA (jury not directed that it must consider whether German consul who was British subject acted with intention of assisting enemy or in belief that duty to assist German subjects; conviction quashed).

4 *R v Casement* [1917] 1 KB 98, 12 Cr App Rep 99, CCA; see also *Joyce v DPP* [1946] AC 347, 31 Cr App Rep 57, HL.

5 1 East PC 78; Fost 217. As to treason by levying war against the Sovereign see para 79 ante.

6 1 East PC 79; Fost 220; *R v Vaughan* (1696) 13 State Tr 485 at 530.

7 It is immaterial that the communications are intercepted and do not reach the enemy: *R v Hensey* (1758) 19 State Tr 1341 at 1372; *R v De la Motte* (1781) 21 State Tr 687 at 808; *R v Gregg* (1708) 14 State Tr 1371; *R v Maclane* (1797) 26 State Tr 721. Communications which are intercepted may constitute treason by compassing the Sovereign's death: see para 81 post.

8 Fost 217; *R v Grahme* (1691) 12 State Tr 645; *R v Gregg* (1708) 14 State Tr 1371; *R v Hensey* (1758) 19 State Tr 1341 at 1344; *R v Maclane* (1797) 26 State Tr 721 at 796, 797; *R v Tyrie* (1782) 21 State Tr 815; *R v Jackson* (1795) 25 State Tr 783; *R v Sheares* (1798) 27 State Tr 255. See also *R v Stone* (1796) 25 State Tr 1155; *R v M* (1915) 11 Cr App Rep 207 at 214 (attempt to communicate information calculated to be useful to the enemy in contravention of the regulations made under the Defence of the Realm

(Consolidation) Act 1914; truth or falsity of information immaterial except as to possible defence of intention to mislead).
9 1 Hale PC 167; *R v Lynch* [1903] 1 KB 444.
10 *R v Evans* (1782) 1 East PC 80.
11 1 Hale PC 159; 3 Co Inst 11; *R v Sheares* (1796) 27 State Tr 255 at 388. Such assistance would, however, be an overt act of levying war or of compassing the Sovereign's death: *R v Townley* (1746) Fost 7, 18 State Tr 329.
12 1 East PC 78; Fost 217. Such incitement would, however, be an overt act of compassing the Sovereign's death: 1 East PC 78; *Story's Case* (1571) 3 Dyer 298b.
13 Fost 217.
14 1 East PC 80.

81. Compassing death of the Sovereign. The treason of compassing, imagining, inventing, devising, or intending the death of the Sovereign, or any bodily harm tending to death, maiming or wounding, imprisonment or restraint of the Sovereign[1] must be proved by overt, that is open, acts or by published writings expressing such compassings etc[2]. It is an overt act of compassing the Sovereign's death, wilfully and deliberately to do or attempt anything whereby the Sovereign's life may be endangered or to conspire, combine, confederate or agree to carry out that purpose[3] or to assent to any overtures for that purpose or to meet with others to kill the Sovereign though no agreement is then come to[4]. It is therefore an overt act of the treason of compassing the death of the Sovereign to enter into measures for deposing or imprisoning Her, or to place Her person in the power of conspirators against Her, or to agree with foreigners to invade Her dominions with force or to go into a foreign country to that end or to levy or conspire to levy war against Her[5] or to raise an insurrection against Her[6] or to destroy the constitution of the country[7], or to enter into communications with the enemy from which he may derive information assisting his attack or defence although the communications are intercepted[8].

Arguments and words of advice or persuasion, uttered in contemplation of some traitorous purpose actually on foot or intended, and in prosecution of it, and consulting together for such a purpose, are also overt acts[9].

1 See para 76 ante.
2 See the Treason Act 1795 s 1 (amended by the Treason Felony Act 1848 s 1). Proof by overt acts was also required of the treason under the 1351 Act of compassing or imagining the death of the Sovereign: see 3 Co Inst 12. Documents, even if not published, may be evidence of treason, if they are connected with other treasonable practices charged in the indictment: Fost 198. See *R v Grahme* (1691) 12 State Tr 645 at 709; *R v Gregg* (1708) 14 State Tr 1371 at 1375; *R v Layer* (1722) 16 State Tr 94 at 205; *R v Hensey* (1758) 19 State Tr 1341.
3 *R v Vane* (1622) 6 State Tr 120; *R v Tonge* (1662) 6 State Tr 225; *R v Parkyns* (1696) 13 State Tr 63; *R v Rookwood* (1696) 13 State Tr 139; *R v Vaughan* (1696) 13 State Tr 485; *R v Layer* (1722) 16 State Tr 94; *Downie's Case* (1794) 24 State Tr 1; *R v Hardy* (1794) 24 State Tr 199; *Watt's Case* (1794) 23 State Tr 1167 at 1186, 1187; *R v Howley* (1803) 28 State Tr 1183; *R v MacIntosh* (1803) 28 State Tr 1215; *R v Lynch* [1903] 1 KB 444.
4 1 East PC 59; *R v Despard* (1803) 28 State Tr 346 at 349, 350.
5 A constructive levying of war (see para 79 ante) is not an overt act of compassing the Sovereign's death: Fost 213; 1 Hale PC 123; *R v Darrel* (1715) 10 Mod Rep 321.
6 See *R v Earls of Essex and Southampton* (1600) 1 State Tr 1334 at 1355 ('In every rebellion the law intends as a consequence the death and deprivation of the Queen').
7 Fost 197, 210; 1 Hale PC 108–128 (where the earlier authorities are fully cited); *R v Hardy* (1794) 24 State Tr 199; *R v Horne Tooke* (1794) 25 State Tr 1; *R v Freind* (1696) 13 State Tr 1; *R v Charnock, King and Keyes* (1696) 12 State Tr 1377; *R v Rookwood* (1696) 13 State Tr 139; *R v Thistlewood* (1820) 33 State Tr 681 at 685; *R v Ings* (1820) 33 State Tr 957.
8 *R v Hensey* (1785) 19 State Tr 1341. Such communications also constitute adherence to the Sovereign's enemies: see para 80 ante.

9 Fost 200; *R v Charnock, King and Keyes* (1696) 12 State Tr 1377 at 1452; *R v Parkyns* (1696) 13 State Tr 63 at 132. Cf *Pine's Case* (1628) 3 State Tr 359 ('loose words, not relative to any act or design . . . are not overt acts').

82. Aiding and abetting treason. All persons who incite, aid or abet an act of treason, or who receive[1] or protect a traitor, are themselves guilty of treason[2].

1 If the husband commits treason and his wife knowingly receives him, she does not herself become guilty of treason: 1 Hale PC 45. There appears to be no authority as to whether she is guilty of misprision of treason (see para 83 post) in these circumstances. However, since treason is an arrestable offence within the meaning of the Police and Criminal Evidence Act 1984 s 24 (1) (see para 703 post), a wife who, knowing or believing her husband to be guilty of treason, does an act with intent to impede his apprehension or prosecution, may be guilty of an offence under the Criminal Law Act 1967 s 4 (as amended): see para 51 ante. As to non-disclosure due to a claim of right made in good faith as applying to the former offence of misprision of felony see *Sykes v DPP* [1962] AC 528 at 564, 45 Cr App Rep 230 at 250, 251, HL per Lord Denning.
2 Fost 341; 1 Hale PC 233. This rule is stated not to have applied to kinds of treason which did not involve the legal notion of compassing the death of the King, Queen or heir apparent: Fost 342; 4 Bl Com (14th Edn) 36. A gaoler who voluntarily permits a person imprisoned for treason to escape, and anyone who rescues such a person, is himself guilty of treason: Fost 344. Although a person who receives and harbours a traitor is himself said to be guilty as a principal traitor, he must be indicted specially for such receiving and harbouring, and not for the principal treason; and he cannot be tried on a separate indictment for the receiving and harbouring, until after the traitor alleged to have been received is convicted; if the receiver is tried for the receiving and harbouring upon the same indictment with the principal offender as he may be, the jury must first be charged to inquire as to the guilt of the latter, and, if he is acquitted, the receiver must also be acquitted: 1 Hale PC 238; Fost 345.

(ii) Misprision of Treason

83. Misprision of treason. It is an offence at common law, punishable by fine and imprisonment at the discretion of the court[1], for a person who knows[2] that treason is being planned or committed not to report it as soon as he can to a justice of the peace or other authority[3].

1 See paras 1200, 1232 post. The offence was formerly also punishable by loss of profits of land during life and forfeiture of goods: see 1 Hale PC 374. Although the abolition of forfeiture under the Forfeiture Act 1870 s 1 (as amended) did not apply to misprision of treason, subsequent provisions to abolish so much of the punishment for an offence as consisted in any general forfeiture of land or of goods and chattels (see the Criminal Law Act 1967 s 7 (5) (repealed)) and the abolition of the distinctions between felony and misdemeanour (see s 1 and para 42 ante) have raised questions as to whether forfeiture is still applicable to misprision of treason.
2 Ie without being a party or consenting to the treason: 1 East PC 139; *R v Tonge* (1662) 6 State Tr 225.
3 1 Hale PC 372; 1 East PC 139. See *Regicides' Case* (1660) 5 State Tr 947 at 985; *R v Tonge* (1662) 6 State Tr 225; *R v Walcot* (1683) 9 State Tr 519 at 553; *R v Thistlewood* (1820) 33 State Tr 681 at 690, 691. To constitute the offence there must be a knowledge of the persons concerned and of the design or offence; merely to be told that there will be a rising and to conceal the information is not misprision of treason: Kel 21; 1 East PC 139.

(iii) Treason and Misprision of Treason; Evidence and Procedure

84. Procedure. The procedure on trials for treason or misprision of treason is the same as that on trials for murder[1]. An indictment for treason or misprision of treason committed in any part of the United Kingdom must be signed within three years from the commission of the offence[2], except in the case of the treason of designing, endeavouring or attempting the assassination of the Sovereign where there is no limitation of time[3]. Treason committed abroad may be tried in England[4].

1 Criminal Law Act 1967 s 12 (6). As to treason being an exception to the general rule of convicting for an offence other than that charged see para 1029 post.
2 See the Treason Act 1695 s 5; the Treason Act 1708 s 1; the Treason (Ireland) Act 1821; the Administration of Justice (Miscellaneous Provisions) Act 1933 s 2 (8), Sch 2, para 1; Fost 249.
3 Treason Act 1695 s 6.
4 See para 634 post.

85. Treason; proof by overt acts. The treason alleged must be proved by overt acts[1]. It seems that the overt acts upon which it is intended to rely must be expressly alleged in the indictment[2] and that no evidence is admissible of any overt act that is not so alleged unless it affords direct proof of the overt acts that are laid[3]. Where the overt acts alleged in the indictment include acts of conspiracy, evidence may be given of acts committed by co-conspirators in execution of the common design even if committed after the date of the overt acts alleged and after the accused's arrest[4].

1 See 3 Co Inst 12.
2 Provision to this effect was contained in the Treason Act 1695 s 8 (repealed). Quaere whether overt acts must be alleged in order to comply with the Indictments Act 1915 s 3 (1): see para 923 post. If the overt acts alleged consist of words or documents, it is sufficient to set out their effect: *R v Francia* (1717) 15 State Tr 897; *R v Watson* (1817) 2 Stark 116 at 132; *R v Vaughan* (1696) 13 State Tr 485 at 498. Several overt acts may be laid in one count: see para 931 note 5 post.
3 See the Treason Act 1695 s 8 (repealed); *R v Rookwood* (1696) 13 State Tr 139 at 217; *R v Layer* (1722) 16 State Tr 94 at 223; *R v Deacon* (1746) 18 State Tr 365; *R v Thistlewood* (1820) 33 State Tr 681 at 686 per Abbott CJ.
4 *R v Horne Tooke* (1794) 1 East PC 98; *R v Hardy* (1794) 1 East PC 99; *R v Watson* (1817) 2 Stark 116 at 127; *R v McCafferty* (1867) 10 Cox CC 603, CCA; *R v Stone* (1796) 25 State Tr 1155.

(iv) Treason Felony

86. Treason felony. Any person who (1) within the United Kingdom[1] or without, compasses, imagines, invents, devises or intends (a) to deprive or depose the Sovereign from the style, honour or royal name of the Crown of the United Kingdom or of any other of Her Majesty's dominions and countries[2]; or (b) to levy war[3] against Her Majesty within any part of the United Kingdom in order by force or constraint to compel Her to change Her measures or counsels or in order to put any force or constraint upon or in order to intimidate or overawe both Houses or either House of Parliament; or (c) to move or stir any foreigner or stranger with force to invade the United Kingdom or any other of Her Majesty's dominions or countries; and (2) expresses, utters or declares such compassings etc by publishing any printing or writing or by any overt act[4] or deed, is guilty of an offence and liable on conviction on indictment to imprisonment for life or for any shorter term[5].

1 'United Kingdom' means Great Britain and Northern Ireland: Interpretation Act 1978 s 5, Sch 1. 'Great Britain' means England, Scotland and Wales: Union with Scotland Act 1706 preamble, art 1; Interpretation Act 1978 s 22 (1), Sch 2 para 5 (a). Neither the Channel Islands nor the Isle of Man are within the United Kingdom.
2 *R v Mitchel* (1848) 6 State Tr NS 599: *R v Gallagher* (1883) 15 Cox CC 291; *Mulcahy v R* (1866) IR 1 CL 12; affd (1868) LR 3 HL 306; *R v Davitt* (1870) 11 Cox CC 676.

3 *R v Gallagher* (1883) 15 Cox CC 291; *R v Mitchel* (1848) 6 State Tr NS 599; *R v Dowling* (1848) 3 Cox CC 509; *Mulcahy v R* (1866) IR 1 CL 12; affd (1868) LR 3 HL 306.
4 Some overt act must be committed within the Sovereign's dominions: see *R v Meany* (1867) 10 Cox CC 506, CCR. Where the accused has conspired with others to commit any offence under the Treason Felony Act 1848 and a co-conspirator commits acts within the Sovereign's dominions in furtherance of the common purpose, it is a sufficient overt act to allege the conspiracy: *R v Meany* supra. See also *Mulcahy v R* (1866) IR 1 CL 12; affd (1868) LR 3 HL 306; *R v Davitt* (1870) 11 Cox CC 676; *R v Deasy* (1883) 15 Cox CC 334. Several overt acts may be alleged in one count: *Mulcahy v R* supra.
5 Treason Felony Act 1848 s 3; Penal Servitude Act 1857 s 2; Penal Servitude Act 1891 s 1; Criminal Justice Act 1948 s 1; Criminal Law Act 1967 s 12 (5) (a). The Treason Felony Act 1848 does not lessen the force of, or in any manner affect anything enacted by, the Treason Act 1351 (see para 76 ante): Treason Felony Act 1848 s 6. If matters alleged in an indictment or proved at the trial for any offence under s 3 amount in law to treason, this does not render the indictment defective or entitle the accused to be acquitted; but an acquittal or conviction for any such offence is a bar to a prosecution for treason on the same facts: s 7; *R v Mitchel* (1848) 6 State Tr NS 599.

(v) Assaults on and Contempt of the Sovereign

87. Assaults on the Sovereign. Any person who (1) with intent to injure the person of the Sovereign or to break public peace or whereby the public peace may be endangered or to alarm the Sovereign (a) wilfully discharges or attempts to discharge or points, aims, or presents at or near to the person of the Sovereign any gun, pistol or any other firearm or other arms, whether the same does or does not contain any explosive or destructive material, or discharges or causes to be discharged or attempts to discharge any explosive substance or material near to the Sovereign's person; (b) wilfully strikes or strikes at or attempts to strike or strike at the Sovereign with any offensive weapon or in any other manner whatsoever; (c) wilfully throws or attempts to throw any substance, matter or thing at or upon the person of the Sovereign; or (2) wilfully produces or has near the person of the Sovereign any gun, pistol or any other description of firearm or other arms whatsoever, or any explosive, destructive, or dangerous matter or thing whatsoever, with intent to use the same to injure the person of the Sovereign or to alarm Her is guilty of high misdemeanour[1] and liable on conviction on indictment to imprisonment for a term not exceeding seven years[2].

1 The anomalous term 'high misdemeanour' is not apparently affected by the Criminal Law Act 1967: see further para 42 ante.
2 Treason Act 1842 s 2 (amended by the Criminal Administration Act 1914 s 44, Sch 4; the Criminal Justice Act 1948 s 83 (3), Sch 10 Pt II); Penal Servitude Act 1857 s 2; Penal Servitude Act 1891 s 1; Criminal Justice Act 1948 s 1.

88. Contempt of the Sovereign. Contempt of the Sovereign[1] is an offence at common law punishable by fine and imprisonment at the discretion of the court[2].

1 See 1 Hawk PC c 6; 2 Hawk PC c 25, s 4; 4 Bl Com (14th Edn) 122; 3 Co Inst 140, where contempts against the King's palaces or courts of justice or against His person, title, prerogative or government are listed under the headings of 'contempts' or 'misprisions'. As to criminal contempt of court see CONTEMPT vol 9 para 97 et seq. No prosecution for a contempt of the Sovereign appears to have been brought since 1840: see *R v Price* (1840) 11 Ad & El 727.
2 See paras 1200, 1232 post.

(2) OFFENCES AGAINST PUBLIC ORDER

(i) Seditious Words and Libel

89. Nature of sedition. Sedition in the common law consists of any act done, or words spoken or written and published, which has or have a seditious tendency and is done or are spoken or written and published with a seditious intention[1]. A person may be said to have a seditious intention if he has any of the following intentions and acts or words may be said to have a seditious tendency if they have any of the following tendencies:

(1) to bring into hatred or contempt, or to excite disaffection against, the Sovereign or the government and constitution of the United Kingdom or either House of Parliament, or the administration of justice[2]; or

(2) to excite the Sovereign's subjects to attempt, otherwise than by lawful means, the alteration of any matter in church or state by law established; or

(3) to incite persons to commit any crime in disturbance of the peace; or

(4) to raise discontent or disaffection amongst the Sovereign's subjects; or

(5) to promote feelings of ill-will and hostility between different classes of those subjects[3].

An intention is not seditious if the object is to show that the Sovereign has been misled or mistaken in Her measures, or to point out errors or defects in the government or constitution with a view to their reformation, or to excite the subjects to attempt by lawful means the alteration of any matter in church or state by law established, or to point out, with a view to their removal, matters which are producing, or have a tendency to produce, feelings of hatred and ill-will between classes of the Sovereign's subjects[4].

The character of the words used may be good evidence of the nature of the intention[5].

1 As to seditious words and seditious libel see para 90 post. It is an offence for an alien to attempt to do any act calculated or likely to cause sedition: see the Aliens Restriction (Amendment) Act 1919 s 3 and BRITISH NATIONALITY AND ALIENAGE vol 4 para 955. For these purposes, 'alien' does not include a British protected person: British Nationality Act 1948 s 3 (3). For the meaning of 'British protected person' see the British Nationality Act 1981 s 50 (1) and BRITISH NATIONALITY AND ALIENAGE.

2 See *R v Lambert and Perry* (1810) 2 Camp 398; *R v Tutchin* (1704) 14 State Tr 1095, CCR; *R v Cobbett* (1804) 29 State Tr 1; *R v Wilkes* (1769) 4 Burr 2527, HL; *R v Harvey* (1823) 2 B & C 257; *R v M'Hugh* [1901] 2 IR 569.

3 *R v M'Hugh* [1901] 2 IR 569 at 578. As to offences relating to racial hatred see para 154 et seq post.

4 See Stephen, Digest of the Criminal Law (9th Edn) 92. The corresponding passage, in substantially the same terms, in the first edition at 55, 56, was adopted in *R v Burns* (1886) 16 Cox CC 355 at 359, 360 per Cave J, and in *R v M'Hugh* [1901] 2 IR 569 at 578. See also *R v Sullivan, R v Pigott* (1868) 11 Cox CC 44. As to the difference between treason and sedition see 1 East PC 48.

5 *R v M'Hugh* [1901] 2 IR 569 at 578. Formerly it was held that if the words used had a direct tendency to cause unlawful meetings and disturbances and to lead to a violation of the laws, they were seditious, as the accused was taken to have intended the natural consequences of what he had done (*R v Lovett* (1839) 9 C & P 462 at 466 per Littledale J; *R v Sullivan, R v Pigott* (1868) 11 Cox CC 44 at 58; see also *R v Horne* (1778) 20 State Tr 651 at 762, HL; *R v Aldred* (1909) 74 JP 55, 22 Cox CC 1); but as to the subjective test see now the Criminal Justice Act 1967 s 8 and para 1061 post.

90. Seditious words and seditious libel. It is an offence at common law, punishable with imprisonment or fine at the discretion of the court[1], to publish orally seditious words with a seditious intention[2] or to publish matter contained in anything capable of being a libel[3] with a seditious intention. In the case of seditious libel there must be an incitement to disorder and violence[4]. Free comment, criticism and censure must, however, be distinguished from seditious words or seditious libel[5].

The defences of absolute[6] and qualified[7] privilege appear to apply to a charge of seditious libel. Qualified privilege ceases if the publication was made with malice[8]. It is uncertain whether the composition of a seditious writing with the intention that it should be published, but without actual publication, constitutes a seditious libel[9].

1 See paras 1200, 1232 post. On a conviction for a seditious libel, the court may make an order for seizure of all copies of the libel: Criminal Libel Act 1819 s 1. As to powers of entry, search and seizure see para 668 et seq post.

2 For the meaning of 'seditious intention' see para 89 ante.

3 The libel may be in writing or print or may be contained in a drawing or engraving, or painted picture, or sculpture, or any permanent representation: *R v Sullivan, R v Pigott* (1868) 11 Cox CC 44 at 55.

4 *R v Collins* (1839) 9 C & P 456; *R v Aldred* (1909) 74 JP 55, 22 Cox CC 1; *R v Caunt* (1947) unreported noted in 64 LQR 203.

5 See *R v Sullivan, R v Pigott* (1868) 11 Cox CC 44 at 49 (the freest public discussion, comment, criticism, and censure, either at meetings or in the press, in relation to all political or party questions, all public acts of the servants of the Crown, all acts of the government, and all proceedings of courts of justice are permissible, and no narrow construction is to be put upon the expressions used in such discussion etc, but the criticism and censure must be without malignity, and must not impute corrupt or malicious motives). See also *R v Collins* (1839) 9 C & P 456 at 460, 461 per Littledale J ('every man has a right to give every public matter a candid, full and free discussion; something must be allowed for feeling in men's minds and for some warmth of expression, but an intention to incite the people to take the power into their own hands and to provoke them to tumult and disorder is a seditious intention'); *R v Burdett* (1820) 1 State Tr NS 1 at 50; *R v Aldred* (1909) 74 JP 55, 22 Cox CC 1.

6 As to statements to which absolute privilege attaches see LIBEL vol 28 paras 98–107.

7 As to statements to which qualified privilege attaches see LIBEL vol 28 paras 108–130.

8 For the meaning of 'malice' see LIBEL vol 28 paras 145–151.

9 *R v Burdett* (1820) 1 State Tr NS 1 at 122, 138. In every case in which any verdict or judgment by default is had against any person for composing, printing or publishing any blasphemous libel (see para 348 post) or any seditious libel tending to bring into hatred or contempt the person of Her Majesty or the government and constitution of the United Kingdom as by law established, or either House of Parliament, or to excite Her Majesty's subjects to attempt the alteration of any matter in Church or State as by law established, otherwise than by lawful means, it is lawful for the judge or the court before whom or in which such verdict has been given, or the court in which judgment by default is had, to make an order for the seizure and carrying away and detaining in safe custody, in such manner as shall be directed in such order, of all copies of the libel which are in the possession of the person against whom such verdict or judgment has been had, or in the possession of any other person named in the order for his use, evidence upon oath having been previously given to the satisfaction of such court or judge that a copy or copies of such libel is or are in the possession of such other person for the use of the person against whom such verdict or judgment has been so had: Criminal Libel Act 1819 s 1. In every such case it is lawful for any justice of the peace, or for any constable or other peace officer, acting under any such order, or for any person or persons acting with or in aid of any such justice of the peace, constable or other peace officer, to search for any copies of such libel in any house, building or other place whatsoever belonging to the person against whom any such verdict or judgment is had, or to any other person so named, in whose possession any copies of any such libel, belonging to the person against whom any such verdict or judgment is had, are; and in case admission is refused or not obtained within a reasonable time after it has first been demanded, to enter by force by day into any such house, building or place whatsoever, and to carry away all copies of the libel there found, and to detain the same in safe custody until the same are restored under the Criminal Libel Act 1819, or disposed of according to any further order made in relation thereto: s 1. As to powers of entry, search and seizure see para 668 et seq post; and as to the power of a constable to use reasonable force see para 659 post.

If in any such case judgment is arrested or if, after judgment has been entered, the same is reversed upon any writ of error, all copies so seized must forthwith be returned to the person or persons from whom the same have been so taken free of all charge and expense, and without the payment of any fees whatever; and in every case in which final judgment is entered upon the verdict so found against the person or persons so charged with having composed, printed or published such libel, then all copies so seized must be disposed of as the court in which such judgment is given orders and directs: s 2. Writs of error were abolished by the Criminal Appeal Act 1907 s 20 (1) (repealed). As to the right to apply to the court for judgment to be arrested see para 1045 post.

The Criminal Libel Act 1819 s 1 appears to treat the composition, printing and publishing of a seditious libel as separate offences. As to evidence of publication see para 91 post.

91. Indictment and evidence in cases of seditious words or seditious libel. In an indictment for seditious words or seditious libel, the words alleged to be seditious must be specified[1]. So much of the words alleged as will support the charge of sedition must be proved at the trial; but, if what is proved substantially constitutes sedition, it is immaterial that a portion is unproved[2].

If the manuscript of a seditious libel is proved to be in the handwriting of the accused, and it is also proved that the same libel was in fact published, this is prima facie evidence for the jury of a publication by the accused, though no evidence is adduced that he directed the publication[3]. To prove that the publication was with an unlawful intent or was not accidental, evidence of the publication of other libels is admissible, provided they expressly refer to the subject matter of the libel which is charged in the indictment[4]. If words spoken or published are seditious, it is no defence that they are true, and evidence to prove their truth is inadmissible[5].

1 See the opinion of the judges in *R v Sacheverell* (1710) 15 State Tr 1 at 466; *R v Sparling* (1722) 1 Stra 497; *Bradlaugh v R* (1878) 3 QBD 607 at 619, CA. It is not essential that the indictment should allege that the words were spoken or published 'seditiously', if it alleges an intent which the law defines to be a seditious intention: *R v M'Hugh* [1901] 2 IR 569.
2 *R v Fussell* (1848) 3 Cox CC 291 at 294. If any part of the speech or writing varied or controlled the sense of the words alleged to be seditious, the onus is on the accused to show it: see *R v Crowe* (1848) 3 Cox CC 123. Where an alleged seditious libel is contained in a newspaper, the accused is entitled to have read in evidence any passage from the same newspaper tending to show his intention in publishing the passage complained of: *R v Lambert and Perry* (1810) 2 Camp 398.
3 *R v Lovett* (1839) 9 C & P 462; *R v Aldred* (1909) 74 JP 55, 22 Cox CC 1. As to what amounts to a publication see further LIBEL.
4 *R v Pearce* (1791) Peake 106, where Lord Kenyon CJ admitted such evidence even to prove the fact of publication and that the accused was the author of a libel; but see *Finnerty v Tipper* (1809) 2 Camp 72; *Chubb v Westley* (1834) 6 C & P 436; *Plunkett v Cobbett* (1804) 5 Esp 136; *Pearson v Lemaitre* (1843) 5 Man & G 700 at 719, 720.
5 *R v Aldred* (1909) 74 JP 55, 22 Cox CC 1. The Libel Act 1843 s 6 and the Newspaper Libel and Registration Act 1881 s 4 (see LIBEL vol 28 para 282) do not apply to seditious libels: *R v Duffy* (1846) 2 Cox CC 45; *Ex p O'Brien* (1883) 15 Cox CC 180; *R v M'Hugh* [1901] 2 IR 569.

(ii) Inciting Disaffection among Her Majesty's Forces and the Police

92. Incitement to mutiny. Any person who maliciously and advisedly[1] endeavours (1) to seduce any person serving in Her Majesty's forces by sea, land or air[2] from his duty and allegiance to Her Majesty; or (2) incites or stirs up such a person to commit any act of mutiny[3] or to make or endeavour to make a mutinous assembly, or to commit any traitorous or mutinous practice, is guilty of an offence and liable on conviction on indictment to imprisonment for life or for any shorter term[4].

1 It must be proved that the accused knew that the person whom he attempted to seduce was a person serving in Her Majesty's forces: *R v Fuller* (1797) 2 Leach 790. However, see also *R v Bowman* (1912) 76 JP 271 (published article addressed to 'persons serving in His Majesty's forces').

2 A person is serving in such forces, although he is at the time in hospital, and not in the receipt of pay, and not liable to be tried by court-martial: *R v Tierney* (1804) Russ & Ry 74, CCR.

3 Mutiny is collective insubordination, collective defiance or disregard of authority, or refusal to obey authority: *R v Grant, Davis, Riley and Topley* [1957] 2 All ER 694, 41 Cr App Rep 173, C-MAC.

4 See the Incitement to Mutiny Act 1797 s 1; the Punishment of Offences Act 1837 s 1; the Penal Servitude Act 1857 s 2; the Penal Servitude Act 1891 s 1; the Air Force (Application of Enactments) (No 2) Order 1918, SR & O 1918/548 (amended by SI 1964/488); the Criminal Justice Act 1948 s 1; the Criminal Law Act 1967 s 12 (5) (a). Cf the Incitement to Disaffection Act 1934 s 1: see para 93 note 1 post.

Any person who is tried and acquitted or convicted of any offence against the Incitement to Mutiny Act 1797 is not liable to be indicted, prosecuted or tried again for the same offence or fact as high treason or misprision of high treason: s 3. See also the Interpretation Act 1978 s 18 and para 970 et seq post.

93. Incitement to disaffection. Any person who (1) maliciously and advisedly endeavours to seduce any member of Her Majesty's forces from his duty or allegiance to Her Majesty[1]; or (2) with intent so to endeavour to seduce or to aid, abet, counsel or procure such endeavour to seduce, has in his possession or under his control any document of such a nature that the dissemination of copies among members of Her Majesty's forces would constitute an endeavour so to seduce[2], is guilty of an offence and liable on conviction on indictment to imprisonment for a term not exceeding two years or a fine, or to both, or on summary conviction to imprisonment for a term not exceeding four months or a fine not exceeding the prescribed sum, or to both[3].

A judge of the High Court, if satisfied by information on oath that there is reasonable ground for suspecting that an offence has been committed and that evidence of the commission is to be found at any premises or place specified in the information may, on the application made by a police officer of a rank not lower than that of inspector, grant a warrant valid for one month authorising entry into the premises or place, by force if necessary, the searching of the premises or place and every person found there and the seizing of anything found which the officer has reasonable ground for suspecting to be evidence of the commission of that offence[4]. No prosecution under the above provisions may take place without the consent of the Director of Public Prosecutions[5]. Where any person is convicted of such an offence, the court dealing with the case may order any documents connected with the offence to be destroyed or dealt with in such other manner as may be specified in the order, but no documents may be so destroyed before the expiration of the period within which an appeal may be lodged; and, if an appeal is lodged, no document may be destroyed until after the appeal has been heard and decided[6].

1 Incitement to Disaffection Act 1934 s 1. Section 1 creates a single offence which is committed by a person who endeavours to seduce members of the forces with a particular intent. The intent may be to seduce them from their duty or from their allegiance or both. A count stating the intent in the alternative is not bad for duplicity: see the Indictment Rules 1971, SI 1971/1253, r 7 and para 929 post. See also *R v Arrowsmith* [1975] 1 All ER 463, 60 Cr App Rep 211, CA. Cf the Incitement to Mutiny Act 1797 s 1 (see para 92 ante) where the offence is endeavouring to seduce from duty and allegiance. There is no basis for reading the words 'without lawful excuse' into the Incitement to Disaffection Act 1934 s 1: see *R v Arrowsmith* supra.

2 Incitement to Disaffection Act 1934 s 2(1). As to causing disaffection amongst the police see para 97 post.

3 Ibid s 3 (1) (amended by the Criminal Law Act 1977 s 32 (1); the Magistrates' Courts Act 1980 s 32 (2)). For the meaning of 'the prescribed sum' see para 807 post.

4 Incitement to Disaffection Act 1934 s 2 (2). A warrant may only be issued in respect of an offence suspected to have been committed within the previous three months; the occupier must be notified

that a search has taken place and of anything removed; and no woman may be searched except by a woman: s 2 (2) provisos (a), (b), (3). Anything seized may be retained for a period not exceeding one month or, if proceedings are commenced within that period, until the conclusion of proceedings; and in relation to property which has come into the possession of the police under s 2(4), the Police (Property) Act 1897 (see POLICE vol 36 para 325) has effect subject to the above provision of the Incitement to Disaffection Act 1934 s 2 (4) (amended by the Criminal Justice Act 1972 s 64 (1), Sch 5) and to the Incitement to Disaffection Act 1934 s 3 (4) (see text to note 6 infra): s 2 (4) (as so amended). As to powers of entry, search and seizure see para 668 et seq post.
5 Ibid s 3 (2). As to the effect of this limitation see para 639 post. Where the Director of Public Prosecutions is carrying on a prosecution under the Act, a court of summary jurisdiction may not deal with the case summarily without his consent: s 3 (3).
6 Ibid s 3 (4).

94. Procuring and assisting desertion from the Royal Navy. Every person who, whether within or without the United Kingdom[1] (1) procures or persuades any person subject to naval discipline[2] to commit an offence of desertion, of absenting himself without leave or of improperly leaving his ship; or (2) knowing that any such person is about to commit such an offence, assists him in so doing; or (3) knowing any such person to have committed such an offence, procures or persuades or assists him to remain a deserter, absentee without leave or improperly absent from his ship, or assists in his rescue from custody, is guilty of an offence and liable on conviction on indictment to imprisonment for a term not exceeding two years or a fine, or to both, or on summary conviction to imprisonment for a term not exceeding three months or a fine not exceeding the prescribed sum, or to both[3].

1 For the meaning of 'United Kingdom' see para 86 note 1 ante.
2 As to persons so subject see the Naval Discipline Act 1957 Pt IV (ss 111–139) and ROYAL FORCES vol 41 para 365 et seq.
3 Naval Discipline Act 1957 s 97 (1), (2) (amended by the Armed Forces Act 1971 s 77 (1), Sch 4; the Armed Forces Act 1976 s 15 (2); the Criminal Law Act 1977 s 32 (1); the Magistrates' Courts Act 1980 s 32 (2)). For the meaning of 'the prescribed sum' see para 807 post.

95. Procuring and assisting desertion from the army or air force. Any person who[1] (1) procures or persuades any officer, warrant officer or non-commissioned officer of the regular forces[2] or the regular air force[3], or any soldier of the regular forces or any airman of the regular air force to desert or to absent himself without leave; or (2) knowing that any such person is about to desert or absent himself without leave, assists him in so doing; or (3) knowing any person to be a deserter or absentee without leave from the regular forces or the regular air force, procures or persuades or assists him to remain such a deserter or absentee, or assists in his rescue from custody, is guilty of an offence and liable on conviction on indictment to imprisonment for a term not exceeding two years or a fine, or to both, or on summary conviction to imprisonment for a term not exceeding three months or a fine not exceeding the prescribed sum, or to both[4].

1 Ie whether within or without Her Majesty's dominions.
2 'Regular forces' means any of Her Majesty's military forces other than the army reserve, the Territorial Army or the Home Guard, and other than forces raised under the law of a colony, provided that an officer of any reserve of officers or an officer who is retired within the meaning of any Royal Warrant, is not to be treated for these purposes as a member of the regular forces save in so far as is expressly provided by the Army Act 1955: s 225 (1). Section 192 (see infra) has effect as if any reference to a member of the regular forces included a reference to a member of a visiting force or of a headquarters to which the Visiting Forces and International Headquarters (Application of Law)

Order 1965, SI 1965/1536 (amended by SI 1987/928) applies (see art 2 (as so amended)): art 14. As to visiting forces see para 40 ante.

3 'Regular air force' means all of Her Majesty's air forces other the the air force reserve and the Royal Auxiliary Air Force, and other than forces raised under the law of a colony, provided that an officer who is retired within the meaning of any order under the Air Force (Constitution) Act 1917 s 2 is not to be treated for these purposes as a member of the regular air force save in so far as is expressly provided by the Air Force Act 1955: s 223 (1).

4 Army Act 1955 s 192; Air Force Act 1955 s 192 (both amended by the Armed Forces Act 1966 s 18 (1); the Criminal Law Act 1977 s 32 (1); the Magistrates' Courts Act 1980 s 32 (2)). For the meaning of 'the prescribed sum' see para 807 post. See further ROYAL FORCES vol 41 para 44.

96. Interfering with military duties. Any person who[1] wilfully obstructs or otherwise interferes with any officer, warrant officer or non-commissioned officer of the regular forces[2] or the regular air force[3] or any soldier of the regular forces or any airman of the regular air force acting in the execution of his duty is liable on summary conviction to imprisonment for a term not exceeding three months or a fine not exceeding level 3 on the standard scale, or to both[4].

Any person who[5]:

(1) produces in an officer, warrant officer, non-commissioned officer, soldier of the regular forces or airman of the regular air force any sickness or disability; or

(2) supplies to or for him any drug or preparation calculated or likely to render him, or lead to the belief that he is, permanently or temporarily unfit for service,

with a view to enabling him to avoid military service, whether permanently or temporarily, is liable on conviction on indictment to imprisonment for a term not exceeding two years or a fine, or to both, or on summary conviction to imprisonment for a term not exceeding three months or a fine not exceeding the prescribed sum, or to both[6].

1 Ie whether in the United Kingdom or any colony. For the meaning of 'United Kingdom' see para 86 note 1 ante.

2 For the meaning of 'regular forces' see para 95 note 2 ante.

3 For the meaning of 'regular air force' see para 95 note 3 ante.

4 Army Act 1955 s 193; Air Force Act 1955 s 193 (both amended by the Criminal Justice Act 1982 ss 38, 46). For the meaning of 'the standard scale' see para 808 post. See further ROYAL FORCES vol 41 para 45.

5 Ie whether within or without Her Majesty's dominions.

6 Army Act 1955 s 194; Air Force Act 1955 s 194 (both amended by the Criminal Law Act 1977 s 32 (1); the Magistrates' Courts Act 1980 s 32 (2)). See further ROYAL FORCES vol 41 para 46. For the meaning of 'the prescribed sum' see para 807 post.

97. Causing disaffection amongst the police. Any person who causes, or attempts to cause, or does any act calculated to cause, disaffection amongst the members of any police force[1], or induces or attempts to induce, or does any act calculated to induce, any member of a police force to withhold his services or to commit breaches of discipline is guilty of an offence and liable on conviction on indictment to imprisonment for a term not exceeding two years or a fine, or to both, or on summary conviction to imprisonment for a term not exceeding six months or a fine not exceeding the prescribed sum, or to both[2].

1 For the meaning of 'police force' see Police Act 1964 s 62 (c), Sch 8 (amended by the Local Government Act 1972 s 272, Sch 30; the Local Government Act 1985 s 37, Sch 11 para 1 (8)) and POLICE vol 36 para 230 note 2.

2 Police Act 1964 s 53 (1) (amended by the Magistrates' Courts Act 1980 s 32 (2)). For the meaning of 'the prescribed sum' see para 807 post. The Police Act 1964 s 53 (1) (as so amended) applies to special constables appointed for a police area as it applies to members of a police force: s 53 (2). For the meaning of 'police area' see s 62 (a), Sch 8 column 1 (as amended: see note 1 supra). See further POLICE vol 36 para 322.

Any person who causes, or attempts to cause, or does any act calculated to cause, disaffection amongst the members of the Ministry of Defence Police, or induces or attempts to induce, or does any act calculated to induce, any member of the Ministry of Defence Police to withhold his services or to commit breaches of discipline, is guilty of an offence and liable on conviction on indictment to imprisonment for a term not exceeding two years or a fine, or to both, or on summary conviction to imprisonment for a term not exceeding six months or a fine not exceeding the statutory maximum, or to both: Ministry of Defence Police Act 1987 s 6. For the meaning of 'the statutory maximum' see para 806 post. See further POLICE.

(iii) Unauthorised Wearing of Naval, Military, Air Force and Police Uniforms

98. Naval, military and air force uniforms. Any person not serving in Her Majesty's naval or military forces[1] or the air force, who (1) without Her Majesty's permission wears the uniform of any of those forces, or any dress having the appearance or bearing any of the regimental or other distinctive marks of any such uniform, in such manner or in such circumstances as to be likely to bring contempt upon that uniform; or (2) employs any other person so to wear that uniform or dress, is guilty of an offence and liable on summary conviction to imprisonment for a term not exceeding one month or a fine not exceeding level 3 on the standard scale[2].

Any person not serving in Her Majesty's military forces or the air force who without Her Majesty's permission wears the uniform of any of those forces, or any dress having the appearance or bearing any regimental or other distinctive marks of any such uniform is guilty of an offence and liable on summary conviction to a fine not exceeding level 3 on the standard scale[3].

Any person who wears the merchant navy uniform[4] or any part of it, or wears anything bearing the appearance of the uniform or any part of it, when not authorised[4] to wear the uniform or that part, is liable on summary conviction to a fine not exceeding level 3 on the standard scale[5].

1 'Her Majesty's naval forces' means the Royal Navy, Queen Alexandra's Royal Naval Nursing Reserve, the Women's Royal Naval Service, the naval reserve force and such of the marine forces, and of the naval forces of a Commonwealth country or raised under the law of any colony, as are for the time being subject to the Naval Discipline Act 1957; and 'Her Majesty's military forces' does not include any Commonwealth force: Uniforms Act 1894 s 4 (substituted by the Armed Forces Act 1981 s 20 (1), Sch 3 Pt II para 5), applying the Naval Discipline Act 1957 s 132 (5) (amended by the Armed Forces Act 1976 s 4, Sch 2 para 4) and the Army Act 1955 s 225 (1).
2 Uniforms Act 1894 s 3 (applied to the air force by the Air Force (Application of Enactments) (No 2) Order 1918, SR & O 1918/548 (amended by SI 1964/ 488); amended by the Criminal Justice Act 1982 ss 38, 46)). For the meaning of 'the standard scale' see para 808 post.
3 Uniforms Act 1894 s 2 (applied to the air force by the Air Force (Application of Enactments) (No 2) Order 1918 (as amended: see note 2 supra); amended by the Criminal Justice Act 1982 ss 38, 46). It is not an offence, however, to wear any uniform or dress in the course of a stage play performed in a place duly licensed or authorised for the public performance of stage plays, or in the course of a music hall or circus performance, or in the course of any bona fide military representation: Uniforms Act 1894 s 2 (1) proviso.
4 Regulations may be made prescribing a uniform, to be known as the merchant navy uniform, for the use of persons serving in ships registered in the United Kingdom and distinguishing marks to be worn, as part of the uniform, by persons so serving in different positions or in different circum-

stances; and regulations so made may prescribe the persons by whom and the circumstances in which the merchant navy uniform or any part of it may be worn: Merchant Shipping Act 1970 s 87 (1), (2). At the date at which this volume states the law no such regulations had been made.

5 Ibid s 87 (3) (amended by the Criminal Justice Act 1982 ss 38, 46). Nothing in the Merchant Shipping Act 1970 s 87 prohibits or restricts the use of the merchant navy uniform or any part of it for the purposes of any stage, film or television performance, unless the use is such as to bring the uniform into disrepute: s 87 (5). See also note 4 supra.

99. Police uniforms. Any person who, not being a constable, wears any article of police uniform[1] in circumstances where it gives him an appearance so nearly resembling that of a member of a police force as to be calculated to deceive[2], is guilty of an offence and liable on summary conviction to a fine not exceeding level 3 on the standard scale[3].

1 For these purposes, 'article of police uniform' means any article of uniform or any distinctive badge or mark or document of identification usually issued to members of police forces or special constables, or anything having the appearance of such an article, badge, mark or document; and 'special constable' means a special constable appointed for a police area: Police Act 1964 s 52 (4). For the meaning of 'police area' see para 97 note 2 ante.

2 The words 'calculated to deceive' are not free from ambiguity, for they may mean 'likely or reasonably likely to deceive' or 'intended to deceive'. It is thought that the phrase has the former meaning: see *Turner v Shearer* [1972] 1 All ER 397, [1973] 1 WLR 1387, DC.

3 Police Act 1964 s 52 (2) (amended by the Criminal Justice Act 1982 ss 38, 46). For the meaning of 'the standard scale' see para 808 post.

Any person who, not being a member of a police force or a special constable, has in his possession any article of police uniform is, unless he proves that he obtained possession of that article lawfully and has possession of it for a lawful purpose, guilty of an offence and liable on summary conviction to a fine not exceeding level 1 on the standard scale: Police Act 1964 s 52 (3) (amended by the Criminal Justice Act 1982 ss 38, 46).

Any person who, not being a member of the Ministry of Defence Police, wears any article of the uniform of the Ministry of Defence Police in circumstances where it gives him an appearance so nearly resembling that of a member as to be calculated to deceive is guilty of an offence and liable on summary conviction to a fine not exceeding level 3 on the standard scale (Ministry of Defence Police Act 1987 s 5 (2)); and any person who, not being a member of the Ministry of Defence Police, has in his possession any article of uniform of the Ministry of Defence Police is, unless he proves that he obtained possession of that article lawfully and has possession of it for a lawful purpose, guilty of an offence and liable on summary conviction to a fine not exceeding level 1 on the standard scale (s 5 (3)). For these purposes, 'article of uniform' means any article of uniform or any distinctive badge or mark or document of identification usually issued to members of the Ministry of Defence Police, or any thing having the appearance of such an article, badge, mark or document: s 5 (4). See further POLICE.

(iv) Political and Quasi-military Organisations

100. Wearing political uniforms. Subject as otherwise provided[1], any person who in any public place[2] or at any public meeting[3] wears uniform[4] signifying his association[5] with any political organisation or with the promotion of any political object is guilty of an offence and liable on summary conviction to imprisonment for a term not exceeding three months or a fine not exceeding level 4 on the standard scale, or to both[6].

Where any person is charged before a court with such an offence, no further proceedings in respect of such offence may be taken against him, except such as are authorised by the Prosecution of Offences Act 1985[7], without the consent of the Attorney General[8]. If such person is remanded in custody, he is entitled, after the expiration of a period of eight days from the date on which he was so remanded, to be released on bail without sureties unless within that period the Attorney General has consented to such further proceedings[9].

1   If the chief officer of police is satisfied that the wearing of any such uniform on any ceremonial, anniversary or other special occasion will not be likely to involve risk of public disorder, he may, with the consent of a Secretary of State, by order permit the wearing of such uniform on that occasion either absolutely or subject to such conditions as may be specified in the order: Public Order Act 1936 s 1 (1) proviso. Any such order may be revoked or varied by a subsequent order: see s 9 (3) (amended by the Public Order Act 1986 s 40 (3), Sch 3).

     The powers conferred on any chief officer of police may, in the event of a vacancy in the office or in the event of the chief officer of police being unable to act owing to illness or absence, be exercised by the person duly authorised in accordance with directions given by a Secretary of State to exercise those powers on behalf of the chief officer of police: Public Order Act 1936 s 9 (4).

     'Chief officer of police' means the Commissioner of the City of London Police, the Commissioner of Police of the Metropolis or the Chief Constable as the case may be: see the Police Act 1964 s 62 (b), Sch 8 (amended by the Local Government Act 1972 s 272 (1), Sch 30; the Local Government Act 1985 s 37, Sch 11 para 1 (8)).

2   For these purposes, 'public place' includes any highway and any other premises or place to which at the material time the public has or is permitted to have access, whether on payment or otherwise: Public Order Act 1936 s 9 (1) (amended by the Criminal Justice Act 1972 s 33). Whether a place is a public place depends upon its status at the material time. Consequently a shop car park was not a public place at 11.30 pm when the shop was shut: *Marsh v Arscott* (1982) 75 Cr App Rep 211, DC (decided under the Public Order 1936 s 5 (repealed)). A public house was a public place even though the landlord could refuse entry to particular people: *Lawrenson v Oxford* [1982] Crim LR 185, DC (decided under the Public Order Act 1936 s 5 (repealed)). The front garden of a house is not a public place because people have access as lawful visitors and as members of the public: *R v Edwards, R v Roberts* (1978) 67 Cr App Rep 228, CA (decided under the Public Order Act 1936 s 5 (repealed)). A 'public place' is public in its entirety though it contains areas to which the public is denied access: *Cawley v Frost* [1976] 3 All ER 743, [1976] 1 WLR 1207, DC (football ground) (decided under the Public Order Act 1936 s 5 (repealed)). Cf the Prevention of Crime Act 1953 s 1 (4) (see para 167 note 4 post); the Firearms Act 1968 s 57 (4) (see para 226 note 3 post); the Prevention of Terrorism (Temporary Provisions) Act 1989 s 3 (3) (see para 112 note 1 post).

3   'Public meeting' includes any meeting in a public place and any meeting which the public or any section of the public is permitted to attend, whether on payment or otherwise; and 'meeting' means a meeting held for the purpose of the discussion of matters of public interest or for the purpose of expression of views on such matters: Public Order Act 1936 s 9 (1).

4   See *O'Moran v DPP* [1975] QB 864, [1975] 1 All ER 473, DC ('uniform' may consist of particular article of clothing (black berets) worn by each member of group to indicate that they are together and in association).

5   See *O'Moran v DPP* [1975] QB 864, [1975] 1 All ER 473, DC (proof may be by evidence (1) that the uniform in question had in the past been used as the uniform of a political organisation; for that purpose it is not necessary to specify the particular organisation; sufficient to show that it had been associated with a political organisation capable of identification in some manner; or (2) that a group of persons assembling together had worn uniform to indicate their association with each other and, furthermore, by their conduct had indicated that the uniform associated them with other activity of a political character).

6   Public Order Act 1936 ss 1 (1), 7 (2) (amended by the Public Order Act 1963 s 1 (2); the Criminal Justice Act 1982 ss 38, 46; the Public Order Act 1986 s 40 (3), Sch 3)). For the meaning of 'the standard scale' see para 808 post. A constable may arrest without warrant any person reasonably suspected by him to be committing such an offence: Public Order Act 1936 s 7 (3). Such power of arrest is preserved by the Police and Criminal Evidence Act 1984: see s 26 (2), Sch 2 and para 708 post. As to powers of arrest see para 693 et seq post. A constable may enter and search any premises for the purpose of arresting a person for an offence under the Public Order Act 1936 s 1 (as amended): Police and Criminal Evidence Act 1984 s 17 (1) (c) (i) (amended by the Public Order Act 1986 s 40 (2), (3), Sch 2 para 7, Sch 3): see para 683 post.

     As to wearing articles of dress indicating membership of a proscribed organisation under the Prevention of Terrorism (Temporary Provisions) Act 1989 see para 112 post.

7 Ie by the Prosecution of Offences Act 1985 s 25: see para 639 post.
8 Public Order Act 1936 s 1 (2) (amended by the Criminal Jurisdiction Act 1975 s 14 (4), Sch 5 para 1); Interpretation Act 1978 s 17 (2) (a). The powers conferred on the Attorney General may, in the event of a vacancy in the office or in the event of the Attorney General being unable to act owing to illness or absence, be exercised by the Solicitor General: Public Order Act 1936 s 9 (2).
9 Ibid s 1 (2) (amended by the Bail Act 1976 s 12, Sch 2 para 10).

101. Quasi-military organisations. Any person who takes part in the control or management[1] of, or in organising or training the members or adherents of, any association of persons, whether incorporated or not, the members or adherents of which are (1) organised or trained or equipped for the purpose of enabling them to be employed in usurping the functions of the police or of the armed forces of the Crown; or (2) organised and trained or organised and equipped either for the purpose of enabling them to be employed for the use or display of physical force in promoting any political object, or in such a manner as to arouse reasonable apprehension[2] that they are organised and either trained or equipped for that purpose, is guilty of an offence and liable on conviction on indictment to imprisonment for a term not exceeding two years or a fine, or to both, or on summary conviction to imprisonment for a term not exceeding six months or a fine not exceeding the prescribed sum, or to both[3]. No prosecution for such an offence may, however, be instituted without the consent of the Attorney General[4].

In any proceedings for any such offence, proof of things done or of words written, spoken or published, whether or not in the presence of any party to the proceedings, by any person taking part in the control or management of the association or in organising, training or equipping members or adherents is admissible as evidence of the purposes for which, or the manner in which, members or adherents of the association, whether those persons or others, were organised or trained or equipped[5].

If satisfied by information on oath that there is reasonable ground for suspecting that such an offence has been committed, and that evidence of its commission is to be found at any premises or place specified in the information, a judge of the High Court may, on an application made by an officer of the police of a rank not lower than that of inspector, grant a search warrant authorising any such officer named in the warrant and any other officers of police to enter the premises or place at any time within one month from the date of the warrant, if necessary by force, and to search the premises or place and every person[6] found there, and to seize anything found there or on any such person which the officer has reasonable ground for suspecting to be evidence of the commission of the offence[7].

If, on the application of the Attorney General, it appears to the High Court that any association is an association of which members or adherents are so organised, trained or equipped, the court may (a) make such order as appears necessary to prevent any disposition without the leave of the court of property held by or for the association; and (b) direct an inquiry and report to be made as to any such property and as to the affairs of the association, and may make such further orders as appear to the court to be just and equitable for the application of such property in or towards (i) the discharge of liabilities of the association lawfully incurred before the date of the application or since that date with the approval of the court; (ii) the repayment of moneys to persons who became subscribers or contributors to the association in good faith and without knowledge of any contravention of the statutory provisions[8]; and (iii) any costs incurred in connection with any such inquiry and report or in winding up or dissolving the association; and the court may order any property which is not directed to be so applied to be forfeited to the Crown[9].

1 In any proceedings against a person charged with an offence under the Public Order Act 1936 s 2 (1) it is a defence to that charge to prove that he neither consented to nor connived at the organisation, training or equipment of members or adherents of the association in contravention of s 2 (1): s 2 (1) proviso.

2 The mere fact that there is no evidence of specific training for attacks on opponents or plans for such attacks does not remove the grounds for reasonable apprehension: *R v Jordan and Tyndall* [1963] Crim LR 124, CCA. It need not be proved that the accused intended the use or display of physical force; reasonable apprehension is the test: *R v Evans* (1969) unreported.

3 Public Order Act 1936 ss 2 (1), 7 (1) (amended by the Magistrates' Courts Act 1980 s 32 (2)). For the meaning of 'the prescribed sum' see para 807 post. Nothing in the Public Order Act 1936 s 2 is to be construed as prohibiting the employment of a reasonable number of persons as stewards to assist in the preservation of order at any public meeting held upon private premises, or the making of arrangements for that purpose or the instruction of the persons to be so employed in their lawful duties as such stewards, or their being furnished with badges or other distinguishing signs: s 2 (6). 'Private premises' means premises to which the public has access, whether on payment or otherwise, only by permission of the owner, occupier or lessee of the premises: s 9 (1). For the meaning of 'public meeting' see para 100 note 3 ante. As to unlawful drilling see para 146 post.

4 Ibid s 2 (2). As to the effect of this limitation see para 639 post. As to the exercise of the Attorney General's powers by the Solicitor General see para 100 note 8 ante.

5 Ibid s 2 (4).

6 No woman may be searched except by a woman: ibid s 2 (5) proviso.

7 Ibid s 2 (5). As to powers of entry, search and seizure see para 668 et seq post.
   Application is in the Chancery Division by originating summons and the accused are such as the Attorney General determines: RSC Ord 93 r 5 (1), (2). The court or a judge may appoint the Official Solicitor to represent any interests not sufficiently represented: r 5 (3).

8 Ie the Public Order Act 1936 s 2 (1): see supra.

9 Ibid s 2 (3).

(v) Prevention of Terrorism

A. EXCLUSION ORDERS

102. Orders excluding persons from Great Britain. If the Secretary of State[1] is satisfied that any person[2] (1) is or has been concerned in the commission, preparation or instigation[3] of acts of terrorism[4]; or (2) is attempting or may attempt to enter Great Britain with a view to being concerned in the commission, preparation or instigation of such acts of terrorism, the Secretary of State may make an exclusion order against him[5]. An exclusion order so made is an order prohibiting the person from being in, or entering, Great Britain[6].

1 The Secretary of State may exercise the powers conferred on him by the Prevention of Terrorism (Temporary Provisions) Act 1989 Pt II (ss 4–8: see infra and paras 103–108 post) in such a way as appears to him expedient to prevent acts of terrorism to which Pt II (ss 4–8) applies (see note 4 infra): s 4 (1).

2 In deciding whether to make an exclusion order under ibid s 5 against a person who is ordinarily resident in Great Britain, the Secretary of State must have regard to the question whether that person's connection with any country or territory outside Great Britain is such as to make it appropriate that such an order should be made: s 5 (3). An exclusion order may not, however, be made under s 5 against a person who is a British citizen and who (1) is at the time ordinarily resident in Great Britain and has then been ordinarily resident in Great Britain throughout the last three years; or (2) is at the time subject to an order under s 6 (order excluding person from Northern Ireland: see para 103 post): s 5 (4). For the meaning of 'British citizen' see the British Nationality Act 1981 Pt I (ss 1–14), s 36, Sch 2 paras 2–6; the British Nationality (Falkland Islands) Act 1983; and BRITISH NATIONALITY AND ALIENAGE.

When any question arises whether a person is exempted from the provisions of the Prevention of Terrorism (Temporary Provisions) Act 1989 s 5, s 6 (see para 103 post) or s 7 (see para 104 post), it is for the person asserting that he is exempt to prove it: s 4 (4), Sch 2 para 9 (1).

A person is not to be treated as ordinarily resident in Great Britain for the purposes of the exemption in s 5 (4) (a) (see head (1) supra) or in Northern Ireland for the purposes of the exemption in s 6 (4) (a) (see para 103 note 2 head (1) post) at a time when he is there in breach of (a) an exclusion order; or (b) the Immigration Act 1971 or any law for purposes similar to that Act in force in the United Kingdom after the passing of the Prevention of Terrorism (Temporary Provisions) Act 1989 (ie 15 March 1989): Sch 2 para 9 (2). In each of those exemptions, 'the last three years' is to be taken as a period amounting in total to three years exclusive of any time during which the person claiming exemption was undergoing imprisonment or detention for a period of six months or more by virtue of a sentence passed for an offence on a conviction in the United Kingdom or in any of the Islands: Sch 2 para 9 (3). 'Sentence' includes any order made on conviction of an offence; two or more sentences for consecutive, or partly consecutive, terms are to be treated as a single sentence; and a person is deemed to be detained by virtue of a sentence (i) at any time when he is liable to imprisonment or detention by virtue of the sentence but is unlawfully at large; and (ii) during any period of custody by which under any relevant enactment the term to be served under the sentence is reduced: Sch 2 para 9 (4). 'Relevant enactment' means the Criminal Justice Act 1967 s 67 (as amended) (computation of sentences of imprisonment: see para 1202 post) and any similar enactment which is for the time being or has, before or after 15 March 1989, been in force in any part of the United Kingdom or in any of the Islands: Prevention of Terrorism (Temporary Provisions) Act 1989 Sch 2 para 9 (5). 'The Islands' means the Channel Islands or the Isle of Man: s 20 (1).

3 Any reference to a person having been concerned in the commission, preparation or instigation of acts of terrorism is to be taken to be a reference to his having been so concerned at any time, whether before or after 15 March 1989: ibid s 20 (4).

4 The acts of terrorism to which ibid Pt II (ss 4–8) applies are acts of terrorism connected with the affairs of Northern Ireland: s 4 (2). 'Terrorism' means the use of violence for political ends, and includes any use of violence for the purpose of putting the public or any section of the public in fear: s 20 (1).

5 Ibid s 5 (1). For the meaning of 'Great Britain' see para 86 note 1 ante.

An order under ss 5, 6 or 7 is referred to in the 1989 Act as an 'exclusion order': ss 4 (3), 20 (1). Any exclusion order in force under any provision of the Prevention of Terrorism (Temporary Provisions) Act 1984 Pt II (ss 3–9) (repealed) has effect as if made under the corresponding provision of the Prevention of Terrorism (Temporary Provisions) Act 1989 Pt II (ss 4–8); and references in the 1989 Act to an exclusion order are to be construed accordingly: s 25 (3).

As to the procedure for making and revoking exclusion orders see para 105 post.

Any document purporting to be an order, notice or direction made or given by the Secretary of State for the purposes of any provision of the Prevention of Terrorism (Temporary Provisions) Act 1989 and to be signed by him or on his behalf must be received in evidence and is deemed, until the contrary is proved, to be made or given by him: s 19 (2). A document bearing a certificate purporting to be signed by or on behalf of the Secretary of State and stating that the document is a true copy of such an order, notice or direction is evidence of the order, notice or direction in any legal proceedings: s 19 (3). The powers conferred by Pt II (ss 4–8), Schs 2, 5 are exercisable notwithstanding the rights conferred by the Immigration Act 1971 s 1 (general principles regulating entry into and staying in the United Kingdom: see BRITISH NATIONALITY AND ALIENAGE vol 4 para 974 et seq): Prevention of Terrorism (Temporary Provisions) Act 1989 s 20 (3).

6 Ibid s 5 (2).

103. Orders excluding persons from Northern Ireland. If the Secretary of State[1] is satisfied that any person[2] (1) is or has been concerned in the commission, preparation or instigation[3] of acts of terrorism[4]; or (2) is attempting or may attempt to enter Northern Ireland with a view to being concerned in the commission, preparation or instigation of such acts of terrorism, the Secretary of State may make an exclusion order against him[5]. An exclusion order so made is an order prohibiting a person from being in, or entering, Northern Ireland[6].

1 As to the exercise by the Secretary of State of the powers conferred on him by the Prevention of Terrorism (Temporary Provisions) Act 1989 Pt II (ss 4–8: see para 102 ante; infra; and paras 104–108 post) see para 102 note 1 ante.

2 In deciding whether to make an exclusion order under ibid s 6 against a person who is ordinarily resident in Northern Ireland, the Secretary of State must have regard to the question whether that person's connection with any country or territory outside Northern Ireland is such as to make it appropriate that such an order should be made: s 6 (3). An exclusion order may not, however, be made under s 6 against a person who is a British citizen and who (1) is at the time ordinarily resident in Northern Ireland and has then been ordinarily resident in Northern Ireland throughout the last three years; or (2) is at the time subject to an order under s 5 (order excluding person from Great Britain: see para 102 ante): s 6 (4). For the meaning of 'British citizen' see the British Nationality Act 1981 Pt I (ss 1–14), s 36, Sch 2 paras 2–6; the British Nationality (Falkland Islands) Act 1983; and BRITISH NATIONALITY AND ALIENAGE.

     As to exemption from exclusion orders see the Prevention of Terrorism (Temporary Provisions) Act 1989 s 4 (4), Sch 2 para 9 and para 102 note 2 ante.

3 For the meaning of references to a person having been concerned in the commission, preparation or instigation of acts of terrorism see para 102 note 3 ante.

4 As to the acts of terrorism to which the Prevention of Terrorism (Temporary Provisions) Act 1989 Pt II (ss 4–8) applies see para 102 note 4 ante.

5 Ibid s 6 (1). For the meaning of 'exclusion order' see para 102 note 5 ante. As to the procedure for the making and revoking of exclusion orders see para 105 post.

6 Ibid s 6 (2).

104. Orders excluding persons from the United Kingdom. If the Secretary of State[1] is satisfied that any person[2] (1) is or has been concerned in the commission, preparation or instigation[3] of acts of terrorism[4]; or (2) is attempting or may attempt to enter Great Britain or Northern Ireland with a view to being concerned in the commission, preparation or instigation of such acts of terrorism, the Secretary of State may make an exclusion order against him[5]. An exclusion order so made is an order prohibiting a person from being in, or entering, the United Kingdom[6].

1 As to the exercise by the Secretary of State of the powers conferred on him by the Prevention of Terrorism (Temporary Provisions) Act 1989 Pt II (ss 4–8: see paras 102, 103 ante; infra; and paras 105–108 post) see para 102 note 1 ante.

2 In deciding whether to make an exclusion order under ibid s 7 against a person who is ordinarily resident in the United Kingdom, the Secretary of State must have regard to the question whether that person's connection with any country or territory outside the United Kingdom is such as to make it appropriate that such an order should be made: s 7 (3). An exclusion order may not, however, be made under s 7 against a person who is a British citizen: s 7 (4). When any question arises whether a person is so exempted, it is for the person asserting that he is exempt to prove it: s 4 (4), Sch 2 para 9 (1). For the meaning of 'British citizen' see the British Nationality Act 1981 Pt I (ss 1–14), s 36, Sch 2 paras 2–6; the British Nationality (Falkland Islands) Act 1983; and BRITISH NATIONALITY AND ALIENAGE.

3 For the meaning of references to a person having been concerned in the commission, preparation or instigation of acts of terrorism see para 102 note 3 ante.

4 As to the acts of terrorism to which the Prevention of Terrorism (Temporary Provisions) Act 1989 Pt II (ss 4–8) applies see para 102 note 4 ante.

5 Ibid s 7 (1). For the meaning of 'exclusion order' see para 102 note 5 ante; and for the meaning of 'Great Britain' see para 86 note 1 ante. As to the procedure for the making and revoking of exclusion orders see para 105 post.

6 Ibid s 7 (2). For the meaning of 'United Kingdom' see para 86 note 1 ante.

105. Procedure for making and revoking exclusion orders. Unless revoked earlier, an exclusion order expires at the end of three years beginning with the day on which it is made[1]. An exclusion order may be revoked at any time by a further order made by the Secretary of State[2]. The fact that an exclusion order against a person has been revoked or has expired does not prevent the making of a further exclusion order against him[3].

As soon as may be after the making of an exclusion order, notice of the making of the order must be served on the person against whom it has been made[4]; and the notice must set out the rights afforded to him to make representations[5] and specify the manner in which those rights are to be exercised[6].

If, after being served with such notice, the person against whom it was made objects to the order, he may (1) make representations in writing to the Secretary of State setting out the grounds of his objections; and (2) include in those representations a request for a personal interview with a nominated person or nominated persons[7]; and such rights must be exercised within seven days of the service of the notice[8]. However, where, before the end of that period, he has consented to his removal[9] from Great Britain, Northern Ireland or the United Kingdom, as the case may be, and he has been removed accordingly, he may exercise his rights within 14 days of his removal; and, where at the time when the notice of an exclusion order is served on a person he is in a part of the United Kingdom other than that from which the order excludes him, he may exercise his rights within 14 days of the service of the notice[10].

If a person exercises such rights within the period within which they are required so to be exercised, the matter must be referred for the advice of one or more persons nominated by the Secretary of State[11]; and, where he is required to exercise his rights within seven days of the service of the notice[12], he must be granted a personal interview with the person or persons so nominated[13]. Where he has consented to his removal and has been so removed[14], or where at the time when the notice was served he is in a part of the United Kingdom other than that from which the order excludes him[15], the person against whom the exclusion order has been made must be granted a personal interview with the person or persons so nominated if it appears to the Secretary of State that it is reasonably practicable to grant him such an interview in an appropriate country or territory[16] within a reasonable period from the date on which he made representations[17].

Where the Secretary of State receives such representations, he must consider the matter as soon as reasonably practicable after receiving the representations and any report of an interview relating to the matter which has been so granted[18]. The Secretary of State must thereafter, if it is reasonably practicable to do so, give notice in writing to the person against whom the exclusion order has been made of any decision he takes as to whether or not to revoke the order[19].

1 Prevention of Terrorism (Temporary Provisions) Act 1989 s 4 (4), Sch 2 para 1 (2).
2 Ibid Sch 2 para 1 (1).
3 Ibid Sch 2 para 1 (3).
4 Ibid Sch 2 para 2 (1) does not impose an obligation to take any steps to serve a notice on a person at a time when he is outside the United Kingdom: Sch 2 para 2 (2).
5 Ie under ibid Sch 2 para 3: see infra.
6 Ibid Sch 2 para 2 (1). The Secretary of State does not have to give reasons for his conclusion that a person was 'concerned in the commission, preparation or instigation of acts of terrorism' when he made an exclusion order restricting a person from entering any part of Great Britain: *R v Secretary of State for the Home Department, ex p Stitt* (1987) Times, 3 February, DC (decided under the Prevention of Terrorism (Temporary Provisions) Acts 1976 and 1984 (repealed)).
    Where the person against whom an exclusion order is made is not for the time being detained by virtue of the Prevention of Terrorism (Temporary Provisions) Act 1989, the notice of the making of the order may be served on him by posting it to him at his last known address: Sch 2 para 2 (3).
7 Ibid Sch 2 para 3 (1). The person or persons are nominated by the Secretary of State under Sch 2 para 3 (5): see infra.
8 Ibid Sch 2 para 3 (2).
9 Ie under ibid Sch 2 para 5: see infra.
10 Ibid Sch 2 para 3 (3), (4). For the meaning of 'Great Britain' and 'United Kingdom' see para 86 note 1 ante.
11 Ibid Sch 2 para 3 (5).

12 Ie where ibid Sch 2 para 3 (2) applies: see supra.
13 Ibid Sch 2 para 3 (6).
14 Ie where ibid Sch 2 para 3 (3) applies: see supra.
15 Ie where ibid Sch 2 para 3 (4) applies: see supra.
16 For these purposes, 'an appropriate country or territory' means (1) Northern Ireland or the Republic of Ireland if the exclusion order was made under ibid s 5 (see para 102 ante); (2) Great Britain or the Republic of Ireland if it was made under s 6 (see para 103 ante); (3) the Republic of Ireland if it was made under s 7 (see para 104 ante): Sch 2 para 3 (8).
    Where it appears to the Secretary of State that it is reasonably practicable to grant a personal interview in more than one appropriate country or territory, he may grant the interview in whichever of them he thinks fit; and it is for the Secretary of State to determine the place in any country or territory at which an interview is so to be granted: Sch 2 para 3 (9), (10).
17 Ibid Sch 2 para 3 (7).
18 Ibid Sch 2 para 4 (1). In so reconsidering a matter, the Secretary of State must take into account everything which appears to him to be relevant and in particular (1) the representations so made to him; (2) the advice of the person or persons to whom the matter was so referred by him; (3) the report of any interview relating to the matter so granted: Sch 2 para 4 (2).
19 Ibid Sch 2 para 4 (3).

106. Failure to comply with an exclusion order. A person who is subject to an exclusion order[1] is guilty of an offence if he fails to comply with the order at a time after he has been, or has become liable to be, removed[2] and is liable on conviction on indictment to imprisonment for a term not exceeding five years or a fine, or to both, or on summary conviction to imprisonment for a term not exceeding six months or a fine not exceeding the statutory maximum, or to both[3].

1 As to exclusion orders see paras 102–105 ante.
2 As to removal under an exclusion order see the Prevention of Terrorism (Temporary Provisions) Act 1989 s 4 (4), Sch 2 paras 5–7 and para 108 post.
3 Ibid s 8 (1), (4). For the meaning of 'the statutory maximum' see para 806 post. Proceedings for such an offence may not be instituted except by or with the consent of the Attorney General: s 19 (1) (a). As to the effect of this limitation see para 639 post.

107. Aiding a person subject to an exclusion order. If a person (1) is knowingly concerned in arrangements for securing or facilitating the entry into Great Britain, Northern Ireland or the United Kingdom of a person whom he knows, or has reasonable grounds for believing, to be an excluded person[1]; or (2) knowingly harbours an excluded person in Great Britain, Northern Ireland or the United Kingdom, he is guilty of an offence and liable on conviction on indictment to imprisonment for a term not exceeding five years or a fine, or to both, or on summary conviction to imprisonment for a term not exceeding six months or a fine not exceeding the statutory maximum, or to both[2].

1 For these purposes, 'excluded person' means (1) in relation to Great Britain, a person subject to an exclusion order made under the Prevention of Terrorism (Temporary Provisions) Act 1989 s 5 (see para 102 ante) who has been, or has become liable to be, removed from Great Britain under s 4 (4), Sch 2 (see para 108 post); (2) in relation to Northern Ireland, a person subject to an exclusion order made under s 6 (see para 103 ante) who has been, or has become liable to be, removed from Northern Ireland under Sch 2 (see para 108 post); and (3) in relation to the United Kingdom, a person subject to an exclusion order made under s 7 (see para 104 ante) who has been, or has become liable to be, removed from the United Kingdom under Sch 2 (see para 108 post): s 8 (3). For the meaning of 'Great Britain' and 'United Kingdom' see para 86 note 1 ante.

2   Ibid s 8 (2), (4). For the meaning of 'the statutory maximum' see para 806 post. Proceedings for such
    an offence may not be instituted except by or with the consent of the Attorney General: s 19 (1) (a).
    As to the effect of this limitation see para 639 post.

108. Power of removal; removal directions. Where an exclusion order has
been made against a person[1] and notice of the making of the order has been served
on him[2], the Secretary of State may have him removed from the relevant territory[3]:

(1) if he consents;

(2) if the relevant period[4] has expired and he has not made representations
     relating to the matter[5]; or

(3) if he has made such representations but the Secretary of State has notified
     him that he has decided not to revoke the order[6].

The Secretary of State may give directions[7] for the removal[8] from the relevant
territory of any person subject to an exclusion order[9]. Directions so given may be:

(a) directions given to the captain[10] of a ship[11] or aircraft[12] about to leave the
     relevant territory requiring him to remove the person in question from that
     territory in that ship or aircraft; or

(b) directions given to the owners or agents of any ship or aircraft requiring
     them to make arrangements for the removal from the relevant territory of
     the person in question in a ship or aircraft specified or indicated in the
     directions; or

(c) directions for the removal from the relevant territory of the person in
     question in accordance with arrangements to be made by the Secretary of
     State;

and any such directions must specify the country or territory to which the person in
question is to be removed[13].

Any person who without reasonable excuse fails to comply with directions so
given to him is guilty of an offence and is liable on summary conviction to
imprisonment for a term not exceeding three months or a fine not exceeding level 4
on the standard scale, or to both[14].

1   As to exclusion orders see paras 102–105 ante.
2   As to service of notice see para 105 ante.
3   For these purposes, 'the relevant territory' means (1) in relation to a person subject to an exclusion
    order under the Prevention of Terrorism (Temporary Provisions) Act 1989 s 5 (see para 102 ante),
    Great Britain; (2) in relation to a person subject to an exclusion order under s 6 (see para 103 ante),
    Northern Ireland; and (3) in relation to a person subject to an exclusion order under s 7 (see para 104
    ante), the United Kingdom: s 4 (4), Sch 2 para 6 (9). For the meaning of 'Great Britain' and 'United
    Kingdom' see para 86 note 1 ante.
4   Ie the period mentioned in ibid Sch 2 para 3 (2): see para 105 ante.
5   Ie in accordance with ibid Sch 2 para 3 (2): see para 105 ante.
6   Ibid Sch 2 para 5.
7   Directions may also be so given for the removal of a person by land to the Republic of Ireland, and
    those directions may be (1) directions given to the driver or owner of any vehicle (being, in the case
    of a private vehicle, one in which that person arrived in Northern Ireland) requiring him to remove
    the person in question to the Republic of Ireland in a vehicle specified in the directions; or (2)
    directions for the removal of the person in question in accordance with arrangements to be made by
    the Secretary of State: Sch 2 para 6 (3).
      No such directions may, however, be for removal of a person to any country or territory other
    than one (a) of which the person in question is a national or citizen; (b) in which he obtained a
    passport or other document of identity; or (c) to which there is reason to believe that he will be
    admitted; and no such directions may be given for the removal of a British citizen, a British
    Dependent Territories citizen, a British Overseas citizen or a British National (Overseas) to a
    country or territory outside the United Kingdom unless he is also a national or citizen of, or has

indicated that he is willing to be removed to, that country or territory: Sch 2 para 6 (4). For the meaning of 'British citizen', 'British Dependent Territories citizen', 'British Overseas citizen' and 'British National (Overseas)' see BRITISH NATIONALITY AND ALIENAGE.

As to the power to give removal directions where a person is found on examination under s 16 (1), Sch 5 to be subject to an exclusion order or an exclusion order is made against a person following such an examination see Sch 2 para 6 (5) and para 121 note 5 post.

A person in respect of whom directions are so given may be placed under the authority of the Secretary of State or an examining officer on board any ship or aircraft or, as the case may be, in or on any vehicle in which he is to be removed in accordance with the directions: Sch 2 para 6 (6). 'Examining officer' has the meaning given in Sch 5 para 1 (see para 121 note 3 post): s 20 (1).

The costs of complying with any directions so given must be defrayed by the Secretary of State: Sch 2 para 6 (7).

As to the offence of failing to comply with removal directions see para 106 ante.

8 A person may not be removed in pursuance of the directions until notice of the making of the order has been served on him and one of the conditions in Sch 2 para 5 (a)–(c) (see text heads (1)–(3) supra) is fulfilled: Sch 2 para 6 (1).
9 Ibid Sch 2 para 6 (1).
10 'Captain' means master of a ship or commander of an aircraft: ibid s 20 (1).
11 'Ship' includes every description of vessel used in navigation: ibid s 20 (1).
12 'Aircraft' includes hovercraft: ibid s 20 (1).
13 Ibid Sch 2 para 6 (2).
14 Ibid Sch 2 para 6 (8). For the meaning of 'the standard scale' see para 808 post.

109. Detention pending removal. A person in respect of whom such directions may be given[1] may be detained[2] pending the giving of such directions and pending removal in pursuance of the directions under the authority of the Secretary of State or, if the directions are to be given or have been given by an examining officer[3], of such an officer[4]. A person liable to be so detained may be arrested without warrant by an examining officer[5]. If a justice of the peace is satisfied that there are reasonable grounds for suspecting that a person liable to be so arrested is to be found on any premises[6], he may grant a search warrant authorising any constable to enter those premises for the purpose of searching for and arresting that person[7]. The captain[8] of a ship[9] or aircraft[10], if so required by an examining officer, must prevent any person placed on board the ship or aircraft[11] from disembarking[12] in the relevant territory[13] or, before the directions for his removal have been fulfilled, elsewhere[14]. The captain of a ship or aircraft who fails to take reasonable steps to comply with such a requirement is guilty of an offence and liable on summary conviction to imprisonment for a term not exceeding six months or a fine not exceeding level 4 on the standard scale, or to both[15].

1 Ie under the Prevention of Terrorism (Temporary Provisions) Act 1989 s 4 (4), Sch 2 para 6: see para 108 ante.
2 A person may be removed from a vehicle for such detention: ibid Sch 2 para 7 (6).
3 'Examining officer' has the meaning given in ibid s 16 (1), Sch 5 para 1 (see para 121 note 3 post): s 20 (1).
4 Ibid Sch 2 para 7 (1). A person so detained is deemed to be in legal custody at any time when he is so detained and, if detained otherwise than on board a ship or aircraft, may be detained in such place as the Secretary of State may from time to time direct: Sch 2 para 8 (4). Where a person is so detained, any examining officer, constable or prison officer, or any other person authorised by the Secretary of State, may take all such steps as may be reasonably necessary for the photographing, measuring or otherwise identifying him: Sch 2 para 8 (5). Any person so detained may be taken in the custody of a constable or an examining officer, or of any person acting under the authority of an examining officer, to and from any place where his attendance is required for the purpose of establishing his nationality or citizenship or for making arrangements for his admission to a country or territory outside the United Kingdom or where he is required to be for any other purposes connected with the operation of the 1989 Act: Sch 2 para 8 (6). For the meaning of 'United Kingdom' see para 86 note 1 ante.

5 Ibid Sch 2 para 7 (2).
6 'Premises' includes any place and in particular includes (1) any vehicle, vessel or aircraft; (2) any offshore installation as defined in the Mineral Workings (Offshore Installations) Act 1971 s 1; and (3) any tent or movable structure: Prevention of Terrorism (Temporary Provisions) Act 1989 s 20 (1). 'Vehicle' includes a train and carriages forming part of a train: s 20 (1).
7 Ibid Sch 2 para 8 (1).
8 For the meaning of 'captain' see para 108 note 10 ante.
9 For the meaning of 'ship' see para 108 note 11 ante.
10 For the meaning of 'aircraft' see para 108 note 12 ante.
11 Ie under the Prevention of Terrorism (Temporary Provisions) Act 1989 Sch 2 para 6: see para 108 ante.
12 Where the captain of a ship or aircraft is so required to prevent a person from disembarking, he may for that purpose detain him in custody on board the ship or aircraft: ibid Sch 2 para 7 (4).
13 In ibid Sch 2 para 7 'relevant territory' has the same meaning as in Sch 2 para 6: Sch 2 para 7 (7). See para 108 note 3 ante.
14 Ibid Sch 2 para 7 (3).
15 Ibid Sch 2 para 7 (5). For the meaning of 'the standard scale' see para 808 post.

110. Supervision of detention pending removal. Where a person is detained pending removal under the authority of an examining officer[1], his detention must be periodically reviewed by a review officer[2] and may not continue unless that officer has authorised it to continue[3]. The reviews must be carried out as follows: (1) the first review must be as soon as practicable after the beginning of the detention; and (2) the subsequent reviews must be at intervals of not more than 12 hours[4]. On any such review the review officer must authorise the continued detention of the person in question if, and only if, he is satisfied that steps for giving directions for his removal or for removing him in pursuance of the directions are being taken diligently and expeditiously[5].

A review may be postponed (a) if, having regard to all the circumstances prevailing[6], it is not practicable to carry out the review at that time; (b) without prejudice to the generality of head (a) above, if at that time the person in detention or being examined is being questioned by a police officer or an examining officer and the review officer is satisfied that an interruption of the questioning for the purpose of carrying out the review would prejudice the investigation in connection with which the person is being detained or examined, or if at that time no review officer is readily available[7].

Before determining whether to authorise a person's continued detention, the review officer must give that person (unless he is asleep), or any solicitor representing him who is available at the time of the review, an opportunity to make representations to him about the detention[8]. The person whose detention is under review or his solicitor may make such representations either orally or in writing[9]; but the review officer may refuse to hear oral representations from the person whose detention is under review if he considers that he is unfit to make such representations by reason of his condition or behaviour[10].

Where the review officer authorises a person's continued detention and at that time that person has not yet exercised his statutory rights[11], the review officer must inform him of those rights and, if their exercise is being delayed[12], that it is being so delayed[13]. Where a review of a person's detention is carried out[14] at a time when the exercise of such rights is being delayed, the review officer must consider whether the reason or reasons for which the delay was authorised continue to subsist, and, if he is not himself the officer who authorised the delay and is of the opinion that the reason or reasons have ceased to subsist, he must inform that officer of his opinion[15].

The review officer carrying out a review must make a written record of the outcome of the review, including, where the continued detention or examination of the person in question is authorised, the grounds for authorisation and, where a review is postponed, the reason for the postponement[16].

1 Ie under the Prevention of Terrorism (Temporary Provisions) Act 1989 s 4 (4), Sch 2 para 7: see para 109 ante.
2 The review officer must be an officer who has not been directly involved in the matter in connection with which the person in question is detained or examined; and (1) in the case of a review carried out within 24 hours of the beginning of that person's detention or in the case of a review under ibid s 4 (5), Sch 3 para 2 (examination without detention: see para 126 post) must be an officer of at least the rank of inspector; (2) in the case of any other review, must be an officer of at least the rank of superintendent: Sch 3 para 4.
   Where the review officer is of a rank lower than superintendent and (a) an officer of higher rank than the review officer gives directions relating to the person detained or examined; and (b) the directions are at variance with any decision made or action taken by the review officer in the performance of a duty imposed on him, or with any decision or action which would but for the directions have been made or taken by him in the performance of that duty, the review officer must refer the matter at once to an officer of the rank of superintendent or above: Sch 3 para 9.
3 Ibid Sch 3 para 1 (1).
4 Ibid Sch 3 para 1 (2).
5 Ibid Sch 3 para 1 (3).
6 Ie at the latest time specified in ibid Sch 3 para 1 (2): see supra.
7 Ibid Sch 3 para 5 (1). If a review is so postponed, it must be carried out as soon as practicable after the latest time specified for it in Sch 3 para 1 (2); and, if a review is so carried out after postponement, the fact that it was so carried out does not affect any requirement in Sch 3 as to the time at which any subsequent review is to be carried out: Sch 3 para 5 (2), (3).
8 Ibid Sch 3 para 6 (1).
9 Ibid Sch 3 para 6 (2).
10 Ibid Sch 3 para 6 (3).
11 Ie the rights conferred on him by the Police and Criminal Evidence Act 1984 s 56 (right of arrested person to have someone informed: see para 726 post) or s 58 (right of arrested person to have access to legal advice: see para 727 post).
12 Ie in accordance with ibid s 56 (see para 729 post) or s 58 (see para 730 post).
13 Prevention of Terrorism (Temporary Provisions) Act 1989 Sch 3 para 7 (1). Where the review officer informs a detained person of the matters mentioned in Sch 3 para 7 (1), he must make a written record of the fact that he has done so: Sch 3 para 8 (4). See also note 16 infra.
14 Ie under ibid Sch 3 para 1: see supra.
15 Ibid Sch 3 para 7 (2). The review officer must also make a written record of his conclusion on the matter which he is required to consider under Sch 3 para 7 (2) (a) and, if he has taken action in accordance with Sch 3 para 7 (2) (b), of the fact that he has done so: Sch 3 para 8 (5). See also note 16 infra.
16 Ibid Sch 3 para 8 (1). The record required by Sch 3 para 8 must be made in the presence of the person detained or examined and, where his continued detention or examination is authorised, he must at that time be told of the grounds for the authorisation: Sch 3 para 8 (2). This requirement does not, however, apply where the person detained or examined is, at the time when the written record is made (1) incapable of understanding what is said to him; (2) violent or likely to become violent; or (3) in urgent need of medical attention: Sch 3 para 8 (3).

B. PROSCRIBED ORGANISATIONS

111. Membership, support and meetings of proscribed organisations. If a person (1) belongs or professes to belong to a proscribed organisation[1]; (2) solicits or invites support for a proscribed organisation other than support with money or other property[2]; or (3) arranges or assists in the arrangement or management of, or addresses, any meeting of three or more persons, whether or not it is a meeting to which the public is admitted, knowing that the meeting is to support a proscribed organisation, to further the activities of such an organisation, or to be addressed by a person belonging or professing to belong to such an organisation, he is guilty of an offence and liable on conviction on indictment to imprisonment for a term not exceeding ten years or a fine, or to both, or on summary conviction to imprisonment for a term not exceeding six months or a fine not exceeding the statutory maximum, or to both[3].

A person belonging to a proscribed organisation is, however, not guilty of such an offence by reason of belonging to the organisation if he shows that he became a member[4] when it was not a proscribed organisation[5] and that he has not, since he became a member, taken part in any of its activities at any time while it was such a proscribed organisation[6].

1 For these purposes, any organisation for the time being specified in the Prevention of Terrorism (Temporary Provisions) Act 1989 s 1 (1), Sch 1 is a proscribed organisation; and any organisation which passes under a name mentioned in Sch 1 is to be treated as proscribed whatever relationship, if any, it has to any other organisation of the same name: s 1 (1). For these purposes, 'organisation' includes any association or combination of persons: s 1 (6).

The Irish Republican Army and the Irish National Liberation Army are proscribed organisations: Sch 1. The Secretary of State may, however, by order made by statutory instrument (1) add to Sch 1 any organisation that appears to him to be concerned in, or in promoting or encouraging, terrorism occurring in the United Kingdom and connected with the affairs of Northern Ireland; (2) remove an organisation from Sch 1: s 1 (2). No such order may be made unless (a) a draft of the order has been laid before and approved by a resolution of each House of Parliament; or (b) it is declared in the order that it appears to the Secretary of State that by reason of urgency it is necessary to make the order without a draft having been so approved: s 1 (3). An order so made of which a draft has not been so approved must be laid before Parliament, and ceases to have effect at the end of the period of 40 days beginning with the day on which it was made unless, before the end of that period, the order has been approved by a resolution of each House of Parliament, but without prejudice to anything previously done or to the making of a new order: s 1 (4). In reckoning any such period of 40 days, no account is to be taken of any such period during which Parliament is dissolved or prorogued or during which both Houses are adjourned for more than four days: s 1 (5). For the meaning of 'United Kingdom' see para 86 note 1 ante.

2 'Property' includes property wherever situated and whether real or personal, heritable or movable and things in action and other intangible or incorporeal property: ibid s 20 (1).

3 Ibid s 2 (1), (2). For the meaning of 'the statutory maximum' see para 806 post. Proceedings for such an offence may not be instituted except by or with the consent of the Attorney General: s 19 (1) (a). As to the effect of this limitation see para 639 post.

4 The reference in ibid s 3 to a person becoming a member of an organisation is a reference to the only or last occasion on which he became a member: s 2 (5).

5 Ie under the current legislation. 'The current legislation', in relation to any time, means whichever of the following was in force at that time: the Prevention of Terrorism (Temporary Provisions) Act 1974; the Prevention of Terrorism (Temporary Provisions) Act 1976; the Prevention of Terrorism (Temporary Provisions) Act 1984; or the Prevention of Terrorism (Temporary Provisions) Act 1989: s 2 (4).

6 Ibid s 2 (3).

112. Display of support for a proscribed organisation in public. Any person who in a public place[1]:

(1) wears any item of dress; or

(2) wears, carries or displays any article,

in such a way or in such circumstances as to arouse reasonable apprehension that he is a member or supporter of a proscribed organisation[2], is guilty of an offence and liable on summary conviction to imprisonment for a term not exceeding six months or a fine not exceeding level 5 on the standard scale, or to both[3].

1 For these purposes, 'public place' includes any highway and any premises to which at the material time the public has, or is permitted to have, access, whether on payment or otherwise: Prevention of Terrorism (Temporary Provisions) Act 1989 s 3 (3).
2 For the meaning of 'proscribed organisation' see para 111 note 1 ante.
3 Prevention of Terrorism (Temporary Provisions) Act 1989 s 3 (1). For the meaning of 'the standard scale' see para 808 post. Proceedings for such an offence may not be instituted except by or with the consent of the Attorney General: s 19 (1) (a). As to the effect of this limitation see para 639 post.

C. ACTS OF TERRORISM; TERRORIST FUNDS

113. Information about acts of terrorism. If a person has information which he knows or believes might be of material assistance (1) in preventing the commission by any other person of an act of terrorism[1] connected with the affairs of Northern Ireland; or (2) in securing the apprehension, prosecution or conviction of any other person for an offence involving the commission, preparation or instigation of such an act, and fails without reasonable excuse to disclose that information as soon as reasonably practicable to a constable, he is guilty of an offence and liable on conviction on indictment to imprisonment for a term not exceeding five years or a fine, or to both, or on summary conviction to imprisonment for a term not exceeding six months or a fine not exceeding the statutory maximum, or to both[2].

1 For the meaning of 'terrorism' see para 102 note 4 ante.
2 Prevention of Terrorism (Temporary Provisions) Act 1989 s 18 (1), (2). For the meaning of 'the statutory maximum' see para 806 post.
    Disclosure in Scotland must be to a constable or the procurator fiscal, and in Northern Ireland to a constable or a member of Her Majesty's Forces: s 18 (1). Proceedings for such an offence may be taken, and the offence may for the purposes of those proceedings be treated as having been committed, in any place where the person to be charged is or has at any time been since he first knew or believed that the information might be of such material assistance: s 18 (3).
    Proceedings for such an offence may not be instituted except by or with the consent of the Attorney General: s 19 (1) (a). As to the effect of this limitation see para 639 post.

114. Contributions to resources of proscribed organisations. If a person:
  (1) solicits or invites any other person to give, lend or otherwise make available, whether for consideration or not, any money or other property[1] for the benefit of a proscribed organisation[2];
  (2) gives, lends or otherwise makes available or receives or accepts, whether for consideration or not, any money or other property for the benefit of such an organisation; or
  (3) enters into, or is otherwise concerned in, an arrangement whereby money or other property is or is to be made available for the benefit of such an organisation,
he is guilty of an offence and liable on conviction on indictment to imprisonment for a term not exceeding 14 years or a fine, or to both, or on summary conviction to imprisonment for a term not exceeding six months or a fine not exceeding the statutory maximum, or to both[3].

In proceedings against a person for an offence under head (2) above it is a defence to prove that he did not know and had no reasonable cause to suspect that the money or property was for the benefit of a proscribed organisation; and in proceedings against a person for an offence under head (3) above it is a defence to prove that he did not know and had no reasonable cause to suspect that the arrangement related to a proscribed organisation[4].

A person who enters into, or is otherwise concerned in, any such transaction or arrangement does not commit such an offence if he is acting with the express consent of a constable, or if (a) he discloses to a constable his suspicion or belief that the money or other property concerned is or is derived from terrorist funds[5] or any matter on which such a suspicion or belief is based; and (b) the disclosure is made after he enters into, or otherwise becomes concerned in, the transactions or arrangement in question but is made on his own initiative and as soon as it is reasonable for him to make it; but heads (a) and (b) above do not apply in a case where, having disclosed any such suspicion, belief or matter to a constable and having been forbidden by a constable to enter into, or otherwise be concerned in, the transaction or arrangement in question, he nevertheless does so[6]. In proceedings against a person for an offence under heads (2) or (3) above it is a defence to prove that he intended to disclose to a constable such a suspicion, belief or matter as is mentioned in head (a) above and that there is a reasonable excuse for his failure to make the disclosure as is mentioned in head (b) above[7].

The court by or before which a person is convicted of such an offence may order (i) in the case of an offence under heads (1) and (2) above, the forfeiture of money or other property which, at the time of the offence, he had in his possession or under his control for the use or benefit of a proscribed organisation[8]; and (ii) in the case of an offence under head (3) above, the forfeiture of money or other property to which the arrangement in question related[9].

1 For the meaning of 'property' see para 111 note 2 ante.
2 For the meaning of 'proscribed organisation' see para 111 note 1 ante. In the Prevention of Terrorism (Temporary Provisions) Act 1989 ss 10, 11, 13 'proscribed organisation' includes a proscribed organisation for the purposes of the Northern Ireland (Emergency Provisions) Act 1978 s 21: Prevention of Terrorism (Temporary Provisions) Act 1989 s 10 (3).

In the Northern Ireland (Emergency Provisions) Act 1978 'proscribed organisation' means an organisation for the time being specified in Sch 2, including an organisation which is to be treated as a proscribed organisation by virtue of s 21 (3): s 31 (1). The proscribed organisations are: The Irish Republican Army; Cumann na mBan; Fianna na hEireann; The Red Hand Commando; Saor Eire; The Ulster Freedom Fighters; The Ulster Volunteer Force; The Irish National Liberation Army: Sch 2 (amended by the Northern Ireland (Emergency Provisions) Act 1978 (Amendment) Order 1979, SI 1979/746). Any organisation which passes under a name mentioned in the Northern Ireland (Emergency Provisions) Act 1978 Sch 2 is to be treated as proscribed, whatever the relationship, if any, it has to any other organisation of the same name: s 21 (3).
3 Prevention of Terrorism (Temporary Provisions) Act 1989 ss 10 (1), 13 (1). For the meaning of 'the statutory maximum' see para 806 post. Proceedings for such an offence may not be instituted except by or with the consent of the Attorney General: s 19 (1) (a). As to the effect of this limitation see para 639 post.
4 Ibid s 10 (2).
5 In ibid ss 11, 12 'terrorist funds' means (1) funds which may be applied or used for the commission of, or in furtherance of or in connection with, acts of terrorism to which s 9 (see para 115 post) applies; (2) the proceeds of the commission of such acts of terrorism or of activities engaged in in furtherance of or in connection with such acts; and (3) the resources of a proscribed organisation: s 11 (3). Head (2) supra includes any property which in whole or in part directly or indirectly represents such proceeds as are there mentioned; and head (3) supra includes any money or other property which is or is to be applied or made available for the benefit of a proscribed organisation: s 11 (4).
6 Ibid s 12 (2).
7 Ibid s 12 (3).
8 Ibid s 13 (4). The court may not under s 13 make an order forfeiting any money or other property unless the court considers that the money or property may, unless forfeited, be applied or used as mentioned in s 9 (1) (see para 115 post), but the court may, in the absence of evidence to the contrary, assume that any money or property may be applied or used as there mentioned: s 13 (5).

Where a person other than the convicted person claims to be the owner of or otherwise interested in anything which can be forfeited by an order under s 13, the court must, before making such an order in respect of it, give him an opportunity to be heard: s 13 (6).

As to forfeiture orders see para 1328 et seq post.

9 Ibid s 13 (3).

115. Contributions towards acts of terrorism. If any person:

(1) solicits or invites any other person to give, lend or otherwise make available, whether for consideration or not, any money or other property[1]; or

(2) receives or accepts from any other person, whether for consideration or not, any money or other property,

intending that it shall be applied or used for the commission of, or in furtherance of or in connection with, specified acts of terrorism[2] or having reasonable cause to suspect that it may be so used or applied, he is guilty of an offence and liable on conviction on indictment to imprisonment for a term not exceeding 14 years or a fine, or to both, or on summary conviction to imprisonment for a term not exceeding six months or a fine not exceeding the statutory maximum, or to both[3].

If a person:

(a) gives, lends or otherwise makes available to any other person, whether for consideration or not, any money or other property; or

(b) enters into, or is otherwise concerned in, an arrangement whereby money or other property is or is to be made available to another person,

knowing or having reasonable cause to suspect that it will or may be applied or used for the commission of, or in furtherance of or in connection with, specified acts of terrorism, he is guilty of an offence and liable on conviction on indictment to imprisonment for a term not exceeding 14 years or a fine, or to both, or on summary conviction to imprisonment for a term not exceeding six months or a fine not exceeding the statutory maximum, or to both[4].

A person who enters into, or is otherwise concerned in, any such transaction or arrangement does not commit such an offence if he is acting with the express consent of a constable, or if (i) he discloses to a constable his suspicion or belief that the money or other property concerned is or is derived from terrorist funds[5] or any matter on which such a suspicion or belief is based; and (ii) the disclosure is made after he enters into, or otherwise becomes concerned in, the transaction or arrangement in question but is made on his own initiative and as soon as it is reasonable for him to make it; but heads (i) and (ii) above do not apply in a case where, having disclosed any such suspicion, belief or matter to a constable and having been forbidden by a constable to enter into, or otherwise be concerned in, the transaction or arrangement in question, he nevertheless does so[6]. In proceedings against a person for an offence under heads (2), (a) or (b) above it is a defence to prove that he intended to disclose to a constable such a suspicion, belief or matter as is mentioned in head (i) above and that there is a reasonable excuse for his failure to make the disclosure as is mentioned in head (ii) above[7].

The court by or before which a person is convicted of such an offence may order the forfeiture of any money or property:

(A) in the case of an offence under heads (1), (2) or (a) above, which, at the time of the offence, he had in his possession or under his control, and which, at that time, in the case of an offence under heads (1) and (2) above, he intended should be applied or used, or had reasonable cause to suspect might be applied or used for the commission of, or in furtherance of or in connection with, specified acts of terrorism, and, in the case of head (a) above, he knew or had reasonable cause to suspect would or might be so applied or used[8];

(B) in the case of an offence under head (b) above, to which the arrangement in question related and which he knew or had reasonable cause to suspect would or might be applied or used for the commisssion of, or in furtherance of or in connection with, specified acts of terrorism[9].

1 For the meaning of 'property' see para 111 note 2 ante.
2 The acts of terrorism to which the Prevention of Terrorism (Temporary Provisions) Act 1989 s 9 applies are (1) acts of terrorism connected with the affairs of Northern Ireland; and (2) acts of terrorism of any other description except acts connected solely with the affairs of the United Kingdom or any part of the United Kingdom other than Northern Ireland: s 9 (3). Head (1) supra does not, however, apply to an act done or to be done outside the United Kingdom unless it constitutes or would constitute an offence triable in the United Kingdom: s 9 (4). In proceedings against a person for an offence under s 9 in relation to an act within head (1) supra done or to be done outside the United Kingdom (a) the prosecution need not prove that that person knew or had reasonable cause to suspect that the act constituted or would constitute an offence triable in the United Kingdom; but (b) it is a defence to prove that he did not know and had no reasonable cause to suspect that the facts were such that the act constituted or would constitute such an offence: s 9 (5). For the meaning of 'United Kingdom' see para 86 note 1 ante.
3 Ibid ss 9 (1), 13 (1). For the meaning of 'the statutory maximum' see para 806 post. Proceedings for such an offence may not be instituted except by or with the consent of the Attorney General: s 19 (1) (a). As to the effect of this limitation see para 639 post.
4 Ibid ss 9 (2), 13 (1). Proceedings for such an offence may not be instituted except by or with the consent of the Attorney General: s 19 (1) (a). As to the effect of this limitation see para 639 post.
5 For the meaning of 'terrorist funds' see para 114 note 5 ante.
6 Prevention of Terrorism (Temporary Provisions) Act 1989 s 12 (2).
7 Ibid s 12 (3).
8 Ibid s 13 (2). See further para 114 note 8 ante. As to forfeiture orders see para 1328 et seq post.
9 Ibid s 13 (3).

116. Assisting in the retention or control of terrorist funds. If a person enters into, or is otherwise concerned in, an arrangement whereby the retention or control by or on behalf of another person of terrorist funds[1] is facilitated, whether by concealment, removal from the jurisdiction, transfer to nominees or otherwise, he is guilty of an offence and liable on conviction on indictment to imprisonment for a term not exceeding 14 years or a fine, or to both, or on summary conviction to imprisonment for a term not exceeding six months or a fine not exceeding the statutory maximum, or to both[2].

In proceedings against a person for an offence under the above provisions it is, however, a defence to prove that he did not know and had no reasonable cause to suspect that the arrangement related to terrorist funds[3].

A person who enters into, or is otherwise concerned in, any such transaction or arrangement does not commit such an offence if he is acting with the consent of a constable, or if (1) he discloses to a constable his suspicion or belief that the money or other property concerned is or is derived from terrorist funds or any matter on which such a suspicion or belief is based; and (2) the disclosure is made after he enters into or otherwise becomes concerned in the transaction or arrangement in question but is made on his own initiative and as soon as it is reasonable for him to make it; but heads (1) and (2) above do not apply in a case where, having disclosed any such suspicion, belief or matter to a constable and having been forbidden by a constable to enter into or otherwise be concerned in the transaction or arrangement in question, he nevertheless does so[4]. In proceedings against a person for an offence under the above provisions it is a defence to prove that he intended to disclose to a constable such a suspicion, belief or matter as is mentioned in head (1) above and that there is a reasonable excuse for his failure to make the disclosure as mentioned in head (2) above[5].

The court by or before which a person is convicted of such an offence may order the forfeiture of the money or other property to which the arrangement in question related[6].

1 For the meaning of 'terrorist funds' see para 114 note 5 ante.
2 Prevention of Terrorism (Temporary Provisions) Act 1989 ss 11 (1), 13 (1). For the meaning of 'the statutory maximum' see para 806 post. Proceedings for such an offence may not be instituted except by or with the consent of the Attorney General: s 19 (1) (a). As to the effect of this limitation see para 639 post.
3 Ibid s 11 (2).
4 Ibid s 12 (2).
5 Ibid s 12 (3).
6 Ibid s 13 (3). See further para 114 note 8 ante.

117. Disclosure of information about terrorist funds. Notwithstanding any restriction on the disclosure of information imposed by contract, a person may disclose to a constable a suspicion or belief that any money or other property is or is derived from terrorist funds[1] or any matter on which such a suspicion or belief is based[2].

1 For the meaning of 'terrorist funds' see para 114 note 5 ante.
2 Prevention of Terrorism (Temporary Provisions) Act 1989 s 12 (1).

D. ENFORCEMENT PROCEDURES

118. Arrest and search of suspected persons. A constable may arrest[1] without warrant a person whom he has reasonable grounds for suspecting to be (1) a person guilty of a specified offence[2]; (2) a person who is or has been concerned in the commission, preparation or instigation of specified[3] acts of terrorism[4]; or (3) a person subject to an exclusion order[5].

In any circumstances in which a constable has such a power to arrest a person, he may also, for the purpose of ascertaining whether that person has in his possession any document or other article which may constitute evidence that he is a person liable to arrest, stop that person and search him[6].

Where a constable has so arrested a person for any reason other than the commission of a criminal offence, he, or any other constable, may search him for the purpose of ascertaining whether he has in his possession any document or other article which may constitute evidence that he is a person liable to arrest[7]. Where a person is so detained, any constable or prison officer, or any other person authorised by the Secretary of State, may take all such steps as may be reasonably necessary for photographing, measuring or otherwise identifying him[8].

1 The provisions of the Prevention of Terrorism (Temporary Provisions) Act 1989 s 14 are without prejudice to any power of arrest apart from s 14: s 14 (7). As to powers of arrest generally see para 693 et seq post.
2 Ie an offence under ibid s 2 (see para 111 ante), s 8 (see paras 106, 107 ante), s 9 (see para 115 ante), s 10 (see para 114 ante) or s 11 (see para 116 ante).
3 The acts of terrorism to which ibid s 14 applies are (1) acts of terrorism connected with the affairs of Northern Ireland; and (2) acts of terrorism of any other description except acts concerned solely with

the affairs of the United Kingdom or any part of the United Kingdom other than Northern Ireland: s 14 (2). For the meaning of 'terrorism' see para 102 note 4 ante; and for the meaning of 'United Kingdom' see para 86 note 1 ante.

4 If a justice of the peace is satisfied that there are reasonable grounds for suspecting that a person whom a constable believes to be liable to arrest under ibid s 14 (1) (b) (see head (2) supra) is to be found on any premises, he may grant a search warrant authorising any constable to enter those premises for the purpose of searching for and arresting that person: s 15 (1). For the meaning of 'premises' see para 109 note 6 ante.

5 Ibid s 14 (1). The power of arrest conferred by s 14 (1) (c) (see head (3) supra) is exercisable only (1) in Great Britain if the order was made under s 5 (see para 102 ante); and (2) in Northern Ireland, if it was made under s 6 (see para 103 ante): s 14 (3). For the meaning of 'Great Britain' see para 86 note 1 ante.

6 Ibid s 15 (3). A search of a person under s 15 (3) or (4) (see infra) may only be carried out by a person of the same sex: s 15 (5).

7 Ibid s 15 (4). See note 6 supra.

8 Ibid s 15 (9). The Police and Criminal Evidence Act 1984 s 61 (1)–(8) (fingerprinting: see para 776 post) applies to the taking of a person's fingerprints by a constable under the Prevention of Terrorism (Temporary Provisions) Act 1989 s 15 (9) as if for the Police and Criminal Evidence Act 1984 s 61 (4) there were substituted:

'An officer may only give an authorisation under s 61 (3) (a) for the taking of a person's fingerprints if he is satisfied that it is necessary to do so in order to assist in determining:

(1) whether that person is or has been concerned in the commission, preparation or instigation of acts of terrorism to which the Prevention of Terrorism (Temporary Provisions) Act 1989 s 14 applies; or

(2) whether he is subject to an exclusion order under that Act;

or if the officer has reasonable grounds for suspecting that person's involvement in an offence under any of the provisions mentioned in s 14 (1) (a) and for believing that his fingerprints will tend to confirm or disprove his involvement': s 15 (10).

119. Detention of suspected persons. A person who has been arrested[1] may not be detained in right of the arrest for more than 48 hours after his arrest[2]. However, the Secretary of State may, in any particular case, extend such period of 48 hours by a period or periods specified by him, but any further period or periods may not exceed five days in all; and, if an application for such an extension is made, the person detained must as soon as practicable be given written notice of that fact and of the time when the application was made[3].

Where a person is so detained, his detention must be periodically reviewed by a review officer[4] and may not continue unless (1) that officer has authorised it to continue; or (2) an application for an extension of the period of detention has been so made to the Secretary of State[5]. The reviews must be carried out as follows: (a) the first review must be as soon as practicable after the beginning of the detention; and (b) the subsequent reviews must be at intervals of not more than 12 hours; and no review may be carried out after an application for an extension of the detention period[6] has been made[7].

On any such review the review officer must authorise the continued detention of the person in question if, and only if, he is satisfied that his continued detention is necessary in order to obtain, whether by questioning him or otherwise, or to preserve evidence which (i) relates to a specified offence[8]; (ii) indicates that he is or has been concerned in the commission, preparation or instigation of acts of terrorism[9]; or (iii) indicates that he is subject to an exclusion order; and that the investigation in connection with which that person is detained is being conducted diligently and expeditiously[10].

The review officer may also authorise the continued detention of the person in question pending consideration of the question whether he is subject to an exclusion order, pending consideration by the Secretary of State whether to make an exclusion order against him or to serve him with notice of a decision to make a deportation order[11], pending a decision by the Director of Public Prosecutions or Attorney General whether proceedings for an offence should be instituted against him, or if he is satisfied as to the specified[12] matters[13].

1 Ie under the Prevention of Terrorism (Temporary Provisions) Act 1989 s 14: see para 118 ante.
2 Ibid s 14 (4). A person detained under s 14 is deemed to be in legal custody at any time when he is so detained, and may be detained in such place as the Secretary of State may from time to time direct: s 15 (6).
　　Any person who immediately before 22 March 1989 was being detained under any provision of the Prevention of Terrorism (Temporary Provisions) Act 1984 (repealed) or of an order made under s 13 (repealed) is to be treated as lawfully detained under the corresponding provision of the Prevention of Terrorism (Temporary Provisions) Act 1989: s 25 (4).
3 Ibid s 14 (5).
4 As to review officers see para 110 note 2 ante.
5 Prevention of Terrorism (Temporary Provisions) Act 1989 s 14 (6), Sch 3 para 3 (1). As to postponement of reviews, representations about detention, the rights of detained persons, records of interviews and interventions by superior officers see Sch 3 paras 5–9 and para 110 ante.
6 Ie an application under ibid s 14 (5): see supra.
7 Ibid Sch 3 para 3 (2).
8 Ie an offence under ibid s 2 (see para 111 ante), s 8 (see paras 106, 107 ante), s 9 (see para 115 ante), s 10 (see para 114 ante) or s 11 (see para 116 ante).
9 Ie acts of terrorism to which ibid s 14 applies: see para 118 ante.
10 Ibid Sch 3 para 3 (3).
11 Ie under the Immigration Act 1971: see BRITISH NATIONALITY AND ALIENAGE vol 4 para 1011 et seq.
12 The matters so specified are (1) that the continued detention of the person in question is necessary (a) pending a decision whether to apply to the Secretary of State for an exclusion order to be made in respect of him or for notice of a decision to make a deportation order under the Immigration Act 1971 to be served on him; or (b) pending the making of such an application; and (2) that consideration of that question is being undertaken, or preparation of the application is being proceeded with diligently and expeditiously: Prevention of Terrorism (Temporary Provisions) Act 1989 Sch 3 para 3(5).
13 Ibid Sch 3 para 3 (4).

120. Use of reasonable force by constables and examining officers. Without prejudice to any provision of the Prevention of Terrorism (Temporary Provisions) Act 1989, or of any instrument made under it, which implies that a person may use reasonable force in connection with that provision, a constable or examining officer[1] may, if necessary, use reasonable force for the purpose of exercising any powers[2] conferred on him by the Act[3].

1 For the meaning of 'examining officer' see para 121 note 3 post.
2 Ie any powers conferred on him under or by virtue of any provision of the Prevention of Terrorism (Temporary Provisions) Act 1989 other than s 16 (1), Sch 5 para 2 (see para 121 post).
3 Ibid s 20 (2).

E. TRAVEL CONTROL

121. Examination on arrival or departure. Any person who has arrived in, or is seeking to leave, Great Britain or Northern Ireland by ship or aircraft[1] may be examined[2] by an examining officer[3] for the purpose of determining:

(1) whether that person appears to be a person who is or has been concerned in the commission, preparation or instigation of acts of terrorism[4]; or
(2) whether any such person is subject to an exclusion order[5]; or
(3) whether there are grounds for suspecting that any such person has committed[6] an offence[7].

An examining officer may:

(a) examine any person who is entering or seeking to enter or leave Northern Ireland by land from, or to go to, the Republic of Ireland for the purpose of determining whether that person is such a person as is mentioned in any of heads (1) to (3) above;

(b) examine any person found in Northern Ireland within a distance of one mile from the border with the Republic of Ireland for the purpose of determining whether he is in the course of entering or leaving Northern Ireland by land;

(c) examine any person entering Northern Ireland by train when he arrives at the first place where the train is scheduled to stop for the purpose of allowing passengers to alight[8].

1 The reference to arrival by ship or aircraft includes a reference to arrival as a transit passenger, member of the crew or other person not seeking to enter Great Britain or Northern Ireland: Prevention of Terrorism (Temporary Provisions) Act 1989 s 16 (1), Sch 5 para 2 (5). For the meaning of 'ship' and 'aircraft' see para 108 notes 11, 12 respectively ante; and for the meaning of 'Great Britain' see para 86 note 1 ante.

2 The period of a person's examination may not exceed 24 hours unless he is detained under ibid Sch 5 para 6 (see para 125 post), and may only exceed 12 hours if an examining officer (1) has reasonable grounds for suspecting that the person examined is or has been concerned in the commission, preparation or instigation of acts of terrorism to which Sch 5 para 2 applies (see note 4 infra); and (2) gives him a notice in writing requiring him to submit to further examination: Sch 5 para 2 (4).

3 The following are examining officers: (1) constables; (2) immigration officers appointed for the purposes of the Immigration Act 1971 s 4 (2), Sch 2 para 1 (see BRITISH NATIONALITY AND ALIENAGE vol 4 para 1003); and (3) officers of customs and excise who are the subject of arrangements for their employment as immigration officers made under Sch 2 para 1 by the Secretary of State: Prevention of Terrorism (Temporary Provisions) Act 1989 Sch 5 para 1 (1). Examining officers must exercise their functions in accordance with such instructions as may from time to time be given to them by the Secretary of State: Sch 5 para 1 (4).

In Northern Ireland members of Her Majesty's Forces may perform such functions conferred on examining officers as the Secretary of State may by order specify: Sch 5 para 1 (2). The power to make such orders is exercisable by statutory instrument subject to annulment in pursuance of a resolution of either House of Parliament: Sch 5 para 1 (3).

4 Ibid Sch 5 para 2 applies to (1) acts of terrorism connected with the affairs of Northern Ireland; and (2) acts of terrorism of any other description except acts connected solely with the affairs of the United Kingdom or any part of the United Kingdom other than Northern Ireland: Sch 5 para 2 (2). For the meaning of 'terrorism' see para 102 note 4 ante; and for the meaning of 'United Kingdom' see para 86 note 1 ante.

5 Where a person is found on examination under the provisions of ibid Sch 5 to be subject to an exclusion order, or an exclusion order is made against a person following such an examination, the power to give directions for his removal under any provision of s 4 (4), Sch 2 para 6 except Sch 2 paras 6 (2) (c) or 6 (3) (b) (see para 108 ante) is exercisable by an examining officer as well as by the Secretary of State; and, where any such person has arrived in a ship or aircraft (including arrival as a transit passenger, member of the crew or other person not seeking to enter Great Britain or Northern Ireland), the countries or territories to which he may be directed to be removed under Sch 2 para 6 (2) (see para 108 ante) include the country or territory in which he embarked on that ship or aircraft: Sch 2 para 6 (5).

As to exclusion orders see paras 102–105 ante.

6 Ie whether he has committed an offence under ibid s 8: see paras 106, 107 ante.

7 Ibid Sch 5 para 2 (1). Without prejudice to the provisions of Sch 5 with respect to persons who enter or leave Northern Ireland by land or who seek to do so, the Secretary of State may by order make such further provision with respect to those persons as appears to him to be expedient; and an order so made may contain transitional provisions and savings and is subject to annulment in pursuance of a resolution of either House of Parliament: s 16 (4), (6). The power to make such orders is exercisable by statutory intrument: s 16 (5).

Schedule 5 para 2 does not apply in relation to a person whose examination under any corresponding provision of an order made under the Prevention of Terrorism (Temporary Provisions) Act 1984 s 13 (repealed) had begun but had not been concluded on 22 March 1989, and s 13 (repealed) continues to apply to him; but any reference in the Prevention of Terrorism (Temporary Provisions)

Act 1989 to examination under Sch 5 para 2 includes a reference to examination under that corresponding provision: s 25 (5).
8 Ibid Sch 5 para 2 (3). Section 20 (2) (use of reasonable force: see para 120 ante) does not apply for the purposes of Sch 5 para 2: s 20 (2).

122. Production of information and documents. It is the duty of any person examined[1] to furnish to the person carrying out the examination all such information in his possession as that person may require for the purpose of his functions as an examining officer[2]. If so required by the examining officer, a person on such examination must (1) produce either a valid passport with photograph or some other document satisfactorily establishing his identity and nationality or citizenship; and (2) declare whether or not he is carrying or conveying documents of any relevant description[3] specified by the examining officer, and produce any documents of that description which he is carrying or conveying[4].

1 Ie under the Prevention of Terrorism (Temporary Provisions) Act 1989 s 16 (1), Sch 5 para 2: see para 121 ante.
2 Ibid Sch 5 para 3 (1). For the meaning of 'examining officer' see para 121 note 3 ante. As to contravention of this provision see para 131 post.
3 For these purposes, 'relevant description' means any description appearing to the examining officer to be relevant for the purposes of the examination: ibid Sch 5 para 3 (3).
4 Ibid Sch 5 para 3 (2).

123. Powers of search etc. An examining officer[1] may, for the purpose of satisfying himself whether there are persons he may wish to examine[2], search any ship[3] or aircraft[4] and anything on board it or anything taken off or about to be taken aboard a ship or aircraft[5]; and an examining officer who examines any person may[6] search that person and any baggage belonging to him or any ship or aircraft and anything on board it or anything taken off or about to be taken aboard a ship or aircraft[7]. An examining officer may detain for the purpose of examining it anything produced[8] by a person on his examination or found on such a search, for a period not exceeding seven days; and, if on examination of anything so produced or found the examining officer is of the opinion that it may be needed in connection with the taking of a decision by the Secretary of State as to whether or not to make an exclusion order or a deportation order[9] or for use as evidence in criminal proceedings, he may detain it until he is satisfied that it will not be so needed[10].

An examining officer may board any ship or aircraft or enter any vehicle[11] for the purpose of exercising[12] his functions[13].

Where an examining officer has power so to search, he may instead authorise the search to be carried out on his behalf by a person who is not an examining officer[14]; and, where a person who is not an examining officer so carries out a search, he may for that purpose board any ship or aircraft or enter any vehicle, and exercise the power[15] of detaining articles; and he may, if necessary, use reasonable force for the purposes of carrying out such functions[16].

1 For the meaning of 'examining officer' see para 121 note 3 ante.
2 Ie under the Prevention of Terrorism (Temporary Provisions) Act 1989 s 16 (1), Sch 5 para 2: see para 121 ante.
3 For the meaning of 'ship' see para 102 note 11 ante.
4 For the meaning of 'aircraft' see para 102 note 12 ante.
5 Prevention of Terrorism (Temporary Provisions) Act 1989 Sch 5 para 4 (1).
6 Ie for the purposes of determining whether he is such a person as is mentioned in ibid Sch 5 para 2 (1) (a)–(c): see para 121 heads (1)–(3) ante.

7 Ibid Sch 5 para 4 (2). Without prejudice to Sch 5 para 4 (1), (2), an examining officer who examines any person in Northern Ireland under Sch 5 para 2 may, for the purpose mentioned in Sch 5 para 4 (2), search any vehicle and anything in or on it or anything taken out of or off it or about to be placed in or on it: Sch 5 para 4 (3).

A search of a person under Sch 5 para 4 may only be carried out by a person of the same sex: Sch 5 para 4 (5).

8 Ie pursuant to ibid Sch 5 para 3 (2) (b): see para 122 ante.

9 Ie under the Immigration Act 1971: see BRITISH NATIONALITY AND ALIENAGE vol 4 para 1011 et seq.

10 Prevention of Terrorism (Temporary Provisions) Act 1989 Sch 5 para 4 (4).

11 For the meaning of 'vehicle' see para 109 note 6 ante.

12 Ie for the purpose of exercising any of his functions under the Prevention of Terrorism (Temporary Provisions) Act 1989.

13 Ibid Sch 5 para 4 (6).

14 Ibid Sch 5 para 4 (7).

15 Ie the power conferred by ibid Sch 5 para 4 (4): see supra.

16 Ibid Sch 5 para 4 (8).

124. Landing, embarkation, entry and departure cards. Any person who disembarks from, or embarks on (1) a ship[1] or aircraft[2] in Great Britain which has come from, or is going to, the Republic of Ireland, Northern Ireland or any of the Islands[3]; or (2) a ship or aircraft in Northern Ireland which has come from, or is going to, Great Britain, the Republic of Ireland or any of the Islands, must, if so required by an examining officer[4], complete and produce to that officer a landing or, as the case may be, an embarkation card in such form as the Secretary of State may direct, which, where the ship or aircraft is employed to carry passengers for reward, must be supplied for the purpose to that person by the owners or agents of that ship or aircraft[5].

1 For the meaning of 'ship' see para 108 note 11 ante.

2 For the meaning of 'aircraft' see para 108 note 12 ante.

3 For the meaning of 'the Islands' see para 102 note 2 ante.

4 For the meaning of 'examining officer' see para 121 note 3 ante.

5 Prevention of Terrorism (Temporary Provisions) Act 1989 s 16 (1), Sch 5 para 5 (1). As to contravention of this provision see para 131 post. Schedule 5 para 5 (1) does not, however, apply to a person disembarking from a ship or aircraft coming from the Republic of Ireland if that person is required to produce a landing card under any order for the time being in force under the Immigration Act 1971 s 4 (2), Sch 2 para 5: Prevention of Terrorism (Temporary Provisions) Act 1989 Sch 5 para 5 (2). See further BRITISH NATIONALITY AND ALIENAGE vol 4 para 1005. For the meaning of 'Great Britain' see para 86 note 1 ante.

Any person who may be examined under Sch 5 para 2 (3) (a) or (c) (see para 121 heads (a), (c) respectively ante) must, if so required by an examining officer, complete and produce to that officer an entry or, as the case may be, a departure card in such form as the Secretary of State may direct: Sch 5 para 5 (3).

125. Detention pending examination etc. A person who is examined[1] may be detained under the authority of an examining officer[2] (1) pending conclusion of his examination; (2) pending consideration by the Secretary of State whether to make an exclusion order against him; or (3) pending a decision by the Director of Public Prosecutions or the Attorney General whether proceedings for an offence should be instituted against him[3]. A person may not, however, be so detained for more than 48 hours from the time when he is first examined[4]. The Secretary of State may, in any particular case, extend the period of 48 hours by a period or periods specified by him, but any such further period or periods may not exceed five days in all; and, if an application for such an extension is made, the person detained must as soon as practicable be given written notice of that fact and of the time when the application was made[5].

A person liable to be so detained may be arrested without warrant by an examining officer[6].

If a justice of the peace is satisfied that there are reasonable grounds for suspecting that a person so liable is to be found on any premises[7], he may grant a search warrant authorising any constable to enter those premises for the purpose of searching for and arresting that person[8].

A person on board a ship[9] or aircraft[10] may, under the authority of an examining officer, be removed from the ship or aircraft for such detention; but, if an examining officer so requires, the captain[11] of the ship or aircraft must prevent from disembarking[12] in the relevant territory[13] any person who has arrived in the ship or aircraft if the examining officer notifies him either that that person is the subject of an exclusion order or that consideration is being given by the Secretary of State to the making of an exclusion order against that person[14].

1   A person may be removed from a vehicle for such detention: Prevention of Terrorism (Temporary Provisions) Act 1989 s 16 (1), Sch 5 para 6 (7).
2   For the meaning of 'examining officer' see para 121 note 3 ante.
3   Prevention of Terrorism (Temporary Provisions) Act 1989 Sch 5 para 6 (1). A person so detained is deemed to be in legal custody at any time when he is so detained and, if detained otherwise than on board a ship or aircraft, may be detained in such a place as the Secretary of State may from time to time direct: Sch 5 para 7 (4). Where a person is so detained, any examining officer, constable or prison officer, or any other person authorised by the Secretary of State, may take all such steps as may be reasonably necessary for photographing, measuring or otherwise identifying him: Sch 5 para 7 (5). Any person so detained may be taken in the custody of an examining officer, or of any person acting under the authority of such an officer, to and from any place where his attendance is required for the purpose of establishing his nationality or citizenship or for making arrangements for his admission to a country or territory outside the United Kingdom or where he is required to be for any other purpose connected with the operation of the 1989 Act: Sch 5 para 7 (7). For the meaning of 'United Kingdom' see para 86 note 1 ante.
       The Police and Criminal Evidence Act 1984 s 61 (1)–(8) (fingerprinting: see para 776 post) applies to the taking of a person's fingerprints by a constable under the Prevention of Terrorism (Temporary Provisions) Act 1989 Sch 5 para 7 (5) as if for the Police and Criminal Evidence Act 1984 s 61 (4) there were substituted:
       'An officer may only give an authorisation under s 61 (3) (a) for the taking of a person's fingerprints if he is satisfied that it is necessary to do so in order to assist in determining:
       (1)   whether that person is or has been concerned in the commission, preparation or instigation of acts of terrorism to which the Prevention of Terrorism (Temporary Provisions) Act 1989 Sch 5 para 2 (see para 121 note 4 ante) applies;
       (2)   whether he is subject to an exclusion order under that Act; or
       (3)   whether there are grounds for suspecting that he has committed an offence under s 8 (see para 106 ante)':
       Sch 5 para 7 (6).
4   Ibid Sch 5 para 6 (2).
5   Ibid Sch 5 para 6 (3).
6   Ibid Sch 5 para 6 (4).
7   For the meaning of 'premises' see para 109 note 6 ante.
8   Prevention of Terrorism (Temporary Provisions) Act 1989 Sch 5 para 7 (1).
9   For the meaning of 'ship' see para 108 note 11 ante.
10 For the meaning of 'aircraft' see para 108 note 12 ante.
11 For the meaning of 'captain' see para 108 note 10 ante.
12 Where the captain of a ship or aircraft is so required to prevent a person from disembarking, he may for that purpose detain him in custody on board the ship or aircraft: Prevention of Terrorism (Temporary Provisions) Act 1989 Sch 5 para 6 (6).
13 For these purposes, 'the relevant territory' has the same meaning as in ibid s 4 (4), Sch 2 para 6 (see para 108 note 3 ante): Sch 5 para 6 (8).
14 Ibid Sch 5 para 6 (5). As to contravention of this provision see para 131 post.

126. Examination without detention. Where a person has been required by a notice[1] to submit to further examination but is not detained[2] pending such examination, his further examination must be reviewed by a review officer[3] not later than 12 hours after the beginning of the examination and may not continue unless that officer has authorised it to continue[4]. The review officer may authorise the examination to continue if, and only if, he is satisfied that the inquiries necessary to complete the examination are being carried out diligently and expeditiously[5].

1 Ie under the Prevention of Terrorism (Temporary Provisions) Act 1989 s 16 (1), Sch 5 para 2 (4): see para 121 ante.
2 Ie under ibid Sch 5 para 6: see para 125 ante.
3 As to review officers see para 110 note 2 ante.
4 Prevention of Terrorism (Temporary Provisions) Act 1989 s 16 (2), Sch 3 para 2 (1). As to post-ponement of reviews, representations about detention, the rights of detained persons, records of interviews and interventions by superior officers see Sch 3 paras 5–9 and para 110 ante.
5 Ibid Sch 3 para 2 (2).

127. Detention for examination. Where a person is detained[1], his detention must be periodically reviewed by a review officer[2] and may not continue unless (1) that officer has authorised it to continue; or (2) an application has been made to the Secretary of State[3] for an extension of the period of detention[4]. The reviews must be carried out as follows: (a) the first review must be as soon as practicable after the beginning of the detention; and (b) the subsequent reviews must be at intervals of not more than 12 hours; and no review can be carried out after an application has been so made[5].

On any such review the review officer may authorise the continued detention of the person in question if, and only if, he is satisfied that his continued detention is necessary in order to obtain, whether by questioning him or otherwise, or to preserve evidence which (i) relates to a specified offence[6]; (ii) indicates that he is or has been concerned in the commission, preparation or instigation of acts of terrorism[7]; or (iii) indicates that he is subject to an exclusion order; and that the investigation in connection with which that person is detained is being conducted diligently and expeditiously[8].

The review officer may also authorise the continued detention of the person in question pending consideration of the question whether he is subject to an exclusion order, pending consideration by the Secretary of State whether to make an exclusion order against him or to serve him with notice of a decision to make a deportation order[9], pending a decision by the Director of Public Prosecutions or Attorney General whether proceedings for an offence should be instituted against him, or if he is satisfied as to the specified[10] matters[11].

1 Ie under the Prevention of Terrorism (Temporary Provisions) Act 1989 s 16 (1), Sch 5 para 6: see para 125 ante.
2 As to review officers see para 110 note 2 ante.
3 Ie under the Prevention of Terrorism (Temporary Provisions) Act 1989 Sch 5 para 6 (3): see para 125 ante.
4 Ibid s 16 (2), Sch 3 para 3 (1). As to postponement of reviews, representations about detention, the rights of detained persons, records of interviews and interventions by superior officers see Sch 3 paras 5–9 and para 110 ante.
5 Ibid Sch 3 para 3 (2).
6 Ie an offence under ibid s 8: see para 107 ante.
7 Ie to which ibid s 14 applies: see para 118 ante.
8 Ibid Sch 3 para 3 (3).
9 Ie under the Immigration Act 1971: see BRITISH NATIONALITY AND ALIENAGE vol 4 para 1011 et seq.

10 The matters so specified are (1) that the continued detention of the person in question is necessary (a) pending a decision whether to apply to the Secretary of State for an exclusion order to be made in respect of him or for notice of a decision to make a deportation order under the Immigration Act 1971 to be served on him; or (b) pending the making of such an application; and (2) that consideration of that question is being undertaken, or preparation of the application is being proceeded with, diligently and expeditiously: Prevention of Terrorism (Temporary Provisions) Act 1989 Sch 3 para 3 (5).

11 Ibid Sch 3 para 3 (4).

128. Designated ports. The owners or agents of a ship[1] or aircraft[2] employed to carry passengers for reward and (1) coming to Great Britain from the Republic of Ireland, Northern Ireland or any of the Islands[3] or going from Great Britain to any other of those places; or (2) coming to Northern Ireland from Great Britain, the Republic of Ireland or any of the Islands or going from Northern Ireland to any other of those places, may not, without the approval of an examining officer[4], arrange for the ship or aircraft to call at a port in Great Britain other than a designated port[5] for the purpose of disembarking or embarking passengers[6].

The captain[7] of an aircraft not employed to carry passengers for reward and (a) coming to Great Britain from the Republic of Ireland, Northern Ireland or any of the Islands or going from Great Britain to any other of those places; or (b) coming to Northern Ireland from Great Britain, the Republic of Ireland or any of the Islands or going from Northern Ireland to any other of those places, may not, without the approval of an examining officer, permit the aircraft to call at or leave a port in Great Britain other than a designated port[8].

1 For the meaning of 'ship' see para 108 note 11 ante.
2 For the meaning of 'aircraft' see para 108 note 12 ante.
3 For the meaning of 'the Islands' see para 102 note 2 ante.
4 For the meaning of 'examining officer' see para 121 note 3 ante.
5 The designated ports for the purposes of the Prevention of Terrorism (Temporary Provisions) Act 1989 s 16 (1), Sch 5 para 8 are those specified in Sch 6; but the Secretary of State may by order add any port to, or remove any port from, Sch 6: s 16 (3). The power so to make an order is exercisable by statutory instrument: s 16 (5). At the date at which this volume states the law no such order had been made.

The designated ports in Sch 6 are:

GREAT BRITAIN

SEAPORTS	AIRPORTS
Ardrossan	Aberdeen
Cairnryan	Biggin Hill
Fishguard	Birmingham
Fleetwood	Blackpool
Heysham	Bournemouth (Hurn)
Holyhead	Bristol
Pembroke Dock	Cambridge
Plymouth	Cardiff
Port of Liverpool	Carlisle
Poole Harbour	Coventry
Portsmouth Continental	East Midlands
Ferry Port	Edinburgh
Southampton	Exeter
Stranraer	Glasgow
Swansea	Gloucester/Cheltenham
Torquay	(Staverton)

SEAPORTS	AIRPORTS
Weymouth	Humberside
	Leeds/Bradford
	Liverpool
	London–City
	London–Gatwick
	London–Heathrow
	Luton
	Lydd
	Manchester
	Manston
	Newcastle
	Norwich
	Plymouth
	Prestwick
	Southampton
	Southend
	Stansted
	Teesside

NORTHERN IRELAND

SEAPORTS	AIRPORTS
Belfast	Aldergrove
Larne	Sydenham
Warrenpoint	

6 Ibid Sch 5 para 8 (1), (3). For the meaning of 'Great Britain' see para 86 note 1 ante. As to contravention of this provision see para 131 post.

7 For the meaning of 'captain' see para 108 note 10 ante.

8 Prevention of Terrorism (Temporary Provisions) Act 1989 Sch 5 para 8 (2), (4). As to contravention of this provision see para 131 post.

129. Control areas. The Secretary of State may from time to time give written notice to the owners or agents of any ships[1] or aircraft[2] designating control areas for the disembarkation or embarkation of passengers in any port[3] in the United Kingdom and specifying the conditions and restrictions, if any, to be observed in any control area; and, where by notice given to any owners or agents a control area is for the time being so designated at any port, the owners or agents must take all reasonable steps to ensure that, in the case of their ships or aircraft, passengers do not disembark or, as the case may be, embark at the port outside the control area and that any conditions or restrictions notified to them are observed[4]. The Secretary of State may also from time to time give to any persons concerned with the management of a port in the United Kingdom written notice designating control areas in the port and specifying facilities to be provided and conditions and restrictions to be observed in any control area; and any such person must take all reasonable steps to secure that any facilities, conditions or restrictions notified to him are provided or observed[5].

1 For the meaning of 'ship' see para 108 note 11 ante.

2 For the meaning of 'aircraft' see para 108 note 12 ante.

3 'Port' includes airport and hoverport: Prevention of Terrorism (Temporary Provisions) Act 1989 s 20 (1).

4 Ibid s 16 (1), Sch 5 para 9 (1). For the meaning of 'United Kingdom' see para 86 note 1 ante. As to contravention of this provision see para 131 post.

5 Ibid Sch 5 para 9 (2). As to contravention of this provision see para 131 post.

130. Embarkation and disembarkation of passengers and crew. The captain[1] of a ship[2] or aircraft[3] employed to carry passengers for reward, or of an aircraft not employed to carry passengers for reward, arriving in Great Britain from the Republic of Ireland, Northern Ireland or any of the Islands[4] or arriving in Northern Ireland from Great Britain, the Republic of Ireland or any of the Islands (1) must, except so far as he may be otherwise required to do so[5], take such steps as may be necessary to secure that passengers on board and members of the crew do not disembark there unless either they have been examined by an examining officer[6] or they disembark in accordance with arrangements approved by an examining officer; and (2) where any examination of persons on board is to be carried out on the ship or aircraft, must take such steps as may be necessary to secure that those to be examined are presented for the purpose in an orderly manner[7]. The captain of a ship or aircraft employed to carry passengers for reward, or of an aircraft not employed to carry passengers for reward, going from Great Britain to the Republic of Ireland, Northern Ireland or any of the Islands or going from Northern Ireland to Great Britain, the Republic of Ireland or any of the Islands, must take such steps as may be necessary to secure that (a) passengers and members of the crew do not embark except in accordance with arrangements approved by an examining officer; and (b) if persons embarking are to be examined on board the ship or aircraft, they are presented for the purpose in an orderly manner[8].

The captain of a ship or aircraft arriving in Great Britain from the Republic of Ireland, Northern Ireland or any of the Islands or arriving in Northern Ireland from Great Britain, the Republic of Ireland or any of the Islands, must[9] comply with the following requirements with respect to the furnishing to the examining officer of the particulars of the passengers on, and crew of, the ship or aircraft: (i) in the case of a ship employed to carry passengers for reward or an aircraft, to furnish to the examining officer, as soon as reasonably practicable after the arrival of the ship or aircraft, a list of the names and of the dates and places of birth of all passengers and members of the crew arriving on the ship or aircraft; and (ii) in the case of a ship not employed to carry passengers for reward, to furnish to the examining officer, within 12 hours of the arrival of the ship, a list of the names, dates and places of birth and the addresses of the destinations in Great Britain or Northern Ireland of all passengers and members of the crew arriving on the ship[10].

1 For the meaning of 'captain' see para 108 note 10 ante.
2 For the meaning of 'ship' see para 108 note 11 ante.
3 For the meaning of 'aircraft' see para 108 note 12 ante.
4 For the meaning of 'the Islands' see para 102 note 2 ante.
5 Ie under the Immigration Act 1971 s 4 (2), Sch 2 para 27 (1): see BRITISH NATIONALITY AND ALIENAGE vol 4 para 1030 note 3.
6 For the meaning of 'examining officer' see para 121 note 3 ante.
7 Prevention of Terrorism (Temporary Provisions) Act 1989 s 16 (1), Sch 5 para 10 (1), (3). For the meaning of 'Great Britain' see para 86 note 1 ante. As to contravention of this provision see para 131 post.
8 Ibid Sch 5 para 10 (2), (3). As to contravention of this provision see para 131 post.
9 Ie unless he is subject to the requirements of an order under the Immigration Act 1971 Sch 2 para 27 (2): see BRITISH NATIONALITY AND ALIENAGE vol 4 para 1030.
10 Prevention of Terrorism (Temporary Provisions) Act 1989 Sch 5 para 10 (4), (5). As to contravention of this provision see para 131 post. An examining officer may dispense with all, or any, of the requirements of Sch 5 para 10 (5) either generally or in respect of such classes of persons as he may specify: Sch 5 para 10 (6). Any passenger on a ship or aircraft must furnish to the captain of the ship or aircraft, as the case may be, any information required by him for the purpose of complying with the provisions of Sch 5 para 10 (5): Sch 5 para 10 (7).

131. Offences. Any person who knowingly contravenes any prohibition or fails to comply with any duty or requirement imposed by or under the provisions relating to travel restrictions[1] is guilty of an offence and liable on summary conviction to imprisonment for a term not exceeding three months or a fine not exceeding level 4 on the standard scale, or to both[2].

1 Ie the provisions contained in the Prevention of Terrorism (Temporary Provisions) Act 1989 s 16 (1), Sch 5: see paras 121–130 ante.
2 Ibid Sch 5 para 11. For the meaning of 'the standard scale' see para 808 post.

F. TERRORIST INVESTIGATIONS

132. Search for material other than excluded or special procedure material. On an application made by a constable, a justice of the peace may issue a warrant if satisfied that a terrorist investigation[1] is being carried out and that there are reasonable grounds for believing:

(1) that there is material on premises[2] specified in the application which is likely to be of substantial value, whether by itself or together with other material, to the investigation;

(2) that the material does not consist of or include items subject to legal privilege[3], excluded material[4] or special procedure material[5]; and

(3) that any of the specified conditions are fulfilled[6].

The specified conditions are:

(a) that it is not practicable to communicate with any person entitled to grant entry to the premises;

(b) that it is practicable to communicate with such a person but it is not practicable to communicate with any person entitled to grant access to the material;

(c) that entry to the premises will not be granted unless a warrant is produced;

(d) that the purpose of a search may be frustrated or seriously prejudiced unless a constable arriving at the premises can secure immediate entry to them[7].

A warrant so issued authorises a constable to enter the premises specified and to search the premises and any person found there and to seize and retain anything found there or on any such person, other than items subject to legal privilege, if he has reasonable grounds for believing:

(i) that it is likely to be of substantial value, whether by itself or together with other material, to the investigation; and

(ii) that it is necessary to seize it in order to prevent it being concealed, lost, damaged, altered or destroyed[8].

1 'Terrorist investigation' means any investigation to which the Prevention of Terrorism (Temporary Provisions) Act 1989 s 17 (1) applies: s 17 (1), Sch 7 para 1.
    For the purposes of s 17, 'terrorist investigation' means (1) an investigation into (a) the commission, preparation or instigation of acts of terrorism to which s 14 applies (see para 118 ante); or (b) any other act which appears to have been done in furtherance of, or in connection with, such acts of terrorism, including any act which appears to constitute an offence under s 2 (see para 111 ante), s 9 (see para 115 ante), s 10 (see para 114 ante) or s 11 (see para 116 ante) or the Northern Ireland (Emergency Provisions) Act 1978 s 21; or (c) without prejudice to head (b) supra, the resources of a proscribed organisation within the meaning of the Prevention of Terrorism (Temporary Provisions) Act 1989 s 1 (see para 111 note 1 ante) or a proscribed organisation for the purposes of the Northern Ireland (Emergency Provisions) Act 1978 s 21 (see para 114 note 2 ante); and (2) an investigation into whether there are grounds justifying the making of an order under the Prevention of Terrorism (Temporary Provisions) Act 1989 s 1 (2) (a) or the Northern Ireland (Emergency Provisions) Act 1978 s 21 (4): Prevention of Terrorism (Temporary Provisions) Act 1989 s 17 (1).

2 For the meaning of 'premises' see para 109 note 6 ante.
3 'Items subject to legal privilege' has the meaning given in the Police and Criminal Evidence Act 1984 s 10 (see para 672 note 5 post): Prevention of Terrorism (Temporary Provisions) Act 1989 Sch 7 para 1.
4 'Excluded material' has the meaning given by the Police and Criminal Evidence Act 1984 s 11 (see para 674 post): Prevention of Terrorism (Temporary Provisions) Act 1989 Sch 7 para 1.
5 'Special procedure material' has the meaning given by the Police and Criminal Evidence Act 1984 s 14 (see para 675 post): Prevention of Terrorism (Temporary Provisions) Act 1989 Sch 7 para 1.
6 Ibid Sch 7 para 2 (1). On an application made by a police officer of at least the rank of superintendent, in relation to a person specified in the application or to property so specified, the Chief Land Registrar must provide the applicant with any information kept by the Registrar under the Land Registration Act 1925 which relates to that person or property: Sch 7 para 9 (1). On such an application the Registrar must be given a certificate stating that there are reasonable grounds for suspecting that there is information kept by him which is likely to be of substantial value, whether by itself or together with other information, to a terrorist investigation: Sch 7 para 9 (2). Such information must be provided by the Registrar in documentary form: Sch 7 para 9 (3). Schedule 7 para 9 is to be repealed on the coming into force of the Land Registration Act 1988: see the Prevention of Terrorism (Temporary Provisions) Act 1989 ss 25 (2), 27 (4), Sch 9. At the date at which this volume states the law no order had been made bringing the Land Registration Act 1988 into force.
7 Prevention of Terrorism (Temporary Provisions) Act 1989 Sch 7 para 2 (2).
8 Ibid Sch 7 para 2 (3). Any power of seizure conferred by Sch 7 is without prejudice to the powers conferred by the Police and Criminal Evidence Act 1984 s 19 (see para 685 post); and for the purposes of ss 21, 22 (access to, and copying and retention of, seized material: see paras 687, 688 respectively post), a terrorist investigation is to be treated as an investigation of or in connection with an offence, and material produced in pursuance of an order under the Prevention of Terrorism (Temporary Provisions) Act 1989 Sch 7 para 3 (see para 133 post) or Sch 7 para 8 (see para 137 post) is to be treated as if it were material seized by a constable: Sch 7 para 10 (1). A search of a person under Sch 7 Pt I (paras 1–9) may only be carried out by a person of the same sex: Sch 7 para 10 (2).

133. Order for production of excluded or special procedure material. For the purposes of a terrorist investigation[1], a constable may apply to a circuit judge for an order in relation to particular material or material of a particular description, being material consisting of or including excluded material[2] or special procedure material[3]. If on such an application the judge is satisfied that the material[4] consists of or includes such material, that it does not include items subject to legal privilege[5] and that the specified conditions are fulfilled, he may make an order[6] that the person who appears to him to be in possession of the material to which the application relates shall (1) produce it to a constable for him to take it away; or (2) give a constable access to it, within such period[7] as the order may specify and, if the material is not in the person's possession (and will not come into his possession within that period), to state to the best of his knowledge and belief where it is[8].

The specified conditions are:

   (a) that a terrorist investigation is being carried out and that there are reasonable grounds for believing that the material is likely to be of substantial value, whether by itself or together with other material, to the investigation for the purposes of which the application is made; and

   (b) that there are reasonable grounds for believing that it is in the public interest, having regard to the benefit likely to accrue to the investigation if the material is obtained, and to the circumstances under which the person in possession of the material holds it, that the material should be produced or that access to it should be given[9].

1 For the meaning of 'terrorist investigation' see para 132 note 1 ante.
2 For the meaning of 'excluded material' see para 132 note 4 ante.

3 Prevention of Terrorism (Temporary Provisions) Act 1989 s 17 (1), Sch 7 para 3 (1). For the meaning of 'special procedure material' see para 132 note 5 ante. Material produced in pursuance of an order under Sch 7 para 3 is to be treated as if it were material seized by a constable: see Sch 7 para 10 (1) and para 132 note 8 ante.

4 Where the material to which such an application relates consists of information contained in a computer: (1) an order under ibid Sch 7 para 3 (2) (a) (see text head (1) infra) has effect as an order to produce the material in a form in which it can be taken away and in which it is visible and legible; and (2) an order under Sch 7 para 3 (2) (b) (see text head (2) infra) has effect as an order to give access to the material in a form in which it is visible and legible: Sch 7 para 4 (4). Where the judge makes an order under Sch 7 para 3 (2) (b) (see text head (2) infra), he may, on the application of the constable, order any person who appears to him to be entitled to grant entry to the premises to allow a constable to enter the premises to obtain access to the material: Sch 7 para 3 (6).

An order may be made under Sch 7 para 3 in relation to material in the possession of a government department which is an authorised government department for the purposes of the Crown Proceedings Act 1947; and any such order, which must be served as if the proceedings were civil proceedings against the department, may require any officer of the department, whether named in the order or not, who may for the time being be in possession of the material concerned, to comply with it: Sch 7 para 4 (6). As to authorised government departments see CROWN PROCEEDINGS.

5 For the meaning of 'items subject to legal privilege' see para 132 note 3 ante.

6 An order so made may relate to material of a particular description which is expected to come into existence or become available to the person concerned in the period of 28 days beginning with the date of the order; and an order made in relation to such material must require that person to notify a named constable as soon as possible after the material comes into existence or becomes available to that person: Prevention of Terrorism (Temporary Provisions) Act 1989 Sch 7 para 3 (3). Provision may be made by Crown Court Rules as to the discharge and variation of orders under Sch 7 para 3 and proceedings relating to such orders: Sch 7 para 4 (1). Pending the coming into force of such Rules, the following provisions have effect under Sch 7 para 4 (1): (1) an order under Sch 7 para 3 may be discharged or varied by a circuit judge on a written application made to the appropriate officer of the Crown Court by any person subject to the order; (2) unless a circuit judge otherwise directs on grounds of urgency, the applicant must, not less than 48 hours before making the application, send a copy of it and a notice in writing of the time and place where the application is to be made to the constable on whose application the order to be discharged or varied was made or on any other constable serving in the same police station: Sch 7 para 4 (2).

An order of a circuit judge under Sch 7 para 3 has effect as if it were an order of the Crown Court: Sch 7 para 4 (3). •

An order under Sch 7 para 3 does not confer any right to production of, or access to, items subject to legal privilege; and has effect notwithstanding any obligation as to secrecy or other restriction on the disclosure of information imposed by statute or otherwise: Sch 7 para 4 (5).

7 The period to be specified in an order so made is seven days from the date of the order or, in the case of an order under ibid Sch 7 para 3 (3) (see note 6 supra), from the notification to the constable unless it appears to the judge that a longer or shorter period would be appropriate in the particular circumstances of the application: Sch 7 para 3 (4).

8 Ibid Sch 7 para 3 (2).

9 Ibid Sch 7 para 3 (5).

134. Search for excluded or special procedure material. A constable may apply to a circuit judge for a warrant in relation to specified premises[1]. On such an application the judge may so issue a warrant if satisfied:

(1) that an order made[2] in relation to material on the premises has not been complied with; or

(2) that there are reasonable grounds for believing that there is on the premises material consisting of or including excluded material[3] or special procedure material[4], that it does not include items subject to legal privilege[5], and that the specified conditions[6] for such an order and the following condition for the issue of such a warrant are fulfilled[7].

The condition is that it would not be appropriate to make such an order[8] in relation to the material because:

(a) it is not practicable to communicate with any person entitled to produce the material; or

(b) it is not practicable to communicate with any person entitled to grant access to the material or entitled to grant entry to the premises on which the material is situated; or

(c) the investigation for the purposes of which the application is made might be seriously prejudiced unless a constable could secure immediate access to the material[9].

A warrant so issued authorises a constable to enter the premises specified in the warrant and to search the premises and any person found there and to seize and retain anything found there or on any such person, other than items subject to legal privilege, if he has reasonable grounds for believing that it is likely to be of substantial value, whether by itself or together with other material, to the investigation for the purposes of which the application was made[10].

1 Prevention of Terrorism (Temporary Provisions) Act 1989 s 17 (1), Sch 7 para 5 (1). For the meaning of 'premises' see para 109 note 6 ante.
2 Ie made under ibid Sch 7 para 3: see para 133 ante.
3 For the meaning of 'excluded material' see para 132 note 4 ante.
4 For the meaning of 'special procedure material' see para 132 note 5 ante.
5 For the meaning of 'items subject to legal privilege' see para 132 note 3 ante.
6 Ie the conditions in the Prevention of Terrorism (Temporary Provisions) Act 1989 Sch 7 para 3 (5): see para 133 heads (a), (b) ante.
7 Ibid Sch 7 para 5 (2).
8 Ie under ibid Sch 7 para 3: see para 133 ante.
9 Ibid Sch 7 para 5 (3).
10 Ibid Sch 7 para 5 (4).

135. Explanation of seized material. On an application made by a constable, a circuit judge may order[1] any person specified in the order to provide an explanation[2] of any material seized in pursuance of a warrant[3] or produced or made available[4] to a constable[5]. A person who, in purported compliance with such a requirement (1) makes a statement which he knows to be false or misleading in a material particular; or (2) recklessly makes a statement which is false or misleading in a material particular, is guilty of an offence and liable on conviction on indictment to imprisonment for a term not exceeding two years or a fine, or to both, or on summary conviction to imprisonment for a term not exceeding six months or a fine not exceeding the statutory maximum, or to both[6].

1 The Prevention of Terrorism (Temporary Provisions) Act 1989 s 17 (1), Sch 7 para 4 (1)–(3), (6) (see para 133 note 6 ante) applies to orders under Sch 7 para 6 as it applies to orders under Sch 7 para 3: Sch 7 para 6 (7).
2 A statement by a person in response to a requirement so imposed on him may only be used in evidence against him on a prosecution for an offence under ibid Sch 7 para 6 (4) (see infra), or on a prosecution for some other offence where in giving evidence he makes a statement inconsistent with it: Sch 7 para 6 (3).
3 Ie under ibid Sch 7 para 2: see para 132 ante.
4 Ie under ibid Sch 7 para 3: see para 133 ante.
5 Ibid Sch 7 para 6 (1). A person may not be required to disclose any information which he would be entitled to refuse to disclose on grounds of legal professional privilege in proceedings in the High Court, except that a lawyer may be required to furnish the name and address of his client: Sch 7 para 6 (2).
6 Ibid Sch 7 para 6 (4), (5). For the meaning of 'the statutory maximum' see para 806 post.

136. Urgent cases. If a police officer of at least the rank of superintendent has reasonable grounds for believing that the case is one of great emergency and that in the interests of the State immediate action is necessary, he may by a written order signed by him give to any constable the authority which may be given[1] by a search warrant[2]. An order so signed may not, however, authorise a search for items subject to legal privilege[3]. Where authority is so given, particulars of the case must be notified as soon as may be to the Secretary of State[4].

If such a police officer has reasonable grounds for believing that the case is as so stated, he may by a notice in writing signed by him require any person specified in the notice to provide an explanation of any materials seized in pursuance of such an order[5]. Any person who without reasonable excuse fails to comply with a notice so signed is guilty of an offence and liable on summary conviction to imprisonment for a term not exceeding six months or a fine not exceeding level 5 on the standard scale, or to both[6].

1 Ie the authority which may be given by a search warrant under the Prevention of Terrorism (Temporary Provisions) Act 1989 s 17 (1), Sch 7 para 2 (see para 132 ante) or para 5 (see para 134 ante).
2 Ibid Sch 7 para 7 (1).
3 Ibid Sch 7 para 7 (3).
4 Ibid Sch 7 para 7 (2).
5 Ibid Sch 7 para 7 (4). Schedule 7 para 6 (2)–(5) (see para 135 ante) applies to a requirement imposed under Sch 7 para 7 (4) as it applies to a requirement under Sch 7 para 6: Sch 7 para 7 (6).
6 Ibid Sch 7 para 7 (5). For the meaning of 'the standard scale' see para 808 post.

137. Orders by the Secretary of State in relation to certain investigations. In relation to a terrorist investigation[1] concerning any act which appears to the Secretary of State to constitute an offence under the provisions relating to financial assistance for terrorism[2], he may by a written order signed by him or on his behalf give to any constable in Northern Ireland the authority which may be given by a search warrant[3] or impose on any person in Northern Ireland any such requirement as may be imposed under the provisions relating to the production of excluded or special procedure material[4] if:

(1) he is satisfied as to the specified matters[5] for the issue of a warrant by a justice of the peace or the making of an order by a county court judge; and
(2) it appears to him that the disclosure of information that would be necessary for an application under those provisions would be likely to prejudice the capability of the Royal Ulster Constabulary in relation to the investigation of specified offences[6] or otherwise prejudice the safety of, or of persons in, Northern Ireland[7].

A person who disobeys an order so made is liable on conviction on indictment to imprisonment for a term not exceeding two years or a fine, or to both, or on summary conviction to imprisonment for a term not exceeding six months or a fine not exceeding the statutory maximum, or to both[8].

The Secretary of State may by a written order signed by him or on his behalf require any person in Northern Ireland to provide an explanation of any material seized or produced in pursuance of an order under the above provisions[9].

1 For the meaning of 'terrorist investigation' see para 132 note 1 ante.
2 Ie the Prevention of Terrorism (Temporary Provisions) Act 1989 Pt III (ss 9–13): see paras 114–117 ante.
3 Ie under ibid s 17 (1), Sch 7 para 2 (see para 132 ante) or para 5 (see para 134 ante).
4 Ie under ibid Sch 7 para 3: see para 133 ante.
5 Ie the matters specified in ibid Sch 7 paras 2, 3 or 5, as the case may be.
6 See note 2 supra.

7 Prevention of Terrorism (Temporary Provisions) Act 1989 Sch 7 para 8 (1), (2). Schedule 7 para 8 is without prejudice to the provisions of Sch 7 paras 1–7: see paras 132–136 ante.

An order so made may be varied or revoked by the Secretary of State; and references in Sch 7 paras 4 (4)–(6) (see para 133 ante) and Sch 7 para 5 (see para 134 ante) to an order under Sch 7 para 3 (see para 133 ante) include references to an order made by the Secretary of State under Sch 7 para 8: Sch 7 para 8 (4). Material produced in pursuance of an order under Sch 7 para 8 is to be treated as if it were material seized by a constable: see Sch 7 para 10 (1) and para 132 note 8 ante.

8 Ibid Sch 7 para 8 (3). For the meaning of 'the statutory maximum' see para 806 post.

9 Ibid Sch 7 para 8 (5). Schedule 7 paras 6 (2)–(5) (see para 135 ante), 7 (5) (see para 136 ante) apply to an order so made as they apply to an order or notice under Sch 7 paras 6 (2)–(5), 7 (5): Sch 7 para 8 (5).

138. Interference with terrorist investigations. Where in relation to a terrorist investigation[1] a warrant or order[2] has been issued or made or has been applied for and not refused, if a person, knowing or having reasonable cause to suspect that the investigation is taking place, (1) makes any disclosure which is likely to prejudice the investigation; or (2) falsifies, conceals or destroys or otherwise disposes of, or causes or permits the falsification, concealment, destruction or disposal of, material which is or is likely to be relevant to the investigation, he is guilty of an offence and liable on conviction on indictment to imprisonment for a term not exceeding five years or a fine, or to both, or on summary conviction to imprisonment for a term not exceeding six months or a fine not exceeding the statutory maximum, or to both[3].

In proceedings against a person for an offence in head (1) above it is a defence to prove that he did not know and had no reasonable cause to suspect that the disclosure was likely to prejudice the investigation, or that he had lawful authority or reasonable excuse for making the disclosure[4]; and in proceedings against a person for an offence in head (2) above it is a defence to prove that he had no intention of concealing any information contained in the material in question from the persons carrying out the investigation[5].

1 For the meaning of 'terrorist investigation' see para 132 note 1 ante.
2 Ie under the Prevention of Terrorism (Temporary Provisions) Act 1989 s 17 (1), Sch 7: see paras 132–137 ante.
3 Ibid s 17 (2), (5). For the meaning of 'the statutory maximum' see para 806 post. Proceedings for such an offence may not be instituted except by or with the consent of the Attorney General: s 19 (1) (a). As to the effect of this limitation see para 639 post.
4 Ibid s 17 (3).
5 Ibid s 17 (4).

G. TAKING OF HOSTAGES

139. Taking of hostages. A person, whatever his nationality, who, in the United Kingdom or elsewhere, detains any other person ('the hostage') and, in order to compel a State, international governmental organisation or person to do or abstain from doing any act, threatens to kill, injure or continue to detain the hostage is guilty of an offence and liable on conviction on indictment to imprisonment for life or for any shorter term[1].

1 Taking of Hostages Act 1982 s 1. Proceedings for such an offence may not, however, be instituted except by or with the consent of the Attorney General: s 2 (1) (a). As to the effect of this limitation see para 639 post.

H. OFFENCES COMMITTED ABROAD

140. Jurisdiction in respect of offences committed abroad. If a person, whether a citizen of the United Kingdom and Colonies[1] or not, does in any convention country[2] any act[3] which, if he had done it in a part of the United Kingdom, would have made him guilty in that part of the United Kingdom of a specified offence[4] or an offence of attempting to commit any such specified offence, he is, in that part of the United Kingdom, guilty of such offence or offences of which the act would have made him guilty if he had done it there[5].

If a person who is a national of a convention country but not a citizen of the United Kingdom and Colonies does outside the United Kingdom and that convention country any act which makes him in that convention country guilty of an offence and which, had he been a citizen of the United Kingdom and Colonies, would have made him in any part of the United Kingdom guilty of a specified offence[6], he is, in any part of the United Kingdom, guilty of such offence or offences of which that act would have made him guilty if he had been such a citizen[7].

Proceedings for an offence which would not be an offence apart from the above provisions may not be instituted except by or with the consent of the Attorney General[8].

1 For the meaning of 'citizen of the United Kingdom and Colonies' see the British Nationality Act 1981 s 51 (3) and BRITISH NATIONALITY AND ALIENAGE.
2 'Convention country' means a country for the time being designated in an order made by the Secretary of State as a party to the European Convention on the Suppression of Terrorism signed at Strasbourg on 27 January 1977: Suppression of Terrorism Act 1978 s 8 (1). For the purposes of s 4, any act done: (1) on board a ship registered in a convention country, being an act which, if the ship had been registered in the United Kingdom, would have constituted an offence within the jurisdiction of the Admiralty; or (2) on board an aircraft registered in a convention country while the aircraft is in flight elsewhere than in or over that country; or (3) on board a hovercraft registered in a convention country while the hovercraft is in journey elsewhere than in or over that country, is to be treated as done in that convention country; and the Civil Aviation Act 1982 s 92 (4) (definition of 'in flight' or, as applied to hovercraft, 'in journey': see AVIATION) applies for these purposes as it applies for the purposes of s 92 (4): Suppression of Terrorism Act 1978 s 4 (7) (amended by the Civil Aviation Act 1982 s 109, Sch 15 para 21). As to the convention countries see EXTRADITION vol 18 para 209. As to the criminal jurisdiction of the Admiralty see para 625 et seq post.
3 For these purposes, 'act' includes omission: Suppression of Terrorism Act 1978 s 8 (1).
4 The specified offences are:
  (1) murder (see para 431 et seq post);
  (2) manslaughter or culpable homicide (see para 436 et seq post);
  (3) kidnapping, abduction or plagium (see paras 493, 529 et seq post);
  (4) false imprisonment (see para 492 post);
  (5) an offence under the Offences against the Person Act 1861 s 55 (repealed) (abduction of unmarried girl under 16) or s 56 (repealed) (child-stealing or receiving stolen child);
  (6) an offence under the Sexual Offences Act 1956 s 20 (abduction of unmarried girl under 16: see para 532 post);
  (7) an offence under the Child Abduction Act 1984 s 2 (abduction of child by person other than parent etc: see para 536 post) or any corresponding provision in force in Northern Ireland;
  (8) an offence under the Offences against the Person Act 1861 s 28 (causing bodily injury by gunpowder: see para 476 post), s 29 (causing gunpowder to explode etc with intent to do grievous bodily harm: see para 477 post), s 30 (placing gunpowder near a building etc with intent to cause bodily injury: see para 481 post);
  (9) an offence under the Explosive Substances Act 1883 s 2 (causing explosion likely to endanger life or property: see para 478 post), s 3 (doing any act with intent to cause such an explosion, conspiring to cause such an explosion, or making or possessing explosive with intent to endanger life or property: see para 479 post);

(10) an offence under the Firearms Act 1968 s 16 (possession of firearm with intent to injure: see para 230 post), s 17 (1) (use of firearm or imitation firearm to resist arrest: see para 231 post) involving the use or attempted use of a firearm within the meaning of s 17;

(11) an offence under the Firearms (Northern Ireland) Order 1981, SI 1981/155, art 17 (person having in his possession any firearm or ammunition with intent by means thereof to endanger life or to enable another person by means thereof to endanger life), art 18 (1) (use of firearm or imitation firearm to resist arrest) involving the use or attempted use of a firearm:

Suppression of Terrorism Act 1978 s 4 (1) (a), Sch 1 (amended by the Child Abduction Act 1984 s 11 (4); the Firearms (Northern Ireland) Order 1981 art 6 (1), Sch 4 para 5; the Aviation Security Act 1982 s 40, Sch 2 para 7). 'Culpable homicide' and 'plagium' are Scottish terms.

5 Suppression of Terrorism Act 1978 s 4 (1). For the meaning of 'United Kingdom' see para 86 note 1 ante.

In the case of any country which, not being a convention country, is either (1) a designated Commonwealth country within the meaning of the Extradition Act 1989; or (2) a foreign state with which there is in force an arrangement of the kind described in the Extradition Act 1870 s 2 (repealed) or in the Extradition Act 1989 with respect to the surrender to that state of fugitive criminals; or (3) a colony, the Secretary of State may by order direct: (a) in the case of a country within heads (1) and (2) supra, that all or any of the provisions to which the Suppression of Terrorism Act 1978 s 5 (1) (i) applies shall apply in relation to that country, subject to such exceptions, if any, as may be specified in the order, as they apply in relation to a convention country; or (b) in the case of a country within head (3) supra, that the provisions of s 4 shall so apply in relation to that country; and, while such an order is in force in the case of any country, the provisions in question apply in relation to it accordingly: s 5 (1) (amended by the Extradition Act 1989 s 36 (4)–(7)). 'Country' includes any territory: Suppression of Terrorism Act 1978 s 8 (1). Section 5 (1) (i) applies (i) to the provisions of the Suppression of Terrorism Act 1978 which would, apart from s 5, apply only in relation to convention countries; and (ii) to the Extradition Act 1989 s 24 (1), (2) (see EXTRADITION): Suppression of Terrorism Act 1978 s 5 (1A) (added by the Extradition Act 1989 s 36 (8)). The Secretary of State may, at any time when the Republic of Ireland is not a convention country, direct that the Suppression of Terrorism Act 1978 s 4 shall apply in relation to the Republic as if it were a convention country; and, while such an order is in force, s 4 applies in relation to the Republic accordingly: s 5 (2).

An order made under s 5 (2) ceases to have effect, unless previously revoked, if the Republic of Ireland subsequently becomes a convention country: s 5 (3). The Republic of Ireland became a convention country on 7 December 1989: Suppression of Terrorism Act 1978 (Designation of Countries) Order 1989, SI 1989/2210, arts 1, 2.

Any power to make an order conferred on the Secretary of State by any provision of the Suppression of Terrorism Act 1978 is exercisable by statutory instrument and includes power to revoke or vary a previous order made under that provision: s 8 (4). No order may, however, be made under s 5 at any time unless a draft of the order has been laid before Parliament and approved by a resolution of each House of Parliament: s 8 (5).

6 The specified offences are:

(1) murder (see para 431 et seq post);

(2) manslaughter or culpable homicide (see 436 et seq post);

(3) an offence under the Explosive Substances Act 1883 s 2 (causing explosion likely to endanger life or property: see para 478 post), s 3 (doing any act with intent to cause such an explosion, conspiring to cause such an explosion, or making or possessing explosive with intent to endanger life or property: see para 479 post);

Suppression of Terrorism Act 1978 s 4 (3), Sch 1.

7 Ibid s 4 (3) (amended by the Internationally Protected Persons Act 1978 s 5 (4)).

8 Suppression of Terrorism Act 1978 s 4 (4). For this purpose the provisions of the Internationally Protected Persons Act 1978 are to be disregarded: Suppression of Terrorism Act 1978 s 4 (4) (as amended: see note 7 supra). As to the effect of this limitation see para 639 post.

141. Attacks and threats of attacks on protected persons. If a person, whether a citizen of the United Kingdom and Colonies[1] or not, does outside the United Kingdom (1) any act[2] to or in relation to a protected person[3] which, if he had done it in any part of the United Kingdom, would have made him guilty of a specified offence[4]; or (2) in connection with an attack on any relevant premises[5] or on any vehicle[6] ordinarily used by a protected person which is made when a protected person is on or in the premises or vehicle, any act which, if he had done it in any part of the United Kingdom, would have made him guilty of a specified offence[7], he is in any part of the United Kingdom guilty of such offences of which the act would have made him guilty if he had done it there[8].

If a person in the United Kingdom or elsewhere, whether a citizen of the United Kingdom and Colonies or not (a) attempts to commit an offence which, by virtue of the above provisions, is an offence mentioned in head (1) above against a protected person or an offence mentioned in head (2) above in connection with an attack so mentioned; or (b) aids, abets, counsels or procures, or is art and part in the commission of such an offence, he is in any part of the United Kingdom guilty of attempting to commit the offence in question or, as the case may be, of aiding, abetting, counselling or procuring, or being art and part in, the commission of the offence or attempt in question[9].

If a person in the United Kingdom or elsewhere, whether a citizen of the United Kingdom and Colonies or not (i) makes to another person a threat that any person will do any act which is an offence mentioned in head (a) above; or (ii) attempts to make or aids, abets, counsels or procures or is art and part in the making of such a threat to another person, with the intention that the other person shall fear that the threat will be carried out, the person who makes the threat or, as the case may be, who attempts to make it or aids, abets, counsels or procures it or is art and part in the making of it, is in any part of the United Kingdom guilty of an offence and liable on conviction on indictment to imprisonment for a term not exceeding ten years and not exceeding the term of imprisonment to which a person would be liable for the offence constituted by doing the act threatened at the place where the conviction occurs and at the time of the offence to which the conviction relates[10].

1 For the meaning of 'citizen of the United Kingdom and Colonies' see the British Nationality Act 1981 s 51 (3) and BRITISH NATIONALITY AND ALIENAGE.

2 For these purposes, 'act' includes omission: Internationally Protected Persons Act 1978 s 1 (5).

3 For these purposes, 'a protected person' means, in relation to an alleged offence, any of the following, namely:

(1) a person who, at the time of the alleged offence, is a Head of State, a member of a body which performs the functions of Head of State under the Constitution of the State, a Head of Government or a Minister for Foreign Affairs and is outside the territory of the State in which he holds office;

(2) a person who, at the time of the alleged offence, is a representative or official of a State or an official or agent of an international organisation of an inter-governmental character, is entitled under international law to special protection from attack on his person, freedom or dignity and does not fall within head (1) supra;

(3) a person who, at the time of the alleged offence, is a member of the family of another person mentioned in either of heads (1), (2) supra and (a) if the other person is mentioned in head (1) supra, is accompanying him; (b) if the other person is mentioned in head (2) supra, is a member of his household:

ibid s 1 (5). If in any proceedings a question arises as to whether a person is or was a protected person, a certificate issued by or under the authority of the Secretary of State and stating any fact relating to the question is conclusive evidence of that fact: s 1 (5).

4 The specified offences are: murder (see para 431 et seq post); manslaughter (see para 436 et seq post); culpable homicide; rape (see para 514 et seq post); assault occasioning actual bodily harm or causing injury (see para 490 post); kidnapping (see para 493 post); abduction (see para 529 et seq post); false imprisonment or plagium (see para 492 post); or an offence under the Offences against the Person Act 1861 s 18 (see para 469 post), s 20 (see para 471 post), s 21 (see para 473 post), s 22 (see para 474 post), s 23 (see para 475 post), s 24 (see para 475 post), s 28 (see para 476 post), s 29 (see para 477 post), s 30 (see para 481 post) or s 56 (repealed) or the Explosive Substances Act 1883 s 2 (see para 478 post): Internationally Protected Persons Act 1978 s 1 (1) (a). 'Culpable homicide' and 'plagium' are Scottish terms.

5 'Relevant premises' means premises at which a protected person resides or is staying or which a protected person uses for the purpose of carrying out his functions as such a person: ibid s 1 (5).
6 'Vehicle' includes any means of conveyance: ibid s 1 (5).
7 The specified offences are offences under: the Explosive Substances Act 1883 s 2 (see para 478 post); the Criminal Damage Act 1971 s 1 (see para 594 post); the Criminal Damage (Northern Ireland) Order 1977, SI 1977/426, art 3, or the offence of wilful fire-raising: Internationally Protected Persons Act 1978 s 1 (1) (b). 'Wilful fire-raising' is a Scottish term.
8 Ibid s 1 (1). For the meaning of 'United Kingdom' see para 86 note 1 ante.
9 Ibid s 1 (2). 'Art and part' is a Scottish term.
10 Ibid s 1 (3).

(vi) Processions and Assemblies

142. Advance notice of public processions. Except where the procession is one commonly or customarily held in the police area[1] (or areas) in which it is proposed to be held or is a funeral procession organised by a funeral director acting in the normal course of his business, written[2] notice[3] must be given of any proposal to hold a public procession[4] intended (1) to demonstrate support for or opposition to the views or actions of any person or body of persons; (2) to publicise a cause or campaign; or (3) to mark or commemorate an event, unless it is not reasonably practicable to give any advance notice of the procession[5].

Where a public procession is held, each of the persons organising it is guilty of an offence if (a) the above requirements as to notice have not been satisfied; or (b) the date when it is held, the time when it starts, or its route, differs from the date, time or route specified in the notice[6]. A person guilty of such an offence is liable on summary conviction to a fine not exceeding level 3 on the standard scale[7]. It is, however, a defence for the accused to prove that he did not know of, and neither suspected nor had reason to suspect, the failure to satisfy the requirements or, as the case may be, the different date, time or route[8]; and, to the extent that an alleged offence turns on a difference of date, time or route, it is a defence for the accused to prove that the difference arose from circumstances beyond his control or from something done with the agreement of a police officer or by his direction[9].

1 For the meaning of 'police area' see the Interpretation Act 1978 s 5, Sch 1 and POLICE vol 36 para 225 note 2.
2 Unless the contrary intention appears, 'writing' includes typing, printing, lithography, photography and other modes of representing or reproducing words in a visible form, and expressions referring to writing are construed accordingly: ibid Sch 1.
3 The notice must specify the date when it is intended to hold the procession, the time when it is intended to start it, its proposed route, and the name and address of the person, or of one of the persons, proposing to organise it: Public Order Act 1986 s 11 (3). Such notice must be delivered to a police station (1) in the police area in which it is proposed the procession will start; or (2) where it is proposed the procession will start in Scotland and cross into England, in the first police area in England on the proposed route: s 11 (4). If delivered not less than six clear days before the date when the procession is intended to be held, the notice may be delivered by post by the recorded delivery service; but the Interpretation Act 1978 s 7 (document sent by post deemed to have been served when posted and to have been delivered in the ordinary course of post) does not apply: Public Order Act 1986 s 11 (5). If not so delivered, the notice must be delivered by hand not less than six clear days before the date when the procession is intended to be held or, if that is not reasonably practicable, as soon as delivery is reasonably practicable: s 11 (6).
4 For these purposes, 'public procession' means a procession in a public place; and 'public place' means (1) any highway; and (2) any place to which at the material time the public or any section of the public has access, on payment or otherwise, as of right or by virtue of express or implied permission: ibid s 16.
5 Ibid s 11 (1), (2).

6 Ibid s 11 (7).
7 Ibid s 11 (10). For the meaning of 'the standard scale' see para 808 post.
8 Ibid s 11 (8).
9 Ibid s 11 (9).

143. Imposing conditions on public processions. If the senior police officer[1], having regard to the time or place at which and the circumstances in which any public procession[2] is being held or is intended to be held and to its route or proposed route, reasonably believes that (1) it may result in serious public disorder, serious damage to property or serious disruption to the life of the community; or (2) the purpose of the persons organising it is the intimidation of others with a view to compelling them not to do an act they have a right to do, or to do any act they have a right not to do, he may give directions imposing on the persons organising or taking part in the procession such conditions as appear to him to be necessary to prevent such disorder, damage, disruption or intimidation, including conditions as to the route of the procession or prohibiting it from entering any public place[3] specified in the directions[4].

A person who organises a public procession and knowingly fails to comply with a condition so imposed is guilty of an offence and liable on summary conviction to imprisonment for a term not exceeding three months or a fine not exceeding level 4 on the standard scale, or to both; but it is a defence for him to prove that the failure arose from circumstances beyond his control[5]. A person who takes part in a public procession and knowingly fails to comply with such a condition is guilty of an offence and liable on summary conviction to a fine not exceeding level 3 on the standard scale; but it is a defence for him to prove that the failure arose from circumstances beyond his control[6]. A person who incites another to commit the latter offence is guilty of an offence and liable on summary conviction to imprisonment for a term not exceeding three months or a fine not exceeding level 4 on the standard scale, or to both[7].

1 For these purposes, 'the senior police officer' means (1) in relation to a procession intended to be held in a case where persons are assembling with a view to taking part in it, the most senior in rank of the police officers present at the scene; and (2) in relation to a procession intended to be held in a case where head (1) supra does not apply, the chief officer of police: Public Order Act 1986 s 12 (2). A direction so given by a chief officer of police must be in writing: s 12 (3). The chief officer of police may delegate, to such extent and subject to such conditions as he may specify, any of his functions under ss 12–14 (see infra and paras 144, 145 post) to a deputy or assistant chief constable or, in the City of London and the metropolitan police district, an assistant commissioner of police: s 15. For these purposes, 'the City of London' means the City as defined for the purposes of the Acts relating to the City of London police; and 'the metropolitan police district' means that district as defined in the London Government Act 1963 s 76: Public Order Act 1986 s 16.
2 For the meaning of 'public procession' see para 142 note 4 ante.
3 For the meaning of 'public place' see para 142 note 4 ante.
4 Public Order Act 1986 s 12 (1).
5 Ibid s 12 (4), (8). For the meaning of 'the standard scale' see para 808 post. A constable in uniform may arrest without warrant anyone he reasonably suspects is committing an offence under s 12 (4), (5) or (6) (see supra and text to notes 6, 7 infra): s 12 (7).
6 Ibid s 12 (5), (9). As to a constable's power of arrest without a warrant see note 5 supra.
7 Ibid s 12 (6), (10). Section 12 (10) applies notwithstanding the Magistrates' Courts Act 1980 s 45 (3) (inciter liable to same penalty as incited: see para 58 note 3 ante): Public Order Act 1986 s 12 (10). As to a constable's power of arrest without a warrant see note 5 supra.

144. Prohibiting public processions. If at any time the chief officer of police[1] reasonably believes that, because of particular circumstances existing in any district or part of a district, the statutory powers to impose conditions on public processions[2] will not be sufficient to prevent the holding of public processions[3] in that district or part from resulting in serious public disorder, he must apply to the council of the district for an order prohibiting for such period not exceeding three months as may be specified in the application the holding of all public processions, or of any class of public processions so specified, in the district or part concerned[4]. On receiving such an application, a council may with the consent of the Secretary of State make an order either in the terms of the application or with such modifications as may be approved by the Secretary of State[5].

A person who organises a public procession the holding of which he knows is prohibited by virtue of such an order[6] is guilty of an offence and liable on summary conviction to imprisonment for a term not exceeding three months or a fine not exceeding level 4 on the standard scale, or to both[7]. A person who takes part in a public procession the holding of which is prohibited by virtue of such an order[8] is guilty of an offence and liable on summary conviction to a fine not exceeding level 3 on the standard scale[9]. A person who incites another to commit the latter offence is guilty of an offence and liable on summary conviction to imprisonment for a term not exceeding three months or a fine not exceeding level 4 on the standard scale, or to both[10].

1 As to the chief officer of police's powers of delegation see para 143 note 1 ante.
2 Ie the powers under the Public Order Act 1986 s 12: see para 143 ante.
3 For the meaning of 'public procession' see para 142 note 4 ante.
4 Public Order Act 1986 s 13 (1). Section 13 (1) does not apply in the City of London or the metropolitan police district: s 13 (3). If at any time the Commissioner of Police for the City of London or the Commissioner of Police of the Metropolis reasonably believes that, because of particular circumstances existing in his police area or part of it, the powers under s 12 (see para 143 ante) will not be sufficient to prevent the holding of public processions in that area or part from resulting in serious public disorder, he may with the consent of the Secretary of State make an order prohibiting for such period not exceeding three months as may be specified in the order the holding of all public processions, or of any class of public procession so specified, in the area or part concerned: s 13 (4). As to the commissioner's powers of delegation see para 143 note 1 ante; and as to the recording, revocation and variation of any such order see note 5 infra. For the meaning of 'the City of London' and 'the metropolitan police district' see para 143 note 1 ante.
5 Ibid s 13 (2). Any order made under s 13 must, if not made in writing, be recorded in writing as soon as practicable after being made; and any such order may be revoked or varied by a subsequent order made in the same way, that is in accordance with s 13 (1), (2) or s 13 (4) (see note 4 supra): s 13 (5), (6). For the meaning of 'writing' see para 142 note 2 ante.
6 Ie an order under ibid s 13 (1), (2) or s 13 (4): see supra.
7 Ibid s 13 (7), (11). For the meaning of 'the standard scale' see para 808 post. A constable in uniform may arrest without warrant anyone he reasonably suspects is committing an offence under s 13 (7), (8) or (9) (see supra and text to notes 9, 10 infra): s 13 (10).
8 See note 6 supra.
9 Public Order Act 1986 s 13 (8), (12). As to a constable's power of arrest without a warrant see note 7 supra.
10 Ibid s 13 (9), (13). Section 13 (13) applies notwithstanding the Magistrates' Courts Act 1980 s 45 (3) (inciter liable to same penalty as incited: see para 58 note 3 ante): Public Order Act 1986 s 13 (3). As to a constable's power of arrest without a warrant see note 7 supra.

145. Imposing conditions on public assemblies. If the senior police officer[1], having regard to the time or place at which and the circumstances in which any public assembly[2] is being held or is intended to be held, reasonably believes that (1) it may result in serious public disorder, serious damage to property or serious disruption to the life of the community; or (2) the purpose of the persons organising it is the intimidation[3] of others with a view to compelling them not to do an act they have a right to do, or to do any act they have a right not to do, he may give directions imposing on the persons organising or taking part in the assembly such conditions as to the place at which the assembly may be, or continue to be, held, its maximum duration, or the maximum number of persons who may constitute it, as appear to him to be necessary to prevent such disorder, damage, disruption or intimidation[4].

A person who organises a public assembly and knowingly fails to comply with a condition so imposed is guilty of an offence and liable on summary conviction to imprisonment for a term not exceeding three months or a fine not exceeding level 4 on the standard scale, or to both; but it is a defence for him to prove that the failure arose from circumstances beyond his control[5]. A person who takes part in a public assembly and knowingly fails to comply with such a condition is guilty of an offence and liable on summary conviction to a fine not exceeding level 3 on the standard scale; but it is a defence for him to prove that the failure arose from circumstances beyond his control[6]. A person who incites another to commit the latter offence is guilty of an offence and liable on summary conviction to imprisonment for a term not exceeding three months or a fine not exceeding level 4 on the standard scale, or to both[7].

1 For these purposes, 'the senior police officer' means (1) in relation to an assembly being held, the most senior in rank of the police officers present at the scene; and (2) in relation to an assembly intended to be held, the chief officer of police: Public Order Act 1986 s 14 (2). A direction so given by a chief officer of police must be given in writing: s 14 (3). For the meaning of 'writing' see para 142 note 2 ante. As to the chief officer of police's powers of delegation see para 143 note 1 ante.

2 For these purposes, 'public assembly' means an assembly of 20 or more persons in a public place which is wholly or partly open to the air: ibid s 16. For the meaning of 'public place' see para 142 note 4 ante.

3 'Intimidation' is not to be equated with discomfort; the police officer must reasonably believe that the organisers acted with a view to compelling: *Police v Reid (Lorna)* [1987] Crim LR 702.

4 Public Order Act 1986 s 14 (1). Cf para 422 post.

5 Ibid s 14 (4), (8). For the meaning of 'the standard scale' see para 808 post. A constable in uniform may arrest without warrant anyone he reasonably suspects is committing an offence under s 14 (4), (5) or (6) (see supra and text to notes 6, 7 infra): s 14 (7).

6 Ibid s 14 (5), (9). As to a constable's power of arrest without a warrant see note 5 supra.

7 Ibid s 14 (6), (10). Section 14 (10) applies notwithstanding the Magistrates' Courts Act 1980 s 45 (3) (inciter liable to same penalty as incited: see para 58 note 3 ante): Public Order Act 1986 s 14 (10). As to a constable's power of arrest without a warrant see note 5 supra.

146. Meetings and assemblies for unlawful drilling. All meetings and assemblies of persons for the purpose of training or drilling themselves, or of being trained or drilled to the use of arms, or for the purpose of practising military exercise, movements or evolutions, without any lawful authority from Her Majesty, or a Secretary of State or any officer deputed by him for the purpose, are prohibited by law[1]. Any person who attends or is present at such a meeting or assembly for the purpose of training or drilling others or who aids or assists therein is guilty of an offence and liable on conviction on indictment to imprisonment for a term not exceeding seven years; and any person who attends or is present at any such meeting or assembly for the purpose of being so trained or drilled is guilty of an offence and liable on conviction on indictment to a fine and imprisonment for a term not exceeding two years[2]. However, no person may be prosecuted for any such offence unless such prosecution is commenced within six months after the commission of the offence[3].

Any justice of the peace or any constable or peace officer, or any other person acting in their aid or assistance, may disperse any such unlawful meeting or assembly and may arrest and detain any person present at or aiding, assisting or abetting any such meeting or assembly[4].

1 Unlawful Drilling Act 1819 s 1; Firearms Act 1920 s 16.
2 Unlawful Drilling Act 1819 s 1; Penal Servitude Act 1857 s 2; Criminal Justice Act 1948 s 1 (1).
3 Unlawful Drilling Act 1819 s 7.
4 Ibid s 2 (amended by the Courts Act 1971 s 56 (4), Sch 11 Pt IV).

(vii) Public Meetings

147. Disturbances at public meetings. Any person who at a lawful public meeting[1] acts in a disorderly manner for the purpose of preventing the transaction of the business for which the meeting was called together, or incites others so to act, is guilty of an offence and liable on summary conviction to imprisonment for a term not exceeding six months or a fine not exceeding level 5 on the standard scale, or to both[2].

If any constable reasonably suspects any person of committing such an offence, he may, if requested to do so by the chairman of the meeting, require that person to declare to him immediately his name and address and, if that person refuses or fails so to declare his name and address or gives a false name and address, he is guilty of an offence and liable on summary conviction to a fine not exceeding level 1 on the standard scale[3].

1 The fact that a meeting is held on a highway is not in itself sufficient to make the meeting unlawful (*Burden v Rigler* [1911] 1 KB 337, DC) nor is the fact that disorderly opposition from other persons occurs (*Beatty v Gillbanks* (1882) 9 QBD 308, DC); see also *Duncan v Jones* [1936] 1 KB 218, DC.
2 Public Meeting Act 1908 s 1 (1), (2) (amended by the Representation of the People Act 1949 s 175 (1), Sch 9; the Public Order Act 1963 s 1 (2); the Criminal Law Act 1977 ss 15 (1), 30, 31 (5), (6), (9), Sch 1; the Criminal Justice Act 1982 ss 38, 46). For the meaning of 'the standard scale' see para 808 post. The Public Meeting Act 1908 s 1 does not, however, apply as respects meetings to which the Representation of the People Act 1983 s 97 (see para 148 post) applies: Public Meeting Act 1908 s 1 (4) (added by the Representation of the People Act 1983 s 206, Sch 8 para 1).
3 Public Meeting Act 1908 s 1 (3) (added by the Public Order Act 1936 s 6; amended by the Criminal Law Act 1977 s 31 (5), (6), (9); the Criminal Justice Act 1982 ss 38, 46; the Police and Criminal Evidence Act 1984 ss 26 (1), 119 (2), Sch 7 Pt I). As to arrest without warrant see para 703 et seq post; and as to the right of the police to be present on private premises in which a public meeting is being held when the commission of any offence or a breach of the peace is anticipated see *Thomas v Sawkins* [1935] 2 KB 249, DC.

148. Disturbances at election meetings. A person who at a lawful public meeting[1] acts, or incites others to act, in a disorderly manner for the purpose of preventing the transaction of the business for which the meeting was called together is guilty of an illegal practice[2] and liable on summary conviction to a fine not exceeding level 5 on the standard scale[3].

If a constable reasonably suspects any person of committing such an offence, he may, if requested to do so by the chairman of the meeting, require that person to declare to him immediately his name and address; and, if that person refuses or fails so to declare his name and address or gives a false name and address, he is guilty of an offence and liable on summary conviction to a fine not exceeding level 1 on the standard scale[4].

1   For these purposes, 'lawful public meeting' means (1) a political meeting held in any constituency between the date of the issue of a writ for the return of a member of Parliament for the constituency and the date at which a return to the writ is made; (2) a meeting held with reference to a local government election in the electoral areas for that election in the period beginning with the last date on which notice of the election may be published in accordance with the rules made under the Representation of the People Act 1983 s 36 (see ELECTIONS) and ending with the day of the election: s 97 (2) (amended by the Representation of the People Act 1985 s 24, Sch 4 para 39).

The statutory provisions relating to disturbances at election meetings apply also to elections to the European Parliament: see the European Parliamentary Elections Regulations 1986, SI 1986/2209, reg 5 (1), Sch 1; the European Communities (Amendment) Act 1986 s 3 (1) (b). In such a case 'lawful public meeting' means a political meeting held in any European parliamentary constituency in connection with an election to the European Parliament between the last date on which notice of election may be published in accordance with the election rules and the date of the poll: European Parliamentary Elections Regulations Sch 1; European Communities (Amendment) Act 1986 s 3 (1) (b). As to elections to the European Parliament see ELECTIONS vol 15 (Reissue) para 303 et seq.

2   As to illegal practices see ELECTIONS vol 15 (Reissue) para 684 et seq.

3   Representation of the People Act 1983 ss 97 (1), 169 (amended by the Representation of the People Act 1985 ss 23, 28 (1), Sch 3 para 9, Sch 5). For the meaning of 'the standard scale' see para 808 post.

4   Representation of the People Act 1983 s 97 (3) (amended by the Police and Criminal Evidence Act 1984 ss 26 (1), 119 (2), Sch 7 Pt I). As to arrest without warrant see para 703 et seq post.

(viii) Riot, Violent Disorder, Affray etc

149. Riot. Where 12 or more persons who are present together use or threaten unlawful violence[1] for a common purpose[2] and the conduct of them, taken together, is such as would cause a person of reasonable firmness present at the scene[3] to fear for his personal safety, each of the persons using unlawful violence for the common purpose is guilty of riot and liable on conviction on indictment to imprisonment for a term not exceeding ten years or a fine, or to both[4]. A person is, however, guilty of riot only if he intends to use violence or is aware that his conduct may be violent[5].

1   It is immaterial whether or not the 12 or more use or threaten unlawful violence simultaneously: Public Order Act 1986 s 1(2). For these purposes, 'violence' means any violent conduct, so that (1) it includes violent conduct towards property as well as violent conduct towards persons; and (2) it is not restricted to conduct causing or intended to cause injury or damage but includes any other violent conduct (eg throwing at or towards a person a missile of a kind capable of causing injury which does not hit or falls short): s 8.

2   The common purpose may be inferred from conduct: ibid s 1 (3).

3   No person of reasonable firmness need actually be, or be likely to be, present at the scene: ibid s 1 (4).

4   Ibid s 1 (1), (6). The common law offences of riot and rout have been abolished: s 9 (1).

Riot may be committed in private as well as in public places: s 1 (5). No prosecution for an offence of riot or incitement to riot may be instituted except by or with the consent of the Director of Public Prosecutions: s 7 (1). As to the effect of this limitation see para 639 post.

For the purposes of the rules against charging more than one offence in the same count or information (see para 922 post), s 1 creates one offence: s 7 (2).

5   Ibid s 6 (1). Section 6 (1) does not affect the determination for the purposes of riot of the number of persons who use or threaten violence: s 6 (7).

For the purposes of s 6, a person whose awareness is impaired by intoxication is to be taken to be aware of that of which he would be aware if not intoxicated, unless he shows either that his intoxication was not self-induced or that it was caused solely by the taking or administration of a substance in the course of medical treatment: s 6 (5). 'Intoxication' means any intoxication, whether caused by drink, drugs or other means, or by a combination of means: s 6 (6). As to self-induced intoxication and involuntary intoxication see paras 28, 29 ante.

150. Violent disorder. Where three or more persons[1] who are present together use or threaten unlawful violence[2] and the conduct of them, taken together, is such as would cause a person of reasonable firmness present at the scene[3] to fear for his personal safety, each of the persons using or threatening unlawful violence is guilty of violent disorder and liable on conviction on indictment to imprisonment for a term not exceeding five years or a fine, or to both, or on summary conviction to imprisonment for a term not exceeding six months or a fine not exceeding the statutory maximum, or to both[4]. A person is, however, guilty of violent disorder only if he intends to use or threaten violence or is aware that his conduct may be violent or threaten violence[5].

1 No mention need be made of the three persons who have to be present in the indictment provided that (1) there is evidence satisfying the jury that there were three or more persons involved in the criminal behaviour, though not necessarily those named in the indictment; and (2) the defence is apprised of what it is the defence has to meet, the best way of achieving this being by putting it in the indictment: *R v Mahroof* (1989) 88 Cr App Rep 317, CA. Where the only persons against whom there is evidence of using or threatening violence are those named in the indictment, the jury should be specifically directed that, if it cannot be sure that three or more of the accused were using or threatening violence, it should acquit every accused of violent disorder, even if satisfied that one or more particular accused was or were unlawfully fighting: *R v Fleming, R v Robinson* (1989) Times, 13 February, CA. The jury should be warned specifically that, if any one of the three accused was acquitted, the other two must also be found not guilty, unless the jury is satisfied that some other person not charged was taking part in the violent disorder: *R v Worton* (1989) Times, 7 November, CA.

2 It is immaterial whether or not the three or more use or threaten unlawful violence simultaneously: Public Order Act 1986 s 2 (2). For the meaning of 'violence' see para 149 note 1 ante.

3 No person of reasonable firmness need actually be, or be likely to be, present at the scene: ibid s 2 (3).

4 Ibid s 2 (1), (5). For the meaning of 'the statutory maximum' see para 806 post. The common law offence of unlawful assembly has been abolished: s 9 (1). As to sentencing for violent disorder see *R v Hebron, R v Spencer* (1989) Times, 12 May, CA.
Violent disorder may be committed in private as well as in public places: Public Order Act 1986 s 2 (4). For the purposes of the rules against charging more than one offence in the same count or information (see para 922 post), s 2 creates one offence: s 7 (2). If on the trial on indictment of a person charged with violent disorder the jury finds him not guilty of the offence charged, the jury may, without prejudice to the Criminal Law Act 1967 s 6 (3) (see para 1029 post), find him guilty of an offence under the Public Order Act 1986 s 4 (see para 152 post): s 7 (3); and see *R v Mahroof* (1989) 88 Cr App Rep 317, CA; *R v Fleming, R v Robinson* (1989) Times, 13 February, CA. The Crown Court has the same powers and duties in relation to a person who is convicted of an offence under the Public Order Act 1986 s 4 by virtue of s 7 (3) as a magistrates' court would have on convicting him of the offence: s 7 (4).

5 Ibid s 6 (2). Section 6 (2) does not affect the determination of the number of persons who use or threaten violence: s 6 (7). As to the position where a person's awareness is impaired by intoxication see para 149 note 5 ante.

151. Affray. If a person uses or threatens[1] unlawful violence[2] towards another and his conduct[3] is such as would cause a person of reasonable firmness present at the scene[4] to fear for his personal safety, he is guilty of affray and liable on conviction on indictment to imprisonment for a term not exceeding three years or a fine, or to both, or on summary conviction to imprisonment for a term not exceeding six months or a fine not exceeding the statutory maximum, or to both[5]. A person is, however, guilty of affray only if he intends to use or threaten violence or is aware that his conduct may be violent or threaten violence[6].

1 For the purposes of the offence of affray, a threat cannot be made by the use of words alone: Public Order Act 1986 s 3 (3).

2 For these purposes, 'violence' means any violent conduct, so that it is not restricted to conduct causing or intended to cause injury or damage but includes any other violent conduct (for example, throwing at or towards a person a missile of a kind capable of causing injury which does not hit or falls short): ibid s 8.

3 For these purposes, where two or more persons use or threaten violence, it is the conduct of them taken together that must be considered: ibid s 3 (2).

4 No person of reasonable firmness need actually be, or be likely to be, present at the scene: ibid s 3 (4).

5 Ibid s 3 (1), (7). For the meaning of 'the statutory maximum' see para 806 post. The common law offence of affray has been abolished: s 9 (1).

  A constable may arrest without warrant anyone he reasonably suspects is committing affray: s 3 (6). As to powers of arrest without warrant see para 703 et seq post.

  Affray may be committed in private as well as in public places: s 3 (5). For the purposes of the rules against charging more than one offence in the same count or information (see para 922 post), s 3 creates one offence: s 7 (2). If on the trial on indictment of a person charged with affray the jury finds him not guilty of the offence charged, the jury may, without prejudice to the Criminal Law Act 1967 s 6 (3) (see para 1029 post), find him guilty of an offence under the Public Order Act 1986 s 4 (see para 152 post): s 7 (3). The Crown Court has the same powers and duties in relation to a person who is convicted of an offence under s 4 by virtue of s 7 (3) as a magistrates' court would have on convicting him of the offence: s 7 (4).

6 Ibid s 6 (2). As to the position where a person's awareness is impaired by intoxication see para 149 note 5 ante.

152. Fear or provocation of violence. If a person:

(1) uses towards another person threatening, abusive or insulting[1] words or behaviour; or

(2) distributes or displays to another person any writing[2], sign or other visible representation which is threatening, abusive or insulting,

with intent to cause that person to believe that immediate unlawful violence will be used against him or another by any person, or to provoke the immediate use of unlawful violence by that person or another, or whereby that person is likely to believe that such violence will be used or it is likely[3] that such violence will be provoked, he is guilty of an offence and liable on summary conviction to imprisonment for a term not exceeding six months or a fine not exceeding level 5 on the standard scale, or to both[4]. A person is, however, guilty of such an offence only if he intends his words or behaviour, or the writing, sign or other visible representation, to be threatening, abusive or insulting, or is aware that it may be threatening, abusive or insulting[5].

1 The words 'threatening, abusive or insulting' were contained in the Public Order Act 1936 s 5 (repealed). It would seem that the decisions on the meaning of that phrase will continue to apply in the Public Order Act 1986 s 4. 'Insulting' is to be given its ordinary meaning and the question whether words or behaviour are insulting is one of fact; this approach applies also to the other words in the phrase: *Brutus v Cozens* [1973] AC 854, 56 Cr App Rep 799, HL. For other decisions on the meaning of that phrase see *Bryan v Robinson* [1960] 2 All ER 173, [1960] 1 WLR 506, DC (words or behaviour might be annoying without being insulting (decided under the Metropolitan Police Act 1839 s 54 para 13 (repealed))); *R v Ambrose* (1973) 57 Cr App Rep 538, CA (words must be insulting, not merely rude or offensive); *Simcock v Rhodes* (1977) 66 Cr App Rep 192, DC (both decided under the Public Order Act 1936 s 5 (repealed). Behaviour which is objectionable may be regarded by another person as insulting by suggesting that he was somebody who would find such conduct in public acceptable: *Masterson v Holden* [1986] 3 All ER 39, 83 Cr App Rep 302, DC (two homosexual men kissing and cuddling at bus stop; convictions upheld (decided under the Metropolitan Police Act 1839 s 54 (13) (repealed))); see also *Parkin v Norman, Valentine v Lilley* [1983] QB 92, [1982] 2 All ER 503, DC. Such decisions are, however, merely illustrative, being decisions on the facts of particular cases. The only principle of law applicable is that enunciated in *Brutus v Cozens* supra. 'It would be unwise to attempt to lay down any positive rules for the recognition of insulting behaviour as such, since the circumstances in which the application of the rules would be called for are almost infinitely variable; the most that can be done is to lay down limits, as was done in *Bryan v Robinson* supra in order to ensure that the statute [the Public Order Act 1936 s 5 (repealed)] is not interpreted more widely than its terms will bear': *Brutus v Cozens* supra at 866, 867 and at 812 per Lord Kilbrandon.

2 For the meaning of 'writing' see para 142 note 2 ante.

3 In *Parkin v Norman, Valentine v Lilley* [1983] QB 92, [1982] 2 All ER 583, DC (decided under the Public Order Act 1936 s 5 (repealed)) the distinction between the words 'likely' and 'liable' was noted.
4 Public Order Act 1986 s 4 (1), (4). For the meaning of 'the standard scale' see para 808 post. A constable may arrest without warrant anyone he reasonably suspects is committing such an offence: s 4 (3). As to powers of arrest without warrant see para 703 et seq post; and as to the common law power of arrest to deal with or prevent a breach of the peace see para 709 post.
  The words 'uses towards' presuppose present physical presence so that a person must perceive with his own senses the threatening words or behaviour; thus, an offence is not committed under s 4 when the threat is made by a person in a dwelling against another person outside that dwelling who has not heard the threat and learned of it only through a third party not under the control or direction of the maker of the threat: *Atkin v DPP* (1989) 89 Cr App Rep 199, DC.
  An offence under the Public Order Act 1986 s 4 may be committed in a public or a private place, except that no offence is committed where the words or behaviour are used, or the writing, sign or other visible representation is distributed or displayed, by a person inside a dwelling and the other person is also inside that or another dwelling: s 4 (2). 'Dwelling' means any structure or part of a structure occupied as a person's home or as other living accommodation, whether the occupation is separate or shared with others, but does not include any part not so occupied; and for this purpose 'structure' includes a tent, caravan, vehicle, vessel or other temporary or movable structure: s 8.
  For the purposes of the rules against charging more than one offence in the same count or information (see para 922 post), s 4 creates one offence: s 7 (2). As to the wording of the information see *Loade v DPP* [1990] 1 All ER 36, [1989] 3 WLR 1281, DC obiter per Neill LJ.
5 Public Order Act 1986 s 6 (3). As to the position where a person's awareness is impaired by intoxication see para 149 note 5 ante; and as to proof of identification and participation under s 4 see *Allan v Ireland* (1984) 79 Cr App Rep 206, DC (decided under the Public Order Act 1936 s 5 (repealed)).

153. Harassment, alarm or distress. If a person:
  (1) uses threatening, abusive or insulting[1] words or behaviour, or disorderly behaviour; or
  (2) displays any writing[2], sign or other visible representation which is threatening, abusive or insulting,
within the hearing or sight of a person likely to be caused harassment, alarm or distress[3] thereby, he is guilty of an offence and liable on summary conviction to a fine not exceeding level 3 on the standard scale[4]. A person is, however, guilty of such an offence only if he intends his words or behaviour, or the writing, sign or other visible representation, to be threatening, abusive or insulting, or is aware that it may be threatening, abusive or insulting or, as the case may be, he intends his behaviour to be or is aware that it may be disorderly[5].
  It is a defence for the accused to prove that:
  (a) he had no reason to believe that there was any person within hearing or sight who was likely to be caused harassment, alarm or distress; or
  (b) he was inside a dwelling and had no reason to believe that the words or behaviour used, or the writing, sign or other visible representation, would be heard or seen by a person outside that or any other dwelling; or
  (c) his conduct was reasonable[6].

1 For the meaning of 'threatening, abusive or insulting' see para 152 note 1 ante.
2 For the meaning of 'writing' see para 142 note 2 ante.
3 A police officer can be a person who is likely to be caused harassment, alarm or distress. However, that is not to say that every police officer is to be assumed to be a person who is caused harassment, alarm or distress: *DPP v Orum* [1988] 3 All ER 449, 88 Cr App Rep 261, DC (only persons present were accused, girlfriend with whom accused was having an argument and the two police constables). It is not necessary that the person alarmed was concerned at physical danger to himself; it might be alarm about the safety of an unconnected third party: *Lodge v DPP* (1988) Times, 26 October, DC.

4 Public Order Act 1986 s 5 (1), (6). For the meaning of 'the standard scale' see para 808 post. Conduct under s 5 does not have to be directed against another person: *R v Ball* [1989] Crim LR 579, CA.

A constable may arrest a person without warrant if (1) he engages in offensive conduct which the constable warns him to stop; and (2) he engages in further offensive conduct immediately or shortly after the warning: Public Order Act 1986 s 5 (4). For these purposes, 'offensive conduct' means conduct the constable reasonably suspects to constitute an offence under s 5; and the conduct mentioned in head (1) supra and the further conduct need not be of the same nature: s 5 (5). If the constable does not reasonably suspect that such an offence has been committed, he has no such power of arrest: *DPP v Orum* [1988] 3 All ER 449, 88 Cr App Rep 261, DC. As to powers of arrest without warrant see para 703 et seq post; and as to the common law power to deal with or prevent a breach of the peace see para 709 post. Such an offence may be committed in a public or a private place, except that no offence is committed where the words or behaviour are used, or the writing, sign or visible representation is displayed, by a person inside a dwelling and the other person is also inside that or another dwelling: Public Order Act 1986 s 5 (2). For the meaning of 'dwelling' see para 152 note 4 ante. For the purpose of the rules against charging more than one offence in the same count or information (see para 922 post), s 5 creates one offence: s 7 (2).

5 Ibid s 6 (4). As to the position where a person's awareness is impaired by intoxication see para 149 note 5 ante.

6 Ibid s 5 (3). The deposit of a letter containing threatening, abusive or insulting words through a letter-box is not an offence under s 5 (1) (a) or (b) because it takes place within a dwelling; but it would be an offence under the Malicious Communications Act 1988 s 1 (1) (see para 375 post): *Chappell v DPP* (1988) 89 Cr App Rep 82, DC.

(ix) Racial Hatred

154. Use of words or behaviour or display of written material. A person[1] who uses threatening, abusive or insulting[2] words or behaviour[3], or displays any written material[4] which is threatening, abusive or insulting, is guilty of an offence if:

(1) he intends thereby to stir up racial hatred[5]; or

(2) having regard to all the circumstances racial hatred is likely to be stirred up thereby,

and is liable on conviction on indictment to imprisonment for a term not exceeding two years or a fine, or to both, or on summary conviction to imprisonment for a term not exceeding six months or a fine not exceeding the statutory maximum, or to both[6].

Such an offence may be committed in a public or a private place, except that no offence is committed where the words or behaviour are used, or the written material is displayed, by a person inside a dwelling[7] and are not heard or seen except by other persons in that or another dwelling[8]. In proceedings for such an offence it is a defence for the accused to prove that he was inside a dwelling and had no reason to believe that the words or behaviour used, or the written material displayed, would be heard or seen by a person outside that or any other dwelling[9].

A person who is not shown to have intended to stir up racial hatred is not guilty of such an offence if he did not intend his words or behaviour, or the written material, to be, and was not aware that it might be, threatening, abusive or insulting[10].

1 Where a body corporate is guilty of such an offence under the Public Order Act 1986 Pt III (ss 17–29) and it is shown that the offence was committed with the consent or connivance of a director, manager, secretary or other similar officer of the body, or a person purporting to act in any such capacity, he as well as the body corporate is guilty of the offence and liable to be proceeded against and punished accordingly: Public Order Act 1986 s 28 (1). Where the affairs of a body corporate are managed by its members, s 28 (1) applies in relation to the acts and defaults of a member in connection with his functions of management as it applies to a director: s 28 (2).

2 For the meaning of 'threatening, abusive and insulting' see para 152 note 1 ante.

3 The Public Order Act 1986 s 18 does not apply to words or behaviour used, or written material displayed, solely for the purpose of being included in a programme broadcast or included in a cable programme service: s 18 (6). As to cable programme services see para 158 post.

4 For these purposes, 'written material' includes any sign or other visible representation: ibid s 29.

5 For these purposes, 'racial hatred' means hatred against a group of persons in Great Britain defined by reference to colour, race, nationality (including citizenship) or ethnic or national origins: ibid ss 17, 29. For the meaning of 'ethnic origin' see *Mandla v Dowell Lee* [1983] 2 AC 548, [1983] 1 All ER 1062, HL (decided under the Race Relations Act 1976 ss 1 (1) (b), 17 (a): see BRITISH NATIONALITY AND ALIENAGE).

6 Public Order Act 1986 ss 18 (1), 27 (3). For the meaning of 'the statutory maximum' see para 806 post. No proceedings for such an offence may be instituted in England and Wales except by or with the consent of the Attorney General: s 27 (1). As to the effect of this limitation see para 639 post. For the purposes of the rules in England and Wales against charging more than one offence in the same count or information (see para 922 post), s 18 creates one offence: s 27 (2). A constable may arrest without warrant anyone he reasonably suspects is committing such an offence: s 18 (3). As to arrest without warrant see para 703 et seq post.

    Nothing in Pt III (ss 17–29) applies to a fair and accurate report of proceedings in Parliament (s 26 (1)); nor does anything in Pt III (ss 17–29) apply to a fair and accurate report of proceedings publicly heard before a court or tribunal exercising judicial authority where the report is published contemporaneously with the proceedings or, if it is not reasonably practicable or would be unlawful to publish a report of them contemporaneously, as soon as publication is reasonably practicable and lawful (s 26 (2)).

    As to the court's power to order forfeiture see para 160 post.

7 For these purposes, 'dwelling' means any structure or part of a structure occupied as a person's home or other living accommodation, whether the occupation is separate or shared with others, but does not include any part not so occupied; and for this purpose, 'structure' includes a tent, caravan, vehicle, vessel or other temporary or movable structure: ibid s 29.

8 Ibid s 18 (2).

9 Ibid s 18 (4).

10 Ibid s 18 (5).

155. Publishing or distributing written material.

A person[1] who publishes or distributes[2] written material[3] which is threatening, abusive or insulting[4] is guilty of an offence if:

(1) he intends thereby to stir up racial hatred[5]; or

(2) having regard to all the circumstances racial hatred is likely to be stirred up thereby,

and is liable on conviction on indictment to imprisonment for a term not exceeding two years or a fine, or to both, or on summary conviction to imprisonment for a term not exceeding six months or a fine not exceeding the statutory maximum, or to both[6].

    In proceedings for such an offence it is a defence for an accused who is not shown to have intended to stir up racial hatred to prove that he was not aware of the content of the material and did not suspect, and had no reason to suspect, that it was threatening, abusive or insulting[7].

1 As to offences by corporations see para 154 note 1 ante.

2 For these purposes, references to the publication or distribution of written material are to its publication or distribution to the public or a section of the public: Public Order Act 1986 s 19 (3). In Pt III (ss 17–29) 'distribute', and related expressions, are to be construed in accordance with s 19 (3) (written material) and s 21 (2) (recordings: see para 157 note 2 post); and 'publish', and related expressions, in relation to written material, are to be construed in accordance with s 19 (3): s 29.

3 For the meaning of 'written material' see para 154 note 4 ante.

4 For the meaning of 'threatening, abusive or insulting' see para 152 note 1 ante.

5 For the meaning of 'racial hatred' see para 154 note 5 ante.

6 Public Order Act 1986 ss 19 (1), 27 (3). For the meaning of 'the statutory maximum' see para 806 post. No proceedings for such an offence in England and Wales may be instituted except by or with

the consent of the Attorney General: s 27 (1). As to the effect of this limitation see para 639 post. For the purposes of the rules against charging more than one offence in the same count or information (see para 922 post), s 19 creates one offence: s 27 (2).

As to the savings for reports of parliamentary or judicial proceedings see para 154 note 6 ante; and as to the court's power to order forfeiture see para 160 post.

7 Ibid s 19 (2).

156. Public performance of play. If a public performance[1] of a play[2] is given which involves the use of threatening, abusive or insulting[3] words or behaviour, any person[4] who presents[5] or directs[6] the performance is guilty of an offence[7] if:

(1) he intends thereby to stir up racial hatred[8]; or

(2) having regard to all the circumstances, and, in particular, taking the performance as a whole, racial hatred is likely to be stirred up thereby,

and is liable on conviction on indictment to imprisonment for a term not exceeding two years or a fine, or to both, or on summary conviction to imprisonment for a term not exceeding six months or a fine not exceeding the statutory maximum, or to both[9].

If a person presenting or directing the performance is not shown to have intended to stir up racial hatred, it is a defence for him to prove:

(a) that he did not know and had no reason to suspect that the performance would involve the use of the offending words or behaviour; or

(b) that he did not know and had no reason to suspect that the offending words or behaviour were threatening, abusive or insulting; or

(c) that he did not know and had no reason to suspect that the circumstances in which the performance would be given would be such that racial hatred would be likely to be stirred up[10].

1 For these purposes, 'public performance' includes any performance in a public place within the meaning of the Public Order Act 1936 (see para 100 note 2 ante) and any performance which the public or any section thereof is permitted to attend, whether on payment or otherwise: Theatres Act 1968 s 18 (1) (applied by the Public Order Act 1986 s 20 (5)).

The Public Order Act 1986 s 20 does not, however, apply to a performance given solely or primarily for one of the following purposes: (1) rehearsal; (2) making a recording of the performance; or (3) enabling the performance to be broadcast or included in a cable programme service; but, if it is proved that the performance was attended by persons other than those directly concerned with the giving of the performance or the doing in relation to it of the things mentioned in heads (2) or (3) supra, the performance is, unless the contrary is shown, to be taken not to have been given solely for the purposes mentioned supra: s 20 (3). As to cable programme services see para 158 post.

2 For these purposes, 'play' means (1) any dramatic piece, whether involving improvisation or not, which is given wholly or in part by one or more persons actually present and performing and in which the whole or a major proportion of what is done by the person or persons performing, whether by way of speech, singing or acting, involves the playing of a role; and (2) any ballet given wholly or in part by one or more persons actually present and performing, whether or not it falls within head (1) supra: Theatres Act 1968 s 18 (1) (applied by the Public Order Act 1986 s 20 (5)).

3 For the meaning of 'threatening, abusive or insulting' see para 152 note 1 ante.

4 As to offences by corporations see para 154 note 1 ante.

5 For these purposes, a person is not to be treated as presenting a performance of a play by reason only of his taking part in it as a performer: Public Order Act 1986 s 20 (4) (a).

6 For these purposes, a person is to be taken to have directed a performance of a play given under his direction notwithstanding that he was not present during the performance: ibid s 20 (4) (c). A person taking part as a performer in a performance directed by another is to be treated as a person who directed the performance if without reasonable excuse he performs otherwise than in accordance with that person's direction: s 20 (4) (b).

7 A person is not to be treated as aiding or abetting the commission of such an offence by reason only of his taking part in a performance as a performer: ibid s 20 (4).

8 For the meaning of 'racial hatred' see para 154 note 5 ante.

9 Public Order Act 1986 ss 20 (1), 27 (3). For the meaning of 'the statutory maximum' see para 806 post. The Theatres Act 1968 s 9 (script as evidence of what was performed: see THEATRES vol 45 para 959), s 10 (power to make copies of script: see THEATRES vol 45 para 960), s 15 (powers of entry and inspection: see THEATRES vol 45 para 961) apply in relation to an offence under the Public Order Act 1986 s 20 as they apply to an offence under the Theatres Act 1968 s 2 (see THEATRES vol 45 para 954): Public Order Act 1986 s 20 (6).

     No proceedings for such an offence may be instituted except by or with the consent of the Attorney General: s 27 (1). As to the effect of this limitation see para 639 post. For the purposes of the rules against charging more than one offence in the same count or information (see para 922 post), s 20 creates one offence: s 27 (2). As to the savings for reports of parliamentary or judicial proceedings see para 154 note 6 ante.

10 Ibid s 20 (2).

157. Distributing, showing or playing a recording.
A person[1] who distributes, or shows or plays[2], a recording[3] of visual images or sounds which are threatening, abusive or insulting[4] is guilty of an offence if:

(1)   he intends thereby to stir up racial hatred[5]; or

(2)   having regard to all the circumstances racial hatred is likely to be stirred up thereby,

and is liable on conviction on indictment to imprisonment for a term not exceeding two years or a fine, or to both, or on summary conviction to imprisonment for a term not exceeding six months or a fine not exceeding the statutory maximum, or to both[6].

In proceedings for such an offence it is a defence for an accused who is not shown to have intended to stir up racial hatred to prove that he was not aware of the content of the recording and did not suspect, and had no reason to suspect, that it was threatening, abusive or insulting[7].

1 As to offences by corporations see para 154 note 1 ante.
2 For these purposes, references to the distribution, showing or playing of a recording are to its distribution, showing or playing to the public or a section of the public: Public Order Act 1986 ss 21 (2), 29.
3 For these purposes, 'recording' means any record from which visual images or sounds may, by any means, be reproduced: ibid s 21 (2). 'Recording' has the meaning given by s 21 (2) and 'play' and 'show', and related expressions, in relation to a recording, are to be construed in accordance with that provision: s 29. However, s 21 does not apply to the showing or playing of a recording for the purposes of enabling the recording to be broadcast or included in a cable programme service: s 21 (4). As to cable programme services see para 158 post.
4 For the meaning of 'threatening, abusive or insulting' see para 152 note 1 ante.
5 For the meaning of 'racial hatred' see para 154 note 5 ante.
6 Public Order Act 1986 ss 21 (1), 27 (3). For the meaning of 'the statutory maximum' see para 806 post. No proceedings for such an offence may be instituted except by or with the consent of the Attorney General: s 27 (1). As to the effect of this limitation see para 639 post. For the purposes of the rules against charging more than one offence in the same count or information (see para 922 post), s 21 creates one offence: s 27 (2).
     As to the savings for reports of parliamentary or judicial proceedings see para 154 note 6 ante; and as to the court's power to order forfeiture see para 160 post.
7 Ibid s 21 (3).

158. Broadcasting or including programme in cable programme service.
If a programme involving threatening, abusive or insulting[1] visual images or sounds is broadcast[2], or included in a cable programme service[3], each of the persons[4] providing the broadcasting or cable programme service, any person by whom the programme[5] is produced or directed, and any person by whom offending words or behaviour are used, is guilty of an offence if:

(1) he intends to stir up racial hatred[6]; or

(2) having regard to all the circumstances racial hatred is likely to be stirred up thereby,

and is liable on conviction on indictment to imprisonment for a term not exceeding two years or a fine, or to both, or on summary conviction to imprisonment for a term not exceeding six months or a fine not exceeding the statutory maximum, or to both[7].

If the person providing the service, or a person by whom the programme was produced or directed is not shown to have intended to stir up racial hatred, it is a defence for him to prove that:

(a) he did not know and had no reason to suspect that the programme would involve the offending material; and

(b) having regard to the circumstances in which the programme was broadcast, or included in a cable programme service, it was not reasonably practicable for him to secure the removal of the material[8].

It is a defence for a person by whom the programme was produced or directed who is not shown to have intended to stir up racial hatred to prove that he did not know and had no reason to suspect:

(i) that the programme would be broadcast or included in a cable programme service; or

(ii) that the circumstances in which the programme would be broadcast or so included would be such that racial hatred would be likely to be stirred up[9].

It is a defence for a person by whom offending words or behaviour were used and who is not shown to have intended to stir up racial hatred to prove that he did not know and had no reason to suspect:

(A) that a programme involving the use of offending material would be broadcast or included in a cable programme service; or

(B) that the circumstances in which a programme involving the use of the offending material would be broadcast, or so included, or in which a programme broadcast or so included would involve the use of the offending material, would be such that racial hatred would be likely to be stirred up[10].

A person who is not shown to have intended to stir up racial hatred is not guilty of such an offence if he did not know, and had no reason to suspect, that the offending material was threatening, abusive or insulting[11].

1 For the meaning of 'threatening, abusive or insulting' see para 152 note 1 ante.

2 For these purposes, 'broadcast' means broadcast by wireless telegraphy (within the meaning of the Wireless Telegraphy Act 1949: see TELECOMMUNICATIONS vol 45 para 503 et seq) for general reception, whether by way of sound broadcasting or television: Public Order Act 1986 s 29. However, s 22 does not apply to the broadcasting of a programme by the British Broadcasting Corporation or the Independent Broadcasting Authority: s 22 (7) (a).

3 For these purposes, 'cable programme service' has the same meaning as in the Cable and Broadcasting Act 1984 s 2 (see para 371 note 2 post): Public Order Act 1986 s 29. Section 22 does not apply to the inclusion of a programme in a cable programme service by the reception and immediate retransmission of a broadcast by either the British Broadcasting Corporation or the Independent Broadcasting Authority: s 22 (7) (b).

4 As to offences by corporations see para 154 note 1 ante.

5 For these purposes, 'programme' means any item which is broadcast or included in a cable programme service: Public Order Act 1986 s 29.

6 For the meaning of 'racial hatred' see para 154 note 5 ante.

7 Public Order Act 1986 ss 22 (1), (2), 27 (3). For the meaning of 'the statutory maximum' see para 806 post. The Cable and Broadcasting Act 1984 ss 33–35 (scripts as evidence, power to make copies of scripts and records, availability of visual and sound records: see TELECOMMUNICATIONS vol 45 para 723) apply to an offence under the Public Order Act 1986 s 22 as they apply to a 'relevant

offence' as defined in the Cable and Broadcasting Act 1984 s 33 (2) (see TELECOMMUNICATIONS vol 45 para 723); and ss 33, 34 apply to an offence under the Public Order Act 1986 s 22 in connection with the broadcasting of a programme as they apply to an offence in connection with the inclusion of a programme in a cable programme service: s 22 (8).

No proceedings for such an offence may be instituted except by or with the consent of the Attorney General: s 27 (1). As to the effect of this limitation see para 639 post. For the purposes of the rules against charging more than one offence in the same count or information (see para 922 post), s 22 creates one offence: s 27 (2).

As to the savings for reports of parliamentary or judicial proceedings see para 154 note 6 ante.
8   Ibid s 22 (3).
9   Ibid s 22 (4).
10 Ibid s 22 (5).
11 Ibid s 22 (6).

159. Possession of racially inflammatory material. A person[1] who has in his possession written material[2] which is threatening, abusive or insulting[3], or a recording[4] of visual images or sounds which are threatening, abusive or insulting, with a view to:

(1) in the case of written material, its being displayed, published[5], distributed[6], broadcast[7] or included in a cable programme service[8], whether by himself or another; or

(2) in the case of a recording, its being distributed or included in a cable programme service, whether by himself or another,

is guilty of an offence if he intends racial hatred[9] to be stirred up thereby or, having regard to all the circumstances, racial hatred is likely to be stirred up thereby, and is liable on conviction on indictment to imprisonment for a term not exceeding two years or a fine, or to both, or on summary conviction to imprisonment for a term not exceeding six months or a fine not exceeding the statutory maximum, or to both[10].

In proceedings for such an offence it is a defence for an accused who is not shown to have intended to stir up racial hatred to prove that he was not aware of the content of the written material or recording and did not suspect, and had no reason to suspect, that it was threatening, abusive or insulting[11].

If in England and Wales a justice of the peace is satisfied by information on oath laid by a constable that there are reasonable grounds for suspecting that a person has possession of such written material or recording, the justice may issue a warrant under his hand authorising any constable to enter and search[12] the premises[13] where it is suspected the material or recording is situated[14].

1   As to offences by corporations see para 154 note 1 ante.
2   For the meaning of 'written material' see para 154 note 4 ante.
3   For the meaning of 'threatening, abusive or insulting' see para 152 note 1 ante.
4   For the meaning of 'recording' see para 157 note 3 ante.
5   For the meaning of 'publish' see para 155 note 2 ante.
6   For the meaning of 'distribute' see para 155 note 2 ante.
7   For the meaning of 'broadcast' see para 158 note 2 ante.
8   For the meaning of 'cable programme service' see para 158 note 3 ante.
9   For the meaning of 'racial hatred' see para 154 note 5 ante.
10 Public Order Act 1986 ss 23 (1), 27 (3). For the meaning of 'the statutory maximum' see para 806 post. For the purposes of s 23, regard must be had to such display, publication, distribution, showing, playing, broadcasting or inclusion in a cable programme service as the accused has, or it may reasonably be inferred that he has, in view: s 23 (2). Section 23 does not apply to the possession of written material or a recording by or on behalf of the British Broadcasting Corporation or the Independent Broadcasting Authority or with a view to its being broadcast by either of those authorities: s 23 (4).

No proceedings for such an offence may be instituted except by or with the consent of the Attorney General: s 27 (1). As to the effect of this limitation see para 639 post. For the purpose of the rules against charging more than one offence in the same count or information (see para 922 post), s 23 creates one offence: s 27 (2).

As to the savings for reports of parliamentary or judicial proceedings see para 154 note 6 ante; and as to the court's power to order forfeiture see para 160 post.

11 Ibid s 23 (3).

12 A constable entering and searching premises in pursuance of a warrant issued under ibid s 24 may use reasonable force if necessary: s 24 (3). As to powers of entry, search and seizure see para 668 et seq ante.

13 For these purposes, 'premises' means any place and, in particular, includes (1) any vehicle, vessel, aircraft or hovercraft; (2) any offshore installation as defined in the Mineral Workings (Offshore Installations) Act 1971 s 1 (3) (b) (see PETROLEUM PRODUCTION vol 35 para 1244); and (3) any tent or movable structure: Public Order Act 1986 s 24 (4).

14 Ibid s 24 (1).

160. Power to order forfeiture. A court by or before which a person is convicted of:

(1) an offence relating to the display of written material[1]; or

(2) an offence of publishing or distributing written material[2], distributing, showing or playing a recording[3] or possessing racially imflammatory material[4],

must order to be forfeited any written material[5] or recordings[6] produced to the court and shown to its satisfaction to be written material or a recording to which the offence relates[7].

An order so made in proceedings in England and Wales does not take effect until the expiry of the ordinary time within which an appeal may be instituted or, where an appeal is duly instituted, until it is finally decided or abandoned[8].

1 Ie under the Public Order Act 1986 s 18: see para 154 ante.
2 Ie under ibid s 19: see para 155 ante.
3 Ie under ibid s 21: see para 157 ante.
4 Ie under ibid s 23: see para 159 ante.
5 For the meaning of 'written material' see para 154 note 4 ante.
6 For the meaning of 'recording' see para 157 note 2 ante.
7 Public Order Act 1986 s 25 (1).
8 Ibid s 25 (2) (a). For these purposes, an application for a case stated or for leave to appeal is to be treated as the institution of an appeal; and, where a decision on appeal is subject to a further appeal, the appeal is not finally determined until the expiry of the ordinary time within which a further appeal may be instituted or, where a further appeal is duly instituted, until the further appeal is finally decided or abandoned: s 25 (3). As to appeals generally see para 1352 et seq post.

(x) Criminal Entry and Trespass

161. Violence for securing entry. Any person who, without lawful authority[1], uses or threatens violence[2] for the purpose of securing entry[3] into any premises[4] for himself or for any other person is guilty of an offence, provided that (1) there is someone present on those premises at the time who is opposed to the entry which the violence is intended to secure; and (2) the person using or threatening the violence knows that this is the case[5]. A person guilty of such an offence is liable on summary conviction to imprisonment for a term not exceeding six months or a fine not exceeding level 5 on the standard scale, or to both[6].

In any proceedings for such an offence it is a defence for the accused to prove that (a) at the time of the alleged offence he or any other person on whose behalf he was acting was a displaced residential occupier[7] of the premises in question; or (b) that part of the premises in question constitutes premises of which he or any other person on whose behalf he was acting was a displaced residential occupier and that the part of the premises to which he was seeking to secure entry constitutes an access[8] of which he or, as the case may be, that other person is also a displaced residential occupier[9].

1 For these purposes, the fact that a person has any interest in or right to possession or occupation of any premises does not constitute lawful authority for the use or threat of violence by him or anyone else for the purpose of securing his entry into those premises: Criminal Law Act 1977 s 6 (2).
2 For these purposes, it is immaterial whether the violence in question is directed against the person or against property: ibid s 6 (4) (a).
3 For these purposes, it is immaterial whether the entry which the violence is intended to secure is for the purpose of acquiring possession of the premises in question or for any other purpose: ibid s 6 (4) (b).
4 For these purposes, 'premises' means any building, any part of a building under separate occupation, any land ancillary to a building, the site comprising any building or buildings together with any land ancillary thereto: ibid s 12 (1) (a).
    References to a building apply also to any structure other than a movable one, and to any movable structure, vehicle or vessel designed or adapted for use for residential purposes; and for these purposes (1) part of a building is under separate occupation if anyone is in occupation or entitled to occupation of that part as distinct from the whole; and (2) land is ancillary to a building if it is adjacent to it and used, or intended for use, in connection with the occupation of that building or any part of it: s 12 (2).
5 Ibid s 6 (1).
6 Ibid s 6 (5) (amended by the Criminal Justice Act 1982 ss 38, 46). For the meaning of 'the standard scale' see para 808 post. A constable in uniform may arrest without warrant anyone who is, or whom he, with reasonable cause, suspects to be, guilty of such an offence: Criminal Law Act 1977 s 6 (6). This power of arrest was preserved by the Police and Criminal Evidence Act 1984 s 26 (2), Sch 2: see para 708 post.
7 For these purposes, any person who was occupying any premises as a residence immediately before being excluded from occupation by anyone who entered those premises, or any access to those premises, as a trespasser is a displaced residential occupier of the premises so long as he continues to be excluded from occupation of the premises by the original trespasser or by any subsequent trespasser; and a person who is such a displaced residential occupier of any premises is to be regarded as a displaced residential occupier also of any access to those premises: Criminal Law Act 1977 ss 6 (7), 12 (3), (5). However, a person who was himself occupying the premises in question as a trespasser immediately before being excluded from occupation is not a displaced residential occupier of the premises in question: ss 6 (7), 12 (4).
8 For these purposes, 'access' means, in relation to any premises, any part of any site or building within which those premises are situated which constitutes an ordinary means of access to those premises, whether or not that is its sole or primary use: ibid s 12 (1) (b).
9 Ibid s 6 (3).

162. Adverse occupation of residential premises. Any person who is on any premises[1] as a trespasser[2] after having entered as such is guilty of an offence if he fails to leave those premises on being required to do so by or on behalf of (1) a displaced residential occupier[3] of the premises; or (2) an individual who is a protected intending occupier[4] of the premises[5]. A person guilty of such an offence is liable on summary conviction to imprisonment for a term not exceeding six months or a fine not exceeding level 5 on the standard scale, or to both[6].

In any proceedings for such an offence it is a defence for the accused to prove:

(a) that he believed that the person requiring him to leave the premises was not a displaced residential occupier or protected intending occupier of the premises or a person acting on behalf of such an occupier[7]; or

(b) that the premises in question are or form part of premises used mainly for non-residential purposes and that he was not on any part of the premises used wholly or mainly for residential purposes[8].

In any such proceedings where the accused was requested to leave the premises by a person claiming to be or to act on behalf of a protected intending occupier of the premises it is a defence for the accused to prove that, although asked to do so by the accused at the time the accused was requested to leave, that person failed at that time to produce to the accused a written statement[9] or certificate[10].

1 For the meaning of 'premises' see para 161 note 4 ante. Any reference in the Criminal Law Act 1977 s 7 (1), (5)–(8) to any premises includes a reference to any access to them, whether or not any such access itself constitutes premises; and a person who is a protected intending occupier of any premises is to be regarded for these purposes as a protected intending occupier also of any access to those premises: s 7 (9). For the meaning of 'access' see para 161 note 8 ante.

2 Anyone who enters or is on or in occupation of any premises by virtue of (1) any title derived from a trespasser; or (2) any licence or consent given by a trespasser or by a person deriving title from a trespasser, is himself to be treated as a trespasser, without prejudice to whether or not he would be a trespasser apart from this provision; and reference to a person's entering or being on or occupying any premises as a trespasser are to be construed accordingly: ibid s 12 (6).

   Anyone who is on any premises as a trespasser does not cease to be a trespasser for these purposes by virtue of being allowed time to leave the premises; nor does anyone cease to be a displaced residential occupier of any premises by virtue of any such allowance of time to a trespasser: s 12 (7).

3 For the meaning of 'displaced residential occupier' see para 161 note 7 ante.

4 For these purposes, an individual is a protected intending occupier of any premises at any time if at that time:

   (1) he has in those premises a freehold interest or a leasehold interest with not less than 21 years still to run and he acquired that interest as a purchaser for money or money's worth; and

   (2) he requires the premises for his own occupation as a residence; and

   (3) he is excluded from occupation of the premises by a person who entered them, or any access to them, as a trespasser; and

   (4) he or a person acting on his behalf holds a written statement (a) which specifies his interest in the premises; and (b) which states that he requires the premises for occupation as a residence for himself; and (c) the prescribed requirements are fulfilled, that is to say, (i) that the statement is signed by the person whose interest is specified in it in the presence of a justice of the peace or commissioner for oaths; and (ii) that the justice of the peace or commissioner for oaths has subscribed his name as a witness to the signature;

   and a person is guilty of an offence and liable on summary conviction to imprisonment for a term not exceeding six months or a fine not exceeding level 5 on the standard scale, or to both, if he makes a statement for the purposes of head (4) supra which he knows to be false in a material particular or if he recklessly makes such a statement which is false in a material particular: ibid s 7 (2), (3), (10) (amended by the Criminal Justice Act 1982 ss 38, 46). For the meaning of 'the standard scale' see para 808 post.

   For these purposes, an individual is also a protected intending occupier of any premises at any time if at that time:

   (a) he has been authorised to occupy the premises as a residence by an authority to which these provisions apply; and;

   (b) he is excluded from occupation of the premises by a person who entered the premises, or any access to them, as a trespasser; and

   (c) there has been issued to him by or on behalf of the authority referred to in head (a) supra a certificate stating that the authority is one to which these provisions apply, being of a description specified in the certificate, and that he has been authorised by the authority to occupy the premises concerned as a residence;

   and the provisions in heads (a)–(c) supra apply to any body mentioned in the Rent Act 1977 s 14 (landlord's interest belonging to local authority etc: see LANDLORD AND TENANT), the Housing Corporation (see HOUSING), Housing for Wales (see HOUSING) and a registered housing association within the meaning of the Housing Associations Act 1985 (see LANDLORD AND TENANT): Criminal Law Act 1977 s 7 (4), (5) (amended by the Housing (Consequential Provisions) Act 1985 s 4, Sch 2 para 36; the Housing Act 1988 s 140 (1), Sch 17 para 101).

   In any proceedings for an offence under the Criminal Law Act 1977 s 7 (1) where the accused was requested to leave the premises by a person claiming to be or to act on behalf of a protected intending occupier of the premises, any document purporting to be a certificate under head (c) supra must be

received in evidence and, unless the contrary is proved, is deemed to have been issued by or on behalf of the authority stated in the certificate: s 7 (8) (b).
5 Ibid s 7 (1).
6 Ibid s 7 (10) (as amended: see note 4 supra). A constable in uniform may arrest without warrant anyone who is, or whom he, with reasonable cause, suspects to be guilty of such an offence: s 7 (11). This power of arrest is preserved by the Police and Criminal Evidence Act 1984 s 26 (2): see para 708 post.
7 Criminal Law Act 1977 s 7 (6).
8 Ibid s 7 (7).
9 Ie under ibid s 7 (2) (d): see note 4 head (4) supra.
10 Ibid s 7 (8) (a). The certificate is such as is referred to in s 7 (4) (c): see note (4) head (c) supra.

163. Trespassing with a weapon of offence. A person who is on any premises[1] as a trespasser[2], after having entered as such, is guilty of an offence if, without lawful authority or reasonable excuse, he has with him on the premises any weapon of offence[3], and is liable on summary conviction to imprisonment for a term not exceeding three months or a fine not exceeding level 5 on the standard scale, or to both[4].

1 For the meaning of 'premises' see para 161 note 4 ante.
2 As to references to a trespasser see para 162 note 2 ante.
3 For these purposes, 'weapon of offence' means any article made or adapted for causing injury to or incapacitating a person, or intended by the person having it with him for such use: Criminal Law Act 1977 s 8 (2).
4 Ibid s 8 (1), (3) (amended by the Criminal Justice Act 1982 ss 38, 46). For the meaning of 'the standard scale' see para 808 post. A constable in uniform may arrest without warrant anyone who is, or whom he, with reasonable cause, suspects to be, in the act of committing such an offence: Criminal Law Act 1977 s 8 (4). This power of arrest is preserved by the Police and Criminal Evidence Act 1984 s 26 (2), Sch 2: see para 708 post.

164. Trespassing on premises of foreign missions etc. A person who enters or is on any specified premises[1] as a trespasser[2] is guilty of an offence and liable on summary conviction to imprisonment for a term not exceeding six months or a fine not exceeding level 5 on the standard scale, or to both[3]. In any proceedings for such an offence it is, however, a defence for the accused to prove that he believed that the premises in question were not specified premises[4].

1 The Criminal Law Act 1977 s 9 applies to any premises which are or form part of (1) the premises of a diplomatic mission within the meaning of the definition in the Vienna Convention on Diplomatic Relations (Cmnd 2565) art 1 (i) as it has effect in the United Kingdom by virtue of the Diplomatic Privileges Act 1964 s 2, Sch 1; (2) the premises of a closed diplomatic mission within the meaning of the definition in the Vienna Convention on Diplomatic Relations art 45 as it has effect in the United Kingdom by virtue of the Diplomatic Privileges Act 1964 s 2, Sch 1; (3) consular premises within the meaning of the definition in the Vienna Convention on Consular Relations (Cmnd 5219) art 1 (1) (j) as it has effect in the United Kingdom by virtue of the Consular Relations Act 1968 s 1, Sch 1; (4) the premises of a closed consular post within the meaning of the definition in the Vienna Convention on Consular Relations art 27 as it has effect in the United Kingdom by virtue of the Consular Relations Act 1968 s 1, Sch 1; (5) any other premises in respect of which any organisation or body is entitled to inviolability by or under any enactment; and (6) any premises which are the private residence of a diplomatic agent, within the meaning of the Vienna Convention on Diplomatic Relations art 1 (e), or of any other person who is entitled to inviolability of residence by or under any enactment: Criminal Law Act 1977 s 9 (2) (amended by the Diplomatic and Consular Premises Act 1987 s 7); and see FOREIGN RELATIONS. For the meaning of 'premises' see para 161 note 4 ante; and for the meaning of 'United Kingdom' see para 86 note 1 ante.
   In any proceedings for such an offence a certificate issued by or under the authority of the Secretary of State stating that any premises were or formed part of premises of any description

mentioned in heads (1)–(6) supra at the time of the alleged offence is conclusive evidence that the premises were or formed part of premises of that description at that time: Criminal Law Act 1977 s 9 (4).

2 As to references to a trespasser see para 162 note 2 ante.

3 Criminal Law Act 1977 s 9 (1), (5) (amended by the Criminal Justice Act 1982 ss 38, 46). For the meaning of 'the standard scale' see para 808 post. Proceedings for such an offence may not be instituted against any person except by or with the consent of the Attorney General: Criminal Law Act 1977 s 9 (6). As to the effect of this limitation see para 639 post.

A constable in uniform may arrest without warrant anyone who is, or whom he, with reasonable cause, suspects to be, in the act of committing such an offence: s 9 (7). This power of arrest is preserved by the Police and Criminal Evidence Act 1984 s 26 (2), Sch 2: see para 708 post.

4 Criminal Law Act 1977 s 9 (3).

165. Power to direct trespassers to leave land. If the senior police officer[1] reasonably believes that two or more persons have entered land[2] as trespassers[3] and are present there with the common purpose of residing there[4] for any period, that reasonable steps have been taken by or on behalf of the occupier[5] to ask them to leave and:

(1) that any of those persons has caused damage to property[6] on the land or used threatening, abusive or insulting words or behaviour towards the occupier, a member of his family or an employee or agent of his; and

(2) that those persons have between them brought 12 or more vehicles[7] on to the land,

he may direct those persons, or any of them, to leave the land[8]. If any person, knowing that such a direction has been given which applies to him:

(a) fails to leave the land as soon as reasonably practicable; or

(b) having left again enters the land as a trespasser within the period of three months beginning with the day on which the direction was given,

he is guilty of an offence and liable on summary conviction to imprisonment for a term not exceeding three months or a fine not exceeding level 4 on the standard scale, or to both[9].

In proceedings for such an offence it is a defence for the accused to show:

(i) that his original entry on the land was not as a trespasser; or

(ii) that he has a reasonable excuse for failing to leave the land as soon as reasonably practicable or, as the case may be, for again entering the land as a trespasser[10].

1 For these purposes, 'senior police officer' means the most senior officer in rank of the police officers present at the scene: Public Order Act 1986 s 39 (5).

2 For these purposes, 'land' does not include (1) buildings other than agricultural buildings within the meaning of the General Rate Act 1967 s 26 (4) (repealed: see now the Local Government Finance Act 1988 s 51, Sch 5 paras 3–7) or scheduled monuments within the meaning of the Ancient Monuments and Archaeological Areas Act 1979; (2) land forming part of a highway: Public Order Act 1986 s 39 (5).

3 For these purposes, 'trespasser', in relation to land, means a person who is a trespasser as against the occupier of land: ibid s 39 (5).

4 For these purposes, a person may be regarded as having the purpose of residing in a place notwithstanding that he has a home elsewhere: ibid s 39 (5).

5 For these purposes, 'occupier' means the person entitled to possession of the land by virtue of an estate or interest held by him: ibid s 39 (5).

6 For these purposes, 'property' means property within the meaning of the Criminal Damage Act 1971 s 10 (1) (see para 597 post): Public Order Act 1986 s 39 (5).

7 For these purposes, 'vehicle' includes a caravan as defined in the Caravan Sites and Control of Development Act 1960 s 29 (1) (see para 192 note 6 post): Public Order Act 1986 s 39 (5).

8 Ibid s 39 (1).

9 Ibid s 39 (2). See *Krumpa v DPP* (1988) Times, 31 December, DC (the Public Order Act 1986 s 39 (2) (a) (see text head (a) supra) is solely concerned with the practicability of moving out and has nothing to do with the belief of the police officer: the sole question for the court was whether the alleged trespasser failed to leave the land as soon as he could reasonably have done so). A constable in uniform who suspects that a person is committing such an offence may arrest him without warrant: s 39 (3).

10 Ibid s 39 (4).

166. Obstruction of court officers executing process against unauthorised occupiers. If a person resists or intentionally obstructs any person who is in fact an officer of a court[1] engaged in executing any process issued by the High Court or any county court for the purpose of enforcing any judgment or order[2] for the recovery of any premises[3] or for the delivery of possession of any premises, he is guilty of an offence and liable on summary conviction to imprisonment for a term not exceeding six months or a fine not exceeding level 5 on the standard scale, or to both[4]. In any proceedings for such an offence it is, however, a defence for the accused to prove that he believed that the person he was resisting or obstructing was not an officer of the court[5].

1 For these purposes, 'officer of a court' means (1) any sheriff, undersheriff, deputy sheriff, bailiff or officer of a sheriff; and (2) any bailiff or other person who is an officer of a county court within the meaning of the County Courts Act 1959 (see now the County Courts Act 1984 s 147): Criminal Law Act 1977 s 10 (6).

2 Ibid s 10 (1) does not apply unless the judgment or order in question was given or made in proceedings brought under any provisions of rules of court applicable only in circumstances where the person claiming possession of any premises alleges that the premises in question are occupied solely by a person or persons, not being a tenant or tenants holding over after the termination of the tenancy, who entered into or remained in occupation of the premises without the licence or consent of the person claiming possession or any predecessor in title of his: s 10 (2).

3 For these purposes, 'premises' means any building, any part of a building under separate occupation, any land ancillary to a building, the site comprising any building or buildings together with any land ancillary thereto, and any other place: ibid s 12 (1) (a). For the meaning of 'building', 'building under separate occupation' and 'land ancillary to a building' see para 161 note 4 ante.

4 Ibid s 10 (1), (4) (amended by the Criminal Justice Act 1982 ss 38, 46). For the meaning of 'the standard scale' see para 808 post. The Criminal Law Act 1977 s 10 (1) is without prejudice to the Sheriffs Act 1887 s 8 (2): Criminal Law Act 1977 s 10 (1). See further SHERIFFS vol 42 para 1132.

A constable in uniform may arrest without warrant anyone who is, or whom he, with reasonable cause, suspects to be, in the act of committing such an offence: s 10 (5). This power of arrest is preserved by the Police and Criminal Evidence Act 1984 s 26 (2), Sch 2: see para 708 post.

5 Criminal Law Act 1977 s 10 (3).

(xi) Offensive Weapons

167. Possession of offensive weapons. Any person who, without lawful authority[1] or reasonable excuse[2], the proof whereof lies on him[3], has with him[4] in any public place[5] any offensive weapon[6] is guilty of an offence and liable on conviction on indictment to imprisonment for a term not exceeding two years or a fine, or to both, or on summary conviction to imprisonment for a term not exceeding six months or a fine not exceeding the prescribed sum, or to both[7].

Where a person is convicted of such an offence, the court may make an order for the forfeiture or disposal of any weapon in respect of which the offence was committed[8].

1 'Lawful authority' covers persons whose duty it is to carry offensive weapons: *Bryan v Mott* (1975) 62 Cr App Rep 71, DC; and see also *Crafter v Kelly* [1941] SASR 237 at 243. However, there is no lawful

authority for security guards to carry truncheons as part of their uniforms: see *R v Spanner, Poulter and Ward* [1973] Crim LR 704, CA. 'Lawful authority' is to be distinguished from a lawful excuse: *Wong Pooh Yin v Public Prosecutor* [1955] AC 93 at 101, [1954] 3 All ER 31 at 34, PC.

2 'Reasonable excuse' is to be identified with the carrying of the weapon and not with its use: *R v Jura* [1954] 1 QB 503, 38 Cr App Rep 53, CCA: *R v Dayle* [1973] 3 All ER 1151, 58 Cr App Rep 100, CA. The expression 'reasonable excuse' is intended to cover the particular moment at which a weapon is carried: see *Evans v Wright* [1964] Crim LR 466, DC. Where a weapon is carried by a person for self-defence if attacked, for the defence of reasonable excuse to be successful it must be shown that there was an imminent particular threat affecting the particular circumstances in which the weapon was carried; constant carrying of a weapon on account of some enduring threat or danger is, however, insufficient: *Evans v Hughes* [1972] 3 All ER 412, 56 Cr App Rep 813, DC (weapon carried seven days after attack could constitute excuse); applying *Evans v Wright* supra (weapon for self-defence when collecting wages; carrying weapon two days after wages last collected not a reasonable excuse) and *Grieve v McLeod* 1967 JC 32 (continuing fear of assault not a reasonable excuse for taxi-driver to carry cosh). See also *Pittard v Mahoney* [1977] Crim LR 169, DC (accused failed to show the kind of imminent danger which could possibly justify the carrying of an offensive weapon; the nature of the weapon had to be taken into account in deciding whether the carrying was justified); *R v Peacock* [1973] Crim LR 639, CA ('it must be very rare that someone not under immediate fear of attack could claim to be entitled to carry a weapon for self-defence on the off chance of being attacked'); *Bradley v Moss* [1974] Crim LR 430, DC (previous threats but no assault; no defence of reasonable excuse available for carrying four weapons for self-defence); *Bryan v Mott* (1975) 62 Cr App Rep 71, DC (accused's intended suicide so remote from the carrying of the offensive weapon that it was not a reasonable excuse); *Malnik v DPP* [1989] Crim LR 451, DC (ordinarily people may not legitimately arm themselves with an offensive weapon to repel unlawful violence which an individual knowingly and deliberately brought about by creating a situation in which violence was liable to be inflicted; but the situation is quite different where the carrying of offensive weapons is by people concerned with security and law enforcement).

Where a weapon, offensive per se, is carried merely as a theatrical property, as part and parcel of a fancy dress worn by a person going to or from a fancy dress party, that does constitute a reasonable excuse for carrying that particular prop: *Houghton v Chief Constable of Greater Manchester* (1987) 84 Cr App Rep 319, CA (wearing police truncheon solely as part of a police uniform for a fancy dress party was a reasonable excuse).

Where a weapon, offensive per se, is carried in order to obtain food for wild birds kept under licence, that may be a reasonable excuse: see *Southwell v Chadwick* (1986) 85 Cr App Rep 235, CA (machete knife in scabbard and catapult for use in killing grey squirrels).

Possession originally unlawful and without excuse may, it seems, by a change of circumstances become possession with reasonable excuse: *Wong Pooh Yin v Public Prosecutor* [1955] AC 93, [1954] 3 All ER 31, PC.

3 The accused must satisfy the jury only on a balance of probabilities and not beyond a reasonable doubt: *R v Brown (DW)* (1971) 55 Cr App Rep 478, CA; and see para 1062 post. The question of lawful authority or reasonable excuse does not arise until it has been established that the accused had with him an offensive weapon: *R v Petrie* [1961] 1 All ER 466, 45 Cr App Rep 72, CCA.

4 This offence is concerned with a person who with no excuse goes out with an offensive weapon: *R v Jura* [1954] 1 QB 503, 38 Cr App Rep 53, CCA (accused, on payment, obtained possession of an air rifle at a shooting gallery for the purposes of firing at a target, but, losing his temper, he fired at and hit a woman who was with him; it was held that he had a reasonable excuse for his possession of the air rifle, and the unlawful use of it did not bring him within the Prevention of Crime Act 1953 s 1 (as amended); but it could have been an offence under the Offences against the Person Act 1861: see para 469 et seq post). This offence is also concerned with a person who, while out, deliberately selects an offensive weapon with the intent of using it without lawful authority or reasonable excuse: *R v Dayle* [1973] 3 All ER 1151, 58 Cr App Rep 100, CA.

The offence is not, however, committed where the accused arms himself with a weapon for instant attack on his victim; the offence is concerned with a person who, possessed of a weapon, forms the necessary intent before an occasion to use actual violence has arisen. The offence is concerned not with the actual use but with the carrying of a weapon with intent to use it if the occasion arises. The accused does not have to have the intention from the moment he set out on his expedition: *Ohlson v Hylton* [1975] 2 All ER 490, [1975] 1 WLR 724, DC (workman attacked fellow passenger with hammer with him for work purposes; no offence under the Prevention of Crime Act 1953 s 1 (as amended)); see also *R v Humphreys* [1977] Crim LR 225, CA (if person happens to have penknife and uses it in desperation, no offence, because not carried in a public place with necessary intent to cause injury). The purport of the Prevention of Crime Act 1953 is to cover the situation where an accused has with him and is carrying an offensive weapon intending that it shall be used, if necessary, for offensive purposes. Actual use is better dealt with by a substantive offence: *Bates v Bulman* [1979] 3 All ER 170, 68 Cr App Rep 21, DC. The distinction between an innocent weapon subsequently used with the intention of an assault and which is being carried innocently, and a similar article which is acquired either by borrowing from somebody else or fortuitously by being picked up in the street, is a rather academic and overly-analytical approach: *Bates v Bulman* supra. Cf *Harrison v Thornton* (1966) 68 Cr App Rep 28, DC (accused picked up a stone and threw it at another person who was fighting with the accused's friend; offence committed); approved in *R v Dayle* supra per Kilner Brown J.

5 'Has with him in any public place' means 'knowingly has with him in a public place' and the prosecution must establish knowledge: *R v Cugullere* [1961] 2 All ER 343, 45 Cr App Rep 108, CCA. A person who forgets he has possession of an offensive weapon continues to have it 'with him': *R v McCalla* (1988) 87 Cr App Rep 372, CA.

Where two or more persons are jointly charged with possession of an offensive weapon, the prosecution must establish that each knew of weapons carried by the other or others and that there was a common purpose: *R v Edmonds* [1963] 2 QB 142, 47 Cr App Rep 114, CCA.

For these purposes, 'public place' includes any highway and any other premises or place to which at the material time the public has or is permitted to have access, whether on payment or otherwise: Prevention of Crime Act 1953 s 1 (4). Justices are entitled to find that premises where there are no barriers or notices restricting access, such as the upper level of a block of flats which could be entered by members of the public without hindrance, are a public place: *Knox v Anderton* (1983) 76 Cr App Rep 156, DC; see also *Sandy v Martin* [1974] Crim LR 258, DC. Cf the Public Order Act 1936 s 9 (1) and para 100 note 2 ante; the Firearms Act 1968 s 57 (4) and para 226 note 3 post; the Prevention of Terrorism (Temporary Provisions) Act 1989 s 3 (3) and para 112 note 1 ante. See also *R v Powell* [1963] Crim LR 511, CCA (part of hospital grounds where visitors to the hospital and their friends were permitted to enter was held to be a public place); *R v Mehmed* [1963] Crim LR 780, CCA (pistol produced by the accused in a private dwelling house; held that the jury, having regard to the accused's defence, was entitled to infer that he brought it to, or took it away from, the house through public streets and had accordingly been in possession of it in a public place).

6 'Offensive weapon' means any article made or adapted for use for causing injury to the person or intended by the person having it with him for such use by him or by some other person: Prevention of Crime Act 1953 s 1 (4) (amended by the Public Order Act 1986 s 40 (2), Sch 2 para 2).

There are three possible categories of offensive weapon: (1) weapons made for use for causing injury to the person, ie a weapon offensive per se eg a bayonet, a stiletto or a gun; (2) a weapon adapted for such a purpose eg a bottle deliberately broken in order that the jagged end may be inserted into the victim's face; (3) an object not so made or adapted but one which the person carrying intends to use for the purpose of causing injury to the person: *R v Simpson* [1983] 3 All ER 789, 78 Cr App Rep 115, CA.

A flick knife is an offensive weapon per se: *Gibson v Wales* [1983] 1 All ER 869, 76 Cr App Rep 60, DC (a flick knife is made for the purpose of causing injury to the person; the accused has the burden of proving that it was used for wholly innocent purposes: see note 3 supra); see also *R v Allamby, R v Medford* [1974] 3 All ER 126, [1974] 1 WLR 1494, CA; *R v Lawrence, R v Pomroy* (1971) 57 Cr App Rep 64, CA. Judicial notice may be taken of the fact that a flick knife is an offensive weapon per se: *R v Simpson* supra. A sword stick is also an offensive weapon per se: *R v Butler* [1988] Crim LR 695, CA; affg *Davis v Alexander* (1970) 54 Cr App Rep 398, DC. The conclusion that a rice flail was a weapon offensive per se was legitimately reached in accordance with the evidence because the only evidence found acceptable was that such an implement is used as a weapon: *Copus v DPP* [1989] Crim LR 577, DC.

Sometimes, it will not be so clear that a weapon is an offensive weapon; in such a case it is a matter of fact for the magistrates or jury: *R v Williamson* (1977) 67 Cr App Rep 35, CA (question of fact whether a sheath knife an offensive weapon); *R v Simpson* supra; (explaining *R v Williamson* supra; not possible to classify all sheath knives as offensive per se unlike flick knives). Where the weapon is offensive per se, intention to use it to cause injury need not be proved: *Davis v Alexander* (1970) 54 Cr App Rep 398, DC.

In *Bryan v Mott* (1975) 62 Cr App Rep 71, DC, the decision of the Crown Court that 'injury to the person' included the accused's own person was not challenged in the Divisional Court. Cf *R v Fleming* [1989] Crim LR 71 (intention to harm oneself cannot sensibly be held to be offensive). See also *Patterson v Block* (1984) Times, 21 June, DC (accused had with him a lock knife (not an offensive weapon per se); only evidence against him was his statement to the police that he carried the knife for his self-defence: held that the justices could properly draw the inference that for the purposes of defending himself he would, if necessary, use the knife to cause injury to the person); *Southwell v*

Chadwick (1986) 85 Cr App Rep 235, CA (no evidence that weapons, a machete knife in its scabbard and a catapult, were made or adapted for causing injury to the person).

The burden of proving intention so to use the weapon lies on the prosecution throughout: *R v Petrie* [1961] 1 All ER 466, 45 Cr App Rep 72, CCA. The use made of the weapon may, but does not necessarily, establish the required intent: see *Harrison v Thornton* (1966) 68 Cr App Rep 28, DC; *R v Dayle* [1973] 3 All ER 1151, 58 Cr App Rep 100, CA; *Ohlson v Hylton* [1975] 2 All ER 490, [1975] 1 WLR 724, DC. It must be proved that, at the time and place charged, the accused had the intent to use the article offensively at some time in the future; proof that he had the intention at some time previously when in possession of the article is insufficient: *R v Allamby, R v Medford* supra. An intention to frighten is not sufficient; an intention to intimidate is more appropriate as a description when the intention was to cause injury by shock; such circumstances are exceedingly rare: *R v Rapier* (1979) 70 Cr App Rep 17, CA.

Any experiment intended to assist in determining the use of a weapon must take place in open court and not in the jury's retiring room: *R v Higgins* (1989) Times, 16 February, CA. See para 1026 post.

7 Prevention of Crime Act 1953 s 1 (1) (amended by the Criminal Law Act 1977 s 32 (1); the Magistrates' Courts Act 1980 s 32 (2); the Criminal Justice Act 1988 s 46 (1)). For the meaning of 'the prescribed sum' see para 807 post. The Prevention of Crime Act 1953 s 1 (1) (as so amended) does not have effect in relation to anything done before 29 September 1988: Criminal Justice Act 1988 ss 46 (3), 171 (6).

An indictment need not contain two counts, one to cover the weapon's being offensive per se and one referring to a weapon being offensive because of the intent: *R v Flynn* (1985) 150 JP 112, CA.

8 Prevention of Crime Act 1953 s 1 (2). An order may be so made even though an offender is placed on probation or discharged absolutely or conditionally: see para 1255 post.

168. Having article with blade or point in public place. Any person who has with him in a public place[1] an article which has a blade or is sharply pointed, except a folding pocketknife[2], is guilty of an offence and liable on summary conviction to a fine not exceeding level 3 on the standard scale[3]. It is a defence, however, for a person charged with such an offence to prove that (1) he had good reason or lawful authority for having the article with him in a public place[4]; or (2) without prejudice to the generality of head (1) above, he had the article with him for use at work, for religious reasons or as part of any national costume[5].

1 For these purposes, 'public place' includes any place to which at the material time the public has or is permitted access, whether on payment or otherwise: Criminal Justice Act 1988 s 139 (7). Cf the Prevention of Crime Act 1953 s 1 (4) and para 167 note 5 ante; the Public Order Act 1936 s 9 (1) (amended by the Criminal Justice Act 1972 s 33) and para 100 note 2 ante; the Firearms Act 1968 s 57 (4) and para 226 note 3 post; the Prevention of Terrorism (Temporary Provisions) Act 1989 s 3 (3) and para 112 note 1 ante.

2 The Criminal Justice Act 1988 s 139 applies to a folding pocketknife if the cutting edge of its blade exceeds three inches: s 139 (3).

3 Ibid s 139 (1), (2), (6). Section 139 has no effect in relation to anything done before 29 December 1988: ss 139 (8), 171 (6). For the meaning of 'the standard scale' see para 808 post. As to a constable's power to stop and search see para 661 post.

4 Ibid s 139 (4).

5 Ibid s 139 (5).

169. Manufacture, sale, hire etc of specified weapons. Any person who manufactures, sells or hires, or offers for sale or hire, exposes or has in his possession for the purpose of sale or hire, or lends or gives to any other person, a specified weapon[1] is guilty of an offence and liable on summary conviction to imprisonment for a term not exceeding six months or a fine not exceeding level 5 on the standard scale, or to both[2]. It is a defence, however, for any person charged in respect of any conduct of his relating to such a weapon to prove that his conduct was only for the purposes of functions carried out on behalf of the Crown or of a visiting force[3]. It is also a defence for any person charged in respect of any conduct of his relating to such a weapon to prove that the conduct in question was only for the purposes of making the weapon available to a museum or gallery[4]; and, if a person acting on behalf of such a museum or gallery is charged with hiring or lending such a weapon, it is a defence for him to prove that he had reasonable grounds for believing that the person to whom he lent or hired it would use it only for cultural, artistic or educational purposes[5].

1 The Secretary of State may by order made by statutory instrument direct that the Criminal Justice Act 1988 s 141 shall apply to any description of weapon specified in the order except (1) any weapon subject to the Firearms Act 1968 (see para 197 et seq post); or (2) crossbows (see paras 170–172 post): Criminal Justice Act 1988 s 141 (2). A statutory instrument containing such an order may not be made unless a draft of the instrument has been laid before Parliament and has been approved by a resolution of each House of Parliament: s 141 (3). The importation of such weapons is prohibited: s 141 (4); and see CUSTOMS AND EXCISE.
  Section 141 applies to the following descriptions of weapons, other than weapons of those descriptions which are antiques:
  (1) a knuckleduster, that is, a band of metal or other hard material worn on one or more fingers, and designed to cause injury, and any weapon incorporating a knuckleduster;
  (2) a swordstick, that is, a hollow walking-stick or cane containing a blade which may be used as a sword;
  (3) the weapon sometimes known as a 'handclaw', being a band of metal or other hard material from which a number of sharp spikes protrude and worn around the hand;
  (4) the weapon sometimes known as a 'belt buckle knife', being a buckle which incorporates or conceals a knife;
  (5) the weapon sometimes known as a 'push dagger', being a knife the handle of which fits within a clenched fist and the blade of which protrudes from between two fingers;
  (6) the weapon sometimes known as a 'hollow kubotan', being a cylindrical container containing a number of sharp spikes;
  (7) the weapon sometimes known as a 'footclaw', being a bar of metal or other hard material from which a number of sharp spikes protrude, and worn strapped to the foot;
  (8) the weapon sometimes known as a 'shruiken', 'shaken' or 'death star', being a hard non-flexible plate having three or more sharp radiating points and designed to be thrown;
  (9) the weapon sometimes known as a 'balisong' or 'butterfly knife', being a blade enclosed by its handle, which is designed to split down the middle, without the operation of a spring or other mechanical means, to reveal the blade;
  (10) the weapon sometimes known as a 'telescopic truncheon', being a truncheon which extends automatically by hand pressure applied to a button, spring or other device in or attached to its handle;
  (11) the weapon sometimes known as a 'blowpipe' or 'blow gun', being a hollow tube out of which hard pellets or darts are shot by the use of breath;
  (12) the weapon sometimes known as a 'kusari gama', being a length of rope, cord, wire or chain fastened at one end to a sickle;
  (13) the weapon sometimes known as a 'kyoketsu shoge', being a length of rope, cord, wire or chain fastened at one end to a hooked knife;
  (14) the weapon sometimes known as a 'manrikigusari' or 'kusari', being a length of rope, cord or wire or chain fastened at each end to a hard weight or hand grip:
Criminal Justice Act 1988 (Offensive Weapons) Order 1988, SI 1988/2019, art 2, Schedule para 1. For these purposes, a weapon is an antique if it was manufactured more than 100 years before the date of any offence alleged to have been committed in respect of that weapon under the Criminal Justice Act 1988 s 141 or the Customs and Excise Management Act 1979 s 50 (2) or (3) (improper importation: see CUSTOMS AND EXCISE): Criminal Justice Act 1988 (Offensive Weapons) Order 1988 Schedule para 2.
2 Criminal Justice Act 1988 s 141 (1). For the meaning of 'the standard scale' see para 808 post. Section 141 has no effect in relation to anything done before 29 July 1988: ss 141 (12), 171 (5).
  If on an application made by a constable a justice of the peace is satisfied that there are reasonable grounds for believing (1) that there are on premises specified in the application knives such as are mentioned in the Restriction of Offensive Weapons Act 1959 s 1 (1) (as amended) (see para 174 post)

or weapons to which the Criminal Justice Act 1988 s 141 applies; and (2) that an offence under the Restriction of Offensive Weapons Act 1959 s 1 (as amended) or the Criminal Justice Act 1988 s 141 has been or is being committed in relation to them; and (3) that any of the specified conditions applies, he may issue a warrant authorising a constable to enter and search the premises: s 142 (1). The specified conditions are: (a) that it is not practicable to communicate with any person entitled to grant entry to the premises; (b) that it is practicable to communicate with a person entitled to grant entry to the premises but it is not practicable to communicate with any person entitled to grant access to the knives or weapons to which the application relates; (c) that entry to the premises will not be granted unless a warrant is produced; (d) that the purpose of a search may be frustrated or seriously prejudiced unless a constable arriving at the premises can secure immediate entry to them: s 142 (3). A constable may seize and retain anything for which a search has been authorised under s 142 (1): s 142 (2).

3 Ibid s 141 (5) (a). It is also a defence for any person charged in respect of any conduct of his relating to such a weapon with an offence under the Customs and Excise Management Act 1979 s 50 (2) or (3) (improper importation: see CUSTOMS AND EXCISE) to prove that his conduct was only for the purposes of functions carried out on behalf of the Crown or of a visiting force: Criminal Justice Act 1988 s 141 (5) (b).

For these purposes, the reference to the Crown includes the Crown in right of Her Majesty's Government in Northern Ireland; and 'visiting force' means any body, contingent or detachment of the forces of a country (1) mentioned in the Visiting Forces Act 1952 s 1 (1) (a) (see ROYAL FORCES vol 41 para 130); or (2) designated for the purposes of any provision of that Act by Order in Council under s 1 (2) (see ROYAL FORCES vol 41 para 130), which is present in the United Kingdom, including United Kingdom territorial waters, or in any place on, under or above an installation in a designated area within the meaning of the Continental Shelf Act 1964 s 1 (7) or any waters within 500 metres of such an installation, on the invitation of Her Majesty's Government in the United Kingdom: Criminal Justice Act 1988 s 141 (6), (7).

4 Ibid s 141 (8) (a). Section 141 (8) applies to a museum or gallery only if it does not distribute profits: s 141 (10). For these purposes, 'museum or gallery' includes any institution which has as its purpose, or one of its purposes, the preservation, display and interpretation of material of historical, artistic or scientific interest and gives the public access to it: s 141 (11).

It is also a defence for any person charged in respect of any conduct of his relating to such a weapon with an offence under the Customs and Excise Management Act 1979 s 50 (2) or (3) (see CUSTOMS AND EXCISE) to prove that the conduct in question was only for the purposes of making the weapon available to a museum or gallery: Criminal Justice Act 1988 s 141 (8) (b).

5 Ibid s 141 (9).

170. Person under seventeen having with him a crossbow. Unless he is under the supervision of a person who is 21 years of age or older, a person under the age of 17 who has with him a crossbow[1] which is capable of discharging a missile, or parts of a crossbow which together, and without any other parts, can be assembled to form a crossbow capable of discharging a missile, is guilty of an offence and liable on summary conviction to a fine not exceeding level 3 on the standard scale[2].

1 The Crossbows Act 1987 does not apply to crossbows with a draw weight of less than 1·4 kilograms: s 5.

2 Ibid ss 3, 6 (2). For the meaning of 'the standard scale' see para 808 post. The court by which a person is convicted of such an offence may make such order as it thinks fit as to the forfeiture or disposal of any crossbow or part of a crossbow in respect of which the offence was committed: s 6 (3).

If a constable suspects with reasonable cause that a person is committing or has committed an offence under s 3, the constable may (1) search that person for a crossbow or part of a crossbow; (2) search any vehicle, or anything in or on a vehicle, in or on which the constable suspects with reasonable cause there is a crossbow, or part of a crossbow, connected with the offence; and a constable may detain a person or vehicle for the purpose of such a search: s 4 (1), (2). For the purposes of exercising the powers conferred by s 4, a constable may enter any land other than a dwelling house: s 4 (4). A constable may seize and retain for the purpose of proceedings for an offence under the Crossbows Act 1987 anything discovered by him in the course of a search under s 4 (1) which appears to him to be a crossbow or part of a crossbow: s 4 (3).

171. Person under seventeen buying or hiring a crossbow. A person under the age of 17 who buys or hires a crossbow[1] or a part of a crossbow is guilty of an offence and liable on summary conviction to a fine not exceeding level 3 on the standard scale[2].

1 For the meaning of 'crossbow' see para 170 note 1 ante.
2 Crossbows Act 1987 ss 2, 6 (2). For the meaning of 'the standard scale' see para 808 post. As to the court's powers of forfeiture or disposal of crossbows or parts of crossbows see para 170 note 2 ante; and as to possession of a crossbow see para 170 ante.

172. Sale and letting on hire of crossbows to persons under seventeen. A person who sells or lets on hire a crossbow[1] or a part of a crossbow to a person under the age of 17 is guilty of an offence and liable on summary conviction to imprisonment for a term not exceeding six months or a fine not exceeding level 5 on the standard scale, or to both, unless he believes him to be 17 years of age or older and has reasonable ground for the belief[2].

1 For the meaning of 'crossbow' see para 170 note 1 ante.
2 Crossbows Act 1987 ss 1, 6 (1). For the meaning of 'the standard scale' see para 808 post. As to the court's powers of forfeiture or disposal of crossbows or parts of crossbows see para 170 note 2 ante; and as to possession of crossbows see para 170 ante.

173. Wearing weapons commonly worn. Apart from statute, it is not an offence for persons to wear common weapons upon occasions on which it is the common practice to wear them, where there can be no suspicion of an intention to commit any act of violence or disturbance of the peace[1].

1 3 Co Inst 160 et seq; 1 Hawk PC c 28 (2) ss 8, 9; Bill of Rights (1688).

174. Manufacture and sale etc of arms and offensive weapons. Any person who manufactures, sells or hires, or offers for sale or hire, or exposes or has for the purpose of sale or hire, or lends or gives to any other person:

(1) any knife which has a blade which opens automatically by hand pressure applied to a button, spring or other device in or attached to the handle of the knife, sometimes known as a 'flick knife' or 'flick gun'; or

(2) any knife which has a blade which is released from the handle or sheath by the force of gravity on the application of centrifugal force and which, when released, is locked in place by means of a button, spring, lever, or other device, sometimes known as a 'gravity knife',

is guilty of an offence and liable on summary conviction to imprisonment for a term not exceeding six months or a fine not exceeding level 5 on the standard scale, or to both[1].

It is an indictable offence at common law punishable by fine and imprisonment[2] to make or sell arms knowing that they are to be used for an unlawful purpose[3].

1 Restriction of Offensive Weapons Act 1959 s 1 (1) (amended by the Restriction of Offensive Weapons Act 1961 s 1; the Criminal Justice Act 1988 s 46 (2)). For the meaning of 'the standard scale' see para 808 post. The Restriction of Offensive Weapons Act 1959 s 1 (1) (as so amended) does not have effect in relation to anything done before 29 September 1988: Criminal Justice Act 1988 ss 46 (3), 171 (6). The importation of any such knife is also prohibited: Restriction of Offensive Weapons Act 1959 s 1 (2). See CUSTOMS AND EXCISE. As to warrants to enter and search premises for

such knives, and as to a constable's power to seize and retain knives for which a search has been so authorised, see para 169 note 2 ante.
2 See paras 1200, 1232 post.
3 *R v Knowles* (1820) 1 State Tr NS 497; *R v Morris* (1820) 1 State Tr NS 521 at 526. As to the control of firearms see also para 197 et seq post.

(xii) Sporting Events

A. CONTROL OF ALCOHOL ETC

175. Alcohol on coaches and trains. A person who knowingly causes or permits intoxicating liquor[1] to be carried on a public service vehicle[2] or railway passenger vehicle which is being used for the principal purpose of carrying passengers for the whole or part of a journey to or from a designated sporting event[3] is guilty of an offence and liable on summary conviction to a fine not exceeding level 4 on the standard scale if (1) the vehicle is a public service vehicle and he is the operator[4] of the vehicle or the servant or agent of the operator; or (2) the vehicle is a hired vehicle and he is the person to whom it is hired or the servant or agent of that person[5].

A person who has intoxicating liquor in his possession while on such a vehicle is guilty of an offence and liable on summary conviction to imprisonment for a term not exceeding three months or a fine not exceeding level 3 on the standard scale, or to both[6]; and a person who is drunk on such a vehicle is guilty of an offence and liable on summary conviction to a fine not exceeding level 2 on the standard scale[7].

1 For the meaning of 'intoxicating liquor' see the Licensing Act 1964 s 201 (1) (amended by the Finance Act 1981 s 11 (1), Sch 8 Pt III para 25) applied by the Sporting Events (Control of Alcohol Etc) Act 1985 s 9 (7). See INTOXICATING LIQUOR vol 26 para 3 note 1.
2 'Public service vehicle' has the same meaning as in the Public Passenger Vehicles Act 1981 (see ROAD TRAFFIC): Sporting Events (Control of Alcohol Etc) Act 1985 s 1 (5).
3 'Designated sporting event' (1) means a sporting event or proposed sporting event for the time being designated, or of a class designated, by order made by the Secretary of State; and (2) includes a designated sporting event within the meaning of the Criminal Justice (Scotland) Act 1980 Pt V (ss 68–77); and an order so made may apply to events or proposed events outside Great Britain as well as those in England and Wales: Sporting Events (Control of Alcohol Etc) Act 1985 s 9 (1), (3). Any power to make an order under s 9 is exercisable by statutory instrument subject to annulment in pursuance of a resolution of either House of Parliament: s 9 (8).
  As to the events and classes so designated see the Sports Grounds and Sporting Events (Designation) Order 1985, SI 1985/1151, art 2 (d)–(f), Sch 2 Pts I–III.
  The Sporting Events (Control of Alcohol Etc) Act 1985 does not apply to any sporting event or proposed sporting event where all competitors are to take part otherwise than for reward, and to which all spectators are to be admitted free of charge: s 9 (1), (6).
4 'Operator' has the same meaning as in the Public Passenger Vehicles Act 1981 (see ROAD TRAFFIC): Sporting Events (Control of Alcohol Etc) Act 1985 s 1 (5).
5 Ibid ss 1 (1), (2), 8 (a). For the meaning of 'the standard scale' see para 808 post. A constable may stop a public service vehicle or a motor vehicle to which s 1A (added by the Public Order Act 1986 s 40 (1), Sch 1 para 2: see para 176 post) applies and may search such a vehicle or a railway passenger vehicle if he has reasonable grounds to suspect that an offence under the Sporting Events (Control of Alcohol Etc) Act 1985 ss 1 or 1A (as so added) is being or has been committed in respect of the vehicle: s 7 (3) (amended by the Public Order Act 1986 Sch 1 para 6).
6 Sporting Events (Control of Alcohol Etc) Act 1985 ss 1 (1), (3), 8 (b).
7 Ibid ss 1 (1), (4), 8 (c).

176. Alcohol on certain other vehicles. A person who knowingly causes or permits intoxicating liquor[1] to be carried on a motor vehicle[2] which is not a public service vehicle[3] but is adapted to carry more than eight passengers, and is being used for the principal purpose of carrying two or more passengers for the whole or part of a journey to or from a designated sporting event[4] is guilty of an offence (1) if he is the driver; or (2) if he is not its driver but is its keeper[5], the servant or agent of its keeper, a person to whom it is made available, by hire, loan or otherwise, by its keeper or the keeper's servant or agent, or the servant or agent of a person to whom it is so made available, and is liable on summary conviction to a fine not exceeding level 4 on the standard scale[6].

A person who has intoxicating liquor in his possession while on such a motor vehicle is guilty of an offence and liable on summary conviction to imprisonment for a term not exceeding three months or a fine not exceeding level 3 on the standard scale, or to both[7]; and a person who is drunk on such a vehicle is guilty of an offence and liable on summary conviction to a fine not exceeding level 2 on the standard scale[8].

1 For the meaning of 'intoxicating liquor' see para 175 note 1 ante.
2 For these purposes, 'motor vehicle' means a mechanically propelled vehicle intended or adapted for use on roads: Sporting Events (Control of Alcohol Etc) Act 1985 s 1A (5) (added by the Public Order Act 1986 s 40 (1), Sch 1 para 2).
3 'Public service vehicle' has the same meaning as in the Public Passenger Vehicles Act 1981: Sporting Events (Control of Alcohol Etc) Act 1985 s 1A (5) (as added: see note 2 supra).
4 For the meaning of 'designated sporting event' see para 175 note 3 ante.
5 'Keeper', in relation to a vehicle, means the person having the duty to take out a licence under the Vehicles (Excise) Act 1971 s 1 (1): Sporting Events (Control of Alcohol Etc) Act 1985 s 1A (5) (as added: see note 2 supra).
6 Ibid ss 1A (1), (2), 8 (a) (respectively added and amended by the Public Order Act 1986 Sch 1 para 2). For the meaning of 'the standard scale' see para 808 post. As to powers of enforcement see para 175 note 5 ante.
7 Sporting Events (Control of Alcohol Etc) Act 1985 ss 1A (1), (3), 8 (b) (respectively added and amended by the Public Order Act 1986 Sch 1 para 2).
8 Sporting Events (Control of Alcohol Etc) Act 1985 ss 1A (1), (4), 8 (c) (respectively added and amended by the Public Order Act 1986 Sch 1 para 2).

177. Possession of intoxicating liquor, containers etc at sports grounds. A person who has intoxicating liquor[1] or a specified article[2] in his possession (1) at any time during the period of a designated sporting event[3] when he is in any area of a designated sports ground[4] from which the event may be directly viewed; or (2) while entering or trying to enter a designated sports ground at any time during the period of a designated sporting event at that ground, is guilty of an offence and liable on summary conviction to imprisonment for a term not exceeding three months or a fine not exceeding level 3 on the standard scale, or to both[5].

A person who is drunk in a designated sports ground at any time during the period of a designated sporting event at that ground or is drunk while entering or trying to enter such a ground at any time during the period of a designated sporting event at that ground is guilty of an offence and liable on summary conviction to a fine not exceeding level 2 on the standard scale[6].

1 For the meaning of 'intoxicating liquor' see para 175 note 1 ante.
2 The Sporting Events (Control of Alcohol Etc) Act 1985 s 2 applies to any article capable of causing injury to a person struck by it, being (1) a bottle, can or other portable container, including such an article when crushed or broken, which is for holding any drink, and is of a kind which, when empty, is normally discarded or returned to, or left to be recovered by, the supplier; or (2) part of an article falling within head (1) supra; but does not apply to anything that is for holding any medicinal product within the meaning of the Medicines Act 1968 (see MEDICINE): Sporting Events (Control of Alcohol Etc) Act 1985 s 2 (3).

3 The period of a designated sporting event is the period beginning two hours before the start of the event or, if earlier, two hours before the time at which it is advertised to start and ending one hour after the end of the event; but (1) where an event advertised to start at a particular time on a particular day is postponed to a later day, the period includes the period in the day on which it is advertised to take place beginning two hours before and ending one hour after that time; and (2) where an event advertised to start at a particular time on a particular day does not take place, the period is the period referred to in head (1) supra: ibid s 9 (1), (4). For the meaning of 'designated sporting event' see para 175 note 3 ante.

In relation to a room in a designated sports ground from which designated sporting events may be directly viewed and to which the general public is not admitted, s 2 (1) (a) (see head (1) supra) and s 3 (1) (a) (see LICENSING) have effect with the substitution for the reference to the period of a designated sporting event of a reference to the restricted period defined in s 5A (2) (added by the Public Order Act 1986 s 40 (1), Sch 1 para 4): Sporting Events (Control of Alcohol Etc) Act 1985 s 5A (1) (added by the Public Order 1986 Sch 1 para 4). The restricted period of a designated sporting event for these purposes is the period beginning 15 minutes before the start of the event or, if earlier, 15 minutes before the time at which it is advertised to start and ending 15 minutes after the end of the event, but (a) where an event advertised to start at a particular time on a particular day is postponed to a later day, the restricted period includes the period in the day on which it is advertised to take place beginning 15 minutes before and ending 15 minutes after that time; and (b) where an event advertised to start at a particular time does not take place, the period is the period referred to in head (a) supra: Sporting Events (Control of Alcohol Etc) Act 1985 s 5A (2) (as so added). However, the Secretary of State may by order provide, in relation to all designated sporting events or in relation to such descriptions of event as are specified in the order (i) that the restricted period shall be such period, shorter than that mentioned in heads (a), (b) supra, as may be specified in the order; or (ii) that there shall be no restricted period: s 5A (3) (added by the Public Order Act 1986 Sch 1 para 4). Any such order must be made by statutory instrument subject to annulment in pursuance of a resolution of either House of Parliament: Sporting Events (Control of Alcohol Etc) Act 1985 s 5A (4) (added by the Public Order Act 1986 Sch 1 para 4).

4 'Designated sports ground' means any place (1) used, wholly or partly, for sporting events where accommodation is provided for spectators; and (2) for the time being designated, or of a class designated, by order made by the Secretary of State; and an order so made may include provision for determining the outer limit of any designated sports ground: Sporting Events (Control of Alcohol Etc) Act 1985 s 9 (1), (2). As to the power to make such orders see para 175 note 3 ante.

As to the sports grounds and classes of sports grounds so designated see the Sports Grounds and Sports Events (Designation) Order 1985, SI 1985/1151, art 2 (a)–(c), Sch 1 Pts I, II.

5 Sporting Events (Control of Alcohol Etc) Act 1985 ss 2 (1), 8 (b). Section 2 (1) (a) (see head (1) supra) has effect subject to s 5A (1) (as added) (see note 3 supra): s 2 (1A) (added by the Public Order Act 1986 Sch 1 paras 1, 5). For the meaning of 'the standard scale' see para 808 post. A constable may, at any time during the period of a designated sporting event at any designated sports ground, enter any part of the ground for the purpose of enforcing the provisions of the Sporting Events (Control of Alcohol Etc) Act 1985: s 7 (1). A constable may search a person he has reasonable grounds to suspect is committing or has committed an offence under the 1985 Act, and may arrest such a person: s 7 (2).

6 Ibid ss 2 (2), 8 (c).

178. Closure of bars. If at any time during the period of a designated sporting event[1] at any designated sports ground[2] it appears to a constable in uniform that the sale or supply of intoxicating liquor[3] at any bar within the ground is detrimental to the orderly conduct or safety of spectators at that event, he may require any person having control of the bar to close it and keep it closed until the end of that period[4]. A person who fails to comply with such a requirement is guilty of an offence and liable on summary conviction to imprisonment for a term not exceeding three months or a fine not exceeding level 3 on the standard scale, or to both, unless he shows that he took all reasonable steps to comply with it[5].

1 For the meaning of 'designated sporting event' and 'the period of a designated sporting event' see paras 175 note 3, 177 note 3 respectively ante.
2 For the meaning of 'designated sports ground' see para 177 note 4 ante.
3 For the meaning of 'intoxicating liquor' see para 175 note 1 ante.

4 Sporting Events (Control of Alcohol Etc) Act 1985 s 6 (1). As to powers of enforcement see para 177 note 5 ante.
5 Ibid ss 6 (2), 8 (b). For the meaning of 'the standard scale' see para 808 post.

179. Possession of fireworks etc at sports grounds. A person is guilty of an offence if he has an article or specified substance[1] in his possession (1) at any time during the period of a designated sporting event[2] when he is in any area of a designated sports ground[3] from which the event may be directly viewed; or (2) while entering or trying to enter a designated sports ground at any time during the period of a designated sporting event at that ground, and is liable on summary conviction to imprisonment for a term not exceeding three months or a fine not exceeding level 3 on the standard scale, or to both[4]. It is a defence, however, for the accused to prove that he had possession with lawful authority[5].

1 The Sporting Events (Control of Alcohol Etc) Act 1985 s 2A (added by the Public Order Act 1986 s 40 (1), Sch 1 para 3) applies to any article or substance whose main purpose is the emission of a flare for purposes of illuminating or signalling, as opposed to igniting or heating, or the emission of smoke or a visible gas; and in particular it applies to distress flares, fog signals, and pellets and capsules intended to be used as fumigators or for testing pipes, but not to matches, cigarette lighters or heaters: Sporting Events (Control of Alcohol Etc) Act 1985 s 2A (3) (as so added). Section 2A (as so added) also applies to any article which is a firework: s 2A (4) (as so added).
2 For the meaning of 'designated sporting event' and 'the period of a designated sporting event' see paras 175 note 3, 177 note 3 respectively ante.
3 For the meaning of 'designated sports ground' see para 177 note 4 ante.
4 Sporting Events (Control of Alcohol Etc) Act 1985 s 2A (1) (as added: see note 1 supra). For the meaning of 'the standard scale' see para 808 post. As to powers of enforcement see para 177 note 5 ante.
5 Ibid s 2A (2) (as added: see note 1 supra).

B. CONTROL OF FOOTBALL SPECTATORS

(A) *National Membership Scheme*

180. The Football Membership Authority. There is a body responsible for the administration of the national football membership scheme[1] which is designated for the purpose by the Secretary of State under the name 'the Football Membership Authority'[2]. The Secretary of State may designate as the Football Membership Authority any body corporate formed for the purpose by the Football Association and the Football League or any body corporate formed by any other persons or, for the purpose, on his behalf[3]. The Secretary of State may withdraw the designation of such a body, whether at the instance of the body or at his own instance[4].

The functions of a body as the Football Membership Authority are assumed or, on withdrawal of its designation, divested on the date specified by the Secretary of State when making or withdrawing the designation[5]. No date other than 1 June in any year may, however, be so specified as the date on which functions are to be assumed or divested, but this does not apply:

(1) to the initial designation of a body as the Football Membership Authority; or
(2) where the Secretary of State withdraws the designation of a body on the ground that the body has failed to discharge its duties as the Football Membership Authority or is being wound up or that a receiver or manager of its property has been appointed[6].

It is the duty of the Football Membership Authority to make to the Secretary of State a report on the discharge of its functions during each period of 12 months beginning with 1 June in any year and the Secretary of State must lay a copy of the report before each House of Parliament[7].

On the withdrawal of the designation of a body as the Football Membership Authority, the scheme ceases to have effect but the Secretary of State may by order provide for the transfer of the body's property, rights and liabilities under the scheme to its successor as the Football Membership Authority on such terms and conditions as may be determined by the Secretary of State[8].

1 For these purposes, the 'national football membership scheme' ('the scheme') means the scheme made and approved and for the time being in force under the Football Spectators Act 1989 s 4 (see para 181 post) for the purpose of restricting the generality of spectators attending designated football matches to persons who are members of the scheme: s 1 (1), (5). 'Designated football match' means any such match of a description for the time being designated for these purposes by order made by the Secretary of State or a particular such match so designated: s 1 (1), (2). The Secretary of State may not so make a designation without giving the Football Membership Authority an opportunity to make representations about the proposed designation, and taking any representations he receives into account: s 1 (1), (3). An order under s 1 (2) may (1) designate descriptions of football matches wherever played or when played at descriptions of ground or in any area specified in the order; and (2) may provide, in relation to the match or description of match designated by the order or any description of match falling within the designation, that spectators admitted to the ground shall be authorised spectators to the extent, and subject to any restrictions or conditions, determined in pursuance of the order by the licensing authority under Pt I (ss 1–13): s 1 (1), (4). For the meaning of 'authorised spectator' see para 182 note 3 post; and for the meaning of 'the licensing authority' see para 186 post. The power so to make an order is exercisable by statutory instrument which is subject to annulment in pursuance of a resolution of either House of Parliament: s 1 (1), (10). At the date at which this volume states the law no such order had been made.

The provisions of Pt I (ss 1–13) apply in relation to association football matches played in England and Wales which are designated football matches: s 1 (1).

2 Ibid s 3 (1). The provisions of the Football Spectators Act 1989 do not come into operation until such day as the Secretary of State may by order made by statutory instrument; and different days may be appointed for different provisions of the Act: s 27 (2), (3). A statutory instrument appointing a commencement date for s 3 (see para 180 ante) or s 13 (licensing authority's powers in relation to safety at football grounds: see PUBLIC HEALTH) is subject to annulment in pursuance of a resolution of either House of Parliament: s 27 (4). The Public Order Act 1986 ss 30–37 (exclusion orders) cease to have effect on the date appointed under the Football Spectators Act 1989 s 27 (2) except for the purposes of the making under the Public Order Act 1986 s 33 of applications after that date to terminate exclusion orders and the communication of termination orders under s 34 (2): Football Spectators Act 1989 s 27 (5). At the date at which this volume states the law no orders had been made bringing any of the provisions of the 1989 Act into force.

3 Ibid s 3 (2). The Secretary of State may not designate any body corporate as the Football Membership Authority, however, unless he is satisfied that its articles of association make provision securing:

(a) that its Board shall comprise a chairman and six other members, of whom the chairman and four of the other members are persons approved by the Secretary of State before their election as chairman or as member, as the case may be, and the remaining two members are persons nominated by the Secretary of State; and

(b) that the chairman shall be a person who has no financial or other interest as is likely to affect prejudicially the performance of his functions as chairman;

and all the members of the Board hold office in accordance with the articles of association of the body corporate: s 3 (4).

4 Ibid s 3 (3). The Secretary of State may withdraw the designation of a body corporate as the Football Membership Authority if he ceases to be satisfied of the matters mentioned in s 3 (4) (see note 3 supra): s 3 (5).

Where the Secretary of State withdraws the designation of a body as the Football Membership Authority, he must, as soon as it appears to him to be appropriate to do so, lay before each House of Parliament a report stating his reasons for the withdrawal: s 3 (10).

5 Ibid s 3 (6).

6 Ibid s 3 (7).

7 Ibid s 3 (8). Where a body assumes or is divested of its functions as the Football Membership Authority on a date other than 1 June, s 3 (8) has effect as if it required a report to be made for such period as the Secretary of State directs: s 3 (9).

8 Ibid s 3 (11). The power to make such an order is exercisable by statutory instrument: s 3 (12).

181. Making, approval etc of the scheme. The Football Membership Authority[1] must, as soon as reasonably practicable after its designation takes effect, prepare a draft scheme which fulfils the statutory requirements[2]. Before exercising any of its functions under these provisions, the Football Membership Authority must (1) consult the Football Association, the Football Association of Wales and the Football League; and (2) give such persons as appear to it to represent the interests of football supporters an opportunity to make representations[3].

When the draft scheme is complete, the Football Membership Authority must submit it to the Secretary of State for his approval and the Secretary of State, if satisfied that the draft scheme fulfils those requirements, may, if he thinks fit, by order approve it either as submitted or with any modifications that may be agreed and, if he does so, he must lay a copy of the scheme as approved before each House of Parliament[4]. Where the Secretary of State so approves the scheme[5], the scheme enters into force on such date as may be agreed between the Secretary of State and the Football Membership Authority[6].

At any time during the currency of the scheme, the Secretary of State and the Football Membership Authority may agree to modify the scheme or to replace the scheme with another scheme in accordance with the statutory provisions[7]. Where the Secretary of State and the Football Membership Authority agree to modify the scheme, the Secretary of State must lay a copy of the modifications before each House of Parliament and the modifications agreed on enter into force on such date as may be agreed and the scheme has effect accordingly[8]. Where the Secretary of State and the Football Membership Authority agree to replace the scheme, the Secretary of State must by order confirm his agreement to the new scheme and must lay a copy of it before each House of Parliament; and the new scheme enters into force and the existing scheme ceases to be in force on such date as may be agreed[9].

1 As to the Football Membership Authority see para 180 ante.
2 Football Spectators Act 1989 s 4 (1). The statutory provisions referred to are s 5: see para 182 post.
3 Ibid s 4 (2).
4 Ibid s 4 (3). The powers of the Secretary of State to make orders under s 4 are exercisable by statutory instrument which is subject to annulment in pursuance of a resolution of either House of Parliament: s 4 (8).
5 For the meaning of 'the scheme' see para 180 note 1 ante.
6 Football Spectators Act 1989 s 4 (4).
7 Ibid s 4 (5). The statutory provisions referred to are s 5: see para 182 post.
8 Ibid s 4 (6).
9 Ibid s 4 (7).

182. Contents and penalties. The national football membership scheme[1] must include provision:

(1) securing that the only spectators permitted to attend at designated football matches[2] are authorised spectators[3];

(2) providing for temporary membership of the scheme, including, in particular, the temporary membership of football club guests;

(3) providing for the admission as spectators at designated football matches, without their being members of the scheme, of disabled persons and accompanied children[4] in such circumstances and subject to such conditions as are specified in the scheme;

(4) securing that persons who are disqualified[5] are excluded from membership while so disqualified;

(5) providing for the exclusion from membership, for an appropriate period not exceeding two years determined under the scheme, of persons who are, by reference to circumstances specified in the scheme, determined under the scheme to be unfit for membership and for notifying persons who are excluded from membership of the grounds for the exclusion;

(6) imposing pecuniary penalties on any persons having functions under the scheme for failure to discharge those functions;

(7) imposing requirements as respects the procedure to be followed in dealing with applications for membership of the scheme and requiring that in Wales any application form for membership of the scheme shall also be available in Welsh;

(8) imposing requirements on responsible persons[6] as respects the procedure to be followed and equipment to be used in relation to any designated football match to secure that, except in an emergency, the only spectators admitted to and permitted to remain on the premises are authorised spectators;

(9) to such effect, in relation to the admission of spectators to the premises, as the Secretary of State may specify in writing;

(10) establishing and maintaining a central register of members of the scheme;

(11) regulating the form and contents of membership cards; and

(12) establishing procedures for the making and consideration of representations against decisions made under the scheme refusing or withdrawing membership of it and for the independent review of the decisions in the light of the representations[7].

The scheme may make provision:

(a) for the discharge of functions under the scheme by persons specified in the scheme on such terms as may be agreed with the Football Membership Authority[8] and approved by the Secretary of State;

(b) for the imposition of charges under the scheme, including different charges for different cases, in connection with the issue of membership cards to persons becoming members of the scheme; and

(c) providing for the admission as spectators at designated football matches, without their being members of the scheme, of descriptions of person specified in the scheme in such circumstances and subject to such conditions as are so specified[9].

Any person who, for the purpose of being admitted to membership of the national football membership scheme:

(i) makes a statement which he knows to be false or misleading in a material particular or recklessly makes a statement which is false or misleading in a material particular; or

(ii) produces, furnishes, signs or otherwise makes use of a document which he knows to be false or misleading in a material particular or recklessly produces, furnishes, signs or otherwise makes use of a document which is false or misleading in a material particular, is guilty of an offence and liable on summary conviction to a fine not exceeding level 3 on the standard scale[10].

1 For the meaning of 'the national football membership scheme' see para 180 note 1 ante.
2 For the meaning of 'designated football match' see para 180 note 1 ante.
3 For these purposes, a person is, in relation to any designated football match, an 'authorised spectator' if (1) he is a member of the national football membership scheme or is otherwise authorised by the scheme to attend the match; or (2) he is an authorised spectator by virtue of the Football Spectators Act 1989 s 1 (4) (b) (see para 180 note 1 head (2) ante); and a person is not be be treated as a 'spectator' in relation to such a match if the principal purpose of his being on the premises is to provide services in connection with the match or to report on it: s 1 (1), (6). The imposition under Pt I (ss 1–13) of restrictions on the persons who may attend as spectators at any designated football match does not affect any other right of any person to exclude persons from admission to the premises at which the match is played: s 1 (1), (11).
4 For these purposes, 'accompanied children' means persons under the age of 10 years in the charge of an authorised spectator: ibid s 5 (2).
5 Ie under ibid s 7: see para 184 post.
6 For these purposes, a person is a 'responsible person' in relation to any designated football match at any premises if he is a person concerned in the management of the premises or in the organisation of the match: ibid s 1 (1), (9).
7 Ibid s 5 (2). The requirements for a national football membership scheme referred to in s 4 (1), (5) (see para 181 ante) are those specified in s 5 (2): s 5 (1).
   Information obtained from persons under the national football membership scheme is to be treated as not obtained under an enactment for the purposes of the Data Protection Act 1984 s 2 (1), Sch 1 Pt II para 1 (2) (which treats information obtained under enactments as fairly obtained): Football Spectators Act 1989 s 5 (5). Nothing in the Data Protection Act 1984 s 28 (1), (2) (which exempts personal data relating to crime from the subject access provisions in certain cases) applies to personal data held by the Football Membership Authority for the purposes of the national football membership scheme: Football Spectators Act 1989 s 5 (6).
8 As to the Football Membership Authority see para 180 ante.
9 Football Spectators Act 1989 s 5 (3). The scheme may make different provision for different circumstances: s 5 (4).
10 Ibid s 5 (7), (8). For the meaning of 'the standard scale' see para 808 post.

183. Phased application of the scheme. The Secretary of State, in exercising his functions of designating football matches[1] as matches in relation to which the national football membership scheme[2] applies, must have regard to whether it is desirable to achieve a phased application of the scheme[3]. For this purpose, the Football Membership Authority[4] must consider the possibility of a phased application of the scheme and may make recommendations to the Secretary of State; and the Secretary of State must have regard to any recommendations so made[5].

1 Ie under the Football Spectators Act 1989 s 1 (2): see para 180 note 1 ante.
2 For the meaning of 'the national football membership scheme' see para 180 note 1 ante.
3 Football Spectators Act 1989 s 6 (1).
4 As to the Football Membership Authority see para 180 ante.
5 Football Spectators Act 1989 s 6 (2).

184. Disqualification for membership of the scheme. Any person who is subject to an exclusion order[1] whenever made is disqualified from becoming or continuing to be a member of the national football membership scheme[2] and, while he is so subject, he may not be admitted as a member of the scheme or, if he is a member, his membership must be withdrawn[3].

Any person convicted[4] of a relevant offence[5] is disqualified from becoming or continuing to be a member of the national football membership scheme, and the following provisions have effect in relation to such a person[6].

The period during which a person's disqualification continues is:

(1) in a case where he was sentenced to a period of imprisonment taking immediate effect, five years; and

(2) in any other case, two years,

beginning with the date of the conviction[7].

During the period for which a person is disqualified he may not be admitted as a member of the scheme or, if he is a member, his membership ceases on the date of the conviction[8].

1 Ie under the Public Order Act 1986 s 30 (repealed): see para 180 note 2 ante.

2 For the meaning of 'the national football membership scheme' see para 180 note 1 ante.

3 Football Spectators Act 1989 s 7 (1).

4 A person in relation to whom a probation order was made under the Powers of Criminal Courts Act 1973 Pt I (ss 1–46: see para 1242 et seq post) is to be treated, notwithstanding anything in s 13 (as amended) (see para 1255 post), as having been convicted of the offence for these purposes: Football Spectators Act 1989 s 7 (9).

5 The offences relevant for these purposes are those specified in ibid s 7 (5), Sch I as relevant offences, with or, as the case may be, without a declaration of relevance: s 7 (5). The offences relevant for these purposes are:

(1) any offence under s 2 (1) (see para 185 ante) or s 5 (7) (see para 182 ante);

(2) any offence under the Sporting Events (Control of Alcohol Etc) Act 1985 s 2 (see para 177 ante) committed by the accused at any designated football match or while entering or trying to enter the ground;

(3) any offence under the Public Order Act 1986 s 5 (see para 153 ante) or any provision of Pt III (ss 17–29: see para 154 et seq ante) committed during a period relevant to a designated football match at any premises while the accused was at, or was entering or leaving or trying to enter or leave, the premises;

(4) any offence involving the use or threat of violence by the accused towards another person committed during a period relevant to a designated football match at any premises while the accused was at, or was entering or leaving or trying to enter or leave, the premises;

(5) any offence involving the use or threat of violence towards property committed during a period relevant to a designated football match at any premises while the accused was at, or was entering or leaving or trying to enter or leave, the premises;

(6) any offence under the Licensing Act 1872 s 12 (persons found to be drunk in public places etc: see INTOXICATING LIQUOR vol 26 paras 411, 412) of being found drunk in a highway or other public place committed while the accused was on a journey to or from a designated football match, being an offence as respects which the court makes a declaration of relevance;

(7) an offence under the Criminal Justice Act 1967 s 91 (1) (disorderly behaviour while drunk in a public place: see INTOXICATING LIQUOR vol 26 para 412) committed in a highway or other public place while the accused was on a journey to or from a designated football match, being an offence as respects which the court makes a declaration of relevance;

(8) any offence under the Sporting Events (Control of Alcohol Etc) Act 1985 s 1 (see para 175 ante) committed while the accused was on a journey to or from a designated football match, being an offence as respects which the court makes a declaration of relevance;

(9) any offence under the Public Order Act 1986 s 5 (see para 153 ante) or any provision of Pt III (ss 17–29: see para 154 et seq ante) committed while the accused was on a journey to or from a designated football match, being an offence as respects which the court makes a declaration of relevance;

(10) any offence under the Road Traffic Act 1988 ss 4 or 5 (driving etc when under the influence of drink or drugs or with an alcohol concentration above the prescribed limit: see ROAD TRAFFIC) committed while the accused was on a journey to or from a designated football match, being an offence as respects which the court makes a declaration of relevance;

(11) any offence involving the use or threat of violence by the accused towards another person committed while one or each of them was on a journey to or from a designated football match, being an offence as respects which the court makes a declaration of relevance;

(12) any offence involving the use or threat of violence towards property committed while the accused was on a journey to or from a designated football match, being an offence as respects which the court makes a declaration of relevance:

Football Spectators Act 1989 Sch 1. In the application of Sch 1 for the purposes of Pt I (ss 1–13), the references in Sch 1 to designated football matches include in heads (8), (9), (11), (12) supra references to football matches designated for the purposes of Pt II (ss 14–22: see para 1343 note 1 post): s 7 (6). For the meaning of 'relevant to' see para 185 note 2 post. For these purposes, 'declaration of relevance', in relation to an offence, means a declaration that the offence related to football matches; and 'imprisonment' includes any form of detention or, in the case of a person under 21 years of age sentenced to custody for life, custody: s 7 (10) (a), (b). A court may not make a declaration of relevance as respects any offence unless it is satisfied that the prosecutor gave notice to the accused, at least five days before the first day of the trial, that it was proposed to show that the offence related to football matches: s 23 (1). A court may, in any particular case, make a declaration of relevance notwithstanding that notice to the accused as so required has not been given if he consents to waive the giving of full notice or the court is satisfied that the interests of justice do not require more notice to be given: s 23 (2).

Any notice or other document required or authorised by or by virtue of the Football Spectators Act 1989 to be served on any person may be served on him either by delivering it to him or by leaving it at his proper address or by sending it by post: s 25 (1). Any notice or other document so required or authorised to be served on a body corporate or a firm is duly served if it is served on the secretary or clerk of that body or a partner of that firm: s 25 (2). For these purposes, and for the purpose of the Interpretation Act 1978 s 7 (references to service by post: see STATUTES vol 44 para 854) in its application to the Football Spectators Act 1989 s 25, the proper address of a person, in the case of a secretary or clerk of a body corporate, is that of the registered office or principal office of that body, in the case of a partner of a firm is that of the principal office of the firm and in any other case is the last known address of the person to be served: s 25 (3). Section 25 and the Interpretation Act 1978 s 7 in its application to the Football Spectators Act 1989 s 25 is subject to s 21 (4), (7) (see para 1348 note 7 post): s 25 (4).

Where a court convicts a person of a relevant offence:

(a)   the court must, except in the case of an offence under s 2 (1) (see para 185 post) or s 5 (7) (see para 182 ante), certify that the offence is a relevant offence and must explain to him in ordinary language the effect of the conviction on his membership of the national football membership scheme; and

(b)   the clerk of the court, in the case of a magistrates' court, or the appropriate officer, in the case of the Crown Court:

     (i)   must, as soon as reasonably practicable, send to the Football Membership Authority and to the chief officer of police for the police area in which the offence was committed notice of the conviction and sentence and of the giving of any certificate that the offence is a relevant offence; and

     (ii)   must give a copy of the notices to the person who was convicted of the offence:

s 7 (7). For these purposes, the reference to a clerk of a magistrates' court is to be construed in accordance with the Magistrates' Courts Act 1980 s 141 (see MAGISTRATES), reading references to that Act as references to the Football Spectators Act 1989 s 7: s 7 (10) (c).

6   Ibid s 7 (2). Where, on appeal against a person's conviction of the relevant offence or against a sentence of imprisonment imposed on him in dealing with him for the offence, his conviction is quashed or the sentence is reduced to one which is not a sentence of imprisonment taking immediate effect, the court which determines the appeal or, as the case may be, the court to which the case is remitted, must cause notice of the quashing of the conviction or of the sentence imposed to be sent to the persons specified in s 7 (7) (b) (i), (ii) (see note 5 head (b) (i), (ii) supra) and, where his conviction is quashed, the Football Membership Authority must readmit him to membership of the scheme, but without prejudice to any proceedings under the scheme to exclude him from membership: s 7 (8).

7   Ibid s 7 (3).

8   Ibid s 7 (4).

185. Unauthorised attendance at designated football matches. If a person who is not, in relation to the match, an authorised spectator[1] enters or remains on premises as a spectator during a period relevant to[2] a designated football match[3], that person and any person who attempts to commit such an offence of entering premises is guilty of an offence and liable on summary conviction to imprisonment for a term not exceeding one month or a fine not exceeding level 3 on the standard scale, or to both[4].

A constable who reasonably suspects that a person has committed any such offence may arrest him without a warrant[5].

Where a person is charged[6] with an offence of entering or remaining on premises, and was at the time of the alleged offence not disqualified from being a member of the national football membership scheme[7], it is a defence to prove that he was allowed to enter the premises as a spectator by a person reasonably appearing to him to have lawful authority to do so[8].

1 For the meaning of 'authorised spectator' see para 182 note 3 ante.
2 Each of the following periods is 'relevant to' a designated football match, that is to say:
  (1) the period beginning:
    (a) two hours before the start of the match; or
    (b) two hours before the time at which it is advertised to start; or
    (c) with the time at which spectators are first admitted to the premises,
  whichever is the earliest, and ending one hour after the end of the match;
  (2) where a match advertised to start at a particular time on a particular day is postponed to a later day, or does not take place, the period in the advertised day beginning two hours before and ending one hour after that time:
  Football Spectators Act 1989 s 1 (1), (8).
3 For the meaning of 'designated football match' see para 180 note 1 ante.
4 Football Spectators Act 1989 s 2 (1), (3). For the meaning of 'the standard scale' see para 808 post. As to restriction orders see para 1343 et seq post.
5 Ibid s 2 (4). As to arrest without warrant see para 703 et seq post.
6 Ie under ibid s 2 (1): see supra.
7 For the meaning of 'the national football membership scheme' see para 180 note 1 ante.
8 Football Spectators Act 1989 s 2 (2).

(B) *Licences to Admit Spectators*

186. The Football Licensing Authority. There is a body called the Football Licensing Authority ('the licensing authority')[1] which must perform the functions assigned[2] to it[3]. The licensing authority consists of a chairman and not less than four nor more than eight other members[4]; and the chairman and other members must be appointed by the Secretary of State[5]. It is the duty of the Secretary of State:
  (1) to satisfy himself, before he appoints a person to be a member of the licensing authority, that he will have no such financial or other interest as is likely to affect prejudicially the performance of his functions as a member; and
  (2) to satisfy himself from time to time with respect to each member that he has no such interest[6].
The quorum of the licensing authority and the arrangements relating to its meetings are such as the licensing authority may determine[7].

The licensing authority may appoint such inspectors as it may determine to perform such functions as are assigned to them[8]; and it may appoint a secretary and such other officers, and take into its employment such other persons, as it may determine[9].

1 The licensing authority is a body corporate: Football Spectators Act 1989 s 8 (4), Sch 2 para 1 (1). It is not to be regarded as the servant or agent of the Crown, or as enjoying any status, privilege or immunity of the Crown; and its property is not to be regarded as property of, or property held on behalf of, the Crown: Sch 2 para 1 (2). It is not exempt from any tax, duty, rate, levy or other charge whatsoever, whether general or local; and it has power to do anything which is calculated to facilitate the discharge of its functions, or is incidental or conducive to their discharge: Sch 2 para 1 (3), (4). Its expenses must be paid by the Secretary of State: s 8 (5).
  The application of the seal of the licensing authority is authenticated by the signature of the chairman of the authority or some other person authorised by the authority to act for that purpose

and that of one other member: Sch 2 para 29. Any document purporting to be an instrument issued by the licensing authority and to be so sealed, or to be signed on behalf of the authority, must be received in evidence and is deemed to be such an instrument without further proof unless the contrary is shown: Sch 2 para 30.

2 Ie by ibid Pt I (ss 1–13).

3 Ibid s 8 (1). As to the licensing authority's powers in relation to safety at football grounds see s 13 and PUBLIC HEALTH; and as to the licensing authority's duty to keep proper accounts and records and the audit of such accounts see Sch 2 paras 23–28.

4 Ibid s 8 (2).

5 Ibid s 8 (3). A person holds and vacates office as a member or the chairman of the licensing authority in accordance with the terms of his appointment; and a person may not be appointed as a member of the licensing authority for more than three years at a time: Sch 2 paras 4, 5. A person may at any time resign his office as a member or chairman of the licensing authority by giving the Secretary of State a signed notice in writing stating that he resigns that office: Sch 2 para 6. Where a member becomes or ceases to be the chairman, the Secretary of State may vary the terms of his appointment as a member of the licensing authority so as to alter the date on which he is to vacate office as a member: Sch 2 para 7.
   If the Secretary of State is satisfied that a member of the licensing authority (1) has been absent from meetings of the licensing authority for a period longer than three consecutive months without the permission of the licensing authority; or (2) has become bankrupt or made an arrangement with his creditors; or (3) is unable or unfit to discharge the functions of a member, the Secretary of State may declare his office as a member of the licensing authority vacant, and notify the declaration in such manner as he thinks fit; and thereupon the office becomes vacant: Sch 2 para 8.
   A person who ceases to be a member, or ceases to be chairman, of the licensing authority is eligible for reappointment: Sch 2 para 9.
   The licensing authority may pay to each member such remuneration and allowances as the Secretary of State may determine; and it may pay, or make provision for paying, to or in respect of any member such sums by way of pensions, allowances or gratuities as the Secretary of State may determine: Sch 2 paras 10, 11. Where a person ceases to be a member otherwise than on the expiry of his term of office and it appears to the Secretary of State that there are special circumstances which make it right for him to receive compensation, the licensing authority may make to him a payment of such amount as the Secretary of State may determine: Sch 2 para 12. The approval of the Treasury is, however, required for any determination under Sch 2 paras 10, 11 or 12: Sch 2 para 13.

6 Ibid Sch 2 para 2. Any person who is, or whom the Secretary of State proposes to appoint to be, a member of the licensing authority must, whenever requested by the Secretary of State to do so, furnish to him such information as the Secretary of State considers necessary for the performance by him of his duties under Sch 2 para 2: Sch 2 para 3.

7 Ibid Sch 2 para 15. A member of the licensing authority who is in any way directly or indirectly interested in any matter which falls to be considered by the authority must disclose the nature of his interest at a meeting of the licensing authority and the disclosure must be recorded in the minutes of the meeting: Sch 2 para 16 (1). The member may not take part after the disclosure in any deliberation or decision with respect to the matter: Sch 2 para 16 (2). The validity of any proceedings of the licensing authority is not affected by any vacancy among the members or by any defect in the appointment of a member or by any failure to comply with the requirements of Sch 2 para 16: Sch 2 para 17.

8 Ibid Sch 2 para 18. The terms and conditions of appointments under Sch 2 paras 18, 19 (see infra) require the approval of the Secretary of State and the consent of the Treasury: Sch 2 para 20. As to the payment of pensions, allowances and gratuities to inspectors, officers and employees see Sch 2 paras 21, 22.

9 Ibid Sch 2 para 19. See note 8 supra.

187. Licences to admit spectators; in general. The licensing authority[1] may, on an application duly made by a responsible person[2], grant a licence to admit spectators[3] to any premises for the purpose of watching any designated football match[4] played at those premises[5]. An application for a licence in respect of any premises must be made in such manner, in such form and accompanied by such fee as may be determined by the Secretary of State[6]. The licensing authority may not refuse to grant a licence without notifying the applicant in writing of the proposed refusal and of the grounds for it, giving him an opportunity to make representations about them within the period of 28 days beginning with the service of the notice[7] and taking any representations so made into account in making its decision[8].

A licence to admit spectators to any premises may authorise the admission of spectators to watch all designated football matches or specified[9] descriptions of designated football matches or a particular such match[10]; and it may also include conditions requiring specified descriptions of spectators to be refused admittance to the premises to watch designated football matches or specified descriptions of designated football matches or a particular such match[11]. Such a licence must be in writing and may be granted on such terms and conditions as the licensing authority considers appropriate and, if the Secretary of State gives to the licensing authority a direction in respect of seating arrangements[12], the conditions may include conditions imposing requirements as respects the seating of spectators[13].

It is a condition of every licence that any authorised person[14] shall be entitled, on production, if so required, of his authority:

(1) to enter at any reasonable time any premises on which a designated football match is being or is to be played;

(2) to make such inspection of the premises and such inquiries relating to them as he considers necessary for these purposes; or

(3) to examine any records relating to the operation of the national football membership scheme[15] on the premises, and take copies of such records[16].

A licence to admit spectators remains in force, unless revoked or suspended[17] or surrendered, for a specified period[18]. The licensing authority may at any time, by notice in writing to the licence holder, vary[19] the terms and conditions of the licence[20]. However, the licensing authority may not vary the terms or conditions of a licence without:

(a) notifying the licence holder in writing of the proposed alterations or additions;

(b) giving him an opportunity to make representations about them within the period of 21 days beginning with the service of the notice; and

(c) taking any representations so made into account in making the decision[21].

In taking any decision under the above provisions the licensing authority must have regard, among the other relevant circumstances, to the following matters or to such of them as are applicable to the decision:

(i) whether the premises and the equipment provided and procedures used at the premises are such as to secure that, except, in the case of the procedures, in an emergency, only authorised spectators are admitted to designated football matches;

(ii) whether and to what extent the requirements imposed for that purpose by the national football membership scheme on responsible persons have been complied with;

(iii) whether the equipment provided, procedures used and other arrangements in force at the premises are such as are reasonably required to prevent the commission or minimise the effects of offences at designated football matches; and

(iv) such other considerations as the Secretary of State determines from time to time and notifies to the licensing authority[22].

If any term or condition of a licence is contravened, any responsible person is guilty of an offence and liable on summary conviction to a fine not exceeding level 5 on the standard scale[23]. Where a person is charged with such an offence, it is a defence to prove that the contravention took place without his consent and that he took all reasonable precautions and exercised all due diligence to avoid the commission of such an offence[24].

1 For the meaning of 'the licensing authority' see para 186 ante.
2 For the meaning of 'responsible person' see para 182 note 6 ante.
3 For these purposes, a 'licence to admit spectators' is a licence granted in respect of any premises by the licensing authority under the Football Spectators Act 1989 Pt I (ss 1–13) authorising the admission to the premises of spectators for the purpose of watching any designated football match played at those premises: s 1 (1), (7). For the meaning of 'spectator' see para 182 note 3 ante.
4 For the meaning of 'designated football match' see para 180 note 1 ante.
5 Football Spectators Act 1989 s 10 (1). The fees charged on the issue of licences may be fixed so as to reimburse the licensing authority its expenses under Pt I (ss 1–13) and must be paid by the licensing authority to the Secretary of State: s 10 (16).
6 Ibid s 10 (2).
7 As to the mode of service of notices see para 184 note 5 ante.
8 Football Spectators Act 1989 s 10 (3).
9 For these purposes, 'specified' means specified in the licence: ibid s 10 (17).
10 Ibid s 10 (4). Where a designation order includes the provision authorised by s 1 (4) (b) (see para 180 note 1 head (2) ante) as respects the admission of spectators to any ground as authorised spectators, the licensing authority may, by notice in writing to the licence holder, direct that, for the purposes of any match or description of match specified in the direction, the licence shall be treated as including such specified terms and conditions as respects the admission of spectators as authorised spectators as the licensing authority considers appropriate; and the licence has effect, for that purpose, subject to those terms and conditions: s 10 (7). For the meaning of 'authorised spectator' see para 182 note 3 ante.
11 Ibid s 10 (6).
12 Ie under ibid s 11. The Secretary of State may by order direct the licensing authority to include in any licence to admit spectators to any specified premises a condition imposing requirements as respects the seating of spectators at designated football matches at the premises; and it is the duty of the authority to comply with the direction: s 11 (1). The power to make an order containing such a direction is exercisable by statutory instrument which is subject to annulment in pursuance of a resolution of either House of Parliament: s 11 (6). The requirements imposed by such a condition may relate to the accommodation to be provided at, or the arrrangements to be made as respects the spectators admitted to, the premises: s 11 (2). A direction may require the licensing authority to include the condition in the licence when granting it or by way of varying the conditions of a licence: s 11 (3). Before so giving a direction in relation to any premises, the Secretary of State must consult the licensing authority which may, if it thinks fit, make recommendations to him: s 11 (4). The licensing authority may not, however, so make any recommendations without consulting the local authority in whose area the premises are situated: s 11 (5). For these purposes, 'local authority' has the same meaning as in the Safety of Sports Grounds Act 1975 (see PUBLIC HEALTH): Football Spectators Act 1989 s 11 (7).
13 Ibid s 10 (5).
14 For these purposes, 'authorised person' means any person authorised by the Secretary of State, the licensing authority or the Football Membership Authority: ibid s 10 (17). As to the Football Membership Authority see para 180 ante.
15 For the meaning of 'national football membership scheme' see para 180 note 1 ante.
16 Football Spectators Act 1989 s 10 (8).
17 Ie under ibid s 12: see para 188 post.
18 Ibid s 10 (9).
19 For these purposes, 'vary', in relation to a licence, includes the addition of further terms or conditions: ibid s 10 (17).
20 Ibid s 10 (10).
21 Ibid s 10 (11).
22 Ibid s 10 (12).
23 Ibid s 10 (13), (15). For the meaning of 'the standard scale' see para 808 post. Where an offence under the Football Spectators Act 1989 which has been committed by a body corporate is proved to have been committed with the consent or connivance of, or to be attributable to any neglect on the part of, a director, manager, secretary or similar officer of the body corporate, or any person purporting to act in that capacity, he, as well as the body corporate, is guilty of that offence and is liable to be proceeded against and punished accordingly: s 24 (1). Where the affairs of a body corporate are

managed by its members, s 24 (1) applies to the acts and defaults of a member in connection with his functions of management as if he were a director of the body corporate: s 24 (2).

24 Ibid s 10 (14).

188. Revocation and suspension of licences. The licensing authority[1] may at any time, by notice in writing to the holder of a licence to admit spectators[2], revoke the licence or suspend the licence indefinitely or for such period as the authority considers appropriate[3]. The licensing authority may not, however, so suspend or revoke a licence unless satisfied that it is necessary to do so having regard to the relevant[4] matters[5]. Nor may the licensing authority revoke or suspend a licence to admit spectators without:

(1) notifying the licence holder of the proposed revocation or suspension and of the grounds for it;

(2) giving him an opportunity to make representations about the matter within the period of 21 days beginning with the date of service of the notice; and

(3) taking any representations so made into account in making the decision[6].

The licensing authority may, however, if satisfied that the urgency of the case so requires, suspend a licence without observing the requirements of heads (1) to (3) above; but the authority must, as soon as is practicable, notify the person to whom the licence was granted of the grounds for the suspension[7]. A licence suspended under the above provisions is during the time of suspension of no effect[8].

Where a licence has been so suspended, the person to whom the licence was granted may at any time apply to the licensing authority to terminate the suspension; and the licensing authority may terminate the suspension if it appears to be appropriate to do so having regard to the relevant matters and after taking into account any representations made by the applicant[9].

1 For the meaning of 'licensing authority' see para 186 ante.
2 For the meaning of 'licence to admit spectators' see para 187 note 3 ante.
3 Football Spectators Act 1989 s 12 (1). As to the mode of service of notices see para 184 note 5 ante.
4 The matters which are relevant for these purposes are (1) the matters specified in ibid s 10 (12) (a)–(c) (see para 187 heads (i)–(iii) ante); and (2) such other considerations as the Secretary of State determines from time to time and notifies to the licensing authority: s 12 (3).
5 Ibid s 12 (2).
6 Ibid s 12 (4).
7 Ibid s 12 (5).
8 Ibid s 12 (6).
9 Ibid s 12 (7).

189. Admitting spectators to unlicensed premises. If persons are admitted as spectators[1] to, or permitted to remain as spectators on, any premises during a period relevant to[2] a designated football match[3] without a licence to admit spectators[4] being in force, any responsible person[5] is guilty of an offence and liable on conviction on indictment to imprisonment for a term not exceeding two years or a fine, or to both, or on summary conviction to a fine not exceeding the statutory maximum[6].

Where a person is charged with such an offence, it is a defence to prove that the spectators were admitted in an emergency or that the spectators were admitted without his consent and that he took all reasonable precautions and exercised all due diligence to avoid the commission of such an offence[7].

1 For the meaning of 'spectator' see para 182 note 3 ante.

2 For the meaning of 'relevant to' see para 185 note 2 ante.
3 For the meaning of 'designated football match' see para 180 note 1 ante.
4 For the meaning of 'licence to admit spectators' see para 187 note 3 ante.
5 For the meaning of 'responsible person' see para 182 note 6 ante.
6 Football Spectators Act 1989 s 9 (1), (3). For the meaning of 'the statutory maximum' see para 806 ante. As to offences by bodies corporate see para 187 note 23 ante.
7 Ibid s 9 (2).

(xiii) Unlawful Eviction and Harassment

190. Unlawful eviction of occupier. If any person[1] unlawfully deprives[2] the residential occupier[3] of any premises[4] of his occupation of the premises or any part thereof, or attempts to do so, he is guilty of an offence and liable on conviction on indictment to imprisonment for a term not exceeding two years or a fine, or to both, or on summary conviction to imprisonment for a term not exceeding six months or a fine not exceeding the prescribed sum, or to both, unless he proves that he believed[5], and had reasonable cause to believe, that the residential occupier had ceased to reside in the premises[6].

1 Where an offence under the Protection from Eviction Act 1977 s 1 (see infra and para 191 post) committed by a body corporate is proved to have been committed with the consent or connivance of, or to be attributable to any neglect on the part of, any director, manager or secretary or other similar officer of the body corporate or any person who was purporting to act in any such capacity, he as well as the body corporate is guilty of that offence and liable to be proceeded against and punished accordingly: s 1 (6).
2 Cases properly described as 'locking out' or not admitting the occupier on one or even more isolated occasions, so that in effect he continues to occupy the premises but is then unable to enter, do not fall within the offence under ibid s 1 (2), but more appropriately within the offence under s 1 (3) (see para 191 post): *R v Yuthiwattana* (1984) 80 Cr App Rep 55, CA. See also *Costelloe v London Borough of Camden* [1986] Crim LR 249, DC.
3 For these purposes, 'residential occupier', in relation to any premises, means a person occupying the premises as a residence, whether under a contract or by virtue of any enactment or rule of law giving him the right to remain in occupation or restricting the right of any other person to recover possession of the premises: Protection from Eviction Act 1977 s 1 (1). 'Residential occupier' does not, however, include a contractual licensee whose licence has expired: *R v Blankley* [1979] Crim LR 166 (decided under the Rent Act 1965 s 30 (repealed)). 'Occupying the premises as a residence' has the same meaning as in the Rent Act 1977 (see LANDLORD AND TENANT): *Schon v London Borough of Camden* (1986) 53 P & CR 361, DC.
4 'Premises' is to be given its normal wide meaning: *Thurrock UDC v Shina* (1972) 23 P & CR 205, DC (decided under the Rent Act 1965 s 30 (repealed); single room may constitute 'premises').
5 The accused's belief that a couple had ceased to reside in the house is a question for the jury to decide; and the trial judge errs if he takes away from the jury and himself decides the questions as to the time and existence of the accused's belief: *R v Davidson-Acres* [1980] Crim LR 50, CA.
6 Protection from Eviction Act 1977 s 1 (2), (4) (amended by the Magistrates' Courts Act 1980 s 32 (2)). For the meaning of 'the prescribed sum' see para 807 post. Nothing in the Protection from Eviction Act 1977 s 1 is to be taken to prejudice any liability or remedy to which a person guilty of such an offence may be subject in civil proceedings: s 1 (5). As to the possibility of a civil action arising from a criminal offence under s 1 (2) see *Ashgar v Ahmed* (1984) 17 HLR 25, CA and LANDLORD AND TENANT; and as to the payment of damages by a landlord for unlawfully depriving a residential occupier of any premises of his occupation of the whole or part of the premises see the Housing Act 1988 ss 27, 28, 33 and LANDLORD AND TENANT.

191. Unlawful harassment of occupier. If any person[1] with intent[2] to cause the residential occupier[3] of any premises (1) to give up the occupation of the premises or any part thereof[4]; or (2) to refrain from exercising any right or pursuing any remedy in respect of the premises or any part thereof, does acts[5] likely[6] to interfere with the peace or comfort of the residential occupier or members of his household, or persistently[7] withdraws or withholds services reasonably required for the occupation of the premises as a residence, he is guilty of an offence and liable on conviction on indictment to imprisonment for a term not exceeding two years or a fine, or to both, or on summary conviction to imprisonment for a term not exceeding six months or a fine not exceeding the prescribed sum, or to both[8].

If the landlord[9] of a residential occupier or an agent of the landlord (a) does acts likely to interfere with the peace or comfort of the residential occupier or members of his household; or (b) persistently withdraws or withholds services reasonably required for the occupation of the premises in question as a residence, and, in either case he knows, or has reasonable cause to believe, that that conduct is likely to cause the residential occupier to give up the occupation of the whole or part of the premises or to refrain from exercising any right or pursuing any remedy in respect of the whole or part of the premises, he is guilty of an offence and liable on conviction on indictment to imprisonment for a term not exceeding two years or a fine, or to both, or on summary conviction to imprisonment for a term not exceeding six months or a fine not exceeding the prescribed sum, or to both[10]. A person is not guilty of such an offence, however, if he proves that he had reasonable grounds for doing the acts or withdrawing or withholding the services in question[11].

1 As to offences committed by bodies corporate see para 190 note 1 ante.
2 A specific intent to cause the residential occupier either to give up the premises or to refrain from exercising some right in respect of the premises must be proved before the offence is complete; it is not sufficient to establish indifference to, and unconcern for, the tenant nor is it sufficient to establish a hopeful inactivity over services on the part of the landlord: *McCall v Abelesz* [1976] QB 585, [1976] 1 All ER 727, CA (decided under the Rent Act 1965 s 30 (repealed)). The facts of an earlier incident of harassment may be admissible eg to show animosity by the landlord to the tenant; evidence of the previous conviction is not normally so admissible: *R v Shepherd* (1980) 124 Sol Jo 290, CA.
3 For the meaning of 'residential occupier' see para 190 note 3 ante.
4 The consequence of doing building work thus affecting the peace or comfort of the occupier is not to be equated with the intent to evict, which must be established: *R v AMK (Property Management) Ltd* [1985] Crim LR 600, CA. The effect upon the occupier (the actus reus) and the intention (the mens rea) must coincide in point of time: *R v AMK (Property Management) Ltd* supra. An intention to persuade the occupier to leave for a limited period of time in order to enable work to be done, and thereafter to allow her to return, is not an intent to cause her to give up the occupation of the premises; but it would be an intent falling within head (2) supra: *Schon v London Borough of Camden* (1986) 53 P & CR 361, DC.
5 Although the plural is used, a single 'act' suffices: *R v Evangeles Polycarpou* (1978) 9 HLR 129, CA (decided under the Rent Act 1965 s 30 (repealed)). It is not necessary that the acts in question should constitute a breach of contract or a tort; it was sufficient that the accused's act, a refusal to replace a missing door key for the occupier of a bed-sitting room in her house, was an act calculated to interfere with the occupier's peace and comfort and was an act intended to cause him to give up his occupation of the premises: *R v Yuthiwattana* (1984) 80 Cr App Rep 55, CA. The words 'does acts' do not impose a responsibility to rectify damage already caused by an act done innocently without either of the necessary intentions in the offence: *R v Ahmad* (1987) 84 Cr App Rep 64, CA. As to acts of omission generally see para 9 ante. There was conduct in *R v Yuthiwattana* supra in addition to the refusal to provide a front door key and it seems not to have been argued that the failure to provide a key was a mere omission: *R v Ahmad* supra.
6 In the Protection from Eviction Act 1977 s 1 (3) the word 'likely' was substituted for the word 'calculated' in respect of acts done after 15 January 1989: see the Housing Act 1988 ss 29 (1), 141 (3). 'Calculated to' meant 'likely to': *R v AMK (Property Management) Ltd* [1985] Crim LR 600, CA. The word 'calculated' required that there had to be proved the element of calculated acts or of persistent withdrawal or withholding of services, as the case might be: *Westminster City Council v Peart* (1968) 19 P & CR 736, DC; *R v Abrol* [1972] Crim LR 318, CA (both decided under the Rent Act 1965 s 30 (repealed)).

7 'Persistently' refers to the offence of withholding as well as to that of withdrawing services: *Westminster City Council v Peart* (1968) 19 P & CR 736, DC (decided under the Rent Act 1965 s 30 (repealed)). The prosecution must prove that there is an element of deliberate continuity in withholding the services, coupled with the necessary intent: *R v Abrol* [1972] Crim LR 318, CA (decided under the Rent Act 1965 s 30 (repealed)).

8 Protection from Eviction Act 1977 s 1 (3), (6) (amended by the Magistrates' Courts Act 1980 s 32 (2); the Housing Act 1988 s 29 (1)). For the meaning of 'the prescribed sum' see para 807 post. The Protection from Eviction Act 1977 s 1 (3) (as so amended) creates only one offence: *Schon v London Borough of Camden* (1986) 53 P & CR 361, DC.

  Nothing in the Protection from Eviction Act 1977 s 1 is to be taken to prejudice any liability or remedy to which a person guilty of such an offence may be subject in civil proceedings: s 1 (5). As to the possibility of a civil action arising from a criminal offence under s 1 (3) (as so amended) see *Ashgar v Ahmed* (1984) 17 HLR 25, CA and LANDLORD AND TENANT.

9 For these purposes, 'landlord', in relation to a residential occupier of any premises, means the person who, but for (1) the residential occupier's right to remain in occupation of the premises; or (2) a restriction on the person's right to recover possession of the premises, would be entitled to occupation of the premises and any superior landlord under whom that person derives title: Protection from Eviction Act 1977 s 1 (3C) (added by the Housing Act 1988 s 29 (2)).

10 Protection from Eviction Act 1977 s 1 (3A) (added by the Housing Act 1988 s 29 (2)).

11 Protection from Eviction Act 1977 s 1 (3B) (added by the Housing Act 1988 s 29 (2)).

192. Residential occupiers of caravans. A person[1] is guilty of an offence[2] if:

  (1) during the subsistence of a residential contract[3], he unlawfully deprives the occupier[4] of his occupation on a protected site[5] of any caravan[6] which the occupier is entitled by the contract to station and occupy, or to occupy, as his residence thereon; or

  (2) after the expiration or determination of a residential contract, he enforces, otherwise than by proceedings in the court[7], any right to exclude the occupier from the protected site or from any such caravan, or to remove or exclude any such caravan from the site; or

  (3) whether during the subsistence or after the expiration or determination of a residential contract, with intent to cause the occupier to abandon the occupation of the caravan or remove it from the site, or to refrain from exercising any right or pursuing any remedy in respect thereof,

he does acts calculated to interfere with the peace or comfort of the occupier or persons residing with him, or persistently[8] withdraws or withholds services or facilities reasonably required for the occupation of the caravan as a residence on the site[9]. A person guilty of such an offence is liable on summary conviction to imprisonment for a term not exceeding six months or a fine not exceeding level 5 on the standard scale, or to both[10].

  In proceedings for an offence under heads (1) or (2) above it is, however, a defence to prove that the accused believed, and had reasonable cause to believe, that the occupier of the caravan had ceased to reside on the site[11].

1 Where an offence committed by a body corporate is proved to have been committed with the consent or connivance of, or to be attributable to any neglect on the part of, any director, manager, secretary or other similar officer of the body corporate or any person who is purporting to act in any such capacity, he as well as the body corporate is guilty of that offence and is liable to be proceeded against and punished accordingly: Caravan Sites Act 1968 s 14 (1).

2 Nothing in ibid s 3 applies to the exercise by any person of a right to take possession of a caravan of which he is the owner, other than a right conferred by or arising on the expiration or determination of a residential contract, or to anything done pursuant to the order of any court: s 3 (5).

3 Ibid Pt I (ss 1–5) applies in relation to any licence or contract under which a person is entitled to station a caravan on a protected site and occupy it as his residence, or to occupy as his residence a caravan stationed on any such site; and any such licence or contract is referred to as a residential

contract, and the person so entitled as the occupier: s 1 (1). For the meaning of 'protected site' see note 5 infra; and for the meaning of 'caravan' see note 6 infra.

4 For these purposes, 'occupier' includes the person who was the occupier under a residential contract which has expired or been determined and, in the case of the death of the occupier, whether during the subsistence or after the expiration or determination of the contract, includes any person then residing with the occupier being the widow or widower of the occupier, or, in default of a widow or widower so residing, any member of the occupier's family: ibid s 3 (2).

5 For these purposes, a protected site is any land in respect of which a site licence is required under the Caravan Sites and Control of Development Act 1960 Pt I (ss 1–32), or would be so required if Sch 1 para 11 (exemption of land occupied by local authorities) were omitted, not being land in respect of which the relevant planning permission or site licence is expressed to be granted for holiday use only, or is otherwise so expressed or subject to such conditions that there are times of the year when no caravan may be stationed on the land for human habitation: Caravan Sites Act 1968 s 1 (2). The site must be one in respect of which planning permission has been granted for the stationing of one or more caravans: *Balthasar v Mullane* (1985) 17 HLR 561, CA. The land can be a protected site where the reason that there is no site licence is the accused's fault in not having acquired planning permission: *Hooper v Eaglestone* (1977) 34 P & CR 311, DC.

6 'Caravan' means any structure designated or adapted for human habitation which is capable of being moved from one place to another, whether by being towed or by being transported on a motor vehicle or trailer, and any motor vehicle so designed or adapted, but does not include (1) any railway rolling stock which is for the time being on rails forming part of a railway system; or (2) any tent: Caravan Sites and Control of Development Act 1960 s 29 (1) (applied by the Caravan Sites Act 1968 s 16). As to the exclusion of twin-unit caravans see s 13.

7 If in proceedings by the owner of a protected site the court makes an eviction order, it may suspend the enforcement of the order for such period not exceeding 12 months from the date of the order as the court thinks reasonable: ibid s 4 (1).

8 Cf para 191 note 7 ante.

9 Caravan Sites Act 1968 s 3 (1).

10 Ibid s 3 (3) (amended by the Criminal Justice Act 1982 ss 35, 38, 46). For the meaning of 'the standard scale' see para 808 post. Proceedings for any such offence may be instituted by any local authority: s 14 (2). Section 3 (3) is without prejudice to any liability or remedy to which a person guilty of an offence may be subject in civil proceedings: s 3 (3).

11 Ibid s 3 (4).

(3) CONTAMINATION OF OR INTERFERENCE WITH GOODS

193. Contamination of or interference with goods with intention of causing public alarm or anxiety etc. A person who (1) contaminates or interferes with goods[1]; or (2) makes it appear that goods have been contaminated or interfered with; or (3) places goods which have been contaminated or interfered with, or which appear to have been contaminated or interfered with, in a place where goods of that description are consumed, used, sold or otherwise supplied with the intention:

  (a) of causing public alarm or anxiety; or
  (b) of causing injury to members of the public consuming or using the goods; or
  (c) of causing economic loss to any person by reason of the goods being shunned by members of the public; or
  (d) of causing economic loss to any person by reason of steps taken to avoid any such alarm or anxiety, injury or loss,

is guilty of an offence and liable on conviction on indictment to imprisonment for a term not exceeding ten years or a fine, or to both, or on summary conviction to imprisonment for a term not exceeding six months or a fine not exceeding the statutory maximum, or to both[2].

A person who, with any such intention as is mentioned in heads (a), (b) or (d) above, threatens that he or another will do, or claims that he or another has done[3], any of the acts mentioned in heads (1) to (3) above is also guilty of an offence and liable on conviction on indictment to imprisonment for a term not exceeding ten years or a fine, or to both, or on summary conviction to imprisonment for a term not exceeding six months or a fine not exceeding the statutory maximum, or to both[4].

1 For these purposes, 'goods' includes substances whether natural or manufactured and whether or not incorporated in or mixed with other goods: Public Order Act 1986 s 38 (5).
2 Ibid s 38 (1), (4). For the meaning of 'the statutory maximum' see para 806 post.
3 The reference in ibid s 38 (2) to a person claiming that certain acts have been committed does not include a person who in good faith reports or warns that such acts have been, or appear to have been, committed: s 38 (6).
4 Ibid s 38 (2), (4).

194. Possession of articles with a view to committing an offence in relation to contamination of or interference with goods etc. A person who is in possession[1] of any of the following articles:
   (1) materials to be used for contaminating or interfering with goods[2] or making it appear that goods have been contaminated or interfered with; or
   (2) goods which have been contaminated or interfered with, or which appear to have been contaminated or interfered with,
with a view to the commission of an offence of contamination of or interference with goods with the intention of causing public alarm or anxiety etc[3], is guilty of an offence and liable on conviction on indictment to imprisonment for a term not exceeding ten years or a fine, or to both, or on summary conviction to imprisonment for a term not exceeding six months or a fine not exceeding the statutory maximum, or to both[4].

1 As to the meaning of 'possession' in relation to statutory offences see *Warner v Metropolitan Police Comr* [1969] 2 AC 256, 52 Cr App Rep 373, HL.
2 For the meaning of 'goods' see para 193 note 1 ante.
3 Ie an offence under the Public Order Act 1986 s 38 (1): see para 193 ante.
4 Ibid s 38 (3), (4). For the meaning of 'the statutory maximum' see para 806 post.

(4) BIOLOGICAL WEAPONS

195. Prohibition on development etc of certain biological agents etc. No person[1] may develop, produce, stockpile, acquire or retain:
   (1) any biological agent[2] or toxin[3] of a type and in a quantity that has no justification for prophylactic, protective or other peaceful purpose;
   (2) any weapon, equipment or means of delivery designed to use biological agents or toxins for hostile purposes or in armed conflict[4].
Any person contravening the above provisions is guilty of an offence and liable on conviction on indictment to imprisonment for life or for any shorter term[5].

Proceedings for any such offence may not be instituted except by or with the consent of the Attorney General[6].

1 Where such an offence which is committed by a body corporate is proved to have been committed with the consent and connivance of, or to be attributable to any negligence on the part of, any

director, manager, secretary or other similar officer of the body corporate, or any person who was purporting to act in any such capacity, he as well as the body corporate is guilty of that offence and liable to be proceeded against and punished accordingly: Biological Weapons Act 1974 s 3.

2 For these purposes, 'biological agent' means any microbial or other biological agent: ibid s 1 (2).

3 For these purposes, 'toxin' means any toxin, whatever its origin or method of production: ibid s 1 (2).

4 Ibid s 1 (1).

5 Ibid s 1 (3).

6 Ibid s 2 (1) (a). As to the effect of this limitation see para 639 post.

196. Power to search and obtain evidence. If a justice of the peace is satisfied on information on oath that there is reasonable ground for suspecting that an offence under the Biological Weapons Act 1974[1] has been, or is about to be, committed, he may grant a search warrant authorising a constable:

(1) to enter, at any time within one month from the date of the warrant, any premises or place named therein, if necessary by force, and to search the premises or place and every person found therein;

(2) to inspect any document found in the premises or place or in the possession of any person found therein, and to take copies of, or seize or detain any such document;

(3) to inspect, seize and detain any equipment so found; and

(4) to inspect, sample, seize and detain any substance so found[2].

A warrant so issued may also authorise any person named in the warrant to accompany the constable and assist him in taking any of the above steps[3].

1 Ie under the Biological Weapons Act 1974 s 1: see para 195 ante.

2 Ibid s 4 (1) (amended by the Police and Criminal Evidence Act 1984 s 119 (2), Sch 7 Pt I). As to powers of entry, search and seizure see para 668 et seq post.

3 Biological Weapons Act 1974 s 4 (2).

(5) FIREARMS, AMMUNITION AND AIR WEAPONS

(i) Acquisition, Purchase and Possession

A. RESTRICTIONS ON ACQUISITION, PURCHASE AND POSSESSION

197. Meaning of 'firearm'. 'Firearm' means a lethal[1] barrelled weapon of any description from which any shot, bullet or other missile can be discharged[2], and includes (1) any prohibited weapon[3], whether it is such a lethal weapon or not; and (2) any component part of such a lethal or prohibited weapon; and (3) any accessory to any such weapon designed or adapted to diminish the noise or flash caused by firing the weapon[4]. 'Firearm' includes an imitation firearm, that is to say anything which has the appearance of being a firearm, other than a prohibited weapon, whether or not it is capable of discharging any shot, bullet or other missile, but only if it has the appearance of being a firearm requiring a firearm certificate[5], and it is so constructed or adapted as to be readily convertible[6] into a firearm[7].

1 A weapon is lethal if it is capable, irrespective of the maker's intentions, of causing injury: *Read v Donovan* [1947] KB 326, [1947] 1 All ER 37, DC (signal pistol, capable of killing at short range); *Muir v Cassidy* 1953 SLT 4 (double-barrelled pistol with holes bored in the sides of the barrels; holes might be filled up so as to make it effective with live ammunition); *R v Freeman* [1970] 2 All ER 413, [1970] 1

WLR 788, CA (starting pistol capable of discharging bullets if barrel was drilled; barrel partially drilled); *Cafferata v Wilson* [1936] 3 All ER 149, DC (dummy revolver capable of conversion by drilling into weapon capable of killing man at a range of five feet); *Moore v Gooderham* [1960] 3 All ER 575, [1960] 1 WLR 1308, DC (air gun capable, if misused, of causing injury from which death might result); *Herron v Flockhart* 1969 SLT (Sh Ct) 37 (air gun); *R v Thorpe* [1987] 2 All ER 108, 85 Cr App Rep 107, CA (six-chamber revolver, loaded with .177 air pellets, propelled by release of compressed carbon dioxide; applying *Read v Donovan* supra and *Moore v Gooderham* supra; when misused capable of causing injury from which death might result). In determining whether a particular weapon is a 'firearm' there are two issues: (1) whether it is a weapon from which any shot etc can be discharged or whether it can be adapted so as to discharge any such missile; (2) if so, whether it is a lethal barrelled weapon: *Grace v DPP* [1989] Crim LR 365, DC. The earlier cases do not establish that a particular weapon is, as a matter of law, a lethal weapon: *Grace v DPP* supra.

2   It is presumed, unless the contrary is shown, that a firearm has been rendered incapable of discharging any shot, bullet or other missile, and has consequently ceased to be a firearm within the meaning of the Firearms Act 1968 and the Firearms (Amendment) Act 1988, if (1) it bears a mark which has been approved by the Secretary of State for denoting that fact and which has been made either by one of the two companies mentioned in the Firearms Act 1968 s 58 (1) (para 200 note 1 post) or by such other person as may be approved by the Secretary of State for these purposes; and (2) that company or person has certified in writing that work has been carried out on the firearm in a manner approved by the Secretary of State for rendering it incapable of discharging any shot, bullet or other missile: Firearms (Amendment) Act 1988 s 8.

3   Ie within the meaning of the Firearms Act 1968 s 5 (1), (2): see para 221 post.

4   Ibid s 57 (1). Where a judge determines that a hand–held signalling discharger is capable of amounting to a firearm, he is entitled to leave to the jury the question whether it does so amount, since the matter is a question of mixed fact and law: *R v Singh* (1989) Times, 29 May, CA.

5   Ie under the Firearms Act 1968 s 1 (as amended): see para 200 post.

6   For these purposes, an imitation firearm is to be regarded as readily convertible into a firearm to which ibid s 1 applies if (1) it can be so converted without any special skill on the part of the person converting it in the construction or adaptation of firearms of any description; and (2) the work involved in converting it does not require equipment or tools other than such as are in common use by persons carrying out works of construction and maintenance in their own homes: Firearms Act 1982 s 1 (6).

7   Ibid s 1 (1), (3); Firearms Act 1968 s 57 (4). Subject to the Firearms Act 1982 ss 1 (3)–(6), 2 (2), the Firearms Act 1968 applies in relation to an imitation firearm to which the 1982 Act applies as it applies in relation to a firearm to which the Firearms Act 1968 s 1 (as amended) (see para 200 post) applies: Firearms Act 1982 s 1 (2), (3). References in the Firearms Act 1968, and in any order made under s 6 (see para 223 post) to firearms (without qualification) or to firearms to which s 1 (as amended) (see para 200 post) applies are to be read as including imitation firearms to which the Firearms Act 1982 applies: s 2 (1). However, the following provisions of the Firearms Act 1968 do not apply by virtue of the Firearms Act 1982 to an imitation firearm to which the 1982 Act applies: (1) the Firearms Act 1968 s 4 (3), (4) (offence to convert anything having appearance of firearm into a firearm and aggravated offence under s 1 (as amended) involving a converted firearm: see para 233 post); and (2) the provisions of the 1968 Act which relate to, or to the enforcement of control over, the manner in which a firearm is used or the circumstances in which it is carried, viz s 16 (as amended) (see para 230 post), s 17 (as amended) (see paras 231, 232 post), s 18 (see para 234 post), s 19 (see para 235 post), s 20 (see para 236 post), s 47 (see para 238 post); but without prejudice, in the case of the provisions mentioned in head (2) supra, to the application to such an imitation firearm of such of those provisions as apply to imitation firearms apart from the Firearms Act 1982: s 2 (2), (3). However, for the purposes of s 1 and the 1968 Act as it applies by virtue of the Firearms Act 1982 s 1, the definition of 'air weapon' in the Firearms Act 1968 s 1 (3) (b) (see para 199 post) includes such weapons declared by the Secretary of State to be specially dangerous (see para 199 note 2 post); and the definition of 'firearm' in the Firearms Act 1968 s 57 (1) (see supra) does not include s 57 (1) (b), (c) (see heads (2), (3) supra): Firearms Act 1982 s 1 (4).

In any proceedings brought by virtue of s 1 for an offence under the Firearms Act 1968 involving an imitation firearm to which the Firearms Act 1982 applies, it is a defence for the accused to show that he did not know and had no reason to suspect that the imitation firearm was so constructed or adapted as to be readily convertible into a firearm to which the Firearms Act 1968 s 1 (as amended) applies: Firearms Act 1982 s 1 (5).

The provisions of the Firearms (Amendment) Act 1988 other than s 15 (see para 214 post), s 17 (see para 216 post) are to be treated as contained in the Firearms Act 1968 for the purposes of the Firearms

Act 1982 (imitation firearms readily convertible into firearms to which the Firearms Act 1968 s 1 (as amended) applies: Firearms (Amendment) Act 1988 s 25 (7).

198. Meaning of 'shot gun'. 'Shot gun' means a smooth-bore gun, not being an air gun, which (1) has a barrel not less than 24 inches in length[1] and does not have any barrel with a bore exceeding two inches in diameter; (2) either has no magazine or has a non-detachable magazine incapable of holding more than two cartridges; and (3) is not a revolver[2] gun[3]. A gun which has been adapted to have such a magazine as is mentioned in head (2) above is not to be regarded as falling within that head unless the magazine bears a mark approved by the Secretary of State for denoting that fact and that mark has been made, and the adaptation has been certified in writing as having been carried out in a manner approved[4] by him[5].

1 The length of the barrel of a firearm must be measured from the muzzle to the point at which the charge is exploded on firing: Firearms Act 1968 s 57 (6) (a).
2 For these purposes, 'revolver', in relation to a smooth-bore gun, means a gun containing a series of chambers which revolve when the gun is fired: ibid s 57 (2B) (added by the Firearms (Amendment) Act 1988 s 25 (2)).
3 Firearms Act 1968 ss 1 (3) (a), 57 (4) (substituted by the Firearms (Amendment) Act 1988 s 2 (1), (2)). As to shot guns whose barrels have been shortened see para 233 post.
    Any weapon which (1) has at any time since 1 July 1989 been a weapon to which the Firearms Act 1968 s 1 (as amended) applies; or (2) would at any previous time have been such a weapon if those provisions had then been in force, is to be treated, if it has or at any time has had, a rifle barrel less than 24 inches in length, as a weapon to which s 1 (as amended) applies notwithstanding anything done for the purpose of converting it into a shot gun or an air weapon: Firearms (Amendment) Act 1988 s 7 (2). For these purposes, there is to be disregarded the shortening of a barrel by a registered firearms dealer for the sole purpose of replacing part of it so as to produce a barrel not less than 24 inches in length: s 7 (3).
4 Ie approved either by one of the two companies mentioned in the Firearms Act 1968 s 58 (1) (see para 200 note 1 post) or by such other person as may be approved by him for that purpose.
5 Ibid s 1 (3A) (added by the Firearms (Amendment) Act 1988 s 2 (1), (3)).

199. Meaning of 'air weapon'. 'Air weapon' means an air rifle, air gun or air pistol not of a type declared by rules made by the Secretary of State[1] to be specially dangerous[2]. 'Air weapon' carries the ordinary meaning of a weapon in which the propulsion is caused by, or derived from, the use of air[3].

1 Ie under the Firearms Act 1968 s 53. The Secretary of State may by statutory instrument make rules (1) prescribing the form of certificates under the Firearms Acts 1968–1988, and the register required under the Firearms Act 1968 s 40 (register of transactions: see TRADE AND LABOUR vol 47 para 375) and other documents; (2) prescribing any other thing which is to be prescribed; and (3) generally carrying the Firearms Acts 1968–1988 into effect; and rules so made may make different provision for different cases: Firearms Act 1968 s 53; Firearms (Amendment) Act 1988 s 25 (6). Rules so made may (1) regulate the manner in which chief officers of police are to carry out their duties under the Firearms Act 1968 and the Firearms (Amendment) Act 1988; (2) enable all or any of the functions of a chief officer of police to be discharged by deputy in the event of his illness or of a vacancy in the office of chief officer of police: Firearms Act 1968 s 55 (1); Firearms (Amendment) Act 1988 s 25 (6). Without prejudice to head (2) supra, the functions of a chief officer of police are so exercisable on any occasion by a person, or a person of a particular class, authorised by the chief officer of police to exercise that function on that occasion, or on occasions of that class or on all occasions: Firearms Act 1968 s 55 (2); Firearms (Amendment) Act 1988 s 25 (6). In exercise of such power the Secretary of State made the Firearms Rules 1989, SI 1989/854, which came into force on 1 July 1989: see r 1 (1).
2 Firearms Act 1968 ss 1 (3) (b), 57 (4). An air weapon, that is to say an air rifle, air gun or air pistol, capable of discharging a missile so that the missile has, on being discharged from the muzzle of the weapon, kinetic energy in excess, in the case of an air pistol, of 6 ft lb or, in the case of an air weapon other than an air pistol, of 12 ft lb, is specially dangerous, except where it is designed for use only

when submerged in water: Firearms (Dangerous Air Weapons) Rules 1969, SI 1969/47, arts 2, 3. For the purposes of the Firearms Act 1982 s 1 'air weapon' includes such specially dangerous weapons: see para 197 note 7 ante.

3 Where propulsion arises from the compression of a gas such as carbon dioxide, the weapon is not an air weapon: *R v Thorpe* [1987] 2 All ER 108, [1987] 1 WLR 383, CA.

200. Firearms and ammunition for firearms. Subject to any statutory exemptions[1], it is an offence for a person to have in his possession[2], or to purchase or acquire[3] (1) any firearm[4], except[5] a shot gun[6] or an air weapon[7], without holding a firearm certificate[8] in force at the time, or otherwise than as authorised by such a certificate; (2) any ammunition[9] for a firearm, except (a) cartridges containing five or more shot, none of which exceeds .36 inch in diameter; (b) ammunition for an air gun, air rifle or air pistol; and (c) blank cartridges not more than one inch in diameter[10], without holding a firearm certificate in force at the time, or otherwise than as authorised by such a certificate or in quantities in excess of those so authorised[11].

A person guilty of such an offence is liable on conviction on indictment to imprisonment for a term not exceeding three years or a fine, or to both, or on summary conviction to imprisonment for a term not exceeding six months or a fine not exceeding the prescribed sum, or to both[12]. However, on conviction on indictment a person guilty of such an offence in an aggravated form by having in his possession or purchasing or acquiring a shortened shot gun[13] or a converted firearm[14] without holding a firearm certificate authorising him to do so is liable to imprisonment for a term not exceeding five years or a fine, or to both[15].

It is an offence for a person to fail to comply with a condition subject to which a firearm certificate is held by him; and a person guilty of such an offence is liable on summary conviction to imprisonment for a term not exceeding six months or a fine not exceeding level 5 on the standard scale, or to both[16].

1 Ie under the Firearms Act 1968 s 7 (see para 209 post); s 8 (1) (see para 210 post); s 9 (see para 211 post); s 10 (see para 212 post); s 11 (see para 213 post); s 12 (1) (see para 217 post); and s 13 (see para 218 post); and under the Firearms (Amendment) Act 1988 s 15 (see para 214 post); s 16 (see para 215 post); s 17 (see para 216 post); s 18 (see para 219 post); and s 19 (see para 220 post). The Firearms Act 1968 s 1 (see infra), s 2 (see para 201 post), ss 7–13 (see paras 209–218 post), ss 26–32 (registration of firearms dealers: see POLICE vol 36 para 332 et seq) in so far as those provisions relate to the purchase and acquisition of firearms, but not so far as they relate to possession of firearms, apply to persons in the service of Her Majesty, including special constables appointed on the nomination of the United Kingdom Atomic Energy Authority, in their capacity as such, except that such a person, if duly authorised in writing in that behalf, may purchase or acquire firearms and ammunition for the public service without holding a certificate under the 1968 Act: s 54 (1), (2) (a); Atomic Energy Authority (Special Constables) Act 1976 s 1 (1) (a). For the purpose of the Firearms Act 1968 s 54, a member of a police force is deemed to be a person in the service of Her Majesty: s 54 (3). A person in the naval, military or air service of Her Majesty is entitled, if he satisfies the chief officer of police on an application under s 26 that he is required to purchase a firearm or ammunition for his own use in his capacity as such, without payment of any fee to the grant of a firearm certificate authorising the purchase or acquisition or, as the case may be, to the grant of a shot gun certificate: s 54 (2) (b). If a person possesses a firearm otherwise than in his capacity as a servant of Her Majesty or a police officer, a firearm certificate is necessary: *Heritage v Claxon* (1941) 85 Sol Jo 323, DC; *Tarttelin v Bowen* [1947] 2 All ER 837. As to the application of the Firearms Act 1968 s 54 (1), (2) (a) to members of a visiting force and headquarters see the Visiting Forces and International Headquarters (Application of Law) Order 1965, SI 1965/1536, arts 3, 12, Schs 2, 3 (amended by SI 1987/928).

Nothing in the 1968 Act applies to the proof houses of the Master, Wardens and Society of the Mystery of Gunmakers of the City of London and the Guardians of the Birmingham Proof House or the rifle range at Small Heath in Birmingham where firearms are sighted and tested, so as to interfere in any way with the operations of those two companies in proving firearms under the provisions of the Gun Barrel Proof Act 1868 or any other Acts for the time being in force, or to any person carrying firearms to or from any such proof house when being taken to such proof house for the purposes of proof or being removed therefrom after proof; and nothing in the 1968 Act relating to firearms applies to an antique firearm which is sold, transferred, purchased, acquired or possessed as a curiosity or ornament: s 58 (1), (2). What is an antique firearm is a question of fact and degree depending upon the article in question: *Richards v Curwen* [1977] 3 All ER 426, 65 Cr App Rep 95, DC; *Bennett v Brown* (1980) 71 Cr App Rep 109, DC. This question is for the jury to decide: *R v Burke* (1978) 67 Cr App Rep 220, CA. The article must in fact be an antique weapon; it is not sufficient for the accused to have an honest and reasonable belief that it is such: *R v Howells* [1977] QB 614, 65 Cr App Rep 86, CA.

2 For the meaning of 'possession' see *Woodage v Moss* [1974] 1 All ER 584, [1974] 1 WLR 411, DC (firearm handed to accused by unknown man to deliver to dealer as surrendered weapon; accused in possession of the firearm); *Sullivan v Earl of Caithness* [1976] QB 966, 62 Cr App Rep 105, DC (owner in possession of firearms kept in another's custody; physical possession not necessary); *Hall v Cotton* [1987] QB 504, 83 Cr App Rep 257, DC (accused does not have to have physical control or be physically present where firearms are in order to be in possession; cases depend upon their own facts; there can be custodial possession and physical possession residing in different persons); *R v Hussain* [1981] 2 All ER 287, 72 Cr App Rep 143, CA (applying *Warner v Metropolitan Police Comr* [1969] 2 AC 256, 52 Cr App Rep 373, HL (see para 596 post) accused has firearm in possession if he knows that he has an article with him which in fact is a firearm; immaterial that accused did not know the nature of the article).

3 For these purposes, 'acquire' means hire, accept as a gift or borrow; and 'acquisition' is to be construed accordingly: Firearms Act 1968 s 57 (4). As to the restrictions on the manufacture of, and dealing in, firearms see s 3 and para 203 et seq post.

4 For the meaning of 'firearm' see para 197 ante.

5 So much of the Firearms Act 1968 s 1 as excludes any description of firearm from the category of firearms to which s 1 applies is to be construed as excluding component parts of, and accessories to, firearms of that description: s 57 (1).

6 For the meaning of 'shot gun' see para 198 ante.

7 For the meaning of 'air weapon' see para 199 ante.

8 'Firearm certificate' means a certificate granted by a chief officer of police under the Firearms Act 1968 (as amended) in respect of any firearm or ammunition to which s 1 applies and includes a certificate granted in Northern Ireland under the Firearms (Northern Ireland) Order 1981, SI 1981/155, Pt III (arts 27–44): Firearms Act 1968 s 57 (4); Interpretation Act 1978 s 17 (2). A certificate for a firearm covers its component parts eg a telescopic sight; the only accessory which must be separately mentioned is one designed or adapted to diminish the noise or flash caused by firing the weapon: *Watson v Herman* [1952] 2 All ER 70, DC. Component parts not made up so as to be part of a firearm may, it seems, be required to be covered by a certificate: *Watson v Herman* supra. See also *Broome v Walter* [1989] Crim LR 725, DC.

A firearm certificate is a specific, and not a general, certificate: see *Wilson v Coombe* [1989] 1 WLR 78, 88 Cr App Rep 322, DC. For the prescribed form of certificate see the Firearms Rules 1989, SI 1989/854, r 3 (5), Sch 1 Pt II. As to a constable's power to require production of a certificate see para 205 post.

9 'Ammunition' means ammunition for any firearm and includes grenades, bombs and other like missiles, whether capable of use with a firearm or not, and also includes prohibited ammunition (see para 221 post): Firearms Act 1968 s 57 (2). Blank cartridges are within the definition of ammunition: *Burfitt v Kille* [1939] 2 KB 743, [1939] 2 All ER 372, DC. The provisions of the Firearms Act 1968 relating to ammunition are in addition to, and not in derogation of, any concurrent enactment relating to the keeping or sale of explosives: s 58 (3). The sale of certain ammunition to which s 1 does not apply is restricted: see para 208 post.

10 Ie measured immediately in front of the rim or cannelure of the base of the cartridge.

11 Firearms Act 1968 s 1 (1), (3), (4). The offence is one of strict liability and thus proof of mens rea is unnecessary: *R v Howells* [1977] QB 614, 65 Cr App Rep 86, CA; *R v Hussain* [1981] 2 All ER 287, 72 Cr App Rep 143, CA. Possession etc of prohibited weapons requires an authority of the Secretary of State: see para 221 post. As to the requirement of shot gun certificates see para 201 post; and as to possession etc of firearms by, and supply to, minors see para 224 et seq post.

12 Firearms Act 1968 s 51, Sch 6 Pt I (amended by the Magistrates' Courts Act 1980 s 32 (2)). For the meaning of 'the prescribed sum' see para 807 post. As to powers of search see para 237 post; as to the limitation period for summary proceedings see para 240 post; and as to the court's power to order forfeiture or disposal of firearms and ammunition see para 241 post.

13 Ie a shot gun which has been shortened contrary to the Firearms Act 1968 s 4 (1): see para 233 post.

14 Ie a firearm which has been converted as mentioned in ibid s 4 (3) (see para 233 post), whether by a registered firearms dealer or not.
15 Firearms Act 1968 s 4 (4), Sch 6 Pt I (amended by the Firearms (Amendment) Act 1988 s 23 (1)). This offence does not apply to imitation firearms to which the Firearms Act 1982 applies: s 2 (2) (a).
16 Firearms Act 1968 s 1 (2), Sch 6 Pt I (amended by the Criminal Justice Act 1982 ss 38, 46). For the meaning of 'the standard scale' see para 808 post.

201. Shot guns. Subject to any statutory exemption[1], it is an offence for a person to have in his possession[2], or to purchase or acquire[3], a shot gun[4] without holding a shot gun certificate[5] authorising him to possess shot guns[6]. A person guilty of such an offence is liable on conviction on indictment to imprisonment for a term not exceeding three years or a fine, or to both, or on summary conviction to imprisonment for a term not exceeding six months or a fine not exceeding the statutory maximum, or to both[7].

It is also an offence for a person to fail to comply with a condition subject to which a shot gun certificate is held by him; and a person guilty of such an offence is liable on summary conviction to imprisonment for a term not exceeding six months or a fine not exceeding level 5 on the standard scale, or to both[8].

1 Ie under the Firearms Act 1968 ss 7–13 (see para 200 note 1 ante), s 15 (see note 6 infra), s 54 (see para 200 note 1 ante), s 58 (see para 200 note 1 ante). See also the Firearms (Amendment) Act 1988 s 17 and para 216 post, s 18 and para 219 post, s 19 and para 220 post.
2 For the meaning of 'possession' in the context of the Firearms Act 1968 s 1 see para 200 note 2 ante.
3 For the meaning of 'acquire' see para 200 note 3 ante.
4 For the meaning of 'shot gun' see para 198 ante.
5 'Shot gun certificate' means a certificate granted by a chief officer of police under the Firearms Act 1968 Pt II (ss 26–45) (amended by the Firearms (Amendment) Act 1988 s 3) and authorising a person to possess shot guns: Firearms Act 1968 s 57 (4). For the prescribed form of certificate see the Firearms Rules 1989, SI 1989/854, r 4 (5), Sch 2 Pt II. As to a constable's power to require production of a certificate see para 239 post.
6 Firearms Act 1968 s 2 (1). Section 2(1) does not apply to a person holding a firearm certificate issued in Northern Ireland authorising him to possess a shot gun: s 15.
7 Ibid s 51, Sch 6 Pt I (amended by the Criminal Justice Act 1988 s 44 (1), (2)). For the meaning of 'the statutory maximum' see para 806 post. Nothing in the Criminal Justice Act 1988 s 44 affects the penalty for an offence committed before 29 September 1988: ss 44 (4), 171 (6). As to possession etc of shot guns by, and supply of shot guns to, minors see para 225 post; as to transfer of shot guns see para 202 post; and as to sale of ammunition for smooth-bore guns see para 208 post. As to powers of search see para 237 post; as to the limitation period for summary proceedings see para 240 post; and as to the court's power to order cancellation of certificates and forfeiture or disposal of firearms and ammunition see para 241 post.
8 Firearms Act 1968 s 2 (2), Sch 6 Pt I (amended by the Criminal Justice Act 1982 ss 38, 46).

202. Transfer of shot guns. Where a person sells, lets on hire or gives a shot gun[1] or lends a shot gun for a period of more than 72 hours to another person in the United Kingdom who is neither a registered firearms dealer[2] nor a person who shows that he is entitled[3] to purchase or acquire the shot gun without holding a shot gun certificate, the transferor must:

(1) comply with any instructions contained in the certificate produced by the transferee; and

(2) within seven days of the transaction send a notice[4] of the transaction to the chief officer of police who issued the transferor's certificate or, if he is entitled[5] to be in possession of the shot gun without holding a certificate, to the chief officer of police who issued the transferee's certificate[6].

The transferee must, within seven days of the transaction, send a notice of the transaction to the chief officer of police who issued his certificate[7].

A person who fails to comply with the above provisions is guilty of an offence and liable on summary conviction to imprisonment for a term not exceeding six months or a fine not exceeding level 5 on the standard scale, or to both[8].

1 For the meaning of 'shot gun' see para 198 ante.
2 For the meaning of 'registered' and 'firearms dealer' see para 203 notes 4, 5 respectively post.
3 Ie by virtue of the Firearms Act 1968 or the Firearms (Amendment) Act 1988.
4 The notice of a transaction under ibid s 4 (2) or (3) (see infra) must contain a description of the shot gun in question, giving the identification number if any, and must state the nature of the transaction and the name and address of the other person concerned; and any such notice must be sent by registered post or the recorded delivery service: s 4 (4).
5 See note 3 supra.
6 Firearms (Amendment) Act 1988 s 4 (1), (2).
7 Ibid s 4 (3). See also note 4 supra.
8 Ibid s 4 (5). For the meaning of 'the standard scale' see para 808 post. As to powers of search see para 237 post; as to the limitation period for summary proceedings see para 240 post; and as to the court's power to order cancellation of certificates and forfeiture or disposal of firearms and ammunition see para 241 post.

203. Trading in firearms without being registered as a firearms dealer. A person commits an offence if, by way of trade or business, he (1) manufactures, sells, transfers[1], repairs, tests or proves any specified firearm or ammunition[2], or a shot gun[3]; or (2) exposes for sale or transfer, or has in his possession for sale, transfer, repair, test or proof any such firearm or ammunition, or a shot gun, without being registered[4] as a firearms dealer[5]. A person guilty of such an offence is liable on conviction on indictment to imprisonment for a term not exceeding three years or a fine, or to both, or on summary conviction to imprisonment for a term not exceeding six months or a fine not exceeding the prescribed sum, or to both[6].

1 For these purposes, 'transfer' includes let on hire, give, lend and part with possession; and 'transferor' and 'transferee' are to be construed accordingly: Firearms Act 1968 s 57 (4).
2 Ie any firearm or ammunition to which ibid s 1 (as amended) applies: see para 200 ante.
3 For the meaning of 'shot gun' see para 198 ante.
4 'Registered', in relation to a firearms dealer, means registered in Great Britain under the Firearms Act 1968 s 33 (see POLICE vol 36 para 338) or in Northern Ireland under corresponding legislation: s 57 (4). For the meaning of 'Great Britain' see para 86 note 1 ante.
5 Ibid s 3 (1). 'Firearms dealer' means a person who, by way of trade or business, manufactures, sells, transfers, repairs, tests or proves firearms or ammunition to which s 1 (as amended) (see para 200 ante) applies, or shot guns: s 57 (4).
    Section 3 (1) has effect subject to any exemption under subsequent provisions of the Firearms Act 1968: s 3 (4). As to exemptions see para 209 et seq post.
6 Ibid s 51, Sch 6 Pt I (amended by the Magistrates' Courts Act 1980 s 32 (2)). For the meaning of 'the prescribed sum' see para 807 post. As to powers of search see para 237 post; as to the limitation period for summary proceedings see para 240 post; and as to the court's power to order forfeiture or disposal of firearms see para 241 post.

204. Selling firearms to person without a certificate. It is an offence for a person to sell or transfer[1] to any other person in the United Kingdom, other than a registered firearms dealer[2], any specified firearm or ammunition[3], or a shot gun[4], unless that other produces a firearm certificate[5] authorising him to purchase or acquire[6] it or, as the case may be, his shot gun certificate[7], or shows that he is entitled to purchase or acquire it without holding a certificate[8]. A person guilty of such an offence is liable on conviction on indictment to imprisonment for a term not exceeding three years or a fine, or to both, or on summary conviction to imprisonment for a term not exceeding six months or a fine not exceeding the prescribed sum, or to both[9].

1 For the meaning of 'transfer' see para 203 note 1 ante.
2 For the meaning of 'registered' and 'firearms dealer' see para 203 notes 4, 5 respectively ante.
3 Ie any firearm or ammunition specified in the Firearms Act 1968 s 1 (as amended): see para 200 ante.
4 For the meaning of 'shot gun' see para 198 ante.
5 For the meaning of 'firearm certificate' see para 200 note 8 ante.
6 For the meaning of 'acquire' see para 200 note 3 ante.
7 For the meaning of 'shot gun certificate' see para 201 note 5 ante.
8 Firearms Act 1968 s 3 (2). For the meaning of 'United Kingdom' see para 86 note 1 ante. 'Certificate', except in a context relating to the registration of firearms dealers, means a firearm certificate or a shot gun certificate: s 57 (4). A firearm certificate does not, unless a variation order has been made, authorise the holder to acquire another firearm, even though it is a replacement; and a dealer exchanging a certificate holder's firearms for firearms of the same type and calibre commits an offence: *Wilson v Coombe* [1989] 1 WLR 78, 88 Cr App Rep 322, DC. The Firearms Act 1968 s 3 (2) has effect subject to any exemption under subsequent provisions of the Firearms Act 1968: s 3 (4). As to exemptions see para 209 et seq post.
  Any reference in the Firearms Act 1968 to a person who is by virtue of that Act entitled to possess, purchase or acquire any weapon or ammunition without holding a certificate includes a reference to a person who is so entitled by virtue of any provision of the Firearms (Amendment) Act 1988: s 25 (4).
9 Firearms Act 1968 s 51, Sch 6 Pt I (amended by the Magistrates' Courts Act 1980 s 32 (2)). For the meaning of 'the prescribed sum' see para 807 post. As to powers of search see para 237 post; as to the limitation period for summary proceedings see para 240 post; and as to the court's power to order forfeiture or disposal of firearms see para 241 post.

205. Repair, test etc of firearm for person without a certificate. It is an offence for a person to undertake the repair, test or proof of a specified firearm or ammunition[1], or of a shot gun[2], for any other person in the United Kingdom other than a registered firearms dealer[3] as such, unless that other produces or causes to be produced a firearm certificate[4] authorising him to have possession of the firearm or ammunition or, as the case may be, his shot gun certificate[5], or shows that he is entitled to have possession of it without holding a certificate[6]. A person guilty of such an offence is liable on conviction on indictment to imprisonment for a term not exceeding three years or a fine, or to both, or on summary conviction to imprisonment for a term not exceeding six months or a fine not exceeding the prescribed sum, or to both[7].

1 Ie a firearm or ammunition to which the Firearms Act 1968 s 1 (as amended) applies: see para 200 ante.
2 For the meaning of 'shot gun' see para 198 ante.
3 For the meaning of 'registered' and 'firearms dealer' see para 203 notes 4, 5 respectively ante.
4 For the meaning of 'firearm certificate' see para 200 note 8 ante.
5 For the meaning of 'shot gun certificate' see para 201 note 5 ante.
6 Firearms Act 1968 s 3 (3). For the meaning of 'certificate' see para 204 note 8 ante; and for the meaning of 'United Kingdom' see para 86 note 1 ante. As to references to persons entitled to possess, purchase or acquire any weapon or ammunition without holding a certificate see para 204 note 8 ante.
  Section 3 (3) has effect subject to any exemption under subsequent provisions of the Firearms Act 1968: s 3 (4). As to exemptions see para 209 et seq post.
7 Ibid s 51, Sch 6 Pt I (amended by the Magistrates' Courts Act 1980 s 32 (2)). For the meaning of 'the prescribed sum' see para 807 post. As to powers of search see para 237 post; as to the limitation period for summary proceedings see para 240 post; and as to the court's power to order forfeiture or disposal of firearms and ammunition see para 241 post.

206. Falsifying certificate etc with view to acquisition of firearm. A person commits an offence if, with a view to purchasing or acquiring[1], or procuring the repair, test or proof of, any specified firearm or ammunition[2], or a shot gun[3], he produces a false certificate[4] or a certificate in which any false entry has been made, or personates a person to whom a certificate has been granted, or makes any false statement[5]. Any person guilty of such an offence is liable on conviction on indictment to imprisonment for a term not exceeding three years or a fine, or to both, or on summary conviction to imprisonment for a term not exceeding six months or a fine not exceeding the prescribed sum, or to both[6].

1 For the meaning of 'acquire' see para 200 note 3 ante.
2 Ie any firearm or ammunition to which the Firearms Act 1968 s 1 (as amended) applies: see para 200 ante.
3 For the meaning of 'shot gun' see para 198 ante.
4 For the meaning of 'certificate' see para 204 note 8 ante.
5 Firearms Act 1968 s 3 (5).
6 Ibid s 51, Sch 6 Pt I (amended by the Magistrates' Courts Act 1980 s 32 (2)). For the meaning of 'the prescribed sum' see para 807 post. As to the limitation period for summary proceedings see para 240 post; and as to the court's power to order cancellation of certificates and forfeiture or disposal of firearms and ammunition see para 241 post.

207. Pawnbroker taking firearm in pawn. It is an offence for a pawnbroker to take in pawn any specified firearm or ammunition[1], or a shot gun[2]. A pawnbroker who commits such an offence is liable on summary conviction to imprisonment for a term not exceeding three months or a fine not exceeding level 3 on the standard scale, or to both[3].

1 Ie a firearm or ammunition to which the Firearms Act 1968 s 1 (as amended) applies: see para 200 ante.
2 Ibid s 3 (6). For the meaning of 'shot gun' see para 198 ante.
3 Ibid s 51, Sch 6 Pt I (amended by the Criminal Justice Act 1982 ss 38, 46). For the meaning of 'the standard scale' see para 808 post. As to powers of search see para 237 post; as to the limitation period for summary proceedings see para 240 post; and as to the court's power to order forfeiture or disposal of firearms and ammunition see para 241 post.

208. Restriction on sale of certain ammunition. It is an offence for a person to sell specified ammunition[1] to another person in the United Kingdom who is neither a registered firearms dealer[2] nor a person who sells such ammunition by way of trade or business unless that other person (1) produces a certificate authorising him to possess a shot gun or a smooth-bore gun; or (2) shows that he is entitled[3] to have possession of such a gun without holding a certificate[4]; or (3) produces a certificate authorising another person to possess such a gun, together with that person's written authority to purchase the ammunition on his behalf[5]. A person guilty of such an offence is liable on summary conviction to imprisonment for a term not exceeding six months or a fine not exceeding level 5 on the standard scale, or to both[6].

1 Ie ammunition to which the Firearms Act 1968 s 1 (as amended) (see para 200 note 9 ante) does not apply and which is capable of being used in a shot gun (see para 198 ante) or in a smooth-bore gun to which s 1 (as amended) applies.
2 For the meaning of 'registered' and 'firearms dealer' see para 203 notes 4, 5 respectively ante.
3 Ie under either the Firearms Act 1968 or the Firearms (Amendment) Act 1988.
4 As to exemptions see para 209 et seq post; and as to references to persons entitled to possess, purchase or acquire any weapon or ammunition without holding a certificate see para 204 note 8 ante.
5 Firearms (Amendment) Act 1988 s 5 (1), (2).
6 Ibid s 5 (1), (3). For the meaning of 'the standard scale' see para 808 post. As to the limitation period for summary proceedings see para 240 post; and as to the court's power to order forfeiture or disposal of firearms and ammunition see para 241 post.

B. EXEMPTIONS

209. Holders of police permits. A person who has obtained from the chief officer of police for the area[1] in which he resides[2] a permit[3] for the purpose may have in his possession, without holding a certificate[4], a firearm[5] or ammunition[6] in accordance with the terms of the permit[7].

It is an offence for a person to make any statement which he knows to be false for the purpose of procuring, whether for himself or for another person, the grant of such a permit[8]. A person guilty of such an offence is liable on summary conviction to imprisonment for a term not exceeding six months or a fine not exceeding level 5 on the standard scale, or to both[9].

1 For these purposes, 'area' means police area: Firearms Act 1968 s 57 (4). For the meaning of 'police area' see para 142 note 1 ante.
2 For the meaning of 'reside' see *Burditt v Joslin* [1981] 3 All ER 203, DC (decided under the Firearms Act 1968 s 26 (1); a person does not reside at an address at a time when that address is let to others and therefore he does not have a right to occupy it). See further POLICE.
3 The permit must be in the prescribed form: ibid s 7 (1). For the prescribed form of permit see the Firearms Rules 1989, SI 1989/854, r 9 (1) (a), Sch 4 Pt I (permit to possess a firearm and/or ammunition), r 9 (1) (b), Sch 4 Pt II (permit to possess shot guns). A chief officer of police may not fetter his discretion in the granting of such permits: *R v Wakefield Crown Court, ex p Oldfield* [1978] Crim LR 164, DC.
4 For the meaning of 'certificate' see para 204 note 8 ante. As to references to persons entitled to possess, purchase or acquire any weapon or ammunition without holding a certificate see para 204 note 8 ante.
5 For the meaning of 'firearm' see para 197 ante.
6 For the meaning of 'ammunition' see para 200 note 9 ante.
7 Firearms Act 1968 s 7 (1).
8 Ibid s 7 (2).
9 Ibid s 51, Sch 6 Pt I (amended by the Criminal Justice Act 1982 ss 38, 46). For the meaning of 'the standard scale' see para 808 post. As to the limitation period for summary proceedings see para 240 post; and as to the court's power to order forfeiture or disposal of firearms and ammunition see para 241 post.

210. Authorised dealing with firearms. A person carrying on the business of a firearms dealer[1] and registered[2] as such, or a servant of such a person may, without holding a certificate[3], have in his possession, or purchase or acquire, a firearm[4] or ammunition[5] in the ordinary course of that business[6].

It is not an offence[7] for a person:

(1) to part with the possession of any firearm or ammunition, otherwise than in pursuance of a contract of sale or hire or by way of gift or loan, to a person who shows he is entitled[8] to have possession of the firearm or ammunition without holding a certificate; or

(2) to return to another person a shot gun which he has lawfully undertaken to repair, test or prove for the other[9].

1 For the meaning of 'firearms dealer' see para 203 note 5 ante.
2 For the meaning of 'registered' see para 203 note 4 ante.
3 For the meaning of 'certificate' see para 204 note 8 ante. As to references to persons entitled to possess, purchase or acquire any weapon or ammunition without holding a certificate see para 204 note 8 ante.
4 For the meaning of 'firearm' see para 197 ante.
5 For the meaning of 'ammunition' see para 200 note 9 ante.
6 Firearms Act 1968 s 8 (1).
7 Ie under ibid s 3 (2): see para 204 ante.

8 Ie by virtue of the Firearms Act 1968.
9 Ibid s 8 (2).

211. Auctioneers, carriers and warehousemen. A person carrying on the business of an auctioneer, carrier or warehouseman, or a servant of such a person may have in his possession, without holding a certificate[1], a firearm[2] or ammunition[3] in the ordinary course of that business[4]. It is an offence for an auctioneer, carrier or warehouseman (1) to fail to take reasonable precautions for the safe custody of any such firearm or ammunition which he or any servant of his has in his possession without holding a certificate; or (2) to fail to report forthwith to the police the loss or theft of any such firearm or ammunition[5]; and a person guilty of such an offence is liable on summary convicton to imprisonment for a term not exceeding six months or a fine not exceeding level 5 on the standard scale, or to both[6].

It is not an offence[7] for an auctioneer to sell by auction, expose for sale by auction or have in his possession for sale by auction a firearm or ammunition without being registered[8] as a firearms dealer[9] if he has obtained from the chief officer of police for the area[10] in which the auction is held a permit[11] for that purpose and complies with its terms[12]. It is, however, an offence for a person to make any statement which he knows to be false for the purpose of procuring the grant of such a permit, either for himself or for another person; and a person guilty of such an offence is liable on summary conviction to imprisonment for a term not exceeding six months or a fine not exceeding level 5 on the standard scale, or to both[13].

It is not an offence[14] for a carrier or warehouseman, or a servant of a carrier or warehouseman, to deliver any firearm or ammunition in the ordinary course of his business or employment as such[15].

1 For the meaning of 'certificate' see para 204 note 8 ante. As to references to persons entitled to possess, purchase or acquire any weapon or ammunition without holding a certificate see para 204 note 8 ante.
2 For the meaning of 'firearm' see para 197 ante.
3 For the meaning of 'ammunition' see para 200 note 9 ante.
4 Firearms Act 1968 s 9 (1).
5 Firearms (Amendment) Act 1988 s 14 (1).
6 Ibid s 14 (2). For the meaning of 'the standard scale' see para 808 post.
7 Ie under the Firearms Act 1968 s 3 (1): see para 203 ante.
8 For the meaning of 'registered' see para 203 note 4 ante.
9 For the meaning of 'firearms dealer' see para 203 note 5 ante.
10 For the meaning of 'area' see para 209 note 1 ante.
11 The permit must be in the prescribed form: Firearms Act 1968 s 9 (2). For the prescribed form of permit see the Firearms Rules 1989, SI 1989/854, r 9 (2) (a), Sch 4 Pt III (auctioneer's shot gun permit).
12 Firearms Act 1968 s 9 (2).
13 Ibid ss 9 (3), 51, Sch 6 Pt I (amended by the Magistrates' Courts Act 1980 s 32 (2); the Firearms (Amendment) Act 1988 s 23 (7)). As to the limitation period for summary proceedings see para 240 post; and as to the court's power to order forfeiture or disposal of firearms and ammunition see para 241 post.
14 Ie under the Firearms Act 1968 s 3 (2): see para 204 ante.
15 Ibid s 9 (4).

212. Slaughter of animals. A person who is duly licensed[1] may, without holding a certificate[2], have in his possession a slaughtering instrument[3] and ammunition therefor in any slaughterhouse or knacker's yard in which he is employed[4].

The proprietor of a slaughterhouse or knacker's yard or a person appointed by him to take charge of slaughtering instruments and ammunition therefor for the purpose of storing them in safe custody at that slaughterhouse or knacker's yard may, without holding a certificate, have in his possession a slaughtering instrument or ammunition therefor for that purpose[5].

1 Ie under the Slaughterhouses Act 1974 s 39 (amended by the Animal Health Act 1981 s 96 (1), Sch 5 para 11 (c)) or the Slaughter of Animals (Scotland) Act 1980: see FOOD vol 18 paras 1334, 1335.
2 For the meaning of 'certificate' see para 204 note 8 ante. As to references to persons entitled to possess, purchase or acquire any weapon or ammunition without holding a certificate see para 204 note 8 ante.
3 'Slaughtering instrument' means a firearm which is specially designed or adapted for the instantaneous slaughter of animals or for the instataneous stunning of animals with a view to the slaughtering of them: Firearms Act 1968 s 57 (4).
4 Ibid s 10 (1) (amended by the Slaughterhouses Act 1974 s 46 (1), Sch 3 para 5; the Slaughter of Animals (Scotland) Act 1980 s 23, Sch 1 para 3). See further FOOD vol 18 para 1344.
5 Firearms Act 1968 s 10 (2).

213. Sports, athletics and other approved activities. Without himself holding a certificate[1]:

(1) a person conducting or carrying on a miniature rifle[2] range, whether for a rifle club or otherwise, or shooting gallery at which no firearms[3] are used, other than air weapons[4] or miniature rifles not exceeding .23 inch calibre may have in his possession[5] or purchase or acquire[6] such miniature rifles and ammunition[7] suitable for them[8];

(2) any person may use any such miniature rifle as is described in head (1) above at such a range or gallery as there described[8];

(3) a member of a cadet corps approved by the Secretary of State may have in his possession a firearm and ammunition when engaged as a member of the corps in, or in connection with, drill or target practice[9];

(4) a person carrying a firearm or ammunition belonging to another person holding a certificate may have in his possession that firearm or ammunition under instructions from, and for the use of, that other person for sporting purposes only[10];

(5) a person may use a shot gun[11] at a time and place approved for shooting at artificial targets by the chief officer of police for the area[12] in which that place is situated[13],

(6) a person may have a firearm in his possession at an athletic meeting for the purpose of starting races at that meeting[14].

1 For the meaning of 'certificate' see para 204 note 8 ante. As to references to persons entitled to possess, purchase or acquire any weapon or ammunition without holding a certificate see para 204 note 8 ante.
2 'Rifle' includes carbine: Firearms Act 1968 s 57 (4) (amended by the Firearms (Amendment) Act 1988 s 25 (3)).
3 For the meaning of 'firearm' see para 197 ante.
4 For the meaning of 'air weapon' see para 199 ante.
5 For the meaning of 'possession' in the context of the Firearms Act 1968 s 1 (as amended) see para 200 note 2 ante.
6 For the meaning of 'acquire' see para 200 note 3 ante.
7 For the meaning of 'ammunition' see para 200 note 9 ante.
8 Firearms Act 1968 s 11 (4).
9 Ibid s 11 (3) (amended by the Firearms (Amendment) Act 1988 s 15 (7)). Any approval of a rifle or miniature rifle club under the Firearms Act 1968 s 11 (3) (as originally enacted) has effect as if it were an approval under the Firearms (Amendment) Act 1988 s 15 (see para 214 post) except that, without

prejudice to renewal, it expires at the end of the period of three years beginning with 1 July 1989: s 15 (9); Firearms Amendment Act 1988 (Commencement No 2) Order 1989, SI 1989/853, art 3 (a), Schedule Pt I.

10 Firearms Act 1968 s 11 (1). Shooting rats is not shooting for sporting purposes only: *Morton v Chaney, Morton v Christopher* [1960] 3 All ER 632, [1960] 1 WLR 1312, DC.

11 For the meaning of 'shot gun' see para 198 ante.

12 For the meaning of 'area' see para 209 note 1 ante.

13 Firearms Act 1968 s 11 (6).

14 Ibid s 11 (2).

214. Rifle and pistol clubs. A member of a rifle[1] club, miniature rifle club or pistol club approved by the Secretary of State[2] may, without holding a firearm certificate[3], have in his possession a firearm[4] and ammunition[5] when engaged as a member of the club in, or in connection with, target practice[6]. A constable duly authorised in writing in that behalf by a chief officer of police may, on producing if required his authority, enter any premises[7] occupied or used by a club so approved and inspect those premises, and anything on them, for the purpose of ascertaining whether this provision and any limitations in the approval are being complied with[8]. It is an offence for a person intentionally to obstruct a constable in the exercise of such powers; and a person guilty of such an offence is liable on summary conviction to a fine not exceeding level 3 on the standard scale[9].

1 For the meaning of 'rifle' see para 213 note 2 ante.

2 Any such approval may be limited so as to apply to target practice with only such types of rifles or pistols as are specified in the approval: Firearms (Amendment) Act 1988 s 15 (2). An approval, unless withdrawn, continues in force for six years from the date on which it is granted but may be renewed for further periods of six years at a time: s 15 (3). On the grant or renewal of an approval a fee of £33 is payable; but this sum may be amended by an order under the Firearms Act 1968 s 43: Firearms (Amendment) Act 1988 s 15 (4). As to approvals under the Firearms Act 1968 s 11 (3) (as originally enacted) see para 213 note 9 ante.

3 For the meaning of 'firearm certificate' see para 200 note 8 ante. As to references to persons entitled to possess, purchase or acquire any weapon or ammunition without holding a certificate see para 204 note 8 ante.

4 For the meaning of 'firearm' see para 197 ante.

5 For the meaning of 'ammunition' see para 200 note 9 ante.

6 Firearms (Amendment) Act 1988 s 15 (1). Whatever might be the situation with regard to shorter lengths of time, it could not on any view possibly be said that the appellant was 'engaged' as a member of a club in or in connection with target practice' one month after an intended day's shooting at Bisley: *R v Wilson (Maxim)* [1989] Crim LR 907, CA (decided under the Firearms Act 1968 s 11 (3) (as originally enacted)).

7 For these purposes, 'premises' includes any land: Firearms Act 1968 s 57 (4) (applied by the Firearms (Amendment) Act 1988 s 25 (1)).

8 Firearms (Amendment) Act 1988 s 15 (5).

9 Ibid s 15 (6). For the meaning of 'the standard scale' see para 808 post. As to the limitation period for summary proceedings see para 240 post.

215. Borrowed shot guns and rifles on private premises. A person may, without holding a shot gun certificate[1], borrow a shot gun[2] from the occupier of private premises[3] and use it on those premises in the occupier's presence[4].

A person of or over the age of 17 may, without holding a firearm certificate[5], borrow a rifle[6] from the occupier of private premises and use it on those premises in the presence either of the occupier or of a servant of the occupier if:

(1) the occupier or servant in whose presence it is used holds a firearm certificate in respect of that rifle; and

(2) the borrower's possession and use of it complies with any conditions as to those matters specified in the certificate[7].

A person so entitled to borrow and use a rifle may also, without holding a firearm certificate, purchase or acquire[8] ammunition[9] for use in the rifle and have it in his possession during the period for which the rifle is borrowed if (a) the firearm certificate held by that other person authorises the holder to have in his possession at that time ammunition for the rifle of a quantity not less than that purchased or acquired by, and in the possession of, the borrower; and (b) the borrower's possession and use of the ammunition complies with any conditions as to those matters specified in the certificate[10].

1 For the meaning of 'shot gun certificate' see para 201 note 5 ante. As to references to persons entitled to possess, purchase or acquire any weapon or ammunition without holding a certificate see para 204 note 8 ante.
2 For the meaning of 'shot gun' see para 198 ante.
3 For the meaning of 'premises' see para 214 note 7 ante.
4 Firearms Act 1968 s 11 (5).
5 For the meaning of 'firearm certificate' see para 200 note 8 ante.
6 For the meaning of 'rifle' see para 213 note 2 ante.
7 Firearms (Amendment) Act 1988 s 16 (1).
8 For the meaning of 'acquire' see para 200 note 3 ante.
9 For the meaning of 'ammunition' see para 200 note 9 ante.
10 Firearms (Amendment) Act 1988 s 16 (2).

216. Visitors' permits. The holder of a visitor's firearm permit[1] may, without holding a firearm certificate[2], have in his possession any firearm[3], and have in his possession, purchase or acquire[4] any specified ammunition[5]; and the holder of a visitor's shot gun permit[6] may, without holding a shot gun certificate[7], have shot guns[8] in his possession and purchase or acquire shot guns[9].

It is an offence for a person (1) to make any statement which he knows to be false for the purpose of procuring the grant of a visitor's firearm or shot gun permit; or (2) to fail to comply with a condition subject to which such a permit is held by him; and a person guilty of such an offence is liable on summary conviction to imprisonment for a term not exceeding six months or a fine not exceeding level 5 on the standard scale, or to both[10].

1 The chief officer of police for an area may, on an application in the prescribed form made by a person resident in that area on behalf of a person specified in the application, grant a permit under the Firearms (Amendment) Act 1988 s 17 to the specified person if satisfied that he is visiting or intending to visit Great Britain and (1) in the case of a visitor's firearm permit, that he has a good reason for having each firearm and the ammunition to which the permit relates in his possession, or, as respects ammunition, for purchasing or acquiring it, while he is a visitor in Great Britain; (2) in the case of a visitor's shot gun permit, that he has a good reason for having each shot gun to which the permit relates in his possession, or for purchasing or acquiring it, while he is such a visitor: Firearms (Amendment) Act 1988 s 17 (2). For the meaning of 'Great Britain' see para 86 note 1 ante.
   No permit may be so granted if the chief officer of police has reason to believe (a) that the visitor's possession of the weapons or ammunition in question would represent a danger to the public safety or to the peace; or (b) that the visitor is prohibited by the Firearms Act 1968 from possessing them: Firearms (Amendment) Act 1988 s 17 (3).
   A permit so granted must be in the prescribed form, must specify the conditions subject to which it is held and (i) in the case of a visitor's firearm permit, must specify the number and description of the firearms to which it relates, including their identification numbers, and, as respects ammunition, the quantities authorised to be purchased or acquired and to be held at any one time; (ii) in the case of a visitor's shot gun permit, must specify the number and description of the shot guns to which it relates, including, if known, their identification numbers: s 17 (4). The chief officer of police by whom a permit is so granted may by notice in writing to the holder vary the conditions subject to which the permit is held, but, in the case of a visitor's shot gun permit, no condition may be imposed or varied so as to restrict the premises where the shot gun or guns to which the permit relates may be used: s 17 (5).

Such a permit comes into force on such date as is specified in it and continues in force for such period, not exceeding 12 months, as is so specified: s 17 (6).

A single application (a 'group application') may be made under these provisions for the grant of not more than 20 permits to persons specified in the application if it is shown to the satisfaction of the chief officer of police that their purpose in having the weapons in question in their possession while visiting Great Britain is using them for sporting purposes on the same private premises during the same period, or participating in the same competition or other event or the same series of competitions or other events: s 17 (7).

On the grant of such a permit a fee of £12 is payable except that, where six or more permits are granted on a group application, the fee is £60 in respect of those permits taken together: s 17 (8). Such fee may be amended by an order under the Firearms Act 1968 s 43: Firearms (Amendment) Act 1988 s 17 (9).

2   For the meaning of 'firearm certificate' see para 200 note 8 ante. As to references to persons entitled to possess, purchase or acquire any weapon or ammunition without holding a certificate see para 204 note 8 ante.
3   For the meaning of 'firearm' see para 197 ante.
4   For the meaning of 'acquire' see para 200 note 3 ante.
5   Ie ammunition to which the Firearms Act 1968 s 1 (as amended) (see para 200 ante) applies.
6   See note 1 supra.
7   For the meaning of 'shot gun certificate' see para 201 note 5 ante.
8   For the meaning of 'shot gun' see para 198 ante.
9   Firearms (Amendment) Act 1988 s 17 (1).
10   Ibid s 17 (10). For the meaning of 'the standard scale' see para 808 post. As to the limitation period for summary proceedings see para 240 post; and as to the court's power to order forfeiture or disposal of firearms and ammunition see para 241 post.

217. Theatre and cinema. A person taking part in a theatrical performance or a rehearsal thereof, or in the production of a cinematograph film, may, without holding a certificate[1], have a firearm[2] in his possession during and for the purpose of the performance, rehearsal or production[3].

Where the Secretary of State is satisfied, on the application of a person in charge of a theatrical performance, a rehearsal of such a performance or the production of a cinematographic film, that a prohibited weapon[4] is required for the purpose of the performance, rehearsal or production, he may[5], if he thinks fit, not only authorise that person to have possession of the weapon but also authorise such other persons as he may select to have possession of it while taking part in the performance, rehearsal or production[6].

1   For the meaning of 'certificate' see para 204 note 8 ante. As to references to persons entitled to possess, purchase or acquire any weapon or ammunition without holding a certificate see para 204 note 8 ante.
2   For the meaning of 'firearm' see para 197 ante.
3   Firearms Act 1968 s 12 (1).
4   For the meaning of 'prohibited weapon' see para 221 post.
5   Ie under the Firearms Act 1968 s 5: see paras 221, 222 post.
6   Ibid s 12 (2) (amended by the Firearms (Amendment) Act 1988 s 23 (2)); Transfer of Functions (Prohibited Weapons) Order 1968/1200.

218. Equipment for ships and aircraft. Without holding a certificate[1], a person:

(1)   may have in his possession a firearm[2] or ammunition[3] on board a ship[4], or a signalling apparatus or ammunition for it on board an aircraft or at an aerodrome, as part of the equipment of the ship, aircraft or aerodrome[5];

(2)   may remove a signalling apparatus or ammunition for it, being part of the equipment of an aircraft from one aircraft to another at an aerodrome, or

from or to an aircraft at an aerodrome, to or from a place appointed for the storage of it in safe custody at that aerodrome, and keep any such apparatus or ammunition at such a place[6]; and

(3) if he has obtained from a constable a permit[7] for the purpose, may remove a firearm from or to a ship, or a signalling apparatus from or to an aircraft or aerodrome, to or from such place and for such purpose as may be specified on the permit[8].

It is an offence for a person to make any statement which he knows to be false for the purpose of procuring the grant of a permit under head (3) above, either for himself or for any other person; and a person guilty of such an offence is liable on summary conviction to imprisonment for a term not exceeding six months or a fine not exceeding level 5 on the standard scale, or to both[9].

1 For the meaning of 'certificate' see para 204 note 8 ante. As to references to persons entitled to possess, purchase or acquire any weapon or ammunition without holding a certificate see para 204 note 8 ante.
2 For the meaning of 'firearm' see para 197 ante.
3 For the meaning of 'ammunition' see para 200 note 9 ante.
4 'Ship' includes hovercraft: Hovercraft (Application of Enactments) Order 1972, SI 1972/971, art 4, Sch 1 Pt A.
5 Firearms Act 1968 s 13 (1) (a).
6 Ibid s 13 (1) (b).
7 The permit must be in the prescribed form: ibid s 13 (1) (c). For the prescribed form of permit see the Firearms Rules 1989, SI 1989/854, r 9(3), Sch 4 Pt V.
8 Firearms Act 1968 s 13 (1) (c) (amended by the Firearms (Amendment) Act 1988 s 23 (3)).
9 Firearms Act 1968 ss 13 (2), 51, Sch 6 Pt I (amended by the Criminal Justice Act 1982 ss 38, 46). For the meaning of 'the standard scale' see para 808 post. As to the limitation period for summary proceedings see para 240 post; and as to the court's power to order forfeiture or disposal of firearms and ammunition see para 241 post.

219. Firearms acquired for export. A person may, without holding a firearm[1] or shot gun certificate[2], purchase a firearm[3] from a registered firearms dealer[4] if (1) that person has not been in Great Britain for more than 30 days in the preceding 12 months; and (2) the firearm is purchased for the purpose only of being exported from Great Britain without first coming into that person's possession[5].

A registered firearms dealer who sells a firearm to a person who shows that he is so entitled to purchase it without holding a certificate must within 48 hours from the transaction send a notice[6] of the transaction to the chief officer of police in whose register the premises[7] where the transaction took place are entered; and it is an offence for a registered firearms dealer to fail to comply with such requirement[8]. A person guilty of such an offence is liable on summary conviction to imprisonment for a term not exceeding six months or a fine not exceeding level 5 on the standard scale, or to both[9].

1 For the meaning of 'firearm certificate' see para 200 note 8 ante. As to references to persons entitled to possess, purchase or acquire any weapon or ammunition without holding a certificate see para 204 note 8 ante.
2 For the meaning of 'shot gun certificate' see para 201 note 5 ante.
3 For the meaning of 'firearm' see para 197 ante.
4 For the meaning of 'registered' and 'firearms dealer' see para 203 notes 4, 5 respectively ante.
5 Firearms (Amendment) Act 1988 s 18 (1).
6 The notice of such a transaction must contain the particulars of the transaction which the dealer is required to enter in the register kept by him under the Firearams Act 1968 s 40; and every notice must be sent by registered post or the recorded delivery service: Firearms (Amendment) Act 1988 s 18 (3). In the case of such a transaction, the particulars to be entered in the register so kept, and accordingly

in the notice so served, must include the number and place of issue of the purchaser's passport, if any: s 18 (4).

7 For the meaning of 'premises' see para 214 note 7 ante.

8 Ibid s 18 (2), (5).

9 Ibid s 18 (5). For the meaning of 'the standard scale' see para 808 post. As to powers of search see para 237 post; as to the limitation period for summary proceedings see para 240 post; and as to the court's power to order forfeiture or disposal of firearms and ammunition see para 241 post.

220. Firearms and ammunition in museums. On an application in writing made on behalf of a museum[1], the Secretary of State may grant a museum firearms licence[2] in respect of that museum[3]. While such a licence is in force, the persons responsible for the management of the museum[4] and their servants:

(1) may without holding a firearm[5] or shot gun certificate[6], have in their possession, and purchase or acquire[7], for the purposes of the museum firearms[8] and ammunition[9] which are or are to be normally exhibited or kept on its premises or on such of them as are specified in the licence; and

(2) if the licence so provides, may, without the authority of the Secretary of State[10], have in their possession, purchase or acquire for those purposes any prohibited weapons[11] and ammunition[12] which are or are to be normally so exhibited or kept[13].

It is an offence (a) for a person[14] to make any statement which he knows to be false for the purpose of procuring the grant, renewal[15] or variation[16] of such a licence; (b) for the persons or any of the persons responsible for the management of a museum to fail to comply or to cause or permit another person to fail to comply with any condition specified in the licence held in respect of that museum[17]. A person guilty of either such offence is liable on summary conviction to imprisonment for a term not exceeding six months or a fine not exceeding level 5 on the standard scale, or to both[18]. In proceedings against any person for an offence under head (b) above, it is a defence, however, for him to prove that he took all reasonable precautions and exercised all due diligence to avoid the commission of the offence[19].

1 The Firearms (Amendment) Act 1988 s 19, Schedule applies to the following museums: The Armouries, HM Tower of London; The National Army Museum; The National Museum of Wales; The Royal Air Force Museum; The Science Museum; The Victoria and Albert Museum; The Royal Marines Museum; The Fleet Air Arm Museum; The Royal Navy Museum; The Royal Navy Submarine Museum; The British Museum; The Imperial War Museum; The National Maritime Museum; The National Museums of Scotland; The National Museums and Galleries on Merseyside; The Wallace Collection; and any other museum or similar institution in Great Britain which has as its purpose, or one of its purposes, the preservation for the public benefit of a collection of historical, artistic or scientific interest which included or is to include firearms and which is maintained wholly or mainly out of money provided by Parliament or by a local authority: Schedule para 5.

2 The Secretary of State may not so grant a licence in respect of a museum unless, after consulting the chief officer of police for the area in which the premises to which the licence is to apply are situated, he is satisfied that the arrangements for exhibiting and keeping the firearms and ammunition in question are or will be such as not to endanger the public safety or the peace: ibid Schedule para 1 (3). Such a licence must be in writing and is subject to such conditions specified in it as the Secretary of State thinks necessary for securing the safe custody of the firearms and ammunition in question: Schedule para 1 (4).

The Secretary of State may by notice in writing to the persons responsible for the management of a museum revoke a licence held in respect of the museum if (1) at any time, after consulting the chief officer of police for the area in which the premises to which it applies are situated, he is satisfied that the continuation of the exemption conferred by the licence would result in danger to the public safety or to the peace; (2) those persons or any of them or any servant of theirs has been convicted of an offence under Schedule paras 1–6; or (3) those persons have failed to comply with a notice requiring them to deliver up the licence: Schedule para 2 (3). Where a licence is so revoked, the Secretary of State must by notice in writing require the persons responsible for the management of the museum in question to surrender the licence to him: Schedule para 2 (4). It is an offence for a person to fail to comply with a notice under Schedule para 2 (4); and a person guilty of such an offence is liable on summary conviction to a fine not exceeding level 3 on the standard scale: Schedule para 4 (3). For the meaning of 'the standard scale' see para 808 post.

3 Ibid Schedule para 1 (1). There is payable (1) on the grant or renewal of a licence, a fee of £200 or of such lesser amount as the Secretary of State may in any particular case determine; (2) on the extension of a licence to additional premises, a fee of £75: Schedule para 3 (1). Schedule para 3 is included in the provisions that may be amended by an order under the Firearms Act 1968 s 43: Firearms (Amendment) Act 1988 Schedule para 3 (2).

4 For these purposes, references to the persons responsible for the management of a museum are to the board of trustees, governing body or other person or persons, whether or not incorporated, exercising corresponding functions: ibid Schedule para 6.

5 For the meaning of 'firearm certificate' see para 200 note 8 ante. As to references to persons entitled to possess, purchase or acquire any weapon or ammunition without holding a certificate see para 204 note 8 ante.

6 For the meaning of 'shot gun certificate' see para 201 note 5 ante.

7 For the meaning of 'acquire' see para 200 note 3 ante.

8 For the meaning of 'firearm' see para 197 ante.

9 For the meaning of 'ammunition' see para 200 note 9 ante.

10 Ie under the Firearms Act 1968 s 5: see para 221 post.

11 For the meaning of 'prohibited weapon' see para 221 post.

12 For the meaning of 'prohibited ammunition' see para 221 post.

13 Firearms (Amendment) Act 1988 Schedule para 1 (2).

14 Where an offence committed by a body corporate is proved to have been committed with the consent or connivance of, or to be attributable to any neglect on the part of, any director, manager, secretary or other similar officer of the body corporate, or any person who was purporting to act in any such capacity, he, as well as the body corporate, is guilty of that offence and liable to be proceeded against and punished accordingly; and, where the affairs of a body corporate are managed by its members, that provision applies in relation to the acts and defaults of a member in connection with his functions of management as if he were a director of the body corporate: ibid Schedule para 4 (5), (6).

15 Unless previously revoked or cancelled, a licence continues in force for five years from the date on which it is granted but is renewable for further periods of five years at a time and the provisions of ibid Schedule para 1 (3) (see note 2 supra) apply to the renewal of a licence as they apply to a grant: Schedule para 1 (5). The Secretary of State may by order substitute for the periods so mentioned such longer or shorter periods as are specified in the order; and the power so to make an order is exercisable by statutory instrument subject to annulment in pursuance of a resolution of either House of Parliament: Schedule para 1 (6), (7).

16 The Secretary of State may by notice in writing to the persons responsible for the management of a museum vary the conditions specified in a licence held in respect of the museum, or vary the licence so as to extend or restrict the premises to which it applies: ibid Schedule para 2 (1). A notice so given may require the persons in question to deliver up the licence to the Secretary of State within 21 days of the date of the notice for the purpose of having it amended in accordance with the variation: Schedule para 2 (2).

17 Ibid Schedule para 4 (1).

18 Ibid Schedule para 4 (2). As to the limitation period for summary proceedings see para 240 post. Where a person is convicted of any offence under the Schedule, no order may be made for the forfeiture of anything in his possession for the purposes of the museum in question: s 25 (5). See further para 241 post.

19 Ibid Schedule para 4 (4).

(ii) Prohibited Weapons and Ammunition

221. Meaning of 'prohibited weapon' and 'prohibited ammunition'. 'Prohibited weapon' means:

(1) any firearm[1] which is so designed or adapted that two or more missiles can be successively discharged without repeated pressure on the trigger[2];

(2) any self-loading or pump-action[3] rifle other than one which is chambered for .22 rim-fire cartridges[4];

(3) any self-loading or pump-action smooth-bore gun which is not chambered for .22 rim-fire cartridges and either has a barrel less than 24 inches in length[5] or, excluding any detachable, folding or retractable or other movable butt-stock, is less than 40 inches in length overall[6];

(4) any smooth-bore revolver[7] gun other than one which is chambered for 9mm rim-fire cartridges or loaded at the muzzle end of each chamber[8];

(5) any rocket launcher, or any mortar, for projecting a stabilised missile, other than a launcher or mortar designed for line-throwing or pyrotechnic purposes or as signalling apparatus[9];

(6) any weapon of whatever description designed or adapted for the discharge of any noxious liquid, gas or other thing[10].

'Prohibited ammunition' means any cartridge with a bullet designed to explode on or immediately before impact, any ammunition[11] containing or designed or adapted to contain any such noxious thing as is mentioned in head (6) above and, if capable of being used with a firearm of any description, any grenade, bomb (or other like missile), or rocket or shell designed so to explode[12].

1 For the meaning of 'firearm' see para 197 ante.
2 Firearms Act 1968 s 5 (1) (a), (2) (substituted by the Firearms (Amendment) Act 1988 s 1 (2)). The purpose of such substitution is to extend the class of prohibited weapons and ammunition (see infra), that is to say weapons and ammunition the possession, purchase, acquisition, manufacture, sale or transfer of which requires the authority of the Secretary of State under the Firearms Act 1968 s 5 (as so amended): Firearms (Amendment) Act 1988 s 1 (1).

   If it appears to the Secretary of State that the provisions of the Firearms Act 1968 relating to prohibited weapons or ammunition should apply to (1) any firearm, not being an air weapon, which is not for the time being specified in s 5 (1) (as so amended), was not lawfully on sale in Great Britain in substantial numbers at any time before 1988 and appears to him to be specially dangerous or wholly or partly composed of material making it not readily detectable by apparatus used for detecting metal objects; or (2) any ammunition which is not for the time being there specified but appears to him to be specially dangerous, he may by order add it to the weapons or ammunition so specified whether by altering the description of any weapon or ammunition for the time being there specified or otherwise: Firearms (Amendment) Act 1988 s 1 (4). The power so to make an order is exercisable by statutory instrument; and no such order may be made unless a draft of it has been laid before and approved by a resolution of each House of Parliament: s 1 (5).

   The following cases decided under the Firearms Act 1968 s 5 (1) (a) as originally enacted may still have some relevance to the new provisions: R v Pannell (1982) 76 Cr App Rep 53, CA (although the three weapons were in parts, the accused was in possession of all the parts of each of three weapons and was therefore in possession of the weapons which were still prohibited weapons since nothing had been done to convert them into weapons of a different kind); R v Clarke [1986] 1 All ER 846, 82 Cr App Rep 308, CA (a firearm which is designed so as to be capable of continuous fire (but now not necessary to be continuous: see Firearms Act 1968 s 5 (1) (a) (as so substituted)) is a prohibited weapon even though an essential component, such as the trigger, is missing).

   In so far as these cases are concerned with conversion see now the Firearms (Amendment) Act 1988 s 7 (1). Any weapon which (a) has at any time, whether before or after 15 November 1988, been a prohibited weapon; and (b) is not a self-loading or pump-action smooth-bore gun which has at any such time been such a weapon by reason only of having had a barrel of less than 24 inches in length, is to be treated as a prohibited weapon notwithstanding anything done for the purposes of converting it into a weapon of a different kind: s 7 (1).
3 For these purposes, 'self-loading' and 'pump-action', in relation to any weapon, mean respectively that it is designed or adapted, otherwise than is mentioned in the Firearms Act 1968 s 5 (1) (a), (2) (as substituted; see note 2 supra) so that it is automatically reloaded or that it is so designed or adapted that it is reloaded by the manual operation of the fore-end or forestock of the weapon: s 57 (2A) (added by the Firearms (Amendment) Act 1988 s 25 (2)).
4 Firearms Act 1968 s 5 (1) (ab), (2) (as substituted: see note 2 supra).
5 As to the measurement of the length of the barrel of a firearm see para 198 note 1 ante.

6 Firearms Act 1968 s 5 (1) (ac), (2) (as substituted: see note 2 supra).
7 For the meaning of 'revolver' see para 198 note 2 ante.
8 Firearms Act 1968 s 5 (1) (ad), (2) (as substituted: see note 2 supra).
9 Ibid s 5 (1) (ae), (2) (as substituted: see note 2 supra).
10 Ibid s 5 (1) (b), (2). The emission of electricity from a hand-held device, known as a Lightning Strike, is the discharge of something from it and therefore the device is capable of being a weapon designed to discharge a noxious thing since electricity was accepted before the courts as properly described, having regard to its effect on the victim, as a noxious thing, contrary to s 5 (1) (b), (2): *Flack v Baldry* [1988] 1 All ER 673, 87 Cr App Rep 130, HL. Water pistols are not weapons designed or adapted for the discharge of a noxious liquid: *R v Titus* [1971] Crim LR 279.
11 For the meaning of 'ammunition' see para 200 note 9 ante.
12 Firearms Act 1968 s 5 (1) (c) (substituted by the Firearms (Amendment) Act 1988 s 1 (3)).

222. Purchase etc of prohibited weapons and ammunition. A person commits an offence if, without the authority of the Secretary of State[1], he has in his possession[2], or purchases or acquires[3], or manufactures, sells or transfers[4] any prohibited weapon[5] or prohibited ammunition[6]. A person guilty of such an offence is liable on conviction on indictment to imprisonment for a term not exceeding five years or a fine, or to both, or on summary conviction to imprisonment for a term not exceeding six months or a fine not exceeding the prescribed sum, or to both[7]. It is an offence for a person to whom an authority is so given to fail to comply with any condition of the authority; and a person guilty of such an offence is liable on summary conviction to imprisonment for a term not exceeding six months or a fine not exceeding level 5 on the standard scale, or to both[8].

The Secretary of State may at any time, if he thinks fit, revoke any authority so given by notice in writing requiring him to deliver up the authority to such person as is specified in the notice within 21 days from the date of the notice; and it is an offence for him to fail to comply with that requirement[9]. A person guilty of such an offence is liable on summary conviction to a fine not exceeding level 3 on the standard scale[10].

1 An authority so given must be in writing and is subject to conditions specified therein; and the condition of the authority must include such as the Secretary of State, having regard to the circumstances of each particular case, thinks fit to impose for the purpose of securing that the prohibited weapon or ammunition to which the authority relates will not endanger the public safety or the peace: Firearms Act 1968 s 5 (3), (4); Transfer of Functions (Prohibited Weapons) Order 1968, SI 1968/1200, art 2.
2 Where a person is knowingly in possession of a prohibited weapon, it is no defence for him to show, even in a 'container' case where the item is concealed by the container, that he neither knew nor suspected, nor should be deemed to have known, that it was such a prohibited weapon: *R v Bradish* (1989) Times, 30 August, CA.
3 For the meaning of 'acquire' see para 200 note 3 ante.
4 For the meaning of 'transfer' see para 203 note 1 ante.
5 For the meaning of 'prohibited weapon' see para 221 ante.
6 Firearms Act 1968 s 5 (1) (amended by the Firearms (Amendment) Act 1988 s 1 (1)–(3)); Transfer of Functions (Prohibited Weapons) Order 1968 art 2. For the meaning of 'prohibited ammunition' see para 221 ante.
   The Secretary of State must, in accordance with a scheme made by him, make payments to persons who surrender or otherwise dispose of firearms (1) which they had, and were entitled to have, in their possession immediately before 23 September 1987 by virtue of firearm or shot gun certificates held by them; or (2) which before that date they had contracted to acquire and were entitled to have in their possession on or after that date by virtue of such certificates held by them, and the possession of which becomes or became unlawful by virtue of the Firearms (Amendment) Act 1988 s 1 (2) (see para 221 ante) or s 7 (1) (see para 221 ante): s 21.
7 Firearms Act 1968 s 51, Sch 6 Pt I (amended by the Magistrates' Courts Act 1980 s 32 (2)). For the meaning of 'the prescribed sum' see para 807 post. As to powers of search see para 237 post; as to the

limitation period for summary proceedings see para 240 post; and as to the court's power to cancel firearm and shot gun certificates and order forfeiture or disposal of firearms and ammunition see para 241 post. The Firearms Act 1968 s 5 (as amended: see note 6 supra) creates an offence of strict liability: *R v Bradish* [1990] 2 WLR 223, CA. As to strict liability see para 18 ante.

8 Firearms Act 1968 ss 5 (5), 51, Sch 6 Pt I (amended by the Criminal Justice Act 1982 ss 38, 46). For the meaning of 'the standard scale' see para 808 post. See also note 7 supra.
9 Firearms Act 1968 s 5 (6); Transfer of Functions (Prohibited Weapons) Order 1968 art 2.
10 Firearms Act 1968 s 51, Sch 6 Pt I (amended by the Criminal Justice Act 1982 ss 38, 46). See also note 7 supra.

(iii) Movement of Firearms and Ammunition

223. Control of movement of firearms and ammunition. The Secretary of State may by order[1] prohibit the removal of firearms[2] or ammunition[3] (1) from one place to another in Great Britain; or (2) for export from Great Britain, unless the removal is authorised by the chief officer of police for the area[4] from which they are to be removed, and unless such other conditions as may be specified in the order are complied with[5]. The Secretary of State may also by order prohibit the removal of firearms or ammunition from Great Britain to Northern Ireland unless (a) the removal is authorised by the chief officer of police for the area from which they are to be removed and by the Chief Constable of the Royal Ulster Constabulary; and (b) such conditions as may be specified in the order or imposed by the chief officer of police or the Chief Constable are complied with[6].

It is an offence to contravene any provision of (i) an order made under the above provisions[7]; (ii) an order made under the Firearms Act 1920[8]; or (iii) any corresponding Northern Ireland order[9] prohibiting the removal of firearms or ammunition from Northern Ireland to Great Britain[10]. A person guilty of such an offence is liable on summary conviction to imprisonment for a term not exceeding three months or, for each firearm or parcel of ammunition in respect of which the offence is committed, a fine not exceeding level 3 on the standard scale, or to both[11].

1 An order so made may apply (1) either generally to all such removals, or to removals from and to particular localities specified in the order; and (2) either to all firearms and ammunition or to firearms and ammunition of such classes and descriptions as may be so specified; and (3) either to all modes of conveyance or to such modes of conveyance as may be so specified; but no such order may prohibit the holder of a firearm certificate from carrying with him any firearm and ammunition authorised by the certificate to be so carried: Firearms Act 1968 s 6 (2). Any such order must be made by statutory instrument and may be varied or revoked by a subsequent order made thereafter by the Secretary of State: s 6 (4).
2 For the meaning of 'firearm' see para 197 ante. References in any order so made to firearms, without qualification, or to firearms to which ibid s 1 (as amended) applies are to be read as including imitation firearms to which the Firearms Act 1982 applies (see para 197 note 7 ante): s 2 (1).
3 For the meaning of 'ammunition' see para 200 note 9 ante.
4 For the meaning of 'area' see para 209 note 1 ante.
5 Firearms Act 1968 s 6 (1) (amended by the Firearms (Amendment) Act 1988 s 20 (1), (3)). For the meaning of 'Great Britain' see para 86 note 1 ante. As to restrictions under other enactments see CUSTOMS AND EXCISE vol 12 paras 723 note 12, 1061.
6 Firearms Act 1968 s 6 (1A) (added by the Firearms (Amendment) Act 1988 s 20 (1), (2)).
7 See the Firearms (Removal to Northern Ireland) Order 1975, SI 1975/760.
8 Ie the Firearms Act 1920 s 9 (repealed). See also the Order of the Secretary of State dated 16 November 1922, SR & O 1922/1263 (prohibition on removal of any firearms or ammunition by any form of conveyance to a ship for export except under licence).
9 Ie an order under the Firearms Act 1920 s 9 (repealed) as extending to Northern Ireland, or under the Firearms Act (Northern Ireland) 1969 s 5 (repealed) or under the Firearms (Northern Ireland) Order 1981, SI 1981/155, art 7 (2).

10 Firearms Act 1968 s 6 (3). It is also an offence to export small arms the barrels of which have not been duly proved and marked (Gun Barrel Proof Act 1868 s 122 (3)) or to import such small arms other than for personal use unless due notice is given to the Proof Masters of the Gunmakers Company of the City of London or the Birmingham Proof House and the barrels duly delivered for proof (s 122 (4)). A person guilty of any such offence is liable on conviction on indictment to a fine or on summary conviction to a fine not exceeding the statutory maximum: s 122 (3), (4) (amended by the Gun Barrel Proof Act 1978 s 1 (2), Sch 3 para 11). For the meaning of 'the statutory maximum' see para 806 post; and for the meaning of 'small arms' and of 'barrel' see para 480 note 2 post.
11 Firearms Act 1968 s 51, Sch 6 Pt I (amended by the Criminal Justice Act 1982 ss 38, 46). For the meaning of 'the standard scale' see para 808 post. As to the limitation period for summary proceedings see para 240 post.

A constable may search for and seize any firearms or ammunition which he has reason to believe are being removed, or to have been removed, in contravention of an order made under the Firearms Act 1968 s 6 (as amended: see notes 5, 6 supra) or of a corresponding Northern Irish order within the meaning of s 6 (3) (c); and a person having the control or custody of any firearms or ammunition in course of transit must, on demand by a constable, allow him all reasonable facilities for the examination and inspection thereof and must produce any documents in his possession relating thereto: s 49 (1), (2) (amended by the Firearms (Amendment) Act 1988 s 23 (3)). A person failing to comply with such a demand is guilty of an offence and liable on summary conviction to imprisonment for a term not exceeding three months or, for each firearm or parcel of ammunition in respect of which the offence is committed, to a fine not exceeding level 3 on the standard scale, or to both: Firearms Act 1968 s 49 (3), Sch 6 Pt I.

In the case of an offence against s 6 (3) (see text to notes 7–10 supra) or s 49 (3) (see supra), the court before which the offender is convicted may, if the offender is the owner of the firearms or ammunition, make such order as to the forfeiture of the firearms or ammunition as the court thinks fit: s 51 (3), Sch 6 Pt II para 2.

(iv) Possession and Acquisition of Firearms by and Supply of Firearms to Minors

224. Firearms and ammunition generally. It is an offence (1) for a person under the age of 17 to purchase or hire any firearm[1] or ammunition[2]; (2) for a person under the age of 14 to have in his possession any specified firearm[3] or ammunition[3] except in circumstances where he is entitled[4] to have possession of it without holding a firearm certificate[5].

It is an offence (a) to sell or let on hire any firearm or ammunition to a person under the age of 17[6]; (b) to make a gift of or lend any specified firearm or ammunition to a person under the age of 14[7]; or (c) to part with the possession of any specified firearm or ammunition to a person under the age of 14 except in circumstances where he is entitled[8] to have possession of it without holding a firearm certificate[9].

A person guilty of any such offence is liable on summary conviction to imprisonment for a term not exceeding six months or a fine not exceeding level 5 on the standard scale, or both[10]. In proceedings for an offence under heads (a) to (c) above it is, however, a defence to prove that the person charged with the offence believed the other person to be of or over the age there mentioned and had reasonable grounds for the belief[11].

1 For the meaning of 'firearm' see para 197 ante.
2 Firearms Act 1968 s 22 (1). For the meaning of 'ammunition' see para 200 note 9 ante.
3 Ie any firearm or ammunition to which ibid s 1 (as amended) applies: see para 200 ante.
4 Ie under ibid s 11 (1), (3), (4) (see para 213 heads (2)–(4) ante) or the Firearms (Amendment) Act 1988 s 15 (see para 214 ante).
5 Firearms Act 1968 s 22 (2) (amended by the Firearms (Amendment) Act 1988 s 23 (4)). For the meaning of 'firearm certificate' see para 200 note 8 ante.

6 Firearms Act 1968 s 24 (1).
7 Ibid s 24 (2) (a).
8 See note 4 supra.
9 Firearms Act 1968 s 24 (2) (b) (amended by the Firearms (Amendment) Act 1988 s 23 (4)).
10 Firearms Act 1968 s 51, Sch 6 Pt I (amended by the Criminal Justice Act 1982 ss 38, 46). For the meaning of 'the standard scale' see para 808 post. Imprisonment may not be imposed on a person under 21 years of age: see para 1195 post. As to powers of search see para 237 post; as to the limitation period for proceedings see para 240 post; and as to the court's powers to cancel firearm certificates and order forfeiture or disposal of firearms or ammunition see para 241 post.
11 Firearms Act 1968 s 24 (5).

225. Shot guns and ammunition. It is an offence (1) for a person under the age of 15 to have with him an assembled shot gun[1] except while under the supervision of a person of or over the age of 21, or while the shot gun is so covered with a securely fastened gun cover that it cannot be fired[2]; or (2) to make a gift of a shot gun or ammunition for a shot gun to a person under the age of 15[3].

A person guilty of any such offence is liable on summary conviction to a fine not exceeding level 3 on the standard scale[4].

In proceedings for an offence under head (2) above it is, however, a defence to prove that the person charged with the offence believed the other person to be of or over the age there mentioned and had reasonable grounds for the belief[5].

1 For the meaning of 'shot gun' see para 198 ante.
2 Firearms Act 1968 s 22 (3). Section 46 (as amended) (power of search with warrant), s 51 (4) (as amended) (limitation period for summary proceedings), s 52 (as amended) (forfeiture of firearms etc) do not apply to offences under s 22 (3): see paras 237 note 1, 240 note 1, 241 note 1 respectively post.
3 Ibid s 24 (3).
4 Ibid s 51, Sch 6 Pt I (amended by the Criminal Justice Act 1982 ss 38, 46 (b). For the meaning of 'the standard scale' see para 808 post.
     The court by which a person is convicted (1) of an offence under the Firearms Act 1968 s 22 (3) may make such order as it thinks as to the forfeiture or disposal of any firearm or ammunition found in his possession; (2) of an offence under s 24 (3) may make such order as it thinks fit as to the forfeiture or disposal of the shot gun or ammunition in respect of which the offence was committed: s 51 (3), Sch 6 Pt II paras 7, 9. As to the limitation period for summary proceedings see para 240 post.
5 Ibid s 24 (5).

226. Air weapons and ammunition. It is an offence (1) for a person under the age of 14 to have with him an air weapon[1] or ammunition for an air weapon[2]; (2) for a person under the age of 17 to have an air weapon with him in a public place[3], except an airgun or air rifle which is so covered with a securely fastened gun cover that it cannot be fired[4].

It is not, however, an offence under head (1) above for a person to have with him an air weapon or ammunition while he is under the supervision of a person of or over the age of 21; but, where a person has with him an air weapon on any premises[5] in circumstances where he would be prohibited from having it with him but for this exception, it is an offence (a) for him to use it for firing any missile beyond those premises; or (b) for the person under whose supervision he is to allow him so to use it[6]. Nor is it an offence under heads (1) or (2) above for a person to have with him an air weapon or ammunition at a time when being a member of an approved[7] rifle club or an approved miniature rifle club, he is engaged as such a member in or in connection with target practice, or he is using the weapon or ammunition at a shooting gallery where the only firearms used are either air weapons or miniature rifles not exceeding .23 inch calibre[8]. It is an offence (i) to make a gift of an air weapon or ammunition for an air weapon to a person under the age of 14; or (ii) to part with the possession of an air weapon or ammunition for an air weapon to a person under that age except where[9] the person is not prohibited from having it with him[10].

A person guilty of any such offence is liable on summary conviction to a fine not exceeding level 3 on the standard scale[11].

In proceedings for an offence under heads (i) and (ii) above it is a defence to prove that the person charged with the offence believed the other person to be of or over the age there mentioned and had reasonable grounds for the belief[12].

1 For the meaning of 'air weapon' see para 199 ante.
2 Firearms Act 1968 s 22 (4).
3 'Public place' includes any highway and any other premises or place to which at the material time the public has or is permitted to have access, whether on payment or otherwise: ibid s 57 (4). Cf the Prevention of Crime Act 1953 s 1 (4) (see para 167 note 5 ante); the Public Order Act 1986 s 16 (see para 142 note 4 ante); the Prevention of Terrorism (Temporary Provisions) Act 1989 s 3 (3) (see para 112 note 1 ante).
4 Firearms Act 1968 s 22 (5).
5 For the meaning of 'premises' see para 214 note 6 ante.
6 Firearms Act 1968 s 23 (1).
7 Ie approved by the Secretary of State for the purposes of ibid s 23 or the Firearms (Amendment) Act 1988 s 15 (see para 214 ante).
8 Firearms Act 1968 s 23 (2) (amended by the Firearms (Amendment) Act 1988 s 23 (4)).
9 Ie by virtue of the Firearms Act 1968 s 23 (as amended): see supra.
10 Ibid s 24 (4).
11 Ibid s 51, Sch 6 Pt I (amended by the Criminal Justice Act 1982 ss 38, 46). For the meaning of 'the standard scale' see para 808 post.
   The court by which a person is convicted of an offence under the Firearms Act 1968 ss 22 (4) or (5), 23 (1) or 24 (4) (see supra) may make such order as it thinks fit as to the forfeiture or disposal of the air weapon or ammunition in respect of which the offence was committed and any firearm or ammunition found in his possession: s 51 (3), Sch 6 Pt II paras 7, 8.
   Section 46 (as amended) (power of search with warrant), s 51 (4) (as amended) (limitation period for summary proceedings), s 52 (as amended) (forfeiture of firearms etc) do not apply to offences relating specifically to air weapons: see paras 237 note 1, 240 note 1, 241 note 1 respectively post.
12 Ibid s 24 (5).

(v) Prevention of Crime and Preservation of Public Safety

227. Supplying firearms or ammunition to persons drunk or of unsound mind. It is an offence for a person to sell or transfer[1] any firearm[2] or ammunition[3] to, or to repair, prove or test any firearm or ammunition for, another person whom he knows or has reasonable cause for believing to be drunk or of unsound mind[4]. A person guilty of such an offence is liable on summary conviction to imprisonment for a term not exceeding three months or a fine not exceeding level 3 on the standard scale, or to both[5].

1 For the meaning of 'transfer' see para 203 note 1 ante.
2 For the meaning of 'firearm' see para 197 ante.
3 For the meaning of 'ammunition' see para 200 note 9 ante.
4 Firearms Act 1968 s 25.
5 Ibid s 51, Sch 6 Pt I (amended by the Criminal Justice Act 1982 ss 38, 46). For the meaning of 'the standard scale' see para 808 post. As to powers of search see para 237 post; as to the limitation period

for summary proceedings see para 240 post; and as to the court's power to cancel firearm and shot gun certificates and order forfeiture or disposal of firearms and ammunition see para 241 post.

228. Possession of firearms by persons previously convicted of crime.

Unless an application for a removal of the prohibition has been granted[1]:

(1) a person who has been sentenced to custody for life or to preventive detention[2] or to imprisonment or to corrective training[2] for a term of three years or more or to youth custody or detention in a young offender institution[3] for such a term, or who has been sentenced to be detained for such a term in a young offenders institution in Scotland, must not at any time have a firearm[4] or ammunition[5] in his possession[6];

(2) a person who has been sentenced to imprisonment for a term of three months or more but less than three years[7] or to youth custody or detention in a young offender institution for such a term, or who has been sentenced to be detained for such a term in a detention centre or in a young offenders institution in Scotland, must not at any time before the expiration of the period of five years from the date of his release[8] have a firearm or ammunition in his possession[9];

(3) a person who is the holder of a specified licence[10], or is subject to a recognisance to keep the peace or to be of good behaviour[11] a condition of which is that he must not possess, use or carry a firearm, or is subject to a probation order[12] containing a requirement that he shall not possess, use or carry a firearm, or has, in Scotland, been ordained to find caution a condition of which is that he shall not possess, use or carry a firearm, must not, at any time during which he holds the licence or is so subject or has been so ordained, have a firearm or ammunition in his possession[13];

(4) a person who is prohibited in Northern Ireland[14] from having a firearm or ammunition in his possession is similarly prohibited in Great Britain[15].

It is an offence for a person to contravene any of the above provisions[16]; and a person guilty of any such offence is liable on conviction on indictment to imprisonment for a term not exceeding three years or a fine, or to both, or on summary conviction to imprisonment for a term not exceeding six months or a fine not exceeding the prescribed sum, or to both[17].

1 Ie under the Firearms Act 1968 s 21 (6) (amended by the Courts Act 1971 s 56 (2), Sch 9 Pt II; the Criminal Justice Act 1972 s 29). Application for removal of prohibition may be made to the Crown Court: s 21 (6) (as so amended). As to the mode of application and the procedure see the Firearms Act 1968 s 21 (7), Sch 3 (amended by the Courts Act 1971 s 56 (2), (4), Sch 9 Pt II, Sch 11 Pt IV).

2 Ie under the Criminal Justice Act 1948 s 21 (1), (2) (repealed). Such sentences were abolished by the Criminal Justice Act 1967 s 37 (1) (repealed).

3 See paras 1271, 1272 post.

4 For the meaning of 'firearm' see para 197 ante.

5 For the meaning of 'ammunition' see para 200 note 9 ante.

6 Firearms Act 1968 s 21 (1) (amended by the Criminal Justice Act 1982 s 77, Sch 14 para 24; the Criminal Justice Act 1988 s 123 (6), Sch 8 para 6).

7 In relation to the Firearms Act 1968 s 21 (2), 'imprisonment' does not include a suspended sentence: *R v Fordham* [1970] 1 QB 77, [1969] 3 All ER 532.

8 For these purposes, 'the date of his release', in the case of a person sentenced to imprisonment with an order under the Criminal Law Act 1977 s 47 (1) (amended by the Criminal Justice Act 1982 s 30) (see para 1207 post) is the date on which he completes service of so much of the sentence as was by that order required to be served in prison: Firearms Act 1968 s 21 (2A) (added by the Criminal Law Act 1977 s 47, Sch 9 para 9).

9 Firearms Act 1968 s 21 (2) (amended by the Criminal Justice Act 1982 Sch 14 para 24; the Criminal Justice Act 1988 s 170 (2), Sch 8 para 6, Sch 16).

10 Ie a person released on licence after being sentenced to be detained under the Children and Young Persons Act 1933 s 53 (as amended) (see paras 1269, 1270 post), or the Children and Young Persons (Scotland) Act 1937 s 57 (repealed: see now the Criminal Procedure (Scotland) Act 1975 s 206 (as amended)). As to the Secretary of State's powers to release on licence see the Criminal Justice Act 1967 s 61 (amended by the Criminal Justice Act 1982 s 77, Sch 14 para 19) and PRISONS vol 37 para 1190.

11 See paras 1233, 1234 post.

12 See para 1242 et seq post.

13 Firearms Act 1968 s 21 (3).

14 Ie by the Firearms Act (Northern Ireland) 1969 s 19 (repealed) or by any other enactment for the time being in force in Northern Ireland and corresponding to the Firearms Act 1968 s 21. See now the Firearms (Northern Ireland) Order 1981, SI 1981/155, art 22.

15 Ibid s 21 (3A) (added by the Criminal Justice Act 1972 s 29).

16 Firearms Act 1968 s 21 (4).

17 Ibid s 51, Sch 6 Pt I (amended by the Criminal Justice Act 1982 ss 38, 46). For the meaning of 'the prescribed sum' see para 807 post. As to powers of search see para 237 post; as to the limitation period for summary proceedings see para 240 post; and as to the court's power to cancel firearms certificates and order forfeiture and disposal of firearms and ammunition see para 241 post.

229. Sale etc of firearms to persons who have been convicted of crime. It is an offence for a person to sell or transfer[1] a firearm[2] or ammunition[3] to, or to repair, test or prove a firearm or ammunition for a person whom he knows or has reasonable ground for believing to be prohibited[4] from having a firearm or ammunition in his possession[5]. A person guilty of such an offence is liable on conviction on indictment to imprisonment for a term not exceeding three years or a fine, or to both, or on summary conviction to imprisonment for a term not exceeding six months or a fine not exceeding the prescribed sum, or to both[6].

1 For the meaning of 'transfer' see para 203 note 1 ante.

2 For the meaning of 'firearm' see para 197 ante.

3 For the meaning of 'ammunition' see para 200 note 9 ante.

4 Ie under the Firearms Act 1968 s 21 (as amended): see para 228 ante.

5 Ibid s 21 (5).

6 Ibid s 51, Sch 6 Pt I (amended by the Criminal Justice Act 1982 ss 38, 46). For the meaning of 'the prescribed sum' see para 807 post. As to the limitation period for summary proceedings see para 240 post; and as to the court's power to cancel firearms certificates and order forfeiture or disposal of firearms and ammunition see para 241 post.

230. Possession of firearms with intent to endanger life. It is an offence for a person to have in his possession[1] any firearm[2] or ammunition[3] with intent[4] by means of it to endanger life or to enable another person by means of it to endanger life[5], whether any injury to property has been caused or not[6]. A person guilty of such an offence is liable on conviction on indictment to imprisonment for life or for any shorter term or a fine, or to both[7].

1 For the meaning of 'possession' in the context of the Firearms Act 1968 s 1 (as amended) see para 200 note 2 ante.

2 For the meaning of 'firearm' see para 197 ante. A firearm for these purposes does not, however, include an imitation firearm to which the Firearms Act 1982 applies, but does include imitation firearms apart from the Firearms Act 1982: s 2 (2), (3).

3 For the meaning of 'ammunition' see para 200 note 9 ante.

4 The intent need not be immediate or unconditional, but the accused must have possession of the firearm and ammunition with a view to using them if and when the occasion arises: *R v Bentham* [1973] QB 357, 56 Cr App Rep 618, CA. On a charge of possession of a firearm with intent to endanger life it is a defence to show that the intent to endanger life had a lawful purpose, although cases where such a defence could be raised are rare: *R v Georgiades* [1989] 1 WLR 759, 89 Cr App Rep

206, CA (issue should have been left to the jury). The intent may be to endanger life outside the United Kingdom: *R v El-Hakkaoui* [1975] 2 All ER 146, [1975] 1 WLR 396, CA; and see note 6 infra.
5	The intention must be to endanger the life of another, not the accused's own life: *R v Norton* [1977] Crim LR 478.
6	Firearms Act 1968 s 16 (amended by the Criminal Damage Act 1971 s 11 (8), Schedule Pt I). An offence under the Firearms Act 1968 s 16 (as so amended) is a serious arrestable offence: see para 704 post. See also *R v El-Hakkaoui* [1975] 2 All ER 146, [1975] 1 WLR 396, CA (the offence is established on proof that the accused had a firearm in his possession in the United Kingdom and at the time of such possession intended by means of it to endanger life; where the intent would have been carried out is irrelevant).
7	Firearms Act 1968 s 51, Sch 6 Pt I (amended by the Criminal Justice Act 1982 ss 38, 46). As to powers of search see para 237 post; and as to the court's power to cancel firearm and shot gun certificates and order forfeiture or disposal of firearms and ammunition see para 241 post.

231. Use of firearm or imitation firearm to resist arrest or detention. It is an offence for a person to make or attempt to make any use whatsoever of a firearm[1] or imitation firearm[2] with intent to resist or prevent the lawful arrest or detention of himself or another person[3]. A person guilty of such an offence is liable on conviction on indictment to imprisonment for life or for any shorter term or a fine, or to both[4].

Where a person commits such an offence in respect of the lawful arrest or detention of himself for any offence committed by him, he is liable to the above penalty in addition to any penalty to which he may be sentenced for that other offence[5].

1	For these purposes, 'firearm' means a lethal barrelled weapon of any description from which any shot, bullet or other missile can be discharged and includes any prohibited weapon, whether it is such a lethal weapon or not: Firearms Act 1968 ss 17 (4), 57 (1) (a). For the meaning of 'prohibited weapon' see para 221 ante.
2	For these purposes, 'imitation firearm' means anything which has the appearance of being a firearm (see note 1 supra), whether or not it is capable of discharging any shot, bullet or other missile: ibid ss 17 (4), 57 (1) (a). It does not, however, include imitation firearms to which the Firearms Act 1982 (see para 197 note 7 ante) applies: s 2 (2), (3).
3	Firearms Act 1968 s 17 (1).
4	Ibid s 51, Sch 6 Pt I (amended by the Criminal Justice Act 1972 s 28 (1), (2)). As to the court's powers to cancel firearm or shot gun certificates and to order forfeiture or disposal of firearms and ammunition see para 241 post.
	On the trial of a person for an offence under the Firearms Act 1968 s 17 (1), the jury, if it is not satisfied that he is guilty of that offence, but is satisfied that he is guilty of an offence under s 17 (2) (see para 232 post), may find him guilty of the offence under s 17 (2): Sch 6 Pt II para 5.
5	Ibid Sch 6 Pt II para 4. Where a person who has attained the age of 17 years is charged before a magistrates' court with an offence specified in the Magistrates' Courts Act 1980 s 17 (1), Sch 1 (offences triable either way: see para 804 post) ('the listed offence'), and is also charged before that court with an offence under the Firearms Act 1968 s 17 (1) or (2) (see para 232 post), the court must proceed as if the listed offence were triable only on indictment and the Magistrates' Courts Act 1980 ss 18–23 (as amended) (procedure for determining mode of trial of offences triable either way: see paras 809–815 post) do not apply in relation to that offence: Firearms Act 1968 Sch 6 Pt II para 3 (1), (2) (amended by the Criminal Law Act 1977 s 65 (4), Sch 12; the Magistrates' Courts Act 1980 s 154, Sch 7 para 73). If the court determines not to commit the accused for trial in respect of the offence under s 17 (1) or (2), or if proceedings before the court for that offence are otherwise discontinued, the Firearms Act 1968 Sch 6 Pt II para 3 (2) (as so amended) ceases to apply as from the time when this occurred and (1) if at that time the court has not yet begun to inquire into the listed offence as examining justices, the court must, in the case of the listed offence, proceed in the ordinary way in accordance with the Magistrates' Courts Act 1980 ss 18–23 (as amended); but (2) if at that time the court has begun so to inquire into the listed offence, ss 18–23 (as amended) continue not to apply and the court must proceed with its inquiry into that offence as examining justices, but has power in accordance with s 25 (3), (4) (as amended) (see para 817 post) to change to summary trial with the accused's consent: Firearms Act 1968 Sch 6 Pt II paras 3 (1), (3) (amended by the Magistrates' Courts Act 1980 Sch 7 para 73).

232. Possession of firearms while committing offences. If a person, at the time of his committing or being arrested for a specified offence[1], has in his possession a firearm[2] or imitation firearm[3], he is guilty of an offence unless he shows that he had it in his possession for a lawful object[4]. A person guilty of such an offence is liable on conviction on indictment to imprisonment for life or for any shorter term or a fine, or to both[5]; and the punishment to which a person is so liable is in addition to any punishment to which he may be liable for the offence he was committing or for which he was being arrested[6].

1 The specified offences are:
   (1) offences under the Criminal Damage Act 1971 s 1 (destroying or damaging property: see para 594 post);
   (2) offences under any of the Offences against the Person Act 1861 s 20–22 (inflicting bodily injury; garrotting; criminal use of stupefying drugs: see paras 471, 473, 474 post), s 30 (laying explosive to building etc: see para 481 post), s 32 (endangering railway passengers by tampering with track: see para 485 post), s 38 (assault with intent to resist arrest: see paras 321, 491 post), s 47 (as amended) (criminal assaults: see para 490 post);
   (3) offences under the Child Abduction Act 1984 Pt I (ss 1–5: see paras 535, 536 post);
   (4) theft (see para 541 et seq post), burglary (see para 552 post), blackmail (see para 566 post) and any offence under the Theft Act 1968 s 12 (1) (taking motor vehicle or other conveyance without owner's consent: see para 556 post);
   (5) offences under the Police Act 1964 s 51 (1) (assaulting constable in the execution of his duty: see para 320 post);
   (6) offences under any of the Sexual Offences Act 1956 s 1 (rape: see para 514 post), ss 17, 20 (abduction of women: see paras 530, 532 post);
   (7) aiding and abetting the commission of any of the offences in heads (1)–(6) supra;
   (8) attempting to commit any offence so specified:
Firearms Act 1968 17 (2), Sch 1 (as amended).
2 For the meaning of 'firearm' see para 231 note 1 ante.
3 For the meaning of 'imitation firearm' see para 232 note 2 ante. For these purposes it does not include an imitation firearm to which the Firearms Act 1982 (see para 197 note 7 ante) applies: s 2 (2), (3).
4 Firearms Act 1968 s 17 (2). Before an accused can be convicted of an offence under s 17 (2), it must be shown that one of the offences specified has in fact been committed, and committed by the accused: *R v Baker* [1962] 2 QB 530, 46 Cr App Rep 47, CCA. As to the procedure where a person who has attained the age of 17 years is charged before a magistrates' court with an offence triable either way and is also charged before that court with an offence under the Firearms Act 1968 s 17 (2) see para 231 note 5 ante. A person is guilty of aggravated burglary if he commits any burglary and at the time has with him, inter alia, any firearm or imitation firearm: see para 553 post.
5 Ibid Sch 6 Pt I (amended by the Criminal Justice Act 1972 s 28 (1), (3); the Criminal Justice Act 1988 s 44 (3)). As to the court's power to cancel firearm and shot gun certificates and to order forfeiture or disposal of firearms and ammunition see para 241 post.
6 Firearms Act 1968 Sch 6 Pt II para 6. A consecutive sentence is the norm because the carrying of arms constitutes an aggravating feature in respect of which Parliament requires that a separate, additional but not necessarily consecutive, sentence be imposed: *R v McGrath* [1987] Crim LR 143, CA. As to sentencing generally see para 1187 et seq post. Offences committed with firearms should attract a minimum sentence of six months: *R v Hackney* (1982) 74 Cr App Rep 194, CA.

233. Shortening or converting weapon. It is an offence (1) to shorten the barrel of a shot gun[1] to a length[2] less than 24 inches[3]; or (2) to shorten to a length less than 24 inches the barrel of any specified smooth-bore gun[4] other than one which has a barrel with a bore exceeding two inches in diameter[5]; or (3) for a person other than a registered firearms dealer[6] to convert into a firearm[7] anything which, though having the appearance of being a firearm, is so constructed as to be incapable of discharging any missile through its barrel[8].

It is not, however, an offence under heads (1) and (2) above for a registered firearms dealer so to shorten the barrel of a shot gun or a gun for the sole purpose of replacing a defective part of the barrel so as to produce a barrel not less than 24 inches in length[9].

A person guilty of an offence under heads (1) or (3) above is liable on conviction on indictment to imprisonment for a term not exceeding five years or a fine, or to both, or on summary conviction to imprisonment for a term not exceeding six months or a fine not exceeding the prescribed sum, or to both[10]; and a person guilty of an offence under head (2) above is liable on conviction on indictment to imprisonment for a term not exceeding five years or a fine, or to both, or on summary conviction to imprisonment for a term not exceeding six months or a fine not exceeding the statutory maximum, or to both[11].

1 For the meaning of 'shot gun' see para 198 ante.
2 As to the measurement of the length of the barrel see para 198 note 1 ante. See also para 198 note 3 ante.
3 Firearms Act 1968 s 4 (1). Such an offence exists because such a weapon has little or no functional use other than to aid serious crime. Mere possession constitutes such an offence without the necessity of an intention to commit such serious crime. Public policy requires the imposition of a custodial sentence for such an offence: *R v Cook* (1987) 9 Cr App Rep (S) 71, CA.
4 Ie a smooth-bore gun to which the Firearms Act 1968 s 1 (as amended) applies: see para 200 ante.
5 Firearms (Amendment) Act 1988 s 6 (1).
6 For the meaning of 'registered' and 'firearms dealer' see para 203 notes 4, 5 respectively ante.
7 For the meaning of 'firearm' see para 197 ante.
8 Firearms Act 1968 s 4 (3). This offence does not apply to imitation firearms to which the Firearms Act 1982 applies (see para 197 note 7 ante): s 2 (2) (a).
9 Firearms Act 1968 s 4 (2); Firearms (Amendment) Act 1988 s 6 (2). As to the conversion of a prohibited weapon not affecting classification of the weapon see para 221 ante; as to the conversion of a weapon to which the Firearms Act 1968 s 1 (as amended) applies not affecting classification of the weapon see para 200 ante; and as to the deactivation of firearms see para 197 note 2 ante.
10 Ibid s 51, Sch 6 Pt I (amended by the Magistrates' Courts Act 1980 s 32 (2)). For the meaning of 'the prescribed sum' see para 807 post.
11 Firearms (Amendment) Act 1988 s 6 (1). For the meaning of 'the statutory maximum' see para 806 post. As to powers of search see para 237 post; as to the limitation period for summary proceedings see para 240 post; and as to the court's power to cancel firearms certificates and order forfeiture or disposal of firearms and ammunition see para 241 post.

234. Carrying firearms or imitation firearms with criminal intent.
It is an offence for a person to have with him[1] a firearm[2] or imitation firearm[3] with intent to commit[4] an indictable offence[5] or to resist arrest or prevent the arrest of another, in either case while he has a firearm or imitation firearm with him[6]. A person guilty of such an offence is liable on conviction on indictment to imprisonment for life or for any shorter term or a fine, or to both[7].

1 The mere fact of possession is not enough; a very close physical link and a degree of immediate control over the weapons are required, although it is not necessary to establish that the accused was carrying the firearm: *R v Kelt* [1977] 3 All ER 1099, 65 Cr App Rep 74, CA.
2 For the meaning of 'firearm' see para 197 ante.
3 For the meaning of 'imitation firearm' see para 197 ante. For these purposes it does not include an imitation firearm to which the Firearms Act 1982 applies (see para 197 note 7 ante): s 2 (2), (3). The question is whether the imitation had the appearance of a firearm at the time of the offence; members of the jury are entitled to have regard to the evidence of witnesses who saw the thing at that time together with their own observation of the thing itself, if they see it: *R v Morris and King* (1984) 79 Cr App Rep 104, CA. See also *R v Sloan* (1974) 19 CCC (2d) 190 (BC.CA) (imitation firearm must be instrument of some sort; finger used to simulate gun barrel not an imitation firearm) considered in *R v Morris and King* supra.
4 It is not essential for the intent to have been formed before the accused pulled the imitation firearm out of the holster: *R v Houghton* [1982] Crim LR 112, CA.
5 For the meaning of 'indictable offence' see para 42 note 6 ante.

6 Firearms Act 1968 s 18 (1). Proof that the accused had a firearm or imitation firearm with him and intended to commit an offence, or to resist or prevent an arrest, is evidence that he intended to have it with him while doing so: s 18 (2). As to a constable's powers to stop and search a person suspected of committing an offence under s 18 (2) see para 238 post.

7 Ibid s 51, Sch 6 Pt I (amended by the Criminal Justice Act 1988 s 44 (3) (b)). The sentence for the firearms offence should normally be consecutive to the sentence for the other offence, subject to the totality of the overall sentence: *R v Faulkner* (1972) 56 Cr App Rep 594, CA; *R v French* (1982) 75 Cr App Rep 1, CA. As to the court's power to cancel firearm and shot gun certificates and order forfeiture or disposal of firearms and ammunition see para 241 post.

235. Possession of firearms in a public place. A person commits an offence if without lawful authority[1] or reasonable excuse[2], the proof whereof lies on him, he has with him in a public place[3] a loaded shot gun[4] or loaded air weapon[5] or any other firearm[6], whether loaded or not, together with ammunition suitable for use in that firearm[7]. A person guilty of such an offence is liable on summary conviction to imprisonment for a term not exceeding six months or a fine not exceeding the prescribed sum, or to both, and, unless the firearm is an air weapon, on conviction on indictment to imprisonment for a term not exceeding five years or a fine, or to both[8].

1 It is not lawful authority for a person who has a loaded gun in a public place to be the holder of a valid shot gun certificate (see para 201 ante) to which no conditions were attached prohibiting such a use: *Ross v Collins* [1982] Crim LR 368, DC.

2 See *Taylor v Mucklow* (1973) 117 Sol Jo 792, DC (quarrel between houseowner and builder; builder thereupon demolishing part of new extension to house; houseowner attempting to stop builder's action by pointing loaded air gun at him from roadway; no reasonable excuse); *Ross v Collins* [1982] Crim LR 368, DC (belief that River Thames was not a public place was not a reasonable excuse because that reason could not amount to an excuse in law).

3 For the meaning of 'public place' see para 226 note 3 ante.

4 For the meaning of 'shot gun' see para 198 ante. A shot gun or an air weapon is to be deemed to be loaded if there is ammunition in the chamber or barrel or in any magazine or other device which is in such a position that the ammunition can be fed into the chamber or barrel by the manual or automatic operation of some part of the gun or weapon: Firearms Act 1968 s 57 (6) (b).

5 For the meaning of 'air weapon' see para 199 ante.

6 For the meaning of 'firearm' see para 197 ante. For these purposes it does not include an imitation firearm to which the Firearms Act 1982 (see para 197 note 7 ante) applies: s 2 (2), (3).

7 Firearms Act 1968 s 19.

8 Ibid s 51, Sch 6 Pt I (amended by the Magistrates' Courts Act 1980 s 32 (2)). For the meaning of 'the prescribed sum' see para 807 post. As to the limitation period for summary proceedings see para 240 post; and as to the court's power to cancel firearm and shot gun certificates and order forfeiture or disposal of firearms and ammunition see para 241 post.

236. Trespassing with firearm. A person commits an offence if, while he has a firearm[1] with him, he enters or is in any building or part of a building as a trespasser and without reasonable excuse, the proof whereof lies on him[2]. A person guilty of such an offence is liable on summary conviction to imprisonment for a term not exceeding six months or a fine not exceeding the prescribed sum, or to both, and, unless the firearm is an air weapon[3], on conviction on indictment to imprisonment for a term not exceeding five years or a fine, or to both[4].

A person commits an offence if, while he has a firearm with him, he enters or is on any land[5] as a trespasser and without reasonable excuse, the proof whereof lies on him[6]. A person guilty of such an offence is liable on summary conviction to imprisonment for a term not exceeding three months or a fine not exceeding level 4 on the standard scale, or to both[7].

1 For the meaning of 'firearm' see para 197 ante. For these purposes, it does not include an imitation firearm to which the Firearms Act 1982 (see para 197 note 7 ante) applies: s 2 (2), (3).
2 Firearms Act 1968 s 20 (1). As to a constable's power to stop and search a person suspected of committing such an offence see para 238 post.
3 For the meaning of 'air weapon' see para 199 ante.
4 Firearms Act 1968 s 51, Sch 6 Pt I (amended by the Magistrates' Courts Act 1980 s 32 (2)). For the meaning of 'the prescribed sum' see para 807 post.
5 For these purposes, 'land' includes land covered with water: Firearms Act 1968 s 20 (3).
6 Ibid s 20 (2). See also note 2 supra.
7 Ibid Sch 6 Pt I (amended by the Criminal Justice Act 1982 ss 38, 46). For the meaning of 'the standard scale' see para 808 post. As to limitation of time for summary proceedings see para 240 post; and as to the court's power to cancel firearm and shot gun certificates and order forfeiture or disposal of firearms and ammunition see para 241 post.

(vi) Enforcement

237. Power of search with warrant. If a justice of the peace is satisfied by information on oath that there is reasonable ground for suspecting that a relevant offence[1] has been, is being, or is about to be, committed, he may grant a search warrant authorising a constable:

(1) to enter at any time any premises[2] or place named in the warrant, if necessary by force, and to search the premises or place and every person found there;

(2) to seize and detain any firearm[3] or ammunition[4] which he may find on the premises or place, or on any such person, in respect of which or in connection with which he has reasonable ground for suspecting that a relevant offence has been, is being, or is about to be, committed;

(3) if the premises are those of a registered firearms dealer[5], to examine any books relating to the business[6].

1 The offences relevant for these purposes are all offences under the Firearms Act 1968 except an offence under s 22 (3) (see para 225 ante) or an offence relating specifically to air weapons: s 46 (2). Section 46 applies also to offences under the Firearms (Amendment) Act 1988: s 25 (5). Offences relating specifically to air weapons are those under the Firearms Act 1968 ss 22 (4), (5), 23 (1), 24 (4) (see para 226 ante): s 57 (3).
2 For the meaning of 'premises' see para 214 note 6 ante.
3 For the meaning of 'firearm' see para 197 ante.
4 For the meaning of 'ammunition' see para 200 note 9 ante.
5 For the meaning of 'registered' and 'firearms dealer' see para 203 notes 4, 5 respectively ante.
6 Firearms Act 1968 s 46 (1) (amended by the Police and Criminal Evidence Act 1984 s 119 (2), Sch 7 Pt I). The power of entry conferred by the Firearms Act 1968 Pt III (ss 46–52) is without prejudice to any power of entry which may exist apart from that Act: s 58 (4). As to powers of entry, search and seizure see para 668 et seq post.

238. Powers of constable to stop and search. A constable may require any person whom he has reasonable cause to suspect:

(1) of having a firearm[1], with or without ammunition[2], with him in a public place[3]; or

(2) to be committing or about to commit, elsewhere than in a public place, a relevant offence[4],

to hand over the firearm or any ammunition for examination by the constable[5].

If a person having a firearm or ammunition with him fails to hand it over when required to do so, he is guilty of an offence and liable on summary conviction to imprisonment for a term not exceeding three months or a fine not exceeding level 4 on the standard scale, or to both[6].

If a constable has reasonable cause to suspect a person of having a firearm with him in a public place, or to be committing or about to commit, elsewhere than in a public place, a relevant offence, the constable may search that person and may detain him for the purpose of doing so[7].

If a constable has reasonable cause to suspect that there is a firearm in a vehicle in a public place, or that a vehicle is being or is about to be used in connection with the commission of a relevant offence elsewhere than in a public place, he may search the vehicle and for that purpose require the person driving or in control of it to stop it[8].

For the purpose of exercising the above powers a constable may enter any place[9].

1 For the meaning of 'firearm' see para 197 ante. For these purposes it does not include an imitation firearm to which the Firearms Act 1982 (see para 197 note 7 ante) applies: s 2 (2), (3).
2 For the meaning of 'ammunition' see para 200 note 9 ante.
3 For the meaning of 'public place' see para 226 note 3 ante.
4 The offences relevant for these purposes are those under the Firearms Act 1968 ss 18 (1), (2) (see para 234 ante), 20 (see para 236 ante): s 47 (6).
5 Ibid s 47 (1). As to powers of stop and search see para 660 et seq post.
6 Ibid ss 47 (2), 51, Sch 6 Pt I (amended by the Criminal Justice Act 1982 ss 38, 46). For the meaning of 'the standard scale' see para 808 post.
7 Ibid s 47 (3).
8 Ibid s 47 (4).
9 Ibid s 47 (5).

239. Production of certificates. A constable may demand, from any person whom he believes to be in possession of a firearm[1] or ammunition[2], or of a shot gun[3], the production of his firearm certificate[4] or, as the case may be, his shot gun certificate[5]. If a person upon whom a demand is so made fails to produce the certificate or to permit the constable to read it, or to show that he is entitled[6] to have the firearm, ammunition or shot gun in his possession without holding a certificate, the constable may detain the firearm, ammunition or shot gun and may require the person to declare to him immediately his name and address[7]. If a person is so required to declare to a constable his name and address and he refuses to declare it or fails to give his true name and address, he is guilty of an offence and liable on summary conviction to a fine not exceeding level 3 on the standard scale[8].

1 For the meaning of 'firearm' see para 197 ante.
2 For the meaning of 'ammunition' see para 200 note 9 ante.
3 For the meaning of 'shot gun' see para 198 ante.
4 For the meaning of 'firearm certificate' see para 200 note 8 ante.
5 Firearms Act 1968 s 48 (1). For the meaning of 'shot gun certificate' see para 201 note 5 ante.
6 Ie by virtue of the Firearms Act 1968 or the Firearms (Amendment) Act 1988.
7 Firearms Act 1968 s 48 (2); Firearms (Amendment) Act 1988 s 25 (4).
8 Firearms Act 1968 ss 48 (3), 51, Sch 6 Pt I (amended by the Criminal Justice Act 1982 ss 38, 46). For the meaning of 'the standard scale' see para 808 post.

240. Limitation period for summary proceedings. Subject to certain exceptions[1], summary proceedings for an offence under the Firearms Act 1968 or the Firearms (Amendment) Act 1988 may[2] be instituted at any time within four years after the commission of the offence[3]; but such proceedings may not be instituted after the expiration of six months after the commission of the offence unless instituted by, or by the direction of, the Director of Public Prosecutions[4].

1 Ie proceedings for an offence under the Firearms Act 1968 s 22 (3) (see para 225 ante) or an offence relating specifically to air weapons (see para 237 note 1 ante): s 51 (4).

2 Ie notwithstanding the Magistrates' Courts Act 1980 s 127 (1) (limitation of time for taking proceedings: see MAGISTRATES).
3 Firearms Act 1968 s 51 (4) (amended by the Magistrates' Courts Act 1980 s 154 (1), Sch 7 para 72); Firearms (Amendment) Act 1988 s 25 (5).
4 Firearms Act 1968 s 51 (4) proviso. As to the effect of this limitation see para 639 post.

241. Forfeiture of firearms; cancellation of certificates. Where a person:

(1) is convicted of an offence under the Firearms Act 1968 or the Firearms (Amendment) Act 1988, other than an offence to which this provision does not apply[1], or is convicted of an offence for which he is sentenced to imprisonment or detention in a young offender institution[2] or in a young offenders' institution in Scotland; or

(2) has been ordered to enter into a recognisance to keep the peace or to be of good behaviour[3], a condition of which is that he shall not possess, use or carry a firearm[4]; or

(3) is subject to a probation order[5] containing a requirement that he shall not possess, use or carry a firearm,

the court by or before which he is convicted, or by which the order is made, may make such order as to the forfeiture or disposal of any firearm or ammunition[6] found in his possession as the court thinks fit and may cancel any firearm certificate[7] or shot gun certificate[8] held by him[9].

1 Ie an offence under the Firearms Act 1968 s 22 (3) (see para 225 ante), or an offence relating specifically to air weapons (see para 237 note 1 ante).
2 See paras 1271, 1272 post.
3 See para 1233 post. This refers only to the common law powers and not to the power under the Justices of the Peace Act 1361: *Goodland v Chief Constable of South Yorkshire* [1978] Crim LR 51.
4 For the meaning of 'firearm' see para 197 ante.
5 See para 1242 et seq post.
6 For the meaning of 'ammunition' see para 214 note 2 ante.
7 For the meaning of 'firearm certificate' see para 200 note 8 ante.
8 For the meaning of 'shot gun certificate' see para 201 note 5 ante.
9 Firearms Act 1968 s 52 (1) (amended by the Criminal Justice Act 1988 ss 123 (6), 170 (2), Sch 8 para 1, Sch 16); Firearms (Amendment) Act 1988 s 25 (5). Where the court so cancels a certificate, the court must cause notice to be sent to the chief officer of police by whom the certificate was granted and the chief officer of police must by notice in writing require the holder of the certificate to surrender it: Firearms Act 1968 s 52 (2) a), (b). A holder who fails to surrender a certificate within 21 days from the date of the notice given him by the chief officer of police is guilty of an offence and liable on summary conviction to a fine not exceeding level 3 on the standard scale: ss 51, 52 (2) (c), Sch 6 Pt I (amended by the Criminal Justice Act 1982 ss 38, 46). For the meaning of 'the standard scale' see para 808 post. A constable may seize and detain any firearm or ammunition which may be the subject of an order for forfeiture (Firearms Act 1968 s 52 (3)); and a magistrates' court may, on the application of the chief officer of police, order any such firearm or ammunition so seized and detained to be destroyed or otherwise disposed of (s 52 (4)). Where, however, a person is convicted of an offence under the Firearms (Amendment) Act 1988 s 19, Schedule (see para 220 ante), no order may be made for the forfeiture of anything in his possession for the purposes of the museum in question: s 25 (5). The Firearms Act 1968 s 52 (3) is not to be taken as prejudicing the power of a constable, when arresting a person for an offence, to seize property found in his possession or any other power of a constable to seize firearms, ammunition or other property, being a power exercisable apart from s 52 (3): s 58 (4). As to the restrictions on the possession of firearms or ammunition by persons who have been convicted of crime see para 228 ante; and as to the power to order deprivation of property used for crime see para 1336 post.

242. Powers on conviction of registered firearms dealer. Where a registered firearms dealer[1] is convicted of a relevant offence[2], the court may order:

(1) that the dealer's name be removed from the register;
(2) that neither the dealer nor any person who acquires the dealer's business nor any person who took part in the management of the business and was knowingly a party to the offence shall be registered as a firearms dealer;
(3) that any person who, after the date of the order, knowingly employs in the management of his business the dealer convicted of the offence, or any person who was knowingly a party to the offence, shall not be registered as a firearms dealer or, if so registered, shall be liable to be removed from the register; and
(4) that any stock-in-hand of the business shall be disposed of by sale or otherwise in accordance with the directions contained in the order[3].

A person aggrieved by such an order may appeal against the order in the same manner as against the conviction; and the court may, if it thinks fit, suspend the operation of the order pending the appeal[4].

1 For the meaning of 'registered' and 'firearms dealer' see para 203 notes 4, 5 respectively ante.
2 Ie an offence relevant for the purposes of the Firearms Act 1968 s 45. The offences so relevant are (1) all offences under the Firearms Act 1968 except an offence under s 2 (see para 201 ante), ss 22 (3), 24 (3) (see para 225 ante); or an offence relating specifically to air weapons (see para 237 note 1 ante); (2) offences against the enactments for the time being in force relating to customs or excise in respect of the import or export of firearms or ammunition to which s 1 (as amended) (see para 200 ante), applies, or of shot guns (see CUSTOMS AND EXCISE vol 12 paras 1061, 1062): s 45 (2) (amended by the Customs and Excise Management Act 1979 s 177 (1), Sch 4 para 12, Table Pt I).
3 Firearms Act 1968 s 45 (1).
4 Ibid s 45 (3). As to appeal on conviction on indictment see para 1352 et seq post; and as to appeal on summary conviction see para 1450 et seq post.

(6) OFFICIAL SECRETS AND COMMUNICATION OF INFORMATION

(i) Offences in respect of Official Secrets

243. Spying and sabotage. If any person for any purpose[1] prejudicial to the safety or interests of the State[2]:
(1) approaches, inspects, passes over or is in the neighbourhood of, or enters any prohibited place[3]; or
(2) makes any sketch[4], plan, model[5], or note which is calculated to be, or might be, or is intended to be, directly or indirectly useful to an enemy[6]; or
(3) obtains[7], collects, records, or publishes, or communicates[8] to any other person any secret official code word, or pass word, or any sketch, plan, model, article, or note, or other document[9] or information[10] which is calculated to be, or might be, or is intended to be, directly or indirectly useful to an enemy,

he is guilty of an offence and liable on conviction on indictment to imprisonment for a term not exceeding 14 years[11].

1 'Purpose' within the meaning of the Official Secrets Act 1911 s 1 (amended by the Official Secrets Act 1920 ss 10, 11 (2), Schs 1, 2) is to be distinguished from the motive for doing an act; and 'any purpose' means or includes the achieving of the consequence which a person intended or desired to follow directly on his act, ie his direct or immediate purpose as opposed to his ultimate aim; and, even if a person had several purposes, his immediate purpose remained one of them and was within the words 'any purpose': *Chandler v DPP* [1964] AC 763, 46 Cr App Rep 347, HL. See also *R v Bettaney* [1985] Crim LR 104, CA (quality of information irrelevant in considering purpose for which it was communicated). As to proof of a purpose prejudicial to the safety or interests of the State see para 267 post.

2 In the phrase 'interests of the State', 'State' means 'the organised community' or 'the organs of government of a national community' and 'interests of the State' means those interests according to the policies of the State as they in fact are, not as it might be argued that they ought to be: *Chandler v DPP* [1964] AC 763, 46 Cr App Rep 347, HL. In that case members of an organisation supporting nuclear disarmament had approached an air base belonging to Her Majesty which was a prohibited place with the admitted purpose of grounding all aircraft, immobilising the airfield and reclaiming the base for civilian purposes. It was held that, where a Secretary of State had declared places within the Official Secrets Act 1911 s 3 (amended by the Official Secrets Act 1920 s 10, Sch 1) (see para 244 post) to be prohibited places in which damage, destruction, obstruction or interference would be useful to an enemy, the accused was not entitled to say or lead evidence to show that, although he had done that which would be useful to an enemy, yet his purpose was not prejudicial to the safety or interests of the State since the Crown (which was for present purposes 'the State') alone was entitled to decide the disposition and armament of the armed forces and the propriety of the decision on such matters could not be questioned in a court of law. See also *Chandler v DPP* supra at 811 and at 389, 390 per Lord Devlin: 'In a case like the present, it may be presumed that it is contrary to the interests of the Crown to have one of its airfields immobilised... The thing speaks for itself... But the presumption is not irrebuttable'. See also *R v Bettaney* [1985] Crim LR 104, CA.

3 For the meaning of 'prohibited place' see para 244 post.

4 'Sketch' includes any photograph or other mode of representing any place or thing: Official Secrets Act 1911 s 12.

5 'Model' includes design, pattern and specimen: ibid s 12.

6 'Enemy' includes a potential enemy with whom there might be war: *R v Parrott* (1913) 8 Cr App Rep 186, CCA.

7 Expressions referring to obtaining or retaining any sketch, plan, model, article, note, or document, include the copying or causing to be copied the whole or any part of any sketch, plan, model, article, note, or document: Official Secrets Act 1911 s 12.

8 Expressions referring to communicating include any communicating, whether in whole or in part, and whether the sketch, plan, model, article, note, document, or information itself or the substance, effect or description thereof only be communicated; and expressions referring to the communication of any sketch, plan, model, article, note or document include the transfer or transmission of the sketch, plan, model, article, note or document: ibid s 12 (amended by the Official Secrets Act 1989 s 16 (4), Sch 2).

9 'Document' includes part of a document: Official Secrets Act 1911 s 12.

10 Where information is communicated, its truth or falsity is, it seems, immaterial: see *R v M* (1915) 32 TLR 1, 11 Cr App Rep 207, CCA (charge of attempting to communicate information to the enemy with the intention of assisting the enemy contrary to the Defence of the Realm (Consolidation) Act 1914 (repealed).

11 Official Secrets Act 1911 s 1 (1) (as amended: see note 1 supra); Official Secrets Act 1920 s 8 (1); Criminal Justice Act 1948 s 1 (1); Criminal Law Act 1967 s 12 (5). As to restrictions on prosecutions see para 264 post; and as to sentencing see *R v Prime* (1983) 5 Cr App Rep (S) 127, CA (series of offences under the Official Secrets Act 1911 s 1 (1) (c) (as so amended): see head (3) supra; consecutive sentences of 14, 14 and seven years upheld having regard to the totality of the sentence); *R v Schulze and Schulze* (1986) 8 Cr App Rep (S) 463, CA (acts preparatory to commission of offence under the Official Secrets Act 1911 s 1 (1) (c) (as so amended); sentence of ten years' imprisonment upheld).

The Official Secrets Act 1911 s 1 (1) (as so amended) is not limited to offences of spying but extends to the saboteur as much as to the spy: *Chandler v DPP* [1964] AC 763, 46 Cr App Rep 347, HL. The Official Secrets Acts 1911, 1920 and 1939 are to be construed as one: see the Official Secrets Act 1920 s 11 (1); the Official Secrets Act 1939 s 2 (1). Archives of a foreign embassy in England can be the subject of a charge under the Acts: See *R v AB* [1941] 1 KB 454; sub nom *R v Kent* (1941) 28 Cr App Rep 23, CCA. As to police powers to obtain information relating to offences under the Official Secrets Act 1911 s 1 (1) (as so amended) see para 261 post; and as to the facts deemed to constitute evidence of obtaining information useful to an enemy see para 266 post.

244. Meaning of 'prohibited place'. 'Prohibited place' means:

(1) any work of defence, arsenal, naval or air force establishment or station, factory, dockyard, mine, minefield, camp, ship[1], or aircraft belonging to or occupied by or on behalf of Her Majesty or any telegraph, telephone, wireless or signal station, or office so belonging or occupied, and any place belonging to or occupied by or on behalf of Her Majesty[2] and used for the

purpose of building, repairing, making, or storing any munitions of war[3], or any sketches[4], plans, models[5], or documents[6], relating thereto, or for the purpose of getting any metals, oil, or minerals of use in time of war[7];

(2) any place not belonging to Her Majesty where any munitions of war, or any sketches, models, plans, or documents relating thereto, are being made, repaired, gotten, or stored under contract with, or with any person on behalf of, Her Majesty, or otherwise on behalf of Her Majesty[8]; and

(3) any place belonging to or used for the purposes of Her Majesty which is for the time being declared by order of a Secretary of State to be a prohibited place on the ground that information with respect thereto, or damage thereto, would be useful to an enemy[9]; and

(4) any railway, road, way, or channel, or other means of communication by land or water, including any works or structures being part thereof or connected therewith, or any place used for gas, water, or electricity works or other works for purposes of a public character, or any place where any munitions of war, or any sketches, models, plans, or documents relating thereto, are being made, repaired, or stored otherwise than on behalf of Her Majesty, which is for the time being declared by order of a Secretary of State to be a prohibited place, on the ground that information with respect thereto, or the destruction or obstruction thereof, or interference therewith, would be useful to an enemy[10];

(5) any office belonging to, or occupied by, the Post Office[11]; and

(6) any station or office belonging to, or occupied by, a public telecommunications operator[12].

For the purposes of head (3) above, any place belonging to or used for the purposes of the United Kingdom Atomic Energy Authority is deemed to be a place belonging to or used for the purposes of Her Majesty[13]; a place belonging to or used for the purpose of the Civil Aviation Authority is deemed to be a place belonging to Her Majesty[14]; and specified nuclear sites[15] are deemed to be a place belonging to or used for the purposes of Her Majesty[16].

1 References in the Official Secrets Acts 1911 and 1920 to ships, vessels, or boats or activities or places connected with them include hovercraft: Hovercraft (Application of Enactments) Order 1972, SI 1972/971, art 4, Sch 1 Pt A.
2 'Place belonging to Her Majesty' includes a place belonging to any department of the government of the United Kingdom or of any British possessions, whether the place is or is not actually vested in Her Majesty: Official Secrets Act 1911 s 12.
3 'Munitions of war' includes the whole or any part of any ship, submarine, aircraft, tank or similar engine, arms and ammunition, torpedo or mine, intended or adapted for use in war, and any other article, material or device, whether actual or proposed, intended for such use: ibid s 12 (amended by the Official Secrets Act 1920 s 9 (2)).
4 For the meaning of 'sketch' see para 243 note 4 ante.
5 For the meaning of 'model' see para 243 note 5 ante.
6 For the meaning of 'document' see para 243 note 9 ante.
7 Official Secrets Act 1911 s 3 (a) (substituted by the Official Secrets Act 1920 s 10, Sch 1).
8 Official Secrets Act 1911 s 3 (b) (amended by the Official Secrets Act 1920 Sch 1).
9 Official Secrets Act 1911 s 3 (c) (amended by the Official Secrets Act 1920 Sch 1). For orders made under the Official Secrets Act 1911 s 3 (c) (as so amended) see the Official Secrets (Prohibited Place) Order 1955, SI 1955/1497; the Official Secrets (Prohibited Places) Order 1975, SI 1975/182.
10 Official Secrets Act 1911 s 3 (d) (amended by the Official Secrets Act 1920 Sch 1). At the date at which this volume states the law, no order under the Official Secrets Act 1911 s 3 (d) (as so amended) had been made.
11 Post Office Act 1969 ss 6, 76, Sch 4 para 21 (1) (amended by the British Telecommunications Act 1981 s 89, Sch 6 Pt II; the Official Secrets Act 1989 s 16 (4), Sch 2). As to the Post Office see POST OFFICE.

12 Telecommunications Act 1984 s 109 (1), Sch 4 para 12 (2); and see TELECOMMUNICATIONS AND BROADCASTING.

13 Atomic Energy Authority Act 1954 s 6 (3). See also the Official Secrets (Prohibited Place) Order 1955; the Official Secrets (Prohibited Places) Order 1975 art 2, Sch 1 Pt II. Any right of entry upon a prohibited place, except by constables and specified officials, is exercisable only with the authority's consent and subject to any conditions the authority imposes: see the Atomic Energy Authority Act 1954 s 6 (3). A right of entry may also be exercised by a person as an inspector of the International Atomic Energy Agency: s 6 (3) (bb) (added by the Nuclear Safeguards and Electricity (Finance) Act 1978 s 2 (3)). See also the Radioactive Substances Act 1960 s 12 (3) proviso. On application by a person aggrieved by a refusal of consent or by conditions imposed, the Secretary of State may authorise the exercise of the right subject to conditions: Atomic Energy Authority Act 1954 s 6 (3) proviso.

14 Civil Aviation Act 1982 ss 2 (1), 18 (2). At the date at which this volume states the law no order had been made under the Official Secrets Act 1911 s 3 (c) as extended by the Civil Aviation Act 1982 s 18 (2). As to the restrictions (similar to those set out in note 13 supra) upon the exercise of any right of entry upon a place which is a prohibited place see s 18 (2)–(4).

15 Ie every site to which applies a permit granted by the Secretary of State to a body corporate in relation to which the Secretary of State has by order directed that the Nuclear Installations Act 1965 s 2, Sch 1 para 3 (1) (added by the Atomic Energy Authority Act 1971 s 17 (6), Schedule), shall have effect: see the Nuclear Installations Act 1965 s 2 (1)–(1D) (amended by the Atomic Energy Authority Act 1971 s 17); and see ELECTRICITY.

16 Nuclear Installations Act 1965 s 2, Sch 1 para 3 (1) (as added: see note 15 supra). See also the Official Secrets (Prohibited Places) Order 1975 Sch 1 Pt I. As to the restrictions (similar to those set out in note 13 supra) upon the exercise of any right of entry except with the consent of, and upon conditions imposed by, the body corporate specified in the Secretary of State's order, or with the authority of the Secretary of State (see note 15 supra) see the Nuclear Installations Act 1965 Sch 1 para 3 (2) (amended by the Nuclear Installations Act 1965 etc (Repeals and Modifications) Regulations 1974, SI 1974/2056, reg 2 (1) (b), Sch 2 para 7; the Nuclear Safeguards and Electricity (Finance) Act 1978 s 2 (3)).

245. Disclosure of security or intelligence information etc. A person who is or has been (1) a member of the security and intelligence services; or (2) a person notified[1] that he is subject to these provisions, is guilty of an offence if without lawful authority[2] he discloses any information[3], document or other article[4] relating to security or intelligence[5] which is or has been in his possession by virtue of his position as a member of any of those services or in the course of his work while the notification is or was in force[6].

A person who is or has been a Crown servant[7] or government contractor[8] is guilty of an offence, if without lawful authority he makes a damaging[9] disclosure of any information, document or other article relating to security or intelligence which is or has been in his possession by virtue of his position[10] as such[11]. It is a defence for a person charged with either of the above offences to prove that at the time of the alleged offence he did not know, and had no reasonable cause to believe, that the information, document or article in question related to security or intelligence or that[12] the disclosure would be damaging[13].

A person guilty of either such offence is liable on conviction on indictment to imprisonment for a term not exceeding two years or a fine, or to both, or on summary conviction to imprisonment for a term not exceeding six months or a fine not exceeding the statutory maximum, or to both[14].

1 Notification that a person is so subject must be effected by a notice in writing served on such a person by a Minister of the Crown; and such a notice may be served if, in the Minister's opinion, the work undertaken by the person in question is or includes work connected with the security and intelligence services and its nature is such that the interests of national security require that he should be so subject: Official Secrets Act 1989 s 1 (6). Such a notification is in force for the period of five years beginning with the day on which it is served, but may be renewed by further notices under s 1 (6) for

periods of five years at a time: s 1 (7). However, such a notification may at any time be revoked by a further notice in writing served by the Minister on the person concerned; and the Minister must serve such further notice as soon as, in his opinion, the work undertaken by that person ceases to be such as is mentioned in s 1 (6): s 1 (8).

2 For the meaning of 'lawful authority' see para 251 post.

3 The reference to disclosing information relating to security or intelligence includes a reference to making any statement which purports to be a disclosure of such information or is intended to be taken by those to whom it is addressed as being such a disclosure: Official Secrets Act 1989 s 1 (2).

4 'Disclose' and 'disclosure', in relation to a document or other article, include parting with possession of it: ibid s 13 (1).

5 For these purposes, 'security or intelligence' means the work of, or in support of, the security and intelligence services or any part of them; and references to information relating to security or intelligence include references to information held or transmitted by those services or by persons in support of, or of any part of, them: ibid s 1 (9). As to the security service see the Security Service Act 1989 and CONSTITUTIONAL LAW.

6 Official Secrets Act 1989 s 1 (1). As to extent of the 1989 Act and the place of trial see para 263 post; as to restrictions on prosecutions see para 264 post; as to the exclusion of the public during a hearing see para 265 post; as to powers of arrest see the Police and Criminal Evidence Act 1984 s 24 (amended by the Official Secrets Act 1989 s 11 (1)) and para 693 et seq post; and as to the power to grant a search warrant see the Official Secrets Act 1911 s 9 (1) (amended by the Official Secrets Act 1989 s 11 (3)) and para 260 post.

Any act done (1) by a British citizen or Crown servant; or (2) by any person in any of the Channel Islands or the Isle of Man or any colony, is, if it would be an offence by that person under any provision of the Official Secrets Act 1989 other than s 8 (1), (4) or (5) (see para 252 post) when done by him in the United Kingdom, an offence under that provision: s 15 (1). For the meaning of 'British citizen' see para 249 note 13 post.

7 'Crown servant' means (1) a Minister of the Crown; (2) a person appointed under the Northern Ireland Constitution Act 1973 s 8; (3) any person employed in the civil service of the Crown, including Her Majesty's Diplomatic Service, Her Majesty's Overseas Civil Service, the civil service of Northern Ireland and the Northern Ireland Court Service; (4) any member of the naval, military or air forces of the Crown, including any person employed by an association established for the purposes of the Reserve Forces Act 1980 (see ROYAL FORCES); (5) any constable and any other person employed or appointed in or for the purposes of any police force (including a police force within the meaning of the Police Act (Northern Ireland) 1970); (6) any person who is a member or employee of a prescribed body or a body of a prescribed class and either is prescribed for these purposes or belongs to a prescribed class of members or employees of any such body; (7) any person who is the holder of a prescribed office or who is an employee of such a holder and either is prescribed for these purposes or belongs to a prescribed class of such employees: Official Secrets Act 1989 s 12 (1).

'Prescribed' means prescribed by an order made by the Secretary of State: s 13 (1). Any such power of the Secretary of State to make orders is exercisable by statutory instrument; and no order may be made by him for the purposes of s 7 (5) (see para 251 post), s 8 (9) (see para 252 post) or s 12 unless a draft of it has been laid before, and approved by a resolution of, each House of Parliament: s 14 (1), (2). If, apart from these provisions, the draft of an order under any of ss 7 (5), 8 (8), 12 would be treated for the purposes of the Standing Orders of either House of Parliament as a hybrid instrument, it must proceed in that House as if it were not such an instrument: s 14 (3).

8 'Government contractor' means any person who is not a Crown servant but who provides, or is employed in the provision of, goods or services (1) for the purposes of any Minister of the Crown or person mentioned in ibid s 12 (1) (a) or (b) (see note 7 heads (1), (2) supra), of any of the services, forces or bodies mentioned in s 12 (1) (see note 7 supra) or of the holder of any office prescribed under s 12 (1); or (2) under an agreement or arrangement certified by the Secretary of State as being one to which the government of a State other than the United Kingdom or an international organisation is a party or which is subordinate to, or made for the purposes of implementing, any such agreement or arrangement: s 12 (2). For the meaning of 'United Kingdom' see para 86 note 1 ante.

Where an employee or class of employees of any body, or of any holder of an office, is prescribed by an order made for the purposes of s 12 (1) (see note 7 supra) (a) any employee of that body, or the holder of that office, who is not prescribed or is not within the prescribed class; and (b) any person who does not provide, or is not employed in the provision of, goods and services for the purposes of the performance of those functions of the body or the holder of the office in connection with which the employee or prescribed class of employees is engaged, is not a government contractor for the purposes of the Official Secrets Act 1989: s 12 (3).

'State' includes the government of a State and any organ of its government; and references to a State other than the United Kingdom include references to any territory outside the United Kingdom: s 13 (1). 'International organisation' means an organisation of which only States are members and includes a reference to any organ of such an organisation: s 13 (1). However, in s 12 (2) (b) (see head (2) supra) the reference to an international organisation includes a reference to any such organisation whether or not one of which only States are members and includes a commercial organisation: s 13 (2). In determining whether only States are members of an organisation, any member which is itself an organisation of which only States are members, or which is an organ of such an organisation, is to be treated as a State: s 13 (3).

9 For these purposes, a disclosure is damaging if (1) it causes damage to the work of, or any part of, the security and intelligence services; or (2) it is of information or a document or other article which is such that its unauthorised disclosure would be likely to cause such damage or which falls within a class or description of information, documents or articles the unauthorised disclosure of which would be likely to have that effect: ibid s 1 (4).

10 Ie but otherwise than as mentioned in ibid s 1 (1): see supra.

11 Ibid s 1 (3). See also note 6 supra.

12 Ie in the case of an offence under ibid s 1 (3): see supra.

13 Ibid s 1 (5).

14 Ibid s 10 (1). For the meaning of 'the statutory maximum' see para 806 post.

246. Damaging disclosure of defence information etc.

A person who is or has been a Crown servant[1] or government contractor[2] is guilty of an offence if without lawful authority[3] he makes a damaging disclosure[4] of any information, document or other article[5] relating to defence[6] which is or has been in his possession by virtue of his position as such[7]. It is a defence for a person charged with such an offence to prove that at the time of the alleged offence he did not know, and had no reasonable cause to believe, that the information, document or article in question related to defence or that its disclosure would be so damaging[8]. A person guilty of such an offence is liable on conviction on indictment to imprisonment for a term not exceeding two years or a fine, or to both, or on summary conviction to imprisonment for a term not exceeding six months or a fine not exceeding the statutory maximum, or to both[9].

1 For the meaning of 'Crown servant' see para 245 note 7 ante.

2 For the meaning of 'government contractor' see para 245 note 8 ante.

3 For the meaning of 'lawful authority' see para 251 post.

4 For these purposes, a disclosure is damaging if (1) it damages the capability of, or of any part of, the armed forces of the Crown to carry out their tasks or leads to loss of life or injury to members of those forces or serious damage to the equipment or installations of those forces; or (2) otherwise than as mentioned in head (1) supra, it endangers the interests of the United Kingdom abroad, seriously obstructs the promotion or protection by the United Kingdom of those interests or endangers the safety of British citizens abroad; or (3) it is of information or of a document or article which is such that its unauthorised disclosure would be likely to have any of those effects: Official Secrets Act 1989 s 2 (2). For the meaning of 'British citizen' see para 249 note 13 post; and for the meaning of 'United Kingdom' see para 86 note 1 ante.

5 For the meaning of 'disclosure' in relation to a document or other article see para 245 note 4 ante.

6 For these purposes, 'defence' means (1) the size, shape, organisation, logistics, order of battle, deployment, operations, state of readiness and training of the armed forces of the Crown; (2) the weapons, stores or other equipment of those forces and the invention, development, production and operation of such equipment and research relating to it; (3) defence policy and strategy and military planning and intelligence; (4) plans and measures for the maintenance of essential supplies and services that are or would be needed in time of war: Official Secrets Act 1989 s 2 (4).

7 Ibid 2 (1). As to extent of the 1989 Act and place of trial see para 263 post; as to restrictions on prosecutions see para 264 post; as to the exclusion of the public during a hearing see para 265 post; as to powers of arrest see the Police and Criminal Evidence Act 1984 s 24 (amended by the Official Secrets Act 1989 s 11 (1)) and para 693 et seq post; as to the power to grant a search warrant see the

Official Secrets Act 1911 s 9 (1) (amended by the Official Secrets Act 1989 s 11 (3)) and para 260 post; and as to acts done abroad see para 245 note 6 ante.

8 Ibid s 2 (3). 'So damaging' means damaging within the meaning of s 2 (1): see supra.

9 Ibid s 10 (1). For the meaning of 'the statutory maximum' see para 806 post.

247. Damaging disclosure of information etc relating to international relations. A person who is or has been a Crown servant[1] or government contractor[2] is guilty of an offence if without lawful authority[3] he makes a damaging disclosure[4] of:

(1) any information, document or other article[5] relating to international relations[6]; or

(2) any confidential[7] information, document or other article which was obtained from a State other than the United Kingdom or an international organisation,

being information or a document or article which is or has been in his possession by virtue of his position as a Crown servant or government contractor[8]. It is a defence for a person charged with such an offence to prove that at the time of the alleged offence he did not know, and had no reasonable cause to believe, that the information, document or article in question was such information as is mentioned above[9] or that its disclosure would be damaging[10].

A person guilty of such an offence is liable on conviction on indictment to imprisonment for a term not exceeding two years or a fine, or to both, or on summary conviction to imprisonment for a term not exceeding six months or a fine not exceeding the statutory maximum, or to both[11].

1 For the meaning of 'Crown servant' see para 245 note 7 ante.

2 For the meaning of 'government contractor' see para 245 note 8 ante.

3 For the meaning of 'lawful authority' see para 251 post.

4 For these purposes, a disclosure is damaging if (1) it endangers the interests of the United Kingdom abroad, seriously obstructs the promotion or protection by the United Kingdom of those interests or endangers the safety of British citizens abroad; or (2) it is of information or of a document or article which is such that its unauthorised disclosure would be likely to have any of those effects: Official Secrets Act 1989 s 3 (2). In the case of information or a document or article within s 3 (1) (b) (see text head (2) infra), the fact that it is confidential, or its nature or contents, may be sufficient to establish for the purposes of s 3 (2) (b) (see head (2) supra) that the information, document or article is such that its unauthorised disclosure would be likely to have any of those effects: s 3 (3). For the meaning of 'British citizen' see para 249 note 13 post; and for the meaning of 'United Kingdom' see para 86 note 1 ante.

5 For the meaning of 'disclosure' in relation to a document or other article see para 245 note 4 ante.

6 For these purposes, 'international relations' means the relations between States, between international organisations or between one or more States and one or more such organisations and includes any matter relating to a State other than the United Kingdom or to an international organisation which is capable of affecting the relations of the United Kingdom with another State or with an international organisation: Official Secrets Act 1989 s 3 (5). For the meaning of 'State', 'international organisation' and 'State other than the United Kingdom' see para 245 note 8 ante.

7 For these purposes, any information, document or article obtained from a State or organisation is confidential at any time while the terms on which it was obtained require it to be held in confidence or while the circumstances in which it was obtained make it reasonable for the State or organisation to expect that it would be so held: ibid s 3 (6).

8 Ibid s 3 (1). As to extent of the 1989 Act and place of trial see para 263 post; as to restrictions on prosecutions see para 264 post; as to the exclusion of the public during a hearing see para 265 post; as to powers of arrest see the Police and Criminal Evidence Act 1984 s 24 (amended by the Official Secrets Act 1989 s 11 (1)) and para 693 et seq post; as to the power to grant a search warrant see the Official Secrets Act 1911 s 9 (1) (amended by the Official Secrets Act 1989 s 11 (3)) and para 260 post; and as to acts done abroad see para 245 note 6 ante.

9 Ie such as is mentioned in ibid s 3 (1): see text heads (1), (2) supra.
10 Ibid s 3 (4). 'Damaging' means damaging within the meaning of s 3 (1) (see supra): s 3 (4).
11 Ibid s 10 (1). For the meaning of 'the statutory maximum' see para 806 post.

248. Disclosure of information etc related to crime and special investigation powers. A person who is or has been a Crown servant[1] or government contractor[2] is guilty of an offence if without lawful authority[3] he discloses any specified information, document or other article[4] which is or has been in his possession by virtue of his position as such[5]. The specified information, document or other article is any information, document or other article:

(1) the disclosure of which (a) results in the commission of an offence; or (b) facilitates an escape from legal custody[6] or the doing of any other act prejudicial to the safekeeping of persons in legal custody; or (c) impedes the prevention or detection of offences or the apprehension or prosecution of suspected offenders; or

(2) which is such that its unauthorised disclosure would be likely to have any of those effects[7].

It is a defence for a person charged with an offence (i) in respect of a disclosure falling within head (1) above to prove that at the time of the alleged offence he did not know, and had no reasonable cause to believe, that the disclosure would have any of the effects there mentioned[8]; (ii) in respect of any other disclosure, to prove that at the time of the alleged offence he did not know, and had no reasonable cause to believe, that the information, document or article in question was information or a document or article to which the above provisions apply[9].

A person guilty of such an offence is liable on conviction on indictment to imprisonment for a term not exceeding two years or a fine, or to both, or on summary conviction to imprisonment for a term not exceeding six months or a fine not exceeding the statutory maximum, or to both[10].

1 For the meaning of 'Crown servant' see para 245 note 7 ante.
2 For the meaning of 'government contractor' see para 245 note 8 ante.
3 For the meaning of 'lawful authority' see para 251 post.
4 For the meaning of 'disclosure' in relation to a document or other article see para 245 note 4 ante.
5 Official Secrets Act 1989 s 4 (1). As to extent of the 1989 Act and place of trial see para 263 post; as to restrictions on prosecutions see para 264 post; as to the exclusion of the public during a hearing see para 265 post; as to powers of arrest see the Police and Criminal Evidence Act 1984 s 24 (amended by the Official Secrets Act 1989 s 11 (1)) and para 693 et seq post; as to the power to grant a search warrant see the Official Secrets Act 1911 s 9 (1) (amended by the Official Secrets Act 1989 s 11 (3)) and para 260 post; and as to acts done abroad see para 245 note 6 ante.
6 For these purposes, 'legal custody' includes detention in pursuance of any enactment or any instrument made under any enactment: ibid s 4 (6).
7 Ibid s 4 (2). Section 4 also applies to: (1) any information obtained by reason of the interception of any communication in obedience to a warrant issued under the Interception of Communications Act 1985 s 2 (see para 271 post), any information relating to the obtaining of information by reason of any such interception and any document or other article which is or has been used or held for use in, or has been obtained by reason of, any such interception; or (2) any information obtained by reason of action authorised by a warrant issued under the Security Service Act 1989 s 3 (see CONSTITUTIONAL LAW), any information relating to the obtaining of information by reason of any such action and any document or other article which is or has been used or held for use in, or has been obtained by reason of, any such action: Official Secrets Act 1989 s 4 (3).
8 Ibid s 4 (4).

9 Ibid s 4 (5).
10 Ibid s 10 (1). For the meaning of 'the statutory maximum' see para 806 post.

249. Disclosure of information etc resulting from unauthorised disclosures or entrusted in confidence. Where:
  (1) any information, document or other article protected against disclosure[1] has come into a person's possession as a result of having been (a) disclosed[2], whether to him or another, by a Crown servant[3] or government contractor[4] without lawful authority[5]; or (b) entrusted to him by a Crown servant or government contractor on terms requiring it to be held in confidence or in circumstances in which the Crown servant or government contractor could reasonably expect that it would be so held; or (c) disclosed, whether to him or another, without lawful authority by a person to whom it was so entrusted[6]; and
  (2) the disclosure without lawful authority of the information, document or article by the person into whose possession it has come is not a specified offence[7],
the person into whose possession the information, document or article has come is guilty of an offence if he discloses it without lawful authority knowing, or having reasonable cause to believe, that it is so protected against disclosure and that it has come into his possession as mentioned above[8].

A person does not commit such an offence (i) in the case of information or a document or article protected against disclosure[9] unless the disclosure is damaging[10] and he makes it knowing, or having reasonable cause to believe, that it would be so damaging[11]; (ii) in respect of information or a document or other article which has come into his possession as a result of having been disclosed[12], unless that disclosure was by a British citizen[13] or took place in the United Kingdom, in any of the Channel Islands or in the Isle of Man or a colony[14].

A person is also guilty of an offence if without lawful authority he discloses any information, document or other article which he knows, or has reasonable cause to believe, to have come into his possession as a result of a contravention of the statutory prohibition[15] on spying and sabotage[16].

A person guilty of any such offence is liable on conviction on indictment to imprisonment for a term not exceeding two years or a fine, or to both, or on summary conviction to imprisonment for a term not exceeding six months or a fine not exceeding the statutory maximum, or to both[17].

1 For these purposes, information or a document or article is protected against disclosure if (1) it relates to security or intelligence, defence or international relations within the meaning of the Official Secrets Act 1989 ss 1–3 (see paras 245–247 ante) or is confidential information within s 3 (1) (b) (see para 247 head (2) ante); or (2) it is information or a document or article to which s 4 (see para 248 ante) applies; and information or a document or article is protected against disclosure by ss 1–3 if it falls within head (1) supra): s 5 (5). Section 5 (5) applies also for the purposes of s 8 (6): see s 8 (8) and para 252 note 17 post.
2 For the meaning of 'disclose' and 'disclosure' in relation to a document or other article see para 245 note 4 ante.
3 For the meaning of 'Crown servant' see para 245 note 7 ante.
4 For the meaning of 'government contractor' see para 245 note 8 ante.
5 For the meaning of 'lawful authority' see para 251 post.
6 Ie as mentioned in the Official Secrets Act 1989 s 5 (1) (a) (ii): see text head (1) (b) supra.
7 Ie an offence under ibid ss 1–4 (see paras 245–248 ante).
8 Ibid s 5 (1), (2). As to extent of the 1989 Act and place of trial see para 263 post; as to restrictions on prosecutions see para 264 post; as to the exclusion of the public during a hearing see para 265 post; as

to powers of arrest see the Police and Criminal Evidence Act 1984 s 24 (amended by the Official Secrets Act 1989 s 11 (1)) and para 693 et seq post; as to the power to grant a search warrant see the Official Secrets Act 1911 s 9 (1) (amended by the Official Secrets Act 1989 s 11 (3)) and para 260 post; and as to acts done abroad see para 245 note 6 ante.

9 Ie by ibid ss 1–3: see paras 245–247 ante.

10 For these purposes, the question of whether a disclosure is damaging is to be determined as it would be in relation to a disclosure of that information, document or article by a Crown servant in contravention of ibid s 1 (3) (see para 245 note 9 ante), s 2 (1) (see para 246 note 4 ante) or s 3 (1) (see para 247 note 4 ante): s 5 (3).

11 Ibid s 5 (3).

12 Ie as mentioned in ibid s 5 (1) (a) (i) (see head (1) (a) supra) by a government contractor, or as mentioned in s 5 (1) (a) (iii) (see head (1) (c) supra).

13 For the meaning of 'British citizen' see the British Nationality Act 1981 Pt I (ss 1–14), s 36, Sch 2 paras 2–6; the British Nationality (Falkland Islands) Act 1983; and BRITISH NATIONALITY AND ALIENAGE.

14 Official Secrets Act 1989 s 5 (4). For the meaning of 'United Kingdom' see para 86 note 1 ante.

15 Ie the Official Secrets Act 1911 s 1: see para 243 ante.

16 Official Secrets Act 1989 s 5 (6). See also note 8 supra.

17 Ibid s 10 (1). For the meaning of 'the statutory maximum' see para 806 post.

250. Damaging disclosure of information entrusted in confidence to other States or international organisations. Where:

(1) any information, document or other article which (a) relates to security or intelligence[1], defence[2] or international relations[3]; and (b) has been communicated in confidence[4] by or on behalf of the United Kingdom to another State[5] or to an international organisation[6], has come into a person's possession as a result of having been disclosed, whether to him or another, without the authority of that State or organisation or, in the case of an organisation, of a member of it; and

(2) the disclosure without lawful authority of the information, document or article by the person into whose possession it has come is not an offence[7],

the person into whose possession the information, document or other article has come is guilty of an offence if he makes a damaging disclosure of it[8] knowing, or having reasonable cause to believe, that it is such information, document or article as is mentioned in heads (1) and (2) above, that it has come into his possession as there mentioned and that its disclosure would be damaging[9].

A person does not commit such an offence if the information, document or article is disclosed by him with lawful authority[10] or has previously been made available to the public with the authority of the State or organisation concerned or, in the case of an organisation, of a member of it[11].

A person guilty of such an offence is liable on conviction on indictment to imprisonment for a term not exceeding two years or a fine, or to both, or on summary conviction to imprisonment for a term not exceeding six months or a fine not exceeding the statutory maximum, or to both[12].

1 For these purposes, 'security or intelligence' has the same meaning as in the Official Secrets Act 1989 s 1 (8): s 6 (4). See para 245 note 5 ante.

2 For these purposes, 'defence' has the same meaning as in ibid s 2 (4): s 6 (4). See para 246 note 6 ante.

3 For these purposes, 'international relations' has the same meaning as in ibid s 3 (5): s 6 (4). See para 247 note 6 ante.

4 For these purposes, information or a document or article is communicated in confidence if it is communicated on terms requiring it to be held in confidence or in circumstances in which the person communicating it could reasonably expect that it would be so held: ibid s 6 (5).

5 For the meaning of 'State' and 'State other than the United Kingdom' see para 245 note 8 ante.

6 For the meaning of 'international organisation' see para 245 note 8 ante.
7 Ie an offence under the Official Secrets Act 1989 ss 1–5: see paras 245–249 ante.
8 For the meaning of 'disclose' and 'disclosure' in relation to a document or other article see para 245 note 4 ante.
9 Official Secrets Act 1989 s 6 (1), (2). For these purposes, the question whether a disclosure is damaging is to be determined as it would be in relation to a disclosure of the information, document or article in question by a Crown servant in contravention of s 1 (3) (see para 245 ante), s 2 (1) (see para 246 ante) or s 3 (1) (see para 247 ante): s 6 (4). As to extent of the 1989 Act and place of trial see para 263 post; as to restrictions on prosecutions see para 264 post; as to the exclusion of the public during a hearing see para 265 post; as to powers of arrest see the Police and Criminal Evidence Act 1984 s 24 (amended by the Official Secrets Act 1989 s 11 (1)) and para 693 et seq post; as to the power to grant a search warrant see the Official Secrets Act 1911 s 9 (1) (amended by the Official Secrets Act 1989 s 11 (3)) and para 260 post; and as to acts done abroad see para 245 note 6 ante. For the meaning of 'United Kingdom' see para 86 note 1 ante.
10 For the meaning of 'lawful authority' see para 251 post.
11 Official Secrets Act 1989 s 6 (3).
12 Ibid s 10 (1). For the meaning of 'the statutory maximum' see para 806 post.

251. Authorised disclosures. A disclosure is made with lawful authority:

(1) by a Crown servant[1] if, and only if, it is made in accordance with his official duty[2];

(2) by a person, not being a Crown servant or government contractor[3], in whose case a notification[4] is in force if, and only if, it is made in accordance with his official duty[5];

(3) by a government contractor if, and only if, it is made in accordance with an official authorisation[6], or for the purposes of the functions by virtue of which he is a government contractor and without contravening an official restriction[7];

(4) by any other person if, and only if, it is made to a Crown servant for the purposes of his functions as such, or in accordance with an official authorisation[8].

It is a defence for a person charged with a relevant offence[9] to prove that at the time of the alleged offence he believed that he had lawful authority to make the disclosure in question and had no reasonable cause to believe otherwise[10].

1 For the meaning of 'Crown servant' see para 245 note 7 ante.
2 Official Secrets Act 1989 s 7 (1) (a).
3 For the meaning of 'government contractor' see para 245 note 8 ante.
4 Ie a notification for the purposes of the Official Secrets Act 1989 s 1 (1): see para 245 ante.
5 Ibid s 7 (1) (b).
6 For these purposes, 'official authorisation' means an authorisation duly given by a Crown servant or government contractor or by or on behalf of a prescribed body or a body of a prescribed class: ibid s 7 (5). For the meaning of 'prescribed' see para 245 note 7 ante. If the disclosure is one falling within s 6 (see para 250 ante), 'official authorisation' includes an authorisation given by or on behalf of the State or organisation concerned or, in the case of an organisation, a member of it: s 7 (6). For the meaning of 'State' see para 245 note 8 ante.
7 Ibid s 7 (2). For these purposes, 'official restriction' means a restriction duly imposed by a Crown servant or government contractor or by or on behalf of a prescribed body or a body of a prescribed class: s 7 (5).
8 Ibid s 7 (3).
9 Ie an offence under ibid ss 1–6: see paras 245–250 ante.
10 Ibid s 7 (4). Under the Official Secrets Act 1911 s 2 (1) (a) (repealed) the onus was on the prosecution to prove that the communicator of the information was not authorised to communicate it: *R v Galvin* (1988) 86 Cr App Rep 85, CA.

252. Safeguarding of information. Where a Crown servant[1] or government contractor[2], by virtue of his position as such, has in his possession or under his control[3] any document or other article which it would be an offence[4] for him to disclose[5] without lawful authority[6], he is guilty of an offence if (1) being a Crown servant, he retains the document or article contrary to his official duty; or (2) being a government contractor, he fails to comply with an official direction[7] for the return or disposal of the document or article, or if he fails to take such care to prevent the unauthorised disclosure of the document or article as a person in his position may reasonably be expected to take[8]. It is a defence, however, for a Crown servant charged with an offence under head (1) above to prove that at the time of the alleged offence he believed that he was acting in accordance with his official duty and had no reasonable cause to believe otherwise[9].

Where a person has in his possession or under his control any document which it would be an offence for him to disclose without lawful authority (a) in the case of information resulting from unauthorised disclosures entrusted in confidence[10], he is guilty of an offence if he fails to comply with an official direction for its return or disposal or, where he obtained it from a Crown servant or government contractor on terms requiring it to be held in confidence or in circumstances in which that servant or contractor could reasonably expect that it would be so held, he fails to take such care to prevent its unauthorised disclosure as a person in his position may reasonably be expected to take[11]; (b) in the case of information entrusted in confidence to other States or international organisations[12], he is guilty of an offence if he fails to comply with an official direction for its return or disposal[13].

A person guilty of any of the above offences is liable on summary conviction to imprisonment for a term not exceeding three months or a fine not exceeding level 5 on the standard scale, or to both[14].

A person is also guilty of an offence if he discloses any official information, document or other article[15] which can be used for the purpose of obtaining access to any information, document or other article protected against disclosure[16], and the circumstances in which it is disclosed are such that it would be reasonable to expect that it might be used for that purpose without authority[17]. A person guilty of such an offence is liable on conviction on indictment to imprisonment for a term not exceeding two years or a fine, or to both, or on summary conviction to imprisonment for a term not exceeding six months or a fine not exceeding the statutory maximum, or to both[18].

1 For the meaning of 'Crown servant' see para 245 note 7 ante. In the Official Secrets Act 1989 s 8 (1), (2) references to a Crown servant include any person, not being a Crown servant or government contractor, in whose case a notification for the purposes of s 1 (1) (see para 245 ante) is in force: s 8 (3).
2 For the meaning of 'government contractor' see para 245 note 8 ante.
3 As to the meaning of 'possession' and 'control' in relation to statutory offences see *Warner v Metropolitan Police Comr* [1969] 2 AC 256, 52 Cr App Rep 373, HL.
4 Ie under the Official Secrets Act 1989 ss 1–6: see paras 245–250 ante.
5 For the meaning of 'disclose' and 'disclosure' in relation to a document or other article see para 245 note 4 ante.
6 For the meaning of 'lawful authority' see para 251 ante.
7 For these purposes, 'official direction' means a direction duly given by a Crown servant or government contractor or by or on behalf of a prescribed body or a body of a prescribed class: Official Secrets Act 1989 s 8 (9). For the meaning of 'prescribed' see para 245 note 7 ante.
8 Ibid s 8 (1). As to extent of the 1989 Act and place of trial see para 263 post; as to restrictions on prosecutions see para 264 post; as to the exclusion of the public during a hearing see para 265 post; as to powers of arrest see the Police and Criminal Evidence Act 1984 s 24 (amended by the Official Secrets Act 1989 s 11 (1)) and para 693 et seq post; as to the power to grant a search warrant see the

Official Secrets Act 1911 s 9 (1) (amended by the Official Secrets Act 1989 s 11 (3)) and para 260 post; and as to acts done abroad see para 245 note 6 ante.
9 Ibid s 8 (2).
10 Ie under ibid s 5: see para 249 ante.
11 Ibid s 8 (4).
12 Ie under ibid s 6: see para 250 ante.
13 Ibid s 8 (5).
14 Ibid s 10 (2). For the meaning of 'the standard scale' see para 808 post.
15 For these purposes, a person discloses information or a document or article which is official if (1) he has or has had it in his possession by virtue of his position as a Crown servant or government contractor; or (2) he knows or has reasonable cause to believe that a Crown servant or government contractor has or has had it in his possession by virtue of his position as such: ibid s 8 (7).
16 Ie under ibid ss 1–7: see paras 245–251 ante.
17 Ibid s 8 (6). Section 5 (5) (see para 249 note 1 ante) applies for the purposes of s 8 (6) as it applies for the purposes of s 5: s 8 (8).
18 Ibid s 10 (1). For the meaning of 'the statutory maximum' see para 806 post.

253. Impersonation etc for gaining admission to prohibited places or other purpose prejudicial to the State. If any person for the purpose of gaining admission, or assisting any other person to gain admission, to a prohibited place[1] or for any other purpose prejudicial to the safety or interests of the State[2]:

(1) uses or wears, without lawful authority, any naval, military, air force, police, or other official uniform, or any uniform so nearly resembling it as to be calculated to deceive, or falsely represents himself to be a person who is or has been entitled to use or wear any such uniform; or

(2) orally, or in writing in any declaration or application, or in any document signed by him or on his behalf, knowingly makes or connives at the making of any false statement or any omission; or

(3) tampers with any official document[3] or has in his possession any forged, altered, or irregular official document; or

(4) personates, or falsely represents himself to be a person holding, or in the employment of a person holding, office under Her Majesty[4], or to be or not to be a person to whom an official document or secret official code word or pass word has been duly issued or communicated, or with intent to obtain an official document, secret official code word or pass word, whether for himself or any other person, knowingly makes any false statement; or

(5) uses, or has in his possession or under his control, without the authority of the government department or the authority concerned, any die, seal, or stamp of or belonging to, or used, made or provided by any government department, or by any diplomatic, naval, military, or air force authority appointed by or acting under the authority of Her Majesty, or any die, seal or stamp so nearly resembling any such die, seal or stamp as to be calculated to deceive, or counterfeits any such die, seal or stamp, or uses, or has in his possession, or under his control, any such counterfeited die, seal or stamp,

he is guilty of an offence and liable on conviction on indictment to imprisonment for a term not exceeding two years, or on summary conviction to imprisonment for a term not exceeding three months or a fine not exceeding the prescribed sum, or to both[5].

1 For the meaning of 'prohibited place' see para 244 ante.
2 In the case of any prosecution under the Official Secrets Act 1920 s 1 involving the proof of a purpose prejudicial to the safety or interests of the State, the Official Secrets Act 1911 s 1 (2) (amended by the

Official Secrets Act 1920 ss 10, 11 (2), Schs 1, 2) applies in like manner as it applies to prosecutions under the Official Secrets Act 1911 s 1 (as so amended): Official Secrets Act 1920 s 1 (3). As to proof of a purpose prejudicial to the safety or interests of the State see para 267 post. See also para 243 note 2 ante.

3 'Official document' means any passport or any naval, military, air force, police, or official pass, permit, certificate, licence, or other document of a similar character: ibid s 1 (1) (c).

4 'Office under Her Majesty' includes any office or employment in or under any department of the government of the United Kingdom or of any British possession: Official Secrets Act 1911 s 12. A police officer holds office under the Sovereign: *Lewis v Cattle* [1938] 2 KB 454, [1938] 2 All ER 368, DC.

5 Official Secrets Act 1920 ss 1 (1), 8 (2) (respectively amended by the Forgery and Counterfeiting Act 1981 s 30, Schedule Pt I; the Magistrates' Courts Act 1980 s 32 (2)); Criminal Justice Act 1948 s 1 (2); Criminal Law Act 1967 s 1. For the meaning of 'the prescribed sum' see para 807 post. As to restrictions on prosecutions see para 264 post.

254. Retention etc of official documents, code words, seals etc. If any person:

(1) retains[1] for any purpose prejudicial to the safety or interests of the State[2] any official document[3], whether or not completed or issued for use, when he has no right to retain it, or when it is contrary to his duty to retain it, or fails to comply with any directions issued by any government department or any person authorised by such department with regard to its return or disposal[4]; or

(2) allows any other person to have possession of any official document issued for his use alone, or communicates[5] any secret official code word or pass word so issued, or, without lawful authority or excuse, has in his possession any official document or secret official code word or pass word issued for the use of some person other than himself, or on obtaining possession of any official document by finding or otherwise, neglects or fails to restore it to the person or authority by whom or for whose use it was issued, or to a police constable[6]; or

(3) without lawful authority or excuse, manufactures or sells or has in his possession for sale any die, seal or stamp[7],

he is guilty of an offence and liable on conviction on indictment to imprisonment for a term not exceeding two years, or on summary conviction to imprisonment for a term not exceeding three months or a fine not exceeding the prescribed sum, or to both[8].

1 For the meaning of 'retain' see para 243 note 7 ante.
2 See para 253 note 2 ante. As to proof of a purpose prejudicial to the safety or interests of the State see para 267 post.
3 For the meaning of 'official document' see para 253 note 3 ante.
4 Official Secrets Act 1920 s 1 (2) (a). As to wrongful retention of documents see also para 252 ante.
5 For the meaning of 'communicate' see para 243 note 8 ante.
6 Official Secrets Act 1920 s 1 (2) (b). As to wrongful disclosure of information etc see paras 245–250 ante; and as to the safeguarding of information see para 252 ante.
7 Ibid s 1 (2) (c). 'Any die, seal or stamp' means any die, seal or stamp referred to in s 1 (1) (e) (see para 253 head (5) ante): s 1 (2) (c).
8 Ibid s 8 (2); Criminal Justice Act 1948 s 1 (2); Criminal Law Act 1967 s 1. For the meaning of 'the prescribed sum' see para 807 post. As to restrictions on prosecutions see para 264 post.

255. Communication of information acquired through Euratom. Where a person, whether a British subject or not, owing either (1) to his duties as a member of any Euratom[1] institution or committee, or as an officer or servant of Euratom; or (2) to his dealings in any capacity official or unofficial with any Euratom institution or installation or with any Euratom joint enterprise, has occasion to acquire, or obtain cognisance of, any classified information[2], he is guilty of an offence if, knowing or having reason to believe that it is classified information, he communicates it to any unauthorised person or makes any public disclosure of it, whether in the United Kingdom or elsewhere, and whether before or after the termination of those duties or dealings, and is liable on conviction on indictment to imprisonment for a term not exceeding two years, or on summary conviction to imprisonment for a term not exceeding three months or a fine not exceeding the prescribed sum, or to both[3].

1 'Euratom' means the European Atomic Energy Community: European Communities Act 1972 s 1 (2), Sch 1 Pt II.
2 For these purposes, 'classified information' means any facts, information, knowledge, documents or objects that are subject to the security rules of a member State or of any Euratom institution: ibid s 11 (2). 'Member' in the expression 'member State' refers to membership of the European Communities: Sch 1 Pt II.
3 Official Secrets Act 1920 s 8 (2) (amended by the Magistrates' Courts Act 1980 s 32 (2)); Criminal Law Act 1967 s 1; European Communities Act 1972 s 11 (2). For the meaning of 'the prescribed sum' see para 807 post; and for the meaning of 'United Kingdom' see para 86 note 1 ante. Section 11 (2) is to be construed, and the Official Secrets Act 1911 to 1939 have effect, as if the European Communities Act 1972 s 11(2) were contained in the Official Secrets Act 1911, but so that ss 10 (1) – (3), 11 (see para 262 post) do not apply: European Communities Act 1972 s 11 (2). As to restrictions on prosecutions see para 264 post; and as to communication of information concerning atomic energy plants see para 269 post.

256. Obstructing police or Her Majesty's forces in or near prohibited places.
If any person in the vicinity[1] of any prohibited place[2] obstructs, knowingly misleads, or otherwise interferes with, or impedes the chief officer or a superintendent[3] or other officer of police, or a member of Her Majesty's forces engaged on guard, sentry, patrol or other similar duty in relation to the prohibited place, he is guilty of an offence and liable on conviction on indictment to imprisonment for a term not exceeding two years, or on summary conviction to imprisonment for a term not exceeding three months or a fine not exceeding the prescribed sum, or to both[4].

1 'In the vicinity of' means 'in or in the vicinity of': *Adler v George* [1964] 2 QB 7, [1964] 1 All ER 628, DC.
2 For the meaning of 'prohibited place' see para 244 ante.
3 'Superintendent of police' includes any police officer of like or superior rank and any person on whom the powers of a superintendent of police are for this purpose conferred by a Secretary of State: Official Secrets Act 1911 s 12 (amended by the Official Secrets Act 1920 s 10, Sch 1).
4 Official Secrets Act 1920 ss 3, 8 (2) (amended by the Magistrates' Courts Act 1980 s 32 (2)); Criminal Justice Act 1948 s 1 (2); Criminal Law Act 1967 s 1. For the meaning of 'the prescribed sum' see para 807 post. As to obstructing a police officer in the execution of his duty see para 320 post; and as to restrictions on prosecutions see para 264 post.

257. Attempts; incitement; preparatory acts.
Any person who attempts[1] to commit any offence under the Official Secrets Acts, or solicits or incites or endeavours to persuade another person to commit an offence, or aids or abets and[2] does any act preparatory to the commission of an offence under those Acts[3] is guilty of an offence and liable on conviction to the same penalty and to be

proceeded against in the same manner as if he had committed the corresponding substantive offence⁴.

1 As to attempts see para 71 et seq ante.
2 In order to produce an intelligible result, the words 'abets and does any act . . .' must be read as if 'or' were substituted for 'and': *R v Oakes* [1959] 2 QB 350, 43 Cr App Rep 114, CCA. See also *R v Bingham* [1973] QB 870, 57 Cr App Rep 439, CA.
3 This ('doing an act preparatory to the commission of an offence . . .') is a very special kind of offence based on a section which . . . contemplates something which is even more remote from the substantive offence than an attempt to commit it: *R v Bingham* [1973] QB 870 at 875, 57 Cr App Rep 439 at 443, 444, CA (approach to foreign embassy by wife with a view to her husband supplying information). In a prosecution for this offence it is sufficient for the prosecution to prove that at the time of doing the act the accused must have realised that the substantive offence might follow; it is not necessary for the prosecution to show that the accused realised that it was a probable consequence of this act: *R v Bingham* supra.
4 Official Secrets Act 1920 s 7; Criminal Law Act 1967 ss 1, 12 (5) (a). As to restrictions on prosecutions see para 264 post.

258. Harbouring offenders. If any person (1) knowingly harbours any person whom he knows, or has reasonable grounds for supposing, to be a person who is about to commit or who has committed an offence under the Official Secrets Acts; or (2) knowingly permits any such persons to meet or assemble in premises in his occupation or under his control; or (3) having harboured any such person or permitted any such persons to meet or assemble in premises in his occupation or under his control, wilfully omits or refuses to disclose to a superintendent of police¹ any information which it is in his power to give in relation to any such person, he is guilty of an offence and liable on conviction on indictment to imprisonment for a term not exceeding two years, or on summary conviction to imprisonment for a term not exceeding three months or a fine not exceeding the prescribed sum, or to both².

1 For the meaning of 'superintendent of police' see para 256 note 3 ante.
2 Official Secrets Act 1911 s 7 (amended by the Official Secrets Act 1920 ss 10, 11 (2), Schs 1, 2); Official Secrets Act 1920 s 8 (2) (amended by the Magistrates' Courts Act 1980 s 32 (2)); Criminal Justice Act 1948 s 1 (2); Criminal Law Act 1967 s 1. As to restrictions on prosecutions see para 264 post.

(ii) Accommodation Addresses

259. Accommodation addresses; registration and regulation. Every person who carries on, whether alone or in conjunction with any other business, the business of receiving for reward letters, telegrams, or other postal packets for delivery or forwarding to the persons for whom they are intended¹:
(1) must send as soon as may be to the chief officer of police² for the district, for registration by him³, notice of the fact together with the address or addresses where the business is carried on⁴;
(2) must from time to time furnish to the chief officer of police notice of any change of address or new address at which the business is carried on, and such other information as may be necessary for maintaining the correctness of the particulars entered in the register⁴;

(3) must cause to be entered in a book kept for the purpose the following
particulars:
  (a) the name and address of every person for whom any postal packet is
      received, or who has requested that postal packets received may be
      delivered or forwarded to him;
  (b) any instructions that may have been received as to the delivery or
      forwarding of postal packets;
  (c) in the case of every postal packet received, the place from which the
      postal packet comes, and the date of posting, as shown by the post-mark,
      and the date of receipt, and the name and address of the sender if shown
      on the outside of the packet, and, in the case of a registered packet, the
      date and office of registration and the number of the registered packet;
  (d) in the case of every postal packet delivered, the date of delivery and the
      name and address of the person to whom it is delivered;
  (e) in the case of every postal packet forwarded, the name and address to
      which, and the date on which, it is forwarded[5];
(4) may not deliver a letter to any person until that person has signed a receipt for
    it in such book, nor, if that person is not the person to whom the postal
    packet is addressed, unless there are left with him instructions signed by the
    last-mentioned person as to its delivery and may not forward any postal
    packet to another address unless there are left with him written instructions
    to that effect signed by the addressee[5].

The books so kept and all postal packets received by a person carrying on any
such business, and any instruction as to the delivery or forwarding of postal packets
received by any such person must be kept at all reasonable times open to inspection
by any police constable[6].

If any person contravenes or fails to comply with any of the above provisions or
furnishes any false information[7] or makes any false entry, he is guilty of an offence
and liable, for each offence, on summary conviction to imprisonment for a term
not exceeding one month or a fine not exceeding level 1 on the standard scale, or to
both[8].

1 The Official Secrets Act 1920 s 5 does not apply to the Post Office (Post Office Act 1969 s 76, Sch 4
   Pt II para 21 (2)), to postal packets addressed to any office where any newspaper or periodical is
   published, being postal packets in reply to advertisements appearing in such newspaper or periodical
   (Official Secrets Act 1920 s 5 (5)), or to any public telecommunications operator (Telecommunications Act 1984 s 109, Sch 4 para 14(1)); nor does it render legal anything which would be in
   contravention of the exclusive privilege conferred on the Post Office by the British Telecommunications Act 1981 s 66 (1) (see POST OFFICE) or an offence under the Telecommunications Act 1984 s 5:
   Official Secrets Act 1920 s 5 (6) (amended by the Telecommunications Act 1984 Sch 4 para 14(2)).
2 For the meaning of 'chief officer of police' see para 261 note 1 post.
3 The chief officer of police must keep a register of the names and addresses of such persons, and must,
   if required by any person who sends such a notice, furnish him on payment of a fee of 38 pence with a
   certificate of registration: Official Secrets Act 1920 s 5 (1) (amended by the Miscellaneous Fees
   (Variation) Order 1970, SI 1970/1954).
4 Official Secrets Act 1920 s 5 (1).
5 Ibid s 5 (2).
6 Ibid s 5 (3).
7 The user, as well as the keeper, of an accommodation address may be guilty of the offence of giving
   false information: *Stevenson v Fulton* [1936] 1 KB 320, DC.
8 Official Secrets Act 1920 s 5 (4) (amended by the Criminal Justice Act 1982 ss 38, 46); Criminal
   Justice Act 1948 s 1 (2). For the meaning of 'the standard scale' see para 808 post.

(iii) Police Powers

260. Powers of arrest and search. Any person who is found committing an offence under the Official Secrets Act 1911[1] or who is reasonably suspected of having committed, or attempted to commit, or being about to commit, such an offence, may be apprehended and detained[2]. Offences under the Official Secrets Act 1920 and, with certain exceptions[3], the Official Secrets Act 1989 are arrestable offences[4].

If a justice of the peace is satisfied by information on oath that there is reasonable ground for suspecting that an offence under the Acts has been or is about to be committed, he may grant a search warrant authorising any constable to enter at any time any premises or place named in the warrant, if necessary by force, and to search the premises or place and every person found there and to seize any sketch[5], plan, model[6], article, note, or document[7] or anything of a like nature or anything which is evidence of an offence under the Acts having been or being about to be committed, which he may find on the premises or place or on any such person, and with regard to or in connection with which he has reasonable ground for suspecting that an offence under the Acts has been or is about to be committed[8].

Where it appears to a superintendent of police[9] that the case is one of great emergency and that in the interests of the State immediate action is necessary, he may by a written order under his hand give to any constable the like authority as may be given by the warrant of a justice[10].

1 An offence under the Official Secrets Act 1911 includes any act, omission or other thing which is punishable under that Act: s 12.
2 Ibid s 6 (amended by the Criminal Law Act 1967 s 10 (2), Sch 3 Pt III). As to powers of arrest see para 693 et seq post.
3 Ie except for the Official Secrets Act 1989 s 8 (1), (4), (5): see para 252 ante.
4 Police and Criminal Evidence Act 1984 s 24 (2) (b), (bb) (as respectively amended and added): see para 703 heads (3) (b), (3) (c) post.
5 For the meaning of 'sketch' see para 243 note 4 ante.
6 For the meaning of 'model' see para 243 note 5 ante.
7 For the meaning of 'document' see para 243 note 9 ante.
8 Official Secrets Act 1911 s 9 (1) (amended by the Police and Criminal Evidence Act 1984 ss 119 (2), 120, Sch 7 Pt I). The Official Secrets Act 1911 s 9 (1) (as so amended) has effect as if references to offences under that Act included references to offences under any provision of the Official Secrets Act 1989 other than s 8 (1), (4) or (5) (see para 252 ante); and the Police and Criminal Evidence Act 1984 s 9 (2) (exclusion of items subject to legal privilege and certain material from powers of search conferred by previous enactments: see para 673 post), and s 9 (1), Sch 1 para 3 (b) (access conditions for the special procedure laid down in that Schedule: see para 677 post) apply to the Official Secrets Act 1911 s 9 (1) as extended by the Official Secrets Act 1989 s 11 (3) as they apply to the Official Secrets Act 1911 s 9 (1) as originally enacted: Official Secrets Act 1989 s 11 (3).
9 For the meaning of 'superintendent of police' see para 256 note 3 ante.
10 Official Secrets Act 1911 s 9 (2). Section 9 (as amended: see note 5 supra) must be read subject to the Police and Criminal Evidence Act 1984 Pt II (ss 8–23): see para 670 et seq post.

261. Power of police to obtain information relating to spying or sabotage. Where a chief officer of police[1] is satisfied that there is reasonable ground for suspecting that an offence[2] has been committed and for believing that any person is able to furnish information as to the offence or suspected offence, he may apply to a Secretary of State for permission to exercise the powers conferred by these provisions; and, if such permission is granted, he may authorise a superintendent of police[3], or any police officer not below the rank of inspector, to require the person believed to be able to furnish information to give any information in his power relating to the offence or suspected offence, and, if so required and on tender of his reasonable expenses, to attend at such reasonable time and place as may be specified by the superintendent or other officer[4]. Where a chief officer of police has reasonable grounds to believe that the case is one of great emergency and that in the interest of the State immediate action is necessary, he may give such authorisation without applying for or being granted the permission of a Secretary of State; but, if he does so, he must forthwith report the circumstances to the Secretary of State[5].

A person who fails to comply with any such requirement or knowingly gives false information is guilty of an offence and liable on conviction on indictment to imprisonment for a term not exceeding two years, or on summary conviction to imprisonment for a term not exceeding three months or a fine not exceeding the prescribed sum, or to both[6].

1 'Chief officer of police' means in England the Commissioner of the City of London Police, the Commissioner of Police of the Metropolis or chief constable as the case may be (Official Secrets Act 1920 s 11 (3) (a), (b); Police Act 1964 s 62 (b), Sch 8 (amended by the Local Government Act 1972 s 272 (1), Sch 30; the Local Government Act 1985 s 37, Sch 11 para 1(8)); and in the Official Secrets Act 1920 s 6 (1), (2) (substituted by the Official Secrets Act 1939 s 1) references to a chief officer of police are to be construed as including references to any other officer of police expressly authorised by a chief officer of police to act on his behalf for these purposes when by reason of illness, absence, or other cause he is unable to do so (Official Secrets Act 1920 s 6 (3) (substituted by the Official Secrets Act 1939 s 1)).
2 Ie under the Official Secrets Act 1911 s 1: see para 243 ante.
3 For the meaning of 'superintendent of police' see para 256 note 3 ante.
4 Official Secrets Act 1920 s 6 (1) (as substituted: see note 1 supra).
5 Ibid s 6 (2) (as substituted: see note 1 supra).
6 Ibid ss 6 (1), 8 (2) (respectively substituted (see note 1 supra) and amended by the Magistrates' Courts Act 1980 s 32 (2)); Criminal Justice Act 1948 s 1 (2); Criminal Law Act 1967 s 1. For the meaning of 'the prescribed sum' see para 807 post. As to restrictions on prosecutions see para 264 post.

(iv) Proceedings and Evidence

262. Official Secrets Acts 1911–1939; extent and place of trial. The Official Secrets Acts apply to all acts which are offences under them when committed in any part of Her Majesty's dominions[1] or when committed by British officers or subjects[2] elsewhere[3]. An offence under the Acts, if alleged to have been committed out of the United Kingdom, may be tried by any competent British court in the place where the offence was committed[4] or in England[5]. For the purposes of the trial of a person for an offence under the Acts, the offence is deemed to have been committed either at the place where it was actually committed or at any place in the United Kingdom where the accused may be found[6].

If by any law made[7] by the legislature of any British possession[8] provisions are made which appear to Her Majesty to be of the like effect to those contained in the Official Secrets Acts, Her Majesty may, by Order in Council, suspend the operation of those Acts or any part of them within that British possession so long as that law continues in force there[9]; but such suspension may not extend to the holder of an office under Her Majesty[10] who is not appointed to the office by the government of that possession[11]. It has been expressly enacted that the Official Secrets Act 1920 is not to apply to Canada, Australia (including Papua and Norfolk Island), and New Zealand[12].

1 For the meaning of 'Her Majesty's dominions' see COMMONWEALTH vol 6 para 803.
2 For the meaning of 'British subject' see para 77 note 2 ante.
3 Official Secrets Act 1911 s 10 (1).
4 Such an offence may not, however, be tried by any court out of the United Kingdom which has not jurisdiction to try offences which involve the greatest penalty allowed by law: see ibid s 10 (3) (amended by the Criminal Law Act 1967 s 10 (2), Sch 3 Pt I). For the meaning of 'United Kingdom' see para 86 note 1 ante.
5 Official Secrets Act 1911 s 10 (2) (amended by the Criminal Justice Act 1948 s 83 (3), Sch 10 Pt I; the Criminal Law Act 1967 s 10 (2), Sch 3 Pt II).
6 Official Secrets Act 1920 s 8 (3).
7 Ie whether before or after the passing of the Official Secrets Act 1911.
8 For the meaning of 'British possession' see COMMONWEALTH vol 6 para 804.
9 Official Secrets Act 1911 s 11. See also the Official Secrets (Commonwealth of Australia) Order in Council 1915, SR & O 1915/1199; the Official Secrets (Jersey) Order in Council 1952, SI 1952/1034.
10 For the meaning of 'office under Her Majesty' see para 253 note 4 ante.
11 Official Secrets Act 1911 s 11 proviso.
12 Official Secrets Act 1920 s 11 (1) proviso (a) (amended by the Burma Independence Act 1947 s 5 (3), Sch 2 Pt I; the Newfoundland (Consequential Provisions) Act 1950 s 1 (2), Schedule Pt II; the South Africa Act 1962 s 2 (3), Sch 5).

263. Official Secrets Act 1989; extent and place of trial. Except as otherwise provided[1], any act done by a British citizen[2] or Crown servant[3], or done by any person in any of the Channel Islands or Isle of Man or any colony, is, if it would be a relevant offence[4] by that person when done by him in the United Kingdom, such an offence[5]. Proceedings for an offence under the Official Secrets Act 1989 may be taken in any place in the United Kingdom[6].

1 The Official Secrets Act 1989 s 15 (1) does not apply to offences under ss 8 (1), (4) or (5) (see para 252 ante): see s 15 (1). As to the normal rules of jurisdiction see para 620 et seq post.
2 For the meaning of 'British citizen' see the British Nationality Act 1981 Pt I (ss 1–14), s 36, Sch 2 paras 2–6; the British Nationality (Falkland Islands) Act 1983; and BRITISH NATIONALITY AND ALIENAGE.
3 For the meaning of 'Crown servant' see para 245 note 7 ante.
4 Ie an offence under any provision of the Official Secrets Act 1989 other than s 8 (1), (4) or (5): see note 1 supra.
5 Ibid s 15 (1). For the meaning of 'United Kingdom' see para 86 note 1 ante.
6 Ibid s 11 (5).

264. Prosecutions for offences under the Official Secrets Acts. Subject to one exception[1], no prosecution for an offence under the Official Secrets Acts 1911 to 1989[2] may be instituted except by or with the consent of the Attorney General[3].

Offences under the Official Secrets Acts 1911–1939 which are punishable on conviction on indictment or on summary conviction[4] may not be dealt with summarily except with the consent of the Attorney General[5].

1 The Official Secrets Act 1989 s 9 (1) does not apply to an offence in respect of any such information, document or article as is mentioned in s 4 (2) (see para 248 ante); but no prosecution for such an offence may be instituted except by or with the consent of the Director of Public Prosecutions: s 9 (2). As to the effect of this limitation see para 639 post.
2 Ie the Official Secrets Acts 1911 to 1939 and the Official Secrets Act 1989: see s 16 (2).
3 Official Secrets Act 1911 s 8 (amended by the Criminal Jurisdiction Act 1975 s 14 (5), Sch 6 Pt I); Official Secrets Act 1989 s 9 (1). As to the effect of this limitation see para 639 post. 'Attorney General' means the Attorney or Solicitor General: Official Secrets Act 1911 s 12.

4 See the Official Secrets Act 1920 s 8 (2) (amended by the Magistrates' Courts Act 1980 s 32 (2)); and the Criminal Law Act 1967 s 1.
5 Official Secrets Act 1920 s 8 (2) proviso; Criminal Law Act 1967 s 1.

265. Exclusion of public during hearing. In addition and without prejudice to any powers which a court may possess to order the exclusion of the public from any proceedings[1], if, in the course of proceedings before a court against any person for an offence under the Official Secrets Acts 1911 to 1989 or the proceedings on appeal, or in the course of the trial of a person for any offence under the Acts, application is made by the prosecution, on the ground that the publication of any evidence to be given or of any statement to be made in the course of the proceedings would be prejudicial to the national safety, that all or any portion of the public be excluded during any part of the hearing, the court may[2] make an order to that effect[3]. The passing of sentence must, however, in any case take place in public[3].

1 See para 995 post.
2 The Official Secrets Act 1920 s 8 (4) does not, however, apply to offences under the Official Secrets Act 1989 s 8 (1), (4) or (5) (see para 252 ante): see s 11 (4).
3 Official Secrets Act 1920 s 8 (4); Criminal Law Act 1967 ss 1, 12 (5) (a); Official Secrets Act 1989 s 11 (4). See further para 995 post; *A-G v Leveller Magazine* [1979] AC 440, 68 Cr App Rep 342, HL; and LIBEL vol 28 para 119. As to appeals against such orders see paras 1420, 1422 post.

266. Evidence of obtaining information useful to an enemy. In any proceedings against a person for spying[1] or sabotage (1) the fact that he has been in communication with, or attempted to communicate with, a foreign agent[2], whether within or outside the United Kingdom, is evidence that he has, for a purpose prejudicial to the safety or interests of the State, obtained or attempted to obtain information which is calculated to be, or might be, or is intended to be, directly or indirectly useful to an enemy[3]; (2) unless he proves the contrary, a person is deemed to have been in communication with a foreign agent if he has, either within or outside the United Kingdom, visited the address[4] of a foreign agent or consorted or associated with a foreign agent; or if, either within or outside the United Kingdom, the name or address of, or any other information regarding, a foreign agent has been found in his possession, or has been supplied by him to, or obtained by him from, any other person[5].

1 Ie for an offence under the Official Secrets Act 1911 s 1: see para 243 ante.
2 'Foreign agent' includes any person who is or has been or is reasonably suspected of being or having been employed by a foreign power either directly or indirectly for the purpose of committing an act, either within or outside the United Kingdom, prejudicial to the safety or interests of the State, or who has or is reasonably suspected of having, either within or outside the United Kingdom, committed, or attempted to commit, such an act in the interests of a foreign power: Official Secrets Act 1920 s 2 (2) (b). The jury must consider the activities of the alleged foreign agent only in so far as evidence of them shows that he was indeed a foreign agent and that the accused was in communication with him: *R v Kent* as reported in (1941) 28 Cr App Rep 23 at 31, CCA.
3 Official Secrets Act 1920 s 2 (1). For the meaning of 'United Kingdom' see para 86 note 1 ante.
4 Any address, whether within or outside the United Kingdom, reasonably suspected of being an address used for the receipt of communications intended for a foreign agent, or any address at which a foreign agent resides, or to which he resorts for the purpose of giving or receiving communications, or at which he carries on any business, is deemed to be the address of a foreign agent, and communications addressed to such an address to be communications with a foreign agent: ibid s 2 (2) (c).
5 Ibid s 2 (2) (a). Section 2 (2) is without prejudice to the generality of s 2 (1): s 2 (2).

267. Proof of purpose prejudicial to the safety or interests of the State. On a prosecution for spying or sabotage[1] or for an offence[2] involving the proof of a purpose prejudicial to the safety or interests of the State, it is not necessary to show that the accused was guilty of any particular act tending to show a purpose prejudical to the safety or interests of the State; and, notwithstanding that no such act is proved against him, he may be convicted if, from the circumstances of the case, or his conduct, or his known character as proved, it appears that the purpose was a purpose prejudicial to the safety or interests of the State; and, if any sketch[3], plan, model[4], article, note, document[5], or information relating to or used in any prohibited place[6] or anything in such a place or any secret official code word or pass word, is made, obtained[7], collected, recorded, published, or communicated[8] by any person other than a person acting under lawful authority, it is deemed to have been made, obtained, collected, recorded, published, or communicated for a purpose prejudicial to the safety or interests of the State unless the contrary is proved[9].

1 Ie a prosecution under the Official Secrets Act 1911 s 1: see para 243 ante.
2 Ie an offence under the Official Secrets Act 1920 s 1 (1) (see para 253 ante) or s 1 (2) (a) (see para 254 ante): see s 1 (3).
3 For the meaning of 'sketch' see para 243 note 4 ante.
4 For the meaning of 'model' see para 243 note 5 ante.
5 For the meaning of 'document' see para 243 note 9 ante.
6 For the meaning of 'prohibited place' see para 244 ante.
7 For the meaning of 'obtain' see para 243 note 7 ante.
8 For the meaning of 'communicate' see para 243 note 8 ante.
9 Official Secrets Act 1911 s 1 (2) (amended by the Official Secrets Act 1920 s 10, Sch 1).

268. Offences by corporations. Where the person guilty of an offence under the Official Secrets Acts 1911 and 1920 is a company or corporation, every director and officer of the company or corporation is guilty of the like offence, unless he proves that the act or omission constituting the offence took place without his knowledge or consent[1].

1 Official Secrets Act 1920 s 8 (5). As to the criminal capacity of corporations see para 35 ante.

(v) Information relating to Atomic Energy

269. Communication of information concerning atomic energy plants. Except as otherwise provided[1], any person[2] who, without the consent of the Secretary of State for Energy[3], communicates to any other person except an authorised person[4] any document, drawing, photograph, plan, model or other information whatsoever which to his knowledge describes, represents or illustrates (1) any existing or proposed plant[5] used or proposed to be used for the purpose of producing or using atomic energy[6]; (2) the purpose or method of operation of any such existing or proposed plant; or (3) any process operated or proposed to be operated in any such existing or proposed plant, is guilty of an offence and liable on conviction on indictment to imprisonment for a term not exceeding five years or a fine[7], or to both, or on summary conviction to imprisonment for a term not exceeding three months or a fine not exceeding the prescribed sum, or to both[8]. Proceedings for such an offence may not be instituted except by or with the consent of the Director of Public Prosecutions[9].

1 It is not an offence under the Atomic Energy Act 1946 s 11 (1) to communicate information with respect to any plant of a type in use for purposes other than the production or use of atomic energy unless the information discloses that plant of that type is used or proposed to be used for the production or use of atomic energy: s 11 (1) proviso. Where any information has been made available to the general public otherwise than in contravention of s 11 (1), any subsequent communication of that information does not constitute an offence: s 11 (4). The Secretary of State may by order grant exemption from s 11 (1) in such classes of cases, and to such extent and subject to such conditions, as may be specified in the order: s 11 (3). Any such order is subject to annulment by resolution of either House of Parliament within 40 days of the order being laid: see s 15 (1). See also the Atomic Energy (Disclosure of Information) (No 1) Order 1947, SR & O 1947/100.
    The Atomic Energy Act 1946 s 11 does not apply to anything done by or to the United Kingdom Atomic Energy Authority: Atomic Energy Authority Act 1954 ss 1 (1), 6 (4), Sch 3.
2 Where an offence has been committed by a body corporate, every person who at the time of the commission of the offence was a director, general manager, secretary or other similar officer of the body corporate, or was purporting to act in any such capacity, is deemed to be guilty of that offence unless he proves that the offence was committed without his consent or connivance and that he exercised all such diligence to prevent the commission of the offence as he ought to have exercised having regard to the nature of his functions in that capacity and to all the circumstances: Atomic Energy Act 1946 s 14 (3).
    As to the criminal capacity of corporations see para 35 ante.
3 The functions of the former Minister of Supply under the Atomic Energy Act 1946 are exercised by the Secretary of State for Energy: see CONSTITUTIONAL LAW vol 8 para 1221 note 7. The Secretary of State may not withhold consent if satisfied that the information proposed to be communicated is not of importance for purposes of defence: s 11 (2).
4 'Authorised person' means a person to whom, by virtue of a general authority granted by the Secretary of State, information on that subject may be communicated: ibid s 11 (1).
5 'Plant' includes any machinery, equipment or appliance whether affixed to land or not: ibid s 18 (1).
6 'Atomic energy' means the energy released from atomic nuclei as a result of any process, including the fission process, but does not include energy released in any process of natural transmutation or radioactive decay which is not accelerated or influenced by external means: ibid s 18 (1). 'Production or use of atomic energy' includes the carrying out of any process preparatory or ancillary to such production or use: s 18 (4).
7 Where a person convicted on indictment of an offence under the Atomic Energy Act 1946 is a body corporate, the provisions of s 14 (1) limiting the amount of the fine which may be imposed do not apply and the body corporate is liable to a fine of such amount as the court thinks just: s 14 (2).
8 Ibid ss 11 (1), 14 (1) (amended by the Criminal Justice Act 1948 s 1 (1), (2); the Criminal Law Act 1977 s 32 (1); the Magistrates' Courts Act 1980 s 32 (2)). For the meaning of 'the prescribed sum' see para 807 post.
9 Atomic Energy Act 1946 s 14 (4). As to the effect of this limitation see para 639 post.
    As to the communication of information acquired through Euratom see para 255 ante.

(vi) Interception of Communications

A. PROHIBITION ON INTERCEPTION

270. Prohibition on interception. A person[1] who intentionally intercepts a communication[2] in the course of its transmission by post or by means of a public telecommunication system[3] is guilty of an offence and liable on conviction on indictment to imprisonment for a term not exceeding two years or a fine, or to both, or on summary conviction to a fine not exceeding the statutory maximum[4].

A person is not guilty of such an offence, however, if (1) the communication is intercepted in obedience to a warrant issued[5] by the Secretary of State[6]; or (2) that person has reasonable grounds for believing that the person to whom, or the person by whom, the communication is sent has consented to the interception[7]; or (3) the communication is intercepted for purposes connected with the provision of postal or public telecommunication services[8] or with the enforcement of any enactment relating to the use of those services[9]; or (4) the communication is being transmitted by wireless telegraphy[10] and is intercepted, with the authority of the Secretary of State, for purposes connected with the issue of licences under the Wireless Telegraphy Act 1949 or the prevention or detection of interference with wireless telegraphy[11].

No proceedings in respect of such an offence may be instituted except by or with the consent of the Director of Public Prosecutions[12].

1 For these purposes, 'person' includes any organisation and any association or combination of persons: Interception of Communications Act 1985 s 10 (1).
2 For these purposes, a communication which is in the course of its transmission otherwise than by means of a public telecommunication system is deemed to be in the course of its transmission by means of such a system if its mode of transmission identifies it as a communication which (1) is to be or has been transmitted by means of such a system; and (2) has been sent from, or is to be sent to, a country or territory outside the British Islands: ibid s 10 (2). 'The British Islands' means the United Kingdom, the Channel Islands and the Isle of Man: Interpretation Act 1978 s 5, Sch 1. For the meaning of 'United Kingdom' see para 86 note 1 ante.
3 The Secretary of State may by order designate as a public telecommunication system any telecommunication system the running of which is authorised by a licence to which the Telecommunications Act 1984 s 8 applies; and any reference to a public telecommunication system is a reference to a telecommunication system which is so designated and the running of which is so authorised: ss 9 (1), 106 (1) (applied by the Interception of Communications Act 1985 s 10 (1)). See further TELECOMMUNICATIONS.
4 Ibid s 1 (1). For the meaning of 'the statutory maximum' see para 806 post. As to the exclusion of evidence see para 1165 post.
5 Ie under ibid s 2: see para 271 post.
6 Ibid s 1 (2) (a).
7 Ibid s 1 (2) (b).
8 'Public telecommunication service' means a telecommunication service provided by means of a public telecommunication system: ibid s 10 (1).
9 Ibid s 1 (3) (a).
10 'Wireless telegraphy' has the same meaning as in the Wireless Telegraphy Act 1949: Interception of Communications Act 1985 s 10 (1). See TELECOMMUNICATIONS vol 45 para 503 note 1.
11 Ibid s 1 (3) (b).
12 Ibid s 1 (4) (a). As to the effect of this limitation see para 639 post.

B. WARRANTS FOR INTERCEPTION

271. Warrants for interception. The Secretary of State may issue[1] a warrant requiring the person to whom it is addressed to intercept, in the course of their transmission by post or by means of a public telecommunication system[2], such communications as are described in the warrant; and such a warrant may also require the person to whom it is addressed to disclose the intercepted material[3] to such persons and in such manner as are described in the warrant[4]. The Secretary of State may not, however, issue such a warrant unless he considers that the warrant is necessary[5] (1) in the interests of national security; (2) for the purpose of preventing or detecting serious crime[6]; or (3) for the purpose of safeguarding the economic well-being of the United Kingdom[7].

1 As to the issue of warrants see para 273 post.
2 For the meaning of 'public telecommunication system' see para 270 note 3 ante.

3 'Intercepted material', in relation to a warrant, means the communications intercepted in obedience to that warrant: Interception of Communications Act 1985 s 10 (1).
4 Ibid s 2 (1).
5 The matters to be taken into account in considering whether a warrant is necessary as mentioned in ibid s 2 (2) (see heads (1)–(3) infra) include whether the information which it is considered necessary to acquire could reasonably be acquired by other means: s 2 (3). However, a warrant is not to be considered necessary as mentioned in s 2 (2) (c) (see head (3) infra) unless the information which it is considered necessary to acquire is information relating to the acts or intentions of persons outside the British Islands: s 2 (4).
6 For these purposes, conduct which constitutes or, if it took place in the United Kingdom, would constitute one or more offences is to be regarded as serious crime if, and only if (1) it involves the use of violence, results in substantial financial gain or is conduct by a large number of persons in pursuit of a common purpose; or (2) the offence or one of the offences is an offence for which a person who has attained the age of 21 and has no previous convictions could reasonably be expected to be sentenced to imprisonment for a term of three years or more: ibid s 10 (3).
7 Ibid s 2 (2). For the meaning of 'United Kingdom' see para 86 note 1 ante.

272. Scope of warrants. The interception required by a warrant[1] is the interception of:
(1) such communications as are sent to or from one or more addresses[2] specified in the warrant, being an address or addresses likely to be used for the transmission of communications to or from (a) one particular person specified or described in the warrant; or (b) one particular set of premises so specified or described;
(2) such other communications, if any, as it is necessary to intercept in order to intercept communications falling within head (1) above[3].
However, the above provisions do not apply to a warrant if:
(a) the interception required by the warrant is the interception, in the course of their transmission by means of a public telecommunication system[4], of (i) such external communications[5] as are described in the warrant; and (ii) such other communications, if any, as it is necessary to intercept in order to intercept such external communications as are so described; and
(b) at the time the warrant is issued, the Secretary of State issues a certificate[6] certifying the descriptions of intercepted material the examination of which he considers[7] necessary[8].

1 References in the Interception of Communications Act 1985 ss 3–9 to a warrant are references to a warrant under s 2: s 2 (5). See para 271 ante.
2 For these purposes, 'address' means any postal or telecommunications address: ibid s 10 (1).
3 Ibid s 3 (1).
4 For the meaning of 'public telecommunication system' see para 270 note 3 ante.
5 For these purposes, 'external communication' means a communication sent or received outside the British Islands: Interception of Communications Act 1985 s 10 (1). For the meaning of 'the British Islands' see para 270 note 2 ante.
6 A certificate so issued may not specify an address in the British Islands for the purpose of including communications sent to or from that address in the certified material unless (1) the Secretary of State considers that the examination of communications sent to or from that address is necessary for the purpose of preventing or detecting acts of terrorism; and (2) communications sent to or from that address are included in the certified material only in so far as they are sent within such a period, not exceeding three months, as is specified in the certificate: ibid s 3 (3). Such a certificate may not be issued except under the hand of the Secretary of State: s 3 (4).
7 Ie which the Secretary of State considers necessary as mentioned in ibid s 2 (2): see para 271 ante.
8 Ibid s 3 (3).

273. Issue and duration of warrants. A warrant[1] may not be issued except (1) under the hand of the Secretary of State; or (2) in an urgent case where the Secretary of State has expressly authorised its issue and a statement of that fact is indorsed thereon, under the hand of an official of his department of or above the rank of Assistant Under Secretary of State[2].

Unless renewed, a warrant ceases to have effect at the end of the relevant period[3]; and for these purposes 'the relevant period' means:

(a) in relation to a warrant which has not been renewed (i) if the warrant was issued under head (1) above, the period of two months beginning with the day on which it was issued; and (ii) if the warrant was issued under head (2) above, the period ending with the second working day[4] following that day;

(b) in relation to a warrant which was last renewed within the period mentioned in head (a) (ii) above, the period of two months beginning with the day on which it was so renewed; and

(c) in relation to a warrant which was last renewed at any other time (i) if the instrument by which it was renewed is indorsed with a statement that the renewal is considered necessary in the interests of national security or for the purpose of safeguarding the economic well-being of the United Kingdom[5], the period of six months beginning with the day on which it was so renewed; and (ii) if that instrument is not so indorsed, the period of one month beginning with that day[6].

At any time before the end of the relevant period the Secretary of State may renew a warrant if he considers[7] that the warrant continues to be necessary[8]; but a warrant may not be so renewed except by an instrument under the hand of the Secretary of State[9]. If, however, at any time before the end of the relevant period the Secretary of State considers that a warrant is no longer necessary[10], he must cancel the warrant[11].

1 For the meaning of 'warrant' see para 272 note 1 ante.
2 Interception of Communications Act 1985 s 4 (1).
3 Ibid s 4 (2).
4 For these purposes, 'working day' means any day other than a Saturday, a Sunday, Christmas Day, Good Friday or a day which is a bank holiday under the Banking and Financial Dealings Act 1971 in any part of the United Kingdom: Interception of Communications Act 1985 s 10 (1). For the meaning of 'United Kingdom' see para 86 note 1 ante.
5 Ie as mentioned in ibid s 2 (2) (a) or (c): see para 271 heads (1), (3) ante.
6 Ibid s 4 (6).
7 Ie if he considers it necessary as mentioned in ibid s 2(2): see para 271 ante.
8 Ibid s 4 (3).
9 Ibid s 4 (5).
10 See note 7 supra.
11 Interception of Communications Act 1985 s 4 (4).

274. Modification of warrants. The Secretary of State may at any time (1) modify a warrant[1] by the insertion of any address[2] which he considers likely to be used[3]; or (2) modify a certificate[4] so as to include in the certified material any material the examination of which he considers[5] necessary[6]. A warrant or certificate may not be so modified except by an instrument under the hand of the Secretary of State or, in an urgent case, (a) under the hand of a person holding office under the Crown who is expressly authorised by the warrant or certificate to modify it on the Secretary of State's behalf; or (b) where the Secretary of State has expressly authorised the modification and a statement of that fact is indorsed on the instrument, under the hand of an official of his department of or above the rank of Assistant Under Secretary of State[7]. An instrument issued under heads (a) or (b) above ceases to have effect at the end of the fifth working day[8] following the day on which it was issued[9].

1 For the meaning of 'warrant' see para 272 note 1 ante.
2 For the meaning of 'address' see para 272 note 2 ante.
3 Ie as mentioned in the Interception of Communications Act 1985 s 3 (1) (a): see para 272 head (1) ante. If at any time the Secretary of State considers that any address specified in a warrant is no longer likely to be so used, he must modify the warrant by the deletion of that address: s 5 (2).
4 References in ibid ss 4–9 to a certificate are references to a certificate such as is mentioned in s 3 (2): s 3 (5). See para 272 ante.
5 Ie which he considers necessary as mentioned in ibid s 2 (2): see para 271 ante.
6 Ibid s 5 (1). If at any time the Secretary of State considers that the material certified by a certificate includes any material the examination of which is no longer necessary as mentioned in s 2 (2) (see para 271 ante), he must modify the certificate so as to exclude that material from the certified material: s 5 (3).
7 Ibid ss 4 (1) (b), 5 (4).
8 For the meaning of 'working day' see para 273 note 4 ante.
9 Interception of Communications Act 1985 s 5 (5).

275. Safeguards. Where the Secretary of State issues a warrant[1], he must, unless such arrangements have already been made, make such arrangements as he considers necessary for the purpose of securing (1) that the statutory requirements are satisfied in relation to the intercepted material[2]; and (2) where a certificate[3] is issued in relation to the warrant, that so much of the intercepted material as is not certified by the certificate is not read, looked at or listened to by any person[4]. The above requirements are satisfied in relation to any intercepted material if each of the following, namely (a) the extent to which the material is disclosed; (b) the number of persons to whom any of the material is disclosed; (c) the extent to which the material is copied[5]; and (d) the number of copies made of any of the material, is limited to the necessary[6] minimum[7]. The above requirements are also satisfied, in relation to any intercepted material, if each copy of any of that material is destroyed as soon as its retention is no longer[8] necessary[9].

1 For the meaning of 'warrant' see para 272 note 1 ante.
2 For the meaning of 'intercepted material' see para 271 note 3 ante.
3 For the meaning of 'certificate' see para 274 note 4 ante.
4 Interception of Communications Act 1985 s 6 (1).
5 For these purposes, 'copy', in relation to intercepted material, means any of the following, whether or not in documentary form: (1) any copy, extract or summary of the material; and (2) any record of the identities of the persons to or by whom the material was sent; and cognate expressions are to be construed accordingly: ibid s 10 (1).
6 Ie the minimum that is necessary as mentioned in ibid s 2 (2): see para 271 ante.
7 Ibid s 6 (2).
8 Ie no longer necessary as mentioned in ibid s 2 (2): see para 271 ante.
9 Ibid s 6 (3).

C. INVESTIGATION OF COMPLAINTS

276. Constitution of the Tribunal. There is a Tribunal which must consist of five members each of whom must be a barrister, advocate or solicitor of not less than ten years' standing[1]. The members of the Tribunal are such persons as Her Majesty may by Letters Patent appoint and they hold office during good behaviour[2]. A member of the Tribunal must vacate office at the end of the period of five years beginning with the day of his appointment but he is eligible for reappointment[3]; however, a member of the Tribunal may be relieved of office by Her Majesty at his own request[4]. A member of the Tribunal may be removed from office by Her Majesty on an Address presented to Her by both Houses of Parliament[5].

1 Interception of Communications Act 1985 s 7 (1), Sch 1 para 1 (1). Her Majesty may by Letters Patent appoint as President or Vice-President of the Tribunal a person who is, or by virtue of those Letters will be, a member of the Tribunal: Sch 1 para 2 (1). If at any time the President of the Tribunal is temporarily unable to carry out the functions of the President, the Vice-President must carry out those functions: Sch 1 para 2 (2). A person ceases to be the President or Vice-President of the Tribunal if he ceases to be a member of the Tribunal: Sch 1 para 2 (3).

2 Ibid Sch 1 para 1 (2). The Secretary of State must pay to the members of the Tribunal out of money provided by Parliament such remuneration and allowances as he may with the approval of the Treasury determine: Sch 1 para 5 (1). Such expenses of the Tribunal must be defrayed by him out of money provided by Parliament: Sch 1 para 5 (2).

   After consultation with the Tribunal and with the approval of the Treasury as to numbers, the Secretary of State may provide the Tribunal with such officers as he thinks necessary for the proper discharge of its functions; and the Tribunal may authorise any such officer to obtain any documents or information on the Tribunal's behalf: Sch 1 para 6.

3 Ibid Sch 1 para 1 (3).
4 Ibid Sch 1 para 1 (4).
5 Ibid Sch 1 para 1 (5).

277. Application to the Tribunal. Any person[1] who believes that communications sent to or by him have been intercepted in the course of their transmission by post or by means of a public telecommunication system[2] may apply to the Tribunal[3] for an investigation[4]. On an application, other than one appearing to the Tribunal to be frivolous or vexatious, the Tribunal must investigate (1) whether there is or has been a relevant warrant[5] or a relevant certificate[6]; and (2) where there is or has been such a warrant or certificate, whether there has been any contravention of the statutory provisions[7] in relation to that warrant or certificate[8].

1 For the meaning of 'person' see para 270 note 1 ante.
2 For the meaning of 'public telecommunication system' see para 270 note 3 ante.
3 As to the Tribunal see para 276 ante.
4 Interception of Communications Act 1985 s 7 (2).
5 For these purposes, a warrant is a relevant warrant in relation to an applicant if (1) the applicant is specified or described in the warrant; or (2) an address used for the transmission of communications to or from a set of premises in the British Islands where the applicant resides or works is so specified: ibid s 7 (9) (a). For the meaning of 'the British Islands' see para 270 note 2 ante.
6 For these purposes, a certificate is a relevant certificate in relation to an applicant if and to the extent that an address used as mentioned in ibid s 7 (9) (a) (ii) (see note 5 head (2) supra) is specified in the certificate for the purpose of including communications sent to or from that address in the certified material: s 7 (9) (b).
7 Ie ibid ss 2–5: see paras 271–274 ante.
8 Ibid s 7 (3).

278. Procedure of the Tribunal. The functions of the Tribunal in relation to any application[1] made to it are capable of being carried out, in any place in the United Kingdom, by any two or more members of the Tribunal designated for the purpose by their President; and different members of the Tribunal may carry out functions in relation to different applications at the same time[2].

It is the duty of every person holding office under the Crown or engaged in the business of the Post Office or in the running of a public telecommunication system[3] to disclose or give to the Tribunal such documents or information as it may require for the purpose of enabling it to carry out its functions[4].

The Tribunal must carry out its functions[5] in such a way as to secure that no document or information which is disclosed or given to the Tribunal is disclosed or given to any person, including an applicant to the Tribunal or a person holding office under the Crown, without the consent of the person who disclosed it or gave it to the Tribunal; and accordingly the Tribunal may not[6] give reasons for any decision made by it[7]. Otherwise, the Tribunal may determine its own procedure[8].

1 As to the application see para 277 ante.
2 Interception of Communications Act 1985 s 7 (1), Sch 1 para 3. For the meaning of 'United Kingdom' see para 86 note 1 ante. As to the exclusion of evidence see para 1165 post.
3 For the meaning of 'public telecommunication system' see para 270 note 3 ante.
4 Interception of Communications Act 1985 Sch 1 para 4 (1).
5 Ie except its functions in relation to reports under ibid s 7 (4): see para 279 post.
6 Ie except in reports under ibid s 7 (4): see para 279 post.
7 Ibid Sch 1 para 4 (2).
8 Ibid Sch 1 para 4 (3).

279. Decisions of the Tribunal. If, on an investigation, the Tribunal, applying the principles applicable on an application for judicial review[1], concludes that there has been a contravention of the statutory provisions[2], it must (1) give notice to the applicant stating that conclusion; (2) make a report of its findings to the Prime Minister; and (3) if the Tribunal thinks fit, make an appropriate order[3]. Such an order may do one or more of the following, namely (a) quash the relevant warrant[4] or the relevant certificate[5]; (b) direct the destruction of copies of the intercepted material[6] or, as the case may be, so much of it as is certified by the relevant certificate; (c) direct the Secretary of State to pay to the applicant such sum by way of compensation as may be specified in the order[7]. If, on an investigation, the Tribunal comes to any other conclusion, it must give notice to the applicant stating that there has been no contravention of the statutory provisions in relation to a relevant warrant or a relevant certificate[8].

The decisions of the Tribunal, including any decisions as to its jurisdiction, are not subject to appeal or liable to be questioned in any court[9].

1 See ADMINISTRATIVE LAW vol 1 (1) (Reissue) para 51 et seq.
2 Ie the Interception of Communications Act 1985 ss 2–5: see paras 270–274 ante.
3 Ibid s 7 (4). A notice or report made under s 7 (4) must state the effect of any order under s 7 (5): s 7 (6). See infra.
4 For the meaning of 'the relevant warrant' see para 277 note 5 ante.
5 For the meaning of 'the relevant certificate' see para 277 note 6 ante.
6 For the meaning of 'copy' and 'intercepted material' see paras 275 note 5, 271 note 3 respectively ante.
7 Interception of Communications Act 1985 s 7 (5).
8 Ibid s 7 (7).
9 Ibid s 7 (8).

280. The Commissioner. The Prime Minister must appoint a person who holds or has held a high judicial office[1] ('the Commissioner') to carry out the following functions:

(1) to keep under review the carrying out by the Secretary of State of his statutory functions in respect of the issue of warrants[2] and the adequacy of any arrangements made in respect of safeguards on the issue of warrants[3]; and

(2) to give to the Tribunal all such assistance as the Tribunal may require for the purpose of enabling it to carry out its statutory functions[4].

It is the duty of every person holding office under the Crown or engaged in the business of the Post Office or in the running of a public telecommunication system[5] to disclose or give to the Commissioner such documents or information as he may require for the purpose of enabling him to carry out his functions[6]. It is the duty of the Tribunal to send to the Commissioner a copy of every report made by it[7]. If at any time it appears to the Commissioner:

(a) that there has been a contravention of the statutory provisions[8] which has not been the subject of a report made[9] by the Tribunal; or

(b) that any arrangements made for the purposes of safeguards on the issue of warrants[10] have proved inadequate,

he must make a report to the Prime Minister with respect to that contravention or those arrangements[11].

As soon as practicable after the end of each calendar year, the Commissioner must make a report to the Prime Minister with respect to the carrying out of his functions[12]; and the Prime Minister must lay before each House of Parliament a copy of every annual report so made together with a statement as to whether any matter has been excluded[13] from that copy[14]. If, however, it appears to the Prime Minister, after consultation with the Commissioner, that the publication of any matter in an annual report would be prejudicial to national security, to the prevention or detection of serious crime[15], or to the economic well-being of the United Kingdom, the Prime Minister may exclude that matter from the copy of the report as laid before each House of Parliament[16].

1 'High judicial office' means any of the following offices, namely the Office of Lord Chancellor of Great Britain or of Judge of one of Her Majesty's superior courts of Great Britain and Ireland; and 'superior courts of Great Britain and Ireland' means and includes, as to England, Her Majesty's High Court of Justice and Her Majesty's Court of Appeal and, as to Northern Ireland, Her Majesty's High Court of Justice in Northern Ireland and Her Majesty's Court of Appeal in Northern Ireland and, as to Scotland, the Court of Session: Appellate Jurisdiction Act 1876 s 25 (as amended) applied by the Interception of Communications Act 1985 s 10 (1).

2 Ie ibid ss 2–5: see paras 271–274 ante.

3 Ie ibid s 6: see para 275 ante.

4 Ibid s 8 (1).

5 For the meaning of 'public telecommunication system' see para 270 note 3 ante.

6 Interception of Communications Act 1985 s 8 (2).

7 Ibid s 8 (3). The reports are made under s 7 (4): see para 279 ante.

8 See note 2 supra.

9 Ie under the Interception of Communications Act 1985 s 7 (4): see para 279 ante.

10 See note 3 supra.

11 Interception of Communications Act 1985 s 8 (5).

12 Ibid s 8 (6).

13 Ie under ibid s 8 (8): see infra.

14 Ibid s 8 (7).

15 For the meaning of 'serious crime' see para 271 note 6 ante.

16 Interception of Communications Act 1985 s 8 (8). For the meaning of 'United Kingdom' see para 86 note 1 ante.

(7) OFFENCES BY AND IN RESPECT OF PUBLIC OFFICERS

(i) Bribery and Obstruction of Public Officers

281. Bribery of judges or other judicial officers. A person who offers or gives a judge, magistrate or other judicial officer, and any judge, magistrate or other judicial officer who takes, any gift or reward to influence his behaviour, or for anything done, in the conduct of his office commits an offence at common law[1]. Any such offence is punishable by fine and imprisonment at the discretion of the court[2], and, in the case of an offender who takes a bribe or reward, by loss of office[3].

1 Bac Abr, Offices and Officers (N); 3 Co Inst 145; 1 Hawk PC c 27; 4 Bl Com (14th Edn) 138, 139. See also *R v Gurney* (1867) 10 Cox CC 550. The offence is punishable whether the bribe is accepted or not: 3 Co Inst 147. As to embracery see para 313 post; and as to bribery of public officers other than judicial officers see paras 282, 283 post.
2 See paras 1200, 1232 post.
3 Bac Abr, Offices and Officers (N); 3 Co Inst 145, 147; 12 Hawk PC c 27.

282. Bribery of public officers. It is an indictable offence at common law for any person to bribe a public officer[1], or for a public officer to accept a bribe, as an inducement to act contrary to his duty or to show favour or forbear to show disfavour in the discharge of his duty[2]. Any such offence is punishable by imprisonment and fine at the discretion of the court[3].

1 A public officer is any officer who discharges any duty in the discharge of which the public is interested: see *R v Whitaker* [1914] 3 KB 1283, 10 Cr App Rep 245, CCA, where it was held that, where such an officer was described as 'a public and ministerial officer', the addition of the words 'and ministerial' did not affect the matter; every officer who is not a judicial officer is a ministerial officer.
2 See *R v Whitaker* [1914] 3 KB 1283, 10 Cr App Rep 245, CCA, where the earlier authorities are reviewed, and where it was held that a colonel of a regiment is a ministerial public officer and was guilty at common law of bribery in accepting sums of money to show favour in the placing of a canteen contract. See also *R v Pollman* (1809) 2 Camp 229 (receipt of a bribe for procuring an appointment to a public office). The giving of bribes to, and the taking of bribes by, members or officers of public bodies is a statutory offence: see para 283 post.
3 See paras 1200, 1232 post. If the holder of a justices' licence bribes or attempts to bribe any constable, he is liable to a fine not exceeding level 2 on the standard scale: Licensing Act 1964 s 178 (c) (amended by the Criminal Justice Act 1982 s 46). For the meaning of 'the standard scale' see para 808 post. See further INTOXICATING LIQUOR vol 26 para 400.

283. Bribery of members and officers of public bodies. A person[1] commits an offence who by himself or by or in conjunction with any other person (1) corruptly[2] solicits or receives, or agrees to receive, for himself, or for any other person, any gift, loan, fee, reward[3], or advantage[4] whatever as an inducement to, or reward for, or otherwise on account of, any member, officer or servant of a public body[5] doing or forbearing to do anything in respect of any matter or transaction whatsoever, actual or proposed, in which such public body is concerned; (2) corruptly gives, promises, or offers any gift, loan, fee, reward, or advantage whatsoever to any person, whether for the benefit of that person or of another person, as an inducement to, or reward for, or otherwise on account of, any member, officer, or servant of any public body doing or forbearing to do anything in respect of any matter or transaction whatsoever, actual or proposed, in which such public body is concerned[6].

A person guilty of any such offence is liable on conviction on indictment to imprisonment for a term not exceeding seven years or a fine, or to both, or on summary conviction to imprisonment for a term not exceeding six months or a fine not exceeding the statutory maximum, or to both[7]. In addition he is liable (a) to be ordered to pay to such public body the amount or value of any gift, loan, fee or reward received by him or any part thereof[8]; (b) to be adjudged incapable of being elected or appointed to any public office[9] for five years from the date of his conviction, and to forfeit any such office held by him at the time of his conviction[10]; and (c) in the event of a second conviction for a like offence, in addition to the above penalties, to be adjudged to be for ever incapable of holding any public office, and to be incapable for five years of being registered as an elector, or voting at a parliamentary election or an election of members of any public body[11]. If he is an officer or servant in the employment of any public body upon such conviction, he is liable, at the discretion of the court, to forfeit his right and claim to any compensation or pension to which he would otherwise have been entitled[12].

1 'Person' includes a body of persons, corporate or unincorporate: Public Bodies Corrupt Practices Act 1889 s 7.
2 'Corruptly' appears in both the Public Bodies Corrupt Practices Act 1889 s 1 and the Prevention of Corruption Act 1906 s 1 (as amended) which, with the Prevention of Corruption Act 1916, may be cited together as the Prevention of Corruption Acts 1889–1916: Prevention of Corruption Act 1916 s 4 (1). It has the same meaning in each Act: *R v Wellburn, R v Nurdin, R v Randel* (1979) 69 Cr App Rep 254 at 265, CA (decided under the Prevention of Corruption Act 1906); *R v Parker* (1985) 82 Cr App Rep 69 at 73, 74, CA (decided under the Public Bodies Corrupt Practices Act 1889). 'Corruptly' denotes that the person making the offer did so deliberately and with the intention that the person to whom it was addressed should enter into a corrupt bargain whether or not the offeror intended to follow it through: *R v Smith* [1960] 2 QB 423 at 428, 44 Cr App Rep 55 at 60, 61, CCA (decided under the Public Bodies Corrupt Practices Act 1889). In *R v Wellburn, R v Nurdin, R v Randel* supra 'corruptly' was described as being a simple English adverb meaning purposefully doing an act which the law forbids as tending to corrupt.
    If a person accepts a gift, knowing that it is a bribe, and intends to keep it, he enters into a corrupt bargain even though he may not intend to carry out and does not carry out his corrupt act: *R v Carr* [1956] 3 All ER 979, 40 Cr App Rep 188, CA; *R v Mills* (1978) 68 Cr App Rep 154 at 158, 159, CA (both cases decided under the Prevention of Corruption Act 1906). If the bribe is innocently received, the recipient does not act corruptly: *R v Millray Window Cleaning Co Ltd* [1962] Crim LR 99, CCA. If the money is received in order to entrap someone or to provide evidence to a listening policeman, the person does not intend to keep the money and it would not be corrupt: *R v Mills* supra. Receipt of money for a past favour without there having been an agreement beforehand is part of the meaning of 'corruptly': *R v Parker* supra, applying *R v Wellburn* supra. There should be a link between the payment to a local councillor and his doing something in pursuance of his public duty; not every payment is therefore unlawful: *R v Parker* supra. It is not a defence if a councillor thought that what he was doing was not against the interests of the authority: *R v Parker* supra. As to the presumption of corruption in instances where the offence charged relates to a contract or proposed contract with Her Majesty, a government department or a public body see para 284 post. Receipt of an extra payment from a public authority for extra duties would not constitute this offence: *Edwards v Salmon* (1889) 23 QBD 531, CA (decided under the Public Health Act 1875 s 189 (repealed)).
3 'Reward' includes the receipt of money for a past favour without any antecedent agreement: *R v Andrews Weatherfoil Ltd* [1972] 1 All ER 65, [1972] 1 WLR 118, CA.
4 'Advantage' includes any office or dignity, and any forbearance to demand any money or money's worth or valuable thing, and includes any aid, vote, consent, or influence, or pretended aid, vote, consent, or influence, and also includes any promise or procurement of or agreement or endeavour to procure, or the holding out of any expectation of any gift, loan, fee, reward, or advantage, as before defined: Public Bodies Corrupt Practices Act 1889 s 7.
5 'Public body', in the Prevention of Corruption Act 1916 (see para 284 post) and in the Public Bodies Corrupt Practices Act 1889 includes, in addition to the bodies mentioned in the latter Act, local and public authorities of all descriptions: Prevention of Corruption Act 1916 s 4 (2). The bodies mentioned in the Public Bodies Corrupt Practices Act 1889 are 'any council of a county or county of a city or town, any council of a municipal borough, also any board, commissioners, select vestry, or other body which has power to act under and for the purposes of any Act relating to local government, or the public health, or to poor law or otherwise to administer money raised by rates in pursuance of any public general Act, but does not include any public body as above defined existing elsewhere than in the United Kingdom': s 7. 'Public general Act' includes the Metropolitan Police Acts (see POLICE): *R v Silbertson* (1899) 129 CC Ct Cas 372. For the purposes of the Prevention of Corruption Acts 1889–1916, the Civil Aviation Authority (see the Civil Aviation Act 1982 ss 2,

19 (1)) and the Housing Corporation (see the Housing Associations Act 1985 s 74, Sch 6 para 1 (2)) are public bodies as were the Gas Council (*R v Joy and Emmony* (1974) 60 Cr App Rep 132) and the Gas Board (*DPP v Holly, DPP v Manners* [1978] AC 43, 64 Cr App Rep 143, HL). The decision that the National Coal Board was not a public body (*R v Newbould* [1962] 2 QB 102, 46 Cr App Rep 247) is wrong and should not be followed: *DPP v Holly* supra. A public body is a body which has public or statutory duties to perform and which performs those duties and carries out its transactions for the benefit of the public and not for private profit: *DPP v Holly* supra.

6 Public Bodies Corrupt Practices Act 1889 s 1; Criminal Law Act 1967 s 1. A person is not exempt from punishment under the Public Bodies Corrupt Practices Act 1889 s 1 by reason of the invalidity of the appointment or election of a person to a public office: s 3 (2). A prosecution for an offence under s 1 may not be instituted except by or with the consent of the Attorney General or the Solicitor General: s 4. As to the effect of this limitation see para 639 post. The giving of bribes to, and the taking of bribes by, public officers is also an offence at common law: see para 282 ante. As to bribery of commissioners or officers of customs and excise see CUSTOMS AND EXCISE vol 12 para 604. An officer or employee of a local government authority who, under colour of his office or employment, accepts any fee or reward other than his proper remuneration is liable on summary conviction to a fine not exceeding level 4 on the standard scale: Local Government Act 1972 s 117 (2), (3) (amended by the Criminal Justice Act 1982 ss 38, 46): and see LOCAL GOVERNMENT. For the meaning of 'the standard scale' see para 808 post. As to corrupt transactions with agents see para 577 post; and as to bribery relating to official contracts see para 284 post.

7 Public Bodies Corrupt Practices Act 1889 s 2 (a) (substituted by the Criminal Justice Act 1988 s 47 (1)). For the meaning of 'the statutory maximum' see para 806 post. Nothing in the Public Bodies Corrupt Practices Act 1889 s 2 (a) (as so substituted) affects the punishment for an offence committed before 29 September 1988: Criminal Justice Act 1988 ss 47 (3), 171 (6).

8 Public Bodies Corrupt Practices Act 1889 s 2 (b).

9 'Public office' means any office or employment of a person as a member, officer, or servant of such public body: ibid s 7.

10 Ibid s 2 (c) (amended by the Representation of the People Act 1948 s 52 (7)).

11 Public Bodies Corrupt Practices Act 1889 s 2 (d) (amended by the Representation of the People Act 1948 s 52 (7)). The enactments for preventing the voting and registration of persons declared by reason of corrupt practices to be incapable of voting (see the Representation of the People Act 1983 and ELECTIONS) apply to a person so adjudged incapable of voting: see the Public Bodies Corrupt Practices Act 1889 s 2 (d).

12 Ibid s 2 (e).

284. Bribery relating to official contracts.

Where in any proceedings against a person for an offence under the Prevention of Corruption Act 1906[1] or the Public Bodies Corrupt Practices Act 1889[2], it is proved that any money, gift, or other consideration[3] has been paid or given to or received by a person in the employment of Her Majesty or any government department or a public body[4] by or from a person, or agent[5] of a person, holding or seeking to obtain a contract from Her Majesty or any government department or public body, the money, gift or consideration is deemed to have been paid or given and received corruptly as such inducement or reward as is mentioned in such Act unless the contrary is proved[6].

1 See para 577 post.

2 See para 283 ante.

3 'Consideration' has the same meaning as in the Prevention of Corruption Act 1906 (see para 577 note 3 post): Prevention of Corruption Act 1916 s 4 (3). 'Consideration' bears its legal meaning and connotes a contract or bargain of some kind: *R v Braithwaite, R v Girdham* [1983] 2 All ER 87, 77 Cr App Rep 34, CA.

4 For the meaning of 'public body' see para 283 note 5 ante.

5 'Agent' has the same meaning as in the Prevention of Corruption Act 1906 (see para 577 note 1 post): Prevention of Corruption Act 1916 s 4 (3).

6 Ibid s 2. The onus or proof that a payment was in fact not a corrupt payment lies upon the accused; however, that onus is only to satisfy the jury of the probability of that which he was called upon to establish and, if he satisfies the jury that the probability is that the gift was made innocently, the statutory presumption is rebutted and he is entitled to be acquitted: *R v Carr-Briant* [1943] KB 607, 29 Cr App Rep 76, CCA.

285. Bribery in connection with grant of honours. If any person:
 (1) accepts or obtains or agrees to accept or attempts to obtain from any person, for himself or for any other person, for any purpose; or
 (2) gives, or agrees or proposes to give, or offers to any person,
any gift, money or valuable consideration[1], as an inducement or reward for procuring or assisting or endeavouring to procure the grant of a dignity or title of honour to any person, or otherwise in connection with such a grant, he is guilty of an offence and liable on conviction on indictment to imprisonment for a term not exceeding two years or a fine, or to both, or on summary conviction to imprisonment for a term not exceeding three months or a fine not exceeding the prescribed sum, or to both; and, where the person convicted, whether on indictment or summarily, received any such gift, money or consideration which is capable of forfeiture, he is in addition to any other penalty liable to forfeit the same to Her Majesty[2].

 1 See CONTRACT vol 9 para 310.
 2 Honours (Prevention of Abuses) Act 1925 s 1 (1)–(3) (amended by the Criminal Law Act 1977 s 32 (1); the Magistrates' Courts Act 1980 s 32 (2)); Criminal Law Act 1967 s 1. For the meaning of 'the prescribed sum' see para 807 post. See also CONTRACT vol 9 para 391 et seq.

286. Bribery at elections. Bribery at a parliamentary[1] or local[2] election was an indictable offence at common law punishable by fine and imprisonment. The common law offence has, however, been superseded by express statutory provisions[3].
 A person is guilty of a corrupt practice[4] if he is guilty of bribery[5]. A person is guilty of bribery if:
 (1) he, directly or indirectly, by himself or by any other person on his behalf:
   (a) gives any money[6] or procures any office[7] to or for any voter[8] or to or for any other person on behalf of any voter or to or for any other person in order to induce any voter to vote or refrain from voting; or
   (b) corruptly does any such act as mentioned in head (a) above on account of any voter having voted or refrained from voting; or
   (c) makes any such gift or procurement to or for any person in order to induce that person to procure, or endeavour to procure, the return of any person at an election[9] or the vote of any voter,
   or if upon or in consequence of any such gift or procurement he procures or engages, promises or endeavours to procure, the return of any person at an election or the vote of any voter[10];
 (2) he advances or pays or causes to be paid any money to or for the use of any other person with the intent that that money or any part of it shall be expended in bribery at an election or knowingly pays or causes to be paid any money to any person in discharge or repayment of any money wholly or in part expended in bribery at any election[11];
 (3) before or during an election, he directly or indirectly by himself or by any other person on his behalf receives, agrees or contracts for any money, gift, loan or valuable consideration, office, place or employment for himself or for any other person for voting or agreeing to vote or refraining or agreeing to refrain from voting[12];
 (4) after an election, he directly or indirectly by himself or by any other person on his behalf receives any money or valuable consideration on account of any

person having voted or refrained from voting or having induced any other person to vote or refrain from voting[13].

A person guilty of a corrupt practice is liable on conviction on indictment to imprisonment for a term not exceeding one year or a fine, or to both, or on summary conviction to imprisonment for a term not exceeding six months or a fine not exceeding the statutory maximum, or to both[14].

Where on an election petition it is shown that corrupt practices[15] committed in reference to the election for the purpose of promoting or procuring the election of any person at that election have so extensively prevailed that they may reasonably be supposed to have affected the result, his election, if he is elected, is void and he is incapable of being elected to fill the vacancy or any of the vacancies for which the election was held[16].

1 *R v Pitt and Mead* (1762) 3 Burr 1335 at 1338.
2 See *R v Plympton* (1724) 2 Ld Raym 1377; *R v Lancaster and Worrall* (1890) 16 Cox CC 737.
3 See infra and ELECTIONS vol 15 (Reissue) para 684.
4 As to the offences constituting corrupt practices see the Representation of the People Act 1983 s 60 (personation), s 75 (5) (as amended) (expenses not authorised by election agent), s 82 (6), Sch 4 para 5 (false declaration of expenses), ss 113–115 (bribery, treating and undue influence) and ELECTIONS vol 15 (Reissue) paras 413, 664, 660, 684 et seq respectively.
5 Ibid s 113 (1); and see ELECTIONS vol 15 (Reissue) para 684. The provisions of s 113 (1)–(3) do not extend nor are they to be construed to extend to any money paid or agreed to be paid for or on account of any legal expenses incurred in good faith at or concerning an election: s 113 (4).
6 For these purposes, references to giving money include references to giving, lending, agreeing to give or lend, offering, promising, or promising to procure or endeavour to procure any money or valuable consideration: ibid s 113 (2) (i).
7 For these purposes, references to procuring any office include references to giving, procuring, agreeing to give or procure, offering, promising, or promising to procure or endeavour to procure any office, place or employment: ibid s 113 (2) (ii).
8 For these purposes, 'voter' includes any person who has or claims to have a right to vote: ibid s 113 (7); and see ELECTIONS vol 15 (Reissue) para 684 note 7.
9 'Election' means a parliamentary election or an election under the Local Government Act 1972: see the Representation of the People Act 1983 ss 202 (1), 203 (1) (as amended). The statutory provisions relating to bribery at elections apply also to elections to the European Parliament: see the European Parliamentary Elections Regulations 1986, SI 1986/2209, reg 5 (1), Sch 1; the European Communities (Amendment) Act 1986 s 3 (1) (b) and ELECTIONS.
10 Representation of the People Act 1983 s 113 (2); and see ELECTIONS.
11 Ibid s 113 (3); and see ELECTIONS vol 15 (Reissue) para 692.
12 Ibid s 113 (5); and see ELECTIONS vol 15 (Reissue) para 694.
13 Ibid s 113 (6); and see ELECTIONS vol 15 (Reissue) para 694.
14 Ibid s 168 (1) (substituted by the Representation of the People Act 1985 s 23, Sch 3 para 8). For the meaning of 'the statutory maximum' see para 806 post. If it appears to the court by which a person holding a licence or certificate under the Licensing Acts (see LICENSING) is convicted of the offence of bribery or treating that the offence was committed on licensed premises (1) the court must direct the conviction to be entered in the proper register of licences; and (2) the entry must be taken into consideration by the licensing authority in determining whether or not it will grant a renewal of the licence or certificate, and may be a ground, if the authority thinks fit, for refusing its renewal: Representation of the People Act 1983 s 168 (7). See ELECTIONS vol 15 (Reissue) para 722.
15 'Corrupt practices' includes bribery: see note 5 supra. Ibid s 164 applies not only to corrupt practices but also to illegal practices or illegal payments, employments or hirings committed in reference to the election for the purpose of promoting or procuring the election of any person at an election: s 164 (1). See ELECTIONS VOL 15 (Reissue) para 724.
16 Ibid s 164 (1). An election is not liable to be avoided otherwise than under s 164 by reason of general corruption, bribery, treating or intimidation: s 164 (2). An election under the Local Government Act 1972 may be questioned on the ground that it is avoided under the Representation of the People Act 1983 s 164: see ss 164 (3), 203 (1) (as amended) and ELECTIONS vol 15 (Reissue) para 724.

287. Obtaining information about spent convictions etc. Any person who obtains specified information[1] from any official record[2] by means of any fraud, dishonesty or bribe is guilty of an offence and liable on summary conviction to imprisonment for a term not exceeding six months or a fine not exceeding level 5 on the standard scale, or to both[3].

  1 For these purposes, 'specified information' means information imputing that a named or otherwise identifiable rehabilitated living person has committed or been charged with or prosecuted for or convicted of or sentenced for any offence which is the subject of a spent conviction: Rehabilitation of Offenders Act 1974 s 9 (1). For the meaning of 'rehabilitated person' and 'spent conviction' see para 1567 post.
  2 For these purposes, 'official record' means a record kept for the purposes of its functions by any court, police force, government department, local or other public authority in Great Britain, or a record kept, in Great Britain or elsewhere, for the purposes of any of Her Majesty's forces, being in either case a record containing information about persons convicted of offences: ibid 9 (1). For the meaning of references to a conviction in the 1974 Act, however expressed, see para 1567 note 2 post.
  3 Ibid s 9 (4), (7) (amended by the Criminal Justice Act 1982 ss 38, 46). For the meaning of 'the standard scale' see para 808 post.

288. Obstruction of public officers. It is an offence at common law to obstruct the execution of powers conferred by a statute[1]. Any such offence is punishable by fine and imprisonment at the discretion of the court[2].

  1 See *R v Smith* (1780) Doug KB 441.
  2 See paras 1200, 1232 post.

(ii) Sale of Public Offices

289. Sale or purchase of public offices. If any person sells, purchases, bargains or gives or receives any money or reward for any office, commission, place or employment in the gift of the Crown or in or under the appointment of any public department in the United Kingdom or in a British possession abroad or any participation in its profits, or if he gives or receives or contracts to give or receive any reward or profit for any interest or recommendation or pretended interest or recommendation concerning appointment to or resignation of any such office, commission, place or employment[1], or, if he opens or keeps any office for negotiating any business relating to vacancies in, or the sale or purchase of, any offices, commissions, places or employments in or under any public department[2], he is guilty of an offence and liable on conviction on indictment to imprisonment for a term not exceeding two years[3], and forfeiture of, and permanent disqualification from holding, the office etc in question[4].

  1 See the Sale of Offices Act 1809 ss 3, 4; the Criminal Law Act 1967 s 1. The Sale of Offices Act 1809 ss 3, 4 are expressed to apply to all offices specified or described in the Sale of Offices Act 1551, or the Sale of Offices Act 1809, or within the true intent and meaning of those Acts: see the Sale of Offices Act 1809 ss 1, 3, 4, 9. As to the construction of the Acts see *Hopkins v Prescott* (1847) 4 CB 578; *Graeme v Wroughton* (1855) 11 Exch 146; *Sterry v Clifton* (1850) 9 CB 110; *Samo v R* (1847) 2 Cox CC 178. The Sale of Offices Act 1809 was extended to the air force by the Air Force (Application of Enactments) (No 2) Order 1918, SR & O 1918/548 (amended by SI 1964/488). It is also an indictable offence at common law to offer a bribe to procure, or to receive a reward for procuring, an appointment to an office: see para 282 ante. Purchase or sale of the office of under-sheriff, deputy sheriff, bailiff or any other office appertaining to the office of sheriff is prohibited by the Sheriffs Act 1887: see s 27 and SHERIFFS vol 42 para 1113. As to bribery in connection with the grant of honours see para 285 ante.

2 See the Sale of Offices Act 1809 s 5; the Criminal Law Act 1967 s 1.
3 As no penalty is prescribed by the Sale of Offices Acts, the Powers of Criminal Courts Act 1973 s 18 (1) applies: see para 1200 post.
4 See the Sale of Offices Act 1551 s 1.

(iii) Misconduct in Public Office

290. Oppression. A public officer[1] commits the common law offence of oppression if, while exercising, or under colour of exercising, his office, he inflicts upon any person from an improper motive any bodily harm, imprisonment or injury other than extortion[2]. The offence is not committed if the officer acted in good faith, in the belief that he had the legal right to do the act in question, and without any intention to act corruptly or oppressively[3].

Oppression is an indictable offence punishable by imprisonment and fine at the discretion of the court[4].

1 For the meaning of 'public officer' see para 282 note 1 ante.
2 Stephen, Digest of the Criminal Law (9th Edn) 112; Bac Abr, Offices and Officers (N). In *R v Dytham* [1979] QB 722, 69 Cr App Rep 387, CA the indictment referred to the present offence, but the Court of Appeal decision concerns the offence of neglect of duty by a public officer: see para 292 post. The common law offence of extortion was abolished by the Theft Act 1968 (see s 32 (1) (a)) which also abolished the statutory offences of extortion by coroners (see ss 32 (1) (b), 33 (3), Sch 3 Pt I) and sheriffs (see Sch 3 Pt I). As to acceptance of fees and rewards by officers of local government authorities see para 283 note 2 ante; as to extortion by county court officers see COUNTY COURTS vol 10 para 31; and as to blackmail see para 566 post.
3 *R v Young and Pitts* (1758) 1 Burr 556; *R v Baylis* (1762) 3 Burr 1318; *R v Jackson* (1787) 1 Term Rep 653; *R v Borron* (1820) 3 B & Ald 432; *R v Marshall* (1855) 4 E & B 475; *R v Badger* (1843) 4 QB 468 at 474. See also *R v Llewellyn-Jones* [1968] 1 QB 429 at 435, 51 Cr App Rep 204 at 209, CA.
4 See paras 1200, 1232 post.

291. Breach of trust or fraud. Any public officer[1] who commits a breach of trust or fraud in a matter affecting the public is guilty of an indictable offence at common law even though the same conduct if in a private transaction would, as between individuals, have given rise only to a civil action[2]. The offence is punishable by fine and imprisonment at the discretion of the court[3].

1 For the meaning of 'public officer' see para 282 note 1 ante.
2 *R v Bembridge* (1783) 3 Doug KB 327 at 332; *Leheup's Case* (1755) 3 Doug KB 332n; *R v Jones* (1809) 2 Camp 131; *R v Dale* (1853) Dears CC 37; *R v Dytham* [1979] QB 722, 69 Cr App Rep 387, CA; *R v Llewellyn-Jones* [1968] 1 QB 429, 51 Cr App Rep 204, CA. The common law offence of false accounting by public officers has been abolished: see the Theft Act 1968 s 32 (1) (a). As to the statutory offence of false accounting see para 572 post.
3 See paras 1200, 1232 post.

292. Neglect of duty by public officer. It is an indictable offence at common law for a public officer[1] wilfully and without reasonable excuse or justification[2] to neglect to perform a duty imposed on him either by common law or by statute[3]. The penalty for the offence is fine and imprisonment at the discretion of the court[4] and loss of office[5].

1 For the meaning of 'public officer' see para 282 note 1 ante.
2 *R v Dytham* [1979] QB 722, 69 Cr App Rep 387, CA. The element of culpability is not restricted to corruption or dishonesty, but must be of such a degree that the misconduct impugned is calculated to injure the public interest so as to call for condemnation and punishment: *R v Dytham* supra.

3 Stephen, Digest of the Criminal Law (9th Edn) 114; *R v Wyatt* (1705) 1 Salk 380. This offence was called misconduct in a public office in *R v Dytham* [1979] QB 722, 69 Cr App Rep 387, CA, but this seems to run two apparently separate offences together. The discussion in *R v Dytham* supra concerns the present offence. See also see *R v Pinney* (1832) 3 State Tr NS 11 at 510, 512 ('... the law requires that, whether a man seeks an office or is compelled to accept it, he should do his best ... he may abstain from doing his duty with rigour; he may, with the best intentions, not act to the full extent of his duty ... But it is no justification of the offence'). See also *R v Metropolitan Police Comr, ex p Blackburn* [1968] 2 QB 118, [1968] 1 All ER 763, CA; *R v Metropolitan Police Comr, ex p Blackburn (No 3)* [1973] QB 241, [1973] 1 All ER 324, CA (ascertaining duty of police alleged by applicant for mandamus to be neglected).

4 See paras 1200, 1232 post.

5 1 Hawk PC c 27 s 1; 4 Bl Com (14th Edn) 140.

293. Refusal to serve in public office.

It is an indictable offence at common law for a duly qualified person to refuse to serve in a public office to which he has been appointed and in which he is by law required to serve[1]. Unless some other penalty is imposed by law[2], the offence is punishable by fine and imprisonment at the discretion of the court[3]. Payment of a fine imposed by statute for refusal to accept the office, unless the statute provides that the fine is payable in lieu of service, does not, it seems, affect the liability to indictment for the common law offence[4].

1 Stephen, Digest of the Criminal Law (9th Edn) 118; and see *R v Bower* (1823) 1 B & C 585.

2 See Stephen, Digest of the Criminal Law (9th Edn) 118.

3 See paras 1200, 1232 post.

4 *R v Denison* (1758) 2 Keny 259 at 260; *R v Woodrow* (1788) 2 Term Rep 731; *R v Bower* (1823) 1 B & C 585.

294. Disclosure of spent convictions etc.

Any person who in the course of his official duties has, or at any time has had, the custody of or access to any official record[1], or the information contained therein, is guilty of an offence if, knowing or having reasonable cause to suspect that any specified information[2] he has obtained in the course of those duties is specified information, he discloses it to another person otherwise than in the course of those duties[3], and is liable on summary conviction to a fine not exceeding level 4 on the standard scale[4].

Proceedings for such an offence may not be instituted except by or on behalf of the Director of Public Prosecutions[5]. In such proceedings it is a defence for the accused to show that the disclosure was made (1) to the rehabilitated person[6] or to another person at the express request of the rehabilitated person; or (2) to a person whom he reasonably believed to be the rehabilitated person or to another person at the express request of a person whom he reasonably believed to be the rehabilitated person[7].

The Secretary of State may by order[8] make such provision as appears to him to be appropriate for excepting the disclosure of specified information derived from an official record from the above provisions[9] in such cases or classes of case as may be specified in the order[10].

1 For the meaning of 'official record' see para 287 note 2 ante.

2 For the meaning of 'specified information' see para 287 note 1 ante.

3 Information sent to Interpol, Paris is specified information, but the disclosure of convictions is in the course of official duties because transmission of such information is an obligation accepted by the United Kingdom in the suppression of international crime: *X v Metropolitan Police Comr* [1985] 1 All ER 890, [1985] 1 WLR 420.

4 Rehabilitation of Offenders Act 1974 s 9 (2), (6) (amended by the Criminal Justice Act 1982 ss 38, 46). For the meaning of 'the standard scale' see para 808 post.

5 Rehabilitation of Offenders Act 1974 s 9 (8). As to the effect of this limitation see para 639 post.
6 For the meaning of 'rehabilitated person' see para 1567 post.
7 Rehabilitation of Offenders Act 1974 s 9 (3).
8 As to orders generally under the Rehabilitation of Offenders Act 1974 see para 1570 post.
9 Ie ibid s 9 (2): see supra.
10 Ibid s 9 (5). At the date at which this volume states the law no such order had been made.

295. Disclosure of information. Under a number of statutes the unauthorised disclosure of information obtained by public officers[1] in the exercise of any power conferred or duty imposed by or under the statute or for the purposes of any functions under the statute is an offence[2].

1 For the meaning of 'public officer' see para 282 note 1 ante.
2 Such offences are dealt with under the appropriate titles of this work. As to disclosure of information by a member of the Serious Fraud Office see para 655 post.

(iv) Offences by Particular Officers

296. Persons engaged in the business of the Post Office. If a person engaged in the business of the Post Office[1]:

(1) secretes[2] a postal packet[3] in course of transmission by post[4], he is guilty of an offence and liable on conviction on indictment to imprisonment for a term not exceeding seven years, or on summary conviction to imprisonment for a term not exceeding six months or a fine not exceeding the prescribed sum, or to both[5];

(2) contrary to his duty, opens or procures or suffers to be opened, or wilfully detains or delays, or procures or suffers to be detained or delayed, any such postal packet, he is guilty of an offence and liable on conviction on indictment to imprisonment for a term not exceeding two years or a fine, or to both, or on summary conviction to imprisonment for a term not exceeding six months or a fine not exceeding the prescribed sum, or to both[6];

(3) grants or issues any money order[7] with a fraudulent intent[8], he commits an offence and is liable on conviction on indictment to imprisonment for a term not exceeding seven years[9];

(4) having official duties connected with the Post Office or acting on its behalf, contrary to his duty, discloses, or in any way makes known or intercepts the contents or any part of the contents of any telegraphic messages or any message entrusted to the Post Office for the purposes of transmission, he is guilty of an offence and liable on conviction on indictment to imprisonment for a term not exceeding 12 months, or on summary conviction to imprisonment for a term not exceeding six months or a fine not exceeding the prescribed sum, or to both[10].

1 Ie the authority established under the Post Office Act 1969 s 6 (as amended): see POST OFFICE vol 36 para 601.
2 For the meaning of 'secreting' see *R v Wynn* (1849) 2 Car & Kir 859, CCR (Post Office employee putting unopened letters in water closet to cover up error; secreting letters); *R v Poynton* (1862) Le & Ca 247 (letter kept in a postman's pocket was secreted).
3 'Postal packet' means a letter, postcard, reply postcard, newspaper, printed packet, sample packet, or parcel, and every packet or article transmissible by post, and includes a telegram: Post Office Act 1953 s 87 (1).
4 As to when a postal packet is in course of transmission by post see ibid s 87 (2) and POST OFFICE vol 36 para 788 note 3. A test letter is a postal packet in course of transmission by post: *Hood v Smith* (1933) 150 LT 477, DC.

5 Post Office Act 1953 s 57 (amended by the Theft Act 1968 ss 33 (1), (3), 36 (2), (3), Sch 2 Pt I paras 1, 7, Sch 3 Pt I; the Post Office Act 1969 ss 76, 88, 139, Sch 4 paras 1, 2 (1); the Criminal Damage Act 1971 s 11 (8), Schedule Pt II); Magistrates' Courts Act 1980 ss 17, 32 (1), Sch 1 para 22 (c). See para 804 post. For the meaning of 'the prescribed sum' see para 807 post. As to the admissibility of statutory declarations in evidence see para 1114 post.

6 Post Office Act 1953 s 58 (1) (amended by the Theft Act 1968 s 33 (1), Sch 2 Pt I paras 1, 6; the Post Office Act 1969 ss 76, 88, 139, Sch 4 paras 1, 2 (1)); Criminal Law Act 1967 s 1; Magistrates' Courts Act 1980 ss 17, 32 (1), Sch 1 para 22 (d). See para 804 post. As to the admissibility of statutory declarations in evidence see para 1114 post; and as to the punishment on summary conviction of Post Office officials for negligence, drunkenness or other misconduct see the Post Office Act 1953 s 59 and POST OFFICE vol 36 para 788.

Nothing in s 58 (1) (as so amended) extends to the opening, detaining or delaying of a postal packet returned for want of a true direction, or returned by reason that the person to whom it is directed has refused it, or has refused or neglected to pay the postage thereof, or that the packet cannot for any other reason be delivered, or to the opening, detaining or delaying of a postal packet under the authority of the 1953 Act or in obedience to a warrant issued by the Secretary of State under the Interception of Communications Act 1985 s 2 (see para 271 ante): Post Office Act 1953 s 58 (1) proviso (amended by the Interception of Communications Act 1985 s 11 (2)).

7 For these purposes, 'money order' includes a postal order: Post Office Act 1969 ss 76, 88, 139, Sch 4 para 2 (9).

8 If any person engaged in the business of the Post Office reissues a money order previously paid, he is deemed to have issued the order with a fraudulent intent for these purposes: Post Office Act 1953 s 22 (2) (amended by the Post Office Act 1969 ss 76, 88, 139, Sch 4 paras 1, 2 (1)).

9 Post Office Act 1953 s 22 (amended by the Theft Act 1968 s 33 (1), Sch 1 Pt I; the Post Office Act 1969 ss 76, 88, 139, Sch 4 paras 1, 2 (1)); Criminal Law Act 1967 s 1.

10 Telegraph Act 1868 s 20 (amended by the Post Office Act 1969 ss 76, 137 (1), Sch 4 Pt II, Sch 8 Pt I); Criminal Law Act 1967 s 1; Magistrates' Courts Act 1980 ss 17, 32 (1), Sch 1 para 6. See para 804 post. If any person in the employment of the Post Office (1) wilfully or negligently omits or delays to transmit or deliver any message; or (2) by any wilful or negligent act or omission prevents or delays the transmission or delivery of any message; or (3) improperly divulges to any person the purport of any message, he is guilty of an offence and liable on summary conviction to a fine not exceeding level 3 on the standard scale: Telegraph Act 1863 s 45 (amended by the Post Office Act 1969 s 76, Sch 4 para 4 (a); the Criminal Justice Act 1982 ss 38, 46; the Telecommunications Act 1984 s 109 (1), Sch 4 para 4) and see TELECOMMUNICATIONS vol 45 para 404. For the meaning of 'the standard scale' see para 808 post. In any proceedings against a person in respect of an offence under the Telegraph Act 1863 s 45 (as so amended) or the Telegraph Act 1868 s 20 (as amended: see supra), it is a defence for him to prove that the act constituting the offence was done in obedience to a warrant issued by the Secretary of State under the Interception of Communications Act 1985 s 2 (see para 271 ante) or in pursuance of a requirement imposed by the Commissioner under s 8 (3) (see para 280 ante): Post Office Act 1969 s 77, Sch 5 para 5 (1) (amended by the Telecommunications Act 1984 s 109 (6), Sch 7 Pt I; the Interception of Communications Act 1985 s 11 (3)).

297. Persons engaged in the running of a public telecommunication system.

A person[1] engaged in the running of a public telecommunication system[2] who otherwise than in the course of his duty intentionally discloses to any person (1) the contents of any message which has been intercepted in the course of its transmission by means of that system; or (2) any information concerning the use made of telecommunication services[3] provided for any other person by means of that system, is guilty of an offence and liable on conviction on indictment to a fine, or on summary conviction to a fine not exceeding the statutory maximum[4].

1 Where a body corporate is guilty of an offence under the Telecommunications Act 1984 and that offence is proved to have been committed with the consent or connivance of, or to be attributable to any neglect on the part of, any director, manager, secretary or other similar officer of the body corporate or any person who was purporting to act in any such capacity, he, as well as the body corporate, is guilty of that offence and is liable to be proceeded against and punished accordingly: Telecommunications Act 1984 s 102.

2 For the meaning of 'public telecommunication system' see para 270 note 3 ante.

3 For the meaning of 'telecommunication services' see TELECOMMUNICATIONS vol 45 para 301.
4 Telecommunications Act 1984 s 45 (1), (4) (substituted by the Interception of Communications Act 1985 s 11 (1), Sch 2). For the meaning of 'the statutory maximum' see para 806 post. As to general restrictions on disclosure of information see the Telecommunications Act 1984 s 101 and TELECOMMUNICATIONS vol 45 para 353.
  Section 45 (1) (as so substituted) does not, however, apply to (1) any disclosure which is made for the prevention or detection of crime or for the purposes of any criminal proceedings; (2) any disclosure or matter falling within s 45 (1) (a) (as so substituted: see text head (1) supra) which is made in obedience to a warrant issued under the Interception of Communications Act 1985 s 2 (see para 271 ante) or in pursuance of a requirement imposed by the Commissioner under s 8 (3) (see para 280 ante); (3) any disclosure of matter falling within the Telecommunications Act 1984 s 45 (1) (b) (as so substituted) (see text head (2) supra) which is made in the interests of national security or in pursuance of the order of a court: s 45 (2) (amended by the Interception of Communications Act 1985 Sch 2). For the purposes of the Telecommunications Act 1984 s 45 (2) (c) (as so substituted) (see head (3) supra), a certificate signed by a Minister of the Crown who is a member of the Cabinet, or by the Attorney General or the Lord Advocate, certifying that a disclosure was made in the interests of national security is conclusive evidence of that fact; and a document purporting to be such a certificate must be received in evidence and is deemed to be such a certificate unless the contrary is proved: s 45 (3) (substituted by the Interception of Communications Act 1985 Sch 2).

298. Sheriffs. If a person being a sheriff, under-sheriff, bailiff, or sheriff's officer (1) lets go at large a prisoner who is not bailable; or (2) is guilty of an offence against, or breach of, the Sheriffs Act 1887[1], he is guilty of an offence and liable on conviction on indictment to imprisonment for a term not exceeding one year and a fine, or, if he is unable to pay a fine, to imprisonment for a term not exceeding three years[2].

1 As to sheriffs see SHERIFFS.
2 Sheriffs Act 1887 s 29 (1) (amended by the Criminal Law Act 1967 ss 1, 10 (2), Sch 3 Pt III; the Local Government Act 1972 s 272 (1), Sch 30). Proceedings must be commenced within two years after the alleged offence was committed: Sheriffs Act 1887 s 29 (7). He is also punishable summarily by the High Court or the Crown Court as for contempt (s 29 (3) (amended by the Courts Act 1971 s 56 (4), Sch 11 Pt IV)); proceedings must be taken before the end of the next sitting of the court (Sheriffs Act 1887 s 29 (7)). See further SHERIFFS vol 42 para 1155. As to contempt see CONTEMPT.

(8) OFFENCES RELATING TO THE ADMINISTRATION OF JUSTICE

(i) Perjury and Offences akin to Perjury

A. PERJURY

299. Meaning of 'perjury'. If any person lawfully sworn[1] as a witness[2] or as an interpreter in a judicial proceeding[3] wilfully[4] makes a statement[5], material[6] in that proceeding, which he knows to be false or does not believe to be true[7], he is guilty of perjury and liable on conviction on indictment to imprisonment for a term not exceeding seven years or a fine, or to both[8].

1 For the meaning of 'lawfully sworn' see para 300 post.
2 A person who is not a competent witness, but is sworn by mistake, cannot be indicted for perjury: *R v Clegg* (1868) 19 LT 47. As to competence of witnesses in criminal proceedings see para 1166 post.
3 For the meaning of 'judicial proceeding' and as to statements which must be treated as made in a judicial proceeding see para 301 post.
4 The statement must be made deliberately and not inadvertently or by mistake: *R v Millward* [1985] QB 519, 80 Cr App Rep 280, CA. See also 1 Hawk PC c 27 (4) s 2; *R v Mawbey* (1796) 6 Term Rep

619; *R v Stolady* (1859) 1 F & F 518. Cf *R v London* (1871) 24 LT 232, CCR. The prosecution does not have to prove that the witness knew or believed the statement to be material: *R v Millward* supra. Duress may negative wilfulness: see *R v Hudson, R v Taylor* [1971] 2 QB 202, 56 Cr App Rep 1, CA and para 24 ante.

5　An expression of opinion, if not genuinely held, can found a charge of perjury: *R v Pedley* (1784) 1 Leach 325 per Lord Mansfield; *R v Schlesinger* (1847) 10 QB 670. Cf *R v Crespigny* (1795) 1 Esp 280 per Kenyon CJ (perjury cannot be assigned on evidence stating the opinion of the witness as to the construction of a deed).

6　As to material statements see para 302 post.

7　Swearing to a fact without knowing at the time whether it was true or false has been held to be perjury: see *R v Mawbey* (1796) 6 Term Rep 619 at 637. It seems that it is sufficient if the person does not believe the statement to be true, even if, in fact, it is true: 1 Hawk PC c 27 (4) s 6; 3 Co Inst 166; *Ockley and Whitlesbyes Case* (1622) Palm 294; *Allen v Westley* (1629) Het 97; *R v Rider* (1986) 83 Cr App Rep 207, CA.

8　Perjury Act 1911 s 1 (1); Criminal Justice Act 1948 s 1 (1), (2). Offences under the Perjury Act 1911 s 1 may not be tried summarily: Magistrates' Courts Act 1980 ss 17, 32 (1), Sch 1 para 14 (a). See *R v Simmonds* (1969) 53 Cr App Rep 488 at 489, CA ('perjury is a very serious offence . . . and . . . attracts a severe penalty'); *R v Davies* [1974] Crim LR 613, CA; *R v Shamji* (1989) Times, 21 December, CA (save in a most exceptional case, a custodial sentence should be imposed for perjury). An action does not lie for damages for injury suffered by conviction upon perjured evidence: *Hargreaves v Bretherton* [1959] 1 QB 45, [1958] 3 All ER 122. A child who wilfully gives unsworn false evidence is liable to punishment on summary conviction: see para 1179 note 2 post. A person who aids, abets etc perjury may be proceeded against as if he were a principal: see para 307 post. As to false written statements tendered in evidence in criminal proceedings see para 306 post; and as to false statements on oath made otherwise than in a judicial proceeding see para 303 post. A person, whether a British subject or not, who, in sworn evidence before the European Court, makes any statement which he knows to be false or does not believe to be true is guilty of an offence and may be proceeded against and punished in England and Wales as for an offence against the Perjury Act 1911 s 1 (1): European Communities Act 1972 s 11 (1) (a). See EUROPEAN COMMUNITIES vol 51 para 3·33.

300. Meaning of 'lawfully sworn'.　The forms and ceremonies used in administering an oath[1] are immaterial[2], if the court or person before whom the oath is taken has power to administer an oath for the purpose of verifying the statement in question[3], and if the oath has been administered in a form and with ceremonies which the person taking the oath has accepted without objection, or has declared to be binding on him[4].

1　'Oath' includes 'affirmation' and 'declaration' and the expression 'swear' includes 'affirm' and 'declare': Perjury Act 1911 s 15 (2) (amended by the Criminal Justice Act 1967 s 10 (2), Sch 3 Pt III; the Administration of Justice Act 1977 ss 8 (3), 32 (4), Sch 5 Pt III).

Any person who objects to being sworn is permitted to make his solemn affirmation instead of taking an oath: Oaths Act 1978 s 5 (1). Section 5 (1) applies in relation to a person to whom it is not reasonably practicable without inconvenience or delay to administer an oath in the manner appropriate to his religious beliefs as it applies in relation to a person objecting to be sworn: s 5 (2). A person who may be permitted under s 5 (2) to make his solemn affirmation may also be required to do so: s 5 (3). A solemn affirmation is of the same force and effect as an oath: s 5 (4).

2　Ie for the purposes of the Perjury Act 1911.

3　Every court, judge, justice, officer, commissioner, arbitrator or other person having by law or by consent of parties authority to hear, receive, and examine evidence, is empowered to administer an oath to all such witnesses as are legally called before them: see the Evidence Act 1851 s 16 and EVIDENCE vol 17 para 268.

4　Perjury Act 1911 s 15 (1). See also *R v Shaw* (1911) 104 LT 112, CCA (justices sitting at informal meeting not authorised by statute; no authority to administer oath; accused not lawfully sworn); *R v Wheeler* [1917] 1 KB 283, 12 Cr App Rep 159, CA (accused giving evidence on oath in mitigation of sentence after pleading guilty; accused lawfully sworn); and see para 299 note 2 ante.

301. Statements made in judicial proceedings.　A judicial proceeding includes a proceeding before any court, tribunal or person having by law power to hear, receive and examine evidence on oath[1].

Where a statement made for the purposes of a judicial proceeding is not made before the tribunal itself, but is made on oath before a person authorised by law to administer an oath to the person who makes the statement, and to record or authenticate the statement, it is to be treated[2] as having been made in a judicial proceeding[3].

A statement made by a person lawfully sworn in England for the purposes of a judicial proceeding (1) in another part of Her Majesty's dominions[4]; or (2) in a British tribunal lawfully constituted in any place by sea or land outside Her Majesty's dominions; or (3) in a tribunal of any foreign state, is to be treated as a statement made in a judicial proceeding in England[5].

Except where otherwise provided[6], where, for the purposes of a judicial proceeding in England, a person is lawfully sworn under statutory authority (a) in any other part of Her Majesty's dominions; or (b) before a British tribunal or a British officer in a foreign country, or within the Admiralty jurisdiction[7], a statement made by such person so sworn is to be treated as having been made in the judicial proceeding in England for the purposes of which it was made[8].

1 Perjury Act 1911 s 1 (2). Special Commissioners sitting to hear an income tax appeal constitute a tribunal: *R v Hood-Barrs* [1943] 1 KB 455, 29 Cr App Rep 55, CCA. An action brought against a fictitious person on a fictitious claim may constitute a judicial proceeding: *R v Castiglione and Porteous* (1912) 7 Cr App Rep 233, 106 LT 1023, CCA.
2 Ie for the purposes of the Perjury Act 1911 s 1: see para 299 ante.
3 Ibid s 1 (3).
4 For the meaning of 'Her Majesty's dominions' see COMMONWEALTH vol 6 para 803.
5 Perjury Act 1911 s 1 (4). An Order in Council directing that the Evidence (Proceedings in Other Jursidictions) Act 1975 ss 1–3 (assistance by the High Court in obtaining evidence for proceedings in other jurisdictions: see EVIDENCE) shall have effect in relation to international proceedings specified in the Order (see s 6 (1)–(3) and EVIDENCE vol 17 para 326), may direct that the Perjury Act 1911 s 1 (4) shall have effect in relation to international proceedings to which the order applies as it has effect in relation to a judicial proceeding in a tribunal of a foreign state: Evidence (Proceedings in Other Jurisdictions) Act 1975 s 6 (2). An Order in Council has been made extending the provisions of the Perjury Act 1911 to the Court of Justice of the European Communities: see the Evidence (European Court) Order 1976, SI 1976/478, and EUROPEAN COMMUNITIES vol 51 para 2·220.
   A statement made on oath by a witness outside the United Kingdom and given through a television link by virtue of the Criminal Justice Act 1988 s 32 (see para 1169 post) is to be treated for the purposes of the Perjury Act 1911 s 1 as having been made in the proceedings in which it is given in evidence: Criminal Justice Act 1988 s 32 (3).
6 Ie unless the Act of Parliament under which a statement was made otherwise specifically provides.
7 As to the Admiralty jurisdiction see para 625 et seq post and ADMIRALTY vol 1 (1) (Reissue) para 307 et seq.
8 Perjury Act 1911 s 1 (5).

302. Materiality of statement. The question whether a statement which forms the subject of proceedings for perjury was material is a question of law to be determined by the trial court[1].

1 Perjury Act 1911 s 1 (6). The test for materiality is whether a statement might have affected the outcome of the proceedings, not that it would have done: *R v Lavey* (1850) 3 Car & Kir 26 at 30; *R v Millward* [1985] QB 519, 80 Cr App Rep 280, CA; *R v Sweet-Escott* (1971) 55 Cr App Rep 316 disapproved on this point. The prosecution does not have to prove that the witness knew or believed the statement to be material: *R v Millward* supra. A statement may be material, although it relates to a mere circumstance, if it induces the court to believe the substantial part of the witness's evidence (*R v Tyson* (1867) LR 1 CCR 107) or a more material part (Bac Abr, Perjury (A); 1 Hawk PC c 27 (4) s 8). Evidence may be material if it induces the court to admit other material evidence (*R v Phillpotts* (1851) 21 LJMC 18, CCR) even though that evidence was not strictly admissible (*R v Yates* (1841) Car & M 32) or was withdrawn by counsel (*R v Phillpotts* supra; *R v Gibbon* (1862) Le & Ca 109,

CCR). A statement going solely to a witness's credit may be material: see *R v Griepe* (1697) 1 Ld Raym 256; *R v Overton* (1843) 4 QB 83; *R v Baker* [1895] 1 QB 797, CCR (accused's statement as to plea on previous charge); *R v Lavey* supra (plaintiff's denial of ever having been convicted). Evidence on oath by a convicted person in mitigation of sentence is material: *R v Hewitt* (1913) 9 Cr App Rep 192, CCA; *R v Wheeler* [1917] 1 KB 283, CCA. As to material statements see also *R v Courtney* (1856) 7 Cox CC 111 (evidence at coroner's inquest as to deceased's conduct not relevant to cause of death); *R v Mullany* (1865) Le & Ca 593, CCR (accused's denial that his Christian names were those given in a summons for debt). As to immaterial statements see *R v Townsend* (1866) 4 F & F 1089 (evidence of truth of alleged criminal libel; truth irrelevant to charge at common law); *R v Tate* (1871) 12 Cox CC 7 (charge of assault; evidence of adultery by accused's wife). Denial of an agreement void under the Statute of Frauds has been held immaterial: see *R v Benesech* (1796) Peake Add Cas 93; *R v Dunston* (1824) Ry & M 109. Evidence so collateral as to be almost irrelevant is insufficient to found a charge of perjury: see *R v Holden* (1872) 12 Cox CC 166; *R v Atlass* (1844) 1 Cox CC 17; *R v Southwood* (1858) 1 F & F 356.

B. OFFENCES AKIN TO PERJURY

303. False statements on oath made otherwise than in a judicial proceeding. If any person:

(1) being required or authorised by law to make any statement on oath for any purpose[1], and being lawfully sworn[2], otherwise than in a judicial proceeding[3], wilfully makes a statement which is material for that purpose and which he knows to be false or does not believe to be true; or

(2) wilfully uses any false affidavit for the purposes of the Bills of Sale Acts[4],

he is guilty of an offence and liable on conviction on indictment to imprisonment for a term not exceeding seven years or a fine, or to both, or on summary conviction to imprisonment for a term not exceeding six months or a fine not exceeding the prescribed sum, or to both[5].

1 As to false oaths with reference to marriage see the Perjury Act 1911 s 3 (1) (amended by the Criminal Justice Act 1925 s 28 (1); the Magistrates' Courts Act 1980 s 32 (2); the Marriage (Prohibited Degrees of Relationship) Act 1986 s 4); HUSBAND AND WIFE vol 22 para 937 and REGISTRATION vol 39 para 1022.
2 For the meaning of 'lawfully sworn' see para 300 ante.
3 For the meaning of 'judicial proceeding' see para 301 ante.
4 Ie the Bills of Sale Act 1878 as amended by any subsequent enactment: see BILLS OF SALE vol 4 para 601 et seq.
5 Perjury Act 1911 s 2; Criminal Justice Act 1948 s 1 (1), (2); Criminal Law Act 1967 s 1; Magistrates' Courts Act 1980 ss 17, 32 (1), Sch 1 para 14. See para 804 post. For the meaning of 'the prescribed sum' see para 807 post. See *R v Stokes* [1988] Crim LR 110, CA. As to false statements without oath see para 304 post.

304. False statutory declarations and other false statements without oath. If any person knowingly and wilfully makes, otherwise than on oath[1], a statement false in a material particular, and the statement is made:

(1) in a statutory declaration[2]; or

(2) in an abstract, account, balance sheet, book, certificate, declaration, entry, estimate, inventory, notice, report, return, or other document which he is authorised or required to make, attest, or verify, by any statute for the time being in force; or

(3) in any oral declaration or oral answer which he is required to make by, under, or in pursuance of any statute for the time being in force,

he is guilty of an offence and liable on conviction on indictment to imprisonment for a term not exceeding two years or a fine, or to both, or on summary conviction to imprisonment for a term not exceeding six months or a fine not exceeding the prescribed sum, or to both[3].

If any person, in giving any testimony, either orally or in writing, otherwise than on oath, where required to do so by an order under the Evidence (Proceedings in Other Jurisdictions) Act 1975[4], makes a statement which he knows to be false in a material particular or which is false in a material particular and which he does not believe to be true, he is guilty of an offence and liable on conviction on indictment to imprisonment for a term not exceeding two years or a fine, or to both, or on summary conviction to imprisonment for a term not exceeding six months or a fine not exceeding the prescribed sum, or to both[5].

1 For the meaning of 'oath' see para 300 note 1 ante.
2 'Statutory declaration' means a declaration made by virtue of the Statutory Declarations Act 1835, or of any Act, Order in Council, rule or regulation applying or extending its provisions (see EVIDENCE vol 17 para 266): Perjury Act 1911 s 15 (2). A false statement in writing by a personal representative that he has not made any assent or conveyance renders him liable as if the statement had been contained in a statutory declaration: Administration of Estates Act 1925 s 36 (6); and see EXECUTORS vol 17 para 1353.
3 Perjury Act 1911 s 5; Criminal Justice Act 1948 s 1 (2); Criminal Law Act 1967 s 1; Magistrates' Courts Act 1980 ss 17, 32 (1), Sch 1 para 14. See para 804 post. For the meaning of 'the prescribed sum' see para 807 post. As to false statements etc with reference to marriages see the Perjury Act 1911 s 3 (amended by the Criminal Justice Act 1925 s 28 (1); the Magistrates' Courts Act 1980 s 32 (2); the Marriage (Prohibited Degrees of Relationship) Act 1986 s 4); HUSBAND AND WIFE vol 22 para 937 and REGISTRATION vol 39 para 1022. As to false statements etc with reference to births or deaths see the Perjury Act 1911 s 4 (amended by the Magistrates' Courts Act 1980 s 32 (2)) and REGISTRATION vol 39 para 1023. As to false declarations etc relating to professional registration see para 305 post. Statutes under which the making of a false statement for any purpose connected with its subject matter is made punishable are dealt with under the relevant titles in this work. As to the mens rea required in such cases see *Bloomfield v Williams* [1970] RTR 184, DC.
4 Ie an order under the Evidence (Proceedings in Other Jurisdictions) Act 1975 s 2 (orders by the High Court for obtaining evidence for proceedings in other jurisdictions: see EVIDENCE vol 17 para 327).
5 Perjury Act 1911 s 1A (added by the Evidence (Proceedings in Other Jurisdictions) Act 1975 s 8 (1), Sch 1); Magistrates' Courts Act 1980 ss 17, 32 (1), Sch 1 para 14. See para 804 post.

305. False declarations etc relating to professional registration. If any person:

(1) procures or attempts to procure himself to be registered on any register or roll[1] of persons qualified by law to practise any vocation or calling; or

(2) procures or attempts to procure a certificate of the registration of any person on any such register or roll,

by wilfully making or producing or causing to be made or produced, either verbally or in writing, any declaration, certificate, or representation which he knows to be false or fraudulent, he is guilty of an offence and liable on conviction on indictment to imprisonment for a term not exceeding 12 months or a fine, or to both, or on summary conviction to imprisonment for a term not exceeding six months or a fine not exceeding the prescribed sum, or to both[2].

1 Ie kept under or in pursuance of any Act of Parliament for the time being in force.
2 Perjury Act 1911 s 6; Criminal Law Act 1967 s 1; Magistrates' Courts Act 1980 ss 17, 32 (1), Sch 1 para 14. See para 804 post. For the meaning of 'the prescribed sum' see para 807 post.

306. False written statements tendered in evidence in criminal proceedings. If any person in a written statement[1] tendered in evidence in criminal proceedings[2] or in proceedings before a court-martial[3] wilfully makes a statement material[4] in those proceedings which he knows to be false or does not believe to be true, he is guilty of an offence and liable on conviction on indictment to imprisonment for a term not exceeding two years or a fine, or to both[5].

If any person in a written statement tendered in evidence in committal proceedings[6] wilfully makes a statement material[7] in those proceedings which he knows to be false or does not believe to be true, he is guilty of an offence and liable on conviction on indictment to imprisonment for a term not exceeding two years or a fine, or to both[8].

1 The Criminal Justice Act 1967 s 89 applies to written statements made in Scotland or Northern Ireland as well as to written statements made in England and Wales: Criminal Justice Act 1972 s 46 (1).
2 Ie by virtue of the Criminal Justice Act 1967 s 9 (amended by the Courts Act 1971 s 56 (1), Sch 8 Pt II para 49): see para 1113 post.
3 Ie by virtue of the Criminal Justice Act 1967 s 9 (as amended: see note 2 supra) as extended by s 12 or by the Army Act 1955 s 99A (added by the Armed Forces Act 1976 s 11, Sch 5 para 1) or the Air Force Act 1955 s 99A (added by the Armed Forces Act 1976 Sch 5 paras 1, 2). See ROYAL FORCES vol 41 para 401.
4 As to materiality of statements see para 302 ante.
5 Criminal Justice Act 1967 s 89 (1) (amended by the Armed Forces Act 1976 s 22 (5), Sch 9 para 15; the Magistrates' Courts Act 1980 s 154 (3), Sch 9). The Perjury Act 1911 has effect as if the Criminal Justice Act 1967 s 89 (as so amended) were contained in that Act: s 89 (2).
6 Ie under the Magistrates' Courts Act 1980 s 102: see para 832 post.
7 See note 4 supra.
8 Magistrates' Courts Act 1980 s 106 (1). The Perjury Act 1911 has effect as if the Magistrates' Courts Act 1980 s 106 were contained in that Act: s 106 (2).

C.   AIDING, ABETTING AND INCITING

307. Aiders and abettors. Every person who aids, abets, counsels, procures, or suborns[1] another person to commit an offence against the Perjury Act 1911 is liable to be proceeded against, tried and punished as a principal offender[2].

1 At common law subornation of perjury was the procuring of a man to take a false oath amounting to perjury and the actual taking of such oath by that man: 1 Hawk PC 27 (4) s 10; 2 Chitty's Criminal Law (2nd Edn) 317.
2 Perjury Act 1911 s 7 (1). As to aiding and abetting generally see para 43 et seq ante.

308. Incitement. Every person who incites another person to commit an offence against the Perjury Act 1911 is guilty of an offence and liable on conviction on indictment to imprisonment[1] or a fine, or to both, or on summary conviction to imprisonment for a term not exceeding six months or a fine not exceeding the prescribed sum, or to both[2].

1 The term of imprisonment may not exceed two years: see para 1200 post.
2 Perjury Act 1911 s 7 (2) (amended by the Criminal Attempts Act 1981 s 10, Schedule Pt I); Criminal Law Act 1967 s 1; Magistrates' Courts Act 1980 ss 17, 32 (1), Sch 1 para 14. See para 804 post. For the meaning of 'the prescribed sum' see para 807 post. As to incitement generally see para 58 ante.

D.   PROCEDURE

309. Indictment. In an indictment for an offence under the Perjury Act 1911 it is sufficient to set out the substance of the offence charged and before which court or person, if any, the offence was committed, without setting out the proceedings or any part of the proceedings in the course of which the offence was committed and the authority of any court or person before whom the offence was committed[1].

In an indictment for aiding, abetting, counselling, suborning or procuring any other person, or for conspiring with any other person, to commit any offence within the Act, it is sufficient, where such offence has been committed, to allege that offence and then to allege that the accused procured its commission and, where such offence has not been committed, to set forth the substance of the offence charged against the accused without setting forth anything which it is unnecessary to aver in the case of an indictment for such offence[2].

1 Perjury Act 1911 s 12 (1). See *R v Aylesbury Justices, ex p Wisbey* [1965] 1 All ER 602, [1965] 1 WLR 339, DC (particulars necessary in an information charging perjury). As to joinder of accused in a single indictment see para 934 post and *R v Assim* [1966] 2 QB 249 at 255, [1966] 2 All ER 881 at 884, CCA.
2 Perjury Act 1911 s 12 (2) (amended by the Criminal Attempts Act 1981 s 10, Schedule Pt I).

310. Evidence. A person may not be convicted of any offence under the Perjury Act 1911, or of any offence declared by any other Act to be perjury or subornation of perjury or to be punishable as such, solely upon the evidence of one witness as to the falsity of any statement alleged to be false[1]. It is not essential to have more than one witness, however, if there is something else which confirms his testimony[2]. This requirement would appear not to apply where there is a formal admission either made before the trial or on evidence at the trial by the accused that the statement was false[3]. Nor does the requirement apply in the very rare cases where the prosecution proceeds on the basis that the truth or falsity of the statement forms no part of its case[4].

On a prosecution for perjury alleged to have been committed on a trial on indictment or for procuring or suborning the commission of perjury on any such trial, the fact of the former trial is sufficiently proved by the production of a certificate containing the substance and effect, omitting the formal parts, of the indictment and trial, purporting to be signed by the appropriate officer of the Crown Court or other person having the custody of the court records or either's deputy, without proof of the signature or official character of the person appearing to have signed it[5].

There is no bar to the admission in a subsequent prosecution for perjury of evidence given at the first trial directed to establishing a perjury at that trial, even though that evidence, if accepted at the second trial, would lead to the inference that the accused was guilty of the offence of which he was acquitted at the first trial; the doctrine of issue estoppel has no application in criminal proceedings[6].

1 Perjury Act 1911 s 13.
2 *R v Threlfall* (1914) 10 Cr App Rep 112 at 114, CCA. A letter written by the accused contradicting his sworn evidence may be sufficient (*R v Mayhew* (1834) 6 C & P 315; *R v Threlfall* supra), or clear statements made by him directly contrary to his sworn evidence (*R v Hook* (1858) Dears & B 606, CCR; *R v Knill* (1822) 5 B & Ald 929n). Statements in a deposition before a magistrate differing from the accused's evidence at the trial are not in themselves sufficient: *R v Wheatland* (1838) 8 C & P 238; *R v Hughes* (1844) 1 Car & Kir 519; *R v Jackson* (1823) 1 Lew CC 270. As to what constitutes sufficient corroboration of a single witness at common law see *Champney's Case* (1836) 2 Lew CC 258; *R v Parker* (1842) Car & M 639; cf *R v Yates* (1841) Car & M 132.
   As to corroboration generally see para 1140 et seq post.
3 *R v Rider* (1986) 83 Cr App Rep 207, CA; *R v Stokes* [1988] Crim LR 110, CA.
4 *R v Rider* (1986) 83 Cr App Rep 207, CA.

5 Perjury Act 1911 s 14 (amended by the Criminal Law Act 1967 s 10 (2), Sch 3 Pt III; the Courts Act 1971 s 56 (1), Sch 8 Pt I para 2 (1), Table).
6 *DPP v Humphrys* [1977] AC 1, 63 Cr App Rep 95, HL. See further para 974 note 1 post.

311. Offences committed abroad. Where an offence against the Perjury Act 1911 or any offence punishable under any other Act as perjury or subornation of perjury is committed in any place either on sea or land outside the United Kingdom, the offender may be proceeded against, indicted, tried and punished in England[1].

1 Perjury Act 1911 s 8 (amended by the Criminal Law Act 1967 s 10 (2), Sch 3 Pt III). As to jurisdiction generally see para 616 et seq post.

312. Liability apart from the Perjury Act 1911. Where the making of a false statement is not only an offence under the Perjury Act 1911 but also by virtue of some other Act is a corrupt practice[1] or subjects the offender to any forfeiture or disqualification or to any penalty other than imprisonment or fine, the offender's liability under the Perjury Act 1911 is in addition to, and not in substitution for, his liability under such other Act[2]. In general[3], where the making of a false statement is made punishable by any other Act on summary conviction, proceedings may be taken either under such other Act or under the Perjury Act 1911[4].

1 See generally ELECTIONS.
2 Perjury Act 1911 s 16 (1).
3 Where an offence is by any Act passed before the Perjury Act 1911, as originally enacted, made punishable only on summary conviction, it remains only so punishable: s 16 (3) proviso.
4 Ibid s 16 (3). Acts under which the making of a false statement for any purpose connected with its subject matter is made punishable are dealt with under the appropriate titles in this work.

(ii) Offences relating to Juries

313. Embracery. Embracery is an indictable offence at common law and is committed by any person[1] who attempts to corrupt, influence, or instruct a jury or to incline a jury to favour one side more than the other, whether by money, promises, letters, threats, or persuasion, or by any means other than by evidence and arguments in open court at the trial[2]. To give jurors money after their verdict constitutes embracery, even though there was no previous promise to pay[3]. The offence of embracery is obsolescent: conduct covered by it is more appropriately dealt with as conspiracy to pervert the course of justice or contempt of court[4].

It is also an indictable offence at common law for any person by improper means to procure himself or others to be sworn on a jury for the purpose of giving a verdict favourable to one of the parties[5] or for any person to induce a juror not to appear[6].

The above offences are punishable by imprisonment and fine at the discretion of the court[7].

1 The offence may be committed as well by one of the jury as by a party to the cause or any person acting on his behalf: 1 Hawk PC c 27 (8) ss 1–4.
2 1 Hawk PC c 27 (8); *Jepps v Tunbridge and Wiseman* (1611) Moore KB 815. The offence of embracery was not abolished by the Criminal Law Act 1967: see s 13 (1) (a).
3 1 Hawk PC c 27 (8) s 3.

4 *R v Owen* [1976] 3 All ER 239, 63 Cr App Rep 199, CA.
5 1 Hawk PC c 27 (8) s 4: *R v Opie and Dodge* (1670) 1 Wms Saund 300k; *Hussey v Cooke* (1621) Hob 294. It is an offence under the Juries Act 1974 for a person, knowing he is ineligible or disqualified for jury service, to serve on a jury: see s 20 (5) (d) and JURIES vol 26 para 609. As to personating a juror see para 314 post.
6 1 Hawk PC c 27 (8) s 5; *Hussey v Cooke* (1621) Hob 294.
7 See paras 1200, 1232 post. A sentence of immediate imprisonment is appropriate unless the circumstances are wholly exceptional: *R v Owen* [1976] 3 All ER 239, 63 Cr App Rep 199, CA.

314. Personating a juror. It is an indictable offence at common law to personate a juror[1]. It is not necessary to prove that the accused had any corrupt motive or any specific intention to deceive other than that which is involved in going into the jury box and taking the oath in another's name[1]. It is no answer that he did not know he was doing wrong[1]. Where a person who is not called as a juror personates a juror and sits in his place, the trial is a nullity[2]. The offence is punishable by fine and imprisonment at the discretion of the court[3].

1 *R v Clark* (1918) 82 JP 295. Such personation is also contempt of court: see CONTEMPT vol 9 para 28.
2 *R v Wakefield* [1918] 1 KB 216, 13 Cr App Rep 56, CCA; and see JURIES vol 26 para 633.
3 See paras 1200, 1232 post.

(iii) Obstructing the Course of Justice

315. Perversion of the course of justice. It is an indictable offence at common law to pervert the course of justice[1]. The offence is otherwise referred to as obstructing the course of justice, obstructing or interfering with the administration of justice and defeating the due course or the ends of justice[2]. The offence consists of an act, a series of acts[3] or conduct which has the tendency[4] and is intended[5] to pervert the course[6] of justice[7]. The course of justice may be perverted by discontinuing a criminal prosecution in return for payment[8]; bringing a false charge against a person[9]; making false statements to police officers investigating an offence[10]; doing an act calculated to assist another to avoid arrest[11]; improperly interfering with a witness[12]; a witness deliberately absenting himself from proceedings in return for payment[13]; producing fabricated evidence[14]; publishing articles calculated to interfere with the course of justice[15]; improperly aborting a prosecution[16]; frustrating a statutory procedure which would or could otherwise lead to a prosecution[17].

The offence is punishable by fine and imprisonment at the discretion of the court[18].

1 *R v Vreones* [1891] 1 QB 360, CCR; *R v Rowell* [1978] 1 All ER 665, 65 Cr App Rep 174, CA; *R v Machin* [1980] 3 All ER 151, 71 Cr App Rep 166, CA; *R v Selvage and Morgan* [1982] 1 All ER 96, 73 Cr App Rep 333, CA; *R v Bassi* [1985] Crim LR 671, CA.
2 *R v Machin* [1980] 3 All ER 151, 71 Cr App Rep 166, CA.
3 *R v Rowell* [1978] 1 All ER 665, 65 Cr App Rep 174, CA.
4 The gist of the offence is conduct which may lead and is intended to lead to a miscarriage of justice whether or not a miscarriage actually occurs. Proof of intention alone is not sufficient: *R v Machin* [1980] 3 All ER 151, 71 Cr App Rep 166, CA; *R v Bassi* [1985] Crim LR 671, CA. There must be evidence that what the accused has done is enough for there to be a risk, without further action by him, that injustice will result. In other words, there must be a possibility that what he has done without more might lead to injustice: *R v Murray* [1982] 2 All ER 225, 75 Cr App Rep 58, CA. The prosecution does not have to prove that the tendency in fact materialised: *R v Machin* supra; *R v Murray* supra.

5 The Crown has to prove that each of the accused intended by the act or acts that the course of justice should be interfered with; it cannot be right to say that the only intent which has to be proved is the intent to do the act which may or may not be held to have a tendency to pervert: *R v Selvage and Morgan* [1982] 1 All ER 96, 73 Cr App Rep 333, CA, relying on *R v Vreones* [1891] 1 QB 360, CCR; *R v Machin* [1980] 3 All ER 151, 71 Cr App Rep 166, CA.

6 A course of justice must have been embarked on in the sense that proceedings of some kind are in being or are imminent or investigations which could or might have brought proceedings about are in progress. *R v Vreones* [1891] 1 QB 360, CCR is on the very boundary of the offence: *R v Selvage and Morgan* [1982] 1 All ER 96, 73 Cr App Rep 333, CA (the mere act of altering records kept at DVLC, Swansea, of endorsements on licences cannot by itself be a perversion of the course of justice, because no proceedings, investigations etc imminent or in progress).

7 The offence was at one time thought to consist of only a conspiracy, attempt or incitement to pervert the course of justice. It is now clear that there is a substantive offence: *R v Vreones* [1891] 1 QB 360, CCR; *R v Grimes* [1968] 3 All ER 179n; *R v Panayiotou* [1973] 1 WLR 1032, 57 Cr App Rep 762, CA, approving *R v Grimes* supra; *R v Andrews* [1973] QB 422, 58 Cr App Rep 254, CA; *R v Rowell* [1978] 1 All ER 665, 65 Cr App Rep 174, CA; *R v Thomas* [1979] QB 326; sub nom *R v Thomas, R v Ferguson* (1978) 68 Cr App Rep 275, CA; *R v Machin* [1980] 3 All ER 151, 71 Cr App Rep 166, CA; *R v Selvage and Morgan* [1982] 1 All ER 96, 73 Cr App Rep 333, CA; *R v Murray* [1982] 2 All ER 225, 75 Cr App Rep 58, CA; *R v Bassi* [1985] Crim LR 671, CA. As to attempts see para 71 et seq ante; as to conspiracy see para 59 et seq ante; and as to incitement see para 58 ante. As to related offences see para 299 et seq ante (perjury); the Criminal Law Act 1967 s 4 (as amended) (see para 51 ante), s 5 (see paras 319, 323 post); and para 313 ante (embracery).

8 *R v Kranze and Duffy* (1913) 77 JP Jo 316 (conspiracy to pervert the course of public justice: see now also the Criminal Law Act 1977 s 1 (as amended) and para 59 ante).

9 The older cases all concern conspiracies, but proof of a conspiracy is not essential: see note 7 supra. A single-handed attempt to pervert the course of justice is an offence known to the law; the use of the word 'attempt' is misleading (see note 7 supra): *R v Rowell* [1978] 1 All ER 665, 65 Cr App Rep 174, CA. As to the conspiracy cases see *R v Rispal* (1762) 3 Burr 1320; *R v Spragg* (1760) 2 Burr 993; *R v M'Daniel* (1755) 19 State Tr 745 at 808. See also *Conteh v R* [1956] AC 158, [1956] 2 WLR 277, PC (the gist of the offence of conspiring to accuse another of a crime is that the accusation should be false to the knowledge of the conspirators). If, however, the object of the conspiracy is to extort money, the truth or falsity of the charge is immaterial: *R v Hollingberry* (1825) 4 B & C 329; *R v Jacobs, Tidmarsh and Partridge* (1845) 1 Cox CC 173. As to blackmail see para 566 post. It is no defence to a charge of conspiring to accuse another of a crime that the indictment or other proceedings preferred or intended to be preferred was or were insufficient, or that the court had no jurisdiction or that the charge was not a grave one: 1 Hawk PC c 27 (5) s 3; *R v Rispal* (1762) 3 Burr 1320. See also *Pippet v Hearn* (1822) 5 B & Ald 634. The making of false statements suggesting the commission by T of serious offences, leading to T's arrest and remand in custody for five days was such an offence: *R v Rowell* supra, relying on *R v Bailey* [1956] NI 15; *Kerr v Hill* 1936 2 JC 71, Court of Justiciary.

10 *R v Field* [1965] 1 QB 402 at 417, [1964] 3 All ER 269 at 279, CCA; *Tsang Ping-Nam v R* [1981] 1 WLR 1462, 74 Cr App Rep 139, PC. It is immaterial that proceedings have not been commenced: *R v Sharpe* [1938] 1 All ER 48, 26 Cr App Rep 122, CCA. As to the statutory offence of causing wasteful employment of the police see para 323 post.

11 *R v Thomas* [1979] QB 326, 68 Cr App Rep 275, CA (appellants provided S with the registration numbers of unmarked police cars so that he could avoid being arrested; interference did not have to be dishonest, corrupt or threatening; cf the requirements in relation to improperly interfering with a witness: see note 12 infra).

12 At one time this was thought to be a separate indictable offence, but it is now clear that it is an example of the offence of perverting the course of justice: *R v Grimes* [1968] 3 All ER 179n; *R v Kellett* [1976] QB 372, [1975] 3 All ER 468, CA (threat to bring proceedings for slander; intention to deter witness from giving evidence in divorce suit). The offence is not necessarily committed by a person who tried to persuade a false witness, or even a witness believed to be false, to speak the truth or to refrain from giving false evidence: *R v Kellett* supra. However proper the end, the means must not be improper. The offence is committed if a person meddles by unlawful means, such as threats or bribery or force. The decision will depend upon all the circumstances of the case: *R v Kellett* supra. The exercise of a legal right or the threat of exercising it does not excuse interfering with the administration of justice by deterring a witness from giving evidence which he wishes to give before he has given it: *R v Kellett* supra (right here was to sue for slander). There may be a material difference if the person interfered with is a litigant and not a witness: *R v Kellett* supra; *Webster v Bakewell RDC* [1916] 1 Ch 300; *A-G v Times Newspapers Ltd* [1974] AC 273 at 319, [1973] 3 All ER 54 at 80, HL per Lord Simon of Glaisdale. 'Witness' includes a potential witness: *R v Grimes* supra. The

question whether a person is to be treated as a witness can only be answered by having regard to the proceedings contemplated. Where a person has made a statement to the police and the decision not to prosecute will be made by the police, that person, although the complainant, is to be regarded as a witness: *R v Panayiotou* [1973] 3 All ER 112, 57 Cr App Rep 762, CA. See also *R v Lady Lawley* (1731) 2 Stra 904; *R v Loughran* (1839) 1 Craw & D 79; *Shaw v Shaw* (1861) 31 LJPM & A 35; *Re Hooley, Rucker's Case* (1898) 79 LT 306; *R v Greenberg* (1919) 121 LT 288, CCA; *R v Steventon* (1802) 2 East 362; *R v Hamp* (1852) 6 Cox CC 167.

13 *R v Bassi* [1985] Crim LR 671, CA.

14 *R v Vreones* [1891] 1 QB 360, CCR; *R v Andrews* [1973] QB 422, 57 Cr App Rep 254, CA (appellant offered in consideration for a reward to make a false statement; incitement to pervert the course of justice charged; producing false evidence to pervert the course of justice is a substantive offence); *R v Machin* [1980] 3 All ER 151, 71 Cr App Rep 166, CA; *R v Murray* [1982] 2 All ER 225, 75 Cr App Rep 58, CA (interfering with second blood sample; did have tendency to pervert the course of justice since it was a practical certainty that that information would be communicated either to the solicitor or to the prosecuting authority or to the police). See also *Omealy v Newell* (1807) 8 East 364 (making use of false affidavit). An agreement to produce evidence known to be false is an indictable conspiracy: *R v Mawbey* (1796) 6 Term Rep 619 at 635.

15 *R v Tibbits and Windust* [1902] 1 KB 77 at 90, CCR (newspaper articles about character and conduct of accused published during course of trial).

16 *R v Coxhead* [1986] RTR 411, CA (there is a prosecutorial discretion which may be properly exercised in favour of non-prosecution in trivial cases such as riding a bicycle without lights, failing to switch on car sidelights when leaving a car park at night, failure to sign a driving licence or to have the road fund licence on display when fallen to floor. There is no such discretion in the most serious of cases, such as murder. It is a matter for the jury to decide where in the scale a particular case fell; police sergeant exercised discretion in favour of son of station inspector who had heart condition that sergeant thought would be affected by prosecution of son; conviction not unsafe or unsatisfactory).

17 *R v Britton* [1973] RTR 502, CA (successful use of the 'hip-flask' defence to the Road Safety Act 1967 s 1 (1) (repealed); conviction of attempting to defeat the course of justice upheld). See now the Road Traffic Act 1988 s 4 and ROAD TRAFFIC. The statutory formulation of the 'hip-flask' defence appears to exclude the possibility of such a conviction now: see *R v Britton* supra at 507.

18 See paras 1200, 1232 post; *R v Field* [1965] 1 QB 402 at 417, [1964] 3 All ER 269 at 279, CCA.

316. Unlawful disposal of a dead body. It is an indictable offence at common law to prevent the burial of a dead body or to dispose of a dead body in order to prevent an inquest being held upon it[1]. The offence is punishable by fine and imprisonment at the discretion of the court[2].

1 See CORONERS vol 9 para 1048; CREMATION AND BURIAL vol 10 para 1018.

2 See paras 1200, 1232 post.

317. Acknowledging recognisance etc in name of another. Any person who, without lawful authority or excuse[1], acknowledges in the name of any other person any recognisance[2] or bail or any cognovit actionem[3] or judgment or any deed or other instrument before any court, judge or other person lawfully authorised in that behalf[4] is guilty of an offence and liable on conviction on indictment to imprisonment for a term not exceeding seven years[5].

1 Proof of lawful authority or excuse lies on the accused: Forgery Act 1861 s 34. See also para 1064 post.

2 'Any recognisance' refers to a valid recognisance into which a person may lawfully be required to enter and a recognisance imposing an obligation for which there is no authority is not within ibid s 34: *R v McKenzie* [1971] 1 All ER 729, 55 Cr App Rep 294.

3 Ie a written instrument by which the plaintiff acknowledges the justness of the accused's claim. It has been superseded by orders of the court made by consent and is now obsolete.

4 This includes a commissioner for oaths: see the Commissioners for Oaths Act 1889 s 1 (2) and EVIDENCE vol 17 para 268.

5 Forgery Act 1861 s 34; Criminal Justice Act 1948 s 1 (1); Criminal Law Act 1967 s (5) (a).

(iv) Offences relating to Witnesses at Public Inquiries

318. Threatening etc witnesses at public inquiries. Every person who threatens or in any way punishes, damnifies or injures or attempts to punish, damnify or injure any person for having given evidence upon any inquiry[1], or on account of the evidence which he has given upon any such inquiry, unless such evidence was given in bad faith, is guilty of an offence and liable on summary conviction to imprisonment for a term not exceeding three months or a fine not exceeding level 3 on the standard scale[2]. The offender may also be ordered to pay compensation to the person injured[3].

1 'Inquiry' means any inquiry held under the authority of any Royal Commission or by any committee of either House of Parliament, or pursuant to any statutory authority, whether the evidence of such inquiry is or is not given on oath, but does not include any inquiry by any court of justice: Witnesses (Public Inquiries) Protection Act 1892 s 1.
2 Ibid ss 2, 3 (amended by the Criminal Justice Act 1982 ss 38, 46; the Criminal Law Act 1977 ss 15 (3) (d), 65 (5), Sch 13); Criminal Law Act 1967 s 1. For the meaning of 'the standard scale' see para 808 post.
3 See the Witnesses (Public Inquiries) Protection Act 1892 ss 4, 5.

(9) OFFENCES RELATING TO THE EXECUTION OF CIVIL OR CRIMINAL PROCESS

(i) Concealing Offences

319. Concealing offences. Where a person has committed an arrestable offence[1], any other person who, knowing or believing that the offence or some other arrestable offence has been committed, and that he has information which might be of material assistance in securing the prosecution or conviction of an offender for it, accepts or agrees to accept for not disclosing that information any consideration other than the making good of loss or injury caused by the offence, or the making of reasonable compensation for that loss or injury, is guilty of an offence and liable on conviction on indictment to imprisonment for a term not exceeding two years, or on summary conviction[2] to imprisonment for a term not exceeding six months or a fine not exceeding the prescribed sum, or to both[3].

Proceedings for such an offence may not be instituted except by or with the consent of the Director of Public Prosecutions[4].

1 In the Criminal Law Act 1967 s 5 'arrestable offence' has the meaning assigned to it by the Police and Criminal Evidence Act 1984 s 24 (as amended): Criminal Law Act 1967 s 4 (1A) (added by the Police and Criminal Evidence Act 1984 s 19 (1), Sch 6 para 17). See para 703 post.
2 Ie where the offence to which it relates is triable either way.
3 Criminal Law Act 1967 s 5 (1); Magistrates' Courts Act 1980 ss 17, 32 (1), Sch 1 para 26 (b). See para 804 post. For the meaning of 'the prescribed sum' see para 807 post.
    The compounding of an offence other than treason is not an offence otherwise than under the Criminal Law Act 1967 s 5: s 5 (5). Nor is misprision an offence except in the case of treason (see para 83 ante), the common law offence of misprision of felony having ceased to exist with the abolition (see para 42 ante) of the distinctions between felony and misdemeanour. However, as to advertising rewards on certain terms for the return of lost or stolen goods see para 564 post.
4 Ibid s 5 (3). As to the effect of this limitation see para 639 post.

(ii) Offences relating to Constables

320. Assaulting or obstructing a constable. Any person who assaults a constable[1] in the execution of his duty, or a person assisting a constable in the execution of his duty, is guilty of an offence and liable on summary conviction to imprisonment for a term not exceeding six months or a fine not exceeding level 5 on the standard scale, or to both[2]. A person does not commit such an offence, however, unless the constable was acting in the execution of his duty, that is to say that he was acting strictly within the limits of his powers and legal duty[3]. The justification of self-defence is available to an accused charged with assaulting a constable where the assault occurred in resisting an act on the constable's part which was technically an assault[4].

Any person who resists or wilfully obstructs[5] a constable in the execution of his duty, or a person assisting a constable in the execution of his duty, is guilty of an offence and liable on summary conviction to imprisonment for a term not exceeding one month or a fine not exceeding level 3 on the standard scale, or to both[6].

1 As to the office of constable see POLICE vol 36 para 264. The constable's appointment need not be proved: *Berryman v Wise* (1791) 4 Term Rep 366. Every prison officer while acting as such has all the powers, authority, protection and privileges of a constable: Prison Act 1952 s 8. See also *Pointing v Wilson* [1927] 1 KB 382. A constable or any other person required or authorised by virtue of the Mental Health Act 1983 to take any person into custody, or to convey or detain any person, has, for the purposes of taking him into custody or conveying or detaining him, all the powers, authorities, protection and privileges which a constable has within the area for which he acts as constable: s 137 (2). See MENTAL HEALTH. Knowledge that the person assaulted was a police officer is not necessary; the offence consists in assaulting a constable being in the execution of his duty, not in knowing him to be in the execution of his duty: *R v Forbes and Webb* (1865) 10 Cox CC 362; *R v Maxwell and Clanchy* (1909) 2 Cr App Rep 26, CCA; *Albert v Lavin* [1982] AC 546, 74 Cr App Rep 150, HL; see also *McBride v Turnock* [1964] Crim LR 456, DC. As to an assault where the accused genuinely and reasonably believed the person assaulted was not a constable see *Kenlin v Gardiner* [1967] 2 QB 510, [1966] 3 All ER 931, DC: *R v Mark, Brown and Mark* [1961] Crim LR 173. If the accused is unaware that the person he assaulted was a constable, but believes that he is acting in self-defence or defence of others, he should have a defence: see *R v Williams (Gladstone)* [1987] 3 All ER 411, 78 Cr App Rep 276, CA.

2 Police Act 1964 s 51 (1) (amended by the Criminal Law Act 1977 ss 15, 30, Sch 1; the Criminal Justice Act 1982 s 46). For the meaning of 'the standard scale' see para 808 post. As to the offence committed by a person who at the time of committing or being arrested for an offence under the Police Act 1964 s 51 (1) (as so amended) has in his possession a firearm or imitation firearm see para 232 ante; and as to assault with intent to resist arrest see para 321 post.

3 Where an accused is charged with assaulting an officer in the execution of his duty, the onus is on the prosecution to prove that the officer was so acting: *Chapman v DPP* (1988) 89 Cr App Rep 190, CA. Where an arrest is made by a police officer for assault in the execution of his duty, arising from the arrest of a third party, it is an essential for the later arrest to be lawful that the prior arrest was lawful; and where, therefore, justices are not told of the reason for the prior arrest, it is not open to them to find that the officer was acting in the execution of his duty: *Riley v DPP* (1989) Times, 13 December, DC.

The cardinal principle is that that which is officially done must be done in accordance with the law: *Arthur Yates & Co (Property) Ltd v Vegetable Seeds Committee* (1945) 72 CLR 37 at 66 (Aust HC) per Sir John Latham CJ. Thus, if an arrest is not lawful, a constable is not acting in the execution of his duty: *Wershof v Metropolitan Police Comr* [1978] 3 All ER 540, 68 Cr App Rep 82; *Grant v Gorman* [1980] RTR 119, DC; *G v Chief Superintendent of Police, Stroud* (1986) 86 Cr App Rep 92, DC; *Nicholas v Parsonage* [1987] Crim LR 474, DC. Where a person is arrested upon a warrant, the fact that the constable making the arrest is not in possession of the warrant at the time does not necessarily mean he is not acting in the execution of his duty: *Jones v Kelsey* (1987) 85 Cr App Rep 226, DC. If a search is not lawful, a constable is not acting in the execution of his duty: *Lindley v Rutter* [1981] QB 128, 72 Cr App Rep 1, DC; *Brazil v Chief Constable of Surrey* [1983] 3 All ER 537, 77 Cr App Rep 237, DC. As to a constable's power of arrest see paras 705, 707 post; as to powers of search and entry see para 668 et seq post; and as to the duties of a constable see *Rice v Connolly* [1966] 2 QB 414 at 419, [1966] 2

All ER 649 at 651, DC per Lord Parker CJ ('. . . it is part of the obligations and duties of a police constable to take all steps which appear to him necessary for keeping the peace, for preventing crime and for protecting property from criminal injury. There is no exhaustive definition of the powers and obligations of the police, but they are at least those, and they further include the duty to detect crime and to bring an offender to justice'). See also *Coffin v Smith* (1980) 71 Cr App Rep 221, DC (a constable's duty is to be a keeper of the peace and to take all necessary steps with that in view; acting in execution of duty because constable thought presence would assist in the keeping of the peace). Cf *R v Waterfield* [1964] 1 QB 164, [1963] 3 All ER 659, CCA. As to a constable's duty to prevent, and otherwise deal with, a breach of the peace, see *Duncan v Jones* [1936] 1 KB 218; *Thomas v Sawkins* [1935] 2 KB 249, DC; *McGowan v Chief Constable of Kingston upon Hull* [1968] Crim LR 34, DC; *King v Hodges* [1974] Crim LR 424, DC; *Hickman v O'Dwyer* [1979] Crim LR 309, DC (constable must apprehend a breach of the peace otherwise action not justified); *Read v Jones* (1983) 77 Cr App Rep 246, DC; *R v Howell* [1982] QB 416, 73 Cr App Rep 31, CA. A constable who becomes a trespasser is no longer acting in execution of his duty: *Davis v Lisle* [1936] 2 KB 434, [1936] 2 All ER 213; *McArdle v Wallace* [1964] Crim LR 467, DC; *Robson v Hallett* [1967] 2 QB 939, 51 Cr App Rep 307, DC; *Pamplin v Fraser* [1981] RTR 494, DC; *McLorie v Oxford* [1982] QB 1290, 74 Cr App Rep 137, DC. See also *R v Thornley* (1980) 72 Cr App Rep 302, CA (constable on premises at invitation of occupier entitled to remain on premises for reasonable time to investigate complaint; still acting in execution of duty despite request by occupier to leave).

Unless expressly authorised by statute, a constable has no power, short of arrest, of detaining a person for questioning: *Rice v Connolly* supra. As to powers to stop and search see para 660 et seq post; and as to powers of arrest see para 693 et seq post. A constable who detains a person against his will without arresting him is acting outside the course of his duty (*Ludlow v Burgess* (1971) 75 Cr App Rep 227n, DC); but not every trivial interference with a person's liberty amounts to a course of conduct sufficient to take him outside the course of a constable's duty (*Donnelly v Jackman* [1970] 1 All ER 987, [1970] 1 WLR 562, DC; *Squires v Botwright* [1972] Crim LR 106, DC; *Daniel v Morrison* (1979) 70 Cr App Rep 142, DC; *Pedro v Diss* [1981] 2 All ER 59, 72 Cr App Rep 193, DC; *Bentley v Brudzinski* (1982) 75 Cr App Rep 217, DC (whether detention by constable short of arrest is unlawful is a question of fact depending on the circumstances which precede it and the degree of force used); *McBean v Parker* [1983] Crim LR 399, DC; *Collins v Wilcock* [1984] 3 All ER 374, 79 Cr App Rep 229, DC (the word 'detaining' can be used in more than one sense. It is a commonplace that one person may request another to stop and speak to him; whether the latter stops willingly or unwillingly, the first person may be said to be 'stopping and detaining' the latter. There is nothing unlawful in such an act. If a police officer so 'stops and detains' another person, he commits no unlawful act, despite the fact that his uniform may give his request certain authority and so render it more likely to be complied with; the police force officer cannot use force; that would be a battery); *Weight v Long* [1986] Crim LR 746, DC. As to whether a constable is in the execution of his duty when detaining a car after arresting the driver, particularly as part of the duty to ensure that the car is properly looked after, see *Stunt v Bolton* [1972] RTR 435, DC; *Liepins v Spearman* [1986] RTR 24, DC.

If a constable is exceeding his authority, an assault is not within the Police Act 1964 s 51 (1) (as amended: see note 2 supra): see *R v Marsden* (1868) LR 1 CCR 131; *R v Mabel* (1840) 9 C & P 474; *Chapman v DPP* (1988) 89 Cr App Rep 190, DC.

Where reasonably necessary for the protection of life or property, a constable has the power to direct other persons to disobey traffic regulations; in giving such a direction in such circumstances he is acting in the execution of his duty and a refusal to obey constitutes a wilful obstruction: *Johnson v Phillips* [1975] 3 All ER 682, DC.

4 *Kenlin v Gardiner* [1967] 2 QB 510, [1966] 3 All ER 931, DC; *R v Williams (Gladstone)* [1987] 3 All ER 411, 78 Cr App Rep 276, CA. As to assault in self-defence and defence of others see para 498 post. See also *R v Fennell* [1971] 1 QB 428, [1970] 3 All ER 215, CA.

5 *Bastable v Little* [1907] 1 KB 59; *Betts v Stevens* [1910] 1 KB 1; *Duncan v Jones* [1936] 1 KB 218, DC; *Piddington v Bates* [1960] 3 All ER 660, [1961] 1 WLR 162, DC; *Tynan v Balmer* [1967] 1 QB 91, [1966] 2 All ER 133, DC; *Stunt v Bolton* [1972] RTR 435, DC. To 'obstruct' is to do any act which makes it more difficult for the police to carry out their duty: *Hinchcliffe v Sheldon* [1955] 3 All ER 406, [1955] 1 WLR 1207, DC; *Rice v Connolly* [1966] 1 QB 414 at 419, [1966] 2 All ER 649 at 651, DC; *Dibble v Ingleton* [1972] 1 QB 480 at 487, [1972] 1 All ER 275 at 278, DC; *Ricketts v Cox* (1981) 74 Cr App Rep 298, DC (whether silence can amount to obstruction must be approached in a realistic manner); *Moore v Green* [1983] 1 All ER 663, DC; *Lewis v Cox* [1985] QB 509, 80 Cr App Rep 1, DC; *Bennett v Bale* [1986] Crim LR 404, DC. The obstruction must be wilful, that is to say deliberate and intentional, to come within the Police Act 1964 s 51 (3) (amended by the Criminal Justice Act 1982 s 46): *Rice v Connolly* supra; *Willmott v Atack* [1977] QB 498, [1976] 3 All ER 794, DC (need for criminal intention to obstruct constable); *Hills v Ellis* [1983] QB 680, 76 Cr App Rep 217, DC; *Lewis*

v Cox supra (act need not be 'aimed at' or 'hostile to' the police; accused must intend conduct to prevent police from carrying out their duty or to make it more difficult to do so). Motive is irrelevant: *Hills v Ellis* supra; *Lewis v Cox* supra.

6 Police Act 1964 s 51 (3) (as amended: see note 5 supra). As to a constable's powers of arrest for such an offence see para 707 post; as to aiding and abetting such an offence see *Smith v Reynolds, Smith v Hancock, Smith v Lowe* [1986] Crim LR 559, DC and para 44 ante; and as to obstructing an officer in or near a prohibited place within the meaning of the Official Secrets Acts 1911 and 1920 see para 256 ante.

321. Assault with intent to resist or prevent arrest. Any person who assaults another with intent to resist or prevent the lawful apprehension[1] or detainer of himself or of any other person is guilty of an offence and liable on conviction on indictment to imprisonment for a term not exceeding two years, or on summary conviction to imprisonment for a term not exceeding six months or a fine not exceeding the prescribed sum, or to both[2].

1 As to powers of arrest see para 693 et seq post.
2 Offences against the Person Act 1861 s 38 (amended by the Police Act 1964 s 64 (3), Sch 10 Pt I; the Criminal Law Act 1967 s 10 (2), Sch 3 Pt III); Criminal Justice Act 1948 s 1 (2); Criminal Law Act 1967 s 1; Magistrates' Courts Act 1980 ss 17, 32 (1), Sch 1 para 5 (g). See para 804 post. For the meaning of 'the prescribed sum' see para 807 post. An assault with intent to resist arrest is not part of the offence for which the victim is attempting to arrest the offender and should be visited with a consecutive sentence: *R v Wellington* (1988) 10 Cr App Rep (S) 384, CA. As to the offence committed by a person who at the time of committing or being arrested for an offence under the Offences against the Person Act 1861 s 38 (as so amended) has in his possession a firearm or imitation firearm see para 232 ante. A person charged with an offence under s 38 (as so amended) may be convicted of common assault (see para 488 post): *R v Wilson* [1955] 1 All ER 744, 39 Cr App Rep 12, CCA. As to assaulting a constable see para 320 ante.

322. Refusing to assist a constable. A person commits an indictable offence at common law if he refuses, without lawful excuse, to assist a constable who sees a breach of the peace committed or who is assaulted or obstructed when making an arrest, and who, where there is reasonable necessity to do so, calls upon that person to assist him[1]. It is no defence that the assistance, if given, would have been useless[2].

The offence is punishable by imprisonment and fine at the discretion of the court[3].

1 *R v Brown* (1841) Car & M 314; *R v Sherlock* (1866) LR 1 CCR 20.
2 *R v Brown* (1841) Car & M 314.
3 See paras 1200, 1232 post.

323. False reports causing wasteful employment of police. Any person who causes any wasteful employment of the police by knowingly making to any person a false report tending to show that an offence has been committed, or to give rise to apprehension for the safety of any persons or property, or tending to show that he has information material to any police inquiry, is liable on summary conviction to imprisonment for a term not exceeding six months or a fine not exceeding level 4 on the standard scale, or to both[1].

Proceedings for such an offence may be instituted only by or with the consent of the Director of Public Prosecutions[2].

1 Criminal Law Act 1967 s 5 (2) (amended by the Criminal Justice Act 1982 ss 38, 46). For the meaning of 'the standard scale' see para 808 post.
2 Criminal Law Act 1967 s 5 (3). As to the effect of this limitation see para 639 post.

(iii) Offences relating to Prisons

324. Breach of prison. Breach of prison is an indictable offence at common law and is committed by a person who, while in lawful custody for any cause, whether civil or criminal, escapes by the use of force[1] from the prison or other place in which he is confined[2]. Breach of prison is punishable by fine and imprisonment at the discretion of the court[3].

The offence of breach of prison is an offence in itself. It is therefore no answer to a charge that the accused was not guilty of the principal offence; the outcome of the principal offence cannot affect the lawfulness of the custody[4].

1   To constitute the offence there must be an actual breaking; merely getting over walls or passing through a door is an escape (see para 325 post) and not a breach of prison (2 Hawk PC c 18 s 9) but the breaking need not be intentional (see *R v Haswell* (1821) Russ & Ry 458, CCR, where accidental breaking in the course of escape was held to be a breach of prison). If a prisoner breaks out to save his life, as in a case of fire, he is not guilty of prison breach, unless he himself started the fire: 1 Hale PC 611. An escape without the use of force constitutes the common law offence of escape: see para 325 post. On an indictment for prison breach it is, it seems, open to the jury to find an alternative verdict of escape when no force is used: see the Criminal Law Act 1967 s 6 (3) and para 1029 post.

2   2 Hawk PC c 18 ss 1, 4. If an accused has been convicted of escape (see para 325 post), it appears that he cannot subsequently be prosecuted for breach of prison on the same facts (*R v Miles* (1890) 24 QBD 423, 6 TLR 186, CCR); but, where an escape involving the use of force has been dealt with and punished as a matter of prison discipline, this is not a bar to an indictment for breach of prison (*R v Hogan, R v Tomkins* [1960] 2 QB 513, 44 Cr App Rep 255, CCA). An accused may be convicted of breach of prison before being tried for the offence for which he was committed (2 Co Inst 592) but not, it seems, after being tried on indictment and acquitted (1 Hale PC 611); see, however, *R v Frascati* (1981) 73 Cr App Rep 28 at 30, CA, where the latter proposition is doubted. Where examining justices dismiss a charge, the accused may subsequently be convicted of breach of prison committed while he was on remand: *R v Waters* (1873) 12 Cox CC 390. It has been doubted whether there can be a conviction for breach of prison where no offence has in fact been committed by anyone (2 Hawk PC c 18 s 15; 1 Hale PC 610) but see text to note 4 infra. It is immaterial whether the prisoner is actually within a gaol, or is only in the constable's house or a lock-up provided that he is lawfully imprisoned or restrained of his liberty: 2 Hawk PC c 18 s 21.

3   See paras 1200, 1232 post. At common law, if the prisoner was detained on a charge of treason or felony, whether he had been convicted or not, breach of prison amounted to a felony; if he was detained on a lesser charge, to a misdemeanour: see 2 Hawk PC c 18. As to the abolition of the distinction between felonies and misdemeanours see para 42 ante.

4   *R v Frascati* (1981) 73 Cr App Rep 28, CA.

325. Escape. Escape is an indictable offence at common law, punishable by imprisonment and fine at the discretion of the court[1], and is committed by a person (1) who, without the use of force[2], escapes from prison either when serving a sentence or when awaiting trial[3]; or (2) who, having a person in his lawful custody[4], whether before or after conviction, voluntarily or negligently permits him to escape[5].

It is also an indictable offence at common law, similarly punishable, for a person to escape from lawful custody on a criminal charge, without using force but by artifice or similar means[6].

It is an indictable offence at common law, punishable by imprisonment and fine at the discretion of the court, to aid a person to escape from lawful custody on civil process[7].

The offence of escape from lawful custody is an offence in itself. It is, therefore, no answer to a charge that the accused was not guilty of the principal offence; the outcome of the principal offence cannot affect the lawfulness of the custody[8].

1 See paras 1200, 1232 post.
2 A person who escapes from prison, using force, commits breach of prison: see para 324 ante. On an indictment for escape it is, it seems, open to the jury to find an alternative verdict of prison breach where force is used: see the Criminal Law Act 1967 s 6 (3) and para 1029 post.
3 *R v Hinds* (1957) 41 Cr App Rep 143, CCA.
4 A private person who lawfully arrests another must hand him over to a constable; thereupon his liability ceases: see 1 Hale PC 595; 2 Hawk PC c 20. As to a private person's power of arrest see paras 705, 706 post. To render an officer liable for escape, there must have been actual and lawful arrest; if the arrest was of a nature that the prisoner would have been justified in escaping, the officer is justified in releasing him: 2 Hawk PC c 19 ss 2, 3. The lawfulness of the arrest must be proved by the prosecution; there is no presumption that the arrest was lawful: *Dillon v R* [1982] AC 484, 74 Cr App Rep 274, PC (offence charged was that of a constable negligently permitting a prisoner to escape out of his custody: see infra).
5 An officer who voluntarily permits a prisoner guilty of treason to escape is, it seems, guilty of treason; in other cases he was formerly guilty of being an accessory after the fact of felony or for a misdemeanour according to whether the prisoner was guilty of a felony or misdemeanour; with the abolition of the distinction between felonies and misdemeanours (see para 42 ante), he is, it seems, guilty of an offence punishable by imprisonment and fine at the discretion of the court; and see 1 Hale PC 593; 2 Hawk PC c 19 ss 22, 25. An officer who negligently permits his prisoner to escape is liable to be fined: 1 Hale PC 603; 2 Hawk PC c 19 ss 31, 33. A private person is punishable in the same way as the officer: 1 Hale PC 595; 2 Hawk PC c 20. At common law, a head gaoler could be fined when an escape took place through the negligence or voluntary act of his subordinate: 2 Hawk PC c 19 ss 27, 29. At common law an officer is entitled to recapture a prisoner who has escaped by reason of his negligence and, if he does so upon fresh pursuit and without losing sight of him, the officer is not to be convicted of escape, since the law will assume that the prisoner never left his custody: 1 Hale PC 602; 2 Hawk PC c 19 ss 6, 13. As to the recapture of a prisoner by an officer who voluntarily permits his escape see 2 Hawk PC c 19 s 12. As to the statutory offence committed by a person who aids a prisoner to escape from prison see para 327 post.
6 2 Hawk PC c 17 s 5. See also *R v Timmis* [1976] Crim LR 129.
7 *R v Allan* (1841) Car & M 295. See also 2 Co Inst 589.
8 *R v Frascati* (1981) 73 Cr App Rep 28, CA.

326. Rescue. Rescue[1] at common law consists in the forcible freeing of a person from lawful arrest or custody[2], whether that of a constable or other officer or that of a private person; but, where a person is freed from private custody, the rescuer incurs criminal liability only if he knew the person freed was in custody on a criminal charge[3]. In general, rescue is punishable on indictment by a fine and imprisonment at the discretion of the court[4]; but a person who rescues a prisoner he knows to be guilty of treason is himself guilty of treason[5].

1 Or 'rescous': see Co Litt 160b.
2 See, however, *R v Almey and Spencer* (1857) 3 Jur NS 750.
3 2 Hawk PC c 21 ss 1, 2; 1 Hale PC 606. The person freed must be tried before the rescuer is tried for the rescue: see 1 Hale PC 598, 599. As to the offence committed by a prisoner who escapes by the use of force see para 324 ante; and as to the statutory offence committed by a person who aids a prisoner to escape see para 327 post. See also paras 94, 95 ante.
4 See paras 1200, 1232 post. A rescuer was formerly guilty of a felony or a misdemeanour, according to whether the person rescued was in custody for felony or misdemeanour: see 2 Hawk PC c 21 s 1; 1 Hale PC 606; Murder Act 1751 s 9 (repealed). As to the abolition of the distinction between felonies and misdemeanours see para 42 ante.
5 2 Hawk PC c 21 s 7. See also *Bensted's Case* (1640) Cro Car 583 (knowledge that the prisoner was guilty of treason held not to be essential).

327. Aiding a prisoner to escape. Any person who (1) aids any prisoner in escaping or attempting to escape from a prison[1]; or (2) with intent to facilitate the escape of any prisoner, conveys any thing[2] into a prison or to a prisoner or places any thing anywhere outside a prison with a view to its coming into the possession of a prisoner is guilty of an offence and liable on conviction on indictment to imprisonment for a term not exceeding five years[3].

1 'Prison' does not include a naval, military or air force prison: Prison Act 1952 s 53 (1). As to escape from a naval, military or air force prison see ROYAL FORCES vol 41 para 421. Subject to such adaptations and modifications as may be specified in rules made by the Secretary of State, s 39 applies to remand centres and young offender institutions: see s 43 (5) (substituted by the Criminal Justice Act 1982 s 11; amended by the Criminal Justice Act 1988 s 123 (6), Sch 8 para 1) and PRISONS vol 37 para 1213. An escape by a remand prisoner from a police station yard or from a magistrates' court is not an escape from prison: *Nicoll v Catron* (1985) 81 Cr App Rep 339, DC; *R v Moss and Harte* (1986) 82 Cr App Rep 116, CA. An escape by a prisoner working outside the prison is an escape from prison: *R v Abbott* [1956] Crim LR 337.

2 Cf *R v Payne* (1866) LR 1 CCR 27 ('any article or thing' under the Prison Act 1865 s 37 (repealed) included a crowbar).

3 Prison Act 1952 s 39 (amended by the Criminal Justice Act 1961 ss 22 (1), 41 (1), Sch 4); Criminal Law Act 1967 s 12 (5) (a). As to forcibly freeing a prisoner see para 326 ante. A person commits a summary offence if, contrary to the regulations of a prison, he brings in etc any alcoholic drink or tobacco or brings in or takes out etc any letter or other article: see the Prison Act 1952 ss 40, 41 (as amended) and PRISONS vol 37 para 1176. As to the application of ss 40, 41 (as amended) to remand centres and young offender institutions see s 43 (5) (as substituted: see note 1 supra) and note 1 supra. A person who knowingly compels, persuades, incites or assists a child or young person to whom the Child Care Act 1980 s 16 (1) applies to become or continue to be absent commits a summary offence: see s 16 (4) and INFANTS vol 24 para 778.

328. Harbouring an escaped prisoner. If any person (1) knowingly harbours a person who has escaped from a prison or other institution[1] or who, having been sentenced in any part of the United Kingdom or in any of the Channel Islands or the Isle of Man to imprisonment or detention, is otherwise unlawfully at large; or (2) gives to any such person any assistance with intent to prevent, hinder or interfere with his being taken into custody, he is guilty of an offence and liable on conviction on indictment to imprisonment for a term not exceeding two years or a fine, or to both, or on summary conviction to imprisonment for a term not exceeding six months or a fine not exceeding the prescribed sum, or to both[2].

1 Ie an institution to which the Prison Act 1952 s 39 (amended by the Criminal Justice Act 1961 ss 22 (1), 41 (1), Sch 4) applies: see para 327 note 1 ante.

2 Criminal Justice Act 1961 s 22 (2) (amended by the Magistrates' Courts Act 1980 s 32 (2)). For the meaning of 'the prescribed sum' see para 807 post; and for the meaning of 'United Kingdom' see para 86 note 1 ante. Some positive act to provide shelter must be proved in order to establish that an escaped prisoner has been harboured: *Darch v Weight* [1984] 2 All ER 245, 79 Cr App Rep 40, DC.

(iv) Offences relating to Mental Patients

329. Assisting absence without leave or escape and harbouring. Where any person induces or knowingly assists another person who is liable to be detained in a hospital within the meaning of the Mental Health Act 1983[1] or is subject to guardianship under the Act[2] to absent himself without leave, he is guilty of an offence[3].

Where any person induces or knowingly assists another person who is in legal custody[4] to escape from such custody, he is guilty of an offence[5].

Where any person knowingly harbours such a patient who is absent without leave, or is otherwise at large and liable to be retaken under the Act[6], or gives him any assistance with intent to prevent, hinder or interfere with his being taken into custody or returned to the hospital or other place where he ought to be, he is guilty of an offence[7].

A person guilty of any such offence is liable on conviction on indictment to imprisonment for a term not exceeding two years or a fine, or to both, or on summary conviction to imprisonment for a term not exceeding six months or a fine not exceeding the statutory maximum, or to both[8].

1 Ie the Mental Health Act 1983 Pt II (ss 2–34): see MENTAL HEALTH.
2 See MENTAL HEALTH.
3 Mental Health Act 1983 s 128 (1).
4 Ie by virtue of ibid s 137: see MENTAL HEALTH.
5 Ibid s 128 (2).
6 See MENTAL HEALTH.
7 Ibid s 128 (3).
8 Ibid s 128 (4). For the meaning of 'the statutory maximum' see para 806 post.

(v) Pound Breach

330. Pound breach. Pound breach is an indictable offence at common law[1] consisting in the removal of goods impounded upon a distress for rent[2] or damage feasant[3] from the pound against the will of the person impounding them[4] or in forcibly releasing cattle or other animals lawfully placed in a proper pound or forcibly damaging or destroying the pound with that object[5]. The offence is punishable by imprisonment and fine at the discretion of the court[6].

1 See Co Litt 47b; 2 Hawk PC c 10 s 56; *R v Butterfield* (1893) 17 Cox CC 598.
2 As to distress for rent see DISTRESS vol 13 para 205 et seq.
3 The common law right to seize and detain any animal by way of distress damage feasant has been abolished: see the Animals Act 1971 s 7 (1). The common law remedy of distress damage feasant is, however, still available in the case of goods.
4 *R v Butterfield* (1893) 17 Cox CC 598 (pound breach of cattle distrained for rent); *R v Nicholson and King* (1901) 65 JP 298. It is doubtful whether an indictment lies in such a case if a person retakes his own goods which have been unlawfully seized: *R v Walshe* (1876) IR 10 CL 511; *R v Knight* (1908) 1 Cr App Rep 186.
5 *R v Bradshaw* (1835) 7 C & P 233; *Green v Duckett* (1883) 11 QBD 275, DC. In certain circumstances, a person who releases or attempts to release an animal seized for the purposes of being impounded commits a summary offence: see ANIMALS vol 2 para 438.
6 See paras 1200, 1232 post.

(10) OFFENCES AFFECTING THE PROPERTY AND PREROGATIVE OF THE CROWN

(i) Offences relating to Government Marks and Stores

331. Offences relating to government marks. If any person with intent to conceal Her Majesty's property in any stores[1] takes out, destroys or obliterates, wholly or in part, any mark appropriated for use in or on Her Majesty's stores to denote Her Majesty's property in stores so marked[2] or any mark whatsoever denoting the property of Her Majesty in any stores, he is guilty of an offence and liable on conviction on indictment to imprisonment for a term not exceeding seven years, or on summary conviction to imprisonment for a term not exceeding six months or a fine not exceeding the prescribed sum, or to both[3].

If any person without lawful authority, proof of which authority lies on the accused, applies any mark so appropriated in or on any stores, he is guilty of an offence and liable on conviction on indictment to imprisonment for a term not exceeding two years[4].

1 For these purposes, 'stores' includes all goods and chattels, and any single store or article: Public Stores Act 1875 s 2. The Public Stores Act 1875 applies to all stores under the care, superintendence or control of a Secretary of State or any public department or office or any person in Her Majesty's service; and 'Her Majesty's stores' means such stores: s 3 (amended by the Defence (Transfer of Functions) (No 1) Order 1964, SI 1964/488, art 2, Sch 1 Pt II).

2 See the Public Stores Act 1875 s 4, Sch 1.

3 Ibid s 5; Criminal Justice Act 1948 s 1 (1); Criminal Law Act 1967 s 12 (5) (a); Magistrates' Courts Act 1980 ss 17, 32 (1), Sch 1 para 8. See para 804 post. For the meaning of 'the prescribed sum' see para 807 post. The Public Stores Act 1875 s 5 does not apply to stores issued as regimental or air force necessaries: see s 13 (amended by the Territorial Army and Militia Act 1921 s 4 (1), Sch 2; the Air Force (Adaptation of Enactments) (No 2) Order 1918, SR & O 1918/548 (amended by SI 1964/488). A constable of the metropolitan police force, and any constable, if deputed by a public department, may, within the limits for which he is constable, stop, search, and detain any vessel, boat or vehicle in or on which there is reason to suspect that any of Her Majesty's stores stolen or unlawfully obtained may be found, or any person reasonably suspected of having or conveying in any manner any of Her Majesty's stores stolen or unlawfully obtained: Public Stores Act 1875 s 6. For these purposes, a constable is deemed to be deputed by a public department if he is deputed by writing signed by the person who is the head of such department, or who is authorised to sign documents on behalf of such department: s 6. As to powers to stop and search see, however, para 660 et seq post; and as to persons appointed to be special constables within any premises in the possession or under the control of British Nuclear Fuels Limited see para 667 note 3 post.

Any person may arrest without warrant anyone who is, or whom he with reasonable cause suspects to be, in the act of committing or attempting to commit an offence under s 5: s 12 (1) (substituted by the Theft Act 1968 s 33 (2), Sch 2 Pt II). As to a constable's power of arrest see, however, para 693 et seq post. If it is made to appear by information on oath before a justice of the peace that there is reasonable cause to believe that any person has in his custody or possession or on his premises any stores in respect of which an offence against the Public Stores Act 1875 s 5 has been committed, the justice may issue a warrant to a constable to search for and seize the stores as in the case of stolen goods (see para 565 post): s 12 (2) (substituted by the Theft Act 1968 s 33 (2), Sch 2 Pt II). As to powers of entry, search and seizure see, however, para 668 et seq post.

4 Public Stores Act 1875 s 4; Criminal Justice Act 1948 s 1 (2); Criminal Law Act 1967 s 1.

332. Prohibition of sweepings etc near dockyards etc. Any person who without permission in writing from a public department or from some person authorised by a public department in that behalf, proof of which permission lies on the accused, gathers or searches for stores[1], or creeps, sweeps or dredges in the sea or any tidal water, within 100 yards from any vessel belonging to Her Majesty or in Her Majesty's service, or from any mooring place or anchoring place appropriated to such vessels, or from any moorings belonging to Her Majesty, or from any of Her Majesty's wharves, or dock victualling or steam factory yards, or within 1,000 yards from any battery or fort used for the practice of artillery either by the Royal Artillery or by volunteer artillery, or in or on any part of the spaces or distances, whether covered with water or not, from time to time marked out as ranges for artillery practice for the use of Her Majesty's ships, or marked out and appropriated for ranges under the provisions of the Artillery Ranges Act 1862 is guilty of an offence and liable on summary conviction to imprisonment for a term not exceeding two months or a fine not exceeding level 1 on the standard scale[2].

1 For the meaning of 'stores' see para 331 note 1 ante.

2 Public Stores Act 1875 s 8 (amended by the Territorial Army and Militia Act 1921 s 4 (1), Sch 2; the Criminal Justice Act 1982 ss 38, 46); Criminal Justice Act 1948 s 1. For the meaning of 'the standard scale' see para 808 post.

References in the Public Stores Act 1875 to ships, vessels or boats or activities or places connected with them are extended to include hovercraft or activities or places connected with hovercraft: see the Hovercraft (Application of Enactments) Order 1972, SI 1972/971 (amended by SI 1982/715; SI 1983/769; SI 1989/1350). The Public Stores Act 1875 s 8 (as so amended) is extended to the air force by the Air Force (Adaptation of Enactments) (No 2) Order 1918, SR & O 1918/548 (amended by SI 1964/488).

(ii) Coinage Offences

333. Making counterfeit coins. If a person[1] makes a counterfeit[2] of a currency note[3] or of a protected coin[4], intending that he or another will pass or tender[5] it as genuine, he is guilty of an offence and liable on conviction on indictment to imprisonment for a term not exceeding ten years or a fine, or to both, or on summary conviction to imprisonment for a term not exceeding six months or a fine not exceeding the statutory maximum, or to both[6].

If a person makes a counterfeit of a currency note or of a protected coin without lawful authority or excuse, he is guilty of an offence and liable on conviction on indictment to imprisonment for a term not exceeding two years or a fine, or to both, or on summary conviction to imprisonment for a term not exceeding six months or a fine not exceeding the statutory maximum, or to both[7].

1 'Person' includes a body of persons corporate or unincorporate: Interpretation Act 1978 s 5, Sch 1.
2 For these purposes, a thing is a counterfeit of a currency note or of a protected coin (1) if it is not a currency note or a protected coin, but resembles a currency note or protected coin, whether on one side only or on both, to such an extent that it is reasonably capable of passing for a currency note or protected coin of that description; or (2) if it is a currency note or protected coin which has been so altered that it is reasonably capable of passing for a currency note or protected coin of some other description: Forgery and Counterfeiting Act 1981 s 28 (1). For these purposes (a) a thing consisting of one side only of a currency note, with or without the addition of other material, is a counterfeit of such a note; (b) a thing consisting (i) of parts of two or more currency notes; or (ii) of parts of a currency note, or of parts of two or more currency notes, with the addition of other material, is capable of being a counterfeit of a currency note: s 28 (2).
3 For these purposes, 'currency note' means (1) any note which (a) has been lawfully issued in England and Wales, Scotland, Northern Ireland or any of the Channel Islands, the Isle of Man or the Republic of Ireland; and (b) is or has been customarily used as money in the country where it was issued; and (c) is payable on demand; or (2) any note which has been lawfully issued in some country other than those mentioned in head (1) (a) supra and is customarily used as money in that country: ibid s 27 (1).
4 For these purposes, 'protected coin' means any coin which is customarily used as money in any country, or is specified in an order made by the Treasury: ibid s 27 (1). The power of the Treasury so to make an order is exercisable by statutory instrument: s 27 (2). A statutory instrument containing such an order must be laid before Parliament after being made: s 27 (3). 'The Treasury' means the Commissioners of Her Majesty's Treasury: Interpretation Act 1978 Sch 1.
  The following coins have been specified for the purposes of the Forgery and Counterfeiting Act 1981 Pt II (ss 14–28): sovereign; half-sovereign; krugerrand; any coin denominated as a fraction of a krugerrand; Maria-Theresa thaler bearing the date of 1780: Forgery and Counterfeiting (Protected Coins) Order 1981, SI 1981/1505, art 2, Schedule.
5 For these purposes, references to passing or tendering a counterfeit of a currency note or a protected coin are not to be construed as confined to passing or tendering it as legal tender: Forgery and Counterfeiting Act 1981 s 28 (3). For the meaning of 'legal tender' see the Coinage Act 1971 s 2 and CONSTITUTIONAL LAW vol 8 para 1019.
6 Forgery and Counterfeiting Act 1981 ss 14 (1), 22 (1), (2) (a), (6) (a). For the meaning of 'the statutory maximum' see para 806 post. As to powers of search, forfeiture etc see para 339 post.
7 Ibid ss 14 (2), 22 (2), (4) (a), (6) (a). As to 'lawful authority or excuse' cf para 167 note 1 ante; paras 504 note 4, 613 note 9 post; HIGHWAYS vol 21 paras 443, 448; NATIONAL HEALTH vol 33 para 661; POST OFFICE vol 36 para 790; ROYAL FORCES vol 41 para 407.

334. Passing, tendering and delivering counterfeit notes and coins. If a person[1] (1) passes or tenders[2] as genuine any thing which is, and which he knows or believes to be, a counterfeit[3] of a currency note[4] or of a protected coin[5]; or (2) delivers to another any thing which is, and which he knows or believes to be, such a counterfeit, intending that the person to whom it is delivered or another will pass or tender it as genuine, he is guilty of an offence and liable on conviction on indictment to imprisonment for a term not exceeding ten years or a fine, or to both, or on summary conviction to imprisonment for a term not exceeding six months or a fine not exceeding the statutory maximum, or to both[6].

If a person delivers to another, without lawful authority or excuse[7], any thing which is, and which he knows or believes to be, a counterfeit of a currency note or of a protected coin, he is guilty of an offence and liable on conviction on indictment to imprisonment for a term not exceeding two years or a fine, or to both, or on summary conviction to imprisonment for a term not exceeding six months or a fine not exceeding the statutory maximum, or to both[8].

1 For the meaning of 'person' see para 333 note 1 ante.
2 As to references to passing or tendering a counterfeit of a currency note or a protected coin see para 333 note 5 ante.
3 For the meaning of 'counterfeit' see para 333 note 2 ante.
4 For the meaning of 'currency note' see para 333 note 3 ante.
5 For the meaning of 'protected coin' see para 333 note 4 ante.
6 Forgery and Counterfeiting Act 1981 ss 15 (1), 22 (1), (2) (b), (6) (a). For the meaning of 'the statutory maximum' see para 806 post. As to powers of search, forfeiture etc see para 339 post.
7 As to 'lawful authority or excuse' see para 333 note 7 ante.
8 Forgery and Counterfeiting Act 1981 ss 15 (2), 22 (3), (4) (b), (6) (a). See also note 6 supra.

335. Custody or control of counterfeit notes and coins. If a person[1] has in his custody or under his control any thing which is, and which he knows or believes to be, a counterfeit[2] of a currency note[3] or of a protected coin[4], intending either to pass or tender[5] it as genuine or to deliver it to another with the intention that he or another will pass or tender it as genuine, he is guilty of an offence and liable on conviction on indictment to imprisonment for a term not exceeding ten years or a fine, or to both, or on summary conviction to imprisonment for a term not exceeding six months or a fine not exceeding the statutory maximum, or to both[6].

If a person has in his custody or under his control, without lawful authority or excuse[7], any thing which is, and which he knows or believes to be, a counterfeit of a currency note or of a protected coin, he is guilty of an offence and liable on conviction on indictment to imprisonment for a term not exceeding two years or a fine, or to both, or on summary conviction to imprisonment for a term not exceeding six months or a fine not exceeding the statutory maximum, or to both[8].

1 For the meaning of 'person' see para 333 note 1 ante.
2 For the meaning of 'counterfeit' see para 333 note 2 ante.
3 For the meaning of 'currency note' see para 333 note 3 ante.
4 For the meaning of 'protected coin' see para 333 note 4 ante.
5 As to references to passing or tendering a counterfeit of a currency note or a protected coin see para 333 note 5 ante.
6 Forgery and Counterfeiting Act 1981 ss 16 (1), 22 (1), (2) (c), (6) (a). For the meaning of 'the statutory maximum' see para 806 post. For the purposes of s 16 (1), (2) (see infra), it is immaterial that a coin or note is not in a fit state to be passed or tendered or that the making or counterfeiting of a coin or note has not been finished or perfected: s 16 (3). As to powers of search, forfeiture etc see para 339 post.

7 As to 'lawful authority or excuse' see para 333 note 7 ante.
8 Forgery and Counterfeiting Act 1981 ss 16 (2), 22 (3), (4) (c), (6) (a). See also note 6 supra.

336. Making, custody or control of counterfeiting materials and implements. If a person[1] makes, or has in his custody or under his control, any thing which he intends to use, or to permit any other person to use, for the purpose of making a counterfeit[2] of a currency note[3] or of a protected coin[4] with the intention that it be passed or tendered[5] as genuine, he is guilty of an offence and liable on conviction on indictment to imprisonment for a term not exceeding ten years or a fine, or to both, or on summary conviction to imprisonment for a term not exceeding six months or a fine not exceeding the statutory maximum, or to both[6].

If a person without lawful authority or excuse[7] makes, or has in his custody or under his control, any thing which, to his knowledge[8], is or has been specially designed or adapted for the making of a counterfeit of a currency note, he is guilty of an offence and liable on conviction on indictment to imprisonment for a term not exceeding two years or a fine, or to both, or on summary conviction to imprisonment for a term not exceeding six months or a fine not exceeding the statutory maximum, or to both[9].

If a person makes, or has in his custody or under his control, any implement which, to his knowledge, is capable of imparting to any thing a resemblance (1) to the whole or part of either side of a protected coin; or (2) to the whole or part of the reverse of the image on either side of a protected coin, he is guilty of an offence and liable on conviction on indictment to imprisonment for a term not exceeding two years or a fine, or to both, or on summary conviction to imprisonment for a term not exceeding six months or a fine not exceeding the statutory maximum, or to both[10]. It is, however, a defence for the accused to show (a) that he made the implement or, as the case may be, had it in his custody or under his control, with the written consent of the Treasury[11]; or (b) that he had lawful authority otherwise than by virtue of head (a) above, or a lawful excuse, for making it or having it in his custody or under his control[12].

1 For the meaning of 'person' see para 333 note 1 ante.
2 For the meaning of 'counterfeit' see para 333 note 2 ante.
3 For the meaning of 'currency note' see para 333 note 3 ante.
4 For the meaning of 'protected coin' see para 333 note 4 ante.
5 As to references to passing or tendering a counterfeit of a currency note or a protected coin see para 333 note 5 ante.
6 Forgery and Counterfeiting Act 1981 ss 17 (1), 22 (1), (2) (d), (6) (a). For the meaning of 'the statutory maximum' see para 806 post. As to powers of search, forfeiture etc see para 339 post.
7 As to 'lawful authority or excuse' see para 333 note 7 ante.
8 Evidence that the accused had previously uttered counterfeit coins could be given in evidence for the purpose of proving that he knowingly and without lawful excuse had in his custody and possession a mould on which was impressed the figure and apparent resemblance of the obverse side of a half-crown: *R v Weeks* (1861) Le & Ca 18.
9 Forgery and Counterfeiting Act 1981 ss 17 (2), 22 (3), (4) (d), 6 (a). See also note 6 supra.
10 Ibid ss 17 (3), 22 (3), (4) (e), (6) (a). See also note 6 supra.
11 For the meaning of 'the Treasury' see para 333 note 4 ante.
12 Forgery and Counterfeiting Act 1981 s 17 (4). It is an offence at common law to procure coining instruments with intent to make counterfeit coin (*R v Roberts* (1855) Dears CC 539, CCR) or to procure base coin with intent to make counterfeit coin (*R v Fuller and Robinson* (1816) Russ & Ry 308). Any such offence is punishable by imprisonment and fine at the discretion of the court: see paras 1200, 1232 post.

337. Reproduction of British currency notes. If any person[1], unless the relevant authority[2] has previously consented in writing, reproduces on any substance whatsoever, and whether or not on the correct scale, any British currency note[3] or any part of a British currency note, he is guilty of an offence and liable on conviction on indictment to a fine, or on summary conviction to a fine not exceeding the statutory maximum[4].

1 For the meaning of 'person' see para 333 note 1 ante. Where an offence under the Forgery and Counterfeiting Act 1981 s 18 or s 19 (see para 338 post) which has been committed by a body corporate is proved to have been committed with the consent or connivance of, or to be attributable to any neglect on the part of, a director, manager, secretary or other similar officer of the body corporate, or any person who was purporting to act in any such capacity, he, as well as the body corporate, is guilty of that offence and liable to be proceeded against and punished accordingly: s 25 (1). Where the affairs of a body corporate are managed by its members, s 25 (1) applies in relation to the acts and defaults of a member in connection with his functions of management as if he were a director of the body corporate: s 25 (2).

2 For these purposes, 'the relevant authority', in relation to a British currency note of any particular description, means the authority empowered by law to issue notes of that description: ibid s 18 (2); and see CONSTITUTIONAL LAW para 1018 et seq.

3 For these purposes, 'British currency note' means any note which (1) has been lawfully issued in England and Wales, Scotland or Northern Ireland; and (2) is or has been customarily used as money in the country where it was issued; and (3) is payable on demand: ibid s 18 (2).

4 Ibid ss 18 (1), 22 (5), (6) (a). For the meaning of 'the statutory maximum' see para 806 post. As to powers of search, forfeiture etc see para 339 post.

338. Making etc imitation British coins. If a person[1]:

(1) makes an imitation British coin[2] in connection with a scheme intended to promote the sale of any product or the making of any contracts for the supply of any service; or

(2) sells or distributes imitation British coins in connection with any such scheme, or has imitation British coins in his custody or under his control with a view to such sale or distribution,

he is guilty of an offence and liable on conviction on indictment to a fine, or on summary conviction to a fine not exceeding the statutory maximum, unless the Treasury[3] has previously consented in writing[4] to the sale or distribution of such imitation British coins in connection with that scheme[5].

1 For the meaning of 'person' see para 333 note 1 ante. As to the position where an offence under the Forgery and Counterfeiting Act 1981 s 19 has been committed by a body corporate see para 337 note 1 ante.

2 For these purposes, 'British coin' means any coin which is legal tender in any part of the United Kingdom; and 'imitation British coin' means any thing which resembles a British coin in shape, size and the substance of which it is made: ibid s 19 (2). For the meaning of 'legal tender' see para 333 note 5 ante.

3 For the meaning of 'the Treasury' see para 333 note 4 ante.

4 For the meaning of 'writing' see para 142 note 2 ante.

5 Forgery and Counterfeiting Act 1981 ss 19 (1), 22 (5), (6) (a). For the meaning of 'the statutory maximum' see para 806 post. As to powers of search, forfeiture etc see para 339 post.

339. Powers of search, forfeiture etc. If it appears to a justice of the peace, from information given him on oath, that there is reasonable cause to believe that a person has in his custody or under his control (1) any thing which is a counterfeit[1] of a currency note[2] or of a protected coin[3], or which is a specified reproduction[4]; or (2) any thing which he or another has used[5], or intends to use, for the making of any such counterfeit or the making of any such reproduction, the justice may issue a warrant authorising a constable to search for and seize the object in question, and for that purpose to enter any premises specified in the warrant[6].

A constable may at any time after the seizure of any object suspected of falling within heads (1) or (2) above, whether the seizure was effected by virtue of such a warrant or otherwise, apply to a magistrates' court for an order with respect to the object; and the court, if it is satisfied both that the object in fact is such an object and that it is conducive to the public interest to do so, may make such order as it thinks fit for the forfeiture of the object and its subsequent destruction or disposal[7].

The court by or before which a person is convicted of a relevant offence[8] may order any thing shown to the satisfaction of the court to relate to the offence to be forfeited and either destroyed or dealt with in such other manner as the court may order[9].

The court may not, however, order any thing to be forfeited under either of the above provisions where a person claiming to be the owner of or otherwise interested in it applies to be heard by the court, unless an opportunity has been given to him to show cause why the order should not be made[10].

1 For the meaning of 'counterfeit' see para 333 note 2 ante.
2 For the meaning of 'currency note' see para 333 note 3 ante.
3 For the meaning of 'protected coin' see para 333 note 4 ante.
4 Ie a reproduction made in contravention of the Forgery and Counterfeiting Act 1981 s 18 (see para 337 ante) or s 19 (see para 338 ante).
5 Ie whether before or after 28 October 1981 (the date on which the Forgery and Counterfeiting Act 1981 came into force: see s 33).
6 Ibid s 24 (1).
7 Ibid s 24 (2). The powers conferred on the court by s 24 (2), (3) (see infra) include power to direct that any object shall be passed to an authority with power to issue notes or coins or to any person authorised by such an authority to receive the object: s 24 (5).
8 Ie an offence under ibid Pt II (ss 14–28): see para 333 et seq ante.
9 Ibid s 24 (3). See also note 7 supra.
10 Ibid s 24 (4).

340. Prohibition of importation and exportation of counterfeit notes and coins.
The importation, landing or unloading of a counterfeit[1] of a currency note[2] or of a protected coin[3] without the consent of the Treasury[4] is prohibited[5]; and the exportation of a counterfeit or a currency note or of a protected coin without the consent of the Treasury is prohibited[6].

1 For the meaning of 'counterfeit' see para 333 note 2 ante.
2 For the meaning of 'currency note' see para 333 note 3 ante.
3 For the meaning of 'protected coin' see para 333 note 4 ante.
4 For the meaning of 'the Treasury' see para 333 note 4 ante.
5 Forgery and Counterfeiting Act 1981 s 20; and see CUSTOMS AND EXCISE vol 12 para 1054 et seq.
6 Ibid s 21 (1); and see CUSTOMS AND EXCISE vol 12 para 1063 et seq. A counterfeit of a currency note or of a protected coin which is removed to the Isle of Man from the United Kingdom is deemed to be exported from the United Kingdom for the purposes of s 20, and for the purposes of the Customs and Excise Acts, in their application to the prohibition imposed by the Forgery and Counterfeiting Act 1981 s 21: s 21 (2). For the meaning of 'United Kingdom' see para 86 note 1 ante. The expression 'the Customs and Excise Acts' is not defined in the Forgery and Counterfeiting Act 1981; but cf the definition of that expression in the Customs and Excise Management Act 1979 s 1 (1) (see para 343 note 4 post).

(iii) Smuggling

341. Making signals to smugglers. Any person who by any means makes any prohibited signal[1] or transmits any prohibited message[1] from any part of the United Kingdom or from any ship[2] or aircraft for the information of a person[3] in any ship or aircraft or across the boundary is liable on summary conviction to imprisonment for a term not exceeding six months or a fine not exceeding level 3 on the standard scale, or to both, and may be arrested[4]. If in any proceedings for such an offence any question arises as to whether any signal or message was a prohibited signal or message, the burden of proof lies on the accused or claimant[5]. Any equipment or apparatus used for sending the prohibited signal or prohibited message is liable to forfeiture[6]. If any officer[7] or constable or any member of Her Majesty's armed forces[8] or coastguard has reasonable grounds for suspecting that any prohibited signal or message is being or is about to be made or transmitted from any ship, aircraft, vehicle[9], house or place, he may board or enter that ship, aircraft, vehicle, house or place and take such steps as are reasonably necessary to stop or prevent the sending of the signal or message[10].

1 For these purposes, references to a 'prohibited signal' or a 'prohibited message' are references to a signal or message connected with the smuggling or intended smuggling of goods into or out of the United Kingdom: Customs and Excise Management Act 1979 s 84 (1). 'Goods' includes stores and baggage: s 1 (1). As to goods the importation of which is subject to duty or is restricted or prohibited see CUSTOMS AND EXCISE vol 12 para 501 et seq.
   'Smuggling' is not defined in the Customs and Excise Management Act 1979. See, however, *R v Hussain* [1969] 2 QB 567 at 572, 53 Cr App Rep 448 at 452, CA ('there is no reason to suppose the jury would associate the word "smugglers" solely with those who seek to evade customs duty . . . in the ordinary use of language today the verb "to smuggle" is used equally to apply to the importation of goods which are prohibited in import').
2 'Ship' includes any boat or vessel whatsoever and hovercraft: Customs and Excise Management Act 1979 ss 1 (1), 2 (1).
3 Ibid s 84 (2) applies whether or not the person for whom the signal or message is intended is in a position to receive it or is actually engaged at the time in smuggling goods: ibid s 84 (3).
4 Ibid s 84 (2) (amended by the Criminal Justice Act 1982 ss 38, 46; the Police and Criminal Evidence Act 1984 s 114 (1)). For the meaning of 'the standard scale' see para 808 post; and for the meaning of 'United Kingdom' see para 86 note 1 ante. As to arrest see CUSTOMS AND EXCISE vol 12 para 649; and as to proceedings see CUSTOMS AND EXCISE vol 12 para 650 et seq.
5 Customs and Excise Management Act 1979 s 84 (4); and see para 1064 post.
6 Ibid s 84 (2). As to forfeiture see CUSTOMS AND EXCISE vol 12 para 625 et seq.
7 For these purposes, 'officer' means, subject to ibid s 8 (2), a person commissioned by the Commissioners of Customs and Excise: s 1 (1). Any person, whether an officer or not, engaged by the orders or with the concurrence of the commissioners, whether previously or subsequently expressed, in the performance of any act or duty relating to an assigned matter which is by law required or authorised to be performed by or with an officer, is deemed to be the proper officer by or with whom that act or duty is to be performed; and any officer so deemed to be the proper officer has all the powers of an officer in relation to the act or duty so performed or to be so performed by him: s 8 (2), (3).
8 'Armed forces' means the Royal Navy, the Royal Marines, the regular army and the regular air force, and any reserve or auxiliary force of any of those services which has been called out on permanent service or called into actual service, or embodied: ibid s 1 (1).
9 'Vehicle' includes a railway vehicle: ibid s 1 (1).
10 Ibid s 84 (5).

342. Shooting at vessels etc engaged in preventing smuggling. Any person who fires upon any vessel[1], aircraft or vehicle[2] in Her Majesty's service while it is engaged in the prevention of smuggling[3] is liable on conviction on indictment to imprisonment for a term not exceeding five years[4].

1 For these purposes, 'vessel' includes any boat or other vessel whatsoever and any hovercraft: Customs and Excise Management Act 1979 ss 1 (1), 2 (1).
2 For these purposes, 'vehicle' includes any railway vehicle: ibid s 1 (1).
3 As to 'smuggling' see para 341 note 1 ante.
4 Customs and Excise Management Act 1979 s 85 (2). Any person who, save for just and sufficient cause, interferes in any way with any ship, aircraft, vehicle, buoy, anchor, chain, rope or mark which is being used for the purposes of the Commissioners of Customs and Excise under Pts III–VII (ss 19–91: control of importation, exportation, coastwise traffic) is guilty of an offence and liable on summary conviction to a fine not exceeding level 1 on the standard scale: s 85 (1). For the meaning of 'the standard scale' see para 808 post. As to proceedings see CUSTOMS AND EXCISE vol 12 para 650 et seq.

343. Customs offences committed while armed or disguised. Any person who, while concerned in the movement, carriage or concealment of goods (1) contrary to or for the purpose of contravening any prohibition or restriction for the time being in force under or by virtue of any enactment with respect to the importation or exportation thereof; or (2) without payment having been made of or security given for any duty payable thereon[1], is armed[2] with any offensive weapon[3] or disguised in any way, and any person so armed or disguised found in the United Kingdom in possession of any goods liable to forfeiture under any provision of the customs and excise Acts[4] relating to imported goods or prohibited or restricted goods[5], is guilty of an offence and liable on conviction on indictment to imprisonment for a term not exceeding three years, and may be arrested[6].

1 As to goods the importation or exportation of which is restricted or prohibited and as to dutiable goods see CUSTOMS AND EXCISE.
2 'Armed' is an ordinary English word. Normally it will involve either physically carrying arms or proof that, to his knowledge, an accused knows that they are immediately available. It is not necessary to prove an intent to use those arms if the situation should require it: *R v Jones (Keith Desmond)* [1987] 2 All ER 692, 85 Cr App Rep 259, CA (referring to the Firearms Act 1968 s 18 (see para 234 ante)).
3 It has been held that a person armed with a common whip when assisting smugglers was not armed with an offensive weapon (*R v Fletcher* (1742) 1 Leach 23) but that 'bats' (poles used by smugglers to carry tubs of spirits) are offensive weapons (*R v Noakes* (1832) 5 C & P 326). See also *R v Hutchinson* (1784) 1 Leach 339 at 342 where a number of earlier cases are noted.
4 'The customs and excise Acts' means the Customs and Excise Acts 1979 and any other enactment for the time being in force relating to customs or excise; and 'the Customs and Excise Acts 1979' means the Customs and Excise Management Act 1979, the Customs and Excise Duties (General Reliefs) Act 1979, the Alcoholic Liquor Duties Act 1979, the Hydrocarbon Oil Duties Act 1979, the Matches and Mechanical Lighters Duties Act 1979 and the Tobacco Products Duty Act 1979: Customs and Excise Management Act 1979 s 1 (1).
5 See CUSTOMS AND EXCISE vol 12 para 501 et seq.
6 Customs and Excise Management Act 1979 s 86 (amended by the Police and Criminal Evidence Act 1984 s 114(1)). For the meaning of 'United Kingdom' see para 86 note 1 ante. As to arrest see CUSTOMS AND EXCISE vol 12 para 649; and as to proceedings see CUSTOMS AND EXCISE vol 12 para 650 et seq.

344. Offering goods for sale as smuggled goods. If any person offers any goods[1] for sale as having been imported without payment of duty or as having been otherwise unlawfully imported, then, whether or not the goods were so imported or were in fact chargeable with duty, the goods are liable to forfeiture and he is liable on summary conviction to a fine of three times the value of the goods or level 3 on the standard scale, whichever is the greater, and may be arrested[2].

1 For the meaning of 'goods' see para 341 note 1 ante.

2 Customs and Excise Management Act 1979 s 87 (amended by the Criminal Justice Act 1982 ss 38, 46; the Police and Criminal Evidence Act 1984 s 114 (1)). For the meaning of 'the standard scale' see para 808 post. As to arrest see CUSTOMS AND EXCISE vol 12 para 649; and as to proceedings see CUSTOMS AND EXCISE vol 12 para 650 et seq.

(11) SLAVERY

345. Slave-dealing. Any person who:

    (1) deals or trades in slaves[1] or persons intended to be dealt with as slaves; or carries away, imports into any place whatsoever or ships slaves or persons to be dealt with as slaves[2]; or equips, lets or hires any ship for any operation in connection with the slave trade; or contracts to do any of these things;

    (2) knowingly and wilfully makes any loan, secures any loan, guarantees any agent or ships any goods, to be used or employed for any operation in connection with the slave trade; knowingly and wilfully insures any slaves or anything to be used for any operation in connection with the slave trade; or knowingly and wilfully contracts to do any of these things;

    (3) acts or contracts to act as master, mate, surgeon or supercargo[3] of a ship knowing it is used or intended to be used in any operation in connection with the slave trade;

    (4) procures, counsels, aids or abets a person who commits any of the offences in heads (1) to (3) above,

is guilty of an offence and liable on conviction on indictment to imprisonment for a term not exceeding 14 years[4].

1 All operations in connection with the slave trade are declared to be illegal: see the Slave Trade Act 1824 s 2. As to slavery and trade in slaves see FOREIGN RELATIONS vol 18 para 1704 et seq.
2 As to when carrying off etc persons as slaves constitutes piracy see para 347 post.
3 Seamen and persons other than those set out in the Slave Trade Act 1824 s 10 who serve or contract to serve on a ship knowing it is employed or intended to be employed in connection with the slave trade, are guilty of an offence and liable on conviction on indictment to imprisonment for a term not exceeding two years: see s 11; the Criminal Law Act 1967 s 1.
4 See the Slave Trade Act 1824 s 10 (amended by the Forgery Act 1913 s 20, Schedule (repealed)); the Penal Servitude Act 1857 s 2; the Penal Servitude Act 1891 s 1; the Criminal Justice Act 1948 s 1 (1); the Criminal Law Act 1967 s 12 (5) (a). Offenders are also liable to forfeitures and pecuniary penalties: see the Slave Trade Act 1824 ss 3–8, 12 and FOREIGN RELATIONS vol 18 para 1709. As to acts committed abroad by British subjects see para 346 post.

346. Liability of British subjects for acts committed abroad. All the provisions of the Slave Trade Act 1824[1] and the Slave Trade Act 1843 are deemed to extend and to apply to British subjects[2] wheresoever residing or being and whether within the dominions of Her Majesty or of any foreign country; and all the several matters and things prohibited by those Acts, when committed by British subjects, whether within Her Majesty's dominions or in any foreign country, are deemed and taken to be offences committed against those Acts respectively and are to be dealt with and punished accordingly[3].

1 See para 345 ante and para 347 post.
2 For the meaning of 'British subject' see para 77 note 2 ante.
3 Slave Trade Act 1843 s 1.

347. Carrying off persons as slaves or for importation or sale as slaves. If a British subject[1] or any person residing in Her Majesty's dominions[2] who, on the high seas or in any place within the Admiralty jurisdiction[3], knowingly and wilfully carries away or ships, or assists in carrying away or shipping, any person as a slave or for the purpose of his being imported into any place whatsoever as a slave or to be sold or dealt with as a slave, he is to be deemed and judged guilty of piracy and liable on conviction on indictment to imprisonment for life or for any shorter term[4].

1 For the meaning of 'British subject' see para 77 note 2 ante.
2 For the meaning of 'Her Majesty's dominions' see COMMONWEALTH vol 6 para 803.
3 As to the Admiralty jurisdiction see para 625 et seq post.
4 Slave Trade Act 1824 s 9; Punishment of Offences Act 1837 s 1; Penal Servitude Act 1857 s 2; Penal Servitude Act 1891 s 1; Criminal Justice Act 1948 s 1 (1); Criminal Justice Act 1967 s 10 (2), Sch 3 Pt III. Offenders are also liable to forfeitures and pecuniary penalties: see the Slave Trade Act 1824 ss 3, 12 and FOREIGN RELATIONS vol 18 para 1705.
   Carrying off etc persons as slaves also constitutes the offence of slave-dealing: see para 345 ante. As to slavery and trade in slaves generally see FOREIGN RELATIONS vol 18 para 1704 et seq.

(12) OFFENCES AGAINST RELIGION

348. Blasphemy and blasphemous libel. Blasphemy is an indictable offence at common law consisting in a publication of contemptuous, reviling, scurrilous or ludicrous matter relating to God, Jesus Christ, the Bible or the formularies of the Church of England[1]. The publisher must intend to publish, but he need not intend that the words amount to blasphemy[2]. It is immaterial whether the words are spoken or written[3]; but, if written, they constitute blasphemous libel[4]. The offence is punishable by fine and imprisonment at the discretion of the court[5].

1 *Whitehouse v Gay News Ltd, Whitehouse v Lemon* [1979] AC 617 at 665, 68 Cr App Rep 381 at 410, HL per Lord Scarman. It is not blasphemy to attack any religion except Christianity: *Whitehouse v Gay News Ltd, Whitehouse v Lemon* supra; *R v Gathercole* (1838) 2 Lew CC 237. It is perhaps not blasphemy to attack any Christian denomination other than the Anglican: *R v Gathercole* supra; cf *Bowman v Secular Society Ltd* [1917] AC 406 at 460, HL per Lord Sumner. The present formulation is to be compared with what appeared to be the formulation prior to *Whitehouse v Gay News Ltd, Whitehouse v Lemon* supra: the publication of words attacking the Christian religion or the Bible so violent, scurrilous or ribald as to pass the limits of decent controversy and tend to lead to a breach of the peace: *R v Ramsay and Foote* (1883) 48 LT 733; *Bowman v Secular Society Ltd* supra; *R v Waddington* (1822) 1 B & C 26; *R v Hetherington* (1841) 4 State Tr NS 563; *R v Boulter* (1908) 72 JP 188; *R v Gott* (1922) 16 Cr App Rep 87, CCA.
2 *Whitehouse v Gay News Ltd, Whitehouse v Lemon* [1979] AC 617, 68 Cr App Rep 381, HL. See also the decision of the Court of Appeal at [1979] QB 10, 67 Cr App Rep 70, CA.
3 *R v Boulter* (1908) 72 JP 188; *R v Gott* (1922) 16 Cr App Rep 87, CCA.
4 If the accused pleads not guilty to the publication of a (blasphemous) libel, he may rebut evidence of publication where done by the act of another person by his authority on proof of evidence that such publication was made without his authority, consent or knowledge, and that the publication did not arise from want of due care or caution on his part: Libel Act 1843 s 7. A criminal prosecution against any proprietor, editor or any person responsible for the publication of a newspaper for any libel published in it may not be commenced without the order of a judge in chambers: Law of Libel Amendment Act 1888 s 8. See also LIBEL vol 28 para 280. Nothing in s 3 (newspaper reports of proceedings in court privileged: see LIBEL vol 28 para 287) authorises the publication of any blasphemous matter: s 3 proviso.
   As to the power to search for and seize a blasphemous libel, and as to the disposal of any blasphemous libel so seized, see the Criminal Libel Act 1819 ss 1, 2 and para 90 note 9 ante.
5 See *R v Taylor* (1676) 1 Vent 293 and paras 1200, 1232 post. A conviction for such an offence does not amount to a violation of the Convention for the Protection of Human Rights and Fundamental Freedoms (Rome, 4 November 1950; TS 71 (1953); Cmd 8969) arts 9, 10 (freedom of thought and religion and freedom of expression: see FOREIGN RELATIONS vol 18 paras 1693, 1694): Application 8710/79, *Gay News Ltd and Lemon v United Kingdom* (1982) 5 EHRR 123, ECt HR.

349. Obstructing ministers of religion. Any person who (1) by threats or force obstructs or prevents, or endeavours to obstruct or prevent, any clergyman or other minister in or from celebrating divine service or otherwise officiating in any church, chapel, meeting house or other place of divine worship, or in or from the performance of his duty in the lawful burial of the dead in any churchyard or other burial place; or (2) strikes or offers any violence to, or arrests upon any civil process or under the pretence of executing such process, any clergyman or other minister who is engaged in or to the knowledge of the offender is about to engage in any of these rites or duties, or who to his knowledge is going to or returning from their performance, is guilty of an offence and liable on conviction on indictment to imprisonment for a term not exceeding two years, or on summary conviction to imprisonment for a term not exceeding six months or a fine not exceeding the prescribed sum, or to both[1].

1 Offences against the Person Act 1861 s 36; Criminal Justice Act 1948 s 1 (2); Criminal Law Act 1967 s 1; Magistrates' Courts Act 1980 ss 17, 32 (1), Sch 1 para 5 (f). See para 804 post. For the meaning of 'the prescribed sum' see para 807 post. As to riotous or indecent behaviour see ECCLESIASTICAL LAW vol 14 para 1048; as to offences at common law see ECCLESIASTICAL LAW vol 14 para 1050; and as to disturbances at burial services see CREMATION AND BURIAL vol 10 paras 1146, 1239, 1240.

(13) BIGAMY

350. Bigamy. Any person who, being married[1], marries any other person during the life of the former husband or wife, whether the second marriage[2] takes place in England or Northern Ireland or elsewhere[3], is guilty of an offence and liable on conviction on indictment to imprisonment for any term not exceeding seven years, or on summary conviction to imprisonment for a term not exceeding six months or a fine not exceeding the prescribed sum, or to both[4].

The above provisions do not, however, extend to (1) any second marriage contracted elsewhere than in England and Northern Ireland by any other than a British subject[5]; (2) any person marrying a second time whose husband or wife has been continually absent from such person for the space of seven years then last past and has not been known by such person to be living within that time[6]; (3) any person who, at the time of such second marriage, has been divorced from the bond of the first marriage[7]; or (4) any person whose former marriage has been declared void[7] by any court of competent jurisdiction[8]. The partner to a bigamous marriage who knows at the time of such marriage that the other person is married, may, it seems, be convicted of counselling the offence[9].

1 For the meaning of 'being married' see para 351 post; and as to evidence of being married see para 354 post. The place of the marriage is immaterial: 1 Hale PC 192.
2 'Second marriage' means the bigamous marriage charged in the indictment and may be a third or subsequent marriage: see *R v Taylor* [1950] 2 KB 368, 34 Cr App Rep 138, CCA. As to the second marriage see further para 352 post.
3 'Elsewhere' is not limited to the Queen's dominions, but includes any foreign country: *R v Earl Russell* [1901] AC 446, HL; but see also note 5 infra.
4 Offences against the Person Act 1861 s 57 (amended by the Criminal Justice Act 1925 s 49, Sch 3; the Criminal Law Act 1967 s 10 (2), Sch 3 Pt III); Criminal Justice Act 1948 s 1 (1); Magistrates' Courts Act 1980 ss 17, 32 (1), Sch 1 para 5 (i). See para 804 post. For the meaning of 'the prescribed sum' see para 807 post.
5 See *R v Topping* (1856) 25 LJMC 72, CCR (British subject: both marriages in Scotland; guilty of bigamy). For the meaning of 'British subject' see para 77 note 2 ante. As to the limitation of criminal liability of British subjects who are not citizens of the United Kingdom and colonies in respect of acts

done in a foreign country or specified Commonwealth countries see BRITISH NATIONALITY AND ALIENAGE vol 4 para 904.

6 See para 353 post.

7 See para 351 post.

8 Offences against the Person Act 1861 s 57 proviso. As to sentencing for bigamy see *R v Carter* (1967) 52 Cr App Rep 117, CA.

9 *R v Brawn* (1843) 1 Car & Kir 144. As to offences in connection with the solemnisation or registration of marriage see HUSBAND AND WIFE; REGISTRATION.

351. Meaning of 'being married'. For a person to be within the meaning of the words 'being married' there must be a valid marriage subsisting at the date of the second marriage[1]; if the first marriage is void[2] or, at the date of the second marriage, has been declared void by a court of competent jurisdiction[3] or has been dissolved[4], the second marriage is not bigamous. The second marriage is bigamous if the first marriage is voidable and has not been avoided at the date of the second marriage[5], or if at that date a decree nisi of nullity or divorce has not been made absolute[6]. Although the first marriage must be monogamous, a potentially polygamous marriage may become monogamous in character, either by the operation of a relevant foreign law or by the acquisition of an English domicile; if a potentially polygamous marriage has become monogamous at the date of the second marriage, the parties to the first marriage are within the meaning of the words 'being married'[7].

An honest belief, held on reasonable grounds, that the first marriage had been dissolved at the date of the second marriage, or that the first marriage was invalid, is a defence to an indictment for bigamy[8].

1 For the meaning of 'second marriage' see para 350 note 2 ante. As to the defence of seven years' absence see para 353 post.

2 *R v Chadwick* (1847) 11 QB 173 at 205, 235; *R v Willshire* (1881) 6 QBD 366, CCR; *R v Millis* (1844) 10 Cl & Fin 534, HL. See also *R v Lamb* (1934) 150 LT 519, CCA (giving notice to the superintendent registrar in a false name is not of itself sufficient to render invalid a marriage contracted in pursuance of it). As to the grounds which render marriages void see DIVORCE vol 13 paras 534, 538. As to the validity of foreign marriages see CONFLICT OF LAWS vol 8 paras 447–478.

3 See para 350 text to note 8 ante. A decree of nullity before 1 August 1971 in respect of a voidable marriage put the parties retrospectively in the position of never having been married to each other; a decree after 31 July 1971 operates to annul the marriage only as respects any time after the decree has been made absolute: see DIVORCE vol 13 para 542. As to recognition of foreign decrees of nullity see CONFLICT OF LAWS vol 8 paras 500–502.

4 See para 350 text to note 7 ante. As to dissolution of marriage see DIVORCE vol 13 para 501 et seq; and as to the recognition of foreign decrees of divorce see CONFLICT OF LAWS vol 8 para 481 et seq.

5 3 Co Inst 88; *R v Jacobs* (1826) 1 Mood CC 140, CCR; *B v B* (1891) 27 LR Ir 587 at 608; *R v Algar* [1954] 1 QB 279 at 287, 37 Cr App Rep 200 at 208, CCA per Lord Goddard CJ. See also note 3 supra.

6 See *Wiggins v Wiggins (otherwise Brooks) and Ingram* [1958] 2 All ER 555, [1958] 1 WLR 1013 (nullity); *Norman v Villars* (1877) 2 Ex D 359, CA; *Stanhope v Stanhope* (1886) 11 PD 103 at 109, CA (divorce).

7 *R v Sagoo* [1975] QB 885, [1975] 2 All ER 926, CA.

8 *R v Gould* [1968] 2 QB 65, 52 Cr App Rep 152, CA (dissolution); *R v King* [1964] 1 QB 285, 48 Cr App Rep 17, CCA (invalid). See also *R v Connatty* (1919) 83 JP 292; *R v Dolman* [1949] 1 All ER 813, 33 Cr App Rep 128.

352. The second marriage. It is immaterial that the second marriage[1] would have been invalid apart from its bigamous nature; it is the appearing to contract a second marriage and the going through a form of ceremony known to and recognised by the law as capable of producing a valid marriage which constitute the offence[2].

1 For the meaning of 'second marriage' see para 350 note 2 ante.
2 *R v Allen* (1872) LR 1 CCR 367 at 376 (marriage within the prohibited degrees of consanguinity); see also *R v Brawn* (1843) 1 Car & Kir 144 (consanguinity); *R v Rea* (1872) LR 1 CCR 365 (false name); *R v Robinson* [1938] 1 All ER 301, 26 Cr App Rep 129, CCA (consanguinity). Cf *Burt v Burt* (1860) 2 Sw & Tr 88 (marriage in Australia in form not recognised as legal by the local law).

353. Absence for seven years. Where continuous absence for the seven years preceding the second marriage[1] has been shown[2], the onus is on the prosecution to prove that the accused knew the other party to the first marriage to be alive within that period[3]. It is not sufficient to prove that he had the means of such knowledge[4].

Even if the period of seven years has not elapsed, an honest belief at the time of the second marriage that the husband or wife was dead, provided it was based on reasonable grounds, is a defence to an indictment for bigamy[5].

1 For the meaning of 'second marriage' see para 350 note 2 ante.
2 See para 350 ante. The onus of showing seven years' absence is, it seems, on the accused: *R v Jones* (1883) 11 QBD 118, CCR (second marriage 17 years after first; no evidence of separation or as to when, if separated, husband and wife last saw each other; held, presumption that cohabitation continued, and this not displaced). As to presumptions in criminal law see para 1067 et seq post. The defence is available even though the absence was due to the accused's wilful desertion: *R v Faulkes* (1903) 19 TLR 250.
3 *R v Cullen* (1840) 9 C & P 681; *R v Heaton* (1863) 3 F & F 819; *R v Curgerwen* (1865) LR 1 CCR 1; *R v Lund* (1921) 16 Cr App Rep 31, CCA; *R v Peake* (1922) 17 Cr App Rep 22, CCA; see also *R v Jones* (1842) Car & M 614.
4 *R v Briggs* (1856) Dears & B 98, CCR.
5 *R v Tolson* (1889) 23 QBD 168, CCR.

354. Evidence of being married. The prosecution must prove the celebration of the first marriage and the identity of the parties; evidence of cohabitation with the reputation of being husband and wife is not sufficient[1]. If a certified copy of an entry in a marriage register book is produced[2], the accused's identity with the person named in it may be proved by any means and a witness to the register need not be called[3]. It is not, however, essential to prove registration; it is sufficient to call a person who was present at and can describe the ceremony and identify the parties[4]. If the first marriage is proved, its validity will be presumed in the absence of evidence to the contrary[5]; but in the case of a foreign marriage expert evidence of validity is necessary[6].

The prosecution must also prove that the first husband or wife was alive at the date of the second marriage[7]; where there is evidence only that he or she was alive at some time before that marriage, the question whether he or she was alive at the relevant date is one for the jury, and the law makes no presumption as to the continuance of life[8].

In proceedings for bigamy, the accused's wife or husband may be called as a witness for the prosecution or defence and without the consent of the accused[9].

1 *Morris v Miller* (1767) 4 Burr 2057; *Catherwood v Caslon* (1844) 13 M & W 261 at 265. Cf *R v Wilson* (1862) 3 F & F 119 (evidence of prior cohabitation with reputation sufficient where defence alleges invalidity of first marriage). However, see also *R v Naguib* [1917] 1 KB 359, 12 Cr App Rep 187, CCA (defence of prior foreign marriage; held expert evidence necessary).
2 A certified copy of an entry in a marriage register book purporting to be sealed or stamped with the seal of the General Register Office is receivable as evidence of the marriage to which it related without any further or other proof of such entry: Marriage Act 1949 s 65 (3).
3 *R v Tolson* (1864) 4 F & F 103 per Willes J (photograph of accused identified by persons present at wedding); *R v Birtles* (1911) 75 JP 288, CCA (proof from the register of marriage of persons with

names of accused and wife, and evidence of subsequent cohabitation and acknowledgment by accused of the other party to the marriage as his wife).

4 *R v Allison (alias Wilkinson)* (1806) Russ & Ry 109, CCR; *R v Mainwaring* (1856) Dears & B 132, CCR.

5 *R v Cresswell* (1876) 1 QBD 446, CCR. The members of the jury should be directed that, if they have any doubt as to the validity of the first marriage, the accused must be acquitted: *R v Morrison* [1938] 3 All ER 787, 27 Cr App Rep 1, CCA.

6 *R v Naguib* [1917] 1 KB 359 at 361, 12 Cr App Rep 187 at 190, CCA. The evidence must be given by a professional lawyer or by a person who is deemed by virtue of his office to be an expert in the law of the country in question: *R v Moscovitch* (1927) 138 LT 183, CCA.

7 For the meaning of 'second marriage' see para 350 note 2 ante. Except where there has been seven years' absence (see para 353 ante), it is not necessary to prove affirmatively that the accused knew the other party to the first marriage was alive: *R v Ellis* (1858) 1 F & F 309; *R v Jones* (1869) 11 Cox CC 358, CCR.

8 *R v Lumley* (1869) LR 1 CCR 196; *R v Willshire* (1881) 6 QBD 366, CCR. As to presumptions in criminal law see para 1067 et seq post.

9 See para 1184 post. A party to a bigamous marriage is not a wife or husband for the purposes of competence and compellability: see para 1184 note 2 post.

(14) OFFENCES AGAINST DECENCY AND MORALITY

(i) Obscene Publications

355. Publishing an obscene article or having an obscene article for publication for gain. Except as otherwise provided[1], any person (1) who, whether for gain or not, publishes[2] an obscene[3] article[4]; or (2) who has an obscene article for publication[5] for gain[6], whether gain to himself or gain to another, is guilty of an offence and liable on conviction on indictment to imprisonment for a term not exceeding three years or a fine, or to both, or on summary conviction to imprisonment for a term not exceeding six months or a fine not exceeding the prescribed sum[7]. A person publishing an article may not be proceeded against for an offence at common law consisting of the publication of any matter contained or embodied in the article where it is of the essence of the offence that the matter is obscene[8].

1 See paras 357, 358 post. It is no defence that the items were held at a sex establishment licensed with the local authority: Local Government (Miscellaneous Provisions) Act 1982 s 2, Sch 3 para 1; and see THEATRES vol 45 para 1019 et seq.

2 For these purposes, a person publishes an article who (1) distributes, circulates, sells, lets on hire, gives, or lends it, or who offers it for sale or for letting on hire; or (2) in the case of an article containing or embodying matter to be looked at or a record, shows, plays or projects it: Obscene Publications Act 1959 s 1 (3). Section 1 (3) (b) (see head (2) supra) does not apply to anything done in the course of television or sound broadcasting: s 1 (3) proviso (amended by the Criminal Law Act 1977 ss 53 (1), 65 (5), Sch 13). As to the groups into which publication under the Obscene Publications Act 1959 s 1 (3) (a) (see head (1) supra) falls see *R v Barker* [1962] 1 All ER 748, 46 Cr App Rep 227, CCA. A film distributor does not publish a film to a cinema audience because he does nothing which falls within the Obscene Publications Act 1959 s 1 (3) (b) (see head (2) supra) vis-à-vis that audience: see *A-G's Reference (No 2 of 1975)* [1976] 2 All ER 753, [1976] 1 WLR 710, CA.

3 As to the test of obscenity see para 356 post.

4 For these purposes, 'article' means any description of article containing or embodying matter to be read or looked at or both, any sound record, and any film or other record of a picture or pictures: Obscene Publications Act 1959 s 1 (2). Anything which is intended to be used either alone or as one of a set, for the reproduction or manufacture therefrom of articles containing or embodying matter to be read, looked at or listened to, is to be treated as if it were an article containing or embodying that matter, so far as the matter is to be derived from it or from the set: Obscene Publications Act 1964 s 2 (1). A video cassette is an article: see *A-G's Reference (No 5 of 1980)* [1980] 3 All ER 816, 72 Cr App Rep 71, CA. See also para 369 post.

5 An article is deemed to be had or kept for publication if it is had or kept for the reproduction or manufacture therefrom of articles for publication: Obscene Publications Act 1964 s 2 (2).

6 A person is deemed to have an article for publication for gain if with a view to such publication he has the article in his ownership, possession or control: ibid s 1 (2). See also *R v Barton* [1976] Crim LR 514, CA. 'Publication for gain' applies to any publication with a view to gain, whether the gain is to accrue by way of consideration for the publication or in any other way: s 1 (5). A person who has an obscene article in his ownership, possession or control with a view to its being shown, played or projected in the course of a cable programme service is to be taken to have that article for publication for gain: Cable and Broadcasting Act 1984 s 57 (1), Sch 5 para 8 (2).

7 Obscene Publications Act 1959 s 2 (1) (amended by the Obscene Publications Act 1964 s 1 (1); the Magistrates' Courts Act 1980 s 32 (2)). For the meaning of 'the prescribed sum' see para 807 post. A prosecution may not be commenced more than two years after the commission of the offence: Obscene Publications Act 1959 s 2 (3) (amended by the Criminal Law Act 1977 s 65 (5), Sch 13). Proceedings for such an offence may not be instituted except by or with the consent of the Director of Public Prosecutions in any case where the article in question is a moving picture film of a width of not more than 16 millimetres and the relevant publication or the only other publication which followed or could reasonably have been expected to follow from the relevant publication took place or, as the case may be, was to take place in the course of a film exhibition: Obscene Publications Act 1959 s 2 (3A) (added by the Criminal Law Act 1977 s 53 (2); amended by the Cinemas Act 1985 s 24 (1), Sch 2 para 6). As to the effect of this limitation see para 639 post. For these purposes 'the relevant publication' means (1) in the case of any proceedings under the Obscene Publications Act 1959 s 2 (as amended) for publishing an obscene article, the publication in respect of which the accused would be charged if the proceedings were brought; and (2) in the case of proceedings under s 2 (as amended) for having an obscene article for publication for gain, the publication which, if the proceedings were brought, the accused would be alleged to have had in contemplation: s 2 (3A) (as so added). For these purposes, 'film exhibition' means any exhibition of moving pictures which is produced otherwise than by simultaneous reception and exhibition of (a) television programmes broadcast by the British Broadcasting Corporation or the Independent Broadcasting Authority; or (b) programmes included in a cable programme service which is, or does not require to be, licensed under the Cable and Broadcasting Act 1984 s 4 (see TELECOMMUNICATIONS AND BROADCASTING): Cinemas Act 1985 s 21 (1) applied by the Obscene Publications Act 1959 s 2 (7) (substituted by the Cinemas Act 1985 s 24 (1), Sch 2 para 6). Proceedings for an offence under the Obscene Publications Act 1959 s 2 (as amended) for publishing an obscene article (i) may not be instituted in any case where the relevant publication took place in the course of including a programme in a cable programme service; and (ii) may not be instituted except by or with the consent of the Director of Public Prosecutions in any case where the only other publication which followed from the relevant publication took place in the course of including a programme in such a service: Cable and Broadcasting Act 1984 Sch 5 para 8 (1). As to the effect of this limitation see para 639 post. For these purposes, 'the relevant publication' means the publication in respect of which the accused would be charged if the proceedings were brought: Sch 5 para 8 (1). Proceedings for the offence of having an obscene article for publication for gain may not be instituted except by or with the consent of the Director of Public Prosecutions in any case where the relevant publication or the only other publication which could reasonably have been expected to follow from the relevant publication was to take place in the course of including a programme in a cable programme service; and for these purposes 'the relevant publication' means the publication which, if proceedings were brought, the accused would be alleged to have had in contemplation: Sch 5 para 8 (3). As to the effect of this limitation see para 639 post. As to the publication of an obscene article in a cable programme service see para 371 post.

A sentence of imprisonment is appropriate where the offence arises out of the commercial exploitation of pornography. The cases have all concerned the offence of having an obscene publication for gain: see *R v Holloway* (1982) 4 Cr App Rep (S) 128, CA; *R v Zampa* (1984) 6 Cr App Rep (S) 110, CA; *R v Hamilton-Grant* (1984) 6 Cr App Rep (S) 438, CA. See also *R v Anderson* [1972] 1 QB 304, 56 Cr App Rep 115, CA (although prison sentences were at that time rare, there are cases where the Court of Appeal thought they were appropriate).

Where articles are seized (see para 359 post) and a person is convicted of having them for publication for gain, the court on his conviction must order their forfeiture: Obscene Publications Act 1964 s 1 (4). An order for forfeiture so made, including an order so made on appeal, may not take effect until the expiration of the ordinary time within which an appeal in the matter of the proceedings in which the order was made may be instituted or, where an appeal is instituted, until it is fully decided or abandoned; and for this purpose an application for a case to be stated or for leave to appeal is to be treated as the institution of an appeal and, where a decision on appeal is subject to further appeal, the appeal is not to be deemed to be finally decided until the expiration of the ordinary time within which a further appeal may be instituted or, where a further appeal is duly instituted, until the further appeal is finally decided or abandoned: s 1 (4) proviso. As to appeal on conviction on indictment see para 1352 et seq post; and as to appeal on summary conviction see para 1450 et seq post.

   As to publishing etc magazines, books, etc tending to corrupt children and young persons see PRESS vol 37 para 1028; and as to the taking, distribution and possession of indecent photographs of children see paras 365–368 post.
8 Obscene Publications Act 1959 s 2 (4). Without prejudice to s 2 (4), a person may not be proceeded against for an offence at common law in respect of a film exhibition or anything said or done in the course of a film exhibition where it is of the essence of the common law offence that the exhibition or what was said or done is obscene, indecent, offensive, disgusting or injurious to morality; nor may a person be proceeded against for an offence at common law in respect of an agreement to give a film exhibition or to cause anything to be said or done in the course of such an exhibition where the common law offence consists of conspiring to corrupt public morals or to do any act contrary to public morals or decency: s 2 (4A) (added by the Criminal Law Act 1977 s 53; amended by the Cinemas Act 1985 s 24 (1), Sch 2 para 6). As to conspiracy to corrupt public morals and to outrage public decency see paras 62, 63 respectively ante.

356. Test of obscenity. An article[1] is deemed to be obscene for the purposes of the Obscene Publications Acts 1959 and 1964[2] if its effect or, where the article comprises two or more distinct items, the effect of any one of its items[3] is, if taken as a whole, such as to tend to deprave and corrupt[4] persons who are likely[5], having regard to all relevant circumstances, to read, see or hear the matter contained or embodied in it[6].

   In proceedings against a person for publishing an obscene article[7], the question as to whether the article is obscene must be determined without regard to any publication by another person unless it could reasonably have been expected that the publication by that other person would follow from publication by the person charged[8]. In proceedings against a person for having an obscene article for publication for gain[9], the question whether the article is obscene must be determined by reference to such publication for gain of the article as in the circumstances it may reasonably be inferred he had in contemplation and to any further publication that could reasonably be expected to follow from it, but not to any other publication[10].

   The issue of obscenity is entirely one for the jury and expert evidence on the issue is not admissible[11].

1 For the meaning of 'article' see para 355 note 4 ante.
2 See para 355 ante and paras 359, 360 post.
      As to the test of obscenity at common law and under the Theatres Act 1968 see paras 361, 362 note 2 post. Cf the test under the Post Office Act 1953 s 11: see para 373 note 2 post.
3 Where the article comprises a number of separate items, the individual items must be considered separately; and, if one is obscene, that is sufficient to make the whole obscene: *R v Anderson* [1972] 1 QB 304, 56 Cr App Rep 115, CA.
4 See *Knuller (Publishing, Printing and Promotions) Ltd v DPP* [1973] AC 435 at 456, 56 Cr App Rep 633 at 641, HL per Lord Reid ('The Obscene Publications Act [1959] appears to use the words "deprave" and "corrupt" as synonymous, as I think they are. To deprave and corrupt does not merely mean to lead astray morally'). 'Deprave' and 'corrupt' refer to the effect of a pornographic publication on the mind, including the emotions; it is not necessary that any physical (or 'overt') sexual activity should result: *DPP v Whyte* [1972] AC 849, 57 Cr App Rep 74, HL.
      Depravity and corruption are not, however, confined to sexual depravity and corruption: see *John Calder (Publications) Ltd v Powell* [1965] 1 QB 509, [1965] 1 All ER 159, DC (drug taking); see also *DPP v A and BC Chewing Gum Ltd* [1968] 1 QB 159, [1967] 2 All ER 504, DC; *R v Calder and Boyars Ltd* [1969] 1 QB 151, 52 Cr App Rep 706, CA. An article is not necessarily obscene for the purposes of the Act because it is repulsive, filthy, loathsome or lewd: *R v Anderson* [1972] 1 QB 304, 56 Cr App Rep 115, CA. It is open to an accused to show that an article is so unpleasant or disgusting that it

would not corrupt and deprave but cause persons to revolt from the activity it describes: *R v Calder and Boyars Ltd* supra; *R v Anderson* supra. The Obscene Publications Act 1959 is not merely concerned with the corruption of the innocent but protects equally the less innocent from further corruption and the addict from feeding his addiction; the proposition that readers whose morals are already in a state of depravity or corruption are incapable of being further depraved or corrupted is fallacious: *DPP v Whyte* supra. The test of obscenity depends on the article and not upon there being an intention on the part of the author or publisher to corrupt: *Shaw v DPP* [1962] AC 220; sub nom *R v Shaw* [1961] 1 All ER 330, CCA; see also *R v Penguin Books Ltd* [1961] Crim LR 176. The tendency to deprave and corrupt must be determined by reference to the publication (see the Obscene Publications Act 1959 s 1 (3) and para 355 ante) of the article: *A-G's Reference (No 2 of 1975)* [1976] 2 All ER 753, [1976] 1 WLR 710, CA.

5 The article must tend to deprave a significant proportion of those likely to read it (*R v Calder and Boyars Ltd* [1969] 1 QB 151, 52 Cr App Rep 706, CA); but it is not appropriate to consider only the largest category of 'most likely' readers; other categories of persons may be 'likely' readers and should be disregarded only if they are numerically negligible (*DPP v Whyte* [1972] AC 849, 57 Cr App Rep 74, HL; *DPP v Jordan* [1977] AC 699, 64 Cr App Rep 33, HL; *Gold Star Publications v DPP* [1981] 2 All ER 257, 73 Cr App Rep 141, HL (readership abroad)).

6 Obscene Publications Act 1959 s 1 (1). This definition retains in substance the test laid down by Cockburn J in *R v Hicklin* (1868) LR 3 QB 360 at 371.

7 See para 355 ante.

8 Obscene Publications Act 1959 s 2 (6).

9 See para 355 ante.

10 Obscene Publications Act 1964 s1 (3) (b). The question whether an article had or kept for the reproduction or manufacture from it of articles for publication is obscene must be determined as if any reference in s 1 (3) (b) to publication were a reference to publication of articles reproduced or manufactured from it: s 2 (2) (a).

11 *R v Anderson* [1972] 1 QB 304, 56 Cr App Rep 115, CA, distinguishing *DPP v A and BC Chewing Gum Ltd* [1968] 1 QB 159, [1967] 2 All ER 504, DC (where expert evidence as to the effect of the publication on children was held admissible); *DPP v Jordan* [1977] AC 699, 64 Cr App Rep 33, HL (in general no evidence, psychological or medical, may be admitted; there are, however, exceptions such as *DPP v A and BC Chewing Gum Ltd* supra). If expert evidence is not aimed at establishing the tendency to deprave and corrupt but is scientific evidence which is essential to ensure that the members of the jury have the necessary information, it is admissible: *R v Skirving, R v Grossman* [1985] QB 819, 81 Cr App Rep 9, CA. The opinion of experts is admissible in relation to the defence of public good: see para 357 post. As to the issues for the jury where publication is to an individual see *R v Barker* [1962] 1 All ER 748, 46 Cr App Rep 227, CCA.

357. Defence of public good. A person may not be convicted of publishing an obscene article[1] and an order for forfeiture may not be made[2] if it is proved that publication of the article in question is justified as being for the public good on the ground that it is in the interests of science, literature, art or learning[3], or of other objects of general concern[4].

The opinion of experts as to the literary, artistic, scientific or other merits[5] of an article may be admitted in any proceedings either to establish or negative such ground[6].

1 Ie under the Obscene Publications Act 1959 s 2 (1): see para 355 ante.

2 Ie under ibid s 3: see para 360 post.

3 'Learning' is a noun meaning the product of scholarship, something with intrinsic value coming from the work of a scholar: *A-G's Reference (No 3 of 1977)* [1978] 3 All ER 1166, 67 Cr App Rep 393, CA.

4 Obscene Publications Act 1959 s 4 (1). If the article is a moving picture film or soundtrack, the publication must be proved to be justified as being for the public good on the ground that it is in the interests of drama, opera, ballet or any other art or of literature or learning: s 4 (1A) (added by the Criminal Law Act 1977 s 53 (6)). Cf the Theatres Act 1968 s 3: see para 363 post. A decision must first be made on the obscenity and only then does the question of public good fall for decision: *R v Calder and Boyars Ltd* [1969] 1 QB 151, 52 Cr App Rep 706, CA; *Olympia Press Ltd v Hollis* [1974] 1 All ER 108, [1973] 1 WLR 1520, DC. As to the order of witnesses, and the proper direction to the jury, see

R v Calder and Boyars Ltd supra. In considering the defence, the jury should consider on the one hand the number of readers who it believes would tend to be depraved and corrupted by the publication, the strength of the tendency to deprave and corrupt and the nature of the depravity or corruption; on the other hand it should assess the strength of the literary, sociological or ethical merit which it considers the book to possess. Weighing up all these factors, it is required to decide whether on balance the publication is proved to be justified as being for the public good: *R v Calder and Boyars Ltd* supra at 172 and at 716. Any 'other objects of general concern' must fall within the same range of considerations as 'science, literature, art or learning': *DPP v Jordan* [1977] AC 699, 64 Cr App Rep 33, HL.

5 'Other merits' includes ethical merits (*R v Penguin Books Ltd* [1961] Crim LR 176), but does not include therapeutic value (*DPP v Jordan* [1977] AC 699, 64 Cr App Rep 33, HL).

6 Obscene Publications Act 1959 s 4 (2). The evidence is restricted to this question and is not admissible on the issue of obscenity: see para 356 text and note 11 ante. See also *DPP v Jordan* [1977] AC 699, 64 Cr App Rep 33, HL (expert evidence of therapeutic qualities of sexually explicit material held inadmissible as evidence going to the issue of obscenity). Evidence relating to other books may be admitted to establish 'the climate of literature' in order to assess the literary merit of the article in question: *R v Penguin Books Ltd* [1961] Crim LR 176.

358. No reasonable cause to believe article obscene. A person may not be convicted of publishing an obscene article, or of having an obscene article for publication for gain[1] if he proves that he had not examined the article in respect of which he is charged and had no reasonable cause to suspect that it was such that his publication of it or his having it, as the case may be, would make him liable to be convicted of such an offence[2].

1 Ie under the Obscene Publications Act 1959 s 2: see para 355 ante.
2 Ibid s 2 (5); Obscene Publications Act 1964 s 1 (3) (a). As to the burden of proof see para 1062 et seq post.

359. Obscene articles for publication for gain; powers of search and seizure. If a justice of the peace is satisfied by information on oath that there is reasonable ground for suspecting that, in any premises in the petty sessions area for which he acts, or on any stall or vehicle in that area, being premises or a stall or vehicle specified in the information, obscene[1] articles[2] are, or are from time to time, kept for publication for gain[3], he may issue a warrant[4] empowering any constable to enter, if need be by force, and search the premises, stall or vehicle and to seize and remove any articles found therein or thereon which the constable has reason to believe to be obscene articles and to be kept for publication for gain[5].

1 For the meaning of 'obscene' see para 356 text to note 6 ante.
2 For the meaning of 'article' see para 355 note 4 ante.
3 For the meaning of 'publication for gain' see para 355 note 6 ante.
4 A justice of the peace may not issue a warrant under the Obscene Publications Act 1959 s 3 (1) except on an information laid by or on behalf of the Director of Public Prosecutions or by a constable: Criminal Justice Act 1967 s 25.
5 Obscene Publications Act 1959 s 3 (1) (amended by the Police and Criminal Evidence Act 1984 s 119 (2), Sch 7 Pt I). As to powers of entry, search and seizure see para 668 et seq post.

Articles seized must be brought before a justice of the peace: see para 360 post. If any obscene articles are so seized, the warrant also empowers the seizure and removal of any documents found in the premises or, as the case may be, on the stall or vehicle which relate to a trade or business carried on at the premises or from the stall or vehicle: Obscene Publications Act 1959 s 3 (2).

A warrant issued under s 3 (1) (as so amended) authorises only one entry, search and seizure of goods; and, when that is carried out, the warrant is spent; however, where the police act more than once on the same warrant, the judge does not necessarily have a discretion to exclude the articles seized on any subsequent occasion as the Obscene Publications Act 1959 s 2 (1) (as amended) does not require strict compliance with s 3 (1) (as so amended) as a condition of conviction under s 2 (1) (as amended): *R v Adams* [1980] QB 575, 70 Cr App Rep 149, CA (the manner in which the evidence there had been obtained under one warrant could not be said to have been oppressive merely because the police had made an error regarding the validity of the warrant for the purpose of entry on the second occasion). Items for publication outside the jurisdiction may be seized: *Gold Star Publications Ltd v DPP* [1981] 2 All ER 257, 73 Cr App Rep 141, HL.

360. Obscene articles for publication for gain; summary procedure for forfeiture. Except as otherwise provided[1], any articles seized under a search warrant[2] must be brought before a justice of the peace acting for the same petty sessions area as the justice who issued the warrant, and the justice before whom the articles are brought may thereupon issue a summons[3] to the occupier of the premises or, as the case may be, the user of the stall or vehicle to appear on a day specified in the summons before a magistrates' court for that petty sessions area to show cause why the articles or any of them should not be forfeited[4]. If the court is satisfied, as respects any of the articles, that at the time when they were seized they were obscene articles[5] kept for publication for gain[6], the court must[7] order those articles to be forfeited[8]. However, if the person summoned does not appear, the court may not make such an order unless service of the summons is proved[9]. In addition to the person summoned, any other person being the owner, author or maker of any of the articles brought before the court, or any other person through whose hands they had passed before being seized, is entitled to appear before the court on the day specified in the summons to show cause[10] why they should not be forfeited[11].

1 The provisions as to forfeiture do not apply in relation to any article seized under the Obscene Publications Act 1959 s 3 (1) (as amended) (see para 359 ante) which is returned to the occupier of the premises or, as the case may be, to the user of the stall or vehicle in or on which it was found: s 3 (3) proviso (added by the Criminal Law Act 1977 s 65 (4), Sch 12). Without prejudice to the duty of the court to make an order for the forfeiture of an article where the Obscene Publications Act 1964 s 1 (4) (orders made on conviction: see para 355 note 7 ante) applies, in a case where by virtue of s 2 (3A) (added by the Criminal Law Act 1977 s 53; amended by the Cinemas Act 1985 s 24 (1), Sch 2 para 6) proceedings under the Obscene Publications Act 1964 s 2 for having an article for publication for gain could not be instituted except by or with the consent of the Director of Public Prosecutions, no order for the forfeiture of the article may be so made unless the warrant under which the article was seized was issued on an information laid by or on behalf of the Director of Public Prosecutions: s 3 (3A) (added by the Criminal Law Act 1977 s 53 (5)).
2 See para 359 ante.
3 Under the corresponding provisions of the Obscene Publications Act 1857 it was held that the summons should be issued within a reasonable time after the complaint leading to the issue of the warrant had been made: *Cox v Stinton* [1951] 2 KB 1021, [1951] 2 All ER 637, DC. A justice to whom articles are shown for the purpose of issuing a summons is not then precluded from hearing the case: *Morgan v Bowker* [1964] 1 QB 507, [1963] 1 All ER 691, DC.
4 Obscene Publications Act 1959 s 3 (3) (amended by the Criminal Law Act 1977 ss 53, 65 (4), Sch 12). It is the duty of the Director of Public Prosecutions to take over the conduct of all proceedings begun by summons issued under the Obscene Publications Act 1959 s 3: Prosecution of Offences Act 1985 s 3 (2) (d). See para 646 post.
5 For these purposes, the question whether an article is obscene must be determined on the assumption that copies of it would be published in any manner likely having regard to the circumstances in which it was found, but in no other manner: Obscene Publications Act 1959 s 3 (7). The question whether an article had or kept for the reproduction or manufacture from it of articles for publication is obscene must for the purposes of s 3 be determined on the assumption that articles reproduced or manufactured from it would be published in any manner likely having regard to the circumstances in which it was found, but in no other manner: Obscene Publications Act 1964 s 2 (2) (b). The intention of the accused is immaterial, but the nature of the business and the method by which it was carried on, just as much as the nature of the premises, are relevant: *Morgan v Bowker* [1964] 1 QB 507, [1963] 1 All ER 691, DC. See also *Straker v DPP* [1963] 1 QB 926, [1963] 1 All ER 697, DC. For the

meaning of 'obscene' see para 356 ante; and as to the defence of public good see para 357 ante. It is the duty of the magistrates to read or look at the articles themselves and the onus is on the occupier or user to show cause why the publications should not be forfeited: *Thomson v Chain Libraries Ltd* [1954] 2 All ER 616, [1954] 1 WLR 999, DC. See also *Olympia Press Ltd v Hollis* [1974] 1 All ER 108, [1973] 1 WLR 1520, DC (magistrates should make themselves fully acquainted with a book, but need not read the whole); *R v Crown Court at Snaresbrook, ex p Metropolitan Police Comr* (1984) 79 Cr App Rep 184, DC (on an appeal from conviction by magistrates, a Crown Court judge has the jurisdiction to decline to inspect each article which is said to be obscene and may order that the police divide the offending material into categories of pornographic behaviour or sexual perversions; the judge may then take examples at random from each category); *R v Croydon Metropolitan Stipendiary Magistrate, ex p Richman* (1985) Times, 8 March, DC, following *R v Crown Court at Snaresbrook, ex p Metropolitan Police Comr* supra (a magistrate may inspect a sample but cannot decline to inspect the material or a part of the material and rely on the evidence of a police officer as to whether the articles are obscene). An article is obscene even though only part of it is obscene and an order may be made to forfeit the whole: *Paget Publications Ltd v Watson* [1952] 1 All ER 1256.

6 For the meaning of 'publication for gain' see para 6 ante.

7 On a conviction for having, for publication for gain, obscene articles which have been seized by virtue of a warrant issued under the Obscene Publications Act 1959 s 3, forfeiture of those articles must be ordered: Obscene Publications Act 1964 s 1 (4); and see para 355 note 7 ante.

8 Obscene Publications Act 1959 s 3 (3) (as amended: see note 1 supra). Where such an order for forfeiture is made, any person who appeared, or who was entitled to appear, to show cause against the making of the order may appeal to the Crown Court: Obscene Publications Act 1959 s 3 (5) (amended by the Courts Act 1971 s 56 (2), Sch 9 Pt I). See also *Burke v Copper* [1962] 2 All ER 14, [1962] 1 WLR 700, DC (informant entitled to appeal by way of case stated against refusal of forfeiture). No such order may take effect until the expiration of the period within which notice of appeal to the Crown Court may be given against the order, or, if before the expiration thereof notice of appeal is duly given or application made for the statement of a case for the opinion of the High Court, until the final determination or abandonment of the proceedings on the appeal or case: Obscene Publications Act 1959 s 3 (5) (amended by the Courts Act 1971 s 56 (2), Sch 8 para 37). If as respects any articles brought before it the magistrates' court does not order forfeiture, it may if it thinks fit order the person on whose information the warrant for the seizure of the articles was issued to pay such costs as the court thinks reasonable to any person who has appeared before the court to show cause why those articles should not be forfeited; and costs so ordered are enforceable as a civil debt: Obscene Publications Act 1959 s 3 (6). Such a power of forfeiture extends to articles kept for publication outside the jurisdiction of the English courts: *Gold Star Publications Ltd v DPP* [1981] 2 All ER 257, 73 Cr App Rep 141, HL.

9 Obscene Publications Act 1959 s 3 (3) proviso. As to service of summonses and proof of service see paras 695–697 post.

10 As to the defence of public good see para 357 ante.

11 Obscene Publications Act 1959 s 3 (4).

361. Obscene libel at common law. It is an indictable offence at common law to publish obscene matter[1]. However, a person publishing an article may not be proceeded against for an offence at common law consisting of the publication of any matter contained or embodied in the article where it is of the essence of the offence that the matter is obscene[2]. Obscene matter at common law is matter having the tendency to deprave and corrupt those whose minds are open to such immoral influences and into whose hands such publication may fall[3]. It is also an indictable offence at common law to procure obscene prints or libels with intent to publish them[4].

A person guilty of any such offence is liable on conviction on indictment to a fine and imprisonment at the discretion of the court[5].

1 *R v Curl* (1727) 2 Stra 788. See also *R v De Marny* [1907] 1 KB 388, CCR (liability of a newspaper proprietor or editor in relation to the insertion of advertisements for the sale of obscene books and photographs).

2 Obscene Publications Act 1959 s 2 (4); see para 355 ante. 'The obvious purpose of s 2 (4) is to make available, where the essence of the offence is tending to deprave and corrupt, the defences which are

set out in the Act': *Knuller (Publishing, Printing and Promotions) Ltd v DPP* [1973] AC 435 at 456, 56 Cr App Rep 633 at 637, HL per Lord Reid. As to such defences see paras 357, 358 ante.

Conspiracy to publish an obscene libel is an offence: see the Criminal Law Act 1977 s 1 (1) (substituted by the Criminal Attempts Act 1981 s 5 (1)) and para 60 ante. Conspiracy to corrupt public morals is an offence, however, only where the agreement entered into would not constitute a statutory conspiracy: see the Criminal Law Act 1977 s 5 (3) and para 62 ante. It is apprehended that all obscene libels are likely to involve the commission of a substantive offence and that no proceedings could therefore be brought in respect of an agreement to publish an obscene article as a common law conspiracy to corrupt public morals; sed quaere.

The law officers through the then Solicitor General (Sir Peter Rawlinson) gave undertakings to the House of Commons on 3 June 1964 (see 695 H of C Official Report (5th series) col 1212) and 7 July 1964 (see 698 H of C Official Report (5th series) col 314) that conspiracies to corrupt public morals would not be charged so as to circumvent the statutory defence under the Obscene Publications Act 1959 s 4.

3 Ie the test of obscenity laid down in *R v Hicklin* (1868) LR 3 QB 360 at 371. The test was applied in *R v Reiter* [1954] 2 QB 16 at 18, 19, 38 Cr App Rep 62 at 64. See also *R v Martin Secker Warburg Ltd* [1954] 2 All ER 683 at 685, 38 Cr App Rep 124 at 126 (the test should be applied according to current standards). As to matters to be taken into account in determining obscenity at common law see *R v Reiter* supra at 20, 21 and at 65; *Steele v Brannan* (1872) LR 7 CP 261; *R v Thomson* (1900) 64 JP 456. The motive for publication is irrelevant: *R v Hicklin* supra; *Steele v Brannan* supra; but see also *R v De Montalk* (1932) 23 Cr App Rep 182, CCA (that publication was made for the public good may be a defence).

4 *Dugdale v R* (1853) 1 E & B 435, CCR. Mere possession, even with intent to publish, is not an offence at common law: *Dugdale v R* supra; *R v Rosenstein* (1826) 2 C & P 414.

5 See paras 1200, 1232 post.

(ii) Obscene Performances of Plays

362. Obscene performances of plays. Subject to certain exceptions[1], if an obscene performance[2] of a play[3] is given, whether in public[4] or in private, any person[5] who, whether for gain or not, presented or directed the performance[6] is guilty of an offence and liable on conviction on indictment to imprisonment for a term not exceeding three years or a fine, or to both, or on summary conviction to imprisonment for a term not exceeding six months or a fine not exceeding the prescribed sum, or to both[7]. Proceedings for such an offence may be instituted only by or with the consent of the Attorney General[8].

Proceedings may not be brought against a person (1) in respect of a performance of a play or anything said or done in the course of such a performance for an offence at common law where it is of the essence of the offence that the performance or what was said or done was obscene, indecent, offensive, disgusting or injurious to morality; or (2) for an offence at common law of conspiring to corrupt public morals, or to do any act contrary to public morals or decency, in respect of an agreement to present or give a performance of a play, or to cause anything to be said or done in the course of such a performance[9].

1 The exceptions are a performance of a play (1) justified as being for the public good (see para 363 post); (2) given on a domestic occasion in a private dwelling (Theatres Act 1968 s 7 (1)); (3) given solely or primarily for the purpose of rehearsal or to enable a record or cinematograph film to be made from or by means of the performance or the performance to be broadcast or included in a cable programme service which is, or does not require to be, licensed; but, if it is proved that the performance was attended by persons other than persons directly connected with the giving of the performance or the recording, broadcast or transmission, the performance must be taken not to have been given solely or primarily for such a purpose unless the contrary is shown (s 7 (2) (amended by the Cable and Broadcasting Act 1984 s 5 (1), Sch 5 para 21)). See also TELECOMMUNICATIONS and THEATRES.

2 A performance of a play is deemed to be obscene if, taken as a whole, its effect was such as to tend to deprave and corrupt persons who were likely, having regard to all the relevant circumstances, to

attend it: Theatres Act 1968 s 2 (1). As to the test of obscenity under the Obscene Publications Act 1959 and at common law see paras 356, 361 ante. Cf the test under the Post Office Act 1953 s 11: see para 373 note 2 post.
3 'Play' means (1) any dramatic piece, whether involving improvisation or not, which is given wholly or in part by one or more persons actually present and performing and in which the whole or a major proportion of what is done by the person or persons performing, whether by way of speech, singing or acting, involves the playing of a role; and (2) any ballet given wholly or in part by one or more persons actually present and performing, whether or not it falls within head (1) supra: Theatres Act 1968 s 18 (1).
4 'Public performance' includes any performance in a public place within the meaning of the Public Order Act 1936 (see para 100 note 2 ante) and any performance which the public or any section of the public is permitted to attend, whether on payment or otherwise: Theatres Act 1968 s 18 (1).
5 Whether an offence committed by a body corporate is proved to have been committed with the consent or connivance of, or to be attributable to any neglect on the part of, any director, manager, secretary or other similar officer of the body corporate, or any person purporting to act in any such capacity, he as well as the body corporate is guilty of that offence and is liable to be proceeded against and punished accordingly: ibid s 16.
6 A person is not to be treated as presenting a performance by reason only of his taking part in the play as a performer; a person taking part as a performer in a performance of a play directed by another person is to be treated as a person who directed the performance if without reasonable excuse he performs otherwise than in accordance with that person's direction; and a person is to be taken to have directed a performance of a play given under his direction notwithstanding that he was not present during that performance: ibid s 18 (2). A person is not to be treated as aiding and abetting the commission of an offence under s 2 in respect of a performance of a play by reason only of his taking part as a performer: s 18 (2).
7 Ibid s 2 (2) (amended by the Magistrates' Courts Act 1980 s 32 (2)). For the meaning of 'the prescribed sum' see para 807 post.
8 Theatres Act 1968 s 8. As to the effect of this limitation see para 639 post. A prosecution on indictment may not be commenced more than two years after the commission of the offence: s 2 (3). As to scripts as evidence see para 364 post.
9 Ibid s 2 (4) (amended by the Indecent Displays (Control) Act 1981 s 5 (2), Schedule). As to indecent displays see para 376 post; and as to conspiracy to corrupt public morals and to outrage public decency see paras 62, 63 respectively ante.

363. Defence of public good. A person may not be convicted of presenting or directing an obscene performance of a play[1] if it is proved that the giving of the performance in question was justified as being for the public good on the ground that it was in the interests of drama, opera or any other art, or of literature or learning[2]. The opinion of experts as to the artistic, literary or other merits of a performance of a play may be admitted in any proceedings for an offence either to establish or negative such ground[3].

1 Ie under the Theatres Act 1968 s 2 (2) (as amended): see para 362 ante.
2 Ibid s 3 (1). Cf the Obscene Publications Act 1959 s 4 (1); see para 357 ante.
3 Theatres Act 1968 s 3 (2). Cf the Obscene Publications Act 1959 s 4 (2). As to cases decided under s 4 see para 357 notes 4–6 ante.

364. Scripts as evidence. Where a performance of a play[1] was based on a script[2], then, in proceedings for an offence under the Theatres Act 1968[3] alleged to have been committed in respect of that performance, an actual script on which the performance was based or a copy of such script made by virtue of an order relating to that performance[4] is admissible as evidence of what was performed and of the manner in which the performance or any part of it was given[5]. If such a script or copy is given in evidence on behalf of any party to the proceedings, the perform-ance is to be taken to have been given in accordance with that script, except in so far as the contrary is shown by evidence given on behalf of the same or any other party[6].

1 For the meaning of 'play' see para 362 note 3 ante.
2 'Script' in relation to the performance of a play, means the text of the play, whether expressed in words or in musical or other notation, together with any stage or other directions for its performance, whether contained in a single document or not: Theatres Act 1968 s 9 (2).
3 Ie under ibid s 2 (as amended) (see para 362 ante) or s 6 (public performance of a play provoking a breach of the peace: see THEATRES vol 45 para 956).
4 A police officer of or above the rank of superintendent, who has reasonable grounds for suspecting that any such offence has been committed by any person in respect of the performance of a play, or that the performance of a play is to be given and that any such offence is likely to be committed by a person in respect of it, may make a written order in relation to that person and that performance: ibid s 10 (1). The order must be signed by the police officer by whom it is made and must name the person to whom it relates and describe the performance to which it relates in a manner sufficient to enable that performance to be identified: s 10 (2). Where such an order has been made any police officer, on production of the order if so required, may require the person named in it to produce, if such a thing exists, an actual script on which the performance was or will be based, and, if such a script is produced, may require that person to afford him an opportunity of causing a copy to be made: s 10 (3). Any person who without reasonable excuse fails to comply with any such requirement is liable on summary conviction to a fine not exceeding level 3 on the standard scale: s 10 (4) (amended by the Criminal Justice 1982 ss 38, 46). For the meaning of 'the standard scale' see para 808 post.
5 Theatres Act 1968 ss 9 (1) (a), 10 (5) (amended by the Public Order Act 1986 s 40 (3), Sch 3).
6 Theatres Act 1968 ss 9 (1) (b), 10 (5).

(iii) Indecent Photographs of Children

365. Taking and distributing indecent photographs of children. It is an offence for a person[1]:

(1) to take[2], or permit to be taken, any indecent[3] photograph[4] of a child[5]; or
(2) to distribute[6] or show such indecent photographs; or
(3) to have in his possession such indecent photographs, with a view to their being distributed or shown by himself or others; or
(4) to publish or cause to be published any advertisement likely to be understood as conveying that the advertiser distributes or shows such indecent photographs, or intends to do so[7].

Proceedings for any such offence may not be instituted except by or with the consent of the Director of Public Prosecutions[8]. A person guilty of any such offence is liable on conviction on indictment to imprisonment for a term not exceeding three years or a fine, or to both, or on summary conviction to imprisonment for a term not exceeding six months or a fine not exceeding the prescribed sum, or to both[9].

Where a person is charged with an offence under heads (2) or (3) above, it is a defence for him to prove (a) that he had a legitimate reason for distributing or showing the photographs or, as the case may be, having them in his possession; or (b) that he had not himself seen the photographs and did not know, nor had any cause to suspect, them to be indecent[10].

1 Where a body corporate is guilty of an offence under the Protection of Children Act 1978 and it is proved that the offence occurred with the consent or connivance of, or was attributable to any neglect on the part of, any director, manager, secretary or other officer of the body, or any person who was purporting to act in any such capacity, he, as well as the body corporate, is deemed to be guilty of that offence and is liable to be proceeded against and punished accordingly: s 3 (1). Where the affairs of a body corporate are managed by its members, s 3 (1) applies in relation to the acts and defaults of a member in connection with his functions of management as if he were a director of the body corporate: s 3 (2).

2 The accused must deliberately and intentionally take the photograph: *R v Graham-Kerr* [1988] 1 WLR 1098, 88 Cr App Rep 302, CA.
3 It is for the jury to decide whether the photograph is indecent: *R v Owen* [1988] 1 WLR 1098, 86 Cr App Rep 291, CA; *R v Graham-Kerr* [1988] 1 WLR 1098, 88 Cr App Rep 302, CA. In determining whether a photograph is indecent, evidence of the circumstances in which it came to be taken or the motivation of the photographer are irrelevant, though they may be relevant if the issue is raised, eg that the photograph was taken accidentally or the photographer inadvertently included the indecent matter. The only evidence that is relevant is the photographs themselves: *R v Graham-Kerr* supra, applying *R v Stamford* [1972] 2 QB 391, 56 Cr App Rep 398, CA; distinguishing *R v Court* [1989] AC 28, 87 Cr App Rep 144, HL. The jury must know the age of the child and is entitled to have regard to that age when answering the question, 'is this an indecent photograph of a child?': *R v Owen* supra. In deciding whether a photograph is indecent, the appropriate test is by having reference to 'the recognised standard of propriety' upon which the jury must decide by looking at the material in question: *R v Stamford* supra (decided under the Post Office Act 1953 s 11 (1) and applied in *R v Owen* supra); *R v Graham-Kerr* supra. As to the Post Office Act 1953 s 11 (1) see para 373 post.
4 For these purposes, references to an indecent photograph include an indecent film, a copy of an indecent photograph or film, and an indecent photograph comprised in a film: Protection of Children Act 1978 s 7 (1), (2). Photographs, including those comprised in a film, are to be treated, if they show children and are indecent, for all purposes of the Act as indecent photographs of children: s 7 (1), (3).
   References to a photograph include the negative as well as the positive version; and 'film' includes any form of video-recording: s 7 (1), (4), (5).
5 For these purposes, 'child' means a person under the age of 16: ibid s 1 (1) (a). In proceedings under the Protection of Children Act 1978 a person is to be taken as having been a child at any material time if it appears from the evidence as a whole that he was then under the age of 16: s 2 (3).
6 For these purposes, a person is to be regarded as distributing an indecent photograph if he parts with possession of it to, or exposes or offers it for acquisition by, another person: ibid s 1 (2).
7 Ibid s 1 (1). Nothing in the Local Government (Miscellaneous Provisions) Act 1982 s 2, Sch 3 (control of sex establishments) affords a defence to a charge in respect of any offence at common law or under any enactments other than Sch 3: Sch 3 para 1(a). On a trial of a charge alleging the taking of indecent photographs of a child contrary to the Protection of Children Act 1978 s 1 (1), the jury should be directed that (1) it had first to be satisfied that the accused deliberately and intentionally took the photographs of the child in question; and (2) in determining whether the photograph was indecent, it had to apply the recognised standards of propriety: *R v Graham-Kerr* [1988] 1 WLR 1098, 88 Cr App Rep 302, CA.
   As to the summary offence of possession of indecent photographs of children see para 366 post; as to entry, search and seizure see para 367 post; as to forfeiture of such photographs see para 368 post; and as to the competence and compellability of the accused's spouse as a witness see para 1184 post. As to procedural provisions applying to offences under the Protection of Children Act 1978 s 1 (1) (a) see para 882 post.
8 Ibid s 1 (3). As to the effect of this limitation see para 639 post.
9 Ibid s 6 (amended by the Magistrates' Courts Act 1980 s 154 (1), Sch 7 para 171). For the meaning of 'the prescribed sum' see para 807 post.
10 Protection of Children Act 1978 s 1 (4).

366. Possession of indecent photographs of children. It is an offence for a person[1] to have any indecent photographs[2] of a child[3] in his possession[4]. Proceedings for any such offence may not be instituted except by or with the consent of the Director of Public Prosecutions[5].

A person guilty of such an offence is liable on summary conviction to a fine not exceeding level 5 on the standard scale[6].

Where a person is charged with such an offence, it is a defence for him to prove:
(1) that he had a legitimate reason for having the photograph in his possession; or
(2) that he had not himself seen the photograph and did not know, nor had any cause to suspect, it to be indecent; or
(3) that the photograph was sent to him without any prior request made by him or on his behalf and that he did not keep it for an unreasonable time[7].

1 Where a body corporate is guilty of an offence under the Criminal Justice Act 1988 s 160 and it is proved that the offence occurred with the consent or connivance of, or was attributable to any neglect on the part of, any director, manager, secretary or other officer of the body, or any person who was purporting to act in any such capacity, he, as well as the body corporate, is deemed to be guilty of that offence and is liable to be proceeded against and punished accordingly: Protection of Children Act 1978 s 3 (1) (applied by the Criminal Justice Act 1988 s 160 (4)). Where the affairs of a body corporate are managed by its members, the Protection of Children Act 1978 s 3 (1) (as so applied) applies in relation to the acts and defaults of a member in connection with his functions of management as if he were a director of the body corporate: s 3 (2) (as so applied).

2 For these purposes, references to an indecent photograph include an indecent film, a copy of an indecent photograph or film, and an indecent photograph comprised in a film: ibid s 7 (1), (2) (applied by the Criminal Justice Act 1988 s 160 (4)). Photographs, including those comprised in a film, are to be treated, if they show children and are indecent, for all purposes of the Act as indecent photographs of children: Protection of Children Act 1978 s 7 (1), (3) (as so applied). References to a photograph include the negative as well as the positive version; and 'film' includes any form of video-recording: s 7 (1), (4), (5) (as so applied).

3 For these purposes, 'child' means a person under the age of 16: Criminal Justice Act 1988 s 160 (1). In proceedings under s 160 a person is to be taken as having been a child at any material time if it appears from the evidence as a whole that he was then under the age of 16: Protection of Children Act 1978 s 2 (3) (applied by the Criminal Justice Act 1988 s 160 (4)).

4 Ibid s 160 (1). Possession before 29 September 1988 is not an offence: ss 160 (5), 171 (6).

5 Protection of Children Act 1978 s 1 (3) (applied by the Criminal Justice Act 1988 s 160 (4)). As to the effect of this limitation see para 639 post.

6 Criminal Justice Act 1988 s 160 (3). For the meaning of 'the standard scale' see para 808 post.

7 Ibid s 160 (2).

367. Entry, search and seizure. Where a justice of the peace is satisfied by information on oath, laid by or on behalf of the Director of Public Prosecutions or by a constable, that there is reasonable ground for suspecting that, in any premises[1] in the petty sessions area for which he acts, there is an indecent photograph of a child[2], the justice may issue a warrant under his hand authorising any constable to enter, if need be by force, and search the premises within 14 days from the date of the warrant, and to seize and remove any articles which he believes, with reasonable cause, to be or include indecent photographs of children[3].

Articles seized under the authority of the warrant, and not returned to the occupier of the premises, must be brought before a justice of the peace acting for the same petty sessions area as the justice who issued the warrant[4].

1 The Protection of Children Act 1978 ss 4, 5 (see para 368 post) apply in relation to any stall or vehicle, as they apply in relation to premises, with the necessary modifications of references to premises and the substitution of references to use for references to occupation: s 4 (4).

2 See paras 365, 366 ante.

3 Protection of Children Act 1978 s 4 (1), (2) (amended by the Criminal Justice Act 1988 s 170, Sch 15 paras 60, 61, Sch 16). As to powers of entry, search and seizure see para 668 et seq post.

4 Protection of Children Act 1978 s 4 (3).

368. Forfeiture of indecent photographs of children. The justice before whom any articles are brought[1] may issue a summons to the occupier of premises[2] to appear on a day specified in the summons before a magistrates' court for that petty sessions area to show cause why such articles should not be forfeited[3]. If the court is satisfied that the articles are in fact indecent photographs of children, the court must order them to be forfeited; but, if the person summoned does not appear, the court may not make an order unless service of the summons is proved[4]. In addition to the person summoned, any other person being the owner of the articles brought before the court, or the persons who made them, or any other person through whose hands they had passed before being seized, is or are entitled to appear before the court on the day specified in the summons to show cause why such articles should not be forfeited[5]. Where any of the articles are ordered so to be forfeited, any person who appears, or was entitled to appear, to show cause against the making of the order may appeal to the Crown Court[6].

If as respects any articles brought before it the court does not order forfeiture, the court may, if it thinks fit, order the person on whose information the warrant for their seizure was issued to pay such costs as the court thinks reasonable to any person who has appeared before it to show cause why the photographs should not be forfeited; and costs so ordered to be paid are recoverable as a civil debt[7].

Where indecent photographs of children are seized, and a person is convicted of offences[8] in respect of those photographs, the court must order them to be forfeited[9].

An order so made[10], including an order made on appeal, does not take effect until the expiration of the ordinary time within which an appeal is finally decided or abandoned[11].

1 Ie in pursuance of the Protection of Children Act 1978 s 4 (amended by the Criminal Justice Act 1988 s 170, Sch 15 paras 60, 61, Sch 16): see para 367 ante.
2 As to the application of the Protection of Children Act 1978 s 5 to any stall or vehicle see para 367 note 1 ante.
3 Ibid s 5 (1).
4 Ibid s 5 (2) (amended by the Criminal Justice Act 1988 s 170, Sch 15 paras 60, 62 (1), Sch 16).
5 Protection of Children Act 1978 s 5 (3).
6 Ibid s 5 (4).
7 Ibid s 5 (5).
8 Ie under ibid s 1 (1) (see para 365 ante) or the Criminal Justice Act 1988 s 160 (see para 366 ante).
9 Protection of Children Act 1978 s 5 (6) (amended by the Criminal Justice Act 1988 Sch 15 paras 60, 62 (2)).
10 Ie under the Protection of Children Act 1978 s 5 (2) (as amended: see note 4 supra) or s 5 (6) (as amended: see note 9 supra).
11 Ibid s 5 (7). For these purposes, (1) an application for a case to be stated or for leave to appeal is to be treated as the institution of an appeal; and (2) where a decision on appeal is subject to a further appeal, the appeal is not finally decided until the expiration of the ordinary time within which a further appeal may be instituted or, where a further appeal is duly instituted, until the further appeal is finally decided or abandoned: s 5 (7). As to appeal on conviction on indictment see para 1352 et seq post; and as to appeal on summary conviction see para 1450 et seq post.

(iv) Video Recordings and Cable Programme Services

369. Supplying video recording of unclassified work. A person[1] who supplies[2] or offers to supply a video recording[3] containing[4] a video work[5] in respect of which no classification certificate[6] has been issued is guilty of an offence and liable on summary conviction to a fine not exceeding £20,000 unless the supply is, or would if it took place be, an exempted supply[7] or the video work is an exempted work[8].

It is a defence to a charge of committing such an offence to prove that the accused believed on reasonable grounds (1) that the video work concerned or, if the video recording contained more than one work to which the charge relates, each of those works was either an exempted work or a work in respect of which a classification certificate had been issued; or (2) that the supply was, or would if it took place be, an exempted[9] supply[10].

1 Where an offence under the Video Recordings Act 1984 committed by a body corporate is proved to have been committed with the consent or connivance of, or to be attributable to any neglect on the

part of, any director, manager, secretary or other similar officer of the body corporate, or any person who was purporting to act in any such capacity, he as well as the body corporate is guilty of the offence and is liable to be proceeded against and punished accordingly: s 16 (1). Where the affairs of a body corporate are managed by its members, s 16 (1) applies in relation to the acts and defaults of a member in connection with his functions of management as if he were a director of the body corporate: s 16 (2).

2   For these purposes, 'supply' means supply in any manner, whether or not for reward, and therefore includes supply by way of sale, letting on hire, exchange or loan; and references to a supply are to be interpreted accordingly: ibid s 1 (1), (4).

3   For these purposes, 'video recording' means any disc or magnetic tape containing information by the use of which the whole or a part of a video work may be produced: ibid s 1 (1), (3).

4   For these purposes, a video recording contains a video work if it contains information by the use of which the whole or a part of the work may be produced; but, where a video work includes any extract from another video work, that extract is not to be regarded for these purposes as a part of that other work: ibid s 22 (2).

5   For these purposes, 'video work' means any series of visual images, with or without sound (1) produced electronically by the use of information contained on any disc or magnetic tape; and (2) shown as a moving picture: ibid s 1 (1), (2).

6   For these purposes, 'classification certificate' means a certificate issued in respect of a video work in pursuance of arrangements made by the designated authority and satisfying the prescribed requirements: ibid s 7 (1). As to classification certificates and the designated authority see THEATRES vol 45 paras 1058, 1059.

7   Ie an exempted supply within the meaning of ibid s 3: see THEATRES vol 45 para 1064.

8   Ibid ss 9 (1), 15 (1). See further THEATRES vol 45 para 1065 et seq. As to supplying a video recording of a classified work in breach of the classification see THEATRES vol 45 para 1067; as to the supply of specified video recordings otherwise than in a sex shop see THEATRES vol 45 para 1068; and as to breach of labelling etc requirements see THEATRES vol 45 para 1069.

9   Ie by virtue of ibid s 3 (4) or (5): see THEATRES vol 45 para 1064.

10 Ibid s 9 (2).

370. Possession of video recording of unclassified work for the purposes of supply. Where a video recording[1] contains[2] a video work[3] in respect of which no classification certificate[4] has been issued, a person[5] who has the recording in his possession for the purposes of supplying[6] it is guilty of an offence and liable on summary conviction to a fine not exceeding £20,000 unless he has it in his possession for the purpose only of a supply which, if it took place, would be an exempted supply[7] or the video work is an exempted work[8].

It is a defence to a charge of committing such an offence to prove:

(1)   that the accused believed on reasonable grounds that the video work concerned or, if the video recording contained more than one work to which the charge relates, each of those works was either an exempted work or a work in respect of which a classification certificate had been issued;

(2)   that the accused had the video recording in his possession for the purpose only of a supply which he believed on reasonable grounds would, if it took place, be an exempted supply[9]; or

(3)   that the accused did not intend to supply the video recording until a classification certificate had been issued in respect of the video work concerned[10].

1   For the meaning of 'video recording' see para 369 note 3 ante.
2   As to when a video recording contains a video work see para 369 note 4 ante.
3   For the meaning of 'video work' see para 369 note 5 ante.
4   For the meaning of 'classification certificate' see para 369 note 6 ante.
5   As the offences by bodies corporate see para 369 note 1 ante.
6   For the meaning of 'supply' see para 369 note 2 ante.
7   Ie an exempted supply within the meaning of the Video Recordings Act 1984 s 3: see THEATRES vol 45 para 1064.

8 Ibid ss 10(1), 15(1). See further THEATRES vol 45 para 1066.
9 Ie by virtue of ibid s 3 (4) or (5): see THEATRES vol 45 para 1064.
10 Ibid s 10(2).

371. Obscene programmes in cable programme service. If the inclusion of a programme[1] in a cable programme service[2] involves the publication of an obscene article[3], or if a programme included in such a service is such that, if any matter in it were recorded matter, the inclusion of the programme would involve the publication of such an article, the person providing that service is guilty of an offence and liable on conviction on indictment to imprisonment for a term not exceeding three years or a fine, or to both, or on summary conviction to imprisonment for a term not exceeding six months or a fine not exceeding the statutory maximum, or to both[4]. Proceedings for such an offence may not be commenced more than two years after the commission of the offence[5] and may not be instituted in England and Wales except by or with the consent of the Director of Public Prosecutions[6].

A person may not be convicted of such an offence, however, if he proves that (1) he did not know and had no reason to suspect that the programme in question would be such that its inclusion in a cable programme service would make him liable to be convicted of such an offence[7]; or (2) the inclusion in a cable programme service of the programme in question was justified as being for the public good on the ground that it was in the interests of drama, opera, ballet or any other art, or of literature or learning[8].

A person may not be proceeded against for an offence at common law (a) in respect of a programme included in a cable programme service or anything said or done in the course of such a programme where it is of the essence of the common law offence that the programme or, as the case may be, what was said or done was obscene, indecent, offensive, disgusting or injurious to morality; or (b) in respect of an agreement to cause a programme to be included in a cable programme service or to cause anything to be said or done in course of such a programme so included, where the common law offence consists of conspiring to corrupt public morals or decency[9].

1 The Cable and Broadcasting Act 1984 s 25 (1) does not apply in relation to a programme which is included in a cable programme service by the reception and immediate retransmission of a broadcast made by a broadcasting authority: s 25 (3). Expressions used in the 1984 Act have the same meanings as in the Obscene Publications Act 1959: Cable and Broadcasting Act 1984 s 25 (10).
2 For the meaning of 'cable programme service' see TELECOMMUNICATIONS AND BROADCASTING vol 45 para 711.
3 As to the publication of obscene articles see para 355 ante; and as to the test of obscenity see para 356 ante.
4 Cable and Broadcasting Act 1984 ss 25 (1), (2). For the meaning of 'the statutory maximum' see para 806 post.
5 Ibid s 25 (4).
6 Ibid s 25 (5) (a). As to the effect of this limitation see para 639 post.
7 Ibid s 25 (7).
8 Ibid s 25 (8). The opinion of experts as to the artistic, literary or other merits of a programme may be admitted in any such proceedings either to establish or negative this defence: s 25 (9).
9 Ibid s 25 (6). Cf para 361 ante. As to conspiracy to corrupt public morals and to outrage public decency see paras 62, 63 respectively ante.

(v) Outraging Public Decency

372. Outraging public decency. It is an indictable offence at common law[1] for a person to commit in public[2] an act of such a lewd, obscene or disgusting nature as to amount to an outrage to public decency, whether or not it tends to deprave and corrupt those who see it[3]. The offence is punishable by fine and imprisonment at the discretion of the court[4].

1 As to the restrictions on prosecutions for common law offences contained in the Obscene Publications Act 1959 s 2 (4), (4A) (as added and amended), the Theatres Act 1968 s 2 (4) and the Cable and Broadcasting Act 1984 s 25 (6) see paras 355, 362, 371 ante.
2 'In public' means that more than one person must have been able to see the act complained of: *R v Watson* (1847) 2 Cox CC 376; *R v Webb* (1848) 3 Cox CC 183; *R v Farrell* (1862) 9 Cox CC 446; *R v Mayling* [1963] 2 QB 717, 47 Cr App Rep 102, CCA; *R v May (John)* (1989) Times, 21 November, CA. If one person is proved to have seen the act and others might have seen it, that is sufficient: *R v May (John)* supra.
3 *R v Mayling* [1963] 2 QB 717, 47 Cr App Rep 102, CCA; *R v May (John)* (1989) Times, 21 November, CA. See also *Knuller (Publishing, Printing and Promotions) Ltd v DPP* [1973] AC 435, 56 Cr App Rep 633, HL; *Shaw v DPP* [1962] AC 220 at 281, 45 Cr App Rep 113 at 151, HL per Lord Reid. It is not necessary for the prosecution to prove actual disgust or annoyance on the part of any observer: *R v Mayling* supra. It is sufficient if the act is calculated to have that effect: *R v May (John)* supra. Exposure of the naked person or any other lewd act is within the ambit of the offence: *R v Sidney* (1663) 1 Sid 168; *R v Harris* (1871) LR 1 CCR 282; *R v Mayling* supra (homosexual conduct); *R v Crunden* (1809) 2 Camp 89; *R v Reed* (1871) 12 Cox CC 1 (men bathing nude); *R v May (John)* supra (simulated sexual intercourse). The offence is not limited to acts involving a sexual element: see *R v Lynn* (1788) 2 Term Rep 733 (disinterring a corpse); *R v Saunders* (1875) 1 QBD 15, CCR (showing an indecent exhibition in a booth at Epsom races; public admitted on payment). The common law offence may be charged even though the facts may be covered by the Indecency with Children Act 1960 s 1 (1) (as amended) (see para 523 post): *R v May (John)* supra. A conspiracy to outrage public decency is also an indictable offence: *Knuller (Publishing, Printing and Promotions) Ltd v DPP* supra. As to conspiracy to outrage public decency see para 63 ante. Indecent exposure with intent to insult any female is punishable summarily under the Vagrancy Act 1824: see para 418 head (6) post. As to indecent displays see also para 376 post.
4 See paras 1200, 1232 post.

(vi) Indecent Matter sent by Post or Telephone

373. Sending indecent or obscene prints etc by post. A person may not send, attempt to send or procure to be sent a postal packet[1] which:

(1) encloses any indecent or obscene[2] print, painting, photograph, lithograph, engraving, cinematograph film, book, card or written communication, or any indecent or obscene article whether similar to the above or not; or

(2) has on the packet, or on its cover, any words, marks, or designs which are grossly offensive or of an indecent or obscene character[3].

If a person acts in contravention of the above provision, he is guilty of an offence and liable on conviction on indictment to imprisonment for a term not exceeding 12 months, or on summary conviction to a fine not exceeding the prescribed sum[4].

1 For the meaning of 'postal packet' see para 296 note 3 ante.
2 The words 'indecent or obscene' in the Post Office Act 1953 s 11 convey one idea, namely offending against the recognised standards of propriety, indecent being at the lower end of the scale and obscene at the upper end: *R v Stanley* [1965] 2 QB 327, 49 Cr App Rep 175, CCA. 'Obscene' in the Post Office Act 1953 s 11 bears its ordinary or dictionary meaning; it includes things which are shocking, lewd, indecent and so on: *R v Anderson* [1972] 1 QB 304, 56 Cr App Rep 115, CA. The test of obscenity is objective and the character of the addressee is immaterial: *R v Straker* [1965] Crim LR 239, CCA. Cf the test of obscenity under the Obscene Publications Act 1959 (see para 356 ante) and the Theatres Act 1968 (see para 362 ante) and at common law (see para 361 ante). The issue of obscenity or indecency is entirely for the jury to decide and evidence on the issue is not admissible; although the issue is to be determined in relation to recognised standards of propriety, which may vary from age to age, it is entirely for the jury to determine and safeguard the current standards and evidence as to the current standards to be applied is not admissible: *R v Stamford* [1972] 2 QB 391, 56

Cr App Rep 398, CA. Indecency is to be determined solely by considering the article; the surrounding circumstances are relevant only in mitigation: *Kosmos Publications Ltd v DPP* [1975] Crim LR 345, DC.
3 Post Office Act 1953 s 11 (1) (b), (c). Insertion of advertisements of indecent books etc obtainable on postal application may constitute an offence under s 11 (1) (b): see *R v De Marny* [1907] 1 KB 388, CCR.
4 Post Office Act 1953 s 11 (2) (amended by the Magistrates' Courts Act 1980 s 32 (2)). For the meaning of 'the prescribed sum' see para 807 post. Detention by the Post Office of any postal packet on the grounds of a contravention of the Post Office Act 1953 s 11 (as amended) or any provisions of a scheme made under the Post Office 1969 s 28 (see POST OFFICE vol 36 para 687), does not exempt the sender from any proceedings which might have been taken if the packet had been delivered in due course of post: Post Office Act 1953 s 11 (4) (amended by the Post Office Act 1969 ss 76, 88, 139, Sch 4 paras 1, 2 (3)).

374. Sending indecent, obscene or false messages by telephone etc. A person[1] who sends by means of a public telecommunication system[2] a message or other matter that is grossly offensive or of an indecent, obscene[3] or menacing character, or for the purpose of causing annoyance, inconvenience or needless anxiety to another, sends by those means a message that he knows to be false[4] or persistently makes use for that purpose of a public telecommunication system is guilty of an offence and liable on summary conviction to a fine not exceeding level 3 on the standard scale[5].

1 Where a body corporate is guilty of an offence under the Telecommunications Act 1984 and that offence is proved to have been committed with the consent or connivance of, or to be attributable to any neglect on the part of, any director, manager, secretary or other similar officer of the body corporate or any person who was purporting to act in any such capacity, he, as well as the body corporate, is guilty of that offence and liable to be proceeded against and punished accordingly: s 102 (1). Where the affairs of a body corporate are managed by its members, s 102 (1) applies in relation to the acts and defaults of a member in connection with his functions of management as if he were a director of the body corporate: s 102 (2).
2 For the meaning of 'public telecommunication system' see para 270 note 3 ante.
3 For the meaning placed on the words 'indecent or obscene' in the Post Office Act 1953 s 11 see para 373 note 2 ante.
4 As to bomb hoaxes see para 484 post.
5 Telecommunications Act 1984 s 43 (1). For the meaning of 'the standard scale' see para 808 post. Section 43 (1) does not apply to anything done in the course of providing a cable programme service: s 43 (2) (amended by the Cable and Broadcasting Act 1984 s 57 (1), (2), Sch 5 para 45 (4), Sch 6). For the meaning of 'cable programme service' see para 371 note 2 ante. As to threatening telephone calls see also para 434 post.

375. Malicious, including indecent, communications. Any person who sends[1] to another person:
(1) a letter or other article which conveys:
    (a) a message which is indecent[2] or grossly offensive;
    (b) a threat; or
    (c) information which is false and known or believed to be false by the sender; or
(2) any other article which is, in whole or in part, of an indecent or grossly offensive nature,
is guilty of an offence and liable on summary conviction to a fine not exceeding level 4 on the standard scale if his purpose, or one of his purposes, in sending it is that it should cause distress or anxiety to the recipient or to any other person to whom he intends that it or its contents or nature should be communicated[3].

A person is not guilty of an offence under head (1)(b) above, however, if he shows (i) that the threat was used to reinforce a demand which he believed he had reasonable grounds for making; and (ii) that he believed that the use of the threat was a proper means of reinforcing the demand⁴.

1 For these purposes, references to sending include references to delivering and causing to be sent or delivered; and 'sender' is to be construed according: Malicious Communications Act 1988 s 1 (3).
2 For the meaning of 'indecent' in the Post Office Act 1953 s 11 see para 373 note 2 ante.
3 Malicious Communications Act 1988 s 1 (1), (4). For the meaning of 'the standard scale' see para 808 post.
4 Ibid s 1 (2). As to the similar requirements in the offence of blackmail see para 566 post; and as to threats to kill see para 434 post.

(vii) Indecent Displays

376. Indecent displays. If any indecent[1] matter[2] is publicly displayed[3], the person[4] making the display and any person causing or permitting the display to be made is guilty of an offence and liable on conviction on indictment to imprisonment for a term not exceeding two years or a fine, or to both, or on summary conviction to a fine not exceeding the statutory maximum[5].

Nothing in the above provision applies, however, in relation to any matter:

(1) included in a television broadcast by the British Broadcasting Corporation or the Independent Broadcasting Authority or a programme included in a cable programme service[6] which is or does not require to be licensed; or

(2) included in the display of an art gallery or museum and visible only from within the gallery or museum; or

(3) displayed by or with the authority of, and visible only from within a building occupied by, the Crown or any local authority; or

(4) included in a performance of a play[7]; or

(5) included in a film exhibition[8] (a) given in a place which as regards that exhibition is required to be licensed[9] or in specified circumstances[10] is not required to be so licensed; or (b) which is an exhibition[11] given by an exempted[12] organisation[13].

A constable may seize any article which he has reasonable grounds for believing to be or to contain indecent matter and to have been used in the commission of an offence under the above provisions[14]. A justice of the peace, if satisfied on information on oath that there are reasonable grounds for suspecting that such an offence has been or is being committed on any premises, may issue a warrant authorising any constable to enter the premises specified in the information, if need be by force, to seize any article which the constable has reasonable grounds for believing to be or to contain indecent matter and to have been used in the commission of such an offence[15].

1 For these purposes, in determining whether any displayed matter is indecent (1) there is to be disregarded any part of that matter which is not exposed to view; and (2) account may be taken of the effect of juxtaposing one thing with another: Indecent Displays (Control) Act 1981 s 1 (5).
2 For these purposes, 'matter' includes anything capable of being displayed, except that it does not include an actual human body or part thereof: ibid s 1 (5).
3 For these purposes, any matter which is displayed in or so as to be visible from any public place is deemed to be publicly displayed: ibid s 1 (2). 'Public place', in relation to the display of any matter, means any place to which the public has or is permitted to have access, whether on payment or otherwise, while that matter is displayed except (1) a place to which the public is permitted to have access only on payment which is or includes payment for that display; or (2) a shop or any part of a

shop to which the public can only gain access by passing beyond an adequate warning notice; but the exclusions in heads (1), (2) supra only apply where persons under the age of 18 years are not permitted to enter while the display in question is continuing: s 1 (3).

A warning notice is not adequate unless it complies with the following requirements:
(a) the warning notice must contain the following words, and no others:

'WARNING

Persons passing beyond this notice will find material on display which they may consider indecent. No admittance to persons under 18 years of age.'
(b) the word 'WARNING' must appear as a heading;
(c) no pictures or other matter may appear on the notice;
(d) the notice must be so situated that no one could reasonably gain access to the shop or part of the shop in question without being aware of the notice; and it must be easily legible by any person gaining such access:

s 1 (6).

4 Where a body corporate is guilty of an offence under the Indecent Displays (Control) Act 1981 and it is proved that the offence occurred with the consent or connivance of, or was attributable to any neglect on the part of, any director, manager, secretary or other officer of the body, or any person who was purporting to act in any such capacity he, as well as the body corporate, is deemed to be guilty of such an offence and is liable to be proceeded against and punished accordingly: s 3 (1). Where the affairs of a body corporate are managed by its members, s 3 (1) applies in relation to the acts and defaults of a member in connection with his functions of management as if he were a director of the body corporate: s 3 (2).
5 Ibid s 1 (1), 4 (1). For the meaning of 'the statutory maximum' see para 806 post.
6 For the meaning of 'cable programme service' see para 371 note 2 ante.
7 Ie within the meaning of the Theatres Act 1968 s 18 (1): see para 362 note 3 ante.
8 Ie as defined in the Cinemas Act 1985 s 21 (1): see para 355 note 7 ante.
9 Ie under ibid s 1 (licences for film exhibitions: see THEATRES).
10 Ie by virtue only of ibid s 5 (exhibitions in private dwelling houses), s 7 (exhibitions in premises used occasionally) or s 8 (exhibitions in movable buildings etc): see THEATRES.
11 Ie an exhibition to which ibid s 6 (other non-commercial exhibitions) applies: see THEATRES.
12 For the meaning of 'exempted organisation' see ibid s 6 (6) and THEATRES.
13 Indecent Displays (Control) Act 1981 s 1 (4) (amended by the Cable and Broadcasting Act 1984 s 57 (1), Sch 5 para 38; the Cinemas Act 1985 s 24 (1), Sch 2 para 13).
14 Indecent Displays (Control) Act 1981 s 2 (2).
15 Ibid s 2 (3) (amended by the Police and Criminal Evidence Act 1984 s 119 (2), Sch 7 Pt I). As to powers of entry, search and seizure see para 668 et seq post.

(viii) Unsolicited Publications on Human Sexual Techniques

377. Unsolicited matter describing or illustrating human sexual techniques. A person[1] who sends[2] or causes to be sent to another person any book, magazine or leaflet, or advertising material for any such publication[3], which he knows or ought reasonably to know is unsolicited[4] and which describes or illustrates human sexual techniques, is guilty of an offence and liable on summary conviction to a fine not exceeding level 5 on the standard scale[5].

Proceedings for such an offence may not be instituted except by or with the consent of the Director of Public Prosecutions[6].

1 Where such an offence committed by a body corporate is proved to have been committed with the consent or connivance of, or to be attributable to any neglect on the part of, any director, manager, secretary, or other similar officer of the body corporate, or of any person who was purporting to act in any such capacity, he as well as the body corporate is guilty of that offence and liable to be proceeded against and punished accordingly: Unsolicited Goods and Services Act 1971 s 5 (1). Where the affairs of a body corporate are managed by its members, s 5 (1) applies in relation to the acts or defaults of a member in connection with his functions of management as if he were a director of the body corporate: s 5 (2).

2 For these purposes, 'send' includes deliver: ibid s 6 (1).

3 The offence is committed even though the advertising material does not itself describe or illustrate human sexual techniques: *DPP v Beate Uhse (UK) Ltd* [1974] QB 158, [1974] 1 All ER 753, DC.

4 For these purposes, 'unsolicited', in relation to goods sent to any person, means that they are sent without any prior request made by him or on his behalf: Unsolicited Goods and Services Act 1971 s 6 (1).

5 Ibid s 4 (1), (2) (amended by the Criminal Justice Act 1982 s 46). For the meaning of 'the standard scale' see para 808 post.

6 Unsolicited Goods and Services Act 1971 s 4 (3). As to the effect of this limitation see para 639 post.

(ix) Permitting Premises to be used for Unlawful Sexual Intercourse

378. Permitting premises to be used for unlawful sexual intercourse. It is an offence for a person who is the owner or occupier of any premises, or who has, or acts or assists in, the management or control of any premises:

(1) to induce or knowingly suffer a girl under the age of 13 to resort to or be on those premises[1] for the purpose of having unlawful sexual intercourse[2] with men[3] or with a particular man[4];

(2) to induce or knowingly suffer a girl under the age of 16 to resort to or be on those premises for the purpose of having unlawful sexual intercourse with men or with a particular man[5];

(3) to induce or knowingly to suffer a woman[6] who is a defective[7] to resort to or be on those premises for the purpose of having unlawful sexual intercourse with men or with a particular man[8].

The parents of the girl may be convicted of such offences even though she was living at home with them[9].

A person guilty of an offence is liable (a) under head (1) above, on conviction on indictment to imprisonment for life or for any shorter term[10]; (b) under head (2) above, on conviction on indictment to imprisonment for a term not exceeding two years, or on summary conviction to imprisonment for a term not exceeding six months or a fine not exceeding the prescribed sum, or to both[11]; and (c) under head (3) above, on conviction on indictment to imprisonment for a term not exceeding two years[12].

A person is not guilty of an offence under head (3) above because he induces or knowingly suffers a defective to resort to or be on any premises for the purpose there mentioned, if he does not know and has no reason to suspect her to be a defective[13].

1 It is immaterial that the premises are the girl's house: *R v Webster* (1885) 16 QBD 134, CCR.

2 Where, on the trial of any offence under the Sexual Offences Act 1956, it is necessary to prove sexual intercourse, whether natural or unnatural, it is not necessary to prove the completion of the intercourse by the emission of seed, but the intercourse is deemed complete upon proof of penetration only: s 44. See also para 516 post.

3 The use in any provision of the Sexual Offences Act 1956 of the word 'man' without the addition of the word 'boy' or vice versa, does not prevent the provision applying to any person to whom it would have applied if both words had been used: s 46.

4 Ibid s 25. As to procedural provisions applying to offences under s 25 and s 26 (as amended: see note 5 infra) see para 882 post.

5 Ibid s 26 (amended by the Criminal Law Act 1967 s 10 (1), Sch 2 para 14). See also note 4 supra.

6 The use in any provision of the Sexual Offences Act 1956 of the word 'woman' without the addition of the word 'girl', or vice versa, does not prevent the provision applying to any person to whom it would have applied if both words had been used: s 46.

7 For these purposes, 'defective' means a person suffering from a state of arrested or incomplete development of mind which includes severe impairment of intelligence and social functioning: ibid

s 45 (substituted by the Mental Health Act 1959 s 127 (1) (b); amended by the Mental Health (Amendment) Act 1982 s 65 (1), Sch 3 Pt I para 29). The words 'severe impairment of intelligence and social functioning' are ordinary English words and not words of art and were inserted, inter alia, to protect women over 16, if defectives, from exploitation; the severe impairment is to be measured against the standard of normal persons: *R v Hall* (1987) 86 Cr App Rep 159, CA (decided under the Sexual Offences Act 1956 s 14 (4): see para 522 post). Cf the meaning of 'severe mental handicap' in the Sexual Offences Act 1967 s 1 (3A) (added by the Mental Health (Amendment) Act 1982 Sch 3 Pt I para 34 (b)); see para 507 note 4 post.

8 Sexual Offences Act 1956 s 27 (1).

9 *R v Webster* (1885) 16 QBD 134, CCR. As to parents permitting intercourse with the daughter on one occasion to obtain evidence against the man who has previously seduced her see *R v Merthyr Tydfil Justices* (1894) 10 TLR 375, DC.

10 Sexual Offences Act 1956 s 37 (1)–(3), Sch 2 para 6; Criminal Law Act 1967 s 1 (2). As to the competence and compellability of the accused's spouse see para 1184 post; and as to corroboration of the evidence of children see para 1144 post.

11 Sexual Offences Act 1956 Sch 2 para 26; Magistrates' Courts Act 1980 ss 17, 32 (1), Sch 1 para 23 (c). See para 804 post. For the meaning of 'the prescribed sum' see para 807 post.

12 Sexual Offences Act 1956 Sch 2 para 27.

13 Ibid s 27 (2). Where, in any of the Sexual Offences Act 1956 ss 1–46, the description of an offence is expressed to be subject to exceptions there mentioned, proof of the exception lies on the person relying on it: s 47. See further para 1064 post.

(x) Disorderly Houses

379. Disorderly houses. A person commits an indictable offence at common law who keeps[1] a common, ill-governed and disorderly house[2]. A house found to be kept open to, and frequented by, persons who conduct themselves in such a manner as to violate law and good order is a disorderly house[3]. Where, however, the essence of the charge is the taking place of indecent performances or exhibitions, the fact that persons resorting to the premises are merely spectators does not prevent the premises constituting a disorderly house[4]; nor need disorderly conduct be visible from the exterior of the house[5]; nor need there be any spectators when the performance, exhibition or service is performed for one client[6]. A disorderly house may amount to a common nuisance, but this is not an essential ingredient of the offence[7].

Where indecent performances or exhibitions are alleged as rendering premises a disorderly house, it must be shown that the matters performed or exhibited there are of such a character that their performance or exhibition in a place of common resort would (1) amount to an outrage of public decency; or (2) tend to corrupt or deprave; or (3) be otherwise calculated to injure the public interest so as to call for condemnation and punishment[8]. The penalty for keeping a disorderly house is a fine and imprisonment at the discretion of the court[9].

Any person who acts or behaves himself or herself as master or mistress, or as the person having the care, government or management, of any bawdy-house, or other disorderly house, is deemed and taken to be the keeper of it, and is liable to be prosecuted and punished as such, notwithstanding he or she is not in fact the real owner or keeper[10].

1 'Keep' involves some element of persistence: see *R v Brady, R v Ram* [1964] 3 All ER 616n, 47 Cr App Rep 196, CCA.

2 3 Co Inst 205; *R v Higginson* (1762) 2 Burr 1232.

3 *R v Berg, Britt, Carre and Lummies* (1927) 20 Cr App Rep 38, CCA; *R v Tan* [1983] QB 1053, 76 Cr App Rep 300, CA. The house need not, however, be open to the public: *R v Berg, Britt, Carre and Lummies* supra.

4   *R v Quinn* [1962] 2 QB 245, 45 Cr App Rep 279, CCA.
5   *R v Rice and Wilton* (1866) LR 1 CCR 21.
6   *R v Tan* [1983] QB 1053, 76 Cr App Rep 300, CA.
7   *R v Quinn* [1962] 2 QB 245, 45 Cr App Rep 279, CCA.
8   *R v Quinn* [1962] 2 QB 245, 45 Cr App Rep 279, CCA; *R v Tan* [1983] QB 1053, 76 Cr App Rep 300,
    CA. As to the common law offence of outraging public decency see para 372 ante.
9   See paras 1200, 1232 post. See also *R v Goldstein* [1971] Crim LR 300, CA (sentences in respect of
    three counts of running a disorderly house of nine, nine and 12 months were upheld; it depends upon
    nature of exhibition); *R v Brady, R v Ram* [1964] 3 All ER 616n, 47 Cr App Rep 196, CCA (fines
    imposed).
10 Disorderly Houses Act 1751 s 8 (amended by the Betting and Gaming Act 1960 s 15, Sch 6 Pt I). The
    offence is triable either way: see the Magistrates' Courts Act 1980 ss 17, 32 (1), Sch 1 para 2 and
    para 804 post.

(xi) Offences relating to Prostitution

380. Keeping a brothel. It is an offence for a person to keep a brothel[1], or to
manage[2], or act or assist in the management[3] of a brothel[4]. The offence is triable
summarily[5]; and a person guilty of such an offence is liable on a first conviction to
imprisonment for a term not exceeding three months or a fine not exceeding level 3
on the standard scale, or to both; or after a previous conviction[6] to imprisonment
for a term not exceeding six months or a fine not exceeding level 4 on the standard
scale, or to both[7].

1   Whether the premises constitute a brothel is a question of fact and degree: *Stevens and Stevens v
    Christy* (1987) 151 JP 366, DC. A brothel is a place resorted to by persons of opposite sexes where the
    women offer themselves as participants in physical acts of indecency for sexual gratification of men.
    It is not essential that there is evidence that normal sexual intercourse is provided on the premises:
    Kelly v Purvis [1983] QB 663, 76 Cr App Rep 165, DC (evidence of masturbation provided for
    clients); explaining *Winter v Wolfe* [1931] 1 KB 549, CCA and *R v Holland, Lincolnshire Justices* (1882)
    46 JP 312. See, however, note 4 infra. Premises frequented by men for intercourse with only one
    woman are not a brothel (*Singleton v Ellison* [1895] 1 QB 607; *Mattison v Johnson* (1916) 85 LJKB 741)
    whether the woman is the tenant or not (*Caldwell v Leech* (1913) 109 LT 188); but it may amount to
    the keeping of a disorderly house (see para 379 ante). Where two women use the premises for
    prostitution, the fact that one is the tenant does not prevent the premises from being a brothel:
    Gorman v Standen, Palace-Clark v Standen [1964] 1 QB 294, 48 Cr App Rep 30, DC. Where prostitutes
    use the premises, with two receptionists, as a team, but never more than one prostitute is present on
    any given day, the premises are being used as a brothel: *Stevens and Stevens v Christy* supra. It is not
    necessary to prove that the women using the premises are known to the police as prostitutes or that
    payments are made to them (*Winter v Wolfe* supra; *Kelly v Purvis* supra); but evidence that the women
    are prostitutes is admissible on the question of whether the premises are a brothel provided that the
    fact of the women being prostitutes is within the personal knowledge of any deponent who makes
    the assertion (*R v Korie* [1966] 1 All ER 50). Nor is it necessary that the use of the premises should
    have caused a nuisance to neighbours (*R v Holland, Lincolnshire Justices* supra) or that indecency or
    disorderly conduct should be apparent from outside (*R v Rice and Wilton* (1866) LR 1 CCR 21).
    Where premises are used by more than one prostitute for her trade, the question whether the
    premises or part of the premises are or is a brothel is a question of fact in each case to be deduced from
    the circumstances as a whole; the mere fact that individual rooms were let under separate tenancies
    for exclusive occupation by one woman does not of itself preclude the whole or part of a house from
    being a brothel: *Donovan v Gavin* [1965] 2 QB 648, [1965] 2 All ER 611, DC. See also *Durose v Wilson*
    (1907) 71 JP 263 (numbers of flats in block each let to and used by one woman for prostitution; held
    to be a brothel); *Abbott v Smith* [1965] 2 QB 662n, [1964] 3 All ER 762 (house let off in single room
    apartments with exclusive occupation; held to be a brothel). Cf *Strath v Foxon* [1956] 1 QB 67, 39 Cr
    App Rep 162, DC (three-storey house, two floors and one floor let separately to prostitutes; held not
    to be a brothel). For the meaning of 'prostitute' see para 386 note 4 post.
2   'Managing a brothel' means taking an active part in the running of the business; and to establish
    'management' evidence must show something suggesting control not purely menial and routine
    duties: *Abbott v Smith* [1965] 2 QB 662n, [1964] 3 All ER 762. It is not necessary to show that the

accused was the real owner or keeper of the brothel; it is sufficient that he or she acted as such or as the person having the management of it: see para 379 text to note 10 ante. Evidence by police officers of conversations in the absence of the accused in which immoral services are offered by women employed at the premises, as masseuses, is admissible to show the purpose for which the premises are used. Such evidence is not hearsay. The truth of the statements alleged to have been made is not in point; the relevance of the evidence lies in the fact that such offers are made: *Woodhouse v Hall* (1980) 72 Cr App Rep 39, DC; *R v Wilson (DT)* (1983) 78 Cr App Rep 247, CA.

3 See *Gorman v Standen, Palace-Clark v Standen* [1964] 1 QB 294, [1963] 3 All ER 627, DC (the mere fact that a woman participates in the activities being conducted in the brothel does not make her a person assisting in the management of a brothel). Where women in a massage parlour not only performed lewd acts, but (inter alia) discussed the nature of the acts to be performed and negotiated the terms of payment for their services, they were assisting in the management of a brothel; the tasks went considerably beyond the menial tasks, such as cleaning and removing rubbish from the premises, which could be done without taking part in the management: *Elliott v DPP, Dublides v DPP* (1989) Times, 19 January.

4 Sexual Offences Act 1956 s 33. For the purposes of ss 33, 34, 35 (see para 381 post) premises are to be treated as a brothel if people resort to them for the purpose of lewd homosexual practices in circumstances in which resort thereto for lewd heterosexual practices would have led to their being treated as a brothel for the purposes of ss 33–35: Sexual Offences Act 1967 s 6.

5 Sexual Offences Act 1956 s 37 (1), (2), Sch 2 para 33 (amended by the Criminal Law Act 1977 s 65, Sch 13).

6 A previous conviction under the Sexual Offences Act 1956 ss 34–36 (see paras 381, 382 post) is to be taken into account: see s 37 (1), (4), (5), Sch 2 para 33.

7 Ibid s 37 (1), (3), Sch 2 para 33 (amended by the Criminal Justice Act 1982 ss 38, 46). For the meaning of 'the standard scale' see para 808 post. As to the competence and compellability of the accused's spouse as a witness see para 1184 post.

381. Use of premises as a brothel. It is an offence for the lessor or landlord of any premises or his agent (1) to let the whole or part of the premises with the knowledge that it is to be used, in whole or in part, as a brothel[1]; or (2) where the whole or part of the premises is used as a brothel, to be wilfully a party to that use continuing[2].

It is an offence for the tenant[3] or occupier, or person in charge, of any premises knowingly to permit the whole or part of the premises to be used as a brothel[4]. Where the tenant or occupier of any premises is so convicted and either (a) the lessor or landlord, after having the conviction brought to his notice, fails to exercise his statutory rights[5] in relation to the lease or contract under which the premises are held by the person convicted; or (b) the lessor or landlord, after exercising his statutory rights so as to determine that lease or contract, grants a new lease or enters into a new contract of tenancy of the premises to, with or for the benefit of the same person, without having all reasonable provisions to prevent the recurrence of the offence inserted in the new lease or contract, then, if subsequently an offence under these provisions is committed in respect of the premises during the subsistence of the lease or contract or during the subsistence of the new lease or contract, the lessor or landlord is deemed to be a party to that offence unless he shows that he took all reasonable steps to prevent the recurrence of the offence[6].

The above offences are triable summarily[7]; and a person guilty of such an offence is liable on a first conviction to imprisonment for a term not exceeding three months or a fine not exceeding level 3 on the standard scale, or to both; or after a previous conviction[8] to imprisonment for a term not exceeding six months or a fine not exceeding level 4 on the standard scale, or to both[9].

1 For the meaning of 'brothel' see para 380 note 1 ante. For the purposes of the Sexual Offences Act 1956 ss 34, 35, the Sexual Offences Act 1967 s 6 (premises resorted to for homosexual practices) applies: see para 380 note 4 ante.

2 Sexual Offences Act 1956 s 34. As to the competence and compellability of the accused's spouse as a witness see para 1184 post.

3 See *Siviour v Napolitano* [1931] 1 KB 636 (in the Criminal Law Amendment Act 1885 s 13 (repealed) (tenant, lessee or occupier permitting use of premises as a brothel) the word 'lessee' referred to a lessee in occupation and did not cover a landlord who was himself a lessee).

4 Sexual Offences Act 1956 s 35 (1). See also note 1 supra. If the holder of a justices' licence permits the licensed premises to be a brothel, he is guilty of an offence and liable on summary conviction to a fine not exceeding level 2 on the standard scale: Licensing Act 1964 ss 176 (1), 194 (1) (amended by the Criminal Justice Act 1982 s 46). For the meaning of 'the standard scale' see para 808 post. See further INTOXICATING LIQUOR vol 26 para 395.

5 For these purposes, references to the statutory rights of a lessor or landlord refer to his rights under the Sexual Offences Act 1956 s 35 (2), Sch 1: see LANDLORD AND TENANT vol 27 para 49.

6 Ibid s 35 (3).

7 Ibid s 37 (1), (2), Sch 2 paras 34, 35 (amended by the Criminal Law Act 1977 s 65, Sch 13).

8 A previous conviction under the Sexual Offences Act 1956 s 33 (see para 380 ante), s 34, s 35 or s 36 (see para 382 post), is to be taken into account: see s 37 (1), (4), (5), Sch 2 paras 34, 35.

9 Ibid s 37 (1), (3), Sch 2 paras 34, 35 (amended by the Criminal Justice Act 1982 ss 38, 46).

382. Permitting premises to be used for prostitution. It is an offence for the tenant[1] or occupier of any premises knowingly to permit the whole or part of the premises to be used for the purposes of habitual prostitution[2].

The offence is triable summarily[3]; and a person guilty of such an offence is liable on a first conviction to imprisonment for a term not exceeding three months or a fine not exceeding level 3 on the standard scale, or to both; or, after a previous conviction[4] to imprisonment for a term not exceeding six months or a fine not exceeding level 4 on the standard scale, or to both[5].

1 For the meaning of 'tenant' see para 381 note 3 ante.

2 Sexual Offences Act 1956 s 36. For the meaning of 'prostitution' see para 386 note 4 post.

3 Ibid s 37 (1), (2), Sch 2 para 36 (amended by the Criminal Law Act 1977 s 65, Sch 13).

4 A previous conviction under the Sexual Offences Act 1956 s 33 (see para 380 ante) or ss 34, 35 (see para 381 ante) must be taken into account: see s 37 (1), (4), (5), Sch 2 para 36.

5 Ibid s 37 (1), (3), Sch 2 para 36 (amended by the Criminal Justice Act 1982 ss 38, 46). For the meaning of 'the standard scale' see para 808 post. As to the competence and compellability of the accused's spouse see para 1184 post.

383. Allowing a person under sixteen to be in a brothel. If any person having the custody, charge or care[1] of a child or young person who has attained the age of four years and is under the age of 16 years[2] allows that child or young person to reside in or to frequent a brothel[3], he is guilty of an offence and liable on summary conviction to imprisonment for a term not exceeding six months or a fine not exceeding level 2 on the standard scale, or to both[4].

1 For the meaning of 'custody, charge or care' see para 537 note 1 post.

2 As to proof of age see para 1156 post.

3 For the meaning of 'brothel' see para 380 note 1 ante.

4 Children and Young Persons Act 1933 s 3 (1) (amended by the Children and Young Persons Act 1963 s 64 (1), (3), Sch 3; the Criminal Law Act 1977 ss 15, 30, Sch 1; the Criminal Justice Act 1982 s 46). As to the procedural provisions applying to offences under the Children and Young Persons Act 1933 s 3 (1) (as so amended) see para 882 post. As to corroboration of the evidence of children see para 1144 post; and as to the competence and compellability of the accused's spouse as a witness see para 1184 post. As to permitting premises to be used for unlawful sexual intercourse with girls under 16 see para 378 ante.

384. Permitting prostitutes at refreshment house. Every person who knowingly permits common prostitutes[1] to assemble at or continue in any house, shop, room or other place of public resort[2] kept by him for the sale or consumption of refreshments of any kind is guilty of an offence and liable on summary conviction to a fine not exceeding level 1 on the standard scale[3].

1 For the meaning of 'common prostitute' see para 386 note 4 post.
2 'Place of public resort' includes a public house: *Cole v Coulton* (1860) 2 E & E 695.
3 Town Police Clauses Act 1847 s 35 (amended by the Criminal Justice Act 1982 ss 38, 46). For the meaning of 'the standard scale' see para 808 post. It is an offence under the Late Night Refreshment Houses Act 1969 for the licensee of a late night refreshment house knowingly to permit prostitutes to assemble at or continue in his premises (see s 9 (1) and INTOXICATING LIQUOR vol 26 para 255) and it is an offence under the Licensing Act 1964 for the holder of a justices' licence knowingly to allow his premises to be the habitual resort or meeting place of reputed prostitutes (see s 175 (1), (2) and INTOXICATING LIQUOR vol 26 para 396).

385. Detention of a woman for unlawful sexual intercourse in a brothel or other premises. It is an offence to detain[1] a woman[2] against her will on any premises with the intention that she shall have unlawful sexual intercourse with men or a particular man, or to detain a woman against her will in a brothel[3]. A person guilty of such an offence is liable on conviction on indictment to imprisonment for a term not exceeding two years[4].

1 For these purposes, where a woman is on any premises for the purpose of having unlawful sexual intercourse or is in a brothel, a person is deemed to detain her there if, with the intention of compelling or inducing her to remain there, he either withholds from her her clothes or any other property belonging to her or threatens her with legal proceedings in the event of her taking away clothes provided for her by him or on his directions: Sexual Offences Act 1956 s 24 (2). A woman is not liable to any legal proceedings, civil or criminal, for taking away or being found in possession of any clothes she needed to enable her to leave premises on which she was for the purpose of having unlawful sexual intercourse or to leave a brothel: s 24 (3). As to the power to issue a search warrant for any woman alleged to be unlawfully detained for immoral purposes see para 534 post.
2 For the meaning of 'woman' see para 378 note 6 ante.
3 Sexual Offences Act 1956 s 24 (1). For the meaning of 'brothel' see para 380 note 1 ante. As to the procedural provisions applying where an offence under s 24 (1) against a child or young person is charged see para 882 post.
4 Ibid s 37 (1), (2), Sch 2 para 25 (amended by the Courts Act 1971 s 56 (4), Sch 11 Pt IV). As to corroboration of a victim's evidence see para 1141 et seq post; and as to the competence and compellability of the accused's spouse as a witness see para 1184 post.

386. Causing prostitution of a woman. It is an offence for a person (1) to procure[1] a woman[2] to become[3], in any part of the world, a common prostitute[4]; or (2) to procure a woman to leave the United Kingdom, intending her to become an inmate of or frequent a brothel[5] elsewhere; or (3) to procure a woman to leave her usual place of abode in the United Kingdom, intending her to become an inmate of or frequent a brothel in any part of the world for the purposes of prostitution[6]. A person guilty of any such offence or an attempt to commit such an offence is liable on conviction on indictment to imprisonment for a term not exceeding two years[7].

A person may not be convicted of any such offence, however, on the evidence of one witness only, unless the witness is corroborated in some material particular by evidence implicating the accused[8].

1 The word 'procure' is not a term of art and whether an act amounts to an attempt to procure is a question for the jury; a useful guide is to be found in *A-G's Reference (No 1 of 1975)* [1975] QB 773, [1975] 2 All ER 684, CA (see para 43 text to note 10 ante): *R v Broadfoot* [1976] 3 All ER 753, CA (offer of a large sum of money for undertaking tasks could, in the absence of any other pressure, amount to persuasion and therefore an attempt to procure). 'Procure' does not apply to a woman

who acts of her own free will without fraud or persuasion: *R v Christian* (1913) 78 JP 112. As to procurement generally see para 524 post.

2 For the meaning of 'woman' see para 378 note 6 ante.

3 A woman who is already a prostitute cannot be procured to become one: see *R v Gold and Cohen* (1907) 71 JP 360. A person who genuinely believes on reasonable grounds that a woman is already a common prostitute cannot be guilty of attempting to procure her to become one: *R v Brown* [1984] 3 All ER 1013, 80 Cr App Rep 36, CA.

4 'Common prostitute' includes a woman who offers her body for purposes amounting to common lewdness in return for payment; there need not be an act of ordinary sexual intercourse: see *R v De Munck* [1918] 1 KB 635, CCA; *Kelly v Purvis* [1983] QB 663, 76 Cr App Rep 165, DC; *R v Morris-Lowe* [1985] 1 All ER 400, 80 Cr App Rep 114, CA. 'Prostitution' is not confined to cases where a woman offers her body for lewdness in a passive way but includes cases where she offers her body as a participant in physical acts of indecency for the sexual gratification of men: see *R v Webb* [1964] 1 QB 357, [1963] 3 All ER 177, CCA; *Kelly v Purvis* supra. Persuading a woman for reward to offer herself for lewdness with the accused alone does not constitute the offence because she would not commonly offer herself for lewdness and therefore not be a common prostitute: *R v Morris-Lowe* supra.

5 For the meaning of 'brothel' see para 380 note 1 ante.

6 Sexual Offences Act 1956 ss 22 (1), 37 (1), (2), Sch 2 para 23 (amended by the Courts Act 1971 s 56 (4), Sch 11 Pt IV). For the meaning of 'United Kingdom' see para 86 note 1 ante.

7 Sexual Offences Act 1956 s 37 (1), (3), Sch 2 para 23. As to the procedural provisions applying where an offence under s 22 (1), or an attempt to commit such an offence, against a child or young person is charged see para 882 post. As to procuring a woman to have unlawful sexual intercourse see para 524 et seq post.

8 Ibid s 22 (2). As to the competence and compellability of the accused's spouse as a witness see para 1184 post; and as to corroboration see para 1141 et seq post.

387. Causing or encouraging prostitution of a defective. It is an offence for a person to cause or encourage the prostitution[1] in any part of the world of a woman[2] who is a defective[3]. A person guilty of such an offence is liable on conviction on indictment to imprisonment for a term not exceeding two years[4]. A person is not, however, guilty of such an offence if he does not know and has no reason to suspect her to be a defective[5].

1 For the meaning of 'prostitution' see para 386 note 4 ante.

2 For the meaning of 'woman' see para 378 note 6 ante.

3 Sexual Offences Act 1956 ss 29 (1), 37 (1), (2), Sch 2 para 29 (amended by the Courts Act 1971 s 56 (4), Sch 11 Pt IV). For the meaning of 'defective' see para 378 note 7 ante. As to the competence and compellabililty of the accused's spouse as a witness see para 1184 post.

4 Sexual Offences Act 1956 s 37 (1), (3), Sch 2 para 29.

5 Ibid s 29 (2). As to the burden of proving exceptions see para 378 note 13 ante.

388. Causing or encouraging prostitution etc of a girl under sixteen. It is an offence for a person to cause or encourage[1] the prostitution[2] of, or the commission of unlawful sexual intercourse[3] with, or of an indecent assault[4] on, a girl under the age of 16[5] for whom he is responsible[6]. For these purposes the persons who are to be treated as responsible for a girl are (1) any person who is her parent[7] or legal guardian[8]; and (2) any person who has actual possession or control of her, or to whose charge she has been committed by her parent or legal guardian or by a person having the custody of her; and (3) any person who has the custody, charge or care of her[9].

A person guilty of any such offence is liable on conviction on indictment to imprisonment for a term not exceeding two years[10].

1 For these purposes, where a girl has become a prostitute, or has had unlawful sexual intercourse, or has been indecently assaulted, a person is deemed to have caused or encouraged it, if he knowingly

allowed her to consort with, or to enter or continue in the employment of, any prostitute or person of known immoral character: Sexual Offences Act 1956 s 28 (2). For a case in which it was held that there was no evidence fit to be left to the jury see *R v Chainey* [1914] 1 KB 137, CCA. Inactivity may constitute encouragement: see *R v Ralphs* (1913) 9 Cr App Rep 86, CCA; *R v Drury* (1974) 60 Cr App Rep 195, CA.

2 For the meaning of 'prostitution' see para 386 note 4 ante.

3 For the meaning of 'sexual intercourse' see para 378 note 2 ante.

4 As to what constitutes 'indecent assault' in this context see para 521 notes 2, 3 post.

5 If, on the charge of an offence under the Sexual Offences Act 1956 s 28 (1), the girl appears to the court to have been under the age of 16 at the time of the offence charged, she is to be presumed to have been so for these purposes, unless the contrary is proved: s 28 (5). As to proof of age see para 1156 post.

6 Ibid s 28 (1). It is not unlawful for a doctor in the proper exercise of his clinical judgment to give contraceptive advice and treatment to a girl under the age of 16 without parental consent: *Gillick v West Norfolk and Wisbech Area Health Authority* [1986] AC 112, [1985] 3 All ER 402, HL. As to evidence of the victim see para 1142 et seq post; and as to the competence and compellability of the accused's spouse as a witness see para 1184 post.

7 For these purposes, 'parent' does not include, in relation to any girl, a person deprived of the custody of her by order of a court of competent jurisdiction but, subject to that, in the case of a girl who is illegitimate, means her mother and any person who has been adjudged to be her putative father: Sexual Offences Act 1956 s 28 (4) (a) (amended by the Children Act 1975 s 108 (1) (b), Sch 4 Pt I).

8 For these purposes, 'legal guardian' means, in relation to any girl, any person who is for the time being her guardian, having been appointed according to law by deed or will or by order of a court of competent jurisdiction (see INFANTS vol 24 para 526 et seq): Sexual Offences Act 1956 s 28 (4) (b).

9 Ibid s 28 (3). See *R v Drury* (1974) 60 Cr App Rep 195, CA. For the meaning of 'custody, charge or care' in the context of the Children and Young Persons Act 1933 see para 537 note 1 post.

10 Sexual Offences Act 1956 s 37 (1), (3), Sch 2 para 28 (amended by the Courts Act 1971 s 56 (4), Sch 11 Pt IV). As to the procedural provisions applying to an offence under the Sexual Offences Act 1956 s 28 see para 882 post.

389. Woman exercising control over a prostitute. It is an offence for a woman[1] for purposes of gain to exercise control, direction or influence[2] over a prostitute's[3] movements in a way which shows she is aiding, abetting or compelling her prostitution[4]. A woman guilty of such an offence is liable on conviction on indictment to imprisonment for a term not exceeding seven years or on summary conviction to imprisonment for a term not exceeding six months[5].

1 For the meaning of 'woman' see para 378 note 6 ante.

2 'Influence' does not mean encouragement; there must be a persuasion or compulsion: *R v O* [1983] Crim LR 401.

3 For the meaning of 'prostitute' see para 386 note 4 ante.

4 Sexual Offences Act 1956 s 31. As to the competence and compellability of the accused's husband as a witness see para 1184 post.

5 Ibid s 37 (1)–(3), Sch 2 para 31 (amended by the Courts Act 1971 s 56 (4), Sch 11 Pt IV; the Criminal Law Act 1977 Sch 13); Street Offences Act 1959 s 4.

390. Man living on earnings of prostitution. It is an offence for a man[1] knowingly to live wholly or in part on the earnings of prostitution[2]. A person guilty of such an offence is liable on conviction on indictment to imprisonment for a term not exceeding seven years, or on summary conviction to imprisonment for a term not exceeding six months[3].

A man is presumed to be knowingly living on[4] the earnings of prostitution[5], unless he proves the contrary[6] if (1) he lives with, or is habitually in the company of, a prostitute[7]; or (2) he exercises control, direction or influence over a prostitute's movements in a way which shows he is aiding, abetting or compelling her prostitution with others[8].

1 For the meaning of 'man' see para 378 note 3 ante. See also *R v Tan* [1983] QB 1053, 76 Cr App Rep 300, CA (man who had undergone a sex change operation but was born and remained a male was held to be a man for these purposes).

2 Sexual Offences Act 1956 s 30 (1). For the meaning of 'prostitution' see para 386 note 4 ante. A man who is paid by a prostitute for goods or services supplied to her which he would not supply but for the fact that she is a prostitute, commits this offence: *Shaw v DPP* [1962] AC 220, [1961] 2 All ER 446, HL (accepting payment from prostitutes and publishing advertisements of their readiness to prostitute themselves). See also *Calvert v Mayes* [1954] 1 QB 342, [1954] 1 All ER 41, DC (use of house and car hire facilities); *R v Thomas* [1957] 2 All ER 181, 41 Cr App Rep 117; affd [1957] 2 All ER 342n, 41 Cr App Rep 121, CCA (letting premises at inflated rent); *R v Calderhead, R v Bidney* (1978) 68 Cr App Rep 37, CA (landlord charging exorbitant rent to a tenant he knows is a prostitute); *R v Farrugia, Borg, Agius and Gauchi* (1979) 69 Cr App Rep 108, CA (taxi drivers plying for hire where they did because it was to their advantage to drive prostitutes to their customers; agency fee from introducing prostitutes to customers came from the intended prostitution). An approach which will often be useful is for the judge to identify for the jury to flavour of the words 'living off', and then express this general concept in the shape of guidance more directly referable to the case in hand. The word 'parasite', or some expanded equivalent, provides a useful starting point for this exercise. Dealing specifically with an accused who supplies goods and services to a prostitute, a good working test is whether the fact of supply means that the supplier and the prostitutes are engaged in the business of prostitution together and the 'fact of supply' will include the scale of supply, the price charged and the nature of the goods or services. In letting premises mere knowledge of the use to which the premises are put will not be sufficient in itself to found a conviction. The jury's attention must be drawn to factors material to the individual case, which will often include in the context of letting premises, the nature and location of the premises, the involvement of the lessor in adapting, furnishing or outfitting the premises for prostitution, the duration of the letting, the hours during which the premises are occupied, the rent at which they are let, the method of payment of rent, the fact that the prostitute does or does not live as well as work at the premises, the presence or absence of a personal relationship between lessor and lessee, the steps taken by the lessor to remove the prostitutes from his premises, and the steps taken by the lessor to disguise his relationship with the premises and the persons working there: *R v Stewart* (1986) 83 Cr App Rep 327, CA.

The fact that payment is made, not by the prostitute, but by her customers does not preclude the commission of the offence, but the payment must be shown to be closely connected with the exercise of direction, influence and control over her: *R v Ansell* [1975] QB 215, [1974] 3 All ER 568, CA (supplying names and addresses of prostitutes to men for a fee; prostitutes unaware of this business; fees did not constitute earnings of prostitution). As to the power to issue a search warrant for a man living on the earnings of prostitution see para 391 post; and as to living on the earnings of male prostitution see para 392 post.

3 Sexual Offences Act 1956 s 37 (1)–(3), Sch 2 para 30 (amended by the Courts Act 1971 s 56 (4), Sch 11 Pt IV; the Street Offences Act 1959 s 4).

The woman on whose earnings the accused is charged with living is not an accomplice: see *R v King* (1914) 10 Cr App Rep 117. As to the competence and compellability of the accused's wife as a witness see para 1184 post.

4 Where the Sexual Offences Act 1956 s 30 (2) is involved, it is irrelevant to consider the nature and quality of the 'living on'; the presumption and its possible rebuttal are purely matters of evidence and decision on fact: *R v Wilson* (1983) 78 Cr App Rep 247, CA.

5 It is presumed that he is living on immoral earnings and it is presumed that he is doing so knowingly: *R v Clarke* [1976] 2 All ER 696, 63 Cr App Rep 16, CA.

6 As to the burden of proof see para 1062 et seq post. The prosecution must prove beyond reasonable doubt that the accused was, for example, habitually in the company of a prostitute; if the presumption arises, the burden of proving the contrary, on a balance of probabilities, is on the accused: *R v Bell* [1978] Crim LR 233, CA. See also *R v Grant* [1985] Crim LR 387, CA.

7 Whether conversations and association with a prostitute amounts to being habitually in her company is an issue for the jury: *R v Ptohopoulos* (1967) 52 Cr App Rep 47, CA.

8 Sexual Offences Act 1956 s 30 (2); and see *R v Clarke* [1976] 2 All ER 696, 63 Cr App Rep 16, CA.

391. Powers of search for man living on earnings of prostitution. Where it is made to appear by information on oath before a justice of the peace that there is reasonable cause to suspect that a house, or part of a house is used by a woman for the purposes of prostitution[1], and that a man[2] residing in or frequenting the house is living wholly or in part on her earnings[3], the justice may issue a warrant authorising a constable to enter and search the house and to arrest the man[4].

1 For the meaning of 'prostitution' see para 386 note 4 ante.
2 For the meaning of 'man' see para 378 note 3 ante.
3 See para 390 ante.
4 Sexual Offences Act 1956 s 42. As to powers of entry and search see para 668 et seq post; and as to powers of arrest see para 693 et seq post.

392. Person living on the earnings of male prostitution. A man[1] or woman[1] who knowingly lives wholly or in part on the earnings of prostitution of another man is guilty of an offence and liable on conviction on indictment to imprisonment for a term not exceeding seven years or on summary conviction to imprisonment for a term not exceeding six months[2].

Anyone may arrest without warrant a person found committing such an offence[3].

1 The use of the terms 'man' and 'woman' in the Sexual Offences Act 1956 (see para 378 notes 3, 6 respectively ante) applies for the purposes of the Sexual Offences Act 1967: s 11 (3). See *R v Tan* [1983] QB 1053, 76 Cr App Rep 300, CA and para 390 ante.
2 Sexual Offences Act 1967 s 5 (1).
3 Ibid s 5 (3). As to arrest without warrant see para 703 et seq post.

393. Prostitute loitering or soliciting. It is an offence for a common prostitute[1] to loiter or solicit[2] in a street[3] or public place[4] for the purpose of prostitution[5]. A person guilty of such an offence is liable on summary conviction to a fine not exceeding level 2 on the standard scale or, for an offence committed after a previous conviction, to a fine not exceeding level 3 on the standard scale[6].

A constable may arrest without warrant anyone he finds in a street or public place and suspects, with reasonable cause, to be committing such an offence[7].

1 For the meaning of 'prostitute' see para 386 note 4 ante.
2 'Soliciting' involves the physical presence of the prostitute and conduct on her part amounting to an importuning of prospective customers; a prostitute who displays an advertisement in a street or public place that she is available as a prostitute does not 'solicit': *Weisz v Monahan* [1962] 1 All ER 664, [1962] 1 WLR 262, DC. A prostitute sitting scantily clad at a window bathed in red light and in an area where prostitutes were sought was held to be 'soliciting' in the sense of tempting or alluring prospective customers to come in for prostitution and projecting her solicitation to passers by: *Behrendt v Burridge* [1976] 3 All ER 285, [1977] 1 WLR 29, DC. See also *Knight v Fryer* [1976] Crim LR 322, DC, para 395 note 2 post and note 3 infra.
3 For these purposes, 'street' includes any bridge, road, lane, footway, subway, square, court, alley or passage, whether a thoroughfare or not, which is for the time being open to the public; and the doorways and entrances of premises abutting on a street and any ground adjoining and open to a street, are treated as forming part of the street: Street Offences Act 1959 s 1 (4). Conduct amounting to soliciting by prostitutes on a balcony or at a window overlooking the street is 'soliciting in the street': *Smith v Hughes* [1960] 2 All ER 859, [1960] 1 WLR 830, DC; *Behrendt v Burridge* [1976] 3 All ER 285, [1977] 1 WLR 29, DC.
4 'Public place' is not defined in the Street Offences Act 1959, but must presumably be construed ejusdem generis with the extended definition of 'street': see note 3 supra. In *R v Wellard* (1884) 14 QBD 63 at 66, 67, CCR, Grove J said 'A public place is one where the public go, no matter whether they have a right to go or not'. See also *R v Collinson* (1931) 23 Cr App Rep 49, CCA (field to which the public was temporarily admitted held to be a public place); *Elkins v Cartlidge* [1947] 1 All ER 829, DC (an inclosure at the rear of a public house where cars were parked held to be a public place).
5 Street Offences Act 1959 s 1 (1).
6 Ibid s 1 (2) (substituted by the Criminal Justice Act 1982 s 71 (1)). For the meaning of 'the standard scale' see para 808 post.

7 Street Offences Act 1959 s 1 (3). Such power of arrest was preserved by the Police and Criminal Evidence Act 1984: see s 26 (2), Sch 2 and para 708 post.

394. Application to court by a woman cautioned for loitering or soliciting. Where a woman is cautioned[1] by a constable, in respect of her conduct in a street[2] or public place, that, if she persists in such conduct, it may result in her being charged with an offence[3], she may apply to a magistrates' court[4] for an order directing that no entry is to be made in respect of that caution in any record maintained by the police of those so cautioned and that any such entry already made is to be expunged[5]. The court must make the order unless satisfied that on the occasion when she was cautioned she was loitering or soliciting in a street or public place for the purpose of prostitution[6].

1 Cautioning is an extra-statutory procedure. When the Street Offences Act 1959 came into force, a system was introduced under which a woman who had not previously been convicted of loitering or soliciting for the purpose of prostitution is not charged unless she has been cautioned by the police on at least two occasions and such cautions have been formally recorded. See *Collins v Wilcock* [1984] 3 All ER 374, 79 Cr App Rep 229, DC. The Street Offences Act 1959 does not confer power on a police officer to stop and detain a woman who is a prostitute for the purpose of cautioning her: *Collins v Wilcock* supra.
2 For these purposes, references to a street are to be construed in accordance with the Street Offences Act 1959 s 1 (4): s 2 (4). See para 393 note 3 ante.
3 Ie under ibid s 1: see para 393 ante.
4 Application must be made not later than 14 clear days after the caution (ibid s 2 (1)) and must be by way of complaint against the chief officer of police for the area in which the woman is cautioned or against such officer of police as he may designate for the purpose in relation to that area or any part of it (s 2 (2)).
5 Ibid s 2 (1). Subject to any provision to the contrary in rules made under the Magistrates' Courts Act 1980 s 144 (see MAGISTRATES), on the hearing of any such complaint the procedure is the same as if it were a complaint by the police officer against the woman, except that this does not affect the operation of ss 55–57 (non-attendance of parties to a complaint: see MAGISTRATES): Street Offences Act 1959 s 2 (2) (amended by the Magistrates' Courts Act 1980 s 154 (1), Sch 7 para 30).
    The application must be heard and determined in camera unless the woman desires that the proceedings be conducted in public: Street Offences Act 1959 s 2 (3).
6 Ibid s 2 (1).

395. Soliciting by a man for immoral purposes. It is an offence for a man[1] persistently to solicit[2] or importune[3] in a public place[4] for immoral purposes[5]. A man guilty of such an offence is liable on conviction on indictment to imprisonment for a term not exceeding two years, or on summary conviction to imprisonment for a term not exceeding six months[6].

Any person[7] may arrest without warrant a person found committing this offence[8].

1 For the meaning of 'man' see para 378 note 3 ante. See also, it would appear, *R v Tan* [1983] QB 1053, 76 Cr App Rep 300, CA and para 390 ante.
2 A man displaying an advertisement outside a shop indicating he is a male prostitute and where his services can be had does not 'solicit': *Burge v DPP* [1962] 1 All ER 666n, [1962] 1 WLR 265, DC. See also para 393 note 2 ante. Solicitation may be by gestures and need not reach the mind of the person intended to be solicited: see *Horton v Mead* [1913] 1 KB 154.
3 See *Field v Chapman* (1953) Times, 9 October, DC (there seems to be no real distinction to be drawn between persistently soliciting and persistently importuning). See also *Dale v Smith* [1967] 2 All ER

1133, [1967] 1 WLR 700, DC (two separate acts of importuning within the period named in the information or indictment are sufficient to render the importuning persistent).

4 'Public place' is not defined in the Sexual Offences Act 1956; but see para 393 note 4 ante.

5 Ibid s 32. 'Immoral purposes' means immoral in respect of sexual conduct: *Crook v Edmondson* [1966] 2 QB 81, [1966] 1 All ER 833, DC. Lawful sexual activity, such as an homosexual act, is capable of being conduct involving immoral purposes; it is for the jury to decide as a matter of fact whether it did involve immoral purposes: *R v Ford* [1978] 1 All ER 1129, 66 Cr App Rep 46, CA; *R v Gray* (1982) 74 Cr App Rep 324, CA (*Crook v Edmondson* supra is doubted to the extent that it suggests the contrary). Soliciting girls under the age of 14 is soliciting for immoral purposes, and would also be a criminal offence contrary to the Sexual Offences Act 1956 s 6 (see para 527 post): *R v Dodd* (1977) 66 Cr App Rep 87, CA. It is not an offence under the Sexual Offences Act 1956 s 32 for a man to solicit common prostitutes: *Crook v Edmondson* supra.

6 Sexual Offences Act 1956 s 37 (1)–(3), Sch 2 para 32 (amended by the Courts Act 1971 s 56 (4), Sch 11 Pt IV).

7 A constable may only do so in accordance with the Police and Criminal Evidence Act 1984 s 25 (see para 707 post): Sexual Offences Act 1956 s 41 (amended by the Police and Criminal Evidence Act 1984 s 119 (1), Sch 6 para 9).

8 Sexual Offences Act 1956 s 41 (amended by the Criminal Law Act 1967 s 10 (2), Sch 3 Pt III). As to arrest without warrant see para 703 et seq post.

396. Soliciting by men of women for prostitution.

A man[1] commits an offence if he solicits a woman[2], or different women, for the purpose of prostitution[3] (1) from a motor vehicle[4] while it is in a street[5] or public place; or (2) in a street or public place while in the immediate vicinity of a motor vehicle that he has just got out of or off, persistently[6] or in such manner or in such circumstances as to be likely to cause annoyance to the woman, or any of the women, solicited, or nuisance to other persons in the neighbourhood[7]. A man also commits an offence if in a street or public place he persistently solicits a woman, or different women, for the purpose of prostitution[8]. A person guilty of either such offence is liable on summary conviction to a fine not exceeding level 3 on the standard scale[9].

1 The Interpretation Act 1978 s 6 (a), (b) (words importing the masculine gender to include the feminine, and vice versa) does not apply to the Sexual Offences Act 1985: s 4 (3). For these purposes, the use of the word 'man' without the addition of the word 'boy' does not prevent the provision applying to any person to whom it would have applied if both words had been used, and similarly with the words 'woman' and 'girl': s 4 (2).

2 See note 1 supra.

3 For these purposes, references to a man soliciting a woman for the purpose of prostitution are references to his soliciting her for the purpose of obtaining her services as a prostitute: Sexual Offences Act 1985 s 4 (1). For the meaning of 'solicit' and 'prostitution' which may apply for these purposes see paras 393 note 2, 395 note 2, 386 note 4 respectively ante.

4 For these purposes, 'motor vehicle' has the same meaning as in the Road Traffic Act 1988: Sexual Offences Act 1985 s 1 (3) (amended by the Road Traffic (Consequential Provisions) Act 1988 s 4, Sch 3 para 29). See ROAD TRAFFIC.

5 For these purposes, 'street' includes any bridge, road, lane, footway, subway, square, court, alley or passage, whether a thoroughfare or not, which is for the time being open to the public; and the doorways and entrances of premises abutting on a street, and any ground adjoining and open to a street, are to be treated as forming part of the street: Sexual Offences Act 1985 s 4 (4).

6 There must be a degree of repetition, either of invitations to one woman or to different women, but two invitations may be sufficient to support a charge: see *Dale v Smith* [1967] 2 All ER 1133, [1967] 1 WLR 700, DC (decided under the Sexual Offences Act 1956 s 32: see para 395 note 3 ante).

7 Sexual Offences Act 1985 s 1 (1). In convicting a man of so called kerb-crawling contrary to s 1, justices are entitled to apply their local knowledge of the area where the offence occurred and conclude that his activities would have been likely to cause a nuisance to other persons in the neighbourhood even though there was no direct evidence that a nuisance had actually been caused to anyone: *Paul v Luton Justices, ex p Crown Prosecution Service* (1989) JP 512, [1989] Crim LR 660, DC.

8 Sexual Offences Act 1985 s 2 (1).

9 Ibid ss 1 (2), 2 (2). For the meaning of 'the standard scale' see para 808 post.

(15) OFFENCES RELATING TO CONTROLLED DRUGS, DRUG TRAFFICKING AND INTOXICATING SUBSTANCES

(i) Controlled Drugs

397. Unlawful possession of a controlled drug. It is an offence[1] for a person[2] (1) to have a controlled drug[3] in his possession[4] unlawfully[5]; or (2) to incite another to commit an offence under head (1) above[6]. A person guilty of such an offence is liable on conviction on indictment or on summary conviction to imprisonment or a fine, or to both; the maximum term of imprisonment, and, in the case of summary conviction, the maximum fine, is dependent upon the controlled drug in relation to which the offence was committed[7].

In any proceedings for an offence under head (1) above in which it is proved that the accused had a controlled drug in his possession, it is a defence for him to prove that, knowing or suspecting it to be a controlled drug:

(a) he took possession of it for the purpose of preventing another from committing or continuing to commit an offence in connection with that drug and, as soon as possible after taking possession of it, took all such steps as were reasonably open to him to destroy the drug or to deliver it into the custody of a person lawfully entitled to take custody of it; or

(b) he tool possession of it for the purpose of delivering it into the custody of a person lawfully entitled to take custody of it and, as soon as possible after taking possession of it, took all such steps as were reasonably open to him to deliver it into the custody of such a person[8].

1 On the authority of *R v Courtie* [1984] AC 463, 78 Cr App Rep 292, HL (cited in para 505 note 5 post) it is submitted that there is more than one offence, because of the difference in penalties imposed: see note 7 infra. *R v Courtie* supra has been applied to the Customs and Excise Management Act 1979 s 170: see CUSTOMS AND EXCISE.

2 Where any offence under the Misuse of Drugs Act 1971 committed by a body corporate is proved to have been committed with the consent or connivance of, or to be attributable to any neglect on the part of, any director, manager, secretary or other similar officer of the body corporate, or any person purporting to act in such capacity, he as well as the body corporate is guilty of that offence and liable to be proceeded against accordingly: s 21.

3 'Controlled drug' means any substance or product for the time being specified in ibid s 2 (1) (a), Sch 2 Pts I, II or III: s 2 (1) (a). Her Majesty may by Order in Council amend Sch 2: see s 2 (2)–(5). As to Sch 2 and the Orders in Council made under s 2 (2)–(5) see MEDICINE vol 30 para 737 et seq. Unlawful possession of any controlled drug described in Sch 2 by its scientific name is not established by proof of possession of naturally occurring material of which the described drug is one of the unseparated constituents; and this is so whether or not the naturally occurring material is also included as another item in the list of controlled drugs: *DPP v Goodchild* [1978] 2 All ER 161, 67 Cr App Rep 56, HL. As to the admissibility as evidence of an admission by an accused that the substance in his possession is a controlled drug see *R v Chatwood* [1980] 1 All ER 467; sub nom *R v Chatwood, R v Egan, R v Flaherty, R v Proctor, R v Walker* (1979) 70 Cr App Rep 39, CA.

4 For these purposes, the things which a person has in his possession are to be taken to include any thing subject to his control which is in the custody of another: Misuse of Drugs Act 1971 s 37 (3). It is for the prosecution to prove basic possession: *R v McNamara* (1988) 87 Cr App Rep 246, CA. As to possession see para 398 post.

The offence is an absolute offence, in the sense that, in order to be satisfied of guilt, there is no need for the jury to be satisfied of any mental elements in the ingredients of the offence, such as used to be described as mens rea: *R v Lewis* (1988) 87 Cr App Rep 270, CA.

5 Ie in contravention of the Misuse of Drugs Act 1971 s 5 (1). For these purposes, 'contravention' includes failure to comply; and 'contravene' has a corresponding meaning: s 37 (1). Subject to any regulations under s 7 for the time being in force (see MEDICINE vol 30 para 741), it is not lawful for a

person to have a controlled drug in his possession: s 5 (1). As to the statutory defences see infra and para 404 post. As to transporting or storing a controlled drug where possession of the drug contravenes s 5 (1) see para 408 note 2 post.

The Secretary of State may by regulations made by statutory instrument make provision for excluding in such cases as may be prescribed the application of any provision of the Act which creates an offence: see ss 22 (a) (i), 31 (1)–(3) and MEDICINE vol 30 para 741. Notwithstanding anything in the Magistrates' Courts Act 1980 s 127 (1) (limitation of time: see MAGISTRATES), a magistrates' court may try an information for an offence under the 1971 Act if the information was laid at any time within 12 months from the commission of the offence: Misuse of Drugs Act 1971 s 25 (4) (amended by the Magistrates' Courts Act 1980 s 154, Sch 7 para 103). As to possession of a controlled drug with intent to supply another unlawfully see para 399 post.

6   Misuse of Drugs Act 1971 ss 5 (2), 19 (amended by the Criminal Attempts Act 1981 ss 10, 11, Schedule Pt I). See also note 5 supra. An offence under the Misuse of Drugs Act 1971 s 19 (as so amended) is punishable on summary conviction, on indictment or in either way according to whether, under Sch 4 (as amended) (see note 7 infra), the substantive offence is punishable on summary conviction, on indictment or in either way; and the penalties which may be imposed on a person so convicted are the same as those which under Sch 4 (as so amended) may be imposed on a person convicted of the substantive offence (ie the offence to which the incitement mentioned in s 19 (as so amended) was directed): s 25 (3) (amended by the Criminal Attempts Act 1981 ss 10, 11, Schedule Pt I). As to incitement see para 58 ante.

7   Misuse of Drugs Act 1971 s 25 (1), (2), Sch 4 (amended by the Criminal Law Act 1977 ss 27, 28, Sch 5; the Magistrates' Courts Act 1980 ss 31, 32). In the case of a Class A drug, the maxima are, on conviction on indictment, imprisonment for seven years or a fine, or both, or on summary conviction, imprisonment for six months or the prescribed sum, or both; in the case of a Class B drug, on conviction on indictment, imprisonment for five years or a fine, or both, or on summary conviction, imprisonment for three months or £500, or both; in the case of a Class C drug, on conviction on indictment, imprisonment for two years or a fine, or both, or on summary conviction, imprisonment for three months or £200, or both: Misuse of Drugs Act 1971 Sch 4 (as so amended). For the meaning of 'the prescribed sum' see para 807 post. 'Class A drug', 'Class B drug' and 'Class C drug' mean any of the substances and products for the time being specified respectively in Sch 2 Pts I, II and III (see MEDICINE vol 30 para 738 et seq): s 2 (1) (b).

As to the power to order forfeiture of anything shown to relate to the offence see para 1327 post.

8   Ibid s 5 (4). Nothing in s 5 (4) prejudices any defence which it is open to a person charged with an offence under s 5 to raise apart from s 5 (4): s 5 (6). As to the statutory defence available to a person charged with an offence under s 5 (2) (see text to note 5 supra) see para 404 post.

398. Meaning of 'possession'. The question of what constitutes possession is an illusive concept at common law[1]. A person has a controlled drug[2] in his possession when he has physical control or custody of a thing plus knowledge that he has it in his custody and control. He may possess a controlled drug without knowing or comprehending its nature; but he does not possess it unless he knows he has it[3].

The quantity of the drug is important in two respects: (1) whether the quantity is sufficient to enable the court to find as a matter of fact that it amounts to something[4]; (2) if the quantity is minute, whether the accused knew that he possessed something[5]. It is no defence that the presence of the drug has been forgotten[6]; nor will ignorance or mistake as to the quality of a substance prevent the accused from being in possession of it if that substance turns out to be a controlled drug[7].

If the accused orders a controlled drug and directs that it be sent by post to his address, he is in possession of such drug from the time it arrives through the letter box[8]. If the drug is in a container, the accused does not automatically possess the drug, although he possesses the container[9].

Where several drugs are specified in the particulars of charge, proof of possession of any of them is sufficient[10].

Where accused are jointly charged, joint possession must be established; mere knowledge of the existence of the drugs on the part of an accused does not amount to possession by him[11].

1 *R v Lewis* (1988) 87 Cr App Rep 270, CA.
2 For the meaning of 'controlled drug' see para 397 note 3 ante.
3 *R v Boyesen* [1982] AC 768, 75 Cr App Rep 51, HL; *Warner v Metropolitan Police Comr* [1969] 2 AC 256, 52 Cr App Rep 373, HL; *R v Lewis* (1988) 87 Cr App Rep 270, CA.
4 If it is visible, touchable and measurable, it is certainly something: *R v Boyesen* [1982] AC 768, 75 Cr App Rep 51, HL; explaining *Bocking v Roberts* [1974] QB 307, [1973] 3 All ER 962, DC. See also *R v Worsell* [1969] 2 All ER 1183, 53 Cr App Rep 322, CA; *R v Graham* [1969] 2 All ER 1181, [1970] 1 WLR 113n, CA (scrapings in accused's pockets sufficient to be measured).
5 See *Police v Emirali* [1976] 1 NZLR 286; *R v Colyer* [1974] Crim LR 243; *R v Hierowski* [1978] Crim LR 563; *R v Boyesen* [1982] AC 768, 75 Cr App Rep 51, HL, overruling *R v Carver* [1978] QB 472, 67 Cr App Rep 352, CA. A small trace of a drug may prove earlier possession (*R v Worsell* [1969] 2 All ER 1183, 53 Cr App Rep 322, CA; *R v Graham* [1969] 2 All ER 1181, [1970] 1 WLR 113n, CA), but care must be taken in bringing charges (*R v Pragliola* [1977] Crim LR 612 (pipe contained drug trace; pipe returned to accused; accused charged with possession of drug; charge oppressive and not justifiable). An accused is not in possession of a drug when a trace of amphetamine powder is found in a urine sample, because of the changed character of the substance; but a sample may prove possession at an earlier time: *Hambleton v Callinan* [1968] 2 QB 427, [1968] 2 All ER 943, DC. The admissibility as evidence of a urine sample required by the police, to determine possession, is at the discretion of the trial judge depending on the facts of the particular case: *R v Beet* (1977) 66 Cr App Rep 188, CA; and see para 1060 post. If a man smokes cannabis resin, he does have cannabis resin in his possession at the time of the smoking: *Chief Constable of Cheshire Constabulary v Hunt* (1983) 147 JP 567, DC.
6 *R v Martindale* [1986] 3 All ER 25, 84 Cr App Rep 31, CA, following *R v Buswell* [1972] 1 All ER 75, CA and not following *R v Russell* (1984) 81 Cr App Rep 315, CA.
7 *Searle v Randolph* [1972] Crim LR 779, DC; *Lockyer v Gibb* [1967] 2 QB 243, [1966] 2 All ER 653, DC; *R v Marriott* [1971] 1 All ER 595, 55 Cr App Rep 82, CA; *R v McNamara* (1988) 87 Cr App Rep 246, CA; *R v Lewis* (1988) 87 Cr App Rep 270, CA.
8 *R v Peaston* (1978) 69 Cr App Rep 203, CA.
9 *Warner v Metropolitan Police Comr* [1969] 2 AC 256, 52 Cr App Rep 373, HL. Possession of the container leads to a strong inference that the accused was in possession of the contents: *R v McNamara* (1988) 87 Cr App Rep 246, CA. It would appear that the accused is not in possession of a drug in a container when (1) he is completely mistaken as to the nature of the contents of the container (confirmed in *R v McNamara* supra); (2) he does not suspect that there is anything wrong with those contents: *Warner v Metropolitan Police Comr* supra (decided under the Drugs (Prevention of Misuse) Act 1964 s 1 (1) (repealed); *R v Wright* (1976) 62 Cr App Rep 169 (not in possession when drug in tin which the accused was handed and did not know or suspect what it contained and was told to throw it away which he did immediately); *R v Ashton-Rickardt* [1978] 1 All ER 173, 65 Cr App Rep 67, CA; *R v Peaston* (1978) 69 Cr App Rep 203, CA.
   The prosecution has the initial burden of proving that the accused had, and knew that he had, the box in his control and also that the box contained something. That establishes the necessary possession. The prosecution must also prove that the box in fact contained the drug alleged: *R v McNamara* supra. As to the statutory defence which may then arise see para 404 post. Cf the approach to possession of drugs in a house rather than a container: see *R v Lewis* (1988) 87 Cr App Rep 270, CA. A man does not possess something put into his house or pocket without his knowledge: *R v McNamara* supra.
10 *R v Peevey* (1973) 57 Cr App Rep 554, CA.
11 *R v Searle* [1971] Crim LR 592, CA. An appropriate direction would be to invite the jury to consider whether the drugs formed a common pool from which all had the right to draw at will and whether there was a joint enterprise to consume drugs together because then the possession of drugs by one in pursuance of that common enterprise might well be possession on the part of all: *R v Searle* supra. See also *R v Wright* (1975) 119 Sol Jo 825, CA; *R v Strong, R v Berry* [1989] 10 LS Gaz R 41, CA (mere presence in the same vehicle as the drug and in particular where there was no evidence of knowledge cannot amount to evidence from which the jury can properly infer possession, whether individual or joint).

399. Controlled drugs; unlawful production or supply and possession with intent to supply unlawfully. It is an offence for a person[1]:

(1) to produce[2] a controlled drug[3] unlawfully[4] or to be concerned in the production of such a drug unlawfully[5];

(2) to supply[6] or offer to supply a controlled drug[7] to another[8] unlawfully or to be concerned[9] in the supplying of such a drug to another unlawfully or to be concerned in the making to another unlawfully of an offer to supply such a drug[10];

(3) to have a controlled drug in his possession[11], whether lawfully or not, with intent to supply[12] it to another unlawfully[13];

(4) to incite another to commit an offence under heads (1)–(3) above[14].

A person guilty of any such offence is liable on conviction on indictment or on summary conviction to imprisonment or a fine, or to both; the maximum term of imprisonment, and in the case of summary conviction the maximum fine, is dependent upon the controlled drug in relation to which the offence was committed[15].

1 As to the liability of directors and officers where an offence is committed by a body corporate see para 397 note 2 ante.

2 For these purposes, 'produce', where the reference is to producing a controlled drug, means producing it by manufacture, cultivation or any other method; and 'production' has a corresponding meaning: Misuse of Drugs Act 1971 s 37 (1).

3 For the meaning of 'controlled drug' see para 397 note 3 ante.

4 Ie in contravention of the Misuse of Drugs Act 1971 s 4 (1). As to producing or supplying a controlled drug in contravention of s 4 (1) see para 408 note 2 post. For the meaning of 'contravention' see para 397 note 5 ante. Subject to any regulations under s 7 for the time being in force (see MEDICINE vol 30 para 754), it is not lawful for a person (1) to produce a controlled drug; or (2) to supply or offer to supply a controlled drug to another: s 4 (1).

5 Ibid s 4 (2). As to the statutory defence see para 404 post. The Secretary of State may by regulations made by statutory instrument make provision for excluding in such cases as may be prescribed the application of any provision of the Act which creates an offence: ss 22 (a) (i), 31 (1)–(3). See MEDICINE vol 30 para 742. As to the time limit for trying an information see para 397 note 5 ante. An offence under ss 4 (2), (3), 5 (3) (see infra) is a drug trafficking offence for the purposes of the Drug Trafficking Offences Act 1986: see s 38 (1) and para 1305 note 2 post.

6 For these purposes, 'supplying' includes distributing: Misuse of Drugs Act 1971 s 37 (1). The word 'supply' appears in s 4 (1) (b) which is referred to for the purposes of creating the offences under heads (1), (2) supra. The meaning of the word is, therefore, the same for both offences. 'Supplying' must be given its ordinary natural meaning: *Holmes v Chief Constable Merseyside Police* [1976] Crim LR 125, DC; *R v Maginnis* [1987] AC 303, 85 Cr App Rep 127, HL. The word 'supply' in its ordinary natural meaning conveys the idea of furnishing or providing to another something which is wanted or required in order to meet the wants or requirements of that other. It connotes more than the mere transfer of physical control of some chattel or object from one person to another. The additional concept is that of enabling the recipient to apply the thing handed over to purposes for which he desires or has a duty to apply it: *R v Maginnis* supra. There is no problem in the obvious case where a person transfers both custody and control of a controlled drug to another: *R v Mills* [1963] 1 QB 522, 47 Cr App Rep 49, CCA. A person who places drugs in temporary custody with another person is not supplying, because the person having custody of them will not use the drugs for his own use: *R v Maginnis* supra, approving *R v Dempsey* (1985) 82 Cr App Rep 291, CA (accused, a registered drug addict, asked the other accused to hold some drugs for him while he went to the toilet; accused's conviction for supplying other accused quashed). The person having custody supplies when he hands back the controlled drugs to the person who had deposited them with him so as to enable those persons to apply the drugs to their own purposes: *R v Maginnis* supra, approving *R v Delgado* [1984] 1 All ER 449, 78 Cr App Rep 175, CA (accused had drugs in a holdall; said he had them for safe-keeping; accused did intend to transfer the drugs to another at an agreed time; thus he had committed offence contrary to the Misuse of Drugs Act 1971 s 5 (3)) and *Donnelly v HM Advocate* 1985 SLT 243. Injecting another with a drug in the latter's possession is not 'supplying': *R v Harris* [1968] 2 All ER 49n, 52 Cr App Rep 277, CA. The division of drugs in joint possession may be a supply: *Holmes v Chief Constable Merseyside Police* supra. Distribution of drugs purchased after pooling of money is a supply: *R v Buckley, R v Lane* (1979) 69 Cr App Rep 371, approving *Holmes v Chief Constable Merseyside Police* supra. Where the accused offered two girls a reefer cigarette to smoke, it was held that there was an offer to supply: *R v Moore* [1979] Crim LR 789. There is, however, no possession with intent to supply when the accused makes reefer cigarettes which are passed round a group of people, because taking a puff and passing on a cigarette does not amount to a

supply: *R v King* [1978] Crim LR 228. It is not a necessary element in the conception of supply that the provision should be made out of the personal resources of the person who does the supplying: *R v Maginnis* supra. As to making an offer to supply, offering to supply a substance which the accused believes is a controlled drug is sufficient, even though the substance is not a controlled drug: *Haggard v Mason* [1976] 1 All ER 337, [1976] 1 WLR 187, DC.

7 As to supply of intoxicating substances other than controlled drugs see the Intoxicating Substances (Supply) Act 1985 and para 413 post; and as to offences relating to the supply of articles for administering controlled drugs see the Misuse of Drugs Act 1971 s 9A (added by the Drug Trafficking Offences Act 1986 s 34) and para 402 post.

8 'Another' cannot be a person in the indictment: *R v Lubren and Adepoju* [1988] Crim LR 378, CA.

9 It is the duty of the judge to assist the jury as to the meaning of the word 'concerned': *R v Hughes* (1985) 81 Cr App Rep 344, CA. A person may be concerned by being involved at a distance in making an offer to supply a controlled drug: *R v Blake, R v O'Connor* (1978) 68 Cr App Rep 1, CA.

10 Misuse of Drugs Act 1971 s 4 (3). See also note 5 supra. In *R v Hughes* (1985) 81 Cr App Rep 344, CA, the three ingredients of the offence were listed as (1) the supply of a drug to another, or as the case may be, the making of an offer to supply the drug to another; (2) participation by the accused in an enterprise involving such a supply or, as the case may be, such an offer to supply; (3) knowledge by the accused of the nature of the enterprise, either knowledge that it is a venture to supply or to make an offer to supply the drug in question.

11 For the meaning of 'possession' see para 398 ante.

12 'Intent to supply' predicates that it should be the intent by the possessor of the drugs and not the intent of some other person: *R v Greenfield* (1983) 78 Cr App Rep 179n, CA. A person has an intention to supply a controlled drug to another if his intention is to return the drug to the person who deposited it with him: *R v Maginnis* [1987] AC 303, 85 Cr App Rep 127, HL (the intention to supply therefore relies upon the meaning of 'supply': see note 6 supra).

13 Misuse of Drugs Act 1971 s 5 (3). See also note 5 supra. As to possession of controlled drugs see para 397 ante.

14 Ibid s 19 (amended by the Criminal Attempts Act 1981 s 10, Schedule Pt I). As to incitement see para 58 ante.

15 Misuse of Drugs Act 1971 s 25 (1), (2), Sch 4 (amended by the Criminal Law Act 1977 ss 27, 28, Sch 5; the Magistrates' Courts Act 1980 ss 31 (1)–(3), 32; the Controlled Drugs (Penalties) Act 1985 s 1 (1)). In the case of a Class A drug, the maxima are, on conviction on indictment, life imprisonment or a fine, or both, or on summary conviction, six months or the prescribed sum, or both; in the case of a Class B drug, on conviction on indictment, imprisonment for 14 years or a fine, or both, or on summary conviction, imprisonment for six months or the prescribed sum, or both; and in the case of a Class C drug, on conviction on indictment, imprisonment for five years or a fine, or both, or on summary conviction, imprisonment for three months or £500, or both: Misuse of Drugs Act 1971 Sch 4 (as so amended). For the meaning of 'Class A drug', 'Class B drug' and 'Class C drug' see para 397 note 7 ante; and for the meaning of 'the prescribed sum' see para 807 post. As to the penalties for incitement see para 397 note 6 ante; and as to the power to order forfeiture of anything shown to relate to the offence see para 1327 post. As to sentencing see also *R v Singh* (1988) 10 Cr App Rep (S) 402, CA.

400. Cultivation of cannabis. It is an offence for a person[1]: (1) to cultivate any plant of the genus Cannabis[2] unlawfully[3]; or (2) to incite another to commit an offence under head (1) above[4]. A person guilty of any such offence is liable on conviction on indictment to imprisonment for a term not exceeding 14 years or a fine, or to both, or on summary conviction to imprisonment for a term not exceeding six months or a fine not exceeding the prescribed sum, or to both[5].

1 As to the liability of directors and officers where an offence is committed by a body corporate see para 397 note 2 ante.

2 Except in so far as the context otherwise requires, 'cannabis', except in the expression 'cannabis resin', means any plant of the genus Cannabis or any part of any such plant, by whatever name designated, except that it does not include cannabis resin or any of the following products after separation from the rest of the plant, namely (1) mature stalk of any such plant: (2) fibre produced from mature stalk of any such plant; and (3) seed of any such plant: Misuse of Drugs Act 1971 s 37 (1) (amended by the Criminal Law Act 1977 s 52).

3 Misuse of Drugs Act 1971 s 6 (2). Subject to any regulations under s 7 for the time being in force (see MEDICINE vol 30 para 754), it is not lawful for a person to cultivate any plant of the genus Cannabis:

s 6 (1). The prosecution does not have to prove that the accused knew that the plant being cultivated was cannabis: *R v Champ* (1981) 73 Cr App Rep 367, CA. As to the statutory defence see para 404 post. The Secretary of State may by regulations made by statutory instrument make provision for excluding in such cases as may be prescribed the application of any provision of the Act which creates an offence: Misuse of Drugs Act 1971 ss 22 (a) (i), 31 (1)–(3); and see MEDICINE vol 30 para 742. As to the time limit for trying an information see para 397 note 5 ante.

4 Ibid s 19 (amended by the Criminal Attempts Act 1981 ss 10, 11, Schedule Pt I). See further note 3 supra. As to incitement see para 58 ante.

5 Misuse of Drugs Act 1971 s 25 (1), (2), Sch 4 (amended by the Criminal Law Act 1977 ss 27, 28, Sch 5; the Magistrates' Courts Act 1980 ss 31 (1)–(3), 32). For the meaning of 'the prescribed sum' see para 807 post. As to the penalties for incitement see para 397 note 6 ante; and as to the power to order forfeiture of anything shown to relate to the offence see para 1327 post.

401. Activities etc relating to opium. It is an offence for a person[1]:
(1) to smoke or otherwise use prepared opium[2]; or
(2) to frequent a place used for the purpose of opium smoking; or
(3) to have in his possession[3] (a) any pipes or other utensils made or adapted for use in connection with the smoking of opium, being pipes or utensils which have been used by him or with his knowledge and permission in that connection or which he intends to use or permit others to use in that connection; or (b) any utensils which have been used by him or with his knowledge and permission in connection with the preparation of opium for smoking[4]; or
(4) to incite another to commit an offence under heads (1)–(3) above[5].

A person guilty of any such offence is liable on conviction on indictment to imprisonment for a term not exceeding 14 years or a fine, or to both, or on summary conviction to imprisonment for a term not exceeding six months or a fine not exceeding the prescribed sum, or to both[6].

1 As to the liability of directors and officers where an offence is committed by a body corporate see para 397 note 2 ante.
2 'Prepared opium' means opium prepared for smoking and includes dross and any other residues remaining after opium has been smoked: Misuse of Drugs Act 1971 s 37 (1).
3 For the meaning of 'possession' see para 398 ante.
4 Misuse of Drugs Act 1971 s 9. As to the statutory defence see para 404 post. The Secretary of State may by regulations made by statutory instrument make provision for excluding in such cases as may be prescribed the application of any provision of the Act which creates an offence: ss 22 (a) (i), 31 (1)–(3); and see MEDICINE vol 30 para 742. As to the time limit for trying an information see para 397 note 5 ante.
5 Ibid s 19 (amended by the Criminal Attempts Act 1981 ss 10, 11, Schedule Pt I). As to incitement see para 58 ante.
6 Misuse of Drugs Act 1971 s 25 (1), (2), Sch 4 (amended by the Criminal Law Act 1977 ss 27, 28, Sch 5; the Magistrates' Courts Act 1980 ss 31 (1)–(3), 32). For the meaning of 'the prescribed sum' see para 807 post. As to the penalties for incitement see para 397 note 6 ante; and as to the power to order forfeiture of anything shown to relate to the offence see para 1327 post.

402. Prohibition of supply etc of articles for administering or preparing controlled drugs. A person[1] who:
(1) supplies or offers to supply any article[2] which may be used or adapted to be used, whether by itself or in combination with another article or other articles, in the administration by any person of a controlled drug[3] to himself[4] or another, believing that article, or the article as adapted, is to be so used in circumstances where the administration is unlawful[5]; or
(2) supplies or offers to supply any article which may be used to prepare a controlled drug for administration by any person to himself or another

believing that the article is to be so used in circumstances where the administration is unlawful; or

(3) incites another to commit an offence under heads (1) or (2) above,

is guilty of an offence and liable on summary conviction to imprisonment for a term not exceeding six months or a fine not exceeding level 5 on the standard scale, or to both[6].

1 As to the liability of directors and officers where an offence is committed by a body corporate see para 397 note 2 ante.
2 It is not an offence under the Misuse of Drugs Act 1971 s 9A (1) (added by the Drug Trafficking Offences Act 1986 s 34) to supply or offer to supply a hypodermic syringe, or any part of one: Misuse of Drugs Act 1971 s 9A (2) (added by the Drug Trafficking Offences Act 1986 s 34).
3 For the meaning of 'controlled drug' see para 397 note 3 ante.
4 For these purposes, references to administration by any person of a controlled drug to himself include a reference to his administering it to himself with the assistance of another: Misuse of Drugs Act 1971 s 9A (5) (added by the Drug Trafficking Offences Act 1986 s 34).
5 For these purposes, any administration of a controlled drug is unlawful except (1) the administration by any person of a controlled drug to another in circumstances where the administration of the drug is not unlawful under the Misuse of Drugs Act 1971 s 4 (1) (see para 399 ante); or (2) the administration by any person of a controlled drug to himself in circumstances where having the controlled drug in his possession is not unlawful under s 5 (1) (see para 397 ante): s 9A (4) (added by the Drug Trafficking Offences Act 1986 s 34).
6 Misuse of Drugs Act 1971 ss 9A (1), (3), 19, 25 (1), (2), Sch 4 (amended and added by the Criminal Law Act 1977 ss 27, 28, Sch 5; the Magistrates' Courts Act 1980 ss 31 (1)–(3), 32; the Criminal Attempts Act 1981 ss 10, 11, Schedule Pt I; the Drug Trafficking Offences Act 1986 s 34 (2)). For the meaning of 'the standard scale' see para 808 post. As to incitement generally see para 58 ante; as to the penalties for incitement see para 397 note 6 ante; as to the time limit for trying an information see para 397 note 5 ante; and as to the power to order forfeiture of anything shown to relate to the offence see para 1327 post.

403. Offences by occupiers or managers of premises. A person[1] commits an offence if, being the occupier[2] or concerned in the management[3] of any premises, he knowingly[4] permits[5] or suffers any of the following activities to take place on those premises: (1) producing[6] or attempting to produce a controlled drug[7] unlawfully[8]; (2) supplying[9] or attempting to supply a controlled drug to another unlawfully or offering to supply a controlled drug to another unlawfully; (3) preparing opium for smoking; (4) smoking cannabis[10], cannabis resin[11] or prepared opium[12]. It is also an offence to incite another to commit an offence under heads (1)–(4) above [13].

A person guilty of any such offence is liable on conviction on indictment or on summary conviction to imprisonment or a fine, or to both; the maximum term of imprisonment, and in the case of summary conviction, the maximum fine is dependent upon the controlled drug in relation to which the offence was committed[14].

1 As to the liability of directors and managers where an offence is committed by a body corporate see para 397 note 2 ante.
2 The phrase 'the occupier' should be given a commonsense interpretation. A person 'in occupation' such that he has the requisite degree of control over the premises to exclude from them those who might otherwise smoke cannabis, or engage in other activity is covered by this provision. A person can have exclusive possession without being a tenant or having an estate in the land: *R v Tao* [1977] QB 141, 63 Cr App Rep 163, CA (undergraduate had an exclusive contractual licence from college which gave him not merely a right to use but a sufficient exclusivity of possession; he was an occupier; appeal against conviction dismissed); disapproving the principle in, but agreeing with the decision on facts of *R v Mogford* [1970] 1 WLR 988 (for persons to be 'occupiers' under the Dangerous Drugs Act 1965 s 5 (repealed) they had to have legal possession of and control over the premises; two daughters not occupiers for the purposes of the Act when parents temporarily away on holiday).

3 If the accused is managing the premises in the sense that he is running them, organising them and planning them, the fact that he has no lawful right or title to be on the premises and is a mere squatter does not prevent him from coming within the terms of the Misuse of Drugs Act 1971 s 8: *R v Josephs, R v Christie* (1977) 65 Cr App Rep 253, CA.

4 Knowledge is essential to permission: it can be either actual or inferred from wilful blindness, but not mere suspicion: *R v Thomas* (1976) 63 Cr App Rep 65, CA.

5 'Permit' involves knowledge: *R v Thomas* (1976) 63 Cr App Rep 65, CA.

6 For the meaning of 'produce' see para 399 note 2 ante. An occupier permitting another to cultivate cannabis plants is permitting or suffering their production: *Taylor v Chief Constable of Kent* [1981] 1 WLR 606, 72 Cr App Rep 318, DC. As to cultivation of cannabis see para 400 ante.

7 For the meaning of 'controlled drug' see para 397 note 3 ante.

8 Ie in contravention of the Misuse of Drugs Act 1971 s 4(1): see para 397 note 4 ante.

9 For the meaning of 'supply' see para 399 note 6 ante.

10 For the meaning of 'cannabis' see para 400 note 2 ante.

11 'Cannabis resin' means the separated resin, whether crude or purified, obtained from any plant of the genus Cannabis: Misuse of Drugs Act 1971 s 37(1).

12 Ibid s 8. Cf *R v Ashdown* (1974) 59 Cr App Rep 193, CA (co-tenant permitting another co-tenant to smoke cannabis is guilty of the offence). For the meaning of 'prepared opium' see para 401 note 2 ante. The Secretary of State may by regulations made by statutory instrument make provision for excluding in such cases as may be prescribed the application of any provision of the Misuse of Drugs Act 1971 which creates an offence: ss 22 (a) (i), 31 (1)–(3); and see MEDICINE vol 30 para 742. As to the time limit for trying an information see para 397 note 5 ante.

13 Ibid s 19 (amended by the Criminal Attempts Act 1981 ss 10, 11, Schedule Pt I). As to incitement see para 58 ante.

14 Misuse of Drugs Act 1971 s 25 (1), (2), Sch 4 (amended by the Criminal Law Act 1977 ss 27, 28, Sch 5; the Magistrates' Courts Act 1980 ss 1 (1)–(3), 32). In the case of a Class A drug or a Class B drug, the maxima are, on conviction on indictment, imprisonment for 14 years or a fine, or both, or on summary conviction, six months or the prescribed sum, or both; in the case of a Class C drug, on conviction on indictment, imprisonment for five years or a fine, or both, or on summary conviction, three months or £500, or both: Misuse of Drugs Act 1971 Sch 4 (as so amended). For the meaning of 'Class A drug', 'Class B drug' and 'Class C drug' see para 397 note 7 ante; and for the meaning of 'the prescribed sum' see para 807 post. Opium is a Class A drug and cannabis and cannabis resin are Class B drugs: see s 2, Sch 2 Pts I, II (as amended) and MEDICINE. As to the penalties for incitement see para 397 note 6 ante; and as to the power to order forfeiture of anything shown to relate to the offence see para 1327 post.

404. Defence of lack of knowledge in proceedings for certain offences.

Where in any specified proceedings[1] it is necessary, if the accused is to be convicted of the offence charged, for the prosecution to prove that some substance or product involved in the alleged offence was the controlled drug[2] which the prosecution alleges it to have been, and it is proved that the substance or product in question was that controlled drug, the accused must be acquitted if he proves (1) that he neither believed nor suspected nor had reason to suspect[3] that the substance or product in question was a controlled drug; or (2) that he believed the substance or product in question to be a controlled drug, or a controlled drug of a description, such that, if it had in fact been that controlled drug or a controlled drug of that description, he would not at the material time have been committing any specified[4] offence[5]; but he must not be acquitted of the offence charged by reason only of proving that he neither knew nor suspected nor had reason to suspect that the substance or product in question was the particular controlled drug alleged[6]. However, in any proceedings for a specified offence it is a defence for the accused to prove that he neither knew of nor suspected nor had reason to suspect the existence of some fact alleged by the prosecution which it is necessary for the prosecution to prove if he is to be convicted of the offence charged[7].

1 Ie proceedings in respect of offences under the Misuse of Drugs Act 1971 ss 4 (2), (3), 5 (3) (see para 399 ante), s 5 (2) (see para 397 ante), s 6 (2) (see para 400 ante), s 9 (see para 401 ante). Nothing in s 28

prejudices any defence which it is open to a person charged with an offence to which s 28 applies to raise apart from s 28: s 28 (4).

2　For the meaning of 'controlled drug' see para 397 note 3 ante.

3　The test of whether the accused had no 'reason to suspect' the substance was a controlled drug is objective and not subjective; voluntary intoxication (see para 28 ante) which makes the accused unable to hold a belief or register a suspicion is not a relevant consideration in the exercise of this statutory defence: *R v Young* [1984] 2 All ER 164, 78 Cr App Rep 288, C-MAC.

4　Ie any offence to which the Misuse of Drugs Act 1971 s 28 applies: see note 1 supra.

5　Ibid s 28 (3) (b).

6　Ibid s 28 (3) (a).

7　Ibid s 28 (2). The burden of proving knowledge of the article rests on the prosecution; this is not affected by s 28 (2): *R v Ashton-Rickardt* [1978] 1 All ER 173, 65 Cr App Rep 67, CA. The Misuse of Drugs Act 1971 s 28 (2) does not cast upon the accused the burden of disproving all facts adduced by the prosecution in support of the charges. Once the prosecution has proved that the accused had control of the box, knew that he had control and knew that the box contained something which was in fact the drug alleged, the burden is cast upon the accused to bring himself within s 28: *R v McNamara* (1988) 87 Cr App Rep 246, CA.

405. Assisting in or inducing commission outside the United Kingdom of an offence punishable under a corresponding law. A person[1] commits an offence if (1) in the United Kingdom he assists in or induces[2] the commission[3] in any place outside the United Kingdom of an offence punishable under the provisions of a corresponding law[4] in force in that place[5]; or (2) incites another to commit the offence in head (1) above[6].

A person guilty of any such offence is liable on conviction on indictment to imprisonment for a term not exceeding 14 years or a fine, or to both, or on summary conviction to imprisonment for a term not exceeding six months or a fine not exceeding the prescribed sum, or to both[7].

1　As to the liability of directors and officers where an offence is committed by a body corporate see para 397 note 2 ante.

2　'Assisting or inducing' is to be construed in its natural broad sense: *R v Vickers* [1975] 2 All ER 945, 61 Cr App Rep 48, CA; *R v Evans* (1976) 64 Cr App Rep 237, CA.

3　On the true construction of this provision a person cannot be guilty of commissioning an offence in a place outside the United Kingdom unless the offence outside the United Kingdom was committed: *R v Panayi and Karte* (1987) 86 Cr App Rep 261, CA. For the meaning of 'United Kingdom' see para 86 note 1 ante.

4　For these purposes, 'corresponding law' means a law stated in a certificate purporting to be issued by or on behalf of the government of a country outside the United Kingdom to be a law providing for the control and regulation in that country of the production, supply, use, export and import of drugs and other substances in accordance with the provisions of the Single Convention on Narcotic Drugs signed at New York on 30 March 1961 (Cmnd 1580, Miscellaneous No 1 1962) or a law providing for the control and regulation in that country of the production, supply, use, export and import of dangerous or otherwise harmful drugs in pursuance of any treaty, convention or other agreement or arrangement to which the government of that country and Her Majesty's government in the United Kingdom are for the time being parties: Misuse of Drugs Act 1971 s 36 (1). A statement in any such certificate to the effect that any facts constitute an offence against the law mentioned in the certificate is evidence of the matters stated: s 36 (2).

5　Ibid s 20. The offence is not one of strict liability: *R v Vickers* [1975] 2 All ER 945, 61 Cr App Rep 48, CA. The Secretary of State may by regulations made by statutory instrument make provision for excluding in such cases as may be prescribed the application of any provision of the Act which creates an offence: Misuse of Drugs Act 1971 ss 22 (a) (i), 31 (1)–(3); and see MEDICINE vol 30 para 742. As to the time limit for trying an information see para 397 note 5 ante.

6　Misuse of Drugs Act 1971 s 19 (amended by the Criminal Attempts Act 1981 ss 10, 11, Schedule Pt I). As to incitement see para 58 ante.

7　Misuse of Drugs Act 1971 s 25 (1), (2), Sch 4 (amended by the Criminal Law Act 1977 ss 27, 28, Sch 5; the Magistrates' Courts Act 1980 ss 31 (1)–(3), 32). For the meaning of 'the prescribed sum' see para 807 post. As to the penalties for incitement see para 397 note 6 ante; and as to the power to order forfeiture of anything shown to relate to the offence see para 1327 post. An offence under the Misuse of Drugs Act 1971 s 20 is a drug trafficking offence for the purposes of the Drug Trafficking Offences Act 1986: see s 38 (1) and para 1305 note 2 post.

406. Powers of search and seizure. If a constable has reasonable grounds to suspect that any person is in possession[1] of a controlled drug[2] in contravention of the Misuse of Drugs Act 1971 or of any regulations made thereunder, the constable may:

(1) search that person and detain him[3] for the purpose of searching him;

(2) search any vehicle or vessel[4] in which the constable suspects that the drug may be found, and for that purpose require the person in control of the vehicle or vessel to stop it;

(3) seize and detain anything found in the course of the search which appears to the constable to be evidence of an offence under the Act[5].

If a justice of the peace is satisfied by information on oath that there is reasonable ground for suspecting:

(a) that any controlled drugs are, in contravention of the Act or any regulations made thereunder, in the possession of a person on any premises; or

(b) that a document directly or indirectly relating to, or connected with, a transaction or dealing which was, or an intended transaction or dealing which would if carried out be an offence under the Act, or in the case of a transaction or dealing carried out or intended to be carried out in a place outside the United Kingdom, an offence against the provisions of a corresponding law[6] in force in that place, is in the possession of a person on any premises,

he may grant a warrant authorising any constable[7] to enter and search[8] the premises named in it and any person found there and to seize and detain any controlled drugs or document found if there is reasonable ground for suspecting that an offence under the Act has been committed in relation to such drugs or that a document is such as mentioned under head (b) above, as the case may be[9].

A person who intentionally obstructs a person in the exercise of the above powers of search and seizure is guilty of an offence and liable on conviction on indictment to imprisonment for a term not exceeding two years or a fine, or to both, or on summary conviction to imprisonment for a term not exceeding six months or a fine not exceeding the prescribed sum, or to both[10].

1 For the meaning of 'possession' see para 397 ante.

2 For the meaning of 'controlled drug' see para 397 note 3 ante.

3 The power conferred by the Misuse of Drugs Act 1971 s 23 (2) (a) does not, however, authorise a search by a constable of a person in police detention at a police station or an intimate search of a person by a constable: see the Police and Criminal Evidence Act 1984 s 53 (1) and para 765 post.

4 For these purposes, 'vessel' includes a hovercraft within the meaning of the Hovercraft Act 1968: Misuse of Drugs Act 1971 s 23 (2).

5 Ibid s 23 (2). Section 23 (2) is without prejudice to any other power of search or any power to seize or detain property which is exercisable by a constable: s 23 (2). As to powers of stop and search see para 660 et seq post.

6 For the meaning of 'corresponding law' see para 405 note 3 ante.

7 Ie any constable acting for the police area in which the premises are situated.

8 Such a warrant authorises entry, if need be by force, and search at any time or times within one month from the date of the warrant: Misuse of Drugs Act 1971 s 23 (3).

9 Ibid s 23 (3).

10 Ibid ss 23 (4) (a), 25 (1), (2), Sch 4. For the meaning of 'the prescribed sum' see para 807 post.

407. Misuse of controlled drugs. Offences in connection with the Secretary of State's powers to prevent the misuse of controlled drugs[1] are dealt with elsewhere[2].

1 Ie under the Misuse of Drugs Act 1971 ss 10–17, 22.
2 See MEDICINE vol 30 para 742 et seq.

(ii) Drug Trafficking

408. Assisting another to retain the benefit of drug trafficking. If a person enters into or is otherwise concerned in an arrangement whereby:

(1) the retention or control by or on behalf of another ('A') of A's proceeds[1] of drug trafficking[2] is facilitated, whether by concealment, removal from the jurisdiction, transfer to nominees or otherwise; or

(2) A's proceeds of drug trafficking are used to secure that funds are placed at A's disposal or are used for A's benefit to acquire property[3] by way of investment,

knowing or suspecting that A is a person who carries on or has carried on drug trafficking or has benefited from drug trafficking[4], he is guilty of an offence and liable on conviction on indictment to imprisonment for a term not exceeding 14 years or a fine, or to both, or on summary conviction to imprisonment for a term not exceeding six months or a fine not exceeding the statutory maximum, or to both[5].

Where a person discloses to a constable[6] a suspicion or belief that any funds or investments are derived from or used in connection with drug trafficking or any matter on which such a suspicion or belief is based:

(a) the disclosure is not to be treated as a breach of any restriction upon the disclosure of information imposed by contract;

(b) if he does any act in contravention of heads (1) or (2) supra and the disclosure relates to the arrangement concerned, he does not commit an offence if the disclosure is made in accordance with the following provisions, that is to say (i) it is made before he does the act concerned, being an act done with the consent of the constable; or (ii) it is made after he does the act, but is made on his initiative and as soon as it is reasonable for him to make it[7].

In proceedings against a person for such an offence it is a defence to prove:

(i) that he did not know or suspect that the arrangement related to any person's proceeds of drug trafficking; or

(ii) that he did not know or suspect that by the arrangement the retention or control by or on behalf of A of any property was facilitated or, as the case may be, that by the arrangement any property was used as mentioned in heads (1) or (2) above; or

(iii) that he intended to disclose to a constable such a suspicion, belief or matter[8] in relation to the arrangement but there is reasonable excuse for his failure to make[9] disclosure[10].

1 For these purposes, references to any person's proceeds of drug trafficking include a reference to any property which in whole or in part directly or indirectly represented in his hands his proceeds of drug trafficking: Drug Trafficking Offences Act 1986 s 24 (2).

In the Act, any payments or other rewards received by a person at any time in connection with drug trafficking carried on by him or another are his proceeds of drug trafficking: ss 2 (1) (a), 24 (2). References to anything received in connection with drug trafficking include a reference to anything received both in that connection and in some other connection: s 38 (5).

2 For these purposes, 'drug trafficking' means doing or being concerned in any of the following, whether in England and Wales or elsewhere: (1) producing or supplying a controlled drug where the production or supply contravenes the Misuse of Drugs Act 1971 s 4 (1) (see para 399 ante) or a corresponding law; (2) transporting or storing a controlled drug where possession of the drug contravenes s 5 (1) (see para 397 ante) or a corresponding law; (3) importing or exporting a controlled drug where the importation or exportation is prohibited by s 3 (1) (see MEDICINE vol 30 para 745) or a corresponding law; and includes a person doing the following, whether in England and Wales or elsewhere, that is entering into or being otherwise concerned in an arrangement whereby (a) the retention or control by or on behalf of another person of the other person's proceeds of drug trafficking is facilitated; or (b) the proceeds of drug trafficking by another person are used to secure that funds are placed at the other person's disposal or are used for the other person's benefit to acquire property by way of investment: Drug Trafficking Offences Act 1986 s 38 (1).

'Corresponding law' has the same meaning as in the Misuse of Drugs Act 1971 (see para 405 note 3 ante): Drug Trafficking Offences Act 1986 s 38 (1).

3 For these purposes, 'property' includes money and all other property, real or personal, heritable or movable, including things in action and other intangible or incorporeal property: ibid s 38 (1). The Act applies to property whether it is situated in England and Wales or elsewhere: s 38 (3).

4 For these purposes, a person who has at any time received any payment or other reward in connection with drug trafficking carried on by him or another has benefited from drug trafficking: ibid ss 1 (3), 38 (2).

5 Ibid s 24 (1), (5). For the meaning of 'the statutory maximum' see para 806 post. An offence under s 24 is a drug trafficking offence for the purposes of the Drug Trafficking Offences Act 1986: see s 38 (1) and para 1305 note 2 post. A person convicted under s 24 is not eligible for early release: see the Criminal Justice Act 1982 s 32 (2), Sch 1 Pt II (amended by the Drug Trafficking Offences Act 1986 s 24 (6)) and PRISONS.

6 'Constable' includes a person commissioned by the Commissioners of Customs and Excise: Drug Trafficking Offences Act 1986 s 38 (1).

7 Ibid s 24 (3).

8 Ie such a suspicion, belief or matter as is mentioned in ibid s 24 (3): see supra.

9 Ie failure to make disclosure in accordance with ibid s 24 (3) (b): see head (b) supra.

10 Ibid s 24 (4).

409. Orders to make material available. A constable[1] may, for the purpose of an investigation into drug trafficking[2], apply to a circuit judge for an order in relation to particular material or material of a particular description[3].

If on such an application the judge is satisfied that the prescribed conditions are fulfilled, he may make an order that the person who appears to him to be in possession of the material to which the application relates shall (1) produce it to a constable for him to take away[4]; or (2) give a constable access to it[5], within such period[6] as the order may specify[7].

The prescribed conditions are:

(1) that there are reasonable grounds for suspecting that a specified person has carried on or has benefited[8] from drug trafficking;

(2) that there are reasonable grounds for suspecting that the material to which the application relates:

(a) is likely to be of substantial value, whether by itself or together with other material, to the investigation for the purpose of which the application is made; and

(b) does not consist of or include items subject to legal privilege[9] or excluded material[10]; and

(3) that there are reasonable grounds for believing that it is in the public interest, having regard:

(a) to the benefit likely to accrue to the investigation if the material is obtained; and

(b) to the circumstances under which the person in possession of the material holds it,

that the material should be produced or that access to it should be given[11].

Where any such order has been made, the person required to comply with it may apply[12] in writing to the appropriate officer of the Crown Court for the order to be discharged or varied; and on hearing such an application a circuit judge may discharge the order or make such variations to it as he thinks fit[13].

1 For the meaning of 'constable' see para 408 note 6 ante.
2 For the meaning of 'drug trafficking' see para 408 note 2 ante. For the purposes of the Police and Criminal Evidence Act 1984 ss 21, 22 (see paras 687, 688 post), an investigation into drug trafficking is to be treated as if it were an investigation of or in connection with an offence: Drug Trafficking Offences Act 1986 s 29 (1) (a). Where material produced under s 27 (see infra) is retained under the Police and Criminal Evidence Act 1984 s 22, the constable retaining it may make information contained in such material available to a foreign law enforcement agency: *R v Crown Court at Southwark, ex p Customs and Excise Comrs* [1989] 3 All ER 673, [1989] 3 WLR 1054, DC.
3 Drug Trafficking Offences Act 1986 s 27 (1). An order of a circuit judge made under s 27 has effect as if it were an order of the Crown Court: s 27 (7). Provision may be made by the Crown Court rules as to the discharge and variation of orders under s 27 and proceedings relating to such orders (see infra): s 27 (6). The power to make an order under s 27 (1) is not limited to an investigation conducted by customs officers in the United Kingdom; but an information laid in support of an application for such an order made solely or partly to assist an investigation by a foreign law enforcement agency must so indicate on its face: *R v Crown Court at Southwark, ex p Customs and Excise Comrs* [1989] 3 All ER 673, [1989] 3 WLR 1054, DC.
4 Drug Trafficking Offences Act 1986 s 27 (2) (a). Where the material to which such an application relates consists of information contained in a computer, an order under s 27 (2) (a) has effect as an order to produce the material in a form in which it can be taken away and in which it is visible and legible: s 27 (8) (a). For the purposes of the Police and Criminal Evidence Act 1984 ss 21, 22 (see paras 687, 688 post), material produced in pursuance of an order under the Drug Trafficking Offences Act 1986 s 27 (2) (a) is to be treated as if it were material seized by a constable: s 29 (1) (b).
   If the prescribed conditions for making a production order are satisfied, the judge has a discretion whether to make such an order; but only in exceptional circumstances is it appropriate to require undertakings from the applicant before making an order: *R v Crown Court at Southwark, ex p Customs and Excise Comrs* [1989] 3 All ER 673, [1989] 3 WLR 1054, DC.
5 Drug Trafficking Offences Act 1986 s 27 (2) (b). Where the material to which such an application relates consists of information contained in a computer, an order under s 27 (2) (b) has effect as an order to give access to the material in a form in which it is visible and legible: s 27 (8) (b). Where the judge makes an order under s 27 (2) (b) in relation to material on any premises, he may, on the application of a constable, order any person who appears to him to be entitled to grant entry to the premises to allow a constable to enter the premises to obtain access to the material: s 27 (5).
6 The period so to be specified must be seven days unless it appears to the judge that a longer or shorter period would be appropriate in the particular circumstances of the application: ibid s 27 (3).
7 Ibid s 27 (2). Section 27 (2) is subject to s 30 (1): s 27 (2). See further para 411 post.
   An order under s 27 (2) does not confer any right to production of, or access to, items subject to legal privilege (see note 9 infra) or excluded material (see note 10 infra), has effect notwithstanding any obligation as to secrecy or other restriction upon the disclosure of information imposed by statute or otherwise and may be made in relation to material in the possession of an authorised government department: s 27 (9). For these purposes, 'authorised government department' means a government department which is an authorised department for the purposes of the Crown Proceedings Act 1947 (see CROWN PROCEEDINGS): Drug Trafficking Offences Act 1986 s 38 (1).
8 For the meaning of 'benefited from drug trafficking' see para 408 note 4 ante.
9 For these purposes, 'item subject to legal privilege' has the same meaning as in the Police and Criminal Evidence Act 1984 (see para 672 note 5 post): Drug Trafficking Offences Act 1986 s 29 (2).
10 For these purposes, 'excluded material' has the same meaning as in the Police and Criminal Evidence Act 1984 (see para 674 post): Drug Trafficking Offences Act 1986 s 29 (2).
11 Ibid s 27 (4).
12 Where a person proposes so to make an application, he must give a copy of the application, not later than 48 hours before the making of the application, to a constable at the police station from which the application for the order was made, together with a notice indicating the time and place at which the application for discharge or variation is to be made: Crown Court Rules 1982, SI 1982/1109,

r 25B (2) (added by SI 1986/2151). For these purposes, 'constable' includes a person commissioned by the Commissioners of Customs and Excise; and 'police station' includes a place for the time being occupied by Her Majesty's Customs and Excise: r 25B (4) (added by SI 1986/2151). A circuit judge may, however, direct that r 25B (2) (as so added) need not be complied with if he is satisfied that the person making the application has good reason to seek a discharge or variation of the order as soon as possible and it is not practicable to comply with r 25B (2) (as so added): r 25B (3) (added by SI 1986/2151).

13 Ibid r 25B (1) (added by SI 1986/2151).

410. Authority for search. A constable[1] may, for the purpose of an investigation into drug trafficking[2], apply to a circuit judge for a warrant in relation to specified premises[3]. On such an application the judge may issue a warrant authorising a constable to enter and search the premises if he is satisfied that the order made[4] in relation to material on the premises has not been complied with, or that either of the two sets of prescribed conditions[5] is fulfilled[6].

The first set of prescribed conditions is:

(1) that there are reasonable grounds for suspecting that a specified person has carried on or has benefited[7] from drug trafficking; and

(2) that the statutory conditions[8] are fulfilled in relation to any material on the premises; and

(3) that it would not be appropriate to make an order to make material available because:

   (a) it is not practicable to communicate with any person entitled to produce the material; or

   (b) it is not practicable to communicate with any person entitled to grant access to the material or entitled to grant entry to the premises on which the material is situated; or

   (c) the investigation for the purposes of which the application is made might be seriously prejudiced unless a constable could secure immediate access to the material[9].

The second set of prescribed conditions is:

(i) that there are reasonable grounds for suspecting that a specified person has carried on or has benefitted from drug trafficking; and

(ii) that there are reasonable grounds for suspecting that there is on the premises material relating to the specified person or to drug trafficking which is likely to be of substantial value, whether by itself or together with other material, to the investigation for the purpose of which the application is made, but that the material cannot at the time of the application be particularised; and

(iii) that:

   (a) it is not practicable to communicate with any person entitled to grant entry to the premises; or

   (b) entry to the premises will not be granted unless a warrant is produced; or

   (c) the investigation for the purpose of which the application is made might be seriously prejudiced unless a constable arriving at the premises could secure immediate entry to them[10].

Where a constable has entered premises in the execution of a warrant so issued, he may seize and retain any material, other than items subject to legal privilege[11] and excluded material[12], which is likely to be of substantial value, whether by itself or together with other material, to the investigation for the purpose of which the warrant was issued[13].

1 For the meaning of 'constable' see para 408 note 6 ante.

2 For the meaning of 'drug trafficking' see para 408 note 2 ante.

3 Drug Trafficking Offences Act 1986 s 28 (1). For these purposes, 'premises' has the same meaning as in the Police and Criminal Evidence Act 1984 (see para 671 note 3 post): Drug Trafficking Offences Act 1986 s 29 (2).

4 Ie an order under ibid s 27: see para 409 ante.

5 Ie the conditions in ibid s 28 (3) or (4): see infra.

6 Ibid s 28 (2).

7 For the meaning of 'benefited from drug trafficking' see para 408 note 4 ante.

8 Ie the conditions in the Drug Trafficking Offences Act 1986 s 27 (4) (b), (c): see para 409 heads (2), (3) ante.

9 Ibid s 28 (3).

10 Ibid s 28 (4).

11 For the meaning of 'items subject to legal privilege' see para 409 note 9 ante.

12 For the meaning of 'excluded material' see para 409 note 10 ante.

13 Drug Trafficking Offences Act 1986 s 28 (5).

411. Disclosure of information held by government departments. On an application by the prosecutor, the High Court may order[1] any specified material which is in the possession of an authorised government department[2] to be produced to the court within such period as the court may specify[3]. Specified material is any material which:

(1) has been submitted to an officer of an authorised government department by the accused or by a person who has at any time held property[4] which was realisable property[5];

(2) has been made by an officer of an authorised government department in relation to the accused or such a person; or

(3) is correspondence which passed between an officer of an authorised government department and the accused or such a person;

and an order so made may require the production of all such material or of a particular description of such material, being material in the possession of the department concerned[6].

The court may by order authorise the disclosure to any member of the police force, any member of the Crown Prosecution Service or any officer within the meaning of the Customs and Excise Management Act 1979[7] of any material produced or any part of such material; but the court may not so make an order unless a reasonable opportunity has been given for an officer of the department to make representations to the court and it appears to the court that the material is likely to be of substantial value in exercising functions relating to drug trafficking[8].

1 An order so made may not require the production of any material unless it appears to the High Court that the material is likely to contain information that would facilitate the exercise of the powers conferred on the court by the Drug Trafficking Offences Act 1986 ss 8–11 (see para 1314 et seq post) or on a receiver appointed under ss 8 or 11 or in pursuance of a charging order (see para 1317 post): s 30 (4). The court may by order authorise the disclosure to such a receiver of any material produced under s 30 (1) or any part of such material; but the court may not so make an order unless a reasonable opportunity has been given for an officer of the department to make representations to the court: s 30 (5). Material disclosed in pursuance of such an order may, subject to any conditions contained in the order, be further disclosed for the purposes of the functions under the Drug Trafficking Offences Act 1986 of the receiver or the Crown Court: s 30 (6).

2 For the meaning of 'authorised government department' see para 409 note 7 ante. As to power to inspect the Land Register see ibid s 33.

3 Ibid s 30 (1). The power to make an order under s 30 (1) is exercisable if (1) the powers conferred on the court by s 8 (1) (see para 1314 post) and s 9 (1) (see para 1317 post) are exercisable by virtue of s 7 (1) (see para 1312 post); or (2) those powers are exercisable by virtue of s 7 (2) (see para 1312 post) and the court has made a restraint or charging order which has not been discharged; but, where the

power to make an order under s 30 (1) is exercisable by virtue of only s 30 (2) (b) (see head (2) supra), s 7 (3) (see para 1312 post) applies for the purposes of s 30 as it applies for the purposes of ss 8, 9: s 30 (2).

An order under s 30 (1) and, in the case of material in the possession of an authorised government department, an order under s 27 (2) (see para 409 ante) may require any officer of the department, whether named in the order or not, who may for the time being be in possession of the material concerned to comply with it; and such an order must be served as if the proceedings were civil proceedings against the department: s 30 (11). The person on whom such an order is served (a) must take all reasonable steps to bring it to the attention of the officer concerned; and (b) if the order is not brought to that officer's attention within the period referred to in s 30 (1), must report the reasons for the failure to the court; and it is the duty of any other officer of the department in receipt of the order to take such steps as are mentioned in head (a) supra: s 30 (12).

4 For the meaning of 'property' see para 408 note 3 ante.
5 For the meaning of 'realisable property' see para 1307 note 14 post.
6 Drug Trafficking Offences Act 1986 s 30 (3). Material may be produced or disclosed in pursuance of s 30 notwithstanding any obligation as to secrecy or other restriction upon the disclosure of information imposed by statute or otherwise: s 30 (10).
7 For the meaning of 'officer' in the Customs and Excise Management Act 1979 s 1 see para 341 note 7 ante.
8 Drug Trafficking Offences Act 1986 s 30 (7), (8). Material disclosed in pursuance of an order under s 30 (7) may, subject to any conditions contained in the order, be further disclosed for the purposes of functions relating to drug trafficking: s 30 (9). For the meaning of 'drug trafficking' see para 408 note 2 ante.

412. Prejudicing investigation. Where, in relation to an investigation into drug trafficking[1], an order[2] to make material available has been made or has been applied for and has not been refused or a warrant[3] to enter and search has been issued, a person who, knowing or suspecting that the investigation is taking place, makes any disclosure which is likely to prejudice the investigation is guilty of an offence and liable on conviction on indictment to imprisonment for a term not exceeding five years or a fine, or to both, or on summary conviction to imprisonment for a term not exceeding six months or a fine not exceeding the statutory maximum, or to both[4].

In proceedings against a person for such an offence it is a defence to prove that he did not know or suspect that the disclosure was likely to prejudice the investigation or that he had lawful authority or reasonable excuse for making the disclosure[5].

1 For the meaning of 'drug trafficking' see para 408 note 2 ante.
2 Ie under the Drug Trafficking Offences Act 1986 s 27: see para 409 ante.
3 Ie under ibid s 28: see para 410 ante.
4 Ibid s 31 (1), (3). For the meaning of 'the statutory maximum' see para 806 post.
5 Ibid s 31 (2).

(iii) Intoxicating Substances

413. Supply of intoxicating substances. If a person supplies or offers to supply a substance other than a controlled drug[1]:

(1) to a person under the age of 18 whom he knows, or has reasonable cause to believe, to be under that age; or

(2) to a person who is acting on behalf of a person under that age and whom he knows, or has reasonable cause to believe, to be so acting,

he is guilty of an offence, if he knows or has reasonable cause to believe that the substance is, or its fumes are, likely to be inhaled by the person under the age of 18 for the purposes of causing intoxication, and is liable on summary conviction to imprisonment for a term not exceeding six months or a fine not exceeding level 5 on the standard scale, or to both[2].

In proceedings against any person for such an offence it is a defence for him to show that at the time he made the supply or offer he was under the age of 18 and was acting otherwise than in the course or furtherance of a business[3].

1 For these purposes, 'controlled drug' has the same meaning as in the Misuse of Drugs Act 1971 (see para 397 note 3 ante): Intoxicating Substances (Supply) Act 1985 s 1 (4).
2 Ibid s 1 (1), (3). For the meaning of 'the standard scale' see para 808 post.
3 Ibid s 1 (2).

(16) HUMAN ORGAN TRANSPLANTS

414. Prohibition of commercial dealings in human organs. Any person[1] who in Great Britain:

(1) makes or receives any payment[2] for the supply of, or for an offer to supply, an organ[3] which has been or is to be removed from a dead or living person and is intended to be transplanted into another person whether in Great Britain or elsewhere;

(2) seeks to find a person willing to supply for payment such an organ as is mentioned in head (1) above or offers to supply such an organ for payment;

(3) initiates or negotiates any arrangement involving the making of any payment for the supply of, or for an offer to supply, such an organ; or

(4) takes part in the management or control of a body of persons corporate or unincorporate whose activities consist of or include the initiation or negotiation of such arrangements,

is guilty of an offence and liable on summary conviction to imprisonment for a term not exceeding three months or a fine not exceeding level 5 on the standard scale, or to both[4].

Without prejudice to head (2) above, if a person causes to be published or distributed, or knowingly publishes or distributes, in Great Britain an advertisement[5]:

(a) inviting persons to supply for payment any such organs as are mentioned in head (1) above or offering to supply any such organs for payment; or

(b) indicating that the advertiser is willing to initiate or negotiate any such arrangement as is mentioned in head (3) above,

he is guilty of an offence and liable on summary conviction to a fine not exceeding level 5 on the standard scale[6].

1 Where an offence under the Human Organ Transplants Act 1989 committed by a body corporate is proved to have been committed with the consent or connivance of, or to be attributable to any neglect on the part of, any director, manager, secretary or other similar officer of the body corporate or any person who was purporting to act in any such capacity, he as well as the body corporate is guilty of the offence and is liable to be proceeded against and punished accordingly: s 4 (1). Where the affairs of a body corporate are managed by its members, s 4 (1) applies to the acts and defaults of a member in connection with his functions of management as if he were a director of the body corporate: s 4 (2).
2 For these purposes, 'payment' means payment in money or money's worth but does not include any payment for defraying or reimbursing: (1) the cost of removing, transporting or preserving the organ to be supplied; or (2) any expenses or loss of earnings incurred by a person so far as reasonably and directly attributable to his supplying an organ from his body: ibid s 1 (3).
3 For these purposes, 'organ' means any part of a human body consisting of a structured arrangement of tissues which, if wholly removed, cannot be replicated by the body: ibid s 7 (2).

4 Ibid s 1 (1), (5). For the meaning of 'the standard scale' see para 808 post. No proceedings for such an offence may be instituted in England and Wales except by or with the consent of the Director of Public Prosecutions: s 5. As to the effect of this limitation see para 639 post.

As to removal of parts of bodies see also the Human Tissue Act 1961 s 1 (as amended); as to the use of bodies for anatomical examination see the Anatomy Act 1984 s 4; and see generally MEDICINE.

5 For these purposes, 'advertisement' includes any form of advertising whether to the public generally, to any section of the public or individually to selected persons: Human Organ Transplants Act 1989 s 1 (4).

6 Ibid s 1 (2), (5). No proceedings for such an offence may be instituted in England and Wales except by or with the consent of the Director of Public Prosecutions: s 5.

415. Restriction on transplants between persons not genetically related. If a person[1]:

(1) removes from a living person an organ[2] intended to be transplanted into another person; or

(2) transplants an organ removed from a living person into another person,

he is guilty of an offence and liable on summary conviction to imprisonment for a term not exceeding three months or a fine not exceeding level 5 on the standard scale, or to both, unless the person into whom the organ is to be or, as the case may be, is transplanted is genetically related[3] to the person from whom the organ is removed[4].

1 As to offences by bodies corporate see para 414 note 1 ante.

2 For the meaning of 'organ' see para 414 note 3 ante.

3 For these purposes, a person is genetically related to (1) his natural parents and children; (2) his brothers and sisters of the whole or half blood; (3) the brothers and sisters of the whole or half blood of either of his natural parents; and (4) the natural children of his brothers and sisters of the whole or half blood or of the brothers and sisters of the whole or half blood of either of his natural parents; but persons may not in any particular case be treated as related in any of those ways unless the fact of the relationship has been established by such means as are specified by regulations made by the Secretary of State: Human Organ Transplants Act 1989 s 2 (2). The power so to make regulations is exercisable by statutory instrument; and regulations under s 2 (2) are subject to annulment in pursuance of a resolution of either House of Parliament: s 2 (6), (7).

The means by which the fact of a genetic relationship is to be established for the purposes of s 2 are the carrying out by a tester of the appropriate tests described in the Human Organ Transplants (Establishment of Relationship) Regulations 1989, SI 1989/2107, reg 2 (2) (see infra): reg 2 (1). The tester must carry out on the donor and the recipient and on such relatives of each as appear to the tester to be necessary:

    (a) tests for the antigenic products of the Human Major Histocompatibility system HLA-A, HLA-B and HLA-DR, using conventional serological techniques; and

    (b) tests to establish HLA-DR beta and HLA-DQ beta gene restriction fragment length polymorphisms; and

    (c) where the tests in heads (a), (b) supra do not establish a genetic relationship between the donor and the recipient, tests to establish DNA polymorphisms, using at least two multilocus gene probes; and

    (d) where the tests in heads (a)–(c) supra do not establish a genetic relationship between the donor and the recipient, further tests to establish DNA polymorphisms, using at least five single locus polymorphic probes:

reg 2 (2). For these purposes, 'donor' means a living person from whom an organ is proposed to be removed which is intended to be transplanted into another person; 'recipient' means the person into whom the organ is intended to be transplanted; and 'tester' means a person approved by the Secretary of State to carry out the tests described in reg 2: reg 1 (2).

The Human Organ Transplants (Establishment of Relationship) Regulations 1989 come into force on 1 April 1990: reg 1 (1).

4 Human Organ Transplants Act 1989 s 2 (1), (5). For the meaning of 'the standard scale' see para 808 post. No proceedings for such an offence may be instituted in England and Wales except by or with the consent of the Director of Public Prosecutions: s 5. As to the effect of this limitation see para 639 post. Section 2 (1) comes into force on 1 April 1990: s 7 (3); Human Organ Transplants Act 1989 (Commencement) Order 1989, SI 1989/2106, art 1.

The Secretary of State may by regulations provide that the the prohibition in the Human Organ Transplants Act 1989 s 2 (1) shall not apply in cases where (1) such authority as is specified in or constituted by the regulations is satisfied (a) that no payment has been or is to be made in contravention of s 1 (see para 414 ante); and (b) that such other conditions as are specified in the regulations are satisfied; and (2) such other requirements as may be specified in the regulations are complied with: s 2 (3). The expenses of any such authority must be defrayed by the Secretary of State out of money provided by Parliament: s 2 (4). The power so to make regulations is exercisable by statutory instrument; and no regulations may be made under s 2 (3) unless a draft of them has been laid before and approved by a resolution of each House of Parliament: s 2 (6), (7).

For the purposes of s 2 (3) there is constituted an authority called the Unrelated Live Transplants Regulatory Authority ('the Authority'): Human Organ Transplants (Unrelated Persons) Regulations 1989, SI 1989/2480, regs 1 (3), 2 (1). The Authority consists of a chairman appointed by the Secretary of State and of such number of other members appointed by him, not being less than seven or more than 11, as he thinks fit: reg 2 (2). The chairman and at least three other members of the Authority must be registered medical practitioners and at least four members of the Authority must be persons who are not, and have not at any time been, registered medical practitioners: reg 2 (3). The tenure of office of the chairman and any other member of the Authority is on such terms and for such period as the Secretary of State specifies on appointing him: reg 2 (4). The procedure of the Authority is such as the Authority may determine: reg 2 (5).

The prohibition in the Human Organ Transplants Act 1989 s 2 (1) does not apply in cases where a registered medical practitioner has caused the matter to be referred to the Authority and where the Authority is satisfied:

(i) that no payment has been, or is to be, made in contravention of s 1 (see para 414 ante);
(ii) that the registered medical practitioner who has caused the matter to be referred to the Authority has clinical responsibility for the donor; and
(iii) except in a case where the primary purpose of removal of an organ from a donor is the medical treatment of that donor, that the specified conditions are satisfied:

Human Organ Transplants (Unrelated Persons) Regulations 1989 reg 3 (1).

The specified conditions are that:

(A) a registered medical practitioner has given the donor an explanation of the nature of the medical procedure for, and the risk involved in, the removal of the organ in question;
(B) the donor understands the nature of the medical procedure and the risks, as explained by the registered medical practitioner, and consents to the removal of the organ in question;
(C) the donor's consent to the removal of the organ in question was not obtained by coercion or the offer of an inducement;
(D) the donor understands that he is entitled to withdraw his consent if he wishes, but has not done so;
(E) the donor and the recipient have both been interviewed by a person who appears to the Authority to have been suitably qualified to conduct such interviews and who has reported to the Authority on the conditions contained in heads (A)–(D) supra and has included in his report an account of any difficulties of communication with the donor or the recipient and an explanation of how those difficulties were overcome:

reg 3 (2).

For these purposes, 'donor' means a living person from whom it is proposed to remove an organ; and 'recipient' means a person into whom it is proposed to transplant an organ: reg 1 (3).

Regulations 1, 2 came into force on 1 January 1990 and reg 3 comes into force on 1 April 1990: reg 1 (2).

416. Information about transplant operations. The Secretary of State may make regulations requiring such persons as are specified in the regulations to supply to such authority as is so specified such information as may be so specified with respect to transplants that have been or are proposed to be carried out in Great Britain using organs[1] removed from dead or living persons[2]. Any such authority must keep a record of information supplied to it in pursuance of the regulations so made[3].

Any person who without reasonable excuse fails to comply with those regulations is guilty of an offence and liable on summary conviction to a fine not exceeding level 3 on the standard scale; and any person who, in purported compliance with those regulations, knowingly or recklessly supplies information which is false or misleading in a material respect is guilty of an offence and liable on summary conviction to a fine not exceeding level 5 on the standard scale[4].

1 For the meaning of 'organ' see para 414 note 3 ante.
2 Human Organ Transplants Act 1989 s 3 (1). The power so to make regulations is exercisable by statutory instrument subject to annulment in pursuance of a resolution of either House of Parliament: s 3 (4).
   A registered medical practitioner who has removed a relevant organ from a dead or living person which is proposed to be transplanted into another person must supply the prescribed information to the South Western Regional Health Authority and:
   (1) where the removal of the relevant organ was carried out in England and Wales:
       (a) to the District Health Authority for the district in which the removal of the relevant organ was carried out; or
       (b) where the removal was carried out in a hospital managed by a special health authority, to that authority;
   (2) where the removal was carried out in Scotland, to the Health Board for the area in which the removal of the relevant organ was carried out:
   Human Organ Transplants (Supply of Information) Regulations 1989, SI 1989/2108, reg 2 (1). For the prescribed information see reg 2 (1), Schedule Pt I and MEDICINE.
   A registered medical practitioner who has received a relevant organ removed from a dead or living person which is proposed to be transplanted into another person must supply the prescribed information to the South Western Regional Health Authority and:
   (i) where the organ was received in England and Wales, to the District Health Authority for the district in which the relevant organ was received or, where the organ was received in a hospital managed by a special health authority, to that authority;
   (ii) where the organ was received in Scotland, to the Health Board for the area in which the organ was received:
   reg 2 (2). For the prescribed information see reg 2 (2), Schedule Pt II and MEDICINE.
   For these purposes, 'District Health Authority' means a District Health Authority within the meaning of the National Health Service Act 1977; 'Health Board' means a Health Board within the meaning of the National Health Service (Scotland) Act 1978; 'relevant organ' means any of the following, namely, kidney, heart, lung, pancreas or liver; 'special health authority' means a special health authority established in pursuance of the National Health Service Act 1977 s 11 (as amended); and 'South Western Regional Health Authority' means the authority of that name constituted in accordance with the National Health Service (Constitution of Regional Health Authorities) Order 1975, SI 1975/1100: Human Organ Transplants (Supply of Information) Regulations 1989 reg 1 (2). See further MEDICINE.
   The Human Organ Transplants (Supply of Information) Regulations 1989 come into force on 1 April 1990: reg 1 (1).
3 Human Organ Transplants Act 1989 s 3 (2).
4 Ibid s 3 (3). For the meaning of 'the standard scale' see para 808 post.

(17) THE VAGRANCY ACTS 1824–1935

417. Idle and disorderly persons. Every person wandering abroad, or placing himself or herself in any public place, street, highway, court, or passage, to beg or gather alms, or causing or procuring or encouraging any child or children so to do[1], is deemed to be an idle and disorderly person and is liable on summary conviction to imprisonment for a term not exceeding one month, or, if convicted before one justice or before justices sitting in an occasional courthouse, for a term not exceeding 14 days, save that, where a person is convicted of wandering abroad, or placing himself in any public place, street, highway, court or passage, to beg or gather alms, the court may not sentence him to imprisonment but has power to fine him[2]. A fine not exceeding £400, or, if the person is convicted before one justice or before justices sitting in an occasional courthouse, a fine of £1, may be imposed in lieu of imprisonment[3].

1 This does not include a person who collects alms in an orderly manner for a specific purpose: *Pointon v Hill* (1884) 12 QBD 306; *Mathers v Penfold* [1915] 1 KB 514, DC; *R v Dalton* [1982] Crim LR 375. If the accused offers something in return for the money given by passers-by, it could not be regarded as begging or gathering alms: *Gray v Chief Constable of Greater Manchester* [1983] Crim LR 45 (busking). As to begging by children see the Children and Young Persons Act 1933 s 4 (amended by the Children and Young Persons Act 1963 s 64 (1), (3), Sch 3 para 4, Sch 5; the Criminal Justice Act 1982 ss 38, 46) and INFANTS vol 24 para 696.

2 Vagrancy Act 1824 s 3 (amended by the National Assistance Act 1948 s 62, Sch 7 Pt I; the Criminal Justice Act 1948 s 1 (2); the Criminal Justice Act 1982 s 77, Sch 14 para 1); Magistrates' Courts Act 1980 s 121 (5); Criminal Justice Act 1982 s 70 (1).

3 See the Magistrates' Courts Act 1980 s 34 (3) (b), Sch 4 para 1 (amended by the Criminal Penalties etc (Increase) Order 1984, SI 1984/447) and MAGISTRATES.

418. Rogues and vagabonds. The following persons are deemed to be rogues and vagabonds:

(1) every person committing an offence for which the offender is deemed to be an idle and disorderly person[1], having been previously convicted as an idle and disorderly person[2];

(2) every person apprehended as an idle and disorderly person and violently resisting any constable or other police officer so apprehending him or her, and being subsequently convicted of the offence for which he or she was apprehended[2];

(3) every person going about as a gatherer or collector of alms, or endeavouring to procure charitable contributions of any nature or kind, under any false or fraudulent pretence[2];

(4) every person wandering abroad and endeavouring by the exposure of wounds or deformities to obtain or gather alms[2];

(5) every person wandering abroad and lodging in any barn or outhouse, or in any deserted or unoccupied building, or in the open air, or under a tent, or in any cart or waggon, and not giving a good account of himself or herself[3];

(6) every person wilfully, openly, lewdly, and obscenely exposing his person with intent to insult any female[4];

(7) every person found in or upon any dwelling house, warehouse, coach-house, stable, or outhouse, or in any enclosed yard, garden, or area for any unlawful purpose[5].

A person committing any of these offences is liable on summary conviction to imprisonment for a term not exceeding three months, or, if convicted before one justice or before justices sitting in an occasional courthouse, for a term not exceeding 14 days, save that, where a person is convicted of wandering abroad and lodging in any barn or outhouse, or in any deserted or unoccupied building, or in the open air, or under a tent, or in any cart or waggon, and not giving a good account of himself or of wandering abroad, and endeavouring by the exposure of wounds and deformities to obtain and gather alms, the court may not sentence him to imprisonment but has power to fine him[6]. A fine not exceeding £400, or, if the person is convicted before one justice or before justices sitting in an occasional courthouse, a fine of £1, may be imposed in lieu of imprisonment[7].

1 See para 417 ante.

2 Vagrancy Act 1824 s 4 (amended by the Criminal Justice Act 1925 ss 42, 49 (4), Sch 3; the Vagrancy Act 1935 s 1 (2); the National Assistance Act 1948 s 62, Sch 7 Pt I; the Criminal Justice Act 1948 s 1 (2); the Theft Act 1968 s 33 (3), Sch 3 Pt I; the Indecent Displays (Control) Act 1981 s 5 (2), Schedule; the Criminal Attempts Act 1981 ss 8, 10, Schedule Pt II; the Criminal Justice Act 1982 s 77, Sch 14 para 1; the Public Order Act 1986 s 40 (3), Sch 3).

3 Vagrancy Act 1824 s 4 (as amended: see note 2 supra). The reference to a person lodging under a tent or in a cart or waggon is not to be deemed to include a person lodging under a tent or in a cart or waggon with or in which he travels: Vagrancy Act 1935 s 1 (4). A person wandering abroad and so lodging is not to be deemed a rogue and vagabond within the meaning of the Vagrancy Act 1824 s 4 (as so amended) unless it is proved either:

(1) that in relation to the occasion on which he so lodged, he had been directed to a reasonably accessible place of shelter and failed to apply for or refused accommodation there;

(2) that he is a person who persistently wanders abroad and, notwithstanding that a place of shelter is reasonably accessible, lodges or attempts so to lodge; or

(3) that by or in the course of so lodging, he caused damage to property, infection with vermin, or other offensive consequence, or that he so lodged in such circumstances as to appear to be likely so to do:

Vagrancy Act 1935 s 1 (3)). For these purposes, 'a place of shelter' means a place where provision is regularly made for giving, free of charge, accommodation for the night to such persons as apply therefor: s 1 (3).

4 Vagrancy Act 1824 s 4 (as amended: see note 2 supra), 'Person' refers to penis and not to other parts of the body: *Evans v Ewels* [1972] 2 All ER 22, 56 Cr App Rep 377, DC. 'Openly' means 'without concealment' and the offence can be committed in other than a public place: *Ford v Falcone* [1971] 2 All ER 1138, 55 Cr App Rep 372, DC. As to the circumstances in which the accused may be cross-examined as to other similar offences see *Perkins v Jeffery* [1915] 2 KB 702, DC. As to similar fact evidence generally see para 1091 et seq post.

5 Vagrancy Act 1824 s 4 (as amended: see note 2 supra). There must be a purpose to commit an offence punishable as a crime, and not a mere offence against eg morality: *Hayes v Stevenson* (1860) 3 LT 296; *Smith v Chief Superintendent, Woking Police Station* (1983) 76 Cr App Rep 234, DC (unlawful purpose; assault in criminal cause; victim in terror of some immediate violence; accused in enclosed garden staring through window of bed-sitting room). Actual arrest on the premises etc where found is not necessary to constitute the offence: *Moran v Jones* (1911) 27 TLR 421. 'Found' means discovered or seen: *R v Goodwin* [1944] KB 518, 30 Cr App Rep 20, CCA (decided under the Prevention of Crimes Act 1871). See also *R v Parkin* [1950] 1 KB 155, 34 Cr App Rep 1, CCA; *R v Lumsden* [1951] 2 KB 513, 35 Cr App Rep 57, CCA (both decided under the Larceny Act 1916 s 28 (4) (repealed)). 'Dwelling house' includes the common hall of a block of flats: *Hollyhomes v Hind* [1944] KB 571, [1944] 2 All ER 8, DC. 'Area' means that part of the basement of a house which is open to the air: *Knott v Blackburn* [1944] KB 77, [1944] 1 All ER 116, DC. A railway yard inclosed on all sides except across the tracks is not an inclosed area: *Knott v Blackburn* supra. A yard may be an inclosed area even though there are gaps in the surrounding walls etc: *Goodhew v Morton* [1962] 2 All ER 771, [1962] 1 WLR 210, DC. The fact that a place is described as a railway yard, shipyard etc does not make it a 'yard' for the purposes of the Vagrancy Act 1824 s 4 (as so amended); *Quatromini v Peck* [1972] 3 All ER 521 at 525, [1972] 1 WLR 1318 at 1322, DC. For the meaning of 'warehouse' see *Holloran v Haughton* (1976) 120 Sol Jo 116, DC.

6 Vagrancy Act 1824 s 4 (as amended: see note 2 supra); Magistrates' Courts Act 1980 s 121 (5); Criminal Justice Act 1982 s 70 (1).

7 See the Magistrates' Courts Act 1980 s 34 (3) (b), Sch 4 para 1 (amended by the Criminal Penalties etc (Increase) Order 1984, SI 1984/447) and MAGISTRATES.

419. Incorrigible rogues. Every person committing any offence which subjects him or her to be dealt with as a rogue and vagabond[1], such person having been at some former time adjudged so to be and duly convicted thereof[2], is deemed to be an incorrigible rogue and on conviction of any such offence may be committed, in custody or on bail, to the Crown Court for sentence[3].

However, if a person deemed a rogue and a vagabond is thereafter:

(1) convicted[4] of wandering abroad, or placing himself in any public place, street, highway, court, or passage, to beg or gather alms; or

(2) convicted[5] (a) of wandering abroad and lodging in any barn or outhouse, or in any deserted or unoccupied building, or in the open air, or under a tent, or in any cart or waggon, and not giving a good account of himself; or (b) of wandering abroad, and endeavouring by the exposure of wounds and deformities to obtain or gather alms,

he must be convicted of that offence and accordingly is not deemed to be an incorrigible rogue and may not be committed to the Crown Court by reason only of that conviction[6].

When a person has been committed to the Crown Court as an incorrigible rogue, the court may examine into the circumstances of the case[7] and, if it thinks fit, may order that the offender be imprisoned for a term not exceeding one year from the time of making such order[8]. Subject to one exception[9], this is the only order the court has power to make[10].

1 Ie any offence under the Vagrancy Act 1824 s 4 (as amended): see para 418 ante.
2 There must be a previous conviction under ibid s 4 (as amended). Previous convictions as an idle and disorderly person (see para 417 ante) are insufficient: *R v Johnson* [1909] 1 KB 439, 2 Cr App Rep 13, CCA. However, on the conviction under the Vagrancy Act 1824 s 4 (as amended) a person need not have been expressly adjudged a rogue or vagabond: *R v Teesdale* (1927) 138 LT 160, 20 Cr App Rep 113, CCA.
3 Vagrancy Act 1824 s 5 (amended by the Criminal Justice Act 1948 s 83 (3), Sch 10; the Criminal Justice Act 1967 s 103, Sch 6; the Courts Act 1971 s 56 (1), Sch 8 Pt II; the Criminal Justice Act 1982 s 77, Sch 14 para 1 (b)).
4 Ie under the Vagrancy Act 1824 s 3 (as amended) or s 4 (as amended): see paras 417, 418 respectively ante.
5 Ie under ibid s 4 (as amended): see para 418 ante.
6 Criminal Justice Act 1982 s 70 (2).
7 The court must satisfy itself that the offender has been convicted of an offence under the Vagrancy Act 1824 s 5 (as amended: see note 3 supra) (*R v Evans* [1915] 2 KB 762, 11 Cr App Rep 178, CCA) and should inquire into the circumstances of the conviction (*R v Holding* (1934) 104 LJKB 28, 25 Cr App Rep 28, CCA). As to methods of proving convictions see paras 1116, 1117 post. The examination into the circumstances of the case must take place in the offender's presence (*R v Cope* (1925) 94 LJKB 662, 18 Cr App Rep 181, CCA) and he should be given an opportunity of cross-examining any witness called by the Crown and of addressing the court (*R v Holding* supra).
8 Vagrancy Act 1824 s 10 (amended by the Criminal Justice Act 1948 s 83 (3), Sch 10; the Criminal Justice Act 1967 s 103 (2), Sch 7 Pt I; the Courts Act 1971 s 56 (1), Sch 8 Pt II para 5 (b)); Criminal Justice Act 1948 s 1 (2).
9 Where the court would have power to make a hospital order if the offender had been convicted before the court, ie where the requirements of the Mental Health Act 1983 s 37 (see para 1257 post) are satisfied, it may make a hospital order, with or without a restriction order: s 43 (5). As to restriction orders see para 1261 post.
10 See *R v Jackson* [1974] QB 517, 59 Cr App Rep 23, CA. The offender must be sentenced as an incorrigible rogue and not for the offences for which he was convicted: *R v Walters* [1969] 1 QB 255, 53 Cr App Rep 9, CA. It is open to the court to make no order at all: *R v Jackson* supra.

420. Appeals. An appeal against a conviction under the Vagrancy Act 1824[1] lies to the Crown Court[2]. An appeal against a sentence imposed by the Crown Court on a person adjudged to be an incorrigible rogue[3] lies to the Court of Appeal[4].

1 See paras 417–419 ante.
2 Vagrancy Act 1824 s 14 (amended by the Courts Act 1971 s 56 (1), Sch 8). As to appeals to the Crown Court see para 1450 et seq post.
3 See para 419 ante.
4 See para 1357 text and note 11 post.

421. Powers of arrest and search. It is lawful for any person whatsoever to apprehend any person found offending against the Vagrancy Act 1824[1] and forthwith to take and convey him before a justice or deliver him to a constable for that purpose[2].

1 See paras 417, 418 ante. A person arrested must be actually committing one of the offences specified in the Vagrancy Act 1824: *Horley v Rogers* (1860) 2 E & E 674. As to arrest generally see para 691 et seq post.
2 Vagrancy Act 1824 s 6.

(18) INTIMIDATION AND HARASSMENT

422. Intimidation. Every person who, with a view to compel[1] any other person to abstain from doing, or to do, any act which such other person[2] has a legal right to do or abstain from doing, wrongfully[3] and without legal authority:

(1) uses violence to or intimidates[4] such other person or his wife or children or injures his property; or

(2) persistently follows[5] such other person about from place to place; or

(3) hides any tools, clothes or other property owned or used by such other person, or deprives him of or hinders him in the use thereof[6]; or

(4) watches or besets the house or other place where such other person resides, or works, or carries on business, or happens to be, or the approach to such house or place[7]; or

(5) follows such other person with two or more other persons in a disorderly manner in or through any street or road[8],

is guilty of an offence and liable on summary conviction to imprisonment for a term not exceeding six months or a fine not exceeding level 5 on the standard scale, or to both[9].

1 It does not matter whether the compulsion was effective: *Agnew v Munro* 1891 28 SLR 335.
2 Ie any other person: *J Lyons & Sons v Wilkins* [1899] 1 Ch 255, CA.
3 The conduct must amount to a civil wrong separately from the existence of the statutory offence: *Ward, Lock & Co Ltd v Operative Printers' Assistants' Society* (1906) 22 TLR 327, CA; *Fowler v Kibble* [1922] 1 Ch 487, CA; *Thomas v National Union of Mineworkers (South Wales Area)* [1986] Ch 20, [1985] 2 All ER 1. Cf *J Lyons & Sons v Wilkins* [1896] 1 Ch 811, CA.
4 'Intimidate' includes putting persons in fear by the exhibition of force or violence or the threat of force or violence; there is no limitation restricting the meaning of 'intimidate' to cases of violence or threats of violence to the person: *R v Jones (John)* [1974] ICR 310, CA (considering *Judge v Bennett* (1887) 52 JP 247; *Connor v Kent, Gibson v Lawson, Curran v Treleaven* [1891] 2 QB 545, CCR). Abuse, swearing and jostling may constitute intimidation if such threats are serious and taken seriously by those who receive them: *News Group Newspapers Ltd v SOGAT 82 (No 2)* [1987] ICR 181.
5 Whether following is persistent is a question of fact: *Smith v Thomasson* (1891) 16 Cox CC 740; *Elsey v Smith* [1983] IRLR 292, High Court of Justiciary.
6 As to deprivation of property see *Fowler v Kibble* [1922] 1 Ch 487, CA.
7 See *J Lyons & Sons v Wilkins* [1899] 1 Ch 255, CA; *Charnock v Court* [1899] 2 Ch 35; *Walters v Green* [1899] 2 Ch 696; *Farmer v Wilson* (1900) 69 LJQB 496, DC; *Ward, Lock & Co Ltd v Operative Printers' Assistants' Society* (1906) 22 TLR 327, CA; *Hubbard v Pitt* [1976] QB 142, [1975] 3 All ER 1, CA; *Galt v Philp* [1984] IRLR 156, High Court of Justiciary. See also *R v Bonsall* [1985] Crim LR 150.
8 See *R v McKenzie* [1892] 2 QB 519, DC; *Elsey v Smith* [1983] IRLR 292, High Court of Justiciary.
9 Conspiracy and Protection of Property Act 1875 s 7 (amended by the Trade Disputes Act 1906 s 2 (2); the Public Order Act 1986 s 40 (2), Sch 2 para 1). For the meaning of 'the standard scale' see para 808 post. It is lawful for a person in contemplation or furtherance of a trade dispute to attend (1) at or near his own place of work; or (2) if he is an official of a trade union, at or near the place of work of a member of that union whom he is accompanying and whom he represents, for the purpose only of peacefully obtaining or communicating information, or peacefully persuading any person to work or abstain from working: Trade Union and Labour Relations Act 1974 s 15 (1) (substituted by the Employment Act 1980 s 16 (1)). See further TRADE AND LABOUR vol 47 para 579 et seq.

423. Harassment of debtors. If a person, with the object of coercing another person to pay money claimed from the other as a debt due under a contract:

(1) harasses the other with demands for payment which, in respect of their frequency or the manner or occasion of making any such demand, or of any

threat or publicity by which any demand is accompanied, are calculated to subject him or members of his family or household to alarm, distress or humiliation;

(2) falsely represents, in relation to the money claimed, that criminal proceedings lie for failure to pay it;

(3) falsely represents himself to be authorised in some official capacity to claim or enforce payment; or

(4) utters a document falsely represented by him to have some official character or purporting to have some official character which he knows it has not,

he is guilty of an offence and liable on summary conviction to a fine not exceeding level 5 on the standard scale[1].

A person may be guilty of an offence by virtue of head (1) above if he concerts with others in the taking of such action as is there described, notwithstanding that his own course of conduct does not by itself amount to harassment[2]. Head (1) above does not apply, however, to anything done by a person which is reasonable, and otherwise permissible in law, for the purpose of (a) securing the discharge of an obligation due, or believed by him to be due, to himself or to persons for whom he acts, or protecting himself or them from future loss; or (b) the enforcement of any liability by legal process[3].

1 Administration of Justice Act 1970 s 40 (1), (4) (amended by the Criminal Justice Act 1982 ss 38, 46). For the meaning of 'the standard scale' see para 808 post.
2 Administration of Justice Act 1970 s 40 (2).
3 Ibid s 40 (3).

3. OFFENCES AGAINST THE PERSON

(1) GENOCIDE

424. Genocide. If a person, with intent to destroy, in whole or in part, a national, ethnical, racial or religious group, as such (1) kills members of the group; (2) causes serious bodily or mental harm to members of the group; (3) deliberately inflicts on members of the group conditions of life calculated to bring about its physical destruction in whole or in part; (4) imposes measures intended to prevent births within the group; or (5) forcibly transfers children of the group to another group, he is guilty of the offence of genocide and is liable on conviction on indictment (a) if the offence consists of the killing of any person, to imprisonment for life[1]; and (b) in any other case, to imprisonment for a term not exceeding 14 years[2]. Proceedings for such an offence may not be instituted except by or with the consent of the Attorney General[3].

1 The sentence is fixed by law and cannot be appealed against under the Criminal Appeal Act 1968 s 9: see para 1355 post.
2 Genocide Act 1969 s 1 (1), (2), Schedule. The definition of 'genocide' is taken from the Convention on the Prevention and Punishment of the Crime of Genocide approved by the General Assembly of the United Nations on 9 December 1948 (Cmnd 4421); see the Genocide Act 1969 ss 1 (1), 4 (2).
  Her Majesty may, by Order in Council, make provision for extending ss 1, 4, with such exceptions, adaptations or modifications as may be specified in the Order, to any of the Channel Islands, the Isle of Man or any colony, other than a colony for whose external relations a country other than the United Kingdom is responsible: s 3 (2). An Order in Council so made may be varied or revoked by a subsequent Order in Council: s 3 (3). The Genocide Act 1969 has been so extended

by the Genocide Act (Guernsey) Order 1969, SI 1969/739, the Genocide Act 1969 (Overseas Territories) Order 1970, SI 1970/146 (as to Bermuda, the British Virgin Islands, the Falkland Islands and Dependencies, the Seychelles, the Turks and Caicos Islands), the Genocide Act 1969 (Isle of Man and Jersey) Order 1974, SI 1974/1113 and the Genocide (Anguilla) Order 1987, SI 1987/453.
3 Genocide Act 1969 s 1 (3). As to the effect of this limitation see para 639 post.

(2) OFFENCES INVOLVING BODILY INJURY

(i) Homicide

A. IN GENERAL

425. Classification of homicide. The term homicide is used to describe the killing of a human being by a human being[1]. Such a killing may be lawful[2] or it may be unlawful and criminal.

Unlawful homicide includes murder[3], manslaughter[4], causing death by reckless driving[5], killing in pursuance of a suicide pact[6], and infanticide[7].

1 As to whether a corporation may be indicted for unlawful homicide see para 35 note 4 ante.
2 Formerly lawful homicide was classified as either justifiable (eg a killing in pursuance of a sentence of a court) or excusable (eg a killing by accident) but the distinction is now without substance: in either case no offence is committed.
3 As to murder see paras 431–435 post. Where the killing is done with intent to destroy, in whole or in part, a national, ethnical, racial or religious group as such, the offence may be charged as genocide: see para 424 ante.
4 See paras 436–450 post.
5 See para 449 post.
6 See para 442 post.
7 See para 451 post. As to alternative verdicts on indictments for murder, manslaughter or infanticide see para 1030 post.

426. Definition and proof. It is murder for a person of sound memory[1] and of the age of discretion[2], unlawfully to kill any human creature in being and under the Queen's peace, with malice aforethought, either express or implied by law, provided the victim dies of the injury inflicted within a year and a day of the injury[3].

Manslaughter differs from murder only in relation to the mental element which is necessary to support the charge[4].

To establish a case of murder the prosecution must prove (1) the death of the victim as the result of a voluntary[5] act or omission[6] of the accused; and (2) malice, express or implied[7]. The burden of proof remains throughout on the prosecution and, apart from the special defences of insanity and diminished responsibility and the anomalous case of suicide pacts, it is at no time incumbent upon the accused to establish any defence, or partial defence, to the charge[8].

1 As to the liability of persons of unsound mind see paras 31–33 ante; as to the defence of diminished responsibility see paras 440, 441 post; and as to acts done under the influence of alcohol or drugs see paras 28–30 ante.
2 See para 34 ante.
3 3 Co Inst 47, 50. As to malice aforethought see para 431 post; as to death within a year and a day see para 429 post; and as to the procedural provisions relating to prosecutions for the murder or manslaughter of a child or young person see para 882 post.
4 See para 436 post.
5 See para 6 ante.

6 See para 9 ante.
7 *Woolmington v DPP* [1935] AC 462, 25 Cr App Rep 72, HL; *Mancini v DPP* [1942] AC 1, 28 Cr App Rep 65, HL.

There is no statutory definition of 'express malice' or 'implied malice' in the Homicide Act 1957 s 1 (see para 431 post) which abolished the doctrine of 'constructive malice'; at common law 'express malice' in the conduct of murder means intention to kill and 'implied malice' intention to do grievous bodily harm: *R v Moloney* [1985] AC 905 at 921, 81 Cr App Rep 93 at 102, HL, approving *R v Vickers* [1957] 2 QB 664, 41 Cr App Rep 189, CCA. See para 431 post.
8 *Chan Kau v R* [1955] AC 206, [1955] 1 All ER 266, PC. See also *R v Wheeler* [1967] 3 All ER 829, 52 Cr App Rep 28, CA; *R v Abraham* [1973] 3 All ER 694, [1973] 1 WLR 1270, CA.

427. Person in being. On a charge of murder or manslaughter it must be shown that the person killed was one who was in being. It is neither murder nor manslaughter to kill an unborn child while still in its mother's womb[1] although it may be the statutory offences of child destruction or abortion[2]. If, however, the child is born alive and afterwards dies by reason of an unlawful act done to it in the mother's womb or in the process of birth, the person who committed that act is guilty of murder or manslaughter according to the intent with which the act is done[3].

A child is not considered in law to be in being, so as to be the subject of a charge of murder or manslaughter, until the whole body of the child is extruded from the womb and has an existence independent of the mother. Whether the child has an independent existence turns upon whether it has an independent circulation, and has breathed or had a capacity for independent breathing[4].

A child may have an independent existence, however, even though it has not drawn breath and even though the umbilical cord is not severed[5].

In relation to the law of homicide a person continues in being until his being is extinguished by death[6].

1 3 Co Inst 50; 1 Hale PC 433; 1 Hawk PC c 13 s 16.
2 See paras 452, 462 post.
3 3 Co Inst 50; 1 Hawk PC c 13 s 16; *R v West* (1848) 2 Car & Kir 784; *R v Senior* (1832) 1 Mood CC 346, CCR.
4 *R v Poulton* (1832) 5 C & P 329 per Littledale J; *R v Enoch* (1833) 5 C & P 539 per Park J; *R v Brain* (1834) 6 C & P 349 per Park J (where it was held that a child born alive could be the subject of a murder, although it had not in fact breathed); *R v Crutchley* (1837) 7 C & P 814 per Parke B; *R v Sellis* (1837) 7 C & P 850 per Coltman J (where it was laid down that the fact that a child had breathed was not conclusive proof that it was born alive, as it might have breathed and died before birth); *R v Wright* (1841) 9 C & P 754 per Gurney B. See further para 467 note 2 post; and see *C v S* [1988] QB 135, [1987] 1 All ER 1230, CA (foetus of gestational age between 18 and 21 weeks incapable of being born alive); *Rance v Mid-Downs Health Authority* (1990) Times, 15 February (27-week foetus capable of being born alive).
5 *R v Crutchley* (1837) 7 C & P 814; *R v Trilloe* (1842) 2 Mood CC 260, CCR; *R v Reeves* (1839) 9 C & P 25 per Vaughan J.
6 As to whether disconnection of a life support machine causes death see *R v Malcherek, R v Steel* [1981] 2 All ER 422, 73 Cr App Rep 173, CA (cited in para 430 note 10 post).

428. Person under the Queen's peace. On a charge of murder or manslaughter it must be shown that the person killed was under the Queen's peace. The Queen's peace extends to all persons in Her Majesty's territories, whether British subjects or aliens, except rebels and alien enemies who are at the time actually engaged in hostile operations against the Crown[1]. An alien who is not at the time of his murder within Her Majesty's territories is not within Her peace, unless the territory has been effectually occupied by Her forces[2].

If a person is criminally stricken, poisoned or otherwise hurt upon the sea or at any place out of England or Northern Ireland, and dies of such hurt in England or Northern Ireland, or being so stricken, poisoned or otherwise hurt, in any place in England or Northern Ireland dies of such hurt upon the sea or at any place out of England or Northern Ireland, the offence, whether it amounts to murder or manslaughter, may be dealt with, inquired into, tried, determined and punished, in England or Northern Ireland[3].

Where a subject of Her Majesty commits a murder or manslaughter on land out of the United Kingdom, whether within the Queen's territories or without, and whether the person killed was a subject of Her Majesty or not, he may be tried in England[4]. Subject to certain exceptions, a person subject to military law may be tried by court-martial for a murder or other offence wherever committed, even though the victim was not within the Queen's peace[5].

1 3 Co Inst 50; 1 Hale PC 433; 1 East PC 227; 4 Bl Com (14th Edn) 198.
2 *R v Page* [1954] 1 QB 170, 37 Cr App Rep 189, C-MAC.
3 Offences against the Person Act 1861 s 10 (amended by the Irish Free State (Consequential Adaptation of Enactments) Order 1923, SR & O 1923/405, art 2; the Criminal Law Act 1967 s 10 (1), (2), Sch 2 para 6, Sch 3 Pt III). The Offences against the Person Act 1861 s 10 (as so amended) does not apply to a foreigner who causes the death of another person by an act committed outside the jurisdiction of the Queen: *R v Lewis* (1857) Dears & B 182, CCR. The reference to England in the Offences against the Person Act 1861 s 10 (as so amended) includes Wales and Berwick upon Tweed: see CONSTITUTIONAL LAW vol 8 para 802. As to the ambit of criminal jurisdiction see para 620 et seq post; and as to the jurisdiction of the Crown Court see paras 618, 942 post.
4 See para 634 text and note 13 post.
5 *R v Page* [1954] 1 QB 170, 37 Cr App Rep 189, C-MAC. See ROYAL FORCES vol 41 para 433.

429. Death within a year and a day. If death does not follow until after the expiration of a year and a day from the date when the injury was inflicted, it is an irrebuttable presumption of law[1] that the death is attributable to some other cause, and the person who inflicted the injury is not punishable for either murder or manslaughter[2].

1 As to irrebutable presumptions of law see para 1068 post.
2 3 Co Inst 53; 1 Hawk PC c 13 s 9; 1 East PC 343, 344; see also *R v Dyson* [1908] 2 KB 454, 1 Cr App Rep 13, CCA. The day of the infliction of the injury is reckoned as the first day: 1 East PC 344. This rule probably applies to statutory forms of homicide, such as infanticide and causing death by reckless driving: see *R v Inner West London Coroner, ex p De Luca* [1989] 1 QB 249 at 252, [1988] 3 WLR 286 at 288, DC obiter per Bingham LJ and at 254 and at 290 per Hutchison J (the rule 'undoubtedly' applies to infanticide).

430. Causation. For the purposes of offences of homicide, a person causes the death of another where by any act or omission[1] he accelerates the death of that other[2]. The act or omission need not be the sole or the substantial cause but it must be one of the causes[3], and one that is more than minimal[4]. It is therefore possible to have two or more independent operative causes of death, and any person whose conduct constitutes a cause may be convicted of an offence in respect of the death[5].

It is not necessary that the death should have been caused in the way intended or foreseen by the accused[6]. It is enough that the death was a foreseeable or natural consequence of the accused's conduct; if, therefore, the accused threatened the victim who accidentally killed himself in trying to make his escape, the accused is liable for murder or manslaughter according to his mens rea[7].

If a wound is inflicted and death results, the person who inflicted the wound will be held to have caused the death although the victim may have neglected to use proper remedies[8], or have refused to undergo a necessary operation[9]. Similarly, where a wound or hurt has necessitated medical treatment and such treatment is unsuccessful, or improper or negligent so that death ensues, the wound will be regarded as causing the death if it continues to be an operative cause at the time of death[10]; but, if the original wound is merely the setting in which another cause operates, or has become merely part of the history of the case, an ensuing death cannot be said to result from the wound and the person who inflicted it cannot be said to have caused the death[11].

1 For an instance of causing death by omission see *R v Gibbins, R v Proctor* (1918) 13 Cr App Rep 134, CCA; and see also para 9 ante.

2 *R v Martin* (1832) 5 C & P 128; *R v Murton* (1862) 3 F & F 492; *R v Dyson* [1908] 2 KB 454, 1 Cr App Rep 13, CCA. A doctor properly administering pain-killing drugs does not cause the death of the patient merely because an incidental effect of the drugs may be some marginal acceleration of death: see Devlin J's summing up in *R v Adams* (1957, unreported) summarised at [1957] Crim LR 375.

3 *R v Dalloway* (1847) 3 Cox CC 273 (driver not guilty of manslaughter where his negligent driving did not contribute to death of child who ran into the path of vehicle).

4 *R v Hennigan* [1971] 3 All ER 133, 55 Cr App Rep 262, CA. See also *R v Cato* [1976] 1 All ER 260, 62 Cr App Rep 41, CA.

5 *R v Benge* (1865) 4 F & F 504. See also *R v Mitchell* [1983] QB 741, 76 Cr App Rep 293, CA (accused's act caused victim to fall and suffer injury; she later died in hospital).

6 Where the accused assaults the victim intending to kill, he may be convicted of murder notwithstanding that the victim's death is caused by subsequent acts done for the purpose of making the victim's death appear to have been an accident (*Thabo Meli v R* [1954] 1 All ER 373, [1954] 1 WLR 228, PC), or done for the purpose of getting rid of the supposed corpse (*R v Church* [1966] 1 QB 59, [1965] 2 All ER 72, CCA). See also *R v Moore and Dorn* [1975] Crim LR 229, CA. As to death caused by a series of acts see para 444 text and note 2 post.

7 *R v Hickman* (1831) 5 C & P 151; *R v Pitts* (1842) Car & M 284; *R v Hayward* (1908) 21 Cox CC 692; *R v Curley* (1909) 2 Cr App Rep 109, CCA; *R v MacKie* (1973) 57 Cr App Rep 453, CA, applied in *DPP v Daley* [1980] AC 237; sub nom *DPP v Daley, DPP v McGhie* (1978) 69 Cr App Rep 39, PC. See also *R v Michael* (1840) 9 C & P 356, CCR (intent to murder victim; poison administered by innocent third party); *R v Towers* (1874) 12 Cox CC 530 (infant said to have died from convulsions brought on by attack on its mother); *R v Halliday* (1889) 61 LT 701, CCR (threats against life resulting in injury sustained in escaping through window); *R v Beech* (1912) 107 LT 461, 2 Cr App Rep 197, CCA; *R v Lewis* [1970] Crim LR 647, CA (similar facts); *R v Roberts* (1971) 56 Cr App Rep 95, CA (girl terrified by sexual advances and threats injured in jumping from car). See also *Cartledge v Allen* [1973] Crim LR 530, DC; *R v Pagett* (1983) 76 Cr App Rep 279, CA (accused fired at police and used victim as a shield: victim killed by police bullets; accused convicted of manslaughter).

8 1 Hale PC 428; 1 East PC 344; *R v Rew* (1662) Kel 26; *R v Wall* (1802) 28 State Tr 51; *R v Flynn* (1867) 16 WR 319, CCR.

9 *R v Holland* (1841) 2 Mood & R 351; *R v Blaue* [1975] 3 All ER 446, [1975] 1 WLR 1411, CA (victim refused to have a blood transfusion because of her religious beliefs).

10 *R v Smith* [1959] 2 QB 35, 43 Cr App Rep 121, C-MAC; *R v Pym* (1846) 1 Cox CC 339; *R v McIntyre* (1847) 2 Cox CC 379; *R v Davis and Wagstaffe* (1883) 15 Cox CC 174. See also *R v Malcherek, R v Steel* [1981] 2 All ER 422, 73 Cr App Rep 173, CA (disconnection of life support machine did not break chain of causation).

11 *R v Smith* [1959] 2 QB 35, 43 Cr App Rep 121, C-MAC; cf *R v Jordan* (1956) 40 Cr App Rep 152, CCA (said by the C-MAC in *R v Smith* supra to be a special case depending upon its particular facts; that case is presumably to be regarded as one where the original wound was merely the setting for subsequent events).

B. MURDER

431. Malice aforethought. The mental element of murder, traditionally called malice aforethought, may take the form of an intention to kill[1] or an intention to cause grievous[2] bodily harm[3]. Intent is the essential element in both forms of malice aforethought[4]. When directing juries, judges should not elaborate on what intent means but should rely upon the good sense of juries to decide whether the accused acted with intent, unless some further explanation or elaboration is strictly necessary to avoid misunderstanding[5].

1 The doctrine of transferred malice applies (see para 13 ante): see Bract, De Corona, c 36; Fost 261; *R v Saunders and Archer* (1573) 2 Plowd 473; *R v Hunt* (1825) 1 Mood CC 93, CCR; *R v Bernard* (1858) 1 F & F 240 per Campbell CJ.

2 'Grievous bodily harm' means really serious bodily harm: *DPP v Smith* [1961] AC 290, 44 Cr App Rep 261, HL; *R v Metharam* [1961] 3 All ER 200, 45 Cr App Rep 304, CCA; *R v Cunningham* [1982] AC 566, 73 Cr App Rep 253, HL. See also *R v Saunders* [1985] Crim LR 230, CA (decided under the Offences against the Person Act 1861 s 20: see para 471 post).

3 *R v Cunningham* [1982] AC 566, 73 Cr App Rep 253, HL. This form of malice aforethought is commonly referred to as implied malice; it is 'implied' in the sense that it is not necessary to prove that the accused either intended or foresaw the death of the victim. Hence this form of malice aforethought was unaffected by the Homicide Act 1957 s 1 which abolished constructive malice while leaving implied malice unaffected: *R v Vickers* [1957] 2 QB 664, 41 Cr App Rep 189, CCA; approved in *R v Moloney* [1985] AC 905 at 921, 81 Cr App Rep 93 at 102, HL. It must, however, be proved that the accused intended to cause grievous bodily harm (cf the Criminal Justice Act 1967 s 8: see para 16 ante), and to that extent use of the expression 'implied malice' may be misleading.

4 See *R v Hancock, R v Shankland* [1986] AC 455 at 471, 82 Cr App Rep 264 at 274, HL.

5 See *R v Moloney* [1985] AC 905 at 926, 81 Cr App Rep 93 at 106, HL per Lord Bridge. If it is necessary to direct the jury as to inferring intent by reference to foresight of consequences, the direction should not follow the guidelines laid down by Lord Bridge in *R v Moloney* supra, but should refer to the probable as well as the natural consequences of the accused's act. The probability of a consequence is only a factor in the evidence to be considered in determining the accused's intention: *R v Hancock, R v Shankland* [1986] AC 455, 82 Cr App Rep 264, HL. See also *R v Nedrick* [1986] 3 All ER 1, 83 Cr App Rep 267, CA and para 16 ante.

As to the appropriate direction on a charge of attempted murder see *R v Walker and Hayles* (1989) Times, 11 August, CA.

As to proof of malice see para 460 post.

432. Penalty for murder. The penalty for murder is imprisonment for life[1]. On sentencing a person convicted of murder to imprisonment for life, the court may recommend that a minimum period should elapse before the Secretary of State orders the release[2] of that person[3]. No appeal lies against any such recommendation made by the court[4].

1 Murder (Abolition of Death Penalty) Act 1965 s 1 (1) (made permanent by resolution of both Houses of Parliament: see 793 H of C Official Report (5th series) 16 December 1969 col 1297; 306 HL Official Report (5th series) 18 December 1969 col 1321). As to sentences on persons under the age of 18 see para 1269 post; and as to murder committed in connection with the hijacking of aircraft see AVIATION vol 2 para 1363.

The sentence is fixed by law and cannot be appealed against under the Criminal Appeal Act 1968 s 9: see para 1355 post.

2 Ie on licence under the Criminal Justice Act 1967 s 61. As to the effect of release on licence see *R v Foy* [1962] 2 All ER 246, 46 Cr App Rep 290, CCA.

3 See the Murder (Abolition of Death Penalty) Act 1965 s 1 (2); the Interpretation Act 1978 s 17 (2) (a), Sch 2 para 3. It has been suggested that no such recommendation should be for a period of less than 12 years: see *R v Flemming* [1973] 2 All ER 401, 57 Cr App Rep 524, CA.

4 *R v Aitken* [1966] 2 All ER 453n, 50 Cr App Rep 204, CCA; *R v Bowden, R v Begley* (1983) 77 Cr App Rep 66, CA. Counsel must be permitted to plead in mitigation before such recommendation is made: *R v Todd* [1966] Crim LR 557, CCA. As to grants of pardon see para 1449 post.

433. Incitement to murder. Any person who solicits, encourages, persuades or endeavours to persuade, or proposes to[1] any person to murder any other person[2], whether he is a subject of Her Majesty or not and whether he is within the jurisdiction or not, is guilty of an offence and liable on conviction on indictment to imprisonment for life or for any shorter term[3].

An article or letter in a newspaper may amount to an incitement to murder, although no particular person is named, so long as the proposed victims belong to a definable class[4]. The communication containing the incitement must be proved to have reached the person intended to be incited, although it is not necessary to show that the latter's mind was affected by it[5]. If the communication cannot be proved to have reached him, the accused may be convicted of an attempt to incite[6].

1 As to incitement see para 58 ante; and as to conspiracy see para 59 et seq ante.
2 'Person' may include an unborn child in the womb: *R v Shephard* [1919] 2 KB 125, 14 Cr App Rep 26, CCA (solicitation of pregnant woman to murder infant after birth).
3 Offences against the Person Act 1861 s 4 (amended by Criminal Law Act 1977 s 5 (10), 65 (5), Sch 13).
4 *R v Most* (1881) 7 QBD 244, CCR; *R v Antonelli and Barberi* (1905) 70 JP 4.
5 *R v Fox* (1870) 19 WR 109, CCR; *R v Krause* (1902) 66 JP 121; *R v Diamond* (1920) 84 JP 211.
6 *R v Krause* (1902) 66 JP 121. See also *R v Ransford* (1874) 13 Cox CC 9, CCR; *R v McCarthy, Holland and O'Dwyer* [1903] 2 IR 146.

434. Threatening to kill. Any person who without lawful excuse[1] makes to another a threat[2], intending that that other would fear it would be carried out[3], to kill that other or a third person[4] is guilty of an offence and liable on conviction on indictment to imprisonment for a term not exceeding ten years, or on summary conviction to imprisonment for a term not exceeding six months or a fine not exceeding the prescribed sum, or to both[5].

1 Self-defence or the prevention of crime may constitute a lawful excuse provided that it was reasonable in the circumstances to make such a threat; and it is for the prosecution to prove the absence of lawful excuse and for the jury to decide what was reasonable: see *R v Cousins* [1982] QB 526, 74 Cr App Rep 363, CA. Lawful excuse does not depend on whether the life of the accused was in immediate jeopardy when he made the threat: *R v Cousins* supra. The reasonableness of the accused's belief that he had lawful excuse is judged on the facts as he believed them to be: see *R v Williams* [1987] 3 All ER 411, 78 Cr App Rep 276, CA; *Beckford v R* [1988] AC 130, 85 Cr App Rep 378, PC and para 21 ante.
2 The threat may be conditional and it may be implied as well as express: *R v Solanke* [1969] 3 All ER 1383, [1970] 1 WLR 1, CA. It would seem that the threat may be made by any means: see eg *R v Williams* (1986) 84 Cr App Rep 299, CA (threatening telephone calls). As to threatening letters see also the Malicious Communications Act 1988 s 1 and para 375 ante.
3 Evidence of the accused's previous history is admissible to prove that he intended his threats to be taken seriously: *R v Williams* (1986) 84 Cr App Rep 299, CA.
4 Where a person threatens a pregnant woman with the words 'I am going to kill your baby' and the threat is to the foetus in utero, no offence under the Offences against the Person Act 1861 s 16 (substituted by the Criminal Law Act 1977 s 65 (4), Sch 12) is made out since the foetus is not another person distinct from its mother: *R v Tait* [1989] 3 All ER 682, [1989] 3 WLR 891, CA. Where, however, the threat is to kill the child after its birth, it seems that such an offence may be made out: *R v Tait* supra (obiter); and see para 433 note 2 ante.
5 Offences against the Person Act 1861 s 16 (as substituted: see note 4 supra); Magistrates' Courts Act 1980 ss 17, 32 (1), Sch 1 para 5 (a). See para 804 post. For the meaning of 'the prescribed sum' see para 807 post.

435. Joint enterprise. The normal principles of criminal liability in joint enterprise[1] apply in cases of homicide so that a person who participates[2] in a joint enterprise which results in the unlawful killing of the victim, and who is a party[2] to the acts of the person who carries out the killing, is guilty of either murder or manslaughter[3]. In order for such a person to be guilty of murder three elements must be proved: (1) a common unlawful joint enterprise; (2) that what was done by the person who carried out the killing was within the scope of that common joint enterprise; and (3) that that action must have been seen as a possible result of that unlawful joint enterprise[4]. Where, however, two or more persons embark on an unlawful joint enterprise but one goes far beyond the scope of that enterprise, and goes on to commit something beyond the contemplation or foresight of the others, those other persons are not in law responsible for that act of the first[4].

When directing a jury on a charge of murder against a co-accused who did not carry out the actual killing, the precise form of words used is not important, but the judge must make it clear that for the co-accused to be guilty he must be proved to have lent himself to a criminal enterprise involving the infliction, if necessary, of serious harm or death, or to have had an express or tacit understanding with the killer that such harm or death should, if necessary, be inflicted[5].

1 See paras 44, 47 ante. The well-established principles of joint enterprise are unaffected by the decisions in *R v Moloney* [1985] AC 905, 81 Cr App Rep 93, HL and *R v Hancock, R v Shankland* [1986] AC 455, 82 Cr App Rep 264, HL: see *R v Ward* (1986) 85 Cr App Rep 71, CA: *R v Slack* [1989] QB 775, 89 Cr App Rep 252, CA.
2 As to complicity in crime see para 43 et seq ante; and see also *R v Anderson, R v Morris* [1966] 2 QB 110, 50 Cr App Rep 216, CCA.
3 Ie according to his mens rea: see para 436 post.
4 *R v Ward* (1986) 85 Cr App Rep 71 at 77, CA. See also *Chan Wing-Siu v R* [1985] AC 168, 80 Cr App Rep 117, PC; *R v Slack* [1989] QB 775, 89 Cr App Rep 252, CA (not following *R v Barr* (1986) 88 Cr App Rep 362, CA).
5 *R v Slack* [1989] QB 775, 89 Cr App Rep 252, CA; and see *Chan Wing-Siu v R* [1985] AC 168, 80 Cr App Rep 117, PC.

C. MANSLAUGHTER

436. In general. Manslaughter differs from murder only in relation to the mental element necessary to support the charge[1]. Manslaughter may be classified as voluntary or involuntary, the distinction being that in cases of voluntary manslaughter a person may be convicted of the offence notwithstanding that he may have the malice aforethought of murder, if he kills (1) under provocation[2]; (2) suffering from diminished responsibility by reason of abnormality of mind[3]; or (3) in pursuance of a suicide pact[4]. Involuntary manslaughter is committed (a) where death results from an unlawful act which any reasonable person would recognise as likely to expose another to the risk of injury[5]; and (b) where death is caused by a reckless or grossly negligent act or omission[6].

1 *R v Doherty* (1887) 16 Cox CC 306 at 307. See also *R v Taylor* (1834) 2 Lew CC 215; *R v Hughes* (1857) Dears & B 248, CCR. As to the effect of alcohol or drugs see paras 28–30 ante; and as to procedural provisions relating to prosecutions for the manslaughter of a child or young person see para 882 post.
2 As to provocation see paras 438, 439 post.
3 As to diminished responsibility see paras 440, 441 post.
4 See para 442 post.
5 See para 444 post.
6 See para 445 post.

437. Penalty for manslaughter. The penalty for manslaughter is imprisonment for life or for any shorter term[1].

1 Offences against the Person Act 1861 s 5 (amended by the Criminal Justice Act 1948 ss 1 (1), 83 (3),
Sch 10 Pt I). There is no power, as there is in a case of murder, to recommend a minimum period of
imprisonment: see *R v Flemming* [1973] 2 All ER 401, 57 Cr App Rep 524, CA. When sentencing an
offender in a simple case of manslaughter, the judge should pass a determinate sentence: *R v Picker*
[1970] 2 QB 161, [1970] 2 All ER 226, CA. A life sentence should be imposed only when the public
requires protection from the offender for a considerable time: *R v Picker* supra. Where death results
from an unlawful act, such as an assault, the fact of death should not be dissociated from the
accused's conduct. It follows that it is wrong to regard the maximum sentence for the unlawful act as
the maximum for the involuntary manslaughter: *R v Ruby* [1987] Crim LR 785, CA. As to the
appropriate sentence for the manslaughter of a baby see *R v Bashford* (1988) 10 Cr App Rep (S) 359,
CA; and as to the appropriate sentence where death results from drunken group violence see *R v
Eaton* (1989) Times, 14 October, CA.
  As to disqualification for driving and endorsement of licence where the driver of a motor vehicle is
convicted of manslaughter see the Road Traffic Offenders Act 1988 ss 34 (2), 97 (2), Sch 2 Pt II and
ROAD TRAFFIC. As to 'motor manslaughter' see paras 445 text to note 8, 449 post.

438. Provocation as defence to murder charge. Provocation may reduce a
charge of murder[1] to one of manslaughter[2]. It consists of conduct[3] which would
cause in any reasonable person, and actually causes in the accused, a sudden and
temporary loss of self-control[4], making him so subject to passion that he is not the
master of his mind[5]. Where on a charge of murder there is evidence on which the
jury can find that the person charged was provoked[6], whether by things done or by
things said[7], or by both together, to lose his self-control, the question whether the
provocation was enough to make a reasonable man do as he did must be left to be
determined by the jury[8]. In determining that question the jury must take into
account everything both done and said according to the effect which, in the jury's
opinion, it would have on a reasonable man[9].

1 Provocation may be a defence only to a charge of murder: *R v Cunningham* [1959] 1 QB 288, 43 Cr
App Rep 79, CCA; *R v Bruzas* [1972] Crim LR 367.
2 The defence of provocation is available even though there exists in the accused's mind such malice as
would support a charge of murder: see *A-G of Ceylon v Kumarasinghege Don John Perera* [1953] AC
200 at 206, [1953] 2 WLR 238 at 243, PC; *Lee Chun-Chuen v R* [1963] AC 220, [1963] 1 All ER 73, PC;
Parker v R [1964] AC 1369, [1964] 2 All ER 641, PC; *R v Martindale* [1966] 3 All ER 305, 50 Cr App
Rep 273, C-MAC. If the facts are not in dispute, it is open to the judge to direct the jury that it may
return only a verdict of murder or manslaughter, ie it may not return a verdict of not guilty: *R v
Larkin* as reported in [1943] 1 All ER 217, CCA.
3 Conduct constituting provocation may include spoken words: see infra. It is not essential that the
conduct be directed at the accused himself. A man may be provoked by finding another raping his
wife (1 Hale PC 486; *R v Millward* (1931) 23 Cr App Rep 119, CCA), or committing an unnatural
offence with his son (*R v Fisher* (1837) 8 C & P 182), or committing an assault on a member of his
family (*R v Harrington* (1886) 10 Cox CC 370). Adultery may also constitute provocation: see 1 Hale
PC 486; *R v Manning* (1671) T Raym 212; *R v Pearson* (1835) 2 Lew CC 216. In general provocation is
a defence when it causes the accused to kill the person giving the provocation (see *R v Simpson* (1915)
84 LJKB 1893, 11 Cr App Rep 218, CCA), but it may provide a defence even where it causes him to
kill a third person (see *R v Davies* [1975] QB 691, 60 Cr App Rep 253, CA; and see also the Homicide
Act 1957 s 3: see infra). As to self-induced provocation see para 439 text and note 7 post.
4 It is essential to the defence that the accused should in fact have lost his self-control at the time of the
killing. In considering whether there was such a genuine loss of self-control the jury may have
regard to the time elapsing between the provocation and the killing (*R v Hayward* (1833) 6 C & P 157;
Kwaku Mensah v R [1946] AC 83, PC; *R v Duffy* [1949] 1 All ER 932n, CCA; *R v Ibrams* (1981) 74 Cr
App Rep 154, CA), and to the manner of the killing itself which may support or negative
contrivance or design (1 Hale PC 454; Fost 291; 1 Hawk PC c 13 s 42; 1 East PC 235; *R v Thorpe*
(1829) 1 Lew CC 171; *R v Shaw* (1834) 6 C & P 372; *R v Thomas* (1837) 7 C & P 817; *Mancini v DPP*
[1942] AC 1, 28 Cr App Rep 65, HL; *R v Gilbert* (1977) 66 Cr App Rep 237, CA). See also *R v Cocker*
[1989] Crim LR 740, CA (husband gave way to wife's entreaties that he should kill her; loss of
self-restraint but not of self-control; no evidence of provocation).
5 See *R v Duffy* [1949] 1 All ER 932n, CCA, approving the direction given to the jury by Devlin J; *R v
Whitfield* (1976) 63 Cr App Rep 39 at 42, CA.

6   Where there is any evidence of provocation which would, if accepted, justify the jury in returning a verdict of manslaughter, the judge must leave that issue to the jury whatever the line of defence adopted at the trial (*R v Hopper* [1915] 2 KB 431, 11 Cr App Rep 136, CCA; *Kwaku Mensah v R* [1946] AC 83, PC; *Bullard v R* [1957] AC 635, 42 Cr App Rep 1, PC; *R v Porritt* [1961] 3 All ER 463, 45 Cr App Rep 348, CCA; *Rolle v R* [1965] 3 All ER 582, [1965] 1 WLR 1341, PC; *R v Cascoe* [1970] 2 All ER 833, 54 Cr App Rep 401, CA; see also *Knowles v R* [1930] AC 366, PC; *Mancini v DPP* [1942] AC 1, 28 Cr App Rep 65, HL); and even if, in the opinion of the trial judge, on the evidence a verdict of manslaughter would be perverse (*R v Gilbert* (1977) 66 Cr App Rep 237, CA). Where the evidence discloses a possible defence of provocation, the burden of proof remains on the prosecution, and it is not for the accused to establish the defence; this must be made clear to the jury: *Chan Kau v R* [1955] AC 206, [1955] 1 All ER 266, PC; *R v McPherson* (1957) 41 Cr App Rep 213, CCA; *R v Cascoe* supra. If there is reasonable doubt whether or not there was provocation, the accused is entitled to a verdict of manslaughter: *R v Prince* [1941] 3 All ER 37, 28 Cr App Rep 60, CCA; *R v McPherson* supra.

     Evidence which was adduced in support of an unsuccessful defence, eg self-defence, may be relied on in whole or in part as affording provocation: see *Bullard v R* supra; *R v Porritt* supra.

7   At common law the defence of provocation tended to be limited to certain particular situations (such as physical attack or finding of spouse in adultery) and it was held in *Holmes v DPP* [1946] AC 588, 31 Cr App Rep 123, HL that words alone, save in extreme and exceptional cases, would not amount to provocation. The effect of the Homicide Act 1957 s 3 is to remove these limitations upon the defence; anything, whether things done or words said or both together, which causes a loss of self-control in the accused may be considered by the jury in determining whether it is capable of amounting to provocation: *R v Davies* [1975] QB 691, 60 Cr App Rep 253, CA. See also *R v Doughty* (1986) 83 Cr App Rep 319, CA (baby's continuous crying may constitute evidence of provocation).

8   Homicide Act 1957 s 3. As to the effect of provocation on a reasonable man see para 439 post.

9   Ibid s 3.

439. Provocation; the criterion of the reasonable man. In order to set up provocation as a defence it is not enough to show that the accused was provoked into losing his self-control; it must be shown that the provocation was such as would in the circumstances have caused a reasonable man to lose his self-control[1]. For these purposes, 'the reasonable man' means an ordinary person of either sex, not exceptionally excitable or pugnacious, but possessed of such powers of self-control as everyone is entitled to expect that his fellow citizens will exercise in society[2]. In determining the question, the jury may consider, along with other factors, the nature of the retaliation by the accused, having regard to the nature of the provocation. There is no rule of law that the retaliation must be proportionate to the provocation: it is merely a matter to be considered by the jury in determining whether a reasonable man would have acted as the accused did[3]. The jury must consider the effect of the provocation on a reasonable man, not a drunken man[4], loss of self-control arising from the taking of alcohol or drugs not being in itself an excuse for crime[5]. Where, however, a person, owing to the taking of alcohol or drugs, makes a mistake of fact, he is entitled, for the purposes of the defence of provocation, to be treated as though the supposed fact was true; hence, if owing to his drunkenness he believed that another was about to make an attack upon him, the jury ought to take that into consideration in determining the issue of provocation[6].

     A person may rely on self-induced provocation where his own conduct causes a reaction in another which in turn causes him to lose his own self-control[7].

1   See para 438 ante.

2   *DPP v Camplin* [1978] AC 705, 67 Cr Ap Rep 14, HL. The judge should direct the jury that the reasonable man is a person with the power of self-control to be expected of an ordinary person of the sex and age of the accused, but in other respects sharing such of the accused's characteristics as the jury thinks would affect the gravity of the provocation to him. The question for the jury is not merely whether such a person would in like circumstances be provoked to lose his self-control but

whether he would also react to the provocation as the accused did: *DPP v Camplin* supra; not following *Bedder v DPP* [1954] 2 All ER 801, 38 Cr App Rep 133, HL. See also *R v Newell* (1980) 71 Cr App Rep 331, CA (characteristics to be taken into account are those with a sufficient degree of permanence which can be regarded as part of an individual's character); *R v Burke* [1987] Crim LR 336, CA (not mandatory to rehearse exact words used in *DPP v Camplin* supra); *R v Ali* [1989] Crim LR 736, CA (accused's age not relevant in circumstances; no need for express allusion to age in direction to jury).

At common law the judge might withdraw the issue of provocation from the jury where, upon the evidence, no reasonable jury could find that a reasonable man would have been provoked (see eg *Holmes v DPP* [1946] AC 588, 31 Cr App Rep 123, HL), but the Homicide Act 1957 s 3 makes it clear that the judge may no longer withdraw the issue on this ground. If there is evidence that the accused was in part provoked, the issue must be left to be determined by the jury. For instances where the court has considered provocation and its effect on a reasonable man after the Homicide Act 1957 see eg *R v Simpson* [1957] Crim LR 815 (threats and nagging constituting provocation); *R v Fantle* [1959] Crim LR 584 (taunts by deceased of having spent the night with accused's wife constituting provocation); *R v Doughty* (1986) 83 Cr App Rep 319, CA (baby's continuous crying capable of constituting provocation).

The Criminal Justice Act 1967 s 8 (see para 16 ante), has not affected the operation of the Homicide Act 1957 s 3: *R v Williams* [1968] Crim LR 678, CA.

3 *Phillips v R* [1969] 2 AC 130, 53 Cr App Rep 132, PC; *R v Walker* [1969] 1 All ER 767, 53 Cr App Rep 195, CA; *R v Brown* [1972] 2 QB 229, 56 Cr App Rep 564, CA.

4 See *R v Wardrope* [1960] Crim LR 770.

5 *R v McCarthy* [1954] 2 QB 105 at 112, 38 Cr App Rep 74 at 82, CCA; and see further paras 28–30 ante.

6 *R v Letenock* (1917) 12 Cr App Rep 221, CCA; *R v Wardrope* [1960] Crim LR 770. See, however, *DPP v Majewski* [1977] AC 443, 62 Cr App Rep 262, HL and para 28 ante.

7 *R v Johnson* [1989] 2 All ER 839, 89 Cr App Rep 148, CA (the mere fact that the accused caused a reaction in others which in turn led him to lose his self-control does not result in the issue of provocation being kept outside the jury's consideration); *Edwards v R* [1973] AC 648, 57 Cr App Rep 157, PC (blackmailer not generally entitled to rely on predictable reaction of person blackmailed as constituting provocation, but may do so where the victim's reaction goes to extreme lengths; explained in *R v Johnson* supra).

440. Diminished responsibility as defence to murder charge. Where a person kills or is a party to the killing of another, he may not be convicted of murder if he was suffering from such abnormality of mind[1] as substantially impaired his mental responsibility[2] for his acts and omissions in doing or being a party to the killing[3]. A person who but for the defence of diminished responsibility would be liable[4] to be convicted of murder is liable instead to be convicted of manslaughter[5]. The fact that one party to a killing is by virtue of such defence not liable to be convicted of murder does not, however, affect the question whether the killing amounted to murder in the case of any other party to it[6].

The onus is on the defence to prove that by reason of diminished responsibility the accused is not liable to be convicted of murder[7], but the burden is not so heavy as the burden of proof on the prosecution and is only that of showing a preponderance of probabilities[8]. As a rule of practice, a plea of guilty of manslaughter on the ground of diminished responsibility should not generally be accepted; the issue of diminished responsibility should be left to the jury[9]. Where such a plea is tendered, however, and the medical evidence plainly shows that the plea can properly be accepted, it is permissible for the court to accept it and thus avoid a trial for murder[10]. Where the defence seeks a verdict of manslaughter on the ground of diminished responsibility and on another ground[11] and the jury returns such a verdict, the judge may ask the jury on which ground its verdict is based or whether it was based on both grounds[12].

1 It is immaterial whether the abnormality of mind arises from a condition of arrested or retarded development of mind or any inherent causes or is induced by disease or injury: Homicide Act 1957 s 2 (1). Abnormality of mind induced by alcohol or drugs is not due to inherent causes: see *R v Gittens* [1984] QB 698, 79 Cr App Rep 272, CA; *R v Fenton* (1975) 61 Cr App Rep 261, CA. If, however, the imbibing of alcohol has reached the stage that the accused's brain has been damaged so that there is gross impairment of judgment and emotional responses, or the accused's use of alcohol is involuntary because he can no longer resist the impulse to drink, the defence of diminished responsibility is available: see *R v Tandy* [1989] 1 All ER 267, 87 Cr App Rep 45, CA. Unless an alleged abnormality of the mind can be shown to fall within one of the causes specified in the Homicide Act 1957 s 2 (1), the defence of diminished responsibility cannot be sustained: *R v King* as reported in [1965] 1 QB 443 at 450, CCA.

'Abnormality of mind', which has to be contrasted with the expression 'defect of reason', means a state of mind so different from that of ordinary human beings that the reasonable man would term it abnormal; it appears to be wide enough to cover the mind's activities in all its aspects, not only the perception of physical acts and matters, and the ability to form a rational judgment whether an act is right or wrong, but also the ability to exercise will-power to control physical acts in accordance with that rational judgment: *R v Byrne* [1960] 2 QB 396 at 403, 44 Cr App Rep 246 at 252, CCA. To establish mental abnormality under the Homicide Act 1957 s 2 (1), it is not necessary to show that the accused's abnormality existed from birth: *R v Gomez* [1964] 48 Cr App Rep 310, CCA.

2 The expression 'mental responsibility for his acts' points to a consideration of the extent to which the accused's mind is answerable for his physical acts which must include a consideration of the extent of his ability to exercise will-power to control his physical acts: *R v Byrne* [1960] 2 QB 396 at 403, 44 Cr App Rep 246 at 252, CCA. Such abnormality as 'substantially impairs his mental responsibility' involves a mental state which in popular language a jury would regard as amounting to partial insanity or being on the borderline of insanity: *R v Byrne* supra at 404 and at 253; see also *Rose v R* [1961] AC 496 at 507, 45 Cr App Rep 102 at 106, PC, where a warning was given about directing a jury that 'borderline of insanity' could be equated with 'abnormality of mind' (cited in *R v Seers* (1984) 79 Cr App Rep 261, CA (case of chronic reactive depression)). As to 'substantially' see *R v Lloyd* [1967] 1 QB 175, 50 Cr App Rep 61, CCA.

3 Homicide Act 1957 s 2 (1). Where on a trial for murder the accused contends (1) that at the time of the alleged offence he was insane so as not to be responsible according to law for his actions; or (2) that at that time he was suffering from abnormality of the mind as is specified in s 2 (1), the court must allow the prosecution to adduce or elicit evidence tending to prove the other of those contentions, and may give directions as to the stage of the proceedings at which the prosecution may adduce such evidence: Criminal Procedure (Insanity) Act 1964 s 6. If, however, the accused does not raise insanity or diminished responsibility, and in no way suggests any abnormality of mind, the prosecution may not introduce evidence tending to establish insanity or diminished responsibility: see *R v Dixon* [1961] 3 All ER 460n, [1961] 1 WLR 337. As to whether the judge may raise the issue of diminished responsibility see *R v Kooken* (1982) 74 Cr App Rep 30, CA; *R v Campbell* (1986) 84 Cr App Rep 255, CA.

When a plea of diminished responsibility is raised, the matter must be fully tested and the jury must be properly satisfied before a verdict of manslaughter is brought in: *R v Ahmed Din* [1962] 2 All ER 123, 46 Cr App Rep 269, CCA (prosecution criticised for supporting pleas); *R v Russell* [1964] 2 QB 596, 48 Cr App Rep 62 (prosecution raising issue of insanity). As to the relative functions of judge and jury in relation to diminished responsibility see para 441 post.

4 Ie whether as principal or as accessory: Homicide Act 1957 s 2 (3).

5 Ibid s 2 (3).

6 Ibid s 2 (4).

7 Ibid s 2 (2). Although the Homicide Act 1957 does not provide that a defence of diminished responsibility must be based on medical evidence, such a defence is not likely to succeed without such evidence: *R v Dix* (1982) 74 Cr App Rep 306, CA.

8 *R v Dunbar* [1958] 1 QB 1, 41 Cr App Rep 182, CCA. As to the burden of proof see para 1062 et seq post.

9 *R v Matheson* [1958] 2 All ER 87, 42 Cr App Rep 145, CCA.

10 *R v Cox* [1968] 1 All ER 386, 52 Cr App Rep 130, CA.

11 Eg provocation: see paras 438, 439 ante.

12 *R v Matheson* [1958] 2 All ER 87, 42 Cr App Rep 145, CCA.

441. Diminished responsibility; functions of judge and jury. In his summing up the judge must give a proper explanation of the terms contained in the statutory provisions[1] to the jury[2].

Whether or not the accused was suffering from an abnormality of the mind at the time of the killing is for the jury to decide[3] and while the medical evidence is important, the jury is not bound to accept it if other evidence is adduced which conflicts with or outweighs it[4]. The question whether the accused's abnormality of mind was sufficiently substantial to impair his mental responsibility is a question of degree; and it should also be decided by the jury[5]. However, the aetiology[6] of the abnormality of the mind is a matter to be determined by medical evidence[7].

The judge should review the evidence in detail for the jury[8]. When directing the jury on burden of proof, the judge must point out that the burden on the defence of establishing diminished responsibility is not so great as the burden on the prosecution[9]. Comment by the judge on the failure of the accused to give evidence in such cases is only rarely proper[10].

1　Ie the Homicide Act 1957 s 2 (1): see para 440 ante. As to explanations of the terms see para 440 notes 1, 2 ante.
2　*R v Terry* [1961] 2 QB 314, 45 Cr App Rep 180, CCA; *R v Gomez* (1964) 48 Cr App Rep 310, CCA. Cf *R v Spriggs* [1958] 1 QB 270, 42 Cr App Rep 69, CCA, as explained in *R v Walden* [1959] 3 All ER 203, 43 Cr App Rep 201, CCA; *R v Terry* supra.
3　*R v Dunbar* [1958] 1 QB 1 at 9, 41 Cr App Rep 182 at 186, CCA: *R v Spriggs* [1958] 1 QB 270, 42 Cr App Rep 69, CCA. The jury should approach this task in a broad common sense way: *Walton v R* [1978] AC 788, 66 Cr App Rep 25, PC.
4　The jury is entitled to consider all the evidence including the acts and statements of the accused and his demeanour: *R v Byrne* [1960] 2 QB 396 at 403, 44 Cr App Rep 246 at 253, CCA. The decision on the issue of diminished responsibility is entrusted to the jury, after proper direction, most obviously when there is a conflict of medical evidence: *R v Jennion* [1962] 1 All ER 689, 46 Cr App Rep 212, CCA. The jury may return a verdict contrary to the medical evidence if the verdict is otherwise supportable: *R v Latham* [1965] Crim LR 434, CCA; *Walton v R* [1978] AC 788, 66 Cr App Rep 25, PC; *R v Kiszko* (1978) 68 Cr App Rep 62, CA. Where, however, the verdict entirely lacks support from the evidence adduced it will be reversed on appeal, eg a verdict of manslaughter will be substituted for one of murder: *R v Matheson* [1958] 2 All ER 87, 42 Cr App Rep 145, CCA; *R v Bailey* (1961) reported in (1977) 66 Cr App Rep 31n, CCA. The principle that mental responsibility is a matter for the jury is the same whether the defence pleads insanity or diminished responsibility: *R v Jennion* supra at 692 and at 217. As to the issue of insanity being left to the jury see para 31 ante.
5　*R v Byrne* [1960] 2 QB 396 at 402, 403, 44 Cr App Rep 246 at 253, CCA. For the direction to be given where abnormality resulted from a combination of alcohol or drugs and inherent causes see *R v Gittens* [1984] QB 698, 79 Cr App Rep 272, CA; disapproving *R v Turnbull* (1977) 65 Cr App Rep 242, CA; and as to alcoholism see para 440 note 1 ante.
6　Ie whether the abnormality arose from a condition of arrested or retarded development of mind or any inherent causes, or was induced by disease or injury: cf para 440 note 1 ante.
7　*R v Byrne* [1960] 2 QB 396 at 403, 44 Cr App Rep 246 at 253, CCA.
8　*R v Terry* [1961] 2 QB 314, 45 Cr App Rep 180, CCA; *R v Gomez* (1964) 48 Cr App Rep 310, CCA. It is bad practice, and normally constitutes an inadequate direction, for the judge merely to hand transcripts of the medical evidence to the jury: *R v Terry* supra.
9　See para 15 ante.
10　*R v Bathurst* [1968] 2 QB 99, 52 Cr App Rep 251, CA. See, however, *R v Bradshaw* (1985) 82 Cr App Rep 79, CA.

442. Suicide pacts. Suicide, which was self-murder at common law, is no longer an offence[1]. However, where a person, acting in pursuance of a suicide pact between himself and another, kills the other or is a party to the other being killed by a third party, he is guilty of manslaughter[2]. For these purposes, 'suicide pact' means a common agreement between two or more persons having for its object the death of all of them, whether or not each is to take his own life, but nothing done by a person who enters into a suicide pact is to be treated as done by him in pursuance of the pact unless it is done while he has the settled intention of dying in pursuance of the pact[3]. Where a person charged with the murder of another killed the other or was a party to his being killed, it is for the defence to prove that the person charged was acting in pursuance of a suicide pact between him and the other[4].

1 See the Suicide Act 1961 s 1.
2 Homicide Act 1957 s 4 (1) (amended by the Suicide Act 1961 s 3 (2), Sch 2). As to complicity in another's suicide see para 443 post; and see *R v Sweeney* (1986) 8 Cr App Rep (S) 419, CA (it is the policy of the law to make suicide pacts unlawful; those who enter into such pacts and survive when the other party thereto dies should expect to be punished). As to the penalty for manslaughter see para 437 ante.
3 Homicide Act 1957 s 4 (3).
4 Ibid s 4 (2) (amended by the Suicide Act 1961 s 3 (2), Sch 2).   •

443. Complicity in suicide. Although suicide is no longer an offence in itself[1], any person who aids, abets, counsels or procures[2] the suicide of another, or an attempt by another to commit suicide, is guilty of an offence and liable on conviction on indictment to imprisonment for a term not exceeding 14 years[3]. No proceedings for this offence may be instituted except by or with the consent of the Director of Public Prosecutions[4].

1 See para 442 ante.
2 As to what constitutes aiding, abetting, counselling and procuring see para 45 et seq ante. It is necessary for the requisite mens rea to be proved in each case of the offence of aiding, abetting, counselling or procuring suicide: *A-G v Able* [1984] QB 795, 78 Cr App Rep 197 (supply of booklets describing methods of suicide).
3 Suicide Act 1961 s 2 (1). In *R v McShane* (1977) 66 Cr App Rep 97, CA a conviction for an attempt to commit an offence under the Suicide Act 1961 s 2 (1) was upheld, notwithstanding that the crime therein defined is itself in the nature of an attempt. Quaere whether the position is affected by the Criminal Attempts Act 1981 s 1 (4) (b) (see para 71 note 1 ante).
   If on the trial of an indictment for murder or manslaughter it is proved that the accused aided, abetted, counselled or procured the suicide of the person in question, the jury may find him guilty of that offence: Suicide Act 1961 s 2 (2). As to procedural provisions relating to prosecutions for aiding etc the suicide of a child or young person see para 882 post.
4 Ibid s 2 (4) (amended by the Criminal Law Act 1967 s 10 (2), Sch 3, Pt II; the Criminal Jurisdiction Act 1975 s 14 (5), Sch 6 Pt I). As to the effect of this limitation see para 639 post.

444. Killing by unlawful act. Where death is caused by an unlawful act, the person doing that act is guilty of manslaughter only if any reasonable person would inevitably recognise that the act would expose the victim to the risk of at least some harm[1]. Where the victim is killed by one or other of two different acts, each of which if it caused the death is sufficient to establish manslaughter, it is not necessary to prove which act caused the death[2].

Although it need not be proved that the accused himself intended, or even foresaw, harm to another, the requirement of an unlawful act will ordinarily require proof that he had the requisite mens rea to render the act unlawful[3]. Thus where, for example, the unlawful act alleged is an assault, a verdict of manslaughter cannot be supported unless it is shown that the accused had the mens rea for an assault[4].

Where a person accidentally kills another while playing a lawful game, the killing is not manslaughter[5]. A contestant who causes the death of his opponent in wrestling or boxing is not guilty of manslaughter if the death results from conduct ordinarily incident to the sport[6]; but prize-fighting[7] is by its nature illegal and, if death results, the survivor is guilty of manslaughter while those who are present encouraging the fight are guilty of manslaughter as abettors[8]. If two persons fight a duel and one is killed, the survivor is guilty of murder or manslaughter according to his mens rea, while the seconds and other persons giving encouragement are liable as abettors[9].

It would appear that to cause death by an unlawful abortion would amount at least to manslaughter[10].

If a person in the course of inflicting lawful correction[11] unintentionally kills the person who is being corrected, the killing is not manslaughter. The death is regarded as having occurred by misadventure if, having regard to the circumstances, the correction was inflicted moderately and with a proper instrument not likely to cause death or serious injury[12]. If the correction exceeds the bounds of what is proper and reasonable in the circumstances and death is caused, the killing amounts at least to manslaughter[13].

An unlawful act does not include an act which becomes unlawful merely because of the negligent manner in which it is performed. Thus a person who causes the death of another while committing the offence of careless driving[14] is not necessarily[15] guilty of manslaughter[16]. It would also seem that a distinction is to be drawn between acts of omission and acts of commission; only in the case of an unlawful act of commission is the resulting death necessarily manslaughter[17].

1   *R v Church* [1966] 1 QB 59 at 70, [1965] 2 All ER 72 at 76, CCA; *R v Larkin* as reported in [1943] 1 All ER 217, CCA; *R v Lamb* [1967] 2 QB 981, 51 Cr App Rep 417, CA; *R v Cato* [1976] 1 All ER 260, 62 Cr App Rep 41, CA; *R v Goodfellow* (1986) 83 Cr App Rep 23, CA; *R v Dawson, R v Nolan, R v Walmsley* (1985) 81 Cr App Rep 150, CCA; *R v Ball* [1989] Crim LR 730, CA; *R v Watson* [1989] 2 All ER 865, 89 Cr App Rep 211, CA.
2   *A-G's Reference (No 4 of 1980)* [1981] 2 All ER 617, 73 Cr App Rep 40, CA.
3   See *R v Church* [1966] 1 QB 59 at 79, [1965] 2 All ER 72 at 76, CCA. Cf *R v Lipman* [1970] 1 QB 152 at 159, 53 Cr App Rep 600 at 607, CA. An accused is guilty of manslaughter if it is proved that he intentionally did an act which was unlawful and dangerous and that act inadvertently caused death; it need not be proved that he knew that the act was unlawful or dangerous, the test being whether sober and reasonable people would recognise its danger: *DPP v Newbury, DPP v Jones* [1977] AC 500, 62 Cr App Rep 291, HL; applying dicta in *R v Larkin* as reported in [1943] 1 All ER 217, CCA; *R v Church* supra; disapproving dictum in *Gray v Barr* [1971] 2 QB 554, [1971] 2 All ER 949, CA. The accused's mistaken belief that what he was doing was not dangerous is irrelevant for these purposes: *R v Ball* [1989] Crim LR 730, CA. The act must be likely to cause immediate injury, however slight, but need not be directed at the victim provided that there is no fresh and intervening cause between the act and the victim's death: *R v Goodfellow* (1986) 83 Cr App Rep 23, CA, explaining *R v Dalby* [1982] 1 All ER 916, 74 Cr App Rep 348; applying dicta in *R v Larkin* supra; *DPP v Newbury, DPP v Jones* supra. Harm may be caused if an unlawful act so shocks a victim that it causes him physical injury: *R v Dawson, R v Nolan, R v Walmsley* (1985) 81 Cr App Rep 150, CA. As to the effect of alcohol or drugs on offences where death is caused see paras 28–30 ante.
4   *R v Lamb* [1967] 2 QB 981, 51 Cr App Rep 417, CA. As to an assault causing death see also *R v Hopley* (1860) 2 F & F 202; *R v Alabaster* (1912) 47 L Jo 397; *R v Woods* (1921) 85 JP 272; *R v Larkin* [1943] KB 174, 29 Cr App Rep 18, CCA; *R v Mitchell* [1983] QB 741, 76 Cr App Rep 293, CA. For the meaning of 'assault' see para 488 et seq post.
5   Fost 259, 260; 1 Hawk PC c 11 ss 6, 7; *R v Bradshaw* (1878) 14 Cox CC 83; *R v Moore* (1898) 14 TLR 229. Nor is a person guilty of manslaughter merely because he has broken the rules of the game: *R v Moore* supra. As to accidental killing see para 450 post.
6   *R v Canniff* (1840) 9 C & P 359; *R v Young* (1866) 10 Cox CC 371.
7   For the meaning of 'prize-fighting' see *R v Coney* (1882) 8 QBD 534, CCR.
8   *R v Canniff* (1840) 9 C & P 359; *R v Hargrave* (1831) 5 C & P 170; *R v Murphy* (1833) C & P 103; *R v Orton* (1878) 14 Cox CC 226, CCR; *R v Coney* (1882) 8 QBD 534, CCR.
9   1 Hale PC 442; 1 Hawk PC c 13 ss 21, 22; Fost 297; *R v Mawgridge* (1706) 17 State Tr 57; *R v Oneby* (1727) 17 State Tr 29; *R v Rice* (1803) 3 East 581; *R v Cuddy* (1843) 1 Car & Kir 210; *R v Young* (1838) 8 C & P 644.

10 *R v Buck and Buck* (1960) 44 Cr App Rep 213; *R v Creamer* [1966] 1 QB 72, 49 Cr App Rep 368, CCA.
11 As to cases in which correction by personal chastisement is lawful see para 497 post.
12 1 Hale PC 473.
13 1 Hale PC 473, 474; Fost 262; 1 Hawk PC c 11 s 5; *R v Turner* (undated), cited in Comb 407; *R v Gray* (1666) Comb 408; *R v Wall* (1802) 28 State Tr 51 at 145 (colonial governor convicted of murder for ordering an excessive flogging which caused death); *R v Conner* (1836) 7 C & P 438; *R v Cheeseman* (1836) 7 C & P 455; *R v Bird* (1851) 5 Cox CC 20, CCR; *R v Hopley* (1860) 2 F & F 202. The chastisement of a child of very tender years must be of the very lightest description: see *R v Griffin* (1869) 11 Cox CC 402 (father causing death of his child aged two and a half years by beating it with a strap; manslaughter). Where on a charge of murder it appears that the injury which caused death may have resulted indirectly and not directly from the violence used by the accused, the question whether it so resulted and whether a reasonable man would have foreseen such a consequence of the violence used is a matter for the jury: see *R v Rymell* [1954] Crim LR 60, CCA (child struck brutally on face; subsequent death from rupture of liver, possibly caused by falling from bed; manslaughter).
14 Ie contrary to the Road Traffic Act 1988 s 3.
15 If the driving is grossly negligent, however, the driver may be guilty of manslaughter on that account: see para 446 post. As to the statutory offence of causing death by reckless driving see para 449 post.
16 *Andrews v DPP* [1937] AC 576, 26 Cr App Rep 34, HL. See also *R v Lowe* [1973] QB 702, 57 Cr App Rep 365, CA (parent not guilty of manslaughter merely because he was guilty of the offence of wilfully neglecting the child contrary to the Children and Young Persons Act 1933 s 1 (1) (as amended) (see para 537 post), and death had resulted from that neglect). It is submitted that *R v Sheppard* [1981] AC 394, 72 Cr App Rep 82, HL does not overrule *R v Lowe* supra on this point.
17 *R v Lowe* [1973] QB 702 at 709, 57 Cr App Rep 365 at 371, CA. An act of omission may give rise to liability for manslaughter if it is grossly negligent: *R v Waters* (1849) 1 Den 356, CCR; *R v Walters* (1841) Car & M 164; *R v Plummer* (1844) 1 Car & Kir 600; *R v Bubb* (1850) 4 Cox CC 455; *R v Smith* (1865) Le & Ca 607, CCR; *R v Conde* (1867) 10 Cox CC 547; *R v Nicholls* (1874) 13 Cox CC 75; *R v Instan* [1893] 1 QB 450, CCR; *R v Chattaway* (1922) 17 Cr App Rep 7, CCA; *R v Bonnyman* (1942) 28 Cr App Rep 131, CCA. Cf *R v Shepherd* (1862) Le & Ca 147, CCR; *R v Hall* (1919) 122 LT 31, 14 Cr App Rep 58, CCA. See also *R v Marriott* (1838) 8 C & P 425. See further paras 445, 446 post.

445. Killing by recklessness or gross negligence. A person upon whom the law imposes a duty or who has taken upon himself any duty, tending to the preservation of life, and who, regardless of the life, safety, welfare and health of others, neglects to perform that duty or performs it negligently and thereby causes the death of another person may be guilty of manslaughter[1]; as may a person who acts recklessly[2] in such a manner as to create an obvious and serious risk of causing physical injury to some person, and who thereby causes the death of another person[3]. A higher degree of negligence is necessary to render a person guilty of manslaughter than to establish civil liability against him[4]; and mere carelessness is not enough[5]. Whether negligence is to be regarded as of such a nature is a question for the jury, after it has been properly directed by the judge as to the standard to be applied, and depends on the facts of the particular case[6]. The number of persons affected by a single act of negligence does not affect the degree of negligence[7]. Negligence sufficient to support a conviction for a criminal offence such as careless driving will not necessarily support a conviction for manslaughter[8].

1 The non-contractual duties imposed by law are either statutory duties or those which arise at common law out of the relation in which persons stand towards each other or towards the public.
2 For the meaning of 'recklessly' see para 14 ante.
3 *R v Goodfellow* (1986) 83 Cr App Rep 23, CA, following *R v Seymour* [1983] 2 AC 493, 77 Cr App Rep 215, HL; *Kong Cheuk Kwan v R* (1985) 82 Cr App Rep 18, PC in adopting the test of recklessness laid down in *R v Lawrence* [1982] AC 510, 73 Cr App Rep 1, HL.
4 *R v Noakes* (1866) 4 F & F 920; *R v Doherty* (1887) 16 Cox CC 306 at 309; *R v Bateman* (1925) 94 LJKB 791 at 793, 796, 19 Cr App Rep 8 at 11–13, CCA (where the difference was described as a difference in kind); *Akerele v R* [1943] AC 255 at 262, [1943] 1 All ER 367 at 371, PC ; *The People (A-G) v Dunleavy* [1948] IR 95.

5 *R v Large* [1939] 1 All ER 753, 27 Cr App Rep 65, CCA; *R v Bateman* (1925) 94 LJKB 791 at 794, 19 Cr
App Rep 8 at 11, 12, CCA per Hewart LCJ; *Andrews v DPP* [1937] AC 576 at 582, 583, 26 Cr App
Rep 34 at 46–48, HL; *Akerele v R* [1943] AC 255 at 262, [1943] 1 All ER 367 at 371, PC; see also *R v
Bonnyman* (1942) 28 Cr App Rep 131, CCA.

The dictum of Hewart LCJ in *R v Bateman* supra was criticised in *Kong Cheuk Kwan v R* (1985) 82
Cr App Rep 18 at 26, PC as no longer necessary or helpful in directing juries in cases of reckless
manslaughter. Quaere to what extent that case, and the cases cited in note 3 supra, have assimilated
the test of gross negligence to that of recklessness; see eg *R v Goodfellow* (1986) 83 Cr App Rep 23 at
26, CA per Lord Lane CJ ('the question for the jury was whether or not the accused had been guilty
of recklessness (or gross negligence)'; suggestive of two separate tests unless tautologous). In *R v
Stone, R v Dobinson* [1977] QB 354, 64 Cr App Rep 186, CA, however, a submission that foresight of
the possibility of death or serious injury had to be proved to establish involuntary manslaughter
based on gross negligence was rejected; proof of recklessness, although not mere inadvertence, was
held to be sufficient; and see *R v West London Coroner, ex p Gray* [1988] QB 467, [1987] 2 All ER 129,
DC (when directing a jury on manslaughter comprising unlawful killing because of neglect on the
part of the police, the coroner must direct that the jury had to be satisfied, inter alia, that there was a
failure amounting to recklessness to do what should have been done for the health and welfare of the
deceased).

6 *R v Bateman* (1925) 94 LJKB 791 at 796, 19 Cr App Rep 8 at 13, CCA; *Akerele v R* [1943] AC 255 at
262, [1943] 1 All ER 367 at 371, PC. If on a trial for murder a verdict of manslaughter by negligence
is as a matter of law a possible verdict in view of the facts of the case, the judge should direct the jury
that such a verdict is open to it: *R v Roberts* [1942] 1 All ER 187, 28 Cr App Rep 102, CCA. As to the
proper direction in cases of reckless manslaughter see *R v Goodfellow* (1986) 83 Cr App Rep 23, CA.
See also note 5 supra.

7 *Akerele v R* [1943] AC 255 at 264, [1943] 1 All ER 367 at 372, PC.

8 See para 444 text to notes 14–16 ante. The test of recklessness is, however, the same in manslaughter
as in causing death by reckless driving: *R v Seymour* [1983] 2 AC 493, 77 Cr App Rep 215, HL. See
note 3 supra. Manslaughter should not, however, be charged unless the risk of death being caused by
the manner of the accused's driving is very high: *R v Seymour* supra. As to the statutory offence of
causing death by reckless driving see para 449 post.

446. Examples of recklessness or gross negligence. A person, whether he is a
medical man or not, who deals with dangerous medicines or undertakes a dangerous operation may be guilty of manslaughter if death is occasioned by his criminal
negligence[1]. A person may be guilty of manslaughter by reason of criminal
negligence in driving a motor vehicle or other vehicle or in riding or navigating a
vessel[2]. A driver, fireman or other railway employee may be guilty of the manslaughter of persons killed as a result of the criminally negligent performance of his
duties[3]. The negligent use of a dangerous weapon or other dangerous thing likely
to cause death in an improper place or without taking proper precautions to avoid
injury will, if the degree of negligence is such as to constitute criminal negligence,
render the owner guilty of manslaughter[4]. A person who is in charge of a mine or
of machinery is guilty of manslaughter if a fatal accident occurs as a result of his
criminal negligence[5]. In general, if a person causes death by his criminally negligent act or omission, he is guilty of manslaughter[6].

1 As to the standard to be applied in determining whether negligence is criminal see *R v Bateman* (1925)
94 LJKB 791, 19 Cr App Rep 8, CCA (dangerous operation; alleged delay in sending patient to
hospital); *Akerele v R* [1943] AC 255, [1943] 1 All ER 367, PC (injection of overdose). See also *R v
Van Butchell* (1829) 3 C & P 629 (genuine attempt to cure patient; not manslaughter); *R v Willamson*
(1807) 3 C & P 635 (midwife; not guilty of manslaughter); *R v Spiller* (1832) 5 C & P 333 (death from
incompetent treatment; manslaughter); *R v Simpson* (1829) 1 Lew CC 172, 262 (medicine administered by untrained person; guilty of manslaughter); *R v Ferguson* (1830) 1 Lew CC 181; *R v
Tessymond* (1828) 1 Lew CC 169; *R v Webb* (1834) 2 Lew CC 196; *R v Spilling* (1838) 2 Mood & R 107
(incautious use of dangerous instrument; manslaughter); *R v Crick* (1859) 1 F & F 519; *R v Crook*
(1859) 1 F & F 521; *R v Bull* (1860) 2 F & F 201 (dangerous medicine; manslaughter); *R v Markuss*
(1864) 4 F & F 356; *R v Chamberlain* (1867) 10 Cox CC 486; *R v Spencer* (1867) 10 Cox CC 525; *R v*

Noakes (1866) 4 F & F 920 (error of chemist in making up medicine; not manslaughter); *R v Finney* (1874) 12 Cox CC 625 (patient scalded in bath); *R v Burdee* (1916) 12 Cr App Rep 153, CCA (unqualified man giving a patient fasting and cold water treatment and accelerating death).

2 As to the standard of negligence necessary to constitute manslaughter see *Andrews v DPP* [1937] AC 576, 26 Cr App Rep 34, HL; *R v Seymour* [1983] 2 AC 493, 77 Cr App Rep 215, HL (adopting *R v Lawrence* [1982] AC 510, 73 Cr App Rep 1, HL); and see para 445 note 5 ante. See also *R v Walker* (1824) 1 C & P 320 (where the deceased was drunk); *R v Murray* (1852) 5 Cox CC 509 (streets unusually crowded); *R v Grout* (1834) 6 C & P 629 (near-sighted driver); *R v Timmins* (1836) 7 C & P 499 (buses racing); *R v Mastin* (1834) 6 C & P 396 (accused and deceased said to be racing); *R v Swindall and Osborne* (1846) 2 Car & Kir 230 (inciting to furious driving); *R v Dalloway* (1847) 3 Cox CC 273 (driving a cart without holding reins); *R v Jones* (1870) 11 Cox CC 544 (contributory negligence); *R v Taylor and West* (1840) 9 C & P 672 (negligent navigation of river or at too great speed); *R v Spence* (1846) 1 Cox CC 352 (liability of pilot); *R v Allen* (1835) 7 C & P 153; *R v Green* (1835) 7 C & P 156 (liability of captain); *R v Williamson* (1844) 1 Cox CC 97 (overloading and mismanagement of boat); *R v Gylee* (1908) 73 JP 72, CCA (motor car in collision with bicycle); *R v Dalloz* (1908) 1 Cr App Rep 258 (motor car); *R v Baldessare* (1930) 144 LT 185, 22 Cr App Rep 70, CCA ('joy ride'; common purpose of reckless driving; driver and companion both guilty of manslaughter); *Kong Cheuk Kwan v R* (1985) 82 Cr App Rep 18, PC (liability of captain of hydrofoil for collision causing death; jury should have been directed in accordance with *R v Lawrence* supra; conviction quashed).

3 See *R v Trainer* (1864) 4 F & F 105 at 111 (an inferior officer, acting honestly, justified in obeying the directions of a superior); *R v Gray* (1865) 4 F & F 1098 (no evidence whether deceased or accused had duty of looking for signals; acquittal directed); *R v Pargeter* (1848) 3 Cox CC 191; *R v Birchall* (1866) 4 F & F 1087 (engine driver and fireman); *R v Elliott* (1889) 16 Cox CC 710 (guard); *R v Benge* (1865) 4 F & F 504; *R v Smith* (1869) 11 Cox CC 210 (private tramway; no statutory obligation to watch); and see *R v Pittwood* (1902) 19 TLR 37 (gatekeeper failing to close level-crossing gates).

4 *R v Salmon* (1880) 6 QBD 79, CCR (firing rifle in a field near roads and houses held to be manslaughter; cf *R v Hutchinson* (1864) 9 Cox CC 555 (artillery practice); *R v Campbell* (1869) 11 Cox CC 323 (firing a gun at deceased, the jury apparently believing that accused did not know it was loaded); *R v Jones* (1874) 12 Cox CC 628 (where Lush J directed the jury that, if the accused pointed the gun at deceased without examining whether it was loaded or not, he was guilty of manslaughter; cf *R v Lamb* [1967] 2 QB 981, 51 Cr App Rep 417, CA (understandable mistake in amateur being unaware of mechanism of revolver)); *R v Weston* (1879) 14 Cox CC 346 at 352 (gun levelled by a poacher at a gamekeeper, but without intention of discharging it); *R v Archer* (1858) 1 F & F 351 (where during a struggle for a loaded gun, to the possession of which accused was entitled, it went off, and Lord Campbell CJ directed a verdict of guilty on the ground that the accused had no right to take the gun by force); *R v Skeet* (1866) 4 F & F 931 (a similar case, but deceased, a gamekeeper, was entitled to take the gun); *R v Burton* (1721) 1 Stra 481 (firing a pistol in a street); *R v Carr* (1832) 8 C & P 163 (negligent manufacture of a cannon or gun). See also *R v Roberts* [1942] 1 All ER 187, 28 Cr App Rep 102, CCA (accused convicted of murder of girl by shooting with rifle; defence that shooting accidental; judge should have directed jury that verdict of manslaughter might be returned).

5 See *R v Gregory* (1860) 2 F & F 153 (explosion on ship owing to inefficient valve); *R v Lowe* (1850) 4 Cox CC 449 (leaving incompetent person in charge of colliery machinery; cf *R v Hilton* (1838) 2 Lew CC 214 (leaving stopped machinery, subsequently started by another person; acquittal directed)); *R v Haines* (1847) 2 Car & Kir 368 (neglecting ventilation of mine); *R v Hughes* (1857) 7 Cox CC 301, CCR (omission to place a stage over shaft of mine).

6 There is a duty upon workmen and others who throw rubbish etc or allow it to fall from a height, not to endanger the lives of persons who may reasonably be expected to be in a place of public resort below. If they throw down such things without giving a sufficient warning which is likely to be heard, they may be guilty of manslaughter: see 1 Hale PC 472, 475; Fost 262, 263; *R v Hull* (1664) Kel 40; *R v Fenton* (1830) 1 Lew CC 179 (throwing stones down a mine); *R v Rigmaidon* (1833) 1 Lew CC 180 (where death was caused by casks which had been insufficiently secured falling into the road). For other cases of manslaughter arising out of a duty imposed by law to do or not to do certain things see *R v Franklin* (1883) 15 Cox CC 163; *R v Bruce* (1847) 2 Cox CC 262 (causing death by rough play with a third person, which was held by Erle J not to be manslaughter); *R v Sullivan* (1836) 7 C & P 641 (causing a cart to upset); *R v Martin* (1827) 3 C & P 211 (giving a very young child a considerable quantity of spirits to drink; see now the Children and Young Persons Act 1933 s 5 and INFANTS vol 24 para 701); *R v Packard* (1841) Car & M 236; *R v Kempson* (1893) 28 L Jo 477 (where causing death by selling diseased meat was held to be manslaughter); *R v Wild* (1837) 2 Lew CC 214 (where death was

caused by kicking at a trespasser); *R v Errington* (1838) 2 Lew CC 217 (where the accused set fire to straw intending only to frighten and death ensued).

A man had a horse which he knew to be so vicious as to be dangerous; he turned it out in a place where there were paths on which he knew people were likely to be; the horse killed such a person and he was convicted of manslaughter: see *R v Dant* (1865) Le & Ca 567.

447. Responsibility for recklessness or gross negligence. To render a person guilty of manslaughter the recklessness or negligence must have been a substantial cause of the death[1], and there must have been personal misconduct or personal negligence on the part of the accused[2]. The accused is not responsible criminally if the death was directly caused in his absence by the negligence of his employees or others[3].

It is no defence that the death was caused by the negligence of others as well as of the accused; if death is occasioned by the act or default of several, they are all guilty of manslaughter[4]. The particular negligence imputed to the accused must, however, have been a substantial cause of the death[5].

Several persons in pursuit of a common purpose may be guilty of negligence and so guilty of manslaughter even if only one of their number commits the actual negligent act[6].

   1 See *R v Hennigan* [1971] 3 All ER 133, 55 Cr App Rep 262, CA (causing death by reckless driving (see para 449 post); 'substantial' merely implies 'more than minimal'); *R v Cato* [1976] 1 All ER 260 at 265, 62 Cr App Rep 41 at 46, CA (causing death by injecting heroin). See also *R v Pocock* (1851) 17 QB 34 (where road trustees liable to repair a road were held by the Court of Queen's Bench not chargeable with manslaughter of a person who had been killed in consequence of their neglect to make a contract for the repair of it); *R v Ledger* (1862) 2 F & F 857.
   2 *R v Allen* (1835) 7 C & P 153 at 156; *R v Green* (1835) 7 C & P 156.
   3 *R v Bennett* (1858) Bell CC 1, CCR (where the accused had unlawfully kept in his house a quantity of fireworks, which, through the negligence of his employees, were set on fire, and thus caused the death of the deceased, and it was held that the accused could not be convicted of manslaughter). As to whether a corporation may be indicted for manslaughter see para 35 note 4 ante.
   4 *R v Haines* (1847) 2 Car & Kir 368; *R v Benge* (1865) 4 F & F 504 at 509 per Pigott B; *R v Salmon* (1880) 6 QBD 79, CCR. See also *R v Gibbins and Proctor* (1918) 13 Cr App Rep 134, CCA; *R v Stone, R v Dobinson* [1977] QB 354, 64 Cr App Rep 186, CA.
   5 *R v Ledger* (1862) 2 F & F 857; *R v Bennett* (1858) Bell CC 1, CCR; and see text and note 1 supra.
   6 *R v Swindall and Osborne* (1846) 2 Car & Kir 230; *R v Longbottom* (1849) 13 JP 270; *R v Baldessare* (1930) 144 LT 185, 22 Cr App Rep 70, CCA.

448. Contributory negligence. If the accused's negligent act or omission was a substantial cause of death, the fact that the deceased was himself negligent and so contributed to the accident or other circumstances by which the death was occasioned does not afford a defence to an indictment for manslaughter[1].

   1 *R v Longbottom* (1849) 3 Cox CC 439; *R v Walker* (1824) 1 C & P 320 (where deceased was intoxicated); *R v Swindall and Osborne* (1846) 2 Car & Kir 230; *R v Hutchinson* (1864) 9 Cox CC 555 at 557 per Byles J; *R v Jones* (1870) 11 Cox CC 544; *R v Kew and Jackson* (1872) 12 Cox CC 355; cf *R v Waters* (1834) 6 C & P 328; see also *R v Hennigan* [1971] 3 All ER 133, 55 Cr App Rep 262, CA (causing death by dangerous driving (now reckless driving: see para 449 post); the accused is guilty if the dangerous driving is more than a minimal factor in causing death and even if in a civil action he might be held to be only partly to blame).

449. Causing death by reckless driving. A person who causes[1] the death of another person by driving[2] a motor vehicle[3] on a road[4] recklessly[5] is guilty of an offence and liable on conviction on indictment to imprisonment for a term not exceeding five years[6]; and the court must order him to be disqualified for such period not less than two years as the court thinks fit, unless the court for special reasons[7] thinks fit to order him to be disqualified for a shorter period or not to order him to be disqualified[8].

Where on a person's trial on indictment for the above offence the jury finds him not guilty of the offence specifically charged in the indictment it may[9] find him guilty[10] of driving without due care and attention or without reasonable consideration for other persons using the road[11].

1 The driving must be a cause of the death and something more than minimal; contributory negligence by another driver is then irrelevant; see *R v Hennigan* [1971] 3 All ER 133, 55 Cr App Rep 262, CA and para 448 ante.
2 A person drives a motor vehicle if he can control it so as to direct its movements: see *McQuaid v Anderton* [1980] 3 All ER 540, [1981] 1 WLR 154, DC.
3 'Motor vehicle' means, subject to the Chronically Sick and Disabled Persons Act 1970 s 20 (special provisions for invalid carriages: see ROAD TRAFFIC), a mechanically propelled vehicle intended or adapted for use on roads: Road Traffic Act 1988 s 185 (1).
4 'Road', in relation to England and Wales, means any highway and any other road to which the public has access, and includes bridges over which a road passes: ibid s 192 (1). A public car park may be a road: see *R v Waterfield* [1964] 1 QB 164, 48 Cr App Rep 42, CCA.
5 For the meaning of 'recklessly' see *R v Lawrence* [1982] AC 510 at 527, 73 Cr App Rep 1 at 12, HL per Lord Diplock and para 14 ante. When directing juries as to what amounts to recklessness, judges should follow the principles enunciated by Lord Diplock in *R v Lawrence* supra: *R v Madigan* (1982) 75 Cr App Rep 145, CA. Evidence of alcoholic consumption sufficient to impair control is admissible to strengthen the inference of recklessness or to displace any explanation advanced by the driver: *R v Griffiths* (1984) 88 Cr App Rep 6, CA.
6 Road Traffic Act 1988 s 1; Road Traffic Offenders Act 1988 s 9, Sch 2 Pt I. As to road traffic offences generally see ROAD TRAFFIC. The statutory offence has not abolished the common law offence of 'motor manslaughter': *Government of the United States of America v Jennings* [1983] 1 AC 624, 75 Cr App Rep 367, HL; but the latter offence (as to which see para 445 note 8 ante) should be charged only in very serious cases where the risk of death being caused is very high and the two offences should not be joined in the same indictment: *R v Seymour* [1983] 2 AC 493, 77 Cr App Rep 215, HL. As to sentencing in cases of causing death by reckless driving see *R v Hudson* [1989] RTR 206, CA; *A-G's References (Nos 3 and 5 of 1989)* (1989) Times, 18 October, CA.
7 For a definition of 'special reason' see *Whittall v Kirby* [1947] KB 194, [1946] 2 All ER 552, DC (reason must be special to the facts which constitute the offence, not to the accused); applied in *R v Wickins* (1958) 42 Cr App Rep 236; *McCormick v Hitchins* (1986) 83 Cr App Rep 11, DC. The onus of proving the facts upon which it is alleged that special reasons exist lies upon the accused on the balance of probabilities, unless the prosecution formally admits the facts: see *Jones v English* [1951] 2 All ER 853, DC; *Brown v Dyerson* [1969] 1 QB 45, 52 Cr App Rep 630, DC.
8 Road Traffic Offenders Act 1988 s 34 (1), (4): see para 1339 post.
9 Ie without prejudice to the Criminal Law Act 1967 s 6 (3): see para 1029 post.
10 Ie guilty of an offence under the Road Traffic Act 1988 s 3: see ROAD TRAFFIC.
11 Road Traffic Offenders Act 1988 s 24 (1) (a).

450. Accidental killing. Killing by misadventure or misfortune, where the act causing death is not unlawful or culpably negligent, is not a crime[1].

1 1 Hale PC 492; Fost 264, 282; *R v Knock* (1877) 14 Cox CC 1 at 2.

D. INFANTICIDE AND CHILD DESTRUCTION

451. Infanticide. Where a woman by any wilful act or omission causes the death of her child under the age of 12 months, but at the time of the act or omission the balance of her mind was disturbed by reason of her not having fully recovered from the effect of giving birth to the child or by reason of the effect of lactation consequent upon the birth of the child, then, notwithstanding that the circumstances were such that the offence would have amounted to murder[1], she is guilty of infanticide and may be punished as if she had been guilty of the manslaughter of the child[2].

1 Ie but for the Infanticide Act 1938.
2 Ibid s 1 (1); Criminal Law Act 1967 s 12 (5) (a). As to the penalty for manslaughter see para 437 ante. On a trial for murder the jury may in the circumstances mentioned return a verdict of infanticide: s 1 (2). Where the evidence on which there has been a committal on a charge of murder does not indicate that the mother's mind had been disturbed by the birth, the prosecution should proceed with the charge of murder and a plea of guilty of infanticide should not be accepted: *R v Soanes* [1948] 1 All ER 289, 32 Cr App Rep 136, CCA.
　　Nothing in the Infanticide Act 1938 affects the power of a jury upon an indictment for the murder of a child to return a verdict of manslaughter or a verdict of not guilty by reason of insanity: s 1 (3) (amended by the Criminal Law Act 1967 s 10 (2), Sch 3 Pt III). On an indictment for infanticide, the mother may be convicted of child destruction: see paras 452, 1030 post. As to alternative verdicts generally see paras 1029–1033 post; and as to procedural provisions relating to infanticide see para 882 post.

452. Child destruction. Any person who, with intent to destroy the life of a child capable of being born alive[1], by any wilful act[2] causes a child to die before it has an existence independent of its mother is guilty of child destruction and liable on conviction on indictment to imprisonment for life or for any shorter term[3]. No person may, however, be found guilty of such an offence unless it is proved that the act which caused the death of the child was not done in good faith for the purpose only of preserving the life of the mother[4].

1 For these purposes, evidence that a woman had at any material time been pregnant for a period of 28 weeks or more is prima facie proof that she was at that time pregnant of a child capable of being born alive: Infant Life (Preservation) Act 1929 s 1 (2). Once a foetus is capable, if born, of breathing and living by reason of its breathing through its own lungs alone, it is 'capable of being born alive': *Rance v Mid-Downs Health Authority* (1990) Times, 15 February. See also *C v S* [1988] QB 135, [1987] 1 All ER 1230, CA.
2 It is presumed that an act of omission would not suffice to support the charge: cf *R v Shepherd* (1862) Le & Ca 147, CCR (mother of pregnant woman under no duty to get midwife).
3 Infant Life (Preservation) Act 1929 s 1 (1); Criminal Justice Act 1948 s 1 (1); Criminal Law Act 1967 s 12 (5) (a).
4 Infant Life (Preservation) Act 1929 s 1 (1) proviso. The words 'preserving the life of the mother' have been widely construed by judges when directing juries: see *R v Bourne* [1939] 1 KB 687 at 692–694, [1938] 3 All ER 615 at 618, 619, CCA per Macnaghten J; *R v Newton and Stungo* [1958] Crim LR 469 at 469 per Ashworth J (both cases on abortion: see para 462 post). Where on the trial of any person for child destruction the jury is of opinion that the person charged is not guilty of that offence but that he is shown by the evidence to be guilty of an offence under the Offences against the Person Act 1861 s 58 (using means to procure an abortion: see para 462 post), the jury may find him guilty of that offence: Infant Life (Preservation) Act 1929 s 2 (3). Nothing in the Abortion Act 1967 affects the provisions of the Infant Life (Preservation) Act 1929: Abortion Act 1967 s 5 (1). See further para 465 post.

E.　DEFENCES TO MURDER AND MANSLAUGHTER

453. Defences in general. Apart from general defences, such as insanity, which are available on a charge of any crime[1], it is a defence to a charge of murder or manslaughter that the killing (1) was done in carrying out the sentence of a court[2];

or (2) was caused by the use of reasonable force in the prevention of crime[3]. Although it is convenient to refer to 'a defence' in this context, the onus of proving that the crime of murder or manslaughter has been committed remains on the prosecution. It is not ordinarily incumbent on the defence to establish, on balance of probability or otherwise, that a particular answer to a charge is made out[4]. The prosecution must negative any tenable answer[4].

1 See para 19 et seq ante.
2 See para 454 post.
3 See paras 455–457 post.
4 See para 1062 post.

454. Lawful execution. If a person is sentenced to death[1] by a court having authority to pass such a sentence, his execution in the proper manner and by the proper officer is justifiable; but, if the execution is by an officer upon whom that duty is not cast, or if it is carried out in a different manner from that which is authorised by the form of the sentence, it is murder[2].

1 Sentence of death may be imposed on conviction on indictment for two offences only, namely high treason and piracy with violence: see para 78 ante and para 1199 post; FOREIGN RELATIONS vol 18 para 1543.
2 3 Co Inst 52: 1 Hale PC 501. It was, as Hale points out, in former times common to modify the form of execution for high treason from that directed by the express terms of the sentence: see Fost 267 et seq.

455. Killing in the prevention of crime. A person may use such force as is reasonable in the circumstances in the prevention of crime or in effecting or assisting in the lawful arrest of offenders or persons unlawfully at large[1]; no criminal liability is incurred even though the use of such force results in the death of another.

At common law the rules relating to the use of force in such circumstances were not altogether clear and appear to have varied according to the situation in which the force was used. Under the present law the same requirement, namely that the force used should be reasonable in the circumstances, is applicable to all cases where force is used in the prevention of crime and the common law rules are to that extent superseded[2]. In determining whether the force used was reasonable the court will take into account all the circumstances of the case, including the nature and degree of force used, the seriousness of the evil to be prevented and the possibility of preventing it by other means,. This statutory provision is of general application[3] and is not limited to arrestable or any other class of offences[4], but it would not be reasonable to use even slight force to prevent very trivial offences[5]. The circumstances in which it can be considered reasonable to kill another in the prevention of crime must be of an extreme kind; they could probably arise only in the case of an attack against the person which is likely to cause death or serious bodily injury and where killing the attacker is the only practicable means of preventing the harm. It cannot be reasonable to kill another merely to prevent a crime which is directed only against property[6].

The ordinary rules relating to mistake of fact[7] are applicable so that where the force used is reasonable having regard to the facts as the accused supposed them to have been, the accused commits no offence although the force used is excessive having regard to the facts as they were. The accused is not entitled to rely on facts unknown to him in order to show that the force used by him was reasonable in the circumstances; the reasonableness of the force must be assessed in relation to facts which the accused knew or believed to have existed[8].

Where the force used is unreasonable and death results, the accused is liable to be convicted of murder or manslaughter according to his mens rea; there is no special rule to the effect that death caused by the use of excessive force in the prevention of crime can only be manslaughter[9].

1 Criminal Law Act 1967 s 3 (1): see para 706 post.
2 Ibid s 3 (2): see para 706 note 2 post.
3 As to the particular provisions relating to police officers see the Police and Criminal Evidence Act 1984 ss 24, 25, 117 and paras 705, 707, 658 respectively post.
4 For the meaning of 'arrestable offence' see para 703 post.
5 See the Criminal Law Revision Committee, Seventh Report, Felonies and Misdemeanours, May 1965 (Cmnd 2659) paras 20–23. As to the abolition of the distinction between felonies and misdemeanours see para 42 ante.
6 See *R v McKay* [1957] VR 560, [1957] ALR 648, where the accused, who had shot and killed a chicken thief, was convicted of manslaughter; the trial judge ruled that the jury should answer two questions: (1) did the accused honestly believe on reasonable grounds that it was necessary to do what he did in order to prevent the crime or the escape of the criminal; and (2) would a reasonable man in his position have considered that what he did was out of proportion to the mischief to be prevented? As to 'honest belief', however, see infra and para 21 ante; and as to defence of property see para 457 post.
7 See para 21 ante.
8 See *R v Dadson* (1850) 2 Den 35, 4 Cox CC 358, CCR.
9 *R v McInnes* [1971] 3 All ER 295, 55 Cr App Rep 551, CA; *Palmer v R* [1971] AC 814, 55 Cr App Rep 223, PC. See also *R v Shannon* (1980) 71 Cr App Rep 192, CA.

456. Self-defence. A person acting in self-defence is normally acting to prevent the commission of a crime, as is a person acting in defence of another. The test to be applied in such cases is now established[1] to be the same as for cases of prevention of crime[2], that is the force used in self-defence or in defence of another must be reasonable in the circumstances. However, a genuine belief in facts which would justify the accused using force in self-defence may be relied upon even if there are no reasonable grounds for the belief and it results in the use of force which is in fact unreasonable[3].

Provided the force used is reasonable, a person is entitled to defend not only himself or a member of his family, but even a complete stranger if the stranger is subject to unlawful attack by others[4]. Acts of self-defence are not limited to spontaneous acts done in response to actual violence, but the threatened danger must be reasonably imminent and must be of a nature which could not be met by more pacific means[5].

In deciding whether the force used was reasonable, all the circumstances may be considered. The matter is one of fact and not one of law, hence it cannot be ruled that a person who is attacked must retreat before retaliating. A person's opportunity to retreat with safety is a factor to be taken into account in deciding whether his conduct was reasonable, as is his willingness to temporise or disengage himself before resorting to force[6]. A man is not obliged to refrain from going where he may lawfully go because he has reason to believe that he may be attacked, and is not thereby deprived of his right of self-defence[7].

At the trial the judge need not leave the issue of self-defence to the jury if it is not raised by the defence and there is no evidence to support it[8].

1 *R v McInnes* [1971] 3 All ER 295, 55 Cr App Rep 551, CA.

2 See para 455 ante.
3 *R v Williams* [1987] 3 All ER 411, 78 Cr App Rep 276, CA; *Beckford v R* [1988] AC 130, 85 Cr App Rep 378, PC; *Ansell v Swift* [1987] Crim LR 194; *R v Fisher* [1987] Crim LR 334, CA; and see para 21 ante. The accused may not, however, rely upon an honest belief which results from a drunken mistake: *R v O'Grady* [1987] QB 995, 85 Cr App Rep 315, CA.
4 *R v Rose* (1884) 15 Cox CC 540; *R v Duffy* [1967] 1 QB 63, 50 Cr App Rep 68, CCA.
5 *A-G's Reference (No 2 of 1983)* [1984] QB 456, 78 Cr App Rep 183, CA (possession of petrol bombs to defend person and property from attack). See also *R v Shannon* (1980) 71 Cr App Rep 192, CA.
6 *R v Julien* [1969] 2 All ER 856, 53 Cr App Rep 407, CA; *Palmer v R* [1971] AC 814 at 827, 55 Cr App Rep 223 at 236, PC; *R v McInnes* [1971] 3 All ER 295, 55 Cr App Rep 551, CA. See also *R v Deana* (1909) 2 Cr App Rep 75, CCA (self-defence not limited to warding off blows); *R v Whyte* [1987] 3 All ER 416, 85 Cr App Rep 283, CA. An accused may rely on a plea of self-defence even though he has failed to demonstrate unwillingness to fight; but the best evidence to cast doubt on an allegation that he was the attacker, retaliator or acting in revenge is that he tried to call off the fight: *R v Bird* [1985] 2 All ER 513, 81 Cr App Rep 110, CA.
7 *R v Field* [1972] Crim LR 435, CA. As to the burden of proof, and as to the direction to the jury where self-defence is raised, see paras 1065, 1015 respectively post.
8 *DPP v Walker* [1974] 1 WLR 1090, PC (force used far greater than that needed for self-defence).

457. Defence of property. Where a person in defending his property is also acting in the prevention of crime, he may use such force as is reasonable in the circumstances[1]. Where no crime is involved, as where there is merely a trespass, the same rule of reasonable force in the circumstances is applicable. If in using reasonable force the accused should accidentally kill another, the killing would not amount to murder or manslaughter. It would not, in general, be reasonable to kill in defence of property alone[2], although it has been held that a man may lawfully kill a trespasser who would forcibly dispossess him of his house[3].

1 See para 455 ante.
2 See para 455 text and note 6 ante.
3 See *R v Hussey* (1924) 18 Cr App Rep 160, CCA; it would appear that the accused was acting in the prevention of crime (forcible entry), but it is doubtful whether such a killing would now be regarded as reasonable having regard to the fact that summary proceedings are available for the recovery of land: see RSC Ord 113; CCR 1981 Ord 24.

F.   EVIDENCE AND PROCEDURE IN HOMICIDE CASES

458. Indictment for murder or manslaughter. In an indictment[1] for murder or manslaughter or for being an accessory thereto it is not necessary to set forth the manner in which or the means by which the death was caused, or to allege malice aforethought[2]. It is sufficient in an indictment for murder to charge that the accused murdered the deceased, and in an indictment for manslaughter to charge that he unlawfully killed the deceased[2]. The name of the deceased must, if it is known or can be ascertained with reasonable diligence, be stated in the indictment; if it cannot be so ascertained, the deceased must be described as 'a person unknown'[3].

1 As to indictments generally see para 913 et seq post.
2 For useful guidance on the form of indictments see the Indictments Rules 1915, Appendix, Forms 1, 3 (both revoked) and para 921 note 3 post. At the date at which this volume states the law, no forms have, however, been prescribed pursuant to the Indictment Rules 1971, SI 1971/1253, r 5 (2). As to the joinder of counts for two murders or the joinder of a count for murder with counts for other offences see para 932 post.
3 *R v Hicks* (1840) 2 Mood & R 302; and see *R v Campbell* (1843) 1 Car & Kir 82.

459. Circumstantial evidence and absence of body in homicide cases. In murder, as in other criminal cases, a jury may convict on circumstantial evidence alone[1]. Even where no body or part of a body has been found, the death of the victim may be proved by circumstantial evidence; and the jury is entitled to convict where the evidence is consistent with no other rational conclusion than that the victim is dead and that his death was caused by the accused[2].

Where the victim has been killed by one of two or more acts of the accused, each of which is sufficient to establish manslaughter, there is no need to establish which act caused the death and the absence of a body is therefore immaterial[3].

1 *R v Robertson* (1913) 9 Cr App Rep 189, CCA. Evidence afforded by the accused himself is sufficient: *R v Davidson* (1934) 25 Cr App Rep 21, CCA. See further para 1061 post.
2 *R v Onufrejczyk* [1955] 1 QB 388, 39 Cr App Rep 1, CCA. However, where no body or part of a body has been found, it has long been considered that a jury should use caution before convicting, particularly in those cases in which death is relied upon from the fact of the disappearance of the deceased: see *Upington v Saul Solomon & Co* (1879) Buch 240 at 276, Cape SC.
3 *A-G's Reference (No 4 of 1980)* [1981] 2 All ER 617, 73 Cr App Rep 40, CA.

460. Proof of malice. On an indictment for murder, evidence of the existence of a bad feeling between the parties, or of former threats of violence by the accused against the deceased, or of other attempts made by him on the life of the deceased is admissible to prove malice[1].

Evidence showing the commission by the accused of other similar murders either before or after the death which is the subject of the indictment, although inadmissible for the purpose of showing that the accused was a person likely from his criminal conduct or character to be guilty of the offence for which he is being tried, may nevertheless be admissible to show that the act charged in the indictment was designed and not accidental, or to prove intent[2], or to identify the accused as the person who committed the murder[3].

1 *R v Clewes* (1830) 4 C & P 221; *R v Hagan* (1873) 12 Cox CC 357; *R v Weston* (1879) 14 Cox CC 346 at 350 per Cockburn CJ. As to malice aforethought as the mental element of murder see para 431 ante.
2 *Makin v A-G for New South Wales* [1894] AC 57 at 65, PC; *R v Mortimer* (1936) 25 Cr App Rep 150, CCA; *Noor Mohamed v R* [1949] AC 182, [1949] 1 All ER 365, PC. See also *R v Smith* (1915) 114 LT 239, CCA (evidence admitted of the murders, in similar circumstances, of two other women in their baths alleged to have been committed at later dates and of the surrounding circumstances of their deaths ie insurance on their lives etc). As to evidence of similar facts in general see *DPP v Boardman* [1975] AC 421 at 435, 60 Cr App Rep 165, HL and para 1091 post; and as to evidence of similar facts rebutting a defence otherwise available see further para 1094 post.
3 See para 1095 post.

461. Statements by deceased. Statements by the deceased made immediately upon the occurrence which caused the death, but not under such circumstances as would render them admissible as dying declarations[1], may be admitted in evidence as part of the res gestae[2].

1 As to dying declarations see para 1104 post.
2 Such statements are admissible if made in conditions sufficiently spontaneous and sufficiently contemporaneous with the event to preclude the possibility of concoction or distortion; the possibility of error in the facts narrated by the victim goes to the weight to be attached to the statement by the jury and not to admissibility: *R v Andrews* [1987] AC 281, 84 Cr App Rep 382, HL, applying *Ratten v R* [1972] AC 378, 56 Cr App Rep 18, PC. See also *Thompson v Trevanion* (1693) Skin 402 where Holt CJ allowed 'what the wife said immediately upon the hurt received, and before she had time to devise or contrive anything for her own advantage' to be given in evidence; and see para 1105 post.
   In *R v Foster* (1834) 6 C & P 325, upon an indictment for manslaughter by furious driving, Gurney B and Park J admitted as evidence a statement made by the deceased in the absence of the accused to a

person immediately after the accident, upon the authority of *Aveson v Lord Kinnaird* (1805) 6 East 188 at 193; in *R v Lunny* (1854) 6 Cox CC 477 (a case of murder), Monahan CJ admitted evidence of a statement made by the deceased to the first person who saw him after, though apparently not immediately after, the blows which caused death. In *Ratten v R* supra evidence was admitted of a telephone call apparently made by the victim shortly before her death; in *R v Andrews* supra the victim's statement identifying his assailants and made soon after the attack was admitted in evidence. A statement made by the deceased before the injury causing the death may be admitted to prove his condition of health at the time of the statement (*R v Johnson* (1847) 2 Car & Kir 354; *R v Gloster* (1888) 16 Cox CC 471 at 473 per Charles J, followed in *R v Thomson* [1912] 3 KB 19, 7 Cr App Rep 276, CCA), or where it is made in the course of the office or business of the deceased (*R v Buckley* (1873) 13 Cox CC 293, in which case the deceased was a police officer, and the statement admitted was a verbal report to his superior as to where he was about to go); but not where it is a statement of intention, not made by the deceased in the course of duty (*R v Wainwright* (1875) 13 Cox CC 171; and see *R v Pook* (1871) 13 Cox CC 172n), nor where it is a statement as to the person by whom, or the manner in which, certain symptoms were caused (*R v Gloster* supra); see also *R v Nicholas* (1846) 2 Car & Kir 246 at 248, and *R v Horsford* (1898) cited in 62 JP Jo 459 by Hawkins J. In *R v Edwards* (1872) 12 Cox CC 230 (murder), Quain J admitted evidence of a statement made by the deceased to her neighbour eight days before the murder as to threats which she said the accused had used towards her (a decision which is open to criticism). See also *R v Podmore* (1930) 46 TLR 365, 22 Cr App Rep 36, CCA and EVIDENCE.

(ii) Procuring Abortion

462. Unlawfully procuring abortion. Any woman, being with child, who, with intent to procure her own miscarriage, unlawfully[1] administers to herself any poison or other noxious thing, or unlawfully uses any instrument or other means whatsoever with the like intent, and any person who, with intent to procure the miscarriage of any woman, whether or not she is with child, unlawfully administers to her or causes to be taken by her any poison or other noxious thing, or unlawfully uses any instrument or other means whatsoever with the like intent is guilty of an offence and liable on conviction on indictment to imprisonment for life or for any shorter term[2].

1 Not all abortions are unlawful: see para 465 post. As to the position at common law see *R v Bourne* [1939] 1 KB 687, [1938] 3 All ER 615, CCA; see also *R v Newton and Stungo* [1958] Crim LR 469; on appeal (1958) Times, 15 October, CCA. For the purposes of the law relating to abortion ie the Offences against the Person Act 1861 ss 58, 59, and any rule of law relating to the procurement of abortion, anything done with intent to procure the miscarriage of a woman is unlawfully done unless authorised by the Abortion Act 1967 s 1: ss 5 (2), 6. As to s 1 see para 465 post.
  Where death results from a criminal abortion, this constitutes manslaughter at least: see para 444 ante. The unlawful use of an instrument as a result of which death results constitutes a single offence: *R v Newton and Stungo* (1958) Times, 15 October, CCA. As to the constituents of unlawfully procuring an abortion see para 463 post.
2 Offences against the Person Act 1861 s 58; Criminal Justice Act 1948 s 1 (1); Criminal Law Act 1967 s 12 (5) (a). The jury may acquit of this offence and convict of child destruction: Infant Life (Preservation) Act 1929 s 2 (2); see also para 452 note 4 ante.

463. Constituents of unlawfully procuring abortion. In order to constitute the statutory offence of unlawfully procuring an abortion[1], the thing supplied or administered must be proved to be noxious[2], although it need not be proved to be an abortifacient[3].

A woman who takes a substance which is in fact harmless, believing it to be a noxious thing and with intent to procure her miscarriage, does not commit the offence[4].

Where a substance procures a miscarriage, it is clearly a noxious thing[5]; even if it does not, it may still be a noxious thing[6]. Provided that an intent to procure a miscarriage is proved, it is immaterial that a miscarriage did not occur or that the acts were not likely to produce such an effect[7].

If a person procures poison for a woman with intent to procure her miscarriage, to which intent she is a party, and she takes it, although in his absence, he may be convicted of causing it to be taken by the woman, and not merely of procuring it with that intent[8].

A woman cannot be convicted of administering poison to herself with intent to procure her own miscarriage, or of procuring poison with such intent, unless she is in fact with child; but even if she is not pregnant, she may be convicted of conspiracy to procure abortion[9], or of aiding and abetting others in administering poison or some noxious thing to her with intent to procure her miscarriage[10].

To prove the intent with which the noxious thing was administered or the instrument or other means used, evidence showing that the accused had on previous occasions used similar means with the avowed intention of procuring an abortion, or that he or she had previously admitted having often done the same thing, is admissible[11]. On a charge of using an instrument to procure an abortion, evidence of the administration of drugs to other women for that purpose may be admitted in order to rebut the defence of innocent user[12].

1 See para 462 ante.
2 *R v Isaacs* (1862) Le & Ca 220, CCR; *R v Hollis* (1873) 12 Cox CC 463 at 467, CCR per Bramwell B; *R v Osborn* (1919) 84 JP 63.
3 *R v Marlow* (1964) 49 Cr App Rep 49; see also *R v Douglas* [1966] NZLR 45, Wellington CA.
4 *R v Osborn* (1919) 84 JP 63; but see *R v Brown* (1899) 63 JP 790 (woman guilty of attempt). In such circumstances a woman may be guilty of an attempt to commit the offence (see the Criminal Attempts Act 1981 s 1 (2), (4) and para 71 ante), but in practice such a charge would not be brought.
5 *R v Hollis* (1873) 12 Cox CC 463, CCR. The quantity of an otherwise noxious drug may be so small as to be innocuous (*R v Perry* (1847) 2 Cox CC 223); conversely a large dose of a drug which is harmless when taken in small quantities may be noxious (*R v Cramp* (1880) 5 QBD 307, CCR); cf *R v Hennah* (1877) 13 Cox CC 547; *R v Marcus* [1981] 2 All ER 833, 73 Cr App Rep 49, CA (both decided under the Offences against the Person Act 1861 s 24: see para 475 post).
6 *R v Marlow* (1964) 49 Cr App Rep 49; cf *R v Hollis* (1873) 12 Cox CC 463 at 467, CCR per Bramwell B.
7 *R v Spicer* (1955) 39 Cr App Rep 189 (manual interference which could not, in the circumstances, have induced a miscarriage).
8 *R v Wilson* (1856) Dears & B 127, CCR; *R v Farrow* (1857) Dears & B 164, CCR.
9 *R v Whitchurch* (1890) 24 QBD 420, CCR.
10 *R v Sockett* (1908) 72 JP 428, 1 Cr App Rep 101, CCA.
11 *R v Bond* [1906] 2 KB 389 at 405, 417, CCR. Such evidence should be admitted with great caution: it should be admitted only where the accused has suggested that the administration of the drug or the use of the instrument was legitimate or accidental on his part, and not where the defence is a denial of the act itself; and proof of only one other similar case, without any special connection with the case charged in the indictment, the object of such evidence being to prove a systematic course of conduct by the accused and so to negative the defence that his action on the particular occasion was legitimate or accidental, ought not to be admitted: *R v Bond* supra at 405, 417. Where a witness who is permitted to give such evidence is in the position of being an accomplice to the illegal acts the jury should be warned as to acting on the evidence in the absence of corroboration: *R v Mohamed Farid* (1945) 30 Cr App Rep 168, CCA. Even where he is not an accomplice and corroboration is not strictly necessary, the jury should be advised to approach the evidence with care: *R v Sanders* (1961) 46 Cr App Rep 60, C-MAC. See further para 1143 post. See also para 1094 post.
12 *R v Starkie* [1922] 2 KB 275, 16 Cr App Rep 61, CCA.

464. Procuring noxious thing. Any person who unlawfully supplies or procures[1] any poison or other noxious thing, or any instrument or thing whatsoever, knowing that it is intended to be unlawfully used or employed with intent to procure the miscarriage of any woman, whether or not she is with child, is guilty of an offence and liable on conviction on indictment to imprisonment for a term not exceeding five years[2].

A person who supplies something which he believes to be noxious for the purpose of procuring a miscarriage cannot be convicted of this offence unless it is shown as a fact that the substance in question is noxious for that purpose[3]. If he knows the article supplied to be harmless, he cannot be convicted of inciting the woman to commit an offence[4], although he knows that she will take it in the belief that it is noxious and with intent to procure abortion[5].

The fact that medicine supplied by the accused is followed by illness and a miscarriage is evidence that the thing supplied is noxious[6].

The offence of supplying a noxious drug is complete even if the intention to use it for the purpose of procuring abortion exists only in the mind of the person supplying it[7].

1 For the purposes of the Offences against the Persons Act 1861 s 59 'procure' means to get possession from another person of something which the accused has not got. If the accused already has it in his possession, eg in a cupboard, he does not procure it if he takes it out in order to sterilise it or for some other purpose: see *R v Mills* [1963] 1 QB 522, 47 Cr App Rep 49, CCA.

2 Offences against the Person Act 1861 s 59; Penal Servitude Act 1891 s 1 (1); Criminal Justice Act 1948 s 1 (1); Criminal Law Act 1967 s 1.

3 *R v Isaacs* (1862) Le & Ca 220, CCR. Presumably he may now be convicted of an attempt: see the Criminal Attempts Act 1981 s 1 (2), (4) and para 71 ante.

4 Ie the Offences against the Person Act 1861 s 58: see para 463 ante.

5 *R v Brown* (1899) 63 JP 790.

6 *R v Hollis* (1873) 12 Cox CC 463 at 467, CCR per Bramwell B.

7 *R v Hillman* (1863) Le & Ca 343, CCR.

465. Medical termination of pregnancy. A person is not guilty of an offence under the law relating to abortion[1] where a pregnancy is terminated by a registered medical practitioner[2] if two medical practitioners are of the opinion, formed in good faith[3] (1) that the continuance of the pregnancy would involve risk to the life of the pregnant woman or of injury to the physical or mental health of the pregnant woman or any existing children of her family, greater than if the pregnancy were terminated[4]; or (2) that there is a substantial risk that, if the child were born, it would suffer from such physical or mental abnormalities as to be seriously handicapped[5].

A man has no right to prevent his wife or girlfriend from having a legal abortion[6] and the foetus, while unborn, cannot be a party to legal proceedings instituted for that purpose[7].

1 'The law relating to abortion' means the Offences against the Person Act 1861 ss 58, 59 (see paras 462–464 ante) and any rule of law relating to the procurement of abortion: Abortion Act 1967 s 6. For the purposes of the law relating to abortion, anything done with intent to procure the miscarriage of a woman is unlawfully done unless authorised by s 1: s 5 (2). Nothing in the Abortion Act 1967 affects the provisions of the Infant Life (Preservation) Act 1929: Abortion Act 1967 s 5 (1). See para 452 ante.

As to the legality of participation in termination by nurses see *Royal College of Nursing of the United Kingdom v Department of Health and Social Security* [1981] AC 800, [1981] 1 All ER 545, HL. As to the meaning of 'participation' see also *Janaway v Salford Area Health Authority* [1988] 3 All ER 1079, [1988] 3 WLR 1350, HL.

2 For the meaning of 'registered medical practitioner' see the Medical Act 1983 s 56 (1), Sch 6 para 11, in conjunction with s 55 (1). As to what constitutes termination by a registered medical practitioner

see *Royal College of Nursing of the United Kingdom v Department of Health and Social Security* [1981] AC 800, [1981] 1 All ER 545, HL.

The Secretary of State must by statutory instrument make regulations to provide: (1) for requiring any such opinion as is referred to in the Abortion Act 1967 s 1 to be certified by the practitioners or practitioner concerned in such form and at such time as may be prescribed by the regulations, and for requiring the preservation and disposal of certificates made for the purposes of the regulations; (2) for requiring any registered medical practitioner who terminates a pregnancy to give notice of the termination and such other information relating to the termination as may be prescribed; (3) for prohibiting the disclosure, except to such persons or for such purposes as may be prescribed, of notices given or information furnished pursuant to the regulations: s 2 (1). Any person who wilfully contravenes or wilfully fails to comply with the requirements of such regulations is liable on summary conviction to a fine not exceeding level 5 on the standard scale: s 2 (3) (amended by the Criminal Justice Act 1982 ss 38, 46). For the meaning of 'the standard scale' see para 808 post. The regulations so made are the Abortion Regulations 1968, SI 1968/390 (amended by SI 1969/636; SI 1976/15; SI 1980/1724). See further MEDICINE.

3 The question of good faith is to be decided by the jury, which may take medical evidence but should not determine the question on the medical evidence alone: see *R v Smith (John)* [1974] 1 All ER 376, 58 Cr App Rep 106, CA.

4 In determining whether the continuance of a pregnancy would involve such risk of injury to health as is mentioned in head (1) supra, account may be taken of the pregnant woman's actual or reasonably foreseeable environment: Abortion Act 1967 s 1 (2).

5 Ibid s 1 (1). Except as provided by s 1 (4) (see infra), any treatment for the termination of pregnancy must be carried out in a hospital vested in the Secretary of State for the purpose of his functions under the National Health Service Act 1977 or in a place approved for those purposes by him: Abortion Act 1967 s 1 (3). Section 1 (3), and so much of s 1 (1) as relates to the opinion of two registered medical practitioners, do not apply to the termination of a pregnancy by a registered medical practitioner in a case where he is of the opinion, formed in good faith, that the termination is immediately necessary to save the life or to prevent permanent injury to the physical or mental health of the pregnant woman: s 1 (4).

As to the application of the Abortion Act 1967 to visiting forces etc see s 3 and MEDICINE.

6 *Paton v British Pregnancy Advisory Service Trustees* [1979] QB 276, [1978] 2 All ER 987, DC (husband refused injunction to prevent legal termination); *C v S* [1988] QB 135, [1987] 1 All ER 1230, CA (injunction refused to putative father).

7 *C v S* [1988] QB 135, [1987] 1 All ER 1230, CA.

(iii) Concealment of Birth

466. Concealment of birth. If any woman has been delivered of a child, any person who, by any secret disposition of the dead body of the child, whether such child died before, at, or after its birth, endeavours to conceal its birth, is guilty of an offence and liable on conviction on indictment to imprisonment for a term not exceeding two years, or on summary conviction to imprisonment for a term not exceeding six months or a fine not exceeding the prescribed sum, or to both[1].

1 Offences against the Person Act 1861 s 60; Criminal Justice Act 1948 s 1 (2); Criminal Law Act 1967 ss 1, 10, Sch 2 para 13 (1), Sch 3 Pt III; Magistrates' Courts Act 1980 ss 17, 32 (1), Sch 1 para 5 (j). See para 804 post. For the meaning of 'the prescribed sum' see para 807 post. As to the constituents of concealing a birth see para 467 post; as to registration of births and deaths and offences in that connection see REGISTRATION; and as to unlawful disposal of a corpse see para 316 ante.

467. Constituents of concealing birth. In order to constitute concealment of birth a woman must have been delivered of something which may properly be called a child, and not the unformed subject of a premature miscarriage[1]. The child must be so far developed that in the ordinary course of events it would have had a fair chance of life when born[2].

There must be a concealment of the fact of birth, carried out by a secret disposition of the body[3], and this implies some act of concealment[4]. Proof that a woman still had the body of her child in her possession, although about to dispose of it[5], or that she allowed others to take away the body, unless it was at her request or with her knowledge and consent[6], or that she merely denied that she had given birth to a child[7], is not sufficient to support a conviction for concealment.

There is a concealment when the child is placed where it is not likely to be found; and the most complete exposure of the body in a secluded place where it would not be likely to be found may be a concealment[8]. Leaving it in a street, although it may amount to a public nuisance, is not a concealment of birth[9].

The secret disposition need not be in a place where it is intended finally to leave the body; a temporary place of concealment is sufficient[10].

The dead body must be found and identified as that of the child the attempted concealment of whose birth is alleged[11].

A person does not commit the offence of endeavouring to conceal the birth of a child, if such person puts it while it is still alive in a place of concealment, even though it may subsequently die[12]; but, if such person later on visits the place, and, finding the child dead, replaces the clothes or other things with which it was concealed, she commits this offence[13].

The offence does not consist in the concealment of the birth of a child from any particular individual, but in such a concealment as would keep the world at large in ignorance of the birth[14].

1 *R v Hewitt and Smith* (1866) 4 F & F 1101.
2 It has been said that, although no specific limit can be assigned to the period when the chance of life begins, it may perhaps be safely assumed that, in the case of a child which has been less than seven months in the womb, the great probability is that it would not be born alive: *R v Berriman* (1854) 6 Cox CC 388; but see *R v Colmer* (1864) 9 Cox CC 506 (where Martin B held that a foetus not bigger than a man's finger, but having the shape of a child, might be a child within the meaning of the statute; in this case the woman had been confined in the fourth or fifth month after pregnancy, and Martin B expressed the opinion at 507 that, as soon as a foetus which had the outward appearance of a child was born, the offence of concealment of birth could be committed); and see Stephen's Digest of the Criminal Law (9th Edn) 227. See also para 452 note 1 ante. It is submitted that the question of whether that which was concealed was 'the dead body of a child' is in each case a question of fact for the jury. See also *R v Kersey* (1908) 1 Cr App Rep 260, CCA (mother confessing to killing her newly-born child and disposing of body; murder charge insupportable in absence of evidence that child had existence separate from its mother and had breathed; conviction for concealment of birth despite absence of body).
3 *R v Rosenberg* (1906) 70 JP 264 (where the child's body was on the bed on which accused lay, it being covered with a petticoat, an acquittal was directed). Cf *R v Perry* (1855) Dears CC 471, CCR (where the accused put the body under a bolster on which she put her head, the conviction was upheld). See also *R v —— (1906) 70 JP Jo 545; *R v Veaty* (1910) 74 JP Jo 352.
4 *R v Derham* (1843) 1 Cox CC 56 (where it was held that the fact that the accused had left the body in a privy where she said she had been confined was not evidence of concealment).
5 *R v Snell* (1837) 2 Mood & R 44.
6 *R v Bate* (1871) 11 Cox CC 686; *R v Douglas* (1836) 1 Mood CC 480; *R v Bird* (1849) 2 Car & Kir 817; *R v Skelton* (1850) 3 Car & Kir 119.
7 *R v Turner* (1839) 8 C & P 755.
8 *R v Brown* (1870) LR 1 CCR 244; see also *R v Sleep* (1864) 9 Cox CC 559; *R v Cook* (1870) 11 Cox CC 542; *R v Rosenberg* (1906) 70 JP 264; *R v George* (1868) 11 Cox CC 41; *R v Waterage* (1846) 1 Cox CC 338.
9 *R v Clark* (1883) 15 Cox CC 171.
10 *R v Perry* (1855) Dears CC 471.
11 *R v Williams* (1871) 11 Cox CC 684. Cf *R v Kersey* (1908) 1 Cr App Rep 260, CCA.
12 *R v May* (1867) 10 Cox CC 448, CCR; but, according to the circumstances, the woman would be guilty of murder or manslaughter or infanticide, or of cruelty to the child.

13 *R v Hughes* (1850) 4 Cox CC 447.
14 *R v Morris* (1848) 2 Cox CC 489; *R v Higley* (1830) 4 C & P 366.

468. Questions for judge and jury on concealing birth. It is a question of law for the judge whether there is evidence that the place where the body was put was such that the body might have been disposed of there so as to conceal it. It is for the jury to say whether the body had in fact been so disposed of by the accused, and with intent to conceal the birth[1].

1 *R v Clarke* (1866) 4 F & F 1040.

(iv) Wounding with Intent

469. Wounding with intent. Any person who unlawfully and maliciously by any means whatsoever wounds or causes any grievous bodily harm to any person with intent to do some grievous bodily harm to any person, or with intent to resist or prevent the lawful apprehension or detainer of any person, is guilty of an offence and liable on conviction on indictment to imprisonment for life or for any shorter term[1].

1 Offences against the Person Act 1861 s 18; Criminal Justice Act 1948 s 1 (1); Criminal Law Act 1967 ss 10 (2), 12 (5) (a), Sch 3 Pt III. This offence may be constituted by an act done in connection with the offence of hijacking committed or attempted on board an aircraft: see AVIATION vol 2 para 1363. The offence may also constitute an 'act of violence' to which the Aviation Security Act 1982 applies: see AVIATION vol 2 para 1035. As to the constituents of wounding with intent see para 470 post. As to procedural provisions applying where an offence involving bodily injury to a child or young person is charged see para 882 post; as to the finding of causing grievous bodily harm with intent to do so on a charge of murder see para 1030 post; and as to the general power to convict of an offence other than that charged see para 1029 post, particularly at note 12. See also *R v Monger* [1973] Crim LR 301.

    Where several accused inflict injuries on a victim, in which a serious injury such as a broken nose is sustained, it is the totality of the injuries which is to be considered in relation to a charge of causing grievous bodily harm with intent contrary to the Offences against the Person Act 1861 s 18; it is immaterial that one accused joins in the attack slightly after the others have begun to inflict injuries, which may have included the broken nose; he is aiding the commission of the offence and participating as soon as he joins in: *R v Grundy, R v Gerrard, R v Patterson* (1989) 89 Cr App Rep 333, CA.

    A defence of drunkenness must be very extreme before it induces the prosecution to accept a plea of guilty to the lesser offence of unlawful wounding (see para 471 post): *R v Stubbs* (1988) 88 Cr App Rep 53, CA. As to voluntary intoxication see para 28 ante.

470. Constituents of wounding etc with intent. In order to constitute a wounding there must be an injury to the person by which the skin is broken[1]; the continuity of the whole skin must be severed, not merely that of the cuticle or upper skin[2]. The skin severed need not, however, be external[3], but it is not sufficient to prove merely that a flow of blood was caused[4], unless there is evidence to show where the blood came from[5]. It is not necessary that any instrument should have been used, as an injury caused for instance by a kick may be a wounding[6].

'Grievous bodily harm' simply means bodily harm of a serious character[7].

The word 'maliciously' imports intention or recklessness in the sense of deliberate risk-taking[8]. Malice against the individual actually injured is not essential; general malice, namely an intention to do an unlawful act, is sufficient[9].

On an indictment for wounding with intent the actual intent must be proved[10].

In considering what will amount to evidence of an intent to do grievous bodily harm, regard must be had to the weapon, if any, used, and the conditions under which it was used. The mere striking of the blow with a fist, even though grievous bodily harm is done, is not of itself sufficient evidence to show an intent to do grievous bodily harm[11].

Where the distance at which a gun is fired is so great that serious injury does not and was not likely to result, the shooting, although the gun is aimed at the complainant, may not of itself be evidence of a shooting with intent to do grievous bodily harm[12].

The intent need not be an intent to do grievous bodily harm to the person actually injured, the offence being complete if there is an intent to do grievous bodily harm to any person[13].

Where the intent is to resist or prevent lawful apprehension, it is negatived if the attempted apprehension is believed to be unlawful and is either unlawful in fact[14] or would be unlawful if the facts had been as the accused honestly but mistakenly believed them to be[15].

1 *R v Wood and McMahon* (1830) 1 Mood CC 278; *Moriarty v Brooks* (1834) 6 C & P 684; *R v Beckett* (1836) 1 Mood & R 526.
2 *R v M'Loughlin* (1838) 8 C & P 635; *C (a minor) v Eisenhower* [1984] QB 331, 78 Cr App Rep 48 (decided under the Offences against the Person Act 1861 s 20: see para 471 post).
3 *R v Smith* (1837) 8 C & P 173 ('skin' within mouth).
4 *R v Jones* (1849) 3 Cox CC 441.
5 *R v Waltham* (1849) 3 Cox CC 442.
6 *R v Duffill* (1843) 1 Cox CC 49.
7 *DPP v Smith* [1961] AC 290 at 334, 44 Cr App Rep 261 at 291, HL per Viscount Kilmuir LC. It is undesirable to attempt any further definition: see *DPP v Smith* supra at 334 and at 291. See also *R v Metharam* [1961] 3 All ER 200, 45 Cr App Rep 304, CCA; *R v Cunningham* [1982] AC 566, 73 Cr App Rep 253, HL; *R v Saunders* [1985] Crim LR 230, CA.
8 See *R v Cunningham* [1957] 2 QB 396, 41 Cr App Rep 155, CCA, applied in *R v Morrison* (1988) 89 Cr App Rep 17, CA; and para 10 note 5 ante. See also para 471 note 1 post.
9 *R v Hunt* (1825) 1 Mood CC 93, CCR.
10 *R v Cox* (1859) 1 F & F 664; *Yardy v Greenwood* (1935) 79 Sol Jo 363, CA: and see further para 1061 post. Foresight of or recklessness as to the consequences of wounding is not sufficient to constitute intent: *R v Belfon* [1976] 3 All ER 46, 63 Cr App Rep 59, CA: but it is a factor to be taken into account in determining whether intent to do grievous bodily harm can properly be inferred: see *R v Bryson* [1985] Crim LR 669: *R v Hancock, R v Shankland* [1986] AC 455, 82 Cr App Rep 264, HL; *R v Donnelly* [1989] Crim LR 739, CA.
11 *R v Wheeler* (1844) 1 Cox CC 106.
12 *R v Abraham* (1845) 1 Cox CC 208 (where the accused was only 40 or 50 yards distant, and fired at the complainant intentionally, and the jury was directed to acquit of this offence and convict of a common assault only, a direction which upon the facts seems difficult to understand); and see *R v Ward* (1872) LR 1 CCR 356 (decided under the Offences against the Person Act 1861 s 20: see para 471 post).
13 Ibid s 18; cf *R v Stopford* (1870) 11 Cox CC 643; *R v Lynch* (1846) 1 Cox CC 361 (where the accused mistook the complainant for another person); and *R v Fretwell* (1864) Le & Ca 443, CCR (where the accused fired at a group of persons intending generally to do grievous bodily harm).
14 *R v Walker* (1854) Dears CC 358, CCR; *R v Sanders* (1867) LR 1 CCR 75.
15 See *R v Williams* [1987] 3 All ER 411, 78 Cr App Rep 276, CA and para 21 ante.

(v) Unlawful Wounding etc

471. Unlawful wounding. Any person who unlawfully and maliciously[1] wounds[2] or inflicts[3] any grievous bodily harm[4] upon any other person, either with or without any weapon or instrument[5], is guilty of an offence and liable on conviction on indictment to imprisonment for a term not exceeding five years, or on summary conviction to imprisonment for a term not exceeding six months or a fine not exceeding the prescribed sum, or to both[6].

Although no specific intention need be alleged or proved, the prosecution must nonetheless prove that the act was committed unlawfully and maliciously[7].

Provocation is no defence to a charge of unlawful wounding[8].

1 For the meaning of 'maliciously' see generally para 470 text to note 8 ante. As to the direction to be given on the meaning of 'maliciously' in the context of the Offences against the Person Act 1861 s 20 (see infra) see *R v Mowatt* [1968] 1 QB 421, 51 Cr App Rep 402, CA, which should now be read in the light of the Criminal Justice Act 1967 s 8 (see para 1061 post). See also *Wilkins v An Infant* [1965] Crim LR 730, DC; *Flack v Hunt* (1979) 123 Sol Jo 751 (accused guilty of malicious wounding if reckless, but must be able to foresee risk of causing personal injury in order to be reckless); *W (a minor) v Dolbey* (1983) 88 Cr App Rep 1, DC; *R v Grimshaw* [1984] Crim LR 108, CA; *R v Rainbird* [1989] Crim LR 505, CA.
2 For the meaning of 'wound' see para 470 ante.
3 'Inflicts' does not necessarily imply an assault but may do so: see *R v Wilson, R v Jenkins* [1983] 3 All ER 448 at 455, 77 Cr App Rep 319 at 327, HL.
4 For the meaning of 'grievous bodily harm' see para 470 text and note 7 ante.
5 As to whether the offence may be committed by releasing a dog which bites the victim see *R v Dume* (1986) Times, 16 October.
6 Offences against the Person Act 1861 s 20; Penal Servitude Act 1891 s 1 (1); Criminal Justice Act 1948 s 1 (1); Criminal Law Act 1967 s 1; Magistrates' Courts Act 1980 ss 17, 32 (1), Sch 1 para 5 (b). See para 804 post. For the meaning of 'the prescribed sum' see para 807 post. As to sentencing where the victim is a young child see *R v Durkin* (1989) Times, 20 June, CA; and as to procedural provisions applying where an offence involving bodily injury to a child or young person is charged see para 882 post. As to the offence committed by a person who at the time of committing or being arrested for an offence under the Offences against the Person Act 1861 s 20 has in his possession a firearm or imitation firearm see para 232 ante; and as to the general power to convict of an offence other than that charged see para 1029 post, particularly at note 12.
   The offence may be constituted by an act done in connection with the offence of hijacking committed or attempted on board an aircraft: see AVIATION vol 2 para 1363. The offence may also constitute an 'act of violence' to which the Aviation Security Act 1982 applies: see AVIATION vol 2 para 1035.
7 See eg *R v Kemp* [1957] 1 QB 399, 40 Cr App Rep 121; *R v Bailey* [1983] 2 All ER 503, 77 Cr App Rep 76, CA. As to 'unlawfully' in the Offences against the Person Act 1861 s 20 see *R v Clarence* (1888) 22 QBD 23 at 40, 41, CCR per Stephen J.
8 *R v Cunningham* [1959] 1 QB 288, 43 App Rep 79, CCA; and see para 438 ante.

472. Causation. Where a person unlawfully and maliciously does an act calculated to cause a panic in a public assembly, for example places a bar across the door in such a way as to cause a crush in which persons are injured, he may be convicted of the offence of inflicting grievous bodily harm[1].

Where one person produces in the mind of another such a sense of immediate danger as causes the other to endeavour to escape, the person responsible for the creation of that state of mind is also responsible for any injuries which may result to the person who endeavours to escape[2].

It is immaterial whether the person actually struck is the person whom the accused intended to strike[3].

1 *R v Martin* (1881) 8 QBD 54, CCR; followed in *R v Chapin* (1909) 74 JP 71 (where a woman, in attempting to damage ballot papers, caused injury to the presiding officer at a polling station). For the meaning of 'grievous bodily harm' see para 470 text and note 7 ante.
2 See para 430 ante.
3 *R v Latimer* (1886) 17 QBD 359, CCR; *R v Monger* [1973] Crim LR 301. Cf para 470 text and note 13 ante.

473. Attempt to choke etc. Any person who by any means whatsoever attempts to choke, suffocate or strangle any other person or by any means calculated to produce that effect attempts to render any other person insensible, unconscious or incapable of resistance, with intent to enable himself or any other person to commit, or with intent to assist any person in committing, any indictable offence is guilty of an offence and liable on conviction on indictment to imprisonment for life or for any shorter term[1].

> 1 Offences against the Person Act 1861 s 21; Criminal Justice Act 1948 s 1 (1); Criminal Law Act 1967 s 12 (5) (a). This offence may be constituted by an act done in connection with the offence of hijacking committed or attempted on board an aircraft: see AVIATION vol 2 para 1363. The offence may also constitute an 'act of violence' to which the Aviation Security Act 1982 applies: see AVIATION vol 2 para 1035.
>
> As to the offence committed by a person who at the time of committing or being arrested for an offence under the Offences aaginst the Person Act 1861 s 21 has in his possession a firearm or imitation firearm see para 232 ante; and as to procedural provisions applying where an offence involving bodily injury to a child or young person is charged see para 882 post.

(vi) Administering Drugs or Poison

474. Administering drugs. Any person who unlawfully applies or administers[1] to or causes to be taken by, or attempts to cause to be administered to or taken by, any person any chloroform, laudanum or other stupefying or overpowering drug, matter or thing, with intent to enable himself or any other person to commit, or with intent to assist any other person in committing, any indictable offence, is guilty of an offence and liable on conviction on indictment to imprisonment for life or for any shorter term[2].

> 1 'Administer' does not necessarily involve the application of direct physical force and covers eg the spraying of tear gas from a distance: see *R v Gillard* (1988) 87 Cr App Rep 189, CA. However, cf *R v Dones* [1987] Crim LR 682 (squirting an ammonia solution at a person is not 'administering' a noxious thing; 'administer' should be construed in a 'quasi-medical' sense). Both cases were decided under the Offences against the Person Act 1861 s 24: see para 475 post.
> 2 Ibid s 22; Criminal Justice Act 1948 s 1 (1); Criminal Law Act 1967 s 12 (5) (a).
>
> As to the offence committed by a person who at the time of committing or being arrested for an offence under the Offences against the Person Act 1861 s 22 has in his possession a firearm or imitation firearm see para 232 ante; as to the administration of drugs etc to a woman for the purpose of facilitating intercourse see para 525 post; as to the administration of poisons etc with intent to annoy see para 475 post; and as to offences in relation to controlled drugs see para 397 et seq ante.
>
> An offence under s 22 may be constituted by an act done in connection with the offence of hijacking committed or attempted on board an aircraft: see AVIATION vol 2 para 1363. The offence may also constitute an 'act of violence' to which the Aviation Security Act 1982 applies: see AVIATION vol 2 para 1035.

475. Administering poison etc. Any person who unlawfully and maliciously[1] administers[2] to or causes to be administered to or taken by any other person any poison or other destructive or noxious thing so as thereby either to endanger the life of such person, or so as to inflict upon him any grievous bodily harm, is guilty of an offence and liable on conviction on indictment to imprisonment for a term not exceeding ten years[3].

Any person who unlawfully and maliciously administers to or causes to be administered to or taken by any other person any poison or other destructive or noxious thing, with intent to injure, aggrieve, or annoy such person, is guilty of an offence and liable on conviction on indictment to imprisonment for a term not exceeding five years[4].

If, in fact, grievous bodily harm is caused by the noxious thing, the accused commits the first-mentioned offence, although the intent was merely to injure or annoy[5].

The drug or thing administered must be noxious or the accused cannot be convicted, although there may have been an intent to injure or annoy[6]; but it is sufficient that the actual amount administered is enough to cause injury, even though when taken in smaller quantities the particular thing given would be harmless[7]. If the thing administered is a recognised poison, the quantity used may be immaterial[8]. The administering does not necessarily consist in the actual giving of the poison to the victim by the accused. It is sufficient if poison is placed by the accused where it will be taken[9], or if it is handed to a third person in order that it may be given to another, although it may ultimately reach and be taken by someone for whom it was not intended[10].

The administration of a drug to a woman with the intention of exciting her sexual passion is an administration of a noxious thing with intent to injure or annoy[11].

1 'Maliciously', where harm is done indirectly, postulates foresight of consequences and requires either an intention to do the particular kind of harm that was done or recklessness whether such harm occurs or not: *R v Cunningham* [1957] 2 QB 396, 41 Cr App Rep 155, CCA (causing escape of coal gas); distinguished in *R v Cato* [1976] 1 All ER 260, 62 Cr App Rep 41, CA (deliberately injecting heroin into victim 'malicious' without proof of intention or recklessness as to harm caused thereby). See also paras 10 note 5, 470 text to note 8 ante.

2 For the meaning of 'administer' see para 474 note 1 ante and text to notes 9, 10 infra.

3 Offences against the Person Act 1861 s 23; Criminal Justice Act 1948 s 1 (1); Criminal Law Act 1967 s 12 (5) (a). For the meaning of 'grievous bodily harm' see para 470 text and note 7 ante.

   As to the finding of a verdict of maliciously administering poison with intent to injure, aggrieve or annoy on a charge of maliciously administering poison so as to endanger life see para 1033 post; and as to procedural provisions applying where an offence involving bodily injury to a child or young person is charged see para 882 post.

   This offence may be constituted by an act done in connection with the offence of hijacking committed or attempted on board an aircraft: see AVIATION vol 2 para 1363. The offence may also constitute an 'act of violence' to which the Aviation Security Act 1982 applies: see AVIATION vol 2 para 1035.

4 Offences against the Person Act 1861 s 24; Criminal Justice Act 1948 s 1 (1); Criminal Law Act 1967 s 1. Where an accused is charged under the Offences against the Person Act 1861 s 24, the jury should convict only if sure that the accused intended to injure in the sense of causing physical harm: *R v Hill* (1986) 83 Cr App Rep 386, HL. The purpose for which a substance is administered may be relevant in determining whether or not it causes harm: *R v Hill* supra at 390 per Lord Griffiths.

   An offence under the Offences against the Person Act 1861 s 24 may also constitute an 'act of violence' to which the Aviation Security Act 1982 applies: see AVIATION vol 2 para 1035.

5 *Tulley v Corrie* (1867) 10 Cox CC 584, 640.

6 *R v Hennah* (1877) 13 Cox CC 547.

7 *R v Cramp* (1880) 5 QBD 307, CCR (decided under the Offences against the Person Act 1861 s 58: see para 463 ante). See also *R v Cato* [1976] 1 All ER 260, 62 Cr App Rep 41, CA; *R v Marcus* [1981] 2 All ER 833, 73 Cr App Rep 49, CA (sedatives added to bottle of milk; whether noxious a question of fact and degree). Cf *R v Weatherall* [1968] Crim LR 115 (small quantity of sedative not noxious).

8 *R v Cramp* (1880) 5 QBD 307 at 309, 316, CCR per Field J.

9 *R v Harley* (1830) 4 C & P 369.

10 *R v Michael* (1840) 9 C & P 356, CCR; *R v Lewis* (1833) 6 C & P 161.

11 *R v Wilkins* (1861) Le & Ca 89, CCR. As to the administration of stupefying drugs see para 474 ante and para 525 post.

(vii) Injury by Explosion, Corrosives, Mantraps etc

476. Causing bodily injury by explosion. Any person who unlawfully and maliciously[1] by the explosion of gunpowder or other explosive substance burns, maims, disfigures, disables or does any grievous bodily harm[2] to any person is guilty of an offence and liable on conviction on indictment to imprisonment for life or for any shorter term[3].

1 For the meaning of 'maliciously' see para 470 text to note 8 ante.
2 For the meaning of 'grievous bodily harm' see para 470 text and note 7 ante.
3 Offences against the Person Act 1861 s 28; Criminal Justice Act 1948 ss 1 (1), 83 (3), Sch 10 Pt I; Criminal Law Act 1967 s 12 (5) (a). As to procedural provisions applying where an offence involving bodily injury to a child or young person is charged see para 882 post.
    This offence may be constituted by an act done in connection with the offence of hijacking committed or attempted on board an aircraft: see AVIATION vol 2 para 1363. The offence may also constitute an 'act of violence' to which the Aviation Security Act 1982 applies: see AVIATION vol 2 para 1035.

477. Causing explosion. Any person who unlawfully and maliciously[1] (1) causes any gunpowder or other explosive substance to explode; or (2) sends or delivers to or causes to be taken or received by any person any explosive substance or any other dangerous or noxious thing; or (3) puts or lays at any place, or casts or throws at or upon or otherwise applies to any person, any corrosive fluid, or any destructive or explosive substance, with intent, in any such case, to burn, maim, disfigure, or disable[2] any person, or to do grievous bodily harm[3] to any person, whether any bodily injury is effected or not, is guilty of an offence and liable on conviction on indictment to imprisonment for life or for any shorter term[4].

1 For the meaning of 'maliciously' see para 470 text to note 8 ante.
2 Where an intent to disable is alleged, the prosecution need not prove that the accused intended to disable permanently: *R v James* (1979) 70 Cr App Rep 215, CA.
3 For the meaning of 'grievous bodily harm' see para 470 text and note 7 ante.
4 Offences against the Person Act 1861 s 29; Criminal Justice Act 1948 ss 1 (1), 83 (3), Sch 10 Pt I; Criminal Law Act 1967 s 12 (5) (a). Boiling water may be a destructive substance for this purpose: *R v Crawford* (1845) 2 Car & Kir 129, CCR.
    An offence under the Offences against the Person Act 1861 s 29 may be constituted by an act done in connection with the offence of hijacking committed or attempted on board an aircraft: see AVIATION vol 2 para 1363. The offence may also constitute an 'act of violence' to which the Aviation Security Act 1982 applies: see AVIATION vol 2 para 1035.

478. Causing explosion likely to endanger life or property. A person who in the United Kingdom[1] or, being a citizen of the United Kingdom and Colonies[2], in the Republic of Ireland unlawfully and maliciously[3] causes by any explosive substance[4] an explosion of a nature likely to endanger life or to cause serious injury to property is guilty of an offence, whether any such injury has been actually caused or not, and is liable on conviction on indictment to imprisonment for life or for any shorter term[5].

1 For the meaning of 'the United Kingdom' see para 86 note 1 ante.
2 For the meaning of 'citizen of the United Kingdom and Colonies' see the British Nationality Act 1981 s 51 (3) (a) and BRITISH NATIONALITY AND ALIENAGE.
3 For the meaning of 'maliciously' see para 470 text to note 8 ante.
4 'Explosive substance' includes any materials for making any such substance and also any apparatus, machine, implement or materials, or any part thereof, used or intended to be used, or adapted for

causing, or aiding in causing, any explosion in or with any explosive substance: Explosive Substances Act 1883 s 9 (1). A petrol bomb is an 'explosive substance': *R v Bouch* [1983] QB 246, 76 Cr App Rep 11, CA. See also *R v Wheatley* [1979] 1 All ER 954, 68 Cr App Rep 287, CA; *R v Elliott* (1984) 81 Cr App Rep 115, CA.

5 Explosive Substances Act 1883 s 2 (substituted by the Criminal Jurisdiction Act 1975 s 7 (1), (3)). An offence under the Explosive Substances Act 1883 s 2 (as so substituted) may constitute an 'act of violence' to which the Aviation Security Act 1982 applies: see AVIATION vol 2 para 1035. No proceedings may be instituted except by or with the consent of the Attorney General: Explosive Substances Act 1883 s 7 (1) (substituted by the Administration of Justice Act 1982 s 63 (1)). As to the effect of this limitation see para 639 post. As to inquiries under the Explosive Substances Act 1883 see EXPLOSIVES vol 18 para 129.

479. Attempting to cause explosion. A person who in the United Kingdom[1] or a dependency[2] or, being a citizen of the United Kingdom and Colonies[3], elsewhere unlawfully and maliciously[4] (1) does any act with intent to cause, or conspires to cause, by an explosive substance[5] an explosion of a nature likely to endanger life or cause serious injury to property, whether in the United Kingdom or the Republic or Ireland; or (2) makes or has in his possession[6] or under his control an explosive substance with intent by means thereof to endanger life or cause serious injury to property, whether in the United Kingdom or the Republic of Ireland, or to enable any other person to do so, is guilty of an offence, whether or not any explosion takes place or any injury to person or property is actually caused, and is liable on conviction on indictment to imprisonment for life or for any shorter term, and forfeiture of the explosive substance[7].

1 For the meaning of 'United Kingdom' see para 86 note 1 ante.
2 'Dependency' means the Channel Islands, the Isle of Man and any colony, other than a colony for whose external relations a country other than the United Kingdom is responsible: Explosive Substances Act 1883 s 3 (2) (substituted by the Criminal Jurisdiction Act 1975 s 7 (1), (3)).
3 For the meaning of 'citizen of the United Kingdom and Colonies' see para 478 note 2 ante.
4 For the meaning of 'maliciously' see para 470 text to note 8 ante.
5 For the meaning of 'explosive substance' see para 478 note 4 ante.
6 In order to convict the accused of an offence under head (2) supra, there must be corroborative evidence that the accused knew the nature of the substance which he acquired, retained possession of or permitted to remain on his premises: *Black v HM Advocate* 1974 SLT 247.
7 Explosive Substances Act 1883 s 3 (1) (substituted by the Criminal Jurisdiction Act 1975 s 7 (1), (3); amended by the Criminal Law Act 1977 s 65 (4), Sch 12; the Criminal Law (Amendment) (Northern Ireland) Order 1977, SI 1977/1249). No proceedings for this offence may be instituted except by or with the consent of the Attorney General: Explosive Substances Act 1883 s 7 (1) (substituted by the Administration of Justice Act 1982 s 63 (1)). As to the effect of this limitation see para 639 post. As to possessing something with intent to destroy or damage property see para 596 post; and as to inquiries under the Explosive Substances Act 1883 see EXPLOSIVES vol 18 para 129.

480. Sending for proof gun barrels containing explosive substances. Any person who (1) knowingly sends for proof[1] any barrel[2] containing any explosive substance or any other matter calculated by explosion or otherwise to occasion injury to any person handling or having to do with the barrel for the purposes of proof or otherwise; or (2) puts in the barrel before or when it is sent such explosive substances or other matter; or (3) causes, procures, or knowingly permits any such offence or an attempt at any such offence; or (4) knowing that any such offence or attempt has been or is to be committed, does not give warning thereof to some officer employed at the proof house in question, is guilty of an offence and liable on conviction on indictment to imprisonment for life or for any shorter term[3].

1 Ie the Proof House of the Gunmakers Company of the City of London or the Birmingham Proof House or any branch proof house: see the Gun Barrel Proof Act 1868 ss 4, 123 (amended by the Gun Barrel Proof Act 1978 s 8 (1), Sch 3 para 12). See further TRADE MARKS vol 48 para 342.
2 For these purposes, 'barrel' includes every barrel of every small arm, and every breech of every small arm, and every small arm which would in the user of the small arm contain all or any part of its charge; every part of every small arm in, from, or through which, in the user of the small arm all or any part of its charge would be exploded or discharged; and every barrel welded, forged, or cast, finished or unfinished or in any other progressive state of manufacture and any and every part of a barrel: see the Gun Barrel Proof Act 1868 s 4. 'Small arms' include small arms of every description (whether 'of present use or of future invention') respectively adapted for the discharge of bullets, shots or other projectiles either by means of the explosion, ignition or other action of gunpowder, gun cotton, fulminating powder or other substance (whether 'of present use or of future invention or application') or by means of the expansion of steam or gas or by any other means not being merely mechanical means, except air guns ('as at present manufactured'): s 4. In the immediately preceding sentence phrases have been printed within inverted commas to draw attention to the historical interpretation which must be given to this definition in the 1868 Act.
3 Ibid s 123 (as amended: see note 1 supra). As to other offences under the Gun Barrel Proof Acts see para 223 ante and para 614 post.

481. Placing or throwing explosive substances. Any person who unlawfully and maliciously[1] places or throws in, into, upon, against, or near any building, ship, or vessel any gunpowder or other explosive substance, with intent to do any bodily injury to any person, whether or not any explosion takes place and whether or not any bodily injury is effected, is guilty of an offence and liable on conviction on indictment to imprisonment for a term not exceeding 14 years[2].

1 For the meaning of 'maliciously' see para 470 text to note 8 ante.
2 Offences against the Person Act 1861 s 30; Criminal Justice Act 1948 ss 1 (1), 83 (3), Sch 10 Pt I; Criminal Law Act 1967 s 12 (5) (a). As to the offence committed by a person who at the time of committing or being arrested for an offence under the Offences against the Person Act 1861 s 30 has in his possession a firearm or an imitation firearm see para 232 ante.

482. Possessing explosive substances etc. Any person who knowingly has in his possession, or makes or manufactures, any gunpowder, explosive substance, or any dangerous or noxious thing, or any machine, engine, instrument or thing, with intent by means of it to commit, or for the purpose of enabling any other person to commit, any of certain offences[1] is guilty of an offence and liable on conviction on indictment to imprisonment for a term not exceeding two years[2].

Any person who makes or knowingly has in his possession or under his control any explosive substance[3], under such circumstances as to give rise to a reasonable suspicion that he is not making it or does not have it in his possession or under his control for a lawful object[4] is, unless he can show that he made it or had it in his possession or under his control for a lawful object, guilty of an offence and liable on conviction on indictment to imprisonment for a term not exceeding 14 years and forfeiture of the explosive substance[5].

A person charged with an offence under the above provisions[6] may plead self-defence as a defence to any such charge[7].

1 The offences specified are the felonies mentioned in the Offences against the Person Act 1861 and any other offence there mentioned for which a person, not previously convicted, may be tried on indictment otherwise than at his own instance: s 64; Criminal Law Act 1967 s 10 (1), Sch 2 para 8

(amended by the Criminal Damage Act 1971 s 11 (8), Schedule). All distinctions between felonies and misdemeanours were abolished by the Criminal Law Act 1967 s 1 (1), and any earlier enactment creating an offence by directing it to be a felony is to be read as directing it to be an offence: see para 42 ante. Nothing in Pt I (ss 1–12) affects the operation of any reference to an offence in earlier enactments specially relating to that offence by reason only of the reference being in terms which are no longer applicable: s 12 (5) (a).

The extant provisions of the Offences against the Person Act 1861 (not all of which are relevant for this purpose) which declare offences to be felonies or so triable on indictment are: ss 4, 5, 16–18, 20–24, 27–33, 35–38, 47, 57–60. To these provisions s 1 must be added: the repeal of s 1 was expressed to be 'without prejudice to the operation of' ss 64, 65, 68: see the Murder (Abolition of Death Penalty) Act 1965 s 3 (2), Schedule. The Offences against the Person Act 1861 ss 64, 65, in so far as they relate to offences mentioned in ss 48, 52–55, 61–63 (all repealed), have been specifically repealed: see the Sexual Offences Act 1956 s 51, Sch 4.

As to offences triable either way see the Magistrates' Courts Act 1980 s 17, Sch 1 (amended by the Criminal Justice Act 1988 s 170 (2), Sch 16) and para 809 et seq post.

2   Offences against the Person Act 1861 s 64; Criminal Justice Act 1948 s 83 (3), Sch 10 Pt I; Criminal Law Act 1967 s 1.
    As to the partial repeal of the Offences against the Person Act 1861 s 64 by the Sexual Offences Act 1956 s 51, Sch 4 see note 1 supra.
3   For the meaning of 'explosive substance' see para 478 note 4 ante.
4   'Lawful object' is not confined to a purpose which takes place in the United Kingdom and the lawfulness of which is to be defined by English law; thus, if an accused is charged with manufacturing in England timers for time bombs to be exploded abroad and cannot show on the balance of probabilities that the timers were to be used for a lawful purpose outside the United Kingdom, he is liable to conviction of an offence: *R v Berry* [1985] AC 246, [1984] 3 All ER 1008, HL.
5   Explosive Substances Act 1883 s 4 (1); Criminal Justice Act 1948 s 1 (1), (2); Criminal Law Act 1967 s 12 (5) (a). No proceedings for this offence may be instituted except by or with the consent of the Attorney General: Explosive Substances Act 1883 s 7 (1) (substituted by the Administration of Justice Act 1982 s 63 (1)). As to the effect of this limitation see para 639 post.
6   Ie an offence under the Explosive Substances Act 1883 s 4: see supra.
7   *A-G's Reference (No 2 of 1983)* [1984] QB 456, 78 Cr App Rep 183, CA (person making petrol bomb with the lawful object of protection against imminent apprehended attack). Once the imminence has passed, however, possession of the explosive substance may cease to be lawful: *A-G's Reference (No 2 of 1983)* supra.

483. Setting mantraps etc. Any person who sets or places, or causes to be set or placed, any spring gun, mantrap, or other engine[1] calculated to destroy human life or inflict grievous bodily harm[2], with the intent that it shall, or whereby it may, destroy or inflict grievous bodily harm on a trespasser or other person coming in contact with it, is guilty of an offence and liable on conviction on indictment to imprisonment for a term not exceeding five years[3].

Any person who knowingly and wilfully permits any such spring gun, mantrap or other engine, which may have been set or placed in any place then being in or afterwards coming into his possession or occupation by some other person, to continue so set or placed is deemed to have set or placed it with the above-mentioned intent[4]. However, nothing in the above provisions makes it illegal to set or place any gin or trap such as may have been or may be usually set or placed with the intent of destroying vermin, or to set or place, or cause to be set or placed, or to be continued set or placed, from sunset to sunrise, any spring gun, mantrap or other engine which is set or placed, or caused or continued to be set or placed, in a dwelling house for its protection[4].

The offence relates only to instruments set with the intention to do grievous bodily harm, or by which grievous bodily harm is actually caused[5].

1   An 'engine' in this context means a mechanical contrivance: *R v Munks* [1964] 1 QB 304, 48 Cr App Rep 56, CCA. It does not include an arrangement of electric wires: *R v Munks* supra.

2 For the meaning of 'grievous bodily harm' see para 470 text and note 7 ante.
3 Offences against the Person Act 1861 s 31; Penal Servitude Act 1891 s 1 (1); Criminal Justice Act 1948 s 1 (1); Criminal Law Act 1967 s 1.
4 Offences against the Person Act 1861 s 31. As to defence of property see also para 457 ante.
5 *Jordin v Crump* (1841) 8 M & W 782 at 786. See also *Wootton v Dawkins* (1857) CBNS 412. Where death is caused by setting such an instrument, the setter is guilty of manslaughter: *R v Heaton* (1896) 60 JP 508.

484. Bomb hoaxes. Any person who (1) places any article[1] in any place whatever, or dispatches any article by post, rail or any other means whatever of sending things from one place to another, with the intention, in either case, of inducing in some other person a belief that it is likely to explode or ignite and thereby cause personal injury or damage to property[2]; or (2) communicates any information which he knows or believes to be false to another person with the intention of inducing in him or any other person a false belief that a bomb or other thing liable to explode or ignite is present in any place or location whatever[3], is guilty of an offence and liable on conviction on indictment to imprisonment for a term not exceeding five years, or on summary conviction to imprisonment for a term not exceeding three months or a fine not exceeding the prescribed sum, or to both[4].

For a person to be guilty of an offence under heads (1) or (2) above, it is not necessary for him to have any particular person in mind as the person in whom he intends to induce the belief there mentioned[5].

1 For these purposes, 'article' includes substance: Criminal Law Act 1977 s 51 (1).
2 Ibid s 51 (1).
3 Ibid s 51 (2).
4 Ibid s 51 (4) (amended by the Magistrates' Courts Act 1980 s 32 (2)). For the meaning of 'the prescribed sum' see para 807 post.
5 Criminal Law Act 1977 s 51 (3). As to threatening to contaminate or interfere with goods see para 193 ante; and as to threatening to destroy or damage property see para 595 post.

(viii) Endangering Railway Passengers

485. Placing wood etc on railway, taking up rails, turning points, showing or hiding signals etc with intent to endanger passengers. Any person who unlawfully and maliciously[1]:

(1) puts or throws upon or across any railway any wood, stone or other matter or thing; or

(2) takes up, removes or displaces any rail, sleeper or other matter or thing belonging to any railway; or

(3) turns, moves or diverts any points or other machinery belonging to any railway; or

(4) makes or shows, hides or removes, any signal or light upon or near to any railway; or

(5) does or causes to be done any other matter or thing,

with intent to endanger the safety of any person travelling or being upon such railway, is guilty of an offence and liable on conviction on indictment to imprisonment for life or for any shorter term[2].

1 For the meaning of 'maliciously' see para 470 text to note 8 ante.
2 Offences against the Person Act 1861 s 32 (amended by the Criminal Justice Act 1948 s 83 (1), Sch 10 Pt I); Criminal Justice Act 1948 s 1 (1). An acquittal on indictment under the Offences against the

Person Act 1861 s 32 (as so amended) is no bar to a subsequent indictment on the same facts for an offence under s 34 (see para 487 post): *R v Gilmore* (1882) 15 Cox CC 85. As to the offence committed by a person who at the time of committing or being arrested for an offence under the Offences against the Person Act 1861 s 32 (as so amended) has in his possession a firearm or an imitation firearm see para 232 ante.

486. Casting stone etc upon a railway carriage, with intent to endanger the safety of any person therein, or in any part of the same train. Any person who unlawfully and maliciously[1] throws, or causes to fall or strike, at, against, into, or upon any engine, tender, carriage or truck used on any railway, any wood, stone, or other matter or thing, with intent to injure or endanger the safety of any person in or upon such engine, tender, carriage or truck or in or upon any other engine, tender, carriage or truck forming part of the same train, is guilty of an offence and liable on conviction on indictment to imprisonment for life or for any shorter term[2].

1 For the meaning of 'maliciously' see para 470 text to note 8 ante.
2 Offences against the Person Act 1861 s 33; Criminal Justice Act 1948 s 1 (1). Throwing a stone at engines or carriages may also be an offence under the Offences against the Person Act 1861 s 34 (see para 487 post): *R v Bowray* (1846) 10 Jur 211.

487. Doing or omitting anything so as to endanger passengers by railway. Any person who, by any unlawful act[1], or by any wilful omission or neglect, endangers or causes to be endangered[2] the safety of any person conveyed or being in or upon a railway, or who aids or assists therein, is guilty of an offence and liable on conviction on indictment to imprisonment for a term not exceeding two years, or on summary conviction to imprisonment for a term not exceeding six months or a fine not exceeding the prescribed sum, or to both[3].

1 Throwing a stone at engines or carriages may be an offence for these purposes (*R v Bowray* (1846) 10 Jur 211) as is playing with a cart on railway premises so as to let it run within a dangerous distance of the track (*R v Monaghan and Granger* (1870) 11 Cox CC 608).
2 Proof of the causation of actual danger is not essential if the facts proved may properly be described as endangering the safety of any person conveyed by railway; and disruption of the automatic signalling system may amount to such endangering of safety: *R v Pearce* [1967] 1 QB 150, 50 Cr App Rep 305, CA.
3 Offences against the Person Act 1861 s 34; Criminal Justice Act 1948 s 1 (2); Criminal Law Act 1967 s 1 (1); Magistrates' Courts Act 1980 ss 17, 32 (1), Sch 1 para 5 (e). See para 804 post. For the meaning of 'the prescribed sum' see para 807 post.

(ix) Assault

A. COMMON ASSAULT

488. Assault and battery. An assault is any act[1] committed intentionally or recklessly, which causes another person to apprehend immediate and unlawful personal violence[2]. If force is actually applied, directly or indirectly, unlawfully or without the consent[3] of the person assaulted, the assault becomes a battery, however slight the force[4]. A battery may or may not include an assault. Although an assault is an independent crime and should be treated as such[5], for practical purposes the term 'assault' is generally synonymous with 'battery' and is used to mean the actual intended use of unlawful force to another person without his consent[6].

There may be an assault without the application of force, but in such cases there must be some threatening act sufficient to raise in the mind of the person threatened a fear of immediate violence; there is thus no assault if a threat is made to strike a person with the fist, at such a distance as to make it impossible for the blow to reach[7], or where a firearm is aimed at a range to which the missile could not possibly carry[8]. There seems no logical reason why mere words should not amount to an assault[9].

The mental element in the offence of battery is satisfied by proof that the accused intentionally or recklessly applied force to the person of another[10]. There must, however, be a positive act; no mere omission to act can amount to a battery[11].

1 Eg an act, compulsion, a threatening gesture or a threat to use violence: see *Beal v Kelley* [1951] 2 All ER 763, 35 Cr App Rep 128, DC; *Fairclough v Whipp* [1951] 2 All ER 834, 35 Cr App Rep 138, DC; *DPP v Rogers* [1953] 2 All ER 644, 37 Cr App Rep 137, DC; *R v Rolfe* (1952) 36 Cr App Rep 4 at 6, CCA. Cf *R v Burrows* [1952] 1 All ER 58n, CCA; *R v McCormack* [1969] 2 QB 442, 53 Cr App Rep 514, CA; *Logdon v DPP* [1976] Crim LR 121, DC.

2 *Fagan v Metropolitan Police Comr* [1969] 1 QB 439 at 444, 52 Cr App Rep 700 at 703, DC per James J; *R v Venna* [1976] QB 421, [1975] 3 All ER 788, CA. For the meaning of 'recklessly' in this context see note 10 infra.

3 As to consent being a defence to a charge see para 494 post.

4 1 Hawk PC c 15 (2) ss 1, 2; and see *Collins v Wilcock* [1984] 3 All ER 374, [1984] 1 WLR 1172, DC. To strike a horse causing the rider to fall is a battery: *Dodwell v Burford* (1669) 1 Mod Rep 24.

5 See eg *R v Rolfe* (1952) 36 Cr App Rep 4, CCA.

6 *Fagan v Metropolitan Police Comr* [1969] 1 QB 439 at 444, 52 Cr App Rep 700 at 703, DC per James J. Except where the context otherwise requires, the term 'assault' is used in this latter sense (ie as meaning assault and battery) in para 489 et seq post but in this paragraph it is used in its strict sense (see text to note 1 supra).

7 See, however, *Smith v Chief Superintendent of Woking Police Station* (1983) 76 Cr App Rep 234, DC (staring through a window at night, intending to frighten elderly occupant of room, constituted assault despite the physical barrier between accused and victim) (decided under the Vagrancy Act 1824 s 4 (as amended): see para 418 note 5 ante).

8 Presenting a loaded firearm at a person within range is prima facie an assault (*R v St George* (1840) 9 C & P 483 at 490; cf *R v Baker* (1843) 1 Car & Kir 254) unless justifiable (*Kwaku Mensah v R* [1946] AC 83 at 91, PC) or done without hostile intent (see *R v Lamb* [1967] 2 QB 981, 51 Cr App Rep 417, CA).

   Assault, with or without battery, and battery may be committed in many ways. For a review of the principles relating to assault see *Wilson v Pringle* [1987] QB 237, [1986] 2 All ER 440, CA; *F v West Berkshire Health Authority (Mental Health Act Commission intervening)* [1989] 2 All ER 545 at 563, 564; sub nom *Re F (Mental Patient: Sterilisation)* [1989] 2 WLR 1025 at 1082, 1083, HL per Lord Goff of Chieveley (civil cases).

9 See *R v Wilson* [1955] 1 All ER 744, 39 Cr App Rep 12, CCA ('Get out the knives'). Cf 1 Hawk PC c 15 (2) s 1; *R v Meade and Belt* (1823) 1 Lew CC 184 (adopting the traditional view that words cannot constitute assault).

10 *R v Venna* [1976] QB 421, [1975] 3 All ER 788, CA; and see *Wilson v Pringle* [1987] QB 237, [1986] 2 All ER 440, CA (it is the act, rather than any injury, which must be intentional). Quaere, however, whether battery implies a 'hostile' touching: see *F v West Berkshire Health Authority (Mental Health Act Commission intervening)* [1989] 2 All ER 545 at 563, 564; sub nom *Re F (Mental Patient: Sterilisation)* [1989] 2 WLR 1025 at 1082, 1083, HL per Lord Goff of Chieveley, disapproving dicta to that effect in *Wilson v Pringle* supra.

   For the meaning of 'recklessness' see *DPP v K (a minor)* [1990] 1 All ER 331, DC, where Parker LJ expressed 'misgivings' about the test in *R v Caldwell* [1982] AC 341, 73 Cr App Rep 13, HL, but apparently accepted that giving no thought to the risk of a particular harm might constitute recklessness in the context of assault causing actual bodily harm (see para 490 post). See further para 14 ante.

11 *Fagan v Metropolitan Police Comr* [1969] 1 QB 439, 52 Cr App Rep 700, DC. With this proposition Bridge J, who dissented from the decision, concurred: see [1969] 1 QB 439 at 446, 52 Cr App Rep 700 at 705. That case illustrates the difficulty in deciding what constitutes a 'mere omission' in this context. A driver of a car drove his vehicle on to the foot of a police constable; this act was not proved

to be deliberate. When the constable remonstrated, the driver indicated in an abusive manner that the constable would have to wait and the engine of the car stopped; after an interval the driver restarted the engine and moved the vehicle. James J, with whom Lord Parker CJ concurred, held that the driver by remaining in the car which was in contact with the constable's foot, by allowing the engine to stop, by maintaining the car on the constable's foot and by using words to indicate his intention to keep the wheel in that position committed a battery. The driver's conduct was not a 'mere omission'. Bridge J, dissenting, regarded the driver's failure to move the vehicle as an omission and as not constituting a battery.

489. Prosecutions for assault; penalty. Common assault and battery are summary offences and a person guilty of either of them is liable on conviction to imprisonment for a term not exceeding six months or a fine not exceeding level 5 on the standard scale, or to both[1].

A count charging a person with common assault may be included in an indictment if the charge is founded on the same facts or evidence as a count charging an indictable offence, or is part of a series of offences of the same or similar character as an indictable offence which is also charged, but only if, in either case, the facts or evidence relating to the offence were disclosed in an examination or deposition taken before a justice in the presence of the person charged[2]. Where a count charging common assault is included in an indictment, the offence must be tried in the same manner as if it were an indictable offence; but the Crown Court may only deal with the offender in respect of it in a manner in which a magistrates' court could have dealt with him[3].

1 Criminal Justice Act 1988 s 39. For the meaning of 'the standard scale' see para 808 post.
2 Ibid s 40 (1), (3) (a). See para 922 post.
3 Ibid s 40 (2), (3) (a). See para 943 post.

B. AGGRAVATED ASSAULT

490. Assault occasioning actual bodily harm. Any person who is convicted on indictment of any assault[1] occasioning actual bodily harm[2] is liable on conviction on indictment to imprisonment for a term not exceeding five years, or on summary conviction to imprisonment for a term not exceeding six months or a fine not exceeding the prescribed sum, or to both[3].

1 As to assault and battery see para 488 ante. The mens rea for the offence of assault occasioning actual bodily harm appears to be identical with that required for common assault: see para 488 text and note 10 ante.
2 An assault occasioning actual bodily harm may be constituted by an assault causing an hysterical and nervous condition: *R v Miller* [1954] 2 QB 282, 38 Cr App Rep 1. It may also be constituted by threats which so terrified the victim that she was injured jumping from a moving vehicle to escape: *R v Roberts* (1971) 115 Sol Jo 809, 56 Cr App Rep 95, CA. For the meaning of 'actual bodily harm' see also *R v Reigate Justices, ex p Counsell* (1983) 148 JP 193, DC. As to criminal liability for injuries caused in attempts to escape from the accused see para 472 ante.
3 Offences against the Person Act 1861 s 47 (amended by the Criminal Justice Act 1988 s 170 (2), Sch 16); Penal Servitude Act 1891 s 1 (1); Criminal Justice Act 1948 s 1 (1); Criminal Law Act 1967 s 1; Magistrates' Courts Act 1980 ss 17, 32 (1), Sch 1 para 5 (h) (amended by the Criminal Justice Act 1988 Sch 16). See para 804 post. For the meaning of 'the prescribed sum' see para 807 post. As to the offence committed by a person who at the time of committing or being arrested for an offence under the Offences against the Person Act 1861 s 47 (as so amended) has in his possession a firearm or an imitation firearm see para 232 ante; and as to procedural provisions applying where an offence involving bodily injury to a child or young person is charged see para 882 post.

491. Aggravated assault; assault committed in certain specified circumstances. Specific statutory provision is made for the punishment of persons who have committed an assault (1) with intent to resist or prevent the lawful apprehension or detainer of the accused or of any other person for any offence[1]; (2) on a constable, or a person assisting a constable, in the execution of his duty[2]; (3) on a magistrate or other lawfully authorised person on account of his preserving a wreck[3]; (4) on a clergyman celebrating divine service[4].

1 See para 321 ante.
2 See para 320 ante.
3 See SHIPPING vol 43 para 1013.
4 See para 349 ante.

C. FALSE IMPRISONMENT; KIDNAPPING

492. False imprisonment. It is an offence at common law punishable by fine and imprisonment[1] to imprison any person without lawful cause[2]. Every restraint of the liberty of one person under the custody of another, either in a prison, house or in the street, is in law an imprisonment[3].

There can be an imprisonment without the detained person knowing that he is being detained[4]. It is not an imprisonment, however, to stop a person from going in one direction if he can without risk go in another[5].

The restraint of a child's freedom of movement by a parent is false imprisonment only if the restraint is unlawful. Unlawfulness is not, however, restricted to actions in contravention of a court order or the wishes of the other parent; it extends to detention which is outside the realms of reasonable parental discipline[6].

1 See paras 1200, 1232 post.
2 Com Dig, Imprisonment (L1); 1 East PC 248; *R v Lesley* (1860) Bell CC 220; and see *Hunter v Johnson* (1884) 13 QBD 225. It is false imprisonment to detain an accused after his acquittal, or after his term of imprisonment has expired: *Mee v Cruickshank* (1902) 20 Cox CC 210.
3 1 Buller's Nisi Prius 22a. A wrongful imprisonment amounts to an assault (1 Hawk PC c 60 s 7: see para 488 ante) even though no violence or threat of violence is actually used (see *R v Linsberg and Leies* (1905) 69 JP 107), and is usually punished as such, there being few reported cases of indictments for false imprisonment simply (but see *R v Hosein and Hosein* (1970) unreported, but cited in Archbold, Criminal Pleading, Evidence and Practice (43rd Edn) para 20–243), as an assault is generally charged in the same indictment and usually in one count with the false imprisonment, as in *R v Lesley* (1860) Bell CC 220, and *R v Hosein and Hosein* supra, although a count for false imprisonment alone without alleging an assault is good. An imprisonment may include a battery, but does not necessarily do so: *Emmett v Lyne* (1805) 1 Bos & PNR 255. As to false imprisonment generally see TORT vol 45 para 1325 et seq.
4 *Meering v Grahame-White Aviation Co Ltd* (1919) 122 LT 44, CA; but see *Herring v Boyle* (1834) 1 Cr M & R 377 to the contrary effect.
5 *Bird v Jones* (1845) 7 QB 742.
6 *R v Rahman* (1985) 81 Cr App Rep 349, CA.

493. Kidnapping. It is an offence at common law punishable by fine and imprisonment[1] to kidnap any person[2]. Kidnapping, which is an aggravated form of false imprisonment[3], consists of the taking or carrying away[4] of one person by another by force or fraud without the consent of the person so taken or carried away and without lawful excuse[5].

The common law offence of kidnapping exists in the case of a victim under the age of 14[6]. It may be committed by a parent who takes away by force or fraud his own unmarried child under the age of 18, without the child's consent[7] and without lawful excuse[8]; and by a husband on his wife if he treats her with hostile force and carries her away from the place where she wishes to remain[9]. Where the offence is committed against a child under the age of 16 and by a person connected with the child[10], no prosecution may be instituted except by or with the consent of the Director of Public Prosecutions[11].

1 See paras 1200, 1232 post.
2 See *R v D* [1984] AC 778, 79 Cr App Rep 313, HL, where the earlier authorities are reviewed.
3 As to false imprisonment see para 492 ante.
4 All that must be proved is a deprivation of liberty and a carrying away from the place where the victim wishes to be; it is unnecessary to prove that the kidnapper carried the victim to the place he intended: *R v Wellard* [1978] 3 All ER 161, 67 Cr App Rep 364, CA.
5 *R v D* [1984] AC 778, 79 Cr App Rep 313, HL. The accused's belief that the victim is an illegal immigrant is not a defence: *R v D* supra.
6 *R v D* [1984] AC 778, 79 Cr App Rep 313, HL.
7 In all cases it is the absence of the child's consent which is material, and this is a question of fact for the jury, although it would not be found at all frequently that a child under the age of 14 had sufficient understanding and intelligence to give its consent: *R v D* [1984] AC 778 at 803, 79 Cr App Rep 313 at 323, HL per Lord Brandon.
8 *R v D* [1984] AC 778, 79 Cr App Rep 313, HL. The giving of consent by a person having custody or care and control of the child may be relevant to a defence of lawful excuse: *R v D* supra.
9 *R v Reid* [1973] QB 299, [1972] 2 All ER 1350, CA. The fact that the parties are cohabiting at the time of the offence is immaterial: *R v Reid* supra.
10 Ie within the meaning of the Child Abduction Act 1984 s 1 (amended by the Family Law Act 1986 s 65): see para 535 post.
11 Child Abduction Act 1984 s 5. As to the effect of this limitation see para 639 post. As to child abduction see paras 535, 536 post; and as to the offence of hostage-taking see para 139 ante.

D. DEFENCES TO ASSAULT

494. Consent to assault. Generally speaking, in order to constitute an assault it is necessary that the act should be done against the will of the person assaulted and, in consequence, consent is generally a good defence to a charge of assault[1]. If, however, the act done is unlawful in itself and its infliction is injurious to the public as well as to the person[2], consent will afford no defence[3]. A prize fight is inherently unlawful and for this reason all persons participating in, or aiding and abetting, a prize fight are guilty of assault[4]. Also unlawful are any fights, whether in private or in public, in which the contestants cause or intend actual bodily harm to each other: each commits an assault on the other[5].

The consent must be that of a rational person who knows the nature of the act consented to[6] and it seems that the act must come within the scope of the consent, whether express or implied[7]. Fraud as to the nature of the act done, or as to the identity of the person doing it, will vitiate consent[8].

The prosecution must prove a lack of consent; but a belief in consent, if honestly though unreasonably held, is a defence[9]. In cases of indecent assault the consent of a person under the age of 16 affords no defence[10]. Consent is not a defence in any proceedings for an indecent assault on a defective if the accused knew or had reason to suspect that the person in respect of whom the offence was committed was a defective[11].

1 *R v Meredith* (1838) 8 C & P 589. As to consent as a defence generally in criminal proceedings see para 23 ante. For the meaning of 'assault' in this paragraph see para 488 note 6 ante.
2 Eg if the act is intended or likely to cause bodily harm.
3 *R v Coney* (1882) 8 QBD 534, CCR; *R v Donovan* [1934] 2 KB 498, 25 Cr App Rep 1, CCA; *R v Lawson* (25 May 1936, unreported), CCA. See also the Prohibition of Female Circumcision Act 1985 ss 1, 2 and para 503 post. Properly conducted games and sports, reasonable surgical interference,

dangerous exhibitions etc may be justified as needed in the public interest: *A-G's Reference (No 6 of 1980)* [1981] QB 715, 73 Cr App Rep 63, CA. As to lawful correction see para 497 post.

4 *R v Coney* (1882) 8 QBD 534, CCR; *R v Perkins* (1831) 4 C & P 537; *R v Brown* (1841) Car & M 314 at 318. Mere presence at a prize fight as a spectator, without taking any part in the proceedings, does not necessarily make a person an aider or abettor, but presence unexplained may be some evidence that such a person was present aiding and abetting: *R v Coney* supra at 552, 558 per Lopes and Hawkins JJ. For the meaning of 'prize fight' see para 444 note 7 ante.

5 *A-G's Reference (No 6 of 1980)* [1981] QB 715, 73 Cr App Rep 63, CA.

6 *R v Lock* (1872) LR 2 CCR 10. See also *Burrell v Harmer* [1967] Crim LR 169, DC (consent by minors to tattooing: see now the Tattooing of Minors Act 1969 s 1 and para 539 post).

7 See eg *R v MacTavish* (1972) 8 CCC (2d) 206 (NB App Div) (fist fight arranged; victim kicked and nose broken); *R v Dix* (1972) 10 CCC (2d) 324 (Ont CA) (fight arranged; onus on prosecution to show that act alleged to be assault goes beyond scope of consent). Quaere, however, whether even the activities consented to in these cases would be lawful: see text to note 5 supra. See also para 23 ante.

8 *R v Clarence* (1888) 22 QBD 23 at 43, CCR (where the majority of the judges held that a wife's consent to her husband having intercourse was not vitiated by his concealing from her the fact that he was suffering from venereal disease); as to a husband's marital rights see further para 495 post. Cf *Hegarty v Shine* (1878) 4 LR Ir 288. As to a man who induces a woman to have intercourse with him by impersonating her husband see para 514 post.

A medical man, or person assuming to act as one, who strips a female patient naked on the pretence that he is diagnosing her case, is guilty of assault: *R v Rosinski* (1824) 1 Mood CC 19. It is also an assault where he has intercourse with her on the pretence that he is treating her medically: *R v Case* (1850) 1 Den 580, CCR. As to consent in relation to rape see para 517 post.

9 *R v Kimber* [1983] 3 All ER 316, 77 Cr App Rep 225, CA; and see para 21 ante.

10 See para 521 et seq post. As to the relevance of age in a finding of indecent assault as an alternative verdict see para 1029 post.

11 See para 521 et seq post.

495. Marital rights. A husband is not entitled to inflict personal chastisement upon his wife, or to imprison her[1]. Although a husband has a right to marital intercourse, and, although, if the husband has intercourse against the will of his wife, it is not as a general rule rape[2], he is not entitled to use force or violence for the purpose of exercising his right and, if he does so, he may be convicted of common assault, assault occasioning actual bodily harm, wounding, indecent assault or such other offence as the facts of the case warrant[3].

1 *R v Jackson* [1891] 1 QB 671 at 679, 683, CA; *R v Lister* (1721) 1 Stra 478. A husband may be guilty of kidnapping his wife even if she is cohabiting with him at the time (*R v Reid* [1973] 1 QB 299, [1972] 2 All ER 1350, CA): see para 493 ante.

2 See para 515 post.

3 *R v Miller* [1954] 2 QB 282, [1954] 2 All ER 529. See also *R v Kowalski* [1988] 1 FLR 447, 86 Cr App Rep 339, CA (husband forced wife to perform fellatio against her will; conviction for indecent assault upheld). As to common assault see paras 488, 489 ante; as to assault occasioning actual bodily harm see para 490 ante; and as to wounding see para 469 et seq ante.

496. Misadventure. It is a defence to a charge of assault that the act alleged was a mere accident[1]; or that it was done while the parties were engaged in a game or sport which was lawful, properly conducted and not intended to cause actual bodily harm[2].

1 *Weaver v Ward* (1616) Hob 134; *Gibbons v Pepper* (1695) 1 Ld Raym 38; *R v Gill* (1719) 1 Str 190; *Wakeman v Robinson* (1823) 1 Bing 213; *Stanley v Powell* [1891] 1 QB 86; see also *Fowler v Lanning* [1959] 1 QB 426, [1959] 1 All ER 290. As to the basis of accident as a defence to a criminal charge see para 22 ante. For the meaning of 'assault' see para 488 note 6 ante.

2 *R v Coney* (1882) 8 QBD 534 at 539, 549, CCR per Cave and Stephen JJ; *A-G's Reference (No 6 of 1980)* [1981] QB 715, 73 Cr App Rep 63, CA.

497. Lawful correction. An act is not an assault if it is done in the course of the lawful correction of a child by its parent or, in certain circumstances, of a pupil by his teacher[1], provided that the correction is reasonable and moderate considering the age and health of the child[2] and administered with a proper instrument, and in the case of a female in a decent manner[3].

Where, in any proceedings, it is shown that corporal punishment has been given[4] to a pupil[5] by or on the authority of a member of the staff[6], giving the punishment cannot be justified on the ground that it was done in pursuance of a right exercisable by the member of staff by virtue of his position as such[7]. A person is not, however, to be so taken as giving corporal punishment by virtue of anything done for reasons that include averting an immediate danger of personal injury to, or an immediate danger to the property of, any person, including the pupil concerned[8]; nor does a person commit an offence by reason of any conduct relating to a pupil which would, apart from the above provisions, be justified on the ground that it is done in pursuance of a right exercisable by a member of the staff by virtue of his position as such[9].

1 *R v Hopley* (1860) 2 F & F 202 at 206 per Cockburn CJ; *R v Griffin* (1869) 11 Cox CC 402; 1 Hawk PC c 28 (1) s 23; 1 Hawk PC c 10 s 4. See also *M'Shane v Paton* 1922 JC 26 and para 444 ante. See, however, text to notes 4–9 infra. For the meaning of 'assault' see para 488 note 6 ante.

2 *R v Mackie* [1973] Crim LR 54.

3 *R v Miles* (1842) 6 Jur 243; *R v Hopley* (1860) 2 F & F 202 at 206; *Cleary v Booth* [1893] 1 QB 465, DC. A parent or person in loco parentis has the right to chastise a child, while under age, in a reasonable manner: see 1 Bl Com 452, 462; 1 Hale PC 473, 474; *R v Conner* (1836) 7 C & P 438. The right of a headmaster to punish a pupil by corporal punishment was regarded as a delegation of this parental right (*Cleary v Booth* supra), and extended to a responsible assistant teacher (*Mansell v Griffin* [1908] 1 KB 947, CA). See also *R v Newport (Salop) Justices, ex p Wright* [1929] 2 KB 416. However, as to the abolition of corporal punishment in the case of specified pupils see the Education (No 2) Act 1986 s 47 and text to notes 4–9 infra.

The right of a parent or other person having the lawful control of a child or young person to administer punishment is recognised and not affected by the Children and Young Persons Act 1933 s 1 (as amended): see para 537 note 9 post. An elder brother, not in loco parentis, has no right to strike a younger brother merely because he is impudent: *R v Woods* (1921) 85 JP 272.

The formerly recognised right to chastise servants, apprentices, mutinous seamen etc may be assumed to have fallen into desuetude; and corporal punishment in prisons was abolished by the Criminal Justice Act 1967 s 65.

4 Subject to the Education (No 2) Act 1986 s 47 (3) (see infra), references in s 47 to giving corporal punishment are references to doing anything for the purposes of punishing the pupil concerned, whether or not there are also other reasons for doing it, which, apart from any justification, would constitute battery: s 47 (2).

5 For these purposes, 'pupil' means a person (1) for whom education is provided (a) at a school maintained by a local education authority; (b) at a special school not so maintained; (c) at a grant-maintained school; or (d) at an independent school which is maintained or assisted by a Minister of the Crown, including a school of which a government department is the proprietor, or assisted by a local education authority and which falls within a prescribed class; (2) for whom primary or secondary education, or education which would be primary or secondary education if it were provided full-time, is provided by a local education authority otherwise than at a school; or (3) a person to whom ibid s 47 (6) (see infra) applies and for whom education is provided at an independent school which does not fall within head (1) (d) supra; but does not include any person who is aged 18 or over: s 47 (5) (amended by the Education Reform Act 1988 s 237, Sch 12 para 35, Sch 13 Pt II). The prescribed classes for the purposes of head (1) (d) supra are (i) any independent school in receipt of grant under the Direct Grant Schools Regulations 1959, SI 1959/1832, regs 4 (1) or 5 (1); (ii) a school maintained by the Ministry of Defence; (iii) a city technology college which is, for the time being, assisted by a Minister of the Crown; and (iv) a city college for the technology of the arts, which is, for the time being, so assisted: Education (Abolition of Corporal Punishment) (Independent Schools) Regulations 1987, SI 1987/1183, reg 2 (amended by SI 1989/1233). The Education (No 2) Act 1986 s 47 (6) applies to a person if (A) he holds an assisted place under a scheme operated by the Secretary of State under the Education Act 1980 s 17; (B) any of the fees or expenses

payable in respect of his attendance at school are paid by the Secretary of State under the Education Act 1944 s 100 or by a local education authority under the Education (Miscellaneous Provisions) Act 1953 s 6; (C) any of the fees payable in respect of his attendance at school are paid by a local education authority under the Education Act 1944 s 81; or (D) he falls within a prescribed category of persons: Education (No 2) Act 1986 s 47 (6). For the purposes of head (D) supra the Secretary of State may prescribe one or more categories of person who appear to him to be persons in respect of whom any fees are paid out of public funds: s 47 (7).

The following is a prescribed category of persons for these purposes, namely any person in respect of whom any of the fees payable in respect of his attendance at an independent school (other than an independent school falling within a prescribed class for the purposes of head (1) (d) supra) are paid by a local authority, an education authority in Scotland within the meaning of the Education (Scotland) Act 1980 or a board constituted by the Education and Libraries (Northern Ireland) Order 1986, SI 1986/594: Education (Abolition of Corporal Punishment) (Independent Schools) (Prescribed Categories of Persons) Regulations 1989, SI 1989/1825, regs 2, 3. For these purposes, 'local authority' means, in relation to England and Wales, a local authority acting in the discharge of any of its functions under any of the enactments specified in the Local Authority Social Services Act 1970 s 2, Sch 1 (as amended: see LOCAL GOVERNMENT vol 28 para 1145) or, so long as an order under s 12 is in force, the Council of the Isles of Scilly: Education (Abolition of Corporal Punishment) (Independent Schools) (Prescribed Categories of Persons) Regulations 1989 reg 2; and see the Isles of Scilly (Local Authority Social Services) Order 1980, SI 1980/328.

6 For these purposes, 'member of the staff' means (1) in relation to a person who is a pupil by reason of the provision of education for him at any school, any teacher who works at the school and any other person who has lawful control or charge of the pupil and works there; and (2) in relation to a person who is a pupil by reason of the provision of education for him by a local education authority at a place other than a school, any teacher employed by the authority who works at that place and any other person employed by that authority who has lawful control or charge of the pupil and works there: Education (No 2) Act 1986 s 47 (10).

7 Ibid s 47 (1). A person may not be debarred from receiving education, whether by refusing him admission to a school, suspending his attendance or otherwise, by reason of the fact that s 47 applies in relation to him, or if he were admitted might so apply: s 47 (8).

8 Ibid s 47 (3).

9 Ibid s 47 (4).

498. Self-defence and defence of others. If the act alleged to be an assault is done in self-defence, it is justified and no unlawful act is committed provided that no more force is used than is necessary for mere defence; and self-defence is a defence even to a charge of assault involving wounding or grievous bodily harm[1]. If an assault is threatened, a person may use such force as is reasonable in the circumstances to repel it[2]; and an honest, even if unreasonable, belief in the existence of facts which, if they existed, would render the use of such force reasonable is a defence[3].

In deciding whether the force used was reasonable, all the circumstances may be considered; the accused's opportunity to retreat with safety and his readiness to disengage are factors to be taken into account in deciding on the justification for the use of force and whether the force used was reasonable[4].

1 *Cockcroft v Smith* (1705) 2 Salk 642; and see *R v Jones* [1978] 3 All ER 1098, 67 Cr App Rep 166, CA (resistance to forcible attempt by police to take fingerprints unlawfully was justified); *R v Shannon* (1980) 71 Cr App Rep 192, CA. For the meaning of 'assault' see para 488 note 6 ante. As to the burden of proof, and as to the direction to the jury where self-defence is raised, see paras 1065, 1015 respectively post.

2 Ie in the prevention of crime: see para 706 post.

3 *R v Williams* (G) [1987] 3 All ER 411, 78 Cr App Rep 276, CA; and see para 21 ante.

4 See para 456 ante. An accused is not disentitled from relying on a plea of self-defence merely because he has failed to demonstrate readiness to disengage: *R v Bird* [1985] 2 All ER 513, 81 Cr App Rep 110, CA.

499. Defence of property. A person is justified in using reasonable force in defence of his property, as for instance in removing a trespasser or preventing his entry or restraining another from taking or destroying his goods[1]. No more force may be used than is necessary for the purpose[2].

1 1 Hawk PC c 28(1) s 23; *Weaver v Bush* (1798) 8 Term Rep 78; *Scott v Matthew Brown & Co Ltd* (1884) 51 LT 746; *Harrison v Duke of Rutland* [1893] 1 QB 142, CA; *R v Hussey* (1924) 89 JP 28, 18 Cr App Rep 160, CCA; cf *Dean v Hogg* (1834) 10 Bing 345; *Holmes v Bagge* (1853) 1 E & B 782 (where the accused had the full enjoyment of the premises, but not the full and exclusive right of possession, and on this ground they were unable to justify the forcible removal of the plaintiffs); and see *Robinson v Balmain New Ferry Co Ltd* [1910] AC 295, PC. See also TORT vol 45 para 1318.

Where the threat to property or the damage amounts to a crime, eg under the Criminal Damage Act 1971 (see para 593 et seq post), a person is entitled to use such force as is reasonable in the circumstances in the prevention of crime; and the rules of the common law on the question when force may be used for such purpose are superseded: see para 706 post.

As to the rescue of goods seized in execution under county court process see COUNTY COURTS vol 10 para 38.

2 *Weaver v Bush* (1798) 8 Term Rep 78; see also *King v Tebbart* (1693) Skin 387; *R v Barrett* (1980) 72 Cr App Rep 212, CA (use of force to prevent entry of bailiffs unjustified unless bailiffs using excessive force). Where force is used in the prevention of crime, it must only be such force as is reasonable in the circumstances: see para 706 post and *Taylor v Mucklow* [1973] Crim LR 750, DC (use of loaded airgun unreasonable in protecting home from criminal damage).

500. Lawful arrest. It is an answer to a charge of assault that the accused was effecting or assisting in a lawful arrest and used no more force than was reasonable in the circumstances[1].

1 See para 706 post. For the meaning of 'assault' see para 488 note 6 ante.

Under certain circumstances it may be a defence to a charge of assault that the accused was using only such force as was necessary to serve civil process: see *Harrison v Hodgson* (1830) 10 B & C 445. Serving process by thrusting a document into the fold of a man's coat is not necessarily an assault: see *Rose v Kempthorne* (1910) 103 LT 730. As to assault on an officer of the county court in the execution of his duty see COUNTY COURTS vol 10 para 38; as to assault on a police officer in the execution of his duty see para 320 ante; and as to resisting arrest see further paras 321, 469, 491 ante.

E. PROCEDURE

501. Alternative verdicts. On a trial for any offence, except treason or murder, if the jury finds the accused not guilty of the offence specifically charged in the indictment, but the allegations in the indictment amount to or include, expressly or by implication, an allegation of another offence falling within the jurisdiction of the trial court, the jury may find him guilty of that other offence or of an offence of which he could be found guilty on an indictment specifically charging that other offence[1].

1 See the Criminal Law Act 1967 s 6 (3) and para 1029 post, particularly at note 12. See also *R v Wilson, R v Jenkins* [1983] 3 All ER 448, 77 Cr App Rep 319, HL, overruling *R v Springfield* (1969) 53 Cr App Rep 608, CA, and approving *R v Lillis* [1972] 2 QB 236, 56 Cr App Rep 432, CA.

502. Effect of summary conviction or dismissal of information. Any person (1) who has been convicted on summary trial of common assault[1] and has either been made the subject of a probation order, been discharged absolutely or conditionally or has undergone the imprisonment awarded and paid any fine and costs; or (2) against whom an information alleging common assault has been heard on the merits[2] and dismissed on summary trial[3], is released from all further or other proceedings, civil or criminal, whether taken by the prosecutor or any other person aggrieved[4], for the same cause[5].

1 As to common assault see paras 488, 489 ante.
2 Where the accused appeared and pleaded not guilty, and the complainant declined to proceed, stating he meant to bring an action, those proceedings were held to constitute a hearing: *Tunnicliffe v Tedd* (1848) 5 CB 553. Similarly, where a complainant purported to withdraw the summons and the accused appeared and asked for a certificate, which was granted, further proceedings were barred: *Vaughton v Bradshaw* (1860) 9 CBNS 103; cf *Reed v Nutt* (1890) 24 QBD 669, DC (where the certificate was held to be no bar to a subsequent action, since there had been no hearing on the merits); *Ellis v Burton* [1975] 1 All ER 395, [1975] 1 WLR 386, DC (wrong to issue certificate after plea of guilty).
3 On dismissal of the information the justices must forthwith deliver a certificate of dismissal to the accused (Offences against the Person Act 1861 s 44 (amended by the Criminal Justice Act 1988 s 170, Sch 15 paras 2, 3, Sch 16); Magistrates' Courts Act 1980 s 50). The certificate is a valid bar to an action for assault although not applied for when the summons was heard and not drawn up until after the parties had left: *Hancock v Somes* (1859) 1 E & E 795. The certificate must be delivered 'forthwith' on demand, not on dismissal (*Costar v Hetherington* (1859) 1 E & E 802); and it should state the grounds on which the charge is dismissed (*Skuse v Davis* (1839) 10 Ad & El 635).
   An employer's disciplinary inquiry into an employee's alleged misconduct does not fall within the ambit of the Offences against the Person Act 1861 s 45 (as amended: see note 5 infra); and a certificate of acquittal does not release the employee from such an inquiry: *Saeed v Inner London Education Authority* [1985] ICR 637.
4 *Masper v Brown* (1876) 1 CPD 97.
5 Offences against the Person Act 1861 s 45 (amended by the Criminal Justice Act 1988 Sch 15 paras 2, 4); Criminal Justice Act 1948 s 1 (2); Powers of Criminal Courts Act 1973 s 13 (4) (a) (amended by the Criminal Justice Act 1982 s 77, Sch 14 para 31). Although the charge may have been of a simple assault, the certificate of dismissal or the conviction is a bar to an indictment for a more serious assault arising out of the same transaction (*R v Walker* (1843) 2 Mood & R 446; *R v Elrington* (1861) 1 B & S 688; *Holden v King* (1876) 46 LJQB 75; *R v Miles* (1890) 24 QBD 423, CCR), but not to an indictment for manslaughter if the person assaulted subsequently dies (*R v Morris* (1867) LR 1 CCR 90) nor probably to an indictment for rape (see *R v Miles* supra at 433 (obiter) per Hawkins J). On conviction for unlawful wounding, the imposition of a sentence of imprisonment and payment to the plaintiff of a sum of money for costs and allowances for loss of time is no bar to an action for damages for bodily suffering, permanent injury and medical expenses arising out of the same assault: *Lowe v Horwarth* (1865) 13 LT 297. The conviction of an employee does not operate as a release of the employer: *Dyer v Munday* [1895] 1 QB 742. As to the effect of the bar on appeals see *Magee v Storey* [1929] NI 134, CA.
   A conviction followed by the accused's entering into recognisances is not sufficient to establish a bar: *Hartley v Hindmarsh* (1866) LR 1 CP 553; *Murray v Fitzpatrick* (1914) 78 JP Jo 521; *Gibbons v Harris* (1956) 106 L Jo 828, County Court. Cf *Jones v Lamond* (1935) 79 Sol Jo 859, CA.

(x) Female Circumcision

503. Female circumcision. Any person who (1) excises, infibulates or otherwise mutilates the whole or any part of the labia majora or labia minora or clitoris of another person; or (2) aids, abets, counsels or procures the performance by another person of any of those acts on that other person's own body, is guilty of an offence and liable on conviction on indictment to imprisonment for a term not exceeding five years or a fine, or to both, or on summary conviction to imprisonment for a term not exceeding six months or a fine not exceeding the statutory maximum, or to both[1].

The provisions in head (1) above do not, however, render unlawful the performance of a surgical operation if that operation (a) is necessary for the physical or mental health[2] of the person on whom it is performed and is performed by a registered medical practitioner; or (b) is performed on a person who is in any stage of labour or has just given birth and is so performed for purposes connected with that labour or birth by a registered medical practitioner or registered midwife or a person undergoing a course of training with a view to becoming a registered medical practitioner or a registered midwife[3].

1 Prohibition of Female Circumcision Act 1985 s 1. For the meaning of 'the statutory maximum' see para 806 post. As to procedural provisions applying where an offence involving infliction of bodily harm on a child or young person is charged see para 882 post.
2 In determining for these purposes whether an operation is necessary for the mental health of a person, no account is to be taken of the effect on that person of any belief on the part of that or any other person that the operation is required as a matter of custom or ritual: ibid s 2 (2). As to the public policy considerations limiting the ability to consent to the infliction of bodily harm see para 23 note 8 ante.
3 Ibid s 2 (1).

(xi) Torture

504. Torture. If, in the United Kingdom or elsewhere, a public official or person acting in an official capacity, whatever his nationality, intentionally inflicts severe pain or suffering[1] on another in the performance or purported performance of his official duties, he is guilty of an offence and liable on conviction on indictment to imprisonment for life or for any shorter term[2].

If any person, whatever his nationality, not being a public official or person acting in an official capacity, (1) in the United Kingdom or elsewhere intentionally inflicts severe pain or suffering on another at the instigation or with the consent or acquiescence of a public official or of a person acting in an official capacity; and (2) the official or other person is performing or purporting to perform his official duties when he instigates the commission of the offence or consents to or acquiesces in it, he is guilty of an offence and liable on conviction on indictment to imprisonment for life or for any shorter term[3].

It is, however, a defence for a person charged with an offence under the above provisions in respect of any conduct of his to prove that he had lawful authority, justification or excuse[4] for that conduct[5].

1 For the purposes of the Criminal Justice Act 1988 s 134, it is immaterial whether the pain or suffering is physical or mental and whether it is caused by an act or an omission: s 134 (3).
2 Ibid s 134 (1), (6). Proceedings for an offence under s 134 may not be begun except by or with the consent of the Attorney General: s 135 (a). As to the effect of this limitation see para 639 post. Sections 134, 135 extend, with the appropriate modifications and exceptions, to the Isle of Man: Criminal Justice Act 1988 (Torture) (Isle of Man) Order 1989, SI 1989/983, art 2, Schedule.
3 Ibid s 134 (2), (6). As to the restriction on the institution of proceedings see note 2 supra.
4 For these purposes, 'lawful authority, justification or excuse' means (1) in relation to pain or suffering inflicted in the United Kingdom, lawful authority, justification or excuse under the law of the part of the United Kingdom where it was inflicted; (2) in relation to pain or suffering inflicted outside the United Kingdom (a) if it was inflicted by a United Kingdom official acting under the law of the United Kingdom or by a person acting in an official capacity under that law, lawful authority, justification or excuse under that law; (b) if it was inflicted by a United Kingdom official acting under the law of any part of the United Kingdom or by a person acting in an official capacity under such law, lawful authority, justification or excuse under the law of the part of the United Kingdom under whose law he was acting; or (c) in any other case, lawful authority, justification or excuse under the law of the place where it was inflicted: ibid s 134 (5).
5 Ibid s 134 (4).

(3) SEXUAL OFFENCES

(i) Unnatural Offences

505. Buggery. At common law it is an indictable offence for a person to commit buggery[1] with an animal or with another person. It is also a statutory offence for a person to commit buggery[2] with another person or with an animal[3]; but it is not an offence for a man to commit buggery with another man in private if both parties consent and have attained the age of 21 years[4]. There are four statutory offences:

(1) buggery with a boy under the age of 16, with a woman or with an animal;

(2) buggery by a man with another man of or over the age of 16 without that other's consent;

(3) buggery by a man of or over the age of 21 with another man under the age of 21 with that other's consent;

(4) buggery by a man with another man with that other's consent where both men are under the age of 21 or both men have attained the age of 21 but the act is not committed in private[5].

Except where otherwise specifically provided[6], consent is no defence[7] and a person who consents to the commission of buggery upon him is also guilty of the offence[8].

There is an irrebuttable presumption of law that a boy under 14 cannot commit buggery[9], although a man who induces a boy under that age to commit buggery with him is guilty of the offence[10]. Where the accused is charged with committing this offence with a consenting party, that party is an accomplice[11] and the jury should be warned that it is dangerous to convict on his uncorroborated evidence[12].

A person guilty of such an offence is liable on conviction on indictment:

(a) in the case of an offence under head (1) above, to imprisonment for life or for any shorter term; and in the case of an attempt to commit an offence under head (1) above, to imprisonment for a term not exceeding ten years[13];

(b) in the case of an offence under head (2) above, to imprisonment for a term not exceeding ten years[14];

(c) in the case of an offence under head (3) above, to imprisonment for a term not exceeding five years[15];

(d) in the case of an offence under head (4) above, to imprisonment for a term not exceeding two years[15].

Where either of the men concerned was under 21 years of age at the time the offence was committed, proceedings in respect of buggery or for aiding, abetting, counselling, procuring or commanding buggery may be instituted only by or with the consent of the Director of Public Prosecutions[16]. No proceedings for an offence of buggery by a man with another man not amounting to an assault on that other man and not being an offence by a man with a boy under the age of 16 may be commenced after the expiration of 12 months from the date on which that offence was committed[17].

1 Buggery consists in sexual intercourse per anum by a man with a man or a woman (*R v Wiseman* (1718) Fortes Rep 91; *R v Reekspear* (1832) 1 Mood CC 342; *R v Barron* [1914] 2 KB 570 at 576, 10 Cr App Rep 81 at 89, CCA) or per anum or per vaginam by a man or a woman with an animal (*R v Cozins* (1834) 6 C & P 351; *R v Brown* (1889) 24 QBD 357, CCA; *R v Bourne* (1952) 36 Cr App Rep 125, CCA). Buggery and rape are separate offences; there is no offence of rape per anum: *R v Gaston* (1981) 73 Cr App Rep 164, CA. Buggery may be committed by a man with his wife: *R v Jellyman* (1838) 8 C & P 604. Other unnatural forms of sexual intercourse do not amount to buggery: *R v Jacobs* (1817) Russ & Ry 331, CCR.

2 'Buggery' is not defined by statute and its elements are governed by the common law: see note 1 supra.

3 Sexual Offences Act 1956 s 12 (1). As to proof of sexual intercourse see para 378 note 2 ante. See also *R v Reekspear* (1832) 1 Mood CC 342. Where an indictment contains counts for indecency offences against males and females, the counts should not ordinarily be tried together: see *R v Sims* [1946] KB 531, 31 Cr App Rep 158, CCA and para 933 post. As to evidence in buggery charges see note 12 infra. An acquittal on a charge of buggery is no bar to a subsequent trial for gross indecency: see *R v Barron* [1914] 2 KB 570, 10 Cr App Rep 81, CCA. As to gross indecency see para 506 post. As to buggery with men patients committed by officers etc of a hospital or home see the Mental Health Act 1959 s 128 (amended by the National Health Service Act 1977 s 129, Sch 15 para 29, Sch 16; the Mental Health Act 1983 s 148 (1), Sch 4 para 15; the Registered Homes Act 1984 s 57 (1), Sch 1 para 2), applied by the Sexual Offences Act 1967 s 1 (4) and MENTAL HEALTH vol 30 para 1107. As to assault with intent to commit buggery see para 509 post.

4 See para 507 post. In any proceedings for such an offence committed between men it is for the prosecution to prove that these three conditions are not satisfied: see para 507 note 5 post.

5 Sexual Offences Act 1956 ss 12 (1), 37 (1), (2), Sch 2 para 3 (a) (amended by the Courts Act 1971 s 56 (4), Sch 11 Pt IV); Criminal Justice Act 1967 s 12 (5) (a); Sexual Offences Act 1967 s 3; *R v Courtie* [1984] AC 463, 78 Cr App Rep 292, HL. References to a person's age, in relation to heads (2)–(4) supra, are references to his age at the time of the commission of the offence: Sexual Offences Act 1967 s 3 (3). As to proof of age see para 1156 post.

6 Ie where ibid s 1 (1) applies: see note 4 supra.

7 Consent may, however, affect sentence: *R v Reakes* [1974] Crim LR 615, CA.

8 See Co Inst 59; 1 Hale PC 670; 1 East PC 480.

9 See *R v Tatam* (1921) 15 Cr App Rep 132, CCA.

10 *R v Allen* (1849) 1 Den 364, CCA.

11 Whether a boy under 14 can be an accomplice even when there is evidence of his guilty knowledge appears doubtful: see *R v Cratchley* (1913) 9 Cr App Rep 232, CCA; *R v Tatam* (1921) 15 Cr App Rep 132, CCA.

12 *R v Jellyman* (1838) 8 C & P 604; *R v Tate* [1908] 2 KB 680, 1 Cr App Rep 39, CCA; and see para 1142 post. As to corroboration see paras 1142, 1143 post; as to the competence and compellability of the accused's spouse as a witness see para 1184 post; as to the evidence of children see paras 1178, 1179 post; as to the admissibility of similar fact evidence see, with regard to homosexual offences, *DPP v Boardman* [1975] AC 421, 60 Cr App Rep 165, HL; and see generally paras 1091–1097 post; as to cases of buggery in which similar fact evidence has been admitted see para 1096 note 7 post; and as to the procedural provisions applying where buggery or attempted buggery with a child or young person is charged see para 882 post.

13 Sexual Offences Act 1956 s 37 (1), (3), Sch 2 para 3 (a), (b). As to the factors which may need to be taken into account when sentencing a man for buggery with a boy under 16 see *R v Willis* [1975] 1 All ER 620, 60 Cr App Rep 146, CA; *R v Gooden* [1980] Crim LR 250, CA (indecent assault case).

   Nothing in the Sexual Offences Act 1956 or Sch 2 excludes, in relation to offences under ss 1–36, the application of (1) the Magistrates' Courts Act 1980 s 24 (summary trial of young offenders for indictable offences: see INFANTS vol 24 para 898:10); (2) s 121 (5) (limitation of punishment which may be imposed by single justice etc: see MAGISTRATES vol 29 para 239); (3) any enactment or rule of law restricting a court's power to imprison; (4) any enactment or rule of law authorising an offender to be dealt with in a way not authorised by the enactments specially relating to his offence; (5) any enactment or rule of law authorising a jury to find a person guilty of an offence other than that with which he is charged: Sexual Offences Act 1956 s 37 (7) (amended by the Magistrates' Courts Act 1980 s 154 (1), Sch 7 para 17).

14 Sexual Offences Act 1967 s 3 (1) (a). As to attempt see para 71 et seq ante.

15 Ibid s 3 (1) (b). See also note 14 supra.

16 Ibid s 8 (amended by the Criminal Jurisdiction Act 1975 s 14 (5), Sch 6 Pt I; and the Criminal Attempts Act 1981 s 10, Schedule Pt I). The limitation applies to proceedings before courts-martial: *Secretary of State for Defence v Warn* [1970] AC 394, 52 Cr App Rep 366, HL. As to the effect of this limitation see para 639 post. Proceedings for incitement to commit buggery are not subject to the limitation: *R v Assistant Recorder of Kingston-upon-Hull, ex p Morgan* [1969] 2 QB 58, [1969] 1 All ER 416, DC.

17 Sexual Offences Act 1967 s 7 (1), (2) (c). The Sexual Offences Act 1956 s 46 (interpretation of 'man', 'boy' and other expressions: see para 378 notes 3, 6 ante) applies for the purposes of the provisions of the Sexual Offences Act 1967 as it applies for the purposes of the provisions of the Sexual Offences Act 1956: Sexual Offences Act 1967 s 11 (3).

In every case to which s 7 (1) applies the judge need not direct the jury that it must be sure the offence was committed within the prescribed period; but he must do so where an issue under s 7 (1) is raised by the defence or where it clearly arises on the evidence: *R v Lewis* [1979] 2 All ER 665, 68 Cr App Rep 310, CA.

There is no statutory time limit for prosecutions involving buggery with animals but delay in prosecution may be a ground for directing acquittal: see *R v Robins* (1844) 1 Cox CC 114.

506. Gross indecency between men. It is an offence[1] for a man[2]:
  (1) to commit an act of gross indecency with[3] another man whether in public or private; or
  (2) to be a party to the commission by a man of such an act with another man; or
  (3) to procure[4] the commission by a man of such an act with another man[5].

It is not an offence, however, for a man to commit an act of gross indecency with another man in private if both parties consent and have attained the age of 21 years[6]. Nor is it an offence for a man to be a party to the commission[6], or to procure the commission with himself[7], of an act of gross indecency which by virtue of the above exception[8] is not an offence.

A person guilty of any such offence or an attempt to commit an offence under head (3) above is liable on conviction on indictment to imprisonment for a term not exceeding two years; but the maximum term of imprisonment which may be imposed on conviction on indictment of a man of or over the age of 21 of committing an act of gross indecency with another man under that age or of being a party to or procuring or attempting to procure the commission by a man under that age of such an act with another man is imprisonment for a term of five years[9]. A person guilty of any such offence is liable on summary conviction to imprisonment for a term not exceeding six months or a fine not exceeding the prescribed sum, or to both[10]. Where either of the men was at the time of the commission of the offence under 21, proceedings for the offence or for aiding, abetting, counselling, procuring or commanding the commission of the offence may not be instituted except by or with the consent of the Director of Public Prosecutions[11]. No proceedings for the above offences may be commenced after the expiration of 12 months from the date on which the offence was committed[12].

1 On the authority of *R v Courtie* [1984] AC 463, 78 Cr App Rep 292, HL (see para 505 note 5 ante), the Sexual Offences Act 1956 s 13 creates more than one offence by reference to the differential penalties that may be imposed: see infra.
2 For the meaning of 'man' see para 505 note 17 ante.
3 The word 'with' is to be construed so that the participation of two men is necessary; it is no such offence if the act is directed towards another without his consent; a man who commits a public act of indecency without the participation of another man may be prosecuted under other provisions of the law, eg indecent exposure (see para 372 ante) and public nuisance (see para 418 ante): *R v Preece, R v Howells* [1977] QB 370, 63 Cr App Rep 28, CA, applying *R v Hornby and Peaple* [1946] 2 All ER 487, 32 Cr App Rep 1, CCA and *R v Hunt* [1950] 2 All ER 291, 34 Cr App Rep 135, CCA and not following *R v Hall* [1964] 1 QB 273, 47 Cr App Rep 253, CCA ('with' means 'against' or 'directed towards' rather than 'with the consent of'; a man may be convicted of such an offence although the other was not a consenting party). It is not essential that there is actual physical contact between the two persons: *R v Hunt* supra. Two persons charged with committing an act of gross indecency must be proved to have been acting in concert (*R v Hornby and Peaple* supra), but it is possible that one may be convicted and the other acquitted (*R v Pearce* [1951] 1 All ER 493, 35 Cr App Rep 17, CCA). A man who persuades a boy to handle him indecently may alone be convicted: *R v Burrows* [1952] 1 All ER 58n, 35 Cr App Rep 180, CCA.
4 Unless the Sexual Offences Act 1967 s 1 (1) (see para 507 post) applies, this includes an accused's procuring the commission of the act with himself: *R v Jones* [1896] 1 QB 4, CCR. Since procuring

the commission of acts of gross indecency is a substantive offence, it is possible to attempt the same; the Criminal Attempts Act 1981 s 1 (4) (b) (see para 71 ante) does not preclude such a charge: *Chief Constable of Hampshire v Mace* (1987) 84 Cr App Rep 40, DC. As to what constitutes an attempt to procure an act of gross indecency see *R v Miskell* [1954] 1 All ER 137, 37 Cr App Rep 214, C–MAC; *R v Gammon* (1959) 43 Cr App Rep 155, CCA; *R v Cope* (1921) 86 JP 78, 16 Cr App Rep 77, CCA. Cf *R v Woods* (1930) 143 LT 311, 22 Cr App Rep 41, CCA. A person may be convicted of inciting to procure the commission of an act of gross indecency although the persons to be procured are not specified individuals: *R v Bentley* [1923] 1 KB 403, CCA.

5 Sexual Offences Act 1956 s 13. As to corroboration see paras 1141–1145 post; as to the competence and compellability of the accused's spouse as a witness see para 1184 post; as to children's evidence see paras 1178, 1179 post; as to admission of similar fact evidence see paras 1091–1097 post and particularly *DPP v Boardman* [1975] AC 421, 60 Cr App Rep 165, HL; and as to procedural provisions applying where offences are committed against children and young persons see para 882 post. As to gross indecency with men patients committed by male officers etc of a hospital or home see the Mental Health Act 1959 s 128 (amended by the Health Service Act 1977 s 129, Sch 15 para 29, Sch 16; the Mental Health Act 1983 s 148 (1), Sch 4 para 15; the Registered Homes Act 1984 s 57 (1), Sch 1 para 2) (applied by the Sexual Offences Act 1967 s 1 (4)) and MENTAL HEALTH vol 30 para 1107. An act of gross indecency with a child under the age of 14 is chargeable as a separate offence: see para 523 post.

6 See para 507 post.

7 Sexual Offences Act 1967 s 4 (3).

8 See notes 6, 7 supra.

9 Sexual Offences Act 1956 s 37 (1), (3), Sch 2 para 16; Sexual Offences Act 1967 s 3 (2), (4); and see para 505 note 13 ante. As to attempts generally see the Criminal Attempts Act 1981 Pt I (ss 1–7) and para 71 et seq ante. References to a person's age are to his age at the time the offence was committed: s 3 (3). As to proof of age see para 1156 post.

10 Sexual Offences Act 1956 s 37 (1), (3), Sch 2; Magistrates' Courts Act 1980 s 17 (1), Sch 1. See para 804 post. For the meaning of 'the prescribed sum' see para 807 post.

11 Sexual Offences Act 1967 s 8 (amended by the Criminal Jurisdiction Act 1975 s 14 (5), Sch 6 Pt I; the Criminal Attempts Act 1981 s 10, Schedule Pt I). As to the effect of this limitation see para 639 post. As to attempts see para 71 et seq ante; and as to proceedings before courts-martial see para 505 note 16 ante.

12 Sexual Offences Act 1967 s 7 (1), (2) (a). There is no compliance with s 7 (1) where the evidence suggests the offence might have been committed more than 12 months before the commencement of the proceedings: *R v Lewis* [1979] 2 All ER 665, 68 Cr App Rep 310, CA.

507. Homosexual acts in private by consenting adults. A homosexual act[1] in private[2] is not an offence[3] provided the parties consent[4] to it and have attained the age of 21 years[5]. It continues to be (1) an offence under statute[6] and at common law for a man to commit buggery with another man in circumstances in which it would not otherwise be an offence; and (2) an offence[7] for a man[8] to commit an act of gross indecency with another man, or to be a party to the commission by a man of such an act, in such circumstances, provided that the act charged is done on a United Kingdom merchant ship[9], wherever it may be, by a man who is a member of the crew[10] of that ship with another man who is a member of the crew of that or any other United Kingdom merchant ship[11]. The statutory exception does not prevent an act from being an offence, other than a civil offence, under naval, military or air force law[12].

1 For these purposes, a man is treated as doing a homosexual act if, and only if, he commits buggery with another man or commits an act of gross indecency with another man or is a party to the commission by a man of such an act: Sexual Offences Act 1967 s 1 (7).

2 An act which would otherwise be treated for the purposes of the Sexual Offences Act 1967 as being done in private is not to be so treated if done (1) when more than two persons take part or are present; or (2) in a lavatory to which the public has or is permitted to have access, whether on payment or otherwise: s 1 (2). Whether the act was done in private is not tested subjectively: *R v Reakes* [1974] Crim LR 615, CA (trial judge's direction 'you look at all the surrounding circumstances, the time of night, the nature of the place including such matters as lighting and you consider further the

likelihood of a third person coming upon the scene' approved; conviction upheld; buggery in an enclosed, unlit 'private' yard at about 1 am).

3 Ie notwithstanding any statutory or common law provision: see paras 505, 506 ante.

4 The issue of consent is one for the jury: *R v Reakes* [1974] Crim LR 615, CA. Although a man who is suffering from severe mental handicap cannot in law give any consent which would prevent a homosexual act from being an offence, a person may not be convicted, on account of the incapacity of such a man to consent, of an offence consisting of such an act if he proves that he did not know and had no reason to suspect that man to be suffering from severe mental handicap: Sexual Offences Act 1967 s 1 (3) (amended by the Mental Health (Amendment) Act 1982 s 65 (1), (2), Sch 3 Pt 1 para 34 (a), Sch 4 Pt 1). For these purposes, 'severe mental handicap' means a state of arrested or incomplete development of mind which includes severe impairment of intelligence and social functioning: Sexual Offences Act 1967 s 1 (3A) (added by the Mental Health (Amendment) Act 1982 s 65 (1), Sch 3 Pt I para 34 (b)). Cf the meaning of 'defective' in the Sexual Offences Act 1956 s 45 (as substituted and amended): see para 378 note 7 ante.

It is open to the prosecutor to support his case not by calling a medical expert to give evidence of the complainant's mental state but by inviting the jury to observe the behaviour and reactions of the complainant and to draw what the jury considers to be an appropriate inference: *R v Robbins* [1988] Crim LR 744, CA.

5 Sexual Offences Act 1967 s 1 (1). Where in any proceedings it is charged that a homosexual act is an offence, the prosecutor has the burden of proving that the act was done otherwise than in private or otherwise than with the consent of the parties or that any of the parties had not attained the age of 21 years: s 1 (6).

6 Ie under the Sexual Offences Act 1956 s 12: see para 505 ante. .

7 For the meaning of 'man' see para 505 note 17 ante.

8 Ie under the Sexual Offences Act 1956 s 13: see para 506 ante.

9 For these purposes, 'United Kingdom merchant ship' means a ship registered in the United Kingdom (see SHIPPING vol 43 para 147 et seq) habitually used or used at the time of the act charged for the purposes of carrying passengers or goods for reward: Sexual Offences Act 1967 s 2 (3).

10 'Member of the crew', in relation to a ship, includes the master of the ship and any apprentice to the sea service serving in that ship: ibid s 2 (3).

11 Ibid s 2 (1), (2).

12 Ibid s 1 (5); and see ROYAL FORCES vol 41 para 428.

508. Procuring a lawful act of buggery. A man[1] who procures another man to commit with a third man an act of buggery which is not an offence[2] commits an offence and is liable on conviction on indictment to imprisonment for a term not exceeding two years, or on summary conviction to imprisonment for a term not exceeding six months or a fine not exceeding the prescribed sum, or to both[3].

1 For the meaning of 'man' see para 505 note 17 ante.

2 Ie by reason of the Sexual Offences Act 1967 s 1: see para 507 ante.

3 Ibid s 4 (1); Magistrates' Courts Act 1980 ss 17, 32 (1), Sch 1 para 27. See para 804 post. For the meaning of 'the prescribed sum' see para 807 post. Procuring the commission of a lawful act of gross indecency with a third man is an offence under the Sexual Offences Act 1956 s 13: see para 506 ante.

509. Assault with intent to commit buggery. It is an offence for a person to assault[1] another person with intent to commit buggery[2]. A person guilty of such an offence is liable on conviction on indictment to imprisonment for a term not exceeding ten years[3].

1 For the meaning of 'assault' see para 488 notes 1, 6 ante.

2 Sexual Offences Act 1956 s 16 (1). For the meaning of 'buggery' see para 505 note 1 ante. As to corroboration of the victim's evidence see para 1142 post; as to the competence and compellability of the accused's spouse as a witness see para 1184 post; as to children's evidence see paras 1178, 1179 post; and as to procedural provisions applying to offences against children and young persons see para 882 post.

3 Sexual Offences Act 1956 s 37 (1), (3), Sch 2 para 19 (amended by the Courts Act 1971 s 56 (4), Sch 11 Pt IV); and see para 505 note 13 ante.

(ii) Incest

510. Incest by a man. It is an offence for a man[1] to have sexual intercourse[2] with a woman[3] whom he knows to be his granddaughter, daughter, sister[4] or mother[5]. It is immaterial that sexual intercourse took place with the consent of the woman[6]. A prosecution for the offence may not be commenced except by or with the consent of the Director of Public Prosecutions[7]; and the same restriction applies to the institution of proceedings for an attempt to commit the offence[8].

On an indictment for the offence the jury may find the accused guilty of sexual intercourse with a girl under 13[9] or with a girl between 13 and 16[10]. A person guilty of such an offence is liable on conviction on indictment (1) if the offence is committed with a girl under the age of 13, and the accused is so charged in the indictment, to imprisonment for life or any shorter term; and (2) otherwise, to imprisonment for a term not exceeding seven years[11]. An attempt to commit such an offence is also an offence and a person guilty of such an attempt is liable on conviction on indictment (a) if the offence is committed with a girl under the age of 13, and the accused is so charged in the indictment, to imprisonment for a term not exceeding seven years; and (b) otherwise, to imprisonment for a term not exceeding two years[12].

1 For the meaning of 'man' see para 378 note 3 ante.
2 For the meaning of 'sexual intercourse' see para 378 note 2 ante.
3 For the meaning of 'woman' see para 378 note 6 ante.
4 For these purposes, 'sister' includes half-sister; and any expression importing a relationship between two people is to be taken to apply notwithstanding that the relationship is not traced through lawful wedlock: Sexual Offences Act 1956 s 10 (2).
5 Ibid s 10 (1). An adoption order does not bring the adopter and the adopted person within the ambit of the law of incest or affect the status of persons for these purposes: see the Adoption Act 1976 s 47 (1).

   A count charging that offences have been committed on divers days between dates several months apart is bad for duplicity: *R v Thompson* [1914] 2 KB 99, 9 Cr App Rep 252, CCA; see further para 931 post. As to the proper course where the accused pleads guilty to a single act of incest, and the trial judge suspects that there may have been a series of acts of incest, see *R v Huchison* [1972] 1 All ER 936, 56 Cr App Rep 307, CA.

   It is for the prosecution to prove not only that the relevant relationship existed, but also that the accused was aware of it at the time of commission of the offence: *R v Carmichael* [1940] 1 KB 630 at 634, 27 Cr App Rep 183 at 189, CCA. An admission by the accused may be sufficient proof: *R v Jones* (1933) 24 Cr App Rep 55, CCA. In the case of a child born during marriage the presumption of legitimacy prevails in the absence of evidence of non-access: *R v Hemmings* [1939] 1 All ER 417, 27 Cr App Rep 46, CCA. In *R v —* (1919) Times, 20 June, a person charged with incest with a person who was alleged to be his daughter, but who was born two months after his marriage to her mother, was allowed to prove that he was not her father. Where the accused was aware of the relationship at the time of commission of the offence, but was under a mistake of fact as to the identity of the person with whom he had intercourse, this may afford a defence: *R v Baillie-Smith* (1976) 64 Cr App Rep 76, CA (father had intercourse with daughter thinking he was in bed with wife). As to the admission of similar fact evidence on charges of incest see para 1096 post; and as to the competence and compellability of the accused's spouse as a witness see para 1184 post.

   As to the course to be adopted when the daughter before trial retracts her allegations against her father see *R v Baillie-Smith* supra.
6 If the act is committed with consent and the woman is called as a witness for the prosecution, her evidence requires corroboration as she is an accomplice: *R v Stone* (1910) 6 Cr App Rep 89, CCA; *R v Draper* (1929) 21 Cr App Rep 147, CCA; as to the corroboration of the evidence of accomplices see para 1143 post. There is a distinction between submission and permission, and the latter is necessary to establish guilt on her part: *R v Dimes* (1911) 76 JP 47, 7 Cr App Rep 43, CCA.

   Where a brother and sister were charged with incest in separate counts of the same indictment, but were tried separately, the acquittal of the sister did not invalidate the conviction of the brother: see *R*

v Gordon (1925) 19 Cr App Rep 20, CCA. See also *R v King* (1920) 15 Cr App Rep 13, CCA. As to the offence committed by a woman who permits incest see para 512 post.
7 Sexual Offences Act 1956 s 37 (1), (2), Sch 2 para 14 (a) (amended by the Criminal Law Act 1977 s 65 (4), Sch 12). As to the effect of this limitation see para 639 post.
8 Sexual Offences Act 1956 Sch 2 para 14 (b) (amended by the Criminal Law Act 1977 Sch 12). See note 7 supra.
9 Ie under the Sexual Offences Act 1956 s 5: see para 526 post.
10 Ibid s 37 (1), (4), Sch 2 para 14 (a) (amended by the Criminal Law Act 1967 s 10 (2), Sch 3 Pt III). As to sexual intercourse with a girl under the age of 16 see the Sexual Offences Act 1956 s 6 and para 527 post. As to alternative verdicts see further para 1029 post.
11 Ibid s 37 (1), (3), Sch 2 para 14 (a). See also para 505 note 13 ante. As to procedural provisions applying to offences under s 10, and attempts to commit such offences, committed against children or young persons see para 882 post; and as to orders divesting the offender of authority over the girl see para 513 post.
    For sentencing guidelines in cases of incest see *A-G's Reference (No 1 of 1989)* [1989] 3 All ER 571, [1989] 1 WLR 1117, CA.
12 Sexual Offences Act 1956 s 37 (1)–(3), Sch 2 para 14 (b) (amended by the Indecency with Children Act 1960 s 2 (3); the Courts Act 1971 s 56 (4), Sch 11 Pt IV). See also the Indecency with Children Act 1960 s 2 (2).

511. Inciting girl under sixteen to have incestuous sexual intercourse. It is an offence for a man[1] to incite to have sexual intercourse with him a girl under the age of 16 whom he knows to be his granddaughter, daughter or sister[2]. A person guilty of such an offence is liable on conviction on indictment to imprisonment for a term not exceeding two years, or on summary conviction to imprisonment for a term not exceeding six months or a fine not exceeding the prescribed sum, or to both[3].

1 For these purposes, 'man' includes boy: Criminal Law Act 1977 s 54 (2).
2 Ibid s 54 (1). For these purposes, 'sister' includes half-sister; and any expression importing a relationship between two people is to be taken to apply notwithstanding that the relationship is not traced through lawful wedlock: s 54 (2).
3 Ibid s 54 (4) (amended by the Magistrates' Courts Act 1980 s 32 (2)). For the meaning of 'the prescribed sum' see para 807 post.
    The Children and Young Persons Act 1933 s 1 (3) (see para 537 post) applies in relation to offences under the Criminal Law Act 1977 s 54 (as so amended): s 54 (3) (amended by the Police and Criminal Evidence Act 1984 s 119 (2), Sch 7 Pt V). As to the competence and compellability of the accused's spouse as a witness see para 1184 post; as to proof of age see para 1156 post; and as to corroboration of the victim's evidence see para 1142 post.

512. Incest by a woman. It is an offence for a woman[1] of the age of 16 or over[2] to permit a man[3] whom she knows to be her grandfather, father, brother[4] or son to have sexual intercourse[5] with her by her consent[6].

A prosecution for this offence may not be commenced except by or with the consent of the Director of Public Prosecutions[7]. The same restriction applies to the institution of proceedings for an attempt to commit this offence[8].

A person guilty of such an offence is liable on conviction on indictment to imprisonment for a term not exceeding seven years[9]. An attempt to commit such an offence is also an indictable offence and a person guilty of such an attempt is liable on conviction on indictment to imprisonment for a term not exceeding two years[10].

1 For the meaning of 'woman' see para 378 note 6 ante.
2 As to proof of age see para 1156 post.
3 For the meaning of 'man' see para 378 note 3 ante.

4 For these purposes, 'brother' includes half-brother; and any expression importing a relationship between two people is to be taken to apply notwithstanding that the relationship is not traced through lawful wedlock: Sexual Offences Act 1956 s 11 (2). See further para 510 note 4 ante.

5 For the meaning of 'sexual intercourse' see para 378 note 2 ante.

6 Sexual Offences Act 1956 s 11 (1). As to the effect of adoption on this prohibition see para 510 note 5 ante. There is a distinction between submission and permission, and the latter is necessary to establish consent: *R v Dimes* (1911) 76 JP 47, 7 Cr App Rep 43, CCA.

7 Sexual Offences Act 1956 s 37 (1), (2), Sch 2 para 15 (a) (amended by the Criminal Law Act 1977 s 65 (4)). As to the effect of this limitation see para 639 post.

8 Sexual Offences Act 1956 Sch 2 para 15 (b) (amended by the Criminal Law Act 1977 Sch 12). See note 7 supra.

9 Sexual Offences Act 1956 s 37 (1), (3), Sch 2 para 15 (a). See also para 505 note 13 ante. As to procedural provisions applying to offences under s 11, and attempts to commit such offences, committed against children or young persons see para 882 post; as to the competence and compellability of the accused's spouse as a witness see para 1184 post; and as to orders divesting the offender of authority over the boy see para 513 post. As to corroboration of the victim's evidence see para 1142 post.

10 Ibid s 37 (1)–(3), Sch 2 para 15 (b) (amended by the Courts Act 1971 s 56 (4), Sch 11 Pt IV).

513. Guardianship of victim of incest. On a person's conviction of incest against a girl under the age of 18[1] or against a boy under that age[2], or of attempting to commit such an offence, the court may by order divest that person of all authority over the girl or boy[3]. If that person is the guardian of the girl or boy, such an order may remove that person from the guardianship[4]; and it may appoint a person to be the guardian of the girl or boy during his or her minority or any less period[5].

1 Ie an offence under the Sexual Offences Act 1956 s 10: see para 510 ante. As to proof of age see para 1156 post.

2 Ie an offence under ibid s 11: see para 512 ante.

3 Ibid s 38 (1) (substituted by the Guardianship Act 1973 ss 1 (8), 15 (3), Sch 1). An order under the Sexual Offences Act 1956 s 38 may be varied from time to time or rescinded by the High Court; and, if such an order is made on conviction of an offence against a girl or boy who is a defective, it may, so far as it has effect for any of the purposes of the Mental Health Act 1983, be rescinded either before or after the defective has attained the age of 18: Sexual Offences Act 1956 s 38 (4) (substituted by the Guardianship Act 1973 ss 1 (8), 15 (3), Sch 1; amended by the Mental Health Act 1983 s 148, Sch 4 para 12). If an order divesting an offender of authority over a defective has been made and not rescinded, the person against whom the order was made may not be taken into account in ascertaining the nearest relative of the defective: see the Mental Health Act 1983 s 26 (5) (d); see further note 5 infra. For the meaning of 'defective' see para 378 note 7 ante.

4 Sexual Offences Act 1956 s 38 (2) (substituted by the Guardianship Act 1973 ss 1 (8), 15 (3), Sch 1).

5 Sexual Offences Act 1956 s 38 (3) (substituted by the Guardianship Act 1973 ss 1 (8), 15 (3), Sch 1). Where a patient who has not attained the age of 18 years is, by virtue of an order made under the Sexual Offences Act 1956 s 38, under the guardianship of a person who is not his nearest relative or is under the joint guardianship of two persons of whom one is not his nearest relative, the person or persons having the guardianship of the patient is or are deemed to be his nearest relative to the exclusion of any other person: see the Mental Health Act 1983 s 28 (1) (a). As to the nearest relatives of patients see ss 26, 28, 148, Sch 5 para 11 and MENTAL HEALTH.

(iii) Rape

514. Rape. It is an offence for a man[1] to rape a woman[2]. For these purposes, a man commits rape if (1) he has unlawful sexual intercourse[3] with a woman who at the time of the intercourse does not consent to it; and (2) at the time he knows that she does not consent to the intercourse or he is reckless as to whether she consents to it[4]. If at a trial for a rape offence[5] the jury has to consider whether a man believed that a woman was consenting to sexual intercourse, the presence or absence of reasonable grounds for such a belief is a matter to which the jury is to have regard, in conjunction with any other relevant matters, in considering whether he so believed[6].

A man who induces a married woman to have sexual intercourse with him by impersonating her husband commits rape[7].

A person guilty of rape or attempted rape is liable on conviction on indictment to imprisonment for life or for any shorter term[8].

1　The Sexual Offences Act 1956 s 46 (meaning of 'man' and 'woman': see para 378 notes 3, 6 respectively ante) has effect as if the reference to that Act included a reference to the Sexual Offences (Amendment) Act 1976 (see infra): s 7 (2). As to the presumption that boys under 14 are incapable of having sexual intercourse see para 34 ante and para 516 post.

2　Sexual Offences Act 1956 s 1 (1). As to the power to convict of other offences on a charge of rape see para 519 post. For the meaning of 'woman' see note 1 supra.

3　References in the Sexual Offences (Amendment) Act 1976 to sexual intercourse are to be construed in accordance with the Sexual Offences Act 1956 s 44 (see para 516 post) so far as it relates to natural intercourse, under which such intercourse is deemed complete on proof of penetration only: Sexual Offences (Amendment) Act 1976 s 7 (2). Sexual intercourse is, however, a continuing act which ends only with withdrawal: see para 516 note 2 post. Sexual intercourse per anum is not rape: *R v Gaston* (1981) 73 Cr App Rep 164, CA.

4　Sexual Offences (Amendment) Act 1976 s 1 (1). Section 1 (1) gives statutory effect to the decision in *DPP v Morgan* [1976] AC 182, 61 Cr App Rep 136, HL, where the mens rea in rape was held to be the intention to have sexual intercourse with a woman without her consent, indifference or recklessness to whether the victim consented being sufficient. See further para 517 post. As to the mens rea in attempted rape see *R v Khan, R v Dhokia, R v Banga, R v Faiz* (1990) Times, 3 February, CA.

'Recklessness' as to whether the woman consents to sexual intercourse means being indifferent to the feelings and wishes of the victim and giving no thought to the possibility that she might not be consenting: *R v Satnam S, R v Kewal S* (1983) 78 Cr App Rep 149, CA, applying *R v Kimber* [1983] 3 All ER 316, 77 Cr App Rep 225, CA (a case of indecent assault); see also *R v Breckenridge* (1983) 79 Cr App Rep 244, CA; *R v Taylor* (1984) 80 Cr App Rep 327, CA.

The Sexual Offences (Amendment) Act 1976 s 1 is merely declaratory of the common law, so that it is not necessary for the prosecution to prove that the consent of the victim of sexual intercourse was vitiated by force, the fear of force or fraud, but merely that the victim did not in fact consent: *R v Olugboja* [1982] QB 320, 73 Cr App Rep 344, CA. As to the direction to the jury on the question of mistaken but genuine belief in consent see *R v Taylor* supra; *R v Haughian* (1985) 80 Cr App Rep 334, CA.

5　'A rape offence' means any of the following, namely rape, attempted rape, aiding, abetting, counselling and procuring rape or attempted rape, incitement to rape, conspiracy to rape and burglary with intent to rape: Sexual Offences (Amendment) Act 1976 s 7 (2) (amended by the Criminal Justice Act 1988 s 158 (6)).

6　Sexual Offences (Amendment) Act 1976 s 1 (2). Evidence of self-induced intoxication is not a relevant matter within the Sexual Offences (Amendment) Act 1976 s 1 (2): *R v Woods* (1981) 74 Cr App Rep 312, CA; *R v Fotheringham* (1988) 88 Cr App Rep 206, CA.

7　Sexual Offences Act 1956 s 1 (2).

8　Ibid s 37 (1), (3), Sch 2 para 1 (amended by the Sexual Offences Act 1985 s 3 (2)). See also para 505 note 13 ante. As to alternative verdicts see para 519 post. As to the offence committed by a man who at the time of committing or attempting rape, or being arrested for such offence has in his possession a firearm or imitation firearm see para 232 ante.

Corroboration of the evidence of the complainant, although not essential in law, is in practice always looked for: see para 1142 post. As to the competence and compellability of the accused's spouse see para 1184 post; and as to restrictions on reporting rape cases see para 520 post.

For guidelines on sentencing see *R v Billam* [1986] 1 All ER 985, 82 Cr App Rep 347, CA. An immediate custodial sentence is normally called for: *R v Roberts* [1982] 1 All ER 609, 74 Cr App Rep 242, CA.

515. Husband and wife. As a general rule, a man cannot be guilty as a principal of rape upon his wife, for the wife is in general unable to retract the consent to sexual intercourse which is a part of the contract of marriage[1]. However, he may be guilty of rape upon the woman who is or was his wife if there is in force a separation order or a decree of judicial separation[2] or a decree nisi of divorce[3], or an injunction restraining him from molesting his wife or an undertaking in lieu of such an injunction[4].

A husband is not entitled to exercise his marital rights by the use of force or violence[5]; and a wife's implied consent to sexual intercourse does not extend to other sexual acts performed against her will, whether or not they are preliminary to sexual intercourse[6].

A husband, who is present and assisting another person to commit a rape upon his wife, may upon an indictment for rape be convicted of aiding and abetting[7], as may a boy under 14[8], or a woman under similar circumstances[9].

1 *R v Miller* [1954] 2 QB 282, 38 Cr App Rep 1; *R v Kowalski* [1988] 1 FLR 447 at 449, 86 Cr Ap Rep 339 at 341, CA. See further 1 Hale PC 629 (intercourse following voidable marriage); *Popkin v Popkin* (1794) 1 Hag Ecc 765n at 767n per Lord Stowell (divorce case where cruelty was charged).
2 *R v Clarke* [1949] 2 All ER 448, 33 Cr App Rep 216.
3 *R v O'Brien* [1974] 3 All ER 663 (decree nisi revokes wife's implied consent to marital intercourse). An agreement to separate, particularly if it contains a non-molestation clause, may constitute revocation of a wife's implied consent: see *R v Miller* [1954] 2 QB 282 at 290, 38 Cr App Rep 1 at 7, 8 per Lynskey J; *R v Roberts* [1986] Crim LR 188, CA (formal deed of separation with no non-cohabitation or non-molestation clause; lack of such a clause did not revive wife's implied consent on termination of injunction restraining molestation).
4 *R v Steele* [1977] Crim LR 290, CA. The issue of proceedings does not of itself vitiate the wife's consent: *R v Steele* supra.
5 See para 495 ante.
6 *R v Kowalski* [1988] 1 FLR 447, 86 Cr App Rep 339, CA (husband forced wife to perform fellatio; convicted of indecent assault).
7 1 Hale PC 629; *R v Lord Audley, Earl of Castelhaven's Case* (1631) 3 State Tr 401, HL. The husband may be convicted notwithstanding that the principal is acquitted on the grounds of mistakenly believing the wife was consenting: *R v Cogan, R v Leak* [1976] QB 217, 61 Cr App Rep 217, CA.
8 *R v Eldershaw* (1828) 3 C & P 396.
9 *R v Lord Baltimore* (1768) 1 Wm Bl 648; *R v Ram and Ram* (1893) 17 Cox CC 609.

516. Meaning of 'sexual intercourse'. It is not necessary to prove the completion of sexual intercourse by the emission of seed; intercourse is deemed complete[1] upon proof of penetration only[2]. The slightest degree of penetration is enough[3]. If penetration cannot be satisfactorily proved, the accused may be convicted of attempted rape; if the intent is not proved, he may be convicted of indecent assault[4].

There is an irrebuttable presumption that a boy under 14 is incapable of sexual intercourse[5]; evidence may not be adduced to show that he is capable[6].

Corroboration of the evidence of the victim is not essential in law but in practice is always looked for except where there is no dispute as to the commission of the offence, but only as to the identity of the offender[7].

1 Ie where, on the trial of any offence under the Sexual Offences Act 1956, it is necessary to prove sexual intercourse, whether natural or unnatural.
2 Ibid s 44. Where there is penetration, intercourse is complete even where emission is disproved: *R v Cox* (1832) 5 C & P 297, CCR; *R v Allen* (1839) 9 C & P 31. Although deemed complete on penetration, sexual intercourse is a continuing act which ends only with withdrawal: *Kaitamaki v R* [1985] AC 147, 79 Cr App Rep 251, PC (accused realised lack of consent after penetration; guilty of rape by continuing intercourse).
3 *R v Hill* (1781) 1 East PC 439; *R v Lines* (1844) 1 Car and Kir 393; *R v Stanton* (1844) 1 Car & Kir 415. It is not necessary that the hymen be ruptured: *R v Jordan and Cowmeadow* (1839) 9 C & P 118; *R v Hughes* (1841) 2 Mood CC 190, CCR.

4 See para 1029 post. As to aiding and abetting see para 519 note 5 post.
5 See para 34 ante.
6 *R v Philips* (1839) 8 C & P 736.
7 See para 1142 post.

517. Consent in relation to rape. To constitute rape, intercourse must have taken place without the consent of the woman[1].

A person accused of rape may raise the defence of consent without putting his own character in issue[2].

Consent obtained by duress is in law no consent[3]. Where the woman is insensible by reason of intoxication the accused cannot successfully plead consent as a defence to a charge of rape[4]. Where the woman is asleep and thus incapable of consent, the accused may be convicted of rape if he knew that she was asleep even though he used no violence[5]. Submission owing to ignorance of, or to a mistake as to the nature of the act done or the person doing it, and induced by the fraud of the accused, does not constitute consent[6]; nor does submission induced by fear, even though no violence was threatened[7].

A person who has sexual intercourse without consent with a woman of unsound mind who is incapable of expressing consent or dissent is guilty of rape[8]. However, if such a woman consents to the act by reason of mere animal instinct, the act does not constitute rape[9].

1 See para 514 ante. There should be clear evidence of the absence of consent: see *R v Bradley* (1910) 74 JP 247, 4 Cr App Rep 225, CCA; *R v Harling* [1938] 1 All ER 307, 26 Cr App Rep 127, CCA. In the case of a girl under 16, the prosecution must prove either that she physically resisted, or, if she did not, that her understanding and knowledge were such that she was not in a position to decide whether to consent or resist: *R v Howard* [1965] 3 All ER 684 at 685, 50 Cr Ap Rep 56 at 58, CCA. Consent after the act, or condonation, affords no defence: 1 Hale PC 631. As to counsel not putting forward an inconsistent defence alleging consent when requested by the accused to do so see *R v Denoel* (1916) 85 LJKB 1756, 12 Cr App Rep 49, CCA. As to consent in relation to a charge of unlawful sexual intercourse with a girl under a specified age see para 526 note 4 post.
    If the accused believed that the woman consented, he cannot be convicted of rape: *DPP v Morgan* [1976] AC 182, 61 Cr App Rep 136, HL. See also the Sexual Offences (Amendment) Act 1976 s 1 and para 514 text and notes 4–6 ante. An accused who aids and abets another man to have intercourse with a woman knowing that she does not consent may be found guilty of aiding and abetting rape notwithstanding that the other man is acquitted on the ground that he mistakenly believed she was consenting: *R v Cogan, R v Leak* [1976] QB 217, 61 Cr App Rep 217, CA.
2 *R v Turner* [1944] KB 463, 30 Cr App Rep 9, CCA; *Selvey v DPP* [1970] AC 304, 52 Cr App Rep 443, HL. As to putting the accused's character in issue under the Criminal Evidence Act 1898 s 1 proviso (f) (ii) see paras 1071 text and note 11, 1088 post.
3 1 Hale PC 631; 1 Hawk PC c 16 (1) s 6; *R v Jones* (1861) 4 LT 154. As to consent as a defence to a criminal charge generally see para 23 ante. As to procuring a woman to have sexual intercourse by threats etc see para 524 post.
4 *R v Camplin* (1845) 1 Cox CC 220, CCR (accused giving drink to girl with intent to excite her): *R v Page* (1846) 2 Cox CC 133 (explaining *R v Camplin* supra); *R v Fletcher* (1859) Bell CC 63 at 71 per Lord Campbell CJ; *R v Lang* (1975) 62 Cr App Rep 50, CA. As to administering drugs etc with intent to stupefy a woman so as to enable a man to have sexual intercourse with her see para 525 post.
5 *R v Mayers* (1872) 12 Cox CC 311; *R v Young* (1878) 14 Cox CC 114, CCR.
6 *R v Case* (1850) 4 Cox CC 220, CCR; *R v Flattery* (1877) 2 QBD 410, CCR; *R v Clarence* (1888) 22 QBD 23 at 43, CCR per Stephen J; *R v Williams* [1923] 1 KB 340, 17 Cr App Rep 56, CCA. The fraud must be as to the nature of the act or the identity of the person committing it: *R v Clarence* supra at 44 per Stephen J. As to the impersonation of a husband see para 514 ante. As to mistakes of identity see further the cases cited at para 23 note 7 ante. As to procuring a woman by false pretences to have unlawful sexual intercourse see para 524 post.
7 *R v Olugboja* [1982] QB 320, 73 Cr App Rep 344, CA.

8 *R v Fletcher* (1859) Bell CC 63 at 70 per Willes J; *R v Fletcher* (1866) LR 1 CCR 39; *R v Barratt* (1873) LR 2 CR 81 (explaining *R v Fletcher* (1866) supra). As to unlawful sexual intercourse with a woman who is a defective see para 528 post.
9 *R v Fletcher* (1866) LR 1 CCR 39.

518. Character of complainant. If at a trial any person is for the time being charged with a rape offence[1] to which he pleads not guilty, then, except with the leave of the judge[2], no evidence and no question in cross-examination may be adduced or asked at the trial, by or on behalf of any accused at the trial, about any sexual experience of a complainant[3] with a person other than the accused[4].

1 For the meaning of 'a rape offence' see para 514 note 5 ante.
2 As to when such leave may be given see para 1071 text and note 7 post.
3 For these purposes, 'complainant' means a woman upon whom, in a charge for a rape offence to which the trial in question relates, it is alleged that rape was committed, attempted or proposed: Sexual Offences (Amendment) Act 1976 s 2 (3).
4 Ibid s 2 (1). The judge may not so give leave for any evidence or question except on an application made to him in the absence of the jury by or on behalf of an accused; and on such an application the judge must give leave if, and only if, he is satisfied that it would be unfair to that accused to refuse to allow the evidence to be adduced or the question to be asked: s 2 (2). Nothing in s 2 authorises evidence to be adduced or a question to be asked which cannot be adduced or asked apart from s 2: s 2 (4). See *R v Mills* (1978) 68 Cr App Rep 327, CA and para 1071 post.

519. Alternative verdicts. On the trial of an indictment for rape the jury may find the accused guilty of: (1) procurement of a woman by threats[1]; (2) procurement of a woman by false pretences[2]; or (3) administering drugs to obtain or facilitate intercourse[3] with her[4].

If penetration is not proved, the accused may be convicted of an attempt to commit rape[5].

On an indictment for rape the accused may be convicted of indecent assault if the victim was under 16; but not of unlawful sexual intercourse[6].

1 Ie under the Sexual Offences Act 1956 s 2: see para 524 post.
2 Ie under ibid s 3: see para 524 post.
3 Ie under ibid s 4: see para 525 post.
4 See para 1032 post.
5 See para 1029 note 6 post. A person charged with aiding and abetting a person in committing rape may be convicted of aiding and abetting him in attempting to commit rape: *R v Hapgood and Wyatt* (1870) LR 1 CCR 221. As to aiding and abetting an attempt see generally para 71 note 1 ante.
  Before a conviction can be secured for aiding and abetting a rape, there must be evidence of participation in the crime beyond mere presence: *R v Clarkson* [1971] 3 All ER 344, 55 Cr App Rep 445, C-MAC; and as to participation by secondary parties see further para 45 ante.
6 See para 1029 text to note 15 post. Where on a trial for rape there is no dispute that penetration took place and the only issue is whether there was consent, the alternative verdict of indecent assault should not be left to the jury: see *R v Touhey* (1960) 45 Cr App Rep 23, CCA. However, where penetration as well as consent is in issue, the alternative verdict may be left to the jury: *R v Gartland* [1962] Crim LR 318, CCA.

520. Restrictions on reporting; anonymity of victim of a rape offence. Except as authorised by a direction given by a judge[1]:
  (1) after an allegation that a woman[2] has been the victim of a rape offence[3] has been made by the woman or by any other person, neither the woman's name nor her address nor a still or moving picture[4] of her may during her lifetime

(a) be published in England and Wales in a written publication[5] available to the public; or (b) be broadcast[6] or included in a cable programme[7] in England and Wales, if that is likely to lead members of the public to identify her as an alleged victim of such an offence; and

(2) after a person is accused of a rape offence[8], no matter likely to lead members of the public to identify a woman as the complainant[9] in relation to that accusation may during her lifetime (a) be published in England and Wales in a written publication available to the public; or (b) be broadcast or included in a cable programme in England and Wales,

but nothing in the above provisions prohibits the publication or broadcasting or inclusion in a cable programme of matter consisting only of a report of criminal proceedings other than proceedings at, or intended to lead to, or on an appeal arising out of, a trial at which the accused is charged with the offence[10].

If, before the commencement of a trial at which a person is charged with a rape offence, he or another person against whom the complainant may be expected to give evidence at the trial applies to a judge of the Crown Court for a direction and satisfies the judge that the direction is required for the purpose of inducing persons to come forward who are likely to be needed as witnesses at the trial and that the conduct of the applicant's defence at the trial is likely to be substantially prejudiced if the direction is not given, the judge must direct that the above reporting restrictions shall not, by virtue of the accusation alleging such offence, apply in relation to the complainant[11].

If at a trial the judge is satisfied that the effect of the reporting restrictions is to impose a substantial and unreasonable restriction upon the reporting of proceedings at the trial and that it is in the public interest to remove or relax the restriction, he must direct that such reporting restrictions shall not apply to such matter as is specified in the direction; but a direction may not be so given by reason only of the outcome of the trial[12].

If any matter is published, broadcast or included in a cable programme in contravention of the above provisions, the following persons, namely:

(i) in the case of a publication in a newspaper or periodical, any proprietor, any editor and any publisher of the newspaper or periodical;

(ii) in the case of any other publication, the person who publishes it;

(iii) in the case of a broadcast, any body corporate which transmits or provides the programme in which the broadcast is made and any person having functions in relation to the programme corresponding to those of an editor of a newspaper; and

(iv) in the case of an inclusion in a cable programme, any body corporate which sends or provides the programme and any person having functions in relation to the programme corresponding to those of an editor of a newspaper,

is guilty of an offence and liable on summary conviction to a fine not exceeding level 5 on the standard scale[13].

Proceedings for such an offence[14] may not be instituted except by or with the consent of the Attorney General[15].

Where a person is charged with such an offence, it is a defence to prove that at the time of the alleged offence he was not aware, and neither suspected nor had reason to suspect, that the publication, broadcast or cable programme was of such matter as is mentioned in heads (1) and (2) above[16].

Where a person is charged with such an offence in respect of the publication or broadcast of any matter or the inclusion of any matter in a cable programme, it is also a defence to prove that the publication, broadcast or cable programme in which the matter appeared was one in respect of which the woman had given written consent to the appearance of matter of that description[17].

Written consent is not, however, a defence if it is proved that any person interfered unreasonably with the woman's peace or comfort with intent to obtain the consent[18].

A person accused of a rape offence has no right to anonymity[19].

1　Ie in pursuance of the Sexual Offences (Amendment) Act 1976 s 4 (2): see infra.
2　For the meaning of 'woman' see para 514 note 1 ante.
3　For the meaning of 'a rape offence' see para 514 note 5 ante.
4　For these purposes, 'picture' includes a likeness however produced: Sexual Offences (Amendment) Act 1976 s 4 (1A) (added by the Criminal Justice Act 1988 s 158 (1), (2)).
5　For these purposes, 'written publication' includes a film, a sound track and any other record in permanent form but does not include an indictment or other document prepared for use in particular legal proceedings: Sexual Offences (Amendment) Act 1976 s 4 (6).
6　For these purposes, 'a broadcast' means a broadcast by wireless telegraphy of sound or visual images intended for general reception, and cognate expressions are to be construed accordingly: ibid s 4 (6).
7　For these purposes, 'cable programme' means a programme included in a cable programme service: ibid s 4 (6) (amended by the Cable and Broadcasting Act 1982 s 57, Sch 5 para 34 (3)). For the meaning of 'cable programme service' see para 371 note 2 ante.
8　For these purposes, a person is accused of a rape offence if (1) an information is laid alleging that he has committed a rape offence; (2) he appears before a court charged with a rape offence; (3) a court before which he is appearing commits him for trial on a new charge alleging a rape offence; or (4) a bill of indictment charging him with a rape offence is preferred before a court in which he may lawfully be indicted for the offence; and references to an accusation alleging a rape offence are to be construed accordingly: Sexual Offences (Amendment) Act 1976 s 4 (6).
9　For these purposes, 'complainant', in relation to a person accused of a rape offence or an accusation alleging a rape offence, means the woman against whom the offence is alleged to have been committed: ibid s 4 (6).
10　Ibid s 4 (1) (substituted by the Criminal Justice Act 1988 s 158 (1), (2)). Nothing in the Sexual Offences (Amendment) Act 1976 s 4: (1) prohibits the publication, broadcasting or inclusion in a cable programme, in consequence of an accusation alleging a rape offence, of matter consisting only of a report of legal proceedings other than proceedings at, or intended to lead to, or on an appeal arising out of, a trial at which the accused is charged with that offence; or (2) affects any prohibition or restriction imposed by virtue of any other enactment upon a publication, broadcast or inclusion in a cable programme; and a direction in pursuance of s 4 (as amended) does not affect the operation of s 4 (1) (as so substituted) at any time before the direction is given: s 4 (7) (amended by the Cable and Broadcasting Act 1984 Sch 5 para 34 (5)).
　　　If a person who has been convicted of an offence and given notice of appeal to the Court of Appeal against the conviction, or notice of an application for leave so to appeal, applies to the Court of Appeal for a direction and satisfies the Court that the direction is required for the purpose of obtaining evidence in support of that appeal and that the applicant is likely to suffer substantial injustice if the direction is not given, the Court must direct that the Sexual Offences (Amendment) Act 1976 s 4 (1) (as so substituted) shall not, by virtue of an accusation which alleges a rape offence and is specified in the direction, apply in relation to a complainant so specified: s 4 (4). In relation to a conviction of an offence tried summarily as mentioned in s 3 (3) (see MAGISTRATES), for references to the Court of Appeal in s 4 (4) there must be substituted references to the Crown Court and the reference to notice of an application for leave to appeal must be omitted: s 5 (3).
11　Ibid s 4 (2). If after the commencement of a trial at which a person is charged with a rape offence a new trial of the person for that offence is ordered, the commencement of any previous trial at which he was charged with that offence must be disregarded for the purposes of s 4 (2): s 5 (2).
12　Sexual Offences (Amendment) Act 1976 s 4 (3) (amended by the Criminal Justice Act 1988 s 158 (1), (4)).
13　Sexual Offences (Amendment) Act 1976 s 4 (5) (amended by the Criminal Justice Act 1982 ss 38, 46; the Cable and Broadcasting Act 1984 Sch 5 para 34 (2), Sch 6). For the meaning of 'the standard scale' see para 808 post. When such an offence which has been committed by a body corporate is proved to have been committed with the consent or connivance of, or to be attributable to any neglect on the part of, any director, manager, secretary or other similar officer of the body corporate or any person who was purporting to act in any such capacity, he as well as the body corporate is guilty of that

offence and liable to be proceeded against and punished accordingly; and, where the affairs of a body corporate are managed by its members, that provision applies in relation to the acts and defaults of a member in connection with his functions of management as if he were a director of the body corporate: Sexual Offences (Amendment) Act 1976 s 5 (4).

14 Ie an offence under ibid s 4 (5) (see supra), including such an offence which is alleged to have been committed by virtue of s 5 (4) (see supra).

15 Ibid s 5 (5). As to the effect of this limitation see para 639 post.

16 Ibid s 5 (5) (amended by the Cable and Broadcasting Act 1984 Sch 5 para 34 (5)).

17 Sexual Offences (Amendment) Act 1976 s 4 (5A) (added by the Criminal Justice Act 1988 s 158 (1), (3)).

18 Sexual Offences (Amendment) Act 1976 s 4 (5B) (added by the Criminal Justice Act 1988 s 158 (1), (3)).

19 The former right of anonymity conferred by the Sexual Offences (Amendment) Act 1976 s 6 was abolished by the Criminal Justice Act 1988 s 158 (5).

(iv) Indecent Assault etc

521. Indecent assault on a man. It is an offence for a person[1] to make an indecent[2] assault[3] on a man[4]. In the case of a man of 16 years of age or over, consent is a defence[5], but a boy under the age of 16 cannot in law give any consent which would prevent an act from being an indecent assault[6]. Similarly a man who is a defective[7] cannot in law give any such consent; but a person is only to be treated as guilty of an indecent assault on a defective by reason of that incapacity to consent, if that person knew or had reason to suspect him to be a defective[8].

A person guilty of such an offence is liable on conviction on indictment to imprisonment for a term not exceeding ten years, or on summary conviction to imprisonment for a term not exceeding six months or a fine not exceeding the prescribed sum, or to both[9].

1 'Person' includes a woman: *R v Hare* [1934] 1 KB 354, 24 Cr App Rep 108, CCA. See also *Faulkner v Talbot* [1981] 3 All ER 468, 74 Cr App Rep 1, DC.

2 As an element of the actus reus of the offence, the assault, or the assault and the circumstances surrounding it, must be capable of being considered by right-minded persons as indecent. Some acts give rise to the irresistible inference that the accused intended to commit an indecent assault; but sometimes the conduct is merely capable of being an indecent assault and whether it is indecent depends on the surrounding circumstances. In the latter case the following factors are clearly relevant in deciding whether or not right-minded persons would think that the assault was indecent: the relationship of the accused to the victim, how the accused had come to embark on this conduct and why he was behaving in this way: *R v Court* [1989] AC 28, 87 Cr App Rep 144, HL (decided under the Sexual Offences Act 1956 s 14: see para 522 post).

As regards the mens rea, the accused must have intended to commit an indecent assault; evidence explaining the accused's conduct is admissible to establish whether he intended to commit such an assault (and possibly to decide whether the assault was an indecent one or not): *R v Court* supra (Lord Goff dissenting).

3 The 'assault' usually relied upon is a battery. However, the 'assault' relied upon need not involve any physical contact but may consist merely of conduct which causes the victim to apprehend immediate and unlawful personal violence: *R v Court* [1989] AC 28, 87 Cr App Rep 144, HL. For these purposes a battery is 'any intentional touching of another person without the consent of that person and without lawful excuse. It need not necessarily be hostile or rude or aggressive, as some cases seem to indicate': *Faulkner v Talbot* [1981] 3 All ER 468 at 471, 74 Cr App Rep 1 at 7, DC per Lord Lane CJ, approved in *R v Court* supra. For the meaning of 'assault' see para 488 ante. See also *R v McCormack* [1969] 2 QB 442, 53 Cr App Rep 514, CA; *R v Thomas* (1985) 81 Cr App Rep 331, CA; and para 522 post. For there to be an assault the accused must do an act to the complainant: *Fairclough v Whipp* [1951] 2 All ER 834, 35 Cr App Rep 138, DC; *R v Mason* (1968) 53 Cr App Rep 12, CA.

4 Sexual Offences Act 1956 s 15 (1). For the meaning of 'man' see para 378 note 3 ante. As to the mens rea for this offence see note 2 supra and *R v Kimber* [1983] 3 All ER 316, 77 Cr App Rep 225, CA (honest belief in victim's consent is a good defence; victim a woman, indecent assault under the Sexual Offences Act 1956 s 14: see para 522 post).

5 See para 23 ante and para 522 note 6 post.
6 Sexual Offences Act 1956 s 15 (2). Where, however, the act of touching is not in itself indecent but takes place in circumstances of indecency, and is consented to, such consent avails to prevent the act from being an indecent assault notwithstanding that the victim is under 16: *R v Sutton* [1977] 3 All ER 476, [1977] 1 WLR 1086, CA. The proper course in such a case is to prosecute under the Indecency with Children Act 1960 (see para 523 post): *R v Sutton* supra. As to proof of age see para 1156 post; as to corroboration of the victim's evidence see para 1142 post; and as to the evidence of children see paras 1178, 1179 post. As to procedural provisions applying where an indecent assault against a child or young person is charged see para 882 post.
7 For the meaning of 'defective' see para 378 note 7 ante.
8 Sexual Offences Act 1956 s 15 (3).
9 Ibid 37 (1)–(3), Sch 2 para 18 (amended by the Courts Act 1971 s 56 (4), Sch 11 Pt IV); Magistrates' Courts Act 1980 ss 17, 32 (1), Sch 1 para 32. See para 804 post. For the meaning of 'the prescribed sum' see para 807 post.

522. Indecent assault on a woman. Subject to one exception[1], it is an offence for any person[2] to make an indecent[3] assault[4] on a woman[5]. In the case of a female of 16 years of age or over, consent is a defence unless it is vitiated, for example by fraud as to the nature of the act. Honest belief in the woman's consent is a good defence[6]. However, a girl under the age of 16 cannot in law give any consent which would prevent an act being an indecent assault[7]. Similarly, a woman who is a defective[8] cannot in law give any such consent; but a person is only to be treated as guilty of an indecent assault on a defective by reason of that incapacity to consent, if that person knew or had reason to suspect her to be a defective[9].

Where a marriage is invalid by reason of the girl being under the age of 16[10], the invalidity does not make the man[11] guilty of an indecent assault by reason of her incapacity to consent while under that age, if he believes her to be his wife and has reasonable cause for the belief[12].

A person guilty of such an offence is liable on conviction on indictment to imprisonment for a term not exceeding ten years, or on summary conviction to imprisonment for a term not exceeding six months or a fine not exceeding the prescribed sum, or to both[13].

1 Ie the exception mentioned in the Sexual Offences Act 1956 s 14 (3): see infra. Where the description of an offence is expressed to be subject to exceptions, proof of the exception lies on the person relying on it: s 47. As to the burden of proof see para 1062 et seq post.
2 The offence can probably be committed by a female: *R v Hare* [1934] 1 KB 354, 24 Cr App Rep 108, CCA. A husband may be guilty of an indecent assault on his wife: *R v Kowalski* [1988] 1 FLR 447, 86 Cr App Rep 339, CA.
3 See para 521 note 2 ante.
4 See para 521 note 3 ante.
5 Sexual Offences Act 1956 s 14 (1). For the meaning of 'woman' see para 378 note 6 ante. An act of gross indecency with or towards a child under the age of 14 is chargeable as an offence in its own right: see para 523 post.
6 *R v Kimber* [1983] 3 All ER 316, 77 Cr App Rep 225, CA; and see para 23 ante. If there is no evidence on an indictment for indecent assault from which the jury might reasonably infer that the complainant consented, it is not necessary that the jury should be given a direction on consent: *R v May* [1912] 3 KB 572, 8 Cr App Rep 63, CCA. As to the direction relating to consent on a charge of indecent assault see *R v Kimber* supra; see also *R v Horn* (1912) 76 JP 270, 7 Cr App Rep 200, CCA; *R v Donovan* [1934] 2 KB 498, 25 Cr App Rep 1, CCA.
   The accused may raise the defence of consent without putting his own character in issue: see para 517 text and note 2 ante. If the complainant denies sexual intercourse with a third party, he cannot be called to contradict her (*R v Holmes* (1871) LR 1 CCR 334); but, if she denies previous sexual intercourse with the accused, evidence to contradict her may be adduced (*R v Riley* (1887) 18 QBD 481, CCR). As to corroboration of the victim's evidence see para 1142 post.
7 Sexual Offences Act 1956 s 14 (2). As to proof of age see para 1156 post. An indictment for indecent assault against a girl aged under 16 is not bad merely because it does not state the girl's age, although

it is better to state it: see *R v Stephenson* [1912] 3 KB 341, 8 Cr App Rep 36, CCA. It is no defence to a charge of indecent assault for the accused to establish that he is aged less than 24, has not previously been charged with a like offence, believed the victim to be more than 16 years old and had reasonable cause for the belief: see para 527 note 7 post. As to the evidence of children see paras 1178, 1179 post.

8 For the meaning of 'defective' see para 378 note 7 ante.
9 Sexual Offences Act 1956 s 14 (4).
10 Ie under the Marriage Act 1949 s 2 or in relation to Scotland under the Age of Marriage Act 1929 s 1. As to the Marriage Act 1949 s 2 see HUSBAND AND WIFE vol 22 para 916.
11 The Sexual Offences Act 1956 s 14 (3) refers to the 'husband'.
12 Ibid s 14 (3). See note 1 supra.
13 Ibid s 37 (1), (3), Sch 2 para 17 (amended by the Magistrates' Courts Act 1980 ss 17, 154, Sch 7; the Sexual Offences Act 1985 s 3 (3)). See also para 505 note 13 ante. For the meaning of 'the prescribed sum' see para 807 post. As to procedural provisions applying to indecent assaults on children and young persons see para 882 post.

523. Indecent conduct towards child. Any person who commits an act of gross indecency[1] with or towards[2] a child under the age of 14[3], or who incites a child under that age to such an act with him or another, is guilty of an offence and liable on conviction on indictment to imprisonment for a term not exceeding two years, or on summary conviction to imprisonment for a term not exceeding six months or a fine not exceeding the prescribed sum, or to both[4].

1 The term 'gross indecency' is not defined by statute. The Indecency with Children Act 1960 was passed to bring within the ambit of the criminal law conduct of an indecent nature which fell short of assault: see eg *Fairclough v Whipp* [1951] 2 All ER 834, 35 Cr App Rep 138, DC; *DPP v Rogers* [1953] 2 All ER 644, 37 Cr App Rep 137, DC; and see para 521 note 6 ante. Inactivity may amount to an act of gross indecency if it amounts to an invitation to the child to continue doing an indecent act: *R v Speck* [1977] 2 All ER 859, 65 Cr App Rep 161, CA. On a charge of gross indecency between men (see the Sexual Offences Act 1956 s 13 and para 506 ante) physical contact is not necessary: *R v Hunt* [1950] 2 All ER 291, 34 Cr App Rep 135, CCA.
2 The words 'with or towards' are a single phrase meaning 'involving' and create only one offence: *DPP v Burgess* [1971] 1 QB 432, [1970] 3 All ER 266, DC. The act must be directed towards the child, at least by the accused deriving satisfaction from the knowledge that he was watching: *R v Francis* (1988) 88 Cr App Rep 127, CA.
3 As to proof of age see para 1156 post.
4 Indecency with Children Act 1960 s 1 (1) (amended by the Magistrates' Courts Act 1980 s 32 (2)). For the meaning of 'the prescribed sum' see para 807 post. The consent of the Director of Public Prosecutions is not required under the Sexual Offences Act 1967 s 8 (see para 506 ante) to the institution of proceedings under the Indecency with Children Act 1960 s 1: see the Criminal Justice Act 1972 s 48. Offences under the Indecency with Children Act 1960 s 1 are deemed to be 'offences against the person' for the purposes of the Visiting Forces Act 1952 s 3: Indecency with Children Act 1960 s 1 (4). Hence, where the accused is a member of a visiting force or a civilian component of such force and the victim had a relevant association with a visiting force of the same country, the accused is not liable to be tried by a United Kingdom court: see the Visiting Forces Act 1952 s 3 (1) (b) and ROYAL FORCES vol 41 para 136.
 Conduct falling within the Indecency with Children Act 1960 s 1 (1) (as so amended) may also constitute the common law offence of outraging public decency (see para 372 ante) and in appropriate cases may be charged as such: see *R v May (John)* (1989) Times, 21 November, CA.
 As to the competence and compellability of the accused's spouse as a witness see para 1184 post; as to procedural provisions applying to acts of gross indecency towards children see para 882 post. As to the offences of taking or permitting to be taken or having in one's possession any indecent photograph of a child under the age of 16 see paras 365, 366 ante.

(v) Unlawful Sexual Intercourse

524. Procurement. It is an offence for a person (1) by threats or intimidation[1] to procure[2] any woman[3] to have unlawful sexual intercourse[4] in any part of the world[5]; (2) by false pretences or false representations to procure any woman to have unlawful sexual intercourse in any part of the world[6]; (3) to procure a girl under the age of 21 to have unlawful sexual intercourse in any part of the world with a third person[7]; (4) to procure any woman who is a defective[8] to have unlawful sexual intercourse in any part of the world[9], except that such an offence[10] is not committed if that person does not know and has no reason to suspect her to be a defective[11]. A person may not, however, be convicted of an offence under heads (1) to (3) above on the evidence of one witness only, unless the witness is corroborated in some material particular by evidence implicating the accused[12].

A person guilty of any such offence or an attempt to commit an offence under heads (1), (3) or (4) above is liable on conviction on indictment to imprisonment for a term not exceeding two years[13].

1 Threats to harm a third person may suffice: *R v Wilson* (1973) 58 Cr App Rep 304 at 307, CA.
2 'Procure' includes procurement to have intercourse with the procurer: *R v Williams* (1898) 62 JP 310. A woman is not procured if she acts on her own initiative: *R v Christian* (1913) 78 JP 112. An offence constituted by procuring a woman to have unlawful sexual intercourse is committed only if unlawful sexual intercourse occurs: *R v Mackenzie and Higginson* (1910) 6 Cr App Rep 64, CCA; *R v Johnson* [1964] 2 QB 404, 48 Cr App Rep 25, CCA. See also para 43 text to note 10 ante. As to procuring a woman to become a common prostitute see para 386 ante.
3 For the meaning of 'woman' see para 378 note 6 ante.
4 For the meaning of 'sexual intercourse' see para 516 ante.
5 Sexual Offences Act 1956 s 2 (1).
6 Ibid s 3 (1).
7 Ibid s 23 (1).
8 For the meaning of 'defective' see para 378 note 7 ante. The jury's attention should be drawn to the meaning of 'defective': *R v Hudson* [1966] 1 QB 448, 49 Cr App Rep 69, CCA (decided under the Sexual Offences Act 1956 s 7 (substituted by the Mental Health Act 1959 s 127 (1) (a) (see para 528 post)).
9 Sexual Offences Act 1956 s 9 (1). See also *R v Cook* [1954] 1 All ER 60, [1954] 1 WLR 125 (accused not shown to have procured the defective to have sexual intercourse).
10 Ie an offence under the Sexual Offences Act 1956 s 9 (1): see supra.
11 Ibid s 9 (2). To set up the defence of absence of knowledge etc that the woman was a defective the accused must establish on a balance of probabilities that he did not know that the woman was a defective: *R v Hudson* [1966] 1 QB 448, 49 Cr App Rep 69, CCA (decided under the Sexual Offences Act 1956 s 7 (as substituted: see note 7 supra). As to the burden of proving exceptions see para 378 note 13 ante.
12 Ibid ss 2 (2), 3 (2), 23 (2). As to corroboration see para 1141 et seq post. For an example where the direction as to corroboration was defective see *R v Shillingford* [1968] 2 All ER 200, 52 Cr App Rep 188, CA. As to procedural provisions applying to offences or attempts to commit offences under the Sexual Offences Act 1956 ss 2, 3, 23 against children or young persons see para 882 post.
13 Ibid s 37 (1), (3), Sch 2 paras 7, 8, 13, 24. See also para 505 note 13 ante. As to attempts to commit an offence under head (2) supra see the Criminal Attempts Act 1981 Pt I (ss 1–7) and para 71 et seq ante.

525. Administering drugs to obtain or facilitate intercourse. Any person who applies or administers to, or causes to be taken by, a woman[1] any drug, matter or thing with intent to stupefy or overpower her so as thereby to enable any man[2] to have unlawful sexual intercourse[3] with her is guilty of an offence and liable on conviction on indictment to imprisonment for a term not exceeding two years[4]. A person may not, however, be convicted of such an offence on the evidence of one witness only, unless the witness is corroborated in some material particular by evidence implicating the accused[5].

1 For the meaning of 'woman' see para 378 note 6 ante.
2 For the meaning of 'man' see para 378 note 3 ante.
3 For the meaning of 'sexual intercourse' see para 516 ante.

4 Sexual Offences Act 1956 ss 4 (1), 37 (1), (3), Sch 2 para 9. See also para 505 note 13 ante. As to procedural provisions applying to such offences committed against children or young persons see para 882 post.

If there is merely a single administration of the drug etc, only one offence is committed even if it is administered for the purpose of more than one man having sexual intercourse: *R v Shillingford* [1968] 2 All ER 200, 52 Cr App Rep 188, CA.

5 Sexual Offences Act 1956 s 4 (2). As to corroboration see para 1141 et seq post. For an example where the direction as to corroboration was defective see *R v Shillingford* [1968] 2 All ER 200, 52 Cr App Rep 188, CA.

526. Unlawful sexual intercourse with girl under thirteen. It is an offence for a man[1] to have unlawful sexual intercourse[2] with a girl under the age of 13[3]; the consent of the girl is immaterial[4]. A person guilty of such an offence is liable on conviction on indictment to imprisonment for life or for any shorter term[5]; and a person guilty of an attempt to commit such an offence is liable on conviction on indictment to imprisonment for a term not exceeding seven years[6].

1 For the meaning of 'man' see para 378 note 3 ante. The irrebuttable presumption that a boy under the age of 14 is incapable of sexual intercourse extends to this offence: *R v Waite* [1892] 2 QB 600. As to whether he might be guilty of an attempt to commit rape and as to indecent assault as an alternative verdict see para 34 ante.
2 For the meaning of 'sexual intercourse' see para 516 ante.
3 Sexual Offences Act 1956 s 5. As to proof of age see para 1156 post; as to corroboration of the evidence of victims of sexual offences see para 1141 post; and as to the evidence of children see paras 1178, 1179 post.
4 *R v Beale* (1865) LR 1 CCR 10; *R v Ryland* (1868) 18 LT 538, CCR. If the sexual intercourse occurred without the victim's consent, an indictment for rape may lie: *R v Dicken* (1877) 14 Cox CC 8; *R v Harling* [1938] 1 All ER 307, 26 Cr App Rep 127, CCA; *R v Howard* [1965] 3 All ER 684, 50 Cr App Rep 56, CCA; see also *R v Ratcliffe* (1882) 10 QBD 74, CCR.

Belief, even if reasonable, that the girl was over 13 years of age is no defence: see *R v Prince* (1875) LR 2 CCR 154. Cf the Sexual Offences Act 1956 s 6 (3) and para 527 post.

A girl under the prescribed age cannot be guilty of inciting a man to have unlawful sexual intercourse with her or of aiding and abetting the commission of the offence in relation to herself: *R v Tyrrell* [1894] 1 QB 710, CCR.
5 Sexual Offences Act 1956 s 37 (1)–(3), Sch 2 para 2 (a). See also para 505 note 13 ante. As to the competence and compellability of the accused's spouse as a witness see para 1184 post; as to alternative verdicts see para 1029 post; and as to procedural provisions applying to offences or attempts to commit offences under s 5 see para 882 post.
6 Ibid Sch 2 para 2 (b) (amended by the Indecency with Children Act 1960 s 2 (3); the Sexual Offences Act 1985 s 5 (2)). See also the Indecency with Children Act 1960 s 2 (1) (amended by the Sexual Offences Act 1985 s 5 (2)). As to permitting premises to be used for unlawful sexual intercourse see para 378 ante.

527. Unlawful sexual intercourse with girl under sixteen. Subject to certain exceptions[1], it is an offence for a man[2] to have unlawful sexual intercourse[3] with a girl under the age of 16[4]; the consent of the girl is immaterial[5].

However, a man is not guilty of such an offence because he has unlawful sexual intercourse with a girl under the age of 16, if he is under the age of 24 and has not previously been charged with a like offence[6], and he believes her to be of the age of 16 or over and has reasonable cause for the belief[7].

Where a marriage is invalid by reason of the girl being under the age of 16[8], the invalidity does not make the man[9] guilty of such an offence because he has sexual intercourse with the girl if he believes her to be his wife and has reasonable cause for the belief[10].

A prosecution for such an offence or an attempt to commit such an offence may not be commenced more than 12 months after the offence charged[11]. Corroboration of the evidence of the girl is not essential in law, but the general rule as to warning the jury in cases of sexual offences of the danger of convicting on the uncorroborated evidence of the victim applies[12].

A person guilty of such an offence or an attempt to commit such an offence is liable on conviction on indictment to imprisonment for a term not exceeding two years, or on summary conviction to imprisonment for a term not exceeding six months or a fine not exceeding the prescribed sum, or to both[13].

1   Ie the exceptions contained in the Sexual Offences Act 1956 s 6 (2), (3): see infra. As to the burden of proving exceptions see para 378 note 13 ante.

2   For the meaning of 'man' see para 378 note 3 ante. The irrebuttable presumption that a boy under the age of 14 is incapable of sexual intercourse extends to this offence: see para 526 note 1 ante.

3   For the meaning of 'sexual intercourse' see para 516 ante.

4   Sexual Offences Act 1956 s 6 (1) (amended by the Criminal Law Act 1967 s 10 (1), Sch 2 para 14). As to proof of age see para 1156 post; and as to the evidence of children see paras 1178, 1179 post.

   A doctor who in the exercise of his clinical judgment gives contraceptive advice or treatment to a girl under 16 without her parents' consent does not necessarily commit an offence for these purposes: *Gillick v West Norfolk and Wisbech Area Health Authority* [1986] AC 112, [1985] 3 All ER 402, HL.

5   See para 526 note 4 ante.

6   'A like offence' means an offence under the Sexual Offences Act 1956 s 6 (as amended: see note 4 supra) or an attempt to commit such offence: s 6 (3). 'Charged' means brought before a court having jurisdiction to determine the matter, ie, where examining justices commit an accused for trial, there is no charge until he is tried on indictment: *R v Rider* [1954] 1 All ER 5, 37 Cr App Rep 209. If an accused is committed on two separate occasions on separate charges of unlawful sexual intercourse but both charges are included in one indictment, he may set up the statutory defence: *R v Rider* supra.

7   Sexual Offences Act 1956 s 6 (3). The accused must have reasonable cause for the belief and must believe the girl to be over the age of 16: *R v Banks* [1916] 2 KB 621, 12 Cr App Rep 74, CCA; *R v Harrison* [1938] 3 All ER 134, 26 Cr App Rep 166, CCA. Whether reasonable cause exists is a question of fact for the jury to determine: *R v Forde* [1923] 2 KB 400, 17 Cr App Rep 99, CCA.

   The exception does not apply to the offence of indecent assault: *R v Forde* supra; *R v Laws* (1928) 21 Cr App Rep 45, CCA; *R v Keech* (1929) 21 Cr App Rep 125, CCA; *R v Maughan* (1934) 24 Cr App Rep 130, CCA.

8   Ie under the Marriage Act 1949 s 2 or, in relation to Scotland, under the Age of Marriage Act 1929 s 1. As to the Marriage Act 1949 s 2 see HUSBAND AND WIFE vol 22 para 916. Where a wife under 16 years is validly married by foreign law and the marriage is recognised in England as valid, a prosecution should not be brought under the Sexual Offences Act 1956 s 6 (as amended: see note 4 supra): see *Mohamed v Knott* [1969] 1 QB 1, [1968] 2 All ER 563, DC.

9   The Sexual Offences Act 1956 s 6 (2) refers to 'the husband'.

10 Ibid s 6 (2). See note 1 supra.

11 Ibid s 37 (1), (2), Sch 2 para 10 (amended by the Criminal Law Act 1967 s 10, Sch 2 para 14; the Courts Act 1971 s 56 (4), Sch 11 Pt IV). If the original prosecution upon which the accused was committed for trial was one of rape, and was commenced within the 12 months, the prosecution is in time, even though the accused is tried only on an indictment for unlawful sexual intercourse at a datewhen the 12 months have expired: see *R v West* [1898] 1 QB 174, CCR. The limitation of time does not apply to evidence of other acts and conduct of the accused outside the limitation admissible to prove a charge within the limitation, although that evidence might establish a previous offence for which there could not be a prosecution: *R v Shellaker* [1914] 1 KB 414, 9 Cr App Rep 240, CCA.

12 See para 1142 post.

13 Sexual Offences Act 1956 s 37 (1)–(3), Sch 2 para 10 (a); Magistrates' Courts Act 1980 ss 17, 32 (1), Sch 1 para 23 (a). See para 804 post. For the meaning of 'the prescribed sum' see para 807 post. As to the principles to be applied in determining the appropriate sentence see *R v Taylor* [1977] 3 All ER 527, 64 Cr App Rep 182, CA. As to the competence and compellability of the accused's wife as a witness see para 1184 post; as to procedural provisions applying to offences or attempts to commit offences under the Sexual Offences Act 1956 s 6 see para 882 post; and as to permitting premises to be used for unlawful sexual intercourse see para 378 ante.

528. Unlawful sexual intercourse with a defective. It is an offence for a man[1] to have unlawful sexual intercourse[2] with a woman[3] who is a defective[4] unless he does not know and has no reason to suspect her to be a defective[5].

A person guilty of such an offence or an attempt to commit such an offence is liable on conviction on indictment to imprisonment for a term not exceeding two years[6].

1 For the meaning of 'man' see para 378 note 3 ante.
2 For the meaning of 'sexual intercourse' see para 516 ante.
3 For the meaning of 'woman' see para 378 note 6 ante.
4 Sexual Offences Act 1956 s 7 (1) (substituted by the Mental Health Act 1959 s 127 (1) (a)). For the meaning of 'defective' see para 378 note 7 ante. The jury's attention should be drawn to the meaning of 'defective': *R v Hudson* [1966] 1 QB 448, 49 Cr App Rep 69, CCA. As to unlawful sexual intercourse with women patients committed by officers etc of a hospital or a home see the Mental Health Act 1959 s 128 (amended by the National Health Service Act 1977 s 129, Sch 15 para 29, Sch 16; the Mental Health Act 1983 s 148 (1), Sch 4 para 15; the Registered Homes Act 1984 s 57 (1), Sch 1 para 2) and MENTAL HEALTH vol 30 para 1107.
5 Sexual Offences Act 1956 s 7 (2) (substituted by the Mental Health Act 1959 s 127 (1) (a)). As to the burden of proving exceptions see para 378 note 13 ante.
6 Sexual Offences Act 1956 s 37 (1)–(3), Sch 2 para 11 (amended by the Mental Health Act 1959 s 149 (1), Sch 7). See also para 505 note 13 ante. As to the competence and compellability of the accused's spouse as a witness see para 1184 post; as to corroboration of the evidence of the victim see para 1142 post; and as to procedural provisions applying to offences or attempts to commit offences under the Sexual Offences Act 1956 s 7 (as substituted: see notes 4, 5 supra) committed against children or young persons see para 882 post. As to permitting premises to be used for unlawful sexual intercourse see para 378 ante.

(4) ABDUCTION

529. Abduction. The abduction of a woman or a girl is an offence[1] but in most instances it is necessary to prove a specific intention underlying the abduction[2]. In the case of an unmarried woman under the age of 18[3] or a woman who is a defective[4] the essence of the offence is the taking of her out of the possession of her parent or guardian[5].

For the offence of abduction to be established it must be shown that the accused's acts amounted to a substantial interference with the relationship of parent and child[6]. A manual possession by the parent or guardian need not be shown[7]. If the girl was a member of his family and under his control, it is sufficient; if she leaves her parent's or guardian's house for a particular purpose with his sanction, she cannot legally be said to be out of his possession[7]. The taking need not be by force either actual or constructive[8], and the consent of the girl, if it has been obtained by the accused's persuasions, is immaterial[9]. The accused may be convicted, although he took no part in the actual removal of the girl, if he previously solicited her to leave her parent or guardian and afterwards received and harboured her when she did so[10]. If a girl leaves her parent or guardian of her own accord, the accused taking no active part in the matter and not persuading or advising her to leave, he cannot be convicted of abduction, even though he failed to advise her not to come, or to return, and afterwards harboured her[11]. A person who finds a girl under 16 years of age wandering in the street and takes her away with him cannot be convicted of abducting her, in the absence of evidence that he knew that she was under the lawful care or charge of her parent or guardian[12]. Religious or philanthropic motives are, however, no defence to a charge of abduction of a girl aged under 16[13]; and a mistaken belief that the accused is entitled to her legal custody cannot afford a defence[14].

The offence is committed by anyone who takes a female illegitimate child from the custody of her mother or her putative father[15].

The taking out of possession[16] must be against the will of the parent or guardian[17]. A taking with the consent of the parent or guardian, if the consent is obtained by fraudulent misrepresentations, is taking against his will[18]. The fact that a parent has countenanced a lax, though not necessarily an immoral, course of life by the girl may in some cases be evidence that the taking out of his possession, although unknown to him, was not against his will[19].

1 See the Sexual Offences Act 1956 ss 17, 19–21 and paras 530–533 post.
2 No intention underlying the abduction need be shown in the case of the abduction of an unmarried girl under the age of 16: see para 532 post.
3 In the case of a married woman or a woman over the age of 17 the essence of the offence is the taking away or detention against her will: see para 530 post.
4 For the meaning of 'defective' see para 378 note 7 ante.
5 See paras 531, 532 post. As to abduction of a child see paras 535, 536 post; and as to kidnapping see para 493 ante.
6 *R v Jones (James William)* [1973] Crim LR 621 at 622 per Swanwick J. See also *R v Baillie* (1859) 8 Cox CC 238 (accused inducing girl to leave home for clandestine marriage; girl returning home after an hour or two; accused guilty of abduction); *R v Timmins* (1860) Bell CC 276, CCR (girl cohabiting with accused for three nights before returning to her father; accused guilty of abduction).
7 *R v Manktelow* (1853) Dears CC 159 at 165, CCR per Jervis CJ.
8 *R v Manktelow* (1853) Dears CC 159, CCR; *R v Frazer* (1861) 8 Cox CC 446; *R v Baillie* (1859) 8 Cox CC 238 (where the girl voluntarily left her home for an hour to be married and then returned, the marriage never having been consummated); *R v Mycock* (1871) 12 Cox CC 28. Force may, however, be an ingredient in the abduction of a married woman or a woman aged over 17 (see para 530 post) or in an offence of child abduction (see paras 535, 536 post).
9 *R v Twisleton* (1668) 1 Lev 257; *R v Robins* (1844) 1 Car & Kir 456; *R v Manktelow* (1853) Dears CC 159, CCR. Cf *R v Meadows* (1844) 1 Car & Kir 399 (a case which it would appear difficult to reconcile with these and other authorities but for the fact that the accused was herself a girl, and the two girls wandered away together; see the observations of Maule J on this case in *R v Kipps* (1850) 4 Cox CC 167 at 168). The marginal note to *R v Meadows* supra is misleading: see the observations of the judges in *R v Manktelow* supra; see also *R v Miller* (1876) 13 Cox CC 179 per Lush J.
10 *R v Robb* (1864) 5 F & F 59 per Pollock CB; *R v Handley* (1859) 1 F & F 648 per Wightman J.
11 *R v Olifier* (1866) 10 Cox CC 402; *R v Jarvis* (1903) 20 Cox CC 249; *R v Kauffman* (1904) 68 JP 189; *R v Alexander* (1912) 107 LT 240, 7 Cr App Rep 110, CCA. See also *R v Henkers* (1886) 16 Cox CC 257. Cf *R v Biswell* (1847) 2 Cox CC 279.
12 *R v Green* (1862) 3 F & F 274; *R v Hibbert* (1869) LR 1 CCR 184.
13 *R v Booth* (1872) 12 Cox CC 231; see also *R v Prince* (1875) LR 2 CCR 154 at 174 per Bramwell B; *R v Tegerdine* (1982) 75 Cr App Rep 298, CA.
14 *R v Tegerdine* (1982) 75 Cr App Rep 298, CA (putative father of child had no lawful excuse for taking her from mother despite his belief that the welfare of the child required that he should have custody of her); not following *R v Tinkler* (1859) 1 F & F 513. As to abduction by parents see para 535 post.
15 1 Hawk PC c 16 (3) s 14; 1 East PC 457; *R v Cornfort (or Cornforth)* (1742) 11 East 10n. As to the possession by the mother see *R v Hopkins* (1806) 7 East 579.
16 Ie in the case of an unmarried woman under the age of 18 or a woman who is a defective.
17 See paras 531–533 post. Unwillingness on the part of the parent may be assumed if, had he been asked, he would have refused: *R v Handley* (1859) 1 F & F 648.
18 *R v Hopkins* (1842) Car & M 254.
19 *R v Primelt* (1858) 1 F & F 50.

530. Abduction of women. It is an offence for a person to take away or detain a woman[1] against her will with the intention that she shall marry or have unlawful sexual intercourse[2] with that or any other person, if she is so taken away or detained either by force or for the sake of her property or expectations of property[3]. Since the offence consists in the abduction or detainer[4] of a woman, it is no defence to show that she consented to the original taking away if she afterwards refuses to continue with the accused; and it is immaterial that the woman later consented to be married or defiled[5].

A person guilty of such an offence is liable on conviction on indictment to imprisonment for a term not exceeding 14 years[6].

1 For the meaning of 'woman' see para 378 note 6 ante. As to offences of this nature involving unmarried girls and defectives see paras 531–533 post.
2 For the meaning of 'sexual intercourse' see para 516 ante. 'Unlawful' in juxtaposition to 'sexual intercourse' in relation to abduction means 'illicit', ie outside the bonds of marriage: *R v Chapman* [1959] 1 QB 100, 42 Cr App Rep 257, CCA; *R v Jones* [1973] Crim LR 710, CA.
3 Sexual Offences Act 1956 s 17 (1); Criminal Law Act 1967 s 12 (5) (a). For these purposes, the reference to a woman's expectations of property relates only to property of a person to whom she is next of kin or one of the next of kin; and 'property' includes any interest in property: s 17 (2). As to evidence of the accused's motives see *R v Barratt* (1840) 9 C & P 387. As to the power to search for a woman suspected of being detained for an immoral purpose see para 534 post.
4 Cf para 529 text to notes 3–5 ante.
5 1 Hawk PC c 16 (1) ss 7, 8.
6 Sexual Offences Act 1956 s 37 (1)–(3), Sch 2 para 4. See also para 505 note 13 ante. As to the offence committed by a person who at the time of committing or being arrested for an offence under s 17 (1) has in his possession a firearm or imitation firearm see para 232 ante.

531. Abduction of unmarried girl under eighteen. It is an offence for a person to take an unmarried girl under the age of 18[1] out of the possession of her parent or guardian[2] against his will, if she is so taken with the intention that she shall have unlawful sexual intercourse[3] with men or with a particular man[4]. However, a person is not guilty of the offence because he takes such a girl out of the possession of her parent or guardian in such circumstances, if he believes her to be of the age of 18 or over, and has reasonable cause for the belief[5].

A person guilty of such an offence is liable on conviction on indictment to imprisonment for a term not exceeding two years[6].

1 As to proof of age see para 1156 post.
2 For these purposes, 'guardian' means any person having the lawful care or charge of the girl: Sexual Offences Act 1956 s 19 (3).
3 For the meaning of 'sexual intercourse' see para 516 ante; and for the meaning of 'unlawful' see para 530 note 2 ante.
4 Sexual Offences Act 1956 s 19 (1). For the meaning of 'man' see para 378 note 3 ante. As to the taking of a girl out of the possession of her parent or guardian against his will see para 529 ante; as to the abduction of married women or of women over 17 see para 530 ante; as to the abduction of unmarried girls under 16 or of women who are defectives see paras 532, 533 post; and as to the power to search for a woman suspected of being detained for an immoral purpose see para 534 post.
5 Ibid s 19 (2). As to the burden of proving exceptions see para 378 note 13 ante.
6 Ibid s 37 (1)–(3), Sch 2 para 20. See also para 505 note 13 ante. As to procedural provisions applying to offences under s 19 committed against children or young persons see para 882 post.

532. Abduction of unmarried girl under sixteen. It is an offence for a person acting without lawful authority or excuse[1] to take an unmarried girl under the age of 16[2] out of the possession of her parent or guardian[3] against his will[4]. A person guilty of such an offence is liable on conviction on indictment to imprisonment for a term not exceeding two years[5].

1 The word 'lawful' must be read before the word 'excuse': *R v Tegerdine* (1982) 75 Cr App Rep 298 at 302, CA per Lawton LJ. Motive is therefore irrelevant: see para 529 ante.

2 As to proof of age see para 1156 post.
3 For these purposes, 'guardian' means any person having the lawful care or charge of the girl: Sexual Offences Act 1956 s 20 (2).
4 Ibid 20 (1). As to the taking of a girl out of the possession of her parent or guardian against his will see para 529 ante; and as to the power to search for a woman suspected of being detained for immoral purposes see para 534 post.
   A belief, even with reasonable cause, that the girl is not under the age of 16, is no defence: *R v Booth* (1872) 12 Cox CC 231; *R v Prince* (1875) LR 2 CCR 154. Cf para 531 ante.
5 Sexual Offences Act 1956 s 37 (1)–(3), Sch 2 para 21. See also para 505 note 13 ante. As to the offence committed by a person who at the time of committing or being arrested for an offence under s 20 (1) has in his possession a firearm or imitation firearm see para 232 ante; and as to procedural provisions applying to offences under s 20 see para 882 post.

533. Abduction of a defective. It is an offence for a person to take a woman[1] who is a defective[2] out of the possession of her parent or guardian[3] against his will, if she is so taken with the intention that she shall have unlawful sexual intercourse[4] with men or with a particular man[5]. However, a person is not guilty of the offence because he takes such a woman out of the possession of her parent or guardian in these circumstances, if he does not know and has no reason to suspect her to be a defective[6].

A person guilty of such an offence is liable on conviction on indictment to imprisonment for a term not exceeding two years[7].

1 For the meaning of 'woman' see para 378 note 6 ante.
2 For the meaning of 'defective' see para 378 note 7 ante.
3 For these purposes, 'guardian' means any person having the lawful care or charge of the girl: Sexual Offences Act 1956 s 21 (3).
4 For the meaning of 'sexual intercourse' see para 516 ante; and for the meaning of 'unlawful' see para 530 note 2 ante.
5 Sexual Offences Act 1956 s 21 (1). For the meaning of 'man' see para 378 note 3 ante. As to the taking of a woman out of the possession of her parent or guardian against his will see para 529 ante; and as to the power to search for a woman suspected of being detained for immoral purposes see para 534 post.
6 Ibid s 21 (2). As to the burden of proving exceptions see para 378 note 13 ante.
7 Ibid s 37 (1)–(3), Sch 2 para 21. See also para 505 note 13 ante.

534. Searching for and removal of woman detained for immoral purposes. Where it is made to appear by information on oath laid before a justice of the peace by a woman's[1] parent, relative or guardian[2], or by any other person who in the opinion of the justice is acting in the woman's interests, that there is reasonable cause to suspect that (1) the woman is detained in any place within the justice's jurisdiction in order that she may have unlawful sexual intercourse[3] with men or a particular man[4]; and (2) either she is so detained against her will or she is under the age of 16[5] or is a defective[6], or she is under the age of 18 and is so detained against the will[7] of her parent or guardian, the justice may issue a warrant authorising a constable to search for her and to take her to and detain her in a place of safety until she can be brought before a justice of the peace[8]. A justice before whom a woman is so brought may cause her to be delivered up to her parent or guardian, or otherwise dealt with as circumstances may permit and require[9].

1 For the meaning of 'woman' see para 378 note 6 ante.
2 For these purposes, 'guardian' means any person having the lawful care or charge of the woman: Sexual Offences Act 1956 s 43 (5).
3 For the meaning of 'sexual intercourse' see para 516 ante; and for the meaning of 'unlawful' see para 530 note 2 ante.

4 For the meaning of 'man' see para 378 note 3 ante.
5 As to proof of age see para 1156 post.
6 For the meaning of 'defective' see para 378 note 7 ante.
7 As to acts contrary to the will of a parent or guardian see para 529 ante.
8 Sexual Offences Act 1956 s 43 (1) (amended by the Police and Criminal Evidence Act 1984 s 119 (2), Sch 7 Pt I). The powers conferred by the Sexual Offences Act 1956 s 43 (as so amended) are in addition to, and not in derogation of, those conferred by the Children and Young Persons Act 1933 s 40 (amended by the Children and Young Persons Act 1963 s 64 (1), Sch 3 para 11; the Police and Criminal Evidence Act 1984 Sch 7 Pt I) (issue of warrant to search for child or young person in respect of whom a specified offence has been committed: see INFANTS vol 24 para 780): Sexual Offences Act 1956 s 43 (6).
   The issue of a warrant under s 43 is a judicial act and is an answer to an action for malicious prosecution against the person on whose information the warrant was issued: *Hope v Evered* (1886) 17 QBD 338, DC; *Lea v Charrington* (1889) 23 QBD 45, DC; affd 23 QBD 272, CA.
   A constable executing a warrant so issued must be accompanied by the person applying for it, if that person so desires, unless the justice issuing it directs otherwise: Sexual Offences Act 1956 s 43 (4). A constable may enter (if need be, by force) any premises specified in the warrant, and remove the woman from the premises: s 43 (3).
9 Ibid s 43 (2).

535. Abduction of child by parents or persons connected with child. A person connected with a child[1] under the age of 16 commits an offence if he takes[2] or sends[3] the child out of the United Kingdom without the appropriate consent[4].

A person does not commit such an offence, however, by doing anything without the consent of another person whose consent is so required if (1) he does it in the belief that the other person has consented or would consent if he was aware of all the relevant circumstances; or (2) he has taken all reasonable steps to communicate with the other person but has been unable to communicate with him; or (3) the other person has unreasonably refused to consent; but head (3) above does not apply where what is done relates to a child who is the subject of a custody order[5] made by a court in the United Kingdom, or where the person who does it acts in breach of any direction under the Guardianship of Minors Act 1971[6] or the Guardianship Act 1973[7]. Where, in proceedings for such an offence, there is sufficient evidence to raise an issue as to the application of heads (1) to (3) above, it is for the prosecution to prove that heads (1) to (3) do not apply[8].

A person guilty of such an offence is liable on conviction on indictment to imprisonment for a term not exceeding seven years, or on summary conviction to imprisonment for a term not exceeding six months or a fine not exceeding the statutory maximum, or to both[9]. No prosecution for such an offence may, however, be instituted except by or with the consent of the Director of Public Prosecutions[10].

1 For these purposes, a person is connected with a child if (1) he is a parent or guardian of the child; or (2) there is in force an order of a court in the United Kingdom awarding custody of the child to him, whether solely or jointly with any other person; or (3) in the case of an illegitimate child, there are reasonable grounds for believing that he is the father of the child: Child Abduction Act 1984 s 1 (2) (amended by the Family Law Act 1986 s 65). 'Guardian' means a person appointed by deed or will or by order of a court of competent jurisdiction to be the guardian of the child: Child Abduction Act 1984 s 1 (7) (a).
2 For these purposes, a person is to be regarded as taking a child if he causes or induces the child to accompany him or any other person or causes the child to be taken: ibid s 3 (a).
3 For these purposes, a person is to be regarded as sending a child if he causes the child to be sent: ibid s 3 (b).
4 Ibid s 1 (1). For these purposes, 'the appropriate consent', in relation to a child, means (1) the consent of each person (a) who is a parent or guardian of the child; (b) to whom custody of the child has been awarded, whether solely or jointly with any other person, by any order of a court in the United

Kingdom; or (2) if the child is the subject of a custody order (see note 5 infra), the leave of the court which made the order; or (3) the leave of the court granted on an application for a direction under the Guardianship of Minors Act 1971 s 7 or the Guardianship Act 1973 s 1 (3): Child Abduction Act 1984 s 1 (3) (amended by the Family Law Act 1986 s 65). In the case of a custody order made by a magistrates' court, head (2) supra is to be construed as if the reference to the court which made the order included a reference to any magistrates' court acting for the same petty sessions area as that court: Child Abduction Act 1984 s 1 (4).

As to applications to the police for assistance where danger of removal of the child from the jurisdiction is imminent see *Practice Direction* [1986] 1 All ER 983, [1986] 1 WLR 475.

The Child Abduction Act 1984 s 1 has effect, however, subject to the provisions of s 1 (8), Schedule in relation to a child who is in the care of a local authority or voluntary organisation or who is committed to a place of safety or who is the subject of custodianship proceedings or proceedings or an order relating to adoption: s 1 (8). Such provisions are:

(a) in the case of a child who is in the care of a local authority or voluntary organisation in England or Wales, s 1 has effect as if (i) the reference in s 1 (1) to the appropriate consent were a reference to the consent of the local authority or voluntary organisation in whose care the child is; and (ii) s 1 (3)–(6) were omitted;

(b) in the case of a child who is committed to a place of safety in England or Wales in pursuance of the Children and Young Persons Act 1933 s 40, or the Adoption Act 1976 s 34, or the Children and Young Persons Act 1969 ss 2 (5) or (10), 16 (3) or 28 (1) or (4), or the Foster Children Act 1980 s 12, the Child Abduction Act 1984 s 1 has effect as if (i) the reference in s 1 (1) to the appropriate consent were a reference to the leave of any magistrates' court acting for the area in which the place of safety is; and (ii) s 1 (3)–(6) were omitted;

(c) in the case of a child (i) who is the subject of an order under the Adoption Act 1976 s 18 freeing him for adoption; or (ii) who is the subject of a pending application for such an order; or (iii) who is the subject of a pending application for an adoption order; or (iv) who is the subject of an order under the Adoption Act 1976 s 55 relating to adoption abroad or of a pending application for such an order; or (v) who is the subject of a pending application for a custodianship order, the Child Abduction Act 1984 s 1 has effect as if (A) the reference in s 1 (1) to the appropriate consent were a reference, in a case within head (i) supra, to the consent of the adoption agency which made the application for the order or, if the parental rights and duties in respect of the child have been transferred from that agency to another agency by an order under the Adoption Act 1976 s 21, to the consent of that other agency; in a case within heads (ii), (iii) or (v) supra, to the leave of the court to which the application was made; and in a case within head (iv) supra, to the leave of the court which made the order or, as the case may be, to which the application was made; and (B) the Child Abduction Act 1984 s 1 (3)–(6) were omitted; and for these purposes, references to an order or to an application for an order are references to an order made by, or to an application to, a court in England or Wales, and references to the court are to be construed as including, in any case where the court is a magistrates' court, a reference to any magistrates' court acting for the same petty sessions area as that court;

(d) in the case of a child falling within both heads (a) and (c) supra, the provisions of head (c) supra apply to the exclusion of those in head (a) supra:

Schedule paras 1–4, 5 (3), (4). For the purposes of heads (a)–(d) supra, 'adoption agency' has the same meaning as in the Adoption Act 1976 s 1; 'adoption order' means an order under s 12; 'custodianship order' has the same meaning as in the Children Act 1975 Pt II (ss 33–46); and 'local authority' and 'voluntary organisation' have the same meanings as in the Child Care Act 1980 s 87: Child Abduction Act 1984 Schedule para 5 (1); Interpretation Act 1978 s 17 (2).

5 For these purposes, a reference to a custody order or an order awarding custody includes a reference to an order awarding legal custody and a reference to an order awarding care and control: Child Abduction Act 1984 s 1 (7) (b).

6 Ie the Guardianship of Minors Act 1971 s 7.

7 Child Abduction Act 1984 s 1 (5) (amended by the Family Law Act 1986 s 65).

8 Child Abduction Act 1984 s 1 (6).

9 Ibid s 4 (1). For the meaning of 'the statutory maximum' see para 806 post. As to the offence committed by a person who at the time of committing or being arrested for an offence under s 1 (as amended) has in his possession a firearm or imitation firearm see para 232 ante.

10 Ibid s 4 (2). As to the effect of this limitation see para 639 post. The common law offence of kidnapping may be committed by a parent or person connected with the child: see para 493 ante.

536. Abduction of children by other persons. A person other than one who is connected with a child[1] commits an offence if, without lawful authority or reasonable excuse, he takes[2] or detains[3] a child under the age of 16 so as to remove him from the lawful control of any person having lawful control of the child, or so as to keep him out of the lawful control of any person entitled to lawful control of the child[4].

In proceedings against any person for such an offence it is a defence for that person to show that at the time of the alleged offence he believed that the child had attained the age of 16 or, in the case of an illegitimate child, he had reasonable grounds for believing himself to be the child's father[5].

A person guilty of such an offence is liable on conviction on indictment to imprisonment for a term not exceeding seven years or on summary conviction to imprisonment for a term not exceeding six months or a fine not exceeding the statutory maximum, or to both[6]. No prosecution for such an offence may, however, be instituted except by or with the consent of the Director of Public Prosecutions[7].

1 Ie a person falling within the Child Abduction Act 1984 s 1 (2) (a) or (b) (amended by the Family Law Act 1986 s 65): see para 535 note 1 heads (1), (2) respectively ante.
2 For the meaning of 'taking a child' see para 535 note 2 ante.
3 For these purposes, a person is to be regarded as detaining a child if he causes the child to be detained or induces the child to remain with him or any other person: Child Abduction Act 1984 s 3 (c).
4 Ibid s 2 (1).
5 Ibid s 2 (2).
6 Ibid s 4 (1). For the meaning of 'the statutory maximum' see para 806 post.
7 Ibid s 4 (2). As to the effect of this limitation see para 639 post. As to the common law offence of kidnapping see para 493 ante; and as to the offence committed by a person who at the time of committing or being arrested for an offence under s 2 has in his possession a firearm or imitation firearm see para 232 ante.

(5) CRUELTY TO CHILDREN

537. Cruelty to persons under sixteen. If any person who has attained the age of 16 years and has the custody, charge, or care[1] of any child[2] or young person[3] under that age, wilfully assaults[4], ill-treats, neglects[5], abandons[6], or exposes[7] him, or causes or procures him to be assaulted, ill-treated, neglected, abandoned or exposed in a manner likely to cause him unnecessary suffering or injury[8] to health, he is guilty of an offence and liable on conviction on indictment to imprisonment for a term not exceeding ten years or a fine, or to both, or on summary conviction to imprisonment for a term not exceeding six months or a fine not exceeding the prescribed sum, or to both[9].

A person may by convicted under the above provisions notwithstanding that actual suffering or injury to health, or the likelihood of actual suffering or injury to health, was obviated by the action of another person, and notwithstanding the death of the child or young person in question[10].

1 For these purposes, any person who is the parent or legal guardian of a child or young person or who is legally liable to maintain him is presumed to have the custody of him, and as between the father and mother the father is not deemed to have ceased to have custody of him by reason only that he has deserted, or otherwise does not reside with, the mother and the child or young person; any person to whose charge a child or young person is committed by any person who has the custody of him is presumed to have charge of the child or young person; any other person having actual possession or control of a child or young person is presumed to have the care of him: Children and Young Persons

Act 1933 s 17. See also *R v Connor* [1908] 2 KB 26, CCR (father leaving wife and children and living apart liable for neglect of children); *Shaftesbury Union v Brockway* [1913] 1 KB 159, DC (wife obtaining non-cohabitation order and custody of children; husband liable for neglect of children); *Poole v Stokes* (1914) 110 LT 1020, DC (father voluntarily separated from mother and making her a proper weekly allowance held liable for neglect of children in her custody, being aware of such neglect); *R v Gibbins and Proctor* (1918) 82 JP 287, 13 Cr App Rep 134, CCA (man living with woman not his wife; both responsible for neglect of man's child); *Brooks v Blount* [1923] 1 KB 257, DC (parent cannot by voluntary agreement rebut presumption that he has custody of child); *Henderson v Stewart* 1954 JC 94 (parents separated and child living with mother; accused not contributing to child's maintenance and convicted of neglect although child not in danger of injury to health or suffering); *R v Watson and Watson* (1959) 43 Cr App Rep 111 (where parents are living together both may be held liable for neglect of their child). Where a child in the joint custody and control of both parents sustains unexplained injuries, both may be held liable (*R v Gibson and Gibson* (1984) 80 Cr App Rep 24 at 30, CA per O'Connor LJ) but, where the injuries are inflicted by one parent, the other is only guilty of ill-treatment or neglect if he fails to intervene in circumstances where such a duty arises (*R v Russell and Russell* (1987) 85 Cr App Rep 388, CA). As to the obligations imposed on a parent by the duty to intervene see *R v Beard* (1987) 85 Cr App Rep 395 at 399, CA. A father is not the 'parent' of an illegitimate child: *Butler v Gregory* (1902) 18 TLR 370; see also the National Assistance Act 1948 s 42 (1), (2). Where, however, the father of illegitimate children is living with their mother and them, he may be a person having the custody or care within the Children and Young Persons Act 1933: *Liverpool Society for the Prevention of Cruelty to Children v Jones* [1914] 3 KB 813. As to parental duties generally see INFANTS vol 24 para 502 et seq; as to the protection of children see INFANTS vol 24 para 693 et seq; and as to the National Assistance Act 1948 s 42 see NATIONAL HEALTH vol 33 para 923.

2   For these purposes, 'child' means a person under the age of 14 years: Children and Young Persons Act 1933 s 107 (1).

3   'Young person' means a person who has attained the age of 14 years and is under the age of 17 years: ibid s 107 (1). In this context the term must, however, be read subject to the age limitation referred to in the text.

4   'Wilfully' appears to govern all the following expressions such as 'assaults', 'ill-treats', 'neglects' etc, as they are also qualified by the words 'in a manner likely to cause unnecessary suffering or injury to health'. 'Wilfully' means deliberately and intentionally, not accidentally or inadvertently (*R v Senior* [1899] 1 QB 283 at 290, CCR per Lord Russell CJ), and the jury must be so directed (*R v Walker* (1934) 24 Cr App Rep 117, CCA). In the context of failure to provide medical attention, however, 'wilfully' means deliberately or recklessly: *R v Sheppard* [1981] AC 394, 72 Cr App Rep 82, HL. The offence of wilfully neglecting a child contrary to the Children and Young Persons Act 1933 s 1 (as amended: see notes 5, 9 infra) is not an offence of strict liability and is to be judged by subjective test: *R v Sheppard* supra.

    The Children and Young Persons Act 1933 s 1 (as so amended) does not create five distinct offences of 'assaulting', 'neglecting' etc but one single offence dealing with various forms of cruelty (*R v Hayles* [1969] 1 QB 364, 53 Cr App Rep 36, CA); however, the prosecution should choose with care the word which more precisely and appropriately than any other describes the conduct complained of (*R v Beard* (1987) 85 Cr App Rep 395, CA). To come within the Children and Young Persons Act 1933 s 1 (as so amended) an assault must be one which is likely to cause unnecessary suffering or injury to health: *R v Hatton* [1925] 2 KB 322, 19 Cr App Rep 29, CCA.

5   For these purposes (1) a parent or other person legally liable to maintain a child or young person is deemed to have neglected him in a manner likely to cause injury to his health if he has failed to provide adequate food, clothing, medical aid or lodging for him, or if, being unable to provide it, he fails to take steps to procure it under the enactments applicable in that behalf; (2) where it is proved that the death of an infant under three years of age was caused by suffocation, not being suffocation caused by disease or the presence of any foreign body in the throat or air passages of the infant, while the infant was in bed with some other person who has attained the age of 16 years, that other person, if he was, when he went to bed, under the influence of drink, is deemed to have neglected the infant in a manner likely to cause injury to its health: Children and Young Persons Act 1933 s 1 (2) (amended by the National Assistance (Adaptation of Enactments) Regulations 1950, SI 1950/174).

    'Neglect' may include the refusal to allow a child to undergo an operation to remove adenoids; the question as to whether it does or not is a question of fact dependent for its answer on the circumstances of the case: *Oakey v Jackson* [1914] 1 KB 216. Deliberate or reckless omission to supply medical or surgical relief necessary for a child is within the Children and Young Persons Act 1933 s 1 (as amended: see note 9 infra): *R v Senior* [1899] 1 QB 283, CCR; *R v Sheppard* [1981] AC 394, 72 Cr App Rep 82, HL; and see note 4 supra. The possibility that resort to public assistance by the mother might have obviated the effect of the father's neglect is no answer to a charge under the Children and Young Persons Act 1933 s 1 (as so amended): *Cole v Pendleton* (1896) 60 JP 359.

6 'Abandon' means to leave a child to its fate: *Mitchell v Wright* 1905 SC 568 at 574 per Lord Dunedin; *R v Boulden* (1957) 41 Cr App Rep 105, CCA. Leaving a child in court causing some mental suffering is not an abandonment: *R v Whibley* [1938] 3 All ER 777, 26 Cr App Rep 184, CCA.

7 Any person who unlawfully abandons or exposes any child under the age of two years, whereby his life is endangered or his health is or is likely to be permanently injured is guilty of an offence and liable on conviction on indictment to imprisonment for a term not exceeding five years or on summary conviction to imprisonment for a term not exceeding six months or a fine not exceeding the prescribed sum, or to both: Offences against the Person Act 1861 s 27; Penal Servitude Act 1891 s 1 (1); Criminal Justice Act 1948 s 1 (1); Criminal Law Act 1967 s 1; Magistrates' Courts Act 1980 ss 17, 30, 32, Sch 1 para 5 (d). See para 804 post. For the meaning of 'the prescribed sum' see para 807 post. As to procedural provisions applying to offences under the Offences against the Person Act 1861 s 27 see para 882 post.

For the purposes of an offence under s 27 the exposure need not necessarily consist of the physical placing of the child somewhere with intent to injure him: *R v Williams* (1910) 26 TLR 290, 4 Cr App Rep 89, CCA. See also *R v Falkingham* (1870) LR 1 CCR 222 (five week old child sent by railway in a hamper); *R v White* (1871) LR 1 CCR 331 (nine month old child left outside house from 7 pm to 1 am).

8 'Injury to health' includes injury to or loss of sight, or hearing, or limb, or organ of the body, and any mental derangement: Children and Young Persons Act 1933 s 1 (1).

9 Ibid s 1 (1) (amended by the Children and Young Persons Act 1963 s 64 (1), (3), Sch 3 para 1, Sch 5; the Children Act 1975 s 108 (1) (b), Sch 4 Pt III; the Magistrates' Courts Act 1980 s 32 (2); the Criminal Justice Act 1988 s 45 (1)). Nothing in the Children and Young Persons Act 1933 s 1 (1) (a) (as so amended) affects the punishment for an offence committed before 29 September 1988: Criminal Justice Act 1988 ss 45 (2), 171 (6). The particulars of the offence should include the word 'wilfully': *R v Walker* (1934) 24 Cr App Rep 117, CCA. Where the facts of a case so justify, a prosecution may be brought under an enactment other than the Children and Young Persons Act 1933 s 1 (as so amended) even though this may entail a more severe penalty: *R v Beanland* (1970) 54 Cr App Rep 289, CA. As to procedural provisions applying to offences under the Children and Young Persons Act 1933 s 1 (as so amended) see para 882 post. The former provisions relating to increased sentences in certain circumstances contained in s 1 (5), (6) were repealed by the Criminal Justice Act 1988 s 170 (2), Sch 16.

If a child dies as a result of neglect in respect of which someone is criminally liable under the Children and Young Persons Act 1933 s 1 (as so amended), it does not necessarily follow that the person concerned is guilty of manslaughter: see *R v Lowe* [1973] QB 702, 57 Cr App Rep 365, CA; and para 444 text and note 18 ante.

Nothing in the Children and Young Persons Act 1933 s 1 (as so amended) is to be construed as affecting the right of any parent, teacher, or other person having the lawful control or charge of a child or young person to administer punishment to him: s 1 (7). Section 1 (7) must be read, however, subject to the provisions of the Education (No 2) Act 1986 s 47 (amended by the Education Reform Act 1988 s 237, Sch 12 para 35, Sch 13 Pt II): see para 497 ante.

10 Children and Young Persons Act 1933 s 1 (3).

538. Exposing child under twelve to risk of burning. If any person who has attained the age of 16 years, having the custody, charge of care of any child[1] under the age of 12 years[2], allows the child to be in a room containing an open fire grate, or any heating appliance liable to cause injury to a person by contact with it, which is not sufficiently protected to guard against the risk of the child being burnt or scalded without taking reasonable precautions against that risk, and the child is killed or suffers serious injury for that reason, that person is guilty of an offence and liable on summary conviction to a fine not exceeding level 1 on the standard scale[3].

1 As to custody, charge or care of a child see para 537 note 1 ante.
2 As to proof of age see para 1156 post.
3 Children and Young Persons Act 1933 s 11 (amended by the Children and Young Persons (Amendment) Act 1952 ss 8, 9, Schedule; the Criminal Justice Act 1982 s 46). For the meaning of 'the standard scale' see para 808 post. Neither these provisions nor any proceedings taken under them

affect the liability of any person to be proceeded against by indictment for any indictable offence: Children and Young Persons Act 1933 s 11 proviso. As to procedural provisions applying to offences under s 11 (as so amended) see para 882 post.

539. Tattooing of minors. It is an offence to tattoo[1] a person under the age of 18[2] except when the tattoo is performed for medical reasons by a duly qualified medical practitioner or by a person working under his direction[3]. It is a defence, however, for a person charged to show that at the time the tattoo was performed he had reasonable cause to believe that the person tattooed was of or over the age of 18 and did in fact so believe[3].

A person guilty of such an offence is liable on summary conviction to a fine not exceeding level 3 on the standard scale[4].

1 For these purposes, 'tattoo' means the insertion into the skin of any colouring material designed to leave a permanent mark: Tattooing of Minors Act 1969 s 3.
2 As to proof of age see para 1156 post.
3 Tattooing of Minors Act 1969 s 1.
4 Ibid s 2 (amended by the Criminal Justice Act 1982 ss 38, 46). For the meaning of 'the standard scale' see para 808 post.

(6) OFFENCES AGAINST EMPLOYEES

540. Neglect to provide food etc for employees. Any employer[1] who, being legally liable to provide for an employee[2] necessary food, clothing or lodging, wilfully and without lawful excuse refuses or neglects to provide the same, or unlawfully and maliciously[3] does or causes to be done any bodily harm to him so that his life is endangered or his health is, or is likely to be, permanently injured is guilty of an offence and liable on conviction on indictment to imprisonment for a term not exceeding five years, or on summary conviction to imprisonment for a term not exceeding six months or a fine not exceeding the prescribed sum, or to both[4].

Where an employer[5], being legally liable to provide for his employee[6] necessary food, clothing, medical aid or lodging, wilfully and without lawful excuse refuses or neglects to provide the same, so that the health of the employee is or is likely to be seriously or permanently injured, he is guilty of an offence and liable on summary conviction to imprisonment for a term not exceeding six months or a fine not exceeding level 2 on the standard scale[7].

1 The Offences against the Person Act 1861 s 26 refers to a 'master or mistress'.
2 Ibid s 26 refers to any 'apprentice or servant'.
3 For the meaning of 'maliciously' see para 470 text to note 8 ante.
4 Offences against the Person Act 1861 s 26; Penal Servitude Act 1891 s 1 (1); Criminal Justice Act 1948 s 1 (1); Criminal Law Act 1967 s 1; Magistrates' Courts Act 1980 ss 17, 32 (1), Sch 1 para 5 (c). See para 804 post. For the meaning of 'the prescribed sum' see para 807 post. As to the common law liability of an employer, apart from liability arising from contract, for the wilful neglect to supply necessaries or medical treatment to an employee or apprentice see *R v Gould* (1704) 1 Salk 381; *R v Self* (1776) 1 Leach 137, 1 East PC 226; *R v Wintersett Inhabitants* (1783) Cald Mag Cas 298 at 300 per Buller J; *Newby v Wiltshire* (1785) 2 Esp 739; *Scarman v Castell* (1795) 1 Esp 270; *Simmons v Wilmott* (1800) 3 Esp 91; *Atkins v Banwell* (1802) 2 East 505; *Wennall v Adney* (1802) 3 Bos & P 247; *R v Ridley* (1811) 2 Camp 650; *Sellen v Norman* (1829) 4 C & P 80; *Cooper v Phillips* (1831) 4 C & P 581; *R v Smith* (1837) 8 C & P 153; *R v Crumpton* (1842) Car & M 597; *R v Smith* (1865) Le & Ca 607, CCR. See also *McKeating v Frame* 1921 SC 382.
5 The Conspiracy, and Protection of Property Act 1875 s 6 refers to 'a master'.

6 Ibid s 6 refers to 'servant or apprentice'.
7 Ibid s 6 (amended by the Criminal Justice Act 1982 ss 38, 46); Criminal Justice Act 1948 s 1 (2). For the meaning of 'the standard scale' see para 808 post.

4. OFFENCES AGAINST PROPERTY

(1) UNLAWFUL TAKING OF PROPERTY

(i) Theft

541. Meaning of 'theft'. A person is guilty of theft if he dishonestly[1] appropriates[2] property[3] belonging to another[4] with the intention of permanently depriving[5] the other of it[6]; and 'thief' and 'steal' are to be construed accordingly[7].

It is immaterial whether the appropriation is made with a view to gain or is made for the thief's own benefit[8].

A person guilty of theft is liable on conviction on indictment to imprisonment for a term not exceeding ten years, or on summary conviction to imprisonment for a term not exceeding six months or a fine not exceeding the prescribed sum, or to both[9].

1 For the meaning of 'dishonestly' see para 542 post. The Theft Act 1968 ss 2–6 (paras 542–549 post) have effect as regards the interpretation and operation of s 1 and, except where otherwise provided by the Theft Act 1968, apply only for the purposes of s 1: s 1 (3).
2 For the meaning of 'appropriation' see para 543 post.
3 As to property which is susceptible of theft see paras 544–547 post.
4 For the meaning of 'belonging to another' see para 548 post.
5 For the meaning of 'intention of permanently depriving' another see para 549 post.
6 Theft Act 1968 s 1 (1). Section 1 (1) is not to be construed as though it contained the words 'without having the consent of the owner' or words to that effect (*Lawrence v Metropolitan Police Comr* [1972] AC 626, 55 Cr App Rep 471, HL), but express consent or authorisation may be relevant to the issue of appropriation (see *R v Morris, Anderton v Burnside* [1984] AC 320, 77 Cr App Rep 309, HL; *Dobson v General Accident, Fire and Life Assurance Corpn plc* [1989] 3 All ER 927, [1989] 3 WLR 1066, CA (a civil case) and para 543 post). The offences of theft and obtaining property by deception (see para 567 post) are not mutually exclusive, and sometimes the same facts may support a charge of either offence: see *Lawrence v Metropolitan Police Comr* supra. However, a person cannot be convicted both of theft of a conveyance and of taking the conveyance without the consent of the owner (see the Theft Act 1968 s 12 (1) and para 556 post) where both convictions are founded on the same facts: *R v Gibbs* (1959) 44 Cr App Rep 77, CCA. It is possible for a person to be acquitted on a charge of theft but convicted on a charge of false accounting (see para 572 post) where the charges are founded on the same facts: see *R v Eden* (1971) 55 Cr App Rep 193, CA. It is possible in law for a person to steal and dishonestly handle the same goods: *R v Dolan* (1975) 62 Cr App Rep 36 at 39, CA per Scarman LJ. However, theft and handling (see para 559 post) should be charged as alternatives and the jury should be directed that the accused may not be convicted of both offences on the same facts: *R v Shelton* (1986) 83 Cr App Rep 379 at 384, CA per Lawton LJ. See also *R v Woods* [1969] 1 QB 447, 53 Cr App Rep 30, CA; *R v Smythe* (1980) 72 Cr App Rep 8, CA.
    Evidence of dispatch or receipt may be given by statutory declaration in proceedings for theft of anything in the course of transmission, whether by post or otherwise: see para 1114 post.
    Any number of persons may be charged in one indictment with the same theft: see para 997 note 1 post; and see also para 934 post. It is unnecessary for the prosecution to prove that all the articles specified in the particulars of offence in the indictment have been stolen, but the sentence should relate only to the articles proved to have been stolen: *Machent v Quinn* [1970] 2 All ER 255, DC. If on the trial of an indictment for theft the jury is not satisfied that the accused committed theft but it is proved that he committed an offence under the Theft Act 1968 s 12 (1) (see para 556 post), the jury may find him guilty of the latter offence: s 12 (4). As to the general power to bring in an alternative verdict see para 1029 post.

As to jurisdiction to prosecute offences of stealing a mail bag, postal packet etc in the course of transmission between places in different jurisdictions within the British postal area but outside England and Wales see para 592 post.

7 Ibid s 1 (1). Stealing is a constituent of certain other offences eg robbery (see para 551 post) and burglary (see para 552 post). As to the offence of going equipped for stealing etc see para 554 post.

8 Ibid s 1 (2).

9 Ibid s 7; Magistrates' Courts Act 1980 ss 17, 32 (1), Sch 1 para 28. For the meaning of 'the prescribed sum' see para 807 post. As to the offence committed by a person who at the time of committing or being arrested for theft has in his possession a firearm or imitation firearm see para 232 ante.

For sentencing guidelines in cases of theft see *R v Barrick* (1985) 81 Cr App Rep 78, CA; *R v Dhunay* (1986) 8 Cr App Rep (S) 107, CA; *R v Stewart* [1987] 2 All ER 383, 85 Cr App Rep 66, CA. As to disqualification for driving and endorsement of licence where the accused is convicted of stealing or attempting to steal a motor vehicle see the Road Traffic Offenders Act 1988 ss 34 (2), 97 (2), Sch 2 Pt II and ROAD TRAFFIC.

542. 'Dishonestly'. A person's appropriation[1] of property belonging to another is not to be regarded as dishonest[2] if he appropriates it in the belief: (1) that he has in law the right to deprive the other of it on behalf of himself or of a third person[3]; or (2) that he would have the other's consent if the other knew of the appropriation and the circumstances of it[4]; or (3) that the person to whom the property belongs cannot be discovered by taking reasonable steps[5], except where the property came to him as a trustee or personal representative[6]. In determining whether the accused acted dishonestly the test is (a) whether his actions were dishonest according to the ordinary standards of reasonable and honest people; and (b) if so, whether he himself realised that his actions were, according to those standards, dishonest[7]. A person's appropriation of property may be dishonest notwithstanding that he is willing to pay for the property[8].

1 For the meaning of 'appropriation' see para 543 post.

2 Whether the accused acted dishonestly is a question of fact for the jury: *R v Feely* [1973] QB 530, 57 Cr App Rep 312, CA. As to the test to be applied in determining that question see text and note 7 infra.

3 Theft Act 1968 s 2 (1) (a). The test of dishonesty is the mental element of belief; and, if a person believes that he has a right within the meaning of s 2 (1) (a), albeit there is none, no offence is committed: *R v Turner (No 2)* [1971] 2 All ER 441, 55 Cr App Rep 336, CA. The belief must be belief in a legal, not merely a moral, right: see *Harris v Harrison* [1963] Crim LR 497.

4 Theft Act 1968 s 2 (1) (b). A person is not to be regarded as acting dishonestly if he appropriates another's property believing that the other person, with full knowledge of the circumstances, agreed to the appropriation: *Lawrence v Metropolitan Police Comr* [1972] AC 626, 55 Cr App Rep 471, HL. However, the belief must be an honest one in a true consent, honestly obtained: *R v Lawrence* [1971] 1 QB 373, 55 Cr App Rep 73, CA. A person in sole control of a limited liability company, or two or more persons in such control, are capable in law of stealing the company's property: see *A-G's Reference (No 2 of 1982)* [1984] QB 624, 78 Cr App Rep 131, CA.

5 Theft Act 1968 s 2 (1) (c); see also para 543 post. If a person finds property that has been lost, or is believed by him to have been lost, and appropriates it with the intent to take entire dominion over it, believing that the owner cannot be found, he lacks the mens rea for theft; but, if he appropriates it with the like intent, but believing that the owner can be found, he commits theft. Cf *R v Thurborn* (1849) 1 Den 387, CCR. Where property has not been abandoned, but the finder thinks that it has, he has a defence to a charge of theft: *Ellerman's Wilson Line Ltd v Webster* [1952] 1 Lloyd's Rep 179, DC. See also *Digby v Heelan* (1952) 102 L Jo 287, DC. It is a misdirection to tell the jury that the accused's belief that the owner cannot be found must be reasonable: *R v Small* (1987) 86 Cr App Rep 170, CA. Property which has been abandoned by the owner and which has not passed into the lawful possession of some other person (eg the occupier of the place where the property was found) is not capable of being stolen: see para 548 note 1 post. As to what amounts to abandonment see para 548 note 1 post.

It is the duty of railway employees to report the finding of articles which are left accidentally, as distinct from being intentionally abandoned, by a passenger in a railway carriage to their superiors and to deliver them up; and, if, instead of doing so, they dishonestly appropriate them to their own use, they may be guilty of theft: *R v Pierce* (1852) 6 Cox CC 117. The same principle applies in the case of taxi-cab drivers and bus drivers and conductors: *R v Lamb* (1694) 2 East PC 644; *R v Wynne* (1786) 1 Leach 413; *R v Sears* (1786) 1 Leach 415n; see also *R v Thurborn* supra. The custody and disposal of property found in public transport is largely regulated by statutes or instruments or byelaws made under statutory powers: see eg the Metropolitan Public Carriage Act 1869 s 9 (5); the London Cab Order 1934, SR & O 1934/1346, para 51; the London Transport (Lost Property) Regulations 1971, SI 1971/2125 (amended by SI 1978/1791); the Public Service Vehicles (Lost Property) Regulations 1978, SI 1978/1684 (amended by SI 1981/1623) and ROAD TRAFFIC vol 40 paras 715, 937. See also AVIATION vol 2 para 1035. As to the duty of a person who finds a stray dog see ANIMALS vol 2 para 377.

6 Theft Act 1968 s 2 (1) (c). Property which comes to a person acting in the capacity of a trustee or legal personal representative is held by him for the benefit of the beneficiaries of the trust or estate of the deceased and not for his own benefit. If the beneficiary cannot be discovered or dies intestate and leaves nobody in whom his interest can vest, his estate will vest in the Crown as bona vacantia, unless the trust instrument or the will clearly shows that the trustee or the personal representative is to take beneficially. Accordingly, if the trustee or personal representative appropriates bona vacantia when he knows he has no right to do so, he commits the offence of theft against the Crown. As to bona vacantia generally see EXECUTORS vol 17 para 941 et seq; and as to breach of trust see TRUSTS vol 48 para 935 et seq.

7 *R v Ghosh* [1982] QB 1053, 75 Cr App Rep 154, CA; *R v Small* (1987) 86 Cr App Rep 170, CA. It is unnecessary, however, to give the jury a direction as to the meaning of 'dishonestly' in these terms unless the accused raises the issue that he did not realise that his actions were, according to ordinary standards, dishonest: *R v Roberts* (1987) 84 Cr App Rep 117, CA (decided under the Theft Act 1968 s 22: see para 559 post); *R v Price* (1989) Times, 28 October, CA per Lord Lane CJ. Dishonesty must exist at the time of the appropriation: see *R v Hall* [1973] QB 126, 56 Cr App Rep 547, CA.

8 Theft Act 1968 s 2 (2).

543. Appropriation. Any assumption by a person of the rights of an owner[1] amounts to an appropriation[2], and this includes, where he has come by the property, innocently or not, without stealing it, any later assumption of a right to it by keeping or dealing with it as an owner[3].

Where property or a right or interest in property is or purports to be transferred for value to a person acting in good faith, no later assumption by him of rights which he believed himself to be acquiring amounts to theft by reason of any defect in the transferor's title[4].

1 There need not be an assumption of all the rights of the owner; adverse interference with or usurpation of some right of the owner suffices: *R v Morris, Anderton v Burnside* [1984] AC 320, 77 Cr App Rep 309, HL. It is immaterial that such an assumption has no legally efficacious result: *Chan Man-sin v A–G of Hong Kong* [1988] 1 All ER 1, [1988] 1 WLR 196, PC (use of forged cheques an appropriation of debts by owners' bank to owners, even though bank had no authority to honour such cheques).

2 Removal of goods from the shelves of a supermarket does not, without more, amount to appropriation, since it is done with the express or implied consent of the owner; but, where such goods are placed into the customer's own bag, or where a label showing a lesser price is substituted for one showing the correct price, there is an appropriation: *R v Morris, Anderton v Burnside* [1984] AC 320, 77 Cr App Rep 309, HL; *R v McPherson* (1972) 117 Sol Jo 13, [1973] Crim LR 191, CA; *Eddy v Niman* (1981) 73 Cr App Rep 237, CA. Cf *Dip Kaur v Chief Constable for Hampshire* [1981] 2 All ER 430, 72 Cr App Rep 359, DC. Where the accused has in fact paid the lesser price, he may also be guilty of obtaining the property by deception (see para 567 post): *R v Morris, Anderton v Burnside* supra. As to whether an act done with the express authority of the owner of property may amount to an appropriation of that property see *Lawrence v Metropolitan Police Comr* [1972] AC 626, 55 Cr App Rep 471, HL; *R v Skipp* [1975] Crim LR 114, CA (accused posed as haulage contractor; obtained instructions to collect goods; no appropriation until goods loaded and probably none until diverted from proper destination); *R v Morris, Anderton v Burnside* supra; *R v Fritschy* [1985] Crim LR 745, CA (accused's intentions in relation to Krugerrands dishonest throughout but no evidence of any act of his within the jurisdiction not expressly authorised by the owner; 'fatal' to charge of theft); *R v McHugh, R v Tringham* (1988) 88 Cr App Rep 385, CA; *R v Philippou* (1989) 89 Cr App Rep 290, CA;

Dobson v General Accident, Fire and Life Assurance Corpn plc [1989] 3 All ER 927, [1989] 3 WLR 1066, CA.

Payment for goods with a stolen cheque which is then dishonoured is an appropriation when the 'buyer' removes the goods in circumstances where the property in them is clearly intended to pass, not on contract, but on payment: *Dobson v General Accident, Fire and Life Assurance Corpn plc* supra.

Tugging at a bag so that the owner no longer has physical control of it may be an appropriation, although the accused does not obtain possession (*Corcoran v Anderton* (1980) 71 Cr App Rep 104, DC); but 'conditional' appropriation of a handbag in order to examine its contents and, finding them worthless, leaving the bag for the owner to repossess, is probably not sufficient (*R v Easom* [1971] 2 QB 315, 55 Cr App Rep 410; the accused's activities in that case might now constitute attempted theft: see the Criminal Attempts Act 1981 Pt I (ss 1–7) and para 71 et seq ante). As to the intention permanently to deprive the owner of property as a constituent of theft see para 549 post.

Appropriation may also occur when a person not in possession of property assumes the rights of an owner even though he does not take or touch it at all (see eg *R v Bloxham* (1943) 29 Cr App Rep 37, CCA, where a person sold another's property pretending it was his own to a third party by merely pointing it out and not touching it; *R v Pitham, R v Hehl* (1977) 65 Cr App Rep 45, CA).

Where an agent dishonestly sells the principal's property to a third party at an undervalue, that amounts to an appropriation: *A–G of Hong Kong v Nai-Keung* [1987] 1 WLR 1339, 86 Cr App Rep 174, PC.

Where there is a joint dishonest enterprise, appropriation by one party is sufficient to sustain the other party's conviction for theft: *R v Bhachu* (1976) 65 Cr App Rep 261, CA. Appropriation is a continuous act (*R v Hale* (1978) 68 Cr App Rep 415, CA); and in a criminal enterprise involving theft there can be more than one appropriation (*R v Gregory* (1981) 77 Cr App Rep 41, CA; *R v Meech* [1974] QB 549, 58 Cr App Rep 74, CA).

Use of a cheque card to guarantee payment of a cheque drawn on an account with inadequate funds is not an assumption of the rights of the bank and thus not an appropriation: *R v Navvabi* [1986] 3 All ER 102, 83 Cr App Rep 271, CA. Theft of money from a bank account is complete when the cheque is dishonestly drawn on the account without authority: see *R v Governor of Pentonville Prison, ex p Osman* (1988) Times, 13 April, DC.

A dishonest supermarket cashier who puts money in the till but does not ring up the customer's purchases appropriates the money at that time: *R v Monaghan* [1979] Crim LR 673, CA.

Property which the accused obtained by deception may subsequently be appropriated by him if he sells or disposes of it: *R v Hircock* (1978) 67 Cr App Rep 278, CA.

3 Theft Act 1968 s 3 (1). Where the evidence of how the accused came into possession of property is inconclusive but the court is satisfied that possession was acquired dishonestly and that the accused intended to keep the property, dishonest appropriation of the property is established: *Stapylton v O'Callaghan* [1973] 2 All ER 782, DC; and see *Davies v Leighton* (1978) 68 Cr App Rep 4, CA.

Generally speaking, the Theft Act 1968 s 3 makes dishonest misappropriation of property by a person in possession of it a theft. A person is guilty of theft if he comes by property in any following manner and subsequently, with the intention of permanently depriving the owner of it, dishonestly keeps or disposes of it: (1) by finding, if he believes that the owner can be found either at the time of the finding or at any time prior to keeping or disposing of it dishonestly (see also para 542 note 5 ante); (2) through a mistake of which he is initially ignorant but which he discovers prior to keeping or disposing of it dishonestly (see *R v Ashwell* (1885) 16 QBD 190, CCR); (3) under a mistake on the part of the owner of which the recipient is aware even if he did nothing to cause the mistake (see *R v Middleton* (1873) LR 2 CCR 38; *R v Gilks* [1972] 3 All ER 280, 56 Cr App Rep 734, CA); (4) wrongfully, eg by trespass (see *R v Riley* (1853) Dears CC 149; *Ruse v Read* [1949] 1 KB 377, [1949] 1 All ER 398, DC; *R v Kindon* (1957) 41 Cr App Rep 208, CCA. In the above cases the accused took property when they were incapable of forming an intention to steal, but they afterwards misappropriated the property with that intention); (5) not knowing it is stolen and discovering it is stolen prior to keeping or disposing of it dishonestly (see *R v Johnson* (1911) 6 Cr App Rep 218, CCA); (6) which he knows is stolen and at first intends to hand over to the true owner or the police and then keeps (see *R v Mathews* [1950] 1 All ER 137, 34 Cr App Rep 55, CCA, where the offence under the present law would be theft); (7) from a child who is under the age of criminal responsibility (see *Walters v Lunt* [1951] 2 All ER 645, 35 Cr App Rep 94, DC); (8) as a bailee; in this instance it is theft if he offers or attempts to dispose of it even though no sale takes place (see *Rogers v Arnott* [1960] 2 QB 244, [1960] 2 All ER 417, DC; *R v Hircock* (1978) 67 Cr App Rep 278, CA). As to property which is susceptible of theft see paras 544–547 post.

4 Theft Act 1968 s 3 (2). Thus, where a person purchases property for value, in good faith, and it subsequently appears that the seller had no, or only a defective, title to it, eg because the seller or

some other person had stolen the property, s 3 (2) protects the buyer to the extent that he exercises rights over the property which he believes he had acquired.

An innocent purchaser who sells the property when he subsequently suspects it to have been stolen is not guilty of handling stolen property: *R v Bloxham* [1982] 1 AC 109, 74 Cr App Rep 279, HL. See further para 559 post.

544. Property in general. 'Property' includes money and all other property, real or personal, including things in action and other intangible property[1].

1 Theft Act 1968 s 4 (1). As to land, growing plants and wild creatures see paras 545–547 post.

Section 4(1) applies generally for the purposes of the Theft Act 1968 as it applies for the purposes of s 1: s 34 (1). To be the subject of theft, the property must belong to another: see further para 548 post. For the purposes of the Theft Act 1968 'goods' includes, except in so far as the context otherwise requires, money and every other description of property except land, and includes things severed from the land by stealing: s 34 (2) (b). As to things in action see CHOSES IN ACTION vol 6 paras 1–8. A credit in a bank account is a thing in action (*A–G's Reference (No 1 of 1983)* [1985] QB 182, 79 Cr App Rep 288, CA), so that an employee who draws, presents and negotiates dishonestly a forged cheque on his employer's account is guilty of the theft of his employer's rights to the credit in his account: see *Chan Man-Sin v A–G of Hong Kong* [1988] 1 All ER 1, [1988] 1 WLR 196, PC; *R v Wille* (1988) 86 Cr App Rep 296, CA. However, an apparent credit balance in a bank account brought about by fraud which could immediately be defeated by a plea of fraud is not a thing in action and therefore not 'property': *R v Thompson* [1984] 3 All ER 565, 79 Cr App Rep 191, CA. See also *R v Kohn* (1979) 69 Cr App Rep 395, CA; *R v Tomsett* [1985] Crim LR 369, CA; *R v Governor of Pentonville Prison, ex p Osman* (1988) Times, 13 April, DC; *R v Shadrokh-Cigari* [1988] Crim LR 465, CA; *R v Davis* (1988) 88 Cr App Rep 347, CA.

Export quotas transferable for value are intangible property (*A–G of Hong Kong v Nai-Keung* [1987] 1 WLR 1339, 86 Cr App Rep 174, PC) but confidential information is not (*Oxford v Moss* (1978) 68 Cr App Rep 183, DC). For the meaning of 'personal property' see PERSONAL PROPERTY vol 35 para 1101 et seq.

Gas and water can be the subject of theft, but electricity is not 'property' within the meaning of s 4 (see *Low v Blease* [1975] Crim LR 513, DC) and has been provided for separately by the offence of abstracting electricity: see para 558 post. The obtaining of gas by an arrangement of pipes so that a quantity consumed does not pass through the meter is theft (see *R v White* (1853) Dears CC 203, CCR; *R v Firth* (1869) LR 1 CCR 172); similarly with water (see *Ferens v O'Brien* (1883) 11 QBD 21; see also *Longhurst v Guildford, Godalming and District Water Board* [1963] AC 265 at 273, 274, [1961] 3 All ER 545 at 547, HL per Lord Reid, at 277, 278 and at 549, 550 per Lord Guest (as to water being an 'article')). For further offences relating to gas and water supply see GAS and WATER. As to property in water see EASEMENTS vol 14 paras 185–201 and WATER.

Articles in which no person has any determinate proprietary right will, in general, not be the subject of theft, eg a corpse cannot be stolen, although a dead body may in some circumstances be the subject of ownership, as in the case of a mummy: see CREMATION AND BURIAL vol 10 para 1019. However, theft may be committed in respect of the shroud in which the body is wrapped (see *R v Haynes* (1614) 12 Co Rep 113) and the coffin (see 2 East PC 652). As to unauthorised disinterment see CREMATION AND BURIAL vol 10 para 1196.

545. Land. A person cannot steal land[1], or things forming part of land and severed from it by him or by his directions, except in the following cases:

(1) when he is a trustee or personal representative, or is authorised by power of attorney, or as liquidator of a company, or otherwise, to sell or dispose of land belonging to another, and he appropriates[2] the land or anything forming part of it by dealing with it in breach of the confidence reposed in him[3];

(2) when he is not in possession of the land and appropriates anything forming part of the land by severing it or causing it to be severed, or after it has been severed[4];

(3) when he, being in possession of the land under a tenancy[5], appropriates the whole or any part of any fixture or structure let to be used with the land[6].

1 For these purposes, 'land' does not include incorporeal hereditaments: Theft Act 1968 s 4 (2). Accordingly incorporeal hereditaments such as easements, profits à prendre, rentcharges and rights of common can be subject to theft. For the meaning of 'incorporeal hereditaments' see REAL PROPERTY vol 39 para 382. With regard to 'things forming part of land' the general maxim of law is that what is annexed to the land becomes part of the land, and what constitutes annexation sufficient for this purpose depends on the circumstances of each case including the degree, and object, of annexation: see *Holland v Hodgson* (1872) LR 7 CP 328, Ex Ch. As to fixtures see LANDLORD AND TENANT vol 27 para 142 et seq.
2 For the meaning of 'appropriate' see para 543 ante.
3 Theft Act 1968 s 4 (2) (a).
4 Ibid s 4 (2) (b).
5 For these purposes, 'tenancy' means a tenancy for years or any less period and includes an agreement for such a tenancy; but a person who after the end of a tenancy remains in possession as statutory tenant or otherwise is to be treated as having possession under the tenancy, and 'let' is to be construed accordingly: ibid s 4 (2). As to the subject matter of tenancy, agreement for a tenancy, and the distinction between a tenancy and a licence see LANDLORD AND TENANT vol 27 para 1 et seq. As to statutory tenants see the Rent Act 1977 and LANDLORD AND TENANT vol 27 para 590 et seq. As to other instances where security of tenure is given to tenants whose tenancies are otherwise validly terminated see the Landlord and Tenant Act 1954 s 64 (business tenancies: see LANDLORD AND TENANT vol 27 para 496 et seq); and the Rent Act 1977 s 155 (3), Sch 24 para 6 (furnished tenancies: see LANDLORD AND TENANT vol 27 para 562).
6 Theft Act 1968 s 4 (2) (c).

546. Growing plants and mushrooms. A person who picks mushrooms[1] growing wild on any land, or who picks flowers, fruit or foliage from a plant[2] growing wild on any land does not, although not in possession of the land, steal what he picks, unless he does it for reward or for sale or other commercial purpose[3].

1 For these purposes, 'mushroom' includes any fungus: Theft Act 1968 s 4 (3).
2 For these purposes 'plant' includes any shrub or tree: ibid s 4 (3). Taking the whole plant would, however, be theft since the exception relates only to picking flowers, fruit or foliage *from* a plant. A person who intentionally picks, uproots or destroys a protected wild plant is guilty of an offence under the Wildlife and Countryside Act 1981: see s 13, Sch 8 and AGRICULTURE.
3 Theft Act 1968 s 4 (3).

547. Wild creatures. Wild creatures, tamed or untamed, are regarded as property[1]; but a person cannot steal a wild creature not tamed or not ordinarily kept in captivity, or the carcase of any such creature, unless it has been reduced into possession by or on behalf of another person and possession of it has not since been lost or abandoned, or another person is in course of reducing it into possession[2].

1 As to the classification of animals into wild and domestic, and the property in such animals, see ANIMALS vol 2 para 201 et seq; and as to the protection of certain wild animals under the Wildlife and Countryside Act 1981 see s 9, Sch 5 and ANIMALS vol 2 para 347.
2 Theft Act 1968 s 4 (4). Poaching in so far as it is concerned with taking or killing creatures is, in general, not the subject of theft although taking and destroying fish is dealt with in s 32, Sch 1 para 2: see FISHERIES vol 18 para 654. As to the taking of deer see the Deer Act 1980 s 1 and ANIMALS vol 2 para 321.
   The mere act of taking over an existing natural mussel bed does not amount to a reduction into possession of the mussels: *R v Howlett and Howlett* [1968] Crim LR 222, CA. As to property in living fish see FISHERIES vol 18 para 652.

548. Property belonging to another. Property is regarded as belonging to any person having possession or control of it, or having any proprietary right or interest in it, not being an equitable interest arising only from an agreement to transfer or grant an interest[1].

Where property is subject to a trust, the persons to whom it belongs are regarded as including any person having a right to enforce the trust, and an intention to defeat the trust is regarded accordingly as an intention to deprive of the property any person having that right[2]. Where a person receives property from or on account of another, and is under an obligation to the other to retain and deal with that property or its proceeds in a particular way, the property or proceeds are regarded, as against him, as belonging to that other[3].

Where a person gets property by another's mistake, and is under an obligation to make restoration, in whole or in part, of the property or its proceeds[4] or of its value, then to the extent of that obligation the property or proceeds are to be regarded, as against him, as belonging to the person entitled to restoration, and an intention not to make restoration is to be regarded accordingly as an intention to deprive that person of the property or proceeds[5].

Property of a corporation sole is regarded as belonging to the corporation notwithstanding a vacancy[6].

The Theft Act 1968 applies in relation to the parties to a marriage, and to property belonging to the wife or husband whether or not by reason of an interest derived from the marriage, as it would apply if they were not married and any such interest subsisted independently of the marriage[7].

1 Theft Act 1968 s 5 (1). Section 5 (1) applies generally for the purposes of the Theft Act 1968: s 34 (1). As to property which is susceptible of theft see paras 544–547 ante. Civil law principles are sometimes applied by the courts in determining questions relating to title to goods for the purposes of the Theft Act 1968: see *R v Walker* [1984] Crim LR 112, CA; *Dobson v General Accident, Fire and Life Assurance Corpn plc* [1989] 3 All ER 927 at 937, 938, [1989] 3 WLR 1066 at 1079, CA per Bingham LJ (a civil case); but cf *R v Morris, Anderton v Burnside* [1984] AC 320 at 334, 77 Cr App Rep 309 at 317, HL per Lord Roskill.

An owner may steal his own goods if such goods are in the possession of his bailee and he has the intention either dishonestly to charge the bailee with the loss of the goods or, in cases where the bailee has a right to possession as against the owner, to deprive the bailee of his special property in the goods: see 1 Hale PC 513; *R v Wilkinson and Marsden* (1821) Russ & Ry 470, CCR; *Rose v Matt* [1951] 1 KB 810, 35 Cr App Rep 1, DC; *R v Turner (No 2)* [1971] 2 All ER 441, 55 Cr App Rep 336, CA (owner of motor car left it with garage for repairs; surreptitiously and dishonestly he collected it without paying for the repairs; guilty of theft). For the meaning of 'possession or control' see *R v Turner (No 2)* supra. Partnership property can be stolen by a partner (*R v Bonner* [1970] 2 All ER 97n, [1970] 1 WLR 838, CA) and persons in control of a limited company are capable of stealing the company's property (*A–G's Reference (No 2 of 1982)* [1984] QB 624, 78 Cr App Rep 131, CA; *R v Phillipou* (1989) 89 Cr App Rep 290, CA). Cf *R v McHugh, R v Tringham* (1988) 88 Cr App Rep 385, CA. If property has been abandoned by the owner, there can be no theft of it: see *R v Thurborn* (1849) 1 Den 387, CCR. However, the occupier of the land on which the abandoned property is found or in whose possession or control, actual or constructive, the property is can claim sufficient title to protect it from strangers: *R v Rowe* (1859) Bell CC 93 (canal company had sufficient property in iron found in canal); *Hibbert v McKiernan* [1948] 2 KB 142, [1948] 1 All ER 860, DC (golf club had special property in golf balls abandoned on course); *Williams v Phillips* (1957) 41 Cr App Rep 5, DC (local authority had constructive possession of rubbish collected by refuse collectors employed by authority); *R v Woodman* [1974] QB 754, [1974] 2 All ER 955, CA (company in control of disused factory site from which trespassers excluded; company had control of articles on site of the existence of which it was unaware). Cf *R v White* (1912) 7 Cr App Rep 266, CCA. As to what may amount to 'abandonment' by the owner see *R v Edwards and Stacey* (1877) 13 Cox CC 384, CCR (carcases of animals buried by owner on his land with intention of not moving them; carcases not abandoned); *Williams v Phillips* supra (refuse put out for collection by local authority not abandoned by original owner). As to instances where the finder of lost or abandoned property has not been found to have the requisite mens rea to commit an offence by appropriating the property see para 542 note 5 ante.

The question whether the property alleged to have been stolen is treasure trove (in which the Crown has a proprietary interest) is one of fact for the jury to decide, applying the ordinary criminal burden and standard of proof; and the lack of a coroner's inquisition does not prevent a prosecution for and conviction of theft of treasure trove: *R v Hancock* (1989) Times, 3 August, CA. As to treasure trove see CORONERS vol 9 paras 1177, 1178.

Where the subject matter of the offence is incorrectly stated in the indictment to be the property of a person, the indictment may be amended if no injustice is caused to the accused: see *R v Tirado* (1974) 59 Cr App Rep 80, CA (bank draft stated in indictment to be the property of person who gave instructions for it to be drawn; amendment made to show draft as property of bank). However, an amendment may not be essential: see *Etim v Hatfield* [1975] Crim LR 234, DC. As to the amendment of indictments generally see further para 937 post.

Where an employee makes a secret profit for which he will be held accountable, the secret profit, if it can be described as a trust, is not such as to give the employer a proprietary right or interest for the purposes of the Theft Act 1968 s 5 (1): *A-G's Reference (No 1 of 1985)* [1986] QB 491, 83 Cr App Rep 70, CA (public house manager selling own beer in breach of contract). A bribe received by an employee is not the property of his employers for the purposes of the Theft Act 1968 s 5: *Powell v MacRae* [1977] Crim LR 571, DC.

It is theft for a person to take goods from a shop without paying for them notwithstanding that possession has been granted to him, because the property in the goods does not pass until payment is made: *Davies v Leighton* (1978) 68 Cr App Rep 4, DC. It is not theft, however, to leave a petrol station without paying as the property in the petrol passes when the fuel enters the customer's tank: *Edwards v Ddin* [1976] 3 All ER 705, [1976] 1 WLR 942, DC. See also *R v McHugh* (1976) 64 Cr App Rep 92, CA (taking petrol possibly not theft as driver might have formed intention after passing of property to him). However, under the Theft Act 1978 s 3 it is an offence to make off without payment: see para 571 post.

Property may pass at the moment of appropriation: see *Dobson v General Accident, Fire and Life Assurance Corpn plc* [1989] 3 All ER 927 at 937, 938, [1989] 3 WLR 1066 at 1079, CA per Bingham LJ (a civil case).

Where a person indorses a cheque to another without knowing that it is a cheque that he is signing, property in the cheque does not pass; it is not, however, necessary to establish a plea of non est factum in order to establish that the property has not passed: *R v Davies* [1982] 1 All ER 513, 74 Cr App Rep 94, CA.

2 Theft Act 1968 s 5 (2).

3 Ibid s 5(3). For general observations on s 5 (3) and, in particular, for consideration of 'obligation' see *R v Hall* [1973] QB 126, 56 Cr App Rep 547, CA (travel agent received money from clients as deposits and payments for air trips, which he paid into his firm's general trading account; none of the flights took place and none of the money was refunded; it was not established either that the clients expected him 'to retain and deal with that property or its proceeds in a particular way', or that an 'obligation' to do so was undertaken by him; there was an absence of such a special arrangement between the accused and his clients as would give rise to an 'obligation' within the Theft Act 1968 s 5 (3)). Whether a person is under an obligation to retain and deal with money received from a customer in a particular way so that it will be regarded under s 5 (3) as belonging to that customer depends on the particular facts of each case: *R v Hall* supra; see also *Wakeman v Farrar* [1974] Crim LR 136, DC; *R v Hayes* (1976) 64 Cr App Rep 82, CA; *R v Brewster* (1979) 69 Cr App Rep 375, CA; *Davidge v Bunnett* [1984] Crim LR 297, DC. It is for the jury to establish the facts and the judge should direct the jury as to whether, on a particular finding of facts, a legal obligation under the Theft Act 1968 s 5 (3) arises: *R v Mainwaring* (1981) 74 Cr App Rep 99 at 107, CA per Lawton LJ. There is a distinction between this type of case and eg the treasurer of a solitary fund, as for instance a holiday fund, where the treasurer is in law the owner of the property, but the Theft Act 1968 s 5 (3) treats the property, as against him, as belonging to the persons to whom he owes the duty to retain and deal with the property as agreed: see *R v Hall* supra. Cf *R v Hassall* (1861) Le & Ca 56, CCR (where the treasurer of a money club misappropriated money paid to him by club members; his conviction of larceny as a bailee was quashed, fraudulent conversion then not having been created; his dishonest misappropriation would now amount to theft under the Theft Act 1968 s 5 (3)). In *R v Hall* supra the money was paid into the firm's general trading account but this was not itself decisive of the question whether or not an obligation under the Theft Act 1968 s 5 (3) arose; see also *R v Yule* [1964] 1 QB 5, 47 Cr App Rep 229, CCA. The Theft Act 1968 s 5 (3) does not apply unless there is an obligation on the accused to account for the particular property he has received or its proceeds. If he can do what he likes with the property having no obligation other than to account for a similar sum at a later date, there is no theft: see *Lewis v Lethbridge* [1987] Crim LR 59, DC; *DPP v Huskinson* [1988] Crim LR 620, DC (recipient of housing benefit under no obligation to use that benefit directly for payment of rent). Where an obligation under the Theft Act 1968 s 5 (3) is assumed and the one who assumes it subsequently discovers that by reason of a prior fraud the obligation is legally

unenforceable, he remains liable to be convicted of theft if he dishonestly fails to fulfil that obligation: *R v Meech* [1974] QB 549, 58 Cr App Rep 74, CA. A person selling his own goods on his employer's premises eg a public house in breach of contract does not receive the money paid for them on account of his employers within the Theft Act 1968 s 5 (3): *A–G's Reference (No 1 of 1985)* [1986] QB 491, 83 Cr App Rep 70, CA.

4 Where the payee of a cheque exchanges that cheque with a third party for cash before the cheque is presented, the cash received represents the 'proceeds' of the cheque for these purposes: *R v Davis* (1988) 88 Cr App Rep 347, CA.

5 Theft Act 1968 s 5 (4). The obligation must be an obligation in law; a social or moral obligation will not suffice: *R v Gilks* [1972] 3 All ER 280, 56 Cr App Rep 734, CA. See also *A–G's Reference (No 1 of 1983)* [1985] QB 182, 79 Cr App Rep 288, CA (money credited in error to employee's bank account by direct debit system; employee aware of mistake but not repaying money; obliged to make restitution); *R v Shadrokh-Cigari* [1988] Crim LR 465, CA (banker's drafts issued by mistake; recipient obliged to restore either proceeds or value of the drafts; moreover, because of the mistake the bank retained an equitable proprietary interest in the drafts within the meaning of the Theft Act 1968 s 5 (1) (see supra)).

The facts of the following cases under the pre-existing law would now bring them within the ambit of the Theft Act 1968 s 5 (4): *R v Middleton* (1873) LR 2 CCR 38 (bank clerk consulted wrong letter of advice and handed the accused much larger sum than he was entitled to); *R v Ashwell* (1885) 16 QBD 190, CCR (accused asked prosecutor to lend him a shilling; in the dark prosecutor handed him sovereign which they both thought was a shilling; accused, discovering mistake later, kept the sovereign); *Moynes v Coopper* [1956] 1 QB 439, 40 Cr App Rep 20, DC (employee given a paypacket which contained more than was due to him; he kept it all when he discovered the mistake on opening the packet). The former two cases would also fall within the provisions of the Theft Act 1968 s 3 (1): see para 543 ante. In *Lacis v Cashmarts* [1969] 2 QB 400, [1969] 2 WLR 329, DC, the accused went to a 'cash and carry' shop, selected goods worth £185 and took them to the till which was capable of registering up to £100 only, and, when the goods had been 'rung up', it accordingly showed a total of only £85; he was mistakenly asked for this sum and, knowing of the mistake, paid it and took the goods away; his conviction of larceny under the pre-existing law was quashed, the court observing that the facts would fall within the provisions of the Theft Act 1968 s 5 (4).

6 Ibid s 5 (5). As to corporations sole see CORPORATIONS vol 9 para 1206 et seq.

7 Ibid s 30 (1). As to the institution of proceedings for stealing or doing unlawful damage to the property of the accused's spouse see para 550 post.

549. Intention to deprive owner permanently. In every case of theft the dishonest appropriation must be accompanied by the intention of permanently depriving the owner of his property[1]. A person appropriating property belonging to another without meaning the other permanently to lose the thing itself is nevertheless to be regarded as having the intention of permanently depriving the other of it if his intention is to treat the thing as his own to dispose of regardless of the other's rights; and a borrowing or lending of it may amount to so treating it if, but only if, the borrowing or lending is for a period and in circumstances making it equivalent to an outright taking or disposal[2]. Without prejudice to the generality of the above provisions, where a person, having possession or control, whether lawfully or not, of property belonging to another, parts with the property under a condition as to its return which he may not be able to perform, this amounts, if done for purposes of his own and without the other's authority, to treating the property as his own to dispose of regardless of the other's right[3].

1 See the Theft Act 1968 s 1 (1) and para 541 ante. As to conditional intention see para 12 note 1 ante. For the meaning of 'dishonest' and 'appropriation' see paras 542, 543 respectively ante.

2 Ibid s 6 (1). Section 6 applies for the purposes of s 15 (see para 567 post) with any necessary adaptation of the reference to appropriating: see s 15 (3). As to the meaning of 'outright taking or disposal' see *R v Coffey* [1987] Crim LR 498, CA.

The purpose of the Theft Act 1968 s 6 is to clarify, but not to restrict, the meaning of the phrase 'with the intention of permanently depriving' and is not meant to contain an exhaustive definition of those words but rather to give illustrations of what can amount to the dishonest intention required by s 1 (1): *R v Warner* (1970) 55 Cr App Rep 93, CA. The Theft Act 1968 s 6 (1) should be referred to in exceptional cases only, and in the vast majority of cases need not be referred to or considered at all: *R v Lloyd, R v Bhuee, R v Ali* [1985] QB 829 at 835, 81 Cr App Rep 182 at 187, CA per Lord Lane CJ. The acquisition of a cheque by way of a loan which it is intended to repay amounts to a 'permanent deprivation'; if the cheque is looked upon as a thing in action (see the Theft Act 1968 s 4 (1) and para 544 ante), it loses its character as such on presentation; alternatively, if it is regarded as a mere piece of paper which after presentation is returned to the drawer, its character changes completely on payment and it ceases to be in substance the same thing as it was previously: see *R v Duru* [1973] 3 All ER 715, 58 Cr App Rep 151, CA; *R v Downes* (1983) 77 Cr App Rep 260, CA (Inland Revenue sub-contractor vouchers). A mere borrowing is insufficient to constitute the necessary guilty mind unless the intention is to return the thing taken to the owner in such a changed state as to have lost all its practical value: *R v Lloyd, R v Bhuee, R v Ali* supra (films taken temporarily from cinema for making copies in breach of copyright). See also *R v Bagshaw* [1988] Crim LR 321, CA; *R v Velumyl* [1989] Crim LR 299, CA. As to 'conditional' appropriation of another's property see para 543 note 2 ante.

3 Theft Act 1968 s 6 (2).

550. Institution of proceedings for theft etc of property of accused's spouse. Proceedings may not be instituted against a person for any offence of stealing or doing unlawful damage to property which, at the time of the offence, belongs to that person's spouse or for any attempt, incitement or conspiracy to commit such an offence, unless the proceedings are instituted by or with the consent of the Director of Public Prosecutions[1]. The above provisions do not apply, however, to proceedings against a person for an offence (1) if that person is charged with committing the offence jointly with his or her spouse; or (2) if, by virtue of any judicial decree or order, wherever made, the spouses are at the time of the offence under no obligation to cohabit[2].

1 Theft Act 1968 s 30 (4) (amended by the Criminal Jurisdiction Act 1975 s 14 (4), (5), Sch 5 para 2 (2), Sch 6 Pt 1). As to the effect of this limitation see para 639 post. See also *R v Withers* [1975] Crim LR 647.
   Notwithstanding the Prosecution of Offences Act 1985 s 25 (requirement of consent to institution of proceedings does not prevent arrest: see para 639 post), the Theft Act 1968 s 30 (4) (as so amended) applies to an arrest, if without warrant, made by the wife or husband and to a warrant of arrest issued on an information laid by the wife or husband: s 30 (5) (added by the Criminal Jurisdiction Act 1975 s 14 (4), Sch 5 para 2 (1); amended by the Prosecution of Offences Act 1979 s 11 (1), Sch 1); Interpretation Act 1978 s 17 (2) (a). Subject also to the Theft Act 1968 s 30 (4) (as so amended), a person has the same right to bring proceedings against his or her spouse for any offence (ie whether or not under that Act), as if they were not married: s 30 (2).
2 Ibid s 30 (4) proviso. 'Judicial decree or order' includes a non-molestation order: see *Woodley v Woodley* [1978] Crim LR 629, DC.

(ii) Other Offences involving or related to Stealing

551. Robbery. A person is guilty of robbery if he steals[1], and immediately before or at the time of[2] doing so, and in order to do so, he uses force on any person[3] or puts or seeks to put any person in fear of being then and there subjected to force[4]. A person guilty of robbery, or of an assault[5] with intent to rob, is liable on conviction on indictment to imprisonment for life or for any shorter term[6].

1 For the meaning of 'steal' see para 541 ante.
2 For the meaning of 'immediately before or at the time of' stealing see *R v Hale* (1978) 68 Cr App Rep 415, CA cited in para 543 note 2 ante.
3 This may include a person who has no proprietary right or interest in the property stolen.
4 Theft Act 1968 s 8 (1). Stealing is an ingredient of robbery and, if the accused believes that he has in law a claim of right to the property which he takes by force, the offence of robbery is not committed:

R v Hall (1828) 3 C & P 409; *R v Boden* (1844) 1 Car & Kir 395 (assault with intent to rob); *R v Hemmings* (1864) 4 F & F 50; *R v Skivington* [1968] 1 QB 166, 51 Cr App Rep 167, CA; *R v Robinson* [1977] Crim LR 173, CA. See also the Theft Act 1968 s 2 (1) (a) and para 542 head (1) ante.

The use of force or the putting in fear is not sufficient to constitute robbery if its purpose is to enable the accused to get away or to prevent the owner from recovering his property: *R v Harman* (1620) 1 Hale PC 534; *R v Gnosil* (1824) 1 C & P 304. 'The sole question is whether the accused used force on any person in order to steal': *R v Dawson, R v James* (1976) 64 Cr App Rep 170 at 172, CA per Lawton LJ. See also *R v Clouden* [1987] Crim LR 56, CA; *R v Shendley* [1970] Crim LR 49, CA. The degree of violence need not be excessive nor need the injury be serious to constitute robbery: *R v Harrison* (1930) 22 Cr App Rep 82, CCA; *R v Dawson, R v James* supra (jostling a person so as to make him lose his balance may be sufficient to constitute robbery). A continuing threat of force may suffice: *R v Donaghy and Marshall* [1981] Crim LR 644.

As to jurisdiction to prosecute offences of stealing a mail bag, postal packet etc in the course of transmission between places in different jurisdictions within the British postal area but outside England and Wales involving robbery, attempted robbery etc see para 592 post. As to the offence committed by a person who at the time of committing or being arrested for robbery has in his possession a firearm or imitation firearm see para 232 ante.

5 For the meaning of 'assault' see para 488 ante.

6 Theft Act 1968 s 8 (2). Offences under s 8 may not be tried summarily: Magistrates' Courts Act 1980 s 17, Sch 1 para 28 (a). For sentencing guidelines in cases of robbery see *R v Edwards, R v Larter* (1987) Times, 3 February, CA; *R v Richardson* (1988) Times, 10 February, CA. A person charged with robbery may be convicted of theft: *R v Shendley* [1970] Crim LR 49, CA. As to the general power to bring in an alternative verdict see para 1029 post.

552. Burglary. A person is guilty of burglary if:

(1) he enters[1] any building[2] or part of a building[3] as a trespasser[4] and with intent to steal[5] anything in the building or part of a building in question, to inflict on any person in it any grievous bodily harm[6] or to rape[7] any woman in it, or to do unlawful damage[8] to the building or anything in it[9]; or

(2) having entered any building or part of a building as a trespasser, he steals or attempts to steal anything in the building or that part of it or inflicts or attempts to inflict on any person in it any grievous bodily harm[10].

A person guilty of burglary is liable on conviction on indictment to imprisonment for a term not exceeding 14 years, or on summary conviction[11] to imprisonment for a term not exceeding six months or a fine not exceeding the prescribed sum, or to both[12].

1 See *R v Collins* [1973] QB 100, 56 Cr App Rep 554, CA ('effective and substantial entry' by the accused required); see also the general observations on entry in *R v Collins* supra at 104 and at 559. Cf *R v Brown* [1985] Crim LR 212, CA (jury should be directed to consider only whether entry was 'effective').

2 For these purposes, references to a building apply also to an inhabited vehicle or vessel, and to any such vehicle or vessel at times when the person having a habitation in it is not there as well as at times when he is: Theft Act 1968 s 9 (3).

3 A counter area in a shop is part of a building for the purposes of ibid s 9: *R v Walkington* [1979] 2 All ER 716, 68 Cr App Rep 427, CA.

4 There can be no conviction for entering a building as a trespasser unless the person entering did so knowing that he was a trespasser and nevertheless deliberately entered, or was reckless whether or not he was entering the premises of another without the other's consent: *R v Collins* [1973] QB 100, 56 Cr App Rep 554, CA. A person who has a general permission to enter premises belonging to another is a trespasser if he enters knowing that, or being reckless whether, he is exceeding that permission: *R v Jones, R v Smith* [1976] 3 All ER 54, 63 Cr App Rep 47, CA. The common law doctrine of trespass ab initio has no application to burglary: *R v Collins* supra. As to the nature of trespass, trespass to land and trespass ab initio see TORT vol 45 para 1384 et seq.

5 For the meaning of 'steal' see para 541 ante. If at the time of entry the trespasser intends to steal, such an intention is sufficient for a conviction and it is immaterial that there is in fact nothing worth stealing: *R v Walkington* [1979] 2 All ER 716, 68 Cr App Rep 427, CA; *A-G's References (Nos 1 and 2 of 1979)* [1980] QB 180, 69 Cr App Rep 266, CA.

6 As to offences involving grievous bodily harm see the Offences against the Person Act 1861 s 18 (wounding or causing grievous bodily harm with intent: see para 469 ante), s 20 (unlawfully and maliciously inflicting grievous bodily harm: see para 471 ante), s 23 (unlawfully and maliciously administering poison so as to inflict grievous bodily harm: see para 475 ante). For the meaning of 'grievous bodily harm' see para 470 text and note 7 ante.

7 As to rape see the Sexual Offences Act 1956 s 1, the Sexual Offences (Amendment) Act 1976 s 1 and para 514 et seq ante.

8 As to criminal damage see para 593 et seq post.

9 Theft Act 1968 s 9 (1) (a), (2). As to the relationship between s 9 (1) (a) and s 9 (1) (b) see note 10 infra.

10 Ibid s 9 (1) (b). It is open to a jury on a charge under s 9 (1) (b) to bring in a verdict under s 9 (1) (a): *R v Whiting* (1987) 85 Cr App Rep 78, CA, not following *R v Hollis* [1971] Crim LR 525, CA.

As to alternative verdicts see para 1029 post particularly at note 12. As to the offence of going equipped for burglary, theft or cheat see para 554 post. Since electricity cannot be appropriated by switching on current, and is not 'property' within the meaning of the Theft Act 1968 s 4, entering premises and using the telephone is not burglary: *Low v Blease* [1975] Crim LR 513, DC. See also para 544 note 1 ante.

11 Burglary comprising the commission of, or an intention to commit, an offence which is triable only on indictment and burglary in a dwelling if any person in the dwelling was subjected to violence or the threat of violence may not be tried summarily: see the Magistrates' Courts Act 1980 s 17, Sch 1 para 28 (b), (c).

12 Theft Act 1968 s 9 (4); Magistrates' Courts Act 1980 ss 17, 32 (1), Sch 1 para 28. For the meaning of 'the prescribed sum' see para 807 post. Burglary is a specified offence for the purposes of the Police and Criminal Evidence Act 1984 s 1 (2) (as amended) (power to search for prohibited articles: see para 661 et seq post). As to the offence committed by a person who at the time of committing or being arrested for burglary has in his possession a firearm or imitation firearm see para 232 ante. See also para 553 post. When the indictment alleges that goods have been stolen, it is not necessary for the prosecution to prove that all the goods referred to have been stolen: see para 541 note 6 ante.

For sentencing guidelines in cases of burglary see *R v O'Driscoll* [1986] Crim LR 701, CA; *R v Stratton* (1988) Times, 15 January, CA; *R v Robinson* (1988) Times, 10 February, CA.

553. Aggravated burglary. A person who commits any burglary[1] and at the time[2] has with him[3] any firearm[4] or imitation firearm[5], any weapon of offence[6], or any explosive[7] is guilty of aggravated burglary and liable on conviction on indictment to imprisonment for life or for any shorter term[8].

1 For the meaning of 'burglary' see para 552 ante.

2 If the charge is one of entry with intent (see para 552 head (1) ante), it is axiomatic that the accused must have with him the article of aggravation at the time of entering. However, if, having entered, the accused is charged with committing or attempting to commit a specified offence (see para 552 head (2) ante), he must have had the article of aggravation with him at the time of the commission of the offence, unless entry is accompanied by one of the specified intents. If the accused, having no such intent at the time of entry, discards his weapon, he is not guilty of aggravated burglary, but he would be if he rearmed himself for this purpose: *R v Francis* [1982] Crim LR 363, CA. See also *R v O'Leary* (1986) 82 Cr App Rep 341, CA (accused, having entered house as a trespasser, picked up a knife, proceeded upstairs and forced victim to hand over property).

3 Ie 'knowingly has with him': see *R v Stones* [1989] 1 WLR 156, 89 Cr App Rep 26, CA; and see para 167 note 5 ante.

4 'Firearm' includes an air gun or air pistol: Theft Act 1968 s 10 (1) (a).

5 'Imitation firearm' means anything which has the appearance of being a firearm, whether capable of being discharged or not: ibid s 10 (1) (a).

6 'Weapon of offence' means any article made or adapted for use for causing injury to or incapacitating a person, or intended by the person having it with him for such use: ibid s 10 (1) (b). Provided that the accused had the weapon with him at the time of entering (see note 2 supra), it is not necessary to prove that he intended to use it in the course of the burglary: *R v Stones* [1989] 1 WLR 156, 89 Cr App Rep 26, CA.

7 Theft Act 1968 s 10 (1). 'Explosive' means any article manufactured for the purpose of producing a practical effect by explosion, or intended by the person having it with him for that purpose: s 10 (1) (c).

8 Ibid s 10 (2). As to the appropriate direction to the jury on a charge of aggravated burglary see *R v O'Sullivan and Lewis* [1989] Crim LR 506, CA. Offences under the Theft Act 1968 s 10 may not be tried summarily: Magistrates' Courts Act 1980 s 17, Sch 1 para 28(a).

554. Going equipped for burglary, theft or cheat. A person is guilty of an offence if, when not at his place of abode[1], he has with him[2] any article for use in the course of or in connection[3] with any burglary[4], theft[5] or cheat[6]. Where a person is charged with such an offence, proof that he had with him any article made or adapted for use in committing a burglary, theft or cheat is evidence that he had it with him for such use[7].

A person guilty of such an offence is liable on conviction on indictment to imprisonment for a term not exceeding three years, or on summary conviction to imprisonment for a term not exceeding six months or a fine not exceeding the prescribed sum, or to both[8].

1 For the meaning of 'place of abode' see *R v Bundy* [1977] 2 All ER 382, 65 Cr App Rep 239, CA.
2 The words 'has with him' in the Prevention of Crime Act 1953 s 1 (1) mean 'knowingly has with him': see para 167 note 5 ante. The mere fact that a person was a passenger in a car containing such articles is not enough to constitute possession on his part: see *R v Lester, R v Byast* (1955) 39 Cr App Rep 157, CCA; *R v Harris* [1961] Crim LR 256, CCA; see also *R v Harran* [1969] Crim LR 662, CA. Although such articles in the physical possession of one person may be held jointly with other persons, it would be difficult for a jury so to find if those others are wholly ignorant of the existence of the articles: see *R v Webley* (1967) 111 Sol Jo 111, CA. It is not necessary to prove that the accused intended to use the article himself: *R v Ellames* [1974] 3 All ER 130, 60 Cr App Rep 7, CA.
3 The connection between the burglary, theft or cheat and the use of the article must not be too remote: *R v Mansfield* [1975] Crim LR 101, CA (documents used to obtain a job which might provide accused with opportunity to steal; use of documents too remote). Nor does the use of the article in connection with a burglary, theft or cheat before it came into the accused's possession constitute a use contemplated by the Theft Act 1968 s 25 (1): *R v Ellames* [1974] 3 All ER 130, 60 Cr App Rep 7, CA. However, it is not necessary to prove that the article is intended for use by the accused in any particular burglary, theft or cheat: *R v Ellames* supra.
4 For the meaning of 'burglary' see para 552 ante.
5 For the meaning of 'theft' see para 541 ante. For these purposes, an offence under s 12 (1) (taking a conveyance without authority: see para 556 post) is treated as theft: s 25 (5).
6 Ibid s 25 (1). 'Cheat' means an offence under s 15 (see para 567 post): s 25 (5). As to the position of an employee, not being at his place of abode, having in his possession articles of his own which dishonestly he intends to sell as his employer's contrary to s 15 see *R v Rashid* [1977] 2 All ER 237, 64 Cr App Rep 201, CA; *R v Doukas* [1978] 1 All ER 1061, 66 Cr App Rep 228, CA; *R v Corboz* [1984] Crim LR 629, CA; *R v Cooke* [1986] AC 909, 83 Cr App Rep 359, HL. As to the requisite direction to the jury where a person has counterfeit articles with him which he intends to sell in breach of copyright see *R v Whiteside, R v Antoniou* [1989] Crim LR 436, CA.
7 Theft Act 1968 s 25 (3).
8 Ibid s 25 (2); Magistrates' Courts Act 1980 ss 17, 32 (1), Sch 1 para 28. For the meaning of 'the prescribed sum' see para 807 post. The offence should attract a significant sentence: see *R v Person* (1969) 53 Cr App Rep 640, CA. As to disqualification for driving and endorsement of licence where the accused is convicted of an offence under the Theft Act 1968 s 25 with reference to the theft or taking of motor vehicles see the Road Traffic Offenders Act 1988 ss 34 (2), 97 (4), Sch 2 Pt II and ROAD TRAFFIC.
 Any person may arrest without warrant anyone who is, or whom he with reasonable cause suspects to be, committing an offence under the Theft Act 1968 s 25: s 25 (4). As to a constable's power of arrest, however, see para 693 et seq post.

555. Removal of articles from places open to the public. Where the public has access to a building in order to view it[1] or part of it, or a collection[2] or part of a collection housed in it, any person who without lawful authority removes from the building or its grounds the whole or part of any article displayed or kept for display to the public in the building or that part of it or in its grounds is guilty of an offence and liable on conviction on indictment to imprisonment for a term not exceeding five years, or on summary conviction to imprisonment for a term not exceeding six months or a fine not exceeding the prescribed sum, or to both[3].

A person does not commit such an offence if he believes that he has lawful authority for the removal or would have had it if the person entitled to give it knew of the removal and the circumstances of it[4].

1 The purpose or purposes of those responsible for the public being given access, and not the purposes of individual visitors, are relevant in deciding whether the public has access in order to view: *R v Barr* [1978] Crim LR 244.

2 For these purposes, 'collection' includes one got together for a temporary purpose; but references to a collection do not apply to one made or exhibited for the purpose of effecting sales or other commercial dealings: Theft Act 1968 s 11 (1).

3 Ibid s 11 (1), (4); Magistrates' Courts Act 1980 ss 17, 32 (1), Sch 1 para 28. For the meaning of 'the prescribed sum' see para 807 post.

For these purposes, it is immaterial that the public's access to a building is limited to a particular period or occasion; but, where anything removed from a building or its grounds is there otherwise than as forming part of, or being on loan for exhibition with, a collection intended for permanent exhibition to the public, the person removing it does not thereby commit the offence unless he removes it on a day when the public has access to the building: Theft Act 1968 s 11 (2). A 'collection intended for permanent exhibition to the public' is simply one intended to be permanently available to the public: *R v Durkin* [1973] QB 786, 57 Cr App Rep 637, CA.

4 Theft Act 1968 s 11 (3).

556. Taking motor vehicle or other conveyance without authority. A person is guilty of an offence if, without having the consent of the owner[1] or other lawful authority, he takes[2] any conveyance[3] for his own or another's use or, knowing that any conveyance has been taken without such authority[4], drives it or allows himself to be carried[5] in or on it[6]. A person guilty of such an offence is liable on summary conviction to imprisonment for a term not exceeding six months or a fine not exceeding level 5 on the standard scale, or to both[7].

A person who, without having the consent of the owner or other lawful authority, takes a pedal cycle for his own or another's use, or rides a pedal cycle knowing it to have been taken without such authority, is guilty of an offence and liable on summary conviction to a fine not exceeding level 3 on the standard scale[8].

A person does not, however, commit either of the above offences by anything done in the belief that he has lawful authority to do it or that he would have the owner's consent if the owner knew of his doing it and the circumstances of it[9].

1 For these purposes, 'owner', in relation to a conveyance which is the subject of a hiring agreement or hire-purchase agreement, means the person in possession of the conveyance under that agreement: Theft Act 1968 s 12 (7) (b).

2 Unauthorised assumption of possession of a vehicle is insufficient to constitute the offence; there must be some movement of the vehicle, however small (*R v Bogacki* [1973] QB 832, 57 Cr App Rep 593, CA) which must be voluntary with the intention of putting the vehicle in motion (*Blayney v Knight* [1975] RTR 279, DC). Where the vehicle is moved in a way which necessarily involves its use as a conveyance, the offence is made out and the taker's motive is irrelevant: *R v Bow* (1976) 64 Cr App Rep 541, CA (moving a vehicle causing obstruction). The offence is committed even though the vehicle has not been used as a conveyance: *R v Marchant, R v McCallister* (1984) 80 Cr App Rep 361,CA (vehicle pushed to another place to be used later).

3 For these purposes, 'conveyance' means any conveyance constructed or adapted for the carriage of a person or persons whether by land, water or air, except that it does not include a conveyance constructed or adapted for use only under the control of a person not carried in or on it; and 'drive' is to be construed accordingly: Theft Act 1968 s 12 (7) (a). A horse is not a conveyance: *Neal v Gribble* (1978) 68 Cr App Rep 9, DC. Nor is a pedal cycle a conveyance for the purposes of the Theft Act 1968 s 12 (1): s 12 (5).

4 This includes knowledge that it has been stolen: *Tolley v Giddings* [1964] 2 QB 354, 48 Cr App Rep 105, DC.
5 There must be some movement of the conveyance for the accused to be carried in it: *R v Diggin* (1981) 72 Cr App Rep 204, CA, following *R v Bogacki* [1973] QB 832, 57 Cr App Rep 593, CA.
6 Theft Act 1968 s 12 (1). As to the power to join in an indictment a count for an offence under s 12 (1) see para 922 post. Taking a motor or other conveyance without authority is a specified offence for the purposes of the Police and Criminal Evidence Act 1984 s 1 (2) (as amended) (power to search for prohibited articles: see para 661 et seq post). Possession of an article for use in committing an offence under the Theft Act 1968 s 12 (1) or (5) (see infra) is itself an offence: see s 25 (1), (5) and para 554 ante. As to interference with a vehicle see para 557 post.
   If on the trial of an indictment for theft the jury is not satisfied that the accused committed theft, but it is proved that the accused committed an offence under s 12 (1), the jury may find him guilty of the offence under s 12 (1), and, if he is found guilty of it, he is liable as he would have been liable under s 12 (2) (amended by the Criminal Justice Act 1988 s 37 (1) (a)) (see infra) on summary conviction: Theft Act 1968 s 12 (4) (amended by the Criminal Justice Act 1988 s 37 (1) (b)).
7 Theft Act 1968 s 12 (2) (as amended: see note 6 supra). For the meaning of 'the standard scale' see para 808 post. As to disqualification and endorsement of licence see the Road Traffic Offenders Act 1988 ss 34 (2), 97 (2), Sch 2 Pt II and ROAD TRAFFIC. As to the commission of the offence by an employee using his employer's vehicle of which he had conditional custody see *R v Wibberley* [1966] 2 QB 214, 50 Cr App Rep 51, CCA (employee using such a vehicle after working hours guilty of the offence), followed in *R v Phipps* (1970) 54 Cr App Rep 300, CA and *McKnight v Davies* [1974] RTR 4, DC; but see *R v Peart* [1970] 2 QB 672, 54 Cr App Rep 374, CA (consent, although obtained by misrepresentation as to the destination and purpose of the journey, was not vitiated). See also *Whittaker v Campbell* [1983] 3 All ER 582, 77 Cr App Rep 267, DC (owner gave de facto consent; consent not vitiated by reason of its having been obtained by fraud), distinguished in *Singh v Rathour* [1988] 2 All ER 16, [1988] 1 WLR 422, CA (limited consent given by owner). As to the offence committed by a person who at the time of committing or being arrested for an offence under the Theft Act 1968 s 12 (1) has in his possession a firearm or imitation firearm see para 232 ante.
8 Ibid s 12 (5) (amended by the Criminal Justice Act 1982 ss 38, 46). See also note 6 supra.
9 Theft Act 1968 s 12 (6). If an issue arises as to the accused's belief, the onus is on the prosecution to prove that the accused did not have the relevant belief: *R v MacPherson* [1973] RTR 157, CA.

557. Interference with vehicles. A person is guilty of an offence if he interferes with a motor vehicle[1] or trailer[2] or with anything carried in or on a motor vehicle or trailer with the intention that the offence of (1) theft of the vehicle or trailer or part of it; or (2) theft of anything carried in or on the vehicle or trailer; or (3) taking a conveyance without authority[3], is committed by himself or some other person[4]. A person guilty of such an offence is liable on summary conviction to imprisonment for a term not exceeding three months or a fine not exceeding level 4 on the standard scale, or to both[5].

1 'Motor vehicle' means, subject to the Chronically Sick and Disabled Persons Act 1970 (special provisions for invalid carriages), a mechanically propelled vehicle intended or adapted for use on roads: Road Traffic Act 1988 s 185 (1) applied by the Criminal Attempts Act 1981 s 9 (5) (amended by the Road Traffic (Consequential Provisions) Act 1988 s 4, Sch 3 para 23).
2 'Trailer' means a vehicle drawn by a motor vehicle: Road Traffic Act 1988 s 185 (1) applied by the Criminal Attempts Act 1981 s 9 (5) (as amended: see note 1 supra).
3 See para 556 ante.
4 Criminal Attempts Act 1981 s 9 (1), (2). If it is shown that a person accused of such an offence intended that one of the offences in text heads (1)–(3) supra should be committed, it is immaterial that it cannot be shown which it was: s 9 (2).
5 Ibid s 9 (3) (amended by the Criminal Justice Act 1982 ss 38, 46). For the meaning of 'the standard scale' see para 808 post.

558. Abstracting electricity. A person who dishonestly[1] uses without due authority, or dishonestly causes to be wasted or diverted, any electricity[2], is liable on conviction on indictment to imprisonment for a term not exceeding five years,

or on summary conviction to imprisonment for a term not exceeding six months
or a fine not exceeding the prescribed sum, or to both[3].

1   Use is not dishonest if the person believed he was acting honestly: *Boggeln v Williams* [1978] 2 All ER
    1061, 67 Cr App Rep 50, DC. The Theft Act 1968 s 2 (meaning of 'dishonestly': see para 542 ante)
    does not apply for the purposes of s 13: see s 1 (3) and para 541 note 1 ante. See, however, *R v Melwani*
    [1989] Crim LR 565, CA (cited in para 567 note 3 post).
2   Electricity is not property and therefore cannot be the subject of theft under the general law: *Low v
    Blease* (1975) 119 Sol Jo 695, [1975] Crim LR 513, DC.
3   Theft Act 1968 s 13; Magistrates' Courts Act 1980 ss 17, 32 (1), Sch 1 para 28. For the meaning of 'the
    prescribed sum' see para 807 post.

(2) STOLEN GOODS

559. Handling stolen goods.   A person handles stolen goods[1] if, otherwise than
in the course of stealing[2], knowing or believing[3] them to be stolen goods, he
dishonestly[4] receives[5] the goods, or dishonestly undertakes or assists in their
retention[6], removal, disposal or realisation[7] by or for the benefit of another
person[8], or if he arranges to do so[9].

A person guilty of handling stolen goods is liable on conviction on indictment to
imprisonment for a term not exceeding 14 years, or on summary conviction to
imprisonment for a term not exceeding six months or a fine not exceeding the
prescribed sum, or to both[10].

1   For the meaning of 'stolen goods' see para 560 post.
2   The prosecution is not normally required to prove that the accused was not the thief or a party to the
    theft; but, where it is established that he was simply a party to the theft, he must not be convicted of
    handling: *R v Cash* [1985] QB 801, 80 Cr App Rep 314, CA. See also *R v Pitham and Hehl* (1977) 65 Cr
    App Rep 45, CA.
3   As to knowledge or belief see para 561 post.
4   As to dishonesty see para 562 post.
5   As to receiving see para 563 post.
6   'Retention' corresponds with the dictionary definition of 'retain', namely 'keep possession of, not to
    lose, continue to have'; an accused's conduct in permitting money to remain in his bank account after
    he learnt that it had been stolen constituted such retention: see *R v Pitchley* (1972) 57 Cr App Rep 30,
    CA, distinguishing *R v Brown* [1970] 1 QB 105, 53 Cr App Rep 527, CA. Assisting in the retention
    of stolen goods is more than the mere use of them; the accused must be proved to have done some
    act, such as hiding them or making identification more difficult: see *R v Sanders* (1982) 75 Cr App
    Rep 84, CA. Verbal representations made to conceal that the goods were stolen may constitute the
    offence: *R v Kanwar* [1982] 2 All ER 528, 75 Cr App Rep 87, CA.
7   A purchase of goods is not a 'realisation' by the purchaser: *R v Bloxham* [1983] 1 AC 109 at 114, 74 Cr
    App Rep 279 at 283, HL per Lord Bridge; not following *R v Deakin* [1972] 3 All ER 803, 56 Cr App
    Rep 841, CA. Merely accepting the benefit of the disposition of stolen goods is insufficient to
    amount to assisting in the disposal of stolen goods: *R v Coleman* (1985) 150 JP 175, [1986] Crim LR
    56, CA.
8   'By or for the benefit of another person' governs 'retention', 'removal', 'disposal' and 'realisation'
    and should be included in the particulars of the offence when a charge under the second part of the
    Theft Act 1968 s 22 (1) is laid in an indictment: *R v Sloggett* [1972] 1 QB 430, 55 Cr App Rep 532, CA.
    A purchaser cannot be 'another person': *R v Bloxham* [1983] 1 AC 109, 74 Cr App Rep 279, HL.
9   Theft Act 1968 s 22 (1). In order to constitute such an arrangement the goods must have been stolen
    at the time the arrangement was made: *R v Park* (1987) 87 Cr App Rep 164, CA. Where an
    arrangement is made before the theft, the appropriate charge is conspiracy (see para 59 et seq ante): *R
    v Park* supra. The Theft Act 1968 s 22 (1) creates two distinct offences, one of receiving and one of
    dishonestly undertaking etc: *R v Bloxham* [1983] 1 AC 109 at 113, 74 Cr App Rep 279 at 282, HL per
    Lord Bridge; but cf *Griffiths v Freeman* [1970] 1 All ER 1117, [1970] 1 WLR 659, DC; and see the cases
    cited in para 931 note 1 post. Particulars should be given to enable the accused to understand the
    ingredients of the charge: *Griffiths v Freeman* supra; *R v Nicklin* [1977] 2 All ER 44, 64 Cr App Rep

205, CA. An indictment containing two separate counts, one in respect of receiving and one in respect of some or all the other forms of handling is not bad for duplicity: *R v Nicklin* supra; *R v Bloxham* supra. As to charging theft and handling as alternatives see para 541 note 6 ante. As to separate counts in an indictment see *R v Bellman* [1989] 1 All ER 22, 88 Cr App 252, HL and para 931 note 1 post. Where the accused is found in possession of property stolen from a number of different burglaries or robberies which he is alleged to have received on separate occasions, each occasion should be the subject of a separate count: *R v Smythe* (1980) 72 Cr App Rep 8, CA. As to similar fact evidence on a charge of handling stolen goods see the Theft Act 1968 s 27 (3) and para 1076 post. As to joint indictments see s 27 (1), (2) and para 997 note 1 post.

10 Theft Act 1968 s 22 (2); Magistrates' Courts Act 1980 ss 17, 32 (1), Sch 1 para 28. For the meaning of 'the prescribed sum' see para 807 post. To secure a conviction it need not be shown that the accused knew the nature of the goods which are the subject matter of the charge: *R v McCullum* (1973) 57 Cr App Rep 645, CA.

560. Meaning of 'stolen goods'. The provisions of the Theft Act 1968[1] relating to goods[2] which have been stolen apply whether the stealing occurred in England or Wales or elsewhere, provided that the stealing, if not an offence under the Act, amounted to an offence where and at the time when the goods were stolen; and references to stolen goods are to be construed accordingly[3]. For the purposes of those provisions[4], goods obtained in England and Wales or elsewhere either by blackmail[5] or by deception[6] are to be regarded as stolen; and 'steal', 'theft' and 'thief' are to be construed accordingly[7].

For the purposes of such provisions, references to stolen goods include, in addition to the goods originally stolen and parts of them, whether in their original state or not: (1) any other goods which directly or indirectly represent or have at any time represented the stolen goods in the hands of the thief as being the proceeds of any disposal or realisation[8] of the whole or part of the goods stolen or of goods so representing the stolen goods[9]; and (2) any other goods which directly or indirectly represent or have at any time represented the stolen goods in the hands of a handler of the stolen goods or any part of them as being the proceeds of any disposal or realisation of the whole or part of the stolen goods handled by him or of goods so representing them[10].

It must be proved that the goods were stolen; the proof may be by direct evidence of the theft or the circumstances in which the accused handled the goods may of themselves prove that the goods were stolen; there is no rule that there must be other evidence of the theft[11]. However, no goods are to be regarded as having continued to be stolen goods after they have been restored to the person from whom they were stolen or to other lawful possession or custody[12], or after that person and any other person claiming through him have otherwise ceased as regards those goods to have any right to restitution in respect of the theft[13]. Thus, where stolen goods are recovered by the prosecutor and subsequently returned to the thief for the purpose of trapping any person who might later handle them, a charge of handling stolen goods will fail[14].

1 Ie the Theft Act 1968 ss 22–24, 26–28, 32 (2). Sections 26, 27, are expressly stated to be construed in accordance with s 24: ss 26 (5), 27 (5). As to s 26 see para 565 post; and as to s 27 see paras 997, 1076, 1114 post. References in s 28 to stealing are to be construed in accordance with s 24 (1), (4): s 28 (6). See para 1337 post.
2 For the meaning of 'goods' see para 544 note 1 ante.
3 Theft Act 1968 s 24 (1).
4 Ie the provisions referred to in note 1 supra. In ibid s 24 (4), those provisions are stated expressly to include s 24 (1)–(3).
5 See para 566 post.
6 Ie under the Theft Act 1968 s 15 (1): see para 567 post.

7 Ibid s 24 (4).

8 For the meaning of 'realisation' see para 559 note 7 ante.

9 Theft Act 1968 s 24 (2) (a). The proceeds of any disposal or realisation may include cheques and bank account balances: *A-G's Reference (No 4 of 1979)* [1981] 1 All ER 1193, 71 Cr App Rep 341, CA.

10 Theft Act 1968 s 24 (2) (b). Thus eg where stolen savings stamps have been converted into cash, the cash or bank notes fall within the term 'stolen goods': see *D'Andrea v Woods* [1953] 2 All ER 1028, 37 Cr App Rep 182, DC.

11 *R v Sbarra* (1918) 13 Cr App Rep 118, CCA; *R v Fuschillo* [1940] 2 All ER 489, 27 Cr App Rep 193, CCA. However, the accused's knowledge or belief that a payment of money represented stolen goods is not conclusive evidence of that fact: *A-G's Reference (No 4 of 1979)* [1981] 1 All ER 1193, 71 Cr App Rep 341, CA. As to similar fact evidence on a charge of handling stolen goods see para 1076 post. If the alleged thief of goods is a child under the age of criminal responsibility, a person handling the goods cannot be guilty of handling stolen goods although an indictment for theft may lie against him: see *Walters v Lunt* [1951] 2 All ER 645, 35 Cr App Rep 94, DC.

12 Whether goods are so restored depends primarily on the intention of the person allegedly restoring them and is a matter for the jury: *A-G's Reference (No 1 of 1974)* [1974] QB 744, 59 Cr App Rep 203, CA; *Metropolitan Police Comr v Streeter* (1980) 71 Cr App Rep 113, DC.

13 Theft Act 1968 s 24 (3). As to restitution orders see para 1337 post.

14 See *R v Dolan* (1855) 6 Cox CC 449; *R v Schmidt* (1866) LR 1 CCR 15; *R v Hancock and Baker* (1878) 14 Cox CC 119, CCR; *R v Villensky* [1892] 2 QB 597, CCR; see also *Haughton v Smith* [1975] AC 476, 58 Cr App Rep 198, HL; cf *R v King* [1938] 2 All ER 662, CCA; *R v Curbishley* (1970) 55 Cr App Rep 310, CA.

561. Knowledge or belief that the goods have been stolen. Knowledge or belief that the goods have been stolen is an essential ingredient in a charge of handling stolen goods[1]. This knowledge or belief must exist at the time when the accused received or otherwise handled the goods[2]. The test of knowledge or belief is subjective; but, if there is evidence that the accused deliberately shut his eyes to the obvious, the inference may be drawn that he did so because he knew or believed the goods to be stolen[3]. The circumstances in which the accused handled the goods may show that he knew that they were stolen[4] but the fact that he lied to the police as to the manner in which the goods came into his possession is not necessarily evidence that he knew that they were stolen[5].

The possession by a person of goods which have been recently stolen is some evidence, in the absence of a reasonable explanation by him as to how they came into his possession, that he either stole them or received them knowing them to be stolen depending on the particular circumstances[6]. The weight attributable to the evidence depends on the nature of the goods and the length of time which has elapsed from the time when they were stolen to the time when they are proved to have been in the possession of the accused[7]. If a person is accused of receiving stolen goods and recent possession of them by him is established, he may be convicted of handling stolen goods in the absence of any explanation by him of the way in which they came into his possession which might reasonably be true, and which is consistent with innocence; but, if he gives such an explanation, even though the jury is not convinced of its truth, the accused is entitled to be acquitted in the absence of other evidence, because the prosecution has failed to discharge the duty of satisfying the jury that it is sure of the guilt of the accused; that onus remains on the prosecution[8]. Evidence that an accused charged with handling stolen goods has had in his possession stolen goods from any theft in the 12 months before the offence charged may be admitted and evidence of any convictions for theft or handling stolen goods in the previous five years may also be given[9].

1 See para 559 ante.

2 See *Atwal v Massey* [1971] 3 All ER 881, 56 Cr App Rep 6, DC; *R v Alt* (1972) 56 Cr App Rep 457, CA; *R v Grainge* [1974] 1 All ER 928, 59 Cr App Rep 3, CA; see also para 562 post.

3 *Atwal v Massey* [1971] 3 All ER 881, 56 Cr App Rep 6, DC; *R v Grainge* [1974] 1 All ER 928, 59 Cr App Rep 3, CA; *R v Griffiths* (1974) 60 Cr App Rep 14, CA. As to the difference between 'knowledge' and 'belief' see *R v Hall* (1985) 81 Cr App Rep 260, CA ('knowledge' is actual knowledge; 'belief', although short of actual knowledge, is appreciation that the goods must have been stolen in the absence of any reason to the contrary). In most cases there is no need to give the jury any direction as to the meaning of 'knowledge or belief': *R v Harris* (1986) 84 Cr App Rep 75, CA. A mere suspicion, not amounting to knowledge or belief, is inadequate to constitute the offence: *R v Grainge* supra. An erroneous belief that the goods are stolen goods is irrelevant (*Haughton v Smith* [1975] AC 476, 58 Cr App Rep 198, HL); but a person who dishonestly handles goods in such a mistaken belief may be convicted for attempted handling (*R v Shivpuri* [1987] AC 1, 83 Cr App Rep 178, HL, overruling *Anderton v Ryan* [1985] AC 560, 81 Cr App Rep 166, HL). As to attempts see para 71 et seq ante.

4 *R v Sbarra* (1918) 13 Cr App Rep 118, CCA; *R v Fuschillo* [1940] 2 All ER 489, 27 Cr App Rep 193, CCA; and see para 560 note 11 ante.

5 See *Cohen v March* [1951] 2 TLR 402, DC; cf *R v Young* [1953] 1 All ER 21, 36 Cr App Rep 200, CCA. An admission made by the thief in the accused's presence may be admissible, eg to show that the accused knew that the goods were stolen, against the accused: *R v Turner* (1832) 1 Mood CC 347; *R v Cox* (1858) 1 F & F 90; as to the extent that such admissions may be evidence against the accused see para 1121 post. Proof of the conviction of the thief is not admissible to show that the accused knew that the goods were stolen: see *R v Kelly* (1900) 64 JP Jo 84; cf *R v Blick* (1830) 4 C & P 377. A plea of guilty by a co-accused is not admissible to show that the accused knew that the goods were stolen: see *R v Fallows* (1948) 65 TLR 93, CCA. As to treating the evidence of the thief as requiring corroboration see para 1143 post.

6 *R v Langmead* (1864) Le & Ca 427, CCR. Guilty knowledge may similarly be inferred where the accused has merely assisted in the disposal of the goods: *R v Ball, R v Winning* [1983] 2 All ER 1089, 77 Cr App Rep 131, CA.

7 *R v Schama, R v Abramovitch* (1914) 84 LJKB 396, 11 Cr App Rep 45, CCA; *R v Loughlin* (1951) 35 Cr App Rep 69, CCA; *R v Seymour* [1954] 1 All ER 1006, 38 Cr App Rep 68, CCA.

8 See *R v Schama, R v Abramovitch* (1914) 84 LJKB 396, 11 Cr App Rep 45, CCA; *R v Norris* (1916) 86 LJKB 810, 12 Cr App Rep 156, CCA; *R v Grinberg* (1917) 33 TLR 428, CCA; *R v Badash* (1917) 87 LJKB 732, 13 Cr App Rep 17, CCA; *R v Hamilton* (1917) 87 LJKB 734, 13 Cr App Rep 32, CCA; *R v Bailey* (1917) 13 Cr App Rep 27 at 31, CCA; *R v Brain* (1918) 13 Cr App Rep 197, CCA; *R v Ketteringham* (1926) 19 Cr App Rep 159, CCA; *R v Booth* (1946) 175 LT 306, CCA; *Practice Note* [1946] WN 101, CCA; *R v Garth* [1949] 1 All ER 773, 33 Cr App Rep 100, CCA; *R v Aves* [1950] 2 All ER 330, 34 Cr App Rep 159, CCA; *R v Hepworth and Fearnley* [1955] 2 QB 600, 39 Cr App Rep 152, CCA; *R v Smythe* (1980) 72 Cr App Rep 8, CA; *R v Cash* [1985] QB 801, 80 Cr App Rep 314, CA; *R v Raviraj* (1987) 85 Cr App Rep 93, CA. Failure to give an explanation after a caution may not, however, be relied upon as evidence of guilt: *R v Raviraj* supra at 101. As to the need for a careful direction to the jury in cases of handling stolen goods see *R v Currell* (1935) 25 Cr App Rep 116, CCA; *R v Smith* (1935) 25 Cr App Rep 119, CCA. As to directions on the burden of proof generally see para 1015 post.

9 See further para 1076 post.

562. Dishonesty in receiving stolen goods. Dishonesty is an essential ingredient in the offence of handling stolen goods[1]. If, at the time when the stolen goods were received, the accused intended to hand them to the owner or to the police, the receipt is innocent and the accused is not guilty of handling even if he subsequently changes his mind[2].

1 See para 559 ante. The Theft Act 1968 s 2 (meaning of 'dishonestly': see para 542 ante) does not apply for the purposes of s 22: see s 1 (3) and para 541 note 1 ante. See, however, *R v Melwani* [1989] Crim LR 565, CA (cited in para 567 note 3 post). Where the accused is found in possession of the goods and the jury is directed as to knowledge or belief that they have been stolen (see para 561 ante), there is no need to give any direction on dishonesty: *R v Ball, R v Winning* [1983] 2 All ER 1089, 77 Cr App Rep 131, CA. As to the appropriate direction where dishonesty is the principal issue see *R v Roberts* (1985) 84 Cr App Rep 117, CA.

2 See *R v Matthews* [1950] 1 All ER 137, 34 Cr App Rep 55, CCA. In such instances misappropriation of property probably amounts to theft: see para 543 note 3 ante.

563. Receiving stolen goods. The dishonest receiving of stolen goods knowing or believing them to be stolen goods is one of the ways in which the offence of handling stolen goods may be committed[1]. A receiving imports possession, sole or joint[2], actual or constructive[3], and control over the stolen goods[4]. The mere presence of stolen goods in the accused's house or other place to which he has access is not in itself sufficient evidence of receipt or possession by him[5]. If the accused is absent when they are delivered, then, before he can be found to have actual or constructive possession of goods found on his premises, it must be shown that since his return he has become aware of them and exercised some control over them or that the goods came, albeit in his absence, at his invitation or by arrangement[6].

1 See para 559 ante. Cf *R v Bloxham* [1983] 1 AC 109 at 113, 74 Cr App Rep 279 at 282, HL per Lord Bridge: see para 559 note 9 ante. As to the framing of the indictment where handling stolen goods in this manner is alleged see para 931 note 1 post.

2 Where a husband and wife are jointly indicted for handling stolen goods, the wife may be convicted if there is evidence of a handling by her separate and apart from that of the husband: *R v Baines* (1900) 69 LJQB 681, CCA. If stolen goods are received by the wife without her husband's knowledge, and he, on becoming aware of it, passively assents, he is not guilty of handling: *R v Dring* (1857) Dears & B 329, CCR; *R v Pritchard* (1913) 9 Cr App Rep 210, CCA. However, the husband is guilty of handling stolen goods if he subsequently ratifies what she has done even though he does not touch the goods: *R v Woodward* (1862) Le & Ca 122, CCR. A husband may be convicted of the offence of handling goods which have been stolen by the wife: see *R v M'Athey* (1862) Le & Ca 250, CCR. As to marital coercion as a defence to a criminal charge see para 25 ante. As to joint possession, other than between husband and wife, see *R v Smith* (1855) Dears CC 494, CCA; *R v Rogers* (1868) LR 1 CCR 136; *R v Payne* (1909) 3 Cr App Rep 259, CCA; *R v Frost, R v Hale* (1964) 48 Cr App Rep 284, CCA. Cf the cases cited as to the possession of the handler being distinct from that of the thief in note 4 infra.

3 Knowledge of the whereabouts of stolen goods, even if they are on the accused's premises, does not necessarily amount to constructive possession: see *R v Orris* (1908) 1 Cr App Rep 199, CCA; as to stolen goods discovered on the accused's premises see further note 4 infra. Similarly, the mere receipt of goods by an employee without authority, instructions or knowledge of the employer does not constitute constructive possession on the part of the employer: *R v Pearson (No 2)* (1908) 72 JP 451, 1 Cr App Rep 79, CCA; *R v Cavendish* [1961] 2 All ER 856, 45 Cr App Rep 374, CCA.

As to subsequent ratification of criminal acts performed by another see note 2 supra. As to constructive possession of stolen goods which are in the hands of an employee, an innocent agent or dealer with the knowledge of the accused see *R v Cryer* (1857) Dears & B 324, CCR; *R v Rogers* (1868) LR 1 CCR 136.

4 *R v Hughes* (1878) Cox CC 223, CCR; *R v Watson* [1916] 2 KB 385, 12 Cr App Rep 62, CCA; *R v Freedman* (1930) 22 Cr App Rep 133, CCA; *R v Smith* (1931) 23 Cr App Rep 135 at 138, CCA. The receipt may be for a temporary purpose, eg concealment: *R v Richardson* (1834) 6 C & P 335. The intention behind the receiving is immaterial, eg the receiving need not be in the hope of profit: see *R v Davis* (1833) 6 C & P 177. The possession of the handler must be distinct from that of the thief; the mere receiving of a thief with stolen goods in his possession does not of itself constitute a receiving of the goods: *R v Wiley* (1850) 2 Den 37 at 48, CCR per Coleridge J and at 50 per Park B; *R v Ashworth* (1911) 6 Cr App Rep 112, CCA; *R v Berger* (1915) 84 LJKB 541, 11 Cr App Rep 72, CCA; *Hawes v Edwards* (1949) 93 Sol Jo 213, DC; *R v Frost, R v Hale* (1964) 48 Cr App Rep 284, CCA. A claim made to the stolen goods does not constitute possession or control of them: *R v Hill* (1849) 1 Den 453, CCR. Actual manual possession need not be proved provided that the goods were under the control of the accused: *R v Hobson* (1854) Dears CC 400, CCR; *R v Smith* (1855) Dears CC 494, CCA; *R v Gleed* (1916) 12 Cr App Rep 32, CCA. However, physically handling goods does not necessarily constitute possession: see *Hobson v Impett* (1957) 41 Cr App Rep 138, DC.

5 *R v Pratt* (1865) 4 F & F 315; *R v Hughes* (1878) 14 Cox CC 223, CCR; *R v Orris* (1908) 1 Cr App Rep 199, CCA; *R v Batty* (1912) 76 JP 388, 7 Cr App Rep 286, CCA; *R v Foreman* (1913) 9 Cr App Rep 216, CCA; *R v Cavendish* [1961] 2 All ER 856, 45 Cr App Rep 374, CCA. Whether such property is there with or without the accused's knowledge and sanction is a question for the jury: *R v Savage* (1906) 70 JP 36.

It has been said that, if stolen goods are found at the accused's house, and he is not the thief, there is a prima facie case against him for receiving them: see *R v Matthews* (1850) 1 Den 596 at 601, CCR per Coleridge J. As to the doctrine of recent possession see para 561 text and note 8 ante.

6 *R v Cavendish* [1961] 2 All ER 856, 45 Cr App Rep 374, CCA. Where evidence as to possession is meagre, the direction to the jury must be carefully worded: see *R v Shaw* [1942] 2 All ER 342, 28 Cr App Rep 138, CCA.

564. Advertising rewards. Where any public advertisement of a reward for the return of any goods which have been stolen[1] or lost uses any words to the effect that no questions will be asked, or that the person producing the goods will be safe from apprehension or inquiry, or that any money paid for the purchase of the goods or advanced by way of loan on them will be repaid, the person advertising the reward and any person who prints or publishes the advertisement is guilty of an offence and liable on summary conviction to a fine not exceeding level 3 on the standard scale[2].

1 For the meaning of 'stolen goods' see para 560 ante.
2 Theft Act 1968 s 23 (amended by the Criminal Justice Act 1982 ss 38, 46). For the meaning of 'the standard scale' see para 808 post. The offence is one of strict liability: see *Denham v Scott* (1983) 77 Cr App Rep 210, DC. As to strict liability see para 18 ante.

565. Warrant to search for stolen goods. If it is made to appear by information on oath before a justice of the peace that there is reasonable cause to believe that any person has in his custody or possession or on his premises any stolen goods[1], the justice may grant a warrant to search for and seize the same; but no such warrant may be addressed to a person other than a constable except under the authority of an enactment expressly so providing[2]. Where a person is so authorised to search premises for stolen goods, he may enter and search the premises accordingly and may seize any goods he believes to be stolen goods[3].

1 For the meaning of 'stolen goods' see para 560 ante.
2 Theft Act 1968 s 26 (1). Section 26 is to be construed in accordance with s 24 (see para 560 ante): s 26 (5). As to the granting of warrants generally see para 670 et seq post.
3 Ibid s 26 (3).

(3) BLACKMAIL

566. Blackmail. A person is guilty of blackmail if, with a view to gain for himself or another or with intent to cause loss to another[1], he makes any unwarranted demand[2] with menaces[3]. For these purposes, a demand with menaces is unwarranted unless the person making it does so in the belief that he has reasonable grounds for making the demand, and that the use of the menaces is a proper means of reinforcing the demand[4]. The nature of the act or omission demanded is immaterial; and it is also immaterial whether the menaces relate to action to be taken by the person making the demand[5].

A person guilty of blackmail is liable on conviction on indictment to imprisonment for a term not exceeding 14 years[6].

1 For the purposes of the Theft Act 1968, 'gain' and 'loss' are to be construed as extending only to gain or loss in money or other property, but as extending to any such gain or loss whether temporary or permanent: s 34 (2) (a). 'Gain' includes a gain by keeping what one has, as well as a gain by getting what one has not; and 'loss' includes a loss by not getting what one might get, as well as a loss by parting with what one has: s 34 (2) (a) (i), (ii). An unwarranted demand with menaces for a debt believed to be due is a 'gain' for this purpose (see *R v Lawrence, R v Pomroy* (1971) 57 Cr App Rep 64,

CA); as is such a demand for an injection of morphine, the morphine plainly being property (*R v Bevans* (1988) 87 Cr App Rep 64, CA).

2 The demand need not be in explicit or express terms but may be implicit in words or conduct: *R v Collister, R v Warhurst* (1955) 39 Cr App Rep 100, CCA. Thus a request imposing conditions may amount to a demand, although a mere request would not: *R v Studer* (1915) 85 LJKB 1017, CCA. A demand contained in a letter is made when the letter is posted: *Treacy v DPP* [1971] AC 537 at 546, 55 Cr App Rep 113 at 117, HL.

3 Theft Act 1968 s 21 (1). 'Menaces' is given a wide meaning: see *Thorne v Motor Trade Association* [1937] AC 797 at 817, 26 Cr App Rep 51 at 67, HL per Lord Wright ('the word menace is to be liberally construed and not as limited to threats of violence, but as including threats of any action detrimental to or unpleasant to the person addressed. It may also include a warning that in certain events such action is intended'). 'Menaces' is an ordinary English word which a jury could be expected to understand: *R v Lawrence, R v Pomroy* (1971) 57 Cr App Rep 64, CA. See also *Treacy v DPP* [1971] AC 537 at 565, 55 Cr App Rep 113 at 146, HL per Lord Diplock ('The Theft Act 1968 . . . is expressed in simple language as used and understood by ordinary literate men and women'); *R v Garwood* [1987] 1 All ER 1032, 85 Cr App Rep 85, CA.

To constitute 'menaces' the threats or conduct of the accused must be of such a nature and extent that the mind of an ordinary person of normal stability and courage might be influenced or made apprehensive so as to accede unwillingly to the demand: *R v Clear* [1968] 1 QB 670, 52 Cr App Rep 58, CA. The term 'an ordinary person of normal stability and courage' in this context should be interpreted literally: see *R v Tomlinson* [1895] 1 QB 706 at 710, CCR per Wills J; *R v Boyle and Merchant* [1914] 3 KB 339, CCA. Where appropriate, the trial judge should direct the jury that menaces are proved either if the threats might have affected a person of ordinary stability but did not affect the person actually addressed or if the threats in fact affected the mind of the victim although they would not have affected a person of ordinary stability provided that the accused was aware of the likely effect of his action on the victim: *R v Garwood* supra. A threat to injure property or character may amount to a menace: *R v Smith* (1850) 2 Car & Kir 882, CCR; *R v Taylor* (1859) 1 F & F 511; *R v Boyle and Merchant* supra. However, a threat to the person or property of another will suffice: *R v Tomlinson* supra. Similarly, a threat to charge a person with a crime (*R v Miard* (1844) 1 Cox CC 22; *R v Tomlinson* supra) or with misconduct not amounting to a crime (*R v Chalmers* (1867) 10 Cox CC 450, CCR; *R v Tomlinson* supra) or with arrest may amount to menaces (*R v Robertson* (1864) Le & Ca 483, CCR). Whether the threats or conduct in a particular case constitute menaces is a matter for the jury: *R v Walton and Ogden* (1863) Le & Ca 288, CCR; *R v Clear* supra; see also *R v Carruthers* (1844) 1 Cox CC 138. As to threats to kill see also para 434 ante; and as to blackmail with an international element see para 624 post.

4 Theft Act 1968 s 21 (1). The test of the accused's belief is subjective; but 'where the threats were to do acts which any sane man knows to be against the laws of every civilised country, no jury would hesitate long before dismissing the contention that the accused genuinely believed the threats to be a proper means of reinforcing even a legitimate demand': *R v Harvey, R v Ulyett, R v Plummer* (1980) 72 Cr App Rep 139 at 142, CA per Bingham J. As to the proper direction to the jury on the question of belief see *R v Harvey, R v Ulyett, R v Plummer* supra. It is for the defence to raise the issue of belief; and, if it is not raised, there is no need for any direction on the question: *R v Lawrence, R v Pomroy* (1971) 57 Cr App Rep 64, CA; *R v Harvey, R v Ulyett, R v Plummer* supra at 142.

5 Theft Act 1968 s 21 (2).

6 Ibid s 21 (3). Offences under s 21 may not be tried summarily: see the Magistrates' Courts Act 1980 s 17, Sch 1 para 28 (a). As to sentencing for blackmail see *R v Hadjou* (1989) 11 Cr App Rep (S) 29, CA; and as to the offence committed by a person who at the time of committing or being arrested for blackmail has in his possession a firearm or imitation firearm see para 232 ante.

The provisions of the Theft Act 1968 relating to stolen goods apply to goods obtained by blackmail: see s 24 (4) and para 560 ante. Similarly, restitution orders are applicable to goods obtained by blackmail: see para 1337 note 2 post.

(4) FRAUD

567. Obtaining property by deception. A person[1] who by any deception[2] dishonestly[3] obtains[4] property belonging to another[5], with the intention of permanently depriving the other of it[6], is guilty of an offence and liable on conviction on indictment to imprisonment for a term not exceeding ten years, or on summary conviction to imprisonment for a term not exceeding six months or a fine not exceeding the prescribed sum, or to both[7].

1 Where an offence committed by a body corporate under the Theft Act 1968 s 15 (see infra), s 16 (see para 568 post) or s 17 (see para 572 post) is proved to have been committed with the consent or connivance of any director, manager, secretary or other similar officer of the body corporate, or any person who was purporting to act in any such capacity, he as well as the body corporate is guilty of that offence and liable to be proceeded against and punished accordingly; and, where the affairs of a body corporate are managed by its members, these provisions apply in relation to the acts and defaults of a member in connection with his functions of management as if he were a director of the body corporate: s 18.

2 For these purposes, 'deception' means any deception, whether deliberate or reckless, by words or conduct as to fact or as to law, including a deception as to the present intentions of the person using the deception or any other person: ibid s 15 (4). As to a reckless deception see *R v Staines* (1974) 60 Cr App Rep 160, CA (recklessness involves an indifference to, or disregard of, whether the statement is true or false). As to recklessness see further para 14 ante. The deception may be by words or conduct: see eg *R v Harris* (1975) 62 Cr App Rep 28, CA; *R v Silverman* (1987) 86 Cr App Rep 213, CA. See also *R v Rashid* [1977] 2 All ER 237, 64 Cr App Rep 201, CA; *R v Doukas* [1978] 1 All ER 1061, 66 Cr App Rep 228, CA (both decided under the Theft Act 1968 s 25: see para 554 ante).

The deception must be the effective cause of obtaining the property (see the Theft Act 1968 s 15) or a pecuniary advantage (see s 16 and para 568 post) or procuring the execution of a valuable security (see s 20 (2) and para 573 post) and must operate on the mind of the person to whom it is directed (*R v Laverty* [1970] 3 All ER 432, 54 Cr App Rep 495, CA; *R v Royle* [1971] 3 All ER 1359, 56 Cr App Rep 131, CA; *R v Kovacs* [1974] 1 All ER 1236, 58 Cr App Rep 412, CA; *R v King* [1987] QB 547, 84 Cr App Rep 357, CA). Otherwise there will only be an attempt to commit the offence: *R v Hensler* (1870) 11 Cox CC 570, CCR; *R v Light* (1915) 84 LJKB 865, 11 Cr App Rep 111, CCA. Even where the prosecutor would not have parted with his money had he been aware that the representation made to him by the accused was false, the deception is not necessarily the effective cause of obtaining the property or securing the advantage: see *R v Clucas* [1949] 2 KB 226, 33 Cr App Rep 136, CCA (bookmaker, induced by false representation to accept a large bet on credit, paying out on it; the effective cause of the payment was the backing of the winning horse). On the facts in *R v Clucas* supra, an offence under the Theft Act 1968 s 16 might now be established. The deception does not necessarily have to be practised on the person suffering the resultant loss: *R v Kovacs* supra (decided under the Theft Act 1968 s 16).

Dishonesty does not necessarily constitute deception: *R v Clucas* supra; *Davies v Flackett* (1972) 116 Sol Jo 526, DC. It is doubtful whether deception can be practised unless there is a human mind to deceive: see *Davies v Flackett* supra (driver avoiding payment at automatic barrier in car park); but making off without having paid as required or expected and with intent to avoid payment of the amount due is an offence under the Theft Act 1978 s 3 (see para 571 post). The deception must precede obtaining the property or the pecuniary advantage or procuring the execution of a valuable security: *R v Collis-Smith* [1971] Crim LR 716, CA. The onus of showing that the property or the pecuniary advantage or the execution of the valuable security was procured by the deception falls on the prosecution and it should normally be proved by direct evidence (*R v Laverty* supra; *R v Tirado* (1974) 59 Cr App Rep 80, CA); but the inducement need not be proved by direct evidence if the facts are such that the alleged deception would have been the only reason why the accused obtained property belonging to another (see *R v Laverty* [1970] 3 All ER 432, 54 Cr App Rep 495, CA; *R v Lambie* [1982] AC 449, 73 Cr App Rep 294, HL).

If a person makes a representation to another, expressly or by implication, and that person subsequently decides not to honour the representation but nevertheless continues in that representation without manifesting any change of intent, he practices deception: *DPP v Ray* [1974] AC 370, 58 Cr App Rep 130, HL (meal ordered in restaurant; accused decided not to pay after he had eaten the meal; accused left restaurant when waiter out of room). By giving a cheque, whether postdated or not, the drawer impliedly represents that the state of facts existing at the date of delivery is such that in the ordinary course of events the cheque will be met on presentation for payment on or after the date specified in it: *R v Gilmartin* [1983] QB 953, 76 Cr App Rep 238, CA; and see *Metropolitan Police Comr v Charles* [1977] AC 177 at 182, 63 Cr App Rep 252 at 260, 261, HL per Lord Diplock; *R v Hazelton* (1874) LR 2 CCR 134; *R v Page* [1971] 2 QB 330n at 333, 55 Cr App Rep 184 at 190, CA. Where a cheque is drawn to cover an application for a large allotment of shares in the knowledge that, if the whole number applied for is in fact allotted, there will not be sufficient funds to meet the cheque, but the drawer's expectation is that he will be allotted only a small proportion of the number of shares applied for, so that with the cheque he will receive in respect of the surplus he can provide a total credit balance to cover his own cheque ('stagging'), the representations implied in drawing the cheque thus constitute a deception: see *R v Greenstein* [1976] 1 All ER 1, 61 Cr App Rep 296, CA. As to the dishonest use of cheque cards and credit cards to obtain the property of another see *Metropolitan Police Comr v Charles* supra (cheque cards); *R v Lambie* supra (credit cards).

3 'Dishonestly' in the Theft Act 1968 ss 15, 16, has replaced the phrase 'intent to defraud' in the pre-existing law and is of wider ambit: *R v Potger* (1970) 55 Cr App Rep 42 at 46, CA. The Theft Act 1968 s 2 (meaning of 'dishonestly': see para 542 ante) does not apply for the purposes of ss 15, 16: see s 1 (3) and para 541 note 1 ante. However, the same test of dishonesty applies throughout the Theft Act 1968: *R v Melwani* [1989] Crim LR 565, CA. The jury should be told that, before convicting, it must be satisfied that the particular deception was dishonest and, where the deception was reckless rather than deliberate, the summing up should normally deal separately with dishonesty as an ingredient of the offence: *R v Potger* supra. The test of an honest belief negativing dishonest intent is subjective: *R v Waterfall* [1970] 1 QB 148, 53 Cr App Rep 596, CA; *R v Potger* supra; *R v Royle* [1971] 3 All ER 1359, [1971] 1 WLR 1764, CA. Honest belief need not be based on reasonable grounds: *R v Lewis* (1975) Times, 16 December, CA; but see *R v Small* (1987) 86 Cr App Rep 170, CA (decided under the Theft Act 1968 s 1: see para 541 ante). The questions for the court are (1) whether the act was dishonest according to the standards of reasonable and honest people; and (2) whether the accused appreciated that what he was doing was by those standards dishonest: see *R v Ghosh* [1982] QB 1053, 75 Cr App Rep 154, CA; *R v Small* supra; *R v Woolven* (1983) 77 Cr App Rep 231, CA. As to the circumstances in which the direction in *R v Ghosh* supra should be given to the jury see *R v Price* (1989) Times, 28 October, CA.

4 For these purposes, a person is to be treated as obtaining property if he obtains ownership, possession or control of it; and 'obtain' includes obtaining for another or enabling another to obtain or to retain: Theft Act 1968 s 15 (2). As to proof that the property was obtained see *Bogdal v Hall* [1987] Crim LR 500, DC. The deception must be the effective cause of the obtaining and must operate on the mind of the person to whom it is directed: see note 2 supra. If the obtaining is for another, it is immaterial that the other is not a party to the deception: *R v Duru* [1973] 3 All ER 715, 58 Cr App Rep 151, CA (accused deceiving local authority into granting loans for house purchase; cheques for the purpose sent to solicitors acting for both the authority and the applicants for loans; cheques 'obtained' within the Theft Act 1968 s 15 (2)). As to jurisdiction in cases involving a foreign element see para 624 post.

5 For the meaning of 'property' see para 544 text and note 1 ante; and for the meaning of 'property belonging to another' see para 548 text and note 1 ante. See also *Etim v Hatfield* [1975] Crim LR 234, DC; *Levene v Pearcey* [1976] Crim LR 63, DC; *R v Thompson* [1984] 3 All ER 565, 79 Cr App Rep 191, CA; *R v Ashbee* [1989] 1 WLR 109, 88 Cr App Rep 357, CA; *Brady v IRC* [1989] STC 178, DC.

6 The Theft Act 1968 s 6 (see para 549 ante) applies for the purposes of s 15, with the necessary adaptation of the reference to appropriating, as it applies for the purposes of s 1: s 15 (3).

7 Ibid s 15 (1); Magistrates' Courts Act 1980 ss 17, 32 (1), Sch 1 para 28. For the meaning of 'the prescribed sum' see para 807 post. Obtaining property by deception is a specified offence for the purposes of the Police and Criminal Evidence Act 1984 s 1 (2) (as amended) (power to search for prohibited articles: see para 661 post). For sentencing guidelines in cases of obtaining property by deception see *R v Barrick* (1985) 81 Cr App Rep 78, CA; *R v Stewart* [1987] 2 All ER 383, 85 Cr App Rep 66, CA. The facts that constitute this offence may also constitute theft: see *Lawrence v Metropolitan Police Comr* [1972] AC 626, 55 Cr App Rep 471, HL. As to the offence of having with one an article for use in connection with an offence under the Theft Act 1968 s 15 when not at one's place of abode see para 554 ante; and as to obtaining property by deception with an international element see para 624 post.

568. Obtaining pecuniary advantage by deception. A person[1] who by any deception[2] dishonestly[3] obtains[4] for himself or another any pecuniary advantage is liable on conviction on indictment to imprisonment for a term not exceeding five years, or on summary conviction to imprisonment for a term not exceeding six months or a fine not exceeding the prescribed sum, or to both[5]. The cases where a pecuniary advantage is to be regarded as so obtained for a person are cases where (1) he is allowed to borrow by way of overdraft[6], or to take out any policy of insurance or annuity contract, or obtains an improvement of the terms on which he is allowed to do so[7]; or (2) he is given the opportunity to earn remuneration or greater remuneration in an office or employment, or to win money by betting[8].

1 As to offences committed by a body corporate see para 567 note 1 ante.
2 For these purposes, 'deception' has the same meaning as in the Theft Act 1968 s 15: s 16 (3). See further para 567 ante.
3 For the meaning of 'dishonestly' see para 567 note 3 ante.
4 The deception must be the effective cause of the obtaining and must operate on the mind of the person to whom it is directed: see para 567 note 2 ante.
5 Theft Act 1968 s 16 (1); Magistrates' Courts Act 1980 ss 17, 32 (1), Sch 1 para 28. For the meaning of 'the prescribed sum' see para 807 post. As to obtaining property by deception see para 567 ante; as to obtaining services by deception see para 569 post; as to the evasion of liability by deception see para 570 post; and as to making off without payment see para 571 post.
6 A person who uses a cheque card and cheque book to run up an overdraft beyond the limits imposed by the bank, or to create an overdraft in the absence of a negotiated and agreed limit, is 'allowed to borrow by way of overdraft' for these purposes: *R v Waites* [1982] Crim LR 369, CA; *R v Bevan* (1987) 84 Cr App Rep 143, CA. A customer who is allowed to borrow from a bank on overdraft obtains a pecuniary advantage at the moment when the overdraft facility is granted to him without need for proof that he drew on that facility: *R v Watkins* [1976] 1 All ER 578.
7 Theft Act 1968 s 16 (2) (b).
8 Ibid s 16 (2) (c).

569. Obtaining services by deception. A person[1] who by any deception[2] dishonestly obtains services[3] from another is guilty of an offence and liable on conviction on indictment to imprisonment for a term not exceeding five years, or on summary conviction to imprisonment for a term not exceeding six months or a fine not exceeding the prescribed sum, or to both[4].

1 For these purposes, the Theft Act 1968 s 18 (liability of company officers for offences by the company: see para 567 note 1 ante) applies: Theft Act 1978 s 5 (1).
2 For these purposes, 'deception' has the same meaning as in the Theft Act 1968 s 15 (see para 567 ante), that is to say, it means any deception, whether deliberate or reckless, by words or conduct as to fact or as to law, including a deception as to the present intentions of the person using the deception or any other person: Theft Act 1978 s 5 (1).
3 It is an obtaining of services where the other is induced to confer a benefit by doing some act, or causing or permitting some act to be done, on the understanding that the benefit has been or will be paid for: ibid s 1 (2). See further *R v Halai* [1983] Crim LR 624, CA (obtaining a benefit); *R v Widdowson* (1986) 82 Cr App Rep 314, CA (obtaining a service).
4 Theft Act 1978 ss 1 (1), 4 (amended by the Magistrates' Courts Act 1980 s 154 (1), Sch 7 para 170). For the meaning of 'the prescribed sum' see para 807 post. The Theft Act 1968 s 30 (1) (husband and wife: see para 550 ante), s 31 (1) (effect on civil proceedings: see para 1111 post), s 34 (interpretation), so far as they are applicable in relation to the Theft Act 1978, apply as they apply in relation to the Theft Act 1968: Theft Act 1978 s 5 (2).

570. Evasion of liability by deception. Where a person[1] by any deception[2]:
(1) dishonestly secures the remission of the whole or part of any existing liability[3] to make a payment, whether his own liability or another's; or
(2) with intent to make a permanent default in whole or in part on any existing liability[4] to make a payment, or with intent to let another do so, dishonestly induces[5] the creditor or any person claiming payment on behalf of the creditor to wait for payment, whether or not the due date for payment is deferred, or to forgo payment; or
(3) dishonestly obtains[6] any exemption from or abatement of liability to make a payment[7],

he is guilty of an offence and liable on conviction on indictment to imprisonment for a term not exceeding five years, or on summary conviction to imprisonment for a term not exceeding six months or a fine not exceeding the prescribed sum, or to both[8].

1 As to the liability of company officers for offences by a company see para 569 note 1 ante.
2 For the meaning of 'deception' see para 569 note 2 ante.
3 For these purposes, 'liability' means legally enforceable liability; and the Theft Act 1978 s 2 (1) (see heads (1)–(3) infra) does not apply in relation to a liability that has not been accepted or established to pay compensation for a wrongful act or omission: s 2 (2).
4 The requirement of an intent to make a permanent default is unique to the offence under head (2) supra; heads (1)–(3) thus create separate offences with substantial differences in the elements of each, but these differences relate principally to the different situations in which the debtor-creditor relationship has arisen, and the features common to all three offences are (a) the use of a deception to a creditor in relation to a liability; (b) dishonesty in the use of deception; and (c) the use of deception to gain some advantage in time or money. There may be situations in which the conduct of the debtor or his agent could fall under more than one of heads (1)–(3) supra: *R v Holt* [1981] 2 All ER 854 at 856, 73 Cr App Rep 96 at 99, CA per Lawson J. See also *R v Sibartie* [1983] Crim LR 470, CA; *R v Jackson* [1983] Crim LR 617, CA.
5 For these purposes, a person induced to take in payment a cheque or other security for money by way of conditional satisfaction of a pre-existing liability is to be treated not as being paid but as being induced to wait for payment: Theft Act 1978 s 2 (3).
6 For these purposes, 'obtains' includes obtaining for another or enabling another to obtain: ibid s 2 (4).
7 The offence under ibid s 2 (1) (c) (see head (3) supra) may be committed irrespective of whether the act is one of commission or omission and may be committed before any liability to pay has come into existence: *R v Firth* (1989) Times, 29 December, CA.
8 Theft Act 1978 ss 2 (1), 4 (amended by the Magistrates' Courts Act 1980 s 154 (1), Sch 7 para 170). For the meaning of 'the prescribed sum' see para 807 post. As to the application of the Theft Act 1968 ss 30 (1), 31 (1), 34 see para 569 note 4 ante.

571. Making off without payment. A person[1] who, knowing that payment on the spot[2] for any goods supplied or services done[3] is required or expected from him, dishonestly makes off[4] without having paid as required or expected and with intent to avoid payment[5] of the amount due is guilty of an offence and liable on conviction on indictment to imprisonment for a term not exceeding two years, or on summary conviction to imprisonment for a term not exceeding six months or a fine not exceeding the prescribed sum, or to both[6].

1 As to the liability of company officers for offences by a company see para 569 note 1 ante.
2 For these purposes, 'payment on the spot' includes payment at the time of collecting goods on which work has been done or in respect of which service has been provided: Theft Act 1978 s 3 (2).
3 Ibid s 3 (1) does not apply, however, where the supply of the goods or the doing of the service is contrary to law, or where the service done is such that payment is not legally enforceable: s 3 (3). See *Troughton v Metropolitan Police* [1987] Crim LR 138, DC (taxi driver broke away from route in breach of contract; accused not liable for payment thereafter).
4 The words 'dishonestly makes off' should be applied in their natural meaning. 'Making off' involves a departure from the spot where payment is required; but, if the accused is stopped before passing that spot, he may be guilty of an attempt to commit the offence: *R v McDavitt* [1981] Crim LR 843; *R v Brooks and Brooks* (1983) 76 Cr App Rep 66, CA.
5 'Intent to avoid payment' means an intent to avoid payment permanently: *R v Allen* [1985] AC 1029, 81 Cr App Rep 200, HL; and see *R v Hammond* [1982] Crim LR 611.
6 Theft Act 1978 ss 3 (1), 4 (amended by the Magistrates' Courts Act 1980 s 154 (1), Sch 7 para 170). For the meaning of 'the prescribed sum' see para 807 post. As to the application of the Theft Act 1968 ss 30 (1), 31 (1), 34 see para 569 note 4 ante.
   Any person may arrest without warrant anyone who is, or whom he, with reasonable cause, suspects to be, committing or attempting to commit an offence under the Theft Act 1978 s 3: s 3 (4). As to powers of arrest see para 693 et seq post.

572. False accounting. Where a person[1] dishonestly, with a view to gain[2] for himself or another or with intent to cause loss[2] to another:
   (1) destroys, defaces, conceals or falsifies[3] any account or any record[4] or document[5] made or required for any accounting purpose; or

(2) in furnishing information for any purpose produces or makes use of any
account, or any such record or document which to his knowledge is or may
be misleading, false or deceptive in a material particular[6],

he is liable on conviction on indictment to imprisonment for a term not exceeding
seven years, or on summary conviction to imprisonment for a term not exceeding
six months or a fine not exceeding the prescribed sum, or to both[7].

1 As to the liability of company officers for offences by a company see para 567 note 1 ante.
2 For the meaning of 'gain' and 'loss' see para 566 note 1 ante. The offence of false accounting may be
  based on the intention to make a temporary gain: *R v Eden* (1971) 55 Cr App Rep 193, CA. Where,
  however, a document is falsified in order to postpone the enforcement of an existing obligation,
  obtaining the creditor's forbearance is not a 'gain' for the purposes of the Theft Act 1968 s 17: *R v
  Golechha* [1989] 3 All ER 908, CA.
3 For these purposes, a person who makes or concurs in making in an account or other document an
  entry which is or may be misleading, false or deceptive in a material particular, or who omits or
  concurs in omitting a material particular from an account or other document is to be treated as
  falsifying the account or document: Theft Act 1968 s 17 (2). A fraud which does not involve any
  entry or omission in an account or other document is not false accounting: *R v Cooke* [1986] AC 909
  at 935, 83 Cr App Rep 339 at 357, HL per Lord Mackay (British Rail steward intending to sell private
  catering supplies as if they were his employers'; such supplies would not show in the account).
4 The word 'record' should be given a wide meaning and includes a meter attached to a turnstile:
  Edwards v Toombs [1983] Crim LR 43, DC.
5 The document need not be made specifically for accounting purposes but it must be required for
  such purpose: *A-G's Reference (No 1 of 1980)* [1981] 1 All ER 366, 72 Cr App Rep 60, CA. Although a
  document is required for an accounting purpose as to part and is falsified as to part, the fact that the
  two parts are not the same does not exonerate the person responsible for the falsification where the
  document constitutes one entire document: *A-G's Reference (No 1 of 1980)* supra. Where there is a
  duty to complete one of a number of standard printed forms, one such form may be a document
  required for an accounting purpose and failure to complete such a form in respect of a transaction
  may constitute falsification of a document for these purposes: *R v Shama* (1990) Times, 18 January,
  CA.
6 There is no need for the material particular to be directly connected with the accounting purpose of
  the document: *R v Mallett* [1978] 3 All ER 10, 67 Cr App Rep 239, CA.
7 Theft Act 1968 s 17 (1); Magistrates' Courts Act 1980 ss 17, 32 (1), Sch 1 para 28. For the meaning of
  'the prescribed sum' see para 807 post.

573. Suppression etc of documents. A person who dishonestly, with a view to
gain[1] for himself or another or with intent to cause loss[1] to another, destroys,
defaces or conceals any valuable security[2], any will or other testamentary document or any original document of or belonging to, or filed or deposited in, any
court of justice or any government department is guilty of an offence and liable on
conviction on indictment to imprisonment for a term not exceeding seven years, or
on summary conviction to imprisonment for a term not exceeding six months or a
fine not exceeding the prescribed sum, or to both[3].

A person who dishonestly, with a view to gain for himself or another or with
intent to cause loss to another, by any deception[4] procures[5] the execution[6] of a
valuable security is guilty of an offence and liable on conviction on indictment to
imprisonment for a term not exceeding seven years, or on summary conviction to
imprisonment for a term not exceeding six months or a fine not exceeding the
prescribed sum, or to both[7].

1 For the meaning of 'gain' and 'loss' see para 566 note 1 ante.
2 For these purposes, 'valuable security' means any document creating, transferring, surrendering or
  releasing any right to, in or over property, or authorising the payment of money or delivery of any
  property, or evidencing the creation, transfer, surrender or release of any such right, or the payment
  of money or delivery of any property, or the satisfaction of any obligation: Theft Act 1968 s 20 (3).

An irrevocable letter of credit is a valuable security within the meaning of s 20: *R v Benstead, R v Taylor* (1982) 75 Cr App Rep 276, CA.

3 Theft Act 1968 s 20 (1); Magistrates' Courts Act 1980 ss 17, 32 (1), Sch 1 para 28. For the meaning of 'the prescribed sum' see para 807 post. As to concealment of documents in cases of serious fraud see para 588 post.

4 For these purposes, 'deception' has the same meaning as in the Theft Act 1968 s 15: s 20 (3). See para 567 note 2 ante.

5 For these purposes, 'procures' bears the common meaning of 'causes' or 'brings about': *R v Beck* [1985] 1 All ER 571, 80 Cr App Rep 355, CA.

6 The Theft Act 1968 s 20 (2) applies also in relation to the making, acceptance, indorsement, alteration, cancellation or destruction in whole or in part of a valuable security, and in relation to the signing or sealing of any paper or other material in order that it may be made or converted into, or used or dealt with as, a valuable security, as if that were the execution of a valuable security: s 20 (2). The word 'acceptance' in s 20 (2) is to be given the meaning prescribed by the Bills of Exchange Act 1882 s 17: see *R v Nanayakkara* [1987] 1 All ER 650, 84 Cr App Rep 125, CA.

See also *R v Beck* [1985] 1 All ER 571, 80 Cr App Rep 355, CA (travellers' cheques forged abroad, honoured in England; acts abroad procured acceptance in England); *R v Kassim, R v Young* [1988] Crim LR 372, CA.

7 Theft Act 1968 s 20 (2); Magistrates' Courts Act 1980 ss 17, 32 (1), Sch 1 para 28. As to the degree of unanimity required of the jury where more than one false statement is alleged see *R v Agbim* [1979] Crim LR 171, CA.

574. Fraudulent practices in connection with conveyancing. Any person disposing of property or any interest therein for money or money's worth to a purchaser, or the solicitor or agent of such a person, who with intent to defraud conceals from the purchaser any instrument or incumbrance material to the title or falsifies any pedigree upon which the title may depend in order to induce the purchaser to accept the title offered or produced is guilty of an offence and liable on conviction on indictment to imprisonment for a term not exceeding two years or a fine, or to both[1].

If any person fraudulently procures, attempts fraudulently to procure, or is privy to the fraudulent procurement of, any entry on, erasure from or alteration of, the register of title kept at the Land Registry, or any land or charge certificate, he is guilty of an offence and liable on conviction on indictment to imprisonment for a term not exceeding two years or a fine, or on summary conviction to imprisonment for a term not exceeding three months or a fine not exceeding the prescribed sum[2].

1 See the Law of Property Act 1925 s 183 and SALE OF LAND vol 42 para 155. No prosecution for such an offence may be commenced without the leave of the Attorney General; and, before leave to prosecute is granted, there must be given to the person intended to be prosecuted such notice of the application for leave to prosecute as the Attorney General may direct: s 183 (4), (5). As to the effect of this limitation see para 639 post. As to suppression of documents see para 573 ante.

2 See the Land Registration Act 1925 ss 116 (1), 117 (amended by the Criminal Law Act 1977 s 32 (1); the Magistrates' Courts Act 1980 s 32 (2)) and LAND REGISTRATION vol 26 paras 1464, 1465.

For the meaning of 'the prescribed sum' see para 807 post. As to the suppression of documents or facts in proceedings before the registrar or the court in pursuance of the Land Registration Act 1925 see ss 115, 117 and LAND REGISTRATION vol 26 paras 1463, 1465.

575. Obtaining property by personation. The personation of another for the purpose of obtaining property, the personation of a person acting in a particular capacity and the personation of another for the purpose of practising deception are made offences under various statutes which are considered elsewhere[1].

1 Eg the Customs and Excise Management Act 1979 s 13 (see CUSTOMS AND EXCISE vol 12 para 602); the Representation of the People Act 1983 ss 60, 168 (1) (substituted by the Representation of the People

Act 1985 s 23, Sch 3 para 8) (see ELECTIONS); the Inland Revenue Regulation Act 1890 s 12 (see INCOME TAXATION vol 23 para 1703); the Pilotage Act 1987 s 3 (8) (see SHIPPING). See also the Official Secrets Act 1920 s 1 and para 253 ante. The common law offence of personation so far as it constituted cheating has been abolished: see the Theft Act 1968 s 32 (1) (a). As to the common law offence of personation of a juror see para 314 ante.

576. Obtaining property by false pretences etc. Specific acts of obtaining sums of money, benefits, grants, subsidies, licences etc or other property by making false statements or representations, knowingly or recklessly, are made offences under various statutes which are considered elsewhere[1].

1 See eg the Agriculture Act 1957 s 7 (3) (as amended) and AGRICULTURE; the Agriculture and Horticulture Act 1964 s 1 (9), Schedule para 3 (amended by the Theft Act 1968 s 33 (3), Sch 3 Pt I; the Criminal Justice Act 1982 ss 38, 46) and AGRICULTURE; the Agriculture Act 1967 s 69 (1) and AGRICULTURE; the Docking and Nicking of Horses Act 1949 s 2 (3), (4) (as amended) and ANIMALS vol 2 para 462; the Riding Establishments Act 1964 s 3 (2) and ANIMALS vol 2 para 358; the Animal Health Act 1981 s 4 (1) and ANIMALS vol 2 para 473; the Social Security Act 1986 s 55 and NATIONAL HEALTH. The constituents of the offence in each instance must be ascertained from the particular statute. In specific instances the making of false statements or provision of false information is itself an offence without there being any need to show that the statement was made or the information was provided for the purpose of obtaining any property eg statements made in connection with betting duty (see the Betting and Gaming Duties Act 1981 s 12 (2), Sch 1, para 13 (3) (amended by the Finance Act 1988 s 12 (4)) and BETTING vol 4 para 170); false statements by a prospective immigrant in course of examination by an immigration officer (see the Immigration Act 1971 s 26 (1) (c) and BRITISH NATIONALITY AND ALIENAGE vol 4 para 1029); fraudulently or negligently making incorrect tax returns (see the Taxes Management Act 1970 ss 95, 97–99 (amended by the Finance Act 1971 ss 37 (1), 38, Sch 6 para 90; the Income and Corporation Taxes Act 1988 s 844, Sch 29 paras 9, 32), CAPITAL GAINS TAXATION vol 5 para 229 and INCOME TAXATION); false statement in application for issue of club registration certificate (see the Licensing Act 1964 s 53 and CLUBS vol 6 para 319); false written statements made with intent to deceive (see the Theft Act 1968 s 19 (1) and COMPANIES vol 7 (1) (Reissue) para 335).

577. Corrupt transactions with agents. If:

(1) any agent[1] corruptly[2] accepts or obtains, or agrees to accept or attempts to obtain, from any person, for himself or for any other person, any gift or consideration[3] as an inducement or reward for doing or forbearing to do, or for having done or forborne to do, any act in relation to his principal's[4] affairs[5] or business; or for showing or forbearing to show favour or disfavour to any person in relation to his principal's affairs or business[6]; or

(2) any person corruptly gives, or agrees to give, or offers any gift or consideration to any agent as an inducement or reward for doing or forbearing to do, or for having done or forborne to do, any such act or for showing or forbearing to show favour or disfavour to any person in relation to his principal's affairs or business; or

(3) any person knowingly gives to any agent, or if any agent knowingly uses with intent to deceive his principal, any receipt, account or other document in respect of which the principal is interested, and which contains any statement which is false or erroneous or defective in any material particular, and which to his knowledge is intended to mislead the principal[7],

such a person is guilty of an offence and liable on conviction on indictment to imprisonment for a term not exceeding seven years or a fine, or to both, or on summary conviction to imprisonment for a term not exceeding six months or a fine not exceeding the statutory maximum, or to both[8].

1　For these purposes, 'agent' includes any person employed by or acting for another: Prevention of Corruption Act 1906 s 1 (2). A person serving under the Crown or under any corporation or any borough, county or district council, or any board of guardians, is an agent within the meaning of the 1906 Act: s 1 (3) (amended by the Local Authorities etc (Miscellaneous Provision) (No 2) Order 1974, SI 1974/595, art 3 (22), Sch 1 Pt I). A person serving under a local or public authority of any description is an agent within the meaning of the Prevention of Corruption Act 1906: Prevention of Corruption Act 1916 s 4 (3). A police constable on duty is an agent (*Graham v Hart* 1908 SC (J) 26) and a complaint alleging conduct which, if shown to have occurred, would constitute an offence under the Prevention of Corruption Act 1906 s 1 (as amended: see note 8 infra) must be referred to the Police Complaints Authority: see the Police (Complaints) (Mandatory Referrals Etc) Regulations 1985, SI 1985/673, reg 4 and POLICE. An employee who is an inspector for his employer and a convenor of shop stewards may be an agent of his employer when acting in relation to union affairs: see *Morgan v DPP* [1970] 3 All ER 1053, DC. See further *Secret Commissions and Bribery Prevention League (Incorporated) v Martin* (1913) 48 L Jo 183; *R v Barrett* [1976] 3 All ER 895, [1976] 1 WLR 946, CA (additional superintendent registrar of births, deaths and marriages a servant of the Crown even though not appointed, paid or liable to be dismissed by the Crown).

2　For the meaning of 'corruptly' in the Public Bodies Corrupt Practices Act 1889 s 1 see para 283 note 2 ante. As to corruption in civil cases see *Industries and General Mortgage Co Ltd v Lewis* [1949] 2 All ER 573.

3　For these purposes, 'consideration' includes valuable consideration of any kind: Prevention of Corruption Act 1906 s 1 (2). The word is used in its legal sense as connoting the existence of some kind of contract or bargain between the parties: *R v Braithwaite, R v Girdham* [1983] 2 All ER 87, 77 Cr App Rep 34, CA.

4　For these purposes, 'principal' includes an employer: Prevention of Corruption Act 1906 s 1 (2).

5　'In relation to his principal's affairs' falls to be construed widely: *R v Dickinson and De Rable* (1948) 33 Cr App Rep 5 at 9, CCA; *Morgan v DPP* [1970] 3 All ER 1053, DC.

6　It is not necessary to show that the recipient of the bribe did what the bribe was given to him to do: *R v Carr* [1956] 3 All ER 979n, 40 Cr App Rep 188. A bribe corruptly given may be innocently received: see *R v Millray Window Cleaning Co Ltd* [1962] Crim LR 99, CCA. See, however, *R v Mills* (1978) 68 Cr App Rep 154, CA (a recipient who takes a gift knowing it is intended to be a bribe and intending to keep it enters into a corrupt bargain despite any mental reservation that he does not intend to carry out his side of the bargain).

7　It is an offence knowingly to give a false document to an agent, although the agent is not corrupted or intended to be corrupted or knows that the document is false: *Sage v Eicholz* [1919] 2 KB 171. The offence under head (3) supra applies only to documents intended to pass between a principal and a third party and does not cover documents such as trading sheets filled in by an agent for his principal, which were never intended to do so: *R v Tweedie* [1984] QB 729, 79 Cr App Rep 168, CA.

8　Prevention of Corruption Act 1906 s 1 (1) (amended by the Criminal Justice Act 1988 s 47 (2)); Criminal Law Act 1967 s 1. For the meaning of 'the statutory maximum' see para 806 post. Nothing in the Prevention of Corruption Act 1906 s 1 (1) (as so amended) affects the punishment for an offence committed before 29 September 1988: Criminal Justice Act 1988 ss 47 (3), 171 (6). A prosecution for an offence under the Prevention of Corruption Act 1906 may not be instituted without the consent of the Attorney General: s 2 (1). As to the effect of this limitation see para 639 post. Every information for such an offence must be upon oath: s 2 (3). As to the presumption of corruption in instances where the offence charged relates to any person employed by Her Majesty, any government department or public body see para 284 ante. A person aggrieved by a summary conviction under the Prevention of Corruption Act 1906 may appeal to the Crown Court: s 2 (6) (amended by the Courts Act 1971 s 56 (1), Sch 8 para 2, Table).

578. Cheating the public revenue. It is an indictable offence at common law[1] for a person to practise a fraud on the public revenue[2]. Any such offence is punishable by fine and imprisonment at the discretion of the court[3].

1　Although the common law offence of cheating is in practice reserved for serious and unusual offences rather than conventional cases, the court should not be inhibited by any statutory provisions from imposing or upholding what would otherwise be a proper sentence: *R v Mavji* [1987] 2 All ER 758, 84 Cr App Rep 34, CA.

2　1 Hawk PC 322; 2 East PC 821; *R v Bembridge* (1783) 3 Doug KB 327; *R v Bradbury, R v Edlin* (1920) [1956] 2 QB 262n; affd on another point [1921] 1 KB 562, 15 Cr App Rep 76, CCA; *R v Hudson* [1956] 2 QB 252, 40 Cr App Rep 55, CCA. Offences relating to the public revenue were expressly saved when the common law offence of cheating was abolished: see the Theft Act 1968 s 32 (1) (a) and *R v Redford* (1988) 89 Cr App Rep 1, CA. A fraud on the public revenue is indictable even though the particular fraud might not have been indictable had it been a fraud on one individual by another: *R v Bembridge* supra, as explained in *R v Hudson* supra at 260 and at 60.

The offence may be committed eg by one who submits incorrect accounts and a certificate of disclosure which he knows to be false to the inspector of taxes: see *R v Hudson* supra. The offence does not require any positive act of deception either by words or conduct, but may include any form of fraudulent conduct which results in diverting money from the revenue: *R v Mavji* [1987] 2 All ER 758, 84 Cr App Rep 34, CA; *R v Redford* supra.

3 See paras 1200, 1232 post.

579. Winning money etc by fraud at gaming. A person who, by any fraud or unlawful device or ill practice[1], wins from any other person to himself, or to any other or others, any sum of money or valuable thing[2] (1) in playing at or with cards, dice, tables[3], or other game; or (2) in bearing a part in the stakes, wagers, or adventures; or (3) in betting on the sides or hands of those who play; or (4) in wagering[4] on the event of any game, sport, pastime or other exercise[5] is guilty of an offence and liable on conviction on indictment to imprisonment for a term not exceeding two years, or on summary conviction to imprisonment for a term not exceeding six months or a fine not exceeding the prescribed sum, or to both[6].

1 Whether a particular incident in a game is a fraud, unlawful device or ill practice is a question of fact for the jury: *R v Moore* (1914) 10 Cr App Rep 54, CCA. The playing of the 'three card trick' is sleight of hand and does not amount to fraud, unlawful device or ill practice: *R v Governor of Brixton Prison, ex p Sjoland and Metzler* [1912] 3 KB 568, DC.
2 Where the victim of a card trick wrote his acceptance for the amount he had lost on a blank bill form provided by one of two confederates, and the bill was subsequently signed by that confederate as drawer, and indorsed by him and the other confederate, there was evidence on which the second confederate could be convicted of winning money in contravention of the Gaming Act 1845 s 17; see *R v Governor of Brixton Prison, ex p Stallmann* [1912] 3 KB 424, DC. It is an essential ingredient of the offence that the money won should be obtained: *R v Harris, R v Turner* [1963] 2 QB 442, 47 Cr App Rep 125, CCA.
3 'Tables' was formerly the ordinary name for backgammon: see the Oxford English Dictionary (2nd Edn, 1989) vol XVII.
4 To place bets with a bookmaker intending to accept winnings but not to pay losses is fraudulent wagering within the Gaming Act 1845 s 17: *R v Leon* [1945] KB 136, 30 Cr App Rep 120, CCA; *R v Clucas, R v O'Rourke* [1959] 1 All ER 438, 43 Cr App Rep 98, CCA. Attempting to get money on forged football pool coupons is attempting to win money by a fraud in wagering: see *R v Butler* (1954) 38 Cr App Rep 57, CCA (although the point that a transaction with a football pool might not be a wager was not taken).
5 Tossing with coins is a 'pastime' or 'exercise' if not a 'game': *R v O'Connor and Brown* (1881) 15 Cox CC 3, CCR. A bet over a sleight of hand or other trick does not fall within 'game, sport, pastime or other exercise': *R v Hudson* (1860) Bell CC 263, CCR. If several persons join together to defraud some other person, as by inducing that person by fraud to play in a game or by any other act which if done by one person is not within the mischief aimed at by the Gaming Act 1845, an indictment lies against the confederates for conspiracy to defraud: *R v Bailey* (1850) 4 Cox CC 390; see also *R v Hudson* supra.
   There must be some fraud or unlawful device or ill practice in the game, sport, pastime or exercise itself; it is not sufficient if fraud is resorted to in order to induce the prosecutor to play in the game: *R v Bailey* (1850) 4 Cox CC 390; *R v Governor of Brixton Prison, ex p Sjoland and Metzler* [1912] 3 KB 568, DC; *R v Moore* (1914) 10 Cr App Rep 54, CCA.
6 Gaming Act 1845 s 17 (amended by the Theft Act 1968 s 33 (2), Sch 2, Pt III; the Magistrates' Courts Act 1980 s 32 (2)). For the meaning of 'the prescribed sum' see para 807 post. It is not necessary to state in the indictment to whom the sum of money or valuable thing belongs (*R v Moss* (1856) Dears & B 104 at 108, CCR per Pollock CB), but it would appear to be necessary for the indictment to contain an allegation to defraud a particular person. However, it does not seem necessary to state the name of the game.

580. Fraudulent mediums. Any person who (1) with intent to deceive purports to act[1] as a spiritualistic medium or to exercise any powers of telepathy, clairvoyance or other similar powers; or (2) in purporting to act as a spiritualistic medium or to exercise such powers, uses any fraudulent device, is guilty of an offence and liable on conviction on indictment to imprisonment for a term not exceeding two years or a fine, or to both, or on summary conviction to imprisonment for a term not exceeding four months or a fine not exceeding the prescribed sum, or to both[2].

1 A person may not be convicted of an offence under the Fraudulent Mediums Act 1951 s 1 unless it is proved that he acted for reward; and for these purposes, a person is deemed to act for reward if any money is paid, or other valuable thing given, in respect of what he does, whether to him or to any other person: s 1 (2). Nothing in s 1 (1) applies, however, to anything done solely for the purpose of entertainment: s 1 (5).

2 Ibid s 1 (1), (3) (amended by the Criminal Law Act 1977 s 32 (1); the Magistrates' Courts Act 1980 s 32 (2)). For the meaning of 'the prescribed sum' see para 807 post. No proceedings for such an offence may be brought except by or with the consent of the Director of Public Prosecutions: Fraudulent Mediums Act 1951 s 1 (4). As to the effect of this limitation see para 639 post.

581. Fraudulent use of telecommunication system. A person who dishonestly obtains any service[1] which is provided by means of a telecommunication system[2] the running of which is authorised by a licence[3], with intent to avoid payment of any charge applicable to the provision of that service, is guilty of an offence and liable on conviction on indictment to imprisonment for a term not exceeding two years or a fine, or to both, or on summary conviction to imprisonment for a term not exceeding six months or a fine not exceeding the statutory maximum, or to both[4].

1 Ie other than a service to which the Cable and Broadcasting Act 1984 s 53 applies: see TELECOMMUNICATIONS vol 45 para 612.
2 For the meaning of 'telecommunication system' see para 270 note 3 ante.
3 Ie a licence granted under the Telecommunications Act 1984 s 7: see TELECOMMUNICATIONS vol 45 para 356.
4 Ibid s 42 (1), (2) (amended by the Cable and Broadcasting Act 1984 s 57 (1), Sch 5 para 45 (2), (3)). For the meaning of 'the statutory maximum' see para 806 post.

582. Making false statement to procure passport. A person who, for the purpose of procuring a passport, whether for himself or any other person, makes a statement which is to his knowledge untrue, is guilty of an offence and liable on conviction on indictment to imprisonment for a term not exceeding two years or a fine, or to both, or on summary conviction to imprisonment for a term not exceeding six months or a fine not exceeding the prescribed sum, or to both[1].

1 Criminal Justice Act 1925 s 36 (amended by the Criminal Law Act 1977 s 32 (1); the Forgery and Counterfeiting Act 1981 s 30, Schedule Pt I); Criminal Law Act 1967 s 1 (1); Magistrates' Courts Act 1980 ss 17, 32 (1), Sch 1 para 19. See para 804 post. For the meaning of 'the prescribed sum' see para 807 post. As to forgery of passports see para 610 post.
  Where, as a result of making a false statement, a passport is in fact obtained and subsequently used, the appropriate charge may be one of obtaining property by deception contrary to the Theft Act 1968 s 15 (1) (see para 567 ante): *R v Ashbee* [1989] 1 WLR 109, 88 Cr App Rep 357, CA.

583. Bankruptcy offences. Where the court has made a bankruptcy order[1] on a bankruptcy petition[2], and whether or not the bankruptcy order is annulled[3], a bankrupt may be liable under the Insolvency Act 1986 for specified offences[4] in respect of his wrongdoing before and after his bankruptcy, as may a person dealing fraudulently with a bankrupt[5].

Proceedings for any such offence may not, however, be instituted after the annulment[6]; nor may they be instituted except by the Secretary of State or by or with the consent of the Director of Public Prosecutions[7].

1 As to bankruptcy orders see BANKRUPTCY vol 3 (2) (Reissue) para 186 et seq.
2 As to bankruptcy petitions see BANKRUPTCY vol 3 (2) (Reissue) para 115 et seq.
3 As to annulment of bankruptcy orders see BANKRUPTCY vol 3 (2) (Reissue) para 598 et seq.
4 Ie under the Insolvency Act 1986 ss 353–362: see BANKRUPTCY vol 3 (2) (Reissue) paras 693–704, 706–708. As to the general provisions in respect of such offences see ss 350–352 and BANKRUPTCY vol 3 (2) (Reissue) para 692.
5 Ie under ibid s 359 (2): see BANKRUPTCY vol 3 (2) (Reissue) para 705.
6 Ibid s 350 (2).
7 Ibid s 350 (5). As to the effect of this limitation see para 639 post.

584. Offences in respect of corporate insolvency. When a company is being wound up, whether by the court or voluntarily, any person, being a past or present officer of the company may be liable under the Insolvency Act 1986 in respect of offences committed in anticipation of winding up[1], for misconduct in the course of winding up[2], for transactions in fraud of creditors[3], for material omissions from the statement relating to a company's affairs[4] or for false representations to creditors[5]. Any officer or contributory may be liable under the Act for falsification of the company's books etc[6].

Whether or not a company has been, or is in the course of being, wound up, if any business of a company is carried on with intent to defraud creditors of the company, every person who was knowingly a party to the carrying on of the business in that manner is guilty of an offence and liable on conviction on indictment to imprisonment for a term not exceeding seven years or a fine, or to both, or on summary conviction to imprisonment for a term not exceeding six months or a fine not exceeding the statutory maximum, or to both[7].

Where it is proposed to wind up a company voluntarily and a director makes a declaration of solvency without having reasonable grounds for the opinion that the company will be able to pay its debts in full, together with interest at the official rate, within such period, not exceeding 12 months from the commencement of the winding up, as may be specified in the declaration, he is guilty of an offence and liable on conviction on indictment to imprisonment for a term not exceeding two years or a fine, or to both, or on summary conviction to imprisonment for a term not exceeding six months or a fine not exceeding the statutory maximum, or to both[8].

1 Ie under the Insolvency Act 1986 s 206: see COMPANIES vol 7 (2) (Reissue) para 1901.
2 Ie under ibid s 208: see COMPANIES vol 7 (2) (Reissue) para 1902.
3 Ie under ibid s 207: see COMPANIES vol 7 (2) (Reissue) para 1904.
4 Ie under ibid s 210: see COMPANIES vol 7 (2) (Reissue) para 1905.
5 Ie under ibid s 211: see COMPANIES vol 7 (2) (Reissue) para 1906.
6 See ibid s 209 and COMPANIES vol 7 (2) (Reissue) para 1903.
7 Companies Act 1985 ss 458, 730, Sch 24: see COMPANIES vol 7 (1) (Reissue) para 1003. For the meaning of 'the statutory maximum' see para 806 post.
8 See the Insolvency Act 1986 ss 89 (1), (4), 430, Sch 10 and COMPANIES vol 7 (2) (Reissue) para 1937.

585. Insider dealing. An individual who contravenes the provisions of the Company Securities (Insider Dealing) Act 1985[1] relating to the prohibition on stock exchange deals by insiders[2], the abuse of information obtained in an official capacity[3], the restriction on off-market deals in advertised securities[4] or the restriction on promoting off-market deals abroad[5] is guilty of an offence and liable on conviction on indictment to imprisonment for a term not exceeding seven years or a fine, or to both, or on summary conviction to imprisonment for a term not exceeding six months or a fine not exceeding the statutory maximum, or to both[6].

Proceedings for any such offence may not be instituted in England and Wales except by the Secretary of State or by or with the consent of the Director of Public Prosecutions[7].

1　As to the Company Securities (Insider Dealing) Act 1985 see COMPANIES vol 7 (1) (Reissue) para 1060 et seq.
2　Ie ibid s 1: see COMPANIES vol 7 (1) (Reissue) para 1060.
3　Ie ibid s 2 (amended by the Financial Services Act 1986 s 173): see COMPANIES vol 7 (1) (Reissue) para 1061.
4　Ie the Company Securities (Insider Dealing) Act 1985 s 4 (amended by the Financial Services Act 1986 s 174 (3)): see COMPANIES vol 7 (1) (Reissue) para 1063.
5　Ie the Company Securities (Insider Dealing) Act 1985 s 5: see COMPANIES vol 7 (1) (Reissue) para 1064.
6　Ibid s 8 (1) (amended by the Criminal Justice Act 1988 s 48 (1)). For the meaning of 'the statutory maximum' see para 806 post. Nothing in the Company Securities (Insider Dealing) Act 1985 s 8 (1) (a) (as so amended) affects the punishment for an offence committed before 29 September 1988: Criminal Justice Act 1988 ss 48 (2), 171 (6).
7　Company Securities (Insider Dealing) Act 1985 s 8 (2). As to the effect of this limitation see para 639 post.

586. Offences under the Financial Services Act 1986. A person who (1) makes misleading statements or engages in misleading practices[1]; or (2) knowingly or recklessly furnishes an auditor appointed by the Secretary of State with information which is false or misleading in a material particular[2]; or (3) makes misleading statements as to insurance contracts[3]; or (4) makes false and misleading statements for the purposes of, or in connection with, any application under, or in purported compliance with any requirement imposed on him by or under, the Financial Services Act 1986[4] may be guilty of an offence under the Act.

1　Ie contrary to the Financial Services Act 1986 s 47 (1): see STOCK EXCHANGE.
2　Ie contrary to ibid s 111 (1): see STOCK EXCHANGE.
3　Ie contrary to ibid s 133 (1): see INSURANCE.
4　Ie contrary to ibid s 200 (1): see STOCK EXCHANGE.

(5) SERIOUS FRAUD

587. Failure to comply with the requirements of the Director of the Serious Fraud Office; making false or misleading statements. Any person who, without reasonable excuse, fails to comply with a requirement imposed on him by the Director of the Serious Fraud Office in connection with his investigative powers[1] is guilty of an offence and liable on summary conviction to imprisonment for a term not exceeding six months or a fine not exceeding level 5 on the standard scale, or to both[2].

A person who, in purported compliance with any such requirement (1) makes a statement which he knows to be false or misleading in a material particular; or (2) recklessly makes a statement which is false or misleading in a material particular, is guilty of an offence and liable on conviction on indictment to imprisonment for a term not exceeding two years or a fine, or to both, or on summary conviction to imprisonment for a term not exceeding six months or a fine not exceeding the statutory maximum, or to both[3].

1 Ie under the Criminal Justice Act 1987 s 2: see para 653 post.
2 Ibid s 2 (13). For the meaning of 'the standard scale' see para 808 post.
3 Ibid s 2 (14), (15). For the meaning of 'the statutory maximum' see para 806 post.

588. Concealment etc of documents. Where any person (1) knows or suspects that an investigation by the police or the Serious Fraud Office[1] into serious fraud or complex fraud is being or is likely to be carried out; and (2) falsifies, conceals, destroys or otherwise disposes of, or causes or permits the falsification, conceal- ment, destruction or disposal of, documents[2] which he knows or suspects are or would be relevant to such an investigation, he is guilty of an offence unless he proves that he had no intention of concealing the facts disclosed by the documents from persons carrying out such an investigation[3]. A person guilty of such an offence is liable on conviction on indictment to imprisonment for a term not exceeding seven years or a fine, or to both, or on summary conviction to imprison- ment for a term not exceeding six months or a fine not exceeding the statutory maximum, or to both[4].

1 As to the Serious Fraud Office see para 652 et seq post.
2 For these purposes, 'document' includes information recorded in any form: Criminal Justice Act 1987 s 2 (18).
3 Ibid s 2 (16).
4 Ibid s 2 (17). For the meaning of 'the statutory maximum' see para 806 post.

(6) OFFENCES RELATING TO MAILS

589. Unlawfully taking away or opening a mail bag etc. If a person unlaw- fully takes away or opens a mail bag[1] sent by any ship, vehicle or aircraft employed by or under the Post Office[2] for the transmission of postal packets[3] under contract, or unlawfully takes a postal packet in course of transmission by post[4] out of a mail bag so sent, he is guilty of an offence and liable on conviction on indictment to imprisonment for a term not exceeding five years, or on summary conviction to imprisonment for a term not exceeding six months or a fine not exceeding the prescribed sum, or to both[5].

1 'Mail bag' includes any form of container or covering in which postal packets in course of transmission by post are conveyed, whether or not it contains any such packets: Post Office Act 1953 s 87 (1) (amended by the Post Office Act 1969 s 141, Sch 11 Pt II).
2 Ie the authority established under the Post Office Act 1969 s 6 (as amended): see POST OFFICE vol 36 para 609 et seq.
3 For the meaning of 'postal packet' see para 296 note 3 ante.
4 For the meaning of 'in course of transmission by post' see para 296 note 4 ante.
5 Post Office Act 1953 s 53 (amended by the Theft Act 1968 s 33 (1), Sch 2 Pt 1 paras 1, 4); Criminal Law Act 1967 s 1; Magistrates' Courts Act 1980 ss 17, 32 (1), Sch 1 para 22 (a). See para 804 post. For the meaning of 'the prescribed sum' see para 807 post. As to the admissibility of statutory declar- ations in evidence see para 1114 post; and as to offences in relation to mails by officers of the Post Office see para 296 ante.

590. Fraudulent retention of mail bag or postal packet. Any person who fraudulently retains, or wilfully secretes[1] or keeps, or detains, or who, when required by a person engaged in the business of the Post Office[2], neglects or refuses to deliver up (1) any postal packet[3] which is in course of transmission by post[4] and which ought to have been delivered to any other person; or (2) any postal packet in course of transmission by post or any mail bag[5] which has been found by him or by any other person, is guilty of an offence and liable on conviction on indictment to imprisonment for a term not exceeding two years, or on summary conviction to imprisonment for a term not exceeding six months or a fine not exceeding the prescribed sum, or to both[6].

1 For the meaning of 'secrete' see para 296 note 2 ante.
2 See para 589 note 2 ante.
3 For the meaning of 'postal packet' see para 296 note 3 ante.
4 For the meaning of 'in course of transmission by post' see para 296 note 4 ante.
5 For the meaning of 'mail bag' see para 589 note 1 ante.
6 Post Office Act 1953 s 55 (amended by the Theft Act 1968 s 33 (1), Sch 2 Pt I paras 1, 6; the Post Office Act 1969 ss 76, 88, 139, Sch 4 paras 1, 2 (1)); Criminal Law Act 1967 s 1; Magistrates' Courts Act 1980 ss 17, 32 (1), Sch 1 para 22 (b). See para 804 post. For the meaning of 'the prescribed sum' see para 807 post. As to the theft of a letter by a postman to whom it had been entrusted for delivery in the course of his duties see *R v Poynton* (1862) Le & Ca 247, CCR; and as to the admissibility of statutory declarations in evidence see para 1114 post.

591. Criminal diversion of letters. If any person[1] not engaged in the business of the Post Office[2] wilfully and maliciously, with intent to injure any other person, opens or causes to be opened any postal packet[3] which ought to have been delivered to that other person, or does any act or thing whereby the due delivery of the packet to that person is prevented or impeded, he is guilty of an offence and liable on summary conviction to imprisonment for a term not exceeding six months or a fine not exceeding level 4 on the standard scale, or to both[4].

1 Nothing in the Post Office Act 1953 s 56 applies to a person who does any act to which these provisions apply where he is parent, or in the position of parent or guardian, of the person to whom the postal packet is addressed: s 56 (2).
2 See para 589 note 2 ante.
3 For these purposes, 'postal packet' means a postal packet which is in course of transmission by post or which has been delivered by post: Post Office Act 1953 s 56 (4). See further para 296 note 3 ante. For the meaning of 'in course of transmission by post' see para 296 note 4 ante.
4 Ibid s 56 (1) (amended by the Post Office Act 1969 ss 76, 88, 139, Sch 4 paras 1, 2 (12); the Criminal Law Act 1977 ss 15, 30, Sch 1; the Criminal Justice Act 1982 s 46); Criminal Law Act 1967 s 1. For the meaning of 'the standard scale' see para 808 post. As to the admissibility of statutory declarations in evidence see para 1114 post; and as to redirection of a bankrupt's letters etc to the responsible insolvency practitioner see BANKRUPTCY vol 3 (2) (Reissue) para 252.

592. Thefts etc of mails from outside England and Wales. Where a person:
  (1) steals or attempts to steal any mail bag[1] or postal packet[2] in the course of transmission[3] as such between places in different jurisdictions in the British postal area[4], or any of the contents of such a mail bag or postal packet; or
  (2) in stealing or with intent to steal any such mail bag or postal packet or any of its contents, commits any robbery, attempted robbery or assault with intent to rob,
then, notwithstanding that he does so outside England and Wales, he is guilty of committing or attempting to commit the offence against the Theft Act 1968 as if he had done so in England and Wales and is accordingly liable to be prosecuted, tried and punished in England and Wales without proof that the offence was committed there[5].

1 For these purposes, 'mail bag' includes any article serving the purpose of a mail bag: Theft Act 1968 s 14 (3). Cf para 589 note 1 ante.
2 'Postal packet' is not defined for the purposes of the Theft Act 1968. Cf para 589 note 3 ante.
3 The Theft Act 1968 does not specify when a postal packet is in the course of transmission. Cf para 296 note 4 ante.
4 For these purposes, the reference to different jurisdictions in the British postal area is to be construed as referring to the several jurisdictions of England and Wales, of Scotland, of Northern Ireland, of the Isle of Man and of the Channel Islands: ibid s 14 (2).
5 Ibid s 14 (1).

(7) CRIMINAL DAMAGE TO PROPERTY

(i) Destroying or Damaging Property

593. Introduction. The Criminal Damage Act 1971 repealed and replaced various statutes relating to damage to property, in particular most of the provisions of the Malicious Damage Act 1861[1]. Where it appears to the Secretary of State that a local statutory provision[2] is inconsistent with or has become unnecessary in consequence of the 1971 Act, he may, after consultation with any person appearing to him to be concerned with that provision, by order[3] amend that provision so as to bring it into conformity with the 1971 Act or repeal it[4]. The 1971 Act abolished the distinctions in the pre-existing law based upon the nature of the property or its situation, upon the means used to destroy or damage it and upon the circumstances in which it is destroyed or damaged[5]. It also clarified the mental element involved in offences of damaging or destroying property[6] and made the absence of lawful excuse a specific constituent of the offences[7].

1 Certain provisions of the Malicious Damage Act 1861 were expressly saved: see the Criminal Damage Act 1971 s 11 (8), Schedule. Those provisions are the Malicious Damage Act 1861 ss 35, 36 (see para 601 post), s 47 (see para 603 post), s 48 (see para 604 post), s 58 (see para 601 note 1 post), and s 72 (see para 625 note 2 post). In addition to the repeal of many statutory offences, the common law offence of arson was abolished: see the Criminal Damage Act 1971 s 11 (1) and para 594 post.

 Where any enactment repealed by the Criminal Damage Act 1971 s 11 (8), Schedule, has been applied by or incorporated in any other Act, the repeal extends so as to repeal that enactment as so applied or incorporated: s 11 (8). The repeal by s 11 or an order made thereunder (see text to notes 2–4 infra) of any enactment relating to procedure or to the jurisdictional powers of any court does not affect the operation of that enactment in relation to offences committed before the repeal took effect or to proceedings for any such offence: s 11 (11). The Criminal Damage Act 1971 came wholly into force on 14 October 1971: see s 12 (1).
2 For these purposes, 'local statutory provision' means a provision of a local Act, including an Act confirming a provisional order, or a provision of a public general Act passed with respect only to a particular area or a particular undertaking or a provision of an instrument made under any such local or public general Act or of an instrument in the nature of a local enactment made under any other Act: ibid s 11 (9).
3 An order so made must be made by statutory instrument which is subject to annulment in pursuance of a resolution of either House of Parliament: ibid s 11 (10). Such orders being local by nature are outside the scope of this work. As to the effect of a repeal made by order see note 1 supra.
4 Ibid s 11 (9).
5 See eg the Malicious Damage Act 1861 s 1 (setting fire to church or chapel), s 2 (setting fire to house with someone in it), s 9 (destroying house by gunpowder with someone in it) (all repealed).
6 The mens rea is now expressed as eg 'intending to destroy or damage any such property or being reckless . . .': see the Criminal Damage Act 1971 s 1 (1) and para 594 post. In the pre-existing law the mens rea was frequently described by the use of 'maliciously'.
7 The expression 'without lawful excuse' has replaced 'unlawfully' which was a common constituent of offences in the pre-existing law. For the meaning of 'lawful excuse' see para 598 post. The points referred to in the text and notes 5, 6 supra may still be relevant in determining the application of cases decided under the pre-existing law to the Criminal Damage Act 1971.

594. Destroying or damaging property. A person who without lawful excuse[1]:

(1) destroys[2] or damages[3] any property[4] belonging to another[5] intending to destroy or damage any such property or being reckless[6] as to whether any such property would be destroyed or damaged is guilty of an offence and liable on conviction on indictment to imprisonment for a term not exceeding ten years, or on summary conviction[7] to imprisonment for a term not exceeding six months or a fine not exceeding the prescribed sum, or to both[8];

(2) destroys or damages any property, whether belonging to himself or another, intending to destroy or damage any property or being reckless as to whether any property would be destroyed or damaged, and intending by the destruction or damage to endanger the life of another or being reckless as to whether the life of another would be thereby endangered[9], is guilty of an offence and liable on conviction on indictment to imprisonment for life or for any shorter term[10].

An offence committed under heads (1) or (2) above by destroying or damaging property by fire[11] is to be charged[12] as arson[13]. A person guilty of arson under head (1) above is liable on conviction on indictment to imprisonment for life or for any shorter term, or on summary conviction to imprisonment for a term not exceeding six months or a fine not exceeding the prescribed sum, or to both; and a person guilty of arson under head (2) above is liable on conviction on indictment to imprisonment for life or for any shorter term[14].

1 For the meaning of 'lawful excuse' see para 598 post.
2 'Destroy' should be given its ordinary and natural meaning: see *Barnet London Borough Council v Eastern Electricity Board* [1973] 2 All ER 319, [1973] 1 WLR 430, DC (decided under the Town and Country Planning Act 1962 s 29 (1) (a) (repealed)).
3 There must be actual damage even if it is only slight: *Gayford v Chouler* [1898] 1 QB 316, DC (injury to pasture on a field to the value of a few pence). A thing may be damaged although nothing is broken: *R v Tacey* (1821) Russ & Ry 452, CCR (removal of a part which renders the whole imperfect and inoperative); *R v Norris* (1840) 9 C & P 241 (running a machine in an improper manner so that impairment results); *R v Foster* (1852) 6 Cox CC 25 (displacement or disarrangement of a machine which causes trifling injury without preventing the machine from working); *R v Fisher* (1865) LR 1 CCR 7 (displacement of parts which prevents the machine from working). It is not necessary that the damage done should be permanent: *R v Fisher* supra; *Roe v Kingerlee* [1986] Crim LR 735, CA ('damage' a matter of fact and degree); *Hardman v Chief Constable of Avon and Somerset Constabulary* [1986] Crim LR 330, CA (washable graffiti; 'damage'); cf *A v R* [1978] Crim LR 689, CA (spittle on policeman's raincoat not 'damage').
4 For the meaning of 'property' see para 597 post.
5 For the meaning of 'property belonging to another' see para 597 post. No offence is committed under the Criminal Damage Act 1971 s 1 (1), however, if the accused honestly, albeit mistakenly, believes that the property is his own; the existence of that belief negatives the necessary mens rea; whether or not that belief is justifiable is irrelevant: *R v Smith (David Raymond)* [1974] QB 354, 58 Cr App Rep 320, CA. Likewise, no offence is committed where the accused, before he inflicts damage, has asserted custody and control over the property: *R v Judge* (1974) 138 JP Jo 649, CA. Nor is any offence of criminal damage committed by a person who sets fire to premises on the instructions of the owner notwithstanding that the accused knew that the instructions were preparatory to the commission of fraud by the employer: *R v Denton* [1982] 1 All ER 65, 74 Cr App Rep 81, CA. Cf *R v Appleyard* (1985) 81 Cr App Rep 319, CA.
6 As to recklessness see para 14 ante and in particular *R v Caldwell* [1982] AC 341, 73 Cr App Rep 13, HL. Intentional or reckless omission of the accused to act to rectify an unintentional act or its consequences may amount to an intentional or reckless act: *R v Fuller* [1974] Crim LR 134, CA (accused broke neighbour's gas pipe attempting to steal from meter; failed to rectify the damage after being warned of the danger; reckless as to whether 'life would be endangered'); *R v Miller* [1983] 2 AC 161, 77 Cr App Rep 17, HL (failure to extinguish a fire started accidentally). As to omissions see para 9 ante. A person may be reckless where the risk must have been obvious to a reasonably prudent

person even though it would not have been obvious to the particular accused because of age, lack of experience etc: *Elliott v C (a minor)* [1983] 2 All ER 1005, 77 Cr App Rep 103, DC; *R v Stephen Malcolm R* (1984) 79 Cr App Rep 334, CA. See also *Chief Constable of Avon and Somerset Constabulary v Shimmen* (1986) 84 Cr App Rep 7, DC; *R v Sangha* [1988] 2 All ER 385, 87 Cr App Rep 88, CA.

7 As to the procedure where offences triable either way are to be tried summarily if the amount is small see para 814 post; and as to the power to join in an indictment a count for an offence mentioned in the Magistrates' Courts Act 1980 Sch 2 column 1 (see para 814 note 1 post) see para 922 post.

8 Criminal Damage Act 1971 ss 1 (1), 4 (2); Magistrates' Courts Act 1980 ss 17, 32 (1), Sch 1 para 29. See para 804 post. For the meaning of 'the prescribed sum' see para 807 post. As to the penalty if the accused is found guilty of arson see infra; as to the offence committed by a person who at the time of committing or being arrested for an offence under the Criminal Damage Act 1971 s 1 has in his possession a firearm or imitation firearm see para 232 ante; and as to evidence in proceedings for an offence under the Criminal Damage Act 1971 see para 1162 post. It is an offence under the Explosive Substances Act 1883 to cause, or to do any act with intent to cause, an explosion likely to endanger life or cause serious injury to property: see ss 2, 3 (substituted by the Criminal Jurisdiction Act 1975 s 7) and paras 478, 479 ante.

9 It is not necessary to prove actual injury; it is sufficient to show such exposure to risk or chance of injury that actual danger to life is caused: *R v McGrath and McKevitt* (1881) 14 Cox CC 598. The prosecution must prove, however, that the danger to life resulted from the destruction of or damage to the property; proof that damage to life resulted from the act which caused the destruction or damage is too remote: *R v Steer* [1987] 2 All ER 833, 85 Cr App Rep 352, HL. As to recklessness see note 6 supra. In relation to recklessness the defence of voluntary intoxication is not available: see para 28 ante.

10 Criminal Damage Act 1971 ss 1 (2), 4 (1). See also notes 7, 8 supra. Section 5 (meaning of 'lawful excuse': see para 598 post) does not apply to offences under s 1 (2): see s 5 (1). Where offences under s 1 (1) and s 1 (2) are charged as alternatives in respect of the same incident and the jury convicts on the more serious charge, the jury should be discharged from giving a verdict on the lesser charge: *R v Haddock* [1976] Crim LR 374, CA. As to joinder of offences see para 932 post.

11 Actual damage by fire must be established but the damage need only be slight: *R v Parker* (1839) 9 C & P 45 (charring of floor sufficient to constitute arson); *R v Russell* (1842) Car & M 541 (scorching of floorboards but no part of the wood consumed by fire; insufficient for arson). There need be no visible flame: *R v Stallion* (1833) 1 Mood CC 398, CCR. Failure to extinguish a fire started accidentally may be arson: *R v Miller* [1983] 2 AC 161, 77 Cr App Rep 17, HL.

12 Ie notwithstanding that the common law offence of arson has been abolished: see the Criminal Damage Act 1971 s 11 (1).

13 Ibid s 1 (3).

14 Ibid s 4 (1); Magistrates' Courts Act 1980 ss 17, 32 (1), Sch 1 para 29. See para 804 post. See also note 7 supra and *R v Calladine* (1975) Times, 3 December, CA (unwise to sentence for arson without seeing psychiatric report). Where an offence under the Criminal Damage Act 1971 s 1 (2) is charged as arson, there should be separate counts of arson with intent to endanger life and reckless arson so that, in relation to sentencing, the court has the verdict of the jury: *R v Hoof* (1981) 72 Cr App Rep 126, CA; seq quaere. An offence under the Criminal Damage Act 1971 s 1 may constitute an 'act of violence' to which the Aviation Security Act 1982 applies: see AVIATION vol 2 para 1035.

595. Threats to destroy or damage property. A person who without lawful excuse[1] makes to another a threat, intending that that other would fear it would be carried out (1) to destroy[2] or damage[3] any property[4] belonging to that other[5] or to a third person; or (2) to destroy or damage his own property in a way which he knows is likely to endanger the life[6] of that other or of a third person, is guilty of an offence and liable on conviction on indictment to imprisonment for a term not exceeding ten years, or on summary conviction to imprisonment for a term not exceeding six months or a fine not exceeding the prescribed sum, or to both[7].

1 For the meaning of 'lawful excuse' see para 598 post. The Criminal Damage Act 1971 s 5 (see para 598 post) does not apply to offences under head (2) infra: see s 5 (1).

2 For the meaning of 'destroy' see para 594 note 2 ante.

3 For the meaning of 'damage' see para 594 note 3 ante.

4 For the meaning of 'property' see para 597 post.

5 For the meaning of 'property belonging to another' see para 597 post.
6 See para 594 note 9 ante.
7 Criminal Damage Act 1971 ss 2, 4 (2); Magistrates' Courts Act 1980 ss 17, 32 (1), Sch 1 para 29. See para 804 post. For the meaning of 'the prescribed sum' see para 807 post. As to evidence see para 1162 post; as to bomb hoaxes see para 484 ante; and as to threatening to contaminate or interfere with goods see para 193 ante.

596. Possessing something with intent to destroy or damage property. A person who has anything in his custody or under his control[1] intending without lawful excuse[2] to use it or cause or permit[3] another to use it (1) to destroy[4] or damage[5] any property[6] belonging to some other person[7]; or (2) to destroy or damage his own or the user's property in a way which he knows is likely to endanger the life[8] of some other person, is guilty of an offence and liable on conviction on indictment to imprisonment for a term not exceeding ten years, or on summary conviction to imprisonment for a term not exceeding six months or a fine not exceeding the prescribed sum, or to both[9].

1 'Custody' means physical custody and 'control' imports the notion of the power to direct what is to be done with the property in question: see *Warner v Metropolitan Police Comr* [1969] 2 AC 256, 52 Cr App Rep 373, HL.
2 For the meaning of 'lawful excuse' see para 598 post.
3 To 'cause' a user involves some degree of dominance or control, or some express or positive mandate from the person 'causing': *McLeod (or Houston) v Buchanan* [1940] 2 All ER 179 at 187, HL per Lord Wright; *Shave v Rosner* [1954] 2 QB 113, [1954] 2 All ER 280, DC; *Lovelace v DPP* [1954] 3 All ER 481, [1954] 1 WLR 1468, DC; *Shulton (Great Britain) Ltd v Slough Borough Council* [1967] 2 QB 471, [1967] 2 All ER 137, DC. A person cannot be said to have 'caused' another to do or omit to do something unless he either knows or deliberately chooses not to know what it is that the other is doing or failing to do: *James & Son Ltd v Smee* [1955] 1 QB 78, [1954] 3 All ER 273, DC; *Ross Hillman Ltd v Bond* [1974] QB 435, 59 Cr App Rep 42, DC. See also *Watkins v O'Shaughnessy* [1939] 1 All ER 385, CA (liability of auctioneer for use of car driven without insurance after auction).
  To 'permit' involves a general or particular permission; the permission may be express or implied: *McLeod (or Houston) v Buchanan* supra. To 'permit' involves a knowledge of the facts constituting the user; but shutting one's eyes to the obvious is sufficient: *James & Son Ltd v Smee* supra; *Grays Haulage Co Ltd v Arnold* [1966] 1 All ER 896, [1966] 1 WLR 534, DC; *Ross Hillman Ltd v Bond* supra; see also *Evans v Dell* [1937] 1 All ER 349, DC; *Churchill v Norris* (1938) 158 LT 255, DC. A person cannot 'permit' unless he is in a position to forbid: *Goodbarne v Buck* [1940] 1 KB 771, [1940] 1 All ER 613, CA; *Lloyd v Singleton* [1953] 1 QB 357, [1953] 1 All ER 291, DC. For a corporation to be liable for 'permitting' it must be shown that some person for whose criminal acts the corporation would be liable permitted the commission of the offence: *James & Son Ltd v Smee* supra. Knowledge on the part of an ordinary employee is not sufficient to make a corporation liable: *Magna Plant v Mitchell* [1966] Crim LR 394, DC; see also *Tesco Supermarkets Ltd v Nattrass* [1972] AC 153, [1971] 2 All ER 127, HL; cf *Prosser v Richings* [1936] 2 All ER 1627, DC; *Forsyth v Phillips* [1964] Crim LR 229, DC. As to the criminal capacity of corporations see para 35 ante.
  Both the offence of 'causing' and that of 'permitting' require mens rea: *Ross Hillman Ltd v Bond* supra.
4 For the meaning of 'destroy' see para 594 note 2 ante.
5 See para 594 note 3 ante.
6 For the meaning of 'property' see para 597 post.
7 For the meaning of 'property belonging to another' see para 597 post.
8 See para 594 note 9 ante.
9 Criminal Damage Act 1971 ss 3, 4 (2); Magistrates' Courts Act 1980 ss 17, 32 (1), Sch 1 para 29. See para 804 post. For the meaning of 'the prescribed sum' see para 807 post. An intention to use the article to cause damage at any time in the future or only if it becomes necessary is sufficient mens rea: *R v Buckingham* (1976) 63 Cr App Rep 159, CA. As to the issue of warrants to search for things intended for use without lawful excuse to destroy or damage property see para 599 post; and as to evidence on proceedings for the offence see para 1162 post.
  It is an offence under the Explosive Substances Act 1883 for a person to have in his possession or control an explosive substance with intent to endanger life or cause serious injury to property or

enable another to do so: see s 3 (substituted by the Criminal Jurisdiction Act 1975 s 7) and para 479 ante; and it is an offence under the Public Order Act 1986 for a person to be in possession of material to be used for contaminating or interfering with goods: see s 38 (3) and para 194 ante.

597. Meaning of 'property'. 'Property' means property of a tangible nature[1], whether real or personal, including money and (1) including wild creatures[2] which have been tamed or are ordinarily kept in captivity, and any other wild creatures or their carcases if, but only if, they have been reduced into possession which has not been lost or abandoned or are in the course of being reduced into possession; but (2) not including mushrooms[3] growing wild on any land or flowers, fruit or foliage of a plant[4] growing wild[5] on any land[6].

Property is to be treated as belonging to any person (a) having custody or control[7] of it; (b) having in it any proprietary right or interest, not being an equitable interest arising only from an agreement to transfer or grant an interest; or (c) having a charge on it[8]. Where property is subject to a trust, the persons to whom it belongs are to be so treated as including any person having a right to enforce the trust[9]. Property of a corporation sole is to be so treated as belonging to the corporation notwithstanding a vacancy in the corporation[10].

1 Erasure of a computer program from the plastic circuit card of a computerised saw so as to render the saw inoperable is damage for the purposes of Criminal Damage Act 1971 since, although the program itself is not property of a tangible nature, the erasure constitutes damage both to the card and to the saw: *Cox v Riley* (1986) 83 Cr App Rep 54, CA.
2 As to the application of the Criminal Damage Act 1971 to animals which fall within the scope of the Act see ANIMALS vol 2 paras 235–238, 265, 380, 401; and as to the destruction of or damage to wild animals specifically excluded from the Act and the prevention of cruelty to animals see ANIMALS vol 2 paras 268–283, 316–347, 383–423. As to destroying fish see FISHERIES vol 18 para 654.
3 For these purposes, 'mushroom' includes any fungus: ibid s 10 (1).
4 For these purposes, 'plant' includes any shrub or tree: ibid s 10 (1).
5 Although wild plants are excluded from the Criminal Damage Act 1971, provision for the prevention of damage to them may be covered by byelaws made under legislation relating to the protection of the countryside: see eg the National Parks and Access to the Countryside Act 1949 s 90 and OPEN SPACES vol 34 para 449. Certain wild plants are protected for the purposes of the Wildlife and Countryside Act 1981 and a person who intentionally picks, uproots or destroys such plants commits an offence: see s 13, Sch 8 and AGRICULTURE.
6 Criminal Damage Act 1971 s 10 (1).
7 As to custody and control see para 596 note 1 ante.
8 Criminal Damage Act 1971 s 10 (2).
9 Ibid s 10 (3).
10 Ibid s 10 (4). As to corporations sole see CORPORATIONS vol 9 para 1206 et seq.

598. Meaning of 'lawful excuse'. A person charged with a specified offence[1] under the Criminal Damage Act 1971 is to be treated as having a lawful excuse, whether or not he would otherwise be so treated for the purposes of the Act:
  (1) if at the time of the act or acts alleged to constitute the offence he believed[2] that the person or persons whom he believed to be entitled to consent to the destruction or damage to the property[3] in question had so consented, or would have so consented to it if he or they had known of the destruction or damage and its circumstances[4]; or
  (2) if he destroyed or damaged or threatened to destroy or damage the property in question, or intended[5] to use or cause or permit the use of something to destroy or damage it, in order to protect property belonging to himself or another or a right or interest in property[6] which was or which he believed to

be vested in himself or another, and at the time of the act or acts alleged to constitute the offence he believed (a) that the property, right or interest was in immediate need of protection; and (b) that the means of protection adopted or proposed to be adopted were or would be reasonable having regard to all the circumstances[7].

1 The Criminal Damage Act 1971 s 5 (see infra) applies to any offence under s 1 (1) (see para 594 ante) and any offence under s 2 (see para 595 ante) or s 3 (see para 596 ante) other than one involving a threat by the person charged to destroy or damage property in a way which he knows is likely to endanger the life of another or involving an intent by the person charged to use or cause or permit the use of something in his custody or under his control so to destroy or damage property: s 5 (1). Section 5 is not to be construed, however, as casting doubt on any defence recognised by law as a defence to criminal charges: s 5 (5). As to general defences see para 19 et seq ante.
2 For these purposes, it is immaterial whether a belief is justified or not if it is honestly held: ibid s 5 (3). A belief may be honestly held for these purposes even if it is induced by intoxication: *Jaggard v Dickinson* [1981] QB 527, 72 Cr App Rep 33, CA.
3 For the meaning of 'property' see para 597 ante.
4 Criminal Damage Act 1971 s 5 (2) (a). See further *R v Denton* [1982] 1 All ER 65, 74 Cr App Rep 81, CA.
5 Ie in relation to an offence charged under the Criminal Damage Act 1971 s 3: see para 596 ante.
6 For these purposes, a right or interest in property includes any right or privilege in or over land, whether created by grant, licence or otherwise: ibid s 5 (4).
7 Ibid s 5 (2) (b). Section 5 (2) (b) effectively overrules *Gott v Measures* [1948] 1 KB 234, [1947] 2 All ER 609, DC. The acts done or proposed to be done must, however, be acts which protect or are capable of protecting property: see *R v Hunt* (1978) 66 Cr App Rep 105, CA (accused set fire to bed in old people's flats to demonstrate that fire alarms were faulty; defence set out in head (2) supra unavailable); *R v Hill, R v Hall* (1988) 89 Cr App Rep 74, CA (campaigners for nuclear disarmament charged with possession of hacksaw blades; intending to cut part of perimeter fence of United States naval base; protection of property from nuclear attack too remote an aim to constitute defence of lawful excuse).

599. Warrant to search for goods used to inflict criminal damage. If it is made to appear by information on oath before a justice of the peace that there is reasonable cause to believe that any person has in his custody[1] or under his control[1] or on his premises anything which there is reasonable cause to believe has been used or is intended for use without lawful excuse to destroy or damage property belonging to another[2] or to destroy or damage any property in a way likely to endanger the life of another, the justice may grant a warrant authorising any constable to search for and seize that thing[3]. A constable who is so authorised to search premises for anything, may enter, if need be by force, and search the premises accordingly and may seize anything which he believes to have been so used or to be intended to be so used[4].

1 For the meaning of 'custody' and 'control' see para 596 note 1 ante.
2 For the meaning of 'property belonging to another' see para 597 ante.
3 Criminal Damage Act 1971 s 6 (1).
4 Ibid s 6 (2). As to search warrants see para 670 et seq post. The Police (Property) Act 1897 (as amended) (disposal of property in the possession of the police: see POLICE vol 36 para 325) applies to property which has come into the possession of the police under the Criminal Damage Act 1971 s 6 as it applies to property which has come into the possession of the police in circumstances mentioned in the 1897 Act: Criminal Damage Act 1971 s 6 (3).

600. Institution of proceedings for criminal damage to property of accused's spouse. Subject to certain exceptions, proceedings may not be instituted against a person for any offence of doing unlawful damage to property which, at the time of the offence, belongs to that person's spouse unless the proceedings are instituted by or with the consent of the Director of Public Prosecutions[1].

1 See para 550 ante. See also *R v Withers* [1975] Crim LR 647.

(ii) Other Offences involving Damage to Property

601. Obstructing railways. Any person who unlawfully and maliciously[1]:

(1) puts, places, casts or throws upon or across any railway any wood, stone or other matter or thing; or

(2) takes up, removes or displaces any rail, sleeper or other matter or thing belonging to any railway; or

(3) turns, moves or diverts any points or other machinery belonging to any railway; or

(4) makes or shows, hides or removes, any signal or light on or near to any railway; or

(5) does or causes to be done any other matter or thing,

with intent to obstruct, upset, overthrow, injure or destroy any engine, tender, carriage or truck using the railway[2] is guilty of an offence and liable on conviction on indictment to imprisonment for life or for any shorter term[3].

Any person who, by any unlawful act[4], or by any wilful omission or neglect[5], obstructs or causes to be obstructed any engine or carriage using any railway, or who aids or assists therein is guilty of an offence and liable on conviction on indictment to imprisonment for a term not exceeding two years, or on summary conviction to imprisonment for a term not exceeding six months or a fine not exceeding the prescribed sum, or to both[6].

1 The term 'maliciously' means wilfully or intentionally and without lawful excuse: *R v Solanke* [1969] 3 All ER 1383, [1970] 1 WLR 1, CA. Malice may also be constituted by a wilful act performed mischievously or recklessly: see *R v Holroyd* (1841) 2 Mood & R 339; *R v Upton and Gutteridge* (1851) 5 Cox CC 298; *R v Welch* (1875) 1 QBD 23, CCR; *Re Borrowes* [1900] 2 IR 593. The precise meaning of the term depends on the context in which it is used: see para 10 note 5 ante. If an act which constitutes an offence occurs in a manner unintended and unforeseen, the accused is guilty of the offence: see para 13 ante. As to drawing inferences about the intention or foresight of the accused see para 1061 post.

Malice in its legal import does not necessitate spite or ill-will: see *Bromage v Prosser* (1825) 4 B & C 247; *M'Pherson v Daniels* (1829) 10 B & C 263 at 268 per Littledale J; *Roper v Knott* [1898] 1 QB 868. It is not a necessary ingredient of offences against the Malicious Damage Act 1861 that the act charged should have been committed from malice conceived against the owner of the property in respect of which the offence is committed: see s 58. See also *R v Newill* (1836) 1 Mood CC 458; *R v Davies* (1858) 1 F & F 69.

In an appropriate case, a claim of right made in good faith will negative malice: see *R v James* (1837) 8 C & P 131; *R v Matthews and Twigg* (1876) 14 Cox CC 5; *R v Twose* (1879) 14 Cox CC 327; *Leyson v Williams* (1890) 54 JP 631, DC; *R v Clemens* [1898] 1 QB 556, CCR; *Heaven v Crutchley* (1903) 68 JP 53, DC; *R v Rutter* (1908) 1 Cr App Rep 174, CCA; *R v Dyer* (1952) 36 Cr App Rep 155, CCA. However, the extent of the damage must be reasonably related to the right which is asserted: see *R v Clemens* supra; *Heaven v Crutchley* supra.

2 Ie whether a public or a private railway: *O'Gorman v Sweet* (1890) 54 JP 663.

3 Malicious Damage Act 1861 s 35 (amended by the Criminal Justice Act 1948 s 83 (3), Sch 10 Pt I); Criminal Justice Act 1948 s 1 (1); Criminal Law Act 1967 s 12 (5)(a). An employer is liable for offences of obstructing a railway committed by his employees: *Roberts v Preston* (1860) 9 CBNS 208. As to vicarious liability see para 54 et seq ante.

If any person without lawful excuse, the proof whereof lies on him (1) wilfully interferes with, removes or alters any part of a tramway, or of the works connected therewith; (2) wilfully places or throws any stones, dirt, wood, refuse or other material on any part of a tramway; (3) wilfully does or causes to be done anything in such manner as to obstruct any carriage using a tramway, or to endanger the lives of persons therein or thereon; or (4) knowingly aids or assists in the doing of any such thing, he is guilty of an offence and liable on summary conviction, in addition to any proceedings by way of indictment or otherwise to which he may be subject, to a fine not exceeding level 1 on the standard scale: Tramways Act 1870 s 50 (amended by the Criminal Justice Act 1982 s 46). For the meaning of 'the standard scale' see para 808 post.

4 For these purposes, 'any unlawful act' includes each of the matters expressly mentioned in the Malicious Damage Act 1861 s 35: *R v Hardy* (1871) LR 1 CCR 278.

5 To be guilty of wilful neglect the accused must know that his conduct involves the risk of an obstruction to the railway unless he takes reasonable care and yet falls short of exercising such care: *R v Gittins* [1982] Crim LR 584, CA.

6 Malicious Damage Act 1861 s 36; Criminal Justice Act 1948 s 1 (2); Criminal Law Act 1967 s 1; Magistrates' Courts Act 1980 ss 17, 32 (1), Sch 1 para 4. See para 804 post. For the meaning of 'the prescribed sum' see para 807 post.

A person who, otherwise than by accident, leaves on a railway line any substance likely to cause an obstruction commits the offence even though his object may not have been to create an obstruction but merely to give the railway employees the trouble of removing the substance: *R v Holroyd* (1841) 2 Mood & R 339. The offence is committed even though the line has not been opened to the public and even if no actual obstruction took place: see *R v Bradford* (1860) 8 Cox CC 309, CCR; *R v Gatenby* [1960] Crim LR 195. The obstruction contemplated is not confined to physical obstruction; a person who improperly goes on a railway line and by raising his arms induces a driver to slow down commits the offence: *R v Hardy* (1871) LR 1 CCR 278. Similarly, the offence is committed where a train is caused to slow down by the unlawful alteration of signals: *R v Hadfield* (1870) LR 1 CCR 253. As to the offence of trespassing on the railway see the Railway Regulation Act 1840 s 16 (as amended) and RAILWAYS vol 38 para 928. As to endangering passengers on the railway see paras 485–487 ante.

602. Injury to post office letter boxes. A person who places or attempts to place in or against any post office letter box[1] any fire, match, light, explosive substance, dangerous substance, filth, noxious or deleterious substance, or fluid, or commits a nuisance in or against any post office letter box, or does or attempts to do anything likely to injure the box is guilty of an offence and liable on conviction on indictment to imprisonment for a term not exceeding 12 months, or on summary conviction to a fine not exceeding the prescribed sum[2].

1 'Post office letter box' includes any pillar box, wall box or other box or receptacle provided by the permission or under the authority of the Postmaster General or the Post Office for the purpose of receiving postal packets, or any class of postal packets, for transmission by or under the authority of the Postmaster General or the Post Office: Post Office Act 1953 s 87 (1) (amended by the Post Office Act 1969 ss 76, 88, 139, Sch 4 para 2 (22)). The office of Postmaster General was abolished by the Post Office Act 1969 s 1 (1) (repealed).

2 Post Office Act 1953 s 60 (amended by the British Telecommunications Act 1981 s 89, Sch 6 Pt II; the Magistrates' Courts Act 1980 s 32 (2)). For the meaning of 'the prescribed sum' see para 807 post.

603. Altering signals with intent to endanger ship etc. Any person who unlawfully masks, alters or removes any light or signal, or unlawfully exhibits any false light or signal, with intent to bring any ship, vessel or boat into danger, or who unlawfully and maliciously[1] does anything tending to immediate loss or destruction of any ship, vessel or boat, is guilty of an offence and liable on conviction on indictment to imprisonment for life or for any shorter term[2].

1 For the meaning of 'maliciously' see para 601 note 1 ante.

2 Malicious Damage Act 1861 s 47; Criminal Justice Act 1948 ss 1 (1), 83 (3), Sch 10 Pt I; Criminal Law Act 1967 s 12 (5) (a).

604. Cutting away buoys etc. Any person who unlawfully and maliciously[1] cuts away, casts adrift, removes, alters, defaces, sinks or destroys or does any act with intent to cut away, cast adrift, remove, alter, deface, sink or destroy, or who in any other manner unlawfully and maliciously injures or conceals any boat, buoy, buoy rope, perch or mark used or intended for the guidance of seamen, or for the purpose of navigation, is guilty of an offence and liable on conviction on indictment to imprisonment for a term not exceeding seven years[2].

1 For the meaning of 'maliciously' see para 601 note 1 ante.
2 Malicious Damage Act 1861 s 48; Criminal Justice Act 1948 ss 1 (1), 83 (3), Sch 10 Pt 1; Criminal Law Act 1967 s 12 (5) (a).

(8) FORGERY

605. Meaning of 'false' and 'instrument'. For the purposes of the Forgery and Counterfeiting Act 1981, 'instrument' means:

(1) any document, whether of a formal or informal character;
(2) any stamp[1] issued or sold by the Post Office;
(3) any Inland Revenue stamp[2]; and
(4) any disc, tape, sound track or other device on or in which information is recorded or stored by mechanical, electronic or other means[3].

A currency note[4] is not, however, an instrument[5].

For these purposes, an instrument is false:

(a) if it purports[6] to have been made[7] in the form in which it is made by a person who did not in fact make it in that form[8];
(b) if it purports to have been made in the form in which it is made on the authority of a person who did not in fact authorise its making in that form;
(c) if it purports to have been made in the terms in which it is made by a person who did not in fact make it in those terms;
(d) if it purports to have been made in the terms in which it is made on the authority of a person who did not in fact authorise its making in those terms;
(e) if it purports to have been altered in any respect by a person who did not in fact alter it in that respect;
(f) if it purports to have been altered in any respect on the authority of a person who did not in fact authorise the alteration in that respect;
(g) if it purports to have been made or altered on a date on which, or at a place at which, or otherwise in circumstances[9] in which, it was not in fact made or altered; or
(h) if it purports to have been made or altered by an existing person but he did not in fact exist[10].

1 A mark denoting payment of postage which the Post Office authorises to be used instead of an adhesive stamp is to be treated for these purposes as if it were a stamp issued by the Post Office: Forgery and Counterfeiting Act 1981 s 8 (3).
2 For these purposes, 'Inland Revenue stamp' means a stamp as defined in the Stamp Duties Management Act 1891 s 27: Forgery and Counterfeiting Act 1981 s 8 (4). See further STAMP DUTIES vol 44 para 605 note 4.
3 Ibid s 8 (1). Electronic impulses keyed in in the course of computer 'hacking' are not a 'device' within the meaning of s 8 (1)(d); nor is the user segment of the databank; and information, such as a customer identification number and password, which is received, held for a moment while checking takes place and then expunged is not 'recorded and stored' within s 8 (1) (d): _R v Gold, R v Schifreen_ [1987] QB 1116, [1987] 3 All ER 618, CA; affd [1988] AC 1063, [1988] 2 All ER 186, HL.

4 For the meaning of 'currency note' see para 333 note 3 ante.

5 Forgery and Counterfeiting Act 1981 s 8 (2).

6 The consistent use of the word 'purports' throughout ibid s 9 (1) (a)–(h) (see infra) imports a requirement that for an instrument to be false it must tell a lie about itself: *R v More* [1987] 3 All ER 825 at 830, [1987] 1 WLR 1578 at 1585, HL.

7 A person is to be treated for these purposes as making a false instrument if he alters an instrument so as to make it false in any respect, whether or not it is false in some other respect apart from that alteration: ibid s 9 (2).

8 Where documents which purport to have been made by a company come into existence after the company has been wound up, the documents are false within the meaning of ibid s 9 (1) (a): *R v Lack* (1987) 84 Cr App Rep 342, CA.

9 The words 'otherwise in circumstances' expand the ambit of the Forgery and Counterfeiting Act 1981 s 9 (1) (g) beyond dates and places to any case in which an instrument purports to be made when it was not in fact made: *R v Donnelly* [1984] 1 WLR 1017 at 1019, 79 Cr App Rep 76 at 78, CA (valuation certificate stating that jewellery had been examined; the jewellery did not exist and the certificate was a sham to defraud insurers; certificate was a false instrument).

10 Forgery and Counterfeiting Act 1981 s 9 (1). A withdrawal form, signed in a false name by a person who has opened a building society account in that name, is not a false instrument within the meaning of s 9 (1) (h): *R v More* [1987] 3 All ER 825, [1987] 1 WLR 1578, HL.

606. Forgery. If a person makes[1] a false instrument[2], with the intention that he or another will use it to induce somebody to accept it as genuine, and by reason of so accepting it to do or not to do some act to his own or any other person's prejudice[3], he is guilty of forgery[4] and liable on conviction on indictment to imprisonment for a term not exceeding ten years, or on summary conviction to imprisonment for a term not exceeding six months or a fine not exceeding the statutory maximum, or to both[5].

1 For the meaning of 'make a false instrument' see para 605 note 7 ante.

2 For the meaning of 'false' and 'instrument' see para 605 ante.

3 An intention that the instrument should be accepted as genuine is not sufficient; there must also be an intention to induce the recipient to act or omit to act to his own or another person's prejudice: *R v Tobierre* [1986] 1 All ER 346, 82 Cr App Rep 212, CA (decided under the Forgery and Counterfeiting Act 1981 s 3: see para 608 post); *R v Garcia* [1988] Crim LR 115, CA. See also *R v Campbell* (1985) 80 Cr App Rep 47, CA.

For these purposes, an act or omission intended to be induced is to a person's prejudice if, and only if, it is one which, if it occurs (1) will result (a) in his temporary or permanent loss of property; or (b) in his being deprived of an opportunity to earn remuneration or greater remuneration; or (c) in his being deprived of an opportunity to gain a financial advantage otherwise than by way of remuneration; or (2) will result in somebody being given an opportunity (a) to earn remuneration or greater remuneration from him; (b) to gain a financial advantage from him otherwise than by way of remuneration; or (3) will be the result of his having accepted a false instrument as genuine, or a copy of a false instrument as a copy of a genuine one, in connection with his performance of any duty: Forgery and Counterfeiting Act 1981 s 10 (1). For these purposes, 'loss' includes not getting what one might get as well as parting with what one has: s 10 (5). An act which a person has an enforceable duty to do and an omission to do an act which a person is not entitled to do are to be disregarded for these purposes: s 10 (2). References to inducing somebody to accept a false instrument as genuine, or a copy of a false instrument as a copy of a genuine one, include references to inducing a machine to respond to the instrument or copy as if it were a genuine instrument or, as the case may be, a copy of a genuine one: s 10 (3). Where s 10 (3) applies, the act or omission intended to be induced by the machine responding to the instrument or copy is to be treated as an act or omission to a person's prejudice: s 10 (4).

4 Computer 'hacking' does not constitute forgery: see *R v Gold, R v Schifreen* [1987] QB 1116, [1987] 3 All ER 618, CA; affd [1988] AC 1063, [1988] 2 All ER 186, HL, cited in para 605 note 3 ante.

The Forgery and Counterfeiting Act 1981 abolished the offence of forgery at common law for all purposes not relating to offences committed before 28 October 1981: see ss 13, 33.

5 Ibid ss 1, 6 (1)–(3). For the meaning of 'the statutory maximum' see para 806 post. As to evidence of handwriting in a false instrument see para 1138 post; and as to production of a false instrument in court see para 1152 post.

607. Copying a false instrument. If a person makes a copy of an instrument[1] which is, and which he knows or believes to be, a false[2] instrument, with the intention that he or another will use it to induce[3] somebody to accept it as a copy of a genuine instrument, and by reason of so accepting it to do or not to do some act to his own or any other person's prejudice[3], he is guilty of an offence and liable on conviction on indictment to imprisonment for a term not exceeding ten years, or on summary conviction to imprisonment for a term not exceeding six months or a fine not exceeding the statutory maximum, or to both[4].

1 For the meaning of 'instrument' see para 605 ante.
2 For the meaning of 'false' see para 605 ante.
3 For the meaning of 'induce' and 'prejudice' see para 606 note 3 ante.
4 Forgery and Counterfeiting Act 1981 ss 2, 6 (1)–(3). For the meaning of 'the statutory maximum' see para 806 post.

608. Using a false instrument. If a person uses an instrument[1] which is, and which he knows or believes to be, false[2], with the intention of inducing[3] somebody to accept it as genuine, and by reason of so accepting it to do or not to do some act to his own or any other person's prejudice[3], he is guilty of an offence and liable on conviction on indictment to imprisonment for a term not exceeding ten years, or on summary conviction to imprisonment for a term not exceeding six months or a fine not exceeding the statutory maximum, or to both[4].

1 For the meaning of 'instrument' see para 605 ante.
2 For the meaning of 'false' see para 605 ante.
3 For the meaning of 'induce' and 'prejudice' see para 606 note 3 ante.
4 Forgery and Counterfeiting Act 1981 ss 3, 6 (1)–(3). For the meaning of 'the statutory maximum' see para 806 post.

609. Using a copy of a false instrument. If a person uses a copy of an instrument which is, and which he knows or believes to be, a false instrument[1], with the intention of inducing[2] somebody to accept it as a copy of a genuine instrument, and by reason of so accepting it to do or not to do some act to his own or any other person's prejudice[2], he is guilty of an offence and liable on conviction on indictment to imprisonment for a term not exceeding ten years, or on summary conviction to imprisonment for a term not exceeding six months or a fine not exceeding the statutory maximum, or to both[3].

1 For the meaning of 'false' and 'instrument' see para 605 ante.
2 For the meaning of 'induce' and 'prejudice' see para 606 note 3 ante.
3 Forgery and Counterfeiting Act 1981 ss 4, 6 (1)–(3). For the meaning of 'the statutory maximum' see para 806 post.

610. Money orders, share certificates, passports etc. If a person:

    (1)   has in his custody[1] or under his control[1] a specified instrument[2] which is, and which he knows or believes to be, false[3], with the intention that he or another will use it to induce[4] somebody to accept it as genuine, and by reason of so accepting it to do or not to do some act to his own or any other person's prejudice[5]; or

    (2)   has in his custody or under his control, without lawful authority or excuse, a specified instrument which is, and which he knows or believes to be, false[6]; or

(3) makes or has in his custody or under his control a machine or implement, or paper or any other material, which to his knowledge is or has been specially designed or adapted for the making of a specified instrument, with the intention that he or another will make a specified instrument which is false and that he or another will use the instrument to induce somebody to accept it as genuine, and by reason of so accepting it to do or not to do some act to his own or any other person's prejudice[7]; or

(4) makes or has in his custody or under his control any such machine, implement, paper or material, without lawful authority or excuse[8],

he is guilty of an offence and liable:

(a) in the case of an offence under heads (1) and (3) above, on conviction on indictment to imprisonment for a term not exceeding ten years, or on summary conviction to imprisonment for a term not exceeding six months or a fine not exceeding the statutory maximum, or to both[9];

(b) in the case of an offence under heads (2) and (4) above, on conviction on indictment to imprisonment for a term not exceeding two years, or on summary conviction to imprisonment for a term not exceeding six months or a fine not exceeding the statutory maximum, or to both[10].

1 'Custody' means physical custody and 'control' imports the notion of the power to direct what is to be done with the property in question: see *Warner v Metropolitan Police Comr* [1969] 2 AC 256, 52 Cr App Rep 373, HL.

2 The instruments to which the Forgery and Counterfeiting Act 1981 s 5 applies are (1) money orders; (2) postal orders; (3) United Kingdom postage stamps; (4) Inland Revenue stamps; (5) share certificates; (6) passports and documents which can be used instead of passports; (7) cheques; (8) travellers' cheques; (9) cheque cards; (10) credit cards; (11) certified copies relating to an entry in a register of births, adoptions, marriages or deaths and issued by the Registrar General, the Registrar General for Northern Ireland, a registration officer or a person lawfully authorised to register marriages; and (12) certificates relating to entries in such registers: s 5 (5). For these purposes, 'share certificate' means an instrument entitling or evidencing the title of a person to a share or interest in any public stock, annuity, fund or debt of any government or state, including a state which forms part of another state, or in any stock, fund or debt of a body, whether corporate or unincorporated, established in the United Kingdom or elsewhere: s 5 (6). For the meaning of 'Inland Revenue stamp' see para 605 note 2 ante.

3 For the meaning of 'false' see para 605 ante.

4 For the meaning of 'induce' see para 606 note 3 ante.

5 Forgery and Counterfeiting Act 1981 s 5 (1). For the meaning of 'prejudice' see para 606 note 3 ante.

6 Ibid s 5 (2). As to what may constitute 'lawful authority' see *Dickins v Gill* [1896] 2 QB 310, DC; *R v Wuyts* [1969] 2 QB 474, 53 Cr App Rep 417, CA.

7 Forgery and Counterfeiting Act 1981 s 5 (3).

8 Ibid s 5 (4).

9 Ibid s 6 (1)–(3). For the meaning of 'the statutory maximum' see para 806 post.

10 Forgery and Counterfeiting Act 1981 s 6 (1), (2), (4). As to forgery etc of statutory documents under the Mental Health Act 1983 see s 126 and MENTAL HEALTH vol 30 para 1104.

611. Powers of search, forfeiture and seizure. If it appears to a justice of the peace, from information given to him on oath, that there is reasonable cause to believe that a person has in his custody[1] or under his control[1];

(1) any thing which he or another has used, or intends to use, for the making of any false instrument[2] or copy of a false instrument in contravention of the provisions[3] relating to forgery and copying a false instrument; or

(2) any false instrument or copy of a false instrument which he or another has used, or intends to use, in contravention of the provisions[4] relating to using a false instrument or using a copy of a false instrument; or

(3) any thing custody or control of which without lawful authority or excuse is an offence under the provisions[5] relating to offences in connection with specified instruments[6],

the justice may issue a warrant authorising a constable to search for and to seize the object in question, and for that purpose to enter any premises specified in the warrant[7].

At any time after the seizure of any object suspected of falling within any of heads (1) to (3) above, whether the seizure was effected by virtue of a warrant or otherwise, a constable may apply to a magistrates' court for an order with respect to the object; and the court, if it is satisfied both that the object in fact falls within any of heads (1) to (3) above and that it is conducive to the public interest to do so, may make such order as it thinks fit for the forfeiture of the object and its subsequent destruction or disposal[8]. The court by or before which a person is convicted of an offence may order any object shown to the satisfaction of the court to relate to the offence to be forfeited and either destroyed or dealt with in such other manner as the court may order[9]. The court may not, however, order any object to be so forfeited where a person claiming to be the owner of or otherwise interested in it applies to be heard by the court, unless an opportunity has been given to him to show cause why the order should not be made[10].

1 See para 610 note 1 ante.
2 For the meaning of 'false' and 'instrument' see para 605 ante.
3 Ie the Forgery and Counterfeiting Act 1981 s 1 (see para 606 ante) or s 2 (see para 607 ante).
4 Ie ibid s 3 (see para 608 ante) or s 4 (see para 609 ante).
5 Ie ibid s 5: see para 610 ante.
6 See para 610 note 2 ante.
7 Forgery and Counterfeiting Act 1981 s 7 (1). As to search warrants see para 670 et seq post.
8 Ibid s 7 (2).
9 Ibid s 7 (3).
10 Ibid s 7 (4).

612. Indictments under the Forgery and Counterfeiting Act 1981. In an indictment for an offence against the Forgery and Counterfeiting Act 1981 with reference to any instrument, it is sufficient to refer to the instrument, by any name or designation by which it is usually known, or by its purport, without setting out any copy or facsimile of the whole or part of it[1].

It is usual in an indictment for forgery, where the facts so justify, to allege in one count a forgery and in a second count using a false instrument[2].

1 Where the specific offence with which an accused person is charged in an indictment is one created by or under an enactment, the statement of offence must contain a reference to the section of the Act creating the offence; and the particulars must disclose the essential elements of the offence: see the Indictment Rules 1971, SI 1971/1253, r 6 and para 929 post.
2 As to the offences of using false instruments and copies of false instruments see paras 608, 609 ante.

613. Fraudulent printing or mutilation of stamps etc. Any person who does, or procures to be done, or knowingly aids, abets or assists in doing any of the following:

(1) fraudulently prints or makes an impression upon any material[1] from a genuine die[2];

(2) fraudulently cuts, tears or in any way removes from any material any stamp[3] with intent that any use should be made of it or of any part thereof[4];

(3) fraudulently mutilates any stamp, with intent that any use should be made of any part of such stamp[5];

(4) fraudulently fixes or places upon any material or upon any stamp, any stamp or part of a stamp which, whether fraudulently or not, has been cut, torn or in any way removed from any other material, or out of or from any other stamp[6];

(5) fraudulently erases or otherwise really or apparently removes from any stamped material any name, sum, date or other matter or thing whatsoever written on it, with the intent that any use should be made of the stamp upon such material[7];

(6) knowingly sells or exposes for sale or utters or uses any stamp which has been fraudulently printed or impressed from a genuine die[8];

(7) knowingly, and without lawful excuse[9], the proof whereof lies on the person accused, has in his possession any stamp which has been fraudulently printed or impressed from a genuine die, or any stamp or part of a stamp which has been fraudulently cut, torn or otherwise removed from any material, or any stamp which has been fraudulently mutilated, or any stamped material out of which any name, sum, date or other matter or thing has been fraudulently erased or otherwise either really or apparently removed[10],

is guilty of an offence and liable on conviction on indictment to imprisonment for a term not exceeding 14 years, or on summary conviction to imprisonment for a term not exceeding six months or a fine not exceeding the prescribed sum, or to both[11].

1 For these purposes, 'material' includes every sort of material upon which words or figures can be expressed: Stamp Duties Management Act 1891 s 27.

2 Ibid s 13 (3). For these purposes, 'die' includes any plate, type, tool or implement used under the direction of the Commissioners of Inland Revenue for expressing or denoting any duty, or rate of duty, or the fact that any duty or rate of duty or penalty has been paid, or that an instrument is duly stamped, or is not chargeable with any duty or for denoting any fee, and also any part of any such plate, type, tool or implement: s 27.

3 For these purposes, 'stamp' means a stamp impressed by means of a die as well as an adhesive stamp for denoting any duty or fee: ibid s 27.

4 Ibid s 13 (4). See also *R v Field* (1785) 1 Leach 383, CCR.

5 Stamp Duties Management Act 1891 s 13 (5).

6 Ibid s 13 (6).

7 Ibid s 13 (7).

8 Ibid s 13 (8) (amended by the Forgery Act 1913 s 20, Schedule). As to uttering forged stamps by delivery to an employee for forwarding see *R v Collicott* (1812) Russ & Ry 212, CCR. A person who sells a forged stamp commits an offence even though the stamp when sold bore a cancellation mark: *R v Lowden* [1914] 1 KB 144, 9 Cr App Rep 195, CCA.

9 Possession of a die to illustrate a stamp catalogue does not constitute a lawful excuse: *Dickins v Gill* [1896] 2 QB 310, DC. The innocent purchase of fictitious social security stamps from an unauthorised source does not constitute a lawful excuse for the possession of such stamps: *Winkle v Wiltshire* [1951] 1 KB 684, [1951] 1 All ER 479, DC.

10 Stamp Duties Management Act 1891 s 13 (9) (amended by the Forgery Act 1913 Schedule).

11 Stamp Duties Management Act 1891 s 13 (amended by the Forgery Act 1913 Schedule); Criminal Law Act 1967 s 1; Magistrates' Courts Act 1980 ss 17, 32 (1), Sch 1 para 12. See para 804 post. For the meaning of 'the prescribed sum' see para 807 post. As to uttering etc fictitious stamps see POST OFFICE vol 36 para 790; and as to powers of search and seizure see STAMP DUTIES vol 44 para 631.

614. Forgery etc of proof marks on gunbarrels. Any person who:

(1) fraudulently erases, obliterates or defaces, or fraudulently causes to be erased, obliterated or defaced, from any barrel[1] any mark[2] of any stamp[3] or

part of a stamp provided or used by either of the two companies[4] for marking barrels[5]; or

(2) knowingly[6] forges or counterfeits any stamp, or any part of a stamp, provided or used by either of the two companies for marking any barrel[7]; or

(3) knowingly sells or parts with the possession of any such forged or counterfeit stamp or part of a stamp[7]; or

(4) knowingly marks any barrel with any such forged or counterfeit stamp, or with any part of any such forged or counterfeit stamp[7]; or

(5) knowingly makes up any barrel so marked[7]; or

(6) knowingly forges, counterfeits, or by any means whatsoever produces upon any barrel an imitation of any mark of any stamp, or any part of a stamp, provided or used by either of the two companies for marking any barrel[7]; or

(7) knowingly sells or parts with the possession of any such mark[7]; or

(8) knowingly transposes or removes from any barrel to any other barrel, or from one part of a barrel to another part of the same barrel, any mark of any stamp, or any part of a stamp, provided or used by either of the two companies for marking any barrel[7]; or

(9) knowingly has in his possession or who sells or parts with the possession of any mark so transposed or removed[7]; or

(10) knowingly has in his possession any such forged or counterfeit stamp or part of a stamp, or any such forged or counterfeit mark or imitation of a mark, or any such transposed or removed mark[7]; or

(11) knowingly cuts or severs from any barrel any mark of any stamp provided or used by either of the two companies for stamping any barrel, with intent that the mark be placed upon or joined or affixed to any other barrel or any other part of the barrel from which the mark is cut or severed[7]; or

(12) knowingly places upon or joins or affixes to any barrel any such mark so cut or severed[7]; or

(13) with intent to defraud uses any genuine stamp, or part of a genuine stamp, provided or used by either of the two companies for marking any barrel[7],

commits an offence and is liable:

(a) in the case of head (1) above, on conviction on indictment to a fine, or on summary conviction to a fine not exceeding the statutory maximum[8]; and

(b) in the case of heads (2) to (13) above, on conviction on indictment to imprisonment for a term not exceeding two years[9].

1 For the meaning of 'barrel' see para 480 note 2 ante.

2 'Mark' includes every mark and other impression of and made with any stamp, or produced by any other means, on any metal whatsoever: Gun Barrel Proof Act 1868 s 4. For the meaning of 'stamp' see note 3 infra.

3 'Stamp' includes every stamp, die, punch, tool and other instrument by means of which any mark can be made on any metal whatsoever: ibid s 4.

4 'The two companies' means and includes the Gunmakers Company of the City of London and the Birmingham Proof House: see ibid s 4.

5 Ibid s 122 (6) (amended by the Gun Barrel Proof Act 1978 s 8, Sch 4).

6 Where the person charged with an offence under the Gun Barrel Proof Act 1868 s 121 (1) (see heads (2)–(13) infra) was at the time when the offence is alleged to have been committed a gunmaker, a gunbarrel maker, or a maker of or dealer in small arms or barrels (or any part of such), knowledge on his part is presumed until the contrary is shown: s 121 (1) proviso (renumbered and amended by the Gun Barrel Proof Act 1978 s 8 (1), Sch 3 para 10).

7 Gun Barrel Proof Act 1868 s 121 (1) (as renumbered and amended: see note 6 supra). Any person who, with respect to any stamp or mark, or any part of any stamp or mark of a foreign country,

registered by either of the two companies, or with respect to any forgery, counterfeit or imitation of any such stamp or mark or part, or with respect to any barrel marked with any such forged or counterfeited stamp or part of a stamp knowingly commits any such offence as is expressed in s 121 (1) (as so renumbered and amended) with respect to any stamp or any part of any stamp provided or used by either of the two companies for marking any barrel, or with respect to any mark of any such stamp or part of a stamp, is guilty of an offence: s 121 (1) (as so renumbered and amended).

Any person who, with respect to (1) any stamp or part of a stamp provided or used at any time by an official Proof House of any foreign state for impressing upon any barrel a mark which is or at any time was a convention proof mark; (2) any mark of any such stamp or part of a stamp; (3) any forgery, counterfeit or imitation of any such stamp or part of a stamp or of any such mark; or (4) any barrel marked with any such forged or counterfeit stamp or part of a stamp, knowingly does anything which would be an offence under s 121 (1) (as so renumbered and amended) if done with respect to any stamp or any part of a stamp provided or used at any time by either of the two companies for marking any barrel, or with respect to any mark of any such stamp or part of a stamp, is guilty of an offence under s 121 (1) (as so renumbered and amended): s 121 (2) (added by the Gun Barrel Proof Act 1978 Sch 3 para 10 (2)). For these purposes, 'convention proof mark' means any mark, sign or character of which a specimen is for the time being included in the register of proof marks published by the Permanent International Commission for the Proof of Small Arms established under a Convention done at Brussels on 1 July 1969, not being a mark, sign or character included in it as a United Kingdom proof mark: Gun Barrel Proof Act 1868 s 129 (1) (substituted by the Gun Barrel Proof Act 1978 s 1 (1), Sch 1).

8 Gun Barrel Proof Act 1868 s 122 (amended by the Gun Barrel Proof Act 1978 s 8, Sch 3 para 11). For the meaning of 'the statutory maximum' see para 806 post.

9 Gun Barrel Proof Act 1868 s 121 (1) (as renumbered and amended: see note 6 supra). As to the counterfeiting etc of dies and marks under the Hallmarking Act 1973 see s 6 and TRADE MARKS vol 48 para 338.

615. Destroying etc register of births etc. Any person who:

(1) unlawfully destroys, defaces or injures or causes or permits to be destroyed, defaced or injured any register of births, baptisms, marriages, deaths or burials authorised or required by law to be kept in England or Northern Ireland, or any part of any such register, or any certified copy of any such register or any part thereof[1];

(2) knowingly and unlawfully inserts or causes or permits to be inserted in any such register, or in any certified copy of the register any false entry of any matter relating to any birth, baptism, marriage, death or burial[1];

(3) knowingly and unlawfully gives any false certificate relating to any birth, baptism, marriage, death or burial[1];

(4) certifies any writing to be a copy or extract from any such register knowing such writing, or the part of the register from which the copy or extract is so given, to be false in any material particular[1];

(5) offers, utters, disposes of or puts off any such register, entry, certified copy, certificate or any copy of any entry in any such register knowing such entry to be false[1];

(6) knowingly and wilfully inserts or causes or permits to be inserted in any copy of any register directed or required by law to be transmitted to any registrar or other officer any false entry of any matter relating to any baptism, marriage or burial[2];

(7) knowingly and wilfully signs or verifies any copy of any such register so directed or required to be transmitted, which copy is false in any part thereof, knowing the same to be false[2];

(8) unlawfully destroys, defaces or injures or for any fraudulent purpose takes from its place of deposit or conceals any such copy of any register[2],

is guilty of an offence and liable on conviction on indictment to imprisonment for life or for any shorter term[3].

1 Forgery Act 1861 s 36 (amended by the Forgery Act 1931 s 20, Schedule Pt 1); Irish Free State (Consequential Adaptation of Enactments) Order 1923, SR & O 1923/405, art 2. As to the register of births etc see REGISTRATION vol 39 para 1001 et seq.

As to the correction of errors notwithstanding the Forgery Act 1861 s 36 see ECCLESIASTICAL LAW vol 14 paras 1034 note 3, 1116. It is not necessary that the entry should be made with intent to defraud, nor is it necessary (where the matter relates to witnessing a marriage) that the marriage should be legal or the witness a necessary witness: *R v Asplin* (1873) 12 Cox CC 391. Any person who wilfully inserts or causes to be inserted in a register or record any false entry of any birth or baptism, naming or dedication, death or burial, or marriage, or wilfully gives any false certificate, or certifies any writing to be an extract from any register or record knowing the register or record to be false in any part is guilty of an offence: Non-parochial Registers Act 1840 s 8 (amended by the Forgery Act 1913 s 20, Schedule; the Criminal Damage Act 1971 s 11 (8), Schedule Pt 1); Criminal Law Act 1967 s 12 (5)(a). The Non-parochial Registers Act 1840 s 8 (as so amended) also applies to registers and records deposited in the Office of Population Censuses and Surveys (see CONSTITUTIONAL LAW vol 8 para 1240 note 20) under the Births and Deaths Registration Act 1858: s 3.
2 Forgery Act 1861 s 37 (amended by the Forgery Act 1913 s 20, Schedule Pt I).
3 Forgery Act 1861 ss 36, 37 (as amended: see notes 1, 2 supra); Criminal Justice Act 1948 s 1 (1).

5. ORIGINAL CRIMINAL JURISDICTION

(1) COURTS HAVING ORIGINAL CRIMINAL JURISDICTION

616. Courts of ordinary criminal jurisdiction. The courts which exercise original criminal jurisdiction[1], administering the ordinary criminal law in England and Wales, are (1) the magistrates' courts[2]; and (2) the Crown Court[3]. The former are inferior courts; and the latter is a superior court of record[4], and part of the Supreme Court[5].

1 As to any original criminal jurisdiction remaining in the High Court of Parliament see COURTS vol 10 para 732 et seq. The original criminal jurisdiction of the Queen's Bench Division as to trials at bar was abolished by the Criminal Law Act 1967 s 10 (2), Sch 3 Pt III. Courts of assize and courts of quarter sessions were abolished by the Courts Act 1971 ss 1 (2), 3 (repealed).
2 See para 617 post and MAGISTRATES.
3 See para 618 post.
4 Supreme Court Act 1981 s 45 (1). As to the classification of courts into superior and inferior courts, and the characteristics of a court of record, see COURTS vol 10 para 708 et seq.
5 Ibid s 1 (1).

617. Magistrates' courts. In regard to criminal matters it is the function of magistrates[1] to conduct the trial of summary offences[2] and of offences triable either way[3] which are not to be tried on indictment, and to act as examining justices in regard to indictable offences and offences triable either way which are not to be tried summarily[4].

1 As to the jurisdiction of justices of the peace and stipendiary magistrates see paras 801, 802 respectively post; and as to the office of magistrates see MAGISTRATES.
2 As to the trial of summary offences see paras 805–808 post and MAGISTRATES.
3 As to the procedure for offences triable either way see paras 804, 809 et seq post; and as to determining the mode of trial see para 811 post.
4 As to the procedure for offences triable on indictment see para 824 et seq post.

618. The Crown Court. All proceedings on indictment must be brought before the Crown Court[1]. In addition, the Crown Court has jurisdiction to sentence or deal with persons committed to it by a magistrates' court[2] and to deal with appeals from magistrates' courts[3].

1 Supreme Court Act 1981 s 46 (1). As to the Crown Court see COURTS vol 10 para 870 et seq.
2 See paras 1350, 1351 post.
3 See para 1450 et seq post.

619. Courts of special criminal jurisdiction. There are, in addition to those courts administering the ordinary criminal law[1], certain courts having special criminal jurisdiction. These are (1) courts-martial[2] which have jurisdiction in respect of offences committed by persons subject to naval, military and air force law; (2) standing civilian courts[3] for the trial outside the United Kingdom of certain civilians subject to naval, military and air force law; and (3) the ecclesiastical courts[4], exercising jurisdiction of a criminal nature over the clergy and other members of the Church of England.

The courts of the Vice-Chancellors of the universities of Oxford and Cambridge[5], which have limited criminal jurisdiction over resident members of those universities and their employees, though still in existence, are now of no practical importance.

1 See paras 616–618 ante. At a coroner's inquest into the death of a person who came by his death by murder, manslaughter or infanticide, the purpose of the proceedings does not include the finding of any person guilty of the murder, manslaughter or infanticide; and accordingly a coroner's inquisition may in no case charge a person with any of those offences: Coroners Act 1988 s 11 (6). See further CORONERS.
2 See ROYAL FORCES vol 41 paras 365 et seq, 406 et seq, 479 et seq.
3 See ROYAL FORCES vol 41 para 514 et seq.
4 See ECCLESIASTICAL LAW vol 14 para 1272 et seq.
5 See COURTS vol 10 paras 981, 973 respectively.

(2) AMBIT OF CRIMINAL JURISDICTION

(i) The General Rule

620. Territorial jurisdiction. English courts exercise criminal jurisdiction in respect of acts done or omissions made by British subjects[1] or aliens[2] within the territory of England and Wales[3].

1 For the meaning of 'British subject' see the British Nationality Act 1981 s 51 (1), (2) and BRITISH NATIONALITY AND ALIENAGE. Citizens of the Republic of Ireland are not aliens: see the Ireland Act 1949 s 2 (1); the British Nationality Act 1981 ss 31, 50 (1) and BRITISH NATIONALITY AND ALIENAGE.
2 For the meaning of 'alien' see the British Nationality Act 1981 ss 50 (1), 51 (4) and BRITISH NATIONALITY AND ALIENAGE. The wife of an alien is not necessarily an alien: see BRITISH NATIONALITY AND ALIENAGE vol 4 para 919. As to the classes of persons who have personal immunity from jurisdiction see paras 38–40 ante and FOREIGN RELATIONS.
3 As to the territory of England and Wales see para 623 post; as to acts done partly within and partly outside England see para 624 post; and as to the basis of jurisdiction see para 623 post.

621. Extra-territorial jurisdiction. English courts exercise criminal jurisdiction over British subjects[1] and aliens[2] for acts done or omissions made (1) on the open sea within the territorial waters of Her Majesty's dominions[3]; (2) on board British ships on the high seas or in foreign rivers 'where great ships generally go'[4]; (3) on board British-controlled aircraft[5] or, in certain circumstances, on any aircraft in flight[6] anywhere; and also in respect of certain acts done by British subjects and special classes of persons on land abroad or on board non-British ships on the high seas[7].

English courts do not exercise criminal jurisdiction in respect of acts of foreigners on land abroad, except in the case of a crime committed ashore by a foreigner belonging to the crew of a British merchant ship[8] and in certain cases of treason[9]; or at sea, except within the territorial waters of Her Majesty's dominions, or on British ships[10]; or in the case of piracy jure gentium which is triable and punishable wherever and by whomsoever it is committed[11]. If an act is done totally outside England by a foreigner, and neither within British territorial water nor on a British ship, the foreigner is not answerable to English criminal jurisdiction although some consequence of the act may take place in England; for example, if the foreigner strikes someone abroad, and the victim comes to England and dies of the blow, there is no crime cognisable in England[12].

In addition to the extension of territory, principally territorial waters, by statute and under the prerogative, the operation of the criminal law has been extended by various statutes which are designed to protect domestic interests or give effect to international conventions[13].

1 For the meaning of 'British subject' see para 620 note 1 ante. As to the limitation of criminal liability of certain British subjects and citizens of the Republic of Ireland see the British Nationality Act 1948 s 3 (1); the Ireland Act 1949 ss 1 (1), (3), 3 and BRITISH NATIONALITY AND ALIENAGE vol 4 para 904.

2 For the meaning of 'alien' see para 620 note 2 ante.

3 See the Territorial Waters Jurisdiction Act 1878 s 2 and para 626 post. For the meaning of 'Her Majesty's dominions' see COMMONWEALTH vol 6 para 803; and as to the territorial sea of the United Kingdom see the Territorial Sea Act 1987 s 1 and FOREIGN RELATIONS.

Where a British subject is a member of the crew of a foreign public armed ship, the English courts may exercise jurisdiction if the foreign power waives the immunity extended to it in accordance with the principles of international law: *Chung Chi Cheung v R* [1939] AC 160, [1938] 4 All ER 786, PC; and see FOREIGN RELATIONS.

Her Majesty may by Order in Council make provision for securing that, where an offence is alleged to have been committed on board any ship by the master or a member of the crew and the ship belongs to a state specified in the Order, proceedings for the offence instituted otherwise than at the request or with the consent of a consular officer of that State are not entertained by any court in the United Kingdom unless (1) the offence is alleged to have been committed by or against a person who is a citizen of the United Kingdom and colonies or a member of certain classes of British subjects or a British protected person or against a person other than the master or a member of the crew; or (2) the offence is one involving the tranquillity or safety of a port, or the law relating to safety of life at sea, public health, oil pollution, wireless telegraphy, immigration or customs or is of any other description specified in the Order; or (3) the offence is a grave crime: see the Consular Relations Act 1968 ss 1 (2), 5 and FOREIGN RELATIONS vol 18 para 1594. As to the Orders in Council which have been so made see FOREIGN RELATIONS vol 18 para 1594 note 6.

4 See para 625 post.

5 See the Civil Aviation Act 1982 s 92 and AVIATION. Section 92 applies to hovercraft: see the Hovercraft (Application of Enactments) Order 1972, SI 1972/1971, art 5, Sch 2 Pt A; Interpretation Act 1978 ss 17 (2) (a), 23 (2).

6 See the Aviation Security Act 1982 s 1. As to the protection of aircraft generally see Pt II (ss 10–24) and AVIATION.

7 See para 625 post.

8 Merchant Shipping Act 1894 s 687 (amended by the Criminal Law Act 1967 s 10 (2), Sch 3 Pt III); but see *R v Anderson* (1868) LR 1 CCR 161, where the question of construction of the Merchant Shipping Act 1854 s 267 (repealed) (in similar terms to the Merchant Shipping Act 1894 s 687 (as so amended)) was reviewed.

9 See para 634 post.

10　*R v Anderson* (1868) LR 1 CCR 161.

11　See the Tokyo Convention Act 1967 s 4, Schedule (amended by the Aviation Security Act 1982 s 40, Sch 3); AVIATION and FOREIGN RELATIONS vol 18 paras 1536, 1539. See also *R v Keyn* (1876) 2 ExD 63 at 168, CCR; *A-G for Colony of Hong Kong v Kwok-a-Sing* (1873) LR 5 PC 179.

12　*R v Lewis* (1857) Dears & B 182, CCR; *R v Depardo* (1807) 1 Taunt 26, CCR; *R v De Mattos* (1836) 7 C & P 458. The Offences against the Person Act 1861 s 10 (amended by the Criminal Law Act 1967 s 10(1), (2), Sch 2 para 6, Sch 3 Pt III) (see para 428 ante) apparently does not apply in the case of a foreigner: see *R v Lewis* supra; *R v Jameson* [1896] 2 QB 425. As to the liability of a foreigner in the case of a continuing act initiated abroad, some part of which is deemed to be performed in England, see *R v De Marny* [1907] 1 KB 388, CCR and para 624 post.

13　See para 632 post.

622. Sources and rationale of territorial jurisdiction.

Jurisdiction in respect of acts done in England is derived from the common law. Jurisdiction over acts done on British ships on the high seas, or in foreign rivers 'where great ships generally go' is, in general[1], the Admiralty jurisdiction. Jurisdiction over acts done in British-controlled aircraft and hovercraft is conferred by statute[2]. Jurisdiction elsewhere is derived from statute[3] or from the extension of territory under the prerogative[4].

All crime is local and the jurisdiction over the crime belongs to the country where the crime is committed, and, except over British subjects, the Sovereign and the legislature have no power out of this country[5]. The jurisdiction over acts done on a British ship was founded on the fiction that 'a ship which bears a nation's flag is to be treated as a part of the territory of that nation'[6]; however, it now seems that the application of English criminal law to offences committed on British ships afloat is based on the common law principle that they fall under the protection of the Sovereign so that all persons aboard, whether British subjects or foreigners, are subject to the laws of the Sovereign[7]. The jurisdiction over British subjects in respect of acts committed abroad is purely statutory and is based on the allegiance of the subject to the Sovereign, and on the power of the Sovereign, by reason of this allegiance, to pass laws for the regulation of the conduct of subjects wherever they are[8]. Apart from statute the general principle of criminal jurisprudence is that the quality of the act depends on the law of the place where it is done[9]. An alien enemy who is a prisoner of war, it seems, may commit crimes for which he is triable and punishable in England and Wales[10].

1　Ie except for the specific offences created by, and the general provisions relating to offences at sea and jurisdiction in respect of such offences contained in, the Merchant Shipping Acts 1894 to 1988: see SHIPPING.

2　See the Aviation Security Act 1982 Pt I (ss 1–9) and AVIATION.

3　For instances of statutes making acts committed abroad by British subjects punishable in England see para 634 post; and for instances of statutes extending the operation of the criminal law either for the purpose of implementing international conventions or for the purpose of protecting or safe-guarding some particular domestic interest see para 632 post.

4　For an example of the extension of territory under the prerogative see para 632 note 9 post. See also para 626 note 5 post.

5　*Macleod v A-G for New South Wales* [1891] AC 455 at 458, PC per Lord Halsbury LC; *Sirdar Gurdyal Singh v Rajah of Faridkote* [1894] AC 670, PC; *Badische Anilin und Soda Fabrik v Basle Chemical Works, Bindschedler* [1898] AC 200, HL. See also *Treacy v DPP* [1971] AC 537 at 561, 55 Cr App Rep 113 at 140, HL per Lord Diplock (the origin of this rule is based on international comity which leans against the English courts punishing those who in another country did something which has no harmful consequences within England). As to piracy jure gentium see para 621 text and note 11 ante.

6　*R v Anderson* (1868) LR 1 CCR 161 at 163 per Blackburn J and at 166 per Bovill CJ; *Forbes v Cochrane* (1824) 2 B & C 448.

7　*R v Lesley* (1860) Bell CC 220 at 223 per Erle CJ ('although an English ship in some respects carries with her the laws of her country in the territorial waters of a foreign state, yet in other respects she is subject to the laws of that state as to acts done to the subjects thereof'). *R v Anderson* (1868) LR 1 CCR 161, and the other cases cited in note 6 supra, and this note, do not, however, decide that a British ship is part of the United Kingdom: *R v Gordon-Finlayson* [1941] 1 KB 171. See also *Chung Chi Cheung v R* [1939] AC 160, [1938] 4 All ER 786, PC.

8 See *Sussex Peerage Case* (1844) 11 Cl & Fin 85 at 146, HL per Tindal CJ.

9 *A-G for Colony of Hong Kong v Kwok-a-Sing* (1873) LR 5 PC 179 at 199 per Mellish LJ.

10 See *R v Molieres* (1758) Fost 188, and the observations of Lord Ellenborough CJ in *R v Johnson* (1805) 6 East 583 at 593, and *R v Sauvajot* (1799) cited in 1 Taunt 32; *R v Acow* (1806) cited in 1 Taunt 32; and see the following Canadian cases: *R v Krebs* [1943] 4 DLR 533 (prisoner of war held not criminally responsible for his act of breaking and entering premises); this case was not agreed with in *R v Shindler* [1944] 3 WWR 125 (prisoner of war who stole a car held subject to criminal law of Canada); see also *R v Kaehler and Stolski* [1945] 1 WWR 566 (Supreme Court held that prisoner of war who steals a car is not immune from trial and imprisonment under the Canadian Criminal Code).

(ii) Common Law Jurisdiction

623. Acts done in the territory of England. At common law the exercise of criminal jurisdiction is limited to crimes committed within the land of England (which includes Wales but does not include Scotland, Ireland, the Isle of Man or the Channel Islands[1]) with its ports and harbours, bays, gulfs and estuaries, and so much of the outer coast as extends to low-water mark[2]. The common law courts exercised jurisdiction over all persons who committed criminal acts within these territorial limits, whether such subjects were subjects of the Sovereign or resident aliens or mere casual and temporary alien visitors[3]. In respect of acts done outside these limits there was no jurisdiction at common law[4].

1 See the Laws in Wales Act 1535 s 1 and CONSTITUTIONAL LAW vol 8 para 802. See also *Re Mitchell, ex p Cunningham* (1884) 13 QBD 418, CA. Lundy Island is part of Great Britain: *Harman v Bolt* (1931) 47 TLR 219. The Island of Rockall has been incorporated into the United Kingdom but as part of Scotland: Island of Rockall Act 1972 s 1 (amended by the Local Government (Scotland) Act 1973 s 214 (2), Sch 27 Pt II para 202). As to the incorporation of part of the Channel tunnel system into the United Kingdom see the Channel Tunnel Act 1987 s 10.

2 *R v Keyn* (1876) 2 ExD 63 at 162, CCR. As to the Admiralty jurisdiction see para 625 post and ADMIRALTY vol 1(1) (Reissue) para 301 et seq. National or internal waters are legally equivalent to land: see FOREIGN RELATIONS vol 18 para 1454. As to the areas of water comprising national waters see *Post Office v Estuary Radio Ltd* [1968] 2 QB 740, [1967] 3 All ER 663 at 679, CA.

3 *R v Keyn* (1876) 2 ExD 63 at 160, CCR.

4 *R v Keyn* (1876) 2 ExD 63 at 168, CCR.

624. Acts done partly within and partly outside England. An offence may be committed against the criminal law of England though some of the essential elements of the offence are committed abroad; each case depends on the nature of the crime, the definition of the offence, the provisions of the statute creating it or any geographical limitation which is apparent from the nature of the crime itself or from the language of the statute creating it[1]. If a person, being outside England, initiates an offence, part of the essential elements of which take effect in England, he is amenable to English jurisdiction[2]; for instance, a person who, being abroad, procures an innocent agent, or uses the Post Office, to commit a crime in England, if a British subject is, or, if a foreigner may be, amenable to the criminal law of England[3]. Where, however, an agent capable of forming his own judgment has been interposed between the initiation of the crime abroad by a foreigner and its consummation in England, difficulties may arise as to whether that foreigner commits an offence cognisable in the English courts[4].

In respect of the offence of obtaining property by deception[5] the gist of the offence lies in the act of obtaining, which must be in England[6]. Thus a person who practises a deception out of England, and by means of that deception obtains property in England, is triable in England[7]. If the deception is made in a letter written and posted in England and sent to an address abroad and by reason of the deception money is sent from abroad and received in England, a crime is committed which is triable in England[8]; but, where it is agreed that a transaction will be completed by the victim posting a cheque abroad, the act of obtaining takes place abroad and the English courts do not have jurisdiction[9].

When a person makes an unwarranted demand with menaces by letter posted in England and received abroad, he may be tried in England for the offence of blackmail[10]; the same rule applies in the converse case where the blackmailing letter is written and posted abroad to the intended victim in England[11].

Where an offence is committed in England, a person (at least if he is a citizen of the United Kingdom) who counsels or procures the commission of that offence is amenable to English law even though he was not in England when he so counselled or procured the offence or when it was committed[12].

If a person, being outside English territory, were intentionally to fire at and kill a person in English territory in such circumstances that the act amounts to murder, the person who fired could be tried for murder in England[13].

1　See the observations of Lord Diplock in *Treacy v DPP* [1971] AC 537 at 540–564, 55 Cr App Rep 113 at 138–145, HL.

2　*R v Munton* (1793) 1 Esp 62; *R v Oliphant* [1905] 2 KB 67, CCR; *R v Stoddart* (1909) 25 TLR 612, CCA; *R v Baxter* [1972] 1 QB 1 at 12, 55 Cr App Rep 214 at 220, CA (where the statement in the text was approved by the Court of Appeal). See also *R v Markus* [1974] 3 All ER 705, [1974] 3 WLR 645, CA; affd sub nom *Secretary of State for Trade v Markus* [1975] 1 All ER 958, [1975] 2 WLR 708, HL; and see *DPP v Doot* [1973] AC 807, 57 Cr App Rep 600, HL; *R v Raud* [1989] Crim LR 809, CA. As to conspiracies with an international element see para 69 ante.

3　*R v Brisac* (1803) 4 East 164; *R v Johnson* (1805) 29 State Tr 414 at 462, 499; *R v Von Veltheim* (1908) 148 CC Ct Cas 579; *R v Baxter* [1972] 1 QB 1 at 8, 55 Cr App Rep 214, CA (the accused posted letters in Northern Ireland to football promoters in England falsely claiming that he had correctly forecast the results of football matches and was entitled to winnings; held, the English courts had jurisdiction to try the accused for attempting to obtain money by deception contrary to the Theft Act 1968 s 15 (see para 567 ante)).

4　See *Badische Anilin und Soda Fabrik v Basle Chemical Works, Bindschedler* [1898] AC 200 at 205, HL per Lord Halsbury LC.

5　Ie contrary to the Theft Act 1968 s 15: see para 567 ante.

6　*R v Ellis* [1899] 1 QB 230, CCR; *R v Harden* [1963] 1 QB 8, 49 Cr App Rep 90, CCA; but see also *R v Thompson* [1984] 3 All ER 565, 79 Cr App Rep 191, CA; *R v Tomsett* [1985] Crim LR 369, CA; *R v Beck* [1985] 1 All ER 571, 80 Cr App Rep 355, CA; *Re Osman* [1988] Crim LR 611.

7　*R v Ellis* [1899] 1 QB 230, CCR; and see *R v Baxter* [1972] 1 QB 1 at 8, 55 App Rep 214, CA (attempt to obtain property by deception); *DPP v Stonehouse* [1978] AC 55, 65 Cr App Rep 192, HL (attempt to defraud life assurance companies in England by faking death abroad).

8　*R v Holmes* (1883) 12 QBD 23, CCR. See *R v Thompson* [1984] 3 All ER 565, 79 Cr App Rep 191, CA (request in England for transfer to England of sums fraudulently credited abroad to foreign bank accounts amounts to offence of obtaining property by deception).

9　*R v Harden* [1963] 1 QB 8, 49 Cr App Rep 90, CCA. However, in *Treacy v DPP* [1971] AC 537 at 563, 55 Cr App Rep 113 at 143, HL, Lord Diplock expressed the view that his decision (relating to the offence of obtaining by false pretences under the Larceny Act 1916 s 32 (repealed)), will call for re-examination if a similar question should arise in connection with the offence of obtaining by deception under the Theft Act 1968 s 15; and see *R v Tirado* (1974) 59 Cr App Rep 80, CA.

10　*Treacy v DPP* [1971] AC 537, 55 Cr App Rep 113, HL.

11　See *Treacy v DPP* [1971] AC 537, 55 Cr App Rep 113, HL.

12　*R v Robert Millar (Contractors) Ltd, R v Millar* [1970] 2 QB 54 at 66, 54 Cr App Rep 158, CA. The principle that persons who counsel or procure the commission of a crime are guilty as secondary parties to that crime applies. As to secondary parties see para 45 et seq ante. Where a person in

England counsels or procures the commission of a crime abroad, he will not be triable in England as the crime is committed abroad: see *R v Godfrey* [1923] 1 KB 24, DC.

13 See *R v Coombes* (1786) 1 Leach 388 (criticised in *Badische Anilin und Soda Fabrik v Basle Chemical Works, Bindschedler* [1898] AC 200, HL); *R v Rogers* (1877) 3 QBD 28 at 34, CCR per Field J; the Offences against the Person Act 1861 s 10 (amended by the Criminal Law Act 1967 Sch 3 Pt III); sed quaere whether the same rule would apply to manslaughter by negligence (see *R v Keyn* (1876) 2 ExD 63 at 234, CCR, where Cockburn CJ thought that it would).

(iii) Admiralty Jurisdiction

625. Offences on the high seas. At common law acts[1] constituting indictable offences[2] done on British ships[3] on the high seas are subject to the jurisdiction of the Admiralty whether such acts are done by British subjects[4] or foreigners[5].

Acts done on, or by means of, a foreign ship on the high seas, but outside the territorial waters of the United Kingdom, are not within the Admiralty jurisdiction if done by a foreigner, except in the case of piracy jure gentium[6]; and are not within such jurisdiction if done by a British subject, except where so provided by statute[7].

The expression 'high seas' when used with reference to the jurisdiction of the Admiralty includes all oceans, seas, bays, channels, rivers, creeks and waters below low water mark and 'where great ships go', with the exception of such oceans etc as are within the body of some country, namely, national or internal waters[8]. A foreign or colonial port, if it is part of the high seas in the above sense, is within the jurisdiction of the Admiralty[9].

1 It is not necessary that the criminal act should be completed on board the ship if part of it is done on board: *R v Armstrong* (1875) 13 Cox CC 184. See also *The People (A-G) v Thomas* [1954] IR 319.
2 Certain statutory provisions confirm the Admiralty jurisdiction and make indictable offences committed on the high seas punishable as if they had been committed on land: see eg the Offences at Sea Act 1799 s 1 (amended by the Criminal Law Act 1967 s 10 (2), Sch 3 Pt I); the Malicious Damage Act 1861 s 72; the Offences against the Person Act 1861 s 68; the Perjury Act 1911 s 8 (all amended by the Criminal Law Act 1967 s 10 (2), Sch 3 Pt III).
3 For the meaning of 'British ship' see the Merchant Shipping Act 1988 s 2 and SHIPPING. A hulk which retains the general appointments of a British ship, which is registered as a British ship and hoists the British ensign, but which is used as a floating warehouse, is sufficiently a British ship to be within the Admiralty jurisdiction: *R v Armstrong* (1875) 13 Cox CC 184. Cf *R v Serva* (1845) 1 Den 104, CCR (unlawful capture of a Brazilian vessel by a British man-of-war did not make the Brazilian vessel a British ship, and a crime alleged to have been committed on the Brazilian vessel while it was in possession of the British man-of-war was not cognisable in the English courts). The fact that a ship carries the British flag and is registered as a British ship is prima facie evidence that it is a British ship, but if it is in fact owned by a person not qualified to be an owner of a British ship, it is not a British ship and the English courts have no jurisdiction to try an offence committed on the high seas by a foreigner on board such a ship: *R v Bjornsen* (1865) Le & Ca 545, CCR. As to the persons qualified to be owners of British ships see the Merchant Shipping Act 1988 s 3 and SHIPPING.
4 For the meaning of 'British subject' see para 620 note 1 ante.
5 *R v Anderson* (1868) LR 1 CCR 161; *R v Keyn* (1876) 2 ExD 63 at 162, CCR; *R v Carr and Wilson* (1882) 10 QBD 76, CCR; *R v Allen* (1837) 1 Mood CC 494; *R v Liverpool Justices, ex p Molyneux* [1972] 2 QB 384, [1972] 2 All ER 471, DC. It appears that the Admiralty had no jurisdiction over offences at sea other than those committed on board, or by means of, a British ship: see *R v Bates* (1968) Times, 22 October, concerning alleged offences committed on a disused anti-aircraft tower standing off the English coast three miles outside territorial waters. As to the origins of the Admiralty jurisdiction see ADMIRALTY vol 1 (1) (Reissue) para 301. See also *Oteri v R* [1976] 1 WLR 1272, [1977] 1 Lloyd's Rep 105, PC.
6 See para 621 text and note 10 ante. As to indictable offences committed in territorial waters see para 626 post.
7 See eg the Merchant Shipping Act 1894 s 686 and para 629 note 5 post.

8　*The Mecca* [1895] P 95 at 107, CA. See also *R v Carr and Wilson* (1882) 10 QBD 76, CCR; *The Tolten* [1946] P 135; sub nom *United Africa Co Ltd v Tolten (Owners)*, *The Tolten* [1946] 2 All ER 372, CA; *R v Liverpool Justices, ex p Molyneux* [1972] 2 QB 384, [1972] 2 All ER 471, DC.
9　*The Mecca* [1895] P 95 at 107, CA.

626. Offences in the territorial sea of the United Kingdom. Indictable offences committed within the territorial sea of the United Kingdom[1] whether by a British subject[2] or a foreigner or whether committed on, or by means of, a foreign ship[3] are offences within the jurisdiction of the Admiralty and are triable in England[4]. Proceedings against a non-British subject instituted in the United Kingdom[5] require the consent of the Secretary of State and his certificate that the institution of such proceedings is expedient[6].

1　For the meaning of 'the territorial sea' of the United Kingdom see the Territorial Sea Act 1987 s 1; the Territorial Sea (Limits) Order 1989, SI 1989/482; and FOREIGN RELATIONS.
2　For the meaning of 'British subject' see para 620 note 1 ante.
3　'Ship' includes every description of ship, boat or other floating craft: Territorial Waters Jurisdiction Act 1878 s 7. 'Ship' includes hovercraft: Hovercraft (Application of Enactments) Order 1972, SI 1972/971, art 4, Sch 1. 'Foreign ship' means any ship which is not a British ship: Territorial Waters Jurisdiction Act 1878 s 7. Only an offence committed on a 'ship' as so defined is triable under the 1878 Act: see *R v Kent Justices, ex p Lye* [1967] 2 QB 153, [1967] 1 All ER 560, DC. As to the position of foreign public ships see *The Parlement Belge* (1880) 5 PD 197, CA: *Chung Chi Cheung v R* [1939] AC 160, [1938] 4 All ER 786, PC and ADMIRALTY vol 1 (1) (Reissue) para 304. As to foreign sovereign immunity from process and its waiver see FOREIGN RELATIONS. See also *Mortensen v Peters* 1906 8 F 93.
4　See the Territorial Waters Jurisdiction Act 1878 s 2; the Territorial Sea Act 1987 s 1 (5).
5　For these purposes, 'United Kingdom' includes the Isle of Man, the Channel Islands and adjacent islands: Territorial Waters Jurisdiction Act 1878 s 7. For the usual meaning of 'United Kingdom' see CONSTITUTIONAL LAW vol 8 para 802.
6　Ibid s 3. Section 3 does not apply to proceedings for an offence within the Oil and Gas (Enterprise) Act 1982 s 27 (see PETROLEUM PRODUCTION): s 27 (5). An Order in Council applying the Health and Safety at Work etc Act 1974 Pt I (ss 1–54) to persons, premises, work etc outside Great Britain may provide that proceedings for offences under Pt I (ss 1–54) committed outside Great Britain are excluded from the operation of the Territorial Waters Jurisdiction Act 1878 s 3: Health and Safety at Work etc Act 1974 s 84 (4) (d). As to powers to exclude other proceedings see the Employment Protection (Consolidation) Act 1978 s 137 (1), (3) (e); and as to restrictions on the institution of proceedings in certain cases see para 621 note 3 ante.

627. Concurrent jurisdiction in internal waters. As regards so much of the coast of England as is between high and low water mark, and as regards the estuaries of English rivers and bays inter fauces terrae[1], the common law and the Admiralty have concurrent jurisdiction[2].

1　Ie inclosed between promontories or projecting headlands.
2　*R v Keyn* (1876) 2 ExD 63 at 168, CCR. See also *R v Bruce* (1812) Russ & Ry 243; *R v Mannion* (1846) 2 Cox CC 158, CCR; *R v Cunningham* (1859) Bell CC 72; *The Fagernes* [1927] P 311, CA (Bristol Channel). As to the areas of water comprising national waters see para 623 note 2 ante.

628. Trial by the Crown Court. Exclusive jurisdiction in trials on indictment belongs to the Crown Court[1]. This jurisdiction includes jurisdiction in proceedings for offences wherever committed, including in particular proceedings on indictment for offences within the Admiralty jurisdiction[2].

1　Supreme Court Act 1981 s 46 (1).
2　Ibid s 46 (2).

629. Trial abroad of offences within Admiralty jurisdiction. Persons charged with committing offences within the Admiralty jurisdiction may be tried in British colonies, or in places abroad outside Her Majesty's dominions, where the Queen has jurisdiction[1].

All offences against property or persons committed either ashore or afloat out of Her Majesty's dominions by any master, seaman, or apprentice who, when the offence is committed, is, or within three months previously has been, employed in any British ship[2], are punishable and triable as if they were offences committed within the Admiralty jurisdiction[3].

Any court in Her Majesty's dominions with jurisdiction to try an offence committed on board a British ship within the limits of its ordinary jurisdiction may try a British subject charged with committing an offence on board any British ship on the high seas[4] or in any foreign port or harbour or on board any foreign ship to which he does not belong[5], or an alien charged with committing an offence on board a British ship on the high seas, if that person is found within the jurisdiction of the court[6].

1 See the Admiralty Offences (Colonial) Act 1849 s 1; the Foreign Jurisdiction Act 1890 ss 5, 6, Sch 1. For places where Her Majesty exercises jurisdiction by Order in Council see COMMONWEALTH vol 6 para 1175; and see further COMMONWEALTH vol 6 para 1173 et seq.
2 'Ship' for the purposes of the Merchant Shipping Act 1894 means every description of vessel used in navigation not propelled by oars: s 742. Sections 686 (see text to note 5 infra), 687, apply to all British ships of 24 metres or more in length whether registered or not: see s 72 (1), (2) (c) (substituted by the Merchant Shipping Act 1988 s 10, Sch 1 para 44). See also *R v Allen* (1866) 10 Cox CC 405; *R v Seberg* (1870) LR 1 CCR 264. A hovercraft may not, except as otherwise provided by or under the Hovercraft Act 1968 or an enactment passed before 26 July 1968 be treated as, inter alia, a ship for the purpose of any enactment or any instrument having effect by virtue of any enactment: Hovercraft Act 1968 ss 4 (3), 7 (2). See also the Hovercraft (Application of Enactments) Order 1972, SI 1972/971, art 5, Sch 2 Pt A.
3 Merchant Shipping Act 1894 s 687 (amended by the Criminal Law Act 1967 ss 10 (2), 11 (1), (2), Sch 3 Pt III) which applies also to offences under the Merchant Shipping Act 1906: ss 84 (1), 86 (1). See also *R v Dudley and Stephens* (1884) 14 QBD 273 at 281, CCR (which decided, under the corresponding provision of the Merchant Shipping Act 1854 (repealed), that the judge of assize sitting at Exeter had jurisdiction to try seamen formerly belonging to a British ship which had been wrecked who committed murder in an open boat on the high seas).
4 'High seas' in this context has the same meaning as when used in connection with the jurisdiction of the Court of Admiralty (see para 625 ante), and eg an English court has jurisdiction to try an offence committed by a British subject on board a British ship in a port of a Commonwealth country if the port forms part of the high seas in that sense: *R v Liverpool Justices, ex p Molyneux* [1972] 2 QB 384, [1972] 2 All ER 471, DC. 'Offence' means an offence against English law: *R v Kelly* [1981] AC 665, 73 Cr App Rep 310, HL. An Australian district court exercises Admiralty jurisdiction and may therefore try an offence committed on a British ship on the high seas: *Oteri v R* [1976] 1 WLR 1272, [1977] 1 Lloyd's Rep 105, PC.
5 Passengers do not 'belong' to a ship: *R v Kelly* [1981] AC 665, 73 Cr App Rep 310, HL; *R v Cumberworth* (1989) 89 Cr App Rep 187, CA.
6 Merchant Shipping Act 1894 s 686; and see *R v Lopez, R v Sattler* (1858) Dears & B 525, CCR; *R v Menham and Fox* (1858) 1 F & F 369. The Merchant Shipping Act 1894 s 686 applies, even though the accused is a foreigner and has been brought within the jurisdiction of the court against his will (*R v Lopez, R v Sattler* supra), unless the crime is committed merely for the purpose of obtaining his liberation (*R v Lopez, R v Sattler* supra at 547 per Lord Campbell CJ). The Merchant Shipping Act 1894 s 686 does not apply to a foreigner on a foreign ship committing a negligent act which causes a collision with a British ship and the death of a person aboard the British ship in consequence of such collision; such an act is not 'an offence committed on board a British ship': *R v Keyn* (1876) 2 ExD 63, CCR. Where a British subject commits an offence while aboard a foreign ship in her berth in a foreign harbour as a passenger, he does not belong to the foreign ship and may be tried by the Crown Court in respect of such offence: *R v Cumberworth* (1989) 89 Cr App Rep 187, CA.

630. Acts done on British ship in foreign territorial waters. If a person on a British ship[1] in the territorial waters of a foreign state, acting under the lawful

orders of the foreign state, commits an act in respect of subjects of the state which
would be criminal but for those orders (for example if he assaults and arrests such
subjects), such person may not be prosecuted in an English criminal court for that
act, so long as it is covered by the authority of the foreign state; but, if such an act is
continued outside the jurisdiction of the state (for example by bringing the subjects
of the foreign state in confinement to England), then that person may be punished
in respect of so much of the act as is done outside the territory of the foreign state[2].

1 For the meaning of 'British ship' see para 625 note 3 ante.
2 *R v Lesley* (1860) Bell CC 220, CCR. See also *Dobree v Napier* (1836) 2 Bing NC 781.

(iv) Extension of Jurisdiction under Statutory Provisions or by Exercise of the Prerogative

631. In general. At common law no one may be tried in England for a crime
committed on land abroad[1]. A statute, unless its provisions show a contrary
intention, applies only to the United Kingdom; and, if it makes certain acts
criminal, in the absence of provisions to the contrary, those acts are only criminal,
even in the case of British subjects[2], if done within the United Kingdom[3]. An alien[4]
may not be tried in England for acts committed outside Her Majesty's dominions
unless the statute creating the offence expressly so provides[5].

1 See para 623 ante. '... apart from those exceptional cases in which specific provision is made in
   regard to acts committed abroad, the whole body of the criminal law of England deals only with acts
   committed in England': *Cox v Army Council* [1963] AC 48 at 67, 46 Cr App Rep 258 at 262, HL per
   Viscount Simonds.
2 For the meaning of 'British subject' see para 620 note 1 ante.
3 See *R v Jameson* [1896] 2 QB 425 at 430 per Lord Russell CJ; cf *Niboyet v Niboyet* (1878) 4 PD 1 at 19,
   CA. See also *Air India v Wiggins* [1980] 2 All ER 593, 71 Cr App Rep 213, HL. As to construction,
   extent and limitation of statutes and those affecting international law see STATUTES vol 44 para 845 et
   seq.
4 For the meaning of 'alien' see para 620 note 2 ante.
5 See para 621 ante.

632. Extension by statute or by the prerogative. The operation of the criminal law has been extended by statutes designed to protect domestic interests or
giving effect to international conventions. Instances occur in legislation relating to
the regulation of fishing within, and in certain areas outside, fishery limits[1]; to the
control of liquor trafficking in the North Sea[2]; to the protection of submarine
cables against wilful, culpable or negligent damage[3]; to offences committed on,
under or above installations in designated areas over the continental shelf, or on
offshore installations either in territorial waters or in designated areas, or within
500 metres of such installations[4]; to the regulation and control of wireless stations
and apparatus in or over territorial waters[5]; to the suppression of illicit radio
stations broadcasting from, inter alia, any ship or aircraft while in or over the
United Kingdom or within territorial waters or from marine structures in territorial waters[6]; to the prevention of oil pollution by ships in territorial waters, by
British ships registered in the United Kingdom in any part of the sea, and as a result
of exploration and exploitation of the continental shelf[7].

An extension of the territory of England and Wales may be made by the exercise
of the prerogative power of the Crown[8]. The authority of Parliament is not

required for such extension; it may be effected by Order in Council[9] or by the appropriate minister or law officer informing the court of the Crown's claim to sovereignty or jurisdiction over any place[10].

1 See the Sea Fisheries Act 1968 s 14. As to regulation of sea fisheries see FISHERIES vol 18 para 740 et seq.
2 See the North Sea Fisheries Act 1893 and FISHERIES vol 18 para 798.
3 See the Submarine Telegraph Act 1885 (as amended) and TELECOMMUNICATIONS vol 45 para 420 et seq.
4 See the Oil and Gas (Enterprise) Act 1982 s 22 (as amended) and PETROLEUM PRODUCTION.
5 See the Wireless Telegraphy Act 1949 s 6 (as amended) and TELECOMMUNICATIONS vol 45 para 503. Offences under the Wireless Telegraphy Act 1949 are triable summarily (see s 14) whereas the Territorial Waters Jurisdiction Act 1878 (see para 626 ante) applies only to indictable offences.
6 See the Marine etc Broadcasting (Offences) Act 1967 ss 1, 2, 9 (1) and TELECOMMUNICATIONS vol 45 para 613 et seq. Offences under the Marine etc Broadcasting (Offences) Act 1967 are triable summarily (see s 6) whereas the Territorial Waters Jurisdiction Act 1878 (see para 626 ante) applies only to indictable offences.
7 See the Prevention of Oil Pollution Act 1971 ss 1–3 (as amended) and SHIPPING vol 43 para 1175 et seq.
8 See *R v Kent Justices, ex p Lye* [1967] 2 QB 153, [1967] 1 All ER 560, DC; *Post Office v Estuary Radio Ltd* [1968] 2 QB 740, [1967] 3 All ER 663 at 679, CA.
9 See eg the Territorial Waters Order in Council 1964 dated 25 September 1964 and the Territorial Waters (Amendment) Order in Council 1979 dated 23 May 1979.
10 See *The Fagernes* [1927] P 311, CA.

(v) Miscellaneous Matters connected with Offences Committed Abroad

633. Offences committed by special classes of persons. By statutory provisions certain persons may be subject to English criminal law or to some specified part of it in respect of acts done or omissions made abroad. Such persons include (1) members of Her Majesty's Forces[1] and civilians accompanying Her Majesty's Forces abroad[2]; (2) British subjects committing offences in foreign ports or harbours or on board foreign ships to which they do not belong[3]; (3) persons employed or recently employed on British ships who commit offences against persons or property in or at any place ashore or afloat out of Her Majesty's dominions[4]; (4) Crown servants serving abroad[5]; (5) United Kingdom observers and exchanged scientists appointed under the terms of the Antarctic Treaty and members of their staffs while in Antarctica[6].

1 See ROYAL FORCES vol 41 para 433.
2 See ROYAL FORCES vol 41 paras 370, 514 et seq.
3 See the Merchant Shipping Act 1894 s 686 and para 629 text to note 6 ante. Passengers do not 'belong' to a ship: *R v Kelly* [1981] AC 665, 73 Cr App Rep 310, HL; *R v Cumberworth* (1989) 89 Cr App Rep 187, CA.
4 See the Merchant Shipping Act 1894 s 687 (amended by the Criminal Law Act 1967 s 10 (2), Sch 3 Pt III). See also para 629 text to note 3 ante.
5 11 Will 3 c 12 (Crimes by Governors of Colonies) (1698–9); and see the Criminal Jurisdiction Act 1802 s 1; the Sale of Offices Act 1809 s 1; the Criminal Justice Act 1948 s 31 (amended by the Criminal Law Act 1967 s 10 (2), Sch 3 Pt III).
6 See the Antarctic Treaty Act 1967 s 5. Such persons are subject to the law of any part of the United Kingdom while in Antarctica: see s 5. The British Nationality Act 1948 s 3 (1) (limitation on criminal liability of certain persons who are not citizens of the United Kingdom and colonies: see BRITISH NATIONALITY AND ALIENAGE vol 4 para 904) does not have effect in relation to any offence under any provision of the Antarctic Treaty Act 1967: s 10 (8). As to offences under s 1 see ANIMALS vol 2 paras 346, 347. See also the Antarctic Minerals Act 1989 s 11 and MINES.

634. Jurisdiction in respect of crimes committed out of England. British subjects who commit offences abroad are in numerous instances by virtue of statutes subject to English criminal jurisdiction[1]. Exceptionally, aliens[2] may also be tried in England for crimes committed abroad.

Treason is committed by a person owing allegiance to the Crown who engages in, or supports, treasonable activities, whether within the realm or elsewhere[3]. A British subject who has become naturalised as a subject of a foreign country at war with Her Majesty remains liable for treasonable acts even if committed abroad[4]. An alien who has previously lived within Her Majesty's dominions and still owes allegiance to the Crown, for example by being in possession of a British passport, is liable for treason committed abroad[5]. An alien resident within Her Majesty's dominions is guilty of treason if he joins a force of Her Majesty's enemies in a place from which Her Majesty's Forces have temporarily retired and which is in the military occupation of the enemy[6].

Other offences committed abroad for which aliens as well as British subjects may be tried in England include piracy jure gentium[7], grave breaches of the Geneva Conventions of 1949[8], offences on British-controlled aircraft or hovercraft[9], hijacking[10], and other offences against aircraft[11]. Aliens residing or being in Her Majesty's dominions who commit certain slave trade offences[12] are subject to English criminal jurisdiction.

Murder or manslaughter committed by a British subject on land outside the United Kingdom whether within Her Majesty's dominions or not and whether the person killed is or is not a British subject is triable in England[13].

Other crimes committed abroad for which British subjects may be tried in England include offences relating to explosive substances[14], offences against the Merchant Shipping Acts 1894 to 1988[15], official secrets offences[16], electoral offences[17], bigamy[18], false trade descriptions[19], procuration[20], certain aspects of homosexual conduct[21], assisting in or inducing drugs offences punishable abroad[22], slave trade offences[23], foreign enlistment offences[24], killing seals in the Behring sea[25], certain offences concerning illegal immigration[26], and customs and excise offences[27].

A person of any nationality who, in the United Kingdom or elsewhere, takes hostages is guilty of an offence and may be tried in England[28].

1 As to the limitation of criminal liability of certain classes of British subjects see the British Nationality Act 1948 s 3 (1); the Ireland Act 1949 ss 1 (1), (3), 3 and BRITISH NATIONALITY AND ALIENAGE vol 4 para 904. For the meaning of 'British subject' see para 620 note 1 ante.
2 For the meaning of 'alien' see para 620 note 2 ante.
3 See the Treason Act 1351 (as amended) and para 76 et seq ante.
4 R v Lynch [1903] 1 KB 444. Naturalisation in such circumstances is itself an act of treason: R v Lynch supra at 495 per Wills J.
5 Joyce v DPP [1946] AC 347, 31 Cr App Rep 57, HL.
6 De Jager v A-G of Natal [1907] AC 326, PC. See also R v Commanding Officer, 30th Battalion Middlesex Regiment, ex p Freyberger [1917] 2 KB 129, CA (declaration of alienage in time of war for the purpose of evading military service).
    However, an enemy alien who comes into the realm in a hostile way cannot be tried for treason: see R v Warbeck (1500) cited in 7 Co Rep 6b.
7 See para 621 text and note 11 ante.
8 See the Geneva Conventions Act 1957 s 1 (1) and FOREIGN RELATIONS vol 18 para 1864 et seq.
9 See the Civil Aviation Act 1982 s 92: the Hovercraft (Application of Enactments) Order 1972, SI 1972/971, art 5, Sch 2 and AVIATION.
10 See the Aviation Security Act 1982 s 1 and AVIATION.
11 See ibid ss 1, 2 and AVIATION. Certain offences against the person and against property committed abroad by United Kingdom citizens or aliens may be tried in England under the Suppression of

Terrorism Act 1978 s 4 (as amended): see para 140 ante. Attacks abroad on certain protected persons by United Kingdom citizens or aliens are also triable in England under the Internationally Protected Persons Act 1978: see para 141 ante.

12 See the Slave Trade Act 1824 s 9 and para 347 ante.

13 See the Offences against the Person Act 1861 s 9 (amended by the Criminal Law Act 1967 s 10 (2), Sch 3 Pt III); see also the Offences against the Person Act 1861 s 10 (amended by the Criminal Law Act 1967 s 10 (1), (2), Sch 2 para 6, Sch 3 Pt III) (conduct causing death in one country, death resulting in another: see para 428 ante) and the Offences against the Person Act 1861 s 4 (amended by the Criminal Law Act 1977 ss 5 (10) (a), (b), 65 (5), Sch 13) (incitement or solicitation to murder: see para 433 ante). The Offences against the Person Act 1861 s 9 (as so amended) is expressed not to prevent proceedings for murder and manslaughter being taken abroad: see s 9 proviso. On general principles see *R v Page* [1954] 1 QB 170, 37 Cr App Rep 189, C-MAC; *R v Azzopardi* (1843) 2 Mood CC 288, CCA.

14 See the Explosive Substances Act 1883 s 3 (substituted by the Criminal Jurisdiction Act 1975 s 7 (1), (3)) and para 479 ante.

15 See eg the Merchant Shipping Act 1894 ss 684, 687 (amended by the Criminal Law Act 1967 ss 10 (2), 11 (1), (2), Sch 3 Pt III) and SHIPPING vol 43 para 173.

16 See the Official Secrets Act 1911 s 10 (1) and para 262 ante; the Official Secrets Act 1989 s 15 (1) and para 245 note 6 ante.

17 See the Representation of the People Act 1983 s 178 (1) (substituted by the Representation of the People Act 1985 s 24, Sch 4 para 62) and ELECTIONS vol 15 (Reissue) para 880.

18 See the Offences against the Person Act 1861 s 57 (amended by the Criminal Justice Act 1925 s 49, Sch 3; the Criminal Law Act 1967 s 10 (2), Sch 3 Pt III) and para 350 ante; *R v Earl Russell* [1901] AC 446, HL; *R v Audley* [1907] 1 KB 383, CCR.

19 See the Trade Descriptions Act 1968 s 21 and TRADE MARKS vol 48 para 312.

20 See the Sexual Offences Act 1956 ss 2, 3, 9, 22, 23, 29 and paras 524, 386, 387 respectively ante.

21 See the Sexual Offences Act 1967 s 2 and para 507 ante.

22 See the Misuse of Drugs Act 1971 s 20 and para 405 ante.

23 See the Slave Trade Act 1873 s 26 (amended by the Criminal Law Act 1967 s 10 (2), Sch 3 Pt III) and the Criminal Justice Act 1925 s 11 (3) (amended by the Forgery and Counterfeiting Act 1981 s 30, Schedule Pt I).

24 See the Foreign Enlistment Act 1870 ss 16, 17 and FOREIGN RELATIONS vol 18 para 1906.

25 See the Behring Sea Award Act 1894 s 1 (amended by the Criminal Justice Act 1982 ss 38, 46) and FISHERIES vol 18 para 939.

26 See the Immigration Act 1971 s 25 (as amended) and BRITISH NATIONALITY AND ALIENAGE vol 4 para 1028.

27 See the Customs and Excise Management Act 1979 ss 88–91 (amended by the Territorial Sea Act 1987 s 3 (1), Sch 1 para 4 (b), (c)) and CUSTOMS AND EXCISE.

28 See the Taking of Hostages Act 1982 s 1 and para 139 ante. See also the Genocide Act 1969 s 1 and para 424 ante.

635. Doctrine of autrefois convict or autrefois acquit in respect of offences committed abroad. A person who has been tried and convicted or acquitted by a court of competent jurisdiction in a foreign country may not be tried again in England in respect of the same offence[1].

1 *R v Hutchinson* (1677) 3 Keb 785; *R v Roche* (1775) 1 Leach 134; *R v Aughet* (1918) 118 LT 658, 13 Cr App Rep 101, CCA. As to pleas of autrefois convict and autrefois acquit see para 970 et seq post.

A plea of autrefois convict based on a foreign conviction is not available to the accused unless he has been in real jeopardy because there was a real risk or danger of punishment following the foreign conviction. The mere fact of a foreign conviction is not by itself enough to found a plea of autrefois convict; and, where the accused has been convicted abroad in his absence and has taken no part in the foreign proceedings, he may not as a general rule plead autrefois convict if he has not been in reach of the court that tried him: *R v Thomas* [1985] QB 604, 79 Cr App Rep 200, CA.

Where a member of a 'visiting force' (see para 40 ante) has been tried by a competent service court, he is not liable to be tried for the same crime by a United Kingdom court: Visiting Forces Act 1952 s 4 (1). A member of Her Majesty's Forces is not liable to be tried by court-martial or to summary trial in respect of an offence for which he has been tried by a competent civil court, wherever situated, or where he has had such offence taken into consideration when being sentenced by such court: see the Army Act 1955 s 134 (1) (amended by the Armed Forces Act 1966 s 26); the Air Force Act 1955 s 134 (1) (amended by the Armed Forces Act 1966 s 76); the Naval Discipline Act 1957 s 129 (2) (amended by the Armed Forces Act 1966 s 35). See ROYAL FORCES vol 41 para 58. Members of Her Majesty's Forces are likewise protected against trial for an offence in the civil courts of the United Kingdom after being tried by court-martial for that offence: see the Army Act 1955 s 13 (1) (substituted by the Armed Forces Act 1966 s 25 (1)); the Air Force Act 1955 s 133 (1) (substituted by the Armed Forces Act 1966 s 25); the Naval Discipline Act 1957 s 129 (1) (amended by the Armed Forces Act 1966 s 35; the Armed Forces Act 1971 s 55). See ROYAL FORCES vol 41 para 60.

6. LAW OFFICERS; CROWN PROSECUTION SERVICE; SERIOUS FRAUD OFFICE

(1) LAW OFFICERS

(i) In general

636. The Attorney General and the Solicitor General. The Queen may not appear in Her own courts to support Her interests[1] in person, but is represented by Her attorney[2], who bears the title of Her Majesty's Attorney General[3].

The Attorney General is primarily an officer of the Crown and is in that sense an officer of the public[4]. Although he performs to some extent judicial functions[5] both at common law and by statute, he does not constitute a court in the ordinary sense, so that prohibition will not lie against him[6]. It is the duty of the Attorney General to institute prosecutions for offences which have a tendency to disturb the peace of the State or to endanger the government[7].

In the Attorney General's absence or incapacity, his duties devolve upon the Solicitor General[8]. Any functions authorised or required by any enactment[9] to be discharged by the Attorney General may be discharged by the Solicitor General if (1) the office of Attorney General is vacant; or (2) the Attorney General is unable to act owing to absence or illness; or (3) the Attorney General authorises the Solicitor General to act in any particular case[10]. The Solicitor General also represents the Crown where distinct interests require it to be separately represented[11].

The offices of Attorney General and Solicitor General are conferred by patent and are held during pleasure. Neither the Attorney General nor the Solicitor General may engage in private practice[12].

1 In *R v Gregory* (1672) 2 Lev 82, a declaration quod dominus rex venit coram domino rege was allowed after some demur, but characterised by Hale CJ as 'well enough, but unmannerly'.
2 *R v Austen* (1821) 9 Prince 142n: 'the King sues by his attorney' or 'the Attorney sues for the King' are only different forms of expressing the same thing. It is the Sovereign who, by his attorney, gives the court to understand and be informed of the matter which is being brought to its notice: *Wilkes v R* (1770) Wilm 322 at 327, HL. See also *A-G to Prince of Wales v St Aubyn* (1811) Wight 167; and *A-G v Ellis* (1959) Times, 21 January (injunction to restrain publication of information relating to the royal family, in breach of undertaking).
3 Cf note 8 infra. As to the Attorney General see CONSTITUTIONAL LAW vol 8 para 1274 et seq; and as to the precedence of the Attorney General see BARRISTERS vol 3 (1) (Reissue) para 434.
4 *A-G v Brown* (1818) 1 Swan 265 at 294; *R v Wilkes* (1770) 4 Burr 2527 at 2570; on appeal 4 Burr 2576, HL. He may also represent the public: see eg AVIATION vol 2 para 1293.
5 *R v Comptroller-General of Patents, ex p Tomlinson* [1899] 1 QB 909, CA.
6 *Re Van Gelder's Patent* (1888) 6 RPC 22 at 27, CA.

7 See *Ex p Crawshay v Langley* (1860) 8 Cox CC 356.
8 The Solicitor General has always been the general deputy of the Attorney General and subordinate to him: *Wilkes v R* (1770) Wilm 322 at 329, 330, HL; 6 Holdsworth's History of English Law (7th Edn) 462, 463, 469, 470. He has never had any special connection with the Court of Chancery: 6 Holdsworth's History of English Law (7th Edn) 469, 470.
9 The enactments to which the Law Officers Act 1944 s 1 (1) applies are (1) any enactment passed before 31 July 1944 which makes no provision for enabling the Solicitor General to discharge the functions of the Attorney General thereunder, or which makes provision enabling him to discharge them only in certain circumstances defined by the enactment; and (2) any enactment passed after 13 July 1944 which does not expressly provide that s 1 is not to apply thereto: s 1 (1) (i), (ii).

   During any period when the office of the Attorney General is vacant, any certificate, petition, direction, notice, proceeding or other document, matter or thing whatsoever authorised or required, by any enactment passed before 13 July 1944 and any enactment passed after that date which does not expressly provide that s 1 (2) is not to apply thereto, to be given, delivered, served, taken or done to, on or against the Attorney General, may be given, delivered, served, taken or done to, on or against the Solicitor General: s 1 (2).
10 Ibid s 1 (1) (a)–(c). As to the effect of a change of Attorney General during proceedings see *Hamilton v A-G* (1880) 7 LR Ir 223, (1881) 9 LR Ir 271, CA.
11 *A-G v Galway Corpn* (1828) 1 Mol 95 at 101n; *A-G v Dean and Canons of Windsor* (1860) 8 HL Cas 369. See also *Ellis v Duke of Bedford* [1899] 1 Ch 494 at 504, 518, CA; *A-G v Duke of Richmond (No 2)* [1907] 2 KB 940.
12 See BARRISTERS vol 3 (1) (Reissue) para 441.

637. The Director of Public Prosecutions. The Director of Public Prosecutions is head of the Crown Prosecution Service[1]. He must be appointed by, and discharge his functions under the superintendence of, the Attorney General[2]; and he must be a barrister or solicitor of not less than ten years' standing[3].

1 As to the Crown Prosecution Service see para 645 et seq post; and as to the exercise of the functions of the Director of Public Prosecutions by Crown Prosecutors see para 647 post.
2 Prosecution of Offences Act 1985 ss 2 (1), 3 (1). As to the Attorney General see para 636 ante; and as to the duty of the Director of Public Prosecutions to make an annual report to the Attorney General on the discharge of his functions see para 641 post.
3 Ibid s 2 (2). There is to be paid to the Director of Public Prosecutions such remuneration as the Attorney General may, with the approval of the Treasury, determine: s 2 (3).

638. The Director of the Serious Fraud Office. The Attorney General[1] must appoint a person to be the Director of the Serious Fraud Office[2] and he must discharge his functions under the superintendence of the Attorney General[3].

1 As to the Attorney General see para 636 ante.
2 As to the Serious Fraud Office see para 652 et seq post.
3 Criminal Justice Act 1987 s 1 (2). There is to be paid to the Director of the Serious Fraud Office such remuneration as the Attorney General may, with the approval of the Treasury, determine: s 1 (15), Sch 1 para 1. As to the duty of the Director of the Serious Fraud Office to make an annual report on the discharge of his functions see para 642 post.

(ii) Consents to Prosecutions

639. Consents by the Attorney General and the Director of Public Prosecutions to prosecutions. Any person may institute any criminal proceedings[1] or conduct any criminal proceedings to which the Director of Public Prosecutions' duty to take over the conduct of proceedings does not apply[2]; but there are statutory provisions which specifically require that certain criminal proceedings may be undertaken only by order of a judge[3] or by, or by the direction of, or with the consent of, the Attorney General[4], the Director of Public Prosecutions[5] or some other official person or body[6].

Any enactment[7] which prohibits the institution or carrying on of proceedings for any offence except (1) with the consent, however expressed, of a law officer of the Crown or the Director of Public Prosecutions; or (2) where the proceedings are instituted or carried on by or on behalf of a law officer of the Crown or the Director of Public Prosecutions, and so applies whether or not there are exceptions to the prohibition, and whether or not the consent is an alternative to the consent of any other authority or person (a) does not prevent the arrest without warrant, or the issue or execution of a warrant for the arrest, of a person for any offence, or the remand in custody or on bail of a person charged with any offence; and (b) is subject to any enactment concerning the apprehension or detention of children or young persons[8].

Where any enactment, whenever passed (i) prevents any step from being taken without the consent of the Director of Public Prosecutions or without his consent or the consent of another; or (ii) requires any step to be taken by or in relation to the Director, any consent given by or, as the case may be, step taken by or in relation to, a Crown Prosecutor is to be treated, for the purposes of that enactment, as given by or, as the case may be, taken by or in relation to the Director of Public Prosecutions[9].

1 For these purposes, binding over proceedings are to be taken as criminal proceedings: Prosecution of Offences Act 1985 s 15 (4). 'Binding over proceedings' means any proceedings instituted, whether by way of complaint under the Magistrates' Courts Act 1980 s 115 (see MAGISTRATES) or otherwise, with a view to obtaining from a magistrates' court an order requiring a person to enter into a recognisance to keep the peace or to be of good behaviour: s 15 (1).
2 Ibid s 6 (1). Such a person does not, however, have a right of access to police statements, reports and photographs held by the Crown Prosecution Service: *R v DPP, ex p Hallas* (1988) 87 Cr App Rep 340, DC. Where criminal proceedings are so instituted, the Director of Public Prosecutions may nevertheless take over their conduct at any stage: Prosecution of Offences Act 1985 s 6 (2). In appropriate cases the Director of Public Prosecutions may take over proceedings in order to abort them by offering no evidence: see *Turner v DPP* (1978) 68 Cr App Rep 70; *Raymond v A-G* [1982] QB 839, 75 Cr App Rep 34, CA (both decided under the Prosecution of Offences Act 1979 s 4 (repealed)). As to the duty of the Director of Public Prosecutions to take over the conduct of proceedings see para 646 post; as to the Crown Prosecution Service see para 645 et seq post and as to discontinuance of proceedings in magistrates' courts see para 871 post.
3 See eg the Law of Libel Amendment Act 1888 s 8 and LIBEL vol 28 para 280.
4 See eg the Prevention of Terrorism (Temporary Provisions) Act 1989 s 19 and para 102 et seq ante.
5 See eg the Suicide Act 1961 s 2 (4) (amended by the Criminal Law Act 1967 s 10 (2), Sch 3 Pt II; the Criminal Jurisdiction Act 1975 s 14 (5), Sch 6 Pt I) and para 443 ante. As to the exercise of the functions of the Director of Public Prosecutions by Crown Prosecutors see para 647 post.
6 See eg the Customs and Excise Management Act 1979 s 145 (1) and CUSTOMS AND EXCISE.
7 For these purposes, 'enactment' includes any provision having effect under or by virtue of any Act, whenever passed: Prosecution of Offences Act 1985 s 25 (3).
8 Ibid s 25 (1), (2). As to powers of arrest see para 693 et seq post; and as to remand in custody or on bail see para 842 et seq post.
9 Ibid s 1 (7). As to proof of consents to prosecutions see para 1155 post.

640. Consents to prosecutions by the Director of the Serious Fraud Office. Where any enactment, whenever passed, prohibits the taking of any step (1) except by the Director of Public Prosecutions[1] or except by him or another; or (2) without the consent of the Director of Public Prosecutions or without his consent or the consent of another, it does not prohibit the taking of any such step by the Director of the Serious Fraud Office[2].

1 See para 639 ante.
2 Criminal Justice Act 1987 s 1 (15), Sch 1 para 4 (1). As to the Director of the Serious Fraud Office see para 638 ante.

(iii) Reports

641. Reports by the Director of Public Prosecutions to the Attorney General. As soon as practicable after 4 April in any year, the Director of Public Prosecutions[1] must make to the Attorney General[2] a report on the discharge of his functions during the year ending with that date[3]; and the Attorney General must lay before Parliament a copy of every report so received by him and must cause every such report to be published[4]. At the request of the Attorney General, the Director of Public Prosecutions must report to him on such matters as the Attorney General may specify[5].

1 As to the Director of Public Prosecutions see para 637 ante.
2 As to the Attorney General see para 636 ante.
3 Prosecution of Offences Act 1985 s 9 (1).
4 Ibid s 9 (2). As to the inclusion in such report of guidelines for Crown Prosecutors see para 649 post.
5 Ibid s 9 (3).

642. Reports by the Director of the Serious Fraud Office to the Attorney General. As soon as practicable after 4 April in any year, the Director of the Serious Fraud Office[1] must make to the Attorney General[2] a report on the discharge of his functions during the year ending with that date[3]; and the Attorney General must lay before Parliament a copy of every report so received by him and must cause every such report to be published[4].

1 As to the Director of the Serious Fraud Office see para 638 ante.
2 As to the Attorney General see para 636 ante.
3 Criminal Justice Act 1987 s 1 (15), Sch 1 para 3 (1).
4 Ibid Sch 1 para 3 (2).

643. Reports to the Director of Public Prosecutions by chief officers of police. The Attorney General[1] may make regulations[2] requiring the chief officer of any police force to which the regulations are expressed to apply to give to the Director of Public Prosecutions[3] information with respect to every offence of a kind prescribed by the regulations which is alleged to have been committed in his area and in respect of which it appears to him that there is a prima facie case for proceedings[4]. Such regulations may also require every such chief officer to give to the Director of Public Prosecutions such information as he may require with respect to such cases or classes of case as he may from time to time specify[5].

1 As to the Attorney General see para 636 ante.
2 Any such power to make regulations is exercisable by statutory instrument subject to annulment in pursuance of a resolution of either House of Parliament; and any such regulations may make different provisions with respect to different cases or classes of case: Prosecution of Offences Act 1985 s 29.
3 As to the Director of Public Prosecutions see para 637 ante.
4 Prosecution of Offences Act 1985 s 8 (1). The chief officer of police of every police area must give to the Director of Public Prosecutions information with respect to any of the following offences where it appears to him that there is a prima facie case for proceedings: (1) offences in which the prosecution

has by statute to be undertaken by, or requires the consent of, the Attorney General, the Solicitor General or the Director of Public Prosecutions (see para 639 ante); (2) offences where it appears to the chief officer of police that the advice or the assistance of the Director of Public Prosecutions is desirable; (3) offences punishable with death; (4) offences of homicide except offences of causing death by reckless driving; (5) offences of abortion; (6) offences of treason felony, misprision of treason, sedition, seditious libel or libel on holders of public offices; (7) offences under the Offences against the Person Act 1861 ss 21, 23, 28, 29, 32 or 33; (8) conspiracies, attempts or incitements to commit any of the offences in heads (1)–(7) supra; (9) offences which may be the subject of an application for extradition: Prosecution of Offences Regulations 1978, SI 1978/ 1357, art 6 (1) (amended by SI 1978/1846; SI 1985/243; and taking effect under the Prosecution of Offences Act 1985 s 8 by virtue of the Interpretation Act 1978 s 17 (2) (b)). As to the applications for extradition see the Extradition Act 1989 and EXTRADITION. The chief officer of every such police area must give to the Director of Public Prosecutions such information as he may require with respect to such other cases as the Director may from time to time specify as appearing to him to be of importance or difficulty or for any other reason requiring his intervention: Prosecution of Offences Regulations 1978 reg 6 (2) (taking effect under the Prosecution of Offences Act 1985 s 8 by virtue of the Interpretation Act 1978 s 17 (2) (b)). Where a chief officer of police is so required to give information to the Director of Public Prosecutions, he must provide a report of the circumstances together with such further information and material as the Director, having regard to arrangements available locally for the prosecution of criminal offences, may require of him: Prosecution of Offences Regulations 1978 reg 7 (amended by SI 1985/243; and taking effect under the Prosecution of Offences Act 1985 s 8 by virtue of the Interpretation Act 1978 s 17 (2) (b)).

5 Prosecution of Offences Act 1985 s 8 (2).

644. Reports to the Director of the Serious Fraud Office by chief officers of police. The Attorney General[1] may make regulations requiring the chief officer of any police force to which the regulations are expressed to apply to give to the Director of the Serious Fraud Office information with respect to every offence of a kind prescribed by the regulations which is alleged to have been committed in his area and in respect of which it appears to him that there is a prima facie case for proceedings[2]. Such regulations may also require every chief officer to give to the Director such information as the Director may require with respect to such cases or classes of case as he may from time to time specify[3].

1 As to the Attorney General see para 636 ante.
2 Criminal Justice Act 1987 s 1 (15), Sch 1 para 7 (1). Any power so to make regulations is exercisable by statutory instrument subject to annulment in pursuance of a resolution of either House of Parliament; and any such regulations may make different provisions with respect to different cases or classes of case: Sch 1 para 9. At the date at which this volume states the law no such regulations had been made.
3 Ibid Sch 1 para 7 (2).

(2) THE CROWN PROSECUTION SERVICE

645. The Crown Prosecution Service. There is a prosecuting service for England and Wales known as the Crown Prosecution Service ('the Service') consisting of:

(1) the Director of Public Prosecutions ('the Director')[1], who is head of the Service;

(2) the Chief Crown Prosecutors[2], each of whom is the member of the Service responsible to the Director for supervising the operation of the service in his area[3]; and

(3) the other staff appointed by the Director[4].

The Director must appoint such staff for the Service as, with the approval of the Treasury as to numbers, remuneration and other terms and conditions of service, he considers necessary for the discharge of his functions[5].

1 As to the Director of Public Prosecutions see para 637 ante.
2 As to Crown Prosecutors see para 647 post.
3 As to the division of England and Wales into areas see para 647 post.
4 Prosecution of Offences Act 1985 s 1 (1).
5 Ibid s 1 (2). As to the transfer of staff formerly employed in prosecution work for local or police authorities or for certain other authorities or bodies to the staff of the Director of Public Prosecutions see s 11 and the Crown Prosecution Service (Transfer of Staff) Regulations 1985, SI 1985/1846; as to the establishment of a staff commission see the Prosecution of Offences Act 1985 s 12; and as to premises formerly used in connection with the Director's new functions see s 13.

646. Duties of the Director of Public Prosecutions. It is the duty of the Director of Public Prosecutions:

(1) to take over the conduct of all criminal proceedings[1], other than specified proceedings[2], instituted[3] on behalf of a police force[4], whether by a member of that force or by any other person;

(2) to institute and have the conduct of criminal proceedings[5] in any case where it appears to him that (a) the importance or difficulty of the case makes it appropriate that proceedings should be instituted by him; or (b) it is otherwise appropriate for proceedings to be instituted by him;

(3) to take over the conduct of all binding over proceedings instituted on behalf of a police force, whether by a member of that force or by any other person;

(4) to take over the conduct of all proceedings begun by summons issued under the Obscene Publications Act 1959[6];

(5) to give, to such extent as he considers appropriate, advice to police forces on all matters relating to criminal offences;

(6) to appear for the prosecution, when directed by the court[7] to do so, on any appeal under the Administration of Justice Act 1960[8], the Criminal Appeal Act 1968[9] or the Magistrates' Courts Act 1980[10]; and

(7) to discharge such other functions as may from time to time be assigned to him by the Attorney General[11].

1 For these purposes, references to the conduct of any proceedings include references to the proceedings being discontinued and to the taking of any steps, including the bringing of appeals and making of representations in respect of applications for bail, which may be taken in relation to them: Prosecution of Offences Act 1985 s 15 (3).
2 'Specified proceedings' means proceedings which fall within any category for the time being specified by order made by the Attorney General for the purposes of ibid s 3: s 3 (3). The power so to make orders is exercisable by statutory instrument subject to annulment in pursuance of a resolution of either House of Parliament: s 3 (4). The following proceedings have been specified for these purposes: (1) fixed penalty offences within the meaning of the Transport Act 1982 s 27 (5) (repealed): see now the Road Traffic Offences Act 1988 s 51 (1)); (2) the offence under the Vehicles (Excise) Act 1971 s 8 (1); (3) the offences under the Road Traffic Act 1972 ss 18, 20, 21, 30 (1), (2), 33 (2), 33AA (3), 44 (1), 161 (4), (5), 162 (1), 164 (1), 168 (3) (repealed): see now the Road Traffic Act 1988 ss 29, 31, 24, 26, 17 (2), 18 (3), 47 (1), 165 (1)–(3), 168, 172 (3), (4) respectively); (4) all offences under the Road Traffic Regulation Act 1984 other than those under ss 35 (5), 43 (5), (12), 47 (3), 52 (1), 108 (3), 115 (1), (2), 116 (1), 129 (3), Sch 12 para 6 (3) (and now see also the Road Traffic Act 1988 ss 32, 36 (1), (2); the Road Traffic Offenders Act 1988 s 91); (5) the offences arising by contravention of the Royal and other Parks and Gardens Regulations 1977, SI 1977/217, regs 3 (9) (involving a pedal cycle), 4 (27), (28), (30): Prosecution of Offences Act 1985 (Specified Proceedings) Order 1985, SI 1985/2010, art 2 (1), Schedule.

Where a summons has been issued in respect of any such offence, proceedings for that offence cease to be specified when the summons is served on the accused unless the documents described in the Magistrates' Courts Act 1980 s 12 (1) (a), (b) (pleading guilty by post etc) are served upon the accused with the summons: Prosecution of Offences Act 1985 (Specified Proceedings) Order 1985 art 2 (2). Proceedings for an offence cease to be specified if at any time a magistrates' court begins to receive evidence in those proceedings; and for these purposes, nothing read out before the court under the Magistrates' Courts Act 1980 s 12 (4) (accused's submission with a view to mitigation) is to be regarded as evidence: Prosecution of Offences Act 1985 (Specified Proceedings) Order 1985 art 2 (3). See MAGISTRATES.

3 For these purposes, proceedings in relation to an offence are instituted (1) where a justice of the peace issues a summons under the Magistrates' Courts Act 1980 s 1 (see para 695 post), when the information for the offence is laid before him; (2) where a justice of the peace issues a warrant for the arrest of any person under s 1 (see para 695 post), when the information for the offence is laid before him; (3) where a person is charged with the offence after being taken into custody without a warrant, when he is informed of the particulars of the charge; (4) where a bill of indictment is preferred under the Administration of Justice (Miscellaneous Provisions) Act 1933 s 2 in a case falling within s 2 (2) (b) (see para 917 head (3) post), when the bill of indictment is preferred before the court; and, where the application of this provision would result in there being more than one time for the institution of the proceedings, they are to be taken to have been instituted at the earliest of those times: s 15 (2).

4 'Police force' means any police force maintained by a police authority under the Police Act 1964 and any other body of constables for the time being specified by order made by the Secretary of State for the purposes of the Prosecution of Offences Act 1985 s 3: s 3 (3). As to the making of orders see note 2 supra. The following bodies of constables have been specified for these purposes: the British Transport Police; the City of London Police; the Dover Harbour Police; the Falmouth Docks Police; the Felixstowe Dock and Railway Company Police; the Manchester Dock Police Force; the Mersey Tunnel law enforcement officers; the Metropolitan Police Force; the Milford Docks Police; the Ministry of Defence Police; the Port of Bristol Police; the Port of Liverpool Police; the Port of London Authority Police; the Royal Parks Constabulary (England); the Tees and Hartlepool Port Authority Harbour Police; the United Kingdom Atomic Energy Authority Constabulary: Prosecution of Offences Act 1985 (Specified Police Forces) Order 1985, SI 1985/1956, art 2, Schedule.

5 For these purposes, binding over proceedings are to be taken to be criminal proceedings: Prosecution of Offences Act 1985 s 15 (4). For the meaning of 'binding over proceedings' see para 639 note 1 ante.

6 Ie the Obscene Publications Act 1959 s 3 (as amended) (forfeiture of obscene articles: see para 360 ante).

7 'The court' means (1) in the case of an appeal to or from the criminal division of the Court of Appeal, that division; (2) in the case of an appeal from a Divisional Court of the Queen's Bench Division, the Divisional Court; and (3) in the case of an appeal against an order of a magistrates' court, the Crown Court: Prosecution of Offences Act 1985 s 3 (3).

8 Ie the Administration of Justice Act 1960 s 1 (amended by the Criminal Appeal Act 1968 s 54, Sch 7) (appeal from the High Court in criminal cases: see para 1491 post).

9 Ie the Criminal Appeal Act 1968 Pts I, II (ss 1–44) (as amended) (appeals from the Crown Court to the criminal division of the Court of Appeal and thence to the House of Lords: see para 1352 et seq post).

10 Ie the Magistrates' Courts Act 1980 s 108 (right of appeal to the Crown Court: see para 1450 post) as it applies, by virtue of the Contempt of Court Act 1981 s 12 (5), to orders made under s 12 (contempt of magistrates' courts).

11 Prosecution of Offences Act 1985 s 3 (2) (amended by the Criminal Justice Act 1987 s 15, Sch 2 para 13). The Prosecution of Offences Act 1985 s 3 (2) (as so amended) is subject to any provisions contained in the Criminal Justice Act 1987: Prosecution of Offences Act 1985 s 3 (2) (as so amended). Where the Director of the Serious Fraud Office has the conduct of any criminal proceedings in England and Wales, he is not, in relation to those proceedings, subject to any duty by virtue of s 3 (2) (as so amended): Criminal Justice Act 1987 s 1 (15), Sch 1 para 5 (1).

As to the duty imposed by the Prosecution of Offences Act 1985 s 3 (a) (as so amended) see also *R v Ealing Magistrates' Court, ex p Dixon* [1989] 2 All ER 1050, [1989] 3 WLR 1098, DC.

647. Crown Prosecutors. The Director of Public Prosecutions may designate any member of the Crown Prosecution Service who is a barrister or solicitor, and any person so designated is known as a Crown Prosecutor[1]. The Director must divide England and Wales into areas[2] and, for each of those areas, designate a Crown Prosecutor and any person so designated is known as a Chief Crown Prosecutor[3].

Without prejudice to any functions which may have been assigned to him in his capacity as a member of the Service, every Crown Prosecutor has all the powers of the Director as to the institution and conduct of proceedings[4] but must exercise those powers under the direction of the Director[5].

Crown Prosecutors have, in any court, the rights of audience[6] enjoyed by solicitors holding practising certificates and have such additional rights of audience[7] in the Crown Court as may be given[8].

1 Prosecution of Offences Act 1985 s 1 (3).
2 The Director of Public Prosecutions may, from time to time, vary the division of England and Wales so made: ibid s 1 (5).
3 Ibid s 1 (4).
4 For the meaning of references to the conduct of proceedings see para 646 note 1 ante.
5 Prosecution of Offences Act 1985 s 1 (6).
6 The reference in ibid s 4 (1) to rights of audience enjoyed in any court by solicitors includes a reference to rights enjoyed in the Crown Court by virtue of any direction given by the Lord Chancellor under the Supreme Court Act 1981 s 83: Prosecution of Offences Act 1985 s 4 (2). See BARRISTERS vol 3 (1) (Reissue) para 401.
7 For the purpose of giving Crown Prosecutors additional rights of audience in the Crown Court, the Lord Chancellor may give any such direction as respects Crown Prosecutors as he could give under the Supreme Court Act 1981 s 83 in respect of solicitors: Prosecution of Offences Act 1985 s 4 (3).
8 Ibid s 4 (1).

648. Conduct of prosecutions on behalf of the Crown Prosecution Service. The Director of Public Prosecutions may at any time appoint a person who is not a Crown Prosecutor[1] but who is (1) a solicitor; or (2) a barrister who is a member of the staff of a public authority[2], to institute[3] or take over the conduct of such criminal proceedings[4] as the Director may assign to him[5]. Any person conducting proceedings so assigned to him has all the powers of a Crown Prosecutor but must exercise those powers subject to any instructions given to him by a Crown Prosecutor[6].

1 As to Crown Prosecutors see para 647 ante.
2 For these purposes, 'public authority' has the same meaning as in the Prosecution of Offences Act 1985 s 17 (see para 1528 note 5 post): s 15 (1).
3 As to when proceedings are instituted see para 646 note 3 ante.
4 For these purposes, binding over proceedings and proceedings begun by summons issued under the Obscene Publications Act 1959 s 3 (as amended) (see para 360 ante) are to be taken to be criminal proceedings: Prosecution of Offences Act 1985 s 15 (4), (5). For the meaning of 'binding over proceedings' see para 639 note 1 ante; and for the meaning of references to the conduct of proceedings see para 646 note 1 ante.
5 Ibid s 5 (1). As to prosecutions instituted and conducted otherwise than by the Crown Prosecution Service see para 639 ante.
6 Ibid s 5 (2).

649. Guidelines for Crown Prosecutors. The Director of Public Prosecutions must issue a Code for Crown Prosecutors giving guidance on general principles to be applied by them:
   (1) in determining, in any case (a) whether proceedings for an offence should be instituted or, where proceedings have been instituted, whether they should be discontinued; or (b) what charges should be preferred; and

(2) in considering, in any case, representation to be made by them to any magistrates' court about the mode of trial suitable for that case[1].

The Director may from time to time make alterations in the Code[2]. The provisions of the Code must be set out in the Director's report[3] for the year in which the Code is issued and any alteration in the Code must be set out in his report for the year in which the alteration is made[4].

1 Prosecution of Offences Act 1985 s 10 (1). As to the Code for Crown Prosecutors see 83 LS Gaz 2308 et seq.
2 Prosecution of Offences Act 1985 s 10 (2).
3 Ie under ibid s 9: see para 641 ante.
4 Ibid s 10 (3).

650. Control of certain fees and expenses etc paid by the Crown Prosecution Service. The Attorney General may, with the approval of the Treasury, by regulations make such provision as he considers appropriate in relation to:
(1) the fees of counsel briefed to appear on behalf of the Crown Prosecution Service in any criminal proceedings; and
(2) the costs and expenses of witnesses attending to give evidence at the instance of the Service[1].

Such regulations may, in particular, prescribe scales or rates of fees, costs or expenses, and specify conditions for the payment of fees, costs or expenses[2].

1 Prosecution of Offences Act 1985 s 14 (1). As to witnesses' costs and expenses see the Crown Prosecution Service (Witnesses Allowances) Regulations 1988, SI 1988/1862, and para 1551 et seq post.
2 Prosecution of Offences Act 1985 s 14 (2).

651. Delivery of recognisances etc to the Director of Public Prosecutions. Where the Director of Public Prosecutions or any Crown Prosecutor gives notice to any justice of the peace that he has instituted[1], or is conducting, any criminal proceedings[2], the justice must:
(1) at the prescribed[3] time and in the prescribed manner; or
(2) in a particular case, at the time and in the manner directed by the Attorney General,

send him every recognisance, information, certificate, deposition, document and thing connected with those proceedings which the justice is required by law to deliver to the appropriate officer of the Crown Court[4].

The Director or, as the case may be, Crown Prosecutor must cause anything which is so sent to him to be delivered to the appropriate officer of the Crown Court, and is under the same obligation, on the same payment, to deliver to an applicant copies of anything so sent as that officer[5].

It is the duty of every justices' clerk to send to the Director a copy of the information and of any depositions and other documents relating to any case in which:
(a) a prosecution for an offence before the magistrates' court to which he is clerk is withdrawn or is not proceeded with within a reasonable time;
(b) the Director does not have the conduct of the proceedings; and
(c) there is some ground for suspecting that there is no satisfactory reason for the withdrawal or failure to proceed[6].

1 As to when proceedings are instituted see para 646 note 3 ante.

2 For these purposes, binding over proceedings are to be taken to be criminal proceedings: Prosecution of Offences Act 1985 s 15 (4). For the meaning of 'binding over proceedings' see para 639 note 1 ante.
3 The Attorney General may make regulations for the purpose of supplementing the provisions of ibid s 7; and for these purposes 'prescribed' means prescribed by the regulations: s 7 (2).
4 Ibid s 7 (1). Every justice of the peace to whom a notice has been so given must within three days of receipt of the notice deliver or transmit by post or other means to the Director of Public Prosecutions all documents and things which are required to be so transmitted: Prosecution of Offences Regulations 1978, SI 1978/1357, reg 8 (taking effect under the Prosecution of Offences Act 1985 s 7 by virtue of the Interpretation Act 1978 s 17 (2) (b)).
5 Prosecution of Offences Act 1985 s 7 (3).
6 Ibid s 7 (4).

(3) THE SERIOUS FRAUD OFFICE

652. Functions of the Director of the Serious Fraud Office. A Serious Fraud Office must be constituted for England and Wales and Northern Ireland[1]. The Director of the Serious Fraud Office ('the Director')[2] must appoint such staff for the Serious Fraud Office as, with the approval of the Treasury as to numbers, remuneration and other terms and conditions of service, he considers necessary for the discharge of his functions[3]. He may investigate any suspected offence which appears to him on reasonable grounds to involve serious or complex fraud[4]; and he must discharge such other functions in relation to fraud as may from time to time be assigned to him by the Attorney General[5]. If he thinks fit, the Director may conduct any such investigation in conjunction either with the police or with any other person who is, in the opinion of the Director, a proper person to be concerned in it[6]. The Director may (1) institute and have the conduct of any criminal proceedings[7] which appear to him to relate to such fraud; and (2) take over the conduct of any such proceedings at any stage[8]. The Director may designate for these purposes any member of the Serious Fraud Office who is a barrister in England and Wales or Northern Ireland, a solicitor of the Supreme Court or a solicitor of the Supreme Court of Judicature of Northern Ireland[9]; and any member so designated has, without prejudice to any functions which may have been assigned to him in his capacity as a member of that Office, all the powers of the Director as to the institution and conduct of proceedings but must exercise those powers under the direction of the Director[10].

1 Criminal Justice Act 1987 s 1 (1).
2 As to the Director of the Serious Fraud Office see para 638 ante.
3 Criminal Justice Act 1987 s 1 (15), Sch 1 para 2.
4 Ibid s 1 (3). An investigation under s 1 may continue even after the person under investigation has been charged: *R v Director of Serious Fraud Office, ex p Saunders* [1988] Crim LR 837, DC.
5 Criminal Justice Act 1987 s 1 (6).
6 Ibid s 1 (4).
7 For these purposes, references to the conduct of any proceedings include references to the proceedings being discontinued and to the taking of any steps, including the bringing of appeals and making representations in respect of applications for bail, which may be taken in relation to them: ibid s 1 (16).
8 Ibid s 1 (5).
9 Ibid s 1 (7). Any member so designated who is a barrister in England and Wales or a solicitor of the Supreme Court has, in any court, the rights of audience enjoyed by solicitors holding practising certificates and has such additional rights of audience in the Crown Court in England and Wales as may be given by s 1 (11): s 1 (9). For the purpose of giving members so designated who are barristers in England and Wales or solicitors of the Supreme Court additional rights of audience in the Crown Court in England and Wales, the Lord Chancellor may give any direction as respects such members

as he could give under the Supreme Court Act 1981 s 83: Criminal Justice Act 1987 s 1 (11). The reference in s 1 (9) to rights of audience enjoyed in any court by solicitors includes a reference to rights enjoyed in the Crown Court by virtue of any direction given by the Lord Chancellor under the Supreme Court Act 1981 s 83: Criminal Justice Act 1987 s 1 (10). See further BARRISTERS vol 3 (1) (Reissue) para 401.

10 Ibid s 1 (8).

653. Investigative powers of the Director of the Serious Fraud Office. The Director of the Serious Fraud Office[1] may by notice in writing require:

(1) the person to be investigated ('the person under investigation') or any other person whom he has reason to believe has relevant information to answer questions or otherwise furnish information with respect to any matter relevant to the investigation at a specified place and either at a specified time or forthwith[2];

(2) require the person under investigation or any other person to produce at such place as may be specified in the notice and either forthwith, or at such time as may be so specified, any specified documents[3] which appear to the Director to relate to any matter relevant to the investigation or any documents of a specified description which appear to him so to relate; and (a) if such documents are produced the Director may (i) take copies or extracts from them; and (ii) require the person producing them to provide an explanation of any of them; (b) if any such documents are not produced, the Director may require the person who was required to produce them to state, to the best of his knowledge and belief, where they are[4].

The above powers of the Director are exercisable, but only for the purposes of an investigation into any suspected offence which appears to him on reasonable grounds to involve serious or complex fraud[5], or, on a request made by the Attorney General of the Isle of Man, Jersey or Guernsey[6], in any case in which it appears to him that there is good reason to do so for the purpose of investigating the affairs, or any aspect of the affairs, of any person[7].

A person is not required to disclose any information or produce any document which he would be required to refuse to disclose or produce on the grounds of legal professional privilege in proceedings in the High Court, except that a lawyer may be required to furnish the name and address of his client[8]; nor is a person required to disclose information or produce a document in respect of which he owes an obligation of confidence by virtue of carrying on any banking business unless (a) the person to whom the obligation of confidence is owed consents to the disclosure or production; or (b) the Director has authorised the making of the requirement or, if it is impracticable for him to act personally, a member of the Serious Fraud Office designated by him for these purposes has done so[9].

A statement made by a person in response to a requirement imposed under the above provisions may only be used in evidence against him on a prosecution for an offence of making a false or misleading statement[10] or on a prosecution for some other offence where in giving evidence he makes a statement inconsistent with it[11].

1 As to the Director of the Serious Fraud Office see para 638 ante.

2 Criminal Justice Act 1987 s 2 (2) (amended by the Criminal Justice Act 1988 s 170 (1), Sch 15 paras 112, 113 (1)). As to enforcement procedures see para 654 post.

3 For these purposes, 'documents' includes information recorded in any form and, in relation to information recorded otherwise than in legible form, references to its production include references to producing a copy of the information in legible form: Criminal Justice Act 1987 s 2 (18). As to concealment etc of documents see para 588 ante.

4 Ibid s 2 (3) (amended by the Criminal Justice Act 1988 Sch 15 paras 112, 113 (2)). The power to require production of documents remains exercisable even after the person under investigation has been charged: *R v Director of Serious Fraud Office, ex p Saunders* [1988] Crim LR 837, DC (obiter).
5 Ie under the Criminal Justice Act 1987 s 1: see para 652 ante.
6 Ie under legislation corresponding to ibid s 1 and having effect in the Island whose Attorney General makes the request.
7 Ibid s 2 (1) (amended by the Criminal Justice Act 1988 s 143).
8 Criminal Justice Act 1987 s 2 (9).
9 Ibid s 2 (10).
10 Ie under ibid s 2 (14): see para 587 ante.
11 Ibid s 2 (8).

654. Enforcement procedures. Where, on information on oath laid by a member of the Serious Fraud Office, a justice of the peace is satisfied, in relation to any documents[1], that there are reasonable grounds for believing:

(1) that (a) a person has failed to comply with an obligation[2] to produce them; (b) it is not practicable to serve a notice[3] in relation to them; or (c) the service of such a notice in relation to them might seriously prejudice the investigation; and

(2) that they are on premises specified in the information,

he may issue a warrant authorising any constable to enter, using such force as is reasonably necessary for the purpose, and search the premises, and to take possession of any documents appearing to be documents of the description specified in the information or to take in relation to any documents so appearing any other steps which may appear to be necessary for preserving them and preventing interference with them[4]. Unless it is not practicable in the circumstances, a constable executing such a warrant must be accompanied by an appropriate person[5].

Without prejudice to the power of the Director to assign his functions to members of the Serious Fraud Office[6], the Director may authorise any competent investigator, other than a constable, who is not a member of that Office to exercise on his behalf all or any of his investigative powers; but no such authority may be granted except for the purpose of investigating the affairs, or any aspect of the affairs, of a person specified in the authority[7]. However, no person is bound to comply with any requirement imposed by a person exercising powers by virtue of any authority so granted unless he has, if required to do so, produced evidence of his authority[8].

1 For the meaning of 'documents' see para 653 note 3 ante.
2 Ie an obligation under the Criminal Justice Act 1987 s 2 (amended by the Criminal Justice Act 1988 s 170, Sch 15 paras 112, 113): see para 653 ante.
3 Ie under the Criminal Justice Act 1987 s 2 (3) (as amended: see note 2 supra): see para 653 ante.
4 Ibid s 2 (4), (5).
5 Ibid s 2 (6). For these purposes, 'appropriate person' means a member of the Serious Fraud Office or some person who is not a member of that Office but whom the Director of the Serious Fraud Office has authorised to accompany the constable: s 2 (7).
6 See para 652 ante.
7 Criminal Justice Act 1987 s 2 (11).
8 Ibid s 2 (12).

655. Disclosure of information. Where any information subject to an obligation of secrecy under the Taxes Management Act 1970 has been disclosed by the Commissioners of Inland Revenue or an officer of the commissioners to any member of the Serious Fraud Office for the purposes of any prosecution of an offence relating to inland revenue, that information may be disclosed by any member of the Serious Fraud Office:

(1) for the purposes of any prosecution of which that Office has the conduct;

(2) to any member of the Crown Prosecution Service[1] for the purposes of any prosecution for an offence relating to inland revenue; and

(3) to the Director of Public Prosecutions for Northern Ireland for the purposes of any prosecution of an offence relating to inland revenue[2].

Where the Serious Fraud Office has the conduct of any prosecution of an offence which does not relate to inland revenue, the court may not prevent the prosecution from relying on any evidence under the Police and Criminal Evidence Act 1984[3] by reason only of the fact that the information concerned was disclosed by the commissioners or an officer of the commissioners for the purposes of any prosecution of an offence relating to inland revenue[4]. Where any information is subject to an obligation of secrecy imposed by or under any enactment other than an enactment contained in the Taxes Management Act 1970, the obligation does not have effect to prohibit the disclosure of that information to any person in his capacity as a member of the Serious Fraud Office; but any information so disclosed may only be disclosed by a member of the Serious Fraud Office for the purposes of any prosecution in England and Wales, Northern Ireland or elsewhere and may only be disclosed by such a member if he is designated by the Director for such purposes[5].

Without prejudice to his power to enter into agreements apart from this provision, the Director may enter into a written agreement for the supply of information to or by him subject, in either case, to an obligation not to disclose the information concerned otherwise than for a specified purpose[6].

Subject to the above provisions and to any provision of an agreement for the supply of information which restricts the disclosure of the information supplied, information obtained by any person in his capacity as a member of the Serious Fraud Office may be disclosed by any member of that Office designated by the Director for these purposes:

(a) to any government department or Northern Ireland department or other authority or body discharging its functions on behalf of the Crown, including the Crown in right of Her Majesty's government in Northern Ireland;

(b) to any competent authority[7];

(c) for the purposes of any prosecution in England and Wales, Northern Ireland or elsewhere; and

(d) for the purposes of assisting any public or other authority for the time being designated for these purposes by an order[8] made by the Secretary of State to discharge any functions which are specified in the order[9].

1 As to the Crown Prosecution Service see para 645 et seq ante.
2 Criminal Justice Act 1987 s 3 (1).
3 Ie under the Police and Criminal Evidence Act 1984 s 78: see para 1060 post.
4 Criminal Justice Act 1987 s 3 (2).
5 Ibid s 3 (3).
6 Ibid s 3 (4).
7 The following are competent authorities for these purposes: (1) an inspector appointed under the Companies Act 1985 Pt XIV (ss 431—453: see COMPANIES vol 7 (2) (Reissue) para 1213 et seq) or the Companies (Northern Ireland) Order 1986, SI 1986/1032, Pt XV (arts 424–446); (2) an official receiver; (3) the Accountant in Bankruptcy; (4) an Official Assignee; (5) a person appointed to carry out an investigation under the Building Societies Act 1986 s 55; (6) a body administering a compensation scheme under the Financial Services Act 1986 s 54; (7) an inspector appointed under s 94; (8) a person exercising powers by virtue of s 106; (9) an inspector appointed under s 177 or any corre-

sponding enactment having effect in Northern Ireland; (10) a person appointed under the Banking Act 1987 s 41; (11) a person exercising powers by virtue of the Insurance Companies Act 1982 s 44 (2); (12) any body having supervisory, regulatory or disciplinary functions in relation to any profession or any area of commercial activity; and (13) any person or body having, under the law of any country or territory outside the United Kingdom, functions corresponding to any of the functions of any person mentioned in any of heads (1)–(12) supra: Criminal Justice Act 1987 s 3 (6) (amended by the Criminal Justice Act 1988 s 170 (1), Sch 15 para 111).
8 Such an order may impose conditions subject to which, and otherwise restrict the circumstances in which, information may be so disclosed: Criminal Justice Act 1987 s 3 (7).
9 Ibid s 3 (5).

656. Delivery of recognisances to the Director of the Serious Fraud Office. Where the Director of the Serious Fraud Office or any designated member[1] of that Office gives notice to any justice of the peace that he has instituted, or is conducting, any criminal proceedings in England and Wales, the justice must (1) at the prescribed time and in the prescribed manner; or (2) in a particular case, at the time and in the manner directed by the Attorney General, send him every recognisance, information, certificate, deposition, document and thing connected with those proceedings which the justice is required by law to deliver to the appropriate officer of the Crown Court[2].

1 Ie any member designated for the purposes of the Criminal Justice Act 1987 s 1 (5): see para 652 ante.
2 Ibid s 1 (15), Sch 1 para 6 (1) (amended by the Criminal Justice Act 1988 s 170 (1), Sch 15 paras 112, 116). The Attorney General may make regulations for the purpose of supplementing the Criminal Justice Act 1987 Sch 1 para 6 (1) (as so amended); and in Sch 1 para 6 (1) (as so amended) 'prescribed' means prescribed by the regulations: Sch 1 para 6 (3). As to the power to make regulations see para 644 note 2 ante. At the date at which this volume states the law no such regulations had been made.
   The Director of the Serious Fraud Office or, as the case may be, the member so designated (1) must, subject to the regulations, cause anything which is sent to him to be delivered to the appropriate officer of the Crown Court: and (2) is under the same obligation, on the same payment, to deliver to an applicant copies of anything so sent as that officer: Sch 1 para 6 (4).

7. ENFORCEMENT PROCEDURES

(1) INTRODUCTION

657. Introduction. The statutory powers to stop and search[1], of entry, search and seizure[2], arrest[3], detention[4], questioning and treatment by the police[5] are contained in the Police and Criminal Evidence Act 1984 and the codes of practice made thereunder[6]. The Secretary of State must issue codes of practice in connection with:
   (1) the exercise by police officers of statutory powers to search a person without first arresting him, or to search a vehicle without making an arrest[7];
   (2) the detention, treatment, questioning[8] and identification[9] of persons by police officers;
   (3) searches of premises by police officers[10]; and
   (4) the seizure of property[10] found by police officers on persons or premises[11].
It is also the duty of the Secretary of State:
   (a) to issue a code of practice in connection with the tape-recording of interviews[12] of persons suspected of the commission of criminal offences which are held by police officers at police stations; and

(b) to make an order[13] requiring the tape-recording of interviews of persons suspected of the commission of criminal offences, or of such description of criminal offences as may be specified in the order, which are so held, in accordance with the code as it has effect for the time being[14].

Where the Secretary of State proposes so to issue a code of practice, he must prepare and publish a draft of that code, must consider any representations made to him about the draft and may modify the draft accordingly[15].

The Secretary of State must lay before both Houses of Parliament a draft of any code of practice so prepared[16]; and, when he has so laid the draft of a code before Parliament, he may bring the code into operation by order made by statutory instrument[17]. The Secretary of State may from time to time revise the whole or any part of a code of practice and issue that revised code[18]. Persons other than police officers who are charged with the duty of investigating offences or charging offenders must in the discharge of that duty have regard to any relevant provision of such a code[19].

1 See the Police and Criminal Evidence Act 1984 Pt I (ss 1–7) and para 661 et seq post.
2 See ibid Pt II (ss 8–23) and para 669 et seq post.
3 See ibid Pt III (ss 24–33) and para 703 et seq post.
4 See ibid Pt IV (ss 34–52) and para 715 et seq post.
5 See ibid Pt V (ss 53–65) and paras 726 et seq, 765, 766, 776 et seq post.
6 The codes of practice so made (see infra) have superseded the Judges' Rules. The codes are Crown copyright and are reproduced by kind permission of the Controller of Her Majesty's Stationery Office. As to the Judges' Rules see CRIMINAL LAW (4th Edn) vol 11 para 419 et seq.
7 See the Code of Practice for the Exercise by Police Officers of Statutory Powers of Stop and Search and para 661 et seq post.
8 See the Code of Practice for the Detention, Treatment and Questioning of Persons by Police Officers and para 715 et seq post.
9 See the Code of Practice for the Identification of Persons by Police Officers and para 767 et seq post.
10 See the Code of Practice for the Searching of Premises by Police Officers and the Seizure of Property found by Police Officers on Persons or Premises and para 685 et seq post.
11 Police and Criminal Evidence Act 1984 s 66.
12 See the Code of Practice on Tape-recording and para 746 et seq post.
13 An order under the Police and Criminal Evidence Act 1984 s 60 (1) must be made by statutory instrument and is subject to annulment in pursuance of a resolution of either House of Parliament: s 60 (2). At the date at which this volume states the law s 60 (1) (b) (see head (b) infra) and s 60 (2) are not in force.
14 Ibid s 60 (1). In pursuance of s 60 (1) (a) and in exercise of the power in s 67 (4) (see infra), the Secretary of State made the Police and Criminal Evidence Act 1984 (Codes of Practice) Order 1988, SI 1988/1200.
15 Police and Criminal Evidence Act 1984 s 67 (1). Section 67 applies to a code of practice under s 60 or s 66: s 67 (2).
16 Ibid s 67 (3).
17 Ibid s 67 (4). No order under s 67 (4) has effect until approved by a resolution of each House of Parliament: s 67 (5). An order bringing a code of practice into operation may contain such transitional provisions or savings as appear to the Secretary of State to be necessary or expedient in connection with the code of practice thereby brought into operation: s 67 (6). In exercise of the power conferred by s 67 (4), the Secretary of State made the Police and Criminal Evidence Act 1984 (Codes of Practice) (No 1) Order 1985, SI 1985/1937, bringing into force the Codes of Practice cited in notes 7–10 supra on 1 January 1986: art 2.
18 Police and Criminal Evidence Act 1984 s 67 (7).
19 Ibid s 67 (9). A police officer is liable to disciplinary proceedings for a failure to comply with any provision of such a code, unless proceedings are precluded by s 104 (restriction on subsequent proceedings: see POLICE): s 67 (8). A failure on the part: (1) of a police officer to comply with any provision of such a code; or (2) of any person other than a police officer who is charged with the duty of investigating offences or charging offenders to have regard to any relevant provision of such a code in the discharge of that duty, does not of itself render him liable to any criminal or civil proceedings: s 67 (10). For these purposes, 'criminal proceedings' includes (a) proceedings in the

United Kingdom or elsewhere before a court-martial constituted under the Army Act 1955, the Air Force Act 1955 or the Naval Discipline Act 1957 or a disciplinary court constituted under s 50; (b) proceedings before the Courts-Martial Appeal Court; and (c) proceedings before a Standing Civilian Court: Police and Criminal Evidence Act 1984 s 67 (12). As to the admissibility in evidence of any such code see paras 1132–1134 post.

The Code of Practice for the Exercise by Police Officers of Statutory Powers of Stop and Search applies to any search by a police officer which commenced after midnight on 31 December 1985, notwithstanding that the person or vehicle in question may have been detained by him in that behalf before that time: Police and Criminal Evidence Act 1984 (Codes of Practice) (No 1) Order 1985 art 3 (1).

The Code of Practice for the Searching of Premises by Police Officers and the Seizure of Property found by Police Officers on Persons or Premises applies to any application for a warrant to search premises made after 31 December 1985 and to any search of premises or seizure of property taking place after midnight on 31 December 1985, notwithstanding that the search or seizure in question may have taken place in pursuance of a warrant granted or applied for before that time: Police and Criminal Evidence Act 1984 (Codes of Practice) (No 1) Order 1985 art 3 (2).

The Code of Practice for the Detention, Treatment and Questioning of Persons by Police Officers applies (1) in so far as it relates to the exercise of powers conferred by the Police and Criminal Evidence Act 1984 Pt IV (ss 34–52: see para 715 et seq post), to persons who were in police detention where the period of police detention commences after 31 December 1985; and (2) as to its other provisions, to persons in police detention after midnight on 31 December 1985, notwithstanding that their period of detention may have commenced before that time: Police and Criminal Evidence Act 1984 (Codes of Practice) (No 1) Order 1985 art 3 (3).

The Code of Practice for the Identification of Persons by Police Officers applies to any procedures to which the Code relates which are carried out after 31 December 1985: art 3 (4).

658. Power of constable to use reasonable force. Where any provision of the Police and Criminal Evidence Act 1984[1] confers a power on a constable, and does not provide that the power may only be exercised with the consent of some person, other than a police officer, the officer may use reasonable force[2], if necessary, in the exercise of the power[3].

1 See para 661 et seq post.
2 As to the use of 'reasonable force' see also para 455 ante and para 706 post.
3 Police and Criminal Evidence Act 1984 s 117. As to the use of reasonable force in the exercise of any powers conferred by the Prevention of Terrorism (Temporary Provisions) Act 1989 see para 120 ante.

659. Delegation of authority by police officers. For the purpose of any provision of the Police and Criminal Evidence Act 1984 or any other Act under which a power in respect of the investigation of offences[1] or the treatment of persons in police custody[2] is exercisable only by or with the authority of (1) a police officer of at least the rank of superintendent; or (2) an officer of at least the rank of inspector, an officer of the rank of chief inspector is to be treated as holding the rank of superintendent for the purpose of head (1) above, and an officer of at least the rank of sergeant is to be treated as holding the rank of inspector for the purpose of head (2) above, if he has been authorised by an officer of at least the rank of chief superintendent to exercise the power or, as the case may be, to give his authority for its exercise[3].

1 See para 661 et seq post.
2 See para 715 et seq post.
3 Police and Criminal Evidence Act 1984 s 107. The holder of an acting rank is to be treated as if he were the holder of the substantive rank, unless his appointment to the acting rank is a colourable pretence: *R v Alladice* (1988) 87 Cr App Rep 380, CA.

(2) POWERS TO STOP AND SEARCH

660. Code of Practice. A constable's powers to stop and search persons, vehicles etc are governed by the Police and Criminal Evidence Act 1984[1] and by the Code of Practice for the Exercise by Police Officers of Statutory Powers of Stop and Search[2]. The Code must be readily available at all police stations for consultation by police officers, detained persons and members of the public[3].

Nothing in the Code affects the ability of an officer to speak to or question a person in the course of his duties without detaining him or exercising any element of compulsion[4].

1 Ie the Police and Criminal Evidence Act 1984 Pt I (ss 1–7): see para 661 et seq post. As to powers of search under the Prevention of Terrorism (Temporary Provisions) Act 1989 s 16 (1), Sch 5 see para 123 ante.

2 The Code of Practice for the Exercise by Police Officers of Statutory Powers of Stop and Search applies to any search by a police officer which commenced after 31 December 1985 and governs the exercise by police officers of statutory powers to search a person without first arresting him or to search a vehicle without making an arrest: para 1.3. As to the main stop and search powers in existence at the time when the Code was prepared see para 1.3, Annex A. That list should not, however, be regarded as definitive: para 1.3. The Code does not apply to the powers of stop and search in the Aviation Security Act 1982 s 27 (2) (see AVIATION) and the Police and Criminal Evidence Act 1984 s 6 (1) (constables employed by statutory undertakers: see para 667 post): Code of Practice for the Exercise by Police Officers of Statutory Powers of Stop and Search para 1.4.

   The notes for guidance included in the Code are not provisions of the Code, but are guidance to police officers and others about its application and interpretation: para 1.2. Provisions in the Annexes to the Code are, however, provisions of the Code: para 1.2.

   It is important to ensure that powers of stop and search are used responsibly and sparingly and only where reasonable grounds for suspicion genuinely exist: para 1, note 1A. Over use of the powers is as likely to be harmful to police effort in the long term as misuse; both can lead to mistrust of the police among sections of the community: para 1, note 1A. It is also particularly important to ensure that any person searched is treated courteously and considerately if police action is not to be resented: para 1, note 1A.

   As to codes of practice generally see para 657 ante.

3 Ibid para 1.1.

4 Ibid para 1.6.

661. Powers of constable to stop and search persons, vehicles etc. A constable may exercise any of the following powers to stop and search:

(1) in any place to which at the time when he proposes to exercise the power the public or any section of the public has access, on payment or otherwise, as of right or by virtue of express or implied permission; or

(2) in any other place to which people have ready access at the time when he proposes to exercise the power but which is not a dwelling[1].

A constable may search any person or vehicle[2] and anything which is in or on a vehicle for stolen or prohibited articles[3], and may detain a person or vehicle for the purpose of such a search[4]. The above provisions do not, however, give a constable power to search a person or vehicle or anything in or on a vehicle unless he has reasonable grounds for suspecting[5] that he will find stolen or prohibited articles[6].

If a person is in a garden or yard occupied with and used for the purposes of a dwelling or on other land so occupied and used, a constable may not search him in the exercise of the above power unless the constable has reasonable grounds for believing that he does not reside in the dwelling, and that he is not in the place in question with the express or implied permission of a person who resides in the dwelling[7].

If a vehicle is in a garden or yard occupied with and used for the purposes of a dwelling or on other land so occupied and used, a constable may not search the vehicle or anything in or on it in the exercise of the above power unless he has reasonable grounds for believing that the person in charge of the vehicle does not reside in the dwelling and that the vehicle is not in the place in question with the express or implied permission of a person who resides in the dwelling[8].

1 Police and Criminal Evidence Act 1984 s 1 (1).
2 Ibid s 1 applies to vessels, aircraft and hovercraft as it applies to vehicles: s 2 (10). For these purposes, 'vessel' means any ship, boat, raft or other apparatus constructed or adapted for floating on water: s 118 (1).
3 An article is prohibited for these purposes if it is (1) an offensive weapon; or (2) an article made or adapted for use in the course of, or in connection with, a specified offence or intended by the person having it with him for such use by him or by some other person: ibid s 1 (7). 'Prohibited article' includes any article in relation to which a person has committed, or is committing or is going to commit an offence under the Criminal Justice Act 1988 s 139 (having an article with a blade or point in a public place: see para 168 ante): Police and Criminal Evidence Act 1984 s 1 (8A) (added by the Criminal Justice Act 1988 s 140 (1) (c)). The offences so specified are (a) burglary; (b) theft; (c) offences under the Theft Act 1968 s 12 (taking motor vehicle or other conveyance without authority: see para 556 ante); and (d) offences under s 15 (obtaining property by deception: see para 567 ante): Police and Criminal Evidence Act 1984 s 1 (8). For these purposes, 'offensive weapon' means any article (i) made or adapted for use for causing injury to persons; or (ii) intended by the person having it with him for such use by him or by some other person: s 1 (9).
4 Ibid s 1 (2) (amended by the Criminal Justice Act 1988 s 140 (1) (a)). As to a constable's power to seize a stolen or prohibited article see para 664 post.
5 For the meaning of 'reasonable grounds for suspicion' see para 662 post.
6 Police and Criminal Evidence Act 1984 s 1 (3) (amended by the Criminal Justice Act 1988 s 140 (1) (a)).
7 Police and Criminal Evidence Act 1984 s 1 (4).
8 Ibid s 1 (5).

662. Reasonable grounds for suspicion. The exercise of the power to stop and search requires reasonable grounds for suspicion that articles of a particular kind are being carried[1]. Reasonable suspicion does not require certainty that an unlawful article is being carried; nor does the officer concerned have to be satisfied of this beyond reasonable doubt[2]. Reasonable suspicion in contrast to mere suspicion must be founded on fact[2]. There must be some concrete basis for the officer's suspicion, related to the individual person concerned, which can be considered and evaluated by an objective third person[2]. Mere suspicion, in contrast, is a hunch or instinct which cannot be explained or justified to an objective observer[2]. An officer who has such a hunch or instinct may well be justified in continuing to keep the person under observation or speak to him, but additional grounds which bring up mere suspicion to the level of reasonable suspicion are needed before he may exercise his powers to stop and search[2].

Reasonable suspicion may arise from the nature of the property observed or being carried or suspected of being carried coupled with other factors including the time, the place or the suspicious behaviour of the person concerned or those with him[3]. The decision to search must be based on all the facts which, to a careful officer, bear on the likelihood that an article of a certain kind will be found, and not only on what can be seen at the time[3]. Thus an officer with prior knowledge of the behaviour of someone he sees in a certain situation, or acting on information received, such as a description of a suspected offender, may have reasonable grounds for searching him although another officer would not[3].

Reasonable suspicion cannot be supported on the basis simply of a higher than average chance that the person has committed or is committing an offence, for example because he belongs to a group within which offenders of a certain kind are relatively common, or because of a combination of factors such as these[4]. For example, a person's colour of itself can never be a reasonable ground for suspicion[4]. The mere fact alone that a person is carrying a particular kind of property or is dressed in a certain way or has a certain hairstyle is likewise not of itself sufficient[4]. Nor is the fact that a person is known to have a previous conviction for unlawful possession of an article[4]. The degree or level of suspicion required to establish the reasonable grounds justifying the exercise of powers of stop and search is no less than the degree or level of suspicion required to effect an arrest without warrant for any of the suspected offences to which these powers relate[5]. The powers of stop and search provide an opportunity to establish the commission or otherwise of certain kinds of offences without arrest and may therefore render arrest unnecessary[5].

1　Code of Practice for the Exercise by Police Officers of Statutory Powers of Stop and Search para 1.5. As to the statutory power of stop and search see para 661 ante.
2　Ibid para 1.5, Annex B para 1.
3　Ibid Annex B para 2.
4　Ibid Annex B para 3.
5　Ibid Annex B para 4. Annex B para 4 is subject to the principle that, where a police officer has reasonable grounds to suspect that a person is in innocent possession of a stolen or prohibited article, the power of stop and search exists notwithstanding that there would be no power of arrest: Annex B para 5. However, every effort should be made to secure the voluntary production of the article before the power is resorted to: Annex B para 5.

663. Preliminary procedure. Where an officer has the reasonable grounds for suspicion[1] necessary to exercise a power of stop and search[2], he may detain the person concerned for the purposes of, and with a view to, searching him[3]. There is no power to stop or detain a person against his will in order to find grounds for a search[3].

Before carrying out a search the officer may question the person about his behaviour or his presence in circumstances which gave rise to the suspicion[4], since he may have a satisfactory explanation which will make a search unnecessary[5]. If, as a result of any questioning preparatory to a search, or other circumstances which come to the attention of the officer, there cease to be reasonable grounds for suspecting that an article is being carried of a kind for which there is a power of stop and search, no search may take place[5].

The reasonable grounds for suspicion which are necessary for the exercise of the initial power to detain may be confirmed or eliminated as a result of the questioning of a person detained for the purposes of a search, or such questioning may reveal reasonable grounds to suspect the possession of a different kind of unlawful article from that originally suspected; but the reasonable grounds for suspicion without which any search or detention for the purposes of a search is unlawful cannot be retrospectively provided by such questioning during his detention or by his refusal to answer any question put to him[6].

If a constable contemplates a search[7], other than a search of an unattended vehicle[8], it is his duty to take reasonable steps before he commences his search to bring to the attention of the appropriate person[9]:

(1) if the constable is not in uniform, documentary evidence[10] that he is a constable; and

(2) whether he is in uniform or not, (a) his name and the name of the police station to which he is attached; (b) the object of the proposed search; (c) his grounds for proposing to make it; and (d) the effect of certain statutory rights[11], as may be appropriate;

and the constable may not commence the search until he has performed that duty[12].

Unless it appears to the officer that it will not be practicable to make a record of the search, he must also inform the person to be searched, or the owner or person in charge of a vehicle that is to be searched, as the case may be, that he is entitled to a copy of the record of the search if he asks for it within a year[13]. If the person wishes to have a copy and is not given one on the spot, he should be advised to which police station he should apply[14].

If the person to be searched, or in charge of a vehicle to be searched, does not understand what is being said, the officer must take reasonable steps to bring the above information[15] to his attention[16]. If the person has someone with him, then the officer must establish whether that person can interpret[16].

1 For the meaning of 'reasonable grounds for suspicion' see para 662 ante.
2 As to the statutory power of stop and search see para 661 ante.
3 Code of Practice for the Exercise by Police Officers of Statutory Powers of Stop and Search para 2.1.
4 In some circumstances preparatory questioning may be unnecessary; but in general a brief conversation or exchange will be desirable as a means of avoiding unsuccessful searches: ibid para 2, note 2A. Where a person is lawfully detained for the purpose of a search, but no search in the event takes place, the detention will not thereby have been rendered unlawful: para 2, note 2A.
5 Ibid para 2.2. A constable who detains a person or vehicle in the exercise of the power conferred by the Police and Criminal Evidence Act 1984 s 1 (amended by the Criminal Justice Act 1988 s 140 (1)) (see para 661 ante) or of any other power (1) to search a person without first arresting him; or (2) to search a vehicle without making an arrest, need not conduct a search if it appears to him subsequently that no search is needed or that a search is impracticable: Police and Criminal Evidence Act 1984 s 2 (1).
6 Code of Practice for the Exercise by Police Officers of Statutory Powers of Stop and Search para 2.3.
7 Ie in the exercise of the power conferred by the Police and Criminal Evidence Act 1984 s 1 (as amended: see note 5 supra) (see para 661 ante) or of any other power, except the power conferred by s 6 (see para 667 post) and the power conferred by the Aviation Security Act 1982 s 27 (2) (see AVIATION).
8 The Police and Criminal Evidence Act 1984 s 2 applies to vessels, aircraft and hovercraft as it applies to vehicles: s 2 (10). For the meaning of 'vessel' see para 661 note 2 ante.
9 For these purposes, 'the appropriate person' means (1) if the constable proposes to search a person, that person; and (2) if he proposes to search a vehicle, or anything in or on a vehicle, the person in charge of the vehicle: ibid s 2 (5).
10 If the officer is not in uniform, he must show his warrant card: Code of Practice for the Exercise by Police Officers of Statutory Powers of Stop and Search para 2.5.
11 Ie the effect of the Police and Criminal Evidence Act 1984 s 3 (7) or s 3 (8) (see para 665 post). A constable need not bring the effect of s 3 (7) or s 3 (8) to the attention of the appropriate person if it appears to the constable that it will not be practicable to make the record in s 3 (1) (see para 665 post): s 2 (4).
12 Ibid s 2 (2), (3); Code of Practice for the Exercise by Police Officers of Statutory Powers of Stop and Search para 2.4.
13 Ibid para 2.5.
14 Ibid para 2.6.
15 Ie the information contained in ibid paras 2.4–2.6: see supra.
16 Ibid para 2.7.

664. Conduct of the search. Every reasonable effort must be made to reduce to the minimum the embarrassment that a person being searched may experience[1].

Although force may only be used as a last resort, reasonable force may be used if necessary to conduct a search or to detain a person or vehicle for the purposes of a search[2]. A compulsory search may be made only if it has been established that the person is unwilling[3] to co-operate[4].

The length of time for which a person or vehicle may be detained will depend on the circumstances[5], but must in all circumstances be reasonable and not extend beyond the time taken for the search[6]. The thoroughness and extent of a search must depend on what is suspected of being carried, and by whom[6]. If the suspicion relates to a particular article, for example an offensive weapon, which is seen to be slipped into a person's pocket, then, in the absence of other grounds for suspicion or an opportunity for the article to be moved elsewhere, the search must be confined to that pocket[6]. In the case of a small article which can readily be concealed, such as a drug, and which might be concealed anywhere on the person, a more extensive search may be necessary[6].

The search must be conducted at the place where the person or vehicle was first detained or nearby[7].

Searches in public must be restricted to superficial examination of outer clothing[8]. There is no power to require a person to remove any clothing in public[9] other than an outer coat, jacket or gloves[10]. Where on reasonable grounds it is considered necessary to conduct a more thorough search, for example by requiring someone to take off a T-shirt or headgear, this should be done out of public view, for example in a police van or a nearby police station if there is one[11]. Any search involving the removal of more than an outer coat, jacket, gloves, headgear or footwear may only be made by an officer of the same sex as the person searched and may not be made in the presence of anyone of the opposite sex[11].

If in the course of such a search a constable discovers an article which he has reasonable grounds for suspecting to be a stolen or prohibited article[12], he may seize it[13].

1 Code of Practice for the Exercise by Police Officers of Statutory Powers of Stop and Search para 3.1.
2 Ibid para 3.2; and see para 658 ante.
3 Eg by opening a bag.
4 Code of Practice for the Exercise by Police Officers of Statutory Powers of Stop and Search para 3.2.
5 As a search of a person in public should be a superficial examination of outer clothing, such searches should normally be capable of completion within one minute or so: ibid para 3.3, note 3B.
6 Ibid para 3.3. The time for which a person or vehicle may be detained for the purposes of a search is such time as is reasonably required to permit a search to be carried out either at the place where the person or vehicle was first detained or nearby: Police and Criminal Evidence Act 1984 s 2 (8). See infra.
7 Code of Practice for the Exercise by Police Officers of Statutory Powers of Stop and Search para 3.4.
8 Ibid para 3.5.
9 A search in the street itself should be regarded as being in public for the purposes of ibid para 3.5, even though it may be empty at the time a search begins: para 3.5, note 3A. Although there is no power to require a person to do so, there is nothing to prevent an officer from asking a person voluntarily to remove more than an outer coat, jacket or gloves in public: para 3.5, note 3A.
10 Ibid para 3.5. Neither the power conferred by the Police and Criminal Evidence Act 1984 s 1 (amended by the Criminal Justice Act 1988 s 140(1)) (see para 661 ante) nor any other power to detain and search a person without first arresting him or to detain and search a vehicle without making an arrest is to be construed (1) as authorising a constable to require a person to remove any of his clothing in public other than an outer coat, jacket or gloves; or (2) as authorising a constable not in uniform to stop a vehicle: Police and Criminal Evidence Act 1984 s 2 (9).
11 Code of Practice for the Exercise by Police Officers of Statutory Powers of Stop and Search para 3.5.
12 For the meaning of 'prohibited article' see para 661 note 3 ante.
13 Police and Criminal Evidence Act 1988 s 1 (6) (amended by the Criminal Justice Act 1988 s 140 (1) (b)).

665. Action after search. Where a constable has carried out a search in exercise of any statutory power[1], he must make a record of it in writing unless it is not practicable to do so[2].

If a constable is so required to make a record of a search but it is not practicable to make the record on the spot[3], he must make it as soon as practicable after the completion of the search[4].

The record of a search of a person must include a note of his name, if the constable knows it; but a constable may not detain a person to find out his name[5]. If a constable does not know the name of a person whom he has searched, the record of the search must include a note otherwise describing that person[6]. The record of a search of a vehicle[7] must include a note describing the vehicle[8].

The record of a search of a person or a vehicle:

(1) must state:
    (a) the object of the search;
    (b) the grounds for making it;
    (c) the date and time when it was made;
    (d) the place where it was made;
    (e) whether anything, and if so what, was found;
    (f) whether any, and if so what, injury to a person or damage to property appears to the constable to have resulted from the search; and
(2) must identify the constable making it[9].

If a constable who conducted a search of a person made a record of it, the person who was searched is entitled to a copy of the record if he asks for one before the end of the period of 12 months beginning with the date on which the search was made[10]; and, if the owner of a vehicle which has been searched or the person who was in charge of the vehicle at the time when it was searched asks for a copy of the record of the search before the end of the period of 12 months beginning with the date on which the search was made and the constable who conducted the search made a record of it, the person who made the request is entitled to a copy[11].

On completing a search of an unattended vehicle or anything in or on such a vehicle, a constable must leave a notice:

    (i) stating that he has searched it;
    (ii) giving the name of the police station to which he is attached;
    (iii) stating that an application for compensation for any damage caused by the search may be made to that police station;
    (iv) stating the effect of certain statutory rights[12]; and
    (v) stating where a copy of the record of the search may be obtained[13].

The constable must leave the notice inside the vehicle unless it is not reasonably practicable to do so without damaging the vehicle[14]. The vehicle must, if practicable, be left secure[15].

1 Ie under the Police and Criminal Evidence Act 1984 s 2 (1): see para 663 ante. Section 3 (1) does not, however, apply in the case of a search under s 6 (see para 667 post) or under the Aviation Security Act 1982 s 27 (2) (see AVIATION): Police and Criminal Evidence Act 1984 s 3 (1).

2 Ibid s 3 (1); Code of Practice for the Exercise by Police Officers of Statutory Powers of Stop and Search para 4.1. In some cases it may not be possible for an officer who has carried out a search to make such a written record such as in situations involving public disorder occurring in seaside areas during bank holiday weekends or the search of football supporters entering or leaving a ground: para 4.1. Nothing in these provisions, however, affects the routine searching of persons entering sports grounds or other premises with their consent, or as a condition of entry: para 4, note 4A.

Every annual report under the Police Act 1964 s 12 (see POLICE vol 36 para 230) or made by the Commissioner of Police of the Metropolis, must contain information about searches recorded under the Police and Criminal Evidence Act 1984 s 3 which have been carried out in the area to which the report relates during the period to which it relates: s 5 (1) (a), (b) (i). Such information may not include information about specific searches but must include (1) the total number of searches in each month during the period to which the report relates for stolen articles, offensive weapons and other prohibited articles; (2) the total number of persons arrested in each such month in consequence of searches of each of such descriptions: s 5 (2) (amended by the Criminal Justice Act 1988 s 140 (2)). For the meaning of 'prohibited article' see para 661 note 3 ante.

3 Ie unless circumstances eg other immediate duties or very inclement weather make this impracticable: Code of Practice for the Exercise by Police Officers of Statutory Powers of Stop and Search para 4.2.

4 Police and Criminal Evidence Act 1984 s 3 (2). The record must be made on the form provided for this purpose: Code of Practice for the Exercise by Police Officers of Statutory Powers of Stop and Search para 4.3.

5 Police and Criminal Evidence Act 1984 s 3 (3). In order to complete the search record the officer should normally seek the name, address and date of birth of the person searched; but under the search procedures there is no obligation on a person to provide these details and there is no power to detain him if he is unwilling to do so: Code of Practice for the Exercise by Police Officers of Statutory Powers of Stop and Search para 4.4. The following information can always, and must, be included in the record even if the person does not wish to identify himself or give his date of birth:

    (1) the name of the person searched or, if he withholds it, a description of him;

    (2) where the person searched is white, Afro-Caribbean or Asian, a note to that effect;

    (3) when a vehicle is searched, a description of it;

    (4) the object of the search;

    (5) the grounds for making it;

    (6) the date and time it was made;

    (7) the place where it was made;

    (8) its result;

    (9) a note of any injury or damage to property resulting from it;

    (10) the identity of the officer making it; but, where a search is made by more than one officer, the identity of all officers engaged in the search must be recorded on the search record:

para 4.5, note 4B. A record is required for each person and each vehicle searched; if eg a person is in a vehicle and both are searched, two records must be completed: para 4.6. The record of the grounds for making a search must, briefly but informatively, explain the reason for suspecting the person concerned, whether by reference to his behaviour or other circumstances: para 4.7.

6 Police and Criminal Evidence Act 1984 s 3 (4). See further note 5 supra.

7 The requirements imposed by ibid s 3 with regard to records of searches of vehicles apply also to records of searches of vessels, aircraft and hovercraft: s 3 (10). For the meaning of 'vessel' see para 661 note 2 ante.

8 Ibid s 3 (5).

9 Ibid s 3 (6).

10 Ibid s 3 (7), (9).

11 Ibid s 3 (8), (9).

12 Ie the effect of ibid s 3 (8): see supra and para 663 note 11 ante.

13 Ibid s 2 (6); Code of Practice for the Exercise by Police Officers of Statutory Powers of Stop and Search paras 4.8, 4.9.

14 Police and Criminal Evidence Act 1984 s 2 (7). The notice must be left on the vehicle if things in it or on it have been searched without opening it: Code of Practice for the Exercise by Police Officers of Statutory Powers of Stop and Search para 4.8.

15 Ibid para 4.10.

666. Road checks. The following provisions have effect in relation to the conduct of road checks[1] by police officers for the purpose of ascertaining whether a vehicle is carrying:

    (1) a person who has committed an offence other than a road traffic offence or a vehicles excise offence;

    (2) a person who is a witness to such an offence;

    (3) a person intending to commit such an offence; or

(4) a person who is unlawfully at large[2].

There may only be such a road check if a police officer of the rank of superintendent or above[3] authorises it in writing[4].

An officer may only so authorise a road check:

(a) for the purpose specified in head (1) above, if he has reasonable grounds (i) for believing that the offence is a serious arrestable offence[5]; and (ii) for suspecting that the person is, or is about to be, in the locality in which vehicles would be stopped if the road check were authorised;

(b) for the purpose specified in head (2) above, if he has reasonable grounds for believing that the offence is a serious arrestable offence;

(c) for the purpose specified in head (3) above, if he has reasonable grounds (i) for believing that the offence would be a serious arrestable offence; and (ii) for suspecting that the person is, or is about to be, in the locality in which vehicles would be stopped if the road check were authorised;

(d) for the purpose specified in head (4) above, if he has reasonable grounds for suspecting that the person is, or is about to be, in that locality[6].

An officer below the rank of superintendent may, however, authorise such a road check if it appears to him that it is required as a matter of urgency for one of the purposes specified in heads (1) to (4) above[7]. If an authorisation is so given, it is the duty of the officer who gives it to make a written record of the time at which he gives it, and to cause an officer of the rank of superintendent or above to be informed that it has been given[8]. An officer to whom a report is so made may, in writing, authorise the road check to continue[9]. If such an officer considers that the road check should not continue, he must record in writing the fact that it took place and the purpose for which it took place[10].

An officer giving an authorisation under the above provisions must specify the locality in which vehicles are to be stopped; and an officer of the rank of superintendent or above so giving an authorisation must specify a period, not exceeding seven days, during which the road check may continue and may direct that the road check shall be continuous or shall be conducted at specified times, during that period[11].

If it appears to an officer of the rank of superintendent or above that a road check ought to continue beyond the period for which it has been authorised, he may, from time to time, in writing specify a further period, not exceeding seven days, during which it may continue[12].

Where a vehicle is stopped in a road check, the person in charge of the vehicle at the time when it is stopped is entitled to obtain a written statement of the purpose of the road check if he applies for such a statement not later than the end of the period of 12 months from the day on which the vehicle was stopped[13].

1 For these purposes, a road check consists of the exercise in a locality of the power conferred by the Road Traffic Act 1988 s 163 in such a way as to stop during the period for which its exercise in that way in that locality continues all vehicles or vehicles selected by any criterion: Police and Criminal Evidence Act 1984 s 4 (2) (amended by the Road Traffic (Consequential Provisions) Act 1988 s 4, Sch 3 para 27 (1)).

2 Police and Criminal Evidence Act 1984 s 4 (1). Nothing in s 4 affects the exercise by police officers of any power to stop vehicles for purposes other than those specified in s 4 (1): s 4 (16).

Every annual report under the Police Act 1964 s 12 (see POLICE vol 36 para 230) or made by the Commissioner of Police of the Metropolis must contain information about road checks in that area during that period under the Police and Criminal Evidence Act 1984 s 4: s 5 (1) (a), (b) (ii). Such information must include information about the reason for authorising each road check and about the result of each of them: s 5 (3).

3 See para 659 ante.

4 Police and Criminal Evidence Act 1984 s 4 (3). Every written authorisation must specify (1) the name of the officer giving it; (2) the purpose of the road check; and (3) the locality in which vehicles are to be stopped: s 4 (13). The duties to specify the purposes of a road check imposed by s 4 (9) (see text to note 10 infra) and s 4 (13) include duties to specify any relevant serious arrestable offence: s 4 (14).

5 For the meaning of 'serious arrestable offence' see para 704 post.

6 Police and Criminal Evidence Act 1984 s 4 (4).

7 Ibid s 4 (5).

8 Ibid s 4 (6). The duties imposed by s 4 (6) must be performed as soon as it is practicable to do so: s 4 (7).

9 Ibid s 4 (8).

10 Ibid s 4 (9). See also note 4 supra.

11 Ibid s 4 (10), (11).

12 Ibid s 4 (12).

13 Ibid s 4 (15).

667. Statutory undertakers etc. A constable employed by statutory undertakers[1] may stop, detain and search any vehicle before it leaves a goods area[2] included in the premises of the statutory undertakers[3].

1 For these purposes, 'statutory undertakers' means persons authorised by any enactment to carry on any railway, light railway, road transport, water transport, canal, inland navigation, dock or harbour undertaking: Police and Criminal Evidence Act 1984 s 7 (3).

2 For these purposes, 'goods area' means any area used wholly or mainly for the storage or handling of goods: ibid s 6 (2).

3 Ibid s 6 (1). For the purposes of the Public Stores Act 1875 s 6 (see para 331 note 3 ante), any person appointed under the Special Constables Act 1923 to be a special constable within any premises which are in the possession or under the control of British Nuclear Fuels Limited is deemed to be a constable deputed by a public department and any goods and chattels belonging to or in the possession of British Nuclear Fuels Limited are deemed to be Her Majesty's Stores: Police and Criminal Evidence Act 1984 s 6 (3).

(3) POWERS OF ENTRY, SEARCH AND SEIZURE

(i) Code of Practice

668. Code of Practice. A constable's power to search premises and to seize property found by him on persons or premises is governed by the Police and Criminal Evidence Act 1984[1] and by the Code of Practice for the Searching of Premises by Police Officers and the Seizure of Property found by Police Officers on Persons or Premises[2]. The Code must be readily available at all police stations for consultation by police officers, detained persons and members of the public[3].

1 Ie the Police and Criminal Evidence Act 1984 Pt II (ss 8–23): see para 669 et seq post.

2 The Code of Practice for the Searching of Premises by Police Officers and the Seizure of Property found by Police Officers on Persons or Premises applies to the following searches of premises:
   (1) searches of premises undertaken for the purposes of an investigation into an alleged offence, with the occupier's consent, other than routine scenes of crime searches and searches following the activation of burglar or fire alarms or bomb threat calls;
   (2) searches under the powers conferred by the Police and Criminal Evidence Act 1984 s 17 (entry for purpose of arrest etc: see para 683 post), s 18 (entry and search after arrest: see para 684 post) and s 32 (search upon arrest: see para 714 post);
   (3) searches of premises undertaken in pursuance of a search warrant issued in accordance with s 15 (see para 671 post) or Sch 1 (see para 673 et seq post):
Code of Practice for the Searching of Premises by Police Officers and the Seizure of Property found by Police Officers on Persons or Premises para 1.3. As to codes of practice generally see para 657 ante.

The notes for guidance included in the Code are not provisions of the Code, but are guidance to police officers and others about its application and interpretation: para 1.2.
3 Ibid para 1.1.

(ii) Search with Consent

669. Search with consent. If it is proposed to search premises with the consent of a person entitled to grant entry to the premises, the consent must be given in writing[1]. Before seeking consent, the officer in charge must state the purpose of the proposed search and inform the person concerned that he is not obliged to consent and that anything seized may be produced in evidence[2]. If at the time the person is not suspected of an offence, the officer must tell him so when stating the purpose of the search[2]. It is unnecessary, however, to seek such consent where in the circumstances this would cause disproportionate inconvenience to the person concerned[3].

1 Code of Practice for the Searching of Premises by Police Officers and the Seizure of Property found by Police Officers on Persons or Premises para 4.1. Where it is intended to search premises under authority of a warrant or a power of entry and search without warrant, and co-operation of the occupier of the premises is obtained, there is no additional requirement to obtain written consent as at para 4.1: para 4.1, note 4B. In the case of a lodging house or similar accommodation, a search should not be made on the basis solely of the landlord's consent unless the tenant is unavailable and the matter is urgent: para 4, note 4A.
2 Ibid para 4.2.
3 Ibid para 4.3. Para 4.3 is intended in particular to apply eg to circumstances where police have arrested someone in the night after a pursuit and it is necessary to make a brief check of gardens along the route of the pursuit to see whether stolen or incriminating articles have been discarded: para 4.3, note 4C.

(iii) Search Warrants and Production Orders; Preliminary Procedure

670. Action before making application for search warrant or production order. Where information is received which appears to justify an application, the officer concerned must take reasonable steps to check that the information is accurate, recent and has not been provided maliciously or irresponsibly[1]. An application may not be made on the basis of information from an anonymous source where corroboration has not been sought[1]. The officer must ascertain as specifically as is possible in the circumstances the nature of the articles concerned and their location[2].

The officer must also make inquiries to establish what, if anything, is known about the likely occupier of the premises and the nature of the premises themselves; whether they have been previously searched and, if so, how recently; and to obtain any other information relevant to the application[3].

No application for a search warrant may be made without the authority of an officer of at least the rank of inspector or, in the case of urgency where no officer of this rank is readily available, the senior officer on duty[4]. No application for a production order or warrant[5] may be made without the authority of an officer of at least the rank of superintendent[6].

Except in case of urgency, if there is reason to believe that a search might have an adverse effect on relations between the police and the community, then the local police community liaison officer must be consulted before the search takes place[7].

1 Code of Practice for the Searching of Premises by Police Officers and the Seizure of Property found by Police Officers on Persons or Premises para 2.1.

2　Ibid para 2.2.
3　Ibid para 2.3.
4　Ibid para 2.4.
5　Ie under the Police and Criminal Evidence Act 1984 s 9, Sch 1: see para 673 et seq post.
6　Code of Practice for the Searching of Premises by Police Officers and the Seizure of Property found
　by Police Officers on Persons or Premises para 2.4.
7　Ibid para 2.5.

671. Application for search warrant. Where a constable applies for any search warrant[1], it is his duty:

(1)　to state (a) the ground on which he makes the application[2]; and (b) the enactment under which the warrant would be issued;

(2)　to specify the premises[3] which it is desired to enter and search; and

(3)　to identify, so far as is practicable, the articles or persons to be sought[4].

An application for such a warrant must be made ex parte and supported by an information in writing[5].

The constable must answer on oath any question that the justice of the peace or judge hearing the application asks him[6].

If an application is refused, no further application may be made for a warrant to search those premises unless supported by additional grounds[7].

1　The Police and Criminal Evidence Act 1984 ss 15, 16 (see infra and paras 679, 680 post) have effect in
　relation to the issue to constables under any enactment, including an enactment contained in an Act
　passed after the 1984 Act, of warrants to enter and search premises; and an entry on or search of
　premises under a warrant is unlawful unless it complies with ss 15, 16: s 15 (1). See also *R v Longman*
　[1988] 1 WLR 619, 88 Cr App Rep 148, CA.
2　The documents or information upon the strength of which a search warrant is obtained are protected
　by public interest immunity: *Taylor v Anderton* (1986) Times, 21 October. See para 1164 post and
　DISCOVERY vol 13 para 86 et seq.
3　For these purposes, 'premises' includes any place and, in particular, includes (1) any vehicle, vessel,
　aircraft or hovercraft; (2) any offshore installation; and (3) any tent or movable structure: Police and
　Criminal Evidence Act 1984 s 23. 'Offshore installation' means any installation which is or has been
　maintained, or is intended to be established, for the carrying on of any activity to which the Mineral
　Workings (Offshore Installations) Act 1971 applies: s 1 (substituted by the Oil and Gas (Enterprise)
　Act 1982 s 24) applied by the Police and Criminal Evidence Act 1984 s 23. As to offshore workings
　and installations see PETROLEUM PRODUCTION vol 35 para 1242 et seq.
4　Ibid s 15 (2).
5　Ibid s 15 (3). An application for a search warrant must be supported by an information in writing,
　stating (1) the enactment under which the application is made; (2) as specifically as is reasonably
　practicable the premises to be searched and the object of the search; and (3) the grounds on which the
　application is made, including, where the purpose of the proposed search is to find evidence of an
　alleged offence, an indication of how the evidence relates to the investigation: Code of Practice for
　the Searching of Premises by Police Officers and the Seizure of Property found by Police Officers on
　Persons or Premises para 2.6. An application for a search warrant under the Police and Criminal
　Evidence Act 1984 Sch 1 para 12 (a) (see para 678 post) must also, where appropriate, indicate why it
　is believed that service of notice of an application for a production order (see para 676 post) may
　seriously prejudice the investigation: Code of Practice for the Searching of Premises by Police
　Officers and the Seizure of Property found by Police Officers on Persons or Premises para 2.7.
　　　The identity of the informant need not be disclosed when making an application; but an officer
　concerned should be prepared to deal with any questions the magistrate or judge may have about
　the accuracy of previous information provided by that source or other related matters: para 2.6,
　note 2A.
6　Police and Criminal Evidence Act 1984 s 15 (4).
7　Code of Practice for the Searching of Premises by Police Officers and the Seizure of Property found
　by Police Officers on Persons or Premises para 2.8.

(iv) Issue of Search Warrants and Production Orders

A. STANDARD PROCEDURE

672. Power of justice of the peace to authorise entry and search. If, on an application[1] made by a constable, a justice of the peace is satisfied that there are reasonable grounds for believing:

(1) that a serious arrestable offence[2] has been committed; and
(2) that there is material on premises[3] specified in the application which is likely to be of substantial value, whether by itself or together with other material, to the investigation of the offence; and
(3) that the material is likely to be relevant evidence[4]; and
(4) that it does not consist of or include items subject to legal privilege[5], excluded material[6] or special procedure material[7]; and
(5) that any of the specified conditions[8] applies,

he may issue a warrant authorising a constable to enter and search the premises[9]. A constable may seize and retain anything for which a search has been so authorised[10].

The specified conditions are:

(a) that it is not practicable to communicate with any person entitled to grant entry to the premises;
(b) that it is practicable to communicate with a person entitled to grant entry to the premises but it is not practicable to communicate with any person entitled to grant access to the evidence;
(c) that entry to the premises will not be granted unless a warrant is produced;
(d) that the purpose of a search may be frustrated or seriously prejudiced unless a constable arriving at the premises can secure immediate entry to them[11].

1 See para 671 ante.
2 For the meaning of 'serious arrestable offence' see para 704 post.
3 For the meaning of 'premises' see para 671 note 3 ante.
4 For these purposes, 'relevant evidence', in relation to an offence, means anything that would be admissible in evidence at a trial for the offence: Police and Criminal Evidence Act 1984 s 8 (4).
5 For these purposes, 'items subject to legal privilege' means:
    (1) communications between a professional legal adviser and his client or any person representing his client made in connection with the giving of legal advice to the client;
    (2) communications between a professional legal adviser and his client or any person representing his client or between such an adviser or his client or any such representative and any other person made in connection with or in contemplation of legal proceedings and for the purposes of such proceedings; and
    (3) items enclosed with or referred to in such communications and made (a) in connection with the giving of legal advice; or (b) in connection with or in contemplation of legal proceedings and for the purposes of such proceedings, when they are in the possession of a person who is entitled to possession of them:
ibid ss 10 (1), 118 (1).
    The actual conveyance of a house, and records showing how the transaction was financed, are not subject to legal privilege within the meaning of s 10, although correspondence as to how the transaction is to be financed and completed may be: *R v Crown Court at Inner London Sessions, ex p Baines and Baines (a firm)* [1988] QB 579, 87 Cr App Rep 111, DC. See also *R v Guildhall Magistrates' Court, ex p Primlaks Holdings Co (Panama) Inc* [1989] 2 WLR 841, 89 Cr App Rep 215, DC (pre-existing documents sent to solicitors under cover of correspondence not subject to legal privilege unless made in accordance with head (3) supra).
    Items held with the intention of furthering a criminal purpose are not items subject to legal privilege: Police and Criminal Evidence Act 1984 s 10 (2). The criminal purpose of a third party suffices where the accused is the innocent instrument or beneficiary of the third party's criminal

purpose: *R v Central Criminal Court, ex p Francis and Francis (a firm)* [1988] 1 All ER 677, 87 Cr App Rep 104, DC; affd [1989] AC 346 at 357, 88 Cr App Rep 213, HL. Cf *R v Crown Court at Snaresbrook, ex p DPP* [1988] QB 532, 86 Cr App Rep 227, DC (accused charged with attempting to pervert the course of justice after instituting action for assault against police, which was without foundation; form applying for legal aid to pursue that civil action not held by the area office of the Law Society with the intention of furthering a criminal purpose). If, prima facie, legal privilege is lost by virtue of the Police and Criminal Evidence Act 1984 s 10 (2), that result does not mean that no express or implied undertaking to hold in confidence can exist; but such undertaking cannot prevent an order being made pursuant to an application under s 9 (see para 673 et seq post) by a circuit judge who will consider the matter inter partes and in circumstances in which the matter can be fully ventilated: *R v Guildhall Magistrates' Court, ex p Primlaks Holdings Co (Panama) Inc* supra.

6 For the meaning of 'excluded material' see para 674 post.

7 For the meaning of 'special procedure material' see para 675 post.

8 Ie the conditions specified in the Police and Criminal Evidence Act 1984 s 8 (3): see text to note 11 infra.

9 Ibid s 8 (1). The power so to issue a warrant is in addition to any such power otherwise conferred: s 8 (5).

10 Ibid s 8 (2). As to computerised information see para 686 post.

11 Ibid s 8 (3). Section 8 confers a 'Draconian power' and it is for the magistrate to satisfy himself that there are reasonable grounds for believing the matters set out; the fact that a police officer states that there are reasonable grounds is not enough: *R v Guildhall Magistrates' Court, ex p Primlaks Holdings Co (Panama) Inc* [1989] 2 WLR 841, 89 Cr App Rep 215, DC. Where the magistrate cannot be so satisfied that the material sought does not include any items which are prima facie subject to legal privilege or special procedure material, he should refuse the application: *R v Guildhall Magistrates' Court, ex p Primlaks Holdings Co (Panama) Ltd* supra.

As to search warrants issued under the Prevention of Terrorism (Temporary Provisions) Act 1989 s 17, Sch 7 see para 132 ante.

B. SPECIAL PROCEDURE

673. Special provisions as to access. A constable may obtain access to excluded material[1] or special procedure material[2] for the purposes of a criminal investigation by making an application in accordance with the statutory provisions[3].

1 For the meaning of 'excluded material' see para 674 post.

2 For the meaning of 'special procedure material' see para 675 post.

3 Police and Criminal Evidence Act 1984 s 9 (1). As to the procedure for making an application see para 676 et seq post. Any Act, including a local Act, passed before the 1984 Act under which a search of premises for the purposes of a criminal investigation could be authorised by the issue of a warrant to a constable has ceased to have effect so far as it relates to the authorisation of searches (1) for items subject to legal privilege; or (2) for excluded material; or (3) for special procedure material consisting of documents or records other than documents: s 9 (2). For the meaning of 'items subject to legal privilege' see para 672 note 5 ante.

As to the procedure for gaining access to such material for the purposes of a terrorist investigation see paras 133–137 ante.

674. Meaning of 'excluded material'. 'Excluded material' means:

(1) personal records[1] which a person has acquired or created in the course of any trade, business, profession or other occupation or for the purposes of any paid or unpaid office and which he holds in confidence;

(2) human tissue or tissue fluid which has been taken for the purposes of diagnosis or medical treatment and which a person holds in confidence;

(3) journalistic material[2] which a person holds in confidence and which consists of documents[3] or of records other than documents[4].

A person holds material other than journalistic material in confidence for these purposes if he holds it subject:

(a) to an express or implied undertaking to hold it in confidence; or
(b) to a restriction on disclosure or an obligation of secrecy contained in any enactment, including an enactment contained in an Act passed after the Police and Criminal Evidence Act 1984[5].

A person holds journalistic material in confidence for these purposes if:
(i) he holds it subject to such an undertaking, restriction or obligation; and
(ii) it has been continuously held, by one or more persons, subject to such an undertaking, restriction or obligation since it was first acquired or created for the purposes of journalism[6].

1 For these purposes, 'personal records' means documentary and other records concerning an individual, whether living or dead, who can be identified from them and relating (1) to his physical or mental health; (2) to spiritual counselling or assistance given or to be given to him; or (3) to counselling or assistance given or to be given to him, for the purposes of his personal welfare, by any voluntary organisation or by any individual who (a) by reason of his office or occupation has responsibilities for his personal welfare; or (b) by reason of an order of a court has responsibilities for his supervision: Police and Criminal Evidence Act 1984 s 12.
2 For these purposes, 'journalistic material' means material acquired or created for the purposes of journalism: ibid s 13 (1). Material is only journalistic material for these purposes if it is in the possession of a person who acquired or created it for the purposes of journalism: s 13 (2). A person who receives material from someone who intends that the recipient shall use it for the purposes of journalism is to be taken to have acquired it for those purposes: s 13 (3).
3 'Document' includes, in addition to a document in writing (1) any map, plan, graph or drawing; (2) any photograph; (3) any disc, tape, sound track or other device in which sounds or other data, not being visual images are embodied so as to be capable, with or without the aid of some other equipment, of being reproduced therefrom; and (4) any film, negative, tape or other device in which one or more visual images are embodied so as to be so capable of being reproduced therefrom; and 'film' includes a microfilm: Civil Evidence Act 1968 s 10 (1) (applied by the Police and Criminal Evidence Act 1984 s 118 (1)).
4 Ibid s 11 (1).
5 Ibid s 11 (2).
6 Ibid s 11 (3).

675. Meaning of 'special procedure material'. 'Special procedure material' means specified material[1] and journalistic material[2], other than excluded material[3].

For these purposes specified material means material, other than items subject to legal privilege[4] and excluded material, in the possession of a person who:
(1) acquired or created it in the course of any trade, business, profession or other occupation or for the purpose of any paid or unpaid office; and
(2) holds it subject (a) to an express or implied undertaking to hold it in confidence; or (b) to a restriction on disclosure or an obligation of secrecy[5] contained in any enactment, including an enactment contained in an Act passed after the Police and Criminal Evidence Act 1984[6].

Where material is acquired:
(i) by an employee from his employer and in the course of his employment; or
(ii) by a company from an associated company[7],
it is only special procedure material if it was special procedure material immediately before the acquisition[8].

Where material is created by an employee in the course of his employment, it is only special procedure material if it would have been special procedure material had his employer created it[9].

Where material is created by a company on behalf of an associated company, it is only special procedure material if it would have been special procedure material had the associated company created it[10].

1　Ie material to which the Police and Criminal Evidence Act 1984 s 14 (2) applies: see text to notes 5, 6 infra.
2　For the meaning of 'journalistic material' see para 674 note 2 ante.
3　Police and Criminal Evidence Act 1984 s 14 (1).
4　For the meaning of 'items subject to legal privilege' see para 672 note 5 ante.
5　Ie an obligation or restriction such as is mentioned in the Police and Criminal Evidence Act 1984 s 11 (2) (b): see para 674 ante.
6　Ibid s 14 (2). See also *R v Crown Court at Bristol, ex p Bristol Press and Picture Agency Ltd* (1987) 85 Cr App Rep 190, DC (press photographs of riots were special procedure material).
7　For these purposes, a company is to be treated as another's associated company if it would be so treated under the Income and Corporation Taxes Act 1988 s 416: Police and Criminal Evidence Act 1988 s 14 (6); Interpretation Act 1978 s 17 (1) (a).
8　Police and Criminal Evidence Act 1984 s 14 (3).
9　Ibid s 14 (4).
10　Ibid s 14 (5).

676. Notice of making of application for order. An application for an order for production or access[1] must be made inter partes[2]; and notice of an application for such an order may be served on a person either by delivering it to him or by leaving it at his proper address or by sending it by post to him in a registered letter or by the recorded delivery service[3]. Such notice may be served on a body corporate by serving it on the body's secretary or clerk or other similar officer and on a partnership by serving it on one of the partners[4].

Where notice of an application for an order has been served on a person, he may not conceal, destroy, alter or dispose of the material to which the application relates except with the leave of the judge or with the written permission of a constable, until the application is dismissed or abandoned or he has complied with an order made on the application[5].

1　Ie under the Police and Criminal Evidence Act 1984 s 9 (1), Sch 1 para 4: see para 677 post. Such an application is an application in a 'criminal cause or matter': *Carr v Atkins* [1987] QB 963, 85 Cr App Rep 343, CA; *R v Crown Court at Bristol, ex p Bristol Press and Picture Agency Ltd* (1987) 85 Cr App Rep 190, DC.
2　Police and Criminal Evidence Act 1984 Sch 1 para 7. Schedule 1 para 7 applies to the police and the person or institution in whose custody special procedure material is believed to be held; there is thus no requirement under Sch 1 para 8 (see infra) to give notice of the proceedings to the accused or suspected person: *R v Crown Court at Leicester, ex p DPP* [1987] 3 All ER 454, 86 Cr App Rep 254, DC.
3　Police and Criminal Evidence Act 1984 Sch 1 para 8. The applicant should set out in the notice a description of all that was sought to be produced since failure to do so might lead the recipient of the notice to destroy the material unwittingly in breach of his obligations under Sch 1 para 11 (see infra): *R v Central Criminal Court, ex p Adegbesan* [1986] 3 All ER 113, 84 Cr App Rep 219, DC. It may, however, suffice if the information is given orally to the person affected, either at the time the notice is served or beforehand: *R v Crown Court at Manchester, ex p Taylor* [1988] 2 All ER 769, [1988] 1 WLR 705, DC; *Barclays Bank plc v Taylor, Trustee Savings Bank of Wales and Border Counties v Taylor* [1989] 3 All ER 563, [1989] 1 WLR 1066, CA.
　　The police are not obliged to give the respondent advance notice of the evidence upon which they propose to rely: *R v Crown Court at Inner London Sessions, ex p Baines and Baines (a firm)* [1988] QB 579, 87 Cr App Rep 111, DC. Where, however, the application is accompanied by evidence, the party against whom the order is sought should be provided with that evidence before the hearing, or given an opportunity to seek an adjournment of the hearing if evidence is given which cannot adequately be responded to there and then: *R v Crown Court at Inner London Sessions, ex p Baines and Baines (a firm)* supra.
4　Police and Criminal Evidence Act 1984 Sch 1 para 9. For these purposes, and for the purposes of the Interpretation Act 1978 s 7 in its application to the Police and Criminal Evidence Act 1984 Sch 1, the proper address of a person, in the case of the secretary or clerk or other similar officer of a body

corporate, is that of the registered or principal office of that body, in the case of a partner of a firm that of the principal office of the firm, and in any other case the last known address of the person to be served: Sch 1 para 10.
5 Ibid Sch 1 para 11.

677. Making of order by circuit judge. If on an application made by a constable a circuit judge is satisfied that one or other of the sets of access conditions is fulfilled, he may make an order[1].

The first set of access conditions is fulfilled if:
(1) there are reasonable grounds for believing:
    (a) that a serious arrestable offence[2] has been committed;
    (b) that there is material which consists of special procedure material[3] or includes special procedure material and does not also include excluded material[4] on premises[5] specified in the application;
    (c) that the material is likely to be of substantial value, whether by itself or together with other material, to the investigation in connection with which the application is made; and
    (d) that the material is likely to be relevant evidence[6];
(2) other methods of obtaining the material:
    (a) have been tried without success; or
    (b) have not been tried because it appeared that they were bound to fail[7]; and
(3) it is in the public interest, having regard:
    (a) to the benefit likely to accrue to the investigation if the material is obtained; and
    (b) to the circumstances under which the person in possession of the material holds it,
that the material should be produced or that access to it should be given[8].

The second set of access conditions is fulfilled if:
  (i) there are reasonable grounds for believing that there is material which consists of or includes excluded material or special procedure material on premises specified in the application;
 (ii) but for the statutory provision[9], a search of the premises for that material could have been authorised by the issue of a warrant to a constable[10]; and
(iii) the issue of such a warrant would have been appropriate[11].

An order so made is an order that the person who appears to the circuit judge to be in possession of the material to which the application relates shall produce it to a constable for him to take away[12] or give a constable access to it[13], not later than the end of the period of seven days from the date of the order or the end of such longer period as the order may specify[14].

If a person fails to comply with such an order, a circuit judge may deal with him as if he had committed a contempt of the Crown Court[15].

1 Police and Criminal Evidence Act 1984 s 9 (1), Sch 1 para 1. The order is made under Sch 1 para 4: see infra. The judge may hear the application in chambers or in open court at his discretion: *R v Central Criminal Court, ex p DPP* (1988) Times, 1 April, DC.
2 For the meaning of 'serious arrestable offence' see para 704 post.
3 For the meaning of 'special procedure material' see para 675 ante.
4 For the meaning of 'excluded material' see para 674 ante.
5 For the meaning of 'premises' see para 671 note 3 ante.
6 For the meaning of 'relevant evidence' see para 672 note 4 ante.
7 In the absence of evidence as to the conditions laid down in the Police and Criminal Evidence Act 1984 Sch 1 para 2 (b), the access conditions cannot be fulfilled: *R v Crown Court at Inner London*

Sessions, ex p Baines and Baines (a firm) [1988] QB 579 at 585, 87 Cr App Rep 111 at 116, DC per Watkins LJ.
8 Police and Criminal Evidence Act 1984 Sch 1 para 2; and see *R v Crown Court at Bristol, ex p Bristol Press and Picture Agency Ltd* (1987) 85 Cr App Rep 190, DC.
9 Ie the Police and Criminal Evidence Act 1984 s 9 (2): see para 673 note 3 ante.
10 Ie under an enactment other than ibid Sch 1.
11 Ibid Sch 1 para 3.
12 For the purposes of ibid ss 21, 22 (see paras 687, 688 respectively post), material produced in pursuance of an order so made is to be treated as if it were material seized by a constable: Sch 1 para 6. Where the material consists of information contained in a computer, an order so made has effect as an order to produce the material in a form in which it can be taken away and in which it is visible and legible: Sch 1 para 5 (a).
13 Where the material consists of information contained in a computer, an order so made has effect as an order to give a constable access to the material in a form in which it is visible and legible: ibid Sch 1 para 5 (b).
14 Ibid Sch 1 para 4. As to the circuit judge's responsibility for ensuring that the special procedure is not abused see *R v Crown Court at Maidstone, ex p Waitt* (1988) Times, 4 January, DC. As to costs see para 678 post.
15 Police and Criminal Evidence Act 1984 Sch 1 para 15 (1). Any enactment relating to contempt of the Crown Court has effect in relation to such a failure as if it were such a contempt: Sch 1 para 15 (2). See further CONTEMPT.

678. Issue of warrant by circuit judge; costs. If on an application made by a constable a circuit judge:
(1) is satisfied (a) that either set of access conditions[1] is fulfilled; and (b) that any of the further specified conditions[2] is also fulfilled; or
(2) is satisfied (a) that the second set of access conditions is fulfilled; and (b) that an order[3] relating to the material has not been complied with,
he may issue a warrant authorising a constable to enter and search the premises[4]. A constable may seize and retain anything for which a search has been so authorised[5].
The further specified conditions are:
(i) that it is not practicable to communicate with any person entitled to grant entry to the premises to which the application relates;
(ii) that it is practicable to communicate with a person entitled to grant entry to the premises but it is not practicable to communicate with any person entitled to grant access to the material;
(iii) that the material contains information which is subject to a restriction or obligation[6] and is likely to be disclosed in breach of it if a warrant is not issued;
(iv) that service of notice of application for an order[7] may seriously prejudice the investigation[8].
The costs of any application under the special procedure and of anything done or to be done in pursuance of an order are in the discretion of the judge[9].

1 Ie the access conditions contained in the Police and Criminal Evidence Act 1984 s 9 (1), Sch 1 paras 2, 3: see para 677 ante.
2 Ie the further conditions set out in ibid Sch 1 para 14: see heads (i)–(iv) infra.
3 Ie under ibid Sch 1 para 4: see para 677 ante.
4 Ibid Sch 1 para 12. Applications under Sch 1 para 12 should never become a matter of common form; the preferred method of obtaining material for a police investigation is by way of inter partes orders under Sch 1 para 4 (see para 677 ante): *R v Crown Court at Maidstone, ex p Waitt* (1988) Times, 4 January, DC.
5 Police and Criminal Evidence Act 1984 Sch 1 para 13. As to computerised information see para 686 post.
6 Ie a restriction or obligation such as is mentioned in ibid s 11 (2) (b): see para 674 head (b) ante.
7 See note 3 supra.

8 Police and Criminal Evidence Act 1984 Sch 1 para 14.
9 Ibid Sch 1 para 16.

(v) Effect of and Execution of Warrants

679. The warrant. A warrant authorises an entry on one occasion only[1]; and it:

(1) must specify (a) the name of the person who applies for it; (b) the date on which it is issued; (c) the enactment under which it is issued; and (d) the premises[2] to be searched; and

(2) must identify, so far as is practicable, the articles or persons to be sought[3].

Two copies must be made of a warrant[4]; and the copies must be clearly certified as copies[5].

A warrant to enter and search premises may be executed by any constable[6]; and such a warrant may authorise persons to accompany any constable who is executing it[7]. Entry and search under a warrant must be within one month from the date of its issue and at a reasonable hour unless it appears to the constable executing it that the purpose of a search may be frustrated on an entry at a reasonable hour[8].

1 Police and Criminal Evidence Act 1984 s 15 (5); Code of Practice for the Searching of Premises by Police Officers and the Seizure of Property found by Police Officers on Persons or Premises para 5.3. As to the application of ss 15, 16 see para 671 note 1 ante.
2 For the meaning of 'premises' see para 671 note 3 ante.
3 Police and Criminal Evidence Act 1984 s 15 (6).
4 Ibid s 15 (7).
5 Ibid s 15 (8).
6 Ibid s 16 (1).
7 Ibid s 16 (2).
8 Ibid s 16 (3), (4); Code of Practice for the Searching of Premises by Police Officers and the Seizure of Property found by Police Officers on Persons or Premises paras 5.1, 5.2. In determining at what time to make a search, the officer in charge should have regard, among other considerations, to the times of day at which the occupier of the premises is likely to be present, and should not search at a time when he, or any other person on the premises, is likely to be asleep unless not doing so is likely to frustrate the purpose of the search: para 5.2, note 5A.

680. Preliminary procedure. The officer in charge must first attempt to communicate with the occupier or any other person entitled to grant access to the premises by explaining the authority under which he seeks entry to the premises and ask the occupier to allow him to do so, unless:

(1) the premises to be searched are known to be unoccupied;

(2) the occupier and any other person entitled to grant access are known to be absent; or

(3) there are reasonable grounds for believing that to alert the occupier or any other person entitled to grant access by attempting to communicate with him would frustrate the object of the search or endanger the officers concerned or other persons[1].

Where the occupier of premises[2] which are to be entered and searched is present at the time when a constable seeks to execute a warrant to enter and search them, the constable must:

(a) identify himself to the occupier and, if not in uniform, produce to him documentary evidence[3] that he is a constable;

(b) produce the warrant[4] to him; and

(c) supply him with a copy of it[5].

Where the occupier of such premises is not present at the time when a constable seeks to execute such a warrant, but some other person who appears to the constable to be in charge of the premises is present, the above provisions have effect as if any reference to the occupier were a reference to that other person[6]. However, if there is no person present who appears to the constable to be in charge of the premises, he must leave a copy of the warrant in a prominent place on the premises[7].

Reasonable force may be used if necessary to enter premises if the officer in charge is satisfied that the premises are those specified in any warrant or other written authority and where:

  (i) the occupier or any other person entitled to grant access has refused a request to allow entry to his premises;

  (ii) it is impossible to communicate with the occupier or any other person entitled to grant access; or

  (iii) any of the specified conditions in heads (1) to (3) above applies[8].

1 Code of Practice for the Searching of Premises by Police Officers and the Seizure of Property found by Police Officers on Persons or Premises para 5.4.
2 For the meaning of 'premises' see para 671 note 3 ante.
3 Where the premises are occupied, the officer must identify himself and, if not in uniform, must show his warrant card and state the purpose of the search and the grounds for undertaking it, before a search begins: Code of Practice for the Searching of Premises by Police Officers and the Seizure of Property found by Police Officers on Persons or Premises para 5.5. Where entry is effected by the use of force or subterfuge (see infra), the requirements of para 5.5 must be complied with after entry and before search: *R v Longman* [1988] 1 WLR 619, 88 Cr App Rep 148, CA.
4 The occupier must be given an opportunity to inspect the warrant and not merely be shown that the officer has a warrant: *R v Longman* [1988] 1 WLR 619, 88 Cr App Rep 148, CA.
5 Police and Criminal Evidence Act 1984 s 16 (5); Code of Practice for the Searching of Premises by Police Officers and the Seizure of Property found by Police Officers on Persons or Premises para 5.7.
6 Police and Criminal Evidence Act 1984 s 16 (6).
7 Ibid s 16 (7); Code of Practice for the Searching of Premises by Police Officers and the Seizure of Property found by Police Officers on Persons or Premises para 5.7. The warrant itself must be indorsed to show that this has been done: para 5.7.
8 Ibid para 5.6; and see para 658 ante. In such circumstances entry may also be effected by the use of a subterfuge: *R v Longman* [1988] 1 WLR 619, 88 Cr App Rep 148, CA.

681. Conduct of searches; standard procedure. A search under a warrant may only be a search to the extent required for the purpose for which the warrant was issued, having regard to the size and nature of whatever is sought[1]. A search under warrant may not continue under the authority of that warrant once all the things specified in it have been found, or the officer in charge of the search is satisfied that they are not on the premises[2]. Searches must be conducted with due consideration for the property and privacy of the occupier of the premises searched, and with no more disturbance than necessary[3]. Reasonable force may be used only where this is necessary because the co-operation of the occupier cannot be obtained or is insufficient for the purpose[3].

If the occupier wishes to ask a friend, neighbour or other person to witness the search, then he must be allowed to do so, unless the officer in charge has reasonable grounds for believing that this would seriously hinder the investigation[4]. A search need not be delayed for this purpose unreasonably[4].

If premises have been entered by force, the officer in charge must, before leaving them, satisfy himself that they are secure either by arranging for the occupier or his agent to be present or by any other appropriate means[5].

HALSBURY'S
Laws of England

FOURTH EDITION
REISSUE

We have pleasure in sending you the reissue of volume 11 of the fourth edition of Halsbury's Laws of England containing the title CRIMINAL LAW, EVIDENCE AND PROCEDURE. Following the significant increase in the amount of material since the fourth edition volume was published, it has been necessary to publish the title from the fourth edition in two volumes, 11(1) and 11(2).

The title CROWN PROCEEDINGS now appears in the Annual Cumulative Supplement to this work. Pending the reissue of that title in volume 12, subscribers should refer to the Supplement for all matters relating to Crown Proceedings.

In view of the reorganisation of the legal aid system effected by the Legal Aid Act 1988, it is proposed eventually to create a new title LEGAL AID. Until such time as that title is issued, subscribers should refer to the following titles in the Annual Cumulative Supplement: LEGAL AID (legal aid in criminal proceedings); and PRACTICE AND PROCEDURE (legal aid in civil proceedings).

The material in volumes 11(1) and 11(2) supersedes that in volume 11 of the fourth edition.

BUTTERWORTH LAW PUBLISHERS LTD
March 1990

Printed in Great Britain by
Thomson Litho Ltd, East Kilbride, Scotland

1 Police and Criminal Evidence Act 1984 s 16 (8); Code of Practice for the Searching of Premises by Police Officers and the Seizure of Property found by Police Officers on Persons or Premises para 5.8. If the wrong premises are searched by mistake, everything possible should be done at the earliest opportunity to allay any sense of grievance, and in appropriate cases assistance should be given to obtain compensation: para 5, note 5C.
2 Ibid para 5.8.
3 Ibid para 5.9; and see para 658 ante.
4 Ibid para 5.10.
5 Ibid para 5.11.

682. Conduct of searches; special procedure. An officer of the rank of inspector or above must take charge of and be present at any search under a warrant[1] for the production of excluded material or special procedure material[2]. He is responsible for ensuring that the search is conducted with discretion and in such manner as to cause the least possible disruption to any business or other activities carried on in the premises[2]. After satisfying himself that material may not be taken from the premises without his knowledge, the officer in charge of the search must ask for the documents or other records concerned to be produced[3]. He may also, if he considers it to be necessary, ask to see the index to files held on the premises, if there is one; and the officers conducting the search may inspect any files which, according to the index, appear to contain any of the material sought[3]. A more extensive search of the premises may be made only if the person responsible for them refuses to produce the material sought, or to allow access to the index; if it appears that the index is inaccurate or incomplete; or if for any other reason the officer in charge has reasonable grounds for believing that such a search is necessary in order to find the material sought[3].

1 Ie a warrant under the Police and Criminal Evidence Act 1984 s 9 (1), Sch 1 para 12: see para 678 ante.
2 Code of Practice for the Searching of Premises by Police Officers and the Seizure of Property found by Police Officers on Persons or Premises para 5.12.
3 Ibid para 5.13. In asking for documents to be so produced officers should direct the request to a person in authority and with responsibility for the documents: para 5.13, note 5B.

(vi) Entry and Search without Search Warrant

683. Entry for purpose of arrest etc. A constable may[1] enter and search any premises[2] for the purpose:
(1) of executing (a) a warrant of arrest[3] issued in connection with or arising out of criminal proceedings; or (b) a warrant of commitment issued under the Magistrates' Courts Act 1980[4];
(2) of arresting a person for an arrestable offence[5];
(3) of arresting a person for other specified offences[6];
(4) of recapturing a person who is unlawfully at large and whom he is pursuing; or
(5) of saving life or limb or preventing serious damage to property[7].
Except for the purpose specified in head (5) above, such powers of entry and search:
(a) are only exercisable if the constable has reasonable grounds for believing that the person whom he is seeking is on the premises; and
(b) are limited, in relation to premises consisting of two or more separate dwellings, to powers to enter and search (i) any parts of the premises which

the occupiers of any dwelling comprised in the premises use in common with the occupiers of any other such dwelling; and (ii) any such dwelling in which the constable has reasonable grounds for believing that the person whom he is seeking may be[8].

Such power of search is only a power to search to the extent that is reasonably required for the purpose for which the power of entry is exercised[9].

1 Ie subject to the Police and Criminal Evidence Act 1984 s 17 (2)–(6) (see infra) and without prejudice to any other enactment.
2 For the meaning of 'premises' see para 671 note 3 ante.
3 As to warrants of arrest see para 698 et seq post.
4 Ie under the Magistrates' Courts Act 1980 s 76 (as amended): see MAGISTRATES vol 29 para 457.
5 For the meaning of 'arrestable offence' see para 703 post. The power of entry under head (2) supra is exercisable only where a constable not only has reasonable grounds for suspecting or believing, but does in fact suspect or believe, that an arrestable offence has been committed: *Chapman v DPP* (1988) 89 Cr App Rep 190 at 196, DC per Bingham LJ.
6 Ie offences under the Public Order Act 1936 s 1 (prohibition of uniforms in connection with political objects: see para 100 ante), the Public Order Act 1986 s 4 (fear or provocation of violence: see para 152 ante) or under the Criminal Law Act 1977 ss 6–8 or 10 (entering and remaining on property: see para 161 et seq ante). The powers of search conferred by the Police and Criminal Evidence Act 1984 s 17 are only exercisable for the purposes of an offence under the Criminal Law Act 1977 ss 6–8 or 10 by a constable in uniform: Police and Criminal Evidence Act 1984 s 17 (3).
7 Ibid s 17 (1) (amended by the Public Order Act 1986 s 40 (2), (3), Sch 2 para 7, Sch 3); Code of Practice for the Searching of Premises by Police Officers and the Seizure of Property found by Police Officers on Persons or Premises para 3.1. All the rules of common law under which a constable has power to enter premises without a warrant have been abolished: Police and Criminal Evidence Act 1984 s 17 (5). However, nothing in s 17 (5) affects any power of entry to deal with or prevent a breach of the peace: s 17 (6). As to arrest for breach of the peace see para 709 post.
8 Ibid s 17 (2).
9 Ibid s 17 (4).

684. Entry and search after arrest. A constable may[1] enter and search any premises[2] occupied or controlled by a person who is under arrest for an arrestable offence[3], if he has reasonable grounds for suspecting that there is on the premises evidence, other than items subject to legal privilege[4], that relates to that offence or to some other arrestable offence which is connected with or similar to that offence[5]. A constable may seize and retain anything for which he may so search[6].

Such power to search is only a power to search to the extent that is reasonably required for the purpose of discovering such evidence[7]; and such powers may not be exercised unless an officer of the rank of inspector or above[8] has authorised them in writing[9].

A constable may conduct such a search (1) before taking the person to a police station; and (2) without obtaining an authorisation, if the presence of that person at a place other than a police station is necessary for the effective investigation of the offence[10]. If a constable so conducts a search, he must inform an officer of the rank of inspector or above that he has made the search as soon as practicable after he has made it[11].

An officer who authorises a search or is informed of a search must make a record in writing of the grounds for the search and of the nature of the evidence that was sought[12].

If the person who was in occupation or control of the premises at the time of the search is in police detention at the time the record is to be made, the officer must make the record as part of his custody record[13].

1 Ie subject to the Police and Criminal Evidence Act 1984 s 18 (2)–(8): see infra.

2 For the meaning of 'premises' see para 671 note 3 ante.
3 For the meaning of 'arrestable offence' see para 703 post.
4 For the meaning of 'items subject to legal privilege' see para 672 note 5 ante.
5 Police and Criminal Evidence Act 1984 s 18 (1); Code of Practice for the Searching of Premises by Police Officers and the Seizure of Property found by Police Officers on Persons or Premises para 3.3.
6 Police and Criminal Evidence Act 1984 s 18 (2). As to computerised information see para 686 post.
7 Ibid s 18 (3).
8 See para 659 ante.
9 Police and Criminal Evidence Act 1984 s 18 (4). 'Authorised in writing' means more than a mere record of verbal authority. It must be an independent document ie a proper authority in writing. Although nothing is said in [the Police and Criminal Evidence Act 1984], such authority should go with the police officers to the premises to be searched: *R v Badham* [1987] Crim LR 202.
10 Police and Criminal Evidence Act 1984 s 18 (5).
11 Ibid s 18 (6).
12 Ibid s 18 (7).
13 Ibid s 18 (8); Code of Practice for the Searching of Premises by Police Officers and the Seizure of Property found by Police Officers on Persons or Premises para 3.3.

(vii) Seizure and Retention of Property

685. Seizure of property. A constable who is lawfully on any premises[1] may seize anything which is on the premises if he has reasonable grounds for believing:

    (1) that it has been obtained in consequence of the commission of an offence; and

    (2) that it is necessary to seize it in order to prevent it being concealed, lost, damaged, altered or destroyed[2].

A constable who is lawfully on any premises may also seize anything which is on the premises if he has reasonable grounds for believing:

    (a) that it is evidence in relation to an offence which he is investigating or any other offence; and

    (b) that it is necessary to seize it in order to prevent the evidence being concealed, lost, altered or destroyed[3].

A constable who is lawfully on any premises may require any information which is contained in a computer and is accessible from the premises to be produced in a form in which it can be taken away and in which it is visible and legible if he has reasonable grounds for believing:

    (i) that it is evidence in relation to an offence which he is investigating or any other offence; or

    (ii) it has been obtained in consequence of the commission of an offence and that it is necessary to do so in order to prevent it being concealed, lost, tampered with or destroyed[4].

No power of seizure conferred on a constable under any enactment, including an enactment contained in an Act passed after the Police and Criminal Evidence Act 1984, is, however, to be taken to authorise the seizure of an item which the constable exercising the power has reasonable grounds for believing to be subject to legal privilege[5].

An officer who decides that it is not appropriate to seize property because of an explanation given by the person holding it, but who has reasonable grounds for believing that it has been obtained in consequence of the commission of an offence by some person, must inform the holder of his suspicions and must explain that, if he disposes of the property, he may be liable to civil or criminal proceedings[6].

1 Ie under any statutory power or with the consent of the occupier. For the meaning of 'premises' see para 671 note 3 ante.

2 Police and Criminal Evidence Act 1984 s 19 (1), (2); Code of Practice for the Searching of Premises by Police Officers and the Seizure of Property found by Police Officers on Persons or Premises para 6.1. Anything covered by a warrant may also be seized: para 6.1. The powers conferred by the Police and Criminal Evidence Act 1984 s 19 are in addition to any power otherwise conferred: s 19 (5).

3 Ibid s 19 (1), (3); Code of Practice for the Searching of Premises by Police Officers and the Seizure of Property found by Police Officers on Persons or Premises para 6.1.

4 Police and Criminal Evidence Act 1984 s 19 (1), (4); Code of Practice for the Searching of Premises by Police Officers and the Seizure of Property found by Police Officers on Persons or Premises para 6.5. See also para 686 post.

5 Police and Criminal Evidence Act 1984 s 19 (6); Code of Practice for the Searching of Premises by Police Officers and the Seizure of Property found by Police Officers on Persons or Premises para 6.2. For the meaning of 'items subject to legal privilege' see para 672 note 5 ante. As to seizure of property for the purposes of terrorist investigations see para 132 ante; and as to seizure of property for the purposes of investigations into drug trafficking see para 410 ante.

6 Ibid para 6.3.

686. Computerised information. Every power of seizure which is conferred by:

(1) any enactment contained in an Act passed before the Police and Criminal Evidence Act 1984;

(2) specified provisions[1] of the 1984 Act;

(3) any enactment contained in an Act passed after the 1984 Act,

on a constable who has entered premises[2] in the exercise of a power conferred by an enactment are to be construed as including a power to require any information contained in a computer and accessible from the premises to be produced in a form in which it can be taken away and in which it is visible and legible[3].

1 Ie the Police and Criminal Evidence Act 1984 s 8 (see para 672 ante), s 18 (see para 684 ante) and Sch 1 para 13 (see para 678 ante).

2 For the meaning of 'premises' see para 671 note 3 ante.

3 Police and Criminal Evidence Act 1984 s 20.

687. Access and copying. A constable who seizes anything in the exercise of a power conferred by any enactment, including an enactment contained in an Act passed after the Police and Criminal Evidence Act 1984, must, if so requested by a person showing himself:

(1) to be the occupier of premises[1] on which it was seized; or

(2) to have had custody or control of it immediately before the seizure,

provide that person with a record of what he seized[2]. The officer must provide the record within a reasonable time from the making of the request for it[3].

If a request for permission to be granted access to anything which:

(a) has been seized by a constable; and

(b) is retained by the police for the purpose of investigating an offence,

is made to the officer in charge of the investigation by a person who had custody or control of the thing immediately before it was so seized or by someone acting on behalf of such a person, the officer must allow the person who made the request access to it under the supervision of a constable[4].

If a request for a photograph or copy of any such thing is made to the officer in charge of the investigation by a person who had custody or control of the thing immediately before it was so seized, or by someone acting on behalf of such a person, the officer must allow the person who made the request access to it under the supervision of a constable for the purpose of photographing or copying it, or must photograph or copy it, or cause it to be photographed or copied, and supply the photograph or copy to the person who made the request[5].

The photograph or copy must be so supplied within a reasonable time from the making of the request[6], and at the person's own expense[7].

A constable may also photograph or copy, or have photographed or copied, anything which he has power to seize, without a request being so made[8].

There is no duty under the above provisions to grant access to, or to supply a photograph or copy of, anything if the officer in charge of the investigation for the purposes of which it was seized has reasonable grounds for believing that to do so would prejudice:

  (i) that investigation;

  (ii) the investigation of an offence other than the offence for the purposes of investigating which the thing was seized; or

  (iii) any criminal proceedings which may be brought as a result of the investigation of which he is in charge or any such investigation as is mentioned in head (ii) above[9].

1 For the meaning of 'premises' see para 671 note 3 ante.
2 Police and Criminal Evidence Act 1984 s 21 (1); Code of Practice for the Searching of Premises by Police Officers and the Seizure of Property found by Police Officers on Persons or Premises para 6.8.
3 Police and Criminal Evidence Act 1984 s 21 (2); Code of Practice for the Searching of Premises by Police Officers and the Seizure of Property found by Police Officers on Persons or Premises para 6.8.
4 Police and Criminal Evidence Act 1984 s 21 (3); Code of Practice for the Searching of Premises by Police Officers and the Seizure of Property found by Police Officers on Persons or Premises para 6.9.
5 Police and Criminal Evidence Act 1984 s 21 (4), (6); Code of Practice for the Searching of Premises by Police Officers and the Seizure of Property found by Police Officers on Persons or Premises para 6.9. As to access to, and copying of, material seized or produced in the course of a terrorist investigation see para 132 note 8 ante; and as to access to, and copying of, material seized or produced in the course of an investigation into drug trafficking see para 409 note 2 ante.
6 Police and Criminal Evidence Act 1984 s 21 (7).
7 Code of Practice for the Searching of Premises by Police Officers and the Seizure of Property found by Police Officers on Persons or Premises para 6.9.
8 Police and Criminal Evidence Act 1984 s 21 (5); Code of Practice for the Searching of Premises by Police Officers and the Seizure of Property found by Police Officers on Persons or Premises para 6.4.
9 Police and Criminal Evidence Act 1984 s 21 (8); Code of Practice for the Searching of Premises by Police Officers and the Seizure of Property found by Police Officers on Persons or Premises para 6.9. In any such case a record of the grounds must be made: para 6.9. Any such refusal may be challenged by way of judicial review: *Allen v Chief Constable of Cheshire Constabulary* (1988) Times, 16 July, CA. See further ADMINISTRATIVE LAW.

688. Retention of property. Anything which has been seized by a constable or taken away by a constable[1] may be retained so long as is necessary in all the circumstances[2]. Without prejudice to the generality of the above provision:

  (1) anything seized for the purposes of a criminal investigation may be retained for use as evidence at a trial for an offence or for forensic examination or for investigation in connection with an offence; and

  (2) anything may be retained in order to establish its lawful owner, where there are reasonable grounds for believing that it has been obtained in consequence of the commission of an offence[3].

Nothing seized on the ground that it may be used:

  (a) to cause physical injury to any person;

  (b) to damage property;

  (c) to interfere with evidence; or

  (d) to assist in escape from police detention or lawful custody, may be retained when the person from whom it was seized is no longer in police detention or the custody of a court or is in the custody of a court but has been released on bail[4].

1 Ie following a requirement made by virtue of the Police and Criminal Evidence Act 1984 s 19 or s 20: see paras 685, 686 ante.

2 Ibid s 22 (1); Code of Practice for the Searching of Premises by Police Officers and the Seizure of Property found by Police Officers on Persons or Premises para 6.6. Nothing in the Police and Criminal Evidence Act 1984 s 22 affects any power of a court to make an order under the Police (Property) Act 1897 s 1 (amended by the Theft Act 1968 ss 33 (3), 36 (2), (3), Sch 3 Pt III; the Criminal Justice Act 1972 s 58; the Consumer Credit Act 1974 s 192 (3) (b), Sch 5 Pt I) (see POLICE vol 36 para 325): Police and Criminal Evidence Act 1984 s 22 (5); Code of Practice for the Searching of Premises by Police Officers and the Seizure of Property found by Police Officers on Persons or Premises para 6, note 6A. Where appropriate, a person should be advised of this procedure: para 6, note 6A.

3 Police and Criminal Evidence Act 1984 s 22 (2); Code of Practice for the Searching of Premises by Police Officers and the Seizure of Property found by Police Officers on Persons or Premises para 6.6. Nothing may be retained for either of the purposes mentioned in the Police and Criminal Evidence Act 1984 s 22 (2) (a) (see head (1) supra) if a photograph or copy would be sufficient for that purpose: s 22 (4); Code of Practice for the Searching of Premises by Police Officers and the Seizure of Property found by Police Officers on Persons or Premises para 6.7.

4 Police and Criminal Evidence Act 1984 s 22 (3). As to the retention of material seized or produced in the course of a terrorist investigation see para 132 note 8 ante; and as to the retention of material seized or produced in the course of an investigation into drug trafficking see para 409 note 2 ante.

(viii) Action following Search

689. Action following search. Where premises have been searched[1], the officer in charge of the search must, on arrival at a police station, make or have made a record of the search[2]. The record must include:

(1) the address of the premises searched;

(2) the date, time and duration of the search;

(3) the authority under which the search was made; and, where the search was made in the exercise of a statutory power to search premises without warrant[3], the record must include the power under which the search was made; and, where the search was made under warrant[4], or with written consent[5], a copy of the warrant or consent must be appended to the record or kept in a place identified in the record;

(4) the names of the officers who conducted the search;

(5) the names of any persons on the premises if they are known;

(6) either a list of any articles seized or a note of where such a list is kept and, if not covered by a warrant, the reason for their seizure;

(7) whether force was used and, if so, the reason why it was used;

(8) details of any damage caused during the search and the circumstances in which it was caused[6].

A search register must be maintained at each sub-divisional police station; and all records which are required to be made must be made, copied or referred to in the register[7].

1 Ie in circumstances to which the Code of Practice for the Searching of Premises by Police Officers and the Seizure of Property found by Police Officers on Persons or Premises applies other than in the circumstances covered by para 4.3 (see para 669 ante).

2 Ibid para 7.1.

3 See para 683 et seq ante.

4 See para 672 et seq ante.
5 See para 669 ante.
6 Code of Practice for the Searching of Premises by Police Officers and the Seizure of Property found by Police Officers on Persons or Premises para 7.1.
7 Ibid para 8.1.

690. Indorsements on, and return of, warrants. A constable executing a warrant must make an indorsement on it stating:

(1) whether the articles or persons sought were found; and
(2) whether any articles were seized, other than articles which were sought;
(3) the date and time at which it was executed;
(4) the names of the officers who executed it; and
(5) whether a copy was handed to the occupier or left on the premises and, if so, where on them[1].

A warrant which has been executed or has not been executed within the time authorised for its execution[2], must be returned: (a) if it was issued by a justice of the peace[3], to the clerk to the justices for the petty sessions area for which he acts; and (b) if it was issued by a judge[4], to the appropriate officer of the court from which he issued it[5].

A warrant which is so returned must be retained for 12 months from its return by the clerk to the justices, if it was returned under head (a) above, and by the appropriate officer, if it was returned under head (b) above[6].

If during the period for which a warrant is to be retained the occupier of the premises[7] to which it relates asks to inspect it, he must be allowed to do so[8].

1 Police and Criminal Evidence Act 1984 s 16 (9); Code of Practice for the Searching of Premises by Police Officers and the Seizure of Property found by Police Officers on Persons or Premises para 7.2.
2 Ie the time specified in the Police and Criminal Evidence Act 1984 s 16 (3): see para 679 ante.
3 Ie under ibid s 8: see para 672 ante.
4 Ie under ibid s 9 (1), Sch 1 para 12: see para 678 ante.
5 Ibid s 16 (10); Code of Practice for the Searching of Premises by Police Officers and the Seizure of Property found by Police Officers on Persons or Premises para 7.3.
6 Police and Criminal Evidence Act 1984 s 16 (11).
7 For the meaning of 'premises' see para 671 note 3 ante.
8 Police and Criminal Evidence Act 1984 s 16 (12).

8. ARREST AND DETENTION

(1) CODE OF PRACTICE

691. Code of Practice. A constable's powers relating to the arrest, detention, treatment and questioning of persons are governed by the Police and Criminal Evidence Act 1984[1] and by the Code of Practice for the Detention, Treatment and Questioning of Persons by Police Officers[2]. The Code must be readily available at all police stations for consultation by police officers, detained persons and members of the public[3].

Whenever the Code requires a person to be given certain information, he does not have to be given it if he is incapable at the time of understanding what is said to him or is violent or likely to become violent or is in urgent need of medical attention, but he must be given it as soon as practicable[4]. In its application to persons who are in custody at police stations, the Code applies⁵ whether or not they have been arrested for an offence⁶.

1   Ie the Police and Criminal Evidence Act 1984 Pts III–V (ss 24–65): see para 692 et seq post. Sections
    34–51 (see para 715 et seq post) do not apply to a child (as for the time being defined for the purposes
    of the Children and Young Persons Act 1969: see para 34 text and notes 6–8 ante) who is arrested
    without a warrant otherwise than for homicide and to whom s 28 (4), (5) accordingly applies: Police
    and Criminal Evidence Act 1984 s 52. See further INFANTS vol 24 para 777.
        Nothing in Pt IV (ss 34–52) affects:
    (1) the powers conferred on immigration officers by the Immigration Act 1971 s 4, Sch 2 (as
         amended) (administrative provisions as to control on entry etc: see BRITISH NATIONALITY AND
         ALIENAGE vol 4 para 1003 et seq);
    (2) the powers conferred by or by virtue of the Prevention of Terrorism (Temporary Provisions)
         Act 1989 s 14 or ss 4 (4), 16 (1), (3), (4), Sch 2, Sch 5 (powers of arrest and detention and control
         of entry and procedure for removal: see para 118 et seq ante);
    (3) any duty of a police officer under the Army Act 1955 ss 129, 190, 202 or the Air Force Act 1955
         ss 129, 190, 202 (duties of governors of prisons and others to receive prisoners, deserters,
         absentees and persons under escort), the Naval Discipline Act 1957 s 107 (duties of governors of
         civil prisons etc) or the Reserve Forces Act 1980 ss 73, 106, Sch 5 para 5 (duties of governors of
         civil prisons); or
    (4) any right of a person in police detention to apply for a writ of habeas corpus or other prerogative
         remedy:
    Police and Criminal Evidence Act 1984 s 51 (amended by the Prevention of Terrorism (Temporary
    Provisions) Act 1989 s 25 (1), Sch 8 para 6 (1), (4)). As to the duties of police officers under head (3)
    supra see POLICE vol 36 para 324.
2   Ie The Code of Practice for the Detention, Treatment and Questioning of Persons by Police
    Officers: see para 692 et seq post.
        The notes for guidance included in the Code are not provisions of the Code, but are guidance to
    police officers and others about its application and interpretation: para 1.3. Provisions in the
    Annexes to the Code are provisions of the Code: para 1.3.
        The Code does not affect the principle that all citizens have a duty to help police officers to prevent
    crime and discover offenders: para 1, note 1B. This is a civic rather than a legal duty; but, when a
    police officer is trying to discover whether, or by whom, an offence has been committed, he is
    entitled to question any person from whom he thinks useful information can be obtained, subject to
    the restrictions imposed by the Code: para 1, note 1B. A person's declaration that he is unwilling to
    reply does not alter this entitlement: para 1, note 1B.
3   Ibid para 1.2.
4   Ibid para 1.8.
5   Ie except for ibid para 16 which applies solely to persons in police detention: see para 761 post.
6   Ibid para 1.10.

(2) VOLUNTARY ATTENDANCE AT POLICE STATION

692. Voluntary attendance at police station. Where for the purpose of assisting with an investigation a person attends voluntarily at a police station or at any other place where a constable is present or accompanies a constable to a police station or any such other place without having been arrested (1) he is entitled to leave at will unless he is placed under arrest; (2) he must be informed at once that he is under arrest if a decision is taken by a constable to prevent him from leaving at will¹. If he is so informed, he must be brought before the custody officer²; and, if he is not placed under arrest but is cautioned, the officer who gives the caution³ must at the same time inform him that he is not under arrest, that he is not obliged to remain at the police station but that, if he remains at the police station, he may obtain legal advice if he wishes⁴.

1   Police and Criminal Evidence Act 1984 s 29; Code of Practice for the Detention, Treatment and
    Questioning of Persons by Police Officers para 3.9. Although certain sections of the Code (see eg

para 9 and paras 732, 733 post) apply specifically to persons in custody at police stations, those there voluntarily to assist with an investigation should be treated with no less consideration (eg offered refreshments at appropriate times) and enjoy an absolute right to obtain legal advice or communicate with anyone outside the police station: para 1, note 1A.

2 Ibid para 3.9.
3 Ie under ibid para 10: see para 734 post.
4 Ibid para 3.9. If a person who is attending a police station voluntarily asks about his entitlement to legal advice, he should be given a copy of the notice explaining the arrangements for obtaining legal advice: para 3.9, note 3G. As to the notice see para 3.2 and para 722 post.

(3) ARREST

(i) In general

693. Meaning of 'arrest'. Arrest[1] consists in the seizure or touching of a person's body with a view to his restraint; words may, however, amount to arrest if, in the circumstances of the case, they are calculated to bring, and do bring, to a person's notice that he is under compulsion and he thereafter submits to the compulsion[2]. An arrest may be effected with or without a warrant[3].

1 There is nothing in the Police and Criminal Evidence Act 1984 to indicate that those acts which served to effect an arrest at common law have either been changed or abolished: *R v Brosch* [1988] Crim LR 743, CA. Whether an arrest once made is to be treated as valid or not is a separate matter and is addressed by the Police and Criminal Evidence Act 1984 s 28 (see para 710 post): *R v Brosch* supra. As to voluntary attendance at a police station see para 692 ante.
2 *Alderson v Booth* [1969] 2 QB 216, 53 Cr App Rep 301, DC. Whether on the facts of a particular case it has been made clear to a person that he is under arrest is a matter of fact for the jury: see *R v Inwood* [1973] 2 All ER 645, 57 Cr App Rep 529, CA.
3 As to arrest with warrant see para 698 et seq post; and as to arrest without warrant see para 703 et seq post.

694. Privilege from arrest. No person, except the Queen[1], a foreign reigning sovereign[2] and in certain circumstances a foreign ambassador[3] is privileged from arrest on a criminal charge[4].

No place affords any protection from arrest[5].

1 See para 38 ante and CONSTITUTIONAL LAW vol 8 para 955.
2 See para 38 and FOREIGN RELATIONS vol 18 paras 1548, 1549.
3 See para 39 ante and FOREIGN RELATIONS vol 18 para 1566.
4 Members of Parliament are not privileged from criminal process (see *Wellesley v Duke of Beaufort* (1831) 2 Russ & M 639); nor are advocates, witnesses etc (see *Re Freston* (1883) 11 QBD 545, CA; *Ex p Lyne* (1822) 3 Stark 132).
5 The privilege of sanctuary was abolished by 21 Jac 1 (Continuance of Acts) (1623–24) s 7 (repealed). An arrest may be effected within the walls of Parliament: Erskine May, Parliamentary Practice (21st Edn) 95.
  As to royal palaces and courts of justice see *Fitzpatrick v Kelly* (1781) cited in 3 Term Rep 740; *R v Stobbs* (1790) 3 Term Rep 735; and CONSTITUTIONAL LAW vol 8 para 956.

(ii) Summonses and Warrants of Arrest

695. Issue of summons to accused or warrant of arrest. Upon an information[1] being laid before a justice of the peace for any county, London commission area or the City of London that any person has, or is suspected of having, committed an offence, the justice may:

(1) issue a summons directed to that person requiring him to appear before a magistrates' court for that area to answer to the information; or

(2) issue a warrant to arrest that person and bring him before a magistrates' court for that area[2].

A justice of the peace may so issue a summons or warrant:

(a) if the offence was committed or is suspected to have been committed within that area; or

(b) if it appears to the justice necessary or expedient, with a view to the better administration of justice, that the person charged should be tried jointly with, or in the same place as, some other person who is charged with an offence, and who is in custody, or is being or is to be proceeded against, within that area; or

(c) if the person charged resides or is, or is believed to reside or be, within that area; or

(d) if under any enactment a magistrates' court for the area has jurisdiction to try the offence; or

(e) if the offence was committed outside England and Wales and, where it is an offence exclusively punishable on summary conviction[3], if a magistrates' court for the area would have jurisdiction to try the offence if the offender were before it[4].

No warrant may be so issued unless the information is in writing and substantiated on oath[5]; nor may a warrant be issued for the arrest of any person who has attained the age of 17 unless the offence to which the warrant relates is an indictable offence or is punishable with imprisonment, or the person's address is not sufficiently established for a summons to be served on him[6]. Where the offence charged is an indictable offence, a warrant may be issued at any time notwithstanding that a summons has previously been issued[7].

A warrant or summons issued by a justice of the peace does not cease to have effect by reason of his death or his ceasing to be a justice of the peace[8].

1 An information is a statement by which a justice of the peace is informed of an alleged offence: *R v Hughes* (1879) 4 QBD 614 at 633, CCR per Huddleston B. An information may be laid by the prosecutor or complainant in person, or by his solicitor or counsel or other person authorised in that behalf: Magistrates' Courts Rules 1981, SI 1981/552, r 4 (1). Failure to name the police officer laying the information does not invalidate it where it is clear that a police officer has laid the information and that officer's identity is easily ascertainable: *Rubin v DPP* [1989] 2 All ER 241, 89 Cr App Rep 44, DC. Subject to any provision of the Magistrates' Courts Act 1980 and any other enactment, an information need not be in writing or on oath: Magistrates' Courts Rules 1981 r 4 (2). It is not necessary in an information to specify or negative an exception, exemption, proviso, excuse or qualification, whether or not it accompanies the description of the offence or matter of complaint contained in the enactment creating the offence or on which the complaint is founded: r 4 (3). As to the significance of this rule see *R v Edwards* [1975] QB 27, [1974] 2 All ER 1085, CA. For the prescribed form of information see the Magistrates' Courts (Forms) Rules 1981, SI 1981/553, r 2, Sch 2, Form 1.

An information, other than one substantiated on oath, may be laid before the justices' clerk: Justices' Clerks Rules 1970, SI 1970/231, r 3, Schedule para 1.

Generally speaking, any person may lay the information and make the charge before a justice of the peace, except where a statutory provision restricts the power of making a charge to certain persons, or makes the consent or order of some person a condition precedent to the institution of proceedings: *R v Kennedy* (1902) 86 LT 753; *R v Granatelli* (1849) 7 State Tr NS 979. See also paras 639, 640 ante.

2 Magistrates' Courts Act 1980 s 1 (1), (8). A justice of the peace may issue a summons or warrant under s 1 upon an information being laid before him notwithstanding any enactment requiring the information to be laid before two or more justices: s 1 (7). A warrant is not normally issued if a

summons will effect the purpose: *O'Brien v Brabner* (1885) 49 JP Jo 227; *Dumbell v Roberts* [1944] 1 All ER 126, CA.
3 As to offences punishable on summary conviction only see paras 805–808 post and MAGISTRATES.
4 Magistrates' Courts Act 1980 s 1 (2).
5 Ibid s 1 (3).
6 Ibis s 1 (4). Where the offence is not an indictable offence (1) no summons may be issued by virtue only of s 1 (2) (c) (see text head (b) supra); and (2) any warrant issued by virtue only of s 1 (2) (c) must require the person charged to be brought before a magistrates' court having jurisdiction to try the offence: s 1 (5).
7 Ibid s 1 (6). Proceedings for an offence in respect of which a confiscation order may be made are instituted when a justice of the peace issues a summons or warrant under s 1 in respect of that offence: see the Criminal Justice Act 1988 s 102 (11) (a) and para 1291 note 3 post. As to the issue of summonses and warrants by the Crown Court see para 959 post.
8 Magistrates' Courts Act 1980 s 124.

696. The summons. A summons must be signed by the justice issuing it or state his name and be authenticated by the signature of the clerk of a magistrates' court[1]. A summons requiring a person to appear before a magistrates' court to answer an information must state shortly the matter of the information and must state the time and place at which the accused is required by the summons to appear[2].

A single summons may be issued against a person in respect of several informations; but the summons must state the matter of each information separately and has effect as several summonses, each issued in respect of one information[3].

1 Magistrates' Courts Rules 1981, SI 1981/552, r 98 (1). For the prescribed form of summons see the Magistrates' Courts (Forms) Rules 1981, SI 1981/553, r 2, Sch 2, Form 2.
   A summons may be issued by a clerk to the justices in his own right: Justices' Clerks Rules 1970, SI 1970/231, r 3, Schedule para 2. Where a summons is issued by a justice, his facsimile rubber stamp signature may be affixed to it either by the justice or by an employee of the justices' clerk with the justice's general authority: *R v Brentford Justices, ex p Catlin* [1975] QB 455, [1975] 2 All ER 201, DC.
2 Magistrates' Courts Rules 1981 r 98 (2).
3 Ibid r 98(3).

697. Service of summons. Service of a summons issued by a justice of the peace on a person other than a corporation may be effected:
   (1) by delivering it to the person to whom it is directed; or
   (2) by leaving it for him with some person at his last known or usual place of abode; or
   (3) by sending it by post in a letter addressed to him at his last known or usual place of abode[1].
Service of a summons issued by a justice of the peace on a corporation may be effected by delivering it at, or sending it by post to, the registered office of the corporation, if that office is in the United Kingdom or, if there is no registered office in the United Kingdom, any place in the United Kingdom where the corporation trades or conducts business[2].

A summons requiring a person to appear before a court in England and Wales may, in such manner as may be prescribed[3], be served on him in Scotland or Northern Ireland[4].

1 Magistrates' Courts Rules 1981, SI 1981/552, r 99 (1). Where r 99 or any other rule provides that a summons may be sent by post to a person's last known or usual place of abode, that rule has effect as if it provided also for the summons to be sent in the specified manner to an address given by that person for that purpose: r 99 (8). If the person summoned fails to appear, service of a summons in manner authorised by r 99 (1) (b) or (c) (see text heads (2), (3) supra) is not to be treated as proved

unless it is proved that the summons came to his knowledge; and for that purpose any letter or other communication purporting to be written by him or on his behalf in such terms as reasonably to justify the inference that the summons came to his knowledge is admissible as evidence of that fact: r 99 (2).
2 Ibid r 99 (3).
3 Ie by rules of court.
4 Criminal Law Act 1977 s 39 (1).

698. Warrant of arrest. A warrant issued by a justice of the peace for the arrest of any person must require the persons to whom it is directed, that is to say, the constables of the police area in which the warrant is issued, or the authorised persons for the police area specified in the warrant, or any persons named in that behalf in the warrant, to arrest the person against whom the warrant is issued[1]. The warrant must name or otherwise describe the person for whose arrest it is issued and must contain a statement of the offence charged in the information[2] or, as the case may be, the ground on which the warrant is issued[3].

1 Magistrates' Courts Rules 1981, SI 1981/552, r 96 (1). For the prescribed form of warrant see the Magistrates' Courts (Forms) Rules 1981, SI 1981/553, r 2, Sch 2, Form 4.
2 For the meaning of 'information' see para 695 note 1 ante.
3 Magistrates' Courts Rules 1981 r 96 (2). See further para 701 post.

699. Warrant indorsed for bail. On issuing a warrant for the arrest of any person, a justice of the peace may grant him bail by indorsing the warrant for bail, that is to say, by indorsing the warrant with a direction stating that the person arrested is to be released on bail subject to a duty to appear before such magistrates' court and at such time as may be specified in the indorsement[1]. The indorsement must fix the amounts in which any sureties are to be bound[2].

Where a warrant has been so indorsed:

(1) where the person arrested is to be released on bail on his entering into a recognisance without sureties, it is not necessary to take him to a police station; but, if he is so taken, he must be released from custody on his entering into the recognisance; and

(2) where he is to be released on his entering into a recognisance with sureties, he must be taken to a police station on his arrest, and the custody officer[3] there must, subject to his approving any surety tendered in compliance with the indorsement, release him from custody as directed in the indorsement[4].

1 Magistrates' Courts Act 1980 s 117 (1), (2) (a). For the prescribed form of warrant indorsed for bail see the Magistrates' Courts (Forms) Rules 1981, SI 1981/553, r 2, Sch 2, Form 4.
2 Magistrates' Courts Act 1980 s 117 (2).
3 As to custody officers see para 716 post.
4 Magistrates' Courts Act 1980 s 117 (3) (substituted by the Police and Criminal Evidence Act 1984 s 47 (7) (b)).

700. Execution of warrant. A warrant of arrest issued by a justice of the peace remains in force until it is executed or withdrawn[1]. Such a warrant may be executed anywhere in England and Wales by any person to whom it is directed or by any constable acting within his police area[2]. A warrant of arrest issued in England or Wales may be executed in Scotland by any constable appointed for a police area in like manner as any such warrant executed in Scotland[3], and in

Northern Ireland by any member of the Royal Ulster Constabulary or the Royal Ulster Reserve[4]. A warrant so issued may be executed at any time of the day or night[5] by a constable notwithstanding that it is not in his possession[6] at the time; but the warrant must, on the demand of the person arrested, be shown to him as soon as practicable[7].

1 Magistrates' Courts Act 1980 s 125 (1). It seems that a justice of the peace may withdraw his own warrant, and in a proper case the Queen's Bench Division of the High Court has power to order the withdrawal of a warrant: *R v Crossman, ex p Chetwynd* (1908) 98 LT 760. The death or cessation in office of a justice does not affect the validity of a warrant: see para 695 text and note 8 ante.
2 Magistrates' Courts Act 1980 s 125 (2). For the meaning of 'police area' see para 142 note 1 ante.
3 Criminal Law Act 1977 s 38(2).
4 Ibid s 38 (3). The Magistrates' Courts (Northern Ireland) Order 1981, SI 1981/1675, art 158(4), (5) (execution without possession of the warrant and execution on Sundays) applies to the execution in Northern Ireland of any such warrant: Criminal Law Act 1977 s 38 (3) (amended by the Magistrates' Courts (Northern Ireland) Order 1981 art 170 (2), Sch 6 para 45). A warrant may be executed by virtue of the Criminal Law Act 1977 s 38 whether or not it has been indorsed under the Indictable Offences Act 1848 ss 12, 14 or 15 or under the Petty Sessions (Ireland) Act 1851 ss 27, 28 or 29: Criminal Law Act 1977 s 38 (4).
5 See 2 Hale PC 113.
6 A warrant left in a police officer's car some 60 yards from the scene of arrest has been held to be in the officer's possession: see *R v Purdy* [1975] QB 288, [1974] 3 All ER 465, CA.
7 Magistrates' Courts Act 1980 s 125 (3), (4) (a) (respectively amended and added by the Police and Criminal Evidence Act 1984 s 33). In order to obtain the protection of this provision the warrant must be valid and the person arrested must have been charged with an offence punishable under the criminal law: see *Horsfield v Brown* [1932] 1 KB 355.
  As to the power to arrest without warrant see para 703 et seq post.

701. Statement of offence. Every information[1], summons[2] or warrant[3] laid or issued for the purposes of, or in connection with, any proceedings before a magistrates' court for an offence is sufficient if it describes the specific offence with which the accused is charged in ordinary language avoiding so far as possible the use of technical terms and without necessarily stating all the elements of the offence, and gives such particulars as may be necessary for giving reasonable information of the nature of the charge[4].

If the offence is one created by or under an Act, the description of the offence must contain a reference to the section of the Act or, as the case may be, the rule, order, regulation, byelaw or other instrument creating the offence[5].

1 For the meaning of 'information' see para 695 note 1 ante.
2 See para 696 ante.
3 See para 698 ante.
4 Magistrates' Courts Rules 1981, SI 1981/552, r 100 (1). See *Waring v Wheatley* [1951] WN 569, DC (omission of 'wilfully'; information bad); but cf *Lomas v Peek* [1947] 2 All ER 574, DC. See also *Atterton v Browne* [1945] KB 122, DC (omission of reference to section of Act); *Stephenson v Johnson* [1954] 1 All ER 369, [1954] 1 WLR 375, DC (omission of particulars); *Cording v Halse* [1955] 1 QB 63, [1954] 3 All ER 287, DC (defective particulars).
  If process does not give sufficient particulars, an application for particulars may be made at any time after the charge is preferred: *R v Aylesbury Justices, ex p Wisbey* [1965] 1 All ER 602, [1965] 1 WLR 339, DC; cf *Hickmott v Curd* [1971] 2 All ER 1399, 55 Cr App Rep 461, DC.
  It is not necessary in an information to specify or negative an exception, exemption, proviso, excuse or qualification: see para 695 note 1 ante.
5 Magistrates' Courts Rules 1981 r 100 (2). See also *R v Pollock, R v Divers* [1967] 2 QB 195 at 211, 50 Cr App Rep 149 at 161, 162, CCA per Veale J.

702. Discretion of justices to issue summons or warrant of arrest. If application is made to a justice of the peace to issue a summons or a warrant of arrest, he must exercise a judicial discretion in deciding whether to grant or refuse it[1]. If he declines jurisdiction or refuses to grant a summons for a reason which is bad in law, judicial review by way of mandamus may issue to compel him to hear and determine the matter[2]. The discretion whether a more serious charge should be preferred or not in particular circumstances must be left to the prosecutor[3]. If the justice exercises a proper discretion over the application to him, the court will not grant judicial review of his decision refusing to issue a summons[4]. If he refuses to grant a summons or warrant of arrest and assigns several reasons for his refusal, some of which are bad in law, but others good, the court will not grant judicial review[5].

1 As to the impropriety of a justice authorising the issue of a summons without having applied his mind to the information see *R v Brentford Justices, ex p Catlin* [1975] QB 455 at 464, [1975] 2 All ER 201 at 207, DC per Lord Widgery CJ.
2 *R v Byrde and Pontypool Gas Co, ex p Williams* (1890) 60 LJMC 17.
3 *R v Nuneaton Justices, ex p Parker* [1954] 3 All ER 251, [1954] 1 WLR 1318, DC.
4 *R v Bros* (1901) 85 LT 581; *R v Kennedy* (1902) 86 LT 753. Cf *R v Chertsey Justices, ex p Tannock* (1966) 111 Sol Jo 18, DC (justices' clerk had no power to refuse to issue a summons without first referring the matter to a justice).
5 *R v Kennedy* (1902) 86 LT 753. As to when an order of mandamus will issue see ADMINISTRATIVE LAW vol 1 (1) (Reissue) para 128 et seq.

(iii) Arrest without Warrant

703. Meaning of 'arrestable offence'. 'Arrestable offence' means:
(1) an offence for which the sentence is fixed by law[1];
(2) an offence for which a person of 21 years of age or over, not previously convicted, may be sentenced to imprisonment for a term of five years, or might be so sentenced but for the restrictions imposed by the Magistrates' Courts Act 1980[2]; and
(3) any of the following offences:
  (a) offences for which a person may be arrested under the customs and excise Acts[3];
  (b) offences under the Official Secrets Act 1920 that are not arrestable offences by virtue of the term of imprisonment for which a person may be sentenced in respect of them;
  (c) offences under any provision of the Official Secrets Act 1989 other than in respect of safeguarding information[4];
  (d) causing prostitution of women[5] and procuration of a girl under the age of 21[6];
  (e) taking a motor vehicle or other conveyance without authority etc[7] and going equipped for stealing etc[8];
  (f) conspiring to commit any of the offences mentioned in heads (1) to (3) above;
  (g) attempting to commit any such offence, other than an offence of taking a motor vehicle or other conveyance without authority;
  (h) inciting, aiding, abetting, counselling or procuring the commission of any such offence[9].

1 See para 1187 post.
2 Ie by the Magistrates' Courts Act 1980 s 33: see para 814 post.
3 For the meaning of 'the customs and excise Acts' see the Customs and Excise Management Act 1979 s 1(1) (applied by the Police and Criminal Evidence Act 1984 s 24 (2) (a)) and para 343 note 4 ante.

4 Ie offences under any provision of the Official Secrets Act 1989 except s 8 (1), (4) or (5): see para 252 ante.
5 Ie contrary to the Sexual Offences Act 1956 s 22: see para 386 ante.
6 Ie contrary to ibid s 23 (1): see para 524 ante.
7 Ie contrary to the Theft Act 1968 s 12 (1): see para 556 ante.
8 Ie contrary to ibid s 25 (1): see para 554 ante.
9 Police and Criminal Evidence Act 1984 s 24 (1)–(3) (amended by the Sexual Offences Act 1985 s 5 (3), Schedule; the Criminal Justice Act 1988 s 170, Sch 15 paras 97, 98, Sch 16; the Official Secrets Act 1989 s 11 (1)); Police and Criminal Evidence Act 1984 s 118 (1). Section s 24 (3) (see heads (3) (e)–(g) supra) is without prejudice to the Criminal Attempts Act 1981 s 2 (see para 71 ante): Police and Criminal Evidence Act 1984 s 24 (3).

704. Meaning of 'serious arrestable offence'. The following offences are always serious:
(1) an offence, whether at common law or under any enactment, of treason[1], murder[2], manslaughter[3], rape[4], kidnapping[5], incest with a girl under the age of 13[6], buggery with a boy under the age of 16[7] or with a person who has not consented[7] and indecent assault which constitutes an act of gross indecency[8];
(2) any specified drug trafficking offence[9];
(3) the offences of causing an explosion likely to endanger life or property[10], sexual intercourse with a girl under the age of 13[11], possession of firearms with intent to injure[12], use of firearms and imitation firearms to resist arrest[13], carrying firearms with criminal intent[14], causing death by reckless driving[15], hostage taking[16], hijacking[17] or torture[18].
Any other arrestable offence[19] is serious only if its commission:
(a) has led to any of the following consequences:
    (i) serious harm to the security of the State or to public order;
    (ii) serious interference with the administration of justice or with the investigation of offences or of a particular offence;
    (iii) the death of any person;
    (iv) serious injury[20] to any person;
    (v) substantial financial gain to any person; and
    (vi) serious[21] financial loss to any person; or
(b) is intended or is likely to lead to any of those consequences[22].
An arrestable offence which consists of making a threat is serious if carrying out the threat would be likely to lead to any of the consequences specified in head (a) (i) to (vi) above[23].
An offence under the Prevention of Terrorism (Temporary Provisions) Act 1989[24] is always a serious arrestable offence[25] and an attempt or conspiracy to commit any such offence is also always a serious arrestable offence[26].

1 See para 76 et seq ante.
2 See para 431 et seq ante.
3 See para 436 et seq ante.
4 See para 514 ante.
5 See para 493 ante.
6 See para 510 ante.
7 See para 505 ante.
8 See para 521 et seq ante.
9 Ie any of the offences mentioned in the definition of 'drug trafficking offence' in the Drug Trafficking Offences Act 1986 s 38 (1) (a)–(d): see para 1305 note 2 post.
10 Ie contrary to the Explosive Substances Act 1883 s 2 (as substituted): see para 478 ante.
11 Ie contrary to the Sexual Offences Act 1956 s 5: see para 526 ante.
12 Ie contrary to the Firearms Act 1968 s 16 (as amended): see para 230 ante.

13 Ie contrary to ibid s 17 (1): see para 231 ante.
14 Ie contrary to ibid s 18: see para 234 ante.
15 Ie contrary to the Road Traffic Act 1988 s 1: see para 449 ante.
16 Ie contrary to the Taking of Hostages Act 1982 s 1: see para 139 ante.
17 Ie contrary to the Aviation Security Act 1982 s 1: see AVIATION.
18 Police and Criminal Evidence Act 1984 s 116 (1), (2), Sch 5 Pts I, II (amended by the Drug Trafficking Offences Act 1986 s 36; the Road Traffic (Consequential Provisions) Act 1988 s 4, Sch 3 para 27 (5); the Criminal Justice Act 1988 s 170 (1), Sch 15 paras 97, 102). The offence of torture is committed contrary to the Criminal Justice Act 1988 s 134: see para 504 ante.
19 For the meaning of 'arrestable offence' see para 703 ante.
20 For these purposes, 'injury' includes any disease and any impairment of a person's physical or mental condition: Police and Criminal Evidence Act 1984 s 116 (1), (8).
21 For these purposes, loss is serious if, having regard to all the circumstances, it is serious for the person who suffers it: ibid s 116 (1), (7). See also *R v McIvor* [1987] Crim LR 409.
22 Police and Criminal Evidence Act 1984 s 116 (1), (3), (6).
23 Ibid s 116 (1), (4).
24 Ie under the Prevention of Terrorism (Temporary Provisions) Act 1989 ss 2, 8, 9, 10 or 11: see paras 111, 106, 107, 115, 114, 116 respectively ante.
25 Ie for the purposes of the Police and Criminal Evidence Act 1984 s 56 (see para 729 post) or s 58 (see para 730 post).
26 Ibid s 116 (1), (5) (amended by the Prevention of Terrorism (Temporary Provisions) Act 1989 s 25(1), Sch 8 para 6 (1), (7)).

705. Power of arrest for arrestable offence. Any person may arrest without a warrant:

(1) anyone who is in the act of committing an arrestable offence[1];
(2) anyone whom he has reasonable grounds for suspecting to be committing such an offence[2].

Where an arrestable offence has been committed, any person may arrest without a warrant:

(a) anyone who is guilty of the offence;
(b) anyone whom he has reasonable grounds for suspecting to be guilty of it[3].

Where a constable has reasonable grounds for suspecting that an arrestable offence has been committed, he may arrest without a warrant anyone whom he has reasonable grounds for suspecting to be guilty of the offence[4].

A constable may arrest without a warrant:

(i) anyone who is about to commit an arrestable offence;
(ii) anyone whom he has reasonable grounds for suspecting to be about to commit an arrestable offence[5].

1 For the meaning of 'arrestable offence' see para 703 ante.
2 Police and Criminal Evidence Act 1984 s 24 (4). As to the use of force by a person in making an arrest for an arrestable offence see para 706 post.
3 Ibid s 24(5).
4 Ibid s 24 (6). As to a constable's power to use reasonable force see para 658 ante.
    Whether there is reasonable cause for suspecting a person to be guilty of an offence is to be determined objectively: *Castorina v Chief Constable of Surrey* [1988] NLJR 180, CA. As to reasonable suspicion see also *Hussien (Shaabin Bin) v Kam (Chong Fook)* [1970] AC 942, [1969] 3 All ER 1626, PC; and *Holgate-Mohammed v Duke* [1984] AC 437, 79 Cr App Rep 120, HL; *Ward v Chief Constable of Avon and Somerset Constabulary* (1986) Times, 26 June, CA; *Holtham v Commissioner of Police of the Metropolis* (1987) Times, 28 November, CA (all decided under the Criminal Law Act 1967 s 2 (repealed)). See also *Chapman v DPP* (1988) 89 Cr App Rep 190, CA.
5 Police and Criminal Evidence Act 1984 s 24 (7).

706. Use of force in making arrest. A person[1] may use such force as is reasonable in the circumstances in the prevention of crime, or in effecting or assisting in the lawful arrest of offenders or suspected offenders or of persons unlawfully at large[2].

A person arrested may be handcuffed if he attempts to escape or if it is necessary to prevent his escaping[3].

A person who assaults anyone with intent to resist or prevent his own arrest or that of another or who causes grievous bodily harm with intent to prevent arrest commits an offence[4]. Where a person uses force in order to escape from arrest and death results, he may be guilty of manslaughter[5].

1 As to the use of force by a constable see para 658 ante.
2 Criminal Law Act 1967 s 3 (1). Section 3 (1) replaces the rules of common law on the question when force used for a purpose there mentioned is justified by that purpose: s 3 (2).
   As to the use of force see *R v Coroner for Durham County, ex p A-G* (1978) Times, 29 June, DC; *Allen v Metropolitan Police Comr* [1980] Crim LR 441, DC. The only circumstances which are relevant for the purposes of the Criminal Law Act 1967 s 3 (1) are the immediate circumstances in which the force is used: *Farrell (formerly McLaughlin) v Secretary of State for Defence* [1980] 1 All ER 166, 70 Cr App Rep 224, HL. The Criminal Law Act 1967 s 3 (1) may afford a defence to a charge of reckless driving where the intention is to assist arrest: *R v Renouf* [1986] 2 All ER 449, 82 Cr App Rep 344, CA.
3 *Osborn v Veitch* (1858) 1 F & F 317; *Levy v Edwards* (1823) 1 C & P 40 at 43; *Wright v Court* (1825) 4 B & C 596; *Leigh v Cole* (1853) 6 Cox CC 329; *R v Taylor* (1895) 59 JP 393.
4 See paras 320, 321 ante. Obstructing the arrest of a person for an arrestable offence may constitute an offence: see para 51 ante. For the meaning of 'arrestable offence' see para 703 ante. As to escape from lawful custody see para 325 ante.
5 *R v Porter* (1873) 12 Cox CC 444. As to the circumstances in which such action will amount to murder see para 425 et seq ante.

707. Arrest for non-arrestable offence. Where a constable has reasonable grounds for suspecting that any offence which is not an arrestable offence[1] has been committed or attempted, or is being committed or attempted, he may arrest the relevant person[2] if it appears to him that service of a summons is impracticable or inappropriate because any of the general arrest conditions[3] is satisfied[4].

The general arrest conditions are:
(1) that the name of the relevant person is unknown to, and cannot be readily ascertained by, the constable;
(2) that the constable has reasonable grounds for doubting whether a name furnished by the relevant person as his name is his real name;
(3) that (a) the relevant person has failed to furnish a satisfactory address for service[5]; or (b) the constable has reasonable grounds for doubting whether an address furnished by the relevant person is a satisfactory address for service;
(4) that the constable has reasonable grounds for believing that arrest is necessary to prevent the relevant person (a) causing physical injury to himself or any other person; (b) suffering physical injury; (c) causing loss of or damage to property; (d) committing an offence against public decency; or (e) causing an unlawful obstruction of the highway;
(5) that the constable has reasonable grounds for believing that arrest is necessary to protect a child or other vulnerable person from the relevant person[6].

1 For the meaning of 'arrestable offence' see para 703 ante.
2 For these purposes, 'the relevant person' means any person whom the constable has reasonable grounds to suspect of having committed or having attempted to commit the offence or of being in the course of committing or attempting to commit it: Police and Criminal Evidence Act 1984 s 25 (2).

3 Ie the general arrest conditions in ibid s 25 (3): see heads (1)–(5) infra.
4 Ibid s 25 (1). Section 25 does not prejudice any power of arrest conferred apart from s 25: s 25 (6). As to a constable's use of reasonable force see para 658 ante.
5 For these purposes, an address is a satisfactory address for service if it appears to the constable (1) that the relevant person will be at it for a sufficiently long period for it to be possible to serve him with a summons; or (2) that some other person specified by the relevant person will accept service of a summons for the relevant person at it: ibid s 25 (4). As to failure to furnish such an address see *Nicholas v Parsonage* [1987] RTR 199, DC.
6 Police and Criminal Evidence Act 1984 s 25 (3). Nothing in s 25 (3) (d) (see head (4) supra) authorises the arrest of a person under s 25 (3) (d) (iv) (see head (4) (d) supra) except where members of the public going about their normal business cannot reasonably be expected to avoid the person to be arrested: s 25 (5). See *G v DPP* [1989] Crim LR 150, DC.

708. Preserved powers of arrest. Subject to certain exceptions[1], so much of any Act, including a local Act, passed before the Police and Criminal Evidence Act 1984 as enabled a constable:

(1) to arrest a person for an offence without a warrant; or

(2) to arrest a person otherwise than for an offence without a warrant or an order of a court,

has ceased to have effect[2].

1 Nothing in the Police and Criminal Evidence Act 1984 s 26 (1) affects the enactments specified in s 26 (2), Sch 2 (amended by the Representation of the People Act 1985 s 25 (1); the Prevention of Terrorism (Temporary Provisions) Act 1989 s 25 (2), Sch 9 Pt I): Police and Criminal Evidence Act 1984 s 26 (2).
    The enactments so specified are: the Military Lands Act 1892 s 17 (2); the Protection of Animals Act 1911 s 12 (1); the Emergency Powers Act 1920 s 2; the Public Order Act 1936 s 7 (3) (amended by the Public Order Act 1986 s 40 (3), Sch 3); the Prison Act 1952 s 49 (as amended); the Visiting Forces Act 1952 s 13 (amended by the Revision of the Army and Air Force Acts (Transitional Provisions) Act 1955 ss 3, 5 (2), Sch 2 para 17 (1), Sch 4); the Army Act 1955 ss 186, 190B (amended and added by the Armed Forces Act 1971 ss 56 (1), 44 (2) respectively); the Air Force Act 1955 ss 186, 190B (amended and added by the Armed Forces Act 1971 ss 56 (1), 44 (2) respectively); the Naval Discipline Act 1957 ss 104, 105 (amended by the Armed Forces Act 1971 s 56); the Street Offences Act 1959 s 1 (3); the Children and Young Persons Act 1969 ss 28 (2), 32 (as amended); the Immigration Act 1971 ss 2, 5, 24 (2), Sch 2 paras 17 (1), 24, 33, Sch 3 para 7 (added by the Criminal Justice Act 1982 s 64, Sch 10 para 2); the Road Traffic Act 1972 ss 5 (5), 7, 100 (repealed: see now the Road Traffic Act 1988 ss 4 (6), 6, 103 (3)); the Bail Act 1976 s 7 (3); the Criminal Law Act 1977 ss 6 (6), 7 (11), 9 (7), 10 (5); the Child Care Act 1980 s 16; the Reserve Forces Act 1980 ss 73, 106, Sch 5; the Animal Health Act 1981 ss 60 (5), 61 (1) (amended by the Police and Criminal Evidence Act 1984 ss 26 (1), 119, Sch 6 Pt I, Sch 7 Pt I); the Representation of the People Act 1983 s 23, Sch 1 r 36; the Mental Health Act 1983 ss 18, 35 (10), 36 (8), 38 (7), 136 (1), 138; the Repatriation of Prisoners Act 1984 s 5 (5).
2 Police and Criminal Evidence Act 1984 s 26 (1). Section 26 has not repealed the Criminal Justice Act 1967 s 91 (1) (power of any person to arrest without warrant for disorderly behaviour while drunk in a public place: see INTOXICATING LIQUOR vol 26 para 412): *DPP v Kitching* (1989) Times, 17 November, DC.

709. Common law power of arrest to deal with or prevent breaches of the peace. A constable or an ordinary citizen may at common law arrest without warrant (1) a person committing a breach of the peace in his presence; (2) a person who he reasonably believes[1] will commit such a breach of the peace in the immediate future, even though at the time of the arrest such person has not committed any breach; and (3) a person who has committed a breach of the peace where it is reasonably believed that a renewal of the breach is threatened[2]. There is no breach of the peace for these purposes unless an act is done or threatened to be done which (a) actually harms a person or, in his presence, his property; (b) is likely to cause such harm; or (c) puts someone in fear of such harm[3].

Nothing in the Public Order Act 1986 affects this common law power of arrest[4], which may be exercised by a constable on private premises[5] even where no member of the public is present[6].

1 Where the power of arrest is exercised on the basis of a belief that a breach of the peace is imminent, not only must the belief be honest, albeit mistaken, but it must be founded on reasonable grounds: *R v Howell* [1982] QB 416, 73 Cr App Rep 31, CA.
2 *R v Howell* [1982] QB 416, 73 Cr App Rep 31, CA; and see *Hardy v Murphy* (1795) 1 Esp 294; *Levy v Edwards* (1823) 1 C & P 40; *Booth v Hanley* (1826) 2 C & P 288; *R v Bright* (1830) 4 C & P 387; *Timothy v Simpson* (1835) 1 Cr M & R 757; *Baynes v Brewster* (1841) 2 QB 375; *Price v Seeley* (1843) 10 Cl & Fin 28, HL; *R v Walker* (1854) Dears CC 358, CCR; *Derecourt v Corbishley* (1855) 5 E & B 188; *R v Light* (1857) 27 LJMC 1 at 3, CCR per Williams J; *Griffin v Coleman* (1859) 4 H & N 265. As to restraint falling short of arrest see *Albert v Lavin* [1982] AC 546, 74 Cr App Rep 150, CA.
   A constable makes a valid arrest when he reasonably believes a breach of the peace is about to be committed if he says merely, 'I am arresting you for a breach of the peace', and is not to be taken in such a case as referring only to the actual commission of a breach: *R v Howell* supra.
3 *R v Howell* [1982] QB 416, 73 Cr App Rep 31, CA.
4 Public Order Act 1986 s 40 (4). As to a constable's power of arrest without warrant under s 5 see para 153 ante.
5 *R v Chief Constable of Devon and Cornwall Constabulary, ex p Central Electricity Generating Board* [1982] QB 458, [1981] 3 All ER 826, CA; *McConnell v Chief Constable of Greater Manchester Police* (1989) Times, 8 November, CA.
6 *McConnell v Chief Constable of Greater Manchester Police* (1989) Times, 8 November, CA.

(iv) Procedure following Arrest

710. Information to be given on arrest. Where a person is arrested, otherwise than by being informed that he is under arrest, the arrest is not lawful unless the person arrested is informed that he is under arrest as soon as is practicable after his arrest[1].

No arrest is lawful unless the person arrested is informed of the ground for the arrest at the time of, or as soon as is practicable after, the arrest[2].

Where a person is arrested by a constable, the above provisions apply regardless of whether the ground for the arrest is obvious[3].

However, nothing in the above provisions is to be taken to require a person to be informed (1) that he is under arrest; or (2) of the ground for the arrest, if it was not reasonably practicable for him to be so informed by reason of his having escaped from arrest before the information could be given[4].

1 Police and Criminal Evidence Act 1984 s 28 (1); and see *R v Brosch* [1988] Crim LR 743, CA.
2 Police and Criminal Evidence Act 1984 s 28 (3). 'At the time' of the arrest comprehends a short but reasonable period of time around the moment of arrest, both before and after; whether words were spoken at the time of arrest or not is a question of fact: *Nicholas v Parsonage* [1987] RTR 199, DC. It is not sufficient to tell a person that he is being arrested because he has not given his name and address as required (see para 707 ante); there must be an indication in some words of an offence for which the arrest is being made: *Nicholas v Parsonage* supra.
   A person arrested without warrant (see para 703 et seq ante) must be given adequate information of the reason for his arrest; but the question whether a police officer has complied with this obligation must be answered taking into account all the background circumstances; and the officer's conduct must be judged bearing in mind that he is not required to do more than is reasonable in those circumstances: *Abbassy v Metropolitan Police Comr* [1990] 1 All ER 193, CA.
   An arresting officer is under a duty to maintain arrest until it is possible to inform the person arrested of the ground of arrest, but subsequent failure to give this information does not retrospectively make the officer's acts in the intermediate period unlawful: *DPP v Hawkins* [1988] 3 All ER 673, 88 Cr App Rep 166, DC.

3 Police and Criminal Evidence Act 1984 s 28 (2), (4).
4 Ibid s 28 (5).

711. Arrest elsewhere than at police station. Where a person is arrested by a constable for an offence or is taken into custody by a constable after being arrested for an offence by a person other than a constable, at any place other than a police station[1], he must be taken to a police station by a constable as soon as practicable after the arrest[2].

A constable who is working in a locality covered by a police station which is not a designated police station[3] and a constable who belongs to a body of constables maintained by an authority other than a police authority may take an arrested person to any police station unless it appears to the constable that it may be necessary to keep the arrested person in police detention for more than six hours[4].

Any constable may take an arrested person to any police station if:

(1) either of the following conditions is satisfied: (a) the constable has arrested him without the assistance of any other constable and no other constable is available to assist him; (b) the constable has taken him into custody from a person other than a constable without the assistance of any other constable and no other constable is available to assist him; and

(2) it appears to the constable that he will be unable to take the arrested person to a designated police station without the arrested person injuring himself, the constable or some other person[5].

If the first police station to which an arrested person is taken after his arrest is not a designated police station, he must be taken to a designated police station not more than six hours after his arrival at the first police station unless he is released previously[6].

A person arrested by a constable at a place other than a police station must be released if a constable is satisfied, before the person arrested reaches a police station, that there are no grounds for keeping him under arrest[7]. A constable who so releases a person must record the fact that he has done so[8]; and he must make the record as soon as is practicable after the release[9].

1 As to arrest of a juvenile at his place of education see para 741 note 9 post.
2 Police and Criminal Evidence Act 1984 s 30 (1). Subject to s 30 (3), (5) (see infra), the police station to which an arrested person is taken under s 30 (1) must be a designated police station: s 30 (2). Nothing in s 30 (1) prevents a constable delaying taking a person who has been arrested to a police station if the presence of that person elsewhere is necessary in order to carry out such investigations as it is reasonable to carry out immediately: s 30 (10). However, nothing in s 30 (10) is to be taken to affect the Immigration Act 1971 s 4, Sch 2 para 18 (3): Police and Criminal Evidence Act 1984 s 30 (13).
   Where there is delay in taking a person who has been arrested to a police station after his arrest, the reasons for the delay must be recorded when he first arrives at a police station: s 30 (11).
   Nothing in s 30 (1) is to be taken to affect (1) the Immigration Act 1971 Sch 2 paras 16 (3) or 18 (1); (2) the Criminal Justice Act 1972 s 34 (1); or (3) the Prevention of Terrorism (Temporary Provisions) Act 1989 ss 4 (4), 15 (6), (9), 16 (1), (3), (4), Sch 2 paras 7 (4), 8 (4), (5), Sch 5 paras 6 (6), 7 (4), (5): Police and Criminal Evidence Act 1984 s 30 (12) (amended by the Prevention of Terrorism (Temporary Provisions) Act 1989 s 25 (1), Sch 8 para 6 (1), (2)).
3 For the meaning of 'designated police station' see para 715 post.
4 Police and Criminal Evidence Act 1984 s 30 (3), (4).
5 Ibid s 30 (5).
6 Ibid s 30 (6).
7 Ibid s 30 (7).
8 Ibid s 30 (8).
9 Ibid s 30 (9).

712. Arrest for further offence. Where (1) a person has been arrested for an offence and is at a police station in consequence of that arrest; and (2) it appears to a constable that, if he were released from that arrest, he would be liable to arrest for some other offence, he must be arrested for that other offence[1].

1 Police and Criminal Evidence Act 1984 s 31. The purpose of s 31 is to prevent the release and immediate re-arrest of the accused; there is nothing to prevent the constable delaying arrest under s 31 until such time as the accused's release is imminent: *R v Samuel* [1988] QB 615 at 622, 87 Cr App Rep 232 at 238, CA obiter per Hodgson J.

713. Bail after arrest. A release on bail[1] of a person under the Police and Criminal Evidence Act 1984[2] is a release on bail granted in accordance with the Bail Act 1976[3]; but nothing in the Bail Act 1976 prevents the rearrest[4] without warrant of a person released on bail subject to a duty to attend at a police station if new evidence justifying a further arrest has come to light since his release[5].

Where a person arrested for an offence who was released on bail subject to a duty to attend at a police station so attends, he may be detained without charge in connection with that offence only if the custody officer[6] at the police station has reasonable grounds for believing that his detention is necessary to secure or preserve evidence relating to the offence, or to obtain such evidence by questioning him[7].

Where a custody officer has granted bail to a person subject to a duty to appear at a police station, the custody officer may give notice in writing to that person that his attendance at the police station is not required[8].

1 For these purposes, references to 'bail' are references to bail subject to a duty (1) to appear before a magistrates' court at such time and such place; or (2) to attend at such police station at such time, as the custody officer may appoint; Police and Criminal Evidence Act 1984 s 47 (3). Section 47 (3) is subject to s 47 (4) (see infra): s 47 (3).
2 Ie under ibid Pt IV (ss 34–52): see para 714 et seq post.
3 See para 883 et seq post.
4 Where a person who was released on bail subject to a duty to attend at a police station is rearrested, the provisions of the Police and Criminal Evidence Act 1984 Pt IV (ss 34–52) apply to him as they apply to a person arrested for the first time: s 47 (7).
5 Ibid s 47 (1), (2).
6 As to custody officers see para 716 post.
7 Police and Criminal Evidence Act 1984 s 47 (5). Where a person is so detained, any time during which he was in police detention prior to being granted bail is to be included as part of any period which falls to be calculated under Pt IV (ss 34–52): s 47 (6). For the meaning of 'in police detention' see para 716 note 5 post.
8 Ibid s 47 (4).

(4) SEARCH UPON ARREST

714. Search upon arrest. A constable may search an arrested person, in any case where the person to be searched has been arrested at a place other than a police station, if the constable has reasonable grounds for believing that the arrested person may present a danger to himself or others[1].

A constable also has power in any such case:

(1) to search the arrested person for anything (a) which he might use to assist him to escape from lawful custody; or (b) which might be evidence relating to an offence; and

(2) to enter and search any premises[2] in which he was when arrested or immediately before he was arrested for evidence relating to the offence for which he has been arrested[3].

The power to search conferred by heads (1) and (2) above is only a power to search to the extent that is reasonably required for the purpose of discovering any such thing or any such evidence[4]; and the powers conferred by the above provisions to search a person are not to be construed as authorising a constable to require a person to remove any of his clothing in public other than an outer coat, jacket or gloves[5].

A constable may not search a person in the exercise of the power conferred by head (1) above unless he has reasonable grounds for believing that the person to be searched may have concealed on him anything for which a search is so permitted[6]; nor may a constable search premises in the exercise of the power conferred by head (2) above unless he has reasonable grounds for believing that there is evidence for which a search is so permitted on the premises[7].

In so far as the power of search conferred by head (2) above relates to premises consisting of two or more separate dwellings, it is limited to a power to search:

(i) any dwelling in which the arrest took place or in which the person arrested was immediately before his arrest; and

(ii) any parts of the premises which the occupier of any such dwelling uses in common with the occupiers of any other dwellings comprised in the premises[8].

1 Police and Criminal Evidence Act 1984 s 32 (1). Nothing in s 32 is to be taken to affect the power conferred by the Prevention of Terrorism (Temporary Provisions) Act 1989 s 15 (3)–(5) (see para 118 ante): Police and Criminal Evidence Act 1984 s 32 (10) (amended by the Prevention of Terrorism (Temporary Provisions) Act 1989 s 25 (1), Sch 8 para 6 (1), (3)).

   A constable searching a person in the exercise of such power may seize and retain anything he finds, if he has reasonable grounds for believing that the person searched might use it to cause physical injury to himself or to any other person: Police and Criminal Evidence Act 1984 s 32 (8).

2 For the meaning of 'premises' see para 671 note 3 ante.

3 Police and Criminal Evidence Act 1984 s 32 (2); and see *R v Churchill* [1989] Crim LR 226, CA. A constable searching a person in the exercise of the power conferred by the Police and Criminal Evidence Act 1984 s 30 (2) (a) (see head (1) supra) may seize and retain anything he finds, other than an item subject to legal privilege, if he has reasonable grounds for believing: (1) that he might use it to assist him to escape from lawful custody; or (2) that it is evidence of an offence or has been obtained in consequence of the commission of an offence: s 32 (9). For the meaning of 'items subject to legal privilege' see para 672 note 5 ante.

4 Ibid s 32 (3).

5 Ibid s 32 (4).

6 Ibid s 32 (5).

7 Ibid s 32 (6).

8 Ibid s 32 (7).

(5) DETENTION

715. Meaning of 'designated police station'. The chief officer of police for each police area must designate the police stations in his area which[1] are to be the stations in that area to be used for the purpose of detaining arrested persons[2]. A chief officer's duty is to designate police stations appearing to him to provide enough accommodation for that purpose[3]. A chief officer may[4] designate a station which was not previously designated and may direct that a designation of a station previously made shall cease to operate[5].

'Designated police station' means a police station for the time being so designated[6].

1 Ie subject to the Police and Criminal Evidence Act 1984 s 30 (3), (5): see para 711 ante.
2 Ibid s 35 (1).
3 Ibid s 35 (2).
4 Ie without prejudice to the Interpretation Act 1978 s 12 (continuity of duties: see STATUTES vol 44 para 935).
5 Police and Criminal Evidence Act 1984 s 35 (3).
6 Ibid ss 35 (4), 118 (1).

716. Custody officers. One or more custody officers must be appointed for each designated police station[1]. A custody officer for a designated police station must be appointed:

(1) by the chief officer of police for the area in which the designated police station is situated; or

(2) by such other police officer as the chief officer of police for that area may direct[2].

No officer may be appointed a custody officer unless he is of at least the rank of sergeant[3]. However, an officer of any rank may perform the functions of a custody officer at a designated police station if a custody officer is not readily available to perform them[4].

None of the functions of a custody officer in relation to a person may be performed by an officer who at the time when the function falls to be performed is involved in the investigation of an offence for which that person is in police detention[5] at that time[6]; but nothing in that provision is to be taken to prevent a custody officer:

(a) performing any function assigned to custody officers by the Police and Criminal Evidence Act 1984 or by a code of practice[7] issued under the Act;

(b) carrying out the statutory duty[8] imposed on custody officers;

(c) doing anything in connection with the identification of a suspect; or

(d) doing anything[9] under the Road Traffic Act 1988[10].

Where an arrested person is taken to a police station which is not a designated police station, the functions in relation to him which at a designated police station would be the functions of a custody officer must be performed:

(i) by an officer who is not involved in the investigation of an offence for which he is in police detention, if such an officer is readily available; and

(ii) if no such officer is readily available, by the officer who took him to the station or any other officer[11].

Where[12] an officer of a force maintained by a police authority who took an arrested person to a police station is to perform the functions of a custody officer in relation to him, the officer must inform an officer who is attached to a designated police station and is of at least the rank of inspector, that he is to do so[13]. Such duty must be performed as soon as it is practicable to perform it[14].

1 Police and Criminal Evidence Act 1984 s 36 (1). References to a custody officer in ss 36 (9)–122 include references to an officer other than a custody officer who is performing the functions of a custody officer by virtue of s 36 (4) or s 36 (7): s 36 (8); Code of Practice for the Detention, Treatment and Questioning of Persons by Police Officers para 1.9. For the meaning of 'designated police station' see para 715 ante.

2 Police and Criminal Evidence Act 1984 s 36 (2).
3 Ibid s 36 (3); and see para 659 ante.
4 Ibid s 36 (4).
5 For these purposes, a person is in police detention if (1) he has been taken to a police station after being arrested for an offence or after being arrested under the Prevention of Terrorism (Temporary Provisions) Act 1989 s 14 or under s 16 (1), (3), (4), Sch 5 para 6 by an examining officer who is a constable; or (2) he is arrested at a police station after attending voluntarily at the station or accompanying a constable to it, and is detained there or is detained elsewhere in the charge of a constable: Police and Criminal Evidence Act 1984 s 118 (2) (amended by the Prevention of Terrorism (Temporary Provisions) Act 1989 s 25 (1), Sch 8 para 6 (1), (8)); Code of Practice for the Detention, Treatment and Questioning of Persons by Police Officers paras 5.2, 6.2, Annex B, note B3. A person who is at court after being charged is not, however, in police detention for these purposes: Police and Criminal Evidence Act 1984 s 118 (2) (as so amended); Code of Practice for the Detention, Treatment and Questioning of Persons by Police Officers paras 5.2, 6.2, Annex B, note B3. As to voluntary attendance at a police station see para 692 ante.
6 Police and Criminal Evidence Act 1984 s 36 (5). Section 36 (5) is subject to s 36 (6)–(10) (see infra) and s 39 (2) (see para 721 post)): s 36 (5).
7 As to codes of practice see para 657 ante.
8 Ie the duty imposed on custody officers by ibid s 39: see para 721 post.
9 Ie anything under the Road Traffic Act 1988 ss 7, 8: see ROAD TRAFFIC.
10 Police and Criminal Evidence Act 1984 s 36 (6) (amended by the Road Traffic (Consequential Provisions) Act 1988 s 4, Sch 3 para 27 (3)).
11 Police and Criminal Evidence Act 1984 s 36 (7).
12 Ie by virtue of ibid s 36 (7): see supra.
13 Ibid s 36 (8).
14 Ibid s 36 (9).

717. Custody records. A separate custody record must be opened as soon as practicable for each person who is brought to a police station under arrest or is arrested at the police station having attended there voluntarily[1]. All information which has to be recorded[2] must be recorded as soon as practicable in the custody record unless otherwise specified[3]. In the case of any action requiring the authority of an officer of a specified rank, his name and rank must be noted in the custody record[4].

The custody officer[5] is responsible for the accuracy and completeness of the custody record and for ensuring that the record or a copy of the record accompanies a detained person if he is transferred to another police station[6]. The record must show the time of, and reason for, transfer and the time a person is released from detention[6].

When a person leaves police detention, he or his legal representative must be supplied on request with a copy of the custody record as soon as practicable; and this entitlement lasts for 12 months after his release[7].

All entries in custody and written interviews records must be timed and signed by the maker[8].

Any refusal by a person to sign either a custody or an interview record when asked to do so[9] must be recorded[10].

1 Code of Practice for the Detention, Treatment and Questioning of Persons by Police Officers para 2.1.
2 Ie under the Code of Practice for the Detention, Treatment and Questioning of Persons by Police Officers: see para 691 ante.
3 Ibid para 2.1.
4 Ibid para 2.2
5 As to custody officers see para 716 ante.
6 Code of Practice for the Detention, Treatment and Questioning of Persons by Police Officers para 2.3

7 Ibid para 2.4. The person who has been detained, the appropriate adult or legal representative who gives reasonable notice of a request to inspect the original custody record after the person has left police detention should be allowed to do so: para 2.4, note 2A. For these purposes, 'the appropriate adult' means:

(1) in the case of juvenile (a) his parent or guardian, or, if he is in care, the care authority or organisation; (b) a social worker; or (c) failing either of the above, another responsible adult who is not a police officer or employed by the police;

(2) in the case of a person who is mentally ill or mentally handicapped (a) a relative, guardian or other person responsible for his care or custody; (b) someone who has experience of dealing with mentally ill or mentally handicapped persons but is not a police officer or employed by the police; or (c) failing either of the above, some other responsible adult who is not a police officer or employed by the police:

para 1.7. In the case of persons who are mentally ill or mentally handicapped, it may in certain circumstances be more satisfactory for all concerned if the appropriate adult is someone who has experience or training in their care rather than a relative lacking such qualifications; but, if the person himself prefers a relative to a better qualified stranger, his wishes should, if practicable, be respected: para 1.7, note 1C. See also para 741 note 1 post; and see *DPP v Blake* [1989] 1 WLR 432, 89 Cr App Rep 179, DC (justices entitled to find that juvenile's estranged father was not an 'appropriate adult'). 'The appropriate adult cannot be a person with whom the the juvenile had no empathy': *DPP v Blake* supra at 440 and at 187 per Mann LJ.

8 Code of Practice for the Detention, Treatment and Questioning of Persons by Police Officers para 2.5.

9 Ie under the Code of Practice for the Detention, Treatment and Questioning of Persons by Police Officers.

10 Ibid para 2.6.

718. Duties of custody officer before charge. Where (1) a person is arrested for an offence without a warrant or under a warrant not indorsed for bail[1]; or (2) a person returns to a police station to answer to bail, the custody officer[2] at each police station where he is detained after his arrest must determine whether he has before him sufficient evidence to charge that person with the offence for which he was arrested and may detain him at the police station for such period as is necessary to enable him to do so[3].

If the custody officer determines that he does not have such evidence before him, the person arrested must be released either on bail or without bail, unless the custody officer has reasonable grounds for believing that his detention without being charged is necessary to secure or preserve evidence relating to an offence for which he is under arrest or to obtain such evidence by questioning him[4]. If the custody officer has reasonable grounds for so believing he may authorise the person arrested to be kept in police detention[5].

Where a custody officer authorises a person who has not been charged to be kept in police detention, he must, as soon as is practicable, make a written record of the grounds for the detention[6]. The written record must be made in the presence of the person arrested who must at that time be informed by the custody officer of the grounds for his detention[7].

If the custody officer determines that he has before him sufficient evidence to charge the person arrested with the offence for which he was arrested, the person arrested must be charged or must be released[8] without charge, either on bail or without bail[9].

Where an arrested juvenile[10] who was arrested without a warrant is not released and it appears to the custody officer that a decision falls to be taken[11] whether to lay an information in respect of an offence alleged to have been committed by the arrested juvenile, it is the duty of the custody officer to inform him that such a decision falls to be taken and to specify the offence[12]. It is also the duty of the custody officer to take such steps as are practicable to ascertain the identity of a person responsible for the welfare of the arrested juvenile[13]; and, if he ascertains the identity of any such person and it is practicable to give that person the required information[14], to give that person the information as soon as it is practicable to do so[15].

1 For these purposes, 'indorsed for bail' means indorsed with a direction for bail in accordance with the Magistrates' Courts Act 1980 s 117 (2) (see para 699 ante): Police and Criminal Evidence Act 1984 s 37 (15).
2 As to custody officers see para 716 ante.
3 Police and Criminal Evidence Act 1984 s 37 (1). The duty imposed on the custody officer under s 37 (1) must be carried out by him as soon as practicable after the person arrested arrives at the police station or, in the case of a person arrested at the police station, as soon as practicable after the arrest: s 37 (10).
4 Ibid s 37 (2). As to bail after arrest see para 713 ante.
5 Ibid s 37 (3). For the meaning of 'in police detention' see para 716 note 5 ante.
6 Ibid s 37 (4).
7 Ibid s 37 (5). Section 37 (5) does not apply, however, where the person arrested is, at the time when the written record is made (1) incapable of understanding what is said to him; (2) violent or likely to become violent; or (3) in urgent need of medical attention: s 37 (6). As to the application of s 37 (1)–(6) to a person whose detention is under review see para 761 note 4 post.
8 Where a person is so released and at the time of his release a decision whether he should be prosecuted for the offence for which he was arrested has not been taken, it is the duty of the custody officer so to inform him: ibid s 37 (8).
9 Ibid s 37 (7). Section 37 (7) is subject to s 41 (7) (see para 760 post): s 37 (7). If the person arrested is not in a fit state to be dealt with under s 37 (7), he may be kept in police detention until he is: s 37 (9). A police officer carrying out the duties imposed on him by s 37 and s 38 (see para 719 post) when charging an arrested person has no power to perform those duties on behalf of, or to entrust the subsequent prosecution to, a private individual: *R v Ealing Magistrates' Court, ex p Dixon* [1989] 2 All ER 1050, [1989] 3 WLR 1098, DC.
10 For these purposes, 'arrested juvenile' means a person arrested with or without a warrant who appears to be under the age of 17 and is not excluded from the Police and Criminal Evidence Act 1984 Pt IV (ss 34–52) by s 52 (see para 691 note 1 ante): s 37 (15).
11 Ie in pursuance of the Children and Young Persons Act 1969 s 5 (2): see INFANTS vol 24 para 898:2.
12 Police and Criminal Evidence Act 1984 s 37 (11).
13 For these purposes, the persons who may be responsible for the welfare of an arrested juvenile are (1) his parent or guardian; and (2) any other person who has for the time being assumed responsibility for his welfare: ibid s 37 (13).
14 Ie the information required by ibid s 37 (11): see supra.
15 Ibid s 37 (12). If it appears to the custody officer that a supervision order as defined in the Children and Young Persons Act 1969 s 11 (see para 1275 post) is in force in respect of the arrested juvenile, the custody officer must also give the information to the person responsible for the arrested juvenile's supervision, as soon as it is practicable to do so: Police and Criminal Evidence Act 1984 s 37 (14).

719. Duties of custody officer after charge. Where a person arrested for an offence otherwise than under a warrant indorsed for bail[1] is charged with an offence, the custody officer must order his release from police detention, either on bail or without bail, unless:

(1) if the person arrested is not an arrested juvenile[2]:

(a) his name or address cannot be ascertained or the custody officer[3] has reasonable grounds for doubting whether a name or address furnished by him as his name or address is his real name or address;

(b) the custody officer has reasonable grounds for believing that the detention of the person arrested is necessary for his own protection or to prevent him from causing physical injury to any other person or from causing loss of or damage to property; or

(c) the custody officer has reasonable grounds for believing that the person arrested will fail to appear in court to answer to bail or that his detention is necessary to prevent him from interfering with the administration of justice or with the investigation of offences or of a particular offence;

(2) if he is an arrested juvenile:

(a) any of the requirements of head (1) above is satisfied; or

(b) the custody officer has reasonable grounds for believing that he ought to be detained in his own interests[4].

If the release of a person arrested is not so required, the custody officer may authorise him to be kept in police detention[5]. Where a custody officer authorises a person who has been charged to be kept in police detention, he must, as soon as practicable, make a written record of the grounds for the detention[6]. The written record must be made in the presence of the person charged who must at that time be informed by the custody officer of the grounds for his detention[7].

1 For the meaning of 'indorsed for bail' see para 718 note 1 ante.
2 For the meaning of 'arrested juvenile' see para 718 note 10 ante.
3 As to custody of officers see para 716 ante.
4 Police and Criminal Evidence Act 1984 s 38 (1). Where a custody officer authorises an arrested juvenile to be so kept in police detention, the custody officer must, unless he certifies that it is impracticable to do so, make arrangements for the arrested juvenile to be taken into the care of a local authority and detained by the authority; and it is lawful to detain him in pursuance of the arrangements: s 38 (6). A certificate so made in respect of an arrested juvenile must be produced to the court before which he is first brought thereafter: s 38 (7). For these purposes, 'local authority', except in relation to proceedings under the Children and Young Persons Act 1969 s 1 instituted by a local education authority, means the council of a non-metropolitan county or of a metropolitan district or London borough or the Common Council of the City of London: s 70 (1) (amended by the Local Government Act 1972 s 195 (6), Sch 23 para 6) (applied by the Police and Criminal Evidence Act 1984 s 38 (8)). As to bail after arrest see para 713 ante.
5 Ibid s 38 (2). For the meaning of 'in police detention' see para 716 note 5 ante.
6 Ibid s 38 (3).
7 Ibid s 38 (4). Section 38 (4) does not apply where the person charged is, at the time when the written record is made (1) incapable of understanding what is said to him; (2) violent or likely to become violent; or (3) in urgent need of medical attention: s 38 (5).
    As to the application of s 38 (1)–(6) to persons whose detention is under review see para 761 note 4 post.

720. Limitations on police detention. A person arrested for an offence may not be kept in police detention[1] except in accordance with the statutory provisions[2]. All persons in custody must be dealt with expeditiously, and released as soon as the need for detention has ceased to apply[3].

If at any time a custody officer[4]:

(1) becomes aware, in relation to any person in police detention, that the grounds for the detention of that person have ceased to apply; and

(2) is not aware of any other grounds on which the continued detention of that person could be justified under the statutory provisions,

it is the duty of the custody officer to order his immediate release from custody[5]. However, a person who appears to the custody officer to have been unlawfully at large when he was arrested is not to be so released[6].

No person in police detention may be released except on the authority of a custody officer at the police station where his detention was authorised or, if it was authorised at more than one station, a custody officer at the station where it was last authorised[7].

A person whose release is ordered[8] must be released without bail unless it appears to the custody officer:

(a) that there is need for further investigation of any matter in connection with which he was detained at any time during the period of his detention; or

(b) that proceedings may be taken against him in respect of any such matter,

and, if it so appears, he must be released on bail[9].

1 For the meaning of 'in police detention' see para 716 note 5 ante.
2 Police and Criminal Evidence Act 1984 s 34 (1). The statutory provisions referred to are Pt IV (ss 34–52: see para 715 et seq ante; infra; and para 721 et seq post). As to the application of Pt IV (ss 34–52) to children see para 691 note 1 ante. For the purposes of Pt IV (ss 34–52) a person arrested under the Road Traffic Act 1988 s 6 (5) is arrested for an offence: Police and Criminal Evidence Act 1984 s 34 (6) (amended by the Road Traffic (Consequential Provisions) Act 1988 s 4, Sch 3 para 27 (2)). See further ROAD TRAFFIC.
3 Code of Practice for the Detention, Treatment and Questioning of Persons by Police Officers para 1.1.
4 As to custody officers see para 716 ante.
5 Police and Criminal Evidence Act 1984 s 34 (2).
6 Ibid s 34 (4).
7 Ibid s 34 (3).
8 Ie under ibid s 34 (2): see supra.
9 Ibid s 34 (5). As to bail after arrest see para 713 ante.

(6) TREATMENT OF DETAINED PERSONS

(i) Initial Procedure

721. Responsibilities in relation to persons detained. It is the duty of the custody officer[1] at a police station to ensure:

(1) that all persons in police detention[2] at that station are treated in accordance with the Police and Criminal Evidence Act 1984 and any code of practice[3] issued under it and relating to the treatment of persons in police detention; and

(2) that all matters relating to such persons which are required by the Act or by such codes of practice to be recorded are recorded in the custody records relating to such persons[4].

If the custody officer, in accordance with any code of practice issued under the Act, transfers or permits the transfer of a person in police detention:

(a) to the custody of a police officer investigating an offence for which that person is in police detention; or

(b) to the custody of an officer who has charge of that person outside the police station,

the custody officer ceases in relation to that person to be subject to the duty imposed on him by head (1) above; and it is the duty of the officer to whom the transfer is made to ensure that he is treated in accordance with the provisions of the Act and of any such codes of practice[5].

If the person detained is subsequently returned to the custody of the custody officer, it is the duty of the officer investigating the offence to report to the custody officer as to the manner in which these provisions and the codes of practice have been complied with while that person was in his custody[6].

If an arrested juvenile[7] is transferred[8] to the care of a local authority[9], the custody officer ceases in relation to that person to be subject to the duty imposed on him by the above provisions[10]. It is the duty of a local authority to make available to an arrested juvenile who is in the authority's care in pursuance of such arrangements such advice and assistance as may be appropriate in the circumstances[11].

Where:

(i) an officer of higher rank than the custody officer gives directions relating to a person in police detention; and

(ii) the directions are at variance with any decision made or action taken by the custody officer in the performance of a duty imposed on him[12] or with any decision or action which would but for the directions have been made or taken by him in the performance of such a duty,

the custody officer must refer the matter at once to an officer of the rank of superintendent or above[13] who is responsible for the police station for which the custody officer is acting as custody officer[14].

1 As to custody officers see para 716 ante.
2 For the meaning of 'in police detention' see para 716 note 5 ante.
3 As to codes of practice see para 657 ante.
4 Police and Criminal Evidence Act 1984 s 39 (1). As to custody records see para 717 ante.
5 Ibid s 39 (2).
6 Ibid s 39 (3).
7 For the meaning of 'arrested juvenile' see para 718 note 10 ante.
8 Ie in pursuance of arrangements made under the Police and Criminal Evidence Act 1984 s 38 (6): see para 719 ante.
9 For the meaning of 'local authority' see para 719 note 4 ante.
10 Police and Criminal Evidence Act 1984 s 39 (4).
11 Ibid s 39 (5).
12 Ie under ibid Pt IV (ss 34–52).
13 See para 659 ante.
14 Police and Criminal Evidence Act 1984 s 39 (6).

722. Detained persons; normal procedure. When a person is brought to a police station under arrest or is arrested at the police station having attended there voluntarily, the custody officer[1] must inform him of the following rights and of the fact that they need not be exercised immediately:

(1) the right to have someone informed of his arrest[2];

(2) the right to consult a solicitor[3];

(3) the right to consult the Code of Practice for the Detention, Treatment and Questioning of Persons by Police Officers and the other codes of practice[4].

The custody officer must also give the person a written notice setting out the above three rights, the right to a copy of the custody record[5] and the caution in the prescribed[6] terms[7]. The custody officer must ask the person to sign the custody record to acknowledge receipt of this notice[7]. If the custody officer authorises a person's detention, he must inform him of the grounds as soon as practicable and in any case before that person is then questioned about any offence[8]. The person must be asked to sign on the custody record to signify whether or not he wants legal advice at this point[9]. The grounds for a person's detention must be recorded, in his presence if practicable[10].

1 As to custody officers see para 716 ante.
2 Ie in accordance with the Code of Practice for the Detention, Treatment and Questioning of Persons by Police Officers para 5: see para 726 post.
3 Ie in accordance with ibid para 6: see para 727 post.
4 Ibid para 3.1. As to the codes of practice see para 657 ante. The right so to consult the codes of practice does not entitle the person concerned to delay unreasonably necessary investigative or

administrative action while he does so: para 3.1, note 3D. A motorist who declines to provide a specimen of breath at a police station before he is permitted to finish reading the relevant code of practice thereby fails to provide such specimen without reasonable excuse: *DPP v Cornell* (1989) Times, 13 July, DC. See further ROAD TRAFFIC.

5 Ie in accordance with the Code of Practice for the Detention, Treatment and Questioning of Persons by Police Officers para 2.4: see para 717 ante.

6 Ie the terms prescribed by ibid para 10: see para 734 post.

7 Ibid para 3.2. When the custody officer gives the person a copy of such notice, he should also give him a copy of a notice explaining the arrangements for obtaining legal advice: para 3.2, note 3E. As to refusal to sign the custody record see para 717 text to notes 9, 10 ante.

8 Ibid para 3.3.

9 Ibid para 3.4.

10 Ibid para 3.10.

723. Detained persons; special groups. If the person does not understand English or appears to be deaf[1] and the custody officer cannot communicate with him, the custody officer[2] must as soon as practicable call an interpreter[3], and ask him to provide the required information[4].

If the person is a juvenile[5], is mentally handicapped or is suffering from mental illness[6], the custody officer must as soon as practicable inform the appropriate adult[7] of the grounds for his detention and his whereabouts, and ask the adult to come to the police station to see the person[8]. If the appropriate adult is already at the police station when information is given to the person[9], the information must be given to the detained person in his presence[10]. If the appropriate adult is not at the police station when the information is given, the information must be given to the detained person again in the presence of the appropriate adult once that person arrives[10].

If the person is blind or seriously visually handicapped or is unable to read, the custody officer should ensure that his solicitor, relative, the appropriate adult or some other person likely to take an interest in him is available to help in checking any documentation[11]. Where written consent or signification is required[12], the person who is assisting may be asked to sign instead if the detained person so wishes[13]. In the case of a juvenile who is known to be subject to a supervision order[14], reasonable steps must also be taken to notify the person supervising him[15].

Action taken under the above provisions must be recorded[16].

1 If a person appears to be blind or seriously visually handicapped, deaf, unable to read or unable to communicate orally with the officer dealing with him at the time, he should be treated as such for these purposes in the absence of clear evidence to the contrary: Code of Practice for the Detention, Treatment and Questioning of Persons by Police Officers para 1.6. See further *R v Clarke* [1989] Crim LR 892,CA (cited in para 744 note 2 post).

2 As to custody officers see para 716 ante.

3 As to interpreters see para 742 et seq post.

4 Code of Practice for the Detention, Treatment and Questioning of Persons by Police Officers para 3.5. Most local authority Social Services Departments can supply a list of interpreters who have the necessary skills and experience to interpret for the deaf at police interviews: para 3, note 3C. As to the required information see para 722 ante.

5 If anyone appears to be under the age of 17, he must be treated as a juvenile for these purposes in the absence of clear evidence to show that he is older: ibid para 1.5.

6 If an officer has any suspicion, or is told in good faith, that a person of any age may be mentally ill or mentally handicapped, or mentally incapable of understanding the significance of questions put to him or his replies, that person must be treated as a mentally ill or mentally handicapped person for these purposes: ibid para 1.4; and see *R v Lamont* [1989] Crim LR 813, CA.

7 For the meaning of 'the appropriate adult' see para 717 note 7 ante.

8 Code of Practice for the Detention, Treatment and Questioning of Persons by Police Officers para 3.6. If the juvenile is in the care of a local authority or voluntary organisation but is living with

his parents or other adults responsible for his welfare, then, although there is no legal obligation on the police to inform them, they as well as the authority or organisation should normally be contacted unless suspected of involvement in the offence concerned: para 3, note 3A. Even if a juvenile in care is not living with his parents, consideration should be given to informing them as well: para 3, note 3A.

As to the appropriate procedure where the juvenile is a ward of court see *Practice Direction* [1988] 2 All ER 1015, [1988] 1 WLR 989. It is not necessary, however, to inform the wardship court of the arrest or detention of a ward of court who is over the age of 17 years; nor is it necessary for a police authority to seek leave to interview a ward or to seek subsequent approval of the wardship court for interviews which have already taken place between the police and a ward of court over the age of 17: *Re B (a Minor)* (1989) Times, 20 December.

9 Ie as required by the Code of Practice for the Detention, Treatment and Questioning of Persons by Police Officers paras 3.1–3.3: see para 722 heads (1)–(3) ante.
10 Ibid para 3.6.
11 Ibid para 3.7. Blind or seriously visually handicapped persons may be unwilling to sign police documents: para 3.7, note 3F. The alternative of their representative signing on their behalf seeks to protect the interests of both police and suspects: para 3.7, note 3F.
12 Ie by the Code of Practice for the Detention, Treatment and Questioning of Persons by Police Officers.
13 Ibid para 3.7.
14 As to supervision orders see para 1275 et seq post.
15 Code of Practice for the Detention, Treatment and Questioning of Persons by Police Officers para 3.8.
16 Ibid para 3.11.

724. Additional rights of children and young persons. Where a child[1] or young person[2] is in police detention[3], such steps as are practicable must be taken to ascertain the identity of a person responsible[4] for his welfare[5].

If it is practicable so to ascertain the identity of a person responsible for the welfare of a child or young person, that person must be informed[6], unless it is not practicable to do so:

(1) that the child or young person has been arrested:
(2) why he has been arrested; and
(3) where he is being detained[7];

and, if it appears that at the time of his arrest a supervision order[8] is in force in respect of him, the person responsible for his supervision must also be informed as soon as it is reasonably practicable to do so[9].

The rights conferred by the above provisions are in addition to the right[10] not to be held incommunicado[11].

1 For the meaning of 'child' see para 537 note 2 ante.
2 For the meaning of 'young person' see para 537 note 3 ante.
3 For these purposes, the reference to a child or young person who is in police detention includes a reference to a child or young person who has been detained under the terrorism provisions; and 'arrest' includes such detention: Children and Young Persons Act 1933 s 34 (10), (11) (added by the Police and Criminal Evidence Act 1984 s 57). For the meaning of 'the terrorism provisions' see para 726 note 1 post.
   The Children and Young Persons Act 1933 s 34 (2)–(11) (as added) does not apply, however, to children over the age of 17 years: *Re B (a Minor)* (1989) Times, 20 December. As to the position where the child or young person is a ward of court see para 724 note 8 ante.
4 For these purposes, the persons who may be responsible for the welfare of a child or young person are (1) his parent or guardian; (2) any other person who has for the time being assumed responsibility for his welfare; and the reference to a parent or guardian is (a) in the case of a child or young person in the care of a local authority, a reference to that authority; and (b) in the case of a child or young person in the care of a voluntary organisation in which parental rights and duties with respect to him are vested by virtue of a resolution under the Child Care Act 1980 s 64 (1) (see INFANTS), a reference to that organisation: Children and Young Persons Act 1933 s 34 (5), (8) (added by the Police and Criminal Evidence Act 1984 s 57).

5 Children and Young Persons Act 1933 s 34 (2) (substituted by the Police and Criminal Evidence Act 1984 s 57).
6 Where information falls to be given under the Children and Young Persons Act 1933 s 34 (3) (added by the Police and Criminal Evidence Act 1984 s 57) (see infra), it must be given as soon as it is practicable to do so: Children and Young Persons Act 1933 s 34 (4) (added by the Police and Criminal Evidence Act 1984 s 57).
7 Children and Young Persons Act 1933 s 34 (3) (as added: see note 6 supra). See also note 3 supra. If it is practicable to give a person responsible for the welfare of the child or young person the information so required, that person must be given it as soon as it is practicable to do so: s 34 (6) (added by the Police and Criminal Evidence Act 1984 s 57).
8 Ie as defined in the Children and Young Persons Act 1969 s 11: see para 1275 post.
9 Children and Young Persons Act 1933 s 34 (7) (added by the Police and Criminal Evidence Act 1984 s 57).
10 Ie under the Police and Criminal Evidence Act 1984 s 56: see para 726 post.
11 See the Children and Young Persons Act 1933 s 34 (9) (added by the Police and Criminal Evidence Act 1984 s 57). As to the detention of children and young persons see also para 723 ante.

725. Detained persons' property. The custody officer[1] is responsible for:
(1) ascertaining (a) what property a detained person has with him when he comes to the police station, whether on arrest, re-detention on answering to bail, commitment to prison custody on the order or sentence of a court, on lodgment at the police station with a view to his production in court from such custody, or on arrival at a police station on transfer from detention at another station or from hospital; (b) what property he might have acquired for an unlawful or harmful purpose while in custody;
(2) the safekeeping of any property which is taken from him and which remains at the police station[2].

To these ends the custody officer may search him or authorise his being searched to the extent that he considers necessary, provided that a search of intimate parts of the body or involving the removal of more than outer clothing may only be made in accordance with the prescribed procedure[3]; and a search may only be carried out by an officer of the same sex as the person searched[4].

A detained person may retain clothing and personal effects[5] at his own risk unless the custody officer considers that he may use them to cause harm to himself or others, interfere with evidence, damage property or effect an escape or they are needed as evidence[6]. In this event the custody officer can withhold such articles as he considers necessary[6]. If he does so, he must tell the person why[6].

The custody officer is responsible for recording all property brought to the police station that a detained person had with him, or had taken from him on arrest[7]. The detained person must be allowed to check and sign the record of property as correct[7]. If a detained person is not allowed to keep any article of clothing or personal effects the reason must be recorded[8].

1 As to custody officers see para 716 ante.
2 Code of Practice for the Detention, Treatment and Questioning of Persons by Police Officers para 4.1.
3 Ie in accordance with ibid Annex A: see para 766 post.
4 Code of Practice for the Detention, Treatment and Questioning of Persons by Police Officers para 4.1. Paragraph 4.1 is not to be taken as requiring each detained person to be searched: para 4.1, note 4A. Where eg a person is to be detained for only a short period and is not to be placed in a cell, the custody officer may at his discretion decide not to search the person: para 4.1, note 4A. In such a case the custody record will be indorsed 'not searched', para 4.4 (see infra) will not apply, and the person will be invited to sign the entry: para 4.1, note 4A. Where the person detained refuses to sign, the custody officer will be obliged to ascertain what property he has on him in accordance with para 4.1: para 4.1, note 4A. Nor is para 4.1 to be taken as requiring that items of clothing worn by the

person be recorded unless withheld by the custody officer in accordance with para 4.2 (see infra): para 4.1, note 4C.

5 For these puposes, personal effects are those items which a person may lawfully need to use or refer to while in detention but do not include cash and other items of value: ibid para 4.3.

6 Ibid para 4.2.

7 Ibid para 4.4. Paragraph 4.4 does not require the custody officer to record on the custody record property in the possession of the person on arrest, if by virtue of its nature, quantity or size, it is not practicable to remove it to the police station: para 4.4, note 4B.

8 Ibid para 4.5.

(ii) Detained Persons' Rights

726. Right not to be held incommunicado. Where a person has been arrested[1] and is being held in custody in a police station or other premises, he is entitled, if he so requests, to have one friend or relative or other person who is known to him or who is likely to take an interest in his welfare told, as soon as is practicable except to the extent that delay is permitted[2] and at public expense, that he has been arrested and is being detained there[3]. If the person cannot be contacted, the person who has made the request may choose up to two alternatives[4]. If they too cannot be contacted, the custody officer[5] has a discretion to allow further attempts until the information has been conveyed[6]. In any case the person in custody must be permitted to exercise such right within 36 hours from the relevant time[7].

The above rights conferred on a person detained at a police station or other premises are exercisable whenever he is transferred from one place to another; and they apply to each subsequent occasion on which they are exercisable as they apply to the first such occasion[8].

The person may receive visits at the custody officer's discretion[9].

Where an inquiry as to the whereabouts of the person is made by a friend, relative or person with an interest in his welfare, this information must be given, if he agrees and the power[10] to delay notification of arrest or to allow access to legal advice does not apply[11].

The person must be supplied on request with writing materials; and any letter must[12] be sent as soon as practicable[13]. He may[14] also speak on the telephone for a reasonable time to one person[15].

Before any letter or message is sent, or telephone call is made, the person must be informed that what he says in any letter, call or message, other than in the case of a communication to a solicitor, may be read or listened to as appropriate and may be given in evidence[16]. A telephone call may be terminated if it is being abused[16]. The costs can be at public expense at the discretion of the custody officer[16].

A record must be kept of (1) any request made under the above provisions and the action taken on it; (2) any letters or messages sent, calls made or visits received; or (3) any refusal on the part of a person to have information about himself or his whereabouts given to an outside inquirer[17].

1 In the Police and Criminal Evidence Act 1984 s 56 references to a person who has been arrested include references to a person who has been detained under the terrorism provisions: and 'arrest' includes detention under those provisions: s 56 (10). For these purposes, 'the terrorism provisions' means the Prevention of Terrorism (Temporary Provisions) Act 1989 s 14 (1) and any provision of ss 4 (4), 16 (1), (3), (4), Schs 2, 5 conferring a power of arrest or detention; and 'terrorism' has the meaning assigned to it by s 20 (1) (see para 102 note 4 ante): Police and Criminal Evidence Act 1984 s 65 (amended by the Prevention of Terrorism (Temporary Provisions) Act 1989 s 25 (1), Sch 8 para 6 (1), (6)).

2 Ie by the Police and Criminal Evidence Act 1984 s 56: see para 729 post.

3 Ibid s 56 (1); Code of Practice for the Detention, Treatment and Questioning of Persons by Police Officers para 5.1. The exercise of such right in respect of each of the persons nominated may be delayed only in accordance with para 5.2, Annex B (see para 729 post): para 5.2. As to the custody officer's duty to inform a person of this right see para 722 ante.

Paragraph 5.1 applies also to any person who is attending at a police station voluntarily (see para 692 ante): para 5.1. An interpreter may make a telephone call or write a letter on a person's behalf: para 5, note 5A. If the person does not know of anyone to contact for advice or support or cannot contact a friend or relative, the custody officer should bear in mind any local voluntary bodies or other organisations who might be able to offer help in such cases; but, if it is specifically legal advice that is wanted, then para 6.1 (see para 727 post) will apply: para 5.1, note 5C. In some circumstances it may not be appropriate to use the telephone to disclose information under paras 5.1, 5.5 (see text to note 8 infra): para 5.1, note 5D.

4 Ibid para 5.1.

5 As to custody officers see para 716 ante.

6 Code of Practice for the Detention, Treatment and Questioning of Persons by Police Officers para 5.1.

7 Police and Criminal Evidence Act 1984 s 56 (3). For the meaning of 'the relevant time' see para 760 post. In its application to a person who has been arrested or detained under the terrorism provisions, s 56 (3) has effect as if for the words from 'within' onwards there were substituted the words 'before the end of the period beyond which he may no longer be detained without the authority of the Secretary of State': Police and Criminal Evidence Act 1984 s 56 (11) (b).

8 Ibid s 56 (8); Code of Practice for the Detention, Treatment and Questioning of Persons by Police Officers para 5.3.

9 Ibid para 5.4. In the exercise of his discretion the custody officer should allow visits where possible in the light of the availability of sufficient manpower to supervise a visit and any possible hindrance to the investigation: para 5.4, note 5B.

10 Ie the power contained in ibid Annex B: see para 729 post.

11 Ibid para 5.5. See also note 3 supra.

12 Ie unless ibid Annex B applies: see para 729 post.

13 Ibid para 5.6.

14 See note 12 supra.

15 Code of Practice for the Detention, Treatment and Questioning of Persons by Police Officers para 5.7. The telephone call referred to in para 5.7 is in addition to any communication under para 5.1 (see supra) and para 6.1 (see para 727 post); para 5.7, note 5E.

16 Ibid para 5.8.

17 Ibid para 5.9.

727. Right to legal advice. A person arrested[1] and held in custody in a police station or other premises is entitled, if he so requests, to consult a solicitor[2] privately at any time[3]. A request so made and the time at which it was so made must be recorded in the custody record[4]; but such a request need not be so recorded in the custody record of a person who makes it at a time while he is at court after being charged with an offence[5]. If a person makes such a request, he must be permitted to consult a solicitor as soon as is practicable except to the extent that delay is permitted[6]. In any case he must be permitted to consult a solicitor within 36 hours from the relevant time[7].

A person who asks for legal advice may not be interviewed[8] or continue to be interviewed until he has received it unless:

(1) delay is permitted; or

(2) an officer of the rank of superintendent or above has reasonable grounds for believing that:

(a) delay will involve an immediate risk of harm to persons or serious loss of, or damage to, property;

(b) where a solicitor, including a duty solicitor, has been contacted and has agreed to attend, awaiting his arrival would cause unreasonable delay to the processes of investigation; or

(3) the solicitor nominated by the person, or selected by him from a list cannot be contacted, or has previously indicated that he does not wish to be contacted or, having been contacted, has declined to attend; and the person has been advised of the Duty Solicitor Scheme, where one is in operation, but has declined to ask for the duty solicitor, or the duty solicitor is unavailable; or

(4) the person has given his agreement in writing or on tape that the interview may be started at once[9].

Where a person has been permitted to consult a solicitor and the solicitor is available at the time the interview begins or is in progress, he must be allowed to have his solicitor present while he is interviewed[10] The solicitor may only be required to leave the interview if his conduct is such that the investigating officer is unable properly to put questions to the suspect[11]. If the investigating officer considers that a solicitor is acting in such a way, he will stop the interview and consult an officer not below the rank of superintendent, if one is readily available, and otherwise an officer not below the rank of inspector who is not connected with the investigation[12]. After speaking to the solicitor, the officer who has been consulted will decide whether or not the interview should continue in the presence of that solicitor[12]. If he decides that it should not, the suspect will be given the opportunity to consult another solicitor before the interview continues and that solicitor will be given an opportunity to be present at the interview[12]. The removal of a solicitor from an interview is a serious step and, if it occurs, the officer of superintendent rank or above who took the decision will consider whether the incident should be reported to the Law Society[13]. If the decision to remove the solicitor has been taken by an officer below the rank of superintendent, the facts must be reported to an officer of superintendent rank or above who will similarly consider whether a report to the Law Society would be appropriate[13].

If the inspector refuses access to a clerk or legal executive or a decision is taken that such a person should not be permitted to remain at an interview, he must forthwith notify a solicitor on whose behalf the clerk or legal executive was to have acted or was acting, and give him an opportunity of making alternative arrangements[14].

If a person has asked for legal advice and an interview is commenced in the absence of a solicitor or his representative, or the solicitor or his representative has been required to leave an interview, a record must be made in the interview record[15].

Access to a solicitor may not be delayed on the grounds that he might advise the person not to answer any questions or that the solicitor was initially asked to attend the police station by someone else, provided that the person himself then wishes to see the solicitor[16]. A detained person must be permitted to consult a solicitor for a reasonable time before any court hearing[17].

1 The reference in the Police and Criminal Evidence Act 1984 s 58 (1) to a person arrested includes a reference to a person who has been detained under the terrorism provisions: s 58 (12). For the meaning of 'the terrorism provisions' see para 726 note 1 ante.

2 For these purposes, 'solicitor' means a solicitor qualified to practise in accordance with the Solicitors Act 1974: Code of Practice for the Detention, Treatment and Questioning of Persons by Police Officers para 6.9. If a solicitor wishes to send a clerk or legal executive to provide advice on his

behalf, the clerk or legal executive must be admitted to the police station for this purpose unless an officer of the rank of inspector or above considers that such a visit will hinder the investigation of crime and directs otherwise: para 6.9. As to the meaning of 'clerk' for these purposes see *R v Chief Constable of Avon and Somerset Constabulary, ex p Robinson* [1989] 2 All ER 15, [1989] 1 WLR 793, DC. It is not unreasonable for a chief constable to issue instructions to his police force to the effect that there will be very few occasions on which it would be appropriate to allow a named solicitor's clerk access to persons in custody, provided the actual decision whether to deny such access is left to individual custody officers: *R v Chief Constable of Avon and Somerset Constabulary, ex p Robinson* supra. The Law Society has issued a guidance note regarding the provision of advice to persons in custody by solicitors' clerks: see (1989) 86 LS Gaz 19 pp 40, 41.

Once admitted to the police station, the provisions of the Code of Practice for the Detention, Treatment and Questioning of Persons by Police Officers paras 6.3–6.7 (see infra) apply: para 6.9.

3 Police and Criminal Evidence Act 1984 s 58 (1); Code of Practice for the Detention, Treatment and Questioning of Persons by Police Officers para 6.1. The exercise of such right may be delayed only in accordance with para 6.2, Annex B (see para 730 post): para 6.2. Any such person may communicate privately, whether in person, in writing or by telephone with a solicitor: para 6.1. As to the custody officer's duty to inform a person of this right see para 722 ante; and as to custody officers in general see para 716 ante. As to the exclusion at the trial of evidence obtained in breach of the right to legal advice see para 1127 note 3 post.

A person who asks for legal advice should be given an opportunity to consult a specific solicitor, eg his own solicitor or one known to him, or the duty solicitor where a Duty Solicitor Scheme is in operation: para 6.1, note 6B. If advice is not available by these means, or he does not wish to consult the duty solicitor, the person should be given an opportunity to choose a solicitor from a list of those willing to provide legal advice: para 6.1, note 6B. If the solicitor is unavailable, the person may choose up to two alternatives: para 6.1, note 6B. If these attempts to secure legal advice are unsuccessful, the custody officer has discretion to allow further attempts until a solicitor has been contacted who agrees to provide legal advice: para 6.1, note 6B.

4 Police and Criminal Evidence Act 1984 s 58 (2). Any request for legal advice and the action taken on it must be recorded: Code of Practice for the Detention, Treatment and Questioning of Persons by Police Officers para 6.11. As to custody records see para 717 ante.

5 Police and Criminal Evidence Act 1984 s 58 (3).

6 Ibid s 58 (4). As to delay see para 730 post.

7 Ibid s 58 (5). In the application of s 58 (5) to a person who has been arrested or detained under the terrorism provisions, s 58 (5) has effect as if for the words from 'within' onwards there were substituted the words 'before the end of the period beyond which he may no longer be detained without the authority of the Secretary of State': s 58 (13) (a). For the meaning of 'the relevant time' see para 760 post.

8 Procedures undertaken under the Road Traffic Act 1972 s 8 (repealed: see now the Road Traffic Act 1988 ss 7, 8 (provision of specimens for analysis) do not constitute interviewing for the purposes of the Code of Practice for the Detention, Treatment and Questioning of Persons by Police Officers: para 6, note 6C. See also *DPP v Billington* [1988] 1 All ER 435, 87 Cr App Rep 68, DC.

9 Code of Practice for the Detention, Treatment and Questioning of Persons by Police Officers para 6.3. Where head (2) (a) supra applies, once sufficient information to avert the risk has been obtained, questioning must cease until the person has received legal advice or heads (1), (2) (b), (3) or (4) supra apply: para 6.4. In considering whether heads (2) (a) and (2) (b) supra apply, the officer should, where practicable, ask the solicitor for an estimate of the time he is likely to take in coming to the station, and relate this information to the time for which detention is permitted, the time of day (ie whether the period of rest required by para 12.2 (see para 738 post) is imminent) and the requirements of other investigations in progress: para 6.3, note 6A. If it appears that it will be necessary to begin an interview before the solicitor's arrival, he should be given an indication of how long police would be able to wait before heads (2) (a) and (2) (b) apply so that he has an opportunity to make arrangements for legal advice to be provided by someone else: para 6.3, note 6A.

10 Ibid para 6.5.

11 Ibid para 6.6. In considering whether para 6.6 applies, a solicitor is not guilty of misconduct if he seeks to challenge an improper question to his client or the manner in which it is put or he wishes to give his client further legal advice; and he should not be required to leave an interview unless his interference with its conduct clearly goes beyond this: para 6.6, note 6D. In a case where an officer takes the decision to exclude a solicitor, he must be in a position to satisfy the court that the decision was properly made; in order to do this he may need to witness what is happening himself: para 6.6, note 6E.

12 Ibid para 6.7.

13 Ibid para 6.8.
14 Ibid para 6.10. As to refusal of access to solicitors' clerks see *R v Chief Constable of Avon and Somerset Constabulary, ex p Robinson* [1989] 2 All ER 15, [1989] 1 WLR 793, DC cited in note 2 supra.
15 Code of Practice for the Detention, Treatment and Questioning of Persons by Police Officers para 6.12. As to interview records see para 736 post.
16 Ibid Annex B para 2.
17 Ibid Annex B para 4.

728. Rights of citizens of independent Commonwealth countries or foreign nationals. A citizen of an independent Commonwealth country or a national of a foreign country, including the Republic of Ireland, may communicate at any time with his High Commission, embassy or consulate[1].

If a citizen of an independent Commonwealth country has been detained for more than 24 hours, he must be asked if he wishes the police to inform his High Commission of his whereabouts and the grounds for his detention[2]. If so, the custody officer[3] is responsible for ensuring that the High Commission is informed by telephone[4].

If a national of a foreign country with which a consular convention is in force is detained, the appropriate consulate must be informed as soon as practicable[5]. However, notwithstanding the provisions of consular conventions, where the person is a political refugee, whether for reasons of race, nationality, political opinion or religion, or is seeking political asylum, a consular officer must not be informed of the arrest of one of his nationals or given access to or information about him except at the person's express request[6].

Any other foreign national who is detained must be informed as soon as practicable of his right to communicate with his consul if he so wishes[7]. He must also be informed that the police will notify his consul of his arrest if he wishes[7].

Consular officers may visit one of their nationals who is in police detention to talk to him and, if required, to arrange for legal advice[8]. Such visits must take place out of the hearing of a police officer[8].

A record must be made when a person is informed of his rights and of any communications with a High Commission, embassy or consulate[9].

1 Code of Practice for the Detention, Treatment and Questioning of Persons by Police Officers para 7.1. The exercise of the rights in para 7 may not be interfered with even though Annex B (see paras 729, 730 post) applies: para 5, Annex B note B2, para 7, note 7A.
2 Ibid para 7.2.
3 As to custody officers see para 716 ante.
4 Code of Practice for the Detention, Treatment and Questioning of Persons by Police Officers para 7.2.
5 Ibid para 7.3. A list of countries with which a consular convention is in force is set out in the Home Office Consolidated Circular to the Police on Crime and Kindred Matters: Code of Practice for the Detention, Treatment and Questioning of Persons by Police Officers para 7, note 7B.
6 Ibid para 7.6.
7 Ibid para 7.4.
8 Ibid para 7.5.
9 Ibid para 7.7.

729. Grounds for delay in notifying arrest. Where a person has been arrested[1] and is being held in custody in a police station or other premises, delay in the exercise of his right to have another person informed that he has been arrested and is being detained there[2] is only permitted in the case of a person who is in police detention for a serious arrestable offence[3] and if an officer of at least the rank of superintendent[4] authorises it[5]. An officer may give such authorisation orally or in writing but, if he gives it orally, he must confirm it in writing as soon as is practicable[6]. In any case the detained person must be permitted to exercise his right within 36 hours from the relevant time[7].

An officer may only authorise delay where he has reasonable grounds for believing that telling the named person of the arrest:

(1) will lead to interference with or harm to evidence connected with a serious arrestable offence or interference with or physical injury to other persons; or

(2) will lead to the alerting of other persons suspected of having committed such an offence but not yet arrested for it; or

(3) will hinder the recovery of any property obtained as a result of such an offence[8].

An officer may also authorise delay where the serious arrestable offence is a drug trafficking offence[9] or an offence in respect of which a confiscation order may be made[10] and the officer has reasonable grounds for believing:

(a) where the offence is a drug trafficking offence, that the detained person has benefited from drug trafficking[11] and that the recovery of the value of that person's proceeds of drug trafficking will be hindered by telling the named person of the arrest; and

(b) where the offence is one in respect of which a confiscation order may be made, that the detained person has benefited from the offence and that the recovery of the value of the property obtained by that person from or in connection with the offence or of the pecuniary advantage derived by him from or in connection with it will be hindered by telling the named person of the arrest[12].

If delay is so authorised, the detained person must be told the reason for it and the reason must be noted on his custody record[13]; and the duties so imposed must be performed as soon as is practicable[14].

Once the reason for authorising the delay ceases to subsist, there may be no further delay in permitting the exercise of the right to have someone informed when arrested[15].

1 For the meaning of references to a person who has been arrested see para 726 note 1 ante.

2 Ie the right conferred by the Police and Criminal Evidence Act 1984 s 56: see para 726 ante. For the meaning of 'in police detention' see para 716 note 5 ante.

3 For the meaning of 'serious arrestable offence' see para 704 ante.

4 See para 659 ante.

5 Police and Criminal Evidence Act 1984 s 56 (2); Code of Practice for the Detention, Treatment and Questioning of Persons by Police Officers para 5, Annex B para 1. Even if Annex B applies in the case of a juvenile, or a person who is mentally ill or mentally handicapped, action to inform the appropriate adult must nevertheless be taken in accordance with para 3.6 (see para 723 ante): Annex B, note B1. For the meaning of 'the appropriate adult' see para 717 note 7 ante. As to the provisions applicable to Commonwealth citizens and foreign nationals see para 728 ante.

In its application to a person who has been arrested or detained under the terrorism provisions, the Police and Criminal Evidence Act 1984 s 56 (2) (a) has effect as if for the words 'for a serious arrestable offence' there were substituted the words 'under the terrorism provisions': s 56 (11) (a). For the meaning of 'the terrorism provisions' see para 726 note 1 ante.

6 Ibid s 56 (4).

7 Ibid s 56 (3); Code of Practice for the Detention, Treatment and Questioning of Persons by Police Officers Annex B para 3. For the meaning of 'the relevant time' see para 760 post. If the grounds specified in heads (1)–(3) infra cease to apply within the relevant time, the person must as soon as practicable be asked if he wishes to exercise his right and the appropriate action must be taken: Annex B para 3.

Where a person has been arrested or detained under the terrorism provisions, the right conferred by the Police and Criminal Evidence Act 1984 s 56 may be delayed only for as long as is necessary and in no case beyond 48 hours from the time of arrest: Code of Practice for the Detention, Treatment and Questioning of Persons by Police Officers Annex B para 7. If the grounds specified in note 8 heads (4), (5) infra cease to apply within the relevant time, the person must as soon as practicable be asked if he wishes to exercise his right and the appropriate action must be taken: Annex B para 7. Any reply given by a person under Annex B para 7 must be recorded and the person asked to indorse the record in relation to whether he wishes to receive legal advice at this point: Annex B para 9. As to detention under the Prevention of Terrorism (Temporary Provisions) Act 1989 see para 119 et seq ante.

 8 Police and Criminal Evidence Act 1984 s 56 (5); Code of Practice for the Detention, Treatment and Questioning of Persons by Police Officers Annex B para 1. Annex B para 1 applies if the person detained has not yet been charged with an offence (Annex B para 1), and 'an offence' means 'any offence' and not 'that offence' (*R v Samuel* [1988] QB 615, 87 Cr App Rep 232, CA). In its application to a person who has been arrested or detained under the terrorism provisions, the Police and Criminal Evidence Act s 56 (5) has effect as if at the end there were added:
    'or
    (4) will lead to interference with the gathering of information about the commission, preparation or instigation of acts of terrorism; or
    (5) by alerting any person, will make it more difficult to prevent an act of terrorism or to secure the apprehension, prosecution or conviction of any person in connection with the commission, preparation or instigation of an act of terrorism':
    s 56 (11) (c); Code of Practice for the Detention, Treatment and Questioning of Persons by Police Officers Annex B para 6.
 9 'Drug trafficking' and 'drug trafficking offence' have the same meaning as in the Drug Trafficking Offences Act 1986 (see para 408 note 2 ante and para 1305 note 2 post respectively): Police and Criminal Evidence Act 1984 s 65 (amended by the Drug Trafficking Offences Act 1986 s 32 (3)).
10 Ie an offence to which the Criminal Justice Act 1988 Pt VI (ss 71–103) applies: see para 1284 et seq post.
11 For the meaning of 'benefited from drug trafficking' see para 408 note 4 ante.
12 Police and Criminal Evidence Act 1984 s 56 (5A) (added by the Drug Trafficking Offences Act 1986 s 32 (1); amended by the Criminal Justice Act 1988 s 99 (1), (2)).
13 Police and Criminal Evidence Act 1984 s 56 (6); Code of Practice for the Detention, Treatment and Questioning of Persons by Police Officers Annex B paras 5, 8. As to custody records see para 717 ante.
14 Police and Criminal Evidence Act 1984 s 56 (7); Code of Practice for the Detention, Treatment and Questioning of Persons by Police Officers Annex B paras 5, 8.
15 Police and Criminal Evidence Act 1984 s 56 (9).

730. Delay in allowing access to legal advice. Where a person has been arrested[1] and is being held in custody in a police station or other premises, his right to consult a solicitor privately at any time[2] may only be delayed in the case of a person who is in police detention[3] for a serious arrestable offence[4] and if an officer of at least the rank of superintendent[5] authorises it[6]. An officer may give such authorisation orally or in writing but, if he gives it orally, he must confirm it in writing as soon as is practicable[7].

An officer may only authorise delay where he has reasonable grounds for believing that the exercise of such right at the time when the person detained desires to exercise it:

(1) will lead to interference with or harm to evidence connected with a serious arrestable offence or interference with or physical injury to other persons; or

(2) will lead to the alerting of other persons suspected of having committed such an offence but not yet arrested for it; or

(3) will hinder the recovery of any property obtained as a result of such an offence[8].

An officer may also authorise delay where the serious arrestable offence is a drug trafficking offence[9] or an offence in respect of which a confiscation order may be made[10] and the officer has reasonable grounds for believing:

(a) where the offence is a drug trafficking offence, that the detained person has benefited from drug trafficking[11] and that the recovery of the value of that person's proceeds of drug trafficking will be hindered by the exercise of the right[11] to consult a solicitor; and

(b) where the offence is one in respect of which a confiscation order may be made, that the detained person has benefited from the offence and that the recovery of the value of the property obtained by that person from or in connection with the offence or of the pecuniary advantage derived by him from or in connection with it will be hindered by the exercise of the right[12] to consult a solicitor[13].

If delay is so authorised, the detained person must be told the reason for it and the reason must be noted on his custody record[14]; and the duties so imposed must be performed as soon as is practicable[15].

Once the reason for authorising the delay ceases to subsist, there may be no further delay in permitting the exercise of the right of access to legal advice[16]; and in any case the detained person must be permitted to exercise his right within 36 hours from the relevant time[17].

1 For the meaning of references to a person who has been arrested see para 726 note 1 ante.
2 Ie the right conferred by the Police and Criminal Evidence Act 1984 s 58: see para 727 ante.
3 For the meaning of 'in police detention' see para 716 note 5 ante.
4 For the meaning of 'serious arrestable offence' see para 704 ante.
5 See para 659 ante.
6 Police and Criminal Evidence Act 1984 s 58 (6); Code of Practice for the Detention, Treatment and Questioning of Persons by Police Officers Annex B para 1. Even if Annex B applies in the case of a juvenile, or a person who is mentally ill or mentally handicapped, action to inform the appropriate adult must nevertheless be taken in accordance with para 3.6 (see para 723 ante): Annex B, note B1. For the meaning of 'the appropriate adult' see para 717 note 7 ante. As to the provisions applicable to Commonwealth citizens and foreign nationals see para 728 ante.

    In its application to a person who has been arrested or detained under the terrorism provisions, the Police and Criminal Evidence Act 1984 s 58 (6) (a) has effect as if for the words 'for a serious arrestable offence' there were substituted the words 'under the terrorism provisions': s 58 (13) (b). For the meaning of 'the terrorism provisions' see para 726 note 1 ante.
7 Ibid s 58 (7).
8 Ibid s 58 (8); Code of Practice for the Detention, Treatment and Questioning of Persons by Police Officers Annex B para 1. Annex B para 1 applies where the person detained has not yet been charged with an offence (Annex B para 1), and 'an offence' means 'any offence' (*R v Samuel* [1988] QB 615, 87 Cr App Rep 232, CA). As to the exercise of a superintendent's power to delay access to a solicitor see *R v Samuel* supra; *R v Alladice* (1988) 87 Cr App Rep 380, CA. In its application to a person who has been arrested or detained under the terrorism provisions, the Police and Criminal Evidence Act 1984 s 58 (8) has effect as if at the end there were added:
'or
(4) will lead to interference with the gathering of information about the commission, preparation or instigation of acts of terrorism; or
(5) by alerting any person, will make it more difficult to prevent an act of terrorism or to secure the apprehension, prosecution or conviction of any person in connection with the commission, preparation or instigation of an act of terrorism':
s 58 (13) (c); Code of Practice for the Detention, Treatment and Questioning of Persons by Police Officers Annex B para 6. If an officer of at least the rank of Commander or Assistant Chief Constable has reasonable grounds for believing that, unless he gives a direction, the exercise by a person arrested or detained under the terrorism provisions of the right conferred by the Police and Criminal Evidence Act 1984 s 58 (1) (see para 727 ante) will have any of the consequences specified in s 58 (8) as it has effect by virtue of s 58 (13), he may give a direction: s 58 (14), (17). Such a direction is a direction that a person desiring to exercise the right conferred by s 58 (1) may only consult a solicitor

in the sight and hearing of a qualified officer of the uniformed branch of the force of which the officer giving the direction is a member: s 58 (15). An officer is so qualified for these purposes if he is of the rank of inspector and in the opinion of the officer giving the direction he has no connection with the case: s 58 (16). A direction so given ceases to have effect once the reason for giving it ceases to subsist: s 58 (18).

9 For the meaning of 'drug trafficking' and 'drug trafficking offence' see para 729 note 9 ante.
10 Ie an offence to which the Criminal Justice Act 1988 Pt VI (ss 71–103) applies: see para 1284 et seq post.
11 For the meaning of 'benefited from drug trafficking' see para 408 note 4 ante.
12 See note 2 supra.
13 Police and Criminal Evidence Act 1984 s 58 (8A) (added by the Drug Trafficking Offences Act 1986 s 32 (2); amended by the Criminal Justice Act 1988 s 99 (1), (3)).
14 Police and Criminal Evidence Act 1984 s 58 (9); Code of Practice for the Detention, Treatment and Questioning of Persons by Police Officers Annex B paras 5, 8. As to custody records see para 717 ante.
15 Police and Criminal Evidence Act 1984 s 58 (10); Code of Practice for the Detention, Treatment and Questioning of Persons by Police Officers Annex B paras 5, 8.
16 Police and Criminal Evidence Act 1984 s 58 (11).
17 Ibid s 58 (5); Code of Practice for the Detention, Treatment and Questioning of Persons by Police Officers Annex B para 3. For the meaning of 'the relevant time' see para 760 post. If the grounds specified in heads (1)–(3) supra cease to apply within the relevant time, the person must as soon as practicable be asked if he wishes to exercise his right and the appropriate action must be taken: Annex B para 3.

Where a person has been arrested or detained under the terrorism provisions, the right conferred by the Police and Criminal Evidence Act 1984 s 58 may be delayed only for as long as is necessary and in no case beyond 48 hours from the time of arrest: Code of Practice for the Detention, Treatment and Questioning of Persons by Police Officers Annex B para 7. If the grounds specified in note 8 heads (4), (5) supra cease to apply within the relevant time, the person must as soon as practicable be asked if he wishes to exercise his right and the appropriate action must be taken: Annex B para 7. Any reply given by a person under Annex B para 7 must be recorded and the person asked to indorse the record in relation to whether he wishes to receive legal advice at this point: Annex B para 9. As to detention under the Prevention of Terrorism (Temporary Provisions) Act 1989 see para 119 et seq ante.

(iii) Detained Persons' Treatment

731. Conditions of detention. So far as is practicable, not more than one person may be detained in each cell[1]. Cells in use must be adequately heated, cleaned and ventilated; and they must be adequately lit, subject to such dimming as is compatible with safety and security to allow persons detained overnight to sleep[2]. No additional restraints should be used within a locked cell unless absolutely necessary, and then only approved handcuffs[2]. Blankets, mattresses, pillows and other bedding supplied should be of a reasonable standard and in a clean and sanitary condition[3]. Access to toilet and washing facilities must be provided[4].

If it is necessary to remove a person's clothes for the purposes of investigation, for hygiene or health reasons or for cleaning, replacement clothing of a reasonable standard of comfort and cleanliness must be provided[5]. A person may not be interviewed unless adequate clothing has been offered to him[5]. At least two light meals and one main meal must be offered in any period of 24 hours[6]. Whenever necessary, advice must be sought from the police surgeon on medical or dietary matters; and, as far as practicable, meals provided must offer a varied diet and meet any special dietary needs or religious beliefs that the person may have; he may also have meals supplied by his family or friends at his or their own expense[6].

Brief outdoor exercise must be offered daily if practicable[7]. A juvenile must not be placed in a police cell unless no other secure accommodation is available and the custody officer considers that it is not practicable to supervise him if he is not placed in a cell[8]. He may not be placed in a cell with a detained adult[8].

Reasonable force may be used if necessary for the following purposes:
(1) to secure compliance with reasonable instructions, including instructions given in pursuance of the provisions of a code of practice[9]; or
(2) to prevent escape, injury, damage to property or the destruction of evidence[10].

Persons detained should be visited every hour, and those who are drunk, every half hour[11].

A record must be kept of replacement clothing and meals offered[12]; and, if a juvenile is placed in a cell, the reason must be recorded[13].

1 Code of Practice for the Detention, Treatment and Questioning of Persons by Police Officers para 8.1.
2 Ibid para 8.2.
3 Ibid para 8.3. The provisions in paras 8.3, 8.6 (see text to note 6 infra) respectively regarding bedding and a varied diet are of particular importance in the case of a person detained under the Prevention of Terrorism (Temporary Provisions) Act 1989; this is because such a person may well remain in police custody for some time: Code of Practice for the Detention, Treatment and Questioning of Persons by Police Officers paras 8.3, 8.6, note 8B.
4 Ibid para 8.4.
5 Ibid para 8.5.
6 Ibid para 8.6.
7 Ibid para 8.7.
8 Ibid para 8.8.
9 As to the codes of practice see para 657 ante.
10 Code of Practice for the Detention, Treatment and Questioning of Persons by Police Officers para 8.9.
11 Ibid para 8.10. Whenever possible juveniles and other persons at risk should be visited more regularly: para 8.10, note 8A.
12 Ibid para 8.11.
13 Ibid para 8.12.

732. Complaint by detained person about treatment. If a complaint is made by or on behalf of a detained person about his treatment since his arrest, or it comes to the notice of any officer that he may have been treated improperly, a report must be made as soon as practicable to an officer of the rank of inspector or above who is not connected with the investigation[1]. If the matter concerns a possible assault or the possibility of the unnecessary or unreasonable use of force, the police surgeon must also be called as soon as practicable[2].

A record must be made of any arrangements so made for an examination by a police surgeon and of any complaint so reported together with any relevant remarks by the custody officer[3].

1 Code of Practice for the Detention, Treatment and Questioning of Persons by Police Officers para 9.1. All officers dealing with detained persons are, of course, under a duty to observe not only the above provisions but also those set out in the Police Discipline Code: Code of Practice for the Detention, Treatment and Questioning of Persons by Police Officers para 9, note 9D. As to the use of reasonable force see para 731 heads (1), (2) ante.
2 Ibid para 9.1.
3 Ibid para 9.7. As to custody officers see para 716 ante.

733. Medical treatment. The custody officer[1] must immediately call the police surgeon or, in urgent cases, send the person to hospital or call the nearest available medical practitioner if a person brought to a police station or already detained there:

(1) appears to be suffering from physical or mental illness; or

(2) is injured; or

(3) does not show signs of sensibility and awareness or fails to respond normally to questions or conversation, other than through drunkenness alone; or

(4) otherwise appears to need medical attention[2].

This applies even if the person makes no request for medical attention and whether or not he has recently had medical treatment elsewhere, unless brought to the police station direct from hospital[2].

If it appears to the custody officer, or he is told, that a person brought to the police station under arrest may be suffering from an infectious disease of any significance, he must take steps to isolate the person and his property until he has obtained medical directions as to where the person should be taken, whether fumigation should take place and what precautions should be taken by officers who have been or will be in contact with him[3].

If a detained person requests a medical examination, the police surgeon must be called as soon as practicable[4]. He may in addition be examined by a medical practitioner of his own choice at his own expense[4].

If a person is required to take or apply any medication in compliance with medical directions, the custody officer is responsible for its safe keeping and for ensuring that he is given the opportunity to take or apply it at the appropriate times[5]. No police officer may administer controlled drugs subject to the Misuse of Drugs Act 1971 for this purpose[5]. A person may administer such drugs to himself only under the personal supervision of the police surgeon[5].

If a detained person has in his possession or claims to need medication relating to a heart condition, diabetes, epilepsy or a condition of comparable potential seriousness then, even though the above provisions may not apply, the advice of the police surgeon must be obtained[6].

A record must be kept of any such request for a medical examination, of the arrangements for any examination so made, and of any such medical directions to the police[7]. The custody record must[8] include not only a record of all medication that a detained person has in his possession on arrival at the police station but also a note of any such medication he claims he needs but does not have with him[9].

1 As to custody officers see para 716 ante.

2 Code of Practice for the Detention, Treatment and Questioning of Persons by Police Officers para 9.2. The need to call a police surgeon need not apply to minor ailments: para 9.2, note 9A. It is important to remember that a person who appears to be drunk or behaving abnormally may be suffering from illness or the effect of drugs or may have sustained injury, particularly head injury, which is not apparent, and that someone needing or addicted to certain drugs may experience harmful effects within a short time of being deprived of their supply: para 9, note 9B. Police should therefore always call the police surgeon when in any doubt, and act with all due speed: para 9, note 9B. All officers dealing with detained persons are of course under a duty to observe not only the above provisions but also those set out in the Police Discipline Code: Code of Practice for the Detention, Treatment and Questioning of Persons by Police Officers para 9, note 9D.

3 Ibid para 9.3.

4 Ibid para 9.4.

5 Ibid para 9.5.

6 Ibid para 9.6.

7 Ibid para 9.8. If a medical practitioner does not record his clinical findings in the custody record, the record must show where they are recorded: para 9, note 9C. As to custody records see para 717 ante.

8 Ie subject to ibid para 4: see para 725 ante.

9 Ibid para 9.9.

(iv) Cautions

734. Cautions. A person whom there are grounds to suspect of an offence must be cautioned before any questions about it, or further questions if it is his answers to previous questions that provide grounds for suspicion, are put to him for the purpose of obtaining evidence which may be given to a court in a prosecution[1]. He therefore need not be cautioned if questions are put for other purposes, for example, to establish his identity, his ownership of, or responsibility for, any vehicle or the need to search him in the exercise of powers of stop and search[1].

When a person who is not under arrest is initially cautioned before or during an interview at a police station or other premises, he must at the same time be told that he is not under arrest, is not obliged to remain with the officer but that, if he does, he may obtain legal advice if he wishes[2]. A person must be cautioned upon arrest for an offence unless:

(1) it is impracticable to do so by reason of his condition or behaviour at the time; or

(2) he has already been cautioned[3] immediately prior to arrest[4].

The caution must be in the following terms:

'You do not have to say anything unless you wish to do so, but what you say may be given in evidence.'[5]

Minor deviations do not constitute a breach of this requirement provided that the sense of the caution is preserved[5].

When there is a break in questioning under caution, the interviewing officer must ensure that the person being questioned is aware that he remains under caution[6]. If there is any doubt, the caution should be given again in full when the interview resumes[6].

A record must be made when a caution is so given, either in the officer's pocket book or in the interview record as appropriate[7].

1 Code of Practice for the Detention, Treatment and Questioning of Persons by Police Officers para 10.1. As to powers of stop and search see para 660 et seq ante.

2 Ibid para 10.2. It is not necessary to give or repeat a caution when informing a person who is not under arrest that he may be prosecuted for an offence: para 10, note 10B.

3 Ie in accordance with ibid para 10.1: see supra.

4 Ibid para 10.3.

5 Ibid para 10.4. If it appears that a person does not understand what the caution means, the officer who has given it should go on to explain it in his own words: para 10.4, note 10C. In case anyone who is given a caution is unclear about its significance, the officer concerned should explain that the caution is given in pursuance of the general principle of English law that a person need not answer any questions or provide any information which might tend to incriminate him, and that no adverse inferences from this silence may be drawn at any trial that takes place: para 10.3, note 10D. The person should not, however, be left with a false impression that non-co-operation will have no effect on his immediate treatment as, for example, his refusal to provide his name and address when charged with an offence may render him liable to detention: para 10.3, note 10D.

6 Ibid para 10.5. In considering whether or not to caution again after a break, the officer should bear in mind that he may have to satisfy a court that the person understood that he was still under caution when the interview resumed: para 10.5, note 10A. Where a person is asked further questions in a police car on the way to the police station after his arrest, failure to caution him prior to the questioning is a breach of para 10.5: *R v Kingsley Brown* [1989] Crim LR 500.

7 Code of Practice for the Detention, Treatment and Questioning of Persons by Police Officers para 10.6.

(v) Interviews

A. GENERAL PROVISIONS

735. In general. No police officer may try to obtain answers to questions or to elicit a statement by the use of oppression[1], or may indicate, except in answer to a direct question, what action will be taken on the part of the police if the person being interviewed answers questions, makes a statement or refuses to do either[2]. If the person asks the officer directly what action will be taken in the event of his answering questions, making a statement or refusing to do either, the officer may inform the person what action the police propose to take in that event provided that that action is itself proper and warranted[2]. As soon as a police officer who is making inquiries of any person about an offence believes that a prosecution should be brought against him and that there is sufficient evidence for it to succeed, he must without delay cease to question him[3].

1 Questions which are deliberately asked with the intention of producing a disordered state of mind will amount to oppression; but the mere fact that questions addressed to the accused trigger off hallucinations is not indicative of oppression: *R v Miller* [1986] 3 All ER 119, [1986] 1 WLR 1191, CA. As to the admissibility of confessions obtained by oppression see para 1124 post; and as to the trial judge's discretion to exclude confessions obtained in breach of the relevant code of practice see paras 1060, 1127 post.
2 Code of Practice for the Detention, Treatment and Questioning of Persons by Police Officers para 11.1. An offer to an arrested person that, if he is willing to give evidence against a co-accused, he will be used as a prosecution witness and not prosecuted himself may, on rare occasions, be justified; but the arrested person must be given full opportunity to discuss the matter with a solicitor before coming to a decision: *R v Mathias* (1989) Times, 24 August, CA.
3 Code of Practice for the Detention, Treatment and Questioning of Persons by Police Officers para 11.2.
   Nothing in the Code of Practice for the Detention, Treatment and Questioning of Persons by Police Officers prevents a police officer from asking questions at or near the scene of a suspected crime to elicit an explanation which, if true or accepted, would exculpate a suspect: *R v Maguire* [1989] Crim LR 815, CA.

736. Interview records. An accurate record must be made of each interview with a person suspected of an offence, whether or not the interview takes place at a police station[1]. If the interview takes place in the police station or other premises:
(1) the record must state the place of the interview, the time it begin and ends, the time the record is made, if different, any breaks in the interview and the names of all those present; and must be made on the forms provided for this purpose or in the officer's pocket book or in accordance with the Code of Practice on Tape-recording[2];
(2) the record must be made during the course of the interview, unless in the investigating officer's view this would not be practicable or would interfere with the conduct of the interview, and must constitute either a verbatim record of what has been said or, failing this, an account of the interview which adequately and accurately summarises it[3].
If an interview record is not made during the course of the interview, it must be made as soon as practicable after its completion[4]. Written interview records must be timed and signed by the maker[5]. If an interview record is not completed in the course of the interview, the reason must be recorded in the officer's pocket book[6]. Any refusal by a person to sign an interview record when asked to do so must itself be recorded[7].

1 Code of Practice for the Detention, Treatment and Questioning of Persons by Police Officers para 11.3 (a). It is not within the spirit of the Police and Criminal Evidence Act 1984 or the codes of practice that 'interview' should be given a restricted meaning: *R v Matthews, R v Voss, R v Dennison* (1989) Times, 9 November, CA.
2 As to tape-recorded interviews see para 746 et seq post.
3 Code of Practice for the Detention, Treatment and Questioning of Persons by Police Officers para 11.3 (b). The importance of the rules relating to contemporaneous noting of interviews can scarcely be over-emphasised: *R v Canale* (1989) Times, 8 November, CA per Lord Lane CJ (case involving 'flagrant, deliberate and cynical' breaches of the rules by police officers conducting interviews).
4 Code of Practice for the Detention, Treatment and Questioning of Persons by Police Officers para 11.4.
5 Ibid para 11.5.
6 Ibid para 11.6.
7 Ibid para 11.7.

737. Urgent interviews. If, and only if, an officer of the rank of superintendent or above considers that delay will involve an immediate risk of harm to persons or serious loss of or serious damage to property:

(1) a person heavily under the influence of drink or drugs may be interviewed in that state; or

(2) an arrested juvenile or a person who is mentally ill or mentally handicapped may be interviewed in the absence of the appropriate adult[1]; or

(3) a person who has difficulty in understanding English or who has a hearing disability may be interviewed in the absence of an interpreter[2].

Questioning in these circumstances may not continue once sufficient information to avert the immediate risk has been obtained[3].

A record must be made of the grounds for any decision so to interview a person[4].

1 For the meaning of 'the appropriate adult' see para 717 note 7 ante.
2 Code of Practice for the Detention, Treatment and Questioning of Persons by Police Officers Annex C para 1. The special groups referred to in Annex C are all particularly vulnerable; and the provisions of Annex C, which override safeguards designed to protect them and to minimise the risk of interviews producing unreliable evidence, should be applied only in exceptional cases of need: Annex C, note C1.
3 Ibid Annex C para 2.
4 Ibid Annex C para 3.

738. Interviews in police stations; in general. If a police officer wishes to interview, or conduct inquiries which require the presence of, a detained person, the custody officer is responsible for deciding whether to deliver him into his custody[1].

In any period of 24 hours a detained person must be allowed a continuous period of at least eight hours for rest, free from questioning, travel or any interruption arising out of the investigation concerned; and this period should normally be at night[2]. The period of rest may not be interrupted or delayed unless there are reasonable grounds for believing that it would:

(1) involve a risk of harm to persons or serious loss of, or damage to, property;

(2) delay unnecessarily the person's release from custody; or

(3) otherwise prejudice the outcome of the investigation[2].

If a person is arrested at a police station after going there voluntarily[3], the period of 24 hours runs from the time of arrival at the police station and not the time of his arrest[4].

A detained person may not be supplied with intoxicating liquor except on medical directions[5]. No person who is unfit through drink or drugs to the extent that he is unable to appreciate the significance of questions put to him and his answers may be questioned about an alleged offence in that condition except[6] in cases of urgency[7].

As far as practicable interviews must take place in interview rooms which must be adequately heated, lit and ventilated[8].

Persons being questioned or making statements must not be required to stand[9].

Before the commencement of an interview each interviewing officer must identify himself and any other officers present by name and rank to the person being interviewed[10].

Breaks from interviewing must be made at recognised meal times; and short breaks for refreshment must also be provided at intervals of approximately two hours, subject to the interviewing officer's discretion to delay a break if there are reasonable grounds for believing that it would:

(a) involve a risk of harm to persons or serious loss of, or damage to, property;

(b) delay unnecessarily the person's release from custody; or

(c) otherwise prejudice the outcome of the investigation[11].

If in the course of the interview a complaint is made by the person being questioned or on his behalf[12], the interviewing officer must:

(i) record it in the interview record; and

(ii) inform the custody officer, who is then responsible for dealing with it[13].

1 Code of Practice for the Detention, Treatment and Questioning of Persons by Police Officers para 12.1. The purpose of any interview is to obtain from the person concerned his explanation of the facts, and not necessarily to obtain an admission: para 12.1, note 12A. As to custody officers see para 716 ante.

2 Ibid para 12.2.

3 As to voluntary attendance at a police station see para 692 ante.

4 Code of Practice for the Detention, Treatment and Questioning of Persons by Police Officers para 12.2.

5 Ibid para 12.3. The police surgeon can give advice about whether or not a person is fit to be interviewed in accordance with para 12.3: para 12.3, note 12C.

6 Ie except in accordance with ibid Annex C: see para 737 ante.

7 Ibid para 12.3.

8 Ibid para 12.4.

9 Ibid para 12.5.

10 Ibid para 12.6.

11 Ibid para 12.7.

12 Ie concerning the provisions of the Code of Practice for the Detention, Treatment and Questioning of Persons by Police Officers.

13 Ibid para 12.8. As to dealing with complaints see para 732 ante; and as to interview records see para 736 ante and para 739 post.

739. Interviews in police stations; records and written statements. A record must be made of the times at which a detained person is not in the custody of the custody officer, and why; and of the reason for any refusal to deliver him out of that custody[1]. A record must also be made of any intoxicating liquor supplied[2] to a detained person[3]; and any decision to delay a break in an interview must be recorded, with grounds, in the interview record[4].

Where the person interviewed is in the police station at the time that a written record of the interview is made, he must be given the opportunity to read it and to sign it as correct or to indicate the respects in which he considers it inaccurate, but no person may be kept in custody for this sole purpose[5]. If the interview is tape-recorded[6], the arrangements set out in the relevant code of practice apply[7].

All written statements made at police stations under caution must be written on the forms provided for the purpose[8]; and all written statements made under caution must be taken in accordance with the prescribed procedure[9].

Where the appropriate adult[10] or another third party is present at an interview and is still in the police station at the time that a written record of the interview is made, he must be asked to read it, or any written statement taken down by a police officer, and sign it as correct or to indicate the respects in which he considers it inaccurate[11]. If the person refuses to read or sign the record as accurate or to indicate the respects in which he considers it inaccurate, the senior officer present must record on the record itself, in the presence of the person concerned, what has happened[11]. If the interview is tape-recorded, the arrangements set out in the relevant code of practice apply[11].

1 Code of Practice for the Detention, Treatment and Questioning of Persons by Police Officers para 12.9. As to custody officers see para 716 ante.

2 Ie in accordance with ibid para 12.3: see para 738 ante.

3 Ibid para 12.10.

4 Ibid para 12.11. As to breaks from interviewing see para 738 ante.

5 Ibid para 12.12. As to refusal to sign see para 736 text to note 7 ante. Any discussion or talk between a suspect or prisoner and a police officer will normally amount to an 'interview' to which para 12.12 applies: *R v Matthews, R v Voss, R v Dennison* (1989) Times, 9 November, CA. If a police officer shows a statement to a prisoner who refuses to read or sign it, it may be a wise precaution to serve a photostat copy of the statement on the prisoner's solicitor, noting on the custody sheet the time of so doing and the reasons: *R v Matthews, R v Voss, R v Dennison* supra.

The purpose of any interview is to obtain from the person concerned his explanation of the facts, and not necessarily to obtain an admission: Code of Practice for the Detention, Treatment and Questioning of Persons by Police Officers para 12.12, note 12B. If the interview has been contemporaneously recorded and the record signed by the person interviewed in accordance with para 12.12, or has been tape-recorded, it is normally unnecessary to ask for a written statement: para 12.12, note 12B. Statements under caution should normally be taken in these circumstances only at the person's express wish; but an officer may ask him whether or not he wants to make such a statement: para 12.12, note 12B.

Paragraph 12.12. applies wherever the interview has taken place if the accused is in a police station when the note of his interview is written up: *R v Kingsley Brown* [1989] Crim LR 500; cf *R v Parchment* [1989] Crim LR 290.

6 As to tape-recorded interviews see para 746 et seq post.

7 Code of Practice for the Detention, Treatment and Questioning of Persons by Police Officers para 12.12.

8 Ibid para 12.13.

9 Ibid para 12.14. As to written statements made under caution see para 740 post.

10 For the meaning of 'the appropriate adult' see para 717 note 7 ante.

11 Code of Practice for the Detention, Treatment and Questioning of Persons by Police Officers para 12.15.

740. Written statements under caution. A person must always be invited to write down himself what he wants to say[1]. Where the person wishes to write it himself, he must be asked to write out and sign before writing what he wants to say, the following:

'I make this statement of my own free will. I understand that I need not say anything unless I wish to do so and that what I say may be given in evidence.'[2]

Any person writing his own statement must be allowed to do so without any prompting except that a police officer may indicate to him which matters are material or question any ambiguity in the statement[3].

If a person says that he would like someone to write it for him, a police officer must write the statement, but, before starting, he must ask him to sign or make his mark, to the following:

'I . . . wish to make a statement. I want someone to write down what I say. I understand that I need not say anything unless I wish to do so and that what I say may be given in evidence.'[4]

Where a police officer writes the statement, he must take down the exact words spoken by the person making it and he must not edit or paraphrase it[5]. Any questions that are necessary, for example to make it more intelligible, and the answers given must be recorded contemporaneously on the statement form[5]. When the writing of a statement by a police officer is finished, the person making it must be asked to read it and to make any corrections, alterations or additions he wishes[6]. When he has finished reading it, he must be asked to write and sign or make his mark on the following certificate at the end of the statement:

'I have read the above statement, and I have been able to correct, alter or add anything I wish. This statement is true. I have made it of my own free will.'[6]

If the person making the statement cannot read, or refuses to read it, or to write the above-mentioned certificate at the end of it or to sign it, the senior police officer present must read it over to him and ask him whether he would like to correct, alter or add anything and to put his signature or make his mark at the end[7]. The police officer must then certify on the statement itself what has occurred[7].

1　Code of Practice for the Detention, Treatment and Questioning of Persons by Police Officers para 12.14, Annex D para 1.
2　Ibid Annex D para 2.
3　Ibid Annex D para 3.
4　Ibid Annex D para 4.
5　Ibid Annex D para 5.
6　Ibid Annex D para 6.
7　Ibid Annex D para 7.

741. Persons at risk. A juvenile or a person who is mentally ill or mentally handicapped, whether suspected or not, must not be interviewed or asked to provide or sign a written statement in the absence of the appropriate adult[1] except[2] in the case of urgent interviews[3]. If he is cautioned[4] in the absence of the appropriate adult, the caution must be repeated in the adult's presence, unless the interview has by then already finished[5]. If, having been informed of the right to legal advice[6], the appropriate adult considers that legal advice should be taken, the provisions relating to legal advice[7] apply[8]. Juveniles may only be interviewed at their places of education in exceptional circumstances and then only where the principal or his nominee agrees and is present[9].

1　For the meaning of 'the appropriate adult' see para 717 note 7 ante. Where the parents or guardians of a person at risk are themselves suspected of involvement in the offence concerned, or are the victims of it, it may be desirable for the appropriate adult to be some other person: Code of Practice for the Detention, Treatment and Questioning of Persons by Police Officers para 13, note 13A.
2　Ie unless ibid Annex C applies: see para 737 ante.
3　Ibid para 13.1. It is important to bear in mind that, although juveniles or persons who are mentally ill or mentally handicapped are often capable of providing reliable evidence, they may, without knowing or wishing to do so, be particularly prone in certain circumstances to provide information which is unreliable, misleading or self-incriminating: para 13, note 13B. Special care should

therefore always be exercised in questioning such a person, and the appropriate adult involved, if there is any doubt about a person's age, mental state or capacity: para 13, note 13B. Because of the risk of unreliable evidence it is also important to obtain corroboration of any facts admitted whenever possible: para 13, note 13B. The appropriate adult should be informed that he is not expected to act simply as an observer: para 13, note 13C. The purposes of his presence are (1) to advise the person being questioned and to observe whether or not the interview is being conducted properly and fairly; and (2) to facilitate communication with the person being interviewed: para 13, note 13C. See also *DPP v Blake* [1989] 1 WLR 432, 89 Cr App Rep 179, DC (the appropriate adult has an important role to play in any interview which he attends; juvenile's estranged father not appropriate adult for these purposes).

4 Ie in accordance with the Code of Practice for the Detention, Treatment and Questioning of Persons by Police Officers para 10: see para 734 ante.
5 Ibid para 13.1; and see *R v Lamont* [1989] Crim LR 813, CA.
6 Ie under the Code of Practice for the Detention, Treatment and Questioning of Persons by Police Officers para 3.6: see para 723 ante.
7 Ie ibid para 6: see para 727 ante.
8 Ibid para 13.2.
9 Ibid para 13.3. A juvenile should not be arrested at his place of education unless this is unavoidable: para 13, note 13D. In this case the principal or his nominee must be informed: para 13, note 13D.

B. INTERPRETERS

742. Interpreters; in general. All reasonable attempts should be made to make clear to the detained person that interpreters will be provided at public expense[1]. Where the right to access to legal advice exists[2] and the person concerned cannot communicate with the solicitor, whether because of language or hearing difficulties, an interpreter must be called[3]. The interpreter may not be a police officer when interpretation is needed for the purposes of obtaining legal advice[3]. In all other cases a police officer may only interpret if he first obtains the detained person's, or the appropriate adult's[4], agreement in writing or if the interview is tape-recorded[5] in accordance with the prescribed procedure[6]. When a person who has difficulty in understanding English is charged with an offence, and the custody officer[7] cannot himself speak the person's language, arrangements must also be made for an interpreter to explain as soon as practicable the offence concerned and any other information given by the custody officer[8]. Action so taken to call an interpreter and any agreement to be interviewed in the absence of an interpreter must be recorded[9].

1 Code of Practice for the Detention, Treatment and Questioning of Persons by Police Officers para 14.6.
2 Ie where ibid para 6.1 applies: see para 727 ante.
3 Ibid para 14.7. If the interpreter is needed as a prosecution witness at the person's trial, a second interpreter must act as the court interpreter: para 14, note 14A. As to interpreters of foreign languages see para 743 post; and as to interpreters for the deaf see para 744 post.
4 For the meaning of 'the appropriate adult' see para 717 note 7 ante.
5 As to tape-recorded interviews see para 746 et seq post.
6 Code of Practice for the Detention, Treatment and Questioning of Persons by Police Officers para 14.7.
7 As to custody officers see para 716 ante.
8 Code of Practice for the Detention, Treatment and Questioning of Persons by Police Officers para 14.8.
9 Ibid para 14.9.

743. Interpreters; foreign languages. Except in the case of urgent interviews[1], a person must not be interviewed in the absence of a person capable of acting as interpreter if:

(1) he has difficulty in understanding English;
(2) the interviewing officer cannot himself speak the person's own language; and
(3) the person wishes an interpreter to be present[2].

The interviewing officer must ensure that the interpreter makes a note of the interview at the time in the language of the person being interviewed for use in the event of his being called to give evidence, and certifies its accuracy[3]. The person must be given an opportunity to read it or have it read to him and sign it as correct or to indicate the respects in which he considers it inaccurate[3]. If the interview is tape-recorded[4], the arrangements set out in the relevant code of practice apply[5].

In the case of a person making a statement in a language other than English:
(a) the interpreter must take down the statement in the language in which it is made;
(b) the person making the statement must be invited to sign it; and
(c) an official English translation must be made in due course[6].

1 Ie unless the Code of Practice for the Detention, Treatment and Questioning of Persons by Police Officers Annex C applies: see para 737 ante.
2 Ibid para 14.1.
3 Ibid para 14.2.
4 As to tape-recorded interviews see para 746 et seq post.
5 Code of Practice for the Detention, Treatment and Questioning of Persons by Police Officers para 14.2.
6 Ibid para 14.3.

744. Interpreters; the deaf. Except in the case of urgent interviews[1], if a person is deaf or there is doubt about his hearing ability, he must not be interviewed in the absence of an interpreter unless he agrees in writing to be interviewed without one[2].

The interviewing officer must ensure that the interpreter makes a note of the interview at the time for use in the event of his being called to give evidence and certifies its accuracy[3]. The person must be given an opportunity to read it and sign it as correct or to indicate the respects in which he considers it inaccurate[3].

1 Ie unless the Code of Practice for the Detention, Treatment and Questioning of Persons by Police Officers Annex C applies: see para 737 ante.
2 Ibid para 14.4. If police officers are not aware that a person is deaf or have doubts about his hearing ability, it cannot be shown that there has been a breach of para 14.4; it is for the officers to decide whether there is a doubt, but, if a doubt arises during an interview, it would be a breach of para 14.4 to continue with the interview: *R v Clarke* [1989] Crim LR 892, CA.
3 Code of Practice for Detention, Treatment and Questioning of Persons by Police Officers para 14.5. Information on obtaining the services of a suitably qualified interpreter for the deaf is given in para 3, note 3C: para 14.5. See further para 723 note 4 ante.

C. SPECIAL RESTRICTIONS

745. Questioning; special restrictions. If a person has been arrested by one police force on behalf of another and the lawful period of detention in respect of that offence has not yet commenced[1], no questions may be put to him about the offence while he is in transit between the forces except in order to clarify any voluntary statement made by him[2]. If a person is in police detention at a hospital, he may not be questioned without the agreement of a responsible doctor[3].

1 Ie in accordance with the Police and Criminal Evidence Act 1984 s 41: see para 760 post.
2 Code of Practice for the Detention, Treatment and Questioning of Persons by Police Officers para 15.1.
3 Ibid para 15.2. If questioning takes place at a hospital under para 15.2, or on the way to or from a hospital, the period concerned counts towards the total period of detention permitted: para 15.2, note 15A.

D. TAPE-RECORDED INTERVIEWS

746. Code of Practice. The tape-recording by the police of their interviews at police stations with suspected persons is governed by the Police and Criminal Evidence Act 1984[1] and the Code of Practice on Tape-recording[2]. The Code must be readily available for consultation by police officers, detained persons and members of the public at every police station to which an order under the Police and Criminal Evidence Act 1984[3] applies[4].

1 Ie the Police and Criminal Evidence Act 1984 s 60: see para 657 ante.
2 Ie the Code of Practice on Tape-recording: see para 747 et seq post. The notes for guidance included in the Code are not provisions of the Code; they form guidance to police officers and others about its application and interpretation: para 1.2. Nothing in the Code is to be taken as detracting in any way from the requirements of the Code of Practice for the Detention, Treatment and Questioning of Persons by Police Officers (see para 691 et seq ante): Code of Practice on Tape-recording para 1.3.
3 Ie an order under the Police and Criminal Evidence Act 1984 s 60 (1) (b): see para 657 ante. At the date at which this volume states the law no order has been made bringing s 60 (1) (b) into force.
4 Code of Practice on Tape-recording para 1.1.

747. Interviews to be tape-recorded. Tape-recording must be used at police stations for any interview:
(1) with a person who has been cautioned[1] in respect of an indictable offence[2], including an offence triable either way[3];
(2) which takes place as a result of a police officer exceptionally putting further questions to a suspect about an offence described in head (1) above after he has been charged with, or informed he may be prosecuted for, that offence[4]; or
(3) in which a police officer wishes to bring to the notice of a person[5], after he has been charged with, or informed he may be prosecuted for an offence described in head (1) above, any written statement made by another person, or the content of an interview with another person[6].
Tape-recording is not required in respect of the following:
(a) an interview with a person arrested under the Prevention of Terrorism (Temporary Provisions) Act 1989[7] or an interview with a person being questioned in respect of an offence where there are reasonable grounds for suspecting that it is connected to terrorism or was committed in furtherance of the objectives of an organisation engaged in terrorism[8];
(b) an interview with a person suspected on reasonable grounds of an offence[9] under the Official Secrets Act 1911[10].
The custody officer[11] may authorise the interviewing officer not to tape-record the interview:
(i) where it is not reasonably practicable to do so because of failure of the equipment or the non-availability of a suitable interview room or recorder and the authorising officer considers on reasonable grounds that the interview should not be delayed until the failure has been rectified or a suitable room or recorder becomes available; or

(ii) where it is clear from the outset that no prosecution will ensue[12].

In all cases the custody officer must make a note in specific terms of the reasons for not tape-recording[12].

Where an interview takes place with a person voluntarily attending the police station[13] and the police officer has grounds to believe that person has become a suspect[14], the continuation of the interview must be tape-recorded, unless the custody officer gives authority[15] for the continuation of the interview not to be recorded[16].

The whole of each interview must be tape-recorded, including the taking and reading back of any statement[17].

1 Ie in accordance with the Code of Practice for the Detention, Treatment and Questioning of Persons by Police Officers para 10: see para 734 ante.

2 As to trial on indictment see para 942 et seq post.

3 As to offences triable either way see paras 804, 809 et seq post.

4 Circumstances in which a suspect may be questioned about an offence after being charged with it are set out in the Code of Practice for the Detention, Treatment and Questioning of Persons by Police Officers para 17.5 (see para 783 post): Code of Practice on Tape-recording para 3.1, note 3C.

5 Procedures to be followed when a person's attention is drawn after charge to a statement made by another person are set out in the Code of Practice for the Detention, Treatment and Questioning of Persons by Police Officers para 17.4 (see para 783 post): Code of Practice on Tape-recording para 3.1, note 3D. One method of bringing the content of an interview with another person to the notice of a suspect may be to play him a tape-recording of that interview: para 3.1, note 3D.

6 Ibid para 3.1. Nothing in the Code of Practice on Tape-recording is intended to preclude tape-recording at police discretion of interviews at police stations with persons cautioned in respect of offences not covered by para 3.1, or responses made by interviewees after they have been charged with, or informed they may be prosecuted for, an offence, provided that the Code is complied with: para 3.1, note 3A. Attention is drawn to the restrictions in the Code of Practice for the Detention, Treatment and Questioning of Persons by Police Officers para 12.3 (see para 738 ante) on the questioning of persons unfit through drink or drugs to the extent that they are unable to appreciate the significance of questions put to them or of their answers: Code of Practice on Tape-recording para 3.1, note 3B.

7 Ie under the Prevention of Terrorism (Temporary Provisions) Act 1989 s 14 (1) (a): see para 118 ante.

8 The Code of Practice on Tape-recording para 3.2 (a) applies only where the terrorism is connected with the affairs of Northern Ireland or is terrorism of any other description except terrorism connected solely with the affairs of the United Kingdom or any part of the United Kingdom other than Northern Ireland: para 3.2 (a). 'Terrorism' has the meaning given by the Prevention of Terrorism (Temporary Provisions) Act 1989 s 20 (1) (see para 102 note 4 ante): Code of Practice on Tape-recording para 3.2 (a). When it only becomes clear during the course of an interview which is being tape-recorded that the interviewee may have committed an offence to which para 3.2 applies, the interviewing officer should turn off the tape-recorder: para 3.2, note 3H.

It should be noted that the provisions of para 3.2 apply only to those suspected of offences connected with terrorism connected with Northern Ireland, or with terrorism of any other description other than terrorism connected solely with the affairs of the United Kingdom or any part of the United Kingdom other than Northern Ireland, or offences committed in furtherance of such terrorism: para 3.2, note 3G. Any interviews with those suspected of offences connected with terrorism of any other description or in furtherance of the objectives of an organisation engaged in such terrorism should be carried out in compliance with the rest of the Code of Practice on Tape-recording: para 3.2, note 3G.

9 Ie an offence under the Official Secrets Act 1911 s 1 (amended by the Official Secrets Act 1920 ss 10, 11 (2), Schs 1, 2): see para 243 ante.

10 Code of Practice on Tape-recording para 3.2 (b). When it only becomes clear during the course of an interview which is being tape-recorded that the interviewee may have committed an offence to which para 3.2 applies, the interviewing officer should turn off the tape-recorder: para 3.2, note 3H.

11 References to custody officers include those carrying out the functions of a custody officer: ibid para 1.3, note 1B. As to custody officers see para 716 ante.

12 Code of Practice on Tape-recording para 3.3. Where practicable, priority should be given to tape-recording interviews with persons who are suspected of more serious offences: para 3.3, note 3J. A decision not to tape-record an interview for any reason may be the subject of comment in

court; and the authorising officer should therefore be prepared to justify his decision in each case: para 3.3, note 3K.
13 As to voluntary attendance at a police station see para 692 ante.
14 Ie the point at which he should be cautioned in accordance with the Code of Practice for the Detention, Treatment and Questioning of Persons by Police Officers para 10.1: see para 734 ante.
15 Ie in accordance with the Code of Practice on Tape-recording para 3.3: see supra.
16 Ibid para 3.4.
17 Ibid para 3.5.

748. Recording and sealing of master tapes. Tape-recording of interviews must be carried out openly to instil confidence in its reliability as an impartial and accurate record of the interview[1]. One tape[2] ('the master tape'), will be sealed before it leaves the presence of the suspect; and a second tape will be used as a working copy[3]. The master tape is either one of the two tapes used in a twin-deck machine or the only tape used in a single-deck machine[3]. The working copy is either the second tape used in a twin-deck machine or a copy of the master tape made by a single-deck machine[3].

1 Code of Practice on Tape-recording para 2.1. Police officers will wish to arrange that, as far as possible, tape-recording arrangements are unobtrusive: para 2.1, note 2A. It must be clear to the suspect, however, that there is no opportunity to interfere with the tape-recording equipment or the tapes: para 2.1, note 2A.
2 Throughout the Code of Practice on Tape-recording any reference to 'tapes' is to be construed as 'tape', as appropriate, where a single-deck machine is used: para 2.2, note 2C.
3 Ibid para 2.2. The purpose of sealing the master tape before it leaves the presence of the suspect is to establish his confidence that the integrity of the tape is preserved: para 2.2, note 2B. Where a single-deck machine is used, the working copy of the master tape must be made in the presence of the suspect and without the master tape having left his sight: para 2.2, note 2B. The working copy must be used for making further copies where the need arises: para 2.2, note 2B. The recorder will normally be capable of recording voices and have a time coding or other security device: para 2.2, note 2B.

749. Commencement of interview. When the suspect is brought into the interview room, the police officer must without delay, but in the sight of the suspect, load the tape-recorder with previously unused tapes[1] and set it to record[2]. The tapes must be unwrapped or otherwise opened in the presence of the suspect[2]. The police officer must then tell the suspect formally about the tape recording[3]. He must say:
(1) that the interview is being tape-recorded;
(2) his name and rank and the name and rank of any other police officer present;
(3) the name of the suspect and any other party present, for example a solicitor;
(4) the date, time of commencement and place of the interview; and
(5) that the suspect will be given a notice about what will happen to the tapes[3].
The police officer must then caution the suspect in the following terms:

'You do not have to say anything unless you wish to do so, but what you say may be given in evidence.'[4]

Minor deviations do not constitute a breach of this requirement provided that the sense of the caution is preserved[4].

1 For the meaning of 'tapes' see para 746 note 2 ante.
2 Code of Practice on Tape-recording para 4.1. The police officer should attempt to estimate the likely length of the interview and ensure that the appropriate number of unused tapes and labels with which to seal the master copies are available in the interview room: para 4.1, note 4A.

3   Ibid para 4.2. It will be helpful for the purpose of voice identification if the officer asks the suspect
    and any other persons present to identify themselves: para 4.2, note 4B.
4   Ibid para 4.3. If it appears that a person does not understand what the caution means, the officer who
    has given it should go on to explain it in his own words: para 4.3, note 4C. In case anyone who is
    given a caution is unclear about its significance, the officer concerned should explain that the caution
    is given in pursuance of the general principle of English law that a person need not answer any
    questions or provide any information which might tend to incriminate him, and that no adverse
    inferences from this silence may be drawn at any trial that takes place: para 4.3, note 4D. The person
    should not, however, be left with a false impression that non-co-operation will have no effect on his
    immediate treatment as, for example, his refusal to provide his name and address may render him
    liable to detention: para 4.3, note 4D.

750. Interviews with the deaf. If the suspect is deaf or there is doubt about his
hearing ability, the police officer must take a contemporaneous note of the interview[1], as well as tape-record it[2].

1   Ie in accordance with the Code of Practice for the Detention, Treatment and Questioning of Persons
    by Police Officers para 11: see para 736 ante.
2   Code of Practice on Tape-recording para 4.4. This provision is intended to give the deaf equivalent
    rights of first-hand access to the full interview record as other suspects: para 4.4, note 4E. The
    provisions of the Code of Practice for the Detention. Treatment and Questioning of Persons by
    Police Officers paras 14.1, 14.4 and 14.7 (interpreters for the deaf or for interviews with suspects
    who have difficulty in understanding English: see paras 742–744 ante) continue to apply: Code of
    Practice on Tape-recording para 4.4, note 4F. In a tape-recorded interview there is no requirement
    on the interviewing officer to ensure that the interpreter makes a separate note of interview as
    prescribed in the Code of Practice for the Detention, Treatment and Questioning of Persons by
    Police Officers para 14 (see paras 742–744 ante): Code of Practice on Tape-recording para 4.4, note
    4F.

751. Objections and complaints by the suspect. If the suspect raises objections
to the interview being tape-recorded either at the outset or during the interview or
during a break in the interview, the police officer must explain the fact that the
interview is being tape-recorded and that the provisions of the Code of Practice on
Tape-recording require that the suspect's objections should be recorded on tape[1].
When any objections have been recorded on tape or the suspect has refused to have
his objections recorded, the police officer may turn off the recorder[1]. In this
eventuality he must say that he is turning off the recorder and give his reasons for
doing so and then turn it off[1]. The police officer must then make a written record[2]
of the interview[3]. If, however, the police officer reasonably considers that he may
proceed to put questions to the suspect with the tape-recorder still on, he may do
so[3]. If in the course of an interview a complaint is made[4] by the person being
questioned, or on his behalf, the officer must[5] record it in the interview record and
inform the custody officer[6] who is then responsible for dealing with it[7].

If the suspect indicates that he wishes to tell the police officer about matters not
directly connected with the offence of which he is suspected and that he is unwilling
for these matters to be recorded on tape, he must be given the opportunity to tell
the police officer about these matters after the conclusion of the formal interview[8].

1   Code of Practice on Tape-recording para 4.5. The officer should bear in mind that a decision to
    continue recording against the wishes of the suspect may be the subject of comment in court: para
    4.5, note 4G.
2   Ie in accordance with the Code of Practice for the Detention, Treatment and Questioning of Persons
    by Police Officers para 11: see para 736 ante.
3   Code of Practice on Tape-recording para 4.5.

4 Ie a complaint concerning the provisions of the Code of Practice on Tape-recording or the Code of Practice for the Detention, Treatment and Questioning of Persons by Police Officers.
5 Ie in accordance with ibid para 12.8: see para 738 ante.
6 As to custody officers see paras 716, 747 note 11 ante.
7 Code of Practice on Tape-recording para 4.6. Where the custody officer is called immediately to deal with the complaint, wherever possible the tape-recorder should be left to run until the custody officer has entered the interview room and spoken to the person being interviewed: para 4.6, note 4H.

   Continuation or termination of the interview should be at the discretion of the interviewing officer pending action by an inspector under the Code of Practice for the Detention, Treatment and Questioning of Persons by Police Officers para 9.1 (see para 732 ante): Code of Practice on Tape-recording para 4.6, note 4H. Where the complaint is about a matter not connected with the Code of Practice on Tape-recording or the Code of Practice for the Detention, Treatment and Questioning of Persons by Police Officers, the decision to continue with the interview is at the discretion of the interviewing officer: Code of Practice on Tape-recording para 4.6, note 4J. Where the interviewing officer decides to continue with the interview, the person being interviewed must be told that the complaint will be brought to the attention of the custody officer at the conclusion of the interview: para 4.6, note 4J. When the interview is concluded, the interviewing officer must, as soon as practicable, inform the custody officer of the existence and nature of the complaint made: para 4.6, note 4J.
8 Ibid para 4.7.

752. Changing tapes. When the recorder indicates that the tapes[1] have only a short time left to run, the police officer must tell the suspect that the tapes are coming to an end and round off that part of the interview[2]. If the police officer wishes to continue the interview but does not already have a second set of tapes, he must obtain a set[2]. The suspect must not be left unattended in the interview room[2]. The police officer will remove the tapes from the tape-recorder and insert the new tapes which must be unwrapped or otherwise opened in the suspect's presence[2]. The tape-recorder must then be set to record on the new tapes[2]. Care must be taken, particularly when a number of sets of tapes have been used, to ensure that there is no confusion between the tapes[2]. This may be done by marking the tapes with an identification number immediately they are removed from the tape-recorder[2].

1 For the meaning of 'tapes' see para 748 note 2 ante.
2 Code of Practice on Tape-recording para 4.8.

753. Taking a break during interview. When a break is to be taken during the course of an interview and the interview room is to be vacated by the suspect, the fact that a break is to be taken, the reason for it and the time must be recorded on tape[1]. The tapes must then be removed from the tape-recorder and the prescribed procedures for the conclusion of an interview[2] followed[3].

When a break is to be a short one and both the suspect and a police officer are to remain in the interview room, the fact that a break is to be taken, the reasons for it and the time must be recorded on tape[4]. The tape-recorder may be turned off; there is, however, no need to remove the tapes and, when the interview is recommenced, the tape-recording must be continued on the same tapes[4]. The time at which the interview recommences must be recorded on tape[4].

When there is a break in questioning under caution, the interviewing officer must ensure that the person being questioned is aware that he remains under caution[5]. If there is any doubt, the caution must be given again in full when the interview resumes[5].

1 Code of Practice on Tape-recording para 4.9. For the meaning of 'tapes' see para 748 note 2 ante.
2 Ie the procedure set out in ibid para 4.15: see para 756 post.
3 Ibid para 4.9.
4 Ibid para 4.10.
5 Ibid para 4.11. In considering whether to caution again after a break, the officer should bear in mind that he may have to satisfy a court that the person understood that he was still under caution when the interview resumed: para 4.11, note 4K. The officer should bear in mind that it may be necessary to show to the court that nothing occurred during a break in an interview or between interviews which influenced the suspect's recorded evidence: para 4.11, note 4L. The officer should consider, therefore, after a break in an interview or at the beginning of a subsequent interview summarising on tape the reason for the break and confirming this with the suspect: para 4.11, note 4L. As to the caution see para 749 ante.

754. Failure of recording equipment. If there is a failure of equipment which can be rectified quickly, for example by inserting new tapes[1], the prescribed procedures[2] must be followed; and, when the recording is resumed, the officer must explain what has happened and record the time the interview recommences[3]. If, however, it will not be possible to continue recording on that particular tape-recorder and no replacement recorder or recorder in another interview room is readily available, the interview may continue without being tape-recorded[3]. In such circumstances the prescribed procedures[4] for seeking the authority of the custody officer will be followed[5].

1 For the meaning of 'tapes' see para 748 note 2 ante.
2 Ie the procedure set out in the Code of Practice on Tape-recording para 4.8: see para 752 ante.
3 Ibid para 4.12. If one of the tapes breaks during the interview, it should be sealed as a master tape in the presence of the suspect and the interview resumed where it left off: para 4.12, note 4M. The unbroken tape should be copied and the original sealed as a master tape in the suspect's presence, if necessary after the interview: para 4.12, note 4M. If equipment for copying the unbroken tape is not readily available, both tapes should be sealed in the suspect's presence and the interview begun again: para 4.12, note 4M. If the tape breaks when a single-deck machine is being used and the machine is one where a broken tape cannot be copied on available equipment, the tape should be sealed as a master tape in the suspect's presence and the interview begun again: para 4.12, note 4M. For the meaning of 'master tape' see para 748 text to note 3 ante.
4 Ie the procedure set out in ibid para 3.3: see para 747 ante.
5 Ibid para 4.12. As to custody officers see paras 716, 747 note 11 ante.

755. Removing tapes from the recorder. Where tapes[1] are removed from the recorder in the course of an interview, they must be retained and the prescribed procedures[2] followed[3].

1 For the meaning of 'tapes' see para 748 note 2 ante.
2 Ie the procedure set out in the Code of Practice on Tape-recording para 4.15: see para 756 post.
3 Ibid para 4.13.

756. Conclusion of interview. At the conclusion of the interview, the suspect must be offered the opportunity to clarify anything he has said and to add anything he may wish[1]. At the conclusion of the interview, including the taking and reading back of any written statement, the time must be recorded and the tape-recorder switched off[2]. The master tape[3] must be sealed with a master tape label and treated as an exhibit in accordance with the force standing orders[4]. The police officer must sign the label and ask the suspect and any third party present to sign it also[4]. If the suspect or third party refuses to sign the label, an officer of at least the rank of inspector, or if one is not available the custody officer[5], must be called into the interview room and asked to sign it[6].

The suspect must be handed a notice which explains the use which will be made of the tape-recording and the arrangements for access to it[7].

1　Code of Practice on Tape-recording para 4.14.
2　Ibid para 4.15.
3　For the meaning of 'master tape' see para 748 text to note 3 ante.
4　Code of Practice on Tape-recording para 4.15.
5　As to custody officers see paras 716, 747 note 11 ante.
6　Code of Practice on Tape-recording para 4.15.
7　Ibid para 4.16.

757. Procedure after interview. The police officer must make a note in his notebook of the fact that the interview has taken place and has been recorded on tape, its time, duration and date and the identification number of the master tape[1].

Where no proceedings follow in respect of the person whose interview was recorded, the tapes must nevertheless be kept[2] securely[3].

Where such proceedings do follow, the officer must prepare a written record of the interview which will be signed by the officer[4]. The interview record must be exhibited to any written statement prepared by the officer[4].

Where the police officer's evidence of the interview is accepted by the defence, the evidence must refer to the fact that the interview was tape-recorded and may be presented to the court in the form of the interview record[5]. Where the police officer's evidence of the interview is not accepted by the defence, the police officer must refer to the fact that the interview was tape-recorded and must produce the master tape as an exhibit[5]. The officer must inform the court of any transcription which has been made of which he is aware[5].

1　Code of Practice on Tape-recording para 5.1. For the meaning of 'master tape' see para 748 text to note 3 ante.
2　Ie in accordance with ibid para 6.1 and note 6A: see para 758 post.
3　Ibid para 5.2.
4　Ibid para 5.3. Prior to preparing the record of the interview, the officer may refresh his memory by listening to the working copy of the tape: para 5.3, note 5A. The purpose of using the tape will be to act as a check on the accuracy of the interview record: para 5.3, note 5A. The interview record must be prepared on the basis that it is to be used (1) to enable the prosecutor to make informed decisions about the case on the basis of what was said at the interview; (2) to be exhibited to the officer's witness statement and used pursuant to the Criminal Justice Act 1967 s 9 (amended by the Courts Act 1971 s 56 (1), Sch 8 Pt II para 49) (see para 1113 post) and the Magistrates' Court Act 1980 s 102 (amended by the Criminal Justice Act 1988 s 170 (1), Sch 15 para 65, 68) (see para 832 post); (3) to enable the prosecutor to comply with the rules of advance disclosure; and (4) where the record is accepted by the defence, to be used for the conduct of the case by the prosecution, the defence, and the court: Code of Practice on Tape-recording para 5.3, note 5B. The record must, therefore, comprise a balanced account of the interview including points in mitigation and/or defence made by the suspect: para 5.3, note 5B. Where an admission is made, the question as well as the answer containing the admission must be recorded verbatim in the record: para 5.3, note 5B. Care should be taken to bring to the attention of the prosecutor, by means of a covering report, any material on the tape which might be regarded by a court as prejudicial or inadmissible: para 5.3, note 5B. As to the admissibility of evidence see para 1132 et seq post.
5　Ibid para 5.4. Production of the tape as an exhibit will have the effect in court proceedings of producing the content of the whole interview, subject to any decision on editing carried out on the direction of the Crown Prosecutor: para 5.4, note 5C. As to Crown Prosecutors see para 647 ante. As to preparing tape-recorded evidence for court see *Practice Note* [1989] 2 All ER 415; sub nom *Practice Direction* (1989) 89 Cr App Rep 132, CA and para 759 post.

758. Tape security. The officer in charge of each police station at which interviews with suspects are recorded must make arrangements for master tapes[1] to be kept securely and their movements accounted for on the same basis as other material which may be used for evidential purposes, in accordance with force standing orders[2].

A police officer has no authority to break the seal on a master tape which is required for criminal proceedings[3]. If it is necessary to gain access to the master tape, the police officer must arrange for its seal to be broken in the presence of a representative of the Crown Prosecution Service[3]. The accused or his legal adviser must be informed and given a reasonable opportunity to be present[3]. If the accused or his legal representative is present, he must be invited to reseal and sign the master tape[3]. If either refuses or neither is present, this must be done by the representative of the Crown Prosecution Service[3].

Where no criminal proceedings result, it is the responsibility of the chief officer of police to establish arrangements for the breaking of the seal on the master tape, where this becomes necessary[4].

1 For the meaning of 'master tape' see para 748 text to note 3 ante.
2 Code of Practice on Tape-recording para 6.1. Paragraph 6 is concerned with the security of the master tape which will have been sealed at the conclusion of the interview: para 6.1, note 6A. Care should, however, be taken of working copies of tapes since their loss or destruction may lead unnecessarily to the need to have access to master tapes: para 6.1, note 6A.
3 Ibid para 6.2. If the tape has been delivered to the Crown Court for keeping after committal for trial, the Crown Prosecutor will apply to the chief clerk of the Crown Court centre for the release of the tape for unsealing by the Crown Prosecutor: para 6.2, note 6B. For these purposes, reference to the Crown Prosecution Service or to the Crown Prosecutor is taken to mean any other body or person with a statutory responsibility for prosecution for whom the police conduct any tape-recorded interviews: para 6.2, note 6C. As to the Crown Prosecution Service see para 645 et seq ante.
4 Ibid para 6.3.

759. Preparing tape-recorded evidence for court. In order that sufficient notice may be given to allow consideration of any amendment[1] to the record of interview or the preparation of any transcript of a tape-recorded interview, or any editing[1] of a tape for the purpose of playing it back in court[2], the following practice should be followed:

(1) where the defence is unable to agree a record of interview or transcript, where one is already available, the prosecution should be notified[3] no more than 21 days[4] from the date of committal or date of transfer[5] with a view to securing agreement to amend; and a copy of such notice should be supplied within the 21 day period[6];

(2) if agreement is not reached and it is proposed that the tape or part of it be played in court, notice should be given to the prosecution by the defence no more than 14 days[7] after the expiry of the period in head (1) above in order that counsel for the parties may agree those parts of the tape that should not be adduced and that arrangements may be made, by editing or in some other way, to exclude the material; and a copy of such notice should be supplied to the court within the 14 day period[8];

(3) notice of any agreement reached under heads (1) or (2) above should be supplied to the court by the prosecution as soon as is practicable[9];

(4) alternatively, if, in any event, prosecuting counsel proposes to play the tape or part of it, the prosecution should within 28 days[10] of the date of committal or date of transfer notify the defence and the court and the defence should

notify the prosecution and the court within 14 days[10] of receiving the notice if the defence objects to the production of the tape on the basis that a part of it should be excluded; if the objections raised by the defence are accepted, the prosecution should prepare an edited tape or make other arrangements to exclude the material part and should notify the court of the arrangements made[11].

If there is a failure to agree between counsel under heads (1) to (4) above, or there is a challenge to the integrity of the master tape[12], notice and particulars should be given to the court and to the prosecution by the defence as soon as is practicable; the court may then, at its discretion, order a pre-trial review or give such other directions as may be appropriate[13].

If a tape is to be adduced during proceedings before the Crown Court, it should be produced and proved by the interviewing officer[14] or any other officer who was present at the interview[14] at which the recording was made; and the prosecution should ensure that such an officer will be available for this purpose[15]. In order to avoid the necessity for the court to listen to lengthy or irrelevant material before the relevant part of a tape-recording is reached, counsel should indicate to the tape-machine operator[16] those parts of a recording which it may be necessary to play[17].

Once a trial has begun, if, by reason of faulty preparation or for some other cause the above procedures have not been properly complied with, and an application is made to amend the record of interview or transcript or to edit the tape, as the case may be, thereby making necessary an adjournment for the work to be carried out, the court may make at its discretion an appropriate award of costs[18].

1 Whenever editing or amendment or a record of interview or of a tape or of a transcript takes place, the general principles which should be followed are those set out in Archbold's Criminal Pleading, Evidence and Practice (43rd Edn, 1988) paras 4–186, 4–187, 4–188: see *Practice Note* [1989] 2 All ER 415; sub nom *Practice Direction* (1989) 89 Cr App Rep 132, CA. As to the editing of an accused's statements see also para 1122 post; and as to the editing of witness statements generally see *Practice Note* [1986] 2 All ER 511, CA.
2 A case in the Crown Court in which a tape-recording of a police interview with a suspect has been made will normally be conducted using a record of interview if such record has been agreed with the defence: see *Practice Note* [1989] 2 All ER 415; sub nom *Practice Direction* (1989) 89 Cr App Rep 132, CA para 1; and see para 757 ante.
3 The notice must specify the part of the tape to which objection is taken or the part omitted which the defence considers should be included: *Practice Note* [1989] 2 All ER 415; sub nom *Practice Direction* (1989) 89 Cr App Rep 132, CA para 2 (a).
4 Where a case is listed for hearing on a date which falls within the time limits set out in *Practice Note* [1989] 2 All ER 415; sub nom *Practice Direction* (1989) 89 Cr App Rep 132, CA, it is the responsibility of the parties to ensure that all the necessary steps are taken to comply with the required procedure within such shorter period as is available: *Practice Note* supra para 8.
5 Ie the date on which notice of transfer is given in accordance with the Criminal Justice Act 1987 s 4 (1) (c): see para 856 post.
6 *Practice Note* [1989] 2 All ER 415; sub nom *Practice Direction* (1989) 89 Cr App Rep 132, CA para 2 (a). See generally para 746 et seq ante; and Home Office Circular 76/1988.
7 See note 4 supra.
8 *Practice Note* [1989] 2 All ER 415; sub nom *Practice Direction* (1989) 89 Cr App Rep 132, CA para 2 (b).
9 *Practice Note* [1989] 2 All ER 415; sub nom *Practice Direction* (1989) 89 Cr App Rep 132, CA para 2 (c).
10 See note 4 supra.
11 *Practice Note* [1989] 2 All ER 415; sub nom *Practice Direction* (1989) 89 Cr App Rep 132, CA para 2 (d).
12 For the meaning of 'master tape' see para 748 text to note 3 ante.
13 *Practice Note* [1989] 2 All ER 415; sub nom *Practice Direction* (1989) 89 Cr App Rep 132, CA para 3.
14 Where such officer is unable to act as the tape-machine operator, it is for the prosecution to make some other arrangement: *Practice Note* [1989] 2 All ER 415; sub nom *Practice Direction* (1989) 89 Cr App Rep 132, CA para 5.
15 *Practice Note* [1989] 2 All ER 415; sub nom *Practice Direction* (1989) 89 Cr App Rep 132, CA para 4.

16 See text and note 14 supra. Such an indication should, so far as possible, be expressed in terms of the time track or other identifying process used by the interviewing police force and should be given in time for the operator to have located those parts by the appropriate point in the trial: *Practice Note* [1989] 2 All ER 419; sub nom *Practice Direction* (1989) 89 Cr App Rep 132, CA para 6.
17 *Practice Note* [1989] 2 All ER 415; sub nom *Practice Direction* (1989) 89 Cr App Rep 132, CA para 6.
18 *Practice Note* [1989] 2 All ER 415; sub nom *Practice Direction* (1989) 89 Cr App Rep 132, CA para 7. As to costs see para 1526 et seq post.

(vi) Limits on Detention

760. Limits on period of detention without charge. A person may not[1] be kept in police detention[2] for more than 24 hours[3] without being charged[4]. The time from which the period of detention of a person is to be calculated ('the relevant time') is:

(1) in the case of a person to whom this provision applies[5]: (a) the time at which that person arrives at the relevant police station; or (b) the time 24 hours after the time of that person's arrest, whichever is the earlier;

(2) in the case of a person arrested outside England and Wales: (a) the time at which that person arrives at the first police station to which he is taken in the police area in England or Wales in which the offence for which he was arrested is being investigated; or (b) the time 24 hours after the time of that person's entry into England and Wales, whichever is the earlier;

(3) in the case of a person who attends voluntarily at a police station[6] or accompanies a constable to a police station without having been arrested, and is arrested at the police station, the time of his arrest;

(4) in any other case[7], the time at which the person arrested arrives at the first police station to which he is taken after his arrest[8].

If:

(i) a person is in police detention in a police area in England and Wales ('the first area'); and

(ii) his arrest for an offence is sought in some other police area in England and Wales ('the second area'); and

(iii) he is taken to the second area for the purposes of investigating that offence, without being questioned in the first area in order to obtain evidence in relation to it,

the relevant time is the time 24 hours after he leaves the place where he is detained in the first area or the time at which he arrives at the first police station to which he is taken in the second area, whichever is the earlier[9].

When a person who is in police detention is removed to hospital because he is in need of medical treatment, any time during which he is being questioned in hospital or on the way there or back by a police officer for the purpose of obtaining evidence relating to an offence is to be included in any period which falls to be calculated for these purposes, but any other time while he is in hospital or on his way there or back is not to be so included[10]. A person who at the expiry of 24 hours after the relevant time is in police detention and has not been charged must be released at that time either on bail or without bail[11]; but this provision does not apply to a person whose detention for more than 24 hours after the relevant time has been authorised or is otherwise permitted[12]. A person so released may not be re-arrested without a warrant for the offence for which he was previously arrested unless new evidence justifying a further arrest has come to light since his release[13].

1 Ie subject to the Police and Criminal Evidence Act 1984 s 41 (2)–(9) (see infra), s 42 (see para 762 post) and s 42 (see para 763 post).
2 For the meaning of 'in police detention' see para 716 note 5 ante.
3 Any reference in the Police and Criminal Evidence Act 1984 Pt IV (ss 34–52: see para 715 et seq ante; infra; and para 761 et seq post) to a period of time or a time of day is to be treated as approximate only: s 45 (2).
4 Ibid s 41 (1).
5 Ibid s 41 (2) (a) (see head (1) supra) applies to a person if: (1) his arrest is sought in one police area in England and Wales; (2) he is arrested in another police area; and (3) he is not questioned in the area in which he is arrested; and for these purposes 'the relevant police station' means the first police station to which he is taken in the police area in which his arrest was sought: s 41 (3). For the meaning of 'police area' see para 142 note 1 ante.
6 As to voluntary attendance at a police station see para 692 ante.
7 Ie except where the Police and Criminal Evidence Act 1984 s 41 (5) applies: see infra.
8 Ibid s 41 (2). Section s 41 (2) has effect in relation to a person arrested under s 31 (see para 712 ante) as if every reference in it to his arrest or his being arrested were a reference to his arrest or his being arrested for the offence for which he was originally arrested: s 41 (4).
9 Ibid s 41 (5).
10 Ibid s 41 (6).
11 Ibid s 41 (7).
12 Ibid s 41 (8). A person's detention for more than 24 hours may be authorised or otherwise permitted under ss 42, 43: see paras 762, 763 post.
13 Ibid s 41 (9).

761. Review of police detention. Reviews of the detention of each person in police detention[1] in connection with the investigation of an offence must be carried out periodically in accordance with the following provisions:

(1) in the case of a person who has been arrested and charged, by the custody officer[2]; and

(2) in the case of a person who has been arrested but not charged, by an officer of at least the rank of inspector[3] who has not been directly involved in the investigation[4].

The first review must be not later than six hours[5] after the detention was first authorised: the second review must be not later than nine hours after the first; and subsequent reviews must be at intervals of not more than nine hours[6]. A review may, however, be postponed:

(a) if, having regard to all the circumstances prevailing at the latest time for it, it is not practicable to carry out the review at that time;

(b) without prejudice to the generality of head (a) above, (i) if at that time the person in detention is being questioned by a police officer and the review officer[7] is satisfied that an interruption of the questioning for the purpose of carrying out the review would prejudice the investigation in connection with which he is being questioned; or (ii) if at that time no review officer is readily available[8].

If a review is so postponed, it must be carried out as soon as practicable after the latest time specified for it[9]; and, if a review is carried out after such a postponement, the fact that it was so carried out does not affect any statutory requirement[10] as to the time at which any subsequent review is to be carried out[11].

The review officer must record the reasons for any postponement of a review in the custody record[12].

Where an officer of higher rank than the review officer gives directions relating to a person in police detention and the directions are at variance with any decision made or action taken by the review officer in the performance of a duty imposed on him[13] or with any decision or action which would but for the directions have been made or taken by him in the performance of such a duty, the review officer must refer the matter at once to an officer of the rank of superintendent or above who is responsible for the police station for which the review officer is acting as review officer in connection with the detention[14]. Before determining whether to authorise a person's continued detention the review officer must give that person, unless he is asleep, or any solicitor representing him who is available at the time of the review, an opportunity to make representations to him about the detention[15]; and the person whose detention is under review or his solicitor may make such representations either orally or in writing[16]. However, the review officer may refuse to hear oral representations from the person whose detention is under review if he considers that he is unfit to make such representations by reason of his condition or behaviour[17].

1 For the meaning of 'in police detention' see para 716 note 5 ante.
2 As to custody officers see para 716 ante.
3 See para 659 ante.
4 Police and Criminal Evidence Act 1984 s 40 (1). Where the person whose detention is under review has not been charged before the time of the review, s 37 (1)–(6) (see para 718 ante) has effect in relation to him, but with the substitution (1) of references to the person whose detention is under review for references to the person arrested; and (2) of references to the review officer for references to the custody officer: s 40 (8). Where, however, a person has been kept in police detention by virtue of s 37 (9) (see para 718 ante), s 37 (1)–(6) does not have effect in relation to him but it is the duty of the review officer to determine whether he is yet in a fit state: s 40 (9).
     Where the person whose detention is under review has been charged before the time of the review, s 38 (1)–(6) (see para 719 ante) has effect in relation to him, but with the substitution of references to the person whose detention is under review for references to the person arrested: s 40 (10).
5 See para 760 note 3 ante.
6 Police and Criminal Evidence Act 1984 s 40 (3).
7 The officer to whom it falls to carry out a review is referred to in ibid s 40 as a 'review officer': s 40 (2).
8 Ibid s 40 (4).
9 Ibid s 40 (5).
10 Ie any requirement of ibid s 40.
11 Ibid s 40 (6).
12 Ibid s 40 (7). As to custody records see para 717 ante.
13 Ie under ibid Pt IV (ss 34–52).
14 Ibid s 40 (11).
15 Ibid s 40 (12). The review officer is responsible under s 40 for determining whether or not a person's detention continues to be necessary: Code of Practice for the Detention, Treatment and Questioning of Persons by Police Officers para 16.1. If in the circumstances the only practicable way of conducting a review is over the telephone, this is permissible, provided that the requirements of the Police and Criminal Evidence Act 1984 s 40 are observed: Code of Practice for the Detention, Treatment and Questioning of Persons by Police Officers para 16, note 16B. In reaching his decision he must provide an opportunity to the detained person himself to make representations, unless he is unfit to do so because of his condition or behaviour, and to his solicitor or the appropriate adult if available at the time: para 16.1. Other persons having an interest in the person's welfare may make representations at the review officer's discretion: para 16.1. The same persons may make representations to the officer determining whether further detention should be authorised under the Police and Criminal Evidence Act 1984 s 42 (see para 762 post): Code of Practice for the Detention, Treatment and Questioning of Persons by Police Officers para 16.2. For the meaning of 'the appropriate adult' see para 717 note 7 ante. The grounds for, and any delay in, conducting a review must be recorded: para 16.3. Any written representations must be retained: para 16.4. A record must be made as soon as practicable of the outcome of each review and application for a warrant of further detention or its extension: para 16.5.
16 Police and Criminal Evidence Act 1984 s 40 (13).
17 Ibid s 40 (14).

762. Authorisation of continued detention. Where a police officer of the rank of superintendent or above[1] who is responsible for the police station at which a person is detained has reasonable grounds for believing that:

(1) the detention of that person without charge is necessary to secure or preserve evidence relating to an offence for which he is under arrest or to obtain such evidence by questioning him;

(2) an offence for which he is under arrest is a serious arrestable offence[2]; and

(3) the investigation is being conducted diligently and expeditiously,

he may authorise the keeping of that person in police detention[3] for a period expiring at or before 36 hours[4] after the relevant time[5].

Where such an officer has so authorised the keeping of a person in police detention for a period expiring less than 36 hours after the relevant time, such officer may authorise the keeping of that person in police detention for a further period expiring not more than 36 hours after that time if the conditions specified in heads (1)–(3) above are still satisfied when he gives the authorisation[6].

If it is proposed to transfer a person in police detention to another police area, the officer determining whether or not to authorise keeping him in detention must have regard to the distance and the time the journey would take[7].

Where an officer so authorises the keeping of a person in police detention[8], it is his duty (a) to inform that person of the grounds for his continued detention; and (b) to record the grounds in that person's custody record[9].

Before determining whether to authorise the keeping of a person in detention[10], an officer must give that person or any solicitor representing him who is available at the time when it falls to the officer to determine whether to give the authorisation, an opportunity to make representations to him about the detention[11]; and the person in detention or his solicitor may so make representations either orally or in writing[12]. The officer to whom it falls to determine whether to give the authorisation may, however, refuse to hear oral representations from the person in detention if he considers that he is unfit to make such representations by reason of his condition or behaviour[13]. Where an officer authorises the keeping of a person in detention and at the time of the authorisation he has not yet exercised his statutory rights to have someone informed of his whereabouts[14] and to legal advice[15], the officer must:

(i) inform him of that right;

(ii) decide whether he should be permitted to exercise it;

(iii) record the decision in his custody record; and

(iv) if the decision is to refuse to permit the exercise of the right, also record the grounds for the decision in that record[16].

Where an officer has authorised the keeping of a person who has not been charged in detention[17], he must be released from detention, either on bail or without bail, not later than 36 hours after the relevant time, unless he has been charged with an offence or his continued detention is authorised or otherwise permitted[18]. A person so released may not be re-arrested without a warrant for the offence for which he was previously arrested unless new evidence justifying a further arrest has come to light since his release[19].

1 See para 659 ante.
2 For the meaning of 'serious arrestable offence' see para 704 ante.
3 For the meaning of 'in police detention' see para 716 note 5 ante.
4 See para 760 note 3 ante.

5 Police and Criminal Evidence Act 1984 s 42 (1). For the meaning of 'the relevant time' see para 760 ante. No authorisation under s 42 (1) may be given, however, in respect of any person (1) more than 24 hours after the relevant time; or (2) before the second review of his detention under s 40 (see para 761 ante) has been carried out: s 42 (4).
6 Ibid s 42 (2).
7 Ibid s 42 (3). For the meaning of 'police area' see para 142 note 1 ante.
8 Ie under ibid s 42 (1): see supra.
9 Ibid s 42 (5). As to custody records see para 717 ante.
10 Ie under ibid s 42 (1) or (2): see supra.
11 Ibid s 42 (6). As to representations see para 761 note 15 ante.
12 Ibid s 42 (7).
13 Ibid s 42 (8).
14 Ie the right conferred on him by ibid s 56: see para 726 ante.
15 Ie the right conferred on him by ibid s 58: see para 727 ante.
16 Ibid s 42 (9).
17 Ie under ibid s 42 (1) or (2): see supra.
18 Ibid s 42 (10). Warrants of further detention may be issued under s 43: see para 763 post.
19 Ibid s 42 (11).

763. Warrants of further detention. Where, on an application on oath made by a constable and supported by an information, a magistrates' court[1] is satisfied that there are reasonable grounds for believing that the further detention of the person to whom the application relates is justified, it may issue a warrant of further detention authorising the keeping of that person in police detention[2]. A court may not hear an application for such a warrant, however, unless the person to whom the application relates has been furnished with a copy of the information and has been brought before the court for the hearing[3].

The person to whom the application relates is entitled to be legally represented at the hearing and, if he is not so represented but wishes to be so represented, the court must adjourn the hearing to enable him to obtain representation and he may be kept in police detention during the adjournment[4]. A person's further detention is only so justified[5] if:

(1) his detention without charge is necessary to secure or preserve evidence relating to an offence for which he is under arrest or to obtain such evidence by questioning him;

(2) an offence for which he is under arrest is a serious arrestable offence[6]; and

(3) the investigation is being conducted diligently and expeditiously[7].

An application for such a warrant may be made (a) at any time before the expiry of 36 hours[8] after the relevant time[9]; or (b) in a case where it is not practicable for the magistrates' court to which the application will be made to sit at the expiry of 36 hours after the relevant time but the court will sit during the six hours following the end of that period, at any time before the expiry of such period of six hours[10].

If an application for a warrant of further detention is made after the expiry of 36 hours after the relevant time and it appears to the magistrates' court that it would have been reasonable for the police to make it before the expiry of that period, the court must dismiss the application[11].

Where on such an application a magistrates' court is not satisfied that there are reasonable grounds for believing that the further detention of the person to whom the application relates is justified, it is its duty to refuse the application or to adjourn the hearing of it until a time not later than 36 hours after the relevant time[12]. The person to whom the application relates may be kept in police detention during the adjournment[13]. A warrant of further detention must state the time at which it is issued and authorise the keeping in police detention of the person to whom it relates for the period stated in it[14]. The period so stated must be such period as the magistrates' court thinks fit, having regard to the evidence before it[15]; but the period may not be longer than 36 hours[16].

If it is proposed to transfer a person in police detention to a police area other than that in which he is detained when the application for a warrant of further detention is made, the court hearing the application must have regard to the distance and the time the journey would take[17].

Where an application is refused, the person to whom the application relates must forthwith be charged or released, either on bail or without bail[18]. However, a person need not be so released before the expiry of 24 hours after the relevant time or before the expiry of any longer period for which his continued detention is or has been authorised[19]. Where an application is refused, no further application may be made in respect of the person to whom the refusal relates, unless supported by evidence which has come to light since the refusal[20].

Where a warrant of further detention is issued, the person to whom it relates must be released from police detention, either on bail or without bail, upon or before the expiry of the warrant unless he is charged[21]. A person so released may not be re-arrested without a warrant for the offence for which he was previously arrested unless new evidence justifying a further arrest has come to light since his release[22].

1 For these purposes, 'magistrates' court' means a court consisting of two or more justices of the peace sitting otherwise than in open court: Police and Criminal Evidence Act 1984 s 45 (1).
2 Ibid s 43 (1). For the meaning of 'in police detention' see para 716 note 5 ante. Any information submitted in support of such an application must state:
   (1) the nature of the offence for which the person to whom the application relates has been arrested;
   (2) the general nature of the evidence on which that person was arrested;
   (3) what inquiries relating to the offence have been made by the police and what further inquiries are proposed by them;
   (4) the reasons for believing the continued detention of that person to be necessary for the purposes of such further inquiries:
   s 43 (14). An application for a warrant of further detention or its extension (see para 764 post) should be made between 10 am and 9 pm and, if possible, during normal court hours: Code of Practice for the Detention, Treatment and Questioning of Persons by Police Officers para 16, note 16A. It will not be practicable to arrange for a court to sit specially outside the hours of 10 am and 9 pm: para 16, note 16A. If it appears possible that a special sitting may be needed, either at a weekend, bank or public holiday or on a weekday outside normal court hours but between 10 am and 9 pm, the clerk to the justices should be given notice and informed of this possibility, while the court is sitting if possible: para 16, note 16A.
3 Police and Criminal Evidence Act 1984 s 43 (2).
4 Ibid s 43 (3).
5 Ie for the purposes of ibid s 43 or s 44 (see para 764 post).
6 For the meaning of 'serious arrestable offence' see para 704 ante.
7 Police and Criminal Evidence Act 1984 s 43 (4).
8 See para 760 note 3 ante.
9 For the meaning of 'the relevant time' see para 760 ante.
10 Police and Criminal Evidence Act 1984 s 43 (5). In a case to which s 43 (5) (b) (see head (b) supra) applies (1) the person to whom the application relates may be kept in police detention until the application is heard; and (2) the custody officer must make a note in that person's custody record (a) of the fact that he was kept in police detention for more than 36 hours after the relevant time; and (b) of the reason why he was so kept: s 43 (6). As to custody officers and custody records see paras 716, 717 respectively ante.
   Section 43 (5) (b) is not limited to a situation in which the 36 hour period expires at a time when the magistrates are not sitting; where the court is already sitting, the justices have a discretion, on being notified of a constable's intention to make an application, either to hear it straight away or to wait for no longer than six hours after the end of the 36 hours: *R v Slough Magistrates' Court, ex p Stirling*

(1987) 151 JP 603, DC. See also *Re an Application for a Warrant of Further Detention* [1988] Crim LR 296.
11 Police and Criminal Evidence Act 1984 s 43 (7). The requirements of s 43 (7) are mandatory; thus, where an information to support an application was drafted eight minutes before the 36 hour period expired and the court clerk advised that it was not practicable to hear the application at that time and it was adjourned, the application should not in those circumstances have been granted: *R v Slough Magistrates Court, ex p Stirling* (1987) 151 JP 603, DC.
12 Police and Criminal Evidence Act 1984 s 43 (8).
13 Ibid s 43 (9).
14 Ibid s 43 (10).
15 Ibid s 43 (11).
16 Ibid s 43 (12).
17 Ibid s 43 (13).
18 Ibid s 43 (15).
19 Ibid s 43 (16). 'Authorised' means authorised under s 42 (see para 762 ante): s 43 (16).
20 Ibid s 43 (17).
21 Ibid s 43 (18).
22 Ibid s 43 (19).

764. Extension of warrants of further detention. On an application on oath made by a constable and supported by an information a magistrates' court[1] may extend a warrant of further detention[2] if it is satisfied that there are reasonable grounds for believing that the further detention of the person to whom the application relates is justified[3].

The period for which a warrant of further detention may be extended is such period as the court thinks fit, having regard to the evidence before it[4]; but the period may not be longer than 36 hours[5] or end later than 96 hours after the relevant time[6].

Where a warrant of further detention has been extended[7] or further extended[8] for a period ending before 96 hours after the relevant time, a magistrates' court may further extend the warrant if it is satisfied that there are reasonable grounds for believing that the further detention of the person to whom the application relates is justified[9]. A warrant of further detention must, if extended or further extended, be indorsed with a note of the period of the extension[10].

Where an application under the above provisions is refused, the person to whom the application relates must forthwith be charged or released, either on bail or without bail[11]. However, a person need not be so released before the expiry of any period for which a warrant of further detention issued in relation to him has been extended or further extended on an earlier application so made[12].

1 For the meaning of 'magistrates' court' see para 763 note 1 ante.
2 Ie a warrant issued under the Police and Criminal Evidence Act 1984 s 43: see para 763 ante.
3 Ibid s 44 (1). Section 43 (2), (3), (14) (see para 763 ante) applies to an application under s 44 as it applies to an application made under s 43: s 44 (6). As to the time for making application see para 763 note 2 ante.
4 Ibid s 44 (2). For the meaning of 'the relevant time' see para 760 ante.
5 See para 760 note 3 ante.
6 Police and Criminal Evidence Act 1984 s 44 (3).
7 Ie under ibid s 44 (1): see supra.
8 Ie under ibid s 44 (4).
9 Ibid s 44 (4). Section 44 (2), (3) (see supra) applies to such further extension as it applies to extensions under s 44 (1): s 44 (4).
10 Ibid s 44 (5).
11 Ibid s 44 (7). As to release on bail see para 713 ante.
12 Ibid s 44 (8).

(vii) Searches of Detained Persons

765. Searches of detained persons. The custody officer[1] at a police station must ascertain and record or cause to be recorded everything which a person has with him when he is (1) brought to the station after being arrested elsewhere or after being committed to custody by an order or sentence of a court; or (2) arrested at the station or detained[2] there[3]. In the case of an arrested person the record must be made as part of his custody record[4].

A custody officer may seize and retain any such thing or cause any such thing to be seized and retained[5]. However, clothes and personal effects may only be seized if the custody officer:

(a) believes that the person from whom they are seized may use them to cause physical injury to himself or any other person, to damage property, to interfere with evidence or to assist him to escape; or

(b) has reasonable grounds for believing that they may be evidence relating to an offence[6].

Where anything is so seized, the person from whom it is seized must be told the reason for the seizure unless he is violent or likely to become violent, or incapable of understanding what is said to him[7]. A person may be searched if the custody officer considers it necessary for him to carry out his duty and to the extent that the custody officer considers it necessary for that purpose[8].

A person who is in custody at a police station or is in police detention[9] otherwise than at a police station may at any time be searched in order to ascertain whether he has with him anything which he could use for any of the specified[10] purposes[11]. A constable may seize and retain, or cause to be seized and retained, anything found on such a search[12]; but a constable may only seize clothes and personal effects in the circumstances specified in heads (a) and (b) above[13]. A search under the above provisions must be carried out by a constable[14]; and the constable carrying out the search must be of the same sex as the person searched[15]. An intimate search[16] may not, however, be conducted under the above provisions[17].

1 As to custody officers see para 716 ante.
2 Ie under the Police and Criminal Evidence Act 1984 s 47 (5): see para 713 ante.
3 Police and Criminal Evidence Act 1984 s 54 (1) (amended by the Criminal Justice Act 1988 s 147 (a)). There ceases to have effect any Act, including a local Act, passed before the Police and Criminal Evidence Act 1984 in so far as it authorises (1) any search by a constable of a person in police detention at a police station; or (2) an intimate search of a person by a constable; and any rule of common law which authorises such a search as is mentioned in heads (1), (2) supra is abolished: s 53 (1).
4 Ibid s 54 (2). As to custody records see para 717 ante.
5 Ibid s 54 (3).
6 Ibid s 54 (4).
7 Ibid s 54 (5).
8 Ibid s 54 (6). As to the use of reasonable force see para 658 ante.
9 For the meaning of 'in police detention' see para 716 note 5 ante.
10 Ie specified in the Police and Criminal Evidence Act 1984 s 54 (4) (a): see head (a) supra.
11 Ibid s 54 (6A) (added by the Criminal Justice Act 1988 s 147 (b)).
12 Police and Criminal Evidence Act 1984 s 54 (6B) (added by the Criminal Justice Act 1988 s 147 (b)).
13 Police and Criminal Evidence Act 1984 s 54 (6C) (added by the Criminal Justice Act 1988 s 147 (b)).
14 Police and Criminal Evidence Act 1984 s 54 (8).
15 Ibid s 54 (9).
16 For the meaning of 'intimate search' see para 766 note 5 post.
17 Police and Criminal Evidence Act 1984 s 54 (7). As to intimate searches see para 766 post.

766. Intimate and strip searches. If an officer of at least the rank of superintendent[1] has reasonable cause for believing:

(1) that a person who has been arrested and is in police detention[2] may have concealed on him anything which he could use to cause physical injury to himself or to others and he might so use while he is in police detention or in the custody of a court; or

(2) that such a person has a Class A drug[3] concealed on him and was in possession of it with the appropriate criminal intent[4] before his arrest,

he may authorise an intimate search[5] of that person[6]. An officer may give such an authorisation orally or in writing but, if he gives it orally, he must confirm it in writing as soon as practicable[7]. However, an officer may not authorise an intimate search of a person for anything unless he has reasonable grounds for believing that it cannot be found without his being intimately searched[8]. The reasons why an intimate search is considered necessary must be explained to the person before the search takes place[9].

An intimate search may only be carried out by a registered medical practitioner, State Registered Nurse, or State Enrolled Nurse, unless an officer of at least the rank of superintendent considers that this is not practicable and the search is to take place under head (1) above[10]. An intimate search under head (1) above may take place only at a police station, a hospital, a registered medical practitioner's surgery or some other place used for medical purposes[11]. A search under head (2) above may not be carried out at a police station but may take place only at a hospital, surgery or other medical premises[11].

An intimate search at a police station of a juvenile or a mentally ill or mentally handicapped person may take place only in the presence of the appropriate adult[12] of the same sex[13]. In the case of a juvenile, the search may take place in the absence of the appropriate adult only if the juvenile signifies in the presence of the appropriate adult that he prefers the search to be done in his absence and the appropriate adult agrees[13].

A strip search, that is a search involving the removal of more than outer clothing, may take place only if the custody officer[14] considers it to be necessary to remove an article which the detained person would not be allowed to keep[15].

Where an intimate search under head (1) above or a strip search is carried out by a police officer, the officer must be of the same sex as the person searched[16]. No person of the opposite sex who is not a medical practitioner or nurse may be present, nor may anyone whose presence is unnecessary[16].

In the case of an intimate search the custody officer must as soon as practicable record which parts of the person's body were searched, who carried out the search, who was present, the reasons for the search and its result[17]. In the case of a strip search he must record the reasons for the search and its result[18].

If an intimate search is carried out by a police officer, the reason why it is impracticable for a suitably qualified person to conduct it must be recorded[19].

The custody officer at a police station may seize and retain anything which is found on an intimate search of a person, or cause any such thing to be seized and retained:

(a) if he believes that the person from whom it was seized may use it to cause physical injury to himself or any other person, to damage property, to interfere with evidence or to assist him to escape; or

(b) if he has reasonable grounds for believing that it may be evidence relating to an offence[20].

Where anything is so seized, the person from whom it is seized must be told the reason for the seizure unless he is violent or likely to become violent or incapable of understanding what is said to him[21].

1 See para 659 ante.

2 For the meaning of 'in police detention' see para 716 note 5 ante.

3 For these purposes, 'Class A drug' has the meaning assigned to it by the Misuse of Drugs Act 1971 s 2 (1) (b): Police and Criminal Evidence Act 1984 s 55 (17). See para 397 note 7 ante.

4 For these purposes, 'the appropriate criminal intent' means an intent to commit an offence under the Misuse of Drugs Act 1971 s 5 (3) (possession of controlled drug with intent to supply to another: see para 399 ante) or the Customs and Excise Management Act 1979 s 68 (2) (exportation etc with intent to evade a prohibition or restriction: see CUSTOMS vol 12 para 738): Police and Criminal Evidence Act 1984 s 55 (17).

5 For these purposes, 'intimate search' means a search which consists of the physical examination of a person's body orifices: ibid s 118 (1).

6 Ibid s 55 (1) (amended by the Criminal Justice Act 1988 s 170 (1), Sch 15 paras 97, 99); Code of Practice for the Detention, Treatment and Questioning of Persons by Police Officers para 4.1, Annex A para 1.

Every annual report under the Police Act 1964 s 12 (see POLICE vol 36 para 230) or made by the Commissioner of Police of the Metropolis must contain information about searches under the Police and Criminal Evidence Act 1984 s 55 (as so amended) which have been carried out in the area to which the report relates during the period to which it relates: s 55 (14). The information about such searches must include: (1) the total number of searches; (2) the number of searches conducted by way of examination by a suitably qualified person; (3) the number of searches not so conducted but conducted in the presence of such a person; and (4) the result of the searches carried out: s 55 (15). The information must also include, as separate items: (a) the total number of drug offence searches; and (b) the result of those searches: s 55 (16).

7 Ibid s 55 (3).

8 Ibid s 55 (2).

9 Code of Practice for the Detention, Treatment and Questioning of Persons by Police Officers para 4.1, Annex A para 1.

10 Ibid Annex A para 2; Police and Criminal Evidence Act 1984 s 55 (5). An intimate search which is only a drug offence search must be by way of examination by a suitably qualified person: s 55 (4). For these purposes, 'drug offence search' means an intimate search for a Class A drug which an officer has authorised by virtue of s 55 (1) (b) (see head (2) supra); and 'suitably qualified person' means a registered medical practitioner or a registered nurse: s 55 (17).

An intimate search which is not carried out as mentioned in s 55 (5) must be carried out by a constable: s 55 (6).

11 Ibid s 55 (8), (9); Code of Practice for the Detention, Treatment and Questioning of Persons by Police Officers Annex A para 3.

12 For the meaning of 'the appropriate adult' see para 717 note 7 ante.

13 Code of Practice for the Detention, Treatment and Questioning of Persons by Police Officers Annex A para 4.

14 As to custody officers see para 716 ante.

15 Code of Practice for the Detention, Treatment and Questioning of Persons by Police Officers Annex 4 para 5.

16 Police and Criminal Evidence Act 1984 s 55 (7); Code of Practice for the Detention, Treatment and Questioning of Persons by Police Officers Annex A para 6. As to the use of reasonable force by police officers see para 658 ante.

17 Police and Criminal Evidence Act 1984 s 55 (10), (11); Code of Practice for the Detention, Treatment and Questioning of Persons by Police Officers Annex A para 7.

18 Ibid Annex A para 8.

19 Ibid Annex A para 9.

20 Police and Criminal Evidence Act 1984 s 55 (12).

21 Ibid s 55 (13).

(viii) Identification

A. CODE OF PRACTICE

767. Code of Practice. A constable's powers relating to the identification of persons are governed by the Police and Criminal Evidence Act 1984[1] and the Code of Practice for the Identification of Persons by Police Officers[2]. The Code must be readily available at all police stations for consultation by police officers, detained persons and members of the public[3].

Where a record is made under the Code of any action requiring the authority of an officer of specified rank, his name and rank must be included in the record[4]; and all records must be timed and signed by the maker[5]. In the case of a detained person records are to be made in his custody record unless otherwise specified[6].

In the case of any procedure requiring a suspect's consent, the consent of a person who is mentally ill or mentally handicapped[7] is only valid if given in the presence of the appropriate adult[8]; and in the case of a juvenile[9] the consent of his parent or guardian is required as well as his own, unless he is under 14, in which case the consent of his parent or guardian is sufficient in its own right[10]. In the case of any procedure requiring information to be given to a suspect, it must be given in the presence of the appropriate adult if the suspect is mentally ill, mentally handicapped or a juvenile[11]. If the suspect is deaf or there is doubt about his hearing ability or ability to understand English, and the officer cannot himself speak the person's language, the information must be given through an interpreter[11].

Any procedure involving the participation of a person, whether as a suspect or witness, who is mentally ill, mentally handicapped or a juvenile must take place in the presence of the appropriate adult; but the adult must not be allowed to prompt any identification of a suspect by a witness[12].

1 Ie the Police and Criminal Evidence Act 1984 ss 61–65 (amended by the Criminal Justice Act 1988 s 148; the Prevention of Terrorism (Temporary Provisions) Act 1989 s 25 (1), Sch 8 para 6 (1), (5), (6)): see para 768 et seq post.
2 Ie the Code of Practice for the Identification of Persons by Police Officers: see para 768 et seq post. As to the codes of practice see para 657 ante. The notes for guidance included in the Code are not provisions of the Code, but are guidance to police officers and others about its application and interpretation: para 1.2. Provisions in the Annexes to the Code are provisions of the Code: para 1.2. Nothing in the Code affects any procedure under the Road Traffic Act 1972 ss 5–12 (repealed: see now the Road Traffic Act 1988 ss 4–11; the Road Traffic Offenders Act 1988 ss 15, 16), the Immigration Act 1971 s 4, Sch 2 para 18 or the Prevention of Terrorism (Temporary Provisions) Act 1984 Sch 3 para 5 (repealed: see now the Prevention of Terrorism (Temporary Provisions) Act 1989 ss 15 (9), (1), 16 (3), (4), Sch 5 para 7 (5), (6)): Code of Practice for the Identification of Persons by Police Officers para 1.13.
3 Ibid para 1.1.
4 Ibid para 1.7.
5 Ibid para 1.8.
6 Ibid para 1.9. As to custody records see para 717 ante.
7 If an officer has any suspicion, or is told in good faith, that a person of any age may be mentally ill or mentally handicapped, or mentally incapable of understanding the significance of questions put to him or his replies, that person must be treated as a mentally ill or mentally handicapped person for the purposes of the Code of Practice for the Identification of Persons by Police Officers: para 1.3.
8 For these purposes, 'the appropriate adult' means:
   (1) in the case of a juvenile:
      (a) his parent or guardian or, if he is in care, the care authority or organisation;
      (b) a social worker; or
      (c) failing either of the above, another responsible adult who is not a police officer or employed by the police;

(2) in the case of a person who is mentally ill or mentally handicapped:
  (a) a relative, guardian or some other person responsible for his care or custody;
  (b) someone who has experience of dealing with mentally ill or mentally handicapped persons but is not a police officer or employed by the police; or
  (c) failing either of the above, some other responsible adult who is not a police officer or employed by the police:
  ibid para 1.5.
9 If anyone appears to be under the age of 17, he must be treated as a juvenile for the purposes of the Code of Practice for the Identification of Persons by Police Officers in the absence of clear evidence to show that he is older: para 1.4.
10 Ibid para 1.10. For these purposes, consent may be given, in the case of a juvenile in the care of a local authority or voluntary organisation, by that authority or organisation: para 1.10, note 1A.
11 Ibid para 1.11. As to interpreters see paras 742–744 ante.
12 Ibid para 1.12.

B. IDENTIFICATION BY WITNESS

768. Method of identification. In a case which involves disputed identification evidence, an identification parade must be held if the suspect asks for one and it is practicable to hold one[1]. A parade may also be held if the officer in charge of the investigation considers that it would be useful[1]. If the identification officer considers that it is not practicable to hold a parade, he must tell the suspect why and record the reason[2]. Arrangements for the parade and its conduct are the responsibility of an officer in uniform not below the rank of inspector who is not involved with the investigation ('the identification officer')[3]. However, no officer involved with the investigation of the case against the suspect may take any part in the arrangements for, or the conduct of, the parade[3]. A parade need not be held if the identification officer considers that, whether by reason of the unusual appearance of the suspect or for some other reason, it would not be practicable to assemble sufficient people who resembled him to make a parade fair[4]. If a suspect refuses or, having agreed, fails to attend an identification parade or the holding of a parade is impracticable, arrangements must if practicable be made to allow the witness an opportunity of seeing him in a group of people[5].

Such a group identification may also be arranged if the officer in charge of the investigation considers, whether because of fear on the part of the witness or for some other reason, that it is, in the circumstances, more satisfactory than a parade[5]. If neither a parade nor a group identification procedure is arranged, the suspect may be confronted by the witness[6]. Such a confrontation does not require the suspect's consent, but may not take place unless neither a parade nor a group identification is practicable, whether because the suspect has withheld his consent to them or his co-operation, or for some other reason[6]. A witness must not be shown photographs[7] or photofit, identikit or similar pictures for identification purposes if there is a suspect already available to be asked to stand on a parade or participate in a group identification[8].

1 Code of Practice for the Identification of Persons by Police Officers para 2.1; and see *R v Conway (John)* (1990) Times, 30 January, CA. As to identification parades see para 771 et seq post.
2 Code of Practice for the Identification of Persons by Police Officers para 2.14.
3 Ibid para 2.2; and see *R v Gall* [1989] Crim LR 745, CA.
4 Code of Practice for the Identification of Persons by Police Officers para 2.3; and see eg *R v Gaynor* [1988] Crim LR 242.
5 Code of Practice for the Identification of Persons by Police Officers para 2.4. As to group identification see paras 771, 774 post.
6 Ibid para 2.5. As to confrontation by a witness see para 775 post.

7 For these purposes, references to photographs include optical disc computer printouts: ibid para 1.14.
8 Ibid para 2.6. As to identification by photographs etc see para 778 post. As to visual identification see also paras 1147, 1148 post.

769. Notice to suspect. Before an identification parade[1] takes place or a group identification[2] is arranged, the identification officer[3] must explain to the suspect:
(1) the purpose of the parade or group identification;
(2) the procedures for holding it, including his right to have a solicitor[4] or friend present;
(3) where appropriate, the special arrangements for juveniles[5];
(4) where appropriate, the special arrangements for mentally ill and mentally handicapped persons[5];
(5) the fact that he does not have to take part in either procedure and, if it is proposed to hold a group identification, his entitlement to a parade if this can practicably be arranged; and
(6) the fact that, if he does not consent to take part in a parade or other group identification, he may be confronted by a witness[6] and his refusal may be given in evidence in any subsequent trial, where a witness might be given an opportunity of identifying him in court[7].
This information must also be contained in a written notice which must be handed to the suspect[8]. The identification officer must give the suspect a reasonable opportunity to read the notice, after which he must be asked to sign a second copy of the notice to indicate whether or not he is willing to attend the parade or participate in the group identification[8]. The signed copy must be retained by the identification officer[8].

1 As to identification parades see para 771 et seq post.
2 As to group identification see paras 771, 774 post.
3 For the meaning of 'the identification officer' see para 768 text to note 3 ante.
4 For the purposes of the Code of Practice for the Identification of Persons by Police Officers, any reference to a solicitor, except in Annex C para 7 (see para 778 post) includes a clerk or legal executive: para 1.6.
5 See para 767 ante.
6 As to confrontation by a witness see para 775 post.
7 Code of Practice for the Identification of Persons by Police Officers para 2.7.
8 Ibid para 2.8.

770. Street identification. A police officer may take a witness to a particular neighbourhood to observe the persons there to see whether he can identify the person whom he said he saw on the relevant occasion[1]. Care should be taken, however, not to direct the witness's attention to any individual[1].

1 Code of Practice for the Identification of Persons by Police Officers para 2.11. Where the suspect is at a police station, the provisions of paras 2.1–2.10 apply: para 2.11. As to paras 2.1–2.10 see paras 768, 769 ante and para 775 post.

771. Identification parades and group identifications; in general. A suspect must be given a reasonable opportunity to have a solicitor[1] or friend present, and the identification officer[2] must ask him to indicate on a second copy of the notice to suspect whether or not he so wishes[3]. If a parade is held without a solicitor or a friend of the suspect being present, a colour photograph of the parade must be taken unless any of the parade members objects[4]. A copy of the photograph must be supplied on request to the suspect or his solicitors within a reasonable time[4]. Where a photograph is so taken, at the conclusion of the proceedings the negative will be destroyed[5]. A parade may take place either in a normal room or in one equipped with a screen permitting witnesses to see members of the parade without being seen[6]. The procedures for the composition and conduct of the parade are the same in both cases[7], except that a parade involving a screen may take place only when the suspect's solicitor, friend or appropriate adult[8] is present or the parade is recorded on video[9].

1 For the meaning of 'solicitor' see para 769 note 4 ante.
2 For the meaning of 'the identification officer' see para 768 text to note 3 ante.
3 Code of Practice for the Identification of Persons by Police Officers para 2.9, Annex A para 1. As to the notice to suspect see para 769 ante.
4 Ibid Annex A para 20.
5 Ibid Annex A para 21.
6 Ibid Annex A para 2.
7 Ie subject to ibid Annex A para 7: see para 773 post.
8 For the meaning of 'the appropriate adult' see para 767 note 8 ante.
9 Codes of Practice for the Identification of Persons by Police Officers Annex A para 2.

772. Parades involving prison inmates. If an inmate is required for identification, and there are no security problems about his leaving the establishment, he may be asked to participate in a parade[1]. Group identification, however, may not be arranged other than in the establishment or inside a police station[2].

A parade may be held in a Prison Department establishment but must be conducted as far as practicable under normal parade rules[3]. Members of the public must make up the parade unless there are serious security or control objections to their admission to the establishment[3]. In such cases, or if a group identification is arranged within the establishment, other inmates may participate[3]. If prison inmates make up a parade, the circumstances must be recorded[4].

1 Code of Practice for the Identification of Persons by Police Officers para 2.9, Annex A para 3.
2 Ibid Annex A para 3. As to group identification see para 771 ante and para 774 post.
3 Ibid Annex A para 4.
4 Ibid Annex A para 24.

773. Conduct of identification parade. Immediately before the parade, the identification officer[1] must remind the suspect of the procedure governing its conduct and caution him[2]. All unauthorised persons must be strictly excluded from the place where the parade is held[3].

Once the parade has been formed, everything afterwards in respect of it must take place in the presence and hearing of the suspect and of any interpreter, solicitor[4], friend or appropriate adult[5] who is present, unless the parade involves a screen, in which case everything said to or by any witness at the place where the parade is held must be said in the hearing and presence of the suspect's solicitor, friend or appropriate adult or be recorded on video[6].

The parade must consist of at least eight persons, in addition to the suspect, who so far as possible resemble the suspect in age, height, general appearance and position in life[7]. One suspect only may be included in a parade unless there are two suspects of roughly similar appearance in which case they may be paraded together with at least 12 other persons[7]. In no circumstances may more than two suspects be included in one parade and, where there are separate parades, they must be made up of different persons[7].

Where all members of a similar group are possible suspects, separate parades must be held for each member of the group unless there are two suspects of similar appearance when they may appear on the same parade with at least 12 other members of the group who are not suspects[8]. Where police officers in uniform form an identification parade, any numerals or other identifying badge must be concealed[8].

When the suspect is brought to the place where the parade is to be held, he must be asked by the identification officer whether he has any objection to the arrangements for the parade or to any of the other participants in it[9]. The suspect may obtain advice from his solicitor or friend, if present, before the parade proceeds[9]. Where practicable, steps must be taken to remove the grounds for objection[9]. Where it is not practicable to do so, the officer must explain to the suspect why his objections cannot be met[9].

The suspect may select his own position in the line[10]. Where there is more than one witness, the identification officer must tell the suspect, after each witness has left the room, that he can, if he wishes, change position in the line[10]. Each position in the line must be clearly numbered, whether by means of a numeral laid on the floor in front of each parade member or by other means[10].

The identification officer is responsible for ensuring that, before they attend the parade, witnesses are not able to:

(1) communicate with each other about the case or overhear a witness who has already seen the parade;

(2) see any member of the parade;

(3) on that occasion see or be reminded of any photograph[11] or description of the suspect or be given any other indication of his identity; or

(4) see the suspect either before or after the parade[12].

The officer conducting a witness to a parade must not discuss with him the composition of the parade, and in particular he must not disclose whether a previous witness has made any identification[13].

Witnesses must be brought in one at a time[14]. Immediately before the witness inspects the parade, the identification officer must tell him that the person he saw may or may not be on the parade and that, if he cannot make a positive identification, he should say so[14]. The officer must then ask him to walk along the parade at least twice, taking as much care and time as he wishes[14]. When he has done so, the officer must ask him whether the person he saw in person on an earlier relevant occasion is on the parade[14]. The witness should make an identification by indicating the number of the person concerned[15].

If the witness makes an identification after the parade has ended, the suspect and, if present, his solicitor, interpreter, or friend must be informed[16]. Where this occurs, consideration should be given to allowing the witness a second opportunity to identify the suspect[16].

If a witness wishes to hear any parade member speak, adopt any specified posture or see him move, the identification officer must first ask whether he can identify any persons on the parade on the basis of appearance only[17]. When the request is to hear members of the parade speak, the witness must be reminded that the participants in the parade have been chosen on the basis of physical appearance only[17]. Members of the parade may then be asked to comply with the witness's request to hear them speak, to see them move or to adopt any specified posture[17].

When the last witness has left, the suspect must be asked by the identification officer whether he wishes to make any comments on the conduct of the parade[18]. The identification officer must make a record of the parade on the forms provided[19]; and a record must be made of a person's refusal to take part in a parade[20]. If the identification officer asks any person to leave a parade because he is interfering with its conduct, the circumstances must be recorded[21]; and a record must be made of all those present at a parade whose names are known to the police[22].

1 For the meaning of 'the identification officer' see para 768 text to note 3 ante.
2 Code of Practice for the Identification of Persons by Police Officers para 2.9, Annex A para 5. The caution must be given in the terms of the Code of Practice for the Detention, Treatment and Questioning of Persons by Police Officers para 10.4: see para 734 ante.
3 Code of Practice for the Identification of Persons by Police Officers Annex A para 6.
4 For the meaning of 'solicitor' see para 769 note 4 ante.
5 For the meaning of 'the appropriate adult' see para 767 note 8 ante.
6 Code of Practice for the Identification of Persons by Police Officers Annex A para 7.
7 Ibid Annex A para 8.
8 Ibid Annex A para 9.
9 Ibid Annex A para 10.
10 Ibid Annex A para 11.
11 For the meaning of 'photograph' see para 768 note 7 ante.
12 Code of Practice for the Identification of Persons by Police Officers Annex A para 12.
13 Ibid Annex A para 13.
14 Ibid Annex A para 14.
15 Ibid Annex A para 15.
16 Ibid Annex A para 16.
17 Ibid Annex A para 17.
18 Ibid Annex A para 18.
19 Ibid para 2.13, Annex A para 25.
20 Ibid para 2.15.
21 Ibid Annex A para 22.
22 Ibid Annex A para 23.

774. Conduct of group identification. The arrangements for a group indentification are the sole responsibility of the identification officer[1] and must as far as possible satisfy the prescribed requirements in respect of an identification parade[2]. The identification officer must make a record of the group indentification on the forms provided[3]; and a record must be made of a person's refusal to take part in a group identification[4]. A record must be made of all those present at a group identification whose names are known to the police[5].

1 For the meaning of 'the identification officer' see para 768 text to note 3 ante.
2 Code of Practice for the Identification of Persons by Police Officers para 2.9, Annex A para 19. As to the prescribed requirements in respect of an identification parade see para 773 ante.
3 Ibid para 2.13, Annex A para 25.
4 Ibid para 2.15.
5 Ibid Annex A para 23.

775. Confrontation by witness. Any confrontation by a witness must be carried out in accordance with the prescribed procedure[1]. The identification officer[2] is responsible for the conduct of any confrontation of a suspect by a witness[3].

The suspect must be confronted independently by each witness, who must be asked, 'Is this the person?'[4]. Confrontation must take place in the presence of the suspect's solicitor[5], interpreter or friend, where he has one, unless this would cause unreasonable delay[6].

Confrontation may take place either in a normal room or one equipped with a screen permitting a witness to see the suspect without being seen[7]. In both cases the procedures are the same except that a room equipped with a screen may be used only when the suspect's solicitor, friend or appropriate adult is present or the confrontation is recorded on video[7].

1 Code of Practice for the Identification of Persons by Police Officers para 2.10. As to the holding of a confrontation see para 2.5 and para 768 ante.
2 For the meaning of 'the identification officer' see para 768 text to note 3 ante.
3 Code of Practice for the Identification of Persons by Police Officers para 2.10, Annex B para 1.
4 Ibid Annex B para 2.
5 For the meaning of 'solicitor' see para 769 note 4 ante.
6 Code of Practice for the Identification of Persons by Police Officers Annex B para 2.
7 Ibid Annex B para 3.

C. FINGERPRINTS

776. Identification by fingerprints. No person's fingerprints[1] may be taken without the appropriate consent[2]. Consent to the taking of a person's fingerprints must be in writing if it is given at a time when he is at a police station[3].

However, the fingerprints of a person detained at a police station[4] may be taken without the appropriate consent:

(1) if an officer of at least the rank of superintendent[5] authorises them to be taken; or

(2) if he has been charged with a recordable offence[6] or informed that he will be reported for such an offence and he has not had his fingerprints taken in the course of the investigation of the offence by the police[7].

An officer may only give an authorisation under head (1) above if he has reasonable grounds for suspecting the involvement of the person whose fingerprints are to be taken in a criminal offence and for believing that his fingerprints will tend to confirm or disprove his involvement[8]. An officer may give such an authorisation under head (1) above orally or in writing but, if he gives it orally, he must confirm it in writing as soon as practicable[9].

If a person:

(a) has been convicted of a recordable offence;

(b) has not at any time been in police detention for the offence; and

(c) has not had his fingerprints taken in the course of the investigation of the offence by the police or since his conviction,

any constable may at any time not later than one month after the date of the conviction require him to attend a police station in order that his fingerprints may be taken[10]. A requirement so made must give the person a period of at least seven days within which he must so attend and may direct him so to attend at a specified time of day or between specified times of day[11]. Any constable may arrest without warrant a person who has failed to comply with a requirement under heads (a) to (c) above[12]. Any person's fingerprints may be taken without the appropriate consent if he has been convicted of a recordable offence[13].

In a case where a person's fingerprints are taken without the appropriate consent[14] he must be told the reason before his fingerprints are taken and the reason must be recorded as soon as is practicable after the fingerprints are taken[15]. If force is used, a record must be made of the circumstances and those present[16]. If he is detained at a police station when the fingerprints are taken, the reason for taking them must be recorded on his custody record[17].

1 'Fingerprints' includes palmprints: Police and Criminal Evidence Act 1984 s 65; Code of Practice for the Identification of Persons by Police Officers para 3.5.

2 Police and Criminal Evidence Act 1984 s 61 (1); Code of Practice for the Identification of Persons by Police Officers paras 3.1, 3.2. For these purposes, 'appropriate consent' means (1) in relation to a person who has attained the age of 17 years, the consent of that person; (2) in relation to a person who has not attained that age but has attained the age of 14 years, the consent of that person and his parent or guardian; and (3) in relation to a person who has not attained the age of 14 years, the consent of his parent or guardian: Police and Criminal Evidence Act 1984 s 65.

The person must be informed that the fingerprints will be destroyed if the Code of Practice for the Identification of Persons by Police Officers para 3.4 (see para 781 post) applies; and he must be told that he may witness their destruction if he asks to do so within one month of being cleared or informed that he will not be prosecuted: para 3.1. As to the destruction of fingerprints see para 781 post.

Nothing in the Police and Criminal Evidence Act 1984 s 61 affects any power conferred by the Immigration Act 1971 s 4, Sch 2 para 18 (2) or applies to a person arrested or detained under the terrorism provisions, except as provided in the Prevention of Terrorism (Temporary Provisions) Act 1989 ss 15 (10), 16 (1), (3), (4), Sch 5 para 7 (6): Police and Criminal Evidence Act 1984 s 61 (9) (amended by the Prevention of Terrorism (Temporary Provisions) Act 1989 s 25 (1), Sch 8 para 6 (1), (5)). For the meaning of 'the terrorism provisions' see para 726 note 1 ante.

3 Police and Criminal Evidence Act 1984 s 61 (2); Code of Practice for the Identification of Persons by Police Officers para 3.1.

4 As to when a person is detained at a police station see para 716 note 5 ante.

5 See para 659 ante.

6 For these purposes, 'recordable offence' means any offence to which regulations under the Police and Criminal Evidence Act 1984 s 27 (see infra) apply: s 118 (1); Code of Practice for the Identification of Persons by Police Officers para 3, note 3A.

7 Police and Criminal Evidence Act 1984 s 61 (3). Reasonable force may be used if necessary: Code of Practice for the Identification of Persons by Police Officers para 3.2.

8 Police and Criminal Evidence Act 1984 s 61 (4). As to authorisation for the purposes of the Prevention of Terrorism (Temporary Provisions) Act 1989 s 15 (9) see para 118 note 8 ante; and as to authorisation for the purposes of s 16 (1), Sch 5 para 7 (5) see para 125 note 3 ante.

9 Police and Criminal Evidence Act 1984 s 61 (5).

10 Ibid s 27 (1); Code of Practice for the Identification of Persons by Police Officers para 3.3. The Secretary of State may by regulations make provision for recording in national police records convictions for such offences as are specified in the regulations; and any such regulations must be made by statutory instrument and are subject to annulment in pursuance of a resolution of either House of Parliament: Police and Criminal Evidence Act 1984 s 27 (4), (5).

In exercise of the power conferred by s 27 (4), the Home Secretary made the National Police Records (Recordable Offences) Regulations 1985, SI 1985/1941, which came into force on 1 January 1986: reg 1. There may be recorded in national police records convictions for offences punishable with imprisonment and for offences under (1) the Street Offences Act 1959 s 1 (amended by the Criminal Justice Act 1982 s 71) (loitering or soliciting for purposes of prostitution: see para 393 ante); (2) the Telecommunications Act 1984 s 43 (amended by the Cable and Broadcasting Act 1984 s 57 (1), (2), Sch 5 para 45 (4), Sch 6) (improper use of public telecommunications system: see para 374 ante); (3) the Road Traffic Act 1988 s 25 (tampering with motor vehicles: see ROAD TRAFFIC); (4) the Malicious Communications Act 1988 s 1 (see para 375 ante); and (5) the Criminal Justice Act 1988 s 139 (1) (see para 168 ante): National Police Records (Recordable Offences) Regulations 1985 reg 2 (1) (amended by SI 1989/694); Road Traffic (Consequential Provisions) Act 1988 s 2 (4). The reference to offences punishable with imprisonment is to be construed without regard to any prohibition or restriction imposed by or under any enactment on the punishment of young offenders: National Police Records (Recordable Offences) Regulations 1985 reg 2 (2). Where a person's convictions are so recordable, there may also be recorded his convictions for any other offence in the same proceedings: reg 2 (3).

11 Police and Criminal Evidence Act 1984 s 27 (2).

12 Ibid s 27 (3). As to arrest without warrant generally see para 703 et seq ante.

13 Ibid s 61 (6).

14 Ie under ibid s 61 (3) or (6): see supra.

15 Ibid s 61 (7); Code of Practice for the Identification of Persons by Police Officers para 3.6. Where consent is given, the person should be informed of the reason for taking the fingerprints before they are taken: para 3.1
16 Ibid para 3.6. See also note 7 supra.
17 Police and Criminal Evidence Act 1984 s 61 (8). As to custody records see para 717 ante; and as to fingerprint evidence see para 1146 note 2 post.

D. PHOTOGRAPHS

777. Photographs. The photograph of a person who has been arrested may be taken at a police station only with his written consent; but the photograph of a person who has been arrested may be taken without consent if:

(1) he is arrested at the same time as other persons, or at a time when it is likely that other persons will be arrested, and a photograph is necessary to establish who was arrested, at what time and at what place;

(2) he has been charged with or reported for a recordable offence[1] and has not yet been released or brought before a court; or

(3) he is convicted of such an offence and his photograph is not already on record as a result of heads (1) or (2) above[2]. In either case he must be informed of the reason for taking it[3].

Force may not be used to take a photograph[4]. A record must be made as soon as possible of the reason for so taking a person's photograph without consent[5].

1 For the meaning of 'recordable offence' see para 776 note 6 ante.
2 Code of Practice for the Identification of Persons by Police Officers paras 4.1, 4.2. There is no power of arrest to take a photograph in pursuance of para 4.2 which applies only where the person is in custody as a result of the exercise of another power eg arrest for fingerprinting under the Police and Criminal Evidence Act 1984 s 27 (see para 776 ante): Code of Practice for the Identification of Persons by Police Officers para 4.2 (iii).
3 Ibid para 4.1. The person must also be informed that the photograph will be destroyed if para 4.4 (see para 782 post) applies; and he must be told that he may witness the destruction of the photograph if he asks to do so within one month of being cleared or informed that he will not be prosecuted: para 4.1. As to the destruction of photographs see para 782 post.
4 Ibid para 4.3.
5 Ibid para 4.5.

778. Showing of photographs. If photographs[1] or photofit, identikit or similar pictures are shown to a witness for identification purposes, this must be done in accordance with the prescribed procedure[2]. An officer of the rank of sergeant or above is responsible for supervising and directing the showing of photographs; but the actual showing may be done by a constable[3].

Only one witness may be shown photographs at any one time[4]; and he must be given as much privacy as practicable and may not be allowed to communicate with or overhear any other witness in the case[4]. The witness must be shown not less than 12 photographs at a time[5]; and these photographs must either be in an album or loose photographs mounted in a frame and must, as far as possible, all be of a similar type[5]. If the photographs include that of a person suspected by the police of the offence concerned, the other photographs must resemble the suspect as closely as possible[5]. When the witness is shown the photographs, he must be told that the photograph of the person he saw may or may not be amongst them[6]. He may not be prompted or guided in any way, however, but must be left to make any selection without help[6]. If a witness makes a positive identification from photographs, then, unless the person identified is otherwise eliminated from inquiries, other witnesses may not be shown photographs[7]. However, both they and the witness who has made the identification must be asked to attend an identification parade[8] or group identification[9] if practicable unless there is no dispute about the identification of the suspect[10].

Where the use of a photofit, identikit or similar picture has led to there being a suspect available who can be asked to appear on a parade, or participate in a group identification, the picture may not be shown to other potential witnesses[11]. Where a witness attending an identification parade has previously been shown photographs or photofit, identikit or similar pictures, the suspect and his solicitor must be informed of this fact before any committal proceedings or summary trial[12]. Any photographs used must be retained for production in court if necessary, whether or not an identification is made[13]. Whether or not an identification is made, a record must be kept of the showing of photographs and of any comment made by the witness[14].

1 For the meaning of 'photograph' see para 768 note 7 ante.
2 Code of Practice for the Identification of Persons by Police Officers para 2.12.
3 Ibid para 2.12, Annex C para 1.
4 Ibid Annex C para 2.
5 Ibid Annex C para 3.
6 Ibid Annex C para 4.
7 Ibid Annex C para 5.
8 As to identification parades see para 771 et seq ante.
9 As to group identifications see paras 771, 774 ante.
10 Code of Practice for the Identification of Persons by Police Officers Annex C para 5.
11 Ibid Annex C para 6.
12 Ibid Annex C para 7. Paragraph 1.6 (meaning of 'solicitor') does not apply for these purposes: see para 769 note 4 ante.
13 Ibid Annex C para 8.
14 Ibid Annex C para 9. As to identification by the showing of photographs see also para 777 ante and para 1147 note 4 post.

E. BODY SAMPLES

779. Intimate samples. An intimate sample[1] may be taken from a person in police detention[2]: (1) if a police officer of at least the rank of superintendent[3] authorises it to be taken; and (2) if the appropriate consent[4] is given[5]. An officer may only so give an authorisation if he has reasonable grounds for suspecting the involvement of the person from whom the sample is to be taken in a serious arrestable offence[6] and for believing that the sample will tend to confirm or disprove his involvement[7]. An officer may so give an authorisation orally or in writing but, if he gives it orally, he must confirm it in writing as soon as is practicable[8].

Where an authorisation has been so given and it is proposed that an intimate sample shall be taken in pursuance of that authorisation, an officer must inform the person from whom the sample is to be taken (a) of the giving of the authorisation; and (b) of the grounds for giving it[9].

An intimate sample, other than a sample of urine or saliva, may only be taken from a person by a registered medical practitioner[10].

If an intimate sample is taken from a person, the authorisation by virtue of which it was taken, the grounds for giving the authorisation and the fact that the appropriate authorisation was given must be recorded as soon as is practicable after the sample is taken[11]; and, if an intimate sample is taken from a person detained at a police station, the matters required so to be recorded must be recorded in his custody record[12].

Where the appropriate consent to the taking of an intimate sample from a person was refused without good cause, in any proceedings against that person for an offence (i) the court, in determining whether to commit that person for trial or whether there is a case to answer; and (ii) the court or jury, in determining whether that person is guilty of the offence charged, may draw such inferences from the refusal as appear proper; and the refusal may, on the basis of such inferences, be treated as, or as capable of amounting to, corroboration of any evidence against the person in relation to which the refusal is material[13].

1 For these purposes, 'intimate sample' means a sample of blood, semen or any other tissue fluid, urine, saliva or pubic hair, or a swab taken from a person's body orifices: Police and Criminal Evidence Act 1984 s 65 (amended by the Criminal Justice Act 1988 s 170 (1), Sch 15 paras 97, 100); Code of Practice for the Identification of Persons by Police Officers para 5.11 (a).
2 For the meaning of 'in police detention' see para 716 note 5 ante.
3 See para 659 ante.
4 For the meaning of 'the appropriate consent' see para 776 note 2 ante. The appropriate consent must be given in writing: Police and Criminal Evidence Act 1984 s 62 (4); Code of Practice for the Identification of Persons by Police Officers para 5.1. Consent to the taking of a sample or impression must be recorded in writing: para 5.9. Before a person is asked to provide an intimate sample or swab, he must be warned that a refusal may be treated, in any proceedings against him, as corroborating prosecution evidence: para 5.2. In warning a person who refuses so to provide an intimate sample or swab, the following form of words may be helpful:

> 'You do not have to [provide this sample] [allow this swab to be taken], but I must warn you that, if you do not do so, a court may treat such a refusal as supporting any relevant evidence against you':

para 5.2, note 5A. A record must be made of the giving of such a warning: para 5.10.
5 Police and Criminal Evidence Act 1984 s 62 (1); Code of Practice for the Identification of Persons by Police Officers para 5.1. Paragraph 5.1 applies also to dental impressions: para 5.1. Nothing in the Police and Criminal Evidence Act 1984 s 62 affects the Road Traffic Act 1988 ss 4–11: Police and Criminal Evidence Act 1984 s 62 (11) (amended by the Road Traffic (Consequential Provisions) Act 1988 s 4, Sch 3 para 27 (4)).
6 For the meaning of 'serious arrestable offence' see para 704 ante.
7 Police and Criminal Evidence Act 1984 s 62 (2); Code of Practice for the Identification of Persons by Police Officers para 5.1.
8 Police and Criminal Evidence Act 1984 s 62 (3).
9 Ibid s 62 (5); Code of Practice for the Identification of Persons by Police Officers paras 5.1, 5.6. The duty imposed by the Police and Criminal Evidence Act 1984 s 62 (5) (ii) (see head (b) supra) includes a duty to state the nature of the offence in which it is suspected that the person from whom the sample is to be taken has been involved: s 62 (6); Code of Practice for the Identification of Persons by Police Officers paras 5.1, 5.6. The suspect must also be informed that the sample or impression will be destroyed if he is prosecuted for the offence concerned and cleared or if he is not prosecuted, unless he admits the offence and is cautioned for it: paras 5.6, 5.8. As to the destruction of samples see para 781 post.
10 Police and Criminal Evidence Act 1984 s 62 (9). Except for samples of urine or saliva, dental impressions and intimate samples and swabs may be taken only by a registered medical or dental practitioner as appropriate: Code of Practice for the Identification of Persons by Police Officers para 5.3.
   Where clothing needs to be removed in circumstances likely to cause embarrassment to the person, no person of the opposite sex, who is not a medical practitioner or nurse, may be present, nor may anyone whose presence is unnecessary: para 5.12.
11 Police and Criminal Evidence Act 1984 s 62 (7); Code of Practice for the Identification of Persons by Police Officers para 5.9.
12 Police and Criminal Evidence Act 1984 s 62 (8). As to custody records see para 717 ante.
13 Ibid s 62 (10).

780. Non-intimate samples. A non-intimate sample[1] may not be taken from a person without the appropriate consent[2]; and consent to the taking of a non-intimate sample must be given in writing[3]. A non-intimate sample may, however, be taken from a person without the appropriate consent if (1) he is in police detention[4] or is being held in custody by the police on the authority of a court; and (2) an officer of at least the rank of superindendent[5] authorises it to be taken without the appropriate consent[6]. An officer may only so give an authorisation if he has reasonable grounds for suspecting the involvement of the person from whom the sample is to be taken in a serious arrestable offence[7] and for believing that the sample will tend to confirm or disprove his involvement[8]. An officer may so give an authorisation orally or in writing but, if he gives it orally, he must confirm it in writing as soon as is practicable[9].

Where an authorisation has been given and it is proposed that a non-intimate sample shall be taken in pursuance of the authorisation, an officer must inform the person from whom the sample is to be taken: (a) of the giving of the authorisation; and (b) of the grounds for giving it[10].

If a non-intimate sample is taken from a person without the appropriate consent, the authorisation by virtue of which it was taken and the grounds for giving the authorisation must be recorded as soon as is practicable after the sample is taken[11]; and, if a non-intimate sample is taken from a person detained at a police station, the matters so to be recorded must be recorded in his custody record[12].

1 For these purposes, 'non-intimate sample' means (1) a sample of hair other than pubic hair; (2) a sample taken from a nail or from under a nail; (3) a swab taken from any part of a person's body other than a body orifice; (4) a footprint or a similar impression of any part of a person's body other than apart of his hand: Police and Criminal Evidence Act 1984 s 65; Code of Practice for the Identification of Persons by Police Officers para 5.11 (b). As to intimate samples see para 779 ante; and as to fingerprints see para 776 ante.

2 Police and Criminal Evidence Act 1984 s 63 (1); Code of Practice for the Identification of Persons by Police Officers para 5.4. For the meaning of 'the appropriate consent' see para 776 note 2 ante. Consent to the taking of a sample or impression must be recorded in writing: para 5.9. Even if a person consents, an officer of the rank of inspector or above must have reasonable grounds for believing that the sample or impression will tend to confirm or disprove his involvement in a particular offence: para 5.4.

3 Police and Criminal Evidence Act 1984 s 63 (2); Code of Practice for the Identification of Persons by Police Officers para 5.4. Where clothing needs to be removed in circumstances likely to cause embarrassment to the person, no person of the opposite sex, who is not a medical practitioner or nurse, may be present, nor may anyone whose presence is unnecessary: para 5.12.

4 For the meaning of 'in police detention' see para 716 note 5 ante.

5 See para 659 ante.

6 Police and Criminal Evidence Act 1984 s 63 (3); Code of Practice for the Identification of Persons by Police Officers para 5.5.

7 For the meaning of 'serious arrestable offence' see para 704 ante.

8 Police and Criminal Evidence Act 1984 s 63 (4).

9 Ibid s 63 (5); Code of Practice for the Identification of Persons by Police Officers para 5.5. Where para 5.5 applies, reasonable force may be used if necessary to take non-intimate samples and body impressions: para 5.7. As to the use of reasonable force see also para 658 ante.

10 Police and Criminal Evidence Act 1984 s 63 (6); Code of Practice for the Identification of Persons by Police Officers para 5.6. The suspect must also be informed that the sample or impression will be destroyed if he is prosecuted for the offence concerned and cleared or if he is not prosecuted unless he admits the offence and is cautioned for it: paras 5.6, 5.8. As to the destruction of samples see para 781 post. The duty imposed by the Police and Criminal Evidence Act 1984 s 63 (6) (ii) (see head (b) supra) includes a duty to state the nature of the offence in which it is suspected that the person from whom the sample is to be taken has been involved: s 63 (7); Code of Practice for the Identification of Persons by Police Officers para 5.6.

11 Police and Criminal Evidence Act 1984 s 63 (8); Code of Practice for the Identification of Persons by Police Officers para 5.9. If force is used, a record must be made of the circumstances and those present: para 5.9.
12 Police and Criminal Evidence Act 1984 s 63 (9).

F. DESTRUCTION OF FINGERPRINTS ETC

781. Destruction of fingerprints and samples. If fingerprints[1] or samples[2] are taken from a person in connection with the investigation of an offence and he is cleared of that offence, they must be destroyed as soon as is practicable after the conclusion[3] of the proceedings[4].

If fingerprints or samples are taken from a person in connection with such an investigation and it is decided that he will not be prosecuted for that offence and he has not admitted it and been dealt with by way of being cautioned by a constable, they must be destroyed as soon as is practicable after that decision is taken[5].

If fingerprints or samples are taken from a person in connection with the investigation of an offence and that person is not suspected of having committed the offence, they must be destroyed as soon as they have fulfilled the purpose for which they were taken[6].

If fingerprints are destroyed, (1) any copies of the fingerprints must also be destroyed; and (2) any chief officer of police[7] controlling access to computer data relating to fingerprints must make access to the data impossible, as soon as it is practicable to do so[8]. However, if the provisions in head (2) above fall to be complied with and the person to whose fingerprints the data relate asks for a certificate that such provisions have been complied with, such a certificate must be issued to him, not later than the end of the period of three months beginning with the day on which he asks for it, by the responsible chief officer of police[9] or a person authorised by him or on his behalf for these purposes[10].

A person who asks to be allowed to witness the destruction of his fingerprints or copies of them has a right to witness it[11].

A record must be made as soon as possible of the destruction of fingerprints and as soon as practicable of the destruction of samples[12].

1 As to the taking of fingerprints see para 776 ante.
2 As to the taking of intimate samples see para 779 ante; and as to the taking of non-intimate samples see para 780 ante.
3 For these purposes, proceedings which have been discontinued are to be treated as concluded: Police and Criminal Evidence Act 1984 s 64 (4).
4 Ibid s 64 (1); Code of Practice for the Identification of Persons by Police Officers paras 3.4, 5.8. Nothing in the Police and Criminal Evidence Act 1984 s 64 (as amended: see notes 7–10 infra) affects any power conferred by the Immigration Act 1971 s 4, Sch 2 para 18 (2) or applies to a person arrested or detained under the terrorism provisions: Police and Criminal Evidence Act 1984 s 64 (7). For the meaning of 'the terrorism provisions' see para 726 note 1 ante.
5 Ibid s 64 (2); Code of Practice for the Identification of Persons by Police Officers paras 3.4, 5.8.
6 Police and Criminal Evidence Act 1984 s 64 (3).
7 For these purposes, 'chief officer of police' means the chief officer of police for an area mentioned in the Police Act 1964 s 62, Sch 8 (as amended: see POLICE): Police and Criminal Evidence Act 1984 s 64 (6B) (added by the Criminal Justice Act 1988 s 148 (2)).
8 Police and Criminal Evidence Act 1984 s 64 (5) (substituted by the Criminal Justice Act 1988 s 148 (1)).
9 For these purposes, 'the responsible chief officer of police' means the chief officer of police in whose area the computer data were put on to the computer: Police and Criminal Evidence Act 1984 s 64 (6B) (as added: see note 7 supra).
10 Ibid s 64 (6A) (added by the Criminal Justice Act 1988 s 148 (2)).

11 Police and Criminal Evidence Act 1984 s 64 (6). A person may witness the destruction of fingerprints if he asks to do so within one month of being cleared or informed that he will not be prosecuted: Code of Practice for the Identification of Persons by Police Officers paras 3.1, 3.4. As to the obligation to inform a person of this right see para 776 note 2 ante.
12 Code of Practice for the Identification of Persons by Police Officers paras 3.6, 5.9.

782. Destruction of photographs. Where a person's photograph has been taken[1], the photograph, negatives and all copies taken in that particular case must be destroyed if he is prosecuted for the offence and cleared or he is not prosecuted, unless he admits the offence and is cautioned for it[2].

An opportunity of witnessing the destruction must be given to him if he so requests, provided he applies[3] within one month of being cleared or informed that he will not be prosecuted[4].

A record must be made as soon as possible of the destruction of photographs[5].

1 Ie in accordance with the Code of Practice for the Identification of Persons by Police Officers para 4: see para 777 ante.
2 Ibid para 4.4.
3 Ie in accordance with ibid para 4.1: see para 777 ante.
4 Ibid para 4.4. As to the obligation to inform a person of this right see para 777 note 3 ante.
5 Ibid para 4.5.

(ix) Charge

783. Charging of detained persons. When an officer considers that there is sufficient evidence to prosecute a detained person, he should without delay bring him before the custody officer[1] who is then responsible for considering whether or not he should be charged[2]. Any resulting action should be taken in the presence of the appropriate adult[3] if the person is a juvenile or mentally ill or mentally handicapped[4].

When a detained person is charged with or informed that he may be prosecuted for an offence he must be cautioned[5] in the prescribed terms[6].

At the time a person is charged he must be given a written notice showing particulars of the offence with which he is charged and including the name of the officer in the case, his police station and the reference number for the case[7]. So far as possible the particulars of the charge must be stated in simple terms, but they must also show the precise offence in law with which he is charged[7]. The notice must begin with the following words:

'You are charged with the offence(s) shown below. You do not have to say anything unless you wish to do so, but what you say may be given in evidence.'[7]

If the person is a juvenile or is mentally ill or mentally handicapped, the notice must be given to the appropriate adult[7]. If at any time after a person has been charged with or informed he may be prosecuted for an offence a police officer wishes to bring to the notice of that person any written statement made by another person or the content of an interview with another person, he must hand to that person a true copy of any such written statement or bring to his attention the content of the interview record, but may say or do nothing to invite any reply or comment save to caution him[8] in the prescribed terms[9]. If the person cannot read, the officer may read it to him[9]. If the person is a juvenile or mentally ill or mentally handicapped, the copy must also be given to, or the interview record brought to the attention of, the appropriate adult[9]. Questions relating to an offence may not be put to a person after he has been charged with that offence, or informed that he may be prosecuted for it, unless they are necessary for the purpose of preventing or minimising harm or loss to some other person or to the public or for clearing up an ambiguity in a previous answer or statement, or where it is in the interests of justice that the person should have put to him and have an opportunity to comment on information concerning the offence which has come to light since he was charged or informed that he might be prosecuted[10]. Before any such questions are put he must be cautioned[11] in the prescribed terms[12]. Where a juvenile is charged with an offence and the custody officer authorises his continuing detention, he must try to make arrangements for the juvenile to be taken into the care of a local authority to be detained pending appearance in court unless he certifies that it is impracticable[13] to do so[14]. If it is not practicable so to make arrangements for the transfer of a juvenile into local authority care, the custody officer must record the reasons and make out a certificate to be produced before the court together with the juvenile[15].

A record must be made of anything a detained person says when charged[16]. Any questions put after charge and answers given relating to the offence must be contemporaneously recorded in full on the forms provided and the record signed by that person or, if he refuses, by the interviewing officer and any third parties present[17]. If the questions are tape-recorded[18], the arrangements set out in the relevant code of practice apply[19].

1 As to custody officers see para 716 ante.
2 Code of Practice for the Detention, Treatment and Questioning of Persons by Police Officers para 17.1.
3 For the meaning of 'the appropriate adult' see para 717 note 7 ante.
4 Code of Practice for the Detention, Treatment and Questioning of Persons by Police Officers para 17.1.
5 Ie in the terms of ibid para 10.4: see para 734 ante.
6 Ibid para 17.2.
7 Ibid para 17.3.
8 See note 5 supra.
9 Code of Practice for the Detention, Treatment and Questioning of Persons by Police Officers para 17.4.
10 Ibid para 17.5.
11 See note 5 supra.
12 Code of Practice for the Detention, Treatment and Questioning of Persons by Police Officers para 17.5. The right to consult a solicitor may not be delayed once a person has been charged: see para 730 ante.
13 Ie that it is impracticable to do so in accordance with the Police and Criminal Evidence Act 1984 s 38 (6): see para 719 note 4 ante.
14 Code of Practice for the Detention, Treatment and Questioning of Persons by Police Officers para 17.6. Neither a juvenile's unruliness nor the nature of the offence with which he is charged provides grounds for the custody officer to retain him in police custody rather than seek to arrange for his transfer to the care of the local authority: para 17.6, note 17A.
15 Ibid para 17.9.
16 Ibid para 17.7.
17 Ibid para 17.8.
18 As to tape-recorded interviews see para 746 et seq ante.
19 Code of Practice for the Detention, Treatment and Questioning of Persons by Police Officers para 17.8.

784. Detention after charge. Where a person (1) is charged with an offence; and (2) after being charged is kept in police detention[1] or is detained by a local authority[2], he must be brought before a magistrates' court in accordance with the following provisions[3].

If he is to be brought before a magistrates' court for the petty sessions area in which the police station at which he was charged is situated, he must be brought before such a court as soon as is practicable and in any event not later than the first sitting after he is charged with the offence[4]. If no magistrates' court for that area is due to sit either on the day on which he is charged or on the next day, the custody officer[5] for the police station at which he was charged must inform the clerk to the justices for the area that there is a person in the area[6] who must be so brought before a magistrates' court[7].

If the person charged is to be brought before a magistrates' court for a petty sessions area other than that in which the police station at which he was charged is situated, he must be removed to that area as soon as is practicable and brought before such a court as soon as is practicable after his arrival in the area and in any event not later than the first sitting of a magistrates' court for that area after his arrival in the area[8]. If no magistrates' court for that area is due to sit either on the day on which he arrives in the area or on the next day, he must be taken to a police station in the area and the custody officer at that station must inform the clerk to the justices for the area that there is a person in the area[9] who must be so brought before a magistrates' court[10].

Where a clerk to the justices for a petty sessions area has been so informed[11], the clerk must arrange for a magistrates' court to sit not later than the day next following the relevant day[12].

1 For the meaning of 'in police detention' see para 716 note 5 ante.
2 Ie in pursuance of arrangements made under the Police and Criminal Evidence Act 1984 s 38 (6): see para 719 note 4 ante.
3 Ibid s 46 (1). Nothing in s 46 requires a person who is in hospital to be brought before a court if he is not well enough: s 46 (9).
4 Ibid s 46 (2).
5 As to custody officers see para 716 ante.
6 Ie a person to whom the Police and Criminal Evidence Act 1984 s 46 (2) applies: see supra.
7 Ibid s 46 (3).
8 Ibid s 46 (4).
9 Ie a person to whom ibid s 46 (4) applies: see supra.
10 Ibid s 46 (5).
11 Ie informed (1) under ibid s 46 (3) that there is a person in the area to whom s 46 (2) applies; or (2) under s 46 (5) that there is a person in the area to whom s 46 (4) applies.
12 Ibid s 46 (6). For these purposes, 'the relevant day' (1) in relation to a person who is to be brought before a magistrates' court for the petty sessions area in which the police station at which he was charged is situated, means the day on which he was charged; and (2) in relation to a person who is to be brought before a magistrates' court for any other petty sessions area, means the day on which he arrives in the area: s 46 (7). Where the day next following the relevant day is Christmas Day, Good Friday or a Sunday, the duty of the clerk under s 46 (6) is a duty to arrange for a magistrates' court to sit not later than the first day after the relevant day which is not one of those days: s 46 (8). As to the clerk's duty under s 46 (6) see also *R v Avon Magistrates' Courts Committee, ex p Broome* [1988] 1 WLR 1246, DC.

(x) Restrictions on Proceedings

785. Restrictions on vexatious proceedings. If, on an application made by the Attorney General, the High Court is satisfied that any person has habitually and persistently and without any reasonable ground instituted vexatious[1] prosecutions, whether against the same person or different persons, the court may, after hearing that person or giving him an opportunity of being heard, make a criminal proceedings order[2]. An order so made may provide that it is to cease to have effect at the end of a specified period, but otherwise remains in force indefinitely[3]. Leave for the laying of an information or for an application for leave to prefer a bill of indictment by a person who is the subject of such an order may not be given unless the High Court is satisfied that the institution of the prosecution is not an abuse of the criminal process and that there are reasonable grounds for the institution of the prosecution by the applicant[4]. No appeal lies from a decision of the High Court refusing such leave[5].

1 In considering whether any proceedings are vexatious, the court must look at the whole history of the matter; and proceedings may be held to be vexatious notwithstanding that in each individual case taken singly the pleading discloses a cause of action: see *Re Vernazza* [1959] 2 All ER 200; affd [1960] 1 QB 197, [1960] 1 All ER 183, CA; revsd in part on other grounds sub nom *A-G v Vernazza* [1960] AC 965, [1960] 3 All ER 97, HL.
   The court considers the number, general character and result of the proceedings alleged to be vexatious, and may make an order even though there may have been reasonable grounds for the proceedings in each case considered by itself: *Re Chaffers, ex p A-G* (1897) 76 LT 351. See also *Re Jones, Re Vexatious Actions Act* (1902) 18 TLR 476.
2 Supreme Court Act 1981 s 42 (1) (amended by the Prosecution of Offences Act 1985 s 24 (1), (2) (c)). For these purposes, 'criminal proceedings order' means an order that (1) no information may be laid before a justice of the peace by the person against whom the order is made without the leave of the High Court; and (2) no application for leave to prefer a bill of indictment may be made by him without the leave of the High Court: Supreme Court Act 1981 s 42 (1A) (added by the Prosecution of Offences Act 1985 s 24 (1), (3)).
   The High Court may also make an all proceedings order: Supreme Court Act 1981 s 42 (1) (as amended: see note 1 supra). For these purposes, an 'all proceedings order' means an order which has the combined effect of a criminal proceedings order and a civil proceedings order: s 42 (1A) (as so added). As to civil proceedings orders see PRACTICE AND PROCEDURE vol 37 para 143. A copy of any order so made must be published in the London Gazette: s 42 (5).
3 Ibid s 42 (2).
4 Ibid s 42 (3A) (added by the Prosecution of Offences Act 1985 s 24 (1), (5)).
5 Supreme Court Act 1981 s 42 (4) (amended by the Prosecution of Offences Act 1985 s 24 (1), (6)).

786. Limitation of time in criminal proceedings. Except where there are statutory provisions to the contrary[1], criminal prosecutions may be commenced at any time after the commission of the offence[2]. A prosecution is commenced when an information is laid before a justice of the peace[3] or, if there is no information, when the accused is brought before a justice to answer the charge[4] or, if there is no preliminary examination before a justice, when a indictment is preferred[5].

Prolonged delay in starting or conducting criminal proceedings may be an abuse of process as, for example, when substantial delay has been caused by some improper use of procedure by, or inefficiency on the part of, the prosecution and the accused has not himself caused or contributed to it and has been prejudiced by it[6]. The jurisdiction to decline to allow criminal proceedings to continue should be used sparingly[7].

1 See eg the Cable and Broadcasting Act 1984 s 25(4) (proceedings in respect of obscene programmes in cable programme service not to be commenced more than two years after the commission of the offence: see para 371 ante). As to the restrictions on the institution of proceedings for conspiracy see para 68 ante.
2 Where there is a time limited for the commencement of a prosecution, the day on which the offence was committed must be excluded in the computation of the prescribed time: *Radcliffe v Bartholomew* [1892] 1 QB 161; and see *Pellew v Wonford Inhabitants* (1829) 9 B & C 134; *Williams v Burgess* (1840) 12 Ad & El 635. Sundays are to be included in the computation of time, unless the statute prescribing the time expressly excludes them: *R v Middlesex Justices* (1843) 2 Dowl NS 719. In every Act passed

after 1850 'month' means calendar month unless a contrary intention appears: Interpretation Act 1978 s 5, Schs 1, 2 para 4 (1). See also TIME vol 45 para 1109. A period of limitation does not exclude, where otherwise admissible, evidence of other acts done by the accused more than the prescribed period before the prosecution was commenced: *R v Shellaker* [1914] 1 KB 414, 9 Cr App Rep 240, CCA.

3 *R v Willace* (1797) 1 East PC 186, CCR. Where an information, laid in time, is amended after the expiration of the time, the amendment relating to the date when the offence is alleged to have been committed and not charging a different offence from that charged in the information as originally laid, the consequent proceedings are in time: *R v Wakeley* [1920] 1 KB 688, CCA. Proof of the issue of a warrant which is not executed within the time limited for commencing the prosecution is not proof that the prosecution is commenced in time, unless proof is also given of the information: *R v Phillips* (1818) Russ & Ry 369, CCR; *R v Parker and Smith* (1864) Le & Ca 459, CCR; *R v Hull* (1860) 2 F & F 16.

4 *R v Austin* (1845) 1 Car & Kir 621.

5 *R v Killminster* (1835) 7 C & P 228. If an indictment is presented within the time limited and is ignored, it would seem that the prosecution has been commenced in time, and another indictment found after the expiration of the limited time would be valid: *R v Killminster* supra.

6 *R v Grays Justices, ex p Graham* [1982] QB 1239, 75 Cr App Rep 229, DC; *R v Oxford City Justices, ex p Smith* (1982) 75 Cr App Rep 200, DC; *R v West London Stipendiary Magistrate, ex p Anderson* (1984) 80 Cr App Rep 143, DC; *Bell v DPP of Jamaica* [1985] AC 937, [1985] 2 All ER 585, PC.

In criminal proceedings mere delay which gave rise to prejudice and unfairness might by itself amount to an abuse of the process; and in some circumstances prejudice would be presumed from substantial delay; but, in the absence of a presumption, where there was substantial delay, it would be for the prosecution to justify it: *R v Bow Street Stipendiary Magistrate, ex p DPP, R v Bow Street Stipendiary Magistrate, ex p Cherry* (1989) Times, 20 December, DC.

7 *R v Oxford City Justices, ex p Smith* (1982) 75 Cr App Rep 200, DC.

(xi) Extradition

787–800. Extradition. Where extradition procedures[1] are available as between the United Kingdom and a foreign state[2], a person in the United Kingdom who:

(1) is accused in that state of the commission of an extradition crime[3]; or

(2) is alleged to be unlawfully at large after conviction of an extradition crime by a court in that state,

may be arrested and returned[4] to that state[5].

A person in the United Kingdom who is accused of an extradition crime in a designated Commonwealth country[6] or in a colony or who is alleged to be unlawfully at large after conviction of such an offence in any such country or in a colony, may be arrested and returned[7] to that country or colony[8].

1 Ie under the Extradition Act 1989 Pt III (ss 7–17): see EXTRADITION. Where an Order in Council under the Extradition Act 1870 s 2 (repealed) is in force in relation to a foreign state, the Extradition Act 1989 s 1 (3), Sch 1 has effect in relation to that state, but subject to the limitations, restrictions, conditions, exceptions and qualifications, if any, contained in the Order: s 1 (3).

2 For these purposes, 'foreign state' means any state other than (1) the United Kingdom; (2) a country mentioned in the British Nationality Act 1981 s 37, Sch 3 (countries whose citizens are Commonwealth citizens); (3) a colony; or (4) the Republic of Ireland; but a state which is a party to the European Convention on Extradition done at Paris on 13 December 1957 may be treated as a foreign state: Extradition Act 1989 s 3 (2).

3 For these purposes, 'extradition crime' means:

(1) conduct in the territory of a foreign state, a designated Commonwealth country or a colony which, if it occurred in the United Kingdom, would constitute an offence punishable with imprisonment for a term of 12 months, or any greater punishment, and which, however described in the law of the foreign state, Commonwealth country or colony, is so punishable under that law;

(2) an extra-territorial offence against the law of a foreign state, designated Commonwealth country or colony which is punishable under that law with imprisonment for a term of 12

months, or any greater punishment, and which satisfies (a) the condition specified in ibid s 2 (2); or (b) all the conditions specified in s 2 (3): s 2 (1).

The condition mentioned in head (2) (a) supra is that in corresponding circumstances equivalent conduct would constitute an extra-territorial offence against the law of the United Kingdom punishable with imprisonment for a term of 12 months, or any greater punishment: s 2 (2). The conditions mentioned in head (2) (b) supra are (i) that the foreign state, Commonwealth country or colony bases its jurisdiction on the nationality of the offender; (ii) that the conduct constituting the offence occurred outside the United Kingdom; and (iii) that, if it occurred in the United Kingdom, it would constitute an offence under the law of the United Kingdom punishable with imprisonment for a term of 12 months, or any greater punishment: s 2 (3).

For the above purposes:

(A) the law of a foreign state, designated Commonwealth country or colony includes the law of any part of it and the law of the United Kingdom includes the law of any part of the United Kingdom;

(B) conduct in a colony or dependency of a foreign state or of a designated Commonwealth country, or a vessel, aircraft or hovercraft of a foreign state or of such a country, is to be treated as if it were conduct in the territory of that state or country; and

(C) conduct in a vessel, aircraft or hovercraft of a colony of the United Kingdom is to be treated as if it were conduct in that colony:

s 2 (4). For the meaning of 'designated Commonwealth country' see note 6 infra.

4 Ie in accordance with the extradition procedures under ibid Pt III (ss 7–17): see note 1 supra and EXTRADITION.

5 Ibid s 1 (1).

6 Her Majesty may by Order in Council designate for the purposes of ibid s 1 (2) any country for the time being mentioned in the British Nationality Act 1981 Sch 3; and any country so designated is in the Extradition Act 1989 referred to as a 'designated Commonwealth country': s 5 (1). See further EXTRADITION.

7 See note 4 supra.

8 Extradition Act 1989 s 1 (2).

INDEX

Criminal Law, Evidence and Procedure

This Index consolidates entries appearing in Volume 11(1) (paragraphs 1–800) and
Volume 11(2) (paragraphs 801–1592)

arrest warrant—
  bail, indorsed for, 699
  contents, 698
  Crown Court, where bail granted by magistrates' court, 898
  discretion to issue, 702
  execution of, 700
  failure to appear before Crown Court, on, 959
  power to issue, 695
  statement of offence, 701
  witness, as to, 1168
arrestable offence—
  meaning, 51n[1], 703
  concealing, 319
  impeding apprehension or prosecution, 51
  power of arrest, 705
  serious: meaning, 704
arrival, examination under prevention of terrorism provisions on, 121
artillery range, prohibition on dredging etc near, 332
assault—
  meaning, 488
  actual bodily harm, occasioning, 490
  aggravated, 490, 491
  alternative verdicts, 501
  arrest, in course of, 500
  arrest, to resist or prevent, 321
  bar to subsequent action, 502
  buggery, with intent to commit, 509
  certificate of dismissal, 502n[3]
  child's evidence in committal proceedings, 830
  common assault, 488, 489
  consent to, 494
  constable, of, 320
  defences—
    consent, 494
    lawful arrest, 500
    lawful correction, 497
    marital rights, 495
    misadventure, 496
    other persons, in defence of, 498
    property, in defence of, 499
    self-defence, 498
  dismissal of information, effect, 502
  false imprisonment, 492
  indecent—
    actus reus, 521n[2]
    consent, 521, 522
    man, on, 521
    mens rea, 521n[2]
    woman, on, 522
  kidnapping, 493
  lawful correction, 497
  marital rights, 495
  misadventure as defence, 496
  police, on, 320
  probation order and bar to subsequent action, 502
  property, protection, of, 499
  protection of others, in, 498
  self-defence, in, 498
  Sovereign, on, 87
  specified cases of aggravated assault, 491
  summary conviction, effect, 502
assembly—
  public, powers as to, 145
  unlawful drilling, 146
assessor of compensation for miscarriage of justice, 1522

association, quasi-military, offences as to, 101
atomic energy—
  meaning, 269n[6]
  authorised person: meaning, 269n[4]
  exempt information, 269n[1]
  plant—
    meaning, 269n[5]
    communication of information as to, 269
attempt—
  actus reus, 72
  breach of national security, as to, 257
  choke, suffocate or strangle, 473
  complicity in, 71n[1]
  conviction on charge of full offence, 74
  criminal liability, 71
  explosion, to cause, 479
  gross indecency between men, 506n[4,5]
  impossibility, 71n[4]
  mens rea, 73
  penalty for statutory attempt, 75
  prosecution, provisions as to, 71n[3]
  special statutory provision, under, 71n[5]
  suicide and complicity, 443n[3]
  vicarious liability, 57
attendance centre order—
  meaning, 1279n[4]
  breach of, 1280
  breach of probation order, on, 1249
  discharge of, 1281
  number of hours, 1279n[3]
  period of rehabilitation, 1585
  power to make, 1279
  restrictions on making, 1279
  revocation, 1280
  variation, 1281
Attorney General—
  annual reports to—
    Director of Public Prosecutions, 641
    Director of Serious Fraud Office, 642
  appointment, 636
  consent to prosecution. *See* consent to prosecution
  criminal proceedings order, 785
  Crown Prosecution Service fees and expenses, control powers, 650
  fraud witnesses' allowances, power to regulate, 1558
  functions, 636
  nature of office of, 636
  nolle prosequi, 939–941
  prosecution witnesses' allowances, power to regulate, 1551
  quasi-military organisations, powers, 101
  reference to Court of Appeal. *See* criminal appeal (lenient sentence; point of law)
  Serious Fraud Office, superintendence of, 638
  status, 636
auctioneer, firearm certificate exemption, 211
automatism—
  criminal liability, and, 6
  defence, as, 6
  insanity compared, 7
autrefois convict or acquit—
  evidence, 972
  form of plea, 971n[2]
  grounds for successful plea, 973
  offences committed abroad, 635
  pleading, 970
  principles, 970
  proof of plea, 971

certificate of conviction—
  admissibility, 1117
  autrefois convict, plea of, 972
  previous convictions, proof of, 1042
certificate of dismissal as to assault, 502n³
certiorari, order of—
  alteration of sentence, 1489
  bail on application for, 1488
  Crown Court, to, 1486
challenge of juror. *See under* jury
character evidence—
  meaning, 1070
  accused, as to—
    bad character—
      co-accused's evidence, 1075
      general principles, 1074
      handling stolen goods, 1076
    cross-examination. *See* cross-examination of accused *infra*
    general reputation, 1136
    good character, 1073, 1088
  co-accused's evidence as to bad character, 1075
  complainant, as to, 1071
  convictions—
    admissible evidence of spent convictions, 1083, 1084
    commission of offence, as proof of, 1085
    element of offence, as, 1077
    excepted proceedings, 1080
    inadmissibility, 1081, 1082
    interests of justice, 1084
    spent, 1078, 1079
  cross-examination of accused—
    co-accused, evidence against, 1090
    good character or imputations, as to, 1088
    judge's discretion, 1089
    proof of offence, 1087
    statutory prohibitions, 1086
  rehabilitation of offenders, 1078, 1079
  relevance, 1070
  witness, as to, 1072
charge—
  bringing before magistrates' court following, 784
  detained person, of, 783
  detention after, 784
  explanation at committal proceedings, 838
  illiterate person, 783
  juveniles and mentally handicapped, 783
  notice provisions, 783
  questioning after, 783
  record of, 783
charging order to enforce confiscation order. *See under* confiscation order
cheat—
  meaning, 554n⁶
  going equipped for, 554
  public revenue, 578
Chief Land Registrar's duty to assist terrorist investigations, 132n⁶
child—
  meaning, 537n²
  abandoning, 537n⁶,⁷
  abduction of. *See under* abduction
  appeal against order on parent or guardian, 1356
  brothel, residing in or frequenting, 383
  burning, exposure to risk of, 538
  care proceedings in relation to offence, 1263
  concealment of birth, 466–468

child—*continued*
  contraceptive advice to girl under 16 years, 388n⁶
  corroboration of evidence of, 1144
  criminal capacity, 34
  criminal trial, presence at, 995
  cruelty to—
    constituents of, 537
    exposing to risk of burning, 538
    penalty, 537
    persons under 16 years, 537
    tattooing, 539
  custody of—
    abduction, and, 535
    general presumptions, 537n¹
  deposition by, 836, 1110
  destruction. *See* child destruction; infanticide
  evidence in certain committal proceedings, 830
  female circumcision, 503
  gross indecency with, 523
  indecent photographs—
    child: meaning, 365n⁵
    consent to prosecution, 365
    constituents of offence, 365
    corporate offences, 365n¹, 366n¹
    defences, 365
    extradition, 365n⁷
    forfeiture, 368
    indecency, test for, 365n³
    penalty, 365
    photographs etc within scope, 365n⁴
    possession of, 366
    search and seizure, 367
  independent existence, time of, 427
  infanticide. *See* infanticide
  injury to health, 537n⁸
  intoxicating substances, supply to, 413
  kidnapping of, 493
  lawful correction, 497
  neglect: meaning, 537n⁵
  police detention, additional rights on, 724
  prostitution of girl under 16 years, 388
  sentencing. *See* sentence (young offenders)
  sexual offences. *See* sexual offences
  statutory provisions as to committal proceedings for certain offences against, 882
  sworn evidence, 1178
  television link, evidence by, 1169, 1170
  unborn—
    capable of being born alive, 452n¹
    child destruction, 452
    homicide, and, 427
    independent existence, 427
    threat to kill, 434n⁴
  unlawful sexual intercourse with, 526, 527
  unsworn evidence, 1179
child destruction—
  alternative verdicts, 1033
  constituents of, 452
  defence to charge, 452
  murder or manslaughter compared, 427
choke, attempt to, 473
circumcision of women and girls, 503
civil debt, recovery of penalty as, 2
civil proceedings distinguished, 2
clergyman, obstruction of, 349
coach, control of alcohol on, 175

Code of Practice—
  admissibility of, 1132
  arrest, 691
  detention and questioning, 691
  identification of persons, 767
  relevance as to admissibility questions, 1133
  search of premises, 668
  seizure of property, 668, 669n[1]
  stop and search, 660
  tape-recording of police interviews, 746
coercion by spouse as defence, 25
coin—
  British: meaning, 338n[2]
  counterfeit. *See* counterfeit
  imitation coins, 338
  protected: meaning, 333n[4]
collateral acts and complicity, 47
collection—
  meaning (articles), 555n[2]
  stealing articles from, 555
committal—
  proceedings. *See* preliminary inquiry (indictable offences)
  sentence, for. *See under* sentence
  trial, for. *See under* preliminary inquiry (indictable offences)
Command Papers—
  Cmd 8969 (Human Rights Convention), 348n[5]
  Cmnd 424 (sentencing), 1188n[9]
  Cmnd 1289 (sentencing), 1188n[2,6]
  Cmnd 2565 (Diplomatic Relations Convention), 164n[1]
  Cmnd 4421 (genocide), 424n[2]
  Cmnd 4991 (Evidence), 1099n[4]
  Cmnd 5219 (Consular Relations Convention), 164n[1]
Commonwealth citizen's rights on police detention, 728
communication, interception. *See* interception of communications
community service order—
  amendment of, 1219
  breach of, 1220
  breach of probation order, on, 1249
  commencement of work, 1225
  court's powers, 1218
  explanation to offender, 1218
  failure to attend for work, 1227
  group placements, 1224
  information for offenders, 1223
  misconduct, 1227
  Northern Ireland, 1230, 1231
  number of hours, 1218n[5]
  obligations of offender, 1222
  procedure, 1218
  reckoning of time, 1226
  records, 1228
  restrictions, 1218
  revocation of, 1221
  Scotland, 1229, 1231
  substitution of other sentence, 1221
  two or more offences, 1218n[6]
compellability—
  accused's spouse as witness, 1184
  witness, of, 1167
compensation—
  confiscation order, as to, 1304, 1325
  criminal injuries. *See* Criminal Injuries Compensation Board; Criminal Injuries Compensation Scheme

compensation—*continued*
  forfeiture under prevention of terrorism provisions, as to, 1335
  miscarriage of justice. *See* miscarriage of justice
compensation order—
  meaning, 1238
  appeal against, 1363
  award of damages, and, 1241
  court's powers, 1238
  enforcement, 1240
  fine, and, 1238n[1]
  magistrates' court limit, 1238n[11]
  matters to consider, 1238
  offender's means, regard to, 1238n[13]
  review of, 1239
  several offences, 1238n[10]
  suspension pending appeal, 1363
  young offenders, 1282
competence—
  accused's spouse as witness, 1184
  witness, of, 1166
complainant—
  age, of, proof, 1156
  character evidence, 1071
  corroboration of evidence of, 1142
complaint—
  interception of communications, as to. *See* interception of communications (Tribunal)
  police detention, as to, 732
  tape-recorded interview, as to, 751
  See also complainant
complicity—
  attempt, and, 71n[1]
  breach of exclusion order, as to, 107
  buggery, 505
  collateral acts, 47
  conspiracy, 66
  corroboration of evidence, 1143
  entrapment, 48
  escape from prison, 327
  general principles, 43
  indictment of secondary parties, 50
  murder, 435
  official collaboration in crime, 48
  perjury, in, 307
  principal: meaning, 44
  rape, 515, 517n[1]
  secondary parties—
    actus reus, 45
    indictment of, 50
    mens rea, 46
  suicide, 443
  terrorist funds, as to, 116
  treason, 82
  vicarious liability, 57
  victim, by, 49
compulsion as defence, 24
computer data—
  admissibility, 1114, 1158
  hearsay rule and, 1100, 1158n[4]
  seizure powers, 686
concealing offences, 319
concealment of birth, 466–468
conditions of bail, 884
confession—
  admissible, 1128
  cross-examination of accused, 1089

criminal appeal—*continued*
  insanity—*continued*
    substitution of verdict, 1398
  judicial review. *See* judicial review
  leave for—
    application to Court of Appeal, 1376
    Court of Appeal, to, 1364
    Divisional Court, appeal from, 1492
    House of Lords appeal, 1437–1439
  lenient sentence—
    amendment of reference, 1430
    application for leave to refer, 1426
    documents etc, supply of, 1432
    form and content of reference, 1429
    hearing, 1435
    notice of application, 1427
    offender, notice to, 1428
    power to refer, 1425
    powers of Court of Appeal, 1435
    presence of offender at hearing, 1434
    Registrar's powers and duties, 1431
    service, 1433
    unduly lenient: meaning, 1435n[2]
    withdrawal of reference, 1430
  magistrates' court, from, entitlement, 1450
  point of law—
    Attorney General, reference by, 1423
    House of Lords, reference to, 1448
    procedure on reference, 1424
  prerogative of mercy, 1449
  reference to European Court—
    Court of Appeal, by, 1383
    Crown Court, by, 1466
  right of—
    Court of Appeal, to. *See under* Court of Appeal *supra*
    Crown Court, to. *See under* Crown Court *supra*
    Divisional Court, from, 1491
    House of Lords, to, 1437
  sentence, against—
    alteration of sentence, 1401
    Attorney General, by. *See* lenient sentence *supra*
    conviction on indictment, 1355
    Crown Court, to. *See* Crown Court, to *supra*
    parent or guardian, by, 1356
    reduction, principles, 1402
    right of appeal—
      Court of Appeal, to, 1355–1358
      House of Lords, to, 1437
    summary conviction in Crown Court, 1357
    summary offence where committal for offence triable either way, 1358
  time of becoming appellant, 1361n[2]
  verdict, against—
    right of appeal—
      Court of Appeal, to, 1352–1354
      House of Lords, to, 1437
criminal capacity—
  aliens, 41
  ambassadors, 39
  children under 14 years, 34
  corporations, 35
  diplomatic staff, 39
  foreign sovereigns, 38
  members of Parliament, 37
  Sovereign, 38
  unincorporated associations, 36
  visiting forces, 40

criminal conviction—
  absolute discharge, effect, 1255
  appeal against. *See under* criminal appeal
  autrefois convict, plea of. *See* autrefois convict or acquit
  bar to further charge, as, 973
  character evidence. *See* character evidence (convictions)
  circumstances ancillary to, 1078n[8]
  conditional discharge, effect, 1255
  conviction: meaning, 823n[1], 883n[3]
  Court of Appeal, evidence in, 1382
  disqualification on, 1340
  firearms dealer, of, powers on, 242
  indictment, reference in, 930
  material irregularity, 1390
  official record—
    meaning, 287n[2]
    obtaining information from, 287
  period of rehabilitation, during, 1592
  previous, proof of, 1042
  probation order, effect, 1255
  sale or possession of firearms etc, prohibition, 228, 229
  sentence. *See* sentence
  spent. *See under* rehabilitation of offenders
  substitution of alternative offence, 1392
  unsafe or unsatisfactory, 1388
  wrong decision in law, 1389
  wrongful, compensation provisions. *See* miscarriage of justice
criminal damage—
  consent to prosecution where damage to property of accused's spouse, 600
  constituents of, 594
  destroying or damaging property, 594
  lawful excuse: meaning, 598
  legislation, 593
  possession of instrument etc for, 596
  privilege, exception, 1162
  property: meaning, 597
  search for instrument etc, 599
  spouse of accused, property of, 600
  statutory provisions generally, 593
  threat of, 595
criminal entry, 161
Criminal Injuries Compensation Board—
  accounts, 1504
  annual report, 1504
  appointment of staff, 1503
  constitution, 1499
  direction by Secretary of State, 1504
  expenses of, 1499
  functions, 1499
  membership, 1501
  remuneration of members, 1502
  scheme. *See* Criminal Injuries Compensation Scheme
  status, 1500
Criminal Injuries Compensation Scheme—
  additional statutory sum, 1511n[8]
  appeal rights, 1517
  assessment, 1512
  award—
    assessment, 1512
    further award, 1513
    heads of compensation, 1511
  benefit entitlement, reduction for, 1512n[9]
  Board. *See* Criminal Injuries Compensation Board

References are to paragraph numbers; superior figures refer to notes

References are to paragraph numbers; superior figures refer to notes

References are to paragraph numbers; superior figures refer to notes

defence (pleading)—*continued*
  intoxication—
    involuntary, 29
    voluntary, 28
  knowledge of controlled drug, denying, 404
  lawful authority, justification or excuse, 504n[4]
  malicious communications, as to, 375
  marital cœrcion, 25
  mistake of fact, 21
  mistake or ignorance of law, 20
  murder and manslaughter—
    general defences, 453
    lawful execution, 454
    prevention of crime, 455
    property, defence of, 457
    self-defence, 456
  necessity as, 26
  obscene cable programme, as to, 371
  obscene publications, as to, 357, 358
  one accused attacking another, amounting to, 997
  plea in mitigation, 1047
  possession of controlled drug, 397
  preserving life of mother, 452
  provocation to murder, 438, 439
  public good, of, 357, 363
  similar fact evidence to rebut, 1094, 1095
  specified weapons, as to, 169
  standard of proof, 1066
  suicide pact, acting in pursuance of, 442
  summing-up by judge. *See* criminal trial (summing-up)
  superior orders, 27
  tattooing of minor, 539
  unclassified video recordings, as to, 369, 370
  uncontrollable impulse, 32
defendant—
  bail. *See* bail in criminal proceedings
  evidence of. *See* evidence (accused)
deferment of compensation for criminal injuries, 1515
delay—
  access to legal advice, 730
  criminal proceedings, 786
delegation of police powers, 659
delusion as defence, 31n[7]
demurrer—
  meaning, 965n[1]
  practice, 965
dental impression—
  authorisation for taking of, 779
  destruction of, 781
departure—
  departure cards, 124
  examination under prevention of terrorism provisions, 121
deportation—
  absolute or conditional discharge, on, 1252n[2]
  criteria, 1283n[2]
  power to recommend, 1283
deposition—
  meaning, 834
  committal proceedings generally, 834
  hearsay rule and, 1107, 1108, 1110
deprivation order—
  court's powers and procedure, 1336
  matters to be considered, 1336n[6]
  property in police possession, 1336n[7]
description in indictment, 924, 925

desertion—
  assisting etc—
    air force or army, from, 95
    Royal Navy, from, 94
destruction—
  child. *See* child destruction
  fingerprints and samples, 781
  photographs of suspects, of, 782
detention—
  appeal to House of Lords, pending, 909, 1441
  appropriate adult: meaning, 717n[7]
  cautions, 734
  cells, provisions as to, 731
  charge, after, 784
  charging of detainee, 783
  Code of Practice, 691
  Commonwealth citizen's rights, 728
  complaint as to treatment, 732
  conditions of, 731
  continuation beyond time limit, 762, 763, 764
  custody officers, 716
  custody record, 717
  delay in access to legal advice, 730
  delay in notifying arrest, grounds, 729
  detainee's rights—
    access to legal advice, delay in, 730
    Commonwealth citizens, 728
    foreign nationals, 728
    grounds for delay in notifying arrest, 729
    incommunicado, not to be held, 726
    legal advice, 727
  designated police station: meaning, 715
  duties after charge, 719
  duties before charge, 718
  fingerprinting, 776
  food, exercise etc, 731
  foreign national's rights, 728
  friend or relative, notice to, 726
  Her Majesty's pleasure, during, 1269
  House of Lords appeal, pending, 909, 1441
  initial procedure—
    additional rights of children and young persons, 724
    normal procedure, 622
    property of detainees, 725
    responsibilities as to detainees, 721
    special groups, 723
  interpreter—
    deaf persons, 744
    foreign languages, 743
    provisions generally, 742
  interview—
    caution, 734
    conduct of, 738
    general principles, 735
    persons at risk, 741
    purpose of, 739n[5]
    record of, 736, 739
    silence as evidence, 1123
    special restrictions, 745
    statement under caution, 740
    tape-recording. *See* tape-recording *infra*
    time for making record of, 736
    urgent, 737
    written statements, 739
  intimate searches, 766
  juveniles, 719n[4], 723
  legal advice, 727

References are to paragraph numbers; superior figures refer to notes

identification parade—
　conduct of, 773
　confrontation by witness, 775
　identification officer's duties, 768
　legal advice, 771
　notice to suspect, 769
　photograph of, 771
　prison inmates, involving, 772
　procedure, 773
　record of, 773
　requirement for, 768
idle and disorderly person—
　meaning, 417
　penalty, 417
ignorance and criminal liability, 20
illegal practices, alternative verdict, 1033
illness—
　deposition in committal proceedings where witness ill,
　835
　failure of accused to appear before Crown Court, 960
immigration—
　entry cards, 124
　examining officer. *See* examining officer
　prevention of terrorism. *See* prevention of terrorism
　　(travel control)
impeding apprehension or prosecution of arrestable
　offenders, 51
importation—
　counterfeit notes and coins, 340
　offensive weapons, 174
　specified weapons, restrictions, 169n[1]
impossibility and attempt, 71n[4]
imprisonment—
　meaning, 492
　adult: meaning, 1207n[1]
　breach of probation order, on, 1249n[14]
　breach of suspended sentence supervision order, 1216
　cases where no term fixed, 1200
　cessation of suspended sentence supervision order,
　1217
　compensation for. *See* miscarriage of justice
　concurrent sentences, 1201
　conditions for extended sentence, 1206
　consecutive sentences, 1201
　duration, 1202
　extended terms, 1206
　false, as assault, 492
　first sentence, restrictions, 1203
　forfeited recognisances, 1236, 1237
　kidnapping, 493
　partly suspended sentence—
　　conviction, powers on, 1208
　　court's powers to restore, 1209
　　further conviction, procedure, 1210
　　principles generally, 1207
　persons under 21 years, 1264
　relevant period for reduction, 1202
　restrictions—
　　first sentence, 1203
　　offender not legally represented, 1205
　　social inquiry reports, 1204
　sentence of: meaning, 1203n[3]
　social inquiry reports, 1204
　supervision order where suspended sentence, 1215–
　1217
　suspended sentence—
　　conviction, powers on, 1212

imprisonment—*continued*
　suspended sentence—*continued*
　　court's powers to deal with, 1213
　　further conviction, procedure, 1214
　　operational period: meaning, 1211n[3]
　　partly. *See* partly suspended sentence *supra*
　　principles generally, 1211
　　supervision order, 1215–1217
　　unpaid fines, 1236, 1237
　　unrepresented offender, restrictions, 1205
incest—
　adoption order, and, 510n[5]
　guardianship of victim, 513
　incitement of girl under 16 years, 511
　man, by, 510
　woman, by, 512
inchoate crime—
　attempt. *See* attempt
　conspiracy. *See* conspiracy
　incitement, 58
incitement—
　breach of national security, 257
　constituents of, 58
　criminal liability, 58
　disaffection, to—
　　constituents of, 93
　　criminal liability, 93
　　desertion from army and air force, 95
　　desertion from Royal Navy, 94
　　military duties, interfering with, 96
　　police, among, 97
　　search powers, 93n[4]
　disturbance at public meeting, 147, 148
　gross indecency with child, 523
　incest with girl under 16 years, 511
　indictable offence, 58
　murder, 433
　mutiny, 92
　penalty for, 58
　perjury, to commit, 308
　possession of controlled drug, 397
　racial hatred. *See* racial hatred
　statutory conspiracy, as to, 59
indecency—
　disorderly houses, 379
　gross indecency—
　　child, with 523
　　men, between, 506
　in public: meaning, 372n[2]
　indecent assault, 521, 522
　indecent conduct towards child, 523
　indecent exposure, 372, 418
　indecent photographs of children. *See under* child
　malicious communications, 375
　outraging public decency, 372
　post, indecent matter sent by, 373
　public displays, 376
　telephone calls, 374
indecent exposure by rogues and vagabonds, 418
indemnity of surety in criminal proceedings, 912
indictable offence—
　meaning, 42n[6], 803n[1]
　attempt, court's powers, 74
　blasphemy and blasphemous libel, 348
　buggery, 505
　carrying firearms with criminal intent, 234
　complicity, liability, 43

injury—*continued*
  compensation scheme. *See* Criminal Injuries Compensation Scheme
  corrosive fluid, by, 477
  cruelty to children. *See* child (cruelty)
  explosion, by. *See* explosion
  neglect to provide food etc for employees, 540
  See also violence; wounding
Inland Revenue, disclosure of information to Serious Fraud Office, 655
inquest, unlawful disposal of body to prevent, 316
insanity—
  appeal as to. *See under* criminal appeal
  automatism compared, 7
  burden of proof, 33
  defence, as, 31
  drunkenness compared, 30
  failure to appear before Crown Court, 960
  medical evidence, 33
  mode of proof, 33
  verdict where, 31n[9]
  trial of issue of fitness to be tried, 963
  uncontrollable impulse, 32
insider dealing, constituents and penalty, 585
insolvency, corporate offences as to, 584
insolvency practitioner—
  meaning, 1332n[6]
  forfeiture order, protection where, 1334
  restraint order, protection where, 1301, 1322
inspection by jury, 1020
insult—
  insulting: meaning, 152n[1]
  public order offences, 152, 153
insurance policy, obtaining advantage by deception, 568
intention—
  burden of proof, 15, 16
  conditional, 12
  element of crime, 11
  notice of. *See* notice of intention
  seditious, 89
  transferred intention, 13
interception of communications—
  certificate as to intercepted material, 272n[6]
  Commissioner, 280
  communication: meaning, 270n[2]
  complaints. *See* Tribunal *infra*
  disclosure of information as to, 248n[7]
  intercepted material: meaning, 271n[3]
  modification of warrants or certificates, 274
  privilege, 1165
  prohibition, 270
  Tribunal—
    application to, 277
    appointment etc of members, 276
    Commissioner's functions, 280
    constitution, 276
    decisions, 279
    procedure, 278
  warrant—
    Commissioner's functions, 280
    grounds, 271
    issue and duration, 273
    modification, 274
    powers of Secretary of State, 271
    safeguards, 275
    scope of, 272

interference—
  goods, with, 193, 194
  navigation signals, with, 603, 604
  terrorist investigation, with, 138
  vehicles, with, 557
interim hospital order—
  meaning, 907n[2]
  absconding offender, 1258
  bail on quashing of, 907
  court's powers, 1258
  House of Lords appeal, pending, 909n[8]
  renewal, 1258n[13]
international organisation—
  meaning, 245n[8]
  disclosure of information entrusted to, 250
international relations—
  meaning, 247n[6]
  disclosure of information as to, 247
interpreter—
  criminal trials, 1005
  police detainee, for. *See under* detention
intimate sample—
  meaning, 779n[1]
  authorisation and consent, 779
  destruction of, 781
intimidation—
  constituents and penalty, 422
  intimidate: meaning, 422n[4]
  picketing, 422n[9]
intoxicating liquor, control at sporting events. *See under* sporting event
intoxicating substances, supply to minors, 413
intoxication—
  awareness of violence impaired by, 149n[5]
  involuntary, defence, as, 29
  supply of firearm etc to drunk person, 227
  voluntary and criminal liability, 28
  See also drunkenness
investigation—
  crime, as to, disclosure of information, 248
  drug trafficking. *See* drug trafficking
  Serious Fraud Office, by, 653
  special, disclosure of information as to, 248
  terrorism, as to. *See* terrorist investigation
involuntary conduct and criminal liability, 6
Ireland, Republic of—
  attempting to cause explosion, 479
  causing explosions, 478
  exclusion order. *See under* prevention of terrorism
issue estoppel in criminal proceedings, 974
judge—
  bribery of, 281
  comments outside court, 1021
  summing-up. *See under* criminal trial
judgment in criminal cases. *See under* criminal trial
judicial officer—
  bribery of, 281
  exception from rehabilitation provisions, 1575
judicial review (criminal proceedings)—
  alteration of sentence on application for certiorari, 1489
  bail on application for certiorari, 1488
  certiorari, 1486
  costs, 1490
  jurisdiction, 1484
  mandamus, 1485
  prohibition, 1487

References are to paragraph numbers; superior figures refer to notes

notice—*continued*
  grounds of appeal, of, 1377
  group identification, as to, 769
  identification parade, as to, 769
  indecent display, warning of, 376n[3]
  intention, of. *See* notice of intention
  institution of criminal proceedings, of, 651, 656
  outcome of application as to dismissal of transferred
    fraud charges, 867n[3]
  preparatory hearing of fraud case, as to, 950
  public procession, of, 142
  recognisance, as to, 896n[1]
  reference of lenient sentence to Court of Appeal, as to,
    1427, 1428
  respondent's, serious fraud cases, 1411
  transfer, of—
    serious fraud cases. *See* preliminary inquiry (fraud
      cases)
    shot gun, 202
  warning of indecent display, 376n[3]
  withdrawal of reference of lenient sentence, 1430
notice of appeal—
  costs, as to, 1537
  Court of Appeal, to—
    criminal appeals generally, 1376
    serious fraud cases, 1410
  Crown Court, to, 1456
  House of Lords, to, 1438n[1]
  taxing master, to, 1537
notice of application—
  search warrant or production order, for, 676
  unduly lenient sentence, as to, 1427
  witness summons, for, 1168n[2]
notice of hearing of Crown Court appeal, 1460
notice of intention—
  bail application to Court of Appeal, 904n[7]
  dismissal of transferred fraud charges, to apply for, 864
  trial in camera, to apply for, 966
oath—
  false statements not in judicial proceedings, 303
  juror, by, 992
objection—
  indictment, to, 921, 931, 936
  tape-recording of police interview, 751
obscene cable programme, 371
obscene performance—
  consent to prosecution, 362
  criminal liability, 362
  excepted performances, 362
  limitation period, 362n[8]
  obscene: meaning, 362n[2]
  penalty, 362
  play: meaning, 362n[3]
  public good, defence of, 363
  public performance: meaning, 362n[4]
  restriction on proceedings, 362
  script as evidence, 364
obscene publication—
  article: meaning, 355n[4]
  cable programmes, 371
  consent to prosecution, 355n[7]
  constituents of offence, 355
  film exhibition, in, 355n[7,8]
  forfeiture of, 355n[7], 360
  had or kept for publication: meaning, 355n[5]
  limitation period, 355n[7]
  no reasonable cause to believe article obscene, 358

obscene publication—*continued*
  obscene libel, 361
  obscenity, test for, 356
  penalty, 355
  public good, defence of, 357
  publication for gain: meaning, 355n[6]
  publishes: meaning, 355n[2]
  search and seizure, 359
obstructing course of justice—
  acknowledging recognisance in name of another, 317
  constituents of, 315
  penalty, 315
  unlawful disposal of dead body, 316
obstruction—
  constable, of, 320
  justice, of. *See* obstructing course of justice
  minister of religion, of, 349
  public officer, of, 288
occupations excepted from rehabilitation provisions,
    1576
occupier—
  drug offences, 403
  residential: meaning, 190n[3]
  unlawful eviction, 190
  unlawful harrassment, 191
offence—
  assisting—
    verdict of, 1031
    See also complicity
  classification of, 42
  concealing, 319
  indictable. *See* indictable offence
  joinder on indictment, 932
  official secrets, as to. *See under* national security
  public order, against. *See* public order offence
  sheriffs, by, 298
  summary. *See* summary offence
  time of the essence, 926n[4]
  triable either way. *See* offence triable either way
  See also crime
offence triable either way—
  meaning, 42n[8], 803n[5]
  complicity, liability, 43
  Crown Court proceedings. *See* criminal trial
  Crown Court's powers to deal with summary offence
    on committal, 873
  dismissal of information, 820
  impeding arrest or prosecution, 51
  indictment. *See* indictment
  list of, 804
  penalty on summary conviction, 819
  preliminary inquiry by justices. *See under* preliminary
    inquiry
  sentence, appeal to Court of Appeal against, 1358
offensive weapon—
  meaning, 167n[6]
  article with blade or point in public place, 168
  crossbows, 170–172
  gravity knives, 174
  lawful authority: meaning, 166n[1]
  manufacture, sale, hire etc—
    restrictions, 174
    specified weapons, 169
  possession, 167
  reasonable excuse: meaning, 163n[2]
  smuggling while armed, 343
  trespass with, 163
  wearing weapons commonly worn, 173

official contract—
  bribery as to, 284
  national security. *See* national security
official secrets. *See* national security
Official Solicitor, bail applications in criminal proceedings, 903
omission to act and criminal liability, 9
opinion evidence. *See under* evidence
opium—
  offences as to, 401
  prepared: meaning, 401n[2]
  See also controlled drug
oppression—
  confession, to obtain, 1124n[5]
  public officer, by, 290
order—
  all proceedings order, 785n[2]
  attendance centre. *See* attendance centre order
  care order. *See* care order
  certiorari. *See* certiorari, order of
  charging order. *See under* confiscation order
  community service. *See* community service order
  compensation. *See* compensation order
  conditional discharge, for, 1252n[3]
  conditional witness order, 837
  confiscation. *See* confiscation order
  criminal proceedings order, 785
  deprivation. *See* deprivation order
  disqualification order, 1338
  exclusion order—
    licensed premises, 1342
    terrorism, as to. *See under* prevention of terrorism
  forfeiture. *See* forfeiture order
  forfeiture of security, 884n[9]
  guardianship order, 1257
  hospital order, 1257
  interim hospital order. *See* interim hospital order
  mandamus to Crown Court, 1485
  movement of firearms and ammunition, prohibiting, 223
  preparatory hearing of serious fraud case, for, 949
  probation. *See* probation order
  production, for—
    drug trafficking, material as to, 409
    excluded or special procedure material, for, 133
  prohibition, of, 1487
  reporting restrictions, lifting, 826
  restitution order, 1337
  restraint order. *See under* confiscation order
  restriction. *See* restriction order
  retrial, for, 1406
  supervision. *See* supervision order
  suspended sentence supervision order, 1215–1217
  terrorist investigations, as to, 137
  variation or rescission by Crown Court, 1053
  venire de novo, 1405
  witness's attendance at court of trial, requiring, 837
Order in Council extending criminal jurisdiction, 632
organ transplant—
  commercial dealings prohibition, 414
  corporate offences, 414n[1]
  genetically related: meaning, 415n[3]
  information requirements, 416
  organ: meaning, 414n[3]
  payment: meaning, 414n[2]
  persons not genetically related, between, 415
  testing for genetic relationship, 415n[4]

organ transplant—*continued*
  Unrelated Live Transplant Regulatory Authority, 415n[4]
organisation—
  meaning (proscribed), 111n[1]
  proscribed—
    meaning, 111n[1], 114n[2]
    contributions to, 114
    prevention of terrorism, 111, 112
  quasi-military, 101
originating summons—
  taxing master, on appeal from, 1538
  warrant to arrest witness, for, 1168n[4]
overdraft, obtaining facility by deception, 568
overnight allowance—
  central funds, payable from, 1546
  prosecution professional etc witnesses, 1554
  witnesses in serious fraud cases, 1561
parade—
  identification. *See* identification parade
  procession. *See* public procession
pardon—
  grant of, 1449
  pleading, 969
parochial register, false entries, 615
particulars of offence in indictment, 923
party to crime—
  complicity. *See* complicity
  conspiracy, 66
  victim as, 49
passport—
  false statement to obtain, 582
  forgery, 610
pawn, prohibition on firearm etc as, 207
pecuniary advantage, obtaining by deception, 568
penalty—
  civil debt, recoverable as, 2
  offence, for. *See relevant offence*
perjury—
  meaning, 299
  abroad, committed, 311
  admission of, 310
  aiding and abetting, 307
  evidence, 310
  incitement, 308
  indictment, 309
  judicial proceedings: meaning, 301
  lawfully sworn: meaning, 300
  liability apart from 1911 Act, 312
  materiality of statement, 302
  penalty, 299
  similar offences—
    false declaration as to professional registration, 305
    false statement on oath other than in judicial proceedings, 303
    false statutory declarations and false statements without oath, 303
    false written statements in criminal proceedings, 306
  statements made in judicial proceedings, 301
  subornation of, 307n[1]
personal injury compensation scheme. *See* Criminal Injuries Compensation Scheme
personation—
  juror, of, 314, 981n[3]
  obtaining property by, 575

Post Office—
　meaning, 296n[1]
　offences by employees, 296
postage stamp, fraudulent printing or mutilation, 613
postal packet—
　meaning, 296n[3]
　diversion of, 591
　fraudulent retention, 590
　indecent matter, 373
　offences by Post Office employees, 296
　theft outside England and Wales, 592
poundbreach, 330
postponement of sentence, 1046
pregnancy—
　abortion. *See* abortion
　medical termination, 465
　woman convicted of capital offence, 1044
preliminary inquiry—
　children and young persons, offences against, 882
　classification of offences, 803
　corporate offences, committal for trial, 874
　duty to hold, 801
　examining justices: meaning, 801n[6]
　fraud cases—
　　conditions for transfer, 856
　　Crown Court centres available for transfer to, 857n[4]
　　designated authorities, 856n[1]
　　dismissal of transferred charges—
　　　determination of applications, 867
　　　effect of, 870
　　　notice of outcome of application, 867n[3]
　　　oral application for, 864
　　　prosecution reply, 866
　　　provisions generally, 863
　　　reporting restrictions, 869
　　　service of documents, 868
　　　written application for, 865
　　documents required on transfer, 856
　　hospital patient, notice as to, 859
　　notice of transfer, 857
　　prescribed form of notice, 856n[3]
　　service of notice of transfer, 858
　　transfer on bail, 860
　　variation of bail arrangements, 861
　　witness orders, 862
　hearsay rule and accused's evidence, 1106
　indictable offence—
　　meaning, 803n[1]
　　accused, evidence for, 840
　　alibi warning, 839
　　attendance of witnesses, 829
　　child or young person, deposition by, 836
　　committal for trial—
　　　meaning, 872n[3]
　　　corporations, 874
　　　court's powers, 872
　　　functions of justices, 872
　　　notice of, 872n[18]
　　　procedure following, 878–880
　　　without consideration of evidence, 875–877
　　conduct of inquiry generally, 825
　　corporate offences, 874
　　decisions on questions of evidence, 841
　　depositions, 834
　　discharge of accused, powers, 872
　　discontinuance of proceedings, 871
　　evidence of children in special cases, 830

preliminary inquiry—*continued*
　indictable offence—*continued*
　　examination before justices, 827
　　formal admission, proof by, 831
　　ill witness, deposition by, 835
　　inadmissible statements, 833
　　legal aid, 825
　　legal representation, 825
　　lifting of reporting restrictions, 826
　　order of proceedings, 828
　　procedure, 824
　　purpose, 824
　　reading charge to accused, 838
　　remand. *See* remand *infra*
　　reporting restrictions, 826
　　serious fraud cases, transfer of. *See* fraud cases *supra*
　　witness order as to court of trial, 837
　　written statements, evidence by, 832, 833
　jurisdiction—
　　examining justices, 801
　　stipendiary magistrate, 802
　offence triable either way—
　　meaning, 803n[5]
　　absence of accused, procedure, 815
　　advance information, 810
　　application for trial on indictment, 811n[1]
　　committal for custody in young offender institution, 822
　　committal for sentence, 821
　　committal proceedings, power to change to summary trial, 817
　　Crown Court's powers to deal with summary offence, 873
　　dismissal of information, 820
　　list of, 804
　　mode of trial, consideration of, 811
　　procedure, 809
　　remission to another court for sentence, 823
　　summary trial—
　　　committal proceedings, change to, 817
　　　indictable offence by child or young person, 816
　　　indictable offences where small value, 814
　　　information to accused, 812
　　　penalties on conviction, 819
　　　recall of witnesses, 818
　　trial on indictment, procedure, 813
　　written statement, supply of, 810
　place of trial, need to specify, 881
　procedure following—
　　accused committed to custody, 879
　　bail, committal on, 880
　　document and exhibits, 878
　purpose of, 801
　remand—
　　accused already in custody, 850
　　bail, on, 844
　　court's powers, 842
　　custody, in, 843
　　further remand, 847
　　limitation on, 845
　　more than 8 days in custody, 846
　　principles generally, 842
　　transfer of hearings, 848, 849
　scheduled offence—
　　meaning, 814n[1]
　　calculation of value, 814n[3]
　　summary trial, 814

preliminary inquiry—*continued*
  summary offence—
    meaning, 803n³
    procedure generally, 805
premises—
  brothel, use as, 381
  prostitution, permitting use for, 382
  unlawful sexual intercourse, permitting use for, 378
prerogative of mercy, 1449
prevention of terrorism—
  act of terrorism—
    meaning, 115n²
    contributions to proscribed organisations, 114
    contributions towards, 115
    information, failure to disclose, 113
  arrest of suspects, 118
  attacks and threats against protected persons outside
    UK, 141
  convention country: meaning, 140n²
  current legislation: meaning, 111n⁵
  departure cards, 124
  designated Commonwealth country, 140n⁵
  detention of suspects, 119
  embarkation and entry cards, 124
  enforcement—
    arrest and search, 118
    detention, 119
    reasonable force, 120
  exclusion order—
    aiding person subject to, 107
    evidence, as, 102n⁵
    examining officer's duties, 108, 109
    Great Britain, from, 102
    non-compliance, 106
    Northern Ireland, from, 103
    notice of, 105
    procedure, 105
    removal from territory—
      detention pending, 109
      directions, 108
      restriction on, 108n⁷
      supervision, 110
    representations, 105
    review of detention, 110
    revocation, 105
    United Kingdom, from, 104
  fingerprinting, 118n⁸
  force, use of, 120
  foreign state, offences in, 140n⁵
  forfeiture order. *See* forfeiture order (terrorism)
  hostages, taking of, 139
  investigation. *See* terrorist investigation
  land registration information, 132n⁶
  landing cards, 124
  offences committed abroad—
    attacks etc on protected persons, 141
    jurisdiction, 140
    specified offences, 140n⁴,⁶
  proscribed organisation—
    meaning, 111n¹, 114n²
    contributions to, 114
    display of support, 112
    list of, 114n²
    membership, support and meetings, 111
  review of detention of suspects, 119
  search powers, 118
  tape-recording of interviews, 747

prevention of terrorism—*continued*
  terrorism: meaning, 102n⁴
  terrorist funds—
    meaning, 114n⁵
    acts of terrorism, contributions towards, 115
    assisting in retention or control of, 116
    disclosure of information, 117
    proscribed organisations, contributions to, 114
  travel control—
    control areas, 129
    designated ports, 128
    detention—
      examination, for, 127
      examination, pending, 125
    embarkation and disembarkation of passengers and
      crew, 130
    examination—
      arrival or departure, on, 121
      detention for, 127
      detention pending, 125
    landing, embarkation etc cards, 124
    offences, 131
    production of information and documents, 122
    search powers, 123
    transit passengers, 121n¹
  UK dependency, offences in, 140n⁵
prison—
  aiding escape, 327
  breach of, 324
  escape from, 324, 325
  harbouring escaped prisoner, 328
  penalty. *See* imprisonment
  rescue, 326
  taking articles into and out of, 327n³
prison officer—
  assault or obstruction, 320
  constable, as, 320n¹
prisoner, identification parade provisions, 772
private prosecution costs out of central funds, 1528
privilege—
  arrest, from, 694
  exceptions—
    criminal damage, 1162
    theft, 1161
  interception of communications, 1165
  legal professional—
    items subject to: meaning, 132n³
    scope of, 1163
  public policy—
    interception of communications, 1165
    provisions generally, 1164
  racial hatred, as to, 154n⁶
  seditious libel, 90
  self-incrimination, 1160
  spouse of accused, 1186
  spouse of witness, 1186n¹
prize-fighting—
  meaning, 444n⁷
  death from, 444
probation hostel—
  meaning, 884n¹²
  residence as condition of bail, 884n¹²
probation officer—
  functions—
    community service order. *See* community service
      order
    suspended sentence. *See under* imprisonment
  probation order. *See* probation order

References are to paragraph numbers; superior figures refer to notes

probation order—
  additional orders compatible with, 1242
  amendment of, 1247
  attendance requirements, 1245, 1246
  breach of, 1249
  conditional discharge, substitution of, 1248
  copies of, 1242
  court's powers, 1242
  custodial sentence restriction, 1242n^3
  day centre, attendance at, 1246
  discharge of, 1247
  effect, 1255
  explanation to offender, 1242
  general requirements under, 1245
  mental treatment condition, 1244
  offences committed during currency of, 1253, 1254
  participation in activities under, 1245
  period of rehabilitation on breach of, 1591
  probation period: meaning, 1242n^9
  residence requirement, 1243
  Scotland, 1250, 1251
  supervising court: meaning, 1243n^{24}
procession, public. *See* public procession
procuring—
  abortion. *See under* abortion
  unlawful sexual intercourse, 524
production—
  Court of Appeal's power to order, 1379
  drug trafficking investigation, powers, 409
  order for. *See* production order; search warrant
  serious fraud, as to, 653, 654
  specified material as to drug trafficking, 411
production order—
  action prior to application for, 670
  costs, special procedure, 678
  drug trafficking, as to, 409
  procedure for issue. *See* search warrant
professions excepted from rehabilitation provisions,
    1574
prohibition—
  order to Crown Court, 1487
  public procession, of, 144
proof—
  burden of. *See* burden of proof
  copy, of, 1150
  foresight, of, 16
  guilt, of, 19
  intention, of, 15, 16
  kidnapping, of, 493n^4
  marriage, of, 354
  political uniform, of, 100n^5
  quasi-military organisation, of, 101
  recklessness, of, 15
  seditious words or seditious libel, 91
  sexual intercourse, of, 378n^2
  treason, of, 85
  unlawfully procuring abortion, 463
  See also evidence
prop_y—
  assault in defence of, 499
  belonging to another, 548
  burglary. *See* burglary
  criminal damage. *See* criminal damage
  damage to. *See* criminal damage; damage to property
  description in indictment, 928
  destroying or damaging, 594
  explosion likely to endanger, causing, 478

property—*continued*
  false pretences, obtaining by, 576
  fraud. *See* fraud
  killing in defence of, 457
  obtaining by deception, 567
  person detained in police station, of, 725
  personation, obtaining by, 575
  possession or control: meaning, 548n^1
  robbery. *See* robbery
  stolen. *See* stolen goods
  theft. *See* theft
prosecution—
  case for. *See* criminal trial (prosecution case)
  consent to. *See* consent to prosecution
  impeding, 51
prostitution—
  meaning, 386n^4
  application for caution not to be recorded, 394
  brothel. *See* brothel
  cause or encourage: meaning, 388n^1
  caution procedure, 394n^1
  girl under 16, causing etc, 388
  kerb-crawling, 396
  male prostitution—
    living on earnings of, 392
    soliciting, 395
  man living on earnings of, 390
  mental defective, 387
  permitting use of premises for, 382
  procuring woman for, 386
  refreshment house, prostitutes in, 384
  search powers as to man living on earnings of, 391
  soliciting of women by men, 396
  soliciting or loitering, 393
  woman controlling prostitute, 389
protected person—
  meaning, 141n^3
  attack or threat of attack on, 141
  specified offences against, 141n^4
provocation—
  defence, as, 438
  reasonable man criterion, 439
  self-induced, 439
public assembly—
  meaning, 145n^2
  conditions, imposition of, 145
public body—
  meaning, 283n^5
  bribery of members and officers, 283
public decency—
  conspiracy to outrage, 63
  outraging, 372
public house—
  brothel, use as, 381n^4
  prostitutes assembling in, 384n^3
  See also licensed premises
public inquiry—
  inquiry: meaning, 318n^1
  threats to witnesses, 318
public interest, appeal from Divisional Court to House of
    Lords, 1493
public meeting—
  meaning, 100n^3
  disturbances at, 147
  election meetings, disturbances at, 148
  lawful: meaning, 148n^1
  political uniforms, wearing of, 100

recklessness—*continued*
  manslaughter, and. *See under* manslaughter
  mens rea, and, 14
  rape, as to, 514n[4]
  voluntary intoxication, and, 28
recognisance—
  acknowledging where in another's name, 317
  any recognisance: meaning, 317n[2]
  appellate courts' powers, 1236, 1237
  delivery to Crown Court, 651, 656
  forfeited—
    application of, 1237
    court's powers and duties, 1236
    recovery of, 1237
  keep the peace, to—
    breach of condition, 1235
    common law, 1233
    forfeited, 1236, 1237
    statute, by, 1234
  See also under bail in criminal proceedings
record—
  bail decisions, of, 889
  charge, of, 783
  community service order, 1228
  Crown Court proceedings, 944
  custody record, 717
  destruction of fingerprints etc, of, 781, 782
  fingerprints, 776n[10]
  identification by photograph etc, 778
  identification parade, of, 773
  interview with suspect, of, 736, 739
  search of premises, of, 689
  stop and search, of, 665
  trial proceedings, of, for Court of Appeal, 1372
  verification for Court of Appeal, 1374
recovery—
  fines, of, 1237
  recognisances, of, 1237
refreshment house, prostitutes assembling in, 384
register—
  births etc, forgery of entries, 615
  search register, 689
registration—
  accommodation address businesses, 259
  external confiscation orders, 1288, 1310
  firearms dealers, 203, 242
  professional, false declaration, 305
regular forces—
  meaning, 95n[2]
  interference with military duties, 96
  procuring desertion from, 95
regulations—
  power to make—
    costs in criminal cases, 1526
    fees and expenses paid by Crown Prosecution Service, 650
    fraud witnesses' allowances, 1558
    maximum fine, as to, 806n[2]
    police reports to Director of Serious Fraud Office, 644
    police reports to DPP, as to, 643
    prosecution witnesses' allowances, 1551
    time limits as to preliminary stages of proceedings, 851
    witnesses' allowances from central funds, 1541
rehabilitation of offenders—
  circumstances ancillary to a conviction, 1078n[8]

rehabilitation of offenders—*continued*
  compliance with sentence, 1568
  conviction: meaning, 1567n[2]
  disqualification, effect on, 1341
  effect of, 1078, 1571
  exceptions—
    Banking Act 1987, under, 1578
    financial services, 1577
    generally, 1079
    occupations, 1576
    offices and employments, 1574
    professions, 1574
  excluded sentences, 1569
  information as to past convictions, 1572
  method, 1571
  obtaining information about spent convictions etc, 287
  period of—
    absolute discharge, 1582
    approved school order, 1585
    attendance centre order, 1585
    breach of conditional discharge or probation, 1591
    care order, 1584
    conditional discharge etc, 1583, 1591
    conviction during, 1592
    custody in remand home, 1585
    disqualification etc, 1587
    hospital order, 1586
    more than one sentence, 1590
    persons aged 17 and over, 1579
    persons under 17 years, 1580
    probation, breach of, 1591
    single sentence, 1589
    supervision order, 1584
    variation of, 1588
    young offenders, 1581
  principle of, 1566
  rehabilitated person: meaning, 1567
  relevant offences, 1079n[7], 1572n[15]
  specified proceedings, 1079n[6,10]
  spent conviction—
    meaning, 1567
    disclosure of, 1573
    information provisions, 1572
    public officer, disclosure by, 294
  subsidiary legislation, powers, 1570
rehearing, Crown Court appeal by way of, 1468
relative, notification of arrest and detention, 726
remand—
  committal proceedings. *See under* preliminary inquiry
  hospital, to, where mental condition, 1259, 1260
remand centre—
  commitment on committal for trial, 879n[3]
  escape from. *See* prison
remuneration—
  Criminal Injuries Compensation Board members, 1502
  Football Licensing Authority members, 186n[5]
repair of firearms, 205
report—
  antecedents of accused, 1190
  mental condition, as to, remand to hospital for, 1259
  social inquiry. *See* social inquiry report
reporting restrictions—
  appeal against—
    procedure, 1421
    right of, 1420
  committal proceedings, 826

Words and Phrases

Words in parentheses indicate the context in which the word or phrase is used

References are to paragraph numbers; superior figures refer to notes

References are to paragraph numbers; superior figures refer to notes

References are to paragraph numbers; superior figures refer to notes